The Handbook of Applied Linguistics

Blackwell Handbooks in Linguistics

This outstanding multi-volume series covers all the major subdisciplines within linguistics today and, when complete, will offer a comprehensive survey of linguistics as a whole.

Already published:

The Handbook of Child Language
Edited by Paul Fletcher and Brian MacWhinney

The Handbook of Phonological Theory
Edited by John A. Goldsmith

The Handbook of Contemporary Semantic Theory
Edited by Shalom Lappin

The Handbook of Sociolinguistics
Edited by Florian Coulmas

The Handbook of Phonetic Sciences
Edited by William J. Hardcastle and John Laver

The Handbook of Morphology
Edited by Andrew Spencer and Arnold Zwicky

The Handbook of Japanese Linguistics
Edited by Natsuko Tsujimura

The Handbook of Linguistics
Edited by Mark Aronoff and Janie Rees-Miller

The Handbook of Contemporary Syntactic Theory
Edited by Mark Baltin and Chris Collins

The Handbook of Discourse Analysis
Edited by Deborah Schiffrin, Deborah Tannen, and Heidi E. Hamilton

The Handbook of Language Variation and Change
Edited by J. K. Chambers, Peter Trudgill, and Natalie Schilling-Estes

The Handbook of Historical Linguistics
Edited by Brian D. Joseph and Richard D. Janda

The Handbook of Language and Gender
Edited by Janet Holmes and Miriam Meyerhoff

The Handbook of Second Language Acquisition
Edited by Catherine Doughty and Michael H. Long

The Handbook of Bilingualism
Edited by Tej K. Bhatia and William C. Ritchie

The Handbook of Pragmatics
Edited by Laurence R. Horn and Gregory Ward

The Handbook of Applied Linguistics
Edited by Alan Davies and Catherine Elder

The Handbook of
Applied Linguistics

Edited by

Alan Davies and
Catherine Elder

© 2004 by Blackwell Publishing Ltd

BLACKWELL PUBLISHING
350 Main Street, Malden, MA 02148-5020, USA
9600 Garsington Road, Oxford OX4 2DQ, UK
550 Swanston Street, Carlton, Victoria 3053, Australia

First published 2004 by Blackwell Publishing Ltd

2   2005

Library of Congress Cataloging-in-Publication Data

The handbook of applied linguistics / edited by Alan Davies and Catherine Elder.
     p. cm. — (Blackwell handbooks in linguistics ; 17)
  Includes bibliographical references and index.
  ISBN 0–631–22899–3 (alk. paper)
  1. Applied linguistics. I. Davies, Alan, Ph. D. II. Elder, C. (Catherine) III. Title.
IV. Series.

  P129. H33 2004
  418 – dc22

                                           2003021505

  ISBN-13: 978-0-631-22899-8 (alk. paper)

A catalogue record for this title is available from the British Library.

Set in 10/12 pt Palatino
by Graphicraft Ltd, Hong Kong
Printed and bound in the United Kingdom
by TJ International, Padstow, Cornwall

The publisher's policy is to use permanent paper from mills that operate a sustainable
forestry policy, and which has been manufactured from pulp processed using acid-free and
elementary chlorine-free practices. Furthermore, the publisher ensures that the text paper
and cover board used have met acceptable environmental accreditation standards.

For further information on
Blackwell Publishing, visit our website:
www.blackwellpublishing.com

Contents

List of Figures

List of Tables

Notes on Contributors

Bob Adamson is International Director in the TESOL Unit at Queensland University of Technology, Brisbane, Australia. He has published in the fields of curriculum studies, teacher education, higher education and comparative education, with particular interest in English Language education and China.
b.adamson@qut.edu.au

Gary Barkhuizen is a Senior Lecturer in the Department of Applied Language Studies and Linguistics at the University of Auckland, New Zealand. He has taught ESL and has been involved in language teacher education in South Africa, the USA, and New Zealand. His research interests include language-in-education planning, learner perceptions of their learning, and the social context of language learning.
g.barkhuizen@auckland.ac.nz

Helen Basturkmen is a Senior Lecturer in the Department of Applied Language Studies and Linguistics at the University of Auckland, New Zealand, where she teaches courses in discourse analysis and methodology for language teachers. Her research interests are in ESP, spoken discourse, teacher beliefs, and focus on form.
h.basturkmen@auckland.ac.nz

Andrew C. Billings is an Assistant Professor in the Department of Communication Studies at Clemson University, USA. His research interests lie within the persuasive aspects of language attitudes and media portrayals of identity.
acbilng@clemson.edu

David Birdsong is Professor of French at the University of Texas at Austin, USA, having previously held positions in Linguistics and Romance Languages at the University of Florida, Georgetown University, and the Max Planck Institute for Psycholinguistics.
birdsong@ccwf.cc.utexas.edu

Kingsley Bolton is Professor in English Linguistics in the English Department, Stockholm University, Sweden. His interests are in sociolinguistics and world Englishes. He has published a number of books and articles on sociolinguistics, Asian Englishes, Hong Kong English, Chinese pidgin English, and Chinese secret societies.
kingsley.bolton@english.su.se

Kees de Bot is Chair of Applied Linguistics at the University of Groningen, The Netherlands. His recent research interests include foreign language attrition, the maintenance and shift of minority languages, language and aging, and the psycholinguistics of bilingual language processing.
c.l.j.de.bot@let.rug.nl

James Dean (JD) Brown is Professor of Second Language Studies at the University of Hawai'i at Manoa. His recent publications include *Using Surveys in Language Programs* (Cambridge University Press, 2001), *Criterion-Referenced Language Testing* (Cambridge University Press, 2002), *Doing Second Language Research* (Oxford University Press, 2002).
brownj@hawaii.edu

Urszula Clark is Principal Lecturer in English at the University of Wolverhampton, UK, where she teaches undergraduate courses in stylistics, language and power, narrative, twentieth-century fiction and creative writing, and postgraduate courses in stylistics. Her main research interests and publications are in the areas of pedagogical stylistics, detective fiction, and language and identity.
U.Clark@wlv.ac.uk

Timothy J. Curnow is a Postdoctoral Fellow at La Trobe University. He is a descriptive linguist, and has written a grammar of Awa Pit, a language spoken in Colombia. He works primarily on the typology of person marking and evidentiality.
tjcurnow@ozemail.com.au

Alan Davies is Emeritus Professor of Applied Linguistics at the University of Edinburgh, Scotland. His publications include *Principles of Language Testing* (Blackwell, 1990), *An Introduction to Applied Linguistics* (Edinburgh University Press, 1999), and *The Native Speaker: Myth and reality* (Multilingual Matters, 2003).
a.davies@ed.ac.uk

John Edwards is Professor of Psychology at St Francis Xavier University in Nova Scotia, Canada, and is editor of the *Journal of Multilingual and Multicultural Development*. His publications include *Language in Canada* (Cambridge University Press, 1998), *Multilingualism* (Penguin, 1995), and *Language, Society and Identity* (Blackwell, 1985). He is also the author of about 200 articles, chapters, and reviews.
jedwards@stfx.ca

Susan Ehrlich is Professor of Linguistics in the Department of Languages, Literatures and Linguistics at York University, Toronto, Canada. Her books

include *Point of View: A linguistic analysis of literary style* (Routledge, 1990), *Teaching American English Pronunciation* (Oxford University Press, 1992), and *Representing Rape: Language and sexual consent* (Routledge, 2001).
ehrlich@yorku.ca

Catherine Elder is Associate Professor in the Department of Applied Language Studies and Linguistics at the University of Auckland, New Zealand. Her research interests and publications span the areas of language testing, language program evaluation, and bilingualism. She is co-author of the *Dictionary of Language Testing* (Cambridge University Press, 1999) and co-editor of *Experimenting with Uncertainty: Essays in honour of Alan Davies* (Cambridge University Press, 2001).
c.elder@auckland.ac.nz

Rod Ellis is currently Professor and Head of the Department of Applied Language Studies and Linguistics, University of Auckland, New Zealand. His recent publications include *Task-Based Learning and Teaching* (Oxford University Press, 2003) and a text-book, *Impact Grammar* (Pearson Longman, 1999).
r.ellis@auckland.ac.nz

Rod Gardner is Senior Lecturer in Linguistics at the University of New South Wales, Australia. He coordinates the MA in Applied Linguistics program. His main research interests are Conversation Analysis, particularly response tokens. His book on this topic, *When Listeners Talk*, was published by Benjamins in 2001.
rod.gardner@unsw.edu.au

John Gibbons is Professor of Linguistics at the Hong Kong Baptist University. His main research interests are language and the law, and bilingualism. His publications include *Language and the Law* (Longman, 1994), *Learning, Keeping and Using Language* (Benjamins, 1990) and *Forensic Linguistics: Language in the Justice System* (Blackwell, 2003).
jgibbons@hkbu.edu.hk

Howard Giles is a Professor of Communication at the University of California, Santa Barbara, USA. He has had a longstanding interest in language attitude studies around the world. Current work revolves around the theme of intergroup communication, including cross-cultural studies of intergenerational communication and aging and police–citizen interactions.
HowieGiles@aol.com

Paul Gruba is a Lecturer in Computer Science and Software Engineering at The University of Melbourne, Australia. His research interests focus on computer-based learning and the comprehension of digitized video media.
p.gruba@unimelb.edu.au

Richard Johnstone is Professor of Education at the University of Stirling, Scotland, and Director of the Scottish Centre for Information on Language Teaching and Research (Scottish CILT). He is also Director of SCOTLANG, the

languages research network funded by the Scottish Higher Education Funding Council. He writes an annual review of the international research on the teaching and learning of second and foreign languages for the journal *Language Teaching*.
rmj1@stir.ac.uk

John E. Joseph is Professor of Applied Linguistics at the University of Edinburgh, Scotland. He has worked on issues of language standardization and linguistic identity, and their social, political, and educational ramifications in a range of Asian, European, and North American settings. He also works extensively in the history of linguistics and in the theory and practice of translation.
john.joseph@ed.ac.uk

Alan Kirkness is a member of the Department of Applied Language Studies and Linguistics at the University of Auckland, New Zealand. He was previously Professor of German in Auckland 1986–98 and a research linguist and practising lexicographer at the Institute for German Language in Mannheim 1974–86. His research interests are in European historical and pedagogical lexicology and lexicography with particular reference to English, German, and French.
a.kirkness@auckland.ac.nz

Claire Kramsch is Professor of German and Foreign Language Acquisition at the University of California at Berkeley, USA. Her research interests include: language, culture, and identity; discourse analysis and second language acquisition; language and literature. She is the author of *Content and Culture in Language Teaching* (Oxford University Press, 1993) and *Language and Culture* (Oxford University Press, 1998), and the editor of *Redrawing the Boundaries of Language Study* (Heinle and Heinle, 1995) and *Language Acquisition and Language Socialization. Ecological perspectives* (Continuum, 2002).
ckramsch@socrates.Berkeley.edu

Anthony J. Liddicoat is Associate Professor of Languages and Linguistics at Griffith University, Australia. He has worked in both descriptive and applied linguistics and his current research interests include language planning, languages in education, and conversation analysis.
T.Liddicoat@mailbox.gu.edu.au

William Littlewood has taught English, French, and German at secondary and tertiary level in the UK and Hong Kong. He is currently Professor for TESOL and Applied Linguistics at the Hong Kong Baptist University. His publications include *Communicative Language Teaching: An introduction* (Cambridge University Press, 1981) and *Teaching Oral Communication: A methodological framework* (Blackwell, 1992).
blittle@hkbu.edu.hk

Joseph Lo Bianco is Director of Language Australia: The National Languages and Literacy Institute; Visiting Professor, Education, University of Melbourne;

and Adjunct Professor, Languages and Comparative Cultural Studies, University of Queensland. His recent books are: *Teaching Invisible Culture: Classroom practice and theory* (Language Australia Publications, 2003), Voices *from Phnom Penh: Language and development* (Language Australia Publications, 2002), and *Australian Policy Activism in Language and Literacy* (Language Australia Publications, 2001).
joe.lobianco@languageaustralia.com.au

Heather Lotherington is Associate Professor of Multilingual Education at York University in Toronto, Canada, and past co-editor of *The Canadian Modern Language Review*. She has taught in many international contexts, including Australia, Fiji, England, Papua New Guinea, and Singapore. She researches bi- and multilingual education, particularly with regard to multiliteracies.
hlotherington@edu.yorku.ca

Tim McNamara is Professor in the Department of Linguistics and Applied Linguistics at the University of Melbourne, Australia. His research interests include language testing, language and identity, and the history of applied linguistics. He is the author of *Language Testing* (Oxford University Press, 2000), co-author of the *Dictionary of Language Testing* (Cambridge University Press, 1999), and co-editor of the *Routledge Applied Linguistics Reader* (Routledge, forthcoming).
t.mcnamara@linguistics.unimelb.edu.au

John McRae is Special Professor of Language in Literature Study at the University of Nottingham, UK. His recent publications include *The Language of Poetry* (Routledge, 1998), *The Penguin Guide to English Literature* (1995/2001), *The Routledge History of Literature in English* (1997/2001), and *Language, Literature and the Learner* (Longman, 1996).
j.mcab@wanadoo.fr

Anne Pauwels is Professor of Linguistics and Dean of the Faculty of Arts, Humanities and Social Sciences at the University of Western Australia. Her areas of research expertise and interest include language contact and language maintenance, language and gender, and cross-cultural communication.
apauwels@arts.uwa.edu.au

Alastair Pennycook is Professor of Language in Education at the University of Technology, Sydney. He is the author of *The Cultural Politics of English as an International Language* (Longman, 1994) and *English and the Discourses of Colonialism* (Routledge, 1998). He was guest editor of a special edition of *TESOL Quarterly* in 1999 on *Critical Approaches to TESOL*. His *Critical Applied Linguistics: A Critical Introduction* was published by Lawrence Erlbaum in 2001.
alastair.pennycook@uts.edu.au

Kanavillil Rajagopalan is Professor of Linguistics at the State University at Campinas (UNICAMP), Brazil. His research interests include philosophy of

language, linguistic pragmatics, applied linguistics, critical discourse analysis, English language teaching, poststructuralism, and postcolonialism.
rajagopalan@uol.com.br

Monika S. Schmid graduated from the Heinrich-Heine-Universität Düsseldorf with a PhD on L1 attrition among Jewish former citizens of that city. She currently holds a position in the English department of the Vrije Universiteit Amsterdam, The Netherlands, and her native German has almost completely attrited.
ms.schmid@let.vu.nl

Michael Stubbs is Professor of English Linguistics at the University of Trier, Germany. He has published widely in the areas of educational linguistics and corpus linguistics. His most recent books are *Text and Corpus Analysis* (Blackwell, 1996) and *Words and Phrases* (Blackwell, 2001).
stubbs@uni-trier.de

Rachel Sutton-Spence is Lecturer in Deaf Studies at the Centre for Deaf Studies at the University of Bristol, UK. She is co-author, with Bencie Woll, of the introductory textbook *The Linguistics of British Sign Language: An introduction* (Cambridge University Press, 1999). Her current research interest is sign language poetry.
rachel.spence@bristol.ac.uk

Hugh Trappes-Lomax is Deputy Director of the Institute for Applied Language Studies at the University of Edinburgh, Scotland. His interests include pedagogical grammar, learner dictionaries, and language in education in Africa. His publications include the *Oxford Wordfinder Dictionary* (Oxford University Press, 1997) *and Language in Language Teacher Education* (Benjamins, 2003).
H.Trappes-Lomax@ed.ac.uk

Eddie Williams is Senior Lecturer in the Department of Linguistics, University of Wales, Bangor. His interests and publications include psycholinguistic and sociolinguistic perspectives on literacy and language, especially with reference to developing countries.
elseø3@bangor.ac.uk

Bencie Woll joined the Department of Language and Communication Science at City University London, UK, in 1995 to take up the newly created Chair in Sign Language and Deaf Studies. She is the co-author with Rachel Sutton-Spence of *The Linguistics of British Sign Language: An introduction* (Cambridge University Press, 1999) and the winner of the 1999 Deaf Nation Award and of the 2000 BAAL Book Prize.
b.woll@city.ac.uk

Acknowledgments

The editors wish to thank staff and former staff of Blackwell Publishing (Linguistics), especially Tami Kaplan and Sarah Coleman, and our copy-editor Anna Oxbury. We are grateful to all the contributors to the volume for their interest and their patience. Most of all, we are grateful to one another.

The editors and publisher gratefully acknowledge the permission granted to reproduce the copyright material in this book:

Table 18.1 From J. Edwards, Sociopolitical aspects of language maintenance and loss: towards a typology of ethnic minority language situations. In W. Fase, K. Jaspaert, & S. Kroon (eds.), *Maintenance and Loss of Ethnic Minority Languages*, 1992. Amsterdam/Philadelphia: John Benjamins. With kind permission by John Benjamins Publishing Company, www.benjamins.com.

Figure 19.1 From D. Nunan, *Research Methods in Language Learning*, 1992. Cambridge: Cambridge University Press. © Cambridge University Press.

Figure 19.2 From J. D. Brown, *Using Surveys in Language Programs*, 2001. Cambridge: Cambridge University Press. © Cambridge University Press.

Figure 19.3 From D. M. Johnson, *Approaches to Research in Second Language Learning*, 1992. New York: Longman. © 1992 Pearson Education. Reprinted/adapted by permission of Pearson Education Ltd.

Figure 19.4 From L. van Lier, *The Classroom and the Language Learner: Ethnography and second language classroom research*, 1988. London: Longman. © Pearson Education. Reprinted by permission of Pearson Education Ltd.

Table 19.1 From R. Grotjahn, On the methodological basis of introspective methods. In C. Faerch & G. Kasper (eds.), *Introspection in Second Language Research*, 1987. Clevedon, UK: Multilingual Matters. © Multilingual Matters Ltd. Reprinted by permission of Multilingual Matters Ltd.

Table 19.2 From C. Reichardt and T. Cook, Beyond qualitative versus quantitative methods. In T. Cook & C. Reichardt (eds.), *Qualitative and Quantitative Methods in Education Research*, 1979. Beverly Hills, CA: Sage. © Sage Publications Inc. Reprinted by permission of Sage Publications Inc.

Table 19.3 Adapted from A. Lazaraton, Qualitative research in applied linguistics: A progress report, *TESOL Quarterly*, 29 (1995), 455–72.

Table 25.2 From C. A. Chapelle, CALL in search of research paradigms? *Language Learning and Technology*, 1(1), 19–43. Reproduced with the permission of Cambridge University Press and the author.

Figure 29.1 From J. A. Fishman, *Reversing Language Shift*, 1991. Clevedon, UK: Miltilingual Matters. © Multilingual Matters Ltd. Reprinted by permission of Multilingual Matters Ltd.

Figure 31.2 From S. Messick, Validity. In R. L. Linn (ed.), *Educational Measurement*, 1989 (3rd edn.). New York: Macmillan.

Every effort has been made to trace copyright holders and to obtain their permission for the use of copyright material. The publisher apologizes for any errors or omissions in the above list and would be grateful if notified of any corrections that should be incorporated in future reprints or editions of this book.

General Introduction
Applied Linguistics:
Subject to Discipline?

ALAN DAVIES AND CATHERINE ELDER

*'Tis of great use to the sailor to know the length of his line, though he cannot
with it fathom all the depths of the ocean. 'Tis well he knows that it is long
enough to reach the bottom, at such places as are necessary to direct his
voyage, and caution him against running upon shoals that may ruin him.
Our business here is not to know all things, but those which concern our
conduct. If we can find out those measures whereby a rational creature, put in
that state which man is in the world, may and ought to govern his opinions
and actions depending thereon, we need not be troubled that some other things
escape our knowledge.*

John Locke, *An Essay Concerning Human Understanding*, 1695

Role

Applied linguistics is often said to be concerned with solving or at least ameli-
orating social problems involving language. The problems applied linguistics
concerns itself with are likely to be: How can we teach languages better? How
can we diagnose speech pathologies better? How can we improve the training
of translators and interpreters? How can we write a valid language examination? How can we evaluate a school bilingual program? How can we determine the literacy levels of a whole population? How can we helpfully discuss
the language of a text? What advice can we offer a Ministry of Education on a
proposal to introduce a new medium of instruction? How can we compare the
acquisition of a European and an Asian language? What advice should we
give a defense lawyer on the authenticity of a police transcript of an interview
with a suspect?

This tradition of applied linguistics established itself in part as a response
to the narrowing of focus in linguistics with the advent in the late 1950s
of generative linguistics, and has always maintained a socially accountable
role, demonstrated by its central interest in language problems. But there is
another tradition of applied linguistics, which belongs to linguistics; it is

sometimes called Linguistics-Applied (L-A) but perhaps "applications of linguistics" would be a more appropriate title for this tradition. This version has become more noticeable in the last 20 years as theoretical linguistics has moved back from its narrowly formalist concern to its former socially accountable role (for example in Bible translation, developing writing systems, dictionary making). In this way the two traditions have come to resemble one another. Or have they? We discuss below whether there is still a distinction.

For the most part, those who write about applied linguistics accept that the label "applied linguistics" refers to language teaching (in its widest interpretation, therefore including speech therapy, translation and interpreting studies, language planning, etc.). Applied linguistics in this tradition is not new, whether from the more practical perspective: "Throughout the history of formal language teaching there has always been some sort of applied linguistics, as it is known today" (Mackey, 1965, p. 253), or whether we consider its role in the academy: "Applied linguistics is not the recent development that is sometimes supposed, but derives from the involvement of linguists in America, particularly Leonard Bloomfield and Charles C. Fries, in specialized language-teaching programs during and immediately after the second World War" (Howatt, 1984, p. 265). Within that tradition, applied linguistics has an honorable role:

> if there is one single source which has been responsible for stimulating innovation and activity [in language teaching], it is (in one or other of its various guises) applied linguistics. It has not performed miracles, but as a focus of enquiry, critical self-examination, and new ideas, it has enriched the profession at least as much as it has irritated it. (Howatt, 1984, p. 226)

One important source of that enrichment has been the journal *Language Learning*, published from the University of Michigan, providing a chronicle of the development of applied linguistics over the past 50 years (Catford, 1998). In a 1993 editorial the journal gave late recognition to the range of coverage beyond linguistics which applied linguistics embraced. Such recognition is significant. Coming out of the tradition of Charles Fries and Robert Lado at the University of Michigan, *Language Learning*, founded in 1948, was "the first journal in the world to carry the term 'applied linguistics' in its title" (*Language Learning*, 1967, pp. 2–3). But by "applied linguistics" what was meant was the "linguistics applied" version.

In the 1990s, the journal seems to have finally accepted the broader church that represents an Applied-Linguistics (A-L) as distinct from a Linguistics-Applied approach to language problems. The 1993 editors acknowledge "the wide range of foundation theories and research methodologies now used to study language issues." And they state that they intend to:

encourage the submission of more manuscripts from

(a) diverse disciplines, including applications of methods and theories from linguistics, psycholinguistics, cognitive science, ethnography, ethnomethodology. sociolinguistics, sociology, semiotics, educational inquiry, and cultural or historical studies, to address:

(b) fundamental issues in language learning, such as bilingualism, language acquisition, second and foreign language education, literacy, culture, cognition, pragmatics, and intergroup relations.

However, the official recognition of the "wide range of foundation theories and research methodologies now used to study language issues" comes at a price. That price is the abandoning of the term "Applied Linguistics" as a sub-heading in the journal's title. The explanation for this removal is that its replacement title, *Language Learning: A journal of research in language studies*, is now seen to be wider.

Corder (1973) was well aware that in limiting the coverage of applied linguistics to language teaching he was open to criticism. To some extent his defense was the mirror image of the *Language Learning* change of name. There the rationale was that the input was too undefined and therefore it was sensible to remove the label of applied linguistics. Corder argues that it is the output that is without shape and therefore it makes sense to limit the area of concern to one main object, that of language teaching. Such modesty is more appealing than enthusiastic and exaggerated claims such as: "This book is something of an exercise in applied linguistics – in the widest senses of that term in that it comprises all systematic knowledge about language in all its aspects" (Christophersen, 1973, p. 88).

Of course there are voices suggesting that applied linguistics can fulfill a role wider than language teaching (for example Kaplan, 1980; Davies, 1999). This is an attractive view, but it is tenable only if it allows for a clear overall limitation to either the input or the output. Otherwise it slips all too easily into claiming that the whole world is its oyster, that the area of concern is everywhere, the science of everything position, destabilizing the applied linguist who is left both site-less and sightless.

Definitions

Definitions of applied linguistics may take the form of a short statement, such as: "the theoretical and empirical investigation of real-world problems in which language is a central issue" (Brumfit, 1997, p. 93); they may occupy a course leading to a degree or diploma; or they may be instantiated within the covers of a volume or a set of volumes. Of this last there are two kinds: there is the single author book (for example Corder, 1973; Davies, 1999) and there is the collection of edited papers. Collections have the advantage over the single-author volume of wide and often specialist coverage of many areas, but they cannot compete with the single-author volume in terms of offering a coherent view of the field and indeed may give the sense of being assembled somewhat at random. In the last three years at least three edited collections have appeared: Grabe (2000), Schmitt (2002), and Kaplan (2002); and now we have this present volume. Schmitt and Celce-Murcia offer the following definition of Applied Linguistics, (which they place in inverted commas): "'Applied Linguistics' is using what we know about (a) language, (b) how it is learned, and (c) how it is used, in order to achieve some purpose or solve some problem in the real world" (Schmitt & Celce-Murcia, 2002, p. 1). They point out that: "Traditionally, the primary concerns of Applied Linguistics have been second language acquisition theory, second language pedagogy and the interface between the two, and it is these areas which this volume will cover" (Schmitt, 2002, p. 2). Grabe's definition is not far away: "the focus of applied linguistics is on trying to resolve language-based problems that people encounter in the real world, whether they be learners, teachers, supervisors, academics, lawyers, service providers, those who need social services, test takers, policy developers, dictionary makers, translators, or a whole range of business clients" (Grabe, 2002, p. 9).

In both cases – and indeed more generally – the "real world" is contrasted with, presumably, the laboratory or, perhaps, the linguist's intuition. And yet the real world is never accessible to research or teaching, as Labov (1966) has pointed out. And are students being taught a language in a classroom setting experiencing the real world? It has indeed been suggested that language teaching and the methods and materials it employs are no more representative of non-idealized spontaneous language use than are the grammatical examples that the linguist's intuition calls up. In fact, of course (and again Labov makes this point) once language use is focused on for study and analysis it ceases to exist in the real world. We make this point not because we wish to argue against collecting samples of real language use but because we consider that the distinction between real and non-real is a flaky one.

It may be that a helpful way of distinguishing between what linguistics and applied linguistics are concerned with is to distinguish between theory and data. Kaplan proposed that applied linguistics is simply not in the business of developing new theories. Its concern is with new data. Looking forward, Kaplan suggests that applied linguists "are likely to move toward the analysis of new data, rather than continue to argue new theory" (Kaplan, 2002, p. 514). As such, the linguistics that will be of most use to the upcoming applied linguistics will be descriptive linguistics.

Kaplan and Grabe used as the title of an earlier publication: "Applied linguistics as an emerging discipline (Grabe, 2000). How helpful is it to consider applied linguistics as a discipline (rather than say as a subject)? No doubt the labeling is a way of assuming coherence and at the same time of distinguishing between applied linguistics and linguistics.

But is it appropriate to refer to applied linguistics, as Kaplan and Grabe do in their title, as an emerging discipline? It surely makes more sense to use the

The relativization of all knowledge within postmodernism, as well as the critique provided by critical applied linguistics (CAL) (Pennycook, 2001) creates a tension between the desire for an ethics and at the same time a mistrust of what may be regarded as the imposition of a universal ethics. Furthermore (and fortunately) a healthy skepticism among practicing applied linguists makes for quite modest ethical claims, typically "within reason." In this way the profession makes clear that it does not claim what cannot be delivered, thus escaping from the charge of hypocrisy. Of course, there are always ethical issues to be addressed in the projects undertaken by applied linguistics: Why is this being undertaken? Who stands to gain? Where does power lie? Interestingly, these are very similar questions to those asked by critical applied linguistics, which suggests that critical applied linguistics is a postmodern version of an ethics of applied linguistics.

L-A and A-L

We have distinguished between two traditions, that of applied linguistics and that of applications of linguistics. Widdowson presents the question in terms of linguistics applied and applied linguistics:

> The differences between these modes of intervention is that in the case of linguistics applied the assumption is that the problem can be reformulated by the direct and unilateral application of concepts and terms deriving from linguistic enquiry itself. That is to say, language problems are amenable to linguistics solutions. In the case of applied linguistics, intervention is crucially a matter of mediation . . . applied linguistics . . . has to relate and reconcile different representations of reality, including that of linguistics without excluding others. (Widdowson, 2000, p. 5)

The "linguistics applied" view seems to derive from the coming together of two traditions:

1 the European philological tradition which was exported to the USA through scholars such as Roman Jakobson,
2 the North American tradition of linguistic-anthropological field-work which required the intensive use of non-literate informants and the linguistic description of indigenous languages for the purposes of cultural analysis.

The social value of applications of linguistics was widely canvassed. Bloomfield (1933, p. 509) hoped that "The methods and results of linguistics . . . [and] the study of language may help us toward the understanding and control of human affairs." In the 1970s R. H. Robins, representing the European tradition, was eager to encourage the use of linguistic ideas and methods: "The teacher who understands and can make use of the methods of scientific linguistics will find the task of presenting a language to his pupils very much lightened and facilitated" (1971/1980, p. 308). Fifty years after Bloomfield, Douglas Brown (1987) was still making a similar claim: "Applied linguistics has been considered a subset of linguistics for several decades, and it has been interpreted to mean the applications of linguistics principles to certain more or less practical matters" (p. 147).

This tradition represents the "expert" view of knowledge and scholarship. It takes for granted that the methods and findings of linguistics are of value to others to solve their problems. But the applications must be carried out either by linguists themselves or by those who have understood and can make use of the methods of scientific linguistics. There is no place here for Corder's applied linguist as a consumer of theories, in which linguistics is one among a number of different source disciplines, let alone for the extreme proposal made by Widdowson that linguistics is itself part of applied linguistics. Critiques and counter-critiques in the journals suggest that the opposing traditions have become more entrenched. Gregg (1990) argues the case for a unitary position on second language acquisition research, while Ellis (1990) and Tarone (1990) declare themselves in favor of the variationist position. Ellis contrasts two models of research, the research-then-theory position, which is essentially inductive, as against theory-then-research, the mainstream classic tradition, which is essentially deductive. We may surmise that the theory-then-research approach is that of linguistics while the research-then-theory is that of applied linguistics. For Gregg, the research-then-theory approach is not serious because it is not based on theory.

So much for the linguistics-applied tradition. What of the applied-linguistics tradition? The two traditions overlap in the work of Henry Sweet. Howatt claims that "Sweet's work established an applied tradition in language teach-ing which has continued uninterruptedly to the present day" (Howatt, 1984, p. 189). Howatt also refers to the influence of J. R. Firth, holder of the first Chair of General Linguistics in the UK, who had first-hand experience of language learning and teaching in India, and who with the anthropologist Bronislaw Malinowski and their pupil Michael Halliday promoted the notion of the context of situation. No doubt because of Firth's lead, the identity of the context of situation school is still that of linguistics-applied in spite of its strong social orientation. John Trim records his view of the origin of the British Association of Applied Linguistics in an address which represents the view of the linguist looking at society's problems: "Members of Departments of Linguistics were present (at the inaugural meeting) because of their wish to see the findings of their science brought to bear on the social problems of the day" (1988, p. 9).

The real push to a coherent conception of the activity, an applied linguistics view, came from Corder who, while insisting on the centrality of linguistics, accepted the need for other inputs. It came even more strongly from Peter Strevens who was unashamedly eclectic in what he saw as a growing discipline. His account of the founding of the British Association for Applied

Linguistics emphasizes the sociological and institutional reasons for forming a new professional group.

> The fundamental question . . . facing applied linguists in Britain in 1965 was whether they were sufficiently like linguists (i.e. theoretical linguists) to remain within the linguists' organization, or whether they were sufficiently like teachers of foreign languages, including English, to remain within their organizations, or whether they were sufficiently different from both to merit an organization of their own.   (Strevens, 1980, p. 31)

What made those inaugural members interested in founding the new BAAL Association was that they had first-hand experience of the social problems that linguistic applications were addressing. What they looked to "applied linguistics" for was a framework for conceptualizing and contemplating those problems.

This Volume

In preparing this volume, we were struck by the tension between our descriptive responsibility – setting out the range of current interpretations of applied linguistics – and what we may ourselves regard as our normative concern, to attempt to define applied linguistics as being a coherent and limiting enterprise. That is how we see applied linguistics. When we planned this volume, we had in mind the distinction A-L/L-A, where A-L looks outward, beyond language in an attempt to explain, perhaps even ameliorate social problems, while L-A looks inward, concerned not to solve language problems "in the real world" but to explicate and test theories about language itself. So L-A uses language data to develop our linguistic knowledge about language, while A-L studies a language problem (an aphasia, let us say, or a speech impediment, such as a speech therapist studies) with a view to correcting it. The difference is large but, we must admit, not always clear-cut. In our set-up letter for the volume we declared our hand as follows:

> Applied Linguistics is, in our view, a coherent activity which theorizes through speculative and empirical investigations real-world problems in which language is a central issue. By careful selection of topic (and of author) we intend to offer a coherent account of applied linguistics as an independent and coherent discipline, which, like similar vocational activities (for example general medicine, business studies, applied psychology, legal studies) seeks to marry practical experience and theoretical understanding of language development and language in use.
>   We distinguish linguistics and applied linguistics in terms of difference of orientation. While linguistics is primarily concerned with language in itself and with language problems in so far as they provide evidence for better language description or for teaching a linguistic theory, applied linguistics is interested in

language problems for what they reveal about the role of language in people's daily lives and whether intervention is either possible or desirable. What this means is that applied linguistics is as much concerned with context as with language and will therefore be likely to draw on disciplines other than linguistics, for example, anthropology, education, psychology. It also means that the language problems with which applied linguistics concerns itself are often concerned with institutions, for example the school, the work-place, the law-court, the clinic.

So much for our invitation position 3 years ago. With the due passage of time since that letter, our experience with assembling and categorizing the 32 contributory chapters to the volume has tempered our view somewhat. What we have been compelled to realize is that the L-A/A-L distinction is sustainable only at the extremes. Thus the chapters on language attrition or language description may be regarded as largely L-A, while the concerns of second language learning or of computer assisted language learning are mainly to do with A-L. But in between the distinction is hard to make. It is probably easiest for those topics in A-L which deal with issues of language learning and language teaching because they have to do with the "real world," that locution we all refer to when we think of how language is used rather than how it is studied. However, even in the area of language learning and language teaching the distinction falters and changes. Thus the topics of contrastive analysis and error analysis, which were both central to applied linguistics in its concern with language learning and language teaching, have evolved into the highly theoretical concern of Second Language Acquisition (SLA) Research which is now less involved with language learning and language teaching and more concerned with linguistic and cognitive theorizing (see Birdsong, and Rajagopalan, this volume).

To an extent this reflects a wider development in the last 40 or 50 years. Thus contrastive analysis and error analysis have morphed into SLA research not only because researchers working in error analysis and contrastive analysis have become more and more interested in (and successful through) theoretical approaches to language acquisition, but also because researchers with a training and a background in theoretical linguistics have extended their data base to take account of language in use (in that "real world"). There are perhaps two reasons for this. The first reflects a wider philosophical shift from a rational, realist, universalist persuasion to a nominalist, relativist point of view. This, of course, is not a new view of language, simply a return to fashion of the interest in individual languages and in language varieties that was in abeyance during the long years of Chomskyan dominance. The second reason is the emergence of tools and methods for collecting and analyzing "real-world" language events, from the tape-recorder to the computer, with the concomitant development of, for example, Conversation Analysis and corpus linguistics and lexicography. And so, that gap between a linguistics concerned solely with an idealized language and an applied linguistics, which took as its concern not just language learning and language teaching but all areas of language in use, has become increasingly filled by those trained in linguistics, who take for granted that their proper study is language use (in the "real world") and that it is legitimate to have a dual concern for their data, a concern with the "problems" they encounter and a concern with the theory they employ, using their data to test the theory.

Is there, then, still a distinction between L-A and A-L? Our answer is that there is but that it cannot easily be found in the topics of interest. Rather, it is found in the orientation of the researchers, and why they are investigating a problem and collecting their data. Do they regard themselves as linguists applying linguistics or as applied linguists doing applied linguistics? Are they investigating because they wish to validate a theory? If so, that is L-A. Or is it because they seek a practical answer to a language problem? That is A-L. We do, of course, recognize that in some, perhaps many, cases the researcher will have both interests at heart.

We have therefore decided to make two divisions in this volume. The first is that of linguistics-applied; the second that of applied-linguistics. Having said that, we accept that the division is not safe and is in some cases problematic. For example, the chapters on discourse analysis; stylistics; language, culture, and thought: these, now in L-A, as well as others, could just as easily have been placed in the other category. It is revealing that when pressed as to why the chapters on language planning and language maintenance (to take two examples) are in A-L, we lean on the centrality to A-L of language learning and language teaching, taking for granted that language planning and language maintenance are largely concerned with intervention. In the cases of stylistics and of language, culture, and thought, our decision to place them in L-A was based on a judgment that their primary concern is with language; but that judgment could easily have gone the other way because of their importance in language learning and language teaching.

ACKNOWLEDGMENT

This General Introduction draws in part on Davies (1999 and 2003).

REFERENCES

Allen, J., Patrick B. & Corder, S. P. (eds.) (1973–5) *The Edinburgh course in applied linguistics* (vols 1–3). (Vol. 1, 1973: *Readings for applied linguistics*; vol. 2, 1974: *Techniques in applied linguistics*; vol. 3, 1975: *Papers in applied linguistics*.) London: Oxford University Press.

Allen, J., Patrick B. & Davies, A. (1977) *The Edinburgh course in applied linguistics*, vol. 4: *Testing and experiment in applied linguistics*. London: Oxford University Press.

Angelis, P. (2001) The roots of applied linguistics in North America. Colloquium on The Roots of Applied Linguistics in Different Contexts. St Louis: AAAL.

BAAL (1994). *Draft recommendations on good practice in applied linguistics*. Lancaster: British Association of Applied Linguistics.

Baynham, M. (2001) Applied linguistics: imagining the future. *Applied Linguistics Association of Australia Newsletter*, new series 44, 26–8.

Bloomfield, L. (1933) *Language*. London: Allen and Unwin.

Brown, H. D. (1987) *Principles of language learning and teaching*. Englewood Cliffs, NJ: Prentice-Hall.

Brumfit, C. (1997) How applied linguistics is the same as any other science. *International Journal of Applied Linguistics*, 7(1), 86–94.

Catford, J. I. C. (1998) Language learning and applied linguistics: a historical sketch. *Language Learning*, 48(4), 465–96.

Christophersen, P. (1973) *Second language learning: myth and reality*. Harmondsworth: Penguin.

Corder, S. P. (1973) *Introducing applied linguistics*. Harmondsworth: Penguin.

Davies, A. (1999) *An introduction to applied linguistics: from practice to theory*. Edinburgh: Edinburgh University Press.

Davies, A. (2001) British applied linguistics. Colloquium on The Roots of Applied Linguistics in Different Contexts. St Louis: AAAL.

Davies, A. (2003) Applied linguistics: subject to discipline? *New Zealand Studies in Applied Linguistics*, 9(1), 1–17.

Ellis, R. (1990). A response to Gregg. *Applied Linguistics*, 11(4), 384–91.

Grabe, W. (ed.) (2000) Applied linguistics as an emerging discipline. *Annual Review of Applied Linguistics*, 2.

Grabe, W. (2001). Applied linguistics in the 21st Century. *Applied Linguistics Association of Australia Newsletter*, new series 44, 24–6.

Grabe, W. (2002) Applied linguistics: an emerging discipline for the twenty-first century. In R. B. Kaplan (ed.), *The Oxford handbook of applied linguistics* (pp. 3–12). Oxford: Oxford University Press.

Gregg, K. R. (1990) The variable competence model of second language acquisition and why it isn't. *Applied Linguistics*, 11(4), 364–83.

House, E. R. (1990) Ethics of evaluation studies. In H. J. Walburg & G. D. Haerte (eds.), *The international encyclopedia of educational evaluation* (pp. 91–4). Oxford: Pergamon.

Howatt, A. P. R. (1984) *A history of English language teaching*. Oxford: Oxford University Press.

Kaplan, R. B. (1980) On the scope of linguistics, applied and non-. In R. B. Kaplan (ed.), *On the scope of applied linguistics* (pp. 76–80). Rowley, MA: Newbury House.

Kaplan, R. B. (ed.) (2002) *The Oxford handbook of applied linguistics*. Oxford: Oxford University Press.

Kaplan, R. B. and Grabe, W. (2000) Applied linguistics and the Annual Review of Applied Linguistics. In Grabe, W. (ed.), *Applied linguistics as an emerging discipline. Annual Review of Applied Linguistics*, 20, 3–17.

Koehn, D. (1994) *The ground of professional ethics*. London: Routledge.

Labov, W. (1966) *The social stratification of English in New York City*. Washington, DC: Center for Applied Linguistics.

Lewis, M. (2001) Looking ahead in applied linguistics. *Applied Linguistics Association of Australia Newsletter*, new series 44, 18–19.

Mackey, W. F. (1965) *Language teaching analysis*. London: Longman.

McNamara, T. (2001) The roots of applied linguistics in Australia. Colloquium on The Roots of Applied Linguistics in Different Contexts. St Louis: AAAL.

Pennycook, A. (2001) *Critical applied linguistics: a (critical) introduction.* Mahwah NJ/London: Lawrence Erlbaum.

Rampton, B. (1997) Retuning in applied linguistics. *International Journal of Applied Linguistics*, 7(1), 3–25.

Robins, R. H. (1971/1980) *General linguistics: an introductory survey.* London: Longman.

Schmitt, N. (ed.) (2002) *An introduction to applied linguistics.* London: Arnold.

Schmitt, N. & Celce-Murcia, M. (2002) An overview of applied linguistics. In N. Schmitt (ed.), *An introduction to applied linguistics* (pp. 1–16). London: Arnold.

Strevens, P. D. (1980) Who are applied linguists and what do they do? A British point of view on the establishment of the American Association of Applied Linguistics. In R. B. Kaplan, (ed.), *On the scope of applied linguistics* (pp. 28–36). Rowley, MA: Newbury House.

Tarone, E. (1990) On variation in interlanguage: a response to Gregg. *Applied Linguistics*, 11(4), 392–400.

Trim, J. L. M. (1988) Applied linguistics in society. In P. Grunwell (ed.), *Applied linguistics in society* (pp. 3–15). London: CILTR.

Webster, N. (1994). *Ninth new collegiate dictionary of the English language.* New York: Black Dog and Leventhal.

Widdowson, H. (2000) On the limitations of linguistics applied. *Applied Linguistics*, 21(1), 3–25.

Introduction to Part I:
Linguistics Applied (L-A)

ALAN DAVIES

We have argued in our general introduction that while the distinction between Linguistics Applied (L-A) and Applied Linguistics (A-L) is fugitive, it remains necessary and that it is at its most obvious in the orientation of the researchers, why they are investigating a problem and collecting their data. If they regard themselves as linguists applying linguistics because they wish to validate a theory, that is linguistics applied (L-A). If they see themselves as applied linguists because they seek a practical answer to a language problem, that is applied linguistics (A-L). Having made that distinction, we offered the caveat: "We do, of course, recognize that in some, perhaps many, cases the researcher will have both interests at heart." We should also point out that the orientation of the researchers, how they regard themselves, what it is they wish to achieve, is not always obvious. Even when asked, researchers may not be clear.

The L-A chapters that follow in Part I present a tendency, a tendency toward the investigation of language using linguistic or other modes of investigation. What I propose to do is to group the 16 chapters in Part I into six sections; the sections themselves providing a cline from closest to the linguistics of language to the more distant connection. Thus in Section 1 we have the Liddicoat and Curnow chapter (on descriptive linguistics) which offers a descriptive apparatus for the linguistic areas of grammar and phonology. Such a chapter could with ease fit into a handbook dealing with linguistic descriptions. No problem there! The border between L-A and A-L is not marked and just as A-L needs linguistics, so too L-A requires a means of handling its application. Also in Section 1 is the Kirkness chapter on lexicography. The purpose of the Liddicoat and Curnow chapter is "to introduce applied linguists to the broad themes and general concepts with which linguists work in developing descriptive accounts of language". Applied linguists, they argue, need "a certain level of familiarity with the principles of linguistics" so that "the work of applied linguistics can be carried out in an informed and principled way" For Liddicoat and Curnow linguistics is system and while this may not be the driving force in applied linguistics, applied linguists must come to grips with language as a system since "linguistic and language description is basic to applied linguists' work". To that end, Liddicoat and Curnow provide an introduction to phonetics/phonology, grammar, and semantics.

Their chapter therefore is linguistics for applied linguists and as such very much at the linguistic end of L-A. In his chapter on lexicography, Alan Kirkness is similarly more linguistic than applied. Even so, as he points out, lexicology operates at the level of particular languages and while, in doing so, it makes use of linguistic procedures and constructs, it is powerfully concerned with the uses made of lexical research. Kirkness maintains that there is and always has been at the heart of lexicology an interest in application. Most particularly in dictionary making for various purposes. And he ends with a compelling plea for a close link between lexicology and lexicography, between the theoretical and the practical, between the linguistic and the applied. What that means is that lexicology belongs, in our terms, to L-A and, within L-A stands at the linguistic end of that approach.

Section 2 consists of chapters that investigate language in terms of the uses that are made of it. For David Birdsong, second langauge acquisition (SLA, or, as he puts it, L2A) is "a central concern of Applied Linguistics (or more precisely . . . of Linguistics Applied)". Such a view is orthodox among SLA researchers: for them (as for Birdsong), the purpose of SLA research is to further our linguistic understanding, not to develop more effective ways of learning and teaching languages. Of course, such spin-offs may follow, but they would be incidental to the role they envision for SLA research, to model and promote our understanding of language and its acquisition. Birdsong's take on the topic is not mainstream in that instead of the more usual account of initial SLA, he discusses "the end state" or "ultimate attainment." He reminds us that "ultimate attainment data are invaluable for ongoing mainstream research in L2A theory, in that they afford unique perspectives on the limits of L2A . . . Clearly, for educators and social-policy makers, as well as for theorists, it is of compelling interest to know more about the rate of native-like attainment". Such an approach could illumine "the most basic issue on L2A research . . . whether the difference in ends (i.e. final states) implies different means (i.e. learning procedures). As well as the L2-L1 comparison, Birdsong addresses the age factor in SLA. While his orientation is very obviously L-A, it is all too clear that his interest in the basic issues of L1-L2 and of age of acquisition are also of central interest to A-L.

For Mike Stubbs, the advent of computerized corpora provides a kind of paradigm shift in linguistic description and in our understanding of language and its development over time. What corpus study does is to bring together as parameters (and therefore unfalsifiable) populations of language tokens across individuals. In other words, what linguistics has always done manually and partially. For our purposes, then, corpus study necessarily falls into the L-A area: "no linguist" Stubbs claims "can now ignore corpus data". But does corpus study do more, does it have any applied reach? For Stubbs there are areas of application: he mentions language teaching, lexicography, translation studies, stylistics, forensic linguistics, cultural representation, and psycho-linguistics. But his claims are modest. While he is unapologetic regarding the value of corpus study for linguistic descriptions (he calls himself an enthusiast here), he offers a conservative view of applications "arguing that applications are indirect, and that before findings can be applied to real-world problems, they require careful interpretation". What we can be sure of is that corpus studies, like lexicography, like discourse analysis, are good for linguistics. Are they good for applied linguistics?

Trappes-Lomax reminds us that discourse analysis is practiced by scholars in many disciplines and not only by those working in linguistics and applied linguistics. The "linguistic turn" in the social sciences has largely been about this continuing interest in discourse analysis, which recognizes the value of non-experimental and non-quantitative methods in managing evidence. Trappes-Lomax takes us through the five areas he terms "focal issues" in discourse analysis: these are interaction, context, function, instrumentalities, and text. He defines discourse analysis as "the study of language viewed communicatively and/or of communication viewed linguistically". Such a wide lens may be too generous since it can be seen as inflating the claim to our attention of discourse analysis by equating it with applied linguistics. There is a warning here. As with SLA (and indeed critical applied linguistics), the excitement and enthusiasm for the research interest may encourage inflation in the value of the research such that then applied linguistics becomes wholly SLA or CAL, or, in this case discourse analysis. But what cannot be denied is Trappes-Lomax's claim that discourse analysis is necessary "to our under-standing of language, of society, and of ourselves as human beings . . . it is useful – in an ever expanding range of practical and socially beneficial act-ivities . . . (and) it is . . . endlessly interesting".

One of the ways in which linguistic theory can be applied to language problems is by differing ways of linguistic description: we saw that in Sec-tion 1, particularly with the Liddicoat and Curnow chapter which provides a methodology for description at a level more abstract than an individual language. Thus the writing of a grammar of English (or of Japanese) would be a way of describing language at a somewhat less abstract level. The chapter by Sutton-Spence and Woll therefore belongs here since it concerns the descrip-tion of a particular language, in this case British Sign Language (BSL), and what the chapter discusses is how linguistic procedures and methods can be implemented in order to establish a description of BSL. For Sutton-Spence and Woll, BSL is a minority language; but so of course are many oral languages. It is British (as is English, as are the Celtic languages . . .), it has its own speech community, again like all oral languages, but uniquely it is a visual language. In other words, for Sutton-Spence and Woll, BSL is fundamentally a language: the fact that it uses visemes rather than phonemes is, in a profound sense, trivial.

In Section 3 we examine approaches that uncover the connections between speakers and their language, thus Giles and Billings, Schmid and de Bot,

Kramsch, and Gardner. In their chapter ASSESSING LANGUAGE ATTITUDES: SPEAKER EVALUATION STUDIES, Giles and Billings explore the interaction between language, communications, and social judgments, recognizing, as they do, that "the effects of language on social judgment is an integral part of uncovering the communication process". What speakers use language for, in other words, is to make judgments about their interlocutors: the fact that social judgments are often stereotypical emphasizes that it is a language rather than a linguistic evaluation that is being made.

Schmid and de Bot examine in their chapter various approaches to the study of language attrition, pointing out that just as languages are gained/acquired so they are lost: they investigate the phenomenon of loss at the individual and the community level, noting that languages are lost both deliberately and non-deliberately, through migration, contact, aging, and trauma. How far language attrition and SLA are mirror images remains an intriguing question. For our purposes, what Schmid and deBot (like Giles and Billings) are centrally concerned with is the ways in which speakers relate to their (and others') language.

As well as viewing language as a resource and/or commodity, as Schmid and de Bot do, we can also regard it as both vehicle and simulation of thought and culture. This is the concern of Claire Kramsch in her chapter LANGUAGE, THOUGHT, AND CULTURE. Kramsch traces the progress of applied linguistics from its universalist certainty in the 1950s and 1960s through to its more questioning, context-sensitive relativism of today. She takes three areas to demonstrate this shift in linguistics: semantic relativism, linguistic relativism, and discursive relativism and then maintains that this shift has followed on, lagging behind, in applied linguistics. This has, she maintains, affected the orientation of speakers to their language above all in language education: "language relativity suggests reorienting the focus of language teachers from what they do to who they are".

Gardner's chapter on conversation analysis (CA) provides another take on the ways in which speakers use language: as we have seen, they form attitudes toward it, they view it as part culture and part culture bearing, and they lose it. In all cases, what the analyst is doing is focusing on the interaction between the speaker and the language. Here too in Gardner's account of conversation analysis we see a similar focusing. Gardner shows how CA borrowed three basic themes from ethnomethodology: accountability, reflexivity, and indexicality. As well as being grammatical and appropriate, speakers are accountable, reflexive, and indexical for the purpose of effective interaction. And it is these themes that CA studies, what Gardner refers to as "the complexities, local design and quiddity of instances of talk", in other words, how language is used to create language meanings. To what extent the systematic use of conversation should take account of "local design and quiddity of instances" remains unclear. Gardner appears not to take the Kramsch view, and concludes that "ordinary conversation is likely, at least in many of its instances, to be universal".

In Section 4 we place three chapters that concern various functional uses of language: LANGUAGE AND THE LAW, LANGUAGE AND GENDER, and STYLISTICS. In all three cases, while the traffic is both ways, what seems primary is the light thrown by these functions on the language itself. What distinguishes Section 4 from Section 3 is that while Section 3 deals with applied linguistics in terms of language, Section 4 concerns applied linguistics in terms of language use. Gibbons, writing on language and the law (also termed "forensic linguistics") proposes that the law is an applied linguistic issue because the law (unlike, say, medicine) is based on and mediated through language. His chapter examines four sources of the problems that arise: the "genre" issue ("the specialized text structure and procedures used in the law"), the "writtenness" of legal documents (that is, that they are accessible only through reading), the "technicality" of legal discourse (rendering its understanding inaccessible to non-lawyers), and the "interpersonal arena" (given the power imbalance in legal processes). Gibbons presents legal language as a type of code: making that code accessible to those in need ("people who cannot understand the legislation impacting on their lives, witnesses whose testimony is distorted by linguistic pressure tactics, minorities whose language cannot be used or who are subjected to group vilification, or the guilty or innocent convicted by language evidence" is a proper task for L-A.

Susan Ehrlich (LANGUAGE AND GENDER) maintains that people *do* gender through the linguistic choices they make. Gendered language is therefore a (deliberate) choice made by speakers. In the same way that lawyers construct their legal identity through language, so do men and women construct their (gendered) identity through linguistic practices. Interestingly, Ehrlich makes a convincing case for bringing together the two main areas of language and gender research: the study of language use and the study of sexist language. Her argument is that the one is the product of the other, that sexism is an act (doing things with words) with outcomes affecting identity and judgments. This is a relativist neo-Whorfian view and fits well with the Kramsch discussion above on language, thought, and culture.

McRae and Clark recognize that stylistics "has proved notoriously difficult to define, since it functions as an umbrella term". For our purposes, what is of interest in stylistics is its concern with a particular language use (its textness, originally entirely literary, more recently quite general). We might think that stylistics would make a more powerful impact if it was still wholly concerned with literary texts. Even more than language and the law, stylistics is language bound. The authors explain how valuable stylistics can be in the teaching of literature as a foreign language, hardly surprising given the long centuries during which literature featured as a main (perhaps the main) component of language teaching. What this chapter does is to make a case for stylistics as a way of applying linguistics to the educational study and understanding of (literary) texts.

Section 5 contains two chapters dealing with the influence of language in external affairs, notably in politics. Thus Joseph proposes that "the study of language and politics is aimed at understanding the role of linguistic communication in the functioning of social units, and how this role shapes language itself". Language influences the political; equally the political influences language. In the case of language and the law, language is the medium of the law; here, in the case of language and politics, language is substance as well as medium. One of the examples Joseph quotes is that of the globalization of English as an instrument of linguistic imperialism. It is this topic of the spread of English (here called world Englishes) that Kingsley Bolton addresses in his chapter. Bolton helpfully points to the dilemma of applied linguistics in approaching the fact of World Englishes where "considerable problems for applied linguistics still exist in the area of pedagogical principles and practices. He refers to local attitudes and official practices, noting that the way ahead may require "new and creative approaches" which might mean the reorientation of the whole concept of World Englishes from its current L-A status to one that is more A-L.

The last section (Section 6) in this part of the volume has only one chapter. Kanavillil Rajagopalan's THE PHILOSOPHY OF APPLIED LINGUISTICS. His chapter exercises a Janus-like function in the volume, looking back at L-A and forward to A-L. This encompassing embrace is provided by Rajagopalan's historical overview, an account both of periods and ideas. The chapter charts the beginnings in the mid twentieth century when linguistics was the driving force in applied linguistics, through the Chomskyan revolution (bringing with it the long-term emphasis on SLA research and what Rajagopalan calls "the apotheosis of the native speaker"). And so to the sunny uplands of interdisciplinarity where L-A yields to A-L, the underlying topic of our Part II. The story does not end on those uplands, as Rajagopalan makes clear, but moves on to a putative post-A-L, which is what critical applied linguistics claims to be. It is not accidental therefore that the last chapter in our Part II (A-L) and in the volume deals with critical applied linguistics. That is for later. We turn now to the 16 chapters in Part I, the L-A approach to applied linguistics.

1 Language Descriptions

ANTHONY J. LIDDICOAT AND TIMOTHY J. CURNOW

1.1 Introduction

The importance of language description in applied linguistics has sometimes been questioned (e.g. by Widdowson, 1979, 1980) because of a perception that the theoretical insights of descriptive linguistics are different from the practical needs of language pedagogy. Linguistics has increasingly separated itself from a prescriptive view of language, which formulates rules for what should be said or written, in favor of a descriptive view, which seeks to record the language which people actually use. Contemporary language description, therefore, takes a synchronic approach, that is, language is described as it is at a particular moment in time and does not incorporate the history of the language (diachrony), although languages do of course change over time.

The descriptive view has led linguists to new insights about language and new ways of talking about and defining units of language. However, in many cases applied linguistics has required a prescriptive grammar recognizing that language teaching is frequently a case of teaching what should be done (Odlin, 1994). In other words, pedagogical grammar has been equated with prescriptive grammar. Pedagogical grammars have tended to adhere to the concepts and terminology of traditional grammar, based on the linguistic categories found in Latin and Ancient Greek, and, especially in the case of first language teaching, often have had a diachronic perspective, favoring rules based on earlier forms of the language. Recently, however, especially with the introduction of corpus-based materials into language classrooms, pedagogical grammar has taken on a more descriptive focus, with learners being required to deduce rules from linguistic data (cf. Tomlin, 1994; Kennedy & Miceli, 2001).

At the same time, applied linguistics itself is not entirely a pedagogy-focused discipline and many areas of applied linguistics have pursued language description as a central feature of their work. This is especially true of first and second language acquisition, where much work has been done on the description of learner grammars. Moreover, language standardization and vernacular language literacy have both faced the challenges involved in bridging the divide between description and prescription and the development of pedagogical grammars from language descriptions.

Applied linguistics is focused on language, and while many applied linguists are not directly involved with language description, knowledge of the approaches and concepts of linguistic description is an important part of the working knowledge of any applied linguist (cf. Stubbs, 1986). In this chapter, we aim to give a brief overview of the main dimensions of linguistic description and the key concepts involved. The terms we use here are generally accepted, however particular theories may use different terms or define these terms in slightly different ways.

Descriptions of language are often divided into a number of categories and each of these categories has its own principles, concepts, and objects of study. For this paper we have separated language description into the study of the sounds of language (phonetics and phonology), language structures (morphology, syntax, and information structure), and meaning (semantics).

1.2   Phonetics

Most languages are transmitted by sounds and one of the most obvious differences between languages is that they sound different. The study of the sounds that human beings make in their languages is known as phonetics. While sign languages, such as British Sign Language and American Sign Language, are clearly not transmitted by sound, there are units in sign languages which correspond to phonetics and phonology, but these will not be discussed here (other areas of language description apply equally to spoken and sign languages).

1.2.1   Transcribing sounds

We are used to the idea of representing language in writing; however, conventional writing systems are not adequate to represent sounds. We need only consider the problems inherent in English spellings such as *cough, dough*, and *through* or the different pronunciations of words in US and UK English to see the problems involved in using conventional spellings to represent sounds: the sounds of a language are not the same as the letters of a language even in languages with much less irregularity than English. To overcome the deficiencies of conventional spellings, linguists use a phonetic alphabet such as the International Phonetic Alphabet (IPA) to represent sounds. IPA has over 100 symbols each representing different possible sounds. Phonetic transcriptions are usually written between square brackets.

In transcribing language we can use either a narrow transcription or a broad transcription. A narrow transcription contains as much information as possible and records very minor differences between sounds, while a broad transcription contains less information and records only some differences between sounds. For example, a broad transcription of the word *pea* might capture the fact that it has two main sounds [pi], a narrower transcription might show that the consonant is actually unvoiced and aspirated and the vowel is long [pʰiː]. A very narrow transcription might include features of voice quality. Narrow transcriptions are very important in areas such as speech pathology or forensic phonetics where minor differences between sounds are important, but in most cases broad transcriptions are adequate for describing languages.

1.2.2   The sounds of language

The core of phonetics is to identify the characteristics of the sounds which human beings can use in language. Sounds can basically be divided into two types: vowels and consonants. Vowels are produced by altering the shape of the vocal tract by the positioning of the tongue and lips. Consonants are sounds which are produced by a partial or complete constriction of the vocal tract.

1.2.2.1   Vowels

Vowels are usually described by reference to five criteria, and these are adequate as a basic point of reference, although some vowel sounds require more specification:

1   the height reached by the highest point of the tongue (high, mid, low),
2   the part of the tongue which is raised (front, center, back),
3   the shape formed by the lips (unrounded or spread, rounded),
4   the position of the soft palate (raised for oral vowels, lowered for nasal vowels),
5   the duration of the vowel (short, long).

Using these features, linguists have constructed a set of standard reference points for describing vowels. These are called the cardinal vowels and are usually shown on a schematized representation of the mouth, as in Figure 1.1. In this diagram, the first vowel of each pair is rounded, the second unrounded, and all vowels are short. To show a long vowel, the symbol [ː] is written after the vowel. The cardinal vowels are not all of the vowels found in human languages and some, such as [œ], are not even very common. There are many intermediate vowel sounds which fall between the cardinal vowel points, as we can see if we look at the vowel chart for English in Figure 1.2.

English vowels are usually oral. In French, there is a regular series of nasal vowels, that is, vowels which are produced by passing air through the nasal cavity by lowering the soft palate, shown by the symbol [˜] written over the vowel. The nasal vowels of French are [ã] *vent* 'wind', [ɛ̃] *pain* 'bread', [ɔ̃] *pont* 'bridge' and for some speakers [œ̃] *un* 'one'. Another feature of English is that front vowels are unrounded and back vowels are rounded, but this is not true of all languages. French, for example, has a series of front rounded vowels: [y] *tu* 'you', [ø] *peu* 'few' and [œ] *peur* 'fear'.

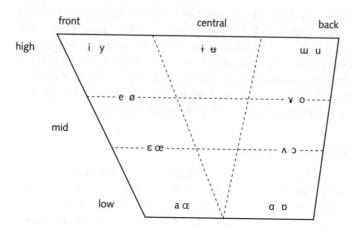

Figure 1.1 Cardinal vowels

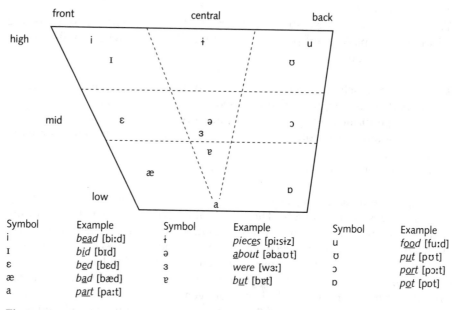

Symbol	Example	Symbol	Example	Symbol	Example
i	b<u>ea</u>d [biːd]	ɨ	piec<u>e</u>s [piːsɨz]	u	f<u>oo</u>d [fuːd]
ɪ	b<u>i</u>d [bɪd]	ə	<u>a</u>bout [əbaʊt]	ʊ	p<u>u</u>t [pʊt]
ɛ	b<u>e</u>d [bɛd]	3	w<u>e</u>re [wɜː]	ɔ	p<u>or</u>t [pɔːt]
æ	b<u>a</u>d [bæd]	ɐ	b<u>u</u>t [bɐt]	ɒ	p<u>o</u>t [pɒt]
a	p<u>ar</u>t [paːt]				

Figure 1.2 English vowels (southern British variety)

In some languages vowels may be voiceless, that is, they are made without vibrating the vocal cords. This is shown by the symbol [̥] written under the vowel, as in Japanese *hito* 'person' [çito̥], *suki* 'like' [su̥ki̥].

1.2.2.2 Diphthongs
Diphthongs are vowels in which the tongue starts in one position and moves to another. Diphthongs are very common in English:

tile [taɪl]   *tail* [teɪl]   *comb* [koʊm]   *shout* [ʃaʊt]
toy [toi]   *hair* [hɛə]   *here* [hiə]   *tour* [tʊə]

It is possible to have vowel sounds in which the tongue moves to more than one additional position during articulation. Some varieties of English in the UK, Australia, and New Zealand have triphthongs with three different tongue positions, for example:

fire [faɪə]   *hour* [aʊə]

1.2.2.3 Consonants

Consonant sounds have three basic features in their articulation: place of articulation, manner of articulation, and voicing.

Place of articulation refers to where in the vocal tract the constriction is made using the tongue or other parts of the mouth. The most commonly used places of articulation are shown in Table 1.1. Manner of articulation refers to how the constriction is produced. The most common manners of articulation are shown in Table 1.2.

When air is passed through the larynx, the vocal cords may either be spread or drawn together. When the vocal cords are drawn together they create a vibration and sounds made with such a vibration are called voiced sounds (e.g. English *z*, *v*), while sounds made with spread vocal cords are called voiceless (e.g. English *s*, *f*). In reality the situation is a bit more complex than a simple distinction between voiced and voiceless consonants, especially in the

Table 1.1   Places of articulation for consonants

Place of articulation	Articulators	Examples
Bilabials	Both lips	English *p*, *b*, *m*
Labio-dental	Upper teeth and the lower lip	English *f*, *v*
Dental	Upper teeth and tongue	French *t*, *d*
Interdental	Tongue between the teeth	English *th*
Alveolar	Tongue and the alveolar ridge (the bony ridge just behind the upper teeth)	English *t*, *d*
Postalveolar	Tongue and the front edge of the hard palate	English *sh*, *r* in some varieties
Palatal	Tongue and the hard palate	Italian *gn*, *gl*, English *y*
Velar	Tongue and the soft palate	English *k*, *g*, *ng*
Uvular	Tongue and the uvula	French *r*
Pharyngeal	Pharynx wall	Arabic ع
Glottal	Glottis (vocal folds)	English *h*, Samoan'

Table 1.2   Manner of articulation for consonants

Manner of articulation	Type of constriction	Examples
Stop	Complete blockage of air flow	English *b*, *d*, *g*
Fricative	Turbulent airflow produced by forcing air through a narrow aperture	English *f*, *s*
Approximant	Partial constriction of airflow, but without turbulence	English *l*, *w*, *y*
Affricate	Blockage of airstream with a delayed release of the block creating turbulence	English *ch*, *j*
Nasal	Blocking of the oral cavity to force air through the nasal cavity	English *m*, *n*, *ng*
Lateral	Air flows around the sides of the tongue	English *l*
Trill	Repeated interruption of the airflow as the result of an articulator vibrating	Spanish *rr*, Italian *r*
Flap or tap	Very brief blockage of the airflow	Spanish *r*, Japanese *r*

case of stops. When a stop is produced, it is possible that voicing will occur throughout the articulation of the stop (voiced), at the moment that the blockage of the airflow is released (unvoiced) or after the moment of release (aspirated). This is known as voice onset time. In some languages such as Khmer, all three voicing contrasts are found: e.g., *baang* /baːŋ/ 'older sibling', *paang*/paːŋ/ 'to expect', *phaang* /pʰaːŋ/ 'too'. English makes a distinction between aspirated and unaspirated stops only, while French distinguishes between voiced and unvoiced stops. The IPA symbols for the main consonants are given in Table 1.3. In addition, in some languages consonants may be long or short: e.g., Italian *notte* 'nights', *note* 'notes'. This is in IPA shown by reduplicating the consonant: [nɔtte], [note].

1.2.2.4   Suprasegmentals

Individual sounds are considered to be discrete segments, however some of the sound properties of languages extend over more than one segment. These are known as suprasegmentals and include stress, pitch, and tone. Stress, tone, and pitch are assigned to syllables or even longer combinations of sounds rather than to individual sounds.

Stress refers to the prominence of a particular syllable in a word, usually the result of a difference in the loudness, pitch, and/or duration. For example, the

Table 1.3 IPA consonant symbols

	Bilabial		Labiodental		Interdental		Dental		Alveolar		Postalveolar	
	−vc	+vc	−vc	+vc	−vc	+vc	−vc	+vc	−vc	+vc	−vc	+vc
Stop	p	b					t̪	d̪	t	d	ʈ	ɖ
Fricative	ɸ	β	f	v	θ	ð	s̪	z̪	s	z	ʂ ʃ	ʐ ʒ
lateral									ɬ	ɮ		
Nasal		m		ɱ				n̪		n		ɳ
Affricate	pɸ	bβ	pf	bv			ts̪	dz̪	ts	dz	tʂ tʃ	dʐ dʒ
lateral								l̪				
Approximant		w ɥ		ʋ						ɹ		ɻ
lateral										l		ɭ
Trill										r		
Tap/Flap									ɾ̥	ɾ		ɽ

	Palatal		Velar		Uvular		Pharyngeal		Glottal	
	−vc	+vc	−vc	+vc	−vc	+vc	−vc	+vc	−vc	+vc
Stop	c	ɟ	k	g	q	ɢ			ʔ	
Fricative	ç	ʝ	x	ɣ	χ	ʁ	ħ	ʕ	h	ɦ
lateral										
Nasal		ɲ		ŋ		ɴ				
Affricate			kx	gɣ	qχ	ɢʁ				
Approximant		j								
lateral		ʎ								
Trill						ʀ				
Tap/Flap										

underlined syllables of the English words *de<u>ve</u>lop* [dɪˈvɛləp], *<u>lan</u>guage* [ˈlæŋgwɪdʒ] and *ab<u>out</u>* [əˈbaʊt] have greater prominence than the other syllables. These underlined syllables are stressed (shown with ['] before the syllable in IPA transcription) and the less prominent ones are unstressed. In English, unstressed syllables are often reduced, as in *about*, where the unstressed vowel is pronounced as [ə]. Longer words may have a secondary stress, a syllable with more prominence than an unstressed syllable, but less prominence than a stressed syllable, as in the underlined syllables of *<u>con</u>troversial* [ˌkʰɒntʰɹəˈvɜːʃl̩]] and *<u>mis</u>demeanour* [ˌmɪsdəˈmiːnə]. Secondary stress is marked by [ˌ] before the syllable.

Tone is a particular pitch which is assigned to the articulation of a syllable. In tone languages such as Mandarin Chinese these changes of pitch serve to distinguish individual words. In Mandarin there are four different tones:

high level	mā	'mother'
rising	má	'hemp'
falling	mà	'scold'
fall-rise	mǎ	'horse'

Some languages have a larger number of tones. For example, Thai has five tones and Cantonese has nine tones.

In some languages, known as pitch accent languages, pitch works in a slightly different way. In these languages, there are commonly two pitches – high (H) and low (L) – either of which is assigned to an individual syllable. In polysyllabic words, the pitch may vary across the word. This can be seen in the following Japanese words:

HL   *kaki*   'oyster'
LH   *kaki*   'fence'

Stress and pitch may also be assigned to larger units of language, such as sentences, in which case we talk about sentence stress and intonation (Cruttenden, 1997). English uses both of these. Sentence stress involves giving additional prominence to a particular lexical item in the sentence. For example compare (1) and (1'):

(1)   I believe <u>John</u> said it.
(1')   I <u>believe</u> John said it.

In each of these sentences, each word has its own particular stress assignment, but one particular word (underlined) has a greater prominence assigned to it than other stressed syllables and the sentence stress has an effect on how the sentence will be interpreted. In some cases, sentence stress may be assigned to syllables which do not receive word stress as in:

(2)   For<u>ty</u> girls and four<u>teen</u> boys.

Intonation refers to a change in a pitch contour across the duration of a sentence, or other large unit of language. One very obvious use of intonation found in many languages is to use a falling pitch contour for declarative utterances and a rising pitch contour for yes/no questions, as in:

(3)   You know how to get there.
(3') You know how to get there?

1.3   Phonology: Speech Sounds as a System

No language has all the speech sounds possible in human languages; each language contains a selection of the possible human speech sounds. As such each language has its own pattern of sounds. This study of sound patterns is known as phonology and the speech sounds are known as phonemes. The focus of phonology is to determine the ways in which speech sounds form meaningful systems within languages.

The essential property of phonemes is that they contrast with each other. For example, we can tell that the sounds [f] and [v] represent two phonemes in English because they contrast in words like *fine* and *vine*, which differ only in terms of the voicing of the initial fricative but which have very different meanings. Two words that contrast in meaning and have only one different sound are known as minimal pairs. The following are minimal pairs in English (we transcribe phonemes using slashes /   /):

bat – vat	/b/ – /v/
bat – pat	/b/ – /p/
pat – fat	/p/ – /f/
hid – heed	/ɪ/ – /i/
hid – head	/ɪ/ – /ɛ/
head – had	/ɛ/ – /æ/

Where many words contrast by replacing one phoneme we call this a minimal series, as in:

hid – heed – head – had – hard – hod – hoard – hood – who'd
/ɪ/ – /i/ – /ɛ/ – /æ/ – /a/ – /ɒ/ – /ɔ/ – /ʊ/ – /u/

When we examine the possible minimal pairs and minimal series in a language, we can determine the phonemic inventory in that language: that is the speech sounds which make up the system of that language. The phonemic inventories of languages differ greatly. Some are quite large and others are quite small (see Table 1.4).

If we examine the words of a language closely, we discover that a single phoneme can have a range of different pronunciations. For example, consider

Table 1.4   Phonemic inventories in four languages

	Vowels	Consonants
Hawai'ian	i e a o u	p k ʔ m n ŋ w h l
English (Southern British)	i ɪ ɛ æ a ə ɜ i ɒ ɔ ʊ u ɐ aɪ eɪ aʊ oi oʊ iə ɛə ʊə	p b t d g k f v θ ð s z ʃ ʒ h m n ŋ ʧ ʤ w l r j
French	i e a o u y ø ɛ̃ ɑ̃ ɔ̃ œ̃	p b t d k g f v s z ʃ ʒ r m n ɲ w l j
Warlbiri (Australia)	i a u	b ḍ d ɟ g m ṇ n ɲ ŋ ḷ l ɭ ɹ r w y

the following English words (note that [l̥] and [n̥] indicate a voiceless [l] and [n]):

/p/   *pin* [pʰɪn]   *spin* [spɪn]
/l/   *leap* [liːp]   *sleep* [sl̥iːp]
/n/   *knees* [niːz]   *sneeze* [sn̥iːz]
/h/   *who* [huː]   *huge* [çjuːʤ]

In each pair of words, the sound is phonetically different because of the different environment (e.g. /p/ is [pʰ] initially but [p] after /s/), but the sounds are still perceived by speakers of English as the same phoneme as there is no meaningful contrast between the sounds, and substituting one for another would not produce a different word, just an unusual pronunciation of the same word. Where two or more sounds represent the same underlying phoneme we call these allophones. It is possible for two languages to have the same sounds but to treat them differently in their phonological system. For example, English and Spanish both have the sounds [d] and [ð], however in English these are two different phonemes (*those* [ðoʊz] = /ðoʊz/ and *doze* [doʊz] = /doʊz/) while in Spanish they are allophones of the same phoneme: [d] occurs at the beginning of words and after consonants and [ð] occurs between vowels (*Dios* 'God' [diɔs] = /diɔs/ and *adiós* 'good-bye' [aðiɔs] = /adiɔs/).

1.3.1 *Phonotactics*

Just as languages have different phonemic inventories and different allophones, they also have different possibilities for combining sounds into syllables, or different phonotactics. Syllables are phonological units consisting of one or more sounds and are made up of a nucleus (the core of the syllable made up of a highly sonorous segment, usually a vowel), with possibly an onset (a less sonorous segment preceding the nucleus) and/or a coda (a less sonorous segment following the nucleus). The nucleus and coda together are known as the rhyme.

We can see an example of a syllable with all three parts in the English word *hat* which is made up of a single consonant (C) followed by a vowel (V) and then another consonant (C):

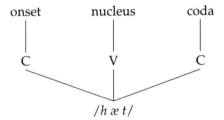

All syllables must have a nucleus. Some languages do not allow syllables to have a coda, e.g. Samoan. Other languages allow for more complex syllables with consonant clusters in the onset and possibly in the coda (Blevins, 1995). English allows for quite complex syllables as in:

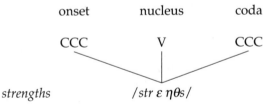

Languages also have phonotactic constraints on what can occur in a particular position in a syllable. For example, English does allow for CCC onsets, but not any three consonants can occur in this position: /tkf/ would not be possible as the beginning of an English syllable. Different languages have different constraints. Some languages allow for some consonants to be nuclei, e.g. Cantonese *m̀h* /m̀/ 'not', *ńgh* /ń/ 'five'. Other languages restrict what can occur in the coda, e.g. Mandarin Chinese allows only /n/ and /ŋ/. Spanish does not allow /s/ + C clusters in onsets and so words borrowed from English add a vowel to the beginning to change the syllable structure, e.g. *estrés* 'stress'. Some languages allow a much larger range of consonant clusters in onsets, e.g. German *schwach* /ʃvax/ 'weak', *straße* /ʃtraːsə/ 'street', French *pneu* /pnø/ 'tyre'.

1.4   Morphology

Morphology deals with the way in which words are made up of morphemes, the smallest meaningful units of language. If we take a word such as *untied*, it is clear that this word consists of three smaller meaningful pieces, three morphemes: the root *tie*, the prefix *un-* and the suffix *-d*.

Morphemes can be divided up into various crosscutting categories. Morphemes can be lexical like *tie*, with full, complex meanings. Or they can be grammatical morphemes, like *-d*, where a speaker does not really have a choice; the grammar of the language simply requires the morpheme to be present if the action occurred in the past. Morphemes can also be divided into free and bound morphemes. Free morphemes are those which can be used on their own, like *tie*; bound morphemes are those which, like *-d*, have to be attached to another morpheme (symbolized by the hyphen). These two categorizations are independent: we have seen the free lexical morpheme *tie* and the bound grammatical morpheme *-d*, but there are also free grammatical morphemes and bound lexical morphemes. An example of a free grammatical morpheme is the English indefinite article *a*. Bound lexical morphemes are not as common in English as in some other languages; in a language like Spanish, the verb morpheme meaning 'eat' has the form *com-*, but this form never appears without some suffix.

Morphemes can also be talked about in terms of their productivity. Some morphemes are highly productive: the past tense morpheme in English can occur on any verb (although it may have different forms, see below). At the other extreme are completely unproductive morphemes. The most famous is the morpheme *cran-* found in the English word *cranberry*. A cranberry is a type of berry, and we can split the morpheme *berry* off, leaving us with *cran-*, which does not occur anywhere else in English. Other morphemes fall between these extremes of productivity, so that *un-* occurs on some, but not all, verbs (*untie* but **ungo*, where the asterisk indicates an ungrammatical word or sentence); and *-hood* occurs on some, but not all, nouns (*motherhood, *tablehood*).

A single morpheme may appear with different forms in different words. The words *horses, cats, dogs,* and *oxen* all have suffixes showing that more than one entity is being talked about, but this plural suffix has different forms, called different allomorphs. Some of these allomorphs are phonologically conditioned, with the form depending on the final phoneme in the root – the form [ɨz] occurs after the sibilant (*s*-like) sound at the end of *horse*, [z] occurs after the final voiced phoneme at the end of *dog*, and [s] occurs after the voiceless phoneme at the end of *cat*. Sometimes allomorphs are lexically conditioned, the form is exceptional and depends simply on the root – we would expect the plural of *ox* to be *oxes* with [ɨz], but it is not, and speakers simply have to learn this about the word *ox*.

Morphemes can be of different types, as well. So far all the bound grammatical morphemes we have seen have been affixes, where a morpheme is attached in front of a root (a prefix like *un-*) or behind a root (a suffix like *-s*).

There is another rarer type of affix, an infix, where a morpheme is placed within a root. For example, in Chamorro, spoken on the island of Guam, there is a root *chocho* meaning 'eat'. In order to use a verb such as this in a sentence like 'I ate', an infix *-um-* must be placed after the first consonant phoneme, giving *chumocho*. It is not the case here that *ch*, *um* and *ocho* are separate morphemes – by themselves, *ch* and *ocho* do not mean anything. The two morphemes are *chocho* and *-um-*, it is just that *-um-* is placed after the first consonant inside the morpheme with which it combines.

As well as the different types of affixes, a morpheme can be shown by root modification, where the idea of the morpheme is expressed by a change of form in the lexical root. We saw above that there is a plural morpheme in English, usually expressed by a suffix such as *-s*. But the plural of *mouse* is *mice* – plurality is shown by changing the vowel of the root. Sometimes the root is changed completely, a process known as suppletion. The past tense morpheme in English is often expressed with a suffix [t], [d] or [ɪd] (depending on the preceding sound), as in *walk* versus *walked*; it is sometimes expressed through root modification, as in *run* versus *ran*; but in the pair *go* and *went*, the past tense is expressed through suppletion, with a completely different form. Because we tend to think of a morpheme as a thing, it can be hard to think of root modification or suppletion as morphemes, and linguists often talk about affixation and root modification as morphological processes rather than morphemes, but the principle is the same – there are two bits of meaning in *mice*, the bit that shows 'mouseness' and the bit that says there is more than one mouse. A simple morpheme such as a suffix can also be thought of as the morphological process of adding a suffix.

An additional complication arises because sometimes the absence of any material in itself can show a particular idea, and be treated as a morpheme. In English, using the root *book* means we are talking about a particular sort of reading matter. We can use this root with the plural suffix *-s* to indicate that we are talking about more than one of the items. But in a sentence such as *the book is red*, the form *book* does not just indicate the general idea of 'bookness' – the use of the form without the suffix *-s* indicates that we are talking about a single book. That is, the absence of the suffix *-s* indicates an additional concept beyond the general idea of 'book', it shows singular. This use of a contrast between no material and an explicit marker, where either choice shows an additional element of meaning, is sometimes talked about as the presence of a zero morpheme (symbolized with Ø). That is, we could say that in *the book is red*, the word *book* actually consists of two morphemes, the lexical root *book* and a singular suffix *-Ø*. While 'zero morphemes' are considered inappropriate by many linguists (how do you tell if there's one, two, or sixty-seven zero morphemes in a word?), it is important to realize that the absence of other (explicit) morphemes can be meaningful. Of course, whether a particular absence is meaningful depends on the language. In the Colombian language Awa Pit, like in many languages but unlike in English, the marking of plural is optional. The root *pashpa* means either 'child' or 'children', depending on context; there is a suffix *-tuzpa* which indicates plurality (*pashpatuzpa* 'children'), but the absence of this suffix does not indicate singular, unlike the absence of the plural suffix in English.

Another morphological process which occurs in some languages is reduplication, which may be full or partial (depending on whether the whole word or only part of the word is reduplicated). For example, *toko* is Indonesian for 'shop', and *toko-toko* means 'shops'. In Ancient Greek, the perfect form of the verb commonly has a partial reduplication of the verb stem, so that the verb root *pau* 'stop' becomes *pepau* (with a repeating of the initial consonant of the root) in a verb form such as *pepau-k-a* 'I have stopped'.

These various morphological processes such as affixation, root modification and reduplication can also be combined in different ways – to form the plural of *child* in English, we add a suffix *-ren* but also change the vowel from the diphthong [aɪ] to [ɪ].

A further morphological process is compounding, where two roots are combined to form a single new word. For example the roots *black* and *bird* can be compounded to form a new word *blackbird* with a different meaning; from *boy* and *friend* we can form *boyfriend*. Some languages have much more productive compounding than English.

Morphological processes are often divided into two types, inflection and derivation, although the distinction is not always clear. Given an English root *consider*, we can make forms like *considers* and *considered*, but also forms like *consideration* and *considerable*. The unsuffixed form and the first two suffixed forms are different forms of the same lexeme – if you want to look *considered* up in a dictionary, you look under *consider*, it's just that if an action happened in the past, the grammar of English forces you to add the inflection *-ed*. On the other hand, *-able* is a derivation, it derives a new lexeme *considerable*, which you would look up by itself in the dictionary. Inflections are highly productive (they apply to all or nearly all roots of a word class), semantically transparent (the meaning of *considered* is 'consider' plus past tense), and do not change word class (*consider* and *considered* are verbs); derivations are not necessarily productive (**goable*), not necessarily semantically transparent (what is the relationship between *consider* and *considerable*?), and may change word class (*considerable* is an adjective).

Languages differ greatly in their use of morphology and the types of morphological processes which they allow. There are two scales that languages are often considered to fall on. One scale is that of isolating, agglutinative, and fusional; the other consists of analytic, synthetic, and polysynthetic. An isolating language is one which does not join morphemes together in one word, agglutination is the process where morphemes join but are easily segmentable (*consider-ed*), and fusion is where morphemes join but are hard to segment (*mice* is 'mouse-plus-plural' but we cannot segment it). An analytic language is one where each word only has one morpheme (and is thus also isolating), a synthetic language has a few morphemes per word, and a polysynthetic language may have many morphemes in a single word. Of course, most languages have a combination of all of these traits, but these scales are used as an overall heuristic of what is most common in a language.

1.5   Syntax

In English, *the boy sees the girl* means something different from *the girl sees the boy*, and **the the boy girl sees* is not a sentence. Syntax deals with how to put words together to form sentences which mean what we want.

1.5.1   *Word classes*

The basis of syntax is the fact that the words of a language come in different classes or parts of speech – nouns, verbs, adjectives, prepositions, and so on. Not all languages have the same classes (English has articles like *a* and *the* showing that a noun phrase is indefinite or definite respectively, Japanese does not), and the same basic meaning can be expressed in different classes in different languages (thus the most basic words corresponding to most kinship terms in the Yuma language of California are verbs; to say 'I am his younger brother', you say literally something like "he younger-brother-calls me," where the equivalent of 'younger-brother-call' is a single verb morpheme). We establish the word classes and which words are in which class on the basis of the way words behave. For example, in English there is a class of words that take an inflection to show past tense (*walked, strolled, ran*) and another class which can follow the word *the* at the end of a sentence (*I saw the book/table/boy*).

Having established the word classes for a particular language, we can then label them. There is always a class which contains most of the words referring to concrete objects, and we call that class 'nouns'. Likewise, there is always a class which contains most of the words referring to actions, and we call that class 'verbs'. It is important to note that the precise list of words which are in any class may differ from language to language; as we noted above, the word corresponding to 'brother' in Yuma is a verb, and while *excitement* is a noun in English, it does not refer to an object. So we cannot say that nouns are words referring to things; rather a noun is any word which is in that class, defined in terms of language-specific behavior, which happens to include most words referring to things (and other words as well).

Many languages also have subclasses within each class. For example, while all verbs in English show marking for tense, they can be distinguished by how many nouns (or arguments) they are associated with. For example, the verb *die* is intransitive, only taking one argument (*Joshua died, *Joshua died the book*); *kill* is transitive, with two arguments (*Sarah killed Moses, *Sarah killed*); and *give* is ditransitive, with three arguments (*Ruth gave Abraham the book*).

Nouns and verbs are the only universal word classes (Schachter, 1985). Many languages have a class of adjectives, but in some languages descriptive words have exactly the same behavior as nouns or as verbs, and consequently in these languages there is no class of adjectives, since there is no special behavior to distinguish them. Different languages have different ways in which their nouns and verbs behave, and so different tests for assigning word class. In English, for example, verbs are marked for tense, but in a language like Indonesian verbs do not inflect for tense, so we cannot use that as a way of establishing the class of verbs in Indonesian (though there are other tests).

It is important to realize that there is no "true" set of features associated with different word classes. As English speakers, we tend to think that the distinction between singular and plural is important, because it shows up in the grammar of English. But there are many languages which do not have this distinction, so when speaking such a language people do not think about it, though they can be more precise if they want to, as English speakers can distinguish *three books* and *four books*, but may just choose to say *books* if the exact number is unimportant. The opposite happens with the English word *we*. When we use this word, we do not indicate if the person we are talking to is part of the group or not, but in many languages there are two separate words translating *we*, depending on whether the addressee is included or not – in Indonesian, for example, *kitu* must be used if the addressee is in the group (inclusive, we-including-you) while *kami* must be used if the addressee is not in the group (exclusive, we-excluding-you). Different languages force their speakers into making different distinctions, with different features being associated with different word classes in different languages.

Despite this, there are some features which are frequently found associated with particular word classes in many different languages. For example, nouns are often marked for number. In English, nouns are either singular or plural; other languages may make more distinctions, so Warlpiri has singular, dual (two) and plural (more than two). And some languages do not mark number at all.

Gender or noun class is another feature commonly associated with nouns. For example, every noun in Spanish is either masculine or feminine, whether human, animate, or inanimate. The gender of a noun affects, for example, the form of the definite article ('the') which is used with the noun – *la mujer* 'the woman', *el hombre* 'the man', *la silla* 'the chair', *el libro* 'the book'. In some languages there are more distinctions than two; Latin has three genders (masculine, feminine, and neuter), while Bantu languages of southern Africa divide their nouns into about ten different 'genders' or noun classes.

A further common noun feature is case, where the form of words changes depending on how they are used in a sentence. For example, Latin nouns are marked for case, and thus *puella* and *puellam* both mean 'girl'. The difference is that the first shows that the word is acting as a subject in the sentence, while the second is acting as an object. This is similar to the distinction between *I* and *me* in English. Some common cases are nominative (primarily used to mark subjects), accusative (objects), dative (recipients), and genitive (possessors). Once again, different languages have different systems of case-marking – English has no cases on nouns, German has four, Latin has six cases, and Finnish has fifteen. Each case may be used for more than one function, so that in German, for example, the dative is used to show a recipient, but is also used on the noun phrase that follows the preposition *mit* 'with'.

Verbs have a different set of features which are often associated with them. These include tense (the marking of when something happened relative to now), aspect (roughly speaking, whether an event is viewed, for example, as completed or on-going), and modality (expressing something about the reality or otherwise of an event, for example indicative and subjunctive verb forms in languages like French and Spanish). In some languages, verbs agree with their subject or object, a process also known as cross-referencing. For example, in Spanish, the difference between *comí, comiste* and *comieron*, all past tense forms of *com-* 'eat', is that the first shows that its subject is first person singular ('I ate'), the second is second person singular ('you (singular) ate'), and the third is third person plural ('they ate').

1.5.2   *Constituent structure*

In most languages, words are not just strung together in any order. Given the sentence *The tall plumber died*, there is no other way of ordering the words to form an English sentence. Also, at an intuitive level, *the tall plumber* seems to go together as a unit, in a way that *plumber died* does not; then the unit *the tall plumber* goes together with the unit *died* to form the sentence.

There are various ways of showing that *the tall plumber* is a unit, without resorting to intuition. This sequence of words can be substituted by a single word, say *Deborah* or *he*. If the sentence is rearranged in some way, this sequence remains together: *It was the tall plumber who died.* And the sequence of an article or determiner such as *the*, followed by none, one or more adjectives, followed by a noun, turns up again and again in English sentences. Using these sorts of tests, we can show that this sequence forms a constituent. Since the most important word in the constituent is the noun, we call this constituent a noun phrase or NP.

Constituent structure can be represented in different ways. Two common ways are through phrase structure trees and phrase structure rules. Phrase structure trees show the constituent structure of a particular sentence, with all the intermediate constituents.

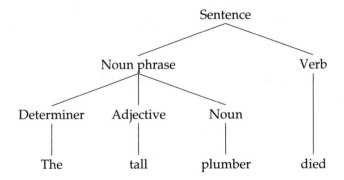

Phrase structure rules are more general representations of possible sentences. We have seen that a noun phrase can consist of a determiner, one or more adjectives, and a noun, with the determiner and adjectives being optional. We can represent this formally as:

NP → (Det) (Adj)* N

Here NP is the noun phrase, Det is a determiner, Adj an adjective and N a noun. The parentheses indicate that the element is optional, while the asterisk tells us we can have more than one of this class of word in this position. We can also devise a rule to make our sentence, S, by having

S → NP V

where V is a verb. Of course, if we want to include the possibility of an NP after the verb (in a sentence like *The boy saw the girl*), we will have to make the rule more complex:

S → NP V (NP)

These rules are clearly not adequate to represent English as a whole, but show the principle of phrase structure rules. Most syntactic theories, such as Government and Binding (Haegeman, 1994), Minimalism (Radford, 1997), Lexical Functional Grammar (Bresnan, 2001), and Role and Reference Grammar (Van Valin & LaPolla, 1997) use some sort of phrase structure rules or trees, although clearly they can be much more complicated than the ones given here.

Different languages have different phrase structure rules (and different trees). For example, in Turkish the verb comes at the end of a transitive sentence, after both NPs, so Turkish would need a phrase structure rule like

S → NP (NP) V

In a few languages, these sorts of phrase structure rules do not work very well. In Latin, the words in a sentence can come in almost any order without changing the basic meaning, so phrase structure rules showing where to put each of the words are not much use; but modifications can be made for languages like these.

1.5.3 *Semantic roles and grammatical relations*

In a sentence like *The farmer is killing the ducklings*, there is a difference in the relationship between the two noun phrases and the verb – we know that the farmer did the killing, and the ducklings ended up dead, and we could talk about them as the 'killer' and the 'thing-killed'. But we know that these are quite similar semantically to the 'hitter' and the 'thing-hit' in *The farmer is hitting the ducklings*. For this reason, more general terms are used to express the semantic role (also called the theta role) which a noun phrase plays in a sentence. Different systems of semantic roles are used, but some of the more common terms are agent (the one who performs something, as the farmer above), patient (the one to whom things happen, the ducklings above), experiencer and theme (*I* and *him* respectively in *I saw him*, where I do not really do anything, and nothing actually happens to him), recipient, and source and goal (where something comes from or goes to respectively, as *house* and *shops* in *she left the house for the shops*).

Semantic roles are needed to talk about sentence construction. For example, in English, if a transitive verb has an agent and a patient, the agent comes before the verb and the patient after, which is how we know who does what in *The farmer is killing the ducklings*. If the sentence is made passive (*The ducklings are being killed by the farmer*), then as well as a change in the verb, the patient now comes before the verb, and the agent is either in a prepositional phrase with *by*, or omitted entirely.

On the other hand, we clearly need more than just semantic roles in language descriptions. In the sentences *The farmer is killing the ducklings*, *The ducklings are being killed*, and *I saw him*, there is something in common between the first noun phrase of each sentence, even though they are respectively agent, patient, and experiencer. This noun phrase comes before the verb; if the verb is present tense it controls the form of the verb (e.g., *is* versus *are*); and if the noun phrase consists of a pronoun it has nominative form (*I* rather than *me*). For this reason we need grammatical relations such as subject, object, and indirect object. These grammatical relations are defined in formal terms, so that in English the subject is that argument which comes directly before the verb, has nominative form if it is a pronoun, and controls the verb form. Because grammatical relations are defined formally, different languages may have different sets of grammatical relations. For example, English does not have an indirect object, although some other languages do – in formal terms, *Mary* acts the same way in English in *John kissed Mary* and in *John gave Mary a book*, so it is the same grammatical relation (object) in both sentences; and *Mary* acts the same in *John gave a book to Mary* and *John went with Mary*, so it is the same grammatical relation in both sentences (oblique or object-of-preposition).

There is a relationship between semantic roles and grammatical relations, in that if a transitive verb has an agent and a patient and the verb is not passive, then the agent will be the subject and the patient will be the object; but agent and subject can be distinct (*The ducklings* (subject) *are being killed by the farmer* (agent)), as can patient and object. In some languages grammatical relations may be signaled by constituent order, as in English; in others, constituent order may be free and grammatical relations signaled by case, as in Latin; in others, cross-referencing on the verb may signal the difference. As in English, more than one technique may be used.

Grammatical relations may have more or less importance in the syntax of a language. In particular, in some languages grammatical relations are very important in complex sentences, while in other languages they are not.

1.5.4   Complex sentences

So far all of the sentences considered have consisted of only a single clause. However it is possible to combine more than one clause in a single sentence. The simplest way of doing this is coordination, where two clauses are joined with a word like *and*. Even here there can be important syntactic effects, however. In English, we can say *Rachel saw Judith and left*. The first clause is complete, with a subject (*Rachel*) and an object (*Judith*), but the second clause contains only *left*, which is missing a subject. Clearly, of course, Rachel is the one who left. But we only know this because English has a syntactic rule which says that if two clauses are coordinated, the subject can be left out of the second clause if it is coreferential (refers to the same entity) as the first subject. In other languages, there can be different rules – in a similar sentence in the Australian language Dyirbal, it would be Judith who left, as the Dyirbal rule is that a subject can be left out of an intransitive second clause if it is coreferential with the object in the first clause. In other languages, grammatical relations are not important here, and in the equivalent sentence either Rachel or Judith could have left, depending simply on context.

As well as coordination, clauses can also be combined using subordination. This is where one clause (the subordinate clause) is somehow less important than the other (the matrix clause). There are three types of subordination – complementation, relative clauses, and adverbial subordination.

Complement clauses are those clauses which substitute for a noun phrase in a sentence. For example, in English we can say *I saw the boy*, with *the boy* the object of the verb *saw*. But we can also say *I saw (that) the boy left*, *I saw the boy leave* and *I saw the boy leaving*. In each case, where we might expect a noun phrase like *the boy*, we have a whole clause, with at least a subject and a verb. Which type of complement clause we get depends on the verb in the matrix clause, so that with *want* rather than *see*, we can have *I wanted the boy to leave*, but not **I wanted that the boy left* or **I wanted the boy leaving*. With *want* we can also leave the subject of the subordinate clause out if it is coreferential with the matrix clause (*I want to leave*) which we cannot do with *see* (*I saw myself leave* versus **I saw leave*). Different languages have different types of complement clauses, and different rules about which complement clause type goes with which verbs.

Relative clauses add some extra information about a noun phrase in a sentence, and in English often begin with *who, which* or *that* – *the man who gave me the book* left contains the relative clause *who gave me the book* (which corresponds to a main clause *the man gave me the book*); this has been added into the sentence *the man left* to specify which man. Different languages differ greatly in how they form their relative clauses. We have seen that one option in English is to leave the common argument (the noun phrase which occurs in both main clauses, *the man*) out of the relative clause, put *who* in the relative clause, and put the relative clause inside the matrix clause after the common argument. An extremely different process is used in the West African language Bambara:

(4) tye ye [ne ye so min ye] san
    man PAST I PAST horse which see buy
    'The man bought the horse which I saw'

Here a relative clause based on the sentence *ne ye so ye* 'I saw the horse' has been inserted in the matrix clause *tye ye so san* 'the man bought the horse' in place of *so* 'horse'. The word *min* has been added in the relative clause after the common argument *so* 'horse', which has been left in the relative clause and left out of the matrix clause (the opposite of English).

The third type of subordination, adverbial subordination, covers those subordinate clauses which are similar in use to adverbs – there are a wide variety of possible constructions in languages, corresponding to English clauses such as *because I went*, *after he came*, *while working*, and so on.

1.5.5 Sentence types

There are three basic types of sentence: declarative, interrogative, and imperative. For example, in English we have a declarative sentence *He opened the window*, the interrogative *Did he open the window?*, and the imperative *Open the window!* While these sentence types broadly correspond to statements, questions, and commands or suggestions, this correspondence is not complete – for example you could issue a command or suggestion with an interrogative utterance (*Could you open the window?*), or ask a question using declarative word order with questioning intonation (*He opened the window?*). Different languages have different ways of forming these three sentence types, by changes in word order, special verb forms, intonation, or special particles.

1.6 Information Structure

One of the functions of syntax is to structure the ways in which information is presented in sentences and this structure is dependent on the context in which the information is presented. As such, the study of language needs to go beyond the level of isolated sentences and treat sequences of sentences, or texts.

1.6.1 Encoding given and new information

Syntax is often sensitive to whether or not information being conveyed can be expected to be known or not by the addressee (Ward & Birner, 2001). In this context, we can distinguish between given information – information which the speaker believes is already available to the hearer, or new information – information which the speaker does not expect the hearer to already know. These two types of information are encoded in sentences in different ways. Consider the exchange in (5).

(5)   A: Who took the book?
      B: Mary did.

In this example, B's utterance is made up of two pieces of information: 'Mary', which is new information, and 'took the book', which is given information. In this case, 'took the book' is encoded as the pro-verb *did*. Given information is often reduced in such a way. Consider the oddity of (5') as a conversational exchange:

(5')   A: Who took the book?
       B: Mary took the book.

Whether information is given or new affects the way in which the information is conventionally introduced into discourse. In English, new information is often introduced in non-subject position, while given information is usually found in subject position. When new information is referred to again in the same discourse, that is when it has become given information, it may be placed in subject position. This can be seen in (6):

(6)   I saw *a really good film* the other day. *It* was about *a man who thought he was going to be killed by some gangsters. He* went into hiding in the hills, but *they* found him.

In this sentence, there are three NPs which begin as new information, but are later used as given information:

New	Given
a really good film (object)	→ *it* (subject)
about *a man who thought he was going to*	→ *he* (subject)
be killed by some gangsters (object of preposition)	
by *some gangsters* (object of preposition)	→ *they* (subject)

In addition, new information is usually introduced in indefinite NPs (*an X*, *some X*), while subsequent references have definite forms such as definite NPs (*the X*) and pronouns. This can be seen in (6).

Sometimes, information which has not previously been mentioned is introduced in definite NPs, as in (7):

(7)   We went to a restaurant. The waiter was rude but the food was good.

In this case both *waiter* and *food* are mentioned for the first time in the discourse but the use of the definite article (*the waiter*, *the food*) seems to indicate that they are being treated as given information. Cultural context has a role here – our knowledge of the world tells us that restaurants have waiters and food, so these things are in a sense given information in the light of other knowledge we have from outside the discourse: that is, while the information is new to the discourse it is not new to the hearer (Prince, 1992; Ward & Birner, 2001). Such information can be easily recovered from context and as such speakers can expect addressees to have such information readily available. Therefore it can be treated as given information in such contexts.

In English, the definite and indefinite articles have an important role in the presentation of given and new information, however other syntactic structures are used in other languages. In Russian, for example, word order is related to given and new information (Comrie, 1979). Rather than having SVO word order, Russian usually presents new information late in the sentence, as can be seen in the contrast between (8) and (9).

(8) *Što koška presleduet?*
     What cat-NOM is chasing
     'What is the cat chasing?'

     Koška presleduet sobaku.
     cat-NOM is chasing dog-ACC
     'The cat is chasing the dog.'

(9) *Što presleduet sobaku?*
     what is chasing dog-ACC
     'What is chasing the dog?'

     Sobaku presleduet koška.
     dog-ACC is chasing cat-NOM
     'The cat is chasing the dog.'

1.6.2 Topic-comment structure

Another way to view information in utterances is in terms of topic and comment. Topic and comment often overlap with given and new information, however the two sets of terminology involve quite different concepts. The topic of the sentence can be considered the central element in the sentence- the thing the sentence is about – while the comment is what is said about it (Chafe, 1970; Lambrecht, 1994). Consider the exchange in (10):

(10) A: What did Mary do?
      B: She took the book.

In B, the topic of the sentence is 'Mary' (*she*) and the comment, the thing said about Mary, is *took the book*. In this case the topic is given information and the comment is new information. However sometimes the topic can be new information, as in (11):

(11)   Virginia always eats her vegetables, but her brother only likes ice cream.

In the second part of this sentence, the brother is the topic, but is also new information. By contrast, in (12) the comment is given information.

(12)   Virginia does not like ice cream, but her brother likes it a lot.

In English, the topic is often but not always related to the subject of the sentence (Li & Thompson, 1976; Tomlin, 1983), but there are other structures which can topicalize an NP. Unlike English, some languages use topic as a basic grammatical category. This is the case in Japanese where the postposition *wa* functions as a topic marker, as in (13) and (14), where in each case the topic is a non-subject constituent.

(13)   *Sakana   wa   tai   ga   ichiban ii.*
       fish   TOP bream NOM   first good
       'Speaking of fish, bream is the best' or 'Bream is the best sort of fish.'

(14)   *Tookyoo kara wa   daremo konakatta.*
       Tokyo   from TOP no-one come-NEG-PAST
       'Speaking of coming from Tokyo, no-one did.' or 'No-one came from Tokyo.'

In other languages word order can be used to indicate topics, as in the Chinese sentence in (15) and the French sentence in (16). Here, placing a constituent at the front of a sentence is a way to mark the topic. The French example differs from the Chinese in that the topicalized NP is repeated later in the sentence as a pronoun (*gare* 'station' is feminine, so the pronoun is 'she').

(15)   *Zhè-ge   zhǎn lǎn huì wǒ kàn dào hěn duò   yóu huàr*
       this-CLASS exhibition I   see very   many painting
       'At this exhibition, I saw very many paintings.'

(16)   *La gare   où   est-elle?*
       the station where is she
       'Where is the station?'

1.7   Semantics

Semantics, that part of linguistic description which deals with meaning, is often divided into lexical semantics, dealing with the meaning of words, and grammatical semantics, how morpheme meanings are combined by grammar to form the meaning of utterances.

1.7.1   *Lexical semantics*

The form which definitions of words should take is a vexed issue in lexical semantics. Different theories take different positions on what definitions should achieve. Some believe that a definition should be sufficiently precise as to include or exclude any particular case, sometimes with a paraphrase approach based on natural language (e.g., Wierzbicka, 1996) or a specially developed metalanguage (e.g., Jackendoff, 1983). Others believe that the lexicon is not structured in this way, but is rather more often similar to a web of prototypes (e.g., Langacker, 1990) or involving a strong use of metaphor (e.g., Lakoff, 1987).

Theories of meaning also differ in terms of whether or not they distinguish between dictionary knowledge and encyclopedic knowledge (Haiman, 1980; Wierzbicka, 1995). For example, many people in our society know that salt is chemically sodium chloride. The question is whether this is part of the meaning of the word *salt*, to be included in a definition, or simply an additional fact about salt (defined in other ways) which many speakers happen to know.

Another important issue which any general theory of lexical semantics must take into account is that the meanings of a far greater proportion of the lexicon than usually imagined, if not the meanings of all words, are language-specific. While this is obvious for words for cultural artifacts, non-equivalence of word-meanings extends throughout the lexicon. The natural world is not divided up the same between different languages, so that the Japanese word *nezumi* covers a collection of animals which in English would be divided into two types, rats and mice. The human body, a physical universal, is divided up in different ways in different languages: in Spanish, the single word *dedos* is used for both fingers and toes, while Japanese has a single word *ashi* corresponding to English leg and foot. Physical aspects of the world are equally different: English has a color category *blue*, but Russians have two terms covering the same range, *goluboj* (lighter) and *sinij* (darker), and these colors are no more closely related for Russians than *green* and *blue* for speakers of English; speakers of Russian are surprised that English only has one word. Human actions may be more or less differentiated: in English we can *hit* someone, but in many languages different verbs must be used depending on whether the action was hit-with-the-open-hand, hit-with-a-fist, hit-with-a-stick, and so on. All facets of the world and events that take place may be encoded differently – the words of different languages divide the world up differently.

As well as looking at the meanings of words, lexical semantics also examines the meaning relations between words. These meaning relations include concepts such as synonymy (where two words have the same, or at least very similar, meanings, as with *couch* and *sofa*), antonymy (opposite meanings as with *good* and *bad* or *tall* and *short*), hyponomy (the meaning of one is included in the meaning of another, as with *boy* and *child*), homonymy (two words having the same form but different meanings, as with a *bank* for money and a *bank* of the river), and polysemy (where a word has two or more related but distinguishable meanings, as with a *chip* of wood, a potato *chip*, and a computer *chip*, where all have the idea of a small piece as part of their meaning).

1.7.2   Grammatical semantics

Some work in grammatical semantics is interested in the meaning of grammatical morphemes, and how systems of grammatical meaning differ across languages. For example, both English and Spanish show tense using verb suffixes, but English has a single past tense corresponding roughly to two different past tenses in Spanish.

As well as the meaning of individual morphemes (lexical and grammatical), there is also the issue of how these meanings combine to form sentences. Even if we know the meaning of the words *boy*, *girl*, and *kiss*, as well as *the* and *-ed*, there is more to the meaning of the sentence *the boy kissed the girl* than the sum of the meanings of the morphemes, since this sentence means something different from *the girl kissed the boy*, which contains exactly the same morphemes.

One way in which semanticists deal with this issue is through the concept of constructions (Goldberg, 1995). Essentially this approach says that, as speakers of English, we have a schema or template such as Noun Phrase – Verb – Noun Phrase, and we have a meaning assigned to this general schema – say, 'the first noun phrase has the more active role, the second the more passive role' – and by combining the meanings of the words with the meaning of the schema, we come up with the meaning of the overall sentence. A different schema would then be used to account for the passive sentence *the girl was kissed by the boy*.

Another approach, Formal Semantics, relies much more on the apparatus of formal logic and grammatical theory. In this approach, the word *kiss* is stored in the lexicon not just with the general meaning of kissing, but with an explicit statement in a formal notation indicating something like 'this verb's (underlying) subject is the agent and its (underlying) object is the patient'. The meaning of the sentence is then created by assigning the appropriate semantic role to the appropriate grammatical relation. The meaning of the passive equivalent is created through rules such as 'make the underlying object into a subject', 'make the underlying subject come after the preposition *by*'. Formal Semantics is associated with the idea of truth-conditional or truth-value semantics, which attempts to establish, given a sentence, what conditions have to hold in the real world for the sentence to be true.

1.8   Conclusion

This chapter can only give a brief outline of what is involved in the description of languages and each area we have discussed has a wealth of literature and a depth of detail which we are unable to address here. However, this brief description should be sufficient to introduce applied linguists to the broad themes and general concepts with which linguists work in developing descriptive accounts of languages.

While language description may not be a core concern for applied linguists, a coherent understanding of the structural features of language is important for applied linguistics research and practice. At all levels of their work, applied linguists must come to grips with language as a system and as such linguistics and language description is basic to applied linguistics work, even if it is not central to the questions which applied linguists pose themselves. We do not claim that linguistic theory is or should be the driving influence in applied linguistics. Rather, we are claiming that a certain level of familiarity with the principles of linguistics provides a framework within which the work of applied linguistics can be carried out in an informed and principled way. The role of linguistics is, therefore, to inform applied linguistics not to determine applied linguistics (cf. Davies, 1999; Widdowson, 2000).

The relationship between language description and applied linguistics is not, however, unidirectional. The insights which applied linguistics gains from confronting real-world language-related problems has great potential to inform the development of linguistic theory and refine our understanding of what needs to be included in language descriptions.

See also 2 LEXICOGRAPHY, 4 LANGUAGE CORPORA, 5 DISCOURSE ANALYSIS, 10 CONVERSATION ANALYSIS.

REFERENCES

Blevins, J. (1995) The syllable in phonological theory. In J. A. Goldsmith (ed.), *Handbook of phonological theory* (pp. 206–44). Cambridge, MA: Blackwell.

Bresnan, J. (2001) *Lexical-functional syntax*. Oxford: Blackwell.

Chafe, W. L. (1970) *Meaning and the structure of language*. Chicago: University of Chicago Press.

Comrie, B. (1979) Russian. In T. Shopen (ed.), *Languages and their status* (pp. 91–207). Philadelphia: University of Pennsylvania Press.

Cruttenden, A. (1997) *Intonation*. Cambridge: Cambridge University Press.

Davies, A. (1999) *An introduction to applied linguistics: from practice to theory*. Edinburgh: The Edinburgh University Press.

Goldberg, A. E. (1995) *Constructions: a construction grammar approach to argument structure*. Chicago: University of Chicago Press.

Haegeman, L. (1994) *Introduction to government and binding theory* (2nd edn.). Oxford: Blackwell.

Haiman, J. (1980) Dictionaries and encyclopedias. *Lingua*, 50, 329–57.

Jackendoff, R. (1983) *Semantics and cognition*. Cambridge, MA: MIT Press.

Kennedy, C. & Miceli, T. (2001) An evaluation of intermediate students' approaches to corpus investigation. *Language Learning and Technology*, 5(3), 77–90.

Lakoff, G. (1987) *Women, fire, and dangerous things: what categories reveal about the mind.* Chicago: University of Chicago Press.

Lambrecht, K. (1994) *Information structure and sentence form: topic, focus and mental representations of discourse referents.* Cambridge: Cambridge University Press.

Langacker, R. W. (1990) *Concept, image, and symbol: the cognitive basis of grammar.* Berlin: Mouton de Gruyter.

Li, C. N. & Thompson, S. (1976) Subject and topic: a new typology of language. In C. N. Li (ed.), *Subject and topic* (pp. 303–34). New York: Academic Press.

Odlin, T. (1994) Introduction. In T. Odlin (ed.), *Perspectives on pedagogical grammar* (pp. 1–22). Cambridge: Cambridge University Press.

Prince, E. F. (1992) The ZPG letter: subjects, definiteness and information status. In S. Thompson & W. C. Mann (eds.), *Discourse description: diverse analyses of a fund-raising text* (pp. 295–325). Amsterdam: Benjamins.

Radford, A. (1997) *Syntax: a minimalist introduction.* Cambridge: Cambridge University Press.

Schachter, P. (1985) Part-of-speech systems. In T. Shopen (ed.), *Language typology and syntactic description*, vol. 1: *Clause structure* (pp. 3–61). Cambridge: Cambridge University Press.

Stubbs, M. (1986) *Educational linguistics.* Oxford: Blackwell.

Tomlin, R. S. (1983) On the interaction of syntactic subject, thematic information and agent in English. *Journal of Pragmatics*, 7, 411–32.

Tomlin, R. S. (1994) Functional grammars, pedagogical grammars and communicative language teaching. In T. Odlin (ed.), *Perspectives on pedagogical grammar* (pp. 140–78). Cambridge: Cambridge University Press.

Van Valin, R. D., Jr., & LaPolla, R. J. (1997) *Syntax: structure, meaning and function.* Cambridge: Cambridge University Press.

Ward, G. & Birner, B. J. (2001) Discourse and information structure. In D. Schiffrin, D. Tannen, & H. H. Hamilton (eds.), *The handbook of discourse analysis* (pp. 119–37). Oxford: Blackwell.

Widdowson, H. G. (1979) *Explorations in applied linguistics.* Oxford: Oxford University Press.

Widdowson, H. G. (1980) Applied linguistics: the pursuit of relevance. In R. B. Kaplan (ed.), *On the scope of applied linguistics.* Rowley, MA: Newbury House.

Widdowson, H. G. (2000) On the limitations of linguistics applied. *Applied Linguistics*, 21, 3–25.

Wierzbicka, A. (1995) Dictionaries vs encyclopaedias: how to draw the line. In P. W. Davis (ed.), *Alternative linguistics: descriptive and theoretical modes* (pp. 289–315). Amsterdam: John Benjamins.

Wierzbicka, A. (1996) *Semantics, primes and universals.* Oxford: Oxford University Press.

FURTHER READING

Akmajian, A., Demers, R. A., Farmer, A. K., & Harnish, R. M. (2001) *Linguistics: an introduction to language and communication* (5th edn.). Cambridge, MA: MIT Press.

Börjars, K. & Burridge, K. (2001) *Introducing English grammar*. London: Arnold.

Brinton L. (2000) *The structure of modern English*. Amsterdam: John Benjamins.

Carnie, A. (2002) *Syntax*. Oxford: Blackwell.

Carr, P. (1999) *English phonetics and phonology*. Oxford, Blackwell.

Crowley, T., Lynch, J., Siegel, J., & Piau, J. (1995) *The design of language: an introduction to descriptive linguistics*. Auckland: Longman Paul.

Fromkin, V. A. et al. (2000) *Linguistics: an introduction to linguistic theory*. Oxford: Blackwell.

Goddard, C. (1998) *Semantic analysis: a practical introduction*. Oxford: Oxford University Press.

Gussenhoven, C. & Jacobs, H. (1998) *Understanding phonology*. London: Arnold.

Hudson, G. (2000) *Essential introductory linguistics*. London: Blackwell.

Kreidler, C. W. (1998) *Introducing English semantics*. London: Routledge.

Ladefoged, P. (2000) *A course in phonetics* (4th edn.). Fort Worth: Harcourt College Publishers.

Ladefoged, P. (2001) *Vowels and consonants: an introduction to the sounds of language*. Oxford: Blackwell.

Lyons, J. (1995) *Linguistic semantics: an introduction*. Cambridge: Cambridge University Press.

Matthews, P. H. (1991) *Morphology* (2nd edn.). Cambridge: Cambridge University Press.

Spencer, A. (1991) *Morphological theory*. Oxford: Blackwell.

Spencer, A. (1995) *Phonology*. Oxford: Blackwell.

Thomas, L. (1993) *Beginning syntax*. Oxford: Blackwell.

2 Lexicography

ALAN KIRKNESS

2.1 Introduction

Lexicography is almost as old as writing. From its beginnings several thousand years ago it has served primarily the real-life needs of written communication between members of human communities using different languages or different varieties of one language. Those needs change just as all living languages constantly change. In many literate societies lexicography has a centuries-old tradition with word lists and word books in scripts based on hieroglyphs, logograms, or letters and in media from clay tablets to the computer. Since print culture replaced scribal culture some five centuries ago and ushered in the modern period in European lexicography, the printed book has predominated. Worldwide, no book on a language or on languages has been and is more widely used in education systems and in communities at large than the dictionary. It has long been and still is an essential source, if not indeed the principal source, of information on language for all members of literate societies who might have questions on any aspect of the form, meaning, and/or use of a word or words in their own or in another language. Lexicographers can be regarded as descriptive linguists in that they empirically analyze and describe (a) language with a traditional emphasis on individual items of vocabulary. However, they do not require linguistic knowledge alone, but according to the particular dictionary project may draw on other non-linguistic disciplines including information technology, publishing, history, and the natural and social sciences amongst others. Nor is their description of (a) language primarily an end in itself. Its aim is not primarily to advance linguistic theory, however much theoretical linguists may and do draw on lexicography for their own purposes and however much lexicographers might seek to apply relevant findings of theoretical linguistics in their work. Rather it is in principle a means to an end, namely to make knowledge about (a) language available to various sectors of the wider public and to mediate between different kinds of language knowledge and different kinds of user needs. This aim is clearly reflected in the vast range of different dictionary types designed to respond to the different needs and interests of different user groups. To a greater or lesser degree depending on the nature and purpose of the particular dictionary project, lexicographers essentially mediate between the community of linguists and the community at large. This is true especially of general-purpose trade dictionaries, less so inevitably of scholarly historical works, which have a more limited audience. In this sense lexicography must be regarded as quite central to applied linguistics, however defined. At the same time, it must also be seen as a complex activity *sui generis* with its own principles, practices, problems, and traditions.

Over the past 20–30 years lexicography has changed fundamentally and irreversibly. The main factor has been the dramatic impact of the computer: the electronic storage of vast textual material in corpora and the varied electronic presentation of lexicological and lexicographical work represent a quantum leap in lexicography, a leap still to be measured (see Section 2.2). A secondary factor has been the rapid emergence of metalexicography or dictionary research as an academic discipline with an explosion of writing on and about dictionaries. As a consequence, this article has to be selective. It is written from a western European perspective and draws primarily on material related to British and other English language lexicographies. Concentrating on English and European lexicography sharpens the focus, but necessarily narrows it; it permits a relative close-up, but inevitably distorts the wider picture.

2.2   What Is Lexicography?

It is difficult to arrive at a succinct and satisfying working definition of lexicography. Even a cursory glance in dictionaries and other reference works and in the secondary literature reveals many variations on a theme, reflecting a variety of standpoints. In a narrow sense lexicography may be described as the art and craft of writing a dictionary. Certainly, a lexicographer is essentially someone who writes or contributes to a dictionary or dictionaries, be it as an individual or a member of a team, as a freelancer or an in-house employee, as a full-time professional or part-time alongside other activities such as university lecturing. *Lexicographer* is also used more generally to refer to writers of other reference works, including encyclopedias. Like other definitions, however, and indeed like much dictionary writing itself, this definition of lexicography is derivative (Landau, 2001), and it is a compromise for the sake of brevity. It raises many questions: why dictionary, why not e.g., thesaurus, lexicon, or encyclopedia and other reference works? Why write, why not, for example, plan, edit, publish or make, produce, compile, let alone study, review, or use? Why art and craft, why not, for example, activity, process, technique, science, job, profession or practice, let alone history, study, use, or theory?

There are justifiable answers to such questions. The dictionary is widely regarded as the prototypical work of lexical reference, but this claim requires much further explication (see Section 2.3). Writing is the essential lexicographic activity, especially writing and rewriting semantic, pragmatic, or etymological descriptions; planning and data collection precede and accompany the writing, editing and publishing follow it. Good lexicography is more than compilation. Extracting meanings and uses from authentic texts and explaining them clearly and fully in a minimum of words is an art, as is the selection of appropriate illustrative examples. Writing with dictionary users uppermost in mind in an attempt to meet their needs is a practical and useful activity, a craft. Defining lexicography in this narrow sense as the art and craft of writing a dictionary is meant to locate it explicitly at the center of the applied linguistic endeavor and to emphasize the high degree of human knowledge, insight, judgment and skill required to produce the text of a successful reference work designed to be of practical use and benefit in real-life situations. Certainly, a dictionary that does not prove useful is unlikely to prove successful. Commercial constraints – the triple nightmare of space, time, and money (Murray, 1977) – have traditionally dictated the relationship between lexicographers and their publishers.

The advent of electronic corpora and media can make the lexicographers' work better, but not necessarily easier. Computers can store and process quantities of textual data quite unmanageable by humans. Where several million manually and painstakingly excerpted citation slips were once considered a sufficient basis for a multi-volume scholarly dictionary, now even one-volume trade dictionaries rest on hundreds of millions of rapidly and automatically entered running words. The differences are not only in quantity, but more importantly in quality. Lexicographers now have at their disposal vastly superior language data. Neutral frequency counts of masses of words can act as a counterbalance to intuition, memory and possible bias in many of the decisions they must make in accordance with the specifications of the particular dictionary project. They help determine which usages are central and which are peripheral, which new items should be included and which items should be excluded as obsolescent or archaic, which combining forms and multi-word items warrant status as main lemmas or headwords rather than as run-ons and sub-lemmas, or how homographs and senses can be ordered, to mention but a few possibilities. Lexicographers have been at the forefront in utilizing language corpora and applying the findings of corpus linguistics (see Stubbs in this volume) to good effect in their analysis and description of lexis and hence to the benefit of their users. The corpus revolution is very real; computerphoria would be misplaced, however. There may be huge savings in storage space and processing time, but it is humans who continue to choose the texts and analyze the vastly increased data, which can now in fact require more time, experience, and skill to process than before. Humans discern and describe sense distinctions in polysemous words and between sets of synonyms, antonyms, and hyponyms. They select appropriate illustrative examples or establish usage and usage restrictions in tune with changing sociocultural conventions. And specialist material from a directed reading program still has a place alongside the mass data entered by means of optical scanners, magnetic tapes, and the like.

Similarly, electronic media open up quite new possibilities for the presentation and use of lexicographical material. They can, for instance, help overcome the constraints of space that have long plagued lexicographers and their editors and limited the coverage, description, and illustration of lexical items even in comprehensive or unabridged dictionaries. The size of the computer screen and of the "search word" box remain limitations, however, and favor directed searches for specific items over the incidental consulting of neighboring entries and the general, even random browsing so dear to word and dictionary buffs brought up on printed books. They can help overcome the tyranny of the printed alphabet that has severely limited accessibility and fostered the modern dominance of the alphabetic mode of presentation over the older thematic or systematic mode. Access through the alphabet has become a practical necessity for most users, however, and modern thesauruses are either arranged alphabetically or have an alphabetical index. Online e-dictionaries and e-cyclopedias available free or by subscription on the Internet and CD-ROM are already vying with and in some cases supplanting conventional printed books. Large and expensive multi-volume reference works seem to be leading the paradigm shift from book to bank and byte. Academic researchers working on and with scholarly historical dictionaries are among the major beneficiaries. At the click of a mouse they can conveniently search from their desks the full resources of the *Oxford English Dictionary Online* in ways simply not possible on visits to the library to consult the 20 large and alphabetically ordered volumes of the *Second Edition*. It is a boon to have *The Century Dictionary Online* in DjVu format available for headword browsing and lookup as well as full text searches rather than have to use the thick and heavy tomes in the library, however much one might delight in them as a bibliophile. Now that wordbanks and wordnets, such as the *British National Corpus* or the *Bank of English*, the Princeton *WordNet*, and the multilingual *EuroWordNet*, can be accessed in full or in part on the Internet, users can effectively become their own lexicographers. The future of lexicography is undoubtedly electronic. Nonetheless, however much the computer can aid lexicographers as dictionary writers, it will not replace them.

The questions raised above also point to a need to understand lexicography in a wider sense as used in the rapidly increasing number of university courses, conferences and workshops, books, journals and articles on the subject. These concern not only lexicography as practice, namely the planning, writing, editing, and publishing of dictionaries and other lexicographical reference works, but also lexicography as theory, notably the study of dictionary history, criticism, typology, structure, and use (Wiegand, 1998). Some scholars distinguish theory, also known as metalexicography or dictionary research, from practice as lexicography proper. Others include all aspects of both theory and practice in their definition of lexicography. Be that as it may, many different sub-branches of lexicography can be distinguished, ranging from computational to pedagogical and terminographical. Postgraduate degree or diploma courses on lexicography aim to provide academic qualifications and professional training for future dictionary writers. However, most lexicographers still train as before in-house or on the job. The literature on lexicography involves university and other scholars as well as lexicographers and ex-lexicographers. The former mediate the findings of research in (theoretical) linguistics and other academic disciplines, which most practicing lexicographers cannot possibly keep abreast of. They also describe and re-edit or reprint historical dictionaries, and make suggestions for the improvement of all aspects of lexicographical description. The latter write from first-hand practical experience and offer an invaluable insider perspective, which sometimes informs an extended introduction in the front matter especially of historical and scholarly dictionaries. All too often, however, it is only half-glimpsed in dictionary prefaces and introductions. The glimpses are tantalizing, and the occasional publication of such material indicates that it can have a general linguistic significance reaching beyond the particular dictionary project or indeed lexicography (e.g., Gove, 1966, 1968). In line with the lexicographers' constant emphasis on utility, the literature on lexicography now devotes much attention to dictionary uses in academic research, educational practice, and leisure activity. It focuses particularly on dictionary users and seeks to ascertain who uses which dictionary when and where, for what purpose and with what result. This focus on the user perspective (Hartmann, 2001, pp. 80–95, pp. 115–20) and the need for empirical studies of what dictionary users do in real look-up situations (Atkins, 1998; Nesi, 2000; Tono, 2001) are important concerns of applied linguistics. Among the scientific commissions of the International Association of Applied Linguistics (AILA) is one devoted to Lexicology and Lexicography as research areas which can contribute to a better understanding and facilitation of language learning and language use and are studied from several perspectives. However, important as it is, the user's perspective is not the only one: lexicographers as dictionary writers, scholars as dictionary researchers, (language) teachers as mediators also offer essential perspectives on the complex and multi-faceted activity that is lexicography, quite apart from publishers, consultants, and others. At the center of this activity is the dictionary itself as text (Hartmann, 2001, pp. 24–5), and the dictionary is thus the focus of the discussion that follows.

Lexicography is in essence an art and a craft. It is also a profession and a hobby, a scholarly and commercial enterprise, and an academic discipline. It is, further, a longstanding cultural practice and an integral part of the intellectual tradition in literate societies. Some idea of this wider sense in which lexicography must be understood can be gained from Hartmann & James (1998) and Hausmann, Reichmann, Wiegand, & Zgusta (1989–91).

2.3 What Is a Dictionary?

2.3.1 *Dictionaries and encyclopedias*

As already mentioned, the dictionary is widely regarded as the prototypical work of lexical reference. It classifies and stores information in print or, increasingly, electronic form and has an access system or systems designed to allow users to retrieve the information in full or in part as readily as possible. The information is essentially linguistic and may include material on the form, meaning, use, origin, and history of words, phrases, and other lexical items (see Section 2.3.3). In a dictionary phonetic and grammatical information is word-related and thus essentially lexical. Put very simply, a dictionary is a book or bank about words.

In theory linguistic or lexical information may be distinguished from extralinguistic or encyclopedic information. Certainly, there are classes of words which lend themselves to either linguistic or encyclopedic treatment. The former include function words such as prepositions, determiners, or conjunctions and discourse-marking chunks such as *you know, I mean*, and many others. They derive their meaning from their function within a linguistic text rather than from any reference to extralinguistic reality and are properly treated in a dictionary. The latter may include proper names of people and places, biographical data, and descriptions of historical events, political, social, and cultural institutions, geographical and geopolitical entities, works of art, literature and music, myths and mythological figures, beliefs and religions, academic disciplines, and the like. A reference work that stores and classifies such factual information on all or some branches of knowledge or a single subject area is generally known as an encyclopedia. Put simply, an encyclopedia is a book or bank about facts. It is notable in this connection that multilingual and especially bilingual dictionaries have long been and continue to be very common, but this is not true of encyclopedias. Conversely, the latter can be and have been translated, but this does not seem to be the case with dictionaries, except perhaps for the fast-developing genre of bilingualized, semi-bilingual, or bridge dictionaries in the area of pedagogical lexicography (see Section 2.5). In practice, however, a hard and fast distinction between lexical and encyclopedic information is not possible. Humans use language to communicate about facts, things, and people; words and the world are inextricably linked. A linguistic description of nouns as names for plants, animals, or insects and of adjectives as names for colors, for instance, necessarily involves encyclopedic information. Such items are entered in both dictionaries and encyclopedias. Their semantic explanation will differ in degree rather than kind, namely in the amount of factual information required or provided to identify and characterize the object referred to according to the intended purpose of the particular reference work. Lexicographers must be concerned with words in their own right as linguistic items and with what words refer to in the world of extralinguistic reality or with their referents as such. Dictionaries and encyclopedias are best seen as two types of reference work, among others, which stand at opposite ends of a continuum, one concerned with words as linguistic or lexical items, the other with facts as such. There are many mixed or blended forms in between (McArthur, 1986, pp. 102–4).

In the titles and/or subtitles of subject-area and biographical reference works, which are most commonly published in one volume, *dictionary* can be used alternatively and synonymously with *encyclopedia*. In this same sense *companion* and *handbook* are also found. In the titles of dictionaries-cum-encyclopedias, which combine lexical and encyclopedic information, the attribute *encyclopedic* sometimes explicitly qualifies the head noun *dictionary*, sometimes not. A successful example of a fully integrated encyclopedic dictionary is the *Reader's Digest Great Illustrated Dictionary*, 1984, which features small color photographs and drawings at the appropriate alphabetical place in the outside columns of virtually every page, color maps, and part- and full-page panels and tables, most also in color. Clearly, the genre of encyclopedic dictionary is established as a blend between the dictionary as a word book/bank on the one hand and the encyclopedia as a fact book/bank on the other. This is certainly true of the American and French traditions, less so in the British and German ones. Equally clearly, the genre is regarded in English as a type of dictionary, and thus belongs to the province of lexicography. The question whether encyclopedias as such also belong has been variously answered. My own view is that it is justifiable to regard encyclopedias as falling within the scope of lexicography in the wider sense discussed above, and it would definitely enhance and advance metalexicography if encyclopedias were given fuller attention. If the present chapter nonetheless restricts itself largely to dictionaries as word books, it is for practical reasons of space, especially as there are so many different types of dictionary.

2.3.2   *Types of dictionary*

Given that dictionaries belong to the oldest, most widespread, and best-selling books in literate societies, it is hardly surprising that their number is legion. Different societies have different lexicographical traditions, and ideas on what might constitute the prototypical dictionary vary accordingly. The range of languages, varieties, and vocabularies, of sizes, formats, and prices, or intended purposes, uses, and users seems inexhaustible. Most dictionaries codify natural languages, but there are also dictionaries of international auxiliary languages, sign languages, shorthands, and braille. The time interval between new impressions and even new editions of popular trade dictionaries grows ever shorter, and their covers and dust jackets resemble ever more strongly billboards advertising the virtues and unique features of their product in a highly competitive market. This is perhaps particularly true of English dictionaries, not least for second/foreign language learners as a reflection of the current worldwide dominance of English as an additional language. What impact electronic publishing will have on this situation is not yet clear. Currently, prospective dictionary users and buyers are faced with a bewildering *embarras de richesses*. Language teachers and librarians are faced with the problem of continuously updating their resources. Dictionary scholars are faced with a rich, diverse, and ever-changing field of study. It is small wonder that dictionary typology has become an integral component of metalexicography, that different criteria, including size, scope of linguistic and subject-area coverage, number of languages, period covered, target groups and intended uses among others, have been advanced as the basis of different typologies, and that no agreed taxonomy has emerged to classify the variety of dictionary types. In the practical typology that underlies the organization of much of their international encyclopedia of lexicography, Hausmann et al. distinguish first between monolingual and multilingual dictionaries. Of the latter, the vast majority are bilingual and cover two national standard languages. Bilingual dictionaries continue to be the most-used reference book in second/foreign language learning at all levels (see Section 2.5). There are specialized bilingual dictionaries, such as dictionaries of deceptive cognates or false friends, subject-specific technical dictionaries, and pictorial dictionaries that feature line drawings largely of thematically grouped concrete objects with their designations in two languages. The prototypical bilingual dictionary, however, is the general translation dictionary. Headwords or lemmas in one (source) language, usually presumed to be the user's first language, are supplied at least with translation equivalents in the other (target) language. Full equivalents may need mere listing, while partial and surrogate equivalents require further explanation or exemplification to ensure sense identification and discrimination. Passive or receptive dictionaries help in decoding or translating from the target/foreign to the source/native language, active or productive dictionaries help in encoding or translating from the source to the target language. For each language pair there are in theory four directions to consider, for example, German-French for French users and French-German for German users (passive), German-French for German users and French-German for French users (active). In practice most bilingual dictionaries are bidirectional: French-German and German-French.

Monolingual dictionaries are divided into general and specialized works. The former are found in two major types, the encyclopedic dictionary (see Section 2.3.1) and above all the semasiological defining dictionary. Aimed at adult native speakers and usually published in a single volume – although the volume may range from compact and portable to very bulky and unwieldy – this latter is the prototypical dictionary of dictionaries in most European lexicographies. Alphabetically ordered lemmas, representing in the main unmarked contemporary standard vocabulary, are supplied with semantic explanations or descriptions of various kinds. Often there is much other information as well. The more than 70 types of specialized dictionaries derive mainly from different types of marked lemmas in the macro-structure or from different types of lexicographic information other than the definitions in the micro-structure (see Section 2.3.3). Marked lemmas include archaisms, neologisms, regionalisms, and internationalisms. There are dictionaries devoted to all these and many other lemma types. Syntagmatic information underlies dictionaries of syntactic patterns or valency, collocations, fixed phrases and idioms, proverbs and quotations. Paradigmatic information underlies onomasiological dictionaries, which move from concepts or word meanings to word forms as the expression of these concepts. They include dictionaries which classify and list synonyms with or without sense discrimination and meaning description – the former are discriminating, the latter cumulative synonymies – reverse and word-family dictionaries, and the thesaurus. From other categories of lexicographic information derive dictionaries of spelling, pronunciation, inflections, frequency and etymology, and chronological dictionaries. There are dictionaries dealing *inter alia* with specific text types, texts by individual authors, and concordances. This essentially phenomenological typology is complemented by a functional one based on the intended use and target group. Included here are children's and learners' dictionaries, both for native and non-native speakers, as well as dictionaries of core vocabulary, all of which are pedagogic in orientation.

   This typology is neither exhaustive nor uncontested. It does not seek explicitly to account for all of the many mixed or hybrid types of lexicographic reference works. Nor can it reflect the fact that different traditions can favor different dictionary types. It also needs to be said that the typology classifies printed dictionaries and that it remains to be seen what impact the electronic presentation of lexicographic information with its different possibilities will have on dictionary typology. The many types of reference works classified in this typology are all dictionaries or word books. The overwhelming majority contain the term *dictionary* (*dictionnaire*, *Wörterbuch*) in the title, and it is this term that is firmly entrenched as the coverall designation of works of lexical or word-centered reference. Few others have survived. *Glossary* is used of an alphabetical list of selected items with definitions and/or translation equivalents as found commonly at the back of subject-area textbooks or language course books. *Vocabulary* can be used similarly, but most commonly refers to the lexical items of a given language, also of a language variety, speaker, or text, taken collectively and studied in lexicology but not necessarily codified and described in lexicography. Part synonyms are *lexis* and *lexicon*, both of which are also used as antonyms of *grammar*. *Lexicon* is used further, often in the collocation or compound *mental lexicon*, for words and vocabulary stored and processed in the speaker's mind. As a label for a lexicographic reference work it is now generally applied in English to specialized or technical works or to dictionaries of classical languages such as Greek or Arabic. It is thus more restricted than its one-time synonym *dictionary*. McArthur's *Longman Lexicon of Contemporary English*, 1981, however, is a type of thesaurus. In modern lexicographic use (Hüllen, 1999), *thesaurus* refers to a word book that classifies and groups lexical items of a language, variety, or subject area according to sense relations, especially synonymy, in semantic sets and arranges and presents them alphabetically and/or thematically or conceptually. All thematic and some alphabetical thesauruses now have alphabetical indexes to ensure easy access, especially when the items are grouped according to a philosophical world view such as those which determined the organization of older thematic encyclopedias. At one level *thesaurus* is used as a hyponym and at another level as an antonym of *dictionary*: the thesaurus is both a type of dictionary and it also contrasts with the dictionary proper, as reflected in the titles of combined dictionaries-cum-thesauruses such as *Collins (Concise, Compact) Dictionary and Thesaurus*. The dictionary proper here is the alphabetical semasiological defining dictionary, and this type represents the stock answer to the question, what is a dictionary?

2.3.3 *Component parts of the dictionary*

Three major component parts may be distinguished in the structure of the dictionary: outside or additional matter, macro-structure, and micro-structure. All can vary very considerably in size and content according to dictionary type and to the specifications of a particular dictionary project, and indeed between successive editions of the same work. They are discussed here with reference only to monolingual general-purpose defining dictionaries, the standard type of trade dictionary.

The components additional to the central word list or the dictionary entries from A to Z consist of front, middle, and back matter, often including the inside covers and, increasingly, the outside covers and dust jacket. The front matter contains most importantly a user's guide or key to the dictionary. The key is now considered essential, but often seems to be ignored by users and reviewers alike. It explains style, structure and content of the dictionary: the metalanguage, symbols and codes used, the punctuation and the complex typography, and the layout of the entries. It often takes the form of reproductions of sample entries with each component of the macro- and micro-structure highlighted and commented on in turn. It sometimes stands alone and sometimes accompanies a longer introduction to the dictionary outlining the editorial principles underlying the work. The middle matter might consist of small, half- or full-page panels devoted to grammar and/or usage notes, frequency charts, word-formation items and patterns, lexical sets or pragmatic conventions; or it might feature inserted study pages, maps, illustrations, and encyclopedic information, sometimes in color and/or on different paper to make the inserts stand out. In many cases the material in such inserts is reserved for appendices in the back matter. These might contain both linguistic and encyclopedic information of all kinds ranging from style guides, prefixes and suffixes, and different alphabets to weights and measures, chemical elements, and countries of the world. Some dictionaries have no back matter, others have as many as 100 pages of appendices. While much of the front matter is essentially similar from one dictionary to the next, the middle and back matter tend to be much more varied and individual.

Macro-structure refers to the list and organization of the lexical items entered in the dictionary, the lemmas or headwords. Lemma is preferred here as it is neutral on the morphological status of the items. In practical terms the lemma list depends on the projected size and scope of the dictionary. It ranges from reasonably comprehensive, as in large unabridged works, to highly selective, as in small pocket dictionaries. Depending on size and intention, current one-volume defining dictionaries tend to emphasize the central core vocabulary of present-day standard usage and to focus as well on new words and senses and on terms from science and technology. The organization of the lemmas is now almost always alphabetical. Decisions must be made on giving each item main lemma status or distinguishing between main lemmas and sub-lemmas. In the latter case, lexicographers must determine on what grounds main lemmas are distinguished from sub-lemmas, how these are grouped or organized in nests or niches, and whether all or some of the sub-lemmas are supplied with a full or partial range of lexicographic information or whether they are simply listed as run-ons. Decisions must also be made on the ordering of homographic lemmas and on the typography of the different types of lemma. Here, as elsewhere, the chief macro-structural criterion must be user-friendliness: the user must be able to find the item looked for as quickly and easily as possible.

Micro-structure refers to the lexicographic information on the lemma contained in the dictionary article. Different dictionaries have different policies on the information they regard as lexically relevant and on the order in which they present it. The micro-structure routinely provides information on the form, meaning and use of the lemma. Formal information may include spelling and pronunciation, usually with accepted variants in different standard varieties; base and inflected forms; syntactic category including part-of-speech and sub-category, e.g., transitive or ergative verb, predicative adjective, or mass noun. Semantic information includes definitions or explanations of literal and figurative, denotative and connotative meanings. These may take the form of synonyms or near-synonyms, for instance, analytical definitions with genus proximum and differentiae specificae, paraphrases or formulae. They are usually supplemented by paradigmatic information on lexical fields involving synonyms, antonyms, or hyponyms; by syntagmatic information on lexical collocation, grammatical colligation and complementation, and on use in idioms, proverbs, and other fixed phrases and chunks; and by pragmatic information or diasystematic marking on register, frequency, currency, style, status, and subject area. They may be complemented by pictorial illustrations, authentic, adapted and constructed textual examples, usage notes and short synonym essays, indications of word-formational activity, especially derivatives and compounds if these are not lemmatised and described separately, and by cross-references to other entries or to extra-textual middle and back matter. As with the macro-structure, the typography and lay-out of the micro-structure must above all be user-friendly.

2.4   Dictionaries in Applied Linguistics

Wherever languages are used and wherever languages are taught and learned, especially in educational settings, dictionaries play a central role. As already discussed (see Section 2.2), lexicography is thus not only a field of professional, commercial, and academic activity in its own right, but also very much an integral part of applied linguistics and its constituent subject areas. The most obvious area is first and second/foreign language teaching and learning at all ages and levels of education, an area that some virtually equate with applied linguistics and that is by common consent certainly one of the core activities of applied linguistics (see Section 2.5). A few examples of other areas of professional applied linguistics must suffice here.

One such area is translation. Professional translators need and use dictionaries of different types according to the nature of the translation, general or specialized, literary or scientific. The dictionaries range from general-purpose dictionaries of the second language and thesauruses and synonym dictionaries of the first language to mono- and bilingual subject-specific technical dictionaries and glossaries. Not for nothing is the general bilingual dictionary known as a translation dictionary, although in this context translation must be seen as a traditional exercise in second/foreign language teaching and learning as well as a professional activity. The work of lexicographers and translators has much in common, and the latter can be expert informants for practicing lexicographers, more so perhaps than linguists. Technical translators must have the combination of linguistic and encyclopedic or content knowledge and an ability at written expression needed by specialist lexicographers. Literary translators must have an ability to extract meaning from text in one language and to arrive at an equivalent formulation in another that could only benefit bilingual lexicographers. They also have a highly developed feeling for sense discrimination and explanation that would make them ideal consultants on or compilers of thesauruses.

Other areas of applied linguistics are communication in the professions and languages for special purposes, both of which have at their disposal a vast range of specialized, subject-specific reference works, be it in law, medicine and engineering, or in the sciences and technologies (Bergenholtz & Tarp, 1995). Both areas draw *inter alia* on terminological lexicography or terminography and use as editors and/or consultants experts in the relevant subject area or areas being treated. Linguistic knowledge as such may or may not play a role. Dictionaries and glossaries of technical terms may be mono- and, increasingly frequently, multilingual, with international standards organizations seeking to establish equivalence of standardized terms and concepts across languages. They tend to be thematic rather than alphabetical in organization and presentation in accordance with their concentration on word meanings rather than word forms and on concepts within a given taxonomy. To handle the problem of the sheer number of terms in some areas they make full use of the possibilities now offered by electronic storage and presentation.

A further area is language planning, both corpus planning and status planning, in which the role of lexicography has been and is as central as it is complex. In the modern period of western European lexicography, mainstream dictionaries have been absolutely instrumental in the establishment of standard varieties of the different vernaculars, especially in written use, and in their gradual emancipation from Latin. Regardless of whether they have been avowedly descriptive or explicitly prescriptive and normative in intention and approach, they have codified and helped standardize spelling, pronunciation, meaning, and usage and they have acquired the status of linguistic authorities in the eyes of many, if not most users. The authoritarian tradition is firmly established, and publishers still often appeal to it in their advertising. Indeed, the history of mainstream dictionaries can be seen *inter alia* as a history of the longstanding and ongoing conflict between the descriptive and the prescriptive, one notable chapter of which was the controversy over *Webster's Third New International Dictionary* in the 1960s (Sledd & Ebbit, 1962; Morton, 1994). The dictionary editors favored a strongly descriptive policy aiming to record and describe authoritatively contemporary English usage as documented in extensive citation files. Where appropriate, they included clear pragmatic information on debated usage, but did not set out to be an authoritarian *arbiter usus*, being concerned to avoid prescribing or proscribing usage. A case in point is the entry on *ain't* reproduced slightly enlarged in Figure 2.1. In some quarters this policy was viewed as a permissive abdication of the alleged responsibility of lexicographers not only to describe what is used and how but also to prescribe what should or should not be used. While attempts to buy out the publishers and remove the dictionary from circulation failed, the controversy produced avowedly rival works such as *The American Heritage Dictionary*, 1969, which featured usage notes informed by a panel of more than 100 representatives of the literary establishment. Its echoes can still be clearly heard in later dictionaries, where a separate usage note on *ain't*, for instance, is often longer than the actual lexicographic description itself. One example is *The Reader's Digest Great Illustrated Dictionary*, 1984 (see Figure 2.2).

The same European dictionaries played as much a role in status planning as in corpus planning, certainly in terms of nation building. The multi-volume

ain't \'ānt\ *also* **an't** \" *also* 'ant *or like* AREN'T\ [prob. contr. of *are not, is not, am not,* & *have not*] **1 a :** are not ⟨you ~ going⟩ ⟨they ~ here⟩ ⟨things ~ what they used to be⟩ **b :** is not ⟨it ~ raining⟩ ⟨he's here, ~ he⟩ **c :** am not ⟨I ~ ready⟩ — though disapproved by many and more common in less educated speech, used orally in most parts of the U. S. by many cultivated speakers esp. in the phrase *ain't I* **2** *sub-stand* **a :** have not ⟨I ~ seen him⟩ ⟨you ~ told us⟩ **b :** has not ⟨he ~ got the time⟩ ⟨~ the doctor come yet⟩

Figure 2.1   Definition of *ain't* from *Webster's Third New International Dictionary* By permission. From *Webster's Third New International® Dictionary, Unabridged,* © 1993 by Merriam-Webster, Incorporated.

ain't (aynt). *Nonstandard.* Contraction of *am not.* Also extended in use to mean *are not, is not, has not,* and *have not.*

> ***Usage:*** Although widely used in colloquial speech, *ain't* is considered nonstandard by educated speakers. It should always be avoided in writing or formal speech, unless you are deliberately trying to create a humorous effect, or using a fixed phrase like *Things ain't what they used to be. Aren't I* (as in *aren't I coming too?*) has sometimes also been attacked on the grounds that it misleadingly suggests a corresponding form *I are.* But the full form, *am I not,* is so formal that in many contexts it may be considered ridiculously stilted, and *aren't I* is therefore a quite acceptable usage in educated British English. The form *amn't I* has some currency in regional English, especially in Scotland and Ireland, but is considered nonstandard.

Figure 2.2 Definition of *ain't* from *The Reader's Digest Great Illustrated Dictionary* By permission of The Readers's Digest Association Limited, *Reader's Digest Great Illustrated Dictionary* (1984).

scholarly and historical dictionaries inaugurated in nineteenth-century Europe, for example, were seen as national dictionaries, and the lexicography of Noah Webster was consciously and patriotically American. Nation building is not just a historical issue, but is equally important in contemporary lexicography. It underlies and supports, for instance, efforts to establish a standardized variety of "lesser-used" European languages such as Luxembourgish or Rhaeto-Romance. It is an important motivation in the lexicographical recording and describing of endangered and indigenous languages by anthropological linguists and also in the planning of comprehensive monolingual dictionaries for languages such as Samoan and Tongan which have previously relied on bilingual dictionaries with English. It is also an integral component of the codification of the different standard varieties of both contiguous and dispersed pluricentric languages. An example of the former is German, where *Österreichisches Wörterbuch*, 1951, 39th edn. 2001, a government sponsored endonormative dictionary used officially in schools, codifies Austrian Standard German as a standard variety distinct from German Standard German and Swiss Standard German. An example of the latter is English, where different native speaker standard varieties are now covered in national dictionaries, for example, *The Australian National Dictionary. A Dictionary of Australianisms on Historical Principles*, 1988; and *The Macquarie Dictionary*, 1981, 3rd edn. 1997, which advertises itself as "the arbiter of Australian English" and as "Australia's National Dictionary."

2.5   Dictionaries in Second/Foreign Language Teaching and Learning

The fundamental importance of language teaching and learning in applied linguistics is beyond dispute. So is the role of dictionaries in languages-in-education planning and policy and in language education of all kinds at all levels, and hence the status of pedagogical lexicography as a significant branch of lexicography. It is concerned with the writing and study of dictionaries for first and second/foreign language education and with the study of dictionary use, especially by language teachers and learners. It involves mono-, bi-, and multilingual works as well as general children's, school, college, and specialized technical dictionaries. Pedagogical lexicography is such a vast field that a sharper focus is necessary here. The present chapter focuses specifically on second/foreign language teaching and learning. It concentrates on monolingual learners' dictionaries, while acknowledging the importance, indeed dominance of bilingual dictionaries and their use particularly in the earlier stages of second/foreign language education (see Section 2.3.2). It concentrates further on English as a second, foreign, or international language, while recognizing that other language communities have their own learners' dictionaries. The current international importance of teaching and learning English as an additional language means that the pedagogical lexicography of English has become a worldwide issue and has been able to sustain a level of activity not matched by other language communities, either quantitatively or qualitatively. The same is true of the very extensive literature on English learners' dictionaries by international scholars. Standard English is a pluricentric language, and it has become common, indeed necessary, to talk about Englishes or the English languages. British English and now American English are the leading varieties, and this is reflected in the coverage of English in monolingual learners' dictionaries or MLDs. Very recently, different English language centers have produced their own MLDs, notably Australia and especially America. These works notwithstanding, the leading center of English MLDs is, without any doubt, Great Britain. For more than half a century it has been home to a tradition of pedagogical lexicography marked by rapid and constant change, technological advance, innovative and creative development and response to users' needs and to teachers' and metalexicographers' suggestions and demands, and an increasingly competitive market (Cowie, 1999; Herbst & Popp, 1999).

The mainstream of modern British pedagogical lexicography is represented by general-purpose MLDs for advanced learners. It dates effectively from 1948, when Oxford University Press published *A Learner's Dictionary of Current English*, edited by A. S. Hornby with E. V. Gatenby and H. Wakefield and renamed *The Advanced Learner's Dictionary of Current English* in 1952. The Oxford dictionary established some of the salient features of MLDs as a distinctive dictionary type. The macro-structure did not seek to be comprehensive, but was restricted and selective with the choice of lemmas based on the classroom experience of practicing language teachers and their knowledge and perception of learner needs, especially those of advanced learners. On the twin principle of frequency and utility, the emphasis was placed on words and meanings current in the standard language. In contrast, the micro-structure was fully developed, with the exception of historical and etymological information. This was omitted, and the MLD has since remained a synchronic record of present-day English concentrating on core vocabulary and opening itself in successive editions to new words. The received British pronunciation (RP) of each lemma was given in the transcriptions of the International Phonetic Association (IPA). IPA offers an international user group from diverse language backgrounds one and the same system and has since established itself, with slight variations, as the dominant phonetic transcription in MLDs. General American pronunciation (GA) is now recorded in addition to RP, and in CD versions learners can listen to native speakers' pronunciations. Grammatical information was given for each lemma to show how it was used in current English and to give directions for productive use or encoding. It included coded complementation patterns for all verbs, distinctions between count and non-count nouns, and detailed treatment of the definite and indefinite articles and other function words. Such grammatical information has since been expanded and refined in succeeding editions and in competing publications, notably in the use of more user-friendly and transparent notations for verb patterns. With the primary aim of meeting decoding or receptive needs, semantic information included an emphasis on explicit synonym discrimination and description, pictorial illustrations, and above all an attempt to explain meanings as simply as possible and to avoid the lexicographic shorthand or lexicographese common in native speaker dictionaries. Stylistic labels or pragmatic markers were used to indicate register, range, and subject field. To illustrate the meanings and uses of words in context, constructed textual examples were included: Hornby was convinced that no word had meaning until placed in context and that illustrative phrases and sentences brought the word to life. This has remained a key principle in all modern MLDs. Further linguistic and some encyclopedic information was provided in appendices.

Hornby published a second edition in 1963 and a third in 1974 together with Anthony Cowie and John Windsor Lewis. It was entitled *Oxford Advanced Learner's Dictionary of Current English* (*OALD*), a title that has been retained since. In 1978 a new advanced MLD appeared, the *Longman Dictionary of Contemporary English* (*LDOCE*), edited by Paul Procter. It was essentially similar to *OALD* in presentation and appearance, but included a more up-to-date lemma list and a number of significant innovations. One was the use of a controlled defining vocabulary of some 2,000 items, not counting derivatives and compounds or different senses of polysemous items. If items not listed in this defining vocabulary (DV) were used in the semantic explanations, they were printed in small capitals and entered as lemmas in the dictionary. A controlled defining vocabulary has since become an integral feature of MLDs. A second innovation was a more transparent alphanumeric notation for verb patterns and the codification of noun and adjective complementation. Further, increased attention was paid to varieties of English other than British English, notably American English, with IPA transcriptions given for both British and American pronunciations. Importantly, computer assistance was used, especially to check the consistency and use of the defining vocabulary.

Longman published a second edition of *LDOCE* in 1987, to be followed in 1989 by the fourth edition of *OALD*, now edited by Anthony Cowie. Both simplified the notation of their verb patterns by using more transparent codes for formal or functional categories. *LDOCE* also extended the use of a computerized citation corpus as the basis for its textual examples, which were adapted by the lexicographers. In 1987 *Collins Cobuild English Language Dictionary* appeared, edited by John Sinclair. It claimed to be an essentially corpus-based dictionary of "real English" with computer assistance fully integrated into all aspects of the lexicographers' work. "Real" was understood in a dual sense: on the one hand, all examples of usage were taken directly from a computerized corpus of some 20 million running words and only very slightly adapted, if at all, by the lexicographers; on the other, meanings and uses were explained in a discursive, full-sentence style similar to teacher talk. This represented a radical departure from traditional defining practices as found in native speaker dictionaries. It was designed to be user-friendly for learners of English as an additional language, who should be met with "real" English sentences rather than lexicographese. A further innovation was the introduction of coded semantic, pragmatic, and especially grammatical information in an extra column with the complex codes explained in the front matter. The dictionary was more strongly oriented to British English than its competitors, and concentrated on a fuller micro-structural description of a smaller number of lemmas from core vocabulary. Unlike its competitors, it had no pictorial illustrations, and alone of all MLDs it has since continued to do without them.

In 1995 *OALD* appeared in a fifth edition with Jonathan Crowther as chief editor, the third edition of *LDOCE* came out under the direction of Della Summers, John Sinclair edited a second edition of *Collins Cobuild English Dictionary* (*CCED*), and Cambridge University Press brought out the *Cambridge International Dictionary of English* (*CIDE*), edited by Paul Procter. The new editions were genuinely new. All included many new words in the macro-structure and refinements and innovations in the micro-structure. *CCED* was now based on a corpus of more than 200 million words. All the illustrative examples were new. So-called "superheadwords" were introduced to give the user an overview of highly polysemous and polyfunctional lemmas. Information on word frequency was added in the extra column in five bands of decreasing frequency, with the marked words together giving a claimed 95 percent coverage of written and spoken English. A defining vocabulary was introduced. Meanings and uses were listed in order of frequency, and pragmatic and grammatical information was revised and refined. *LDOCE* also featured a large corpus basis, the British National Corpus of 100 million words and Longman's own extensive citation files. The most frequent 3,000 words in written and/or spoken English were marked, and extra graphs gave details on differences between written and spoken frequency for selected lemmas. Index-like menus and so-called "signposts" in a different font were introduced to guide users quickly to the different senses of highly polysemous lemmas. Usage notes gave extra grammatical or semantic information, including meaning discrimination of synonyms. Set phrases and fixed collocations were highlighted and defined as lexical units, especially as used in spoken usage. Full-page full-color illustrations were introduced to illustrate prepositions of position and direction, for instance, or lexical/conceptual fields such as adjectives denoting 'broken'. Both the notation of syntactic patterns and the defining vocabulary were further revised. *OALD* now claimed to be "the dictionary that really teaches English." It likewise made extensive use of the British National Corpus and of the Oxford American English Corpus of 40 million words, with most of the textual examples now being corpus-based. It introduced for the first time a defining vocabulary of some 3,500 items. Idioms and phrasal verbs were highlighted. Special notes gave more detailed information on grammatical difficulties and on synonym differentiation. Extralinguistic and cultural-encyclopedic information was provided on glossy-paper inserts, some in full color, in addition to appendices in the back matter. The wholly new *CIDE* brought further innovations to the British MLD tradition. It was based on the Cambridge Language Survey of 100 million words taken from the major standard varieties of English, including Australian English and an equal representation of British and American English. It also drew on a specialized corpus of learner English, which allowed typical learner errors to be specifically targeted, for instance in lists of selected false friends in 16 other, mainly European, languages. The corpus base also allowed detailed treatment of function words and lexical and grammatical collocations. Like *LDOCE*, it used typographically highlighted "guidewords" to help users distinguish between the main senses of polysemous items, which were usually lemmatized separately in a strongly homographic approach, and a controlled defining vocabulary of 2,000 basic items. Grammatical information was given on the lemmas as such and attached in coded form to the many illustrative textual examples. It was also provided together with lexical and stylistic information in full- and part-page language portraits on topics from adjectives and adverbs to linking verbs, varieties of English, and words used together. A necessary innovation was the lengthy phrase index in the back matter. It listed multi-word items under each item a learner might look up and gave a precise reference with page and line number to its location in the dictionary. The index is helpful given the difficulty in locating idioms and phrases under the multiple separate entries for productive and polysemous items like *get*, *go*, or *take*. A further innovation was the use of black-and-white silhouette drawings instead of the more traditional line drawings.

The intervals between editions have since grown even shorter. In 2000 Sally Wehmeier edited the sixth edition of *OALD*. Again, it is a new work with new words, major changes in lemmatization, revisions in the defining vocabulary, and a pronounced emphasis on American English usage. The third edition of *CCED*, with *for Advanced Learners* added to the title, followed in 2001. The Bank of English corpus now counts more than 400 million words, and among the significant changes is a similarly strong emphasis on American English. Longman reissued its third edition in 2001, featuring blue-colored lemmas and usage notes and a 64-page new word supplement. These three works and *CIDE* are all available with extra features including worksheets and vocabulary-learning activities as CD-ROMs and online. The most recent addition to this highly competitive series of MLDs is the *Macmillan English Dictionary for Advanced Learners* published early in 2002 in an English and an American edition as both a printed book and a CD. Clearly, British publishers have become ever more conscious of the market for American English: either they publish separate dictionaries of American English, such as Longman and Cambridge, or they explicitly highlight their treatment of American English in their general MLDs. They have now been joined by American publishers. At the start of the new millennium, teachers and advanced learners of English as a second/foreign or international language have an unparalleled lexicographic offering to choose from. Given the high quality of the dictionaries, each with its own individual features and particular strengths, price and personal prefer-ence will no doubt decide the choice. The sample entries reproduced in Fig-ure 2.3 are intended to illustrate concrete lexicographic practice in MLDs for advanced learners. The entries on the semi-modal verb *used to* illustrate above all differing treatments of the relatively uncommon negative forms *used not to, didn't use to, didn't used to,* which are attested 12, 17, and 25 times respectively in the British National Corpus. Reference grammars of English differ similarly in their description of and pedagogical grammars in their advice on such forms. They are all very much less frequent than *never used to,* which has 141 tokens spread over 96 texts in the British National Corpus and thus appeals as the preferred form to teach learners of English as an additional language. The entries on the item or items *base* illustrate macro-structural differences in lemmatization policy, which ranges from homographic, with items lemmatized separately according to word-class, to polysemous, where different word-classes and different meanings are not reflected in the lemmatization, and also varies in the treatment of derivatives as run-ons or as separate main or sub-lemmas. They likewise illustrate micro-structural variation, for instance, in the descrip-tion and ordering of meanings, the number and use of textual examples, the presentation of grammatical and pragmatic information (e.g., frequency), or in the treatment of phrasal verbs, phrases and idioms.

The mainstream of monolingual English pedagogical lexicography is supported by numerous major and minor tributaries. The leading publishers, especially in Britain, offer a whole range of general learners' dictionaries for all levels from beginner and elementary to upper intermediate as well as advanced. In addition, there are many specialized works, some of which are also available in different formats for different learner levels. They include dictionaries of pronunciation, collocations, and particularly idioms and phrasal verbs. There are also encyclopedic learners' dictionaries, notably *Oxford Advanced Learner's Encyclopedic Dictionary,* 1993; and *Longman Dictionary of English Language and Culture,* 1993, 2nd edn. 2000 (Stark, 1999). In addition, there are learners' thesauruses in a broad sense. McArthur's *Longman Lexicon of Contemporary English,* 1981, is arranged thematically with an alphabetic

base /beɪs/ (bases, basing, based; baser, basest) ◆◆◆◆◆

1 The **base** of something is its lowest edge or part. ◻ *There was a cycle path running along this side of the wall, right at its base... Line the base and sides of a 20cm deep round cake tin with paper.* — N-COUNT: usu the N of n = bottom ≠ top

2 The **base** of something is the lowest part of it, where it is attached to something else. ◻ *The surgeon placed catheters through the veins and arteries near the base of the head.* — N-COUNT: usu the N of n

3 The **base** of an object such as a box or vase is the lower surface of it that touches the surface it rests on. ◻ *Remove from the heat and plunge the base of the pan into a bowl of very cold water.* — N-COUNT: usu with poss = bottom, underneath

4 The **base** of an object that has several sections and that rests on a surface is the lower section of it. ◻ *The mattress is best on a solid bed base... The clock stands on an oval marble base, enclosed by a glass dome.* — N-COUNT: usu with supp, oft n N

5 A **base** is a layer of something which will have another layer added to it. ◻ *Spoon the mixture on to the biscuit base and cook in a pre-heated oven... On many modern wooden boats, epoxy coatings will have been used as a base for varnishing.* — N-COUNT: usu with supp

6 A position or thing that is a **base** for something is one from which that thing can be developed or achieved. ◻ *The post will give him a powerful political base from which to challenge the Kremlin... The family base was crucial to my development.* — N-COUNT: usu sing, with supp = basis, foundation

7 If you **base** one thing on another thing, the first thing develops from the second thing. ◻ *He based his conclusions on the evidence given by the captured prisoners.* ◆ **based** *Three of the new products are based on traditional herbal medicines... The figures are based upon average market prices.* — VERB = found V n on/upon n / ADJ: v-link ADJ on n

8 A military **base** is a place which part of the armed forces works from. ◻ *Gunfire was heard at an army base close to the airport... Lauren Long works in the Air Force motor pool on a massive air base in eastern Saudi Arabia.* — N-COUNT: usu supp N

9 Your **base** is the main place where you work, stay, or live. ◻ *For most of the spring and early summer her base was her home in Scotland.* — N-COUNT: usu poss N

10 If a place is a **base** for a certain activity, the activity can be carried out at that place or from that place. ◻ *The two hotel-restaurants are attractive bases from which to explore southeast Tuscany... Los Angeles was still my financial base. I was still doing business there.* — N-COUNT: usu sing, usu N prep

11 The **base** of a substance such as paint or food is the main ingredient of it, to which other substances can be added. ◻ *Just before cooking, drain off any excess marinade and use it as a base for a pouring sauce... Oils may be mixed with a base oil and massaged into the skin.* — N-COUNT

12 A **base** is a system of counting and expressing numbers. The decimal system uses base 10, and the binary system uses base 2. — N-COUNT: also N num

13 A **base** in baseball, softball, or rounders is one of the places at each corner of the square on the pitch. — N-COUNT

14 **Base** behaviour is behaviour that is immoral or dishonest. [LITERARY] ◻ *Love has the power to overcome the baser emotions.* — ADJ-GRADED

15 If you say that someone is **off base**, you mean that they are wrong. [mainly AM, INFORMAL] ◻ *Am I wrong? Am I way off base? Because I want you to set me straight if you think I'm wrong.* — PHRASE: usu v-link PHR

16 If you **communicate** with someone, especially someone you have not communicated with recently, you can say that you **touch base** with them. [INFORMAL] ◻ *Being there gave me a chance to touch base with three friends whom I had not seen for a year.* — PHRASE: V inflects, oft PHR with n

17 If someone **touches all the bases** or **covers the bases**, they deal with everyone or everything involved in a situation. [INFORMAL] ◻ *He has managed to touch all the bases necessary, and trade goes on... The boss covers all bases when he sets up a job.* — PHRASE

┌─────────── **used** ───────────┐
│ ① MODAL USES AND PHRASES   │
│ ② ADJECTIVE USES   │
└────────────────────────────────┘

① used ◆◆◆◆◇

☑ Pronounced /juːst/ in **used** ①, and /juːzd/ in **used** ②.

1 If something **used to** be done or **used to** be the case, it was done regularly in the past or was the case in the past. ◻ *People used to come and visit him every day... He used to be one of the professors at the School of Education... I feel more compassion and less anger than I used to.* — PHR-MODAL

2 If something **used not to** be done or **used not to** be the case, it was not done in the past or was not the case in the past. The forms **did not use to** and **did not used to** are also found, especially in spoken English. ◻ *Borrowing used not to be recommended... At some point kids start doing things they didn't use to do. They get more independent... He didn't used to like anyone walking on the lawns in the back garden.* — PHR-MODAL: with neg

3 If you **are used to** something, you are familiar with it because you have done it or experienced it many times before. ◻ *I'm used to having my sleep interrupted... It doesn't frighten them. They're used to it.* — PHRASE: V inflects, PHR n/-ing

4 If you **get used to** something or someone, you become familiar with it or get to know them, so that you no longer feel that the thing or person is unusual or surprising. ◻ *This is how we do things here. You'll soon get used to it... He took some getting used to... You quickly get used to using the brakes.* — PHRASE: V inflects

② used ◆◇◇◇◇

☑ Pronounced /juːst/ in **used** ①, and /juːzd/ in **used** ②.

1 A **used** object is dirty or spoiled because it has been used, and usually needs to be thrown away or washed. ◻ *...a used cotton ball stained with makeup... He took a used envelope bearing an Irish postmark.* — ADJ: usu ADJ n ≠ clean

2 A **used** car has already had one or more owners. ◻ *Would you buy a used car from this man?... His only big purchase has been a used Ford.* — ADJ: usu ADJ n = second-hand

---

Figure 2.3 Entries on *base* and *used* in MLDs for advanced learners
(a) Reproduced from *Collins COBUILD English Dictionary* with the permission of HarperCollins Publishers Ltd. © Harper-Collins Publishers Ltd 2001. Updated from the Bank of English. Based on the COBUILD series developed in collaboration with the University of Birmingham. COBUILD® and Bank of English® are registered trademarks of HarperCollins Publishers Ltd.

base BOTTOM /beɪs/ n [C] the bottom part of an object, on which it rests, or the lowest part of something • *This drinking glass is made of crystal and has a heavy base.* • *'Wedgwood' was written on the base of the cup.* • *At the base of the cliff was a rocky beach.* • *This cream provides an excellent base for your make-up* (= a good bottom layer on which other layers can be put). • *(fig.) A strong economy depends on a healthy manufacturing base.* • *(Br specialized)* The **base rate** is the percentage rate decided by the government or the Bank of England which banks use when deciding how much to charge for lending money: *The interest rate on Caroline's mortgage is fixed at two percent above the base rate for five years.* • Ⓟ

base MAIN PLACE /beɪs/ n [C] the main place where a person lives and works, or a place that a company does business from, or a place where there are military buildings and weapons and where members of the armed forces live • *I spend a lot of time in Brussels, but London is still my base.* • *Nice is an excellent base for* (= place to stay when) *exploring the French Riviera.* • *With the ending of the Cold War, a lot of American bases in the UK have been closed.* • In the game of baseball, a base is one of the four positions on a square that a player must reach to score a point. • A **base camp** is a place where food and general supplies are kept, esp. for people climbing a mountain. • Ⓟ

base obj /beɪs/ v [T usually passive; always + adv, prep] • *Where is your firm based?* • *He was based in* (= He lived in or was at a military establishment in) *Birmingham during the war.*

–based /-beɪst/ combining form • *a Manchester-based company* • *community-based programs* • *land-based missiles* (= ones which are fired from the ground)

base MAIN PART /beɪs/ n [C usually sing] the main part of something • *A Manhattan is a cocktail with a whisky base.* • *(specialized)* In grammar, the **base form** of a verb is the simplest form, without a special ending: *The base form of 'calling' is 'call'.* • Ⓟ

base obj /beɪs/ v [T usually passive] • *The film is based on a short story by Thomas Mann* (= the film was developed from the story). • *I feel he's doing something wrong, but I've got nothing to base it on* (= I have no proof).

–based /-beɪst/ combining form • *This is a cream-based sauce* (= Cream is the main thing in it).

base·less /'beɪ·sləs/ adj • A baseless claim or belief is not based on facts: *baseless accusations/allegations/ rumours* ○ *The reports that he has been involved in corruption are completely baseless.*

base NOT HONOURABLE /beɪs/ adj -r, -st literary not honourable and lacking in morals • *I accused him of having base motives.* • *(specialized)* A **base metal** is a common metal such as LEAD, TIN or COPPER which is not a precious metal and which reacts easily with other chemicals. • Ⓟ

base·ly /'beɪ·sli/ adv literary • *I shall lie basely to help them.*

base·ness /'beɪ·snəs/ n [U] literary

base MATHEMATICS /beɪs/ n [C usually sing] specialized the number on which a counting system is built • *The normal counting system uses base 10, but computers use base 2.* • *A binary number is a number written in base 2, using the two numbers 0 and 1.* • *5 in base 10 is 101 in base 2, and 3 in base 10 is 11 in base 2.* • The base is also the number which must be multiplied by itself a particular number of times to produce another number, when you represent the other number using a LOGARITHM: *The logarithm of 1 000 000 is six, if the base is ten.* • Ⓟ

base CHEMISTRY /beɪs/ n [C] specialized a base is a chemical that dissolves in water and combines with an acid to create a SALT • *Caustic soda is a base which reacts with hydrochloric acid to give water and sodium chloride.* • Ⓟ

used IN THE PAST /juːst/ v [+ to infinitive] used to show that a particular thing always happened or was true in the past, esp. if it no longer happens or is no longer true • *Aunt Betty used to live in Australia.* • *You used to be able to walk around the town at night without fear of being mugged.* • *She used to like cats but one attacked her and she doesn't anymore.* • *You don't come and see me like you used* (to). • *(not standard) He did used to work there, didn't he?* • 'Used to' can form negatives and questions in the same way as modal auxiliary verbs: *When we were younger we used not to be allowed to coffee to drink.* ○ *Used he/Didn't he use to read the news on television?* ○ *(fml) Used you to work in banking?* • Used to only has the past simple tense. • LP Auxiliary verbs

use /juːs/ v [+ to infinitive] • 'Use to' can be used instead of 'used to' after 'did' in negatives and questions: *You didn't use to/(slightly fml) You usen't to like cream.* ○ *Didn't he use to be the doctor in 'Star Trek'?*

used NOT NEW /juːzd/ adj [not gradable] that has been put to the purpose it was intended for; not new • *a used airline ticket* • *The blackmailers demanded to be paid in used £20 notes.* • A used car is one that has already been owned by at least one person, and is being sold again: *a used-car salesman*

used to /juːst/ adj [after v] familiar with (something or someone) • *We're used to tourists here.* • *She was not used to speaking Cantonese.* [+ v-ing] • *Eventually you'll get used to the smells in the laboratory.* • *There are some things you never get used to.* • *It'll take a while for people to become used to the new building.*

Figure 2.3 (b) By permission, *Cambridge International Dictionary of English* 1995. © Cambridge University Press.

base¹ /beɪs/ v [T] to establish or use somewhere as the main place for your business or work: *a Denver-based law firm* [S] [1] [W] [1]

base sth **on/upon** sth *phr v* [T often passive] to use particular information or facts as a point from which to develop an idea, plan etc: *The film is based on a novel by Sinclair Lewis.*

base² *n* [S] [2] [W] [2]

1 ► LOWEST PART ◄ [C usually singular] the lowest part of something, or the surface at the bottom of something: [+ of] *There was a chip in the base of the glass.* | *the base of a triangle* | *Waves crashed and pounded at the base of the cliff.*

2 ► KNOWLEDGE/IDEAS ◄ [U] the most important part of something from which new ideas develop: *India has a good scientific research base.* | *This provides a good base for the development of new techniques.*

3 ► COMPANY/ORGANIZATION ◄ [C,U] the main place from which a group, company, or organization controls its activities: *Cuba was seen as a base for Communist activity throughout Latin America.* | *Report back to base as soon as you see anything.*

4 ► MILITARY ◄ [C] a place where people in a military organization live and work: *a naval base*

5 ► PEOPLE/GROUPS ◄ [C usually singular] the people, money, groups etc from which a lot of support or power comes: *an attempt to strengthen the city's economic base* | **tax/customer base** (=all the people who pay tax or buy goods in a particular place) *A reputation for excellent service will expand our customer base.* | **manufacturing base** (=all the factories, companies etc that produce goods in a country) *The country's manufacturing base has shrunk by 20% during the recession.* —see also POWER BASE

6 ► SUBSTANCE/MIXTURE ◄ [singular, U] the main part of a substance to which something else is later added: *paint with an oil base*

7 ► BODY/PLANT ◄ [C usually singular] the point where part of your body or part of a plant joins with the rest: *She had a dull ache at the base of her neck.*

8 ► SPORT ◄ [C] one of the four places that a player must touch in order to get a point in games such as BASEBALL

9 **be off base** *AmE informal* to be completely wrong: *His estimate for painting the kitchen seems way off base.*

10 ► CHEMISTRY ◄ [C] *technical* a chemical substance that combines with an acid to form a SALT¹ (3)

11 ► NUMBERS ◄ [C usually singular] *technical* the number in relation to which a number system or mathematical table is built up

12 **touch base (with sb)** to telephone someone who you live or work with, or make a short visit, while you are spending time somewhere else —see also **cover (all) the bases** (COVER¹ (13))

base³ *adj literary* not having good moral principles: *base passions* —see also BASE METAL

use³ *v negative form of* usedn't, usen't *old-fashioned* [S] [1] [W] [2]
BrE **used to do sth** if something used to happen, it happened regularly or all the time in the past, but does not happen now: *I used to go to the cinema a lot, but I never get the time now.* | *Beth used to like rock 'n' roll when she was young.* | **used to** *"Do you play golf?" "No, but I used to."* | **did not use to** , also **used not to** *BrE old-fashioned: I'm surprised to see you smoking. You didn't use to.* | *The shops usedn't to open on Sundays.* | **used to be** (=something was true in the past but is not true now) *She used to be such a happy lively girl.* | **did there use to be?** also **used there to be?** *formal: Did there use to be a hotel on that corner?*

used /ju:st/ *adj* **be used to** to have experienced something so that it no longer seems surprising, difficult, strange etc: *Lady Whitton wasn't used to people disagreeing with her.* | **get used to** *I'm sure I'll get used to the hard work.* [S] [1] [W] [2]

used /ju:zd/ *adj* **1** **used cars/clothes etc** cars, clothes etc that have already had an owner; SECOND-HAND: *a used car salesman* **2** dirty as a result of use: *a used tissue*

Figure 2.3 (c) Reproduced from the *Longman Dictionary of Contemporary English.* © Longman Group Limited 1995, reprinted by permission of Pearson Education Limited.

index, while other works are arranged alphabetically, for example Trappes-Lomax's *Oxford Learner's Wordfinder Dictionary*, 1997, and *Longman Language Activator*, 1993. The latter is explicitly designed as a production dictionary for encoding in English. Finally, there are a number of technical learners' dictionaries for specific subject areas, notably for Business or Computing English.

An important development in pedagogical lexicography, the bilingualized dictionary, seeks to combine the advantages of both monolingual and bilingual dictionaries. Bilingualized learners' dictionaries, or BLDs, based on different Hornby dictionaries have been available since the 1960s for languages from Hindi and Chinese to Hebrew and Italian. BLDs are most often unidirectional,

base¹ /beɪs/ noun [C] ★★★

1 lowest part of sth	6 main food/substance
2 place where sth is done	7 chemical
3 ideas etc to start from	8 number
4 p ople/businesses	+ PHRASES
5 in baseball/rounders	

1 the bottom part, edge, or surface of something: *a tall cliff, with a narrow footpath at its base* ♦ **+of** *The pituitary gland is at the base of the brain.* ♦ *The manufacturer's name is printed on the base of the vase.* **1a.** the bottom part or section of something, that supports the rest of it: *The statue stands on a large round base.* ♦ **+of** *The base of your bed is as important as the mattress.*
2 a place from which an activity can be planned, started, or carried out: **+for** *Terrorists had been using the warehouse as a base for their operations.* ♦ *Hikers find this a convenient base for their mountain expeditions.*
2a. a place where members of the armed forces live and work: *a US naval base*
3 a set of ideas, facts, achievements etc from which something can develop: *Income from magazine publishing provides the company with a strong financial base.* ♦ **+for** *The report will give us a base for building a better healthcare system.* ♦ **+of** *a broad base of experience/knowledge/expertise*
4 a group of people who use a particular service or do a particular job: *They have built a loyal customer base.* ♦ **+of** *The team has a base of strong players.* **4a.** a group of people who support someone or something, for example with money or votes: *He has a large base of support within the party.* **4b.** a group of businesses or industries that form an important part of an economy: *Britain's manufacturing base was weak and deteriorating.*
5 one of the four places on a baseball or ROUNDERS field that a player must touch in order to score points → FIRST BASE —*picture* → C15
6 a food or substance that is the main food or substance to which other things are added: *Use the stock as a base for your sauce.* ♦ *paint with a water base*
7 *science* a chemical substance that reacts with an acid to form a SALT
8 *technical* a number that is used to form a system of counting. The usual system of counting uses **base 10**, and the BINARY SYSTEM used in computers uses **base 2**.

off base *Am E informal* not right or accurate
touch base to communicate with someone that you have not seen for some time in order to find out how they are, what is happening etc

base² /beɪs/ verb [T often passive] ★★★ to have somewhere as your main office or place of work, or the place where you live: *Where are you based now?* ♦ *a Geneva-based aid agency* ♦ **base sth in** *Our parent company is based in Osaka.* ♦ *We decided to base our training operations in the New York office.*
base on phrasal vb [T usually passive] [**base sth on sth**] **1** to use particular ideas or facts to make a decision, do a calculation, or develop a theory: *The prosecution's case is based largely on evidence from ex-members of the gang.* ♦ *Prices are based on two people sharing a room.* **2** to use something as a model for a film, piece of writing, or work of art: *He bases his designs on Roman mosaics.* ♦ *The film is based on a true story.*
base³ /beɪs/ adj *literary* without any moral principles: WICKED

used to¹ /ˈjuːst tuː/ modal verb ★★★

Used to is usually followed by an infinitive: *We used to swim in the river.* But sometimes the following infinitive is left out: *I don't play golf now, but I used to.*
Used to only exists as a past tense.
Questions and negatives are usually formed with 'did + **use to** (with no 'd'): *Did you use to work here?* ♦ *We didn't use to earn much.* The spelling 'did used to' is sometimes used, but many people think that this is wrong.
In formal English, negatives are often formed with **used not to**: *They used not to allow shops to be open on Sundays.* The short forms **usen't to** and **usedn't to** are sometimes used, but they sound rather formal and old-fashioned.

used for saying what was true or what happened regularly in the past, especially when you want to emphasize that this is not true or does not happen now: *I used to enjoy gardening, but I don't have time for it now.* ♦ *They always used to ring me and say what they were doing.* ♦ *Where did you use to live before you moved here?* ♦ *I didn't use to like him, but now we're good friends.* ♦ *Customers didn't use to want to shop from home.* ♦ *There used not to be so much violence.*

used to² /ˈjuːst tuː/ adj [never before noun] ★★★ familiar with something because you have often experienced it before, so it no longer seems difficult or strange: **be used to (doing) sth** *Deborah was used to working on difficult assignments.* ♦ *I'm tired – I'm not used to these late nights.* ♦ *It's completely different from what people are used to.* ♦ **get used to (doing) sth** *I haven't got used to the new system yet.* ♦ *It took weeks to get used to having someone else around.*

Figure 2.3 (d) Reproduced from the *Macmillan English Dictionary for Advanced Learners*. By permission of Macmillan Publishers Limited.

moving from English as L2 to the user's first language as L1. They generally retain the English lemma list of the English MLD in full, but can differ considerably in their approach to micro-structural information. They may repeat or delete the English definitions and/or examples, translate L2 definitions literally word by word or give translation equivalents in L1. They may translate the illustrative textual examples into L2 or not, try to render different L2

base /beɪs/ *noun, verb, adj.*

■ *noun*

LOWEST PART | **1** [C, usually sing.] the lowest part of sth, especially the part or surface on which it rests or stands: *the base of a column/pyramid/glass* ◇ *a pain at the base of the spine* ◇ *The lamp has a heavy base.*—picture at ARCADE, BED

ORIGINAL IDEA/SITUATION | **2** [C] an idea, a fact, a situation, etc. from which sth is developed: *She used her family's history as a base for her novel.* ◇ *His arguments have a sound economic base.*

OF SUPPORT/INCOME/POWER | **3** [C, usually sing.] the people, activity, etc. from which sb/sth gets most of their support, income, power, etc: *The party's main power base is in the agricultural regions.* ◇ *These policies have a broad base of support.* ◇ *an economy with a solid manufacturing base* ◇ *Our business needs to build up its customer base.*

FIRST/MAIN SUBSTANCE | **4** [C, usually sing.] the first or main part of a substance to which other things are added: *a drink with a rum base* ◇ *Put some moisturizer on as a base before applying your make-up.*

MAIN PLACE | **5** [C] the main place where you live or stay or where a business operates from: *I spend a lot of time in Britain but Paris is still my base.* ◇ *The town is an ideal base for touring the area.* ◇ *The company has its base in New York, and branch offices all over the world.*

OF ARMY/NAVY/AIR FORCE | **6** [C, U] a place where an army, a navy or an air force operates from: *a military/naval base* ◇ *an air base* ◇ *After the attack, they returned to base.*

CHEMISTRY | **7** [C] a chemical substance, for example an ALKALI, that can combine with an acid to form a salt

MATHEMATICS | **8** [C, usually sing.] a number on which a system of counting and expressing numbers is built up, for example 10 in the DECIMAL system and 2 in the BINARY system

IN BASEBALL/ROUNDERS | **9** [C] one of the four positions that a player must reach in order to score points

—see also DATABASE

IDM **off base** (*AmE, informal*) completely wrong about sth: *If that's what you think, you're way off base.*—more at FIRST BASE, TOUCH *v.*

■ *verb* [VN] [usually passive] ~ **sb/sth/yourself in ...** to use a particular city, town, etc. as the main place for a business, holiday/vacation, etc: *They decided to base the new company in York.* ◇ *We're going to base ourselves in Tokyo and make trips from there.*

PHRV ˈ**base sth on/upon sth** to use an idea, a fact, a situation, etc. as the point from which sth can be developed: *What are you basing this theory on?*—see also BASED

■ *adj.* (**baser, bas·est**) (*formal*) not having moral principles or rules: *He acted from base motives.* ▶ **base·ly** *adv.*

used¹ /juːst/ *adj.* ~ **to sth/to doing sth** familiar with sth because you do it or experience it often: *I'm not used to eating so much at lunchtime.* ◇ *I found the job tiring at first but I soon got used to it.* ⇨ note at USED TO

used² /juːzd/ *adj.* [usually before noun] that has belonged to or been used by sb else before **SYN** SECOND-HAND: *used cars*

WHICH WORD?
used to / be used to

Do not confuse **used to do sth** with **be used to sth**.
You use **used to do sth** to talk about something that happened regularly or was the case in the past, but is not now: *I used to smoke, but I gave up a couple of years ago.*
You use **be used to sth/to doing sth** to talk about something that you are familiar with so that it no longer seems new or strange to you: *We're used to the noise from the traffic now.* ◇ *I'm used to getting up early.* You can also use **get used to sth**: *Don't worry — you'll soon get used to his sense of humour.* ◇ *I didn't think I could ever get used to living in a big city after living in the country.*

---

used to /ˈjuːs tə; *before vowels and finally* ˈjuːst tu/ *modal verb* (*negative* **didn't use to** /-ˈjuːs/, *BrE also, old-fashioned or formal* **used not to** *short form* **usedn't to** /ˈjuːsnt tə; *before vowels and finally* ˈjuːsnt tu/) used to say that sth happened continuously or frequently during a period in the past: *I used to live in London.* ◇ *We used to go sailing on the lake in summer.* ◇ *I didn't use to like him much when we were at school.* ◇ *You used to see a lot of her, didn't you?* ⇨ note at MODAL

GRAMMAR POINT
used to

Except in negatives and questions, the correct form is **used to**: *I used to go there every Saturday.* ◇ ~~I use to go there every Saturday.~~
To form questions, use *did*: *Did she use to have long hair?* Note that the correct spelling is **use to**, not 'used to'.
The negative form is usually **didn't use to**, but in *BrE* this is quite informal and is not usually used in writing.
The negative form **used not to** (rather formal) and the question form **used you to...?** (oldfashioned and very formal) are only used in *BrE*, usually in writing.

Figure 2.3 (e) Reproduced by permission of Oxford University Press from the *Oxford Advanced Learner's Dictionary of Current English*, 6th edn. by A. S. Hornby. © Oxford University Press 2000.

registers in the L1 translations or not, or repeat, add or delete grammatical and phonetic information. Some scholars distinguish between semi-bilingual dictionaries, which repeat the English material but translate into L1 only the lemma in its various meanings, and bilingualized works, which repeat and translate more information. The former have been developed since the 1980s particularly by Lionel Kernerman in Israel, whose beginner and intermediate *Password* or *K Dictionaries* are now available in print and/or electronic format for some 30 languages. This type of learners' dictionary has significant potential for further expansion and development, especially in view of the possibilities offered by electronic media.

English language pedagogical lexicography has been quick to utilize computer assistance, both in the establishment and systematic use of large text corpora as the primary basis of different dictionary projects and in the presentation of lexicographical material in electronic form. The major learners' dictionaries are available online, and it is now possible to consult simultaneously all or some of the different works in a publisher's program in an integrated search and to work interactively with them for (second/foreign) vocabulary teaching and learning. Workbooks and work sheets, which have traditionally accompanied learners' dictionaries (Stark, 1990), are now appearing not only in printed form but, increasingly, also as an integral component of CD and online versions. They form an essential part of pedagogical lexicography: whatever form a learners' dictionary takes, whether word book or word bank, its use needs to be taught and learned systematically if it is to be effective. It represents for teachers and learners alike perhaps the single most valuable source of linguistic information on all aspects of the target language. Insofar as word knowledge is inextricably linked to world knowledge (see Section 2.3.1), it is also a source of extralinguistic, cultural information on the society whose language is being studied. Second/foreign language teachers need to learn to use MLDs as a resource (Kipfer, 1984; Wright, 1998), and instruction in the use of learners' dictionaries should be part of language teacher education programs. Such programs need to teach learners not only to use them effectively but also to learn with them independently and autonomously. It is here that the practical interests of publishers and lexicographers, language teachers and learners coincide. It is here too that the research interests of applied linguists, for example in the AILA scientific commission on Lexicology and Lexicography, and metalexicographic studies on dictionary uses and dictionary users have their place (see Section 2.2). Over the past two decades the literature on theoretical and practical issues in (second/foreign) vocabulary teaching and learning has become extensive (Schmitt, 2000; Nation, 2001). It includes some reference to dictionaries and dictionary use, for instance as an important strategy for learning low frequency vocabulary, and to the use in vocabulary teaching and learning of a tool long viewed as essential by lexicographers, the concordance. But it does not yet always show a first-hand awareness of metalexicographic research or of the many different types of learners' dictionaries available and their full potential, not only for teaching and learning, but also for research on vocabulary and on vocabulary teaching and learning. A greater cross-fertilization between pedagogical lexicography and pedagogical lexicology would enhance and benefit the applied linguistic endeavor, certainly in the area of second/foreign language teaching and learning.

See also 1 LANGUAGE DESCRIPTIONS, 4 LANGUAGE CORPORA, 5 DISCOURSE ANALYSIS.

REFERENCES

Atkins, B. T. (ed.) (1998) *Using dictionaries. Studies of dictionary use by language learners and translators.* Tübingen: Max Niemeyer.

Bergenholtz, H. & Tarp, S. (eds.) (1995) *Manual of specialised lexicography. The preparation of specialised dictionaries.* Amsterdam/Philadelphia: John Benjamins.

Cowie, A. P. (1999) *English dictionaries for foreign learners. A history.* Oxford: Clarendon Press.

Gove, P. (1966) Etymology in *Webster's Third New International Dictionary.* Word, 22, 7–82.

Gove, P. (1968) The international scientific vocabulary in *Webster's Third. Journal of English Linguistics,* 2, 1–11.

Hartmann, R. R. K. (2001) *Teaching and researching lexicography.* Harlow: Pearson Education Ltd.

Hartmann, R. R. K. & James, G. (1998) *Dictionary of lexicography.* London/New York: Routledge.

Hausmann, F. J., Reichmann, O., Wiegand, H. E., & Zgusta, L. (eds.) (1989–91) *Wörterbücher Dictionaries Dictionnaires: International encyclopedia of lexicography* (3 vols). Berlin/New York: Walter de Gruyter.

Herbst, T. & Popp, K. (eds.) (1999) *The perfect learners' dictionary (?).* Tübingen: Max Niemeyer.

Hüllen, W. (1999) *English dictionaries, 800–1700: the topical tradition.* Oxford: Clarendon Press.

Kipfer, B. A. (1984) *Workbook on lexicography. A course for dictionary users with a glossary of English lexicographical terms.* Exeter: University of Exeter.

Landau, S. I. (2001) *Dictionaries. The art and craft of lexicography* (2nd edn.). Cambridge: Cambridge University Press.

McArthur, T. (1986) *Worlds of reference: lexicography, learning and language from the clay tablet to the computer.* Cambridge: Cambridge University Press.

Morton, H. C. (1994) *The Story of Webster's Third: Philip Gove's controversial dictionary and its critics.* Cambridge: Cambridge University Press.

Murray, K. M. E. (1977) *Caught in the web of words: James Murray and the* Oxford English Dictionary. New Haven: Yale University Press.

Nation, I. S. P. (2001) *Learning vocabulary in another language.* Cambridge: Cambridge University Press.

Nesi, H. (2000) *The use and abuse of EFL dictionaries: how learners of English as a foreign language read and interpret dictionary entries.* Tübingen: Max Niemeyer.

Schmitt, N. (2000) *Vocabulary in language teaching.* Cambridge: Cambridge University Press.

Sledd, J. & Ebbit, W. R. (1962) *Dictionaries and that dictionary: a casebook on the aims of lexicographers and the targets of reviewers.* Glenview: Scott, Foresman & Co.

Stark, M. P. (1990) *Dictionary workbooks: a critical evaluation of the dictionary workbooks for the foreign language learner.* Exeter: University of Exeter.

Stark, M. P. (1999) *Encyclopedic learners' dictionaries: a study of their design features from the user perspective.* Tübingen: Max Niemeyer.

Tono, Y. (2001) *Research on dictionary use in the context of foreign language learning: focus on reading comprehension.* Tübingen: Max Niemeyer.

Wiegand, H. E. (1998) *Wörterbuchforschung: Untersuchungen zur Wörterbuchbenutzung, zur Theorie,*

*Geschichte, Kritik und Automatisierung
der Lexikographie.* [Dictionary research:
investigations into dictionary use and
the theory, history, criticism and

computerisation of lexicography].
Berlin/New York: Walter de Gruyter.
Wright, J. (1998) *Dictionaries.* Oxford:
Oxford University Press.

FURTHER READING

Barz, I. & Schröder, M. (eds.) (1996)
*Das Lernerwörterbuch Deutsch als
Fremdsprache in der Diskussion*
[Discussing the learner's dictionary
German as a foreign language].
Heidelberg: C. Winter.
Battenburg, J. D. (1991) *English
monolingual learners' dictionaries:
a user-oriented study.* Tübingen:
Max Niemeyer.
Béjoint, H. (1994) *Tradition and innovation
in modern English dictionaries.* Oxford:
Clarendon Press.
Cowie, A. P. (ed.) (1981) *Applied
Linguistics 2, 3: Lexicography and its
pedagogic applications.*
Cowie, A. P. (ed.) (1987) *The dictionary
and the language learner.* Tübingen:
Max Niemeyer.
*Dictionaries: Journal of the Dictionary
Society of North America.* Vol. 1–
(1979–). Terre Haute, IN; Cleveland,
Ohio; Madison, Wisconsin: Dictionary
Society of North America.
Dolezal, F. T. & McCreary, D. R. (eds.)
(1999) *Pedagogical lexicography today:
a critical bibliography on learners'
dictionaries with special emphasis on
language learners and dictionary users.*
Tübingen: Max Niemeyer.
Hartmann, R. R. K. (ed.) (1999)
*Dictionaries in language learning:
recommendations, national reports and
thematic reports from the TNP sub-project
9: dictionaries.* Berlin: Thematic
Network Project in the Area of
Languages, Freie Universität Berlin.
Hausmann, F. J. (1977) *Einführung in die
Benutzung der neufranzösischen*

Wörterbücher [Introduction to the use
of the modern French dictionaries].
Tübingen: Max Niemeyer.
Hupka, W. (1989) *Wort und Bild: Die
Illustrationen in Wörterbüchern und
Enzyklopädien* [Word and picture:
the illustrations in dictionaries and
encyclopedias]. Tübingen: Max
Niemeyer.
International Journal of Lexicography.
Vol. 1– (1988–). Oxford: Oxford
University Press.
Ilson, R. (ed.) (1985) *Dictionaries,
lexicography and language learning.*
Oxford: Pergamon Press.
*Lexicographica: international annual for
lexicography.* Vol. 1– (1985–). Tübingen:
Max Niemeyer.
McCorduck, E. S. (1993) *Grammatical
information in ESL dictionaries.*
Tübingen: Max Niemeyer.
Rey, A. (1977) *Le lexique: images et
modèles. Du dictionnaire à la lexicologie*
[Lexis: images and models. From the
dictionary to lexicology]. Paris:
Armand Colin.
Rey-Debove, J. (ed.) (1970) La
lexicographie [Lexicography]. *Langages,*
19, 1–119.
Schaeder, B. (1987) *Germanistische
Lexikographie* [German lexicography].
Tübingen: Max Niemeyer.
Sinclair, J. (ed.) (1987) *Looking up: an
account of the COBUILD project in
lexical computing and the development of
the Collins COBUILD English Language
Dictionary.* London: HarperCollins.
Svensén, B. (1993) *Practical lexicography:
principles and methods of*

dictionary-making. Oxford/New York: Oxford University Press.

Tickoo, M. L. (ed.) (1989) *Learners' dictionaries: state of the art*. Singapore: SEAMEO Regional Language Centre.

Wiegand, H. E. (ed.) (1998) *Perspektiven der pädagogischen Lexikographie des Deutschen: Untersuchungen anhand von "Langenscheidts Großwörterbuch Deutsch als Fremdsprache"* [Perspectives on the pedagogical lexicography of German: investigations based on Langenscheidt's Dictionary of German as a foreign language]. Tübingen: Max Niemeyer.

Wiegand, H. E. (ed.) (2002) *Perspektiven der pädagogischen Lexikographie des Deutschen II: Untersuchungen anhand des "de Gruyter Wörterbuchs Deutsch als Fremdsprache"* [Perspectives on the pedagogical lexicography of German II: investigations based on de Gruyter's Dictionary of German as a foreign language]. Tübingen: Max Niemeyer.

Zgusta, L. (1971) *Manual of lexicography*. The Hague/Paris: Mouton.

Zöfgen, E. (1994) *Lernerwörterbücher in Theorie und Praxis: Ein Beitrag zur Metalexikographie mit besonderer Berücksichtigung des Französischen* [Learners' dictionaries in theory and practice: a contribution to metalexicography with special reference to French]. Tübingen: Max Niemeyer.

3 Second Language Acquisition and Ultimate Attainment

DAVID BIRDSONG

3.1 Introduction

In second language acquisition (L2A) research, ultimate attainment refers to the outcome or end point of acquisition, and is used interchangeably with the terms final state, end state, and asymptote. "Ultimate" is not to be thought of as synonymous with "native-like," although native-likeness is one of the observed outcomes of L2A.

Most L2A studies have focused on the initial state, stages in L2 development, and rates of acquisition. However, data from such studies do not directly speak to the potential of the learner, which is an inescapable consideration of L2A theory. As we will see, the study of ultimate attainment engages such core L2A issues as native language influence, access to Universal Grammar (UG), maturational effects, and fossilization.

Just as ultimate attainment is a fundamental consideration of L2A research, L2A itself is a central concern of Applied Linguistics (or, more precisely, following the distinction made by this volume's editors, of Linguistics-Applied (L-A)). Since the mid-1950s, the understanding of how linguistic knowledge is acquired and represented mentally has been a cornerstone of linguistic inquiry. Starting with first language acquisition (L1A) and eventually embracing L2A, much of this inquiry has been guided by the heuristic of *constraints*. By hypothesis, language acquisition is constrained epistemologically: learners' hypotheses about the possible forms of language are finite, and are not inconsistent with the range of structural features of natural language grammars. Similarly, it is believed that language acquisition is constrained maturationally: if native-like grammars are to be acquired, the learning must begin at an early developmental stage. One of the basic missions of L-A is to provide empirical data that speak to the adequacy of these elemental premises of modern linguistic theory. The methods recruited for this purpose are varied, and are informed by research in cognitive neuroscience, linguistic theory, and experimental psychology.

We begin the chapter by outlining the reasons why researchers are interested in investigating L2A at the end state. This rationale will provide a context for discussion in the remainder of the chapter, where we will consider a variety of ongoing research efforts relating to ultimate attainment in L2A.

3.2   Why Study Ultimate Attainment?

Ultimate attainment data are invaluable for ongoing mainstream research in L2A theory, in that they afford unique perspectives on the limits of L2A. On the received view of late L2A, the upper limits of competence are not comparable to those of a native monolingual. "Success," construed as attainment of native-likeness, is ruled out in principle by advocates of the Critical Period Hypothesis (e.g., Johnson & Newport, 1989; Long, 1990) and by those who argue that UG and associated learning mechanisms are not available to post-adolescent L2 acquirers (e.g., Bley-Vroman, 1989). Under these views, the typical, if not unique, outcome of L2A is "failure" or non-native-like competence. However, recent research has challenged the notion of universal or near-universal failure (see below, and Birdsong, 1999, for a review). It appears that native-likeness may not be so rare as to be "peripheral to the enterprise of second language acquisition theory" (Bley-Vroman, 1989; see Selinker, 1972). Clearly, for educators and social-policy-makers, as well as for theorists, it is of compelling interest to know more about the rate of native-like attainment. For this purpose, the data *de rigueur* are those from learners at the end state; data from any other acquisitional stage can, at best, address only indirectly the upper limits of attainment.

In the most general terms, L2A theory tackles the question of the resemblance of L2A to L1A. L1A is uniformly successful, with all normal children attaining full competence, whereas in L2A there are various outcomes. As we will see below, the mature grammar may be incomplete vis-à-vis the target grammar, or it may diverge from it. And, unlike L1A, certain L2 learner grammars have been characterized as non-deterministic, or probabilistic. Perhaps the most basic issue in L2A research is whether this difference in ends (i.e., final states) implies different means (i.e., learning procedures), as suggested by Bley-Vroman's (1989) Fundamental Difference Hypothesis. The obverse question can also be posed, namely, whether, in those cases where native-like attainment is observed, L1A-like learning (with access to UG) is necessarily involved.

The age factor in L2A is another domain in which ultimate attainment data figure prominently. It is widely recognized that the age at which L2A begins is reliably the strongest predictor of level of ultimate attainment. At issue, however, is the nature of this function. If there is a linear decrement in performance over all ages of immersion, this suggests a general age effect, with the possibility that experiential factors covarying with age may be implicated.

If, on the other hand, the age effect ceases at a maturationally-defined developmental point, and is not predictive thereafter, this suggests a qualitative change in learning. Researchers also look for evidence of discontinuity in the age function, which would suggest the start of a decline from peak levels of sensitivity (e.g., Flege, 1999).

With end-state data one brings a privileged perspective to the perennial question of native language effects. In particular, one looks at the pairing of different L1s with a single L2 to determine if there is a corresponding varying incidence of native-likeness. In addition, there is the question of whether some areas of the L2 grammar, but not others, are ultimately mastered, and if this asymmetry is a function of the learner's native language (Bialystok & Hakuta, 1999; Bialystok & Miller, 1999).

Ultimate attainment data are useful when investigating other linguistically-motivated distinctions as well. One may compare, for example, learner proficiency on low-level phonetic features, which are presumably learned in a data-driven, frequency-sensitive manner, to the acquisition of morphosyntactic features such as *that*-trace, which are deductive consequences of parameter resetting, and whose acquisition is not dependent on frequency in the input. A similar logic is applied to the acquisition of regular versus irregular verb past and noun plural morphology (Birdsong & Flege, 2001).

In the remainder of this chapter we will consider a number of topics that fall under the umbrella of ultimate attainment in L2A. The emphasis will be on late learners, who typically are defined in terms of having arrived in the target language setting at age 12 or later. (Most studies operationalize age of learning in terms of age of immersion or age of arrival (AOA) in the target country, not in terms of age of first exposure, which typically is brief or sporadic, and which may take the form of school study, watching films or TV, or vacations.)

3.3   Non-Native-Like Outcomes in L2A

As pointed out by Sorace (1993, pp. 23–4), learners at the end state may have a grammar of the L2 that lacks some property P of the target grammar; accordingly this grammar is said to be incomplete. Another type of non-native-like grammatical representation is divergence, whereby property P is instantiated but in a manner that is not consistent with that property of the target grammar. On the basis of grammaticality judgments of Italian unaccusative constructions, Sorace found that French learners of L2 Italian preferred *avere* to *essere* in instances where both auxiliaries are permitted. This outcome was considered divergent with respect to the target grammar. English natives, on the other hand, did not show a principled preference for either *essere* or *avere*, even in contexts where *essere* only was permitted (i.e., sentences with clitic-climbing). Sorace therefore concluded that their grammar was incomplete with respect to the range of features associated with unaccusativity in Italian.

A variant of incompleteness in grammatical representation is indeterminacy. Indeterminate or probabilistic grammars are characterized by variability in intuitions for grammaticality from Time 1 to Time 2. Such inconsistency was observed by Johnson et al. (1996) in a sample of Chinese-speaking adult learners of English at end state (mean length of residence = 6.45 years). By Johnson et al.'s reckoning, some 35 percent of the learner performance in their sample was attributable to guessing, response bias, or problems with retrieving the target form from memory.

As Johnson et al. point out, what appears to be indeterminacy may actually reflect optionality in the grammar, i.e., a representation that allows multiple surface realizations of a single construction, such as the choice of relatives in *There's the boy (that/whom/0) Mary likes*. In L2A, a learner who accepts *John *seeked Fred* at Time 1, then *John sought Fred* at Time 2, might be inconsistent not because of indeterminacy in the grammar, but because the grammar permits both forms optionally. (Observe that optionality in this instance would reflect a grammar that diverges from the English target grammar.)

Non-native-like outcomes have been examined in the context of UG. Schachter (1990) maintains that an L2 learner's access to UG principles is incomplete, that is, it is restricted to those principles that are instantiated in the learner's L1. Johnson and Newport (1991) suggest that subjacency "survives in a weak and probabilistic form" (p. 237) among Sinophone late learners of English. In addition to indeterminacy, Johnson and Newport (1991) find divergence in the form of non-compliance with UG, that is, learner structures that are not consistent with any known natural language (see also E. C. Klein, 1995).

3.4 A Closer Look at the Concept

First let us recall that, as we noted at the beginning of this chapter, "ultimate attainment" is not to be misunderstood as suggesting native-likeness. Rather, it refers to the end point of L2A, irrespective of degree of approximation to the native grammar. Moving beyond this clarification, let us try to pin down conceptually what is meant by the term. At a basic level of understanding, the notion of end state in L2A is no different from its counterpart in L1A, as both denote the mature grammar. However, as we have just seen, the end state of L2A may be non-deterministic, and thereby differ qualitatively from the L1A end state. As a result, the idealization of the mature grammar as a "steady-state grammar" must be finessed: compared with L1, the L2 steady state seems "unsteady," as it admits more variability in surface realizations and more uncertainty of intuitions. This is the nature of an indeterminate end-state L2 grammar, and as such this outcome should not be confused with "backsliding" or ongoing grammatical re-representation, which would suggest learning still in progress (see Johnson et al., 1996, p. 336 for further discussion of this distinction). With this understanding, it should be clear that the labels "end state," "final state," "asymptote," and "ultimate attainment" are not inappropriately applied to the outcome of L2A. (Splitting hairs, the label "asymptote" is often associated with a learning function that continuously approaches but does not reach the horizontal asymptote. This conceptualization of the mature state (in both L1A and L2A) allows for incremental progress, and thus no absolute finality, in learning. This view would accommodate additions of novel lexical items (along with idioms, slang, dialectal variants, technical jargon, etc.) and occasional changes in surface morphological or phonetic forms, but not re-representation of the underlying grammar.)

We are still left with the matter of determining when the end state has been reached. For example, how do we know that the abstract features associated with functional heads have been set, permanently, to native-like or non-native-like values (see, e.g., Lardiere, 1998)? To a large extent, the answer to this question depends on the adequacy of our methods for probing learner grammars. That is, we need reliable data – ideally, convergent evidence from multiple elicitation methods – and sensible interpretation of these data. If the data were longitudinal, researchers would be better able to determine whether dissimilar performance at Time X and Time Y reflects ongoing learning or a probabilistic end-state grammar. Moreover, with a longitudinal approach one could safely conclude that similar performances over Times X, Y, Z, etc. reflect an asymptotic level of attainment. As it happens, however, most studies of ultimate attainment are one-shot observations. In such cases, researchers have arbitrarily, but not unreasonably, established a length-of-exposure proxy for the L2 end state. Thus, for example, Johnson et al. (1996) operationalized the asymptote as a minimum of five years of immersion in the US. In Flege, Yeni-Komshian, and Liu (1999), participants were required to have lived at least eight years in the US. Birdsong and Flege (2001) employed a criterion of ten years or more of residence as a proxy for L2 ultimate attainment.

Common-sense caveats apply. An immigrant with ten years' residence in the target country, yet isolated socially from native speakers, may not have attained the levels of L2 competence he is capable of. Thrust into an immersion situation after these ten years of isolation, this hypothetical learner is likely to go on to higher levels of attainment. Relatedly, one cannot assume that learners with comparable lengths of residence, even if fully immersed, have comparable levels of proficiency. That is – mindful again of the distinction between ultimate attainment and native-likeness – the assumption that the L2 end state has been reached is independent of observable levels of L2 proficiency. With this understanding, one may distinguish conceptually as well as methodologically between L2A studies that refer to their subjects as "near-natives" and those that sample learners at the end state.

3.5   A Note on Fossilization

Since the term was popularized in the L2A context by Selinker (1972), "fossilization" has been understood in various ways, among them, as a process, as a cognitive mechanism, and as a result of learning. Selinker and Han (2000) catalogue various learner behaviors that researchers have associated with fossilization. These include backsliding, low proficiency, errors that are impervious to negative evidence, and persistent non-targetlike performance. They also list a host of proposed explanations for these behaviors, such as simplification, avoidance, end of sensitivity to language data, and lack of understanding, acculturation, input, or corrective feedback.

Unquestionably, the study of various representational and acquisitional facts that might fall under the umbrella of fossilization has advanced our knowledge of L2A. But among researchers there is disagreement at the most basic level, for example, on whether fossilization is an *explanans* or an *explanandum*, whether it is a process or a product, whether its domain extends to L1A, and whether it refers to invariant non-native forms or variable non-native forms (Han, 1998). Fossilization appears to be a protean, catch-all term that fails to capture a unitary or even coherent construct. This being the case, one must recognize the limitations of attempts to characterize the nature of fossilization. For the sake of descriptive and explanatory precision, it may be more reasonable to investigate discrete products, processes, behaviors, and epistemological states of L2A. Imagine, for example, that a given learner at presumed L2A asymptote exemplifies Behavior A (e.g., use of the imperfective to encode progressive past aspect) and Behavior B (e.g., use of the imperfective in telic contexts); Behavior A is native-like and Behavior B is non-native-like. Imagine further that Behavior A appears to be unsystematic, perhaps reflecting a probabilistic grammar, while Behavior B is invariant, suggesting a stable divergent grammar. The unique character of each behavior makes each worthy of investigation in its own right. Trying to decide whether one or both behaviors qualify as "fossilization" is unnecessary. Moreover, such labeling would not meaningfully illuminate matters, and would be likely to provoke unhelpful disputes over "questions of semantics." It is self-defeating to be so bound to a term – which to date has defied attempts at meaningful characterization – that fundamental descriptive and explanatory goals become obscured.

3.6 Ultimate Attainment and the Critical Period Hypothesis: The Age Function

A key feature of the Critical Period Hypothesis for second language acquisition (CPH/L2A) is the prediction that native-like attainment in a second language will not be possible if the start of L2A is delayed past a certain critical age. (For consideration of what the critical age might be, see Long, 1990; Moyer, 1999; and discussion below. For a review of the different formulations of the CPH/L2A, see Birdsong, 1999.) Because the CPH/L2A addresses the upper limits of attainment possible in L2A, the only evidence that is decisively relevant to the adequacy of the CPH/L2A comes from learners at the L2A end state. (Surprisingly, this common-sense requirement is not met in all studies purporting to test the CPH/L2A.)

As a general rule, level of ultimate attainment in L2A is predicted by age of arrival in the target country. Note that other age-related factors such as age of initial exposure, particularly in classroom contexts, are not strongly predictive; see, e.g., Birdsong and Molis, 2001; Johnson and Newport, 1989. After age of arrival, the strongest predictor appears to be amount of L2 input and inter-action (e.g., Birdsong & Molis, 2001; Flege, 1999; Flege, Frieda, & Nozawa, 1997; Flege, Yeni-Komshian, & Liu, 1999). For discussion of other endogenous and exogenous variables, see, e.g., Bialystok and Miller (1999); Hyltenstam and Abrahamsson (2000); W. Klein (1995).

Not all apparent age effects are maturational in nature. Johnson and Newport (1989), articulating the logic of a critical period for L2A, point out that attainment should correlate negatively with age of arrival (AOA), just in cases of learners whose AOAs predate the end of maturation. However, under the CPH/L2A, correlations of AOA with attainment should not be observed in cases where the AOA is later than the end of maturation, since maturational factors could no longer be at play.

With a sample of Chinese and Korean learners of English assumed to be at asymptote ($\geq$ 5 years' residence), Johnson and Newport (1989) obtained exactly this type of result. Participants were asked to provide grammaticality judgments for 276 English sentences presented on an audiotape. Stimuli exemplified basic surface contrasts in English, for example, regular verb morphology:

(1)   Every Friday our neighbor washes her car.
      *Every Friday our neighbor wash her car

irregular noun morphology:

(2)   Two mice ran into the house this morning.
      *Two mouses ran into the house this morning

and particle placement:

(3)   The horse jumped over the fence yesterday.
      *The horse jumped the fence over yesterday

Accuracy on the judgment task varied as a function of age for those subjects whose AOA was less than 16 years ($r = -0.87$), but not for later arrivers ($r = -0.16$). Birdsong and Molis (2001) conducted a replication study of Johnson and Newport (1989). Using the original materials and methods, but Spanish natives as their subjects, Birdsong and Molis obtained very different results. Learners with AOA $\leq$ 16 performed at ceiling ($r = -0.23$), while the performance of later arrivals was predicted by AOA ($r = -0.69$).

Other studies of late learners (e.g., Birdsong, 1992) have observed significant correlations of attainment with AOA. Interestingly, Bialystok and Hakuta (1994, p. 69), reanalyzing the Johnson and Newport (1989) data, found a significant correlation of age and performance among late arrivals if the lower end of the late arrival group was set at 20 years. Many studies, including Johnson and Newport (1989) have found correlations of performance with AOA when later and earlier arrivals are pooled (Bialystok & Hakuta, 1999; DeKeyser, 2000; Flege, 1999; Oyama, 1976). A correlation of AOA with declining performance past the end of maturation – indeed, over the entire life span – has been viewed as a priori evidence for falsification of maturational accounts of L2A (Pulvermüller & Schumann, 1994, p. 684).

Researchers (e.g., Bialystok & Hakuta, 1999; Flege, 1999) have also argued that a distribution of end-state performance, to be consistent with the CPH/ L2A, should incorporate a point of inflection, an "elbow" corresponding to the start of a decline in learning ability, i.e., the offset of the period of peak sensitivity. Flege (1999, p. 104), finding no evidence for such non-linearity in studies of L2 pronunciation, states: "In my view, the lack of a non-linearity in the function relating AOA to degree of foreign accent is inconsistent with the view that a critical period exists for speech learning." Further, a series of regression analyses performed by Birdsong and Molis (2001) on their data suggests that, if there is an inflection point in the age function, it occurs at a point past the end of maturation (> 18 years). That is, the observed decline begins at a developmental point where sensitivity should presumably be already at its lowest level. (For further discussion of the timing of age-related effects and its relevance to the CPH/L2A, see Birdsong & Molis, 2001; Elman et al., 1996, pp. 187–8; Moyer, 1999, p. 100. For consideration of biographical factors that may covary with AOA, and that are unrelated to maturation, see Bialystok & Hakuta, 1999.)

Birdsong (in press) argues that even if one ignores the timing of the age effects in L2A, the shape of the age function is inconsistent with standard conceptions of critical periods. According to Bornstein (1989), one of the characteristic features of a critical period is an end to enhanced receptivity or sensitivity. That is, after the peak of sensitivity, there is a decline – the beginning of the offset phase of the critical period – which culminates at a point of zero or baseline sensitivity marking the end of the offset phase. From this point on, sensitivity should not decline further. The overall age function should resemble a stretched 'Z,' as described by Johnson and Newport (1989, p. 79) and Pinker (1994, p. 293).

In contrast, a meta-analysis of L2A end-state studies (Birdsong, in press) reveals a consistent picture of ongoing declines in attainment over the span of AOA. These indefinitely-persisting age effects usually take the form of a simple straight-line decline or a stretched "7" shape, the bottom end pulled rightward. With no apparent end to the decline of sensitivity, the notion of a bounded time frame, or critical "period" of sensitivity, fails to match up with the ultimate attainment data.

3.7   The Incidence of Native-Like Attainment

Along with post-maturational age effects in ultimate attainment, native-likeness among late learners of L2 has been considered as a criterion for falsification of the CPH/L2A. In fact, Long (1990, p. 255) maintained that a single case of demonstrable native-like proficiency among late learners would be sufficient to refute the CPH/L2A.

Such a standard was not out of keeping with the Zeitgeist of the late 1980s and early 1990s. Non-native-likeness was the presumed end state of post-pubertal L2A, and there was little or no empirical evidence to the contrary (see the comprehensive review by Long, 1990). Estimates of the incidence of native-likeness ranged from near 0 (Bley-Vroman, 1989) to 5 percent (Selinker, 1972). Success in adult L2A was thought to be so rare as to be pathological, in the sense that the rate of native-like attainment could be compared to the rate of failure to acquire a first language (Bley-Vroman, 1989). Mainstream texts deemed a lack of mastery a basic characteristic of late L2A, a fact in need of an explanation (e.g., Towell & Hawkins, 1994).

Two studies in particular contributed to this view: Coppieters (1987) and Johnson and Newport (1989). Coppieters studied 21 near-native speakers of French from varying L1 backgrounds. All were late learners who had resided in France for at least five and a half years. Participants judged the grammaticality of 107 complex French sentences, some of which exemplified language-specific structures, such as the choice of subject pronoun in identificational constructions:

(4)   Qui est Victor Hugo? *Who is Victor Hugo?*
       C'est un grand écrivain.
       He's [identification function] a great writer.
       *Il est un grand écrivain.
       He's [anaphoric function] a great writer.

Other items illustrated universal constraints or principles, for example, use and placement of the clitic *en*, which varies according to the predicate:

(5)   Elle en aime l'auteur.
       She likes its author.
       *Elle en téléphone à l'auteur.
       She telephones its author.

Twenty monolingual native speakers of French served as controls, and the judgments of both groups were compared to acceptability norms. In the Coppieters sample the observed incidence of native-likeness was zero.

A similar result was obtained in the Johnson and Newport (1989) study. Among their 23 late learners, the highest score was 254 out of 276. The lowest score among native controls was 265. The researchers consider this depressed performance to be consistent with the idea of maturational constraints in L2A. Indeed, among late learners, non-native-likeness is thought to be an inevitable outcome: "for adults, later age of acquisition determines that one will not become native or near-native in a language" (Johnson & Newport, 1989, p. 81).

Since the publication of these two highly influential papers, replication studies have been carried out. With tasks and stimuli modeled on Coppieters (1987), Birdsong (1992) looked at the acquisition of French by 20 native speakers of English. All had been exposed to French post-pubertally (range = 11–28 years, mean = 14.9); all had been residing in France for at least three years (range 3–36 years, mean = 11.8 years). Mean age of arrival was 28.5 years (range = 19–48). On scalar grammaticality judgments, the performance of more than half of the 20 experimental subjects was within the range of performance of native controls.

Differences between the two studies are likely the result of variation in procedural controls and subject sampling, details of which are found in Birdsong (1992). It is unlikely that native-like levels of attainment are attributable to stimuli choice. The replication used many of the original stimuli (such as (4) and (5) above), and the additional stimuli exemplified subtle and complex features of the French grammar, for example, prenominal past participle:

(6)   Le très-connu Marcel Proust vient d'arriver.
      The well-known Marcel Proust just arrived.

that-trace:

(7)   *Qui crois-tu qui rendra visite à Marc?
      Who do you think [that] will visit Marc?

adjacency (verb raising):

(8)   Les garçons regardent avec intérêt la télévision.
      The boys look with interest at the television.

Several other studies have attested native-like performance among late learners. For 20 Sinophone and 20 Francophone subjects, all late learners of English, Cranshaw (1997) studied the acquisition of tense and aspect in English. The study involved a series of production and judgment tasks. Over all tasks, three of the Francophones and one Sinophone performed like English native controls. Van Wuijtswinkel (1994), using a grammaticality judgment task based in part on the Johnson and Newport (1989) items, tested Dutch natives who began learning English after age 12. In one group van Wuijtswinkel studied, 8 of 26 participants performed like native English speakers, and in another group 7 of 8 were indistinguishable from natives. White and Genesee (1996) investigated the acquisition of subtle properties of English syntax. Their subjects were Montréal Francophones, whose first significant exposure to English had taken place after age 12. Some 16 of the 45 participants had demonstrated English-native-like performance on various screening measures. These subjects performed like natives on production and judgment tasks involving *wh*-extraction, e.g., *What did the newspaper report the minister had done?* In another study where anglophone subjects were pre-screened for native-like performance (here, screening involved oral interviews and a proficiency test), Montrul and Slabakova (2001) studied the L2 acquisition of the Spanish preterit/ imperfective distinction. Participants' average age of exposure to Spanish was about 15 years (range = 12–24), and they were not living in a Hispanophone country at the time of testing. Across a variety of tasks and sentence types, 35 percent of the sample performed like native controls. A lower rate of native-likeness was observed by Birdsong and Molis (2001), using the Johnson and Newport (1989) instrument. Of the 32 late arrivals (AOA range = 17–44 years), only one scored within the native range of performance. However, 13 of these participants scored at a 92 percent level of accuracy or above.

To allow for meaningful extrapolations to L2 learning generally, the incidence of native-like attainment, expressed as a proportion of the participant sample, must not be established on the basis of a "stacked deck" – a group of subjects who have been pre-screened for demonstrably high attainment (or for having extraordinary motivation, input/interaction with natives, etc.). In unscreened samples of learners at presumed L2 asymptote, the levels of ultimate attainment represented are quite diverse, and desirably so. In this type of sampling, the observed rates of native-like attainment (usually from 5 to 15 percent of the sample) may be more safely generalized to broader populations.

Typically, native-likeness among late learners is observed less frequently in the area of pronunciation than in morphosyntax (e.g., Oyama, 1982; Patkowski, 1980; Scovel, 1988; see also Flege, 1999, for an overview). For example, in Flege, Munro, & MacKay (1995), a 6 percent incidence of unaccented pronunciation was found among late learners. However, none of the participants with AOA greater than 16 years had authentic pronunciation. Such results suggest not only that the incidence of native-like pronunciation is low, but also that the rate continues to decline with increasing AOA, even after the presumed end of maturation.

In contrast to the general pattern of accentedness observed in late L2A, Bongaerts (1999) has demonstrated that Dutch late learners of English and French (age of exposure > 12 years) can speak without accent, though the rate of native-likeness is lower for French L2 than for English L2. Pronunciation was sampled at the sentence level (e.g., *My sister Paula prefers coffee to tea; Avec ce brouillard horrible j'allumerais mes phares*). In addition, for the French study the complete range of nasal and oral vowels was sampled in CV (consonant-vowel) frames (e.g., /u/ in *pou, tout,* and *loup*). Relatedly, Birdsong (2001) performed an instrumental analysis of the pronunciation of late learners of French (AOA ≥ 12 years, mean AOA = 23 years) whose native language was English. Two of the 20 subjects were indistinguishable from native Parisian controls in terms of voice-onset time (VOT) for word-initial consonants (e.g., *le père*), release of word-final obstruents (e.g., *le cap*), and word-final vowel duration (e.g., *le dé*).

To recap the preceding observations about the rate of native-likeness in late L2A: A significant incidence of native-likeness has been found in several studies (in addition to those mentioned above, other studies where native-likeness is observed include Bruhn de Garavito, 1999; Ioup et al., 1994; Juffs & Harrington, 1995; Mayberry, 1993; and White & Juffs, 1997); the rate of native-likeness appears to be lower for features of pronunciation than for morphosyntactic features; and varying rates of native-likeness may result from different L1-L2 pairings.

Some researchers in bilingualism and neurocognitive development dispute the a priori appropriateness of the native standard for the study of the L2 end state. For example, Cook (1997) and Grosjean (1998) note that an L2 learner can never be or become a native speaker. According to this line of thinking, it is ill conceived to peg success in L2A theory to native-likeness. This argument applies as well to social contexts, where immigrants are often stigmatized for non-native-like linguistic behaviors.

Further, one could argue that the criterion of native-likeness sets the bar too high, since late learners routinely attain quite impressive, if not native-like, levels of L2 proficiency and linguistic knowledge. Late L2 learners rarely resemble Genie, whose delayed L1 acquisition was characterized by profound deficits in syntactic and morphology at various levels of analysis (Curtiss, 1977). Nor do they exhibit the extreme pathology of another late L1 learner, Chelsea, whose output included violations of structure dependency, for example, determiners preceding finite verbs (Curtiss, 1989).

From the perspective of research in developmental psychology and language acquisition, however, the native competence level affords a benchmark for comparison that permits ready interpretation of experimental results (see also Mack, 1997). Perhaps most importantly, demonstrations of native-likeness represent dramatic counterpoints to received views of the upper limits of L2A, whereby the outcome of L2A is doomed to be inferior to that of L1A.

3.8   Initial State, End State, and Universal Grammar

Recent research in the UG/L2A framework has stressed the theoretical relationship of initial state competence to final state competence (e.g., Hardin, 2001; White, 2000). In the most basic terms, researchers make predictions about end-state competence based on a theorized initial-state grammar. Thus, for example, if the L2A initial state is not characterized by transfer from the L1, and there is full access to UG, then native-like competence at the end state should be predicted. In contrast, if the initial state of L2A is the full L1 grammar, and there is no access to UG, then a failure to attain native-like competence at L2 ultimate attainment is expected. Under this approach additional aspects of the end-state grammar may also be anticipated, such as the nature of the grammar (e.g., incomplete, divergent, indeterminate), "rogue" or non-UG-compliant features, and effects of L1-L2 pairing.

Hardin (2001) examines in detail the relationships between initial and end states in L2A. Under the Full Transfer/No Access theory of initial state (e.g., Bley-Vroman, 1989; Schachter, 1990), for example, Hardin observes that the end-state grammar could be incomplete, divergent, and indeterminate; it may have optionality in contexts where the L2 does not; the grammar may not conform to constraints given by UG, and there are likely to be L1-L2 pairing effects. Native-likeness, if observed at all, is rare, and would not be attained via direct access to UG and associated domain-specific learning principles but by extraction of universal properties of grammar from the L1 and use of generalized learning principles. In contrast, by the No Transfer/Full Access theory of the initial state (e.g., Epstein, Flynn, & Martohardjono, 1996; Martohardjono & Flynn, 1995), the grammar at the end state should be native-like, at least with respect to the core grammar, and there should be no evidence of incompleteness, divergence, indeterminacy, non-native optionality, UG-non-compliance, or L1-L2 pairing effects. An intermediate position assumes full L1 transfer and complete access to UG (e.g., Schwartz, 1998; Schwartz & Sprouse, 1996). Hardin (2001, p. 113) points out that native-like ultimate attainment is not excluded under this approach, but that L1 influence is understood to persist throughout L2 development. In addition to L1-L2 pairing effects, under the Full Transfer/Full Access theory of the initial state one could expect any number of non-native-like outcomes (incompleteness, divergence, indeterminacy), but the grammar would conform to constraints of UG.

It is important to note that a native-like outcome in L2A does not necessarily imply that UG is accessed. The *raison d'être* of UG is to provide a solution to the logical problem of language acquisition. That is, grammatical knowledge at the end state is underdetermined by the linguistic evidence at the learner's disposal, and it is hypothesized that the constraints on grammatical form given by UG fill in the epistemological gap. This argument applies equally to L2A and L1A. In both instances, to discern a role for UG one must demonstrate that there is in fact a logical problem that is solved by UG. Thus, if one wishes to attribute observed native-likeness at the L2A end state to UG, it must be shown that there was a logical problem in the first place and that the underlying grammatical competence could only have been gained by access to UG.

3.9   Dissociations and Asymmetries

Pinker (e.g., Pinker, 1999) proposes a dual-mechanism model for knowledge of regular inflectional morphology (e.g., verb pasts such as *walk-ed*; noun plurals such as *cup-s*) versus irregular morphology (*run – ran; child – children*). Under this model, computation of regulars involves rule-based, or symbolic, processing of the compositional features *stem + ending*, whereas irregulars are accessed as individual units from associative memory. Unlike regulars, the representation of irregulars is sensitive to the items' frequency in the input. Were verb pasts and noun plurals represented under a single-system connectionist model, on the other hand, then there would be no symbolic manipulation, and all retrieval would require accessing inflected forms from (frequency-sensitive) associative memory.

There is behavioral and neurofunctional evidence of dissociations between rule-based and lexical knowledge. For example, Jaeger et al. (1996) asked native English adults to produce past tense forms of regular, irregular, and nonce verb stems, and found significantly different reaction times for the three types of verbs. In addition, using positron emission tomography (PET) technology, the researchers observed that the regular and irregular computations were subserved by different areas of the brain and required different amounts of cortical activation. Although most research has involved L1 adults and children (e.g., Marcus et al., 1995; Pinker, 1999; Ullman et al., 1997), Beck (1997), Marzilli and O'Brien (2000), and others have obtained experimental evidence for regular-irregular dissociations in L2A short of asymptote (see, however, discussion of Brovetto & Ullman, 2001, below).

The end-state perspective was adopted by Flege, Yeni-Komshian, and Liu (1999), in their study of 240 Korean learners of L2 English. From the Johnson and Newport (1989) instrument they isolated a subset of 44 items to represent rule-based and irregular forms. For late learners (AOA > 12), the participants' accuracy figures revealed a clear dissociation in performance as a function of age, with regulars much less affected by increasing AOA than irregulars.

Taking this finding as their point of departure, Birdsong and Flege (2001) hypothesized that input frequency should be a factor in knowledge of irregular, but not regular forms (e.g., Beck, 1997). Also, regular versus irregular differences should obtain across grammatical categories such as verbs and nouns (e.g., Marzilli & O'Brien, 2000). Most importantly, they expected to replicate the different age of arrival effects for regulars versus irregulars found by Flege, Yeni-Komshian, & Liu (1999). Finally, if (ir)regularity effects are universal, the predicted dissociations should be observed regardless of L1-L2 pairing. The researchers recruited a sample of educated Spanish (n = 30) and Korean (n = 30) natives at L2 asymptote (length of residence ranged between 10 and 16 years). The sample was broken down into groups of 10 based on age of arrival in the US (6–10 years; 11–15 years; 16–20 years). Participants performed a timed multiple-choice judgment task on 80 items exemplifying regularity vs. irregularity, high vs. low stem frequency, and noun plural vs. verb past tense morphology. The following items exemplified low frequency regular noun plural, and high frequency irregular verb past, respectively:

(9)   There are five   a. knuckli   on each hand.
                              b. knuckle
                              c. knuckles
                              d. knackle
                              e. knuckleses

(10) Yesterday the little girl   a. swim   for the first time.
                              b. swam
                              c. swimmed
                              d. swims
                              e. swammed

A series of Analyses of Variance (ANOVAs) was performed on both accuracy and response latency data. For both types of data, several significant effects were obtained. First, the effect of item frequency was found to be significantly higher for irregular items than for regulars. Also, in most respects, the results for noun plurals were comparable to those for verb pasts, the exception being that, among Korean natives, but not among Spanish natives, performance on noun plurals was depressed relative to that for verb pasts. (Birdsong and Flege suggest that this result reflects the fact that Korean typically does not inflect for plurals, but plurality is inferred pragmatically from contextual cues.) Finally, consistent with their principal prediction, Birdsong and Flege found that the accuracy decline and increased response time (RT) with increasing AOA were more pronounced for irregulars than regulars. In fact, no significant age-related declines at all were observed for the regular items. Accuracy and RT data for 20 additional items exemplifying phrasal verbs, e.g., "The student cannot come up with the correct answer" were comparable to performance on irregulars, suggesting that age of arrival effects apply to other varieties of idiosyncratic information in addition to morphological irregularities.

Interestingly, Brovetto and Ullman (2001) in a study of oral production of regular and irregular English pasts by 32 Spanish and 32 Chinese natives (AOA ≥ 17 years) with a minimum of three years' US residence, found that performance on both irregulars and regulars was sensitive to frequency. To reconcile this result with Birdsong and Flege's finding of greater frequency sensitivity for irregulars than regulars, one may hypothesize that, for learners at stages leading up to the end state, many if not most target language forms are bits of idiosyncratic information stored in declarative memory. However, by the L2 end state, computation may take on a more L1-like flavor. As Ullman (2001, p. 118) suggests, "an increasing amount of experience (i.e., practice) with a [second] language should lead to better learning of grammatical rules in procedural memory, which in turn should result in higher proficiency in the language." Thus it may be that the course of attainment of proficiency in an L2 involves a transition from unitary associative L2 processing to a system that exploits both symbolic and associative processes, in procedural and declarative memory respectively, with activation of the corresponding neural substrates. Clearly, this line of reasoning underscores the importance of studying learners at the end state (and, where appropriate, comparing them with learners not yet at asymptote).

One may speculate that declarative memory, which provides for learning and storage of facts, names, and arbitrary and irregular forms, is more susceptible to aging effects than the procedural memory system, which may be responsible for rule-based learning. Evidence of age-related declines in various types of declarative memory is found in the literature on cognitive aging (e.g., Salthouse, 1991), though much of the experimental work relates to short-term memory effects. Moreover, certain well-known histological features associated with cognitive decline over the course of normal aging appear to be concentrated in neural regions implicated in declarative memory. Specifically, neurofibrillary tangles appear mainly in the cortical pyramidal cells of the hippocampus and temporal association areas, and neuritic (senile) plaques are generally found in the hippocampus and second and third layers of the temporal/associative cortex (Scheibel, 1996). These degenerative features of normal neurologic aging – which, in high concentrations characterize the synaptic pathology of Alzheimer's Disease – appear not only to corrupt existing cortical pathways but may impair the work of neurotransmittors, particularly acetylcholine, which are crucial to encoding and consolidation of memories; for overviews, see Hasselmo (1999) and Martin (1999). (This is not to suggest that the aforementioned etiologies and loci of cognitive decline are the only ones associated with aging. For example, declines in dopamine D2 receptors – on the order of 10 percent per decade after 20 years of age – are observed in the basal ganglia, hippocampus, frontal cortex, anterior cingulate cortex, and amygdala regions (Li, Lindenberger, & Sikström, 2001). The relevant issue is the extent to which age-related declines are more severe in some brain areas than in others, and the corresponding effects on specific types of cognitive functions involved in L2A.)

Moving beyond speculation as to the underlying causes of regular-irregular dissociations over the age function, it is clear that the question of age effects in late L2A cannot be approached monolithically. Future investigations should aim for sufficient granularity to take into account not only the moderator variable of L1-L2 pairing, but also principled questions of representation and processing such as those raised by the study of regular versus irregular inflectional morphology.

Another variable that should not be overlooked in the study of ultimate attainment is the participants' dominant language. Interest in the dominance factor goes back to a study by Cutler et al. (1989), who observed an asymmetry in early French-English bilinguals' ability to process spoken words into segments. Those whose self-reported dominant language was French were able to switch back and forth between syllable-based and non-syllable based segmentation routines as a function of the language being processed. In contrast, English-dominant bilinguals controlled only one segmentation strategy, suitable to the processing of English words, and applied it to both French and English speech. Golato (1998) attempted to reproduce the results of Cutler et al. (1989), using late L2 learners at the end state. Twenty-one late bilinguals (English natives n = 10) participated. Overall, they had spent a mean of 8.5 years in an anglophone or francophone country, had an age of immersion ranging from 13 to 33 years, and had a mean age of 30 years at time of testing. Golato found that the English-dominant bilinguals commanded two syllable segmentation routines, and applied the English-appropriate strategy to English stimuli, and the French-appropriate strategy to French words. In contrast, the French-dominants used a single strategy indiscriminately for both French and English stimuli. Different operationalizations of language dominance were considered, and the asymmetry obtained for every operationalization. Provocatively, Golato's results for learners at the L2A end state are opposite to those that Cutler et al. (1989) had reported for early bilinguals; follow-up replications are unquestionably warranted. It is also clear that, as with L1-based and regularity-based dissociations, the study of asymmetries promises to contribute significantly to a finer-grained understanding of the end state of L2A.

3.10   Ultimate Attainment and Cortical Function

Modern technologies such as Functional Magnetic Resonance Imaging (fMRI), Positron Emission Tomography (PET), and Event-Related Brain Potentials (ERPs) allow L2A researchers to investigate the neural systems involved in language processing. In most cases, work does not address the L2A end state specifically, but is concerned with the age at which L2 acquisition was begun and L2 proficiency. A recurrent goal in this research is determining the degree to which L1 processing and L2 processing involve similar neural substrates.

For example, Weber-Fox and Neville (1999), in a study of Sinophone learners of English with over five years' immersion, found that the neural subsystems involved in language processing differ as a function of age of acquisition. Notably, for the processing of phrase structure violations, involvement of both the right and left hemispheres increased as the age of immersion in English was delayed. The researchers also compared the learners' processing of grammatical features (closed-class words and syntactic anomalies) with their processing of semantic features (open-class words and semantic anomalies), and found that these types of activity are differentially affected by age of acquisition. However, an ERP study by Osterhout, Davis, and McLaughlin (in press) has revealed a confound of word length and open versus closed class: "Although the two word classes did elicit distinct ERPs, all of these differences were highly correlated with word length. We conclude that ERP differences between open- and closed-class words are primarily due to quantitative differences in word length rather than qualitative differences in linguistic function" (Osterhout, Davis, & McLaughlin, in press, p. 1).

In a study of highly proficient late L2 learners (mean initial exposure = 12.25 years of age), Illes et al. (1999) used fMRI to investigate the semantic processing of nouns by eight English-Spanish bilinguals. Comparing the scans of processing in the two languages, the researchers found no activity differences in either the left or right inferior frontal gyrus, and both languages seemed to be dominantly lateralized in the left hemisphere. At least with respect to vocabulary, Illes et al. (1999) suggest that, irrespective of the age of acquisition, increasing proficiency in the L2 leads to a common cortical representation of the two languages. An earlier PET study by D. Klein et al. (1995) had reached a similar conclusion for repetition and translation of single words, albeit with early learners. The highly fluent subjects in this instance were 12 anglophone learners of French whose mean age of acquisition was 7.3 years. The researchers determined that semantic processing in the two languages involved similar areas of the front left cortical regions, particularly in the left anterior frontal gyrus.

We note that in the Weber-Fox and Neville (1999) study, the late bilinguals' L2 proficiency (both self-rated and based on standardized tests) was significantly below that of the early learners. In this instance, both late age of acquisition and low proficiency are predictive of processing differences in the relevant neural substrates. However, in the Illes et al. (1999) and D. Klein et al. (1995) research, high proficiency, but not early age of acquisition, is predictive of homotropic cortical representations for the L1 and L2. Thus, for some aspects of semantic processing, the evidence suggests that those late learners who are native-like or near-native-like at end state will have common cortical localization of activity for the L1 and the L2.

In an investigation designed to disentangle the factors of proficiency and age of acquisition, a similar conclusion was reached by Perani et al. (1998). This was a PET study involving monitoring of brain activity of subjects (nine proficient late learners, AOA > 10 years) listening passively to a story in the L1 (Italian) and the L2 (English). In this case, the cortical responses were not only similar in the L1 and L2, but were comparable to the L1 and L2 brain activity of 12 speakers of Catalan and Spanish who had learned both languages early in life. The researchers conclude that "these findings suggest that, at least for pairs of L1 and L2 languages that are fairly close, attained proficiency is more important than age of acquisition as a determinant of the cortical representation of L2" (Perani et al., 1998, p. 1841).

For other tasks, however, the story is somewhat different. Kim et al. (1997) asked bilinguals from various language backgrounds to silently recount events from the previous day. Using fMRI, Kim et al. found a common neural representation for L2 and L1 among early bilinguals, but for late bilinguals (mean age of acquisition = 11.2 years) distinct regions of Broca's area were involved. In Wernike's area, on the other hand, similar cortical regions served both the L1 and the L2. This similarity was observed for each of the various L2s represented in the sample, and across all ages at which L2A was begun. Comparing the results of Kim et al. (1997) with those of their own study, Perani et al.

(1998, p. 1846) ascribe the differences in brain activation to the differences in task. We note further that in Kim et al. (1997), the question of whether proficiency trumps age of acquisition was not addressed, as the proficiency levels of the late acquirers was not specified.

On the general question of cortical function in L2 versus L1, Sanders (2000) reviews several additional studies, which vary in terms of L1-L2 pairings, tasks, measurement techniques, and emphasis on proficiency and age of acquisition. Although none of the studies cited makes specific reference to the L2A asymptote, the early bilinguals in each instance are uncontroversially at the end state, and one can assume that the highly proficient late learners are near if not at the end state. This being the case, it appears that, depending on the task and the L1-L2 pairing, native-likeness among late L2 learners can be observed not only in linguistic behaviors but in cortical function as well. For a recent review of neuroimaging studies of cortical function in bilingualism, see Abutalebi, Cappa, and Perani (2001).

3.11   Conclusion

The study of learners immersed in an L2 for significant lengths of time has led to significant advances in the understanding of the nature of L2A. Researchers recognize that a range of variables – in particular, age of immersion, L1-L2 pairings, and quantity of input – may interactively determine the level of ultimate attainment. As we move forward, we are alert to the need for finer-grained investigation of the limits of bilingualism, as suggested by the discovery of asymmetries at the end state, and their relation to representational variables such as the learner's dominant language. Granularity is further motivated by demonstrations that discrepant effects of AOA are associated with various features of the language, possibly reflecting principled cognitive distinctions such as declarativized versus proceduralized knowledge, or symbolic computation versus lexical retrieval.

A dozen or so years ago the study of ultimate attainment in L2A was in its infancy. The field is now entering adolescence (and, to paraphrase Oscar Wilde's witticism, is no longer young enough to know everything). With additional nourishment from cognitive neuroscience, linguistic theory, and developmental psychology, there is every reason to believe that the spurts of growth – and sophistication – will continue.

See also 8 LANGUAGE ATTRITION, 17 THE NATIVE SPEAKER IN APPLIED LINGUISTICS, 20 LANGUAGE LEARNING, 21 INDIVIDUAL DIFFERENCES IN SECOND LANGUAGE LEARNING.

REFERENCES

Abutalebi, J., Cappa, S. F., & Perani, P. (2001) The bilingual brain as revealed by functional neuroimaging. *Bilingualism: Language and Cognition,* 4, 179–90.

Beck, M.-L. (1997) Regular verbs, past tense and frequency: tracking down a potential source of NS/NNS competence differences. *Second Language Research,* 13, 93–115.

Bialystok, E. & Hakuta, K. (1994) *In other words: the science and psychology of second-language acquisition.* New York: Basic Books.

Bialystok, E. & Hakuta, K. (1999) Confounded age: linguistic and cognitive factors in age differences for second language acquisition. In D. Birdsong (ed.), *Second language acquisition and the Critical Period Hypothesis* (pp. 161–81). Mahwah, NJ: Erlbaum.

Bialystok, E. & Miller, B. (1999) The problem of age in second language acquisition: influences from language, task, and structure. *Bilingualism: Language and Cognition,* 2, 127–45.

Birdsong, D. (1992) Ultimate attainment in second language acquisition. *Language,* 68, 706–55.

Birdsong, D. (1999) Introduction: Whys and why nots of the Critical Period Hypothesis. In D. Birdsong (ed.), *Second language acquisition and the Critical Period Hypothesis* (pp. 1–22). Mahwah, NJ: Erlbaum.

Birdsong, D. (2001) Comprehensive nativelikeness in second language acquisition. Unpublished manuscript, University of Texas-Austin.

Birdsong, D. (in press) Understanding age effects in second language acquisition. In J. Kroll & A. de Groot (eds.), *Handbook of bilingualism: psycholinguistic perspectives.* Oxford: Oxford University Press.

Birdsong, D. & Flege, J. E. (2001) Regular-irregular dissociations in the acquisition of English as a second language. In *BUCLD 25: Proceedings of the 25th Annual Boston University Conference on Language Development* (pp. 123–32). Boston, MA: Cascadilla Press.

Birdsong, D. & Molis, M. (2001) On the evidence for maturational effects in second language acquisition. *Journal of Memory and Language,* 44, 235–49.

Bley-Vroman, R. (1989) What is the logical proglem of foreign language learning? In S. Gass & J. Schachter (eds.), *Linguistic perspectives on second language acquisition* (pp. 41–68). Cambridge: Cambridge University Press.

Bongaerts, T. (1999). Ultimate attainment in foreign language pronunciation: the case of very advanced late foreign language learners. In D. Birdsong (ed.), *Second language acquisition and the Critical Period Hypothesis* (pp. 133–59). Mahwah, NJ: Erlbaum.

Bornstein, M. H. (1989) Sensitive periods in development: Structural characteristics and causal interpretations. *Psychological Bulletin,* 105, 179–97.

Brovetto C. & Ullman, M. T. (2001) First vs. second language: a differential reliance on grammatical computations and lexical memory. In *Proceedings of the Fourteenth Annual CUNY Conference on Human Sentence Processing,* (vol. 14). CUNY Graduate School and University Center, Philadelphia, PA.

Bruhn de Garavito, J. L. S. (1999) The syntax of Spanish multifunctional clitics and near-native competence.

Unpublished doctoral dissertation, McGill University.

Cook, V. J. (1997) Monolingual bias in second language acquisition research. *Revista Canaria de Estudios Ingleses*, 34, 35–49.

Coppieters, R. (1987) Competence differences between native and near-native speakers. *Language*, 63, 544–73.

Cranshaw, A. (1997) A study of anglophone native and near-native linguistic and metalinguistic performance. Unpublished doctoral dissertation, Université de Montréal.

Curtiss, S. (1977) *Genie: a linguistic study of a modern day "wild child."* New York: Academic Press.

Curtiss, S. (1989) The case of Chelsea: a new test case of the critical period for language acquisition. Unpublished ms., University of California, Los Angeles.

Cutler, A., Mehler, J., Norris, D., & Seguí, J. (1989) Limits on bilingualism. *Nature*, 340, 159–60.

DeKeyser, R. M. (2000) The robustness of critical period effects in second language acquisition. *Studies in Second Language Acquisition*, 22, 499–533.

Elman, J. L., Bates, E. A., Johnson, M. H., Karmiloff-Smith, A., Parisi, D., & Plunkett, K. (1996) *Rethinking innateness: a connectionist perspective on development*. Cambridge, MA: MIT Press.

Epstein, S., Flynn, S., & Martohardjono, G. (1996) Second language acquisition: theoretical and experimental issues in contemporary research. *Behavioral and Brain Sciences*, 19, 677–758.

Flege, J. E. (1999) Age of learning and second-language speech. In D. Birdsong (ed.), *Second language acquisition and the Critical Period Hypothesis* (pp. 101–31). Mahwah, NJ: Erlbaum.

Flege, J. E., Frieda, A. M., & Nozawa, T. (1997) Amount of native-language (L1) use affects the pronunciation of an L2. *Journal of Phonetics*, 25, 169–86.

Flege, J. E., Munro, M. J., & MacKay, I. (1995) Factors affecting degree of perceived foreign accent in a second language. *Journal of the Acoustical Society of America*, 97, 3125–34.

Flege, J. E., Yeni-Komshian, G. H., & Liu, S. (1999) Age constraints on second-language acquisition. *Journal of Memory and Language*, 41, 78–104.

Golato, P. (1998) Syllabification processes among French-English bilinguals: a further study of the limits of bilingualism. Unpublished doctoral dissertation, University of Texas-Austin.

Grosjean, F. (1998) Studying bilinguals: methodological and conceptual issues. *Bilingualism: Language and Cognition*, 1, 131–49.

Han, Z.-H. (1998) Fossilization: an investigation into advanced L2 learning of a typologically distant language. Unpublished doctoral dissertation, University of London.

Hardin, C. (2001) Initial state and end state in second language acquisition theory. Unpublished Masters report, University of Texas-Austin.

Hasselmo, M. E. (1999) Neuromodulation: acetylcholine and memory consolidation. *Trends in Cognitive Sciences*, 3, 352–9.

Hyltenstam, K. & Abrahamsson, N. (2000) Who can become native-like in a second language? All, some, or none? On the maturational constraints controversy in second language acquisition. *Studia Linguistica*, 54, 150–66. (Special issue: A selection of papers from the Ninth Annual Conference of the European Second Language Association, EUROSLA 9, Lund, Sweden, June 10–12, 1999, ed. G. Hakansson & A. Viberg).

Illes, J., Francis, W. S., Desmond, J. E., Gabrieli, J. D. E., Glover, G. H., Poldrack, R., Lee, C. J., &

Wagner, A. D. (1999) Convergent cortical prepresentation of semantic processing in bilinguals. *Brain and Language*, 70, 347–63.

Ioup, G., Boustagui, E., El Tigi, M., & Moselle, M. (1994) Reexamining the critical period hypothesis: a case study of successful adult SLA in a naturalistic environment. *Studies in Second Language Acquisition*, 10, 303–37.

Jaeger, J. J., Lockwood, A. H., Kemmerer, D. L., Van Valin, R. D., Murphy, B. W., & Khalak, H. G. (1996) A positron emission tomographic study of regular and irregular verb morphology in English. *Language*, 72, 451–97.

Johnson, J. S. & Newport, E. L. (1989) Critical period effects in second language learning: the influence of maturational state on the acquisition of English as a second language. *Cognitive Psychology*, 21, 60–99.

Johnson, J. S. & Newport, E. L. (1991) Critical period effects on universal properties of language: the status of subjacency in the acquisition of a second language. *Cognition*, 39, 215–58.

Johnson, J., Shenkman, K., Newport, E., & Medin, D. (1996) Indeterminacy in the grammar of adult language learners. *Journal of Memory and Language*, 35, 335–52.

Juffs, A. & Harrington, M. (1995) Parsing effects in second language sentence processing: subject and object asymmetries in wh-extraction. *Studies in Second Language Acquisition*, 17, 483–516.

Kim, K. H. S., Relkin, N. R., Lee, K.-M., & Hirsch, J. (1997) Distinct cortical areas associated with native and second languages. *Nature*, 388, 171–4.

Klein, D., Zatorre, R. J., Milner, B., Moyer, E., & Evans, A. C. (1995) The neural substrates of bilingual language processing: evidence from positron emission tomography. In M. Paradis (ed.), *Aspects of bilingual aphasia* (pp. 23–36). Oxford: Pergamon.

Klein, E. C. (1995) Evidence for a "wild" L2 grammar: when PPs rear their empty heads. *Applied Linguistics*, 16, 87–117.

Klein, W. (1995) Language acquisition at different ages. In D. Magnusson (ed.), *The lifespan development of individuals: behavioral, neurobiological, and psychosocial perspectives. A synthesis* (pp. 244–64). Cambridge: Cambridge University Press.

Lardiere, D. (1998) Case and tense in the "fossilized" steady state. *Second Language Research*, 14, 1–26.

Li, S.-C., Lindenberger, U., & Sikström, S. (2001) Aging cognition: from neuromodulation to representation. *Trends in Cognitive Sciences*, 5, 479–86.

Long, M. H. (1990) Maturational constraints on language development. *Studies in Second Language Acquisition*, 12, 251–85.

Mack, M. (1997) The monolingual native speaker: not a norm, but still a necessity. *Studies in the Linguistic Sciences*, 27, 113–46.

Marcus, G. F., Brinkmann, U., Clahsen, H., Wiese, R., & Pinker, S. (1995) German inflection: the exception that proves the rule. *Cognitive Psychology*, 29, 189–256.

Martin, J. B. (1999) Mechanisms of disease: molecular basis of the neurogenerative disorders. *New England Journal of Medicine*, 340, 1970–80.

Martohardjono, G. & Flynn, S. (1995) Language transfer: what do we really mean? In L. Eubank, L. Selinker & M. Sharwood Smith (eds.), *The current state of Interlanguage: studies in honor of William E. Rutherford* (pp. 205–18). Amsterdam: John Benjamins.

Marzilli, A. & O'Brien, M. G. (2000) Plural morphology of German: a test of Marcus et al. (1995). Unpublished manuscript, University of Texas-Austin.

Mayberry, R. (1993) First-language acquisition after childhood differs from second-language acquisition: the case of American Sign Language. *Journal of Speech and Hearing Research*, 36, 1258–70.

Montrul, S. & Slabakova, R. (2001) Is native-like competence possible in L2 acquisition? In *BUCLD 25: Proceedings of the 25th Annual Boston University Conference on Language Development* (pp. 522–33). Boston, MA: Cascadilla Press.

Moyer, A. (1999) Ultimate attainment in L2 phonology. *Studies in Second Language Acquisition*, 21, 81–108.

Osterhout, L., Allen, M., & McLaughlin, J. (In press) Words in the brain: lexical determinants of word-induced brain activity. *Journal of Neurolinguistics*. (Special issue on the Lexicon and the Brain, ed. A. Caramazza.)

Oyama, S. (1976) A sensitive period for the acquisition of a nonnative phonological system. *Journal of Psycholinguistic Research*, 5, 261–85.

Oyama, S. (1982) A sensitive period for the acquisition of a nonnative phonological system. In S. Krashen, R. Scarcella, & M. Long (eds.), *Child-adult differences in second language acquisition* (pp. 20–38). Rowley, MA: Newbury House.

Patkowski, M. S. (1980) The sensitive period for the acquisition of syntax in a second language. *Language Learning*, 30, 449–72.

Perani, D., Paulesu, E., Galles, N. S., Dupoux, E., Dehaene, S., Bettinardi, V., Cappa, S. F., Fazio, F., & Mehler, J. (1998) The bilingual brain: proficiency and age of acquisition of the second language. *Brain*, 121, 1841–52.

Pinker, S. (1994) *The language instinct: how the mind creates language*. New York: Morrow.

Pinker, S. (1999) *Words and rules*. New York: Basic Books.

Pulvermüller, F. & Schumann, J. H. (1994) Neurobiological mechanisms of language acquisition. *Language Learning*, 44, 681–734.

Salthouse, T. A. (1991) *Theoretical perspectives on cognitive aging*. Hillsdale, NJ: Erlbaum.

Sanders, C. (2000) Functional imaging evidence of cortical overlap in second language acquisition. Unpublished manuscript, University of Texas-Austin.

Schachter, J. (1990) On the issue of completeness in second language acquisition. *Second Language Research*, 6, 93–124.

Scheibel, A. B. (1996) Structural and functional changes in the aging brain. In J. E. Birren & K. W. Schaie (eds.), *Handbook of the psychology of aging* (4th edn.) (pp. 105–28). San Diego, CA: Academic Press.

Schwartz, B. D. (1998) On two hypotheses of "transfer" in L2A: minimal trees and absolute L1 influence. In S. Flynn, G. Martohardjono, & W. O'Neil (eds.), *The generative study of second language acquisition* (pp. 35–59). Mahwah, NJ: Erlbaum.

Schwartz, B. D. & Sprouse, R. A. (1996) L2 cognitive states and the Full Transfer/Full Access model. *Second Language Research*, 12, 40–72.

Scovel, T. (1988) *A time to speak: a psycholinguistic inquiry into the critical period for human speech*. Rowley, MA: Newbury House.

Selinker, L. (1972) Interlanguage. *International Review of Applied Linguistics*, 10, 209–31.

Selinker, L. & Han, Z.-H. (2000) Fossilization: moving the concept into empirical longitudinal study. In E. Elder (ed.), *Studies in language testing/experimenting with uncertainty: essays in honor of Alan Davies*. Cambridge: UCLES.

Sorace, A. (1993) Incomplete vs. divergent representations of unaccusativity in non-native grammars of Italian. *Second Language Research, 9,* 22–47.

Towell, R. & Hawkins, R. (1994) *Approaches to Second Language Acquisition.* Clevedon, UK: Multilingual Matters.

Ullman, M. (2001) The neural basis of lexicon and grammar in first and second language: the declarative/procedural model. *Bilingualism: Language and Cognition,* 4, 105–22.

Ullman, M. T., Corkin, S., Coppola, M., Hickok, G., Growdon, J. H., Koroshetz, W. J., & Pinker, S. (1997) A neural dissociation within language: evidence that the mental dictionary is part of declarative memory, and that grammatical rules are processed by the procedural system. *Journal of Cognitive Neuroscience,* 9, 266–76.

van Wuijtswinkel, K. (1994) Critical period effects on the acquisition of grammatical competence in a second language. Unpublished thesis, Katholieke Universiteit, Nijmegen.

Weber-Fox, C. M. & Neville, H. J. (1999) Functional neural subsystems are differentially affected by delays in second-language immersion: ERP and behavioral evidence in bilingual speakers. In D. Birdsong (ed.), *The Critical Period Hypothesis and second language acquisition* (pp. 23–38). Mahwah, NJ: Erlbaum.

White, L. (2000) Second language acquisition: from initial to final state. In J. Archibald (ed.), *Second language acquisition and linguistic theory* (pp. 130–55). Oxford: Blackwell.

White, L. & Genesee, F. (1996) How native is near-native? The issue of ultimate attainment in adult second language acquisition. *Second Language Research,* 12, 238–65.

White, L. & Juffs, A. (1997) Constraints on wh-movement in two different contexts of non-native language acquisition: competence and processing. In S. Flynn, G. Martohardjono, & W. O'Neil (eds.), *The generative study of second language acquisition* (pp. 111–29). Mahwah, NJ: Erlbaum.

4 Language Corpora

MICHAEL STUBBS

4.1 Introduction

Since the 1990s, a "language corpus" usually means a text collection which is:

- large: millions, or even hundreds of millions, of running words, usually sampled from hundreds or thousands of individual texts;
- computer-readable: accessible with software such as concordancers, which can find, list and sort linguistic patterns;
- designed for linguistic analysis: selected according to a sociolinguistic theory of language variation, to provide a sample of specific text-types or a broad and balanced sample of a language.

Much "corpus linguistics" is driven purely by curiosity. It aims to improve language description and theory, and the task for applied linguistics is to assess the relevance of this work to practical applications. Corpus data are essential for accurately describing language use, and have shown how lexis, grammar, and semantics interact. This in turn has applications in language teaching, translation, forensic linguistics, and broader cultural analysis. In limited cases, applications can be direct. For example, if advanced language learners have access to a corpus, they can study for themselves how a word or grammatical construction is typically used in authentic data. Hunston (2002, pp. 170–84) discusses data-driven discovery learning and gives further references.

However, applications are usually indirect. Corpora provide observable evidence about language use, which leads to new descriptions, which in turn are embodied in dictionaries, grammars, and teaching materials. Since the late 1980s, the influence of this work is most evident in new monolingual English dictionaries (CIDE, 1995; COBUILD, 1995a; LDOCE, 1995; OALD, 1995) and grammars (e.g., COBUILD, 1990), aimed at advanced learners, and based on authentic examples of current usage from large corpora. Other corpus-based reference grammars (e.g., G. Francis, Hunston, & Manning, 1996, 1998; Biber et al., 1999) are invaluable resources for materials producers and teachers.

Corpora are just sources of evidence, available to all linguists, theoretical or applied. A sociolinguist might use a corpus of audio-recorded conversations to study relations between social class and accent; a psycholinguist might use the same corpus to study slips of the tongue; and a lexicographer might be interested in the frequency of different phrases. The study might be purely descriptive: a grammarian might want to know which constructions are frequent in casual spoken language but rare in formal written language. Or it might have practical aims: someone writing teaching materials might use a specialized corpus to discover which grammatical constructions occur in academic research articles; and a forensic linguist might want to study norms of language use, in order to estimate the likelihood that linguistic patterns in an anonymous letter are evidence of authorship.

So, if corpus linguistics is not (necessarily) applied linguistics, and is not a branch of linguistics, then what is it? It is an empirical approach to studying language, which uses observations of attested data in order to make generalizations about lexis, grammar, and semantics. Corpora solve the problem of observing patterns of language use. It is these patterns which are the real object of study, and it is findings about recurrent lexico-grammatical units of meaning which have implications for both theoretical and applied linguistics. Large corpora have provided many new facts about words, phrases, grammar, and meaning, even for English, which many teachers and linguists assumed was fairly well understood.

Valid applications of corpus studies depend on the design of corpora, the observational methods of analysis, and the interpretation of the findings. Applied linguists must assess this progression from evidence to interpretation to applications, and this chapter therefore has sections on empirical linguistics (pre- and post-computers), corpus design and software, findings and descriptions, and implications and applications.

I use these presentation conventions. LEMMAS (LEXEMES) are in upper case. *Word-forms* are lower case italics. 'Meanings' are in single quotes. Collocates of a node are in angle brackets: UNDERGO <surgery>.

4.2   Empirical Linguistics

Since corpus study gives priority to observing millions of running words, computer technology is essential. This makes linguistics analogous to the natural sciences, where it is observational and measuring instruments (such as microscopes, radio telescopes, and x-ray machines) which extended our grasp of reality far beyond "the tiny sphere attainable by unaided common sense" (Wilson, 1998, p. 49).

Observation is not restricted to any single method, but concordances are essential for studying lexical, grammatical, and semantic patterns. Printed concordance lines (see Appendix) are limited in being static, but a computer-accessible concordance is both an observational and experimental tool, since ordering it alphabetically to left and right brings together repeated lexico-grammatical patterns. A single concordance line, on the horizontal axis, is a fragment of language use (*parole*). The vertical axis of a concordance shows repeated co-occurrences, which are evidence of units of meaning in the language system (*langue*).

The tiny sample of concordance lines in the Appendix is not representative. In a real study one might have hundreds or thousands of concordance lines, but I can use this sample for illustration. Concordance data are often especially good at distinguishing words with related propositional meanings, but different connotations and patterns of usage. The Appendix therefore gives examples of *endure, persevere, persist*, and *undergo*, which are all used to talk about unpleasant things which last a long time, but which differ in their surrounding lexis and grammar. For example, we can observe how the word-form *persist* occurs in distinct constructions. When its subject is an abstract noun, it often denotes unpleasant things (*fears, problems*), often medical (*symptoms, headaches*), and often has a time reference (*for over a year, for up to six weeks*). Alternatively, when the subject of *persist in* is animate, it is often used of someone who persists, often unreasonably or *in the face of* opposition, in doing something which is difficult or disapproved of. Such recurrent co-occurrence patterns provide evidence of typical meaning and use.

It is sometimes objected that concordances place words in small, arbitrary contexts, defined by the width of a computer screen, and ignore contexts of communication. However, it is an empirical finding that evidence for the meaning of a node word often occurs within a short span of co-text. In addition, corpora allow individual utterances to be interpreted against the usage of many speakers and the intertextual norms of general language use.

The observation of large publicly available data sets implies (a weak sense of) inductive methods, that is, gathering many observations and identifying patterns in them. This does not imply mechanical methods of generalizing from observations, but (as Fillmore, 1992, pp. 38, 58 puts it) a combination of corpus linguistics (getting the facts right) and armchair linguistics (thinking through the hypotheses that corpus data suggest). It does mean, however, that corpus study belongs to a philosophical tradition of empiricism. Contrary to a loss of confidence, from Saussure to Chomsky, in the ability to observe real language events, corpora show that language use is highly patterned. Although there are limitations on corpus design (see below), and although we can never entirely escape subjective interpretations, corpora allow "a degree of objectivity" about some central questions, "where before we could only speculate" (Kilgarriff, 1997, p. 137). There are no automatic discovery procedures, but inductive generalizations can be tested against observations in independent corpora.

Corpus methods therefore differ sharply from the view, widely held since the 1960s, that native speaker introspection gives special access to linguistic competence. Although linguists' careful analyses of their own idiolects have revealed much about language and cognition, there are several problems with intuitive data and misunderstandings about the relation between observation and intuition in corpus work. Intuitive data can be circular: data and theory have the same source in the linguist who both proposes a hypothesis and invents examples to support or refute it. They can be unreliable or absent: many facts about frequency, grammar, and meaning are systematic and evident in corpora, but unrecorded in pre-corpus dictionaries. They are narrow: introspection about small sets of invented sentences cannot be the sole and privileged source of data.

There is no point in being purist about data, and it is always advisable to compare data from different sources, both independent corpora, and also introspection and experiments. Corpus study does not reject intuition, but gives it a different role. Concordances focus intuition, and this "confirms rather than produces the data" (de Beaugrande, 1999, pp. 247–8). Without this retrospective competence, native speakers could not recognize untypical collocations in literature, advertising, or jokes. We cannot know in advance what kinds of evidence might bear on a theory of linguistic competence (as even Chomsky, 2000, pp. 139–40 admits). Nevertheless, with some striking exceptions (Fillmore, 1992), cognitive approaches have neglected corpus data on recurrent semantic patterns as evidence of cognitive structures.

4.3   Some Brief History

There was corpus study long before computers (W. Francis, 1992) and, from a historical perspective, Saussure's radical uncertainty about the viability of studying *parole*, followed by Chomsky's reliance on introspective data, were short breaks in a long tradition of observational language study. Disregard of quantified textual data was never, of course, accepted by everyone. Corder (1973, pp. 208–23) emphasizes the relevance of frequency studies to language teaching, and language corpora have always been indispensable in studying dead languages, unwritten languages and dialects, child language acquisition, and lexicography. So, within both philological and fieldwork traditions, corpus study goes back hundreds of years, within a broad tradition of rhetorical and textual analysis.

Early concordances were prepared of texts of cultural significance, such as the Bible (Cruden, 1737). Ayscough's (1790) index of Shakespeare is designed "to point out the different meanings to which words are applied." Nowadays we would say that he had a concept of "meaning as use." By bringing together many instances of a word, a concordance provides evidence of its range of uses and therefore of its meanings, and this essential point is still the basis of corpus semantics today.

The other main reason for studying large text collections, which again emphasizes the central concern with meaning, was the attempt to produce comprehensive dictionaries. From Samuel Johnson's dictionary of 1755 onward, lexicographers have used quotations to illustrate the uses and meanings of words. Johnson collected 150,000 illustrative quotations for 40,000 head-words, and the readers for the *Oxford English Dictionary* collected five million quotations to illustrate over 400,000 entries (Kennedy, 1998, pp. 14–15; Winchester, 1998). For example, Johnson's dictionary has these quotes which contain *persist*:

> . . . I would advise neither to persist in refusing
> . . . the sinful act, to continue and persist in it
> . . . thus will persist, relentless in his ire

The collocates of *persist* are observable evidence of its typical semantic features of doing something over time and against opposition. However, there is a limitation here on printed dictionaries: these examples do not occur under the head-word PERSIST, and can therefore be found only by a full text search of a machine-readable version of the dictionary (McDermott, 1996). The Appendix gives further illustrations of observable evidence of meaning. For example, *endure* co-occurs with *compelled* and *forced*, *difficult* and *painful*, with references to long time periods, and also with near synonyms such as *persevere*, *accept*, and *bear*. Semantic features are not abstract, but often realized in co-occurring and observable collocates.

Modern lexicographers use better designed corpora, their methods are more explicit, they use statistical techniques to systematize observations (Church & Hanks, 1990; Clear, 1993; Sinclair et al., 1998), and the theory of "meaning as use" has been developed by Wittgenstein, Austin, and Firth, but the basic approach to semantic analysis is not fundamentally different from that of Cruden, Ayscough, Johnson, and Murray.

Other impressive quantitative corpus analyses, between the 1890s and the 1950s, were possible only with significant expense and personnel, and often had precise institutional and/or educational applications. In order to improve shorthand methods for court transcription, Kaeding (1898) used large numbers of helpers from the Prussian civil service to analyze word frequency in an 11-million-word German corpus. From the 1920s to the 1940s, Thorndike and Lorge (1944) calculated word frequencies in large English language corpora, of up to 18 million words. These word-lists were used to control the vocabulary in foreign language and literacy materials. West's (1953) influential *General Service List* gave also the frequency of different meanings of words.

In a word, corpus-based study of language is much older than its alternatives. Indeed, up until the 1950s, it was assumed that writing a grammar required the study of text collections. Famous examples include: Jespersen (1909–49), based on examples of written English over several centuries; Fries (1952), based on a 250,000-word corpus of telephone conversations; and Quirk et al. (1972), based on the last of the great non-computerized corpora, which was itself overtaken by technology and computerized, and then used in turn for later versions of the grammar (Quirk et al., 1985, and, with substantial additional corpora, Biber et al., 1999).

4.4 Modern Corpora and Software

Modern computer-assisted corpus study is based on two principles.

1 *The observer must not influence what is observed.* What is selected for observation depends on convenience, interests and hypotheses, but corpus data are part of natural language use, and not produced for purposes of linguistic analysis.
2 *Repeated events are significant.* Quantitative work with large corpora reveals what is central and typical, normal and expected. It follows (Teubert, 1999) that corpus study is inherently sociolinguistic, since the data are authentic acts of communication; inherently diachronic, since the data are what has frequently occurred in the past; and inherently quantitative. This disposes of the frequent confusion that corpus study is concerned with "mere" performance, in Chomsky's (1965, p. 3) pejorative sense of being characterized by "memory limitations, distractions, shifts of attention and interest, and errors." The aim is not to study idiosyncratic details of performance which are, by chance, recorded in a corpus. On the contrary, a corpus reveals what frequently recurs, sometimes hundreds or thousands of times, and cannot possibly be due to chance.

4.4.1 Available corpora

Any list of extant corpora would be quickly out of date, but there are two sets of important distinctions between

- small first generation corpora from the 1960s onward and much larger corpora from the 1990s, and
- carefully designed reference corpora, small and large, and other specialized corpora, opportunistic text collections, archives and the like.

The first computer-readable corpora, compiled in the 1960s, are very small by contemporary standards, but still useful because of their careful design. The Brown corpus (from Brown University in the USA) is one million words of written American English, sampled from texts published in 1961: both informative prose, from different text-types (e.g., press and academic writing), and different topics (e.g., religion and hobbies); and imaginative prose (e.g., detective fiction and romance). Parallel corpora were designed to enable comparative research: the LOB corpus (from the universities of Lancaster, Oslo, & Bergen) contains British data from 1961; Frown and FLOB (from Freiburg University, Germany) contain American and British data from 1991; and

ICE (International Corpora of English) contains regional varieties of English, such as Indian and Australian. Similar design principles underlie the Lund corpus of spoken British English (from University College London and Lund University), which contains around half a million words, divided into samples of the usage of adult, educated, professional people, including face-to-face and telephone conversations, lectures and discussions.

By the late 1990s, some corpora consisted of hundreds of millions of words. The Bank of English (at COBUILD in Birmingham, UK) and the British National Corpus (BNC) had commercial backing from publishers, who have used the corpora to produce dictionaries and grammars. The 100-million-word BNC is also carefully designed to include demographically and stylistically defined samples of written and spoken language. The Bank of English arguably over-emphasizes mass media texts, but these are very influential, and it still has a range of text-types and advantages of size: over 400 million words by 2001. Because constructing large reference corpora is so expensive, it may be that huge new corpora cannot again be created in the near future. These corpora will remain standard reference points, which can be supplemented by small specialized corpora, designed by individual researchers, and by large opportunistic collections.

Many other corpora for English, and increasingly for other languages, are available (see Michael Barlow's website: address in the further reading section below).

4.4.2   Corpus design

Some basic principles of corpus design (Kennedy, 1998, pp. 13–87; Hunston, 2002, pp. 25–37) are simple enough. A corpus which claims to be a balanced sample of language use must represent variables of demography, style, and topic, and must include texts which are spoken and written, casual and formal, fiction and non-fiction, which vary in level (e.g., popular and technical), age of audience (e.g., children or adults), and sex and geographical origin of author, and which illustrate a wide range of subject fields (e.g., natural and social sciences, commerce, and leisure). However, no corpus can truly represent a whole language, since no one quite knows what should be represented. It is not even obvious what are appropriate proportions of mainstream text-types such as quality newspapers, literary classics, and everyday conversation, much less text-types such as newspaper ads, business correspondence, and church sermons. (Even carefully designed corpora have odd gaps: despite their influence as a text-type, textbooks are not represented in Brown and LOB.) A realistic aim is a corpus which samples widely, is not biased toward data which are easy to collect (e.g., mass media texts), does not under-represent data which are difficult to collect (e.g., casual conversation), and is not unbalanced by text-types which have over-specialized lexis and grammar (e.g., academic research articles).

Since large quantities of data are necessary in order to study what is typical and probable, an important criterion is size, which is usually measured in terms of running words (tokens). But measures of heterogeneity are also important: How large is the corpus measured as word-types (i.e., different words), or as the number of different texts or text-types it contains? A corpus might be very large, but consist entirely of American newswire texts, with a correspondingly narrow vocabulary. One can also attempt to measure linguistic influence: How large is the audience for the texts in the corpus? Casual conversation is a linguistic universal, but a typical conversation is private, whereas the language of the mass media is public, and therefore much more influential. And whereas some texts are heard once by millions of people (sports commentaries), others (literary classics) are constantly re-read over generations. A reception index, which weights texts by their audience size, can be constructed at least in a rough way.

In summary, any corpus is a compromise between the desirable and the feasible, and although design criteria cannot be operationalized, large balanced corpora reveal major regularities in language use. In any case, there is no reason to rely on any single corpus, and it is often advisable to combine large general corpora designed according to principles of sociolinguistic variation, small corpora from specific knowledge domains (since much lexis is determined by topic), and opportunistic text collections.

Huge text collections (such as the world-wide-web) can be used to study patterns which do not occur even in large reference corpora. For example, concordance lines in the Appendix show that *undergo* is typically used of someone who is forced to undergo something unpleasant, often a medical procedure or a test of some kind, or of a situation which undergoes some profound and often unwelcome change. Typical examples are:

had to *undergo* a stringent medical examination
is about to *undergo* dramatic changes

However generalizations must be checked against potential counter-examples. First, comparison of different text-types shows that, in scientific and technical English, *undergo* usually has no unpleasant connotations. An example from the BNC (which still involves 'change') is:

the larvae *undergo* a complex cycle of 12 stages

Second, people 'unwillingly' undergo unpleasant experiences. But does the collocation *willingly UNDERGO* occur and does it provide a counter-example? Now we have a problem: the lemma UNDERGO is fairly frequent (around 25 occurrences per million words in the BNC), and even *willingly* is not infrequent (around 5 per million), but the combination *willingly UNDERGO* does not occur at all in the 100-million-word BNC. However, a search of the world-wide-web quickly provided 200 examples, which revealed another pattern: people *willingly undergo* a sacrifice for the sake of others or for the sake of religious beliefs. Characteristic examples are:

one can *willingly undergo* some painful experience for one who is dearly loved
sufferings and dangers the early Christians *willingly underwent* for the sake of . . .

A corpus is specifically designed for language study, but other text collections (such as newspapers on CD-ROM) can be useful for some types of study. Again, I see no point in being purist about data, as long as their source is stated in a way which allows findings to be assessed. The world-wide-web has the advantage of enormous size, but it is impossible to characterize its overall range of texts. Words and phrases in the world-wide-web can be searched for directly with search engines, or with a concordancer which uses these engines, such as one developed at the University of Liverpool (http://www.webcorp.org.uk/).

4.4.3   *Raw, lemmatized, and annotated corpora*

A corpus may consist of raw text (strings of orthographic word-forms), or it can be lemmatized, and annotated or tagged, for intonation (for spoken corpora), grammatical or semantic categories. Part-of-speech tagging allows a corpus to be searched for grammatical constructions, such as adjective-noun combinations (*persistent rain*), and make it possible to study the frequency of grammatical categories in different text-types (e.g., see Biber, Conrad, & Reppen, 1998, pp. 59–65 on nominalizations; and Carter & McCarthy, 1999, on passives). Information on the frequencies of lexical and grammatical features can indicate to language teachers where it is worthwhile devoting pedagogical effort (Kennedy, 1998, pp. 88–203).

Nevertheless, a simple example illustrates the value of working with raw text. Many occurrences of the lemmas of the verbs PERSIST and ENDURE share the semantic and pragmatic features that something 'unpleasant' is lasting 'for a long time'. However, although the adjectives *persistent* and *enduring* also share the feature "for a long time", their typical collocates show their very different connotations:

persistent <ambiguity, bleeding, confusion, headaches>
enduring <appeal, legacies, peace, significance, values>

Traditionally, lemmas comprise words within a single part of speech. *Persistent* is an adjective, and shares the connotations of the verb PERSIST. *Enduring* might be considered an adjective, or the *-ing* form of the verb ENDURE, but has very different connotations from the verb.

In addition, the grammatical categories needed for unrestricted naturally occurring text can be very different from those required for the invented data described in abstract syntax. This draws into question centuries-old assumptions about the part-of-speech system (Sinclair, 1991, pp. 81–98; Sampson, 1995; Hallan, 2001). So, tagging may make unwarranted assumptions about appropriate grammatical categories. Again, the principle is that observer and data should be kept independent. The facts never "speak for themselves," but inductive methods aim for the minimum of preconceptions. How to lemmatize words is by no means always obvious, and there are no standardized systems for part-of-speech tagging (Atwell et al., 2000) or full parsing (Sampson, 1995).

4.5   New Findings and Descriptions

The main findings which have resulted from the "vastly expanded empirical base" (Kennedy, 1998, p. 204) which corpora provide concern the association patterns which inseparably relate item and context:

- lexico-grammatical units: what frequently (or never) co-occurs within a span of a few words;
- style and register: what frequently (or never) co-occurs in texts.

Findings about lexico-grammar question many traditional assumptions about the lexis–grammar boundary. The implications for language teaching are, at one level, rather evident. A well-known problem for even advanced language learners is that they may speak grammatically, yet not sound native-like, because their language use deviates from native speaker collocational norms. I once received an acknowledgment in an article by a non-native English-speaking colleague, for my "repeated comments on drafts of this paper," which seemed to connote both irritation at my comments and to imply that they were never heeded. (I suppose this was better than being credited with "persistent comments"!)

Syllabus designers ought to know which words are used frequently in con-ventionalized combinations, and which are used rarely and in special contexts. The importance of collocations for language learners was emphasized in the 1930s and 1940s by H. E. Palmer and A. S. Hornby. More recently corpora have been used to study how learners and native speakers differ in their use of conventionalized expressions (Granger, 1998), and a major topic has been how to represent such information in learners' dictionaries (Cowie, 1998). Pro-posals have also been made about the form of a "lexical syllabus." This concept was discussed in detail by Corder (1973, pp. 315–17), and has been revived in corpus work by Willis (1990) and Lewis (1998), although corresponding teaching materials have been adopted only to a limited extent. The shorthand label for this area is phraseology: the identification of typical multi-word units of language use and meaning.

4.5.1   *Words*

Many corpus studies reject individual words as units of meaning, and propose a theory of abstract phrasal units. Nevertheless, words are a good place to start, since, "a central fact about a word is how frequent it is" (Kilgarriff, 1997,

p. 135), and other things being equal, the more frequent a word is, the more important it is to know it, and to teach it early to learners: hence the interest, since the 1890s, in reliable word-frequency lists for many applications.

Frequency shows that system and use are inseparable (Halliday, 1991). More frequent words tend to be shorter, irregular in morphology and spelling, and more ambiguous out of context: a glance at a dictionary shows that short frequent words require many column inches. A few, mainly grammatical, words are very frequent, but most words are very rare, and in an individual text or smallish corpus, around half the words typically occur only once each. In addition, a word with different senses usually has one meaning which is much more frequent. These relations imply a balance between economy of effort for the speaker and clarity for the hearer, and in the 1930s and 1940s Zipf (1945) tried to formulate statistical relations between word frequency, word length, and number of senses. (These regularities apply to many other aspects of human behavior. In a library, a few books are frequently borrowed, but most books collect dust.)

The simplest frequency lists contain unlemmatized word-forms from a general corpus, in alphabetical or frequency order, but there are considerable differences between even the top ten words from an unlemmatized written corpus (in 1), a spoken corpus (in 2), and a lemmatized mixed written and spoken corpus (in 3):

(1)   the, of, and, a, in, to [infinitive marker], is, to [preposition], was, it
(2)   I, you, it, the, 's, and, n't, a, that, yeah
(3)   the, BE, of, and, a, in, to [infinitive marker], HAVE, it

These examples are from frequency lists for the 100-million-word BNC, made available by Kilgarriff (ftp://ftp.itri.bton.ac.uk/bnc/).

Unlemmatized lists show that different forms of a lemma differ greatly in frequency, and may have very different collocational behavior: see above on *endure* and *enduring*. However, raw frequency lists cannot distinguish words in different grammatical classes (e.g., *firm* as adjective or noun) and the different meanings of a word (e.g., *cold* as 'low temperature' versus 'lacking in feeling'). This requires a grammatically tagged corpus and a method of automatic sense disambiguation, and makes an apparently trivial counting task into a considerable theoretical problem.

Frequency lists require careful interpretation to provide what is really wanted, which is a measure of the relative importance of words, and more important than raw frequency may be even distribution across many text-types. Conversely, we want to know not only what is frequent in general, but what distinguishes a text-type. For example, words may be frequent in academic texts but unlikely in fiction, or vice-versa:

constants, measured, thermal, theoretically
sofa, kissed, damned, impatiently

These examples are from Johansson (1981; discussed also by Kennedy, 1998, p. 106). For important reference data on word frequency and distribution, see W. Francis and Kucera (1982), Johannson and Hofland (1988–9), and Leech, Rayson, and Wilson (2001; and http://www.comp.lancs.ac.uk/ucrel/bncfreq/flists.html).

We come back to the distinction between evidence and interpretation. Frequency and distribution (which are all we have) are indirect objective measures of the subjective concept of salience (which is what we really want). The objective measures have limitations, but allow analysis to be based on public and replicable data. The only alternative is intuition, which may be absent, speculative, or wrong.

A very useful applied frequency study is reported by Coxhead (2000), who used a corpus of 3.5 million words to set up the Academic Word List (AWL). This contains words which have both high frequency and wide distribution in academic texts, irrespective of subject area (but excluding approximately the 2,000 most frequent words in English, from West, 1953). AWL comprises 570 word families: not just word-forms, but head-words plus their inflected and derived forms, and therefore around 3,100 word-forms altogether, e.g.:

> concept: conception, concepts, conceptual, conceptualization, conceptualize, conceptualized, conceptualizes, conceptualizing, conceptually.

Coxhead's corpus comprised texts from academic journals and university textbooks from arts, commerce, law, and natural science. To be included in AWL, a word had to occur at least 100 times altogether in the whole academic corpus, at least ten times in each of the four sub-corpora, and in at least half of 28 more finely defined subject areas, such as biology, economics, history, and linguistics. AWL gives very good coverage of academic texts, irrespective of subject area. Here it must be remembered that words are *very* uneven in their frequency. In a typical academic text, the single word *the* covers around 6 or 7 per cent of running text, the top ten words cover over 20 per cent, and the 2,000 most frequent words cover around 75 per cent. The words in AWL typically cover a further 10 per cent. The remaining 15 per cent will be specialized words which are specific to a given topic, plus proper names, etc. AWL is further divided into ten sub-groups, from most to least frequent. Group 1 covers 3.6 per cent of the corpus, which means that a student reading academic prose could expect to come across *each word* in group 1, on average, once every four pages or so.

A list is, of course, just a list, not teaching materials, and requires interpretation by materials designers and teachers. However, even as a bare list, AWL can provide a check, for teachers or students themselves, on what words students should know.

4.5.2 *Phrases*

Word frequency lists are limited, especially for very common words, since these are common, not in their own right, but because they occur in common phrases. For example, *back* is usually in the top 100 in lemmatized frequency lists, and (including compounds such as *backward* and *backwater*) gets nearly five full pages in the COBUILD (1995a) dictionary. This is not because speakers frequently use *back* to mean a part of the body, but because it occurs in many phrases with only residual relations to this denotation. It has many meanings, but vanishingly few uses with the part-of-body meaning. The following examples are from Cobuild (1995a), and Sinclair (1991, p. 116) gives a detailed analysis of its nominal, prepositional and idiomatic uses.

> lying on his back; the back of the chair; on the back of a postcard; at the back of the house; round the back; do something behind her back; get off my back; you scratch my back . . . ; see the back of someone; turn your back on

In summary: Frequent words are frequent because they occur in frequent phrases. In these phrases, frequent words are often delexicalized, because meaning is dispersed across the whole phrase. Since frequent content words are rarely used with their full lexical meaning, the boundary between content and function words is fuzzy. It is for these reasons that the co-occurrence of words and grammatical constructions has been studied so intensively: the central principle is that it is not words, but phrase-like units, which are the basic units of meaning.

4.5.3   Recurrent phrases, collocations and phrasal schemas

The simplest definition of a phrase is a string of two or more uninterrupted word-forms which occur more than once in a text or corpus: see Altenberg (1998) on "recurrent word-combinations" and Biber et al. (1999) on "lexical bundles." I used a program to identify strings in this sense, in a written corpus of four million words. (Since 2002, when I did this work with a locally written program, excellent n-gram software has been made available by William Fletcher at http://kwicfinder.com/kfNgram/.) The most frequent five-word string, over twice as frequent as any other, was *at the end of the*. And almost 30 out of the top 100 five-word strings had the pattern *PREP* + *the* + *NOUN* + *of* + *the*. Examples included:

> at the end of the; in the middle of the; at the beginning of the; at the bottom of the

The program operationalizes, in a very simple way, the concept of repeated units. It cannot automatically identify linguistic units, but presents data in a way which helps the analyst to see patterns. These findings are not an artifact of my small corpus. I looked at the same strings in the 100-million-word BNC, and found that, normalized to estimated occurrences per million words, the frequencies in the two corpora were remarkably similar. These examples represent only one pattern, of course. Other frequent five-word strings have discourse functions:

> as a matter of fact; it seems to me that; it may well be that; but on the other hand

Altenberg (1998) identifies other recurrent multi-word strings, and some of their typical pragmatic functions.

These multi-word strings are already evidence that recurrent lexico-grammatical units are not fixed phrases, but abstract semantic units. For example, the program above counts separately the strings *on the top of the*, *on the very top of the*, or *on top of the*, although, to the human analyst, they are semantically related.

More abstract again is the concept of collocation, in the sense of the habitual co-occurrence of word-forms or lemmas. A few dozen concordance lines can be manually inspected for patterns, but if we have thousands of lines, then we require a method of summarizing concordances and showing patterns. We can write a program which finds the most frequent collocates of a node, one, two, and three words to the left and right, and lists them in descending frequency. The positional frequency table for *undergo* shows that it often occurs in a passive construction (*was forced to, is required to*), is often followed by an adjective signaling the seriousness of the event (*extensive, major*), and is often used of medical events (*surgery, operation*).

Raw frequency of co-occurrence is important, but we need to check the frequency of collocation relative to the frequency of the individual words. If two words are themselves very frequent, they may co-occur frequently just by chance. Conversely, a word might be infrequent, but when it does occur, it usually occurs with a small set of words. For example, the word *vegetative* is not frequent, but when it occurs, especially in journalism, it often co-occurs with *persistent*, in the phrase *persistent vegetative state*, with reference to patients in a coma.

The variability of phrasal units makes it doubtful whether there could be a useful "phrase frequency list," but corpus studies show that all words occur in habitual patterns which are often much stronger than is evident to intuition. For example, in a 200-million-word corpus, the word-form *persistent* occurred over 2,300 times, with clear semantic preferences, shown by the top 20 collocates, ordered by frequency:

> persistent <offenders, reports, most, rumours, state, vegetative, despite, young, juvenile, problem, injury, problems, rain, allegations, critic, offender, rumors, speculation, amid, cough>

The most frequent single collocate (in 5 percent of cases) was *offenders*; and the most frequent set of collocates were words for *reports, rumors,* and *speculations*.

Table 4.1   Positional frequency table for NODE *undergo* in a span of 3 words to left and right (only collocates occurring five or more times are shown, in descending frequency, independently for each position)

N – 3	N – 2	N – 1	NODE	N + 1	N + 2	N + 3
was	forced	to	*	a	medical	and
is	required	will	*	an	surgery	tests
be	have	and	*	further	testing	examination
are	had	would	*	extensive	tests	of
and	is	must	*	the	treatment	surgery
that	they	he'll	*	major	change	operation
been	about	should	*	surgery	changes	transformation
were	and	who	*	treatment	for	before
where	patients	women	*	medical	heart	test
children	that	often	*	heart	and	medical
he	he		*	his	major	for
in	will		*	testing	operation	in
the	women		*		examination	on
women	due		*		extensive	training
will	ordered		*		transformation	to
for			*		radical	testing
last			*		test	the
not			*		training	a
of			*		the	as
			*			by
			*			changes

Persistent is used of bad situations (collocates include *problem* and *problems*), which include medical conditions (*cough, injury, vegetative*) and criminal activities (*juvenile, offenders*). Some collocates frequently occur in longer phrases (*persistent juvenile offenders, persistent vegetative state*), and most examples involving "crime" and "allegations" are from journalism. With comparable data on a broad sample of words, we can then ask whether *persistent* exerts a stronger than average collocational attraction on its surrounding collocates. The brief answer is that *persistent* is typical of many words in this respect.

The top collocates of a word provide evidence of its characteristic semantic preferences and syntactic frames. Figures for a broad sample of words show how pervasive collocational attraction is, and allow generalizations about its strength and variability. The example of *persistent* is taken from a data-base (COBUILD, 1995b), which provides a suitable sample of node-words and their collocates for quantitative statements about phraseology. For the 10,000 most frequent content words (word-forms) in the 200-million-word corpus, the data-base gives the 20 most frequent collocates in a span of four words to left and right. For each node-collocate pair, it gives 20 randomly selected concordance lines, each with a rough description of its source (e.g., British fiction, American journalism). For individual words, this provides figures on the strength of attraction between node and top collocate:

> undergoing <surgery 11%>, undergo <surgery 9%>, endured <years 6%>, persistent <offenders 5%>

(That is, in 11 percent of occurrences, *undergoing* co-occurs with *surgery*, etc.) The data-base shows that around 75 percent of content words in the central vocabulary of English have a strength of attraction of between 2 and 9 percent. And over 20 percent co-occur with one specific collocate in over 10 percent of occurrences. Conversely, few words have less than one chance in 50 of co-occurring with one specific collocate.

These are figures for the attraction between two single unlemmatized word-forms. Collocational attraction is much stronger if it is calculated between a node and a set of approximate synonyms. For example:

> achieving <goal(s) 7%, success, aim, results, objectives> 15%
> ambitious <plan(s) 7%, project, program(me), scheme> 16%

The strength of attraction between all common content words is surprisingly high, yet not taken into account in most language description. Corpus study shows kinds of linguistic organization which are not predictable by rule, but are recurrent and observable.

4.5.4 *Semantic preference, discourse prosody, and extended lexical units*

A central aim is to make more explicit the semantic and pragmatic features of multi-word units. For example, *enduring, persistent*, and *haunting* are all rough synonyms, which share a propositional meaning, but they co-occur with nouns from different semantic fields and have different evaluative connotations. Characteristic combinations of modifier plus noun include:

> enduring peace; haunting music; persistent headaches

We can also generalize about semantic preferences. In adjective-noun constructions, *persistent* is often used of medical conditions, and *haunting* is usually used of music, words, and images. Different speaker attitudes are also conveyed: *persistent* is used of unpleasant topics, whereas *enduring* and *haunting* are usually used of things which are valued. For some speakers, ENDURE will have further Biblical connotations, since it occurs frequently in the King James translation, often with positive connotations when intransitive (*his mercy endureth for ever*), and often negative when transitive (*endureth temptation*). Louw (1993) was the first important article on how such attitudes are conveyed.

A model of extended lexical units proposed by Sinclair (1998) combines these increasingly abstract relations: (1) collocation (the habitual co-occurrence of individual word-forms or lemmas); (2) colligation (the co-occurrence of words and grammatical categories); (3) semantic preference (the co-occurrence of a word or grammatical construction with words from a well defined semantic field); and (4) discourse prosody (a descriptor of speaker attitude and discourse function). We can also specify: (5) strength of attraction between node and collocates; (6) position of node and collocate, variable or fixed (as in *spick and span*, but not **span and spick*); and (7) distribution, wide occurrence in general English or in broad varieties (e.g., journalism), or restricted to specialized text-types (e.g., recipes: *finely chopped*; or weather forecasts: *warm front*).

In summary: Work on extended lexical units has redrawn the lexis–grammar boundary. Only a few units are fixed phrases; most are recurrent combinations of grammatical constructions with words from restricted lexical fields, but with considerable lexical variation. A good term is "stabilized expressions" (Lenk, 2000). So, the vocabulary of a language is not merely "a list of basic irregularities" (Bloomfield, 1933, p. 274). Relations (1) to (4) correspond to the classic distinctions between syntax (how language units relate to one another), semantics (how linguistic signs relate to the external world), and pragmatics (how linguistic signs relate to their users, here expression of speaker attitude). This model has profoundly influenced dictionary design (Cowie, 1998) and language teaching (Hunston, 2002).

4.5.5   *Grammar, co-text, and text-type*

Corpus work has taken the development of grammars in two directions: description of the pervasive co-selection of grammar and lexis, and of grammatical variation in different text-types.

The examples above of lexico-grammatical units illustrate very briefly the type of patterns which G. Francis, Hunston, and Manning (1996, 1998) document systematically in the first corpus-driven grammars of English. For each verb, noun, and adjective in a large corpus, down to a frequency cut-off point, they show "the patterns that are associated with particular lexical items" (Hunston & Francis, 2000, p. 1). These highly innovative grammars show, for the first time, across the whole language, the intimate interaction between lexis, grammar, and meaning. Starting from individual words, users can find the grammatical patterns in which the words typically occur. Starting from the grammar, users can find the semantically related words which typically occur in the patterns, and therefore the meanings which they typically express.

Corpus methods can also reveal characteristics of whole texts and text-types, such as what proportion of a text consists of repetitions of the same words or new words (its type-token ratio), the ratio of content to function words (its lexical density), or the relative proportions of everyday and academic vocabulary, and can establish the central tendencies and range of variation across text-types. Other things being equal, high type-token ratio, high lexical density, and high percentages of academic vocabulary will make a text more difficult to understand. Biber (1988) used quantitative and distributional techniques to identify words and grammatical constructions which frequently (or never) co-occur in text-types such as conversation, personal letters, and science fiction, and to identify textual dimensions such as informational, narrative, and persuasive.

The grammar of spoken and written English by Biber et al. (1999), based on a 40-million-word corpus of British and American English, shows the frequency and distribution of lexical and grammatical structures in different text-types. Taking just one specific finding, of great potential interest to anyone concerned with designing English language teaching materials, the grammar identifies (pp. 373ff) the twelve most frequent lexical verbs in English. These are activity verbs (*get, go, make, come, take, give*), mental verbs (*know, think, see, want, mean*) and a communication verb (*say*). As a group, these verbs make up only 11 percent of lexical verbs in academic prose, but nearly 45 percent in conversation. Such findings do not translate directly into teaching materials or lesson plans, and applications of such work are still relatively modest, but such grammars indicate aspects of language use on which teachers may need to concentrate.

Although description of language use is inevitably description of language variation, G. Francis, Hunston, and Manning (1996, 1998) do not distinguish text-types, and Biber et al. (1999) differentiate only four broad categories (conversation, fiction, newspaper language, academic prose). Given their need to present "general English," dictionaries and grammars can take only limited account of variation within the language, and, as noted above, it is doubtful whether varieties can be exhaustively classified.

4.6   Applications, Implications, and Open Questions

There are often striking differences between earlier accounts of English usage (pedagogical and theoretical) and corpus evidence, but the applications of corpus findings are disputed. Since I cannot assess the wide range of proposed, rapidly changing, and potential applications, I have tried to set out the principles of data design and methods which applied linguists can use in assessing descriptions and applications. Perhaps especially in language teaching, one also has to assess the vested interests involved: both resistance to change by those who are committed to ways of teaching, and also claims made by publishers with commercial interests in dictionaries and teaching materials.

Apart from language teaching and lexicography, other areas where assessment is required are as follows:

1   Translation studies. By the late 1990s, bilingual corpora and bilingual corpus-based dictionaries had developed rapidly. The main finding (Baker, 1995; Kenny, 2001) is that, compared with source texts, the language of target texts tends to be "simpler," as measured by lower type-token ratios and lexical density, and the proportion of more explicit and grammatically conventional constructions.

2   Stylistics. Corpora are the only objective source of information about the relation between instance and norm, and provide a concrete interpretation of the concept of intertextuality. Burrows (1987) is a detailed literary case study, and Hockey (2001) discusses wider topics. The next category might be regarded as a specialized application of stylistics.

3   Forensic linguistics. Corpus studies can establish linguistic norms which are not under conscious control. Although findings are usually probabilistic, and an entirely reliable "linguistic fingerprint" is currently unlikely, corpus data can help to identify authors of blackmail letters, and test the authenticity of police transcripts of spoken evidence. Progress has also been made with other kinds of text comparison, such as identifying plagiarism and copyright violation (Coulthard, 1994).

4   Cultural representation and keywords. Several studies investigate the linguistic representation of culturally important topics: see Gerbig (1997) on texts about the environment, and Stubbs (1996) and Piper (2000) on culturally important keywords and phrases. Atkinson (1999) combines computational, manual, and historical methods in a detailed study of an influential corpus of scientific writing from the seventeeth to the twentieth century. Channell (2000) shows the importance of correctly representing the cultural connotations of cultural keywords in learner dictionaries.

5   Psycholinguistics. On a broader interpretation of applications, psycholinguistic studies of fluency and comprehension can use findings about the balance of routine, convention, and creativity in language use (Wray, 2002). Corpus-based studies of child language acquisition have also questioned assumptions about word-categories and have far-reaching implications for linguistic description in general (Hallan, 2001).

6   Theoretical linguistics. The implications here lie in revisions or rejection of the *langue/parole* opposition, the demonstration that the tagging and parsing of unrestricted text requires changing many assumptions about the part-of-speech system (Sinclair, 1991, pp. 81–98; Sampson, 1995), and about the lexis/grammar boundary (G. Francis, Hunston, & Manning, 1996, 1998).

Computer-readable corpora became available only in the 1970s, and for many years were limited and inconvenient. They became widely accessible only from the mid-1990s, when linguistics suddenly went from a position of being "starved of adequate data" (Sinclair, 1991, p. 1) to being swamped with data. Development is now (post-2000) very rapid, but it will take time before we can see the wood for the trees, and state with certainty the long-term implications. No linguists can now ignore corpus data. Many severe difficulties in observing language use have been resolved, and although language corpora are not the only way of seeing language, they are a very productive way. With reference to language description, I have taken an enthusiastic view, arguing that language corpora have provided many new findings about lexis, grammar, and semantics. With reference to applications, I have taken a conservative view, arguing that applications are indirect, and that, before findings can be applied to real-world problems, they require careful interpretation.

See also 1 LANGUAGE DESCRIPTIONS, 2 LEXICOGRAPHY, 27 THE PRACTICE OF LSP, 31 LANGUAGE TESTING.

ACKNOWLEDGMENTS

For pointing out to me the interest of the set of words related to PERSIST and PERSE-VERE, I am grateful to Alan Partington and to my student Anne Schmidt. For writing the "strings" and positional frequency programs, I am grateful to my student research assistants, Isabel Barth and Oliver Hardt. I am very grateful to colleagues who have made available the Bank of English (at COBUILD in Birmingham) and the British National Corpus.

REFERENCES

Altenberg, B. (1998) On the phraseology of spoken English. In A. P. Cowie (ed.), *Phraseology: theory, analysis and applications*, (pp. 101–22). Oxford: Oxford University Press.

Atkinson, D. (1999) *Scientific discourse in sociohistorical context*. Mahwah, NJ: Erlbaum.

Atwell, E., Demetriou, G., Hughes, J., Schiffrin, A., Souter, C., & Wilcock, S. (2000) A comparative evaluation of modern English corpus grammatical annotation schemes. *ICAME Journal*, 24, 7–24.

Ayscough, S. (1790) *An index to the remarkable passages and words made use of by Shakespeare*. London: Stockdale.

Baker, M. (1995) Corpora in translation studies. *Target*, 7(2), 223–43.

Beaugrande, R. de (1999) Reconnecting real language with real texts: text linguistics and corpus linguistics. *International Journal of Corpus Linguistics*, 4(2), 243–59.

Biber, D. (1988) *Variation across speech and writing*. Cambridge: Cambridge University Press.

Biber, D., Conrad, S., & Reppen, R. (1998) *Corpus linguistics*. Cambridge: Cambridge University Press.

Biber, D., Johansson, S., Leech, G., Conrad, S., & Finegan, E. (1999) *Longman grammar of spoken and written English*. London: Longman.

Bloomfield, L. (1933) *Language*. London: Allen & Unwin.

Burrows, J. F. (1987) *Computation into criticism*. Oxford: Clarendon.

Carter, R. & McCarthy, M. (1999) The English *get*-passive in spoken discourse. *English Language and Linguistics*, 3(1), 41–58.

Channell, J. (2000) Corpus-based analysis of evaluative lexis. In S. Hunston &

G. Thompson (eds.), *Evaluation in text* (pp. 38–55). Oxford: Oxford University Press.

Chomsky, N. (1965) *Aspects of the theory of syntax*. Cambridge, MA: MIT Press.

Chomsky, N. (2000) *New horizons in the study of language and mind*. Cambridge: Cambridge University Press.

Church, K. W. & Hanks, P. (1990) Word association norms, mutual information and lexicography. *Computational Linguistics*, 16(1), 22–9.

CIDE (1995) *Cambridge international dictionary of English*. Cambridge: Cambridge University Press.

Clear, J. (1993) From Firth principles: computational tools for the study of collocation. In M. Baker, G. Francis, & E. Tognini-Bonelli (eds.), *Text and technology* (pp. 271–92). Amsterdam: Benjamins.

COBUILD (1990) *Collins COBUILD English grammar*. London: HarperCollins.

COBUILD (1995a) *Collins COBUILD English dictionary*. London: HarperCollins.

COBUILD (1995b) *Collins COBUILD English collocations on CD-ROM*. London: HarperCollins.

Corder, P. (1973) *Introducing applied linguistics*. Harmondsworth: Penguin.

Coulthard, M. (1994) On the use of corpora in the analysis of forensic texts. *Forensic Linguistics*, 1, 27–44.

Cowie, A. P. (ed.) (1998) *Phraseology: theory, analysis and applications*. Oxford: Oxford University Press.

Coxhead, A. (2000) A new academic word list. *TESOL Quarterly*, 34(2), 213–38.

Cruden, A. (1737) *A complete concordance to the Holy Scriptures* (10th edn., 1833). London: Tegg.

Fillmore, C. J. (1992) Corpus linguistics or computer-aided armchair linguistics. In J. Svartvik (ed.), *Directions in corpus linguistics* (pp. 35–60). Berlin: Mouton.

Francis, G., Hunston, S., & Manning, E. (1996, 1998) *Grammar patterns* (2 vols: *Verbs* and *Nouns and adjectives*). London: HarperCollins.

Francis, W. N. (1992) Language corpora BC. In J. Svartvik (ed.), *Directions in corpus linguistics* (pp. 17–32). Berlin: Mouton.

Francis, W. N. & Kucera, H. (1982) *Frequency analysis of English usage: lexicon and grammar*. Boston: Houghton Mifflin.

Fries, C. C. (1952) *The structure of English*. New York: Harcourt, Brace & World.

Gerbig, A. (1997) *Lexical and grammatical variation in a corpus*. Frankfurt: Lang.

Granger, S. (ed.) (1998) *Learner English on computer*. London: Longman.

Hallan, N. (2001) Paths to prepositions? A corpus-based study of the acquisition of a lexico-grammatical category. In J. Bybee & P. Hopper (eds.), *Frequency and the emergence of linguistic structure* (pp. 91–120). Amsterdam: Benjamins.

Halliday, M. A. K. (1991) Corpus studies and probabilistic grammar. In K. Aijmer & B. Altenberg (eds.), *English corpus linguistics* (pp. 30–3). London: Longman.

Hockey, S. (2001) *Electronic texts in the humanities*. Oxford: Oxford University Press.

Hunston, S. (2002) *Corpora in applied linguistics*. Cambridge: Cambridge University Press.

Hunston, S. & Francis, G. (2000) *Pattern grammar: a corpus-driven approach to the lexical grammar of English*. Amsterdam: Benjamins.

Jespersen, O. (1909–49) *Modern English grammar*. Vols 1–4, Heidelberg: Winter. Vols 5–7, Copenhagen: Munksgaard.

Johansson, S. (1981) Word frequencies in different types of English texts. *ICAME News*, 5, 1–13.

Johansson, S. & Hofland, K. (1988–9) *Frequency analysis of English vocabulary and grammar* (2 vols). Oxford: Oxford University Press.

Kaeding, F. W. (1898) *Häufigkeitswörterbuch der deutschen Sprache.* Berlin: Steglitz.

Kennedy, G. (1998) *An introduction to corpus linguistics.* London: Longman.

Kenny, D. (2001) *Lexis and creativity in translation: a corpus-based study.* Manchester: St Jerome.

Kilgarriff, A. (1997) Putting frequencies in the dictionary. *International Journal of Lexicography*, 10(2), 135–55.

Leech, G., Rayson, P., & Wilson, A. (2001) *Word frequencies in written and spoken English.* London: Longman.

Lenk, U. (2000) Stabilized expressions in spoken discourse. In C. Mair & M. Hunt (eds.), *Corpus linguistics and linguistic theory* (pp. 187–200). Amsterdam: Rodopi.

LDOCE (1995) *Longman dictionary of contemporary English.* London: Longman.

Lewis, M. (1998) *Implementing the lexical approach.* Hove: Language Teaching Publishers.

Louw, B. (1993) Irony in the text or insincerity in the writer? The diagnostic potential of semantic prosodies. In M. Baker, G. Francis & E. Tognini-Bonelli (eds.), *Text and technology* (pp. 157–76). Amsterdam: Benjamins.

McDermott, A. (ed.) (1996) *Samuel Johnson's Dictionary of the English Language* (1st edn. 1755, 4th edn. 1773). Cambridge: Cambridge University Press in association with University of Birmingham. (CD-ROM)

OALD (1995) *Oxford advanced learner's dictionary.* Oxford: Oxford University Press.

Piper, A. (2000) Lifelong learning, human capital and the soundbite. *Text*, 20(1), 109–46.

Quirk, R., Greenbaum, S., Leech, G., & Svartvik, J. (1972) *A grammar of contemporary English.* London: Longman.

Quirk, R., Greenbaum, S., Leech, G., & Svartvik, J. (1985) *A comprehensive grammar of the English language.* London: Longman.

Sampson, G. (1995) *English for the computer.* Oxford: Clarendon.

Sinclair, J. (1991) *Corpus concordance collocation.* Oxford: Oxford University Press.

Sinclair, J. (1998) The lexical item. In E. Weigand (ed.), *Contrastive lexical semantics* (pp. 1–24). Amsterdam: Benjamins.

Sinclair, J., Mason, O., Ball, J., & Barnbrook, G. (1998) Language independent statistical software for corpus exploration. *Computers and the Humanities*, 31, 229–55.

Stubbs, M. (1996) *Text and corpus analysis.* Oxford: Blackwell.

Teubert, W. (1999) Korpuslinguistik und Lexikographie. *Deutsche Sprache*, 4/1999, 292–313.

Thorndike, E. L. & Lorge, I. (1944) *A teacher's word book of 30,000 words.* New York: Teachers' College, Columbia University.

West, M. (1953) *A general service list of English words.* London: Longman.

Willis, D. (1990) *The lexical syllabus.* London: Collins.

Wilson, E. O. (1998) *Consilience: the unity of knowledge.* London: Little, Brown & Co.

Winchester, S. (1998) *The surgeon of Crowthorne: a tale of murder, madness and the Oxford English Dictionary.* London: Viking.

Wray, A. (2002) *Formulaic language and the lexicon.* Stanford, CA: Cambridge University Press.

Zipf, G. K. (1945) The meaning-frequency relationship of words. *Journal of General Psychology*, 33, 251–6.

FURTHER READING

Altenberg, B. (1998) *ICAME bibliography 3* (1990–8). http://khnt.hit.uib.no/icame/manuals/icamebib3.htm.

Barlow, M. (1996) Corpora for theory and practice. *International Journal of Corpus Linguistics*, 1(1), 1–37.

Barnbrook, G. (1996) *Language and computers: a practical introduction to the computer analysis of language.* Edinburgh: Edinburgh University Press.

Beaugrande, R. de (2000) Text linguistics at the millenium: corpus data and missing links. *Text*, 20(2), 153–95.

Biber, D., Conrad, S., & Reppen, R. (1994) Corpus-based approaches to issues in applied linguistics. *Applied Linguistics*, 15(2), 169–89.

BNC (British National Corpus): http://info.ox.ac.uk/bnc/.

COBUILD (Collins Birmingham University International Language Database): http://titania.cobuild.collins.co.uk/index.html.

Computers and the Humanities (1960s–)

Corpus linguistics web-site (Michael Barlow): http://www.ruf.rice.edu/~barlow/corpus.html.

Corpus linguistics web-site (David Lee): http://devoted.to/corpora.

Cowie, A. P. (1999) Phraseology and corpora: some implications for dictionary-making. *International Journal of Lexicography*, 12(4), 307–323.

Cowie, A. P., Howarth, P. A., Moon, R., et al. (1998) *Phraseology: a select bibliography.* http://www.ims.uni-stuttgart.de/euralex/bibweb.html.

Data-driven learning page (Tim Johns): http://web.bham.ac.uk/Johnstf/timconc.htm.

Fillmore, C. J. & Atkins, B. T. S. (1994) Starting where the dictionaries stop: the challenge of corpus lexicography. In B. T. S. Atkins & A. Zampoli (eds.), *Computational approaches to the lexicon* (pp. 349–93). Oxford: Clarendon.

ICAME (International Computer Archive of Modern and Medieval English): http://www.hd.uib.no/icame.html.

ICAME Journal (1976– previously *ICAME News*).

ICE (International Corpus of English): http://www.ucl.ac.uk/english-usage/ice/index.htm.

International Journal of Corpus Lingustics (1996–)

LDC (Linguistic Data Consortium): http://www.ldc.upenn.edu/.

Literary and Linguistic Computing (1986–, in its present form)

Oxford Text Archive: http://ota/ahds/ac.uk/.

Partington, A. (1998) *Patterns and meanings: using corpora for English language research and teaching.* Amsterdam: Benjamins.

Pawley, A. (2001) Phraseology, linguistics and the dictionary. *International Journal of Lexicography*, 14(2), 122–34.

Stubbs, M. (2001) *Words and phrases: corpus studies of lexical semantics.* Oxford: Blackwell.

APPENDIX: ILLUSTRATIVE CONCORDANCE DATA

These are a very few attested, but purely illustrative, concordance lines. They are not a random or representative sample of the corpora from which they are drawn. Readers could however study larger samples of the node words from other corpora and check whether they find comparable examples, and could also check whether other word-forms of the lemmas (e.g., *endures, endured*) show the same patterns. These examples are taken from the publicly accessible versions of CobuildDirect and the BNC. The concordance lines are ordered alphabetically to the right of the node word.

Word-forms *endure, persevere, persist, and undergo.*

```
01     st that smokers will have to endure 12-hour flights by becoming mo
02   d can remember having had to endure a certain amount of misery bef
03     ng that Romania still had to endure a period of austerity. Rome
04     ht find himself compelled to endure a spartan existence; unlike a
05      so that the rider has had to endure a steady worsening of the trav
06     erced family audience has to endure an hour of his old cine films,
07        the 1,700 prisoners have to endure constant noise from the Garmen
08     dertake forced labour and to endure dehumanizing captivity in the
09      t workers in El Paso, Texas, endure difficult conditions, and comp
10      e felt he had been forced to endure during the last three years. I
11     he birth. These episodes may endure for a few days or may linger f
12     nd the animals often have to endure hours trapped in the midst of
13     do nothing about, other than endure it or enjoy it, but it is alwa
14     lame. At last, when he could endure no more, he jerked his hands a
15      in a dark and cold place, to endure patiently sorrow and weakness
16     ans, for they were forced to endure the indignity of having anothe
17        over, one finds it easier to endure those tedious weekly audiences
18     aving to accept and bear and endure, and because I am quite clever
19      s will be painful for her to endure, and for you to witness, but u
20     ment. But they persevere and endure, rather than come out

21   ying at the moment. But they persevere and endure, rather than com
22      to quit, half determined to persevere he was caught for some mome
23     mething about the ability to persevere in adversity. Koppel: Well,
24   t they produce. And we shall persevere in our efforts to find the
25     them to concentrate on, and persevere in solving problems and pur
26     atient's family as a need to persevere in the face of inevitable l
27      ing and difficult but if you persevere in the most important area
28   raiseworthy, and urge you to persevere in this work of salvation.
29     ting Colonel North failed to persevere through adversity or anythi
30   determined to remain and to persevere until she reaches a working
31        is often quite difficult to persevere with tape-recording during
32   t completely. Be patient and persevere with the inoculation – it m
33     game to get into, but if you persevere you won't be disappointed.
34     ts were fully determined 'to persevere' with the three-strand form
35     stage, but Brian decided to persevere, moving the boat to EDJ Boa
36      earliest efforts, but should persevere, using a single rock sample
37        the ability to do it. If we persevere, we will get there. I accep
38   destroyed his willingness to persevere, yet since Izzy's reawakeni
39   who insisted that she should persevere. One was a bright editor at
40      do this and it works if you persevere. You need to work at it – i
```

41   nsiderable misunderstandings persist about the nature of the handi
42   hat tremendous uncertainties persist about the relative importance
43   appropriate if the movements persist and are causing the child an
44   operation, and that this can persist for five years or more. For
45   ally cold temperatures might persist for over a year. Any survivor
46   n that residual activity may persist for up to six weeks following
47   is it that many commentators persist in calling the Presocratics s
48   portunity, should the regime persist in its ill-advised campaign a
49   the region, parents will not persist in the face of the child's re
50   r-pistol if the dog tries to persist in this antisocial behaviour.
51   ingle wet straws. Why do you persist in this perversity? Why do yo
52   d, dead batteries and if you persist in trying to recharge an
53   the office governments will persist in trying to regulate what we
54   minor ailments. If symptoms persist or are severe please consult
55   like Julie Andrews. Rumours persist that her brother will join he
56   ny smooth passages but fears persist that modern lightweight racin
57   l three weeks ago. And fears persist that the PLO too may be drift
58   is not successful, he should persist until he has got what he want
59   mpassable forest, but if you persist you may find, depending on re
60   orth but the light rain will persist, especially over high ground.

61   lued women would have had to undergo a deep and important change o
62   he old people were likely to undergo a major psychological upheava
63   driving, had been induced to undergo a medical examination to see
64   work, each operative had to undergo a stringent medical examinati
65   racter of the shop seemed to undergo a transformation. The rush wa
66   ate. Mr Forbes was forced to undergo an emergency operation to rem
67   dly take kindly to having to undergo an identity check before bein
68   tually anyone at risk should undergo confidential testing on a tra
69   hospital and insisted that I undergo extensive tests. There was he
70   officers and men have had to undergo great privations. They landed
71   cope with two recessions and undergo immense change in that proces
72   Many of these creatures undergo intolerably cruel conditions
73   titute employees may have to undergo lie detector tests. Rapist w
74   fractured skull may have to undergo neuro-surgery if his conditio
75   g, if they were expecting to undergo surgery, or if they had a his
76   ho find themselves having to undergo the painful dislocation entai
77   ur means he will not have to undergo the punishing marathon of the
78   ronization, and initiative – undergo trial by fire. Holder also ha
79   but they would also need to undergo years of specialized training
80   ree RAF widows would have to undergo 'demeaning means tests' years

Word-forms *enduring, haunting, and persistent* followed immediately by a noun.

81   andist only testified to his enduring ability to draw a crowd. 53
82   becoming a smash hit. The enduring appeal of Unchained Melody to
83   easoned optimism and by their enduring courage press on when lesser
84   also fails to reflect the enduring fascination of sporting it is
85   is the SUN which provides an enduring image of how Mrs Thatcher has

86	daily lives Perhaps the most enduring legacy of Thatcherism is that
87	ries, for the prestige or the enduring legacy of having their name o
88	goofing around, it's about an enduring love of guitars that borders
89	rary education with a work of enduring merit from Everyman's Library
90	intended to study music, an enduring passion of his which is refle
91	Hampshire's winsome charm and enduring popularity have elicited pity
92	the all-time bestsellers. Its enduring popularity is beyond doubt, a
93	of the credit for 'Messiah's" enduring popularity belongs to the
94	rticular, Raeder developed an enduring reverence for the Baumeister
95	overworked person. Given the enduring sense of identity within
96	al" forms of masculinity, the enduring significance of the power of
97	of 1945 was led by men of enduring stature. Do you believe that
98	ars, this tree will become an enduring symbol of your commitment to
99	OUS Kelly Brown displayed her enduring talent when winning the Silk
100	in the 5th century AD – is an enduring tribute to one man's vision.
101	was driving his car. The haunting beauty of the young woman sta
102	Days. Her voice retained its haunting edge, and when she reached fo
103	cold in his body. There was a haunting feeling of familiarity in the
104	e fought, in Matthew Arnold's haunting image, on a darkling plain sw
105	Aztecs. Everything else – the haunting keyboard and nagging soprano
106	ed in black lace, and wails a haunting lament similar to Ofro Haza,
107	useums. We'll see the craggy, haunting land that the Berbers, an
108	es are part of an ancient and haunting landscape, and it is the livi
109	etry of his music has its own haunting lilt, vocabulary and rhythm.
110	ches, and listen to fado, the haunting music so expressive of the
111	d have-not society. This is a haunting novel that should give John M
112	; 14.99) quickly turns into a haunting parable of our times. There i
113	d it contains a sensitive and haunting performance from Rade Serbedz
114	all restrictions. Wistful and haunting piano music by Erik Satie;
115	and Demi Moore danced to the haunting record in the film Ghost – th
116	t imperious, with a dazzling, haunting smile; but the performance is
117	ntingly sung her own, quietly haunting song. Ex-S A Far Cry from
118	t surely have appreciated the haunting sound of the pipes after 280
119	Prevert, Francois Dupeyron's haunting tale of a husband, his wife a
120	ter still, in Luke's fragile, haunting voice, his effortless melodic
121	theft, damage to machinery or persistent absenteeism, and the employ
122	for just 27 runs. Apart from persistent abuse directed at home capt
123	from any body opening, any persistent change in a wart or mole –
124	of Iraqi government. Iraq's persistent claim is that the allies' a
125	diness when confronted with a persistent condition such as traumatic
126	n Wilson of our Science Unit. Persistent fatigue is the fourth most
127	e distressed by her husband's persistent friendship with Diana, whic
128	elay of at least five days. A persistent front of high pressure over
129	ll; If you have suffered from persistent indigestion or chest pains,
130	by the unpopular poll tax and persistent inflation. At the Rome summ
131	freelance scholars. Yet the persistent popularity of the subject i
132	However, if memory loss is a persistent problem, there are exercise

133   mic sound of the train sets a persistent pulse that throws the
134   good, but no more. Under more persistent questioning he admitted tha
135   eam against the ebb tide. The persistent rain had made the river ang
136   had his prayers answered with persistent rain over the last 48 hours
137   economic reinvestment and the persistent recession, while Perot can
138   courts", and about its persistent rejection of international
139   with relish. Yet there is a persistent risk in using these snails.
140   [caption] Slow growth and persistent unemployment are global pro

5 Discourse Analysis

HUGH TRAPPES-LOMAX

5.1 Who Does Discourse Analysis, and Why?

Discourse analysts do what people in their everyday experience of language do instinctively and largely unconsciously: notice patternings of language in use and the circumstances (participants, situations, purposes, outcomes) with which these are typically associated. The discourse analyst's particular contribution to this otherwise mundane activity is to do the noticing consciously, deliberately, systematically, and, as far as possible, objectively, and to produce accounts (descriptions, interpretations, explanations) of what their investigations have revealed.

Since the study of language *in use*, as a goal of education, a means of education, and an instrument of social control and social change, is the principal concern of applied linguistics, indeed its *raison d'être*, it is easy to see why discourse analysis has such a vital part to play in the work that applied linguistics does, and why so much of the work that has been done over the last few decades on developing the theory and practice of discourse analysis been done by applied linguists (Widdowson, Candlin, Swales, for example) or by linguists (notably Halliday and his followers) for whom the integration of theory and practice is a defining feature of the kind of linguistics that they do.

Much of the work, but not by any means all. A great deal of discourse analysis is done by linguists who would not call themselves applied and much by scholars in other disciplines – sociology, psychology, psychotherapy, for example – who would not call themselves linguists. Discourse analysis is part of applied linguistics but does not belong exclusively to it; it is a *multi*-disciplinary field, and hugely diverse in the range of its interests.

For many the interest in discourse is *beyond* language in use (Jaworski & Coupland, 1999, p. 3) to "language use relative to social, political and cultural formations . . . , language reflecting social order but also language shaping social order, and shaping individuals' interaction with society."

That this is no overstatement may quickly be demonstrated by indicating something of the range of discourse-related books published in recent years: discourse and politics (Schäffner & Kelly-Holmes, 1996; Howarth et al., 2000); ideologies (Schäffner, 1997), and national identity (Wodak et al., 1999); environmental discourse (Hajer, 1997; Harre, Brockmeier, & Muhlhausler, 1999); discourse and gender (Walsh, 2001; Wodak, 1997; Romaine, 1998); discourse of disability (Corker & French, 1999) and the construction of old age (Green, 1993); applied discursive psychology (Willig, 1999); professional discourse (Gunnarson, Linell, & Nordberg, 1997) and professional communication across cultural boundaries (Scollon, Scollon, & Yuling, 2001); the discourse of inter-rogation and confession (Shuy, 1998); academic discourse (Swales, 1998); dis-course in cross-cultural communication (Hatim, 2000) and translation (Schäffner, 2002); discourse in everyday life (Locke, 1998; Cameron, 2000; Delin, 2000) and, at some remove from the everyday, divine discourse (Wolterstorff, 1995).

Jaworski and Coupland (1999, pp. 3–6) explain why so many areas of academic study have become so gripped by enthusiasm for discourse analysis in terms, firstly, of a shift in epistemology, "a falling off of intellectual security in what we know and what it means to know . . . The question of *how* we build knowledge has come to the fore, and this is where issues to do with language and linguistic representation come into focus." They point, secondly, to a broadening of perspective in linguistics, with a growth of linguistic interest in analysis of conversation, stories, and written text, in "the subtleties of implied meaning" and in the interaction of spoken language with non-linguistic communication. And, thirdly, they note how, in the changed polit-ical, social and technological environment in which we now live – the postmodern world of service industry, advertising, and communications media – discourse "ceases to be 'merely' a function of work; it becomes work [and the] analysis of discourse becomes correspondingly more important."

5.2 Defining Discourse

Discourse analysis may, broadly speaking, be defined as the study of language viewed communicatively and/or of communication viewed linguistically. Any more detailed spelling out of such a definition typically involves reference to concepts of language *in use*, language *above or beyond the sentence*, language as meaning *in interaction*, and language in *situational and cultural context*. Depending on their particular convictions and affiliations – functionalism, structuralism, social interactionism, etc. – linguists will tend to emphasize one, or some, rather than others in this list. (On the origins and implications of the language in use vs. language above the sentence distinction see for example Schiffrin, 1994, pp. 20–39; Pennycook, 1994a, p. 116; Widdowson, 1995, p. 160; Cameron, 2001, pp. 10–13.)

To illustrate this point, let us imagine four linguists preparing to work with the following small sample:

A: <u>You</u> THREW it so <u>you</u> GET it
B: MOI↓ra + I'll call my MUM

Linguist 1 sees a *text* – the verbal record of a speech event, something visible, palpable and portable, consisting of various bits of linguistic meaning (words, clauses, prosodic features, etc.). This linguist is mainly interested in the way the parts of the text relate to each other to constitute a unit of meaning.

Linguist 2 sees beyond the text to the *event* of which it is the verbal record. Linguist 2 is most likely the person who collected the data; and who made the following note describing some features of the situation in which the exchange took place:

[sunny Sunday afternoon, Edinburgh Botanic Garden, two girls, both aged 7 or 8, on a path; one of them has kicked the ball they are playing with into the bushes]

This linguist is mainly interested in the relationships between the various factors in the event: the participants, their cultural backgrounds, their relationship to each other, the setting, what is going on, the various linguistic choices made, etc.

Linguist 3 sees the text and the event but then beyond both to the *performance* being enacted, the *drama* being played out between the two girls: what has happened, who is responsible, how the girls evaluate these facts (relate them to some existing framework of beliefs and attitudes about how the world – their world – works), how they respond to them, what each is trying to achieve, their strategies for attempting to achieve these objectives, etc. This linguist is mainly interested in the dynamics of the process that makes the event happen.

Linguist 4 sees the text, the event, and the drama; but beyond these, and focally, the *framework of knowledge and power* which, if properly understood, will explain how it is possible for the two children, individually and jointly, to enact and interpret their drama in the way they do.

We may, not unreasonably, imagine that our four linguists are colleagues in the same university department. Each recognizes the validity of the perspective of each of the others, and the fact that, far from there being any necessary conflict or "incommensurability" between them (but cf. Pennycook, 1994a), the perspectives are complementary: all are needed for a full understanding of what discourse is and how it works.

As implied by the above, I do not think there is much to be gained from attempts to achieve a single definition of discourse that is both comprehensive and succinct. (For a list and discussion of such definitions, see for example Jaworski & Coupland 1999: 1–7.) Here instead is a set of definitions in the style of a dictionary entry for "discourse":

discourse

1   the linguistic, cognitive and social processes whereby meanings are expressed and intentions interpreted in human interaction (linguist 3);
2   the historically and culturally embedded sets of conventions which constitute and regulate such processes (linguist 4);
3   a particular event in which such processes are instantiated (linguist 2);
4   the product of such an event, especially in the form of visible text, whether originally spoken and subsequently transcribed or originally written (linguist 1).

5.3   Ways and Means

Each of our linguists will draw, in their own particular fashion and to different degrees, on the theories and techniques of a number of source disciplines for the study of language in use – especially linguistics, psychology, pragmatics, sociolinguistics, sociology, and anthropology. They will tend to favor one or more of a variety of approaches to conducting their research that have developed from these various sources. They are summarized in Table 5.1 and then briefly discussed under four main headings: rules and principles, contexts and cultures, functions and structures, and power and politics.

5.3.1   *Rules and principles of language in use*

Under this heading are grouped approaches which seek to understand the means by which language users – presumably universally, though this is always open to empirical contradiction – make sense, in the light of various contextual factors, of others' utterances and contrive to have their own understood more

Table 5.1   Ways and means of discourse analysis

Rules and principles	• pragmatics (including speech act theory and politeness theory) • conversation analysis
Contexts and cultures	• ethnography of communication • interactional sociolinguistics
Functions and structures	• systemic-functional linguistics (SFL) • Birmingham school discourse analysis • text-linguistics
Power and politics	• pragmatic and sociolinguistic approaches to power in language • critical discourse analysis

or less as they intend. Included here is work in pragmatics (Levinson, 1983; Mey, 1993; Thomas, 1995; Yule, 1996; Grundy, 2000) on:

- speech act theory (Austin, 1962; Searle, 1969);
- context; deixis and reference; shared knowledge (presuppositions) and frameworks of interpretation (schemata);
- cooperativeness in interaction: the "cooperative principle" and its "maxims" (Grice, 1975) and procedures for determining relevance (Sperber & Wilson, 1995);
- indirectness, indeterminacy and implicature and how these derive from particular ways of performing speech acts and manipulating the "maxims";
- politeness or tact (Leech, 1983; Brown & Levinson, 1987; Kasper, 1997). Politeness theory deals with the concept of face, with acts which are potentially damaging to face, and with the linguistic stratagems used for limiting such damage, when it is unavoidable. It is informed not only by linguistic pragmatics but also by social psychology and linguistic anthropology.

Work in conversation analysis (CA) (see Chapter 10, this volume), notably on rules of turn-taking and topic-management, and the sequencing rules governing relations between acts, is also included here. Note that the "rules" that CA is interested in are understood as members' (not analysts') rules: norms of behaviour, discoverable in the recurring patterns of the action itself, to which members orient in order to manage and make sense of what is going on. In this respect CA differs from pragmatics. It also differs in its insistent empirical concern with the minutiae of the textual data.

5.3.2   *Contexts and cultures of language in use*

Here are grouped approaches which focus on the sensitivity of ways of speaking (and writing) to situational and cultural differences. Ethnography of communication (Gumperz & Hymes, 1986; Duranti, 1997, Saville-Troike, 2003):

- offers a framework for the study of speech events, seeking to describe the ways of speaking associated with particular speech communities and to understand the role of language in the making of societies and cultures;
- involves both insider-like ("emic") understanding of culturally specific ways of communicating (both verbal and non-verbal) and of the various beliefs and attitudes which connect with these ways; and outsider object-ivity, encapsulated in Hymes' well-known "SPEAKING" acronym – an "etic" framework of speech event components: setting and scene, particip-ants, ends (purposes, outcomes), act sequences, key (attitudinal aspects), instrumentalities (norms and styles of speech), norms of interaction and interpretation, and genre (the discourse type).

The knowledge that members of communities have of ways of speaking includes knowing when, where and how to speak, what to speak about, with whom, and so forth. The idea that we need, in addition to a theory of grammatical competence, a theory of *communicative* competence (Hymes, 1972) arises from this fact. Speakers need knowledge not only of what is grammatically possible but also of what is appropriate and typically done.

Interactional sociolinguistics (Schiffrin, 1994; Gumperz, 2001) aims at "replicable analysis that accounts for our ability to interpret what participants intend to convey in everyday communicative practice" (Gumperz, 2001). It pays particular attention to culturally specific contextual presuppositions, to the signals – "contextualisation cues" such as code- and style-switching, and prosodic and lexical choices – which signal these, and to the potential for misunderstanding which exists in culturally complex situations. It shares with CA a keen attention to detail and a focus on members' procedures, but differs from it in its interest in processes of inferencing and in the consequences of contextual variation and cultural diversity (for example, Tannen, 1984a).

5.3.3   *Functions and structures of language in use*

Grouped here are text-friendly models of language and grammar-friendly approaches to text.

Systemic-functional linguistics (SFL) (Halliday, 1978; Halliday & Hasan, 1985; Martin, 1992)

- sees language not as an autonomous system but as part of the wider socio-cultural context, as "social semiotic"; the aim is "to look into language from the outside and specifically, to interpret linguistic processes from the standpoint of the social order" (Halliday, 1978, p. 3);
- sees grammar as meaning potential – a "potential" that is functionally determined by the need of speakers and writers to simultaneously represent experience (the ideational function), manage their relationship with their co-participants (the interpersonal function) and produce dialogue or monologue, whether spoken or written, which is cohesive and coherent (the textual function); the realization of these meta-functions can be discerned both at the micro-level of clause structure (e.g., systems of transitivity) and at the macro-level of context (register features of "field," "tenor," and "mode");
- provides a comprehensive theory of text analysis and genre (Martin, 2002).

Sharing much of the theoretical basis of SFL, Birmingham school discourse analysis originated in the analysis of classroom discourse (Sinclair & Coulthard, 1975). This revealed a hierarchical model of discourse structure (lesson, transaction, exchange, move, act), whose most widely exploited insight has been the regular sequence of moves within a teaching exchange: Initiating move (from the teacher), Responding move (from the pupil), Feedback move (from the teacher). This "IRF" pattern can be detected in other domains, including not only other unequal-power institutional domains such as doctor–patient consultations but also casual conversation (Stubbs, 1983; Tsui, 1994; Eggins & Slade, 1997, pp. 45–7). In the latter case, the third move (renamed follow-up) is likely to involve some kind of interpersonally motivated evaluation, for example a positive gloss on a respondent's declining the initiator's invitation.

Text-linguistics (de Beaugrande & Dressler, 1981; Levinson, 1983, p. 288 for the distinction between this and "speech act (or interactional)" approaches;) is not so much a single approach to discourse as a somewhat indeterminate set of interests or predispositions. These include:

- focus on *text*, generally defined as language "above," "beyond" or "longer than" the sentence, and especially on the structure of texts and on their formal (syntactic and lexical), or surface, features;
- achievement – and the role of various kinds of lexis in signalling these (Hoey, 1991); on cohesion generally (e.g., Halliday & Hasan, 1976); on rhetorical patterns of textual meaning such as general-particular and problem-solution (Hoey, 1983, 2001); and on text structure seen in terms of hierarchies of textual relationships (Mann & Thompson, 1987);
- a particular concern with the analysis of *written* texts (see, for example, Connor & Johns, 1990; Mann & Thompson, 1992).

5.3.4 *Power and politics of language in use*

"Critical" approaches to discourse analysis do not hold a monopoly on interest in the power and politics of discourse. Pragmatic and sociolinguistic approaches necessarily share this concern. For example, in Searle's speech act theory "having the authority to do so" is one of the felicity conditions for issuing an order; in Brown and Levinson's politeness theory, difference in power between speaker and hearer is one of the factors in choosing a strategy to manage a face-threatening act; and the mere fact that most forms of discourse analysis invoke, in one way or another, the relationship between language use and social structure ensures that issues of power must always be on the agenda.

What distinguishes critical discourse analysis (CDA) (Fairclough, 1989, 1995; van Dijk, 2001; Luke, 2002) in its approach to language and power is that it:

- aims to lay bare the "hidden effects of power," the kind of effects which may stigmatize the vulnerable, exclude the marginal, naturalize privilege and, through the simple contrivance of presenting ideology as common sense, define the terms of reference of political debate and subvert resistance;
- draws on critical, poststructuralist, feminist and postcolonial theory, on Foucault's anti-essentialist philosophy of knowledge/power and Bourdieu's theory of symbolic capital, among others, as well as on various of the ways and means of discourse analysis listed above, especially SFL;

- concerns itself with issues of identity, dominance and resistance, and with seeking out evidence in text – especially (to date) media and advertising texts, and political documents and speeches – of class, gender, ethnic and other kinds of bias;
- distinguishes crucially between two senses of the word discourse: what Gee calls "discourse" and "Discourse": the former refers to instances of language in use, actual speech events; the latter to (far more abstract) ways of using language: configurations of things that can (in particular cultural and institutional contexts) be spoken about, ways of thinking and speaking about them, and ways of behaving in relation to them.

CDA sees language as "everywhere and always" political (Gee, 1999, p. 1). By politics Gee means "anything and anyplace where human social interactions and relationships have implications for how 'social goods' are or ought to be distributed," and by social goods "anything that a group of people believes to be a source of power, status or worth." When we speak or write we "always take a particular *perspective* on what the 'world' is like. This involves us in taking perspectives on what is 'normal' and not; what is 'acceptable' and not; what is 'right' and not . . . But these are all, too, perspectives on how we believe, wish or act as if potential 'social goods' are, or ought to be distributed."

CDA is a political enterprise in the additional and crucial sense that it is motivated by a particular political agenda – non-conformist, anti-elitist, neo-Marxist, anti-neo-liberal; it seeks not just to understand the social world, but to transform it.

5.4 Some Issues of Approach, Focus, and Method

By approach I mean the adoption of one, or a combination, of the ways and means of discourse analysis outlined above. By focus I mean particular attention to certain aspects of the total discourse reality, either on grounds of theoretical preference or on grounds of perceived relevance to particular issues of practical problem solving. By method, I mean decisions relating to data collection and analysis, quality and quantity, subjectivity and generalizability, etc.

To some these issues are interdependent: a particular focus or approach will imply some particular choices and dilemmas relating to method. To some extent, however, they are separable: there are general issues of research method in discourse analysis which arise whatever the chosen focus or approach.

The latter connect largely to the fact, noted above, that discourse research is basically and predominantly qualitative: *basically*, in that the description of some newly or differently identified *kind* of language-in-use phenomenon, understood as far as possible from the participants' point of view, is usually the starting point, even if some counting up of types and tokens follows on from this; *predominantly*, in that very little quantitative research is actually done. (Lazaraton, 2002 looked at publications in applied linguistics journals over the last five years and found very few purely quantitative studies.) The main exceptions to this statement are the variationist studies of discourse, especially narrative, associated with Labov, a growing body of corpus-based discourse studies (see Conrad, 2002 for an overview), and some discourse-related work in second language acquisition.

Discourse research is mainly qualitative because it is inherently interpretive. It sets out "to make sense of or to interpret phenomena in terms of the meanings people bring to them" (Denzin & Lincoln, 2000, p. 3). There is no "raw: data – qua discourse – for the analyst to work with. There is, of course, the "text-as-record" (Brown & Yule, 1983, p. 6) but even this (in the case of spoken discourse) is subject to a certain amount of "cooking" in the process of transcription (see Ochs 1999 for a discussion of this issue) and part of what the analyst has to do is to re-imagine (i.e., interpret) the actual discourse of which the text-as-record is a very impoverished trace. Discourse analysis thus shares with other forms of interpretive research in the social sciences the many challenges of being qualitative while also being "disciplined."

Qualitative research methods (see for example Holliday, 2002), designed as they are to deal with the complexities of meaning in social context, are natural-istic (not controlled), observational (not experimental), and more focused on problems of validity than on those of reliability and generalizability. Data will be "real, rich, deep" rather than "hard and replicable" (Lazaraton, 2002; and see Pennington, 2002 on dilemmas for discourse analysts in determining what is or is not to be data). Questions about how to deal with subjectivity, how to relate to human subjects ethically, and how, in general, to be methodical and principled in the approach to data and its analysis, while not being blinkered by a priori theorizing, must always be at the forefront of researchers' concerns (Milroy, 1987; Cameron et al., 1992).

One way of dealing with subjectivity is through multiplicity of approach. This is usually referred to as triangulation and is especially characteristic of ethnographic approaches. Triangulation is generally understood to refer to the use of different types or sources of data (for example a participant's account in addition to the analyst's account) as a means of cross-checking the validity of findings, but may also refer to multiple investigators, multiple theories, or multiple methods (Denzin, 1978).

Another is through explicitness of criteria. An example is Sinclair and Coulthard's (1975) set of four criteria for any model of discourse: (1) there should be a finite descriptive apparatus, (2) there should be clear criteria for labeling data, (3) the whole of the data should be describable, and (4) there should be at least one impossible combination of symbols. The difficulty of defining and applying such criteria no doubt explains why, almost 30 years later, Lazaraton (2002) identifies solving the problem of evaluative criteria for qualitative discourse research as the key to ensuring that all published research is *quality* research.

A third way is mechanization. This involves the use of concordancing and other programs to analyze large corpora of textual data. "When correctly instructed, computers make it more difficult to overlook inconvenient instances, and are to that extent a move towards descriptive neutrality. We select what to look for but should then accept as evidence what the computer finds" (Stubbs, 1994, p. 218; Stubbs, 1996).

When all else fails vigorous debate may help to stimulate reflection and to clarify contentious issues. An example is the debate between Widdowson and Fairclough (Widdowson, 1995, 1996; Fairclough, 1996) on CDA (a set of proced-ures "not essentially different from literary criticism," in Widdowson's view), with particular reference to the meaning of "interpretation" in discourse analysis and the implications of ideological commitment. The nub of Widdowson's argu-ment is that "critical" means committed and implies a partial (both biased and selective) interpretation of text, while "analysis . . . seeks to reveal those factors which lead to a divergence of possible meanings, each conditionally valid . . . [and] recognizes its own partiality." CDA is thus a contradiction in terms. Fairclough argues, in reply, that Widdowson is confusing two meanings of inter-pretation: interpretation-1, "an inherent part of ordinary language use, which analysts, like anyone else, necessarily do, [i.e.] make meaning from/with spoken or written texts"; and interpretation-2 (which elsewhere Fairclough calls explana-tion), "a matter of analysts seeking to show connections between properties of texts and practices of interpretation-1 in a particular social space, and wider social and cultural properties of that particular social space." Interpretation-1 is part if the domain of interpretation-2. Fairclough also notes that the political positionings and priorities of CDA are not inevitable: "a CDA of the right is quite conceivable, directed for instance at left-wing or feminist texts."

Moving to issues of "focus," Figure 5.1 summarizes five factors, displaying these in a particular configuration with "interaction" at the center and the four others aligned so as to suggest two principal dimensions in the description of language in use: one (Instrumentalities–Text) oriented more to the linguistic aspects of discourse, the other (Function–Context) more to the social. All the factors are, of course, interconnected. Placing interaction at the center, linked to each of the other factors by double arrows, is intended to represent the reality that, whatever aspect of discourse we may for practical or theoretical reasons focus our attention on, ultimately it must be understood in terms of interaction.

5.4.1 Interaction

It is with the concept of interaction that discourse (for the analyst) comes to life. Entrances are made, intentions are formed, topics are introduced, turns are taken, actions are performed, reactions are prompted and in turn reacted to; understandings are checked, contributions are acknowledged, breakdowns occur, repairs are contrived; exits are negotiated. *People* are at work, doing things with meanings (producing them, interpreting them, negotiating them),

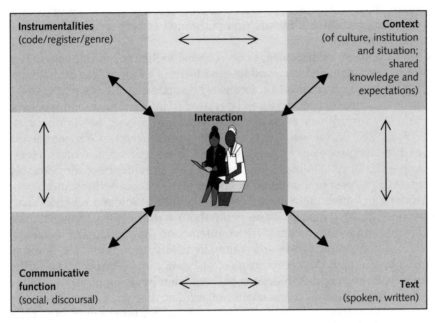

Figure 5.1　Discourse: five factors which focus discussion and analysis

co-creating an event whose trajectory may be clear to none of them until it is complete, and perhaps not even then.

This is discourse seen not as product (a text on a page) but as process, joint action in the making (Clark, 1996), and in consequence most difficult to capture and analyze without losing sight of its essence. The very smallest details – the falling-from-high pitch tone on which B says "Moira" for example – may be the most telling in revealing what is happening and with what intended, or unintended, effect.

The concept of discourse as interaction is present in all current ways and means of doing discourse analysis. In pragmatics, meaning is seen as "a dynamic process, involving the negotiation of meaning between speaker and hearer, the context of utterance (physical, social, and linguistic) and the meaning potential of an utterance" (Thomas, 1995, p. 22). The interactional workings of intention and effect are central to speech act theory; Grice's maxims "are essentially ground rules for the interactive management of intentions" (Widdowson, 1998, p. 13); and the mutual establishment and maintenance of rapport (the avoidance of threats to face) underpins theories of politeness and tact. Conversation analysis and interactional sociolinguistics provide somewhat contrasting approaches to the description of the accomplishment of interaction, the former more focused on the internal (to the text) mechanisms of turn-taking and sequencing, the latter highlighting the links between the micro-processes of the text, for example intonational and other "contextualization cues," and the macro-world of social structures and cultural presuppositions. IRF analysis provides a somewhat static post hoc view of the *accomplished* interaction as a hierarchical patterning of acts, moves, exchanges, and transactions.

The interactionality of discourse is not restricted to the spoken language. "Text is a form of exchange; and the fundamental form of a text is that of dialogue, of interaction between speakers . . . In the last resort, every kind of text in every language is meaningful because it can be related to interaction among speakers, and ultimately to ordinary everyday spontaneous conversation" (Halliday & Hasan, 1985, p. 11). It can be argued that written no less than spoken interaction involves dynamic processes of interaction between readers and writers. Hoey, for example (2001, p. 11) defines text as "the visible evidence of a reasonably self-contained purposeful interaction between one or more writers and one or more readers, in which the writer(s) control the interaction and most of (characteristically all) the language." The point about writer control, however, is a reminder that though monologic written interaction may be likened to spoken interaction as a dynamic process of pragmatic meaning creation (Widdowson, 1995), it is unlike it in the crucial respect of being non-reciprocal. The writer may anticipate the imagined reactions of the reader, but cannot respond to the actual ones. Much that is characteristic of written discourse is explained by this fact. As Widdowson (1979, p. 176) puts it, "the writer assume[s] the roles of both addresser and addressee [and] incorporate[s] the interaction within the process of encoding itself." For the reader, normal Gricean principles operate: "People do not consume texts unthinkingly but process them in normal pragmatic ways, inferring meanings . . ." (Widdowson, 2000, p. 22).

5.4.2   *Context*

The word *interaction* encodes two of our focal factors: *context* ("inter"), the participants, understood in terms of their roles and statuses as well as their uniqueness as individuals, *between whom* the discourse is enacted; and *function* ("action"), the socially recognized purposes to the fulfillment of which the interaction is directed; what Gee (1999, p. 13) calls the *whos* and *whats* of discourse.

> When you speak or write anything, you use the resources of English to project yourself as a certain kind of person, a different kind in different circumstances. If I have no idea who you are or what you are doing, then I cannot make sense of what you have said, written or done . . . What I mean by a "who" is a socially-situated identity, the "kind of person" one is seeking to be and enact here and now. What I mean by a "what" is a socially situated activity that the utterance helps to constitute.

Note that Gee talks of "projecting," "enacting," "seeking," "constituting," as if context is part of what people think and do and create rather than merely a fixed set of circumstances constraining what they may think and may do.

This idea that context is something psychological and dynamic, within the minds of the participants and part of the discourse *process*, is prevalent in most of the ways and means we have discussed. Hymes' model, for example, distinguishes between setting – the physical surroundings – and scene, the participants' understanding of the kind of thing that is going on, the "psychological setting." Context activates prediction-making; SFL offers an explanation of how this happens:

> You [construct] in your mind a model of the context of situation; and you do it in something like these terms. You assign to it a field ..., a tenor ... and a mode. You make predictions about the kinds of meaning that are likely to be fore-grounded in this kind of situation. So you come with your mind alert... (Halliday & Hasan, 1985, p. 28)

In a discussion of theories of context in relation to the needs of teachers and learners, Widdowson (1998, p. 15) criticizes relevance theory for "dissociating inference from interaction, and therefore from the on-line context which is interactionally constructed in the actual activity of interpretation"; i.e. it is not enough for a theory of contextual meaning to be a psychological theory, it must also be an interactional theory.

5.4.3 *Function*

Context and function (Gee's "socially situated activity") are closely inter-connected. Each is at least partly definable in terms of the other, so that we can recognize a context of situation by the kind of communicative functions that are typically realized in it (in church, praying; in the classroom, eliciting, replying, and evaluating) and we can recognize a function by the kind of contexts required for its performance (sentencing: the end of a trial, judge speaking, prisoner being addressed; marrying: wedding ceremony, bride or groom addressing officiating person). Utterance "helps to constitute" these activities – the variously defined "acts" of speech act theory, conversation analysis, ethnography of speaking, and IRF analysis – but they are definable independently of any particular form of expression. To explain to a person who doesn't speak English what an apology is I need only describe the kind of situation that produces an apology, the intention behind it, and its likely effects; I do not need to mention that an apology in English may be performed with expressions such as "I'm so sorry" and "I do apologize." Furthermore, it is only in context that speakers are able to recognize whether, for example, an utterance of "I'm so sorry" is to be taken as an expression of apology, regret, condolence, or sarcastic defiance.

As Hymes' model makes clear, speech events and speech situations are cultural constructs, and the norms of behavior and attitude associated with them belong within particular speech communities. The context of culture defines what is conventionally possible within a speech community, expressed by Halliday as "the institutional and ideological background that give value to the text and constrain its interpretation" (Halliday & Hasan, 1985, p. 49). Critical discourse analysis problematizes the notion of context of culture in terms of discourses and orders of discourse, the power that lies behind these, and the ideologies that they covertly encode. This raises issues of considerable interest and importance about how interaction – the participants interacting – relates to context-function. To what extent are the participants free agents? How far does the Discourse determine the discourse? This is one of the themes of the Widdowson–Fairclough debate referred to above (and see also Pennycook, 1994a). For Widdowson, individuals do not "simply act out social roles . . . Discourse is *individual engagement*. It is individual not social subjects who interact with each other. Of course I do not mean to suggest that they are free agents to do what they will. They are constrained by established conventions and regulations, and restrictions are set on their initiative. But they are not absolutely controlled by them: there is always room for maneuver" (Widdowson, 1996, p. 58; my emphasis). Fairclough's response to this is that Widdowson "assumes too liberal a view of the social as a voluntary association of free individuals." Discourse analysis on this account is

> reduced to pragmatics . . . It takes on the prediscoursal theory of the subject and of context which is general in pragmatics: subjects and contexts are not constituted in discourse, they are constituted before and outside discourse – subjects use contexts to interpret discourse. This cuts discourse analysis off from exploration of the socially and culturally constitutive effects of discourse, and more generally cuts discourse analysis off from treating language as part of the social whole.   (Fairclough, 1996, p. 54)

It is clear from this that it is not only language that is "always and everywhere political." Context is too.

5.4.4   Instrumentalities

By *instrumentalities* (the term is borrowed from Hymes' SPEAKING grid) I mean the resources of the language system (lexico-grammar and intonation), contextually determined or determining registers or styles, and genres.

Some discourse analysis pays, and has paid, relatively little attention to the language side of discourse – instrumentalities and their realization in text – concentrating instead on context-function. This has been criticized both from an applied-linguistics-for-language-teaching point of view (e.g., Widdowson, 1998) and also from a CDA point of view (Fairclough, 1999).

Discourse analysis needs a *functional* model of language, one that can show how the resources of the language system are organized to meet the needs of "whos and whats" (context-function) in actual communication. Two distinct versions of functionalism can be identified here, which we may call "function-external" and "function-internal."

The "function-external" version is essentially an appropriateness model, derived from Hymes' theory of communicative competence, which includes knowledge of what is appropriate use of language for a given context-function. For example, it is appropriate, in some English-speaking cultures, to say "I'm so sorry" – but not "I'm sorry" – when offering condolences (social function) to a friend; it is appropriate (in some kinds of conversational situation) to use the simple present tense when shifting to narrative mode (discourse function).

The "function-internal" version is the systemic model, whose premise, as described above, is that the lexico-grammar is organized, through the ideational, interpersonal, and textual metafunctions, to meet the intrinsic needs of language-mediated communication in whatever situation. In this model, the connection to the external is made through the categories of register and genre.

At some risk of over-generalizing, one might say that function-external description is more favored in discourse analysis applied to language teaching (work of the Sydney School is an exception to this); and function-internal description is more favored in critical discourse analysis, particularly the variety associated with Fairclough. (One of Widdowson's criticisms of CDA, in the debate already mentioned, is what he sees as its tendency to confuse the internal and external concepts of function, and assume that it is possible to "read off" discourse meanings – external – from textual encodings – internal.)

The distinction between register and genre is not always easy to grasp, but may be explained, if somewhat over-simply, as follows. Register is the means whereby contextual predictability (in terms of field, tenor, and mode) is reflected in the lexico-grammar. Genre is the set of purpose-determined conventions in accordance with which the discourse proceeds on a particular occasion. These include the staged patterning of the discourse, typical topics, and features of register. (Genre analysis thus subsumes register analysis.)

Most approaches to discourse explicitly or implicitly address the question of genre. Genre, as already noted, is one of the items in Hymes' SPEAKING grid for the analysis of speech events. In conversation analysis, as Eggins and Slade (1997, p. 30) note, though the focus has tended to be on micro-structural issues rather than on the larger macro-structures of conversation, there is some attention to "global text structure" – i.e., in effect, to genre. Birmingham school discourse analysis, though not normally referred to as genre analysis, in fact is so; Sinclair and Coulthard's (1975) original account of classroom discourse in terms of social purposes, macro-structure, lexico-grammatical choice, etc. is a notable example.

Eggins and Slade (1997) is a detailed study of the genre of, and the genres in (for example gossiping and storytelling) casual conversation, drawing on SFL as well as other approaches to discourse analysis. Their analysis of story-telling episodes draws on Labov's account (Labov, 1972) of narrative structure in terms of abstract, orientation, complicating action, evaluation, result or resolution, and coda. This must be by far the most frequently cited theory of a genre in the discourse literature. A close runner-up would be Hoey's situation-problem-solution-evaluation pattern (Hoey, 1983) which, though not devised as a model specifically of narrative structure and though normally applied to the analysis of written text, bears many resemblances to it. It provides, for example, a neat account of the sequence of events in the Moira incident:

act 1	*situation* (the one created by B as a result of throwing the ball)
(unstated)	*problem* (the ball is lost or difficult to get)
act 2	*solution* (B should get it)
act 3	*evaluation* (the solution is unacceptable to B)

Granted what we said in our first reference to the Moira incident, B's negative evaluation of A's solution defines this particular encounter as, generically, a quarrel (or at least the beginning of one). If we looked not only at this instance of quarreling but at a sufficient sample, we could begin to identify the generic features of children's quarrels in terms of their micro-functions (acts), stages, register features, etc., and to explain them in terms of some overall characterization of who engages in quarrels, in what circumstances, and for what reasons.

There are several current approaches to genre, notably SFL, English for Specific Purposes, new rhetoric, and critical (Hyon, 1996; Hyland, 2002).

Early SFL genre studies were Hasan's (Halliday & Hasan, 1985) and Ventola's (e.g., 1987) studies of service encounters. Later work (especially by Martin and his associates) has been on written genres (reports, narratives, explanations, etc.), especially with the aim of facilitating literacy education in schools (see Section 5.5.2).

The "ESP approach," especially associated with Swales (1990) and Bhatia (1993), is a pedagogically oriented approach to genre, with strong roots in the teaching of English for academic purposes, especially reading and writing. The two most prominent features of this kind of analysis are the description of genre in terms of functionally-defined stages, moves, and steps (in effect Birmingham-style analysis transmuted to the written mode), and the association of genres with particular "discourse communities," i.e., networks of expert users (for example applied linguists) for whom a genre or set of genres (research article, conference paper) constitutes their professionally recognized means of intercommunication.

The new rhetoric approach is less linguistic and text focused than either the SFL or ESP approaches; it is more ethnographic, looking at the ways in which texts are used and at the values, attitudes, and beliefs of the communities of text users (Hyon, 1996, p. 695).

Within the critical discourse framework, Fairclough defines genre as "a socially ratified way of using language in connection with a particular type of social activity (e.g., interview, narrative, exposition)" (1995, p. 14). The distinction he draws between discourse, style and genre is explained, in relation to political language, in his account of the discourse of New Labour (Fairclough, 2000, p. 14):

> Styles (e.g., Tony Blair's style) are to do with political identities and values; discourses (e.g., the discourse of the "Third Way") are to do with political representations; and genres are to do with how language figures as a means of government (so the Green Paper constitutes a particular genre, a particular way of using language in governing).

The critical view of genre is that such "ways," as part of the unequally distributed symbolic capital of society, are empowering to some, oppressive to others.

Oppressive, but not necessarily imprisoning. Genres are historical outcomes, and subject to change through contestation (the resistance of individuals). Widdowson's claim, quoted above, that subjects are not absolutely controlled by conventions, "there is always room for maneuver," represents a widely held view. Genre, like context, is "negotiated" in the process of interaction.

Where the focus of research is on instrumentalities, issues of "quantity" come to the fore. A register is a *variety* of language (like a dialect), a genre is a *type* of speech event. Neither can be described simply on the basis of single instances analyzed qualitatively. Sufficient samples of representative data are needed, and many different features of these samples, and associations between the features (for example between tense usage and stage of discourse), will be subjected to scrutiny. It follows that corpus data and methods are likely to prove particularly useful. In the article cited earlier, Stubbs (1994) outlines a research programme to include (amongst other points) *comparative analysis*, without which "we cannot know what is typical or atypical, or whether features of texts are significant, linguistically or ideologically, or not," and *long texts*, "since some patterns of repetition and variation are only realized across long texts (such as complete books)."

5.4.5 *Text*

Earlier in this chapter I characterized text as the "verbal record of a speech event," "the product of [a speech] event, especially in the form of visible text, whether originally spoken and subsequently transcribed or originally written," and a "unit of meaning." Text is both something produced by interactants in the process of making discourse and something consumed by linguists in the process of making analyses. These two somethings are by no means the same. The first is an inextricable part of a living here-and-now process of meaning-creation and intention-interpretation (i.e., undetachable from interaction), the second is an inert object laid out as if on a slab for dissection by the pathologist. Both are meaningful, but again not in the same way. In the first, meaning is the output of the activity of the participants (they create meaning in the process of text-making); in the second, meaning is the input to the process of analysis (analysts take meanings and work out how they got there). The situation is further complicated by the fact that the relation between participants' text and analysts' text is affected by the original medium of communication. In the case of spoken discourse the thing on the slab bears only a faint resemblance to the original event. In the case of written discourse the two may seem (but in fact for the reasons I have given are not) indistinguishable.

The essential idea is that discourse analysts deal with meanings. They are interested only in forms and they *are* or should be interested in forms as conveyors of meaning. (The attraction to discourse analysts of a systemic model of language is precisely that its approach to grammatical analysis is in terms of the *meaning* potential of forms for use in texts.) The constructs that discourse analysts work with in analyzing texts – function, texture, information structure, macro-structure, cohesion, coherence, text itself – are meaning constructs. This is non-controversial, but it does not get us very far. How can we know (and agree) precisely what the meanings are that we are dealing with? (Recall the debate between Widdowson and Fairclough on the analyst's role in interpretation.) To what extent (and in what respects) are these meanings "in" the text (so all the analyst has to do is to "read them out"), and how far are they "read in" by participants in the light of contextual factors?

In view of all these complexities, it is not surprising that the word *text* is a site – "critical" euphemism for battleground – of considerable theoretical importance. How you think about text will surely determine how you think about context, function, instrumentalities, and interaction. It will also have a profound impact on decisions about method.

It is, for example, partly (but significantly) issues to do with the nature of text – and how text is to be distinguished from discourse – that underlie the debate between Widdowson and Fairclough mentioned earlier. Widdowson's view is that a conceptualization of text as a formal object ("language bigger than the sentence"), disconnected from context and therefore from interpretation as discourse, disposes critical discourse analysts to overlook the possibility of multiple interpretations of text (different discourses which may be found). "There is usually the implication that the single interpretation offered is uniquely validated by the textual facts." (In a separate controversy, Widdowson takes corpus linguistics to task on similar grounds; Widdowson, 2000, 2001; Stubbs, 2001).

In his reply to Widdowson, Fairclough denies the charge, pointing to the way in which his own work "centers the dialectic of structure and action in an account of the subject in discourse" and emphasizes the way in which "shifting discursive practices, manifested in texts which are heterogeneous in forms and meanings, can be analyzed as facets of wider processes of social and cultural change" (Fairclough, 1996, p. 55). He counter-argues that Widdowson's position is "unduly restrictive" especially in failing to take account of intertextuality, "the key to linking the Foucaultian tradition to the tradition in linguistics." This notion – no text is an island – draws attention to the dependence of texts upon society and history and bridges the gap between texts and contexts (Fairclough, 1999). Actual texts mix genres and discourses, or more accurately actual people contrive to mix genres and discourses in the texts they produce. In this way the text is understood as a site of struggle for symbolic resources.

5.5   Discourse Analysis, Language in Education, and Education for Language

Discourse analysis figures prominently in areas of applied linguistics related to language and education. These include both language as a means of education and language as a goal of education, and both first language education and second language education. (By first language education I mean mainstream education, generally state provided, in situations where the medium of education is, typically, the L1 of most of the students. By second language education I mean both the teaching of second/foreign languages and the use of second/foreign languages as media of education. For many learners these two situations are, of course, co-occurrent.)

Figure 5.2 sets out, in accordance with these two dimensions, some of the main areas of discourse-related work in education. Each of these areas has been informed or influenced by discourse research drawing on pragmatics,

Language use	as goal	as means
in the context of second language education	• needs analysis, syllabus design and means of assessment • design of tasks and materials teaching grammar, lexis and intonation • teaching skills: spoken/written, receptive/productive • teaching for specific purposes: academic/professional • pedagogical description and teacher education	• role of classroom interaction and task-fostered interaction in language acquisition • interlanguage pragmatics • the second language as a medium of education: contrastive rhetoric • the second language as medium of education and as prospective medium of communication outside the classroom: issues of language, ideology and power
in the context of first language education	• skills for education and for life • literacy as social practice, critical language awareness (CLA) as a means of empowerment	• structure of classroom discourse • social class codes and educational genres • classroom discourse and textbooks as commodities

Figure 5.2   Discourse analysis and education

conversation analysis, ethnography, and the various other ways and means described earlier in the chapter, some of this research focusing more on the context-function aspects of discourse such as situation types and speech acts, some on instrumentalities such as register and genre, some on the structure and cohesiveness of text, and some on interactional aspects of discourse such as inferencing, predicting, turn-taking, and repair.

5.5.1   Discourse and second language education

Since the beginnings of communicative language teaching (CLT) and especially the teaching of English for specific (academic and professional) purposes, second language teaching and learning has come to be understood increasingly in terms of discourse, so that "today it is rare to find people involved in language teaching who are unaware of the significance of discourse for teaching reading, writing, intonation or spoken language, and for the evaluation of students' communicative competence" (Pennycook, 1994a).

Hymes' concept of communicative competence has been appropriated for language teaching purposes in a series of evolutionary reformulations (Canale & Swain, 1980; Canale, 1983; Bachman, 1990) so as to include grammatical, pragmatic, sociolinguistic, discourse, and strategic competences, *all* of which are in effect discourse competences, since they account for the ability of members of speech communities to put language to use. Defining the goals of language teaching in terms of communicative competence leads naturally to "an integrative view wherein the over-arching perspective of language as discourse will affect every part of the syllabus, including any conventional system components and functional/speech act components, however they are treated, whether as a series of layers of language, or as realizations within general specifications of discourse strategies" (McCarthy & Carter, 1994). Within such a perspective, learner needs, syllabus aims and content, and task goals and procedures will all be specified primarily in discourse terms. Materials (text or audio/video) are selected and presented to meet criteria of communicative authenticity. Tests are constructed to recreate as closely as possible the conditions under which language will be used in real communication in the defined target situation.

But in the context of the classroom it is not easy to be sure what is real, what is authentic. In part this is a text/discourse issue, in part an interaction/learning issue. As the former, it has been around since the earliest years of CLT in the form of the proposition that the most effective input material for learning is "authentic" – i.e., completely or substantially unmodified – instances of native speaker discourse. It has recently been given a new lease of life as a result of the impact (or at least the claims) of corpus-based language teaching publications: dictionaries, reference grammars and course materials (Hunston, 2002, pp. 192–7). The texts on which such learner inputs are based are of course "authentic" in one sense, namely that they are *attested*: they were all produced by real people in real contexts for real communicative purposes. But what we have here are only the "material products of what people do when they use language . . . only . . . the textual traces of the processes whereby meaning is achieved" and what is lost is "the complex interplay of linguistic and contextual factors whereby discourse is enacted" (Widdowson, 2000). Furthermore, what was real for the original participants cannot be similarly "real" for learners, for their context is a different context, that of learning a foreign language. It seems clear (Widdowson, 2002)

> that the language of normal user occurrence has to be pedagogically processed so as to make it appropriate for learning, which means that learners can appropriate it for learning. And this appropriation depends on two conditions: firstly, the language has to key into the learner's reality so that they can realize it as meaningful on their terms; secondly, it has to activate their learning – it has to be language they can learn from.

As to the other issue (interaction/learning) we note that in the language classroom acts of communication using the target language are not merely the hoped for *outcome* of learning but an essential *means* to successful language acquisition.

In their interactions with their peers and with their teachers, learners experience communication breakdowns which prompt negotiation of meaning, accomplished through clarification requests, confirmation checks, and requests for repetition. The resulting modifications are assumed to enhance comprehensibility of input and thence indirectly lead to acquisition itself (Tsui, 1998; Platt & Brookes, 2002).

From this it follows that opportunities for interaction, and involvement in relatively more beneficial types of interaction (if it can be determined what these are), are crucial to success. The attention of researchers thus turns to how questioning is conducted; how and by whom turn-taking is controlled; how tasks are designed in terms of the nature of the interactional demands they make on the learners and how learners "engage" with them (Platt & Brookes, 2002); and how feedback is given in response to learner output. All of these are discourse issues (as well as pedagogic ones), to the analysis of which a variety of approaches, including conversational analysis, ethnography, and genre analysis, can contribute.

Preparation for language teaching, whether in the form of teacher training courses or methodology textbooks, is most commonly organized around the main language areas (phonology, grammar, and lexis) and the four skills (speaking, listening, reading, and writing). A recent example is Hedge (2000). Textbooks on discourse for language teachers (e.g., McCarthy, 1991; Celce-Murcia & Olshtain, 2000) often follow this familiar pattern; Olshtain and Celce-Murcia (2001) and Trappes-Lomax (2002) provide recent overviews. In general this approach is probably effective in meeting the needs and expectations of practitioners, but potential disadvantages of these divisions may surface if

- grammar and lexis are presented as more separate than they really are, thus obscuring their inter-connectedness in lexico-grammar;
- the four skills are presented as more separate than they really are, thus obscuring the fact that they are often co-constitutive of actual speech events (illustrated in Figure 5.1 by the picture of the two nurses who are engaged in the skill-complex social practice of jointly reviewing a patient's notes);
- spoken and written media are conceptualized as discrete types rather than points on a continuum;
- there is a failure to attend to general features of interpretation, on the one hand, and production, on the other, thus obscuring what is common to listening and reading and what is common to speaking and writing;
- text-making features are divided arbitrarily between the spoken and written modes (for example it is sometimes implied that cohesion is mainly a property of written text), thus obscuring those text-making features that are common to discourse of all kinds.

A discourse-based pedagogical description of *phonology* will focus on prosodic aspects including rhythm (especially differences between L1 and L2), the use of tonic stress placement to signal information status (given, new, etc.), and the use of tone and key to signal functional (e.g., question, statement), attitudinal (e.g., concerned, unconcerned), and interactional (e.g., turn and topic management) meanings (Brazil, 1997; Clennell, 1997; Chun, 2002).

A discourse-based description of *grammar* – a "discourse grammar" (Hughes & McCarthy, 1998; McCarthy, 1998) – will treat grammar functionally. It will cover not only the possible realizations in grammar of particular speech act functions such as requesting and suggesting (and their mitigation for reasons of politeness and tact), but the way in which grammatical categories such as tense, aspect and modality pattern across texts, the role of grammar in creating textual cohesion (reference, substitution, conjunction, etc.) and information structure (through devices of thematization such as adverbial placement, the use of the passive and clefting).

One particularly important aspect of the development of discourse grammar in recent years has been work on grammatical descriptions of the spoken language in the light of work on spoken corpora (Carter & McCarthy, 1995; McCarthy, 1998).

A pedagogical discourse grammar may also attend to "critical" or "political" (in Gee's sense) aspects of lexico-grammatical choice. Through grammar we create, whenever we speak or write, "political" perspectives. An example of this is pronoun use. (B's most potent weapon in her rebuff to Moira in our example is the word "my" in "my mum.") As Pennycook has pointed out (1994b) "pronouns are always political in that they always imply relations of power." Another is the use of connectives. (Moira's "so" explicitly evokes the relevant aspect of "the way things are" in children's play.)

A discourse description of *lexis* (see for example Carter & McCarthy, 1988) will cover the ways in which lexis contributes to textual cohesion (through relationships of synonymy, hyponymy, collocation, etc.), textual structuring both spoken and written (through discourse markers), and genre (through lexical features of register). Attention to the role of lexical phrases or "chunks" in relation to functional and contextual features of discourse (Nattinger & de Carrico, 1992) has been hugely significant in recent years, contributing to the development of lexical approaches to language teaching.

In considering discourse aspects of *skills* teaching, "interaction" is central since it is here that we look for accounts of the different kinds of social and cognitive work required of participants depending on whether their role in the interaction is productive (speaking, writing) or receptive (listening, reading) or both alternately (oral interaction or on-line written "chat"), and depending on whether the medium of communication is speech or writing.

Effectiveness in receptive roles, in whatever mode of discourse, can be fostered by (amongst other things):

- activating appropriate knowledge structures (schemata), both formal (genre) and content (knowledge of the topic) through pre-listening/reading activities;
- foregrounding contextually relevant shared knowledge to help in predicting topic development and guessing speaker/writer intentions;
- devising tasks which promote appropriate use of top-down processing (from macro-context to clause, phrase, and lexical item) and bottom-up processing (from lexical item, phrase and clause to macro-context);
- focusing on meta-discoursal signaling devices.

Effectiveness in productive roles can be fostered by building into the cycle of task work attention to:

- salient features of context (setting, scene, the predicted state of knowledge and expectations of the reader/hearer);
- the means whereby a speaker or writer projects himself or herself as a certain kind of person, "a different kind in different circumstances" (Gee, 1999, p. 13);
- function (communicative goals); the "socially situated activity that the utterance helps to constitute" (Gee, 1999, p. 13);
- appropriate instrumentalities (features of register and genre);
- development of effective communication strategies appropriate to the mode of communication.

The teaching of *spoken language skills* draws on our gradually increasing understanding of the structuredness and predictability of some aspects of spoken interaction (openings, closings, adjacency pairs, pre-sequences and insertion sequences, turn-taking work), of differences between spoken genres (e.g., casual conversation, service encounters) and of conversational routines (e.g., for issuing, responding to, and following up responses to, requests, invitations, offers, compliments, apologies, etc.).

One source of potential problems for the learner is cross-cultural differences in ways of speaking. The "cross-culturally relative in communication" (Tannen, 1984b) includes "just about everything": when to talk, what to say, pacing and pausing, showing "listenership" through gaze, backchannelling, etc., intonation, use of formulaic expressions and indirectness. Another is the inherent difficulty of the listening role, which is the one in which learners are likely to feel they have least control: speed of delivery, ellipsis, and implicitness may all contribute to learners' problems.

In the context of the spoken language skills, the importance of strategic competence in the learner's negotiation of meaning is readily apparent: their strategies for coping with potential or actual breakdown need to be developed, and this can be facilitated, though not without difficulty (Hedge, 2000), through appropriate design and management of communication tasks.

In teaching *written language skills*, recognition of the interactional and socially situated nature of the task focuses attention on contextualization: in the case of the reading skill, contextualization of the reader, their purpose in reading a particular text, and what they bring to it in terms of background knowledge and expectations; in the case of the writing skill, contextualization of the writer, their purpose in writing, and the way in which they construct their reader in terms of social role (e.g., membership of a particular discourse community), reading purpose, background knowledge, and expectations.

Much of the work on reading and writing pedagogy has been in the context of English for academic and professional (especially business) purposes. Both reading and writing in a second language are complex skills, capable of causing great difficulties to learners: writing especially, because the output is a product (text) that, in addition to being satisfactory in terms of content, needs to meet reader expectations in terms of register and generic features (overall organization, metadiscourse features, use of cohesion, etc.), and also attain an adequate standard of linguistic accuracy.

The writer's (and reader's) principal support ("scaffolding" in Vygotskyan terms) is genre: this provides a conceptualization of writing purposes within the context of the professional goals and means of the discourse community, a framework of discourse organization (stages, moves, etc.) within which to construct or interpret a text, and guidance on the conventionally accepted and rhetorically effective exploitation of instrumentalities at the micro-level of text construction. The role of the researcher is to find ways of analyzing the real-world tasks that the student faces. These ways will typically involve a combination of genre analysis, corpus linguistic methods, and ethnography (through consulting the experts themselves). Research findings need then to be translated into classroom goals, materials, and procedures. A classic example of the latter, in the context of academic English, is Swales and Feak (1994). A recent example of the former, drawing together many of the threads of recent developments in discourse analysis, is Hyland (2000).

Hyland's book is firmly in the writing-as-social-interaction mould. He notes (p. xi) that "there are two main ways we can study social interaction in writing. We can examine the actions of individuals as they create particular texts, or we can examine the distribution of different features to see how they cluster in complementary distributions." He chooses the second of these and in consequence corpus-quantitative methods feature prominently. His theorizing of writing as social interaction draws on critical insights into the relation between text and social structure as well as Gricean pragmatics and Brown and Levinson's politeness theory; a genre is seen as not merely a text type but an institutional practice. He stresses the importance of interpersonal as well as ideational features of academic text (academic writing involves competition and argument as well as representation). He also, crucially in terms of pedagogic implications, stresses the balance between conventions and choice.

> The notion of reader-writer interaction provides a framework for studying texts in terms of how knowledge comes to be socially constructed by writers acting as members of social groups. It offers an explanation for the ways writers frame their understandings of the world and how they attempt to persuade others of these understandings. But while the norms and ideologies that underpin these interactions provide a framework for writing, they are, essentially, a repertoire of choices rather than a set of binding and immutable constraints. (pp. 18–19)

The English for Academic Purposes context is one of those, mentioned above, in which the L2 may be simultaneously a goal and means of education: students studying English and at the same time studying through English. The texts that they produce in the latter role are English texts not only in the sense that they are written in English but also in the sense that, in terms of rhetorical patterning, they are the *type* of texts that are expected of academic writing in an English-speaking (cultural) environment. Both teachers and students need to understand how the rhetorical features of English texts differ systematically from those of texts from the students' home culture, and reflect on what is to be done about this. There are both descriptive and knowledge/power issues here. The former have been addressed in a growing body of work in contrastive rhetoric (Connor, 1996). The latter are part of the wider body of issues currently addressed within the framework of critical applied linguistics (see Pennycook, this volume).

5.5.2 *Discourse and first language education*

It is, of course, not just second language learners for whom communicative competence is a goal of education. Education generally must acculturate children to new registers and genres, both spoken and written, developing their grammatical, sociolinguistic, discourse, and strategic competences along the way (Verhoeven, 1997). Children bring to their school experience of a variety of standard and non-standard dialects and communicative codes which tend to be valued differently within the commodified "exchange system" of classroom speech (Wortham, 1998). The school, in turn, brings to the children's learning experience an organized process of classroom talk which may promote personal involvement, co-ordinated interaction, and shared meaning (Cazden, 1988 cited in Verhoeven, 1997) or induce the transmission of standardized knowledge through a standardized structure (Wortham, 1998, p. 256). It is often claimed that the standardized structure that does most to induce standardized transmission is the IRF pattern referred to above, but a recent article by Nassaji and Wells (2000) suggests a more complex reality.

The work of Halliday, Martin, Hyon and others in the Sydney School (Johns, 2002; Macken-Horarik, 2002) addresses the issue of genre competence directly, drawing on SFL theory to produce text-based descriptions of school and institutional genres and registers. "Using these insights, practitioners have developed pedagogical frameworks in which genres and registers are related to the goals, values and 'staged' processes of a culture . . . As students become comfortable with particular text types, they are given an increasing amount of independence and encouraged to negotiate text structure and content" (Johns, 2002, p. 5).

Discussing the shift that he detects in applied linguistics (in Britain) toward a more ideological stance and a concern with social issues, Rampton (1995) links this with Street's distinction between "autonomous" (neutral technology) and "ideological" (social practice) models of literacy and with an interest among its practitioners less in English language teaching overseas and more in language education in the UK. It is in this context that critical discourse analysis as a form of applied linguistics (linguistics applied to the remedying of imbalances of power and various forms of social injustice) can perhaps best be understood. Since ideologies – in this view – permeate society by disguising themselves as common sense, the way to resist them is to unmask them. Critical language awareness raising (Fairclough, 1989, p. 236) is proposed as the means to this end, and the key site for developing it is the school. The "critical" is critical. Non-critical awareness raising is criticized for delivering a knowledge only of pragmatic appropriateness, thus further naturalizing existing power relations. Learners have to decide (Clark & Ivanič, 1998, p. 217)

> whether to accommodate to all or some of the dominant practices (including the discoursal and generic conventions) which they encounter or to challenge these by adopting alternative practices. By turning awareness into action – by choosing to adopt alternative practices in the face of pressure to confirm to norms – people can contribute to their own emancipation and that of others by opening up new possibilities for linguistic behavior. These new possibilities can contribute to change not only in the classroom but also in the wider institution of education and within societies as whole.

5.6   Conclusion

My objective in this chapter has been to give some indication of the multidisciplinary range of discourse analysis, to identify and describe some of its gradually emerging landmarks (the "ways and means," the "focusing" factors), to illustrate the range of educational issues that discourse work informs, and to point to some current movements and controversies.

Whether or not discourse analysis can yet be described as a discipline, it must certainly be recognized as a force. It has shown, and increasingly shows, that it is *necessary* – to our understanding of language, of society and of ourselves as human beings; it is *useful* – in an ever-expanding range of practical and socially beneficial activities, from the management of smoking-prevention campaigns to the evaluation of witness statements, from the design of classroom tasks to the unmasking and tackling of social injustices; and, as a mirror to our ever-fascinating selves, it is, as many students who come to it for the first time find, endlessly interesting.

See also 4 LANGUAGE CORPORA, 10 CONVERSATION ANALYSIS, 13 STYLISTICS, 23 LITERACY STUDIES, 26 LANGUAGE TEACHER EDUCATION, 27 THE PRACTICE OF LSP, 32 CRITICAL APPLIED LINGUISTICS.

REFERENCES

Austin, J. (1962) *How to do things with words*. Oxford: Clarendon Press.

Bachman, L. F. (1990) *Fundamental considerations in language testing*. Oxford: Oxford University Press.

de Beaugrande, R. & Dressler, W. (1981) *An introduction to text linguistics*. London: Longman.

Bhatia, V. K. (1993) *Analyzing genre*. London: Longman.

Brazil, D. (1997) *The communicative value of intonation in English*. Cambridge: Cambridge University Press.

Brown, G. & Yule, G. (1983) *Discourse analysis*. Cambridge: Cambridge University Press.

Brown, P. & Levinson, S. (1987) *Politeness: some universals in language usage*. Cambridge: Cambridge University Press.

Cameron, D. (2000) *Good to talk*. London: Sage.

Cameron, D. (2001) *Working with spoken discourse*. London: Sage.

Cameron, D., Frazer, E., Harvey, P., Rampton, B., & Richardson, K. (1992) *Researching language: issues of power and method*. London: Routledge.

Canale, M. (1983) From communicative competence to communicative language pedagogy. In J. C. Richards & R. Schmidt (eds.), *Language and communication* (pp. 2–27). London: Longman.

Canale, M. & Swain, M. (1980) Theoretical bases of communicative approaches to second language teaching and testing. *Applied Linguistics*, 1(1), 1–47.

Carter, R. & McCarthy, M. (1988) *Vocabulary and language teaching*. London: Longman.

Carter, R. & McCarthy, M. (1995) Grammar and the spoken language. *Applied Linguistics*, 16(2), 141–58.

Celce-Murcia, M. & Olshtain, E. (2000) *Discourse and context in language teaching: a guide for language teachers*. Cambridge: Cambridge University Press.

Chun, D. M. (2002) *Discourse intonation in L2: from theory and research to practice*. Amsterdam: John Benjamins.

Clark, H. (1996) *Using language*. Cambridge: Cambridge University Press.

Clark, R. & Ivanič, R. (1998) Critical discourse analysis and educational change. In L. van Lier & D. Corson (eds.), *Encyclopedia of language and education*, vol. 6: *Knowledge about language*. Dordrecht: Kluwer Academic Publishers.

Clennell, C. (1997) Raising the pedagogic status of discourse intonation teaching. *English Language Teaching Journal*, 51(2), 117–25.

Connor, U. (1996) *Contrastive rhetoric: cross-cultural aspects of second language writing*. New York: Cambridge University Press.

Connor, U. & Johns, A. (eds.) (1990) *Coherence in writing: research and pedagogical perspectives*. Alexandria, VA: TESOL.

Conrad, S. (2002) Corpus linguistic approaches for discourse analysis. In M. McGroarty (ed.), *Discourse and dialogue. Annual review of applied linguistics 22* (pp. 75–95). Cambridge: Cambridge University Press.

Corker, M. & French, S. (eds.) (1999) *Disability discourse*. Buckingham, UK: Open University Press.

Delin, J. (2000) *The language of everyday life: an introduction*. London: Sage.

Denzin, N. K. (1978) *The research act: a theoretical introduction to sociological methods*. New York: McGraw Hill.

Denzin, N. K. & Lincoln, Y. S. (2000) *Handbook of qualitative research*. Thousand Oaks, CA: Sage.

Duranti, A. (1997) *Linguistic anthropology*. Cambridge: Cambridge University Press.

Eggins, S. & Slade, D. (1997) *Analyzing casual conversation*. London: Cassell.

Fairclough, N. (1989) *Language and power*. London: Longman.

Fairclough, N. (1995) *Critical discourse analysis*. London: Longman.

Fairclough, N. (1996) A reply to Henry Widdowson's "Discourse analysis: a critical view." *Language and Literature*, 5(1), 49–56.

Fairclough, N. (1999) Linguistic and intertextual analysis within discourse analysis. In A. Jaworski & N. Coupland (eds.), *The discourse reader* (pp. 183–211). London: Routledge.

Fairclough, N. (2000) *New Labour, new language?* London: Routledge.

Gee, J. (1999) *An introduction to discourse analysis*. London: Routledge.

Green, B. S. (1993) *Gerontology and the construction of old age: as study in discourse analysis*. New York: Aldine de Gruyter.

Grice, H. (1975) Logic and conversation. In P. Cole & J. Morgan (eds.), *Syntax and semantics 3: speech acts* (pp. 41–58). New York: Academic Press.

Grundy, P. (2000) *Doing pragmatics*. London: Edward Arnold.

Gumperz, J. (2001) Interactional sociolinguistics: a personal perspective. In D. Schiffrin, D. Tannen & H. E. Hamilton (eds.), *The handbook of discourse analysis* (pp. 215–28). Oxford: Blackwell.

Gumperz, J. & Hymes, D. (eds.) (1986) *Directions in sociolinguistics: the ethnography of speaking*. New York: Basil Blackwell.

Gunnarson, B., Linell, P., & Nordberg, B. (1997) *The construction of professional discourse*. London: Longman.

Hajer, M. A. (1997) *The politics of environmental discourse*. Oxford: Oxford University Press.

Halliday, M. A. K. (1978) *Language as social semiotic*. London: Arnold.

Halliday, M. A. K. & Hasan, R. (1976) *Cohesion in English*. London: Longman.

Halliday, M. A. K. & Hasan, R. (1985) *Language, context and text: aspects of language in a social-semiotic perspective*. Victoria, Australia: Deakin University Press.

Harre, R., Brockmeier, J., & Muhlhausler, P. (1999) *Greenspeak*. London: Sage.

Hatim, B. (2000) *Communication across cultures*. Exeter: University of Exeter Press.

Hedge, T. (2000) *Teaching and learning in the language classroom.* Oxford: Oxford University Press.

Hoey, M. (1983) *On the surface of discourse.* London: Allen and Unwin.

Hoey, M. (1991) *Patterns of lexis in text.* Oxford: Oxford University Press.

Hoey, M. (2001) *Textual interaction: an introduction to written discourse analysis.* London: Routledge.

Holliday, A. (2002) *Doing and writing qualitative research.* London: Sage.

Howarth, D., Norval, A. J., Stavrakakis, Y., & Laclau, E. (eds.) (2000) *Discourse theory and political analysis.* Manchester: Manchester University Press.

Hughes, R. & McCarthy, M. (1998) From sentence to discourse: discourse grammar and English language teaching. *TESOL Quarterly*, 32(2), 263–87.

Hunston, S. (2002) *Corpora in applied linguistics.* Cambridge: Cambridge University Press.

Hyland, K. (2000) *Disciplinary discourses: social interaction in academic writing.* London: Longman.

Hyland, K. (2002) Genre: language, context and literacy. In M. McGroarty (ed.), *Discourse and dialogue. Annual review of applied linguistics 22* (pp. 113–35). Cambridge: Cambridge University Press.

Hymes, D. (1972) On communicative competence. In J. B. Pride & J. Holmes (eds.), *Sociolinguistics* (pp. 269–93). Harmondsworth: Penguin.

Hyon, S. (1996) Genres in three traditions: implications for ESL. *TESOL Quarterly*, 30(4), 693–722.

Jaworski, A. & Coupland, N. (eds.) (1999) *The discourse reader.* London: Routledge.

Johns, A. M. (2002) *Genre in the classroom.* London: Lawrence Erlbaum Associates.

Kasper, G. (1997) Linguistic etiquette. In F. Coulmas (ed.), *The handbook of sociolinguistics* (pp. 374–85). Oxford: Blackwell.

Labov, W. (1972) The transformation of experience in narrative syntax. In W. Labov, *Language in the inner city: studies in the Black English vernacular* (pp. 354–96). Philadelphia: University of Pennsylvania Press.

Lazaraton, A. (2002) Quantitative and qualitative approaches to discourse analysis. In M. McGroarty (ed.), *Discourse and dialogue. Annual review of applied linguistics 22* (pp. 32–51). Cambridge: Cambridge University Press.

Leech, G. (1983) *Principles of pragmatics.* London: Longman.

Levinson, S. (1983) *Pragmatics.* Cambridge: Cambridge University Press.

Locke, J. L. (1998) *The de-voicing of society: why we don't talk to each other anymore.* New York: Simon & Schuster.

Luke, A. (2002) Beyond science and ideology critique: developments in critical discourse analysis. In M. McGroarty (ed.), *Discourse and dialogue. Annual review of applied linguistics 22* (pp. 96–110). Cambridge: Cambridge University Press.

Macken-Horarik, M. (2002) "Something to shot for": a systemic functional approach to teaching genre in secondary school science. In A. M. Johns (ed.), *Genre in the classroom* (pp. 17–42). London: Lawrence Erlbaum Associates.

Mann, W. C. & Thompson, S. A. (1987) *Rhetorical structure theory: a framework for the analysis of texts.* Marina del Rey: University of Southern California, Information Sciences Institute.

Mann, W. C. & Thompson, S. A. (eds.) (1992) *Discourse description: diverse linguistic analyses of a fund-raising text.* Amsterdam: John Benjamins.

Martin, J. R. (1992) *English text: system and structure.* Amsterdam: John Benjamins.

162   *Hugh Trappes-Lomax*

Martin, J. R. (2002) Meaning beyond the clause: SFL perspectives. In M. McGroarty (ed.), *Discourse and dialogue. Annual review of applied linguistics* 22 (pp. 54–74). Cambridge: Cambridge University Press.

McCarthy, M. (1991) *Discourse analysis for language teachers.* Cambridge: Cambridge University Press.

McCarthy, M. (1998) *Spoken language and applied linguistics.* Cambridge: Cambridge University Press.

McCarthy, M. & Carter, R. (1994) *Language as discourse: perspectives for language teaching.* London: Longman.

Mey, J. (1993) *Pragmatics: an introduction.* Oxford: Blackwell.

Milroy, L. (1987) *Observing and analyzing natural language.* Oxford: Blackwell.

Nassaji, H. & Wells, G. (2000) What's the use of "triadic dialogue"?: An investigation of teacher-student interaction. *Applied Linguistics,* 21(3), 376–406.

Nattinger, J. R. & de Carrico, J. S. (1992) *Lexical phrases and language teaching.* Oxford: Oxford University Press.

Ochs, E. (1999/1979) Transcription as theory. In A. Jaworski & N. Coupland (eds.), *The discourse reader* (pp. 167–82). London: Routledge.

Olshtain, E. & Celce-Murcia, M. (2001) Discourse analysis and language teaching. In D. Schiffrin, D. Tannen, & H. E. Hamilton (eds.), *The handbook of discourse analysis* (pp. 707–24). Oxford: Blackwell.

Pennington, M. (2002) Examining classroom discourse frames: an approach to raising language teachers' awareness of and planning for language use. In H. Trappes-Lomax & G. Ferguson (eds.), *Language in language teacher education* (pp. 149–72). Amsterdam: John Benjamins.

Pennycook, A. (1994a) Incommensurable discourses? *Applied Linguistics,* 15(2), 115–38.

Pennycook, A. (1994b) The politics of pronouns. *English Language Teaching Journal,* 48(2), 173–8.

Platt, E. & Brookes, F. (2002) Task engagement: a turning point in foreign language development. *Language Learning,* 52(2), 365–400.

Rampton, B. (1995) Politics and change in research in applied linguistics. *Applied Linguistics,* 16(2), 233–56.

Romaine, S. (1998) *Communicating gender.* London: Lawrence Erlbaum Associates.

Saville-Troike, M. (2003) *Ethnography of communication: an introduction* (3rd edn.). Oxford: Blackwell.

Schäffner, C. (ed.) (1997) *Analyzing political speeches.* Clevedon, UK: Multilingual Matters.

Schäffner, C. (ed.) (2002) *The role of discourse analysis for translation and translator training.* Clevedon, UK: Multilingual Matters.

Schäffner, C. & Kelly-Holmes, H. (eds.) (1996) *Discourse and ideologies.* Clevedon, UK: Multilingual Matters.

Schiffrin, D. (1994) *Approaches to discourse.* Oxford: Blackwell.

Scollon, R., Scollon, S. W., & Yuling, P. (2001) *Professional communication in international settings.* Oxford: Blackwell.

Searle, J. R. (1969) *Speech acts: an essay in the philosophy of language.* Cambridge: Cambridge University Press.

Shuy, R. W. (1998) *The language of confession, interrogation and deception.* London: Sage.

Sinclair, J. McH. & Coulthard, M. (1975) *Towards an analysis of discourse.* Oxford: Oxford University Press.

Sperber, D. & Wilson, D. (1995) *Relevance: communication and cognition* (2nd edn.). Oxford: Blackwell.

Stubbs, M. (1983) *Discourse analysis: the sociolinguistic analysis of natural language.* Oxford: Basil Blackwell

Stubbs, M. (1994) Grammar, text and ideology: computer-assisted methods in the linguistics of representation. *Applied Linguistics*, 15(2), 201–23.

Stubbs, M. (1996) *Text and corpus analysis*. Oxford: Blackwell.

Stubbs, M. (2001) Texts, corpora and problems of interpretation: a response to Widdowson. *Applied Linguistics*, 22(2), 149–72.

Swales, J. (1990) *Genre analysis: English in academic and research settings*. Cambridge: Cambridge University Press.

Swales, J. (1998) *Other floors, other voices: a textography of a small university building*. London: Lawrence Erlbaum Associates.

Swales, J. & Feak, C. B. (1994) *Academic writing for graduate students*. Ann Arbor: The University of Michigan Press.

Tannen, D. (1984a) *Conversational style: analyzing talk among friends*. Norwood, NJ: Ablex.

Tannen, D. (1984b) The pragmatics of cross-cultural communication. *Applied Linguistics*, 5(3), 189–95.

Thomas, J. (1995) *Meaning in interaction*. London: Longman.

Trappes-Lomax, H. (2002) Language in language teacher education: a discourse perspective. In H. Trappes-Lomax & G. Ferguson (eds.), *Language in language teacher education* (pp. 1–21). Amsterdam: John Benjamins.

Tsui, A. (1994) *English conversation*. Oxford: Oxford University press.

Tsui, A. (1998) Awareness raising about classroom interaction. In L. van Lier & D. Corson (eds.), *Encyclopedia of language and education*, vol. 6: *Knowledge about language*. Dordrecht: Kluwer Academic Publishers.

van Dijk, T. A. (2001) Critical discourse analysis. In D. Schiffrin, D. Tannen, & H. E. Hamilton (eds.), *The handbook of discourse analysis* (pp. 352–71). Oxford: Blackwell.

Ventola, E. (1987) *The structure of social interaction: a systemic approach to the semiotics of service encounters*. London: Francis Pinter.

Verhoeven, L. (1997) Sociolinguistics and education. In F. Coulmas (ed.), *The handbook of sociolinguistics*. Oxford: Basil Blackwell.

Walsh, C. (2001) *Gender and discourse*. London: Longman.

Widdowson, H. G. (1979) *Explorations in applied linguistics*. Oxford: Oxford University Press.

Widdowson, H. G. (1995) Discourse analysis: a critical view. *Language and Literature*, 4(3), 157–72.

Widdowson, H. G. (1996) Reply to Fairclough: discourse and interpretation: conjectures and refutations. *Language and Literature*, 5(1), 57–70.

Widdowson, H. G. (1998) The conditions of contextual meaning. In K. Malmkjær & J. Williams (eds.), *Context in language learning and language understanding* (pp. 1–23). Cambridge: Cambridge University Press.

Widdowson, H. G. (2000) On the limitations of linguistics applied. *Applied Linguistics*, 21(1), 3–25.

Widdowson, H. G. (2001) Interpretations and correlations: a reply to Stubbs. *Applied Linguistics*, 22(4), 531–8.

Widdowson, H. G. (2002) Language teaching: defining the subject. In H. Trappes-Lomax & G. Ferguson (eds.), *Language in language teacher education* (pp. 67–81). Amsterdam: John Benjamins.

Willig, C. (ed.) (1999) *Applied discourse analysis: social and psychological interventions*. Buckingham, UK: Open University Press.

Wodak, R. (ed.) (1997) *Gender and discourse*. London: Sage.

Wodak, R., de Cillia, R., Resigi, M., & Liebhart, K. (1999) *The discursive construction of national identity* (trans. A. Hirsch & R. Mitten). Edinburgh: Edinburgh University Press.

Wolterstorff, N. (1995) *Divine discourse.* Cambridge: Cambridge University Press.

Wortham, S. (1998) The commodification of classroom discourse in postmodern contexts. In L. van Lier & D. Corson (eds.), *Encyclopedia of language and education*, vol. 6: *Knowledge about language* (pp. xx–xx). Dordrecht: Kluwer Academic Publishers.

Yule, G. (1996) *Pragmatics.* Oxford: Oxford University Press.

FURTHER READING

Cutting, J. (2002) *Pragmatics and discourse.* London: Routledge.

6 British Sign Language

RACHEL SUTTON-SPENCE AND BENCIE WOLL

6.1 Introduction

The study of British Sign Language (BSL) can inform the field of applied linguistics by providing an insight into a native British minority language with a language community unlike any other. Close and culturally informed study of this often misunderstood language can provide insight into issues of language planning, with its related topics of acquisition, second language learning and testing, language teacher education, language attrition and maintenance, and lexicography. When studying the implications of minority status on any language it is useful to consider the reality facing users of a language whom the majority society frequently sees as disabled English users. The threats facing BSL have important implications for social, regional, and situational variation in a language where native speakers are greatly outnumbered by non-native speakers.

BSL is the language of Britain's deaf community. Within this simple statement are four essential ideas: it is a language, it is British, it is a visual language created by a community of people who cannot hear spoken language under normal conditions, and it is used by an identifiable social language community.

6.1.1 BSL is an independent language, distinct from English

Throughout history the status of BSL and other sign languages has been denied:

> Gesture languages have been observed among the lower-class Neapolitans, among Trappist monks ... among the Indians of our western plains ... and among groups of deaf-mutes ... It seems certain that these gesture languages are merely developments of ordinary gestures and that any and all complicated or

not immediately intelligible gestures are based on the conventions of ordinary speech. (Bloomfield, 1933, p. 39)

Despite extensive linguistic descriptions (e.g., Deuchar, 1984; Brennan, 1992; Sutton-Spence & Woll, 1999) that clearly demonstrate that BSL easily fulfils all linguistic and social requirements of a human language, its status is still misunderstood by many people. In a debate in the House of Lords in 1999 concerning the safeguards for sign language users being interviewed at police stations Lord Williams of Mostyn made the common error of equating BSL with a form of English made visible. "It is correct that the sign language to which the noble Lord [Lord Annaly] referred is a distinct language, but it is based on the English language" (Hansard, February 18, 1999).

6.1.2 BSL is the national sign language of Britain

Its independence from English is demonstrated by the mutual unintelligibility of BSL, American Sign Language, and Irish Sign Language, despite use of English in all three countries. Although many signs in all known sign languages are visually motivated, the sources of visual motivation are rarely transparent (Klima & Bellugi, 1979), are often culturally determined (Pizzuto & Volterra, 2000), and are often metaphorical (Boyes Braem, 1985; Woll, 1983). Cultural differences can be seen: the BSL sign DOOR might be expected to be international, as the hands appear to represent a door opening at its hinges. However, traditional Japanese doors do not have hinges, but slide, and Japanese Sign Language reflects this. Even when cultural elements are not relevant, languages can simply focus on different aspects of a referent. The American sign HORSE represents the ears of a horse, while the BSL sign represents riding. The BSL sign PENCIL is motivated by the action of writing with a pencil, but the Uganda Sign Language sign represents sharpening a pencil.

Not only is the language unintelligible to users of other national sign languages, it is also recognized as a single national language in its own right. The existence of a sign language presupposes a language community and a claim to the existence of a national sign language implies a national sign language community.

Although deaf people have clearly communicated through signs for centuries (Miles, 1988), the modern sign language used in Britain is linked to the development of large towns and cities and the establishment of schools for deaf children in the eighteenth and especially nineteenth centuries. Large numbers of deaf children brought together in deaf schools, where signed language was frequently a mode of instruction, promoted the development of sign language in Britain.

There was not, however, a single source of the language which spread across the country and no written means by which to standardize it, as happened to English. Consequently, regional dialects of BSL were highly distinct. There was no national policy for deaf schools, and no single "parent" school at which teachers were trained before going to teach in other parts of the country. However, there was considerable movement of teachers between schools around the country and this could have helped to unify the language to some extent. For example, Matthew Burns, the first deaf head master of the Bristol deaf school spent time in London, Edinburgh and Aberdeen before his time in Bristol. He later moved to London.

Despite forces that helped to level the regional dialects, the language was recognized in the 1970s as being highly diverse. Nearly a century of oppression by an oral education system had hindered any coherent standardization of the language. When, at this time, linguists named the signing of British deaf people as "British Sign Language," it was more of a social judgment than one based on lexical similarities across the country. Deaf people referred to their language as "deaf signing" and did not recognize the name "British Sign Language."

Over the last 30 years, the language has become much more recognizable as a single national language. Since 1980, television programmes have been broadcast nationally in BSL. The establishment of the Council for the Advancement of Communication with Deaf People (CACDP) to oversee the teaching of BSL and the production of a BSL/English dictionary have also helped to standardize the vocabulary.

Although there is still considerable regional variation in BSL, most members of the British deaf community today would recognize their language as being different from those of other countries.

6.1.3   BSL is a visual language, created by deaf people

As a visual language it makes use of the physical options available for the articulation of linguistically meaningful elements – the two hands, the head, face (including the mouth), and the body. Much of its vocabulary is visually motivated (see above) and much of the language's grammar exploits the possibility of placing and moving signs within a space in front of the signer's body (see, for example, Liddell, 1990). The availability of multiple articulators also allows signers to produce more than one piece of linguistic information at a time. A sign may be produced with one hand, then held, while the other hand produces a second sign that relates to the first. For example, in the BSL sentence "The cat sat under the chair," one hand produces the sign for "chair" while the other produces the sign referring to the "cat" below the first hand to indicate the relationship "under."

Early modern research on sign languages emphasized the underlying structural similarities of spoken and sign languages, but more recent research has moved toward recognition that there are systematic typological differences. These arise mainly from the interaction of language form with modality. Phonological and morphological structures differ, since sign languages exhibit a relatively high degree of systematic correspondence between form and meaning (iconicity or visual motivation) in comparison to spoken languages. There are also consistent grammatical features in which sign languages differ from spoken languages. Sign languages distinguish 1st and non-1st person, while spoken languages usually contrast 1st, 2nd, and 3rd person; sign languages prioritize object agreement while spoken languages prioritize subject agreement. Sign languages exploit the use of space for grammatical purposes, preferring three-dimensionality in syntax, while spoken languages prefer linearization and affixation. Other differences arise from the properties of the articulators (there are two active articulators in sign languages – the hands) and the differing properties of the visual and auditory perceptual systems.

Observation of such differences has led most recently to active consideration of the extent to which the contrasting typological properties of spoken and signed languages indicate that linguistic theory may need to take greater account of modality (Meier, Cormier, & Quinto-Pozos, 2002).

It has also been noted that there is greater typological variation among spoken languages than among sign languages. There are a number of possible explanations for the grammatical similarities among sign languages which still remain to be researched fully. Sign languages are relatively young languages, and indeed, the recent studies of Nicaraguan Sign Language (Kegl, Senghas, & Coppola, 1999) suggest that sign languages can arise and develop spontaneously in deaf communities over three generations. Iconicity as an organizing factor in the lexicon may also result in greater similarity at the lexical level (Woll, 1984). Additionally, the linear syntax found in spoken languages may intrinsically allow greater differences than spatial syntax. Lastly, the relatively low percentage of signers who are themselves the children of signers results in continual recreolization with resulting similarity of grammar (Fischer, 1978). There is evidence to support all of these hypotheses, but a great deal of research remains to be done in this area.

6.1.4   BSL is used by a language community

Membership of the British deaf community is not necessarily defined by a person's hearing ability but rather by identifying with the deaf way of life. This can involve participation in a variety of deaf social networks, use of BSL, or choice of a partner from within the deaf community. For members of the deaf community, being deaf is not a medical condition but an attitudinal state (Woll & Lawson, 1980). An upper-case "D'" is usually used to distinguish "Deaf" as a cultural, linguistic, and social identity from "deaf" as an audiological status. (For simplicity we have used a lower case "d" throughout this chapter.) Ladd (2002) has suggested the use of the term "Deafhood" to reflect the difference between these.

Although most members of the deaf community are deaf, their degree of hearing loss is irrelevant in the same way that darkness of skin color is irrelevant to black community membership. The vast majority of the eight million people in Britain estimated to have a hearing loss, most of whom have lost hearing as part of aging, are not part of the deaf community. These people might rather be considered as "hearing people whose ears don't work" who rely entirely on English for communication. There are some hearing people, such as the hearing children of deaf parents or the hearing partners of deaf people, who may be members of the deaf community. However, they often have marginal status, feeling peripheral to the deaf community or that they straddle deaf and hearing communities (Corker, 1996).

The deaf community is constantly changing. The central position of the deaf club in community life is diminishing as changes in technology (such as SMS (Short Message Service) and captioning on television) mean that deaf people no longer need to meet centrally for information exchange or entertainment (Burns, 1998). Until the 1980s, most deaf children were educated in special schools. Today, most deaf children are educated in mainstream schools. This has had considerable impact on the self-identity of younger deaf people, their attitude to older members of the community, and their use of BSL. However, the deaf community, while different from that of even 20 years ago, is still a central part of the lives of many deaf people, and use of BSL is a defining feature of their identity (Dye & Kyle, 2000).

Deaf children do not automatically acquire BSL. They need to be exposed to linguistic role models, just like any other children. Deaf children exposed to good BSL-using linguistic role models learn BSL in stages similar to those of hearing children acquiring English. For many deaf children, however, access to mature linguistic role models is not straightforward. Approximately 5 percent of British deaf children have deaf parents, and so receive early exposure to BSL (see Dye & Kyle, 2000). The overwhelming majority of deaf children are born to hearing parents with no knowledge of BSL. Increasingly, hearing parents are learning BSL in order to provide an accessible home language. However, for many children, the only BSL users in their environment are hearing teachers and classroom language assistants. Access to deaf BSL-using classroom assistants or to deaf BSL-using teachers is a major linguistic benefit.

6.2 Child-Directed Language

Hearing professionals working with deaf children are increasingly aware of their poor BSL skills. This is a positive development, as in the past deaf children were often blamed for not understanding the teacher's language. Research and training in the area of child-directed BSL, especially to school-age children is still very limited. However, some research has been done on child-directed BSL used with very young children. Gallaway and Woll (1994) have reviewed features of child-directed BSL. Features include: signing on the baby's body; holding and manipulating the baby's hands to articulate a sign; placing the child on the mother's lap, facing away from the mother and signing in front of the child; signing the name of an object on the object; signing the name of an object while holding it; enlarging the movement or increasing the duration of a sign's movement; repeating a sign's movement; using special baby signs.

6.3   Social Dialects in BSL

BSL, like any other living language, has many variants. Variation may be attributable to the social experience and identity of signers or to the setting in which interaction occurs.

6.3.1   *Social class*

Social class does not have the same linguistic defining features for the British deaf community as for British hearing people. Deaf people are more likely to have unskilled and semi-skilled jobs than hearing people, so income is not necessarily a good guide to social class dialect variation. In the American deaf community, there is a recognized elite social class of deaf people who have been to Gallaudet University, the only university for deaf people in the world. The most noticeable social class distinction in BSL is based on family background: whether the signer is from a hearing or deaf family. Those born to deaf parents are more likely to have had early exposure to a good model of adult BSL. Those born to hearing parents may only learn BSL when they start school, or sometimes as late as when they leave school. Consequently, those deaf people coming from deaf families are seen as members of a linguistic elite. There are substantial grammatical differences between the signing of adults from deaf and from hearing families.

Social class in hearing society may also have some effect upon BSL. In the past, children from poorer families were more likely to suffer childhood diseases that cause deafness. Working-class children were also more likely to be sent to deaf schools (often termed "asylums") where education was poor and expectations were low, but where BSL flourished. Children with wealthier parents were more likely to go to private or smaller schools where there was a greater emphasis placed on English skills.

6.3.2   *Men and women's dialect*

In some sign languages (e.g., Irish Sign Language, see Le Master & Dwyer, 1991; Matthews, 1996; and Burns, 1998) the differences between men's and women's signing are substantial. This is not the case in BSL, where gender differences are minimal, and rarely extend beyond stylistic variation. However, as with English speakers, conversational style and lexicon differ between men and women. For example (Coates & Sutton-Spence, 2001), analysis of conversation of deaf same-sex friendship groups found that young men talk about sport (especially football) while young women discuss their family lives and the lives, loves, and behavior of celebrities. Although this may appear self-evident, it is an important issue for language pedagogy, as tutors may not include in their lessons the appropriate lexicon for topics more regularly discussed by members of the opposite sex. Anecdotal observations that men use more "coarse" signing than women received some support in this same conversation sample, with deaf men using more expletives and socially unacceptable sign variants for potentially taboo topics.

Turn-taking also differs among men and women signers. For example, in women's talk, "interruptions" are not really a challenge to take the floor but a supportive reinforcement of what another person has said as part of a collaborative floor. This is less common with men's talk, where mutual support is provided in different ways. Women also provide much more feedback as "backchannel" responses than men do.

6.3.3   Signs linked to sexual orientation

Varieties specific to gay communities are seen within many languages, with distinct lexical items and often their own pronunciation. In Britain, a gay slang, Polari, was used extensively by gay men, especially in London, before the legalization of homosexuality in the late 1960s. Polari was important for creating social identity and ensuring that non-speakers remained outsiders.

Although research has not revealed a BSL equivalent of Polari, F. Elton (personal communication) has researched a variety of BSL which she has called GSV (Gay Sign Variant). GSV contains many signs that are specific to the gay deaf community. Although gay members of the deaf community will occasionally use GSV in the presence of heterosexuals, it is pre-eminently the style or dialect of deaf gay men and its use by heterosexual deaf signers or by those outside the deaf community is frowned upon. A defining feature is a recognizable "camp" pronunciation of BSL. At the sub-lexical level, some signs are characterized by the extension of the little finger. In ASL, "pinky extension" has been identified as a pronunciation variable used especially by women, but its use by men is not specifically equated with homosexuality, and in BSL, extension of the little finger is a stylistic sub-lexical variation not necessarily associated with GSV.

One feature of Polari (and other slangs – e.g., the French Verlan (from *l'envers* – 'backwards') is the use of "backslang" (e.g., *riah*, for *hair*, and *eek*, from *ecaf* for *face*). Some lexical differences in GSV can also be regarded as exemplifying phonological "opposites" to BSL signs, for example, reversing the direction of the palm in BORING, or using the little finger instead of the index finger for signs such as HEARING.

6.3.4   Signs linked to ethnic group

There are dialects of ASL that are identifiable as "Black ASL" and "White ASL." Segregation in American society, including deaf clubs, and separate education for black and white children has resulted in language varying between racial groups. Black signers often know both the white and black varieties of sign, while white signers often only know the white signs (Aramburo, 1989). The variation in the BSL of black and white signers is less marked for a number of reasons. The black deaf community has only recently developed: Deaf people did not immigrate during the first wave of immigration from the West Indies, and black deaf children are in the minority in British deaf schools. Variation in the British black deaf community is mostly limited to isolated lexical items and use of facial expressions and gestures also found in the black hearing community (James, 2001; James & Woll, in press).

The British Asian community is also relatively small and only recently established, but there are now increasing numbers of Asian deaf children in British schools. An "Asian" variety of BSL may emerge if Asian deaf people begin to see themselves as a single, unified social group. This is unlikely, as Asian people in Britain come from many different countries, have many different home languages, and belong to several different religious and cultural groups.

The issue of ethnic minority BSL dialects has enormous practical implications for sign language interpreters and other service providers. Interpreters from traditional white British backgrounds may be unable to cope with words and concepts that are common in Afro-Caribbean English but not in their own dialects. Not only will they not have the signs, but they also will not know either the English words or concepts.

6.3.5   *Religious groups*

There are a few differences in BSL arising from religious identity. There are some differences between Catholic and Protestant signing. The signing of deaf British Catholics has been influenced by Irish Sign Language because of the strong Irish presence in Catholic deaf schools, and Irish-trained priests serve the Catholic deaf communities in Britain. Catholics use many initialized signs with handshapes taken from the Irish manual alphabet (Woll, Sutton-Spence, & Elton, 2001). In Glasgow, the Catholic and Protestant deaf communities have different dialects, reinforced by membership of different deaf clubs and sports teams, as well as churches.

The dialect of Britain's Jewish signers, whether they are seen as an ethnic group or one identified primarily by religious beliefs, may also be traced to their education and community identity. The Residential School for Jewish Deaf Children existed from 1864 to 1965. Although the school used oral communication methods, the children signed among themselves in private and out of the classroom, just as children did in other British deaf schools using oral methods (Weinberg, 1992). Attendance at this school gave children a strong Jewish identity, despite their deafness. In effect, they had a Jewish deaf identity. Today, younger Jewish deaf people sign very differently from older members of the community. Apart from those signs specific to Jewish religion and customs, their signing is the same as the BSL used by other people of their age.

6.3.6   *Age dialect*

The changing experiences and social identities of deaf people have resulted in age-related variation in BSL. As with other language communities, younger people are language innovators; and this role of linguistic innovation is particularly seen in young deaf men (Wardhaugh, 1992; Battison, 1978). As a very broad generalization, older deaf people (for example, those over 70) use more fingerspelling and many fewer English mouthings than younger deaf people (Sutton-Spence, Woll, & Allsop, 1991). Deaf people aged under 20 use a form of BSL that is more heavily influenced by English grammar, with relatively little fingerspelling. There is also lexical variation among signers from different age groups. Some younger deaf people, in a deliberate move to dissociate themselves from English influences, avoid use of English mouthings or fingerspelling.

The age-related differences are due to three major factors. Firstly, as we have seen, there are few signing deaf parents of deaf children. This means that parents cannot transmit their language to their children. This lack of continuity in language transmission between generations results in extensive inter-generational language change.

Secondly, changes in educational policy have had a very large impact on the signing of deaf people. Before the 1940s, English was taught through lip-reading and fingerspelling, resulting in fingerspelling being a dominant feature of the signing of the older age group. Since the 1940s, improvements in hearing aid technology have meant that deaf children have been expected to use their residual hearing to listen to and learn English, although signing was always tolerated outside the classroom in residential schools. Since the 1970s there have been increasingly tolerant attitudes toward the use of signing in deaf school classrooms. At the same time, however, residential schools have been closing, with most deaf children sent to local mainstream schools. This has reduced the size of the community of child signers. It remains to be seen what effect this will have upon young people's BSL.

A third reason for age differences in BSL is technological innovation. Many signs in BSL reflect some aspect of the appearance of referents or their use. As technology has changed, so have signs, to reflect the new appearance of old technology, or how new devices are handled or operated. The BSL sign for "telephone" has changed over time as the appearance and use of telephones has changed. Similar changes may be seen in signs for "train," "camera," and "watch."

Old signs also die out. For example, signs such as PAWN-BROKER and ALMS are no longer in widespread use, although they are illustrated in a very basic list of signs from 100 years ago (see Figure 6.1).

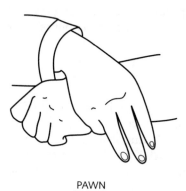

PAWN

Figure 6.1   Sign for PAWN-BROKER

6.4   Regional Dialects in BSL

In a study of regional variation in BSL, signers in Glasgow, Newcastle, Manchester, London, and Bristol were presented with a list of English words to translate (Woll, 1991). Subjects included a wide age range of men and women. Specific groups of words were chosen: some were culturally central to BSL users (e.g., DEAF, HEARING, INTERPRETER); some were everyday words (e.g., BRITISH, BUSINESS, THEATRE); and some had recently entered BSL (e.g., DISCRIMINATION, COMMUNITY). Extensive regional sign differences were recorded, with many signs specific to only one region, including signs for color terms, days of the week and numerals. In most cases, however, one form was used or recognized by signers in all regions. Thus, it appeared that signers were bi-dialectal. National broadcasting of BSL on television only began in 1981 but since that time, signers have had the opportunity to see more varieties of BSL, leading to a greater familiarity with different dialect forms.

Although the recording of different regional signs is interesting for an appreciation of the variation within BSL, these findings are also significant for interpreters and for those working in broadcast media. With only a few BSL/English interpreter training programs in Britain, newly qualified interpreters may very well find themselves working with dialects with which they are not familiar, and facing clients who do not understand their signs.

Regional dialect differences in BSL are most likely related to regional residential deaf schools. We may expect a trend toward dialect leveling now that so many children are mainstreamed or attend Partially Hearing Units near to their homes. Coupled with a decline in attendance at deaf clubs, deaf people's access to regional dialects may be lessened and the "national" signs used by deaf television presenters and hearing interpreters may become more dominant.

The publication of BSL dictionaries may also become a unifying force in BSL. If a regional sign is excluded from a dictionary (or if it is labeled as a "regional sign") its use may decline.

6.5 Situational Dialects: BSL Register

As with all languages, BSL changes according to the situation in which it is being used. The details of BSL situational variants have yet to be researched in depth, but it is clear that there are sub-lexical, lexical, and grammatical differences in BSL, depending on the identity of the addressee, the topic of the utterance, the function of the discourse, and the formality of the situation. In casual BSL, we see the following features when compared to more formal BSL (Deuchar, 1984; Sutton-Spence & Woll, 1999; similar features are described for ASL by Zimmer, 1989):

- Less finger spelling
- More use of non-manual features, especially for grammatical function
- Less evidence of English influence
- Greater use of metaphor and idioms
- Reduction of two-handed signs to one-handed signs (including producing the two-handed manual alphabet with only the dominant hand)
- Reduced specification of the location of signs
- Greater use of "role shift" or characterization used in reported speech
- Greater use of spatial and temporal structures for textual cohesion and segmentation (rather than overt lexical markers such as NOW or the indexing seen in more formal discourse)

When considering register variation in BSL, it is important to note that many deaf people live and work in a society where BSL is used in only a limited range of contexts. The rules of formality in English governing how parents, parents-in-law, teachers, clergy, judges, and higher status work colleagues are addressed are not present in BSL, since for most deaf people, all such interactions are conducted in English. Even more general variants such as "conversing with elders" are not relevant for some signers. James (2001) has described the lack of experience of younger members of the black deaf community in signing to older black deaf BSL users because there is no older generation.

As the use of BSL becomes more accepted and widespread, and as interpreters are more widely used in different settings, new register variants of BSL are developing. Greater use of BSL in higher education settings has led to deaf people and hearing interpreters working together to create new BSL vocabulary for new concepts, and the increased presence of deaf professionals has led to new contexts for BSL use.

6.6   Aesthetic Use of BSL

Just as there are aesthetic uses of English, so there are culturally recognized aesthetic uses of BSL. The British deaf community has a strong tradition of storytelling, and skilled storytellers are known and respected for their use of BSL. Skilled narratives in BSL make great use of characterization, using facial expressions and body movements to give color to the characters in the narratives. BSL stories often contain detailed descriptions of the appearance and behavior of the characters. Narratives generally contain many more "productive" (cf. Brennan, 1992) signs than non-narratives and these productive signs are frequently morphologically complex verbs that are created ad hoc during the narrative to show the location and movement of particular objects in the space of the story. Ability to use detailed spatial description and accurate characterization is important, coupled with clear textual cohesion.

Storytelling was once an important part of school life, as children signed to each other in dormitories away from adults (Ladd, 2002). It was also a part of deaf club life. With the closing of deaf schools and declining attendance at deaf clubs, this is changing. However, national deaf festivals still preserve storytelling and the increased use of video allows the preservation of nationally acclaimed BSL storytelling and its transmission to much wider audiences.

Sign language poetry is also a small but important use of aesthetic BSL. BSL poetry makes use of parallelism at many levels and the form of the language used brings out extra meaning and symbolism.

Because of the essentially simultaneous nature of the sublexical components in sign languages, there are not exact equivalents of "rhyme," "assonance," or "alliteration" in sign language poetry. However, the sign poet may use signs that share the same handshape or the same location or the same patterns of movement in the sublexical components to create equivalent repetitive effects. Dorothy Miles, the first BSL poet, noted in her unpublished notes on poetry composition that repeated handshapes produce stronger "rhymes" than repeated location or movement, although in general the more parameters shared by two signs, the stronger the "rhyme."

Specific timing patterns of signs also create poetic rhythms. Sign poems also make unusually regular use of both hands, as the use of the non-dominant hand is increased to create extra symmetry and balance in the poem.

Sign language poetry not only uses repeated sublexical components to enhance the meaning, but it also selects signs – or elements of signs – that deviate from everyday non-poetic language. Poetic language that is "irregularly deviant" uses neologisms, blends or "morphs" signs in order to create a smooth flow from one to the next, and it can create ambiguous signs whose different possible interpretations lead to extra poetic significance. Neologisms can also be accompanied by unusual use of eye-gaze or unusual use of the signing space. In all these instances, the rules of the language are broken (or sometimes, merely "bent") for poetic effect.

Dorothy Miles, arguably the British deaf community's finest poet, originally began composing ASL poetry during her time in America. Throughout the 1980s, however, until her death in 1993, she composed many fine works in BSL. Her earlier work was quite heavily influenced by English but her later, more "mature" sign poems are entirely free from English influence. A brief description of her BSL poem "To a Deaf Child" (Miles, 1998) will illustrate some of the points made above. The poem celebrates sign language, and its message concerns the ease of communication for deaf signers, contrasting this with the problems caused by the inaccessibility of speech to deaf people.

The poem contains many signs made using the handshape of the closed hand with only the index finger extended. This "pointing" handshape is used for referents that the language treats as being essentially "one-dimensional" (e.g., a person, a fence post, or a screwdriver). Here, by metaphorical extension, the handshape is used for signs relating to the hearing world (such as VOICE, SPEAK, HEAR, EAR, IGNORE, LIP, SAY, and SOUNDS). Another dominant handshape is the flat open hand with fingers spread or together, which is used in BSL for more solid referents (e.g., a table, a wall or a box). These handshapes are used in the poem in signs relating to the deaf world (such as SIGN, HAND, LIGHTLY-GIVE, BUTTERFLY, CLEAR, and MEANING). The clear contrast between the handshapes provides a metaphor for the "thin" hearing world and the "solid" deaf world.

Close "rhymes" are also seen in the simultaneous signs found in the poem. These simultaneous signs occur to link and contrast certain ideas. Thus HEAR and UNDERSTAND are articulated at the same time, as are NOTHING and IGNORE. In the first of these pairs of simultaneous signs, the handshapes are very similar and, additionally, the locations are similar and contrast on opposite sides of the head. The movements also contrast: in HEAR the movement is toward the head and in UNDERSTAND it is away from the head (Figure 6.2). In the second pair, the handshapes are maximally different, the orientation of the palms is maximally contrasting and both move away from the head to be located in opposing locations, balanced in signing space (Figure 6.3). This use of signs is highly "deviant."

HEAR   UNDERSTAND

Figure 6.2 Simultaneous signs for HEAR and UNDERSTAND

IGNORE   NOTHING

Figure 6.3 Simultaneous signs for IGNORE and NOTHING

WORD   WORD-IMPRISONS

Figure 6.4 Metaphor using signs for WORD and IMPRISONS

An example of morphing and ambiguity is seen in the metaphor that Miles uses to describe the way that the spoken word imprisons a person who cannot understand it. The BSL sign WORD is made with the thumb and index finger extended and curved so that together they create a "C" shape (with the remaining three fingers curved to the palm). In the poem, the sign WORD moves and the handshape locks against the wrist of the other hand, literally imprisoning it (Figure 6.4).

Poets on both sides of the Atlantic see Miles' work as the foundation for modern sign language poetry. Sign language poetry is now an area of growing interest for those concerned with the aesthetic use of BSL, and several organizations run sign language poetry workshops to encourage composition. Criticism and metacriticism of sign language poetry is only a recent development in sign linguistics and deaf studies, but it is an area of increasing interest (e.g., Taub, 2001; Sutton-Spence, 2001).

6.7   Encounters between Deaf and Hearing Communities

There are many instances of conflict and misunderstanding arising between deaf and hearing people. Much of the time these arise from their very different experiences of life within British society. The British deaf community shares life experiences and culture, but these are embedded within the hearing world. When hearing people do not appreciate deaf values and the importance of certain behaviors, friction and even hostility can occur.

Perhaps the area where such conflict is greatest is in the area of language. Young, Ackerman, & Kyle (1998) studied the use of sign language in the workplace (in psychiatric units for deaf people and in a school for deaf children), exploring the role of signers as not only service users but also as service providers. The signing skills of deaf staff were far superior to those of their hearing colleagues. These skills were especially important for communicating with mentally ill deaf people or with deaf children. Despite this, the deaf staff had lower-grade jobs than the hearing staff, although the delivery of services depended on deaf staff and their cultural and linguistic skills. They thus had low status, but high value.

Since only a BSL linguistic environment provided deaf staff with full access to information at work, hearing staff were required to use BSL at all times when a deaf person was present or might be present. Deaf and hearing people differed in the way they viewed this policy. For deaf staff, signing promoted involvement, making deaf people feel confident, valued, and respected, and with a sense of well-being; signing promoted the development of personal and social relationships between deaf and hearing people; signing enabled deaf staff to fulfill their professional roles and responsibilities.

In contrast, for hearing staff, signing caused lack of confidence, and worries about linguistic competence; hearing people felt that the pressure to sign was sometimes too great. When they were tired, distracted, or under pressure, they reverted to English.

A clear signing policy, good training, and a supportive environment encouraged hearing people to sign. This increased recognition of the role of sign language within the workplace, for the benefit of both employees and service users, is a positive step.

6.8   Language Planning and Standardization

One of the causes of change in sign languages has been language planning. The great sign language enthusiasts of the eighteenth and nineteenth centuries, such as the Abbé de L'Epée in France, and Thomas and Edward Gallaudet in America, created new signs and morphological markers to create a system of signing which matched the structure of the spoken language of the country.

The changes have not been as long-lasting as the planners expected. Those who have invented new signs or sign systems (new manual alphabets or entirely new communication systems such as the Paget Gorman Sign System or Seeing Essential English (SEE)) have not found them accepted by deaf communities.

There are occasional influences from artificial sign systems on sign languages. For example, the Paget Gorman sign "animal" has been borrowed by some

BSL signers. Other signers have borrowed the sign's form, but with the meaning "the Paget Gorman sign system."

Another cause of language change is standardization, yet it is by no means clear that there is a standard form of BSL. While standard varieties of English are taught to second language learners of English, learners of BSL learn local dialects of BSL, often taught by tutors with no formal training qualifications (Dye & Kyle, 2000). The standard for English is validated by its status in dictionaries (non-standard word forms listed in dictionaries are marked as non-standard). However, there is no written form of BSL, BSL has only recently begun to be taught in schools after a 100-year gap, and it is rarely taught to children by native users. There is only one BSL–English dictionary (Brien, 1992), and it includes a limited number of signs. While standard varieties of English are used on broadcast media, there is no standardized variety of BSL on television and deaf television presenters use their own regional signs (Steiner, 1998).

Despite the degree of variation, there is no doubt that British deaf people recognize BSL as one language. It is possible that some form of Standard BSL is slowly emerging, but as yet there is no certainty of when this will happen or what the standard will be like.

6.9   Learning BSL

Despite the limited acceptance of BSL by educators, there has been an enormous increase in the numbers of hearing people learning BSL in recent years. This can be seen from Figure 6.5, which shows the rise in the numbers of students taking national examinations offered by the Council for the Advancement of Communication with Deaf People at Stage 1, 2, and 3. BSL is now the second most popular vocationally related evening class subject in the UK after First Aid.

Training for teachers of BSL is very limited, with only brief courses, training tutors to deliver a single curriculum to hearing adult learners. There is no formal training for those concerned with teaching BSL to deaf children or their parents, for example.

6.10   BSL–English Interpreters

The increase in numbers of students taking BSL courses has not been matched by an increase in the number of BSL–English interpreters. Indeed, the shortage of interpreters is one of the most serious problems facing the deaf community, since interpreters enable access to communication with the hearing world. The Digital Broadcasting Act requires the provision of BSL on 5 percent of all digital terrestrial programing. The Disabled Students Allowance provides funding for sign language interpretation for undergraduate and postgraduate

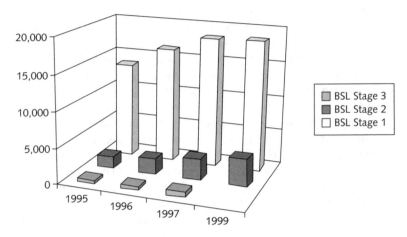

Figure 6.5 Number of students taking BSL exams

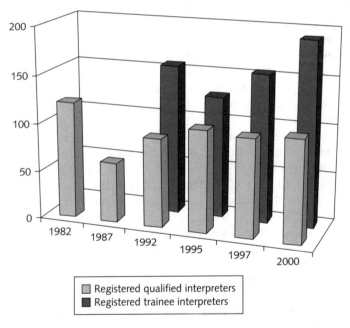

Figure 6.6 Number of registered qualified and registered trainee interpreters

students, and the Disability Discrimination Act requires the provision of sign language interpretation by firms and government for publicly available services. However, as can be seen from Figure 6.6, there has been virtually no increase in the number of qualified sign language interpreters over the past 17 years.

BSL–English interpreting has undergone great changes over the last two decades. In the past, the role of "go-between" between hearing and deaf people was taken by hearing members of a deaf person's family or by missioners to the deaf. The missioner to the deaf was concerned with the welfare of deaf people within his parish and was one of the few members of society with any social standing who could sign. He would be called upon to interpret, for example, when a deaf person went for a job interview or wished to resolve a dispute with hearing neighbors. Deaf people used the missioner as an interpreter and also frequently as an ally, adviser, and advocate. As connections between deaf communities and the church weakened, this task was taken on by social workers for the deaf (Brennan & Brown, 1997). (The sign SOCIAL WORKER is derived from the old sign MINISTER because of their similar role in deaf life.) Social workers for the deaf and missioners for the deaf often came from deaf families and lived and socialized with members of the deaf community. There was no sign INTERPRET at this time in BSL, and deaf people would simply use a phrase such as MISSIONER SIGN FOR ME.

Professional BSL–English interpreting evolved out of this, beginning in the early 1980s, with the establishment of the CACDP (see above). Professional interpreters were seen as a step toward empowerment of deaf people. These interpreters had undergone formal linguistic and interpreting training and did not make decisions for deaf people or advise them, but merely relayed information between the two languages, comparable to spoken language interpreters. Professional BSL–English interpreters were encouraged to operate solely as "conduits" for the languages, and to be socially and emotionally neutral throughout their work.

This shift from the "traditional" style of interpreting to "professional" interpreting did have benefits, especially in avoiding the dangers of patronizing or controlling the deaf client. Modeling professional sign language interpreting on theories taken from the well-established and well-respected fields of spoken language interpreting aimed to raise standards and the status of the language and the interpreters. In many ways this has been successful; however, "professional" interpreting has not been an unqualified success, and the interpreting profession has begun to re-assess the impact of adopting this wholesale application of theory from one field to another.

The effect of this shift has been summarized by Pollitt (2000), an interpreter and interpreter trainer. She notes that many deaf people do not like the professional approach, and see interpreters as "cold" or "unhelpful" and unacceptably "impersonal." Some people (especially older deaf people) *want* advice, support, and explanation that go beyond a mere transference of a message, and they continue to use family members or social workers instead of "professionals" for this reason.

Further problems have arisen from the way that interpreters are trained. With interpreter training moving out from the community and into university settings, many members of the deaf community feel that interpreters (now often from hearing families) no longer have in-depth knowledge of the deaf communities where they work. Subtle language nuances, contextual information, complex social relationships between the parties, and specific language skills of a deaf client are only learned through long-term, committed relationships with a community, such as missioners and social workers had. Interpreters may cover much wider areas of the country and have far less daily interaction with their clients.

Interpreters are now beginning to recognize the need to adapt other models of interpreting to the specific needs of the deaf community today. There is call for a more flexible approach, incorporating ideas from both the "traditional" and the "professional" approaches.

Most discussions of BSL–English interpreting assume that the interpreter will be hearing. Clearly there are many situations where the interpreter must be hearing because translation between spoken English and BSL is required. However, there are increasing numbers of deaf interpreters, particularly in legal and media settings.

In legal settings, deaf interpreters often work as "relay" interpreters. For a variety of reasons, a deaf person in court may not understand the signing of a hearing interpreter (for further consideration of this topic, see Brennan & Brown, 1997). In such situations a deaf relay interpreter may be called upon to act as an interface between the interpreter and the deaf client, modifying the interpreter's BSL so that the deaf client can understand it. The relay interpreter also interprets the deaf client's signing into a form of BSL more easily rendered into spoken English by the hearing interpreter.

Increasingly, deaf interpreters are also working in the media, providing BSL translation of pre-recorded programs or pre-prepared live programs (especially regional television news bulletins). In these settings, the deaf interpreters work from written English scripts and autocue. At present, there has been little formal research on the differences between hearing and deaf interpreters on television from the point of view of audience satisfaction.

Another solution to the chronic shortage of interpreters might lie in the current experimental use of computer generated signing avatars. Although still in early stages of development, research is currently underway to use text-driven computer translation from English to BSL for applications such as alternatives to text on Internet pages (Hanke, 2002).

6.11 Official Recognition of BSL

The British deaf community has been campaigning for many years for official recognition of BSL. With the recent signing by the government of the European Charter for Regional or Minority Languages, the campaign has moved toward seeking the inclusion of BSL on the Charter list of minority languages, in order to ensure adequate funding for training and provision of interpreters and acceptance of BSL in public settings such as the law and education. This campaign has made only limited progress to date, but some official recognition is likely to be extended within the next few years. As well as increasing provision of interpreters and protecting signers' linguistic rights, recognition is likely to lead to standardization.

6.12   Conclusions

The history of BSL, like that of many minority languages, cannot be separated from a study of its relationship with the majority language community which surrounds it. At the beginning of the twenty-first century, there are two contrasting futures. On the one hand, there are pressures, such as the decrease in opportunities for deaf children to use BSL with their peers as a result of the move to mainstream education, and a possible decrease in the deaf population as a result of medical intervention and advances in genetics. On the other hand, there is increased interest and demand from the hearing community for courses in BSL, increased use of BSL in public contexts such as television, and increased pride of the deaf community in their distinctive language and culture. Although the social circumstances of the language are changing, there is every probability that BSL will continue to be a living language.

REFERENCES

Aramburo, A. (1989) Sociolinguistic aspects of the black deaf community. In C. Lucas (ed.), *The sociolinguistics of the deaf community* (pp. 103–21). San Diego: Academic Press.

Battison, R. (1978) *Lexical borrowing in American Sign Language*. Silver Springs, MD: Linstok Press.

Bloomfield, L. (1933) *Language*. New York: Holt, Rinehart and Winston.

Boyes Braem, P. (1985) Studying sign language dialects. In W. Stokoe & V. Volterra (eds.), *SLR'83* (pp. 247–53). Rome/Silver Spring, MD: CNR/Linstok Press.

Brennan, M. (1992) The visual world of BSL. In D. Brien (ed.), *The dictionary of British Sign Language/English* (pp. 1–133). London: Faber & Faber.

Brennan, M. & Brown, R. (1997) *Equality before the law: deaf people's access to justice*. Durham, UK: Deaf Studies Research Unit.

Brien, D. (ed.) (1992) *Dictionary of British Sign Language/English*. London: Faber & Faber.

Burns, S. (1998) Irish Sign Language. Ireland's second minority language. In C. Lucas (ed.), *Pinky extension and eye gaze: language use in deaf communities* (pp. 233–74). Washington, DC: Gallaudet University Press.

Coates, J. & Sutton-Spence, R. (2001) Turn-taking patterns in deaf conversation. *Journal of Sociolinguistics*, 5, 507–29.

Corker, M. (1996) *Deaf transitions*. London: Jessica Kingsley.

Davies, J. (1999) *The Welsh language*. Cardiff: University of Wales Press.

Deuchar, M. (1984) *British Sign Language*. London: Routledge & Kegan Paul.

Dye, M. & Kyle, J. (2000) *Deaf people in the community: demographics of the deaf community in the UK*. Bristol: Deaf Studies Trust.

Fischer, S. (1978) Sign language and Creoles. In P. Siple (ed.), *Understanding language through sign language research* (pp. 309–31) (Perspectives in Neurolinguistics and Psycholinguistics). London: Academic Press.

Gallaway, C. & Woll, B. (1994) Interaction and childhood deafness. In C. Gallaway & Brian J. Richards (eds.), *Input and interaction in language acquisition* (pp. 197–218). Cambridge/ New York: Cambridge University Press.

Hanke, T. (2002) HamNoSys in a sign language generation context. In R. Schulmeister & H. Reinitzer (eds.), *Progress in Sign Language research*. Hamburg: Signum Press.

Hansard (1999) February 18. www.parliament.the-stationery-office.co.uk/pa/cm/cmhansrd.htm

James, M. (2001) Black Deaf or Deaf Black? Unpublished PhD dissertation: City University.

James, M. & Woll, B. (in press) Black Deaf or Deaf Black? In A. Blackledge and A. Pavlenco (eds.), *Negotiation of identities in multilingual contexts*. Clevedon, UK: Multilingual Matters.

Kegl, J., Senghas, A., & Coppola, M. (1999) Creation through contact: sign language emergence and sign language change in Nicaragua. In M. DeGraff (ed.), *Language creation and language change: creolization, diachrony, and development* (pp. 179–237) (Learning, development, and conceptual change). Cambridge, MA: MIT Press.

Klima, E. & Bellugi, U. (1979) *The signs of language*. Cambridge, MA: Harvard University Press.

Ladd, P. (2002) *Understanding deaf culture: in search of deafhood*. Clevedon, UK: Multilingual Matters.

Le Master, B. & Dwyer, J. (1991) Knowing and using female and male signs in Dublin. *Sign Language Studies*, 73, 361–96.

Liddell, S. (1990) Four functions of a locus: re-examining the structure of space in ASL. In C. Lucas (ed.), *Theoretical issues in sign language research* (pp. 176–98). Washington, DC: Gallaudet University Press.

Matthews, P. (1996) *The Irish deaf community* (vol. 1). Dublin: The Linguistics Institute of Ireland.

Meier, R., Cormier, K., & Quinto-Pozos, D. (eds.) (2002) *Modality and structure in signed and spoken language*. Cambridge: Cambridge University Press.

Miles, D. (ed.) (1988) British Sign Language. A beginner's guide. London: BBC Books.

Miles, D. (1998) *Bright memory*. Feltham, Middlesex: British Deaf History Society.

Pizzuto, E. & Volterra, V. (2000) Iconicity and transparency in sign languages: a cross-linguistic cross-cultural view. In K. Emmorey & H. Lane (eds.), *The signs of language revisited* (pp. 261–86). Hillsdale, NJ: Lawrence Erlbaum Associates.

Pollitt, K. (2000) On babies, bathwater and approaches to interpreting. *Deaf Worlds*, 16, 60–4.

Steiner, B. (1998) Signs from the void: The comprehension and production of sign language on television. *Interpreting*, 3(2), 99–146.

Sutton-Spence, R. (2001) British sign language poetry: a linguistic analysis of the work of Dorothy Miles. In V. Dively, M. Metzger, S. Taub, & A. M. Baer (eds.), *Signed languages: discoveries from international research* (pp. 231–43). Washington, DC: Gallaudet University Press.

Sutton-Spence, R. & Woll, B. (1999) *The linguistics of British Sign Language: an introduction*. Cambridge: Cambridge University Press.

Sutton-Spence, R., Woll, B., & Allsop, L. (1991) Variation in fingerspelling in BSL. *Language Variation and Language Change*, 2, 315–32.

Taub, S. (2001) Complex superposition of metaphors in an ASL poem. In V. Dively, M. Metzger, S. Taub, & A. M. Baer (eds.), *Signed languages: discoveries from international research* (pp. 197–230). Washington, DC: Gallaudet University Press.

Wardhaugh, R. (1992) *An introduction to sociolinguistics*. Oxford: Blackwell.

Weinberg, J. (1992) *The history of the residential school for Jewish deaf children*. London: Reunion of the Jewish Deaf School Committee.

Woll, B. (1983) The semantics of British Sign Language signs. In J. Kyle & B. Woll (eds.), *Language in sign: an international perspective on sign language* (proceedings of the Second International Symposium of Sign Language Research, Bristol, UK, July) (pp. 41–55). London: Croom Helm.

Woll, B. (1984) The comparative study of different sign languages. In F. Loncke, Y. LeBrun, & P. Boyes Braem (eds.), *Comparing sign languages: recent research in European Sign Language* (pp. 79–92). Ca Lisse: Swets.

Woll, B. (1991) *Variation and recent change in British Sign Language*. Final Report to Economic and Social Research Council. University of Bristol: Centre for Deaf Studies.

Woll, B. & Lawson, L. (1980) British Sign Language. In E. Haugen, J. Derrick McClure, and D. Thomson (eds.), *Minority languages today* (pp. 218–34), a selection from the papers read at the First International Conference on Minority Languages held at Glasgow University September 8–13. Edinburgh: Edinburgh University Press.

Woll, B., Kyle, J., & Deuchar, M. (eds.) (1984) *Perspectives on British Sign Language and deafness*. London: Croom Helm.

Woll, B., Sutton-Spence, R., & Elton, F. (2001) Multilingualism: the global approach to sign languages. In C. Lucas (ed.), *The sociolinguistics of sign languages* (pp. 8–32). Cambridge: Cambridge University Press.

Young, A., Ackerman, J., & Kyle, J. (1998) *Looking on*. Bristol: Policy Press.

Zimmer, J. (1989) Toward a description of register variation in American Sign Language. In C. Lucas, (ed.), *The sociolinguistics of the deaf community* (pp. 253–72). San Diego: Academic Press.

FURTHER READING

Emmorey, K. & Lane, H. (eds.) (2000) *The signs of language revisited*. Hillsdale, NJ: Lawrence Erlbaum Associates.

Lucas, C. (ed.) (2001) *The sociolinguistics of sign languages*. Cambridge: Cambridge University Press.

7 Assessing Language Attitudes: Speaker Evaluation Studies

HOWARD GILES AND ANDREW C. BILLINGS

7.1 Introduction

Over the past 40 years, a substantial amount of research on attitudes to language variation has emerged around the world and across the disciplines. We have witnessed seminal investigations (e.g., Labov, 1966; Lambert, 1967), programmatic enterprises in Britain (e.g., Giles, 1990), Australia (e.g., Gallois, Callan, & Johnstone, 1984), the United States of America (e.g., Williams, 1976), and New Zealand (e.g., Bayard et al., 2001), journal special issues (e.g., Cooper, 1974, 1975; Giles & Edwards, 1983; Kristiansen, 2001a; Milroy & Preston, 1999; Ryan, Giles, & Bradac, 1994) as well as authored (Baker, 1992; Giles & Powesland, 1975; Lippi-Green, 1997) and edited books (e.g., Shuy & Fasold, 1969; Ryan & Giles, 1982) on the topic that have accumulated into a substantial literature overviewed at regular interviews (e.g., Bourhis & Maas, in press; Bradac, 1990; Bradac, Cargile, & Hallett, 2001; Giles, Hewstone, et al., 1987). This body of work has provided us with a wealth of valuable information concerning how speakers' language choices shape others' impressions of them impacting decision-making processes in an array of critical social and applied arenas.

The study of language attitudes frequently resides at the core of interaction analysis. Social scientists have approached this form of research from the perspective of both the listener and the speaker. While the findings have varied across variables of culture, dialect, accent, and context, scholars have argued that determining the effects of language on social judgment is an integral part of uncovering the *communication* process. As Cargile et al. (1994) argued, "language is a powerful social force that does more than convey intended referential information" (p. 211). From the job applicant who is chosen because of his "cultured" British accent to the Southern-American who is not selected because of their "unintelligent" dialogue, attitudes about specific forms of language can have a significant influence at many levels. At the macro-sociological level, images of cultures and societies are shaped based on the perceptions of language telecast on television and in film; at a micro-sociological level, relationships with friends and family can be permanently altered by the manner of language they employ. Thus, scholars have argued the importance of language attitude research within many domains. The media researcher purports that language influences cognitive images that we use to form collective realities (Lippman, 1922); interpersonal experts employ listener- and speaker-based models to explain the impact of language in one-on-one and group dynamics (Berger & Calabrese, 1975); organizational scholars write of linguistic "first impressions" that impact past, present, and future alliances. In sum, academics from many disciplines agree that language attitudes are an important enterprise. It is the method with which these researchers have chosen to analyze such attitudes that has differed widely.

This chapter explores the intersections between language, communication, and social judgment as, again, such findings directly relate to everyday and applied social interactions. We begin with the earliest studies as they are still heavily cited today and form the foundation for subsequent research, theory, and applications. We shall then examine the differing social meanings of speaking with standard and non-standard accents and the ways they impact applied social decision-making. After paying due attention to sociopolitical contexts and other mediating variables, language attitudes as a process of person perception will be engaged theoretically. Finally, we shall underscore the value of following through on two other (untested) models that frame language attitudes as discursive and linguistic actions. Having overviewed many of the empirical achievements of speaker evaluation research over the years, we will devote some attention to the growing number of recent theoretical frameworks that have begun to enrich the research enterprise.

7.2 Empirical Origins

Empirical research in this area began arguably in the 1930s with Pear's (1931) classic study inviting BBC audiences in Britain to provide personality profiles of various voices heard on the radio, finding that different forms of the British dialect caused integral changes in person perception. Much research followed over the decades to determine whether voice parameters were an external mirror of someone's actual dispositional states. Consequently, the research concluded that there was only a very modest overlap between listener-judges' ratings of "targets'" vocal features and peer-ratings of the latters' personalities. There appeared little advantage in pursuing voice as a cue to actual personality. On the other hand, study after study has shown that there is a quite considerable social consensus among listener-judges about the *stereotypical* traits associated with voices (see Giles & Powesland, 1975).

These stereotype-based judgments of voice are, nonetheless, socially vital and there has been an explosion of research since 1960 showing that people can express definite and consistent attitudes toward speakers who use particular styles of speaking. Encouragingly, the cultural diversity of speech communities studied is ever on the increase, such as in the People's Republic of China (Zhou, 2001) and Cyprus (Papapapvlou, 1998). Although a variety of methods has been fruitfully adopted, most of the research has been contained within the so-called "speaker evaluation paradigm." Its origins can, in large part, be found in the Lambert et al. (1960) study introducing the "matched-guise" technique (MGT). Indeed, many of the roots of the social psychology of language itself can be traced to this seminal investigation.

Lambert was interested in inter-ethnic attitudes in Montreal, more specifically in how French- and English-Canadian people perceive each other. Distrusting people's overt and public ascriptions (as would be the case from direct questionnaire procedures) as a true reflection of their privately held views, he formulated the MGT as a means of eliciting attitudes to users of different language varieties. The procedure is built on the assumption that speech style triggers certain social categorizations that will lead to a set of group-related trait-inferences. In other words, hearing a voice that is classified as "French-Canadian" will predispose listeners (depending, of course, on their own group-memberships) to infer that she or he has a particular set of personality-attributes. Balanced bilinguals (people with equal facility in two languages) were tape-recorded reading a standard (ethnically neutral) passage of prose in both French and in English. These recordings were then used as "stimulus" materials for evaluation. Each speaker's (two or often more) versions were interspersed with other recordings (so-called "filler voices") to avoid them being identified as produced by the same speaker. Care was, and is always, taken to ensure that the "guises" are perceived to be authentic; in other words, in the case we are considering, independent listeners must believe the English guises derive from English-Canadians – and not from French-Canadians speaking English. In this way, considerable care is expended on issues of stimulus control. Prosodic and paralinguistic features of voice (such as pitch, voice quality, and speech rate) as well as other aspects of reading style and expressiveness are kept constant as far as possible across the different recordings (for a discussion of the virtues and limitations of the MGT, see Giles & Bourhis, 1976). By these means, it is argued that reactions to the "speakers" are dependent solely on social expectations based, in turn, on language cues.

Listener-judges are then asked to listen to a series of (supposedly) *different speakers* on audiotape, and then to form an impression of these speakers using a series of person perception rating scales (such as intelligence and sincerity) provided them on a questionnaire. Judges are asked to undertake this task in the same way as people can gain first impressions about speakers that they hear (but cannot see) – say, behind them in a restaurant or on the radio. In the original Lambert et al. (1960) study, the judges were French- and English-Canadian (FC and EC) students, with matching tape-recorded guises. Although there were many facets to this study, and hence a variety of findings emerging, for our present purposes the main results were that: (1) EC listeners judged speakers of their own ethnic group more favorably on half of the 14 traits;

while (2) the FC listeners not only went along in the same evaluative direction, but accentuated this in favoring the "outgroup'" over their own on ten out of 14 traits.

This initial MGT study was valuable for at least six reasons. First, Lambert invented a rigorous and elegant method for eliciting apparently private attitudes that controlled for extraneous variables. Second, it showed how certain individuals can attribute unfavorable traits to members of their own language community. Third, the findings underscored the important role of language (and code and dialect choice) in impression formation. Fourth, the study laid the foundations for an interface between sociolinguistic and sociopsychological analyses of language (see Milroy & Preston, 1999) and was an important factor in establishing the cross-disciplinary field of language attitudes. Arguably, Labov's (1966) exploration into this arena, through his own "subjective reaction test" owes much to the innovations of Lambert. Fifth, the original study spawned an enormous number of studies worldwide, particularly in Britain, Australasia, the United States, The Netherlands, and more recently Denmark (e.g., Jarvella et al., 2001). Indeed, the importance of the Lambert et al. paper can be gauged by the fact that Tajfel (1959) published a critique of it a year before the original was published. Finally, the dependent variables used in the study gave rise to the now pervasively recognized (though often relabeled) judgment-clusters of *status* (e.g., confidence, ambition) versus *solidarity* (e.g., friendly, generous) traits (see, for example, Mulac, Hanley, & Prigge (1974) and Zahn & Hopper (1985) for the addition of dynamism traits such as active, lively, etc.).

The study was far from being a "one-off" affair. For instance, the important role of language in social evaluation was substantiated by introducing variants of the technique across a range of black, French, and Jewish communities in the United States, and in Israel, and the Philippines. Moreover, the roles of listener-variables such as age and interactions between speakers' and listeners' ethnicity-by-gender were also reported (see Lambert, 1967). In the latter respect, Lambert discussed the work of one of his students (Preston) who investigated whether judges react similarly to male and female speakers of the FC and EC guises. It was found that the EC listeners, in general, viewed female speakers more positively in their French guises, but the male speakers more favorably in their English guises. EC female listeners were not quite as resolute as male listeners in their upgrading of FC female listeners, but there was a still a strong tendency in the same direction.

Lambert and his associates also moved beyond "static" varieties of speech styles toward evaluations of language shifts, as in the case of language "convergence" toward and "divergence" away from, speakers (see Bourhis, Giles, & Lambert, 1975), and showed how language could affect other forms of social decision-making in an educational context (see Section 6.3.2). In addition, the original empirical effects were monitored from time to time to appraise the influence of changing sociocultural and historical climates in quasi-replication studies. For instance, Genesee and Holobow (1989) found that although the

downgrading of Québec French was dissipating in the wake of laws to provide the language with better institutional support, widespread improvements
on ratings of status have not really been forthcoming.

7.3   Subsequent Empirical Explosion of Research

Work following through with this basic methodological paradigm, though
modified in one way or another, continues today. Much of it is descriptive to
the extent that it generates valuable base-line data about intergroup attitudes
in particular sociolinguistic communities. Edwards (1982) points out that there
are three broad possibilities for the underlying patterns of speech-style
judgments: they may reflect (1) intrinsic linguistic superiorities/inferiorities;
(2) intrinsic aesthetic differences; or (3) social convention and preference.
It is, however, sociolinguistically unpalatable for languages and language
varieties to be reasonably described, as (1) suggests, as being "better/worse,"
"correct/incorrect," or "logical/illogical." Similarly, with (2), aesthetic judgments of language varieties do not in fact seem to be based on inherent qualities
of beauty," though they may be represented as such by members of speech
communities. A series of studies (see Section 7.1, see Giles & Niedzielski, 1998)
showed that listeners rating totally unfamiliar (foreign) varieties, which judges
could not categorize as class- or status-related varieties, did not discriminate
between them on the grounds of aesthetic criteria, although they *were* perceived
to differ sharply in these qualities within their *own* speech communities. It
seems, therefore, that evaluations of language varieties do not reflect intrinsic
linguistic or aesthetic qualities so much as (3) the levels of status and prestige
that they are *conventionally* associated with in particular speech communities
(Trudgill & Giles, 1978).

7.3.1   *The power of the standard accent*

Empirical studies spanning a range of speaking situations and communities
around world have produced a generally consistent pattern of results relating
to the social evaluation of standard and non-standard speakers. Much of this
has centered around the anglophone world and varieties of (frequently British) English, given the prestige and institutional support for this language (for
the Brazilian case, see El-Dash & Busnardo, 2001). It should be recognized that
notions of "standardness" are not unproblematic (see Edwards & Jacobsen,
1987), can be confusing (Crowley, 1999), and are ever-evolving. As a case in
point, and with the assistance of two empirical studies, Kristiansen (2001b)
claims that there are, in actuality, two Danish standards: one emerging in
the media (Low Copenhagen), and the other, more traditional Copenhagen
spoken in public institutions such as the school and business (see also, Long &
Yim, 2000 regarding the complex standardization situations existing in Japan
& South Korea). Nevertheless, a standard variety is the one that is most often

associated with high socioeconomic status, power, and media usage in a particular community. Received Pronunciation (RP) could reasonably be taken to identify standard British English, as it is most commonly designated. Indeed, the quality of what they espouse too has attracted more favorable content ratings (Giles, 1973). Even speakers of non-standard/"subordinate" varieties will tend to downgrade them (Giles & Powesland, 1975), with the appreciation of such social connotations beginning quite early in life.

Until very recently, RP-like varieties have attracted the most uniformly favorable evaluations in the English-speaking world, not only in Britain, but also in Australia (Ball, 1983), New Zealand (Huygens & Vaughn, 1984), and the United States (Stewart, Ryan, & Giles, 1985). Interestingly though, a study (entitled "Pax Americana") conducted by Bayard et al. (2001) examined reactions to Australian-, New Zealand-, and American-English finding that the most highly regarded voice was the *American* female, followed closely by the *American* male. Even Australian students ranked Australian-English below American-English, and, while New Zealanders ranked their own New Zealand female moderately, all groups disliked the New Zealand male. It will be interesting, in future work, to rediscover the relative prestige of both RP and Standard American dialect in other anglophone settings (see Gill, 1994) and elsewhere (see, for example, El Dash & Busnardo, 2001; Jarvella et al., 2001).

Other dependent measures used to examine the effects of speech style are those of recall and cooperation. In Northern Ireland, Cairns and Dubiez (1976) found that children subsequently recalled more material when it was presented in RP than in other more local guises (see Giles, Henwood, et al., 1992). Giles, Baker, and Fielding (1975) showed that high-school students in South Wales provided more written information to (24 percent), and about (48 percent), an RP-accented speaker than they did to and about a regionally-accented (Birmingham) one. Similarly, matched samples of housewives wrote and provided more ideas on a three-item open-ended questionnaire when it was delivered by an RP speaker than by the same bidialectal researcher using her Cockney dialect (when the respondents' local dialect was also Cockney; Giles & Farrar, 1979). This difference in cooperative behavior actually grew larger as respondents progressed from answering their first to the second and third answers (33 percent, 45 percent, and 72 percent more, respectively). And in a more recent elaboration of this study in a Danish setting, Kristiansen and Giles (1992) found the same overall pattern in favor of standard Danish in the Naevstad area (albeit this effect was influenced by the type of audience which attended particular kinds of films in a multi-screen cinema).

As alluded to in this last study, attributions of the perceived status of standard speakers are mediated by the social context in which evaluations are elicited. Creber and Giles (1983) found that the typical status-upgrading of RP was attenuated significantly when the testing situation was an evening youth club, compared with the (usual) classroom setting. On the other hand, Giles, Harrison, et al. (1983) found that the status connotations of RP were accentu-ated when informants were asked to discuss their speaker-evaluations with each other for 90 seconds before making their ratings. The language of testing in MGT studies has also been shown to be important, as for example when Welsh bilinguals in a study by Price, Fluck, and Giles (1983) made evaluative distinctions between RP and a non-standard Welsh accent on status traits when the experimental procedure was conducted in English, but *not* when it was in the Welsh language. In sum, not only can the status connotations of a standard variety be diminished or exaggerated depending on the nature of the context, but the evaluative criteria brought to bear in them can also vary. While we do not cavalierly dismiss the potency of situational manipulations, the status accorded standard speakers is, nonetheless, extremely robust.

7.3.2   Social decision-making and language attitudes

Speech style is clearly an important social cue in many applied social contexts (Lippi-Green, 1997) including very small portions of it being poignant when requesting housing information from a potential landlord over the telephone (Purnell, Isdardi, & Baugh, 1999). Within the educational setting, Seligman, Tucker, and Lambert (1972) in fact found that speech style was an important cue in teachers' evaluations of pupils, even when combined with other information, such as photographs of the children and examples of their school-work. Choy and Dodd (1976) reported that teachers evaluating standard English and Hawai'ian speakers consistently favored the former. Overall, research indicates that the perception of children's so-called "poor" speech characteristics leads teachers to make negative inferences about their person-alities, social background, and academic abilities. Clearly, these may lead to self-fulfilling prophecies to the disadvantage of non-standard-speaking children. Teachers may themselves induce behavior from children that *confirms* their stereotyped expectations.

Language attitude studies in the medical arena are not as frequent. Fielding and Evered (1980) showed that RP speakers are more likely to be perceived as having psychosomatic symptoms than non-standard accented patients, even when they are voicing exactly the same complaints. Moreover, medical student listener-judges in this study perceived lexical and syntactic differences between two supposed patients they heard on audiotape, despite the fact that these features were in fact held constant. Patients' social class has been shown to affect the frequency of communication difficulties experienced by doctors, with working-class patients being disadvantaged as a consequence.

Legal and judicial settings also offer much scope for language attitudes in crucial social episodes. Seggie (1983) presented voices of speakers (in RP, broad Australian, and Asian-accented English) in the role of defendants. RP speakers were adjudged more guilty when the crime was embezzlement, whereas Australian-accented speakers were more severely judged when the crime was physical assault. In other words, "white-collar" crimes tend to be asso-ciated with prestige speakers whereas crimes of violence are cognitively aligned more with non-standard users. In Britain, recently, Dixon, Mahoney,

& Cocks (2002) asked raters, using the matched-guise technique, to evaluate an audio-taped interrogation by police officers with a criminal suspect who was pleading his innocence. They found that the Birmingham-accented suspect was rated significantly more guilty – and especially so when it related to a blue-collar crime (armed robbery) – than an RP-sounding suspect.

Most research in occupational settings has related to employment interviews (see Hui & Yam, 1987 for a Hong Kong case). Hopper and Williams (1973) showed that speech characteristics (for Standard American, black, Mexican-American, and Southern white speakers) were relevant to employment decisions, but decreased in importance when the interviews were for lower-status jobs. Indeed, Giles, Wilson, and Conway's (1981) study in the British context showed a linear relationship between seven jobs, independently rated as varying in status, and the job suitability of RP and non-standard speakers.

Seggie, Smith, & Hodgins (1986) also elicited evaluations of employment suitability based on ethnic accent in Australia. Two groups of subjects of European descent – owners of small businesses and female shoppers – were asked to decide whether a speaker they heard on tape was suitable to be trained for a low- or high-status job; all the speakers were presented as having identical backgrounds and qualifications. The owners of small businesses heard Asian-, German-, and two (standard and broad) Anglo-Australian voices; the female shoppers heard Asian- and two Anglo-Australian voices. It is interesting that the businessmen did not differentiate between the two Anglo voices, whereas the shoppers regarded the standard speakers as being unsuitable for low-status job training. The businessmen rated the Asian voice equally with the standard Anglo voice, while the shoppers rated it equivalent to the broad Anglo voice. The authors offer an explanation of these findings in terms of the different cognitive schemas of the two groups (see also, Thakerar & Giles, 1981). The businessmen have knowledge of the success of Asian business in Australia, whereas the female shoppers are more likely to think of Asians as restaurant workers; different evaluative profiles, it is suggested, emerge as a consequence.

7.3.3   *The power of non-standard varieties*

While non-standard accented speakers per se attract less prestige than standard accents, and particularly so among older speakers (Giles, Henwood, et al., 1992; but for a different pattern, see the Japanese-American case of Cargile & Giles, 1998), research in a number of cultures shows that a status-hierarchy differentiating *among* non-standard varieties exists. This has been shown to be so for English non-standard varieties (Giles & Powesland, 1975) as well as for regional varieties of Welsh (Garrett, Coupland, & Williams, 1995). Likewise in France, a Parisian guise was rated more favorably along competence traits than a Provincial guise, which was afforded more prestige than a Brittany guise which, in turn, was more highly evaluated than an Alsace guise (Paltridge & Giles, 1984). But beyond this, the degree of accentedness displayed by the non-standard speaker has also been accorded social significance. Ryan, Carranza, and Moffie (1977) found that students' ratings of Spanish-accented American English became less favorable (across nine varieties) the more heavily-accented the speaker sounded. Such fine sociolinguistic discriminations are not made everywhere, however. Cargile & Giles (1997), for instance, found that while the Japaneseness of an American accent did influence person perception and feelings of pleasure, strength of accent did not, nor did it have an effect on listeners' level of arousal. In Costa Rica, Berk-Seligson (1984) also found little evaluative distinctions between mildly-accented and broadly-accented non-standard Spanish, but a considerable evaluative divide between these two and the standard variety.

There is another side to this evaluative coin. In many contexts, including Britain, it has been shown that non-standard speakers are *upgraded* on traits relating to solidarity, integrity, benevolence, and social attractiveness relative to non-standard speakers (Giles & Powesland, 1975), and especially so in contexts, like family ones (Carranza & Ryan, 1975). In Switzerland, for example, Hogg, Joyce, and Abrams (1984) found that judges rated High German and Swiss German speakers equivalently on status dimensions, but Swiss Germans more favorably on solidarity traits. In Ireland, a Donegal speaker was rated the most competent of five Irish guises, but a Dublin speaker, who was regarded the lowest in this regard, was considered the highest in social attractiveness (Edwards, 1977). And in the United States, Luhman (1990) invited Kentucky students to evaluate the personalities of Standard Network American and Kentucky-accented speakers. The former were judged in the high status/low solidarity quadrant, while Kentucky-accented speakers were found in the low status/high solidarity quadrant. Returning to Britain, Garrett, Coupland, and Williams (1999) found that school students' views of RP speakers were far less positive than their teachers'. Indeed, while conceding prestige to speakers of RP, Garrett (2001) overviewed a research program in Wales where RP speakers "are not considered so likeable or fun to be with, or to have interesting things to say, they are 'not like us' and they attract labels like 'posh' and snob' from teenagers" (p. 627).

Such evaluations in favor of the non-standard voice have been extended to powers of persuasiveness in Britain (Giles, 1973) as well as to attributions of dynamism in Hawai'i Creole speakers in comparison to their Standard American counterparts (Ohama, et al., 2000). The persuasiveness of the non-standard variety is particularly potent when speakers of it portray an ideological position that is stereotypically incongruous as in the case where Hispanic-accented speakers in the USA defend the English-only movement (Giles, Williams, et al., 1995). However, pro-non-standard patterns can be qualified on some occasions by speakers' gender, as we have noted already. For instance, while white Australians and Aborigines upgraded male Aboriginal speakers as more friendly, trustworthy, and gentle than white males, Aboriginal female speakers were, in complete contrast, rated less favorably on solidarity traits (Gallois, Callan, & Johnstone, 1984).

7.3.4   *The politics of language attitudes*

Language attitudes are, of course, sensitive to local conditions and changes in the sociopolitical milieu (see Baker, 1992; Giles & Pierson, 1988; Lippi-Green, 1997; St. Clair, 1982). For instance, Bourhis and Sachdev (1984) found that Anglo-Canadian secondary school students had less favorable attitudes toward Italian language usage when the demographic proportions of Anglos and Italians in their immediate school environment were equal, as opposed to when Anglos were the clear majority. Such findings illustrate the notion that negative language attitudes are not as prevalent when there is a clear in-group and out-group. Bourhis (1983) has also shown that the changing political climate in Québec has been associated with modifications in attitudes toward the use of Canadian French and English. In South Wales, at a time when Welsh identity appeared to be particularly strongly sensed in the community, Bourhis, Giles, and Tajfel (1973) found that bilingual speakers were perceived more favorably than RP-accented ones, and in ways that were not evident some years earlier. Tong, et al. (1999) also argued that language attitude profiles in Hong Kong as they were associated with Cantonese and Mandarin speakers reflected listeners adjustments to their new and old identities after the Colony passed back to the People's Republic of China.

An even more vivid illustration of language attitudes comes from Woolard and Gahng (1990) who collected MGT data in Barcelona in 1980 and then again with a matched sample in 1987. They found at the first time of testing that Catalan speakers were accorded more status than Castilian speakers, regardless of whether the listener-judges were Catalan or Castilian speakers themselves. The ethnolinguistic background of the judges was, however, very potent when the solidarity dimension was examined. Castilian judges gave high ratings to fellow Castilians who spoke the in-group language, but severely downgraded them when they were heard to be speaking Catalan (notwithstanding its status in this area of Spain). Catalan listener-judges rated their in-group variety higher on solidarity traits than the outgroup language, but were quite indifferent as to whether Castilians accommodated their language or maintained their Castilian.

Since Woolard and Gahng's first testing widespread changes emerged with respect to language politics. In 1983, a law was passed giving the language co-official status alongside Castilian in government, legal, affairs, education, the media, etc. When replicating the study in the wake of these language policies, Woolard and Gahng found an even stronger status superiority for Catalan yet a "loosening of the bond between the Catalan language and native Catalan ethnolinguistic identity. It no longer matters so much who speaks Catalan, but rather simply that it is spoken" (p. 326). Hence, Castilian listeners no longer downgraded their in-group on solidarity traits for speaking Catalan and Catalan listeners were now more favorably disposed toward Castilians who accommodated them.

Thus, it seems reasonable to propose that when a non-standard speech style is, or becomes, a valued symbol of in-group pride (be it working-class, ethnic, or occupational), individuals who are strongly committed to their social group membership display evaluative preferences for their own variety (Bresnahan, Ohashi, Nebashi, Liu, & Morinaga Shearman, 2002). For instance, Flores and Hopper (1975) found some preference for Mexican-American speech styles among people who identified themselves as "Chicanos," a term associated with cultural and linguistic pride.

7.3.5   *Other intervening and mediating variables*

It is often the case, but not always (as in the case probably of German-accented speech), that non-standard speakers are concentrated in the lower socio-economic strata and are accorded lower prestige as a consequence. Thus, Ryan and Sebastian (1980) suggested that assumptions about social class could lead to the downgrading of ethnically-accented speakers. They were able to demonstrate these interaction effects by presenting social class background information to judges along with the vocal guises of standard and non-standard speakers (in an orthogonal factorial design). The evaluative differences between standard American and Mexican-American speakers were drastically reduced when they were both known to derive from middle-class backgrounds. Yet, this interdependence of accent and social class information has not shown up in more recent studies in other speech communities. For example, Giles and Sassoon (1983) found that whether a speaker was known to be middle class *or* working class, his non-standard speech style still evoked a lower rating on status-traits in comparison with RP speakers.

The meshing of non-verbal, visual cues with vocal and verbal ones is, perhaps surprisingly, an understudied domain and one that holds out much potential for future work. The evaluative potency of accent effects (in this case, Asian versus more standard British accent) was not diminished when visual cues were added to the presentation of vocal styles (Elwell, Brown, & Rutter, 1984). But interestingly, Aboud, Clément, and Taylor (1974) demonstrated in Québec that socioeconomically "incongruous" presentations of photographs of people at work and their voice samples (e.g., a middle-class-looking speaker with a Joual accent) were reported as being a more pleasing combination for potential workmates than "congruous" stimuli (e.g., middle-class-looking and -sounding individuals). The opposite was the case for potential superiors or subordinates.

In fact, relatively few studies have manipulated accent, dialect, or language along with other language factors. Giles, Wilson, and Conway (1981) showed that accent had as significant an effect on listeners' social evaluations as did lexical diversity in Britain, while Bradac and Wisegarver (1984), in a most ambitious design in the United States varying lexical diversity, accent, and social class background information, demonstrated that these factors were additive on status-related dimensions. This "combinatorial model" suggests that the least favorable status-judgments will be made for non-standard speakers, low in lexical diversity, with a known working-class background, and vice versa. Interestingly, accent was a less salient variable than lexical diversity on status-traits in this study.

Message content has rarely been examined alongside speech-style effects, although it has been shown to bear significant consequences (Cargile & Giles, 1997; Giles & Johnson, 1986). For instance, Powesland and Giles (1975) showed an "incongruity" effect, again, where speakers who argued in ways not expected from their voice-patterns (e.g., an RP speaker advocating greater powers to Trade Unions) were upgraded as a consequence of their presumed integrity. Gallois, Callan, and Johnstone (1984) have also discussed the mediating influence of perceived message threat in determining social evaluations, while attaching even greater weight to the role of social distance. Many recent studies have shown that standard listeners infer from a non-standard speech style not only that such speakers would be unsuitable as partners in close personal relationships, but would be likely to hold many dissimilar beliefs (e.g., Stewart, Ryan, & Giles, 1985). Also, they are perceived as being less in *control* communicatively (Bradac & Wisegarver, 1984). Future research needs to explore whether, and the precise ways in which, belief dissimilarity, direct threat, large social distance, low control (and doubtless other factors) mediate the perception of non-standard speech and low-status ratings.

7.4   Speaker Evaluation and Person Perception

Researchers are now beginning to develop theories pertaining to the effects of language on person perception. Ryan, Giles, and Sebastian (1982) provided a framework for understanding the two primary sociostructural factors affecting language attitudes. They articulated speaker assessment as a model with two crossing dimensions: (1) standard vs. non-standard and (2) increasing vitality vs. decreasing vitality. Standardization is defined as the codified form of language that the power elites of society consider to be acceptable. Relatedly, vitality (the second dimension) is termed as the practical use of the language itself and implicitly raises the question of whether people actually speak the standard or non-standard language (see El-Dash & Busnardo, 2001 for an empirical investigation). When viewed as a whole, this model provides an appropriate heuristic for language assessment, as the authors argued that any language or dialect can be placed along these standardization/vitality continua. Giles and Ryan (1982) also provide a complementary model for interpreting perceived language attitude situations and evaluative ratings. Again, they argue for two broad dimensions: (1) status-stressing vs. solidarity-stressing, and (2) person-centered vs. group-centered. This model stressed the context of the situation and the type of study involved as key elements that need to be examined when determining the validity of a study.

A decade later, Cargile, et al. (1994) detailed a general process model of speaker evaluations that has been elaborated further by Cargile and Bradac (2001) with particular attention (among other factors) to how a listener's emotional state (or mood) can influence speaker evaluations, and how these, in turn, can shape raters' social identities – as Americans, women, older, or whatever (see Cargile & Giles, 1997; Giles, Williams, et al., 1995). In addition, these listener-processing models afford considerable theoretical status to information processing. More specifically, the particular social goals listeners bring to bear on the evaluative task to hand, their levels of involvement in and the amount of attention they expend (mindfully or automatically) on it, can be very important for outcomes. This being so, the mechanisms of cognitive work in which listeners can engage in forming their language attitudes are of much value for theorists in designing future research. Furthermore, the contribution which these listener processing models have made to sociolinguistic accounts is the realization that, as the above authors write, ". . . attitudes about language are not a singular, static, phenomenon. Rather, they affect, and are affected by, numerous elements in a virtually endless, recursive fashion" (p. 215). In essence, speaker evaluation may always be viewed as slightly incomplete, as this circular process has no direct beginning or end, making any point of entry for research an intuitively reassured guess. Nonetheless, the authors argue that speaker evaluation can be assessed even within the circular model, noting that the model is a useful heuristic for the study of how language influences evaluations by bisecting the process both linguistically (verbal and non-verbal) and attitudinally (effects on cognitions and behaviors).

The development of speaker evaluation profiles can also be grounded within attribution theory (see Hewstone, 1989). Kelley (1972), one of the pioneers in this area, has coined the term *causal schema*. He argues that people store their schemata cognitively and then implement these mental elements to judge people. Another one of Kelley's (1967) attribution theories, that of covariation, furthers this conceptualization by arguing three applicable principles: consistency, differentiation, and deviation from consensus. More specifically, covariation theory applies to additional judgments in a schema once a first judgment has been made and whether these supplemental judgments support or deviate from the consensus. While these attribution frameworks assist our understanding of how speakers can be evaluated within communication, a model taken from Giles and Powesland (1975) articulates the practical implications of this form of research. The authors argue that once deficiencies in the perceptions of language are pinpointed, speakers of this language can alter the way in which they speak in order to best fit into mainstream society (see also Street & Hopper, 1982).

In sum, the study of language attitudes can be grounded in a range of theoretical positions relating to person perception. These explain how lexical, dialectical, and semantic differences become embedded in language, ultimately altering the way in which cultures and segments of society are viewed.

7.4.1   The MGT paradigm from a more discursive perspective

Several innovative developments are possible if, at least as an alternative design, language attitudes are approached from a *discursive* perspective (Giles & Coupland, 1991; see also, Preston, 1999). That is, one where social meanings (and in this case, language attitudes) are assumed to be inferred by means of *constructive, interpretive* processes drawing upon social actors' reservoirs of contextual and textual knowledge; a perspective which has, of course, much in common with constructivist and pragmatic orientations. Indeed, the matched-guise paradigm is one that seems to have been reluctant to move beyond a static, input-output mechanism.

It is an established tenet of discourse analysis that meanings arise from the interplay of communicative acts and the full range of factors in their contextualization. Another is that texts are never "neutral," although recall in Section 7.2 we noted that this is an avowed and valued control feature of the MGT. Texts inevitably seek to establish or subvert, through complex and often inconsistent means, rhetorical, political, and ideological positions. This may seem an exaggerated claim in the case of texts we researchers may have composed *explicitly* to be uncontroversial or even trivial, and to be politically and socially inert. But to take a case in point, how is it possible to generate a text that is "age-neutral"?

Giles, Coupland, et al. (1990) tried to do precisely this in a matched-guise study which required listeners to evaluate a speaker varying in terms of speech rate (fast, medium, or slow), accent (standard or non-standard), and age (young adult vs. elderly). The passage spoken was supposedly an extract from an interview where the speaker was talking at length about his car. Adopting the traditional rating measures, they found that few effects emerged for speaker's age. However, in addition, the researchers asked textually-interpretive questions and found that when providing listeners with extracts from the text, such as the speaker saying, "I didn't know what to think," the listeners interpreted this variously depending on the speaker's age. Hence, his "not knowing" was more likely to be attributed to his being "confused" if elderly (the speaker was in fact perceived to be in his early sixties), or if young (early thirties). When asked why they rated the speaker as they had done, despite the fact that he said exactly the same thing in each condition, he was described as "arrogant and pompous" when in the guise of a young, standard speaker; "trying to impress" or "using the words of others" when non-standard and young; "egocentric, living in the past, and talking of trivia" when standard and elderly; and even "stupid, and losing his grip" when non-standard and elderly. Even more interestingly, when invited to substantiate these accounts by pinpointing textual information, respondents would very often highlight exactly the *same* utterances to justify their (very disparate) claims.

The evaluative process needs to be separated conceptually from its "reporting," since language attitudes are, after all, appraisals conveyed in a particular context. Indeed, the reporting can come about in many different forms and may, in reality, never be transmitted or even mindfully appraised. Recent work in Britain has begun to challenge – if not deconstruct – the very notion of "attitude" as currently measured and conceptualized in social psychology. And this is the very bedrock upon which language attitude studies are based. Potter and Wetherell (1987) point not only to the variability inherent in people's social attitudes when they are expressed in talk (even within the same conversation), but also question whether attitudes *can* be rarified in the minds of individuals *away from* the assumed objects to which they are targeted in the "outside world." As we know from a myriad of studies in the social psychology of language (e.g., Street & Hopper, 1982), our judgments about how people actually sound and speak – the object of language attitudes – can themselves be a constantly redefining, social construction process and dependent on social cognitive biases. Hence, "language varieties" on the one hand, and "attitudes" on the other, are *symbiotically* related in a subjective sense, rather than the dichotomous entities they are assumed to be in the MGT paradigm. Billig (1987) also considers attitudes in a wider historical context as *positions in an argument* and embedded in particular social controversies. Attitudes in this sense are not only explicit appraisals pro or contra a position, but also include an implicit stance *against counter-positions*. In sum then, we have arguably paid too little attention to the cognitive activities involved in recipiency, and to the complex interrelationships between language and attitudes and the functions of these in discourse (see Cargile et al., 1994).

7.4.2 *Language attitudes and linguistic action*

It is appropriate to conclude this chapter by asking the question: To what extent do people's language attitudes predict their sociolinguistic behavior? Although early social psychological research on attitudes implicitly assumed that by understanding a person's attitudes one could predict behavior, contemporary research is far more critical. Fishbein and Ajzen (1975) proposed that the predictability of a behavior is increased by working with attitudes and behaviors defined at an equivalent level of specificity. According to their "theory of reasoned action," an action is viewed quite simply as a person's *intention to perform* (or not perform) a behavior (e.g., speaking French to a customer in Québec). The basic determinants of a person's intention are also specified. The person's *attitude toward the behavior* is a function of *beliefs* about the consequences of performing a particular behavior and the person's *evaluation* of these consequences. The second determinant of intention, *subjective norms*, are themselves determined by the person's normative beliefs regarding the expectations of others, and the person's *motivation to comply* with these expectations.

Another approach which emphasizes the idea of attitude toward behavior is Jaccard's (1981) "behavioral alternative" model which considers situations in which an individual can perform one of a number of alternative and mutually exclusive behaviors (e.g., one must choose to speak a standard or non-standard dialect, assuming for simplicity, that code-shifting is not possible). According to Jaccard, the individual may be said to possess an attitude toward performing each of the behavioral alternatives available. The individual will decide to perform that alternative for which the most positive attitude is held. Thus, the prediction of behavior is based on an intra-individual comparison of behavioral alternatives, and each person's attitude toward speaking a variety of language might have to be measured (for a variety of situations) in order to predict accurately.

7.5   Epilogue

We have seen how the MGT has blossomed since its inception and language attitude studies are now at the core of the social psychology of language. Indeed, Garrett (2001) argued that "since explanations of sociolinguistic phenomena are most likely to be found in social psychological processes, language attitudes are a key component of sociolinguistic theory-building" (p. 630). Listeners can very quickly stereotype another's personal and social attributes on the basis of language cues and in ways that appear to have crucial effects on important social decisions made about them, as we saw in the medical, occupational, and legal spheres. There are different kinds of evaluative profiles attending individuals who use language in different ways in different contexts, and a wide range of contextual, speaker-, and listener-variables have been shown to interact in this process. We noted that a plethora of theoretical models are beginning to emerge at different levels of analysis, which is timely given the accumulation of findings worldwide (see also, Bradac & Giles' (1991) developmental model of the process whereby language attitudes can be socialized early in life). Moreover, we argued that the evaluation phase of the MGT was indeed a process – a discursive event – and that much active interpretive work gets done during these studies.

In this chapter, we have identified where language attitude research has been over the past 40 years in order to determine where the research will be going in the future. We envision that future research will examine (1) the influence of accent, particularly in regard to content; (2) the heterogeneity of speakers offered as representative of a speech community (Luhman, 1990) and others implanted alongside them in the evaluative frame (Abrams & Hogg, 1987); (3) the influence of language attitudes on self-presentation, accommodative tactics, and argumentation; (4) the role of friendships in molding language attitudes (Bresnahan et al., 2002) together with the integration of information processing at the relational interpersonal (Berger & Bradac, 1982) and intergroup (Ryan, Giles, & Sebastian, 1982) levels into one approach; and (5) how we talk about language varieties (Giles & Coupland, 1991; Preston, 1999). Therefore, much remains to be achieved, not least regarding the relationships between language attitudes and linguistic action. Edwards (1999), alongside Milroy and Preston (1999), calls for bridging gaps between evaluative reactions and speech attributes, therein extolling the virtues of "a more linguistically aware social psychology or a more psychologically aware sociolinguistics" (p. 108). Both arguments are quite valid and are important steps toward making the necessary connections between the plethora of one-shot studies and the inter-disciplinary area this work entails. Much language attitude work has been completed over the past 40 years; now is the time to begin bridging the past studies to ground future endeavors.

REFERENCES

Aboud, F., Clément, R., & Taylor D. M. (1974) Evaluational reactions to discrepancies between social class and language. *Sociometry*, 37, 239–50.

Abrams, D. & Hogg, M. A. (1987) Language attitudes, frames of reference and social identity: a Scottish dimension. *Journal of Language and Social Psychology*, 6, 201–14.

Baker, C. (1992) *Attitudes and language*. Clevedon, UK: Multilingual Matters.

Ball, P. (1983) Stereotypes of Anglo-Saxon and non-Anglo-Saxon accents: some explanatory Australian studies with the matched-guise technique. *Language Sciences*, 5, 163–84.

Bayard, D., Weatherall, A., Gallois, C., & Pittam, J. (2001) Pax Americana? Accent attitudinal evaluations in New Zealand, Australia, and America. *Journal of Sociolinguistics*, 5, 22–49.

Berger, C. R. & Bradac, J. J. (1982) *Language and social knowledge*. London: Edward Arnold.

Berger, C. R. & Calabrese, R. J. (1975) Some explorations in initial interaction and beyond: toward a developmental theory of interpersonal communication. *Human Communication Research*, 1, 99–112.

Berk-Seligson, S. (1984) Subjective reactions to phonological variation in Costa Rican Spanish. *Journal of Psycholinguistic Research*, 13, 415–42.

Billig, M. (1987) *Arguing and thinking: a rhetorical approach to social psychology*. Cambridge: Cambridge University Press.

Bourhis, R. Y. (1983) Language attitudes and self-reports of French-English language usage in Quebec. *Journal of Multilingual and Multicultural Development*, 4, 163–80.

Bourhis, R. Y., Giles, H., & Lambert, W. E. (1975) Social consequences of accommodating one's style of speech: a cross-national investigation. *International Journal of the Sociology of Language*, 6, 55–72.

Bourhis, R. Y., Giles, H., & Tajfel, H. (1973) Language as a determinant of Welsh identity. *European Journal of Social Psychology*, 3, 447–60.

Bourhis, R. Y. & Maas, A. (in press) Linguistic prejudice and stereotypes. In U. Ammon, N. Dittmar, & K. J. Mattheier (eds.), *Sociolinguistics: an international handbook of the science of language and society* (2nd edn.). New York: de Gruyter.

Bourhis, R. Y. & Sachdev, I. (1984) Vitality perceptions and language attitudes. *Journal of Language and Social Psychology*, 3, 97–126.

Bradac, J. J. (1990) Language attitudes and impression formation. In H. Giles & W. P. Robinson (eds.), *Handbook of language and social psychology* (pp. 387–412). Chichester: Wiley.

Bradac, J. J., Cargile, A. C., & Hallett, J. S. (2001) Language attitudes: retrospect, conspect, and prospect. In W. P. Robinson & H. Giles (eds.), *The new handbook of language and social psychology* (pp. 137–55). Chichester: Wiley.

Bradac, J. J. & Giles, H. (1991) Social and educational consequences of language attitudes. *Moderna Sprak*, 85, 1–11.

Bradac, J. J. & Wisegarver, R. (1984) Ascribed status, lexical diversity, and accent: determinants of perceived status, solidarity, and control of speech style. *Journal of Language and Social Psychology*, 3, 239–56.

Bresnahan, M. J., Ohashi, R., Nebashi, R., Liu, W. Y., & Morinaga Shearman, S. (2002) Attitudinal and affective response toward accented English. *Language and Communication*, 22, 171–86.

Cairns, E. & Dubiez, B. (1976) The influence of speaker's accent on recall by Catholic and Protestant schoolchildren in Northern Ireland. *British Journal of Social and Clinical Psychology*, 15, 441–2.

Cargile, A. C. & Bradac, J. J. (2001) Attitudes toward language: a review of speaker-evaluation research and a general process model. In W. B. Gudykunst (ed.), *Communication Yearbook*, 25, 347–82.

Cargile, A. C. & Giles, H. (1997) Understanding language attitudes: exploring listener affect and identity. *Language and Communication*, 17, 195–218.

Cargile, A. C. & Giles, H. (1998) Language attitudes towards varieties of English: an American-Japanese context. *Journal of Applied Communication Research*, 26, 338–56.

Cargile, A. C., Giles, H., Ryan, E. B., & Bradac, J. J. (1994) Language attitudes as a social process: a conceptual model and new directions. *Language and Communication*, 14, 211–36.

Carranza, M. A. & Ryan, E. B. (1975) Evaluative reactions of bilingual Anglo and Mexican-American adolescents towards speakers of English and Spanish. *International Journal of the Sociology of Language*, 6, 83–104.

Choy, S. & Dodd, D. (1976) Standard-English speaking and non-standard Hawaiian-English-speaking children: comprehension of both dialects and teachers' evaluations. *Journal of Educational Psychology*, 68, 184–93.

Cooper, R. L. (ed.) (1974) The study of language attitudes. *International Journal of the Sociology of Language*, 3, 5–19.

Cooper, R. L. (ed.) (1975) The study of language attitudes II. *International Journal of the Sociology of Language*, 6.

Creber, C. & Giles, H. (1983) Social context and language attitudes: the role of formality-informality of the setting. *Language Sciences*, 5, 155–62.

Crowley, T. (1999) Curiouser and curiouser: falling standards in the standard English debate. In T. Bex & R. J. Watts (eds.), *Standard English: the widening debate* (pp. 271–82). London: Routledge.

Dixon, J. A., Mahoney, B., & Cocks, R. (2002) Accents of guilt? Effects of regional accent, race, and crime type on attributions of guilt. *Journal of Language and Social Psychology*, 21, 162–8.

Edwards, J. R. (1977) Students' reactions to Irish regional accents. *Language and Speech*, 20, 280–6.

Edwards, J. R. (1982) Language attitudes and their implications among English speakers. In E. B. Ryan & H. Giles (eds.), *Attitudes towards language variation* (pp. 20–33). London: Edward Arnold.

Edwards, J. R. (1999) Refining our understanding of language attitudes. *Journal of Language and Social Psychology*, 18, 101–10.

Edwards, J. R. & Jacobsen, M. (1987) Standard and regional standard speech: distinctions and similarities. *Language in Society*, 16, 369–80.

El-Dash, L. G. & Busnardo, J. (2001) Brazilian attitudes toward English: dimensions of status and solidarity. *International Journal of Applied Linguistics*, 11, 57–68.

Elwell, C. M., Brown, R. J., & Rutter, D. R. (1984) Effects of accent and visual information on impression formation. *Journal of Language and Social Psychology*, 3, 297–99.

Fielding, G. & Evered, C. (1980) The influence of patients' speech upon doctors. In R. N. St. Clair & H. Giles (eds.), *The social and psychological contexts of language* (pp. 51–72). Hillsdale, NJ: Erlbaum.

Fishbein, M. & Ajzen, I. (1975) *Beliefs, attitude, intention and behavior*. Reading, MA: Addison-Wesley.

Flores, N. & Hopper, R. (1975) Mexican Americans' evaluation of spoken Spanish and English. *Speech Monographs*, 42, 91–8.

Gallois, C., Callan, V., & Johnstone, M. (1984) Personality judgements of Australian Aborigine and white speakers: ethnicity, sex and context. *Journal of Language and Social Psychology*, 3, 39–57.

Garrett, P. (2001) Language attitudes and sociolinguistics. *Journal of Sociolinguistics*, 5, 626–31.

Garrett, P., Coupland, N., & Williams, A. (1995) "City harsh" and "The Welsh version of RP": some ways in which teachers view dialects of Welsh English. *Language Awareness*, 2, 99–107.

Garrett, P., Coupland, N., & Williams, A. (1999) Evaluating dialect in discourse: Teachers' and teenagers' responses to young English speakers in Wales. *Language in Society*, 28, 321–54.

Genesee, F. & Holobow, N. E. (1989) Change and stability in intergroup perceptions. *Journal of Language and Social Psychology*, 8, 17–38.

Giles, H. (1973) Communicative effectiveness as a function of accented speech. *Speech Monographs*, 40, 330–1.

Giles, H. (1990) Social meanings of Welsh-English. In N. Coupland (ed.), *English in Wales: diversity, conflict, and change* (pp. 258–82). Clevedon, UK: Multilingual Matters.

Giles, H., Baker, S., & Fielding, G. (1975) Communication length as a behavioral index of accent prejudice. *International Journal of the Sociology of Language*, 6, 73–81.

Giles, H. & Bourhis, R. Y. (1976) Methodological issues in dialect perception: some social psychological perspectives. *Anthropological Linguistics*, 18, 294–304.

Giles, H. & Coupland, N. (1991) Language attitudes: discursive, contextual and gerontological considerations. In A. G. Reynolds (ed.), *Bilingualism, multiculturalism, and second language learning* (pp. 21–42). Hillsdale, NJ: Erlbaum.

Giles, H., Coupland, N., Henwood, K., Harriman, J., & Coupland, J. (1990) The social meaning of RP: a intergenerational perspective. In S. Ramsaran (ed.), *Studies in the pronunciation of English: a commemorative volume in honor of A. C. Gimson* (pp. 191–221). London: Routledge.

Giles, H. & Edwards, J. R. (eds.) (1983) Language attitudes in multicultural settings. *Journal of Multilingual and Multicultural Development*, 4, 81–236.

Giles, H. & Farrar, K. (1979) Some behavioral consequences of speech and dress styles. *British Journal of Social and Clinical Psychology*, 18, 209–10.

Giles, H., Harrison, C., Creber, C., Smith, P. M., & Freeman, N. H. (1983) Developmental and contextual aspects of British children's language attitudes. *Language and Communication*, 3, 1–6.

Giles, H., Henwood, K., Coupland, N., Harriman, J., & Coupland, J. (1992) Language attitudes and cognitive mediation. *Human Communication Research*, 18, 500–27.

Giles, H., Hewstone, M., Ryan, E. B., & Johnson, P. (1987) Research on language attitudes. In U. Ammon, N. Dittmar & K. J. Mattheier (eds.), *Sociolinguistics: an international handbook of the science of language and society* (pp. 585–97). New York: de Gruyter.

Giles, H. & Johnson, P. (1986) Perceived threat, ethnic commitment and interethnic language behavior. In Y. Kim (ed.), *Interethnic communication: current research* (pp. 91–116). Beverly Hills: Sage.

Giles, H. & Niedzielski, N. (1998) German sounds awful, but Italian is beautiful. In L. Bauer & P. Trudgill (eds.), *Language myths* (pp. 85–93). Harmondsworth, UK: Penguin.

Giles, H. & Pierson, H. D. (1988) Social inferences from language proficiency in Hong Kong: a reinterpretation of Hui and Yam. *British Journal of Social Psychology*, 27, 279–81.

Giles, H. & Powesland, P. F. (1975) *Speech style and social evaluation*. London, Academic Press.

Giles, H. & Ryan, E. B. (1982) Prolegomena for developing a social psychological theory of language attitudes. In E. B. Ryan & H. Giles (eds.), *Attitudes towards language variation* (pp. 208–23). London: Edward Arnold.

Giles, H. & Sassoon, C. (1983) The effects of speakers' accent, social class, background and message style on British listeners' social judgements. *Language and Communication*, 3, 305–13.

Giles, H., Williams, A., Mackie, D. M., & Rosselli, F. (1995) Reactions to Anglo- and Hispanic-American-accented speakers: affect, identity, persuasion, and the English-only controversy. *Language and Communication*, 15, 107–20.

Giles, H., Wilson, P., & Conway, A. (1981) Accent and lexical diversity as determinants of impression formation and employment selection. *Language Sciences*, 3, 92–103.

Gill, M. M. (1994) Accent and stereotypes: their effect on perceptions of teacher and lecture comprehension. *Journal of Applied Communication Research*, 22, 348–61.

Hewstone, M. (1989) *Attribution theory*. Oxford: Blackwell.

Hogg, M., Joyce, N., & Abrams, D. (1984) Diglossia in Switzerland? A social identity analysis of speaker evaluations. *Journal of Language and Social Psychology*, 3, 185–96.

Hopper, R. & Williams, F. (1973) Speech characteristics and employability. *Speech Monographs*, 46, 296–302.

Hui, H. C. & Yam, Y-M. (1987) Effects of language proficiency and physical attractiveness on person perception. *British Journal of Social Psychology*, 26, 257–61.

Huygens, I. & Vaughn, G. M. (1984) Language attitudes, ethnicity, and social class in New Zealand. *Journal of Multilingual and Multicultural Development*, 4, 207–24.

Jaccard, J. (1981) Attitudes and behavior: implications of attitudes toward behavioral alternatives. Journal *of Experimental Social Psychology*, 17, 286–307.

Jarvella, R. J., Bang, E., Jakobsen, A. L., & Mees, I. M. (2001) Of mouths and men: nonnative listeners' identification and evaluation of varieties of English. *International Journal of Applied Linguistics*, 11, 37–56.

Kelley, H. (1967) Attribution theory in social psychology. *Nebraska Symposium on Motivation*, 15, 192–238. Lincoln, NE: University of Nebraska Press.

Kelley, H. (1972) The process of causal attribution. *American Psychologist*, 28, 107–28.

Kristiansen, T. (ed.). (2001a) Changing representations of standardness in late modernity: the case of Denmark. *Language Awareness*, 10, 1–71.

Kristiansen, T. (2001b) Two standards: one for the media and one for school. *Language Awareness*, 10, 9–24.

Kristiansen, T. & Giles, H. (1992) Compliance-gaining as a function of accent: public requests in varieties of Danish. *International Journal of Applied Linguistics*, 2, 17–35.

Labov, W. (1966) *The social stratification of English in New York City.* Washington, DC: Centre for Applied Linguistics.

Lambert, W. E. (1967) A social psychology of bilingualism. *Journal of Social Issues*, 23, 91–109.

Lambert, W. E., Hodgson, R., Gardner, R. C., & Fillenbaum, S. (1960) Evaluational reactions to spoken languages. *Journal of Abnormal and Social Psychology*, 60, 44–51.

Lippi-Green, R. (1997) *English with an accent: language, ideology, and discrimination in the United States.* New York: Routledge.

Lippman, W. (1922) *Public opinion.* New York: Harcourt, Brace.

Long, D. & Yim, Y-C. (2000) Perceptions of regional variation in Korean. *Gengo Kenkyu: Journal of the Linguistics Society of Japan*, 117, 37–69.

Luhman, R. (1990) Appalachian English stereotypes: language attitudes in Kentucky. *Language in Society*, 19, 331–48.

Milroy, L. & Preston, D. (eds.) (1999) Attitudes, perception, and linguistic features. *Journal of Language and Social Psychology*, 18, 4–112.

Mulac, A., Hanley, T. D., & Prigge, D. Y. (1974) Effects of phonological speech foreignness upon three dimensions of attitude of selected American listeners. *Quarterly Journal of Speech*, 60, 411–20.

Ohama, M. L. F., Gotay, C. C., Pagano, I. S., Boles, L., & Craven, D. D. (2000) Evaluations of Hawaii Creole English and standard English. *Journal of Language and Social Psychology*, 19, 357–77.

Paltridge, J. & Giles, H. (1984) Attitudes towards speakers of regional accents of French: Effects of regionality, age and sex of listeners. *Linguistische Berichte*, 90, 71–85.

Papapapvlou, A. N. (1998) Attitudes toward the Greek Cypriot dialect: sociocultural implications. *International Journal of the Sociology of Language*, 134, 15–28.

Pear, T. H. (1931) *Voice and personality.* London: Wiley.

Potter, J. & Wetherell, M. (1987) *Discourse and social psychology: beyond attitude and behavior.* London: Sage.

Powesland, P. & Giles, H. (1975) Persuasiveness and accent-message incompatibility. *Human Relations*, 28, 85–93.

Preston, D. (ed.) (1999) *Handbook of perceptual dialectology* (vol. 1). Amsterdam: John Benjamins.

Price, S., Fluck, M., & Giles, H. (1983) The effects of testing bilingual pre-adolescents' attitudes towards Welsh and varieties of English. *Journal of Multilingual and Multicultural Development*, 4, 149–62.

Purnell, T., Isdardi, W., & Baugh, J. (1999) Perceptual and phonetic experiments on American English dialect identification. *Journal of Language and Social Psychology*, 18, 10–30.

Ryan, E. B. & Giles, H. (eds.) (1982) *Attitudes toward language variation.* London: Edward Arnold.

Ryan, E. B. & Sebastian, R. J. (1980) The effects of speech style and social class background on social judgements of speakers. *British Journal of Social and Clinical Psychology*, 19, 229–33.

Ryan, E. B., Carranza, M. A., & Moffie, R. W. (1977) Reactions towards varying degrees of accentedness in the speech of Spanish-English. *Language and Speech*, 20, 267–73.

Ryan, E. B., Giles, H., & Bradac, J. J. (eds.) (1994) Recent studies in language attitudes. *Language and Communication*, 14, 211–312.

Ryan, E. B., Giles, H., & Sebastian, R. J. (1982) An integrative perspective for the study of attitudes toward language variation. In E. B. Ryan & H. Giles (eds.), *Attitudes towards language variation* (pp. 1–19). London: Edward Arnold.

Seggie, I. (1983) Attribution of guilt as a function of ethnic accent and type of crime. *Journal of Multilingual and Multicultural Development*, 4, 197–206.

Seggie, I., Smith, N., & Hodgins, P. (1986) Evaluations of employment suitability based on accent alone: an Australian case study. *Language Sciences*, 8, 129–40.

Seligman, C., Tucker, G. R., & Lambert, W. E. (1972) The effects of speech style and other attributes on teachers' attitudes toward pupils. *Language in Society*, 1, 131–42.

Shuy, R. & Fasold, R. W. (eds.) (1969) *Language attitudes: current trends and prospects*. Washington, DC: Center for Applied Linguistics.

St. Clair, R. N. (1982) From social history to language attitudes. In E. B. Ryan & H. Giles (eds.), *Attitudes toward language variation* (pp. 164–74). London: Edward Arnold.

Stewart, M. A., Ryan, E. B., & Giles, H. (1985) Accent and social class effects on status and solidarity evaluations. *Personality and Social Psychology Bulletin*, 11, 98–105.

Street, R. L., Jr. & Hopper, R. (1982) A model of speech style evaluation. In E. B. Ryan & H. Giles (eds.), *Attitudes towards language variation* (pp. 175–88). London, Arnold.

Tajfel, H. (1959) A note on Lambert's "Evaluational reactions to spoken language." *Canadian Journal of Psychology*, 13, 86–92.

Thakerar, J. N. & Giles, H. (1981) They are – so they speak: noncontent speech stereotypes. *Language and Communication*, 1, 251–5.

Tong, Y-Y., Hong, Y-Y., Lee, S-L., & Chiu, C-Y. (1999) Language use as a carrier of social identity. *International Journal of Intercultural Relations*, 23, 281–96.

Trudgill, P. & Giles, H. (1978) Sociolinguistics and linguistic value judgements: correctness, adequacy and aesthetics. In F. Coppiertiers & D. Goyvaerts (eds.), *The functions of language and literature studies* (pp. 161–90). Ghent: Story Scientia.

Williams, F. (1976) *Explorations of the linguistic attitudes of teachers*. Rowley, MA: Newbury House.

Woolard, K. A. & Gahng, T-J. (1990) Changing language policies and attitudes in autonomous Catalonia. *Language in Society*, 19, 311–30.

Zahn, C. J. & Hopper, R. (1985) Measuring language attitudes: the speech evaluation instrument. *Journal of Language and Social Psychology*, 4, 113–23.

Zhou, M. (2001) The spread of Putonghua and language attitude changes in Shanghai and Guangzhou, China. *Journal of Asian Pacific Communication*, 11, 231–54.

FURTHER READING

Bourhis, R. Y. (1982) Language policies and language attitudes: Le monde de la Francophonie. In E. B. Ryan & H. Giles (eds.), *Attitudes toward language variation: social and applied contexts* (pp. 34–62). London: Edward Arnold.

Bourhis, R. Y. & Giles, H. (1976) The language of co-operation in Wales: a field study. *Language Sciences*, 42, 13–16.

Farb, P. (1973) *Word play: what happens when people talk.* New York: Knopf.

Fuertes, J. N., Potere, J. C., & Ramirez, K. Y. (2002) Effects of speech accents on interpersonal evaluations: implications for counseling practice and research. *Cultural Diversity and Ethnic Minority Psychology*, 8, 346–56.

Giles, H. & Street, R. (1994) Communicator characteristics and behavior. In M. L. Knapp & G. R. Miller (eds.), *Handbook of interpersonal communication* (2nd edn.) (pp. 103–61). Beverly Hills: Sage.

Jones, E., Gallois, C., Barker, M., & Callan, V. J. (1994) Evaluations of interactions between students and academic staff: Influence of communication accommodation, ethnic group, and status. *Journal of Language and Social Psychology*, 13, 158–91.

Kalin, R. & Rayko, D. (1980) The social significance of speech in the job interview. In R. N. St. Clair & H. Giles (eds.), *The social and psychological contexts of language* (pp. 39–50). Hillsdale, NJ: Erlbaum.

8 Language Attrition

MONIKA S. SCHMID AND
KEES DE BOT

8.1 Introduction

Language attrition (for the purpose of this article, the discussion will be confined to the attrition of an L1) is often considered to be a reversal of language acquisition. On the most general level, this definition is fairly uncontroversial: where language acquisition is a process during which the proficiency in a first or second language increases, in the process of language attrition, lack of contact leads to a reduced level of proficiency in the attriting language. (We find definitions which base language acquisition not only on actual loss of knowledge that can be shown or assumed to have been there at a previous time, but on "incomplete acquisition" as well (Polinsky, 1994, p. 257) to be unhelpful for the description of language attrition.)

The task of the study of language attrition is to provide a more detailed analysis and explanation of this rather idealized picture, to describe the observed process of loss from linguistic as well as sociolinguistic perspectives, and to try and model the (contact) variety of the attriting language within given theoretical frameworks. Such an analysis has to take into account observed differences in the application of rules of grammar and lexical selection between attrited and non-attrited language use (i.e., what are commonly perceived as "mistakes"), but ideally it should also attempt to describe the linguistic behavior of attriters and non-attriters from a more holistic perspective. The analysis should therefore include aspects of the attriting language even where it is not "deviant" in an immediately obvious way, e.g., by establishing factors such as type-token frequency, lexical richness, or grammatical complexity. Any study that focuses merely on "what is lost," i.e., on "mistakes" in the speech of an attriter, fails to take into account avoidance strategies that she might have developed in order to deal with her reduced capabilities. If these strategies are perfected in a simplification of the linguistic system, her speech might very well show up little or no "interferences" at all, and the emerging picture might be skewed if "deviant" utterances are all that is considered.

The picture of the attrited language which thus emerges should help us understand how different linguistic levels are affected by the attritional process, how different sociolinguistic variables affect the attritional process, and whether any of the theoretical models available can account for these observations.

8.2   Models and Theories

There are predominantly four theoretical models and frameworks available to the study of language attrition:

1   Jakobson's regression hypothesis,
2   language contact and language change,
3   Universal Grammar and parameter setting,
4   psycholinguistic questions of accessibility.

However, the division between these frameworks cannot be drawn as neatly as this list might lead one to suspect. Often theories will overlap, or features of an observed attritional variety can equally well be accounted for by several of these theories or by an interaction of them. Moreover, some of the theoretical aspects underlying these different hypotheses are related. For example, in the search for universal linguistic mechanisms, parallels between language change, language acquisition, and (pathological) language loss have been pointed out. This suggests that the evolution of a linguistic system over a long time in a language community and over a short time in an individual might follow some of the same or similar principles (cf. de Bot & Weltens, 1991).

8.2.1   Regression

The regression hypothesis has a tradition that goes back far longer than any other theory in language loss: it was first formulated by Ribot in the 1880s, and taken up again by Freud in connection with aphasia. It was Roman Jakobson who in the 1940s integrated it into a linguistic framework, specifically in the area of phonology (Jakobson, 1941). At the center of this hypothesis is the assumption that

> [t]he pattern of language dissolution in aphasics is similar, but in reverse order, to the pattern of language acquisition in children. Those aspects of language competence acquired last, or, more precisely, those that are most dependent on other linguistic developments, are likely to be the first to be disrupted consequent to brain damage; those aspects of language competence that are acquired earliest and are thus "independent" of later developments are likely to be most resistant to effects of brain damage.   (Caramazza & Zurif, 1978, p. 145)

The regression hypothesis has been the subject of much debate in research on both pathological and non-pathological loss. It is probably generally accepted nowadays that this hypothesis does not provide a conclusive framework for aphasia (Berko-Gleason, 1982, p. 17; Caramazza & Zurif 1978, p. 146). However, the fact that languages are acquired in stages by children has been taken to suggest that language competence is "layered," and that attrition will work its way from the topmost layer to the bottom (Andersen, 1982, p. 97; Berko-Gleason, 1982, p. 14; Caramazza & Zurif, 1978, p. 145; Seliger, 1991, p. 227). A related approach is based on the notion of frequency of reinforcement, hypothesizing that it is not what is learned *first* but what is learned *best* that is least vulnerable to language loss (Berko-Gleason, 1982, p. 21; Jordens et al., 1986, p. 161; Lambert, 1989, p. 7).

The difference between these two lines of thought, as well as the major theoretical problem in connection with the regression hypothesis, can be reduced to the two basic competing frameworks in the theory of L1 acquisition: the nativist (or Chomskyan) and the cognitivist (or Piagetian) approach. If the sequence of L1 acquisition is seen as determined by an innate language learning capacity developing autonomously (Chomsky, 1965, pp. 27–37), then the hypothesis that the loss of this autonomous system will proceed in inverse order appears at least possible. The linguistic system could "atrophy" due to lack of use, and this atrophying process could be the reverse of the acquisitional one. If, on the other hand, the linguistic capacity is seen as being paced by the growth of conceptual and communicative capacities in L1 acquisition, then such an assumption would not make sense: in non-pathological language attrition, it is not the conceptual and communicative skills that are affected, but the lexical and grammatical system. If the cognitive concepts that are seen as the prerequisites for the acquisition of a certain feature – e.g., the concept of singularity and plurality, which the child must have in order to acquire the singular/plural distinction – are not lost, there is no reason why the grammatical features that express them should be.

Studies of language attrition using this framework: Jordens et al. (1986); Jordens, de Bot, and Trapman (1989); Håkansson (1995); Schmid (2002).

8.2.2   *Language contact and language change*

The notion that in situations of language contact and ensuing language change the modifications that can be observed in the linguistic system of one of these languages are entirely or in parts due to one language's encroaching on the other is fairly widespread and probably true to some extent. In the lexical, or open-class domain, at least, it is hard to see where effects like code-switching and code-mixing should come from, if not directly from the linguistic system of the L2.

In the grammatical system, however, a clear distinction of cases of language contact from modifications within the linguistic system of one language that are not due to influences from the other is often problematic. Studies on language death as well as situations of intense language contact, e.g., creolization, have often discovered modifications within a linguistic system that cannot be explained by interlanguage effects alone. The distinction between *externally* and *internally* induced linguistic change in language attrition was made by Seliger & Vago (1991, p. 10), who identified different strategies of linguistic change caused by these two forces.

Studies of attrition within this framework have to be based on a comparison of linguistic features of both languages, trying to isolate phenomena that can only be due to interlanguage effects against mistakes that are internally induced. In this context, the role of contrast between the two languages is clearly a determining factor, but speculations as to its effect are contradictory: it has been hypothesized that features that are cognate in L1 and L2 are more likely to be retained while categories that do not have an equivalent in the L2 will be lost both in language attrition and language death (Andersen, 1982, p. 97; Lambert, 1989, p. 7; Romaine, 1989, p. 75; Sharwood Smith, 1989, p. 193; U. Weinreich, 1953, p. 43). However, an alternative hypothesis is that at a certain stage in language attrition, due to lack of input in the attriting language (AL), the grammar of the non-attriting language (NAL) will become a source of "indirect positive evidence" which will affect grammaticality judgments in the AL (Seliger, 1991, p. 237). The two linguistic systems will interact in those domains where both of them contain a rule which serves the same semantic function, and "that version of the rule which is formally less complex and has a wider linguistic distribution . . . will replace the more complex more narrowly distributed rule" (Seliger, 1989, p. 173). It should be noted that the distinction between interlanguage and language change effects is often very hard, if not impossible, to draw. Analytical structures can develop in contact languages, even where both linguistic systems have highly developed synthetic structures. However, they can also arise out of processes of non-contact-induced linguistic change.

Difficulties in the distinction of processes of interlanguage vs. internal simplification of a system notwithstanding, some processes that were predicted or have been shown to obtain in language attrition are qualitatively different from processes that could be explained by interlanguage alone. (This, however, does not preclude the possibility that, once gaps in the linguistic system of the AL have been created, NAL elements might move in to fill the voids thus created.) Language loss is thus often seen as a form of language change that is speeded up within the individual or within the community. Some of these predictions have been empirically verified (see e.g., Schmidt, 1991 on Dyirbal under the influence of English; Dorian, 1982 on East Sutherland Gaelic under the influence of English; and Håkansson, 1995 on the L1 attrition of Swedish in English/Swedish or French/Swedish bilinguals).

Studies of language attrition using this framework: Altenberg (1991); Kauffman & Aronoff (1991); Köpke (1999); Maher (1991); Major (1992); Vago (1991).

8.2.3   Universal Grammar (UG)

At a very basic level, the UG approach to language attrition is not unrelated to the regression hypothesis, since it also considers acquisitional factors. It is, however, not so much based on an observable sequence of acquisition but on grammatical reasons for this sequence.

The parameter view on language acquisition and language attrition is based on Chomsky's notion of a UG which contains a set of fixed principles and certain open parameters which are set during the acquisitional process (Chomsky, 1981, p. 4; Ingram, 1989, p. 64; Seliger & Vago, 1991, p. 12). This theory is complicated by the assumption that certain parameters carry a pre-ferred or unmarked setting, which, in the absence of evidence to the contrary, will be the value assigned to the specific feature.

The parameter view has instigated many studies into first and second language acquisition, with a view to establishing factors such as:

- Are children born with an innate knowledge about universal properties of the linguistic system?
- If a parameter is set to a specific value, can that setting ever be neutralized (e.g., in L2 acquisition, if the settings for L2 differ from those of L1)?
- the role of markedness in this context: Can a marked parameter be reset to an unmarked setting in L2 acquisition?

Within the framework of L1 attrition, it has been proposed that this process might involve the "unmarking" of parameters that have been set to a marked value in L1 (Håkansson, 1995, p. 155; Sharwood Smith, 1989, p. 199). However, Sharwood Smith & van Buren hypothesize that since parameter settings are influenced by evidence from input, and since language attrition is character-ized by lack of evidence through lack of contact, marked values in the L1 might persist (Sharwood Smith & van Buren, 1991, p. 26). As yet, there are no data to support this view.

Studies of language attrition using this framework: Håkansson (1995); Montrul (2002).

8.2.4   Psycholinguistics

The psycholinguistic model of language attrition augments the perspectives on language internal and acquisitional factors by taking into account features of processing and memory retrieval, dealing with more general psychological issues like the accessing and forgetting of information. It thus reflects the growing emphasis on psycholinguistic processes in bilingual speech production at large that the past decade has witnessed.

For some time now, attrition researchers have attempted to establish whether evidence for attrition is evidence for something being irretrievably "lost" or merely an indication of a temporary problem of accessibility – an issue that is somewhat related to the competence–performance debate in language attrition. The question of whether attrition merely affects procedural knowledge, or whether the actual knowledge of a language can become deteriorated (Ammerlaan, 1996, p. 10) – or, on a more general level, whether knowledge once acquired can ever be lost from memory – has not conclusively been resolved, but evidence overwhelmingly points toward what difficulties there are being only temporary.

Studies of language attrition using this framework: Ammerlaan (1996); Hulsen (2000); Hulsen, de Bot & Weltens (1999); Köpke (1999); Schoenmakers-Klein Gunnewiek (1998).

8.3   Linguistic Levels

Ever since Weinreich's seminal study on language contact (U. Weinreich, 1953), contact linguistics has attempted to provide a classification of linguistic material in terms of likelihood for transfer. It is generally agreed that there is a cline of "borrowability" within the linguistic system; that lexical items are borrowed more easily than functional or grammatical ones; that nouns are more easily borrowed than verbs, and so on (Muysken, 1999; Romaine, 1989, p. 65; Wilkins, 1996). This has led to the assumption that the attritional process might not be an overall decline of linguistic proficiency, but that certain levels or faculties might be affected earlier or more profoundly than others. Consequently, it has often been hypothesized that language attrition will first manifest itself on the level of the lexicon, and only later move on to affect grammatical and syntactic categories.

8.3.1   Lexicon

Where lexical items are concerned, "interferences" of several types can occur. The first and surely most widespread of these is the use of NAL items in AL discourse. This is a frequent feature in the discourse of bilinguals, especially with other bilingual interlocutors, and it is very doubtful whether simple code-switching can be considered evidence for attrition. Suffice it to say that the use of an NAL item does not necessarily license the conclusion that the speaker has "lost" the corresponding AL items (Romaine, 1989, p. 143) or even that she cannot access it within the time span allocated for that task in on-line discourse; she might also feel that the NAL item is for some reason more "appropriate," "sounds better," or is more salient. Some pragmatic functions of code-switching – such as providing "local color" or flagging quotations – have been pointed out by Appel & Muysken (1987) and Romaine (1989, p. 160ff.).

A second area in which the lexicon may be affected in language attrition is that of specificity of meaning. This can manifest itself in different ways, e.g., what has been called "(semantic) extension" (Romaine, 1989, p. 56), "semantic transfer" (de Bot & Clyne, 1994, p. 20) or "loanshift" (Haugen, 1953). In this type of interference, the meaning of a word from the base language is extended so that it corresponds to that of another language, leading to overgeneralizations. Consider the case of English *take* and *break*. In some cases, the German equivalents of these verbs, *nehmen* and *brechen* respectively, are adequate translations, in others they are not, as is illustrated by English *to take a sandwich* and German *ein Brot nehmen*, but English *to take a picture* and German **ein Foto nehmen* (→ *ein Foto machen*). It has been shown that such selectional restrictions are vulnerable to language attrition, in some cases extending to composite items, yielding what has been called a "calque," i.e. a morpheme-by-morpheme translation, as in the case of English *look after* which is translated to German *nachschauen* 'look up' and used instead of the semantic equivalent *sich kümmern* (Altenberg, 1991, p. 198ff.; Clyne, 1981, p. 32).

A further type of mistake that sometimes occurs in the speech of attriters is that an AL word which is homophonous to an NAL item with a different meaning is used in inappropriate contexts (Romaine, 1989, p. 56). An example of such an interference is given by Schmid (2002, p. 33) who found the German verb *zerstreuen* ('to scatter') used with the meaning of English *destroy*, instead of the appropriate German *zerstören*.

Interferences of all these types are easily spotted and analyzed in attrition studies, since they show up on the "surface level" of utterances. Much more difficult to find is evidence for a predicted reduction of the vocabulary, i.e., a loss in lexical richness. It has often been hypothesized that this will be one of the most prominent characteristics of an attriter's speech (Andersen, 1982, p. 94; Grendel, Weltens, & de Bot, 1993, p. 59; Olshtain, 1989, p. 162; Olshtain & Barzilay, 1991, p. 146; Yağmur, 1997, p. 9).

Several studies have attempted to find evidence for or against such a reduction. The hypothesis that it will manifest itself first in low-frequency, highly marked lexical items (Andersen, 1982, p. 94) was tested through a retelling of a picture book (the 'Frog story') and an analysis of overgeneralized use of frequent, general terms in situations where a more specified term is required provided evidence to support this hypothesis (Olshtain & Barzilay, 1991; Yağmur, 1997). A further test that has been conducted in this framework is Fluency in Controlled Association (Waas, 1996; Yağmur, 1997).

Since both these tests establish lexical richness in a specific field only, a broader approach might be desirable. This could be established through type/token ratios of a larger stretch of discourse or (ideally) through an analysis of the distributional frequencies of the tokens used in native speech. This is extremely tedious and time-consuming work, which may account for the fact that few studies to this date have conducted such an analysis on the data collected (de Bot & Clyne, 1994; Schmid, 2002). The only study so far which compares these findings to data from a monolingual control group (Schmid, forthcoming) does find evidence for a significant reduction both of type-token ratios and of word frequencies for all of her attriters.

8.3.2 *Morphology*

Where language attrition in the domain of morphology is concerned, it has been predicted that the attrited variety will exhibit an overall reduction in morphological complexity, resulting in a more analytical structure. Features that have been mentioned in this respect are:

- interlanguage effects in free morphemes,
- reduction in allomorphic variation,
- loss of agreement, especially across phrase boundaries,
- a movement from inflectional devices and allomorphic variation toward more regularized or analytic forms,
- a trend toward periphrastic constructions (e.g., from an inflected future tense to a *go*-future),
- grammatical relations tend to be encoded less by bound morphemes and more by lexemes.

(cf. Andersen, 1982; Hagen & de Bot, 1990; Maher, 1991). The selection of these features is largely based on observations from language contact, language change, and language/dialect death. An interesting hypothesis that has hitherto gone uninvestigated predicts a reduction in morphological distinctions that is dependent on the amount of vital information they contribute to the discourse and suggests that distinctions will be maintained if their loss would result in frequent loss of information (Andersen, 1982, p. 97; Lambert & Moore, 1986, p. 180). This hypothesis presupposes a high awareness of the morphological and functional complexity of the attriting language by the attriter, and it would therefore be interesting to see if it can be verified.

Among these factors, contextually-driven NP inflection appears the stablest in studies on language attrition: Jordens et al. (1986), Jordens, de Bot, and Trapman (1989), Köpke (1999) and Schmid (2002) found little difference between case-marking in German L1 and L2 attriters and non-attrited German. Agreement features that depend on invariable inherent features of the lexical entry (e.g., gender agreement, plural morphology) on the other hand, have been shown to be substantially affected in L1 attrition (Altenberg, 1991; Håkansson, 1995). Bolonyai and Dutkova-Cope (2001) have further shown that late system morphemes, which do not encode semantic relationships but organize sentence constituents into larger morphosyntactic structures and are cross-linguistically less frequent, are more vulnerable to attrition than early system morphemes in the L1 attrition of Hungarian and Czech-English early and late bilinguals.

It has furthermore been shown that free grammatical morphemes, especially function words and articles, are very vulnerable to interlanguage effects (Olshtain, 1989, p. 160; Clyne, 1981, p. 34). Often, one of several possible items is overgeneralized, as was found for the use of the German auxiliary *haben* (Clyne, 1981, p. 34). It has been hypothesized that the domain of morphology might be the linguistic level on which it is hardest for the attriter to develop avoidance strategies. While it seems conceivable that an attriter might come to prefer intransitive over transitive verbs and thus arrive at an overall less complex argument structure than a non-attriter, it is hard to conceive of a strategy that would reduce inherent inflectional categories like gender and plural morphology. Language attrition studies have therefore largely concentrated on the ungrammatical structures that resulted from the overgeneralization of regular or more frequent instances of inflection, e.g., the regular plural allomorph -s in English or the most frequent gender of nouns. However, a more recent study (Schmid, forthcoming) did find evidence to suggest that avoidance strategies to achieve an overall reduction of inflectional morphology can be developed in first language attrition: in comparison with a monolingual control group, her attriters used significantly fewer items in the plural, fewer synthetic tenses, and more nominative vs. oblique cases.

8.3.3   Syntax

The assumption that word order is a domain which is vulnerable to simplification processes in language attrition seems intuitively convincing: many languages offer their speakers the possibility to express what they want to say in structures with a variation in complexity, e.g., hypotactical structures with a large number of embedded clauses vs. straight paratactical constructions. The information load more complex structures carry is generally comparatively low, and a trend away from more elaborate constructions – e.g., avoidance of embedded clauses – will often not result in ungrammatical utterances.

Given these presuppositions, it seems strange that syntax in attrition has hardly been explored to this date. The only studies that have investigated this feature in detail are Yağmur's investigation of Turkish relative clauses, Håkansson's study of the V2 rule in Swedish, and Schmid on verbal placement in German. Yağmur found the late-acquired complex Turkish forms of relative clauses to be most vulnerable to language loss among the features he investigated (Yağmur, 1997, p. 95), while Håkansson's data contained only three violations of the V2 rule in Swedish, all of them occurring in the data from one informant. Furthermore, she found that the distribution of V2 (verb second) and SVO (subject verb object) structures almost exactly paralleled that in monolingual Swedish (Håkansson, 1995, p. 160). Schmid's findings, on the other hand, suggest a slight tendency to overgeneralize the L2 English SVO rule in German L1 attriters (Schmid, 2002, p. 168) and a dispreference for hypotactical, embedded, and long sentences (Schmid, forthcoming).

8.4   Sociolinguistic Factors

It is generally accepted that language attrition is only partly determined by internal linguistic factors. Specific features of a certain language may be more vulnerable to attrition than others – a highly developed inflectional system may be subject to "mistakes" in a contact situation more quickly than SVO word order. However, external and social factors also play a role. Such factors comprise sociolinguistic variables like age, gender, education, etc., as well as the amount of contact the individual has with the attriting language and the length of time elapsed since the onset of attrition. However, language attrition might also be influenced by factors which operate on the level of society, and these are far more elusive to describe, determine, and operationalize. Such factors can largely be subsumed under theories of prestige, (ethnic) identity, and assimilation.

8.4.1   Age at onset of attrition

The "critical period" hypothesis for language acquisition in general and L2 acquisition in particular has been contested in some points; and today, the influence of age on second language acquisition is still very much in doubt. Where language attrition, and especially L1 attrition, is concerned, however, one immediately relevant factor of age is the level of achievement at the onset of attrition. In the hypothetical case of a child emigrating at age six and not being given the chance to speak her first language from that point onward, the linguistic abilities of a six-year-old child will obviously have to be the base-line for comparison in a study of language attrition, and she cannot be compared to an attriter who had reached adult age before her emigration.

To what degree attrition – as opposed to failure to acquire – is influenced by the age at the onset of non-contact beyond this has not been determined so far. There are a number of studies which observe immigrants who had been very young when input in their L1 became reduced (Kauffman & Aronoff, 1991; Seliger, 1991; Turian & Altenberg, 1991; Vago, 1991 – all of these studies investigate children who had been less than six years old at this point). Others use "adult" informants, although the age at which the acquisition of the first language is considered completed varies between 14 (Köpke, 1999), 15 (de Bot & Clyne, 1989, 1994; Clyne, 1973, 1981), 16 (Waas, 1996; Schmid, 2002) and 17 years (de Bot, Gommans, & Rossing, 1991).

Among these researchers, only Köpke and Schmid attempted to determine the effect of age at emigration, but this distinction did not show significant effects on any linguistic level of attrition (Köpke, 1999, p. 203ff.; Schmid, 2002, p. 175). This suggests that, once a linguistic feature has been acquired, the length of time which elapses between the completion of acquisition and the onset of attrition is of little or no consequence to the attritional process.

8.4.2   Education

Very little research has been devoted to the influence of the education level on language attrition. The only studies that included education among their independent variables are those by Jaspaert & Kroon (1989) and Köpke (1999). The results from these two studies are contradictory: In Jaspaert & Kroon's study, education turned out to be the most important explanatory factor for language loss (p. 92). They hypothesize that the reason for this influence might either be purely material – a higher level of education, on the whole, making for a better financial situation and allowing more trips home – or be linked to a higher familiarity with the written code and thus offering more chances for contact. A third hypothesis put forward is that "maybe their education provides them with a better insight in the structure of language," thus making retention easier (p. 92ff.). For Köpke, on the other hand, the level of education did not show significant results for attrition on any linguistic level (Köpke, 1999, p. 204).

Yağmur treats education as an ambivalent factor which might either facilitate the shift to L2 (through better instruction) or be conductive to a higher degree of maintenance of the L1 (Yağmur, 1997, p. 20). A higher level of education has also been cited by Clyne in explanation of the fact that he found a greater tendency toward maintenance of the L1 in pre-war German emigrants to Australia than in an otherwise comparable group of post-war emigrants (1973, p. 97). It may also be the case that the level of education affects the informants' performance on different tests (e.g., free speech vs. metalinguistic judgments). Differences in the test results may therefore not be an adequate reflection of linguistic proficiency for groups with different educational levels, but merely be the outcome of some speakers' being more comfortable with specific test settings.

8.4.3   Time

The findings from several studies suggest that the time span elapsed since the onset of attrition does not matter to the degree one might suspect. In fact, it seems generally agreed for L1 attrition that what attrition of linguistic skills takes place does so within the first decade of emigration (de Bot & Clyne, 1994, p. 17; de Bot, Gommans, & Rossing, 1991). De Bot & Clyne therefore conclude that "first-language attrition does not necessarily take place in an immigrant setting and that those immigrants who manage to maintain their language in the first years of their stay in the new environment are likely to remain fluent speakers of their first language" (1994, p. 17).

Köpke, on the other hand, finds differences in the amount of errors produced on some linguistic levels between her English- and French-speaking L1 German attriters, for whom the average time of emigration shows great variance. However, she points out that this divergence cannot unambiguously be ascribed to these factors, and concludes that her findings do not contradict those of de Bot et al. (Köpke, 1999, p. 342).

8.4.4   Gender

In many studies on language change and variation, the gender of the informants appears to be an important sociolinguistic variable (e.g., Wodak & Benke,

basis of historical accounts on National-Socialist anti-Semitic persecution. For her data, the degree of persecution the individual had suffered proved to be the single most important explanatory factor.

8.4.8 *Data collection*

The unspoken assumption that language attrition leads to a diminished ability to perform certain linguistic tasks, and that this reduction can best be measured on the basis of errors, has been the basis of practically all language attrition studies done so far. It is only in the area of the lexicon that there have occasionally been attempts to provide a picture on the full repertoire, usually on the basis of picture naming or verbal fluency tests (Ammerlaan, 1996; Hulsen, 2000; Schoenmakers-Klein Gunnewiek, 1998; Waas, 1996; Yağmur, 1997). (A slightly different approach was taken by Olshtain & Barzilay (1991) who used re-tellings of the Frog-story picture-book in order to ascertain whether language attrition would lead to less accurate specificity of semantic meaning.) While the validity of fluency tests in assessing verbal retrieval difficulties in adult aphasics has been demonstrated (Goodglass & Kaplan, 1983), it has not proven an adequate tool to assess such difficulties in normal vs. language disordered children by Hall & Jordan (1987), who conclude that "word-finding problems may be symptoms of a variety of language problems and therefore elude any single identification technique" (p. 109). Such tests cannot, therefore, *a priori* be assumed to be a valid instrument in assessing adult non-pathological language loss. It has also not been demonstrated whether findings from such tests adequately represent "difficulties" the subject encounters in the production of unguided discourse. It would therefore be desirable to include further data, which was obtained through less explicit tests, in order to arrive at a realistic assessment of the range of the lexicon which is retained.

All studies which have been conducted on language attrition on the grammatical level (with the exception of Schmid, 2002, forthcoming) have confined their analysis to "mistakes." Some of these studies used "free" data which was produced either through a spontaneous narrative or story-retellings (Bolonyai & Dutkova-Cope, 2001; de Bot & Clyne, 1994; Leisiö, 2001; Schmid, 2002; Søndergaard, 1996), some elicited their data through translations, grammaticality judgments or explicit grammatical tasks, e.g., presenting a noun in the singular and asking the informant to provide the plural (Altenberg, 1991; Köpke, 1999), or presenting a number of linguistic items in scrambled word order which were then to be rearranged as a relative clause (Yağmur, 1997). Elicited data were further used by Grosjean & Py (1991); Hirvonen (1995); Jordens et al. (1986), Jordens, de Bot, and Trapman (1989); Schoenmakers-Klein Gunnewiek (1998). For some studies, a combination of free and elicited data was used (Polinsky 1994; de Bot, Gommans, & Rossing 1991; Köpke 1999).

This difference between the use of free and elicited data is especially important in studies which focus on errors, since it has been demonstrated at least for first language acquisition that elicited data often contain a number of errors which exceeds that found in free discourse. Since most of these studies of grammatical attrition do not establish a non-attrited control group (the exceptions being Köpke, 1999: Schoenmakers-Klein Gunnewiek, 1998: and Yağmur, 1997), it is difficult to accept accounts of "massive" attrition in findings based on elicited data alone.

The fact that the findings on the degree to which language attrition is present in the data under observation vary so radically among studies is partly due to different methods of data collection. The ways in which the material under analysis has been obtained ranges from the collection of free, unguided discourse (Bolonyai and Dutkova-Cope, 2001; de Bot & Clyne, 1994; Schmid, 2002) through elicited "free" discourse by means of picture description (de Bot, Gommans, & Rossing, 1991; Köpke, 1999; Seliger, 1991), requesting the subject to produce a certain linguistic structure (Altenberg, 1991; Yağmur, 1997), to psycholinguistic tests like Fluency in Controlled Association (FiCA) (Ammerlaan, 1996; Waas, 1996; Yağmur, 1997).

It has not, so far, been comparatively assessed whether the results obtained by these different methods are, in fact, comparable. As far as metalinguistic tasks such as grammaticality judgments (e.g., Altenberg, 1991; Jordens et al., 1986; Jordens, de Bot, and Trapman, 1989) are concerned, it has also not, so far, been demonstrated whether there is a significant correlation between misjudgments of expressions that the subject is presented with and "mistakes" she makes in speech production.

It is evident, therefore, that studies which test very different aspects of the individual attriters' linguistic proficiency, may complement each other and have to be comparatively evaluated in order to arrive at a holistic picture of the attritional process.

8.5   What Is "Language Attrition"?

One of the main reasons why the results from studies of language attrition often seem conflicting is that there is no agreed-upon and testable definition of what, exactly, counts as "attrition." There are several ways in which it has been attempted to establish the "significant restriction" and "lack of adherence to the linguistic norm" which supposedly characterize the language use of an attriter in comparison with a linguistically competent speaker (Andersen, 1982, p. 91). One obvious way to achieve this is to collect data from a monolingual control group and test whether the language use of (presumed) attriters and non-attriters shows any statistically significant differences (Andersen, 1982, p. 85; Jaspaert, Kroon, & van Hout, 1986). (This approach was taken e.g., by Köpke, 1999; Yağmur, 1997. Ammerlaan, 1996 used subjects with a shorter emigration span as a control group.) Secondly, data from attrition studies have sometimes been compared to data gleaned from statistical analyses of the distribution of the variable under investigation in "normal" language data (e.g., Håkansson, 1995). However, the majority of studies done on language attrition so far do without comparisons of this kind. Such an approach tacitly assumes the "mistakes'" that occur in the language of attriters to be "competence errors," while non-attrited speakers' language only contains "performance errors" which "are not representative of their ordinary language use, and which can be corrected by them if they are asked to do so" – slips of the tongue.

However, even studies which adopt a comparative perspective often leave us with an unsatisfactory picture of an "attriter." Even if the study can establish that subjects who have lived in an L2 environment for a certain length of time have statistically significantly more errors in free speech than the monolingual control group (as was the case, for example, in Köpke, 1999), it is often not clear to what degree the reduction in proficiency disrupts communicative skills, from the perspective either of the speaker or her native speaking interlocutors.

A second major problem in language attrition studies is that of dialectal or sociolectal variation in the L1. So far, only one study (Schmid, 2002) has been able to collect data from language attriters who originate from the same region and social class in their country of origin. If the informants come from different dialectal regions or social groups in their country of origin, utterances may show deviations from the standard which the researcher is unable to recognize as being part of the informant's L1 variety. Since no native speaker can be assumed to be proficient in all varieties of her L1, the possibility that the attriter produces structures which are unacceptable to the researcher but may be acceptable in the informant's variety cannot be ruled out.

The fact that any classification of such structures as "interferences" or "mistakes" will yield a skewed picture of some individuals' attrition process leads directly to the next methodological problem in research on language attrition: what is to be counted a "mistake"? Most researchers have made these judgments exclusively on the basis of their own native speaker intuition (with the exception of Köpke (1999) and Schmid (2002), who had every utterance judged by several competent speakers of German, and classified those structures as errors that were objected to by at least two of these judges (Köpke, 1999, p. 163ff.; Schmid, 2002, p. 67)). Native speaker judgments vary to the degree that almost no study will not contain at least some examples that were classified as "mistakes," but will appear perfectly acceptable to other readers who are competent speakers of the language under investigation. Although this possibility can never be ruled out – unless one were to use a potentially infinite number of judges – it can at least be minimized if the data under investigation are rated by native speakers other than the researcher herself.

A fourth issue has already been pointed out above: the overwhelming majority of language attrition studies have concentrated on "what is lost" to the exclusion of "what is retained." This, again, is a factor that may potentially give a biased picture of an individual's proficiency: speakers who are prepared to take more risks by using complex structures will potentially make more "mistakes" than speakers who accept that their control over their L1 is not what it was and consequently use a simplified variety. This means that a study of L1 attrition that wishes to come up with a comprehensive picture of the linguistic proficiency of the group under investigation cannot do without an in-depth analysis of factors such as lexical richness and morphological and syntactic complexity of the total data under investigation, or at least part thereof.

These methodological considerations leave us with the following demands for language attrition studies:

1 ideally, a longitudinal study design in order to establish the attriters' proficiency at earlier stages of the attritional process instead of a monolingual control group;
2 comparison of the data to non-attrited speech, either from a monolingual control group or from existing statistical analyses of the language under investigation;
3 exclusion of the possibility of dialectal or sociolectal variety within the group of attriters under investigation;
4 classification of "mistakes" from the data collected by more than one judge;
5 establishment of a "linguistic complexity index'" to augment the data on "what is lost" by "what is retained."

In addition, it might be valuable to have free spoken data collected from the attriters subjectively rated by native speakers in order to establish to what degree the data sound "native" or "foreign" – based on features such as accent, sentence structures, or lexical choices. Such intuitive judgments might provide us with valuable insights into the perception of attrited proficiency. If these data are combined with the overall rate of mistakes, it is possible that a "tolerance saturation point" might be established, i.e., the overall frequency of mistakes up to which listeners are prepared to accept a speaker as native.

A further issue that has been widely debated in the literature on language attrition is whether attrition is a phenomenon of performance or competence (de Bot, 1991, p. 63ff.; Köpke, 1999, p. 105ff.; Seliger & Vago, 1991, p. 7; Sharwood Smith & van Buren, 1991, p. 19; Sharwood Smith, 1983, p. 49). Can the linguistic system an individual has acquired actually be changed in the attrition process, or is the larger number of mistakes found in the speech of attriters merely a surface phenomenon? However, it is hard to see how this is to be established. It would seem that there is no way to test whether an attriter is actually unable to produce a certain structure any longer. While the hypothetical case of all the data collected from one speaker exclusively containing misapplications of a certain rule might point strongly toward her having lost that rule entirely, there would still be no conclusive evidence that she does not, on occasion, apply it correctly. The actual findings from language attrition studies, however, are nowhere near this point: there is not a single case where any individual made any mistake in all possible cases, and most of the time the overwhelming majority of structures are correct.

See also 3 SECOND LANGUAGE ACQUISITION AND ULTIMATE ATTAINMENT, 7 ASSESSING LANGUAGE ATTITUDES, 17 THE NATIVE SPEAKER IN APPLIED LINGUISTICS, 29 LANGUAGE MAINTENANCE.

REFERENCES

Altenberg, E. P. (1991) Assessing first language vulnerability to attrition. In H. W. Seliger & R. M. Vago (eds.) *First language attrition* (pp. 189–206). Cambridge: Cambridge University Press.

Ammerlaan, T. (1996) "You get a bit wobbly . . ." Exploring bilingual lexical retrieval processes in the context of first language attrition. PhD Dissertation, Katholieke Universiteit Nijmegen.

Andersen, R. W. (1982) Determining the linguistic attributes of language attrition. In R. D. Lambert & B. F. Freed (eds.), *The loss of language skills* (pp. 83–118). Rowley, MA: Newbury House.

Appel, R. & Muysken, P. (1987) *Language contact and bilingualism*. London: Arnold.

Berko-Gleason, J. (1982) Insights from child language acquisition for second language loss. In R. D. Lambert & B. F. Freed (eds.), *The loss of language skills* (pp. 13–23). Rowley, MA: Newbury House.

Bolonyai, A. & Dutkova-Cope, L. (2001) L1 attrition of verbal morphology in bilingual children and adults. In X. Bonch-Bruevich, W. J. Crawford, J. Hellermann, C. Higgins, & H. Nguyen (eds.), *The past, present, and future of second language research: selected proceedings of the 2000 Second Language Research Forum* (pp. 104–23). Somerville, MA: Cascadilla.

Bot, K. de (1991) Language attrition: competence loss or performance loss.

In B. Spillner (ed.), *Sprache und Politik* (pp. 63–5). Frankfurt/New York: Peter Lang.

Bot, K. de & Clyne, M. (1989) Language reversion revisited. *Studies in Second Language Acquisition*, 11, 167–77.

Bot, K. de & Clyne, M. (1994) A 16 year longitudinal study of language attrition in Dutch immigrants in Australia. *Journal of Multilingual and Multicultural Development*, 15(1), 17–28.

Bot, K. de & Weltens, B. (1991) Recapitulation, regression, and language loss. In H. W. Seliger & R. M. Vago (eds.), *First language attrition* (pp. 31–51). Cambridge: Cambridge University Press.

Bot, K. de, Gommans, P., & Rossing, C. (1991) L1 loss in an L2 environment: Dutch immigrants in France. In H. W. Seliger & R. M. Vago (eds.), *First language attrition* (pp. 87–98). Cambridge: Cambridge University Press.

Breakwell, G. M. (1983) Identities and conflicts. In: G. M. Breakwell (ed.), *Threatened identities* (pp. 189–213). New York: John Wiley.

Caramazza, A. & Zurif, E. B. (1978) Comprehension of complex sentences in children and aphasics: a test of the regression hypothesis. In A. Caramazza & E. B. Zurif (eds.), *Language acquisition and language breakdown: parallels and divergencies* (pp. 145–61). Baltimore: John Hopkins University Press.

Chomsky, N. (1965) *Aspects of the theory of syntax*. Cambridge, MA: MIT Press.

Chomsky, N. (1981) *Lectures on government and binding: the Pisa lectures.* Dordrecht: Foris.

Clyne, M. (1973) Thirty years later: some observations on "refugee German" in Melbourne. In H. Scholler & H. Reilly (eds.), *Lexicography and dialect geography. Festgabe für Hans Kunath* (pp. 96–106). Wiesbaden: Steiner.

Clyne, M. (1981) *Deutsch als Muttersprache in Australien: Zur Ökologie einer Einwanderersprache.* Wiesbaden: Franz Steiner.

Dorian, N. C. (1982) Language loss and maintenance in language contact situations. In R. D. Lambert & B. F. Freed (eds.), *The loss of language skills* (pp. 44–59). Rowley, MA: Newbury House.

Edwards, J. (1985) *Language, society and identity.* Oxford: Blackwell.

Ervin-Tripp, S. (1973 [1954]) Identification and bilinguslism. In S. Ervin-Tripp (ed.), *Language acquisition and communicative choice.* Stanford: Stanford University Press.

Fishman, J. A. (1989) *Language and ethnicity in minority sociolinguistic perspective.* Clevedon, UK/Philadelphia: Multilingual Matters.

Gardner, R. C. (1982) Social factors in language retention. In R. D. Lambert & B. F. Freed (eds.), *The loss of language skills* (pp. 24–43). Rowley, MA: Newbury House.

Gardner, R. C. & Lambert, W. E. (1972) *Attitudes and motivation in second language learning.* Rowley, MA: Newbury House.

Giles, H., Bourhis, R., & Taylor, D. (1977) Towards a theory of language in ethnic group relations. In H. Giles (ed.), *Language, ethnicity and intergroup relations* (pp. 307–48). London: Academic Press.

Goodglass, H. & Kaplan, E. (1983) *The assessment of aphasia and related disorders.* Philadelphia: Lea & Febiger.

Grendel, M., Weltens, B., & Bot, K. de. (1993) Language attrition: rise and fall of a research topic? *Toegepaste Taalwetenschap in Artikelen,* 46/47, 59–68.

Grosjean, F. & Py, B. (1991) La restructuration d'une première langue: L'intégration de variantes de contact dans la compétence de migrants bilingues. *La Linguistique,* 27(2), 35–60.

Hagen, A. M. & Bot, K. de (1990) Structural loss and levelling in minority languages and dialects. *Sociolinguistica,* 4, 136–49.

Håkansson, G. (1995) Syntax and morphology in language attrition: a study of five bilingual expatriate Swedes. *International Journal of Applied Linguistics,* 5(2), 153–71.

Hall, P. K. & Jordan, L. S. (1987) An assessment of a controlled association task to identify word-finding problems in children. *Language, Speech, and Hearing Services in Schools,* 18, 99–111.

Haugen, E. (1953) *The Norwegian language in America.* Philadelphia: University of Pennsylvania Press.

Hermann, G. (1990) L'Influence de la langue étrangère sur la perception sociale et éthnique: Étude inter-culturelle. *Les Langues Modernes,* 84(2), 57–74.

Hermann, J. (1988) Bilingualism versus identity. In J. N. Jørgensen, E. Hansen, A. Holmen, & J. Gimbel (eds.), *Bilingualism in society and school* (pp. 227–32). Clevedon, UK/Philadelphia: Multilingual Matters.

Hirvonen, P. A. (1995) Phonological and morphological aspects of Finnish language attrition in the United States. In W. Viereck (ed.), *Soziolinguistische Variation* (pp. 181–93). Stuttgart: Steiner.

Hormann, C. (1994) Acts of identity in Aussiedler-German: operationalizing Le Page's sociolinguistic identity theory. PhD Dissertation, University of Texas at Austin.

Hull, P. V. (1991) Bilingualism. Two languages, two personalities? PhD Dissertation, University of California at Berkeley.

Hull, P. V. (1996) Bilingualism: some personality and cultural issues In D. I. Slobin, J. Gerhardt, A. Kyratzis, & J. Guo (eds.), *Social interaction, social context, and language. Essays in honor of Susan Ervin-Tripp* (pp. 419–34). Mahwah, NJ: Lawrence Erlbaum.

Hulsen, M. (2000) Language loss and language processing. Three generations of Dutch migrants in New Zealand. PhD Dissertation, Katholieke Universiteit Nijmegen.

Hulsen, M., Bot, K. de, & Weltens, B. (1999) Language shift, language loss and language processing: an investigation of three generations of Dutch immigrants in New Zealand. In E. Huls & B. Weltens (eds.), *Artikelen van de Derde Sociolinguistische Conferentie* (pp. 221–32). Delft: Eburon.

Hulsen, M., Bot, K. de, & Weltens, B. (2002) "Between two worlds": social networks, language shift and language processing in three generations of Dutch migrants in New Zealand. *International Journal of the Sociology of Language*, 2002, 27–52(1).

Ingram, D. (1989) *First language acquisition: method, description and explanation*. Cambridge: Cambridge University Press.

Jakobson, R. (1941) *Kindersprache, Aphasie und allgemeine Lautgesetze*. Uppsala: Almqvist & Wiksell.

Jaspaert, K. & Kroon, S. (1989) Social determinants of language loss. *Review of Applied Linguistics (ITL)*, 83–4, 75–98.

Jaspaert, K., Kroon, S., & Hout, R. van (1986) Points of reference in first-language loss research. In B. Weltens, K. de Bot & T. van Els (eds.), *Language attrition in progress* (pp. 37–49). Dordrecht: Foris.

Jordens, P., Bot, K. de, & Trapman, H. (1989) Linguistic aspects of regression in German case marking. *Studies in Second Language Acquisition*, 11(2), 179–204.

Jordens, P., Bot, K. de., Os, C. van., & Schumans, J. (1986) Regression in German case marking. In B. Weltens, K. de Bot & T. van Els (eds.), *Language attrition in progress* (pp. 159–76). Dordrecht: Foris.

Kauffman, D. & Aronoff, M. (1991) Morphological disintegration and reconstruction in first language attrition. In H. W. Seliger & R. M. Vago (eds.), *First language attrition* (pp. 175–88). Cambridge: Cambridge University Press.

Khemlani-David, M. (1998) Language shift, cultural maintenance, and ethnic identity: a study of a minority community: the Sindhis of Malaysia. *International Journal of the Sociology of Language*, 130, 67–76.

Köpke, B. (1999) L'attrition de la première language chez le bilingue tardif: implications pour l'étude psycholinguistique du bilinguisme. PhD Dissertation, Université de Toulouse-Le Mirail, France.

Lambert, R. D. (1989) Language attrition. *Review of Applied Linguistics (ITL)*, 83–4, 1–18.

Lambert, R. D. & Moore, S. J. (1986) Problem areas in the study of language attrition. In B. Weltens, K. de Bot, & T. van Els (eds.), *Language attrition in progress* (pp. 177–86). Dordrecht: Foris.

Leets, L. & Giles, H. (1995) Dimensions of minority language survival/non-survival: intergroup cognition and communication climates. In W. Fase, K. Jaspaert, & S. Kroon (eds.), *The state of minority languages: international perspectives on survival and decline* (pp. 37–73). Lisse: Sweets/Zeitlenger.

Leisiö, L. (2001) Morphosyntactic convergence and integration in Finland Russian. PhD Dissertation, University of Tampere, Finland.

Le Page, R. B. & Tabouret-Keller, A. (1985) *Acts of identity. Creole-based approaches to language and ethnicity.* Cambridge: Cambridge University Press.

Maher, J. (1991) A crosslinguistic study of language contact and language attrition. In H. W. Seliger & R. M. Vago (eds.), *First language attrition* (pp. 67–84). Cambridge: Cambridge University Press.

Major, R. C. (1992). Losing English as a first language. *The Modern Language Journal*, 76, 190–209.

Matsumoto, D. & Hull, P. V. (1994) Language and language acquisition. In D. Matsumoto (ed.), *People: psychology from a cultural perspective* (pp. 83–100). Pacific Grove, CA: Brooks & Cole.

Montrul, S. (2002) Incomplete acquisition and attrition of Spansh tense/aspect distinctions in adult bilinguals. *Bilingualism: Language and Cognition*, 5(1), 39–68.

Muysken, P. (1999) *Retrieving the lexicon in language contact.* MS, Universiteit Leiden.

Northover, M. (1988) Bilinguals and linguistic identities. In J. N. Jørgensen et al. (eds.), *Bilingualism in society and school* (pp. 201–31). Clevedon, UK/ Philadelphia: Multilinguals Matters.

Olshtain, E. (1989) Is second language attrition the reversal of second language acquisition? *Studies in Second Language Acquisition*, 11(2), 151–65.

Olshtain, E. & Barzilay, M. (1991) Lexical retrieval difficulties in adult language attrition. In H. W. Seliger & R. M. Vago (eds.), *First language attrition* (pp. 139–50). Cambridge: Cambridge University Press.

Polinsky, M. (1994) Strucutral dimensions of first language loss. In K. Beals, J. Denton, R. Knippen, L. Melnar, H. Suzuku, & E. Zeinfeld (eds.), *CLS 30 – Papers from the 30th Regional Meeting of the Chicago Linguistic Society*, vol. 2: *The parassession on variation in linguistic theory* (pp. 257–76). Chicago: Chicago Linguistic Society.

Ricker, K. (1995) Sprache und Identität – Zur Rekonstruktion und Präsentation von Identität in Migrationsbiographien. *Grazer Linguistische Studien*, 44, 101–12.

Romaine, S. (1989) *Bilingualism.* Oxford: Basil Blackwell.

Schmid, M. S. (2002) *First language attrition, use, and maintenance: the case of German Jews in anglophone countries.* Amsterdam/Philadelphia: John Benjamins.

Schmid, M. S. (forthcoming) *First language attrition: the methodology revised.*

Schmidt, A. (1991) Language attrition in Bouman Fijian and Dyirbal. In H. W. Seliger & R. M. Vago (eds.), *First language attrition* (pp. 113–24). Cambridge: Cambridge University Press.

Schoenmakers-Klein Gunnewiek, M. (1998) Taalverlies door taalkcontact? Een onderzoek bij Portugese migranten. PhD Dissertation, Katholieke Universiteit Brabant.

Seliger, H. W. (1989) Deterioration and creativity in childhood bilingualism In K. Hyltenstam & L. K. Obler (eds.), *Bilingualism across the lifespan* (pp. 173–84). Cambridge: Cambridge University Press.

Seliger, H. W. (1991) Language attrition, reduced redundancy, and creativity. In H. W. Seliger & R. M. Vago (eds.), *First language attrition* (pp. 227–40). Cambridge: Cambridge University Press.

Seliger, H. W. & Vago, R. M. (1991) The study of first language attrition: an overview. In H. W. Seliger & R. M. Vago (eds.), *First language attrition* (pp. 3–15). Cambridge: Cambridge University Press.

Sharwood Smith, M. (1983) On first language loss in the second language acquirer. In S. Gass & L. Selinker (eds.), *Language transfer in language learning* (pp. 222–31). Rowley, MA: Newbury House.

Sharwood Smith, M. (1989) Crosslinguistic influence in language loss. In K. Hyltenstam & L. K. Obler (eds.), *Bilingualism across the lifespan* (pp. 185–201). Cambridge: Cambridge University Press.

Sharwood Smith, M. & van Buren, P. (1991) First language attrition and the parameter setting model. In H. W. Seliger & R. M. Vago (eds.), *First language attrition* (pp. 17–30). Cambridge: Cambridge University Press.

Søndergaard, B. (1996) Language maintenance, code mixing, and language attrition: some observations. *Nowele: North-Western European Language Evolution*, 28–9, 535–55.

Stoessel, S. (2002) Investigating the role of social networks in language maintenance and shift. *International Journal of the Sociology of Language*, 2002(1), 93–131.

Turian, D. & Altenberg, E. P. (1991) Compensatory strategies of child first language attrition. In H. W. Seliger & R. M. Vago (eds.), *First language attrition* (pp. 207–26). Cambridge: Cambridge University Press.

Vago, R. M. (1991) Paradigmatic regularity in first language attrition. In H. W. Seliger & R. M. Vago (eds.), *First language attrition* (pp. 241–51). Cambridge: Cambridge University Press.

Waas, M. (1996) *Language attrition downunder: German speakers in Australia*. Frankfurt/New York: Peter Lang.

Weinreich, P. (1983) Emerging from threatened identities: ethnicity and gender in redefinitions of ethnic identity. In G. M. Breakwell (ed.), *Threatened identities* (pp. 143–85). New York: John Wiley.

Weinreich, U. (1953) *Languages in contact*. The Hague: Mouton.

Wilkins, D. P. (1996) Morphology. In H. Goebl, P. H. Nelde, Z. Stary, & W. Wölck (eds.), *Contact linguistics: an international handbook of contemporary research* (vol. 1) (pp. 109–17). Berlin/New York: Walter de Gruyter.

Wodak, R. & Benke, G. (1997) Gender as a sociolinguistic variable: new perspectives on variation studies. In F. Coulmas (ed.), *The handbook of sociolinguistics* (pp. 127–50). Oxford: Blackwell.

Yağmur, K. (1997) *First language attrition among Turkish speakers in Sydney*. Tilburg: Tilburg University Press.

FURTHER READING

Ammerlaan, T., Hulsen, M., Strating, H., & Yağmur, H. (eds.) (2001) *Sociolinguistic and psycholinguistic perspectives on maintenance and loss of minority languages*. Münster/New York/München/Berlin: Waxmann.

Bot, K. de (1996) Language loss. In H. Goebl, P. H. Nelde, Z. Stary, & W. Wölck (eds.), *Contact linguistics. An international handbook of contemporary research* (vol. 1) (pp. 579–85). Berlin/New York: Walter de Gruyter.

Klatter-Folmer, J. & Avermaet, P. van (eds.) (2001) *Theories on maintenance and loss of minority languages*. Münster/New York/München/Berlin: Waxmann.

Lambert, R. D. & Freed, B. F. (eds.) (1982) *The loss of language skills*. Rowley, MA: Newbury House.

Major, R. C. (1997) L2 acquisition, L1 loss, and the critical period hypothesis. In A. James & J. Leather (eds.), *Second-language speech: structure and process* (pp. 147–59). Berlin: Mouton de Gruyter.

Schmid, M. S., Köpke, B., Keijzer, M., & Weilemar, L. (eds.) (2002) Proceedings of the International Conference on First Language Attrition. Amsterdam, August.

Seliger, H. W. & Vago, R. M. (eds.) (1991) *First language attrition*. Cambridge: Cambridge University Press.

Weltens, B., Bot, K. de, & Els, T. Van. (eds.) (1986) *Language attrition in progress*. Dordrecht: Foris.

9 Language, Thought, and Culture

CLAIRE KRAMSCH

9.1 Introduction

The hypothesis that language both expresses and creates categories of thought that are shared by members of a social group and that language is, in part, responsible for the attitudes and beliefs that constitute what we call "culture," is a hypothesis that various disciplines have focused on in various ways. The field of applied linguistics, born in the fifties, at a time when the relationship of language and mind was the primary concern of formal linguistics, had a natural affinity to the brain sciences as they were developed then. Applied linguistics missed the heydays of empirical linguistics research that had led linguists like Boas, Sapir, and Whorf to investigate the relation of language and culture in pre-industrialized societies. In the rationalist spirit of the fifties and sixties, and its information processing focus, the young field of applied linguistics was at first primarily interested in the psycholinguistic processes at work in language acquisition and testing, and in the cognitive dimensions of language pedagogy. In the eighties, the ascendancy of sociology and anthropology created a favorable climate for applied linguists to explore, in addition, the relation of language and social structure (Halliday, 1978), the social psychological aspects of language acquisition (e.g., Ellis, 1986) and the multiple discursive aspects of language in use in a variety of social contexts (e.g., Gumperz, 1982a & b; Ochs, 1988). It is not before the nineties, however, that advances in cognitive linguistics, linguistic anthropology, and the growing importance given to culture in language education brought a renewed interest in the relation of language, thought, and culture in applied linguistics.

In this essay, I first review the canonical linguistic relativity hypothesis and its current resurgence in various fields related to applied linguistics. I then examine three major strands of thought in the triadic relation – language, thought, and culture – and how they are reflected in applied linguistics research. Finally, I explore the potential enrichment that the principle of language relativity can bring to applied linguistics, both in its theoretical endeavors and in its educational practice.

9.2   Language, Thought, and Culture and the Problem of Linguistic Relativity

The relation of language, thought, and culture was first expressed in the early nineteenth century by the two German philosophers Johann Herder and Wilhelm von Humboldt, and picked up later by the American anthropologists Franz Boas, Edward Sapir, and Sapir's student Benjamin Lee Whorf, in what has come to be called the linguistic relativity or Sapir-Whorf hypothesis.

9.2.1   *Early precursors: Herder and von Humboldt*

In part in reaction to the French political and military hegemony of the time, the German philosopher Johann Herder (1744–1803) expressed the idea that a nation's language reflected the way its people thought according to the equation: one language = one folk = one nation.

> If it be true that we . . . learn to think through words, then language is what defines and delineates the whole of human knowledge . . . In everyday life, it is clear that to think is almost nothing else but to speak. Every nation speaks . . . according to the way it thinks and thinks according to the way it speaks.   (Herder, [1772] 1960, pp. 99–100, my translation)

Around the same time, Wilhelm von Humboldt (1762–1835) expressed the link between language and worldview (or cultural mindset) in the following manner:

> . . . there resides in every language a characteristic world-view . . . By the same act whereby [man] spins language out of himself, he spins himself into it, and every language draws about the people that possesses it a circle whence it is possible to exit only by stepping over at once into the circle of another one. (von Humboldt, [1836] 1988, p. 60)

In these rather stark formulations, the two German philosophers were putting in question the Cartesian claim on the universality of human reason based on the universal human capacity for rational thought, i.e., a messianic universalism that became associated with the imperialist campaigns of Napoleon. They suggested that the motto "I think therefore I am" did not apply in the same manner to all humans, for there is no disembodied thought that is not shaped by language. If human language interferes between a person's existence and her thoughts, then a person's social existence itself is inflected by the grammar of her speech.

In the 30 years preceding the advent of applied linguistics, the Herder/ Humboldt tradition was still alive and well in the fieldwork that Boas, Malinowski, Sapir, and Whorf conducted in small, exotic, homogeneous cultures. Boas showed how a language directs its speakers to attend to the dimensions of experience encoded in its grammar and phonology (Boas, [1911] 1966). For example, even trained speakers of one language cannot reliably hear sound distinctions that are different from those in their own language. Malinowski was the first anthropologist to actually learn the language of the people he was studying and to show the role it played within various "contexts of situation" (Malinowski, 1923) and "contexts of culture" (Malinowski, 1935).

9.2.2   *The Sapir-Whorf hypothesis*

The best known formulation of the relation of language, thought, and culture is that captured by Sapir and Whorf under the term "linguistic relativity."

> Language *is a guide* to "social reality" ... it *powerfully conditions* all our thinking about social problems and processes. Human beings do not live in the objective world alone, nor alone in the world of social activity as ordinarily understood, but are very much *at the mercy* of the particular language which has become the medium of expression for their society. It is quite an illusion to imagine that one adjusts to reality essentially without the use of language and that language is merely an incidental means of solving specific problems of communication or reflection. The fact of the matter is that the "real world" is *to a large extent* unconsciously built up on the language habits of the group. No two languages are ever sufficiently similar to be considered as representing the same social reality. The worlds in which different societies live are distinct worlds, not merely the same world with different labels attached ... We see and hear and otherwise experience *very largely* as we do because the language habits of our community *predispose* certain choices of interpretation.   (Sapir, 1962, pp. 68–9 my emphases)

The emphases show a certain imprecision as to whether Sapir is talking about linguistic relativity (language *is a guide*, language *predisposes*, the world is *to a large extent* ... built up on the language habits of the group), or linguistic determinism (language *powerfully conditions* all our thinking, human beings are *at the mercy* of a particular language). The following famous passage from Whorf does nothing to dispel this uncertainty.

> We dissect nature along lines laid down by our native languages. The categories and types that we isolate from the world of phenomena we do not find there because they stare every observer in the face; on the contrary, the world is presented in a kaleidoscopic flux of impressions which has to be organized by our minds – and this means largely by the linguistic systems of our minds. We

cut nature up, organize it into concepts, and ascribe significances as we do, largely because we are parties to an agreement to organize it in this way – an agreement that holds throughout our speech community and is codified in the patterns of our language. The agreement is, of course, an implicit and unstated one, but its terms are absolutely obligatory. We cannot talk at all except by subscribing to the organization and classification of data which the agreement decrees . . .

From this fact proceeds what I have called the "linguistic relativity principle," which means, in informal terms, that users of markedly different grammars are pointed by their grammars toward different types of observations and different evaluations of externally similar acts of observation, and hence are not equivalent as observers, but must arrive at somewhat different views of the world. (Whorf, [1940] 1956, pp. 212–13, 221)

Whorf's hypothesis encountered virulent scorn and criticism from rationalist circles. Steven Pinker's biting rejection of Whorf's hypothesis is but one recent example.

What led Whorf to this radical position? He wrote that the idea first occurred to him in his work as a fire prevention engineer when he was struck by how language led workers to misconstrue dangerous situations. For example, one worker caused a serious explosion by tossing a cigarette into an "empty" drum that in fact was full of gasoline vapor. But the more you examine Whorf's arguments, the less sense they make. Take the story about the worker and the "empty" drum. The seeds of disaster supposedly lay in the semantics of empty, which, Whorf claimed, means both "without its usual contents" and "null and void, empty, inert." The hapless worker, his conception of reality molded by his linguistic categories, did not distinguish between the "drained" and "inert" sense, hence, flick*boom! But wait. Gasoline vapor is invisible. A drum with nothing but vapor in it looks just like a drum with nothing in it at all. Surely this walking catastrophe was fooled by his eyes, not by the English language . . . His assertions about Apache psychology are based entirely on Apache grammar – making his argument circular. Apaches speak differently, so they must think differently. How do we know that they think different? Just listen to the way they speak!   (Pinker, 1994, pp. 60–1)

To understand the virulence of the debate, we have to understand the historical context in which Whorf was writing. At the end of the thirties, Whorf, who had been studying the Hopi language and culture, went deliberately against the grain of the positivistic, scientific, universalist spirit of his time. Whorf's work, published in 1956 by J. B. Carroll, coincided with Chomsky's vitriolic attack against behaviorism and B. F. Skinner's suggestion that the acquisition of language was a habit forming process, subject to social conditioning. Thus, the times were not propitious for any talk about linguistic relativity (for a comparative historical account of Whorf's and Bakhtin's work, see Schultz, 1990).

9.3 Re-Thinking Linguistic Relativity

The strong version of linguistic relativity, or linguistic determinism, has been pretty much discarded, for a variety of convincing reasons. It is clear that translation is possible amongst languages, even though some meaning does get lost in translation, so the language web that Humboldt refers to does not seem to be spun as tightly as he suggests. Bi- or multilingual individuals are able to use their various languages in ways that are not dictated by the habits of any one speech community. And, with the increasing diversity of speakers within speech communities around the globe, it is increasingly difficult to maintain that all speakers of a language think the same way.

A weak form of the hypothesis has remained generally accepted. But the idea that the grammar we use influences in some way the thoughts that we communicate to others did not affect the young field of applied linguistics at a time when rationalist, experimental, and, moreover, monolingual modes of research dominated all linguistic inquiry, and information processing theories of cognition dominated western psychology. The role of social context in language acquisition and use was a strong component of linguistic research, but western linguists were careful not to suggest in any way that the social context might influence the way people speak and think. A case in point is the debate between Basil Bernstein and William Labov. Bernstein had linked speakers' different ways with words (i.e., elaborated vs. restricted codes) with the social class of these speakers (Bernstein, 1971). He suggested that middle-class speakers use more elaborated codes, i.e., assume less prior knowledge of their listeners, than working-class speakers, who assume greater shared knowledge on the part of their listeners, and thus use more restricted codes. Labov violently rejected Bernstein's views, showing that poor black adolescents in New York's inner city used as "elaborated" codes as Bernstein's middle-class whites, thus dispelling the idea that social context conditions language use (Labov, 1972).

However, since the late eighties, the notion of linguistic relativity has re-appeared in various, more sophisticated forms. In a recent state-of-the-art article on "Language and worldview" (1992), anthropologists Jane Hill and Bruce Mannheim argue that the hypothesis was never a hypothesis, but an axiom that was formulated at the time against "a naive and racist universalism in grammar, and an equally vulgar evolutionism in anthropology and history" (1992, p. 384). The resurgence of the concept in applied linguistics is due to a variety of developments in several related fields in the last 30 years. The first two come from work done in the twenties and thirties by Vygotsky and Bakhtin in the then Soviet Union. Vygotsky's work, translated in the west in 1962 and 1978, became particularly influential in applied linguistics through the neo-Vygotskyian research of psychologist James Wertsch (1985) and linguist James Lantolf (2000). It has foregrounded the role of the sociocultural in cognitive development. The work of Mikhail Bakhtin, discovered and translated in the west in the early eighties (1981, 1986), became influential in all areas of western intellectual life through the work of American literary scholars Michael Holquist (1990) and Gary Morson and Caryl Emerson (1990). Bakhtin's thought has ushered in a period of postmodernism that questions the stable truths on which modern rationalism is based and gives a new meaning to the notion of linguistic relativity within a dialogic perspective.

The other developments come from the emergence of new fields within the established disciplines of the social sciences. Innovative research in cognitive semantics (Lakoff, 1987, Lakoff & Johnson, 1980), cross-cultural semantics (Wierzbicka, 1992), cognitive linguistics (Slobin, 1996; Levinson, 1997; Turner, 1996; Fauconnier, 1985), and gesture and thought (McNeill, 1992) has provided new insights into the relation of language and thought. The social psychological study of talk and interaction as it is explored through discourse and conversation analysis (see Jaworski & Coupland, 1999; Moerman, 1988), discursive psychology (see Edwards & Potter, 1992), cultural psychology (Stigler, Shweder, & Herdt, 1990), and language socialization research (Schieffelin and Ochs, 1986; Jacoby & Ochs, 1995) has opened up new ways of relating thought and action. Advances in linguistic anthropology (e.g., Silverstein, 1976: Gumperz, 1982a and b; Friedrich, 1986; Hanks, 1996; Hymes, 1996; Becker, 2000) have placed discourse at the core of the nexus of language, thought, and culture. Finally, there is a growing body of research on bi- and multilingualism that counteracts the monolingual bias prevalent until now in applied linguistics (e.g., Romaine, 1995: Cook, 2000; Pavlenko, in press). This research is enabling us to consider the conceptual and cultural make-up of people who use more than one language in their daily lives (Pavlenko, 1999).

Three edited volumes give the state of current research on the relation of language, thought, and culture: Duranti and Goodwin (1992), Gumperz and Levinson (1996), and Niemeier and Dirven (2000). In his introduction to this last volume, Lucy makes the distinction between three ways or levels in which language can be said to influence thought. The semiotic or cognitive level concerns the way any symbolic system (versus one confined to iconic-indexical elements) transforms thinking in certain ways. The linguistic or structural level concerns the way particular languages (e.g., Hopi vs. English) influence thinking about reality in particular ways, based on their unique morphosyntactic configurations of meaning. The functional or discursive level concerns the way in which using language in a particular manner (e.g., according to schooled, scientific, or professional "cultures") influences thinking. Semiotic, linguistic, and discursive relativity interact in important ways. For example, semiotic effects are associated with cognitive patterns, that in turn are related to discourse regularities and cultural differences. I examine how these three levels of language relativity have been researched in recent years.

9.4 Semiotic Relativity, or How the Use of a Symbolic System Affects Thought

From a phylogenetic perspective (the development of the human species), the argument has been made by biological anthropologist Terrence Deacon (1997) that the acquisition of symbolic reference, by contrast with iconic or indexical reference, represents a quantum leap in the development of humankind that has led to the development of uniquely human thought. It is this leap that animals have never been able to make. Using a Peircean terminology, Deacon argues that, whereas iconic reference (i.e., a relation of similarity) is based on the negation of the distinction between signs and their objects, and indexical reference (i.e., a relation of contiguity) is based on the associative links between iconic signs and their referents in the world, symbolic reference builds on both iconic and indexical signs, and adds the unique capacity of language as a semiotic system to reflect cognitively upon itself, i.e., to refer to itself as a symbolic system, and link sign to sign, word to word. Symbolic reference represents the core semiotic innovation that distinguishes the human "symbolic species" from other living species. Deacon argues that the ability to manipulate symbols is in a hierarchical relationship with the ability to manipulate iconic and indexical signs. Symbolic reference needs the two others, but goes beyond them, adding an interpretive response to the mere perception of icons and recognition of indexical links. What symbolic activity does is add sense, which is something in the mind, to reference, which is something in the world (Frege, 1879 in Deacon, 1997, p. 61).

Taking the American psychologist James Mark Baldwin as his anchor point in the natural sciences, Deacon argues that the ability to use language symbolically has phylogenetically affected the human brain, not in a direct cause and effect manner, but indirectly through its effect on human behavior and on the changes that human behavior brings about in the environment. Even though the ability to use language as a symbolic system doesn't bring about genetic changes in the nature of the brain, the changes in environmental conditions brought about by human symbolic responses to that environment can, in the long run, bias natural selection and alter the selection of cognitive predispositions that will be favored in the future.

From an ontogenetic perspective (the development of the individual human organism), Vygotsky has shown ([1934] 1962) how language as a social activity influences thought. He argues that the language the child hears and experiences on the social plane becomes internalized in the form of inner speech on the psychological plane, thus leading to both language acquisition and language socialization. Vygotsky's theory turns on its head the traditional, Cartesian, view of the pre-eminence of thought over language. For him, symbolic activity derives from social interaction, according to his "general genetic law of cultural development" formulated as follows:

> Any function in the child's cultural [or, higher mental] development appears twice, or on two planes. First it appears on the social plane, and then on the psychological plane. First it appears between people as an interpsychological category, and then within the child as an intrapsychological category. This is equally true with regard to voluntary attention, logical memory, the formation of concepts, and the development of volition. (Vygotsky, 1981, p. 163)

Vygotsky's theory further claims that human language as a semiotic system links what we say and what we think, for it is both linguistic sign and psychological tool. As semiotic system, it mediates both psychological and social processes, because symbols can only be recognized and interpreted if they are shared by a community of sign users who agree on their meaning, even if sign users differ in the associations and combinations they make of these signs.

If, in Vygotsky's theory, children learn to think and to speak by internalizing the speech of others in the form of conceptual categories that they make their own, is this not a rather strong form of linguistic relativity? How do children transform the meaning resources of the group into their own? We can find an answer to these questions in the comparative study that Lucy and Wertsch (1987) make of Whorf's and Vygotsky's contributions to the theory of linguistic relativity. Both Whorf and Vygotsky share the view that language is a social and cultural phenomenon, and is a primary mediator between the individual and society. But while the linguist Whorf uses a synchronic approach, because he is intent on comparing the worldviews of speakers of different languages, the psychologist Vygotsky uses a diachronic approach, as he is interested in the cognitive development of the child. To use Lucy's terminology, Whorf is interested in linguistic relativity (see Section 9.5 below), Vygotsky is interested in semiotic relativity. Whorf wishes to understand how thought becomes "culturally contextualized, that is, bound to a cultural perspective" (Lucy & Wertsch, 1987, p. 80). For him "it is language which guides thought, although not to a higher level of development but to a culturally specific interpretation of experience" (p. 82). By contrast, Vygotsky is concerned with how thought becomes developmentally transformed through speech, how the child reaches the higher functions of symbolic reference, i.e., functions that are abstract, systematic, and subject to conscious control. By enabling the emergence of these higher mental functions, language transforms thought and "provides the essential ground for the development of human consciousness" (p. 83).

It is Vygotsky's semiotic theory that gives a clue as to how this transformation might take place. Words are both tools and signs. However, as Deacon noted, unlike tools that refer to and act upon objects, signs do not refer only to objects, but point to a multitude of other signs that are all potential candidates for selection and combination in the creation of meaning. The ability to select among all the possible signs provided by the speech community those that are the most relevant to the speaker or listener, and to combine them with other signs, is the hallmark of individual freedom and creativity.

The tension between semiotic determinism and semiotic relativity underlies much of the work done by researchers in cognitive semantics like George Lakoff (1987) and Mark Johnson (1987). They remind us of the way in which language is both "in the mind" and also quintessentially embodied as the "bodily basis of meaning, imagination and reason" (Johnson, 1987). Johnson goes one step further than Vygotsky, to show that symbols have a way of changing not only our ability for abstraction and reason, but also our imagination and emotions (see also Varela, Thompson, & Rosch, 1991: and Shore, 1996). This is nowhere more apparent than in the linguistic "metaphors we live by," i.e., those expressions that we take as representing reality "as it is," but that are, in fact, mental representations or conceptual spaces (Fauconnier, 1985; Turner, 1996) that are constructed by language (Lakoff, 1987; Lakoff & Johnson, 1980). They are so tied up with our bodily presence in the world that they can arouse emotions and passions, and lead people to action (see George Lakoff, 1992; Robin Lakoff, 1990, 2000). The metaphors given by Lakoff and Johnson 1980, for example, THE MIND IS A CONTAINER, are constructed by the language we use to talk about the mind, as in "it slipped my mind," or "you must be out of your mind," or in the phrase "comprehensible input." They permeate the language of the media, the professions, the academic disciplines, and our daily conversations; they are often invisible to us because they are so ever present. Applied linguists like Norman Fairclough, who advocates critical language awareness (1992), and Alastair Pennycook, who calls for a critical applied linguistics (2001), argue that it is the role of applied linguists to demystify these "naturalized" metaphors, whether they occur in the ideology of the media (Fairclough, 1992) or in the ways in which colonial discourses still "adhere" to English as a former colonial language. (Pennycook, 1998). The usefulness of exploring metaphors to study the mind is that metaphors are also linguistic and discursive constructs, crafted and used at the intersection of language and thought and of language and society. Because they juxtapose two domains of experience that don't normally belong together, as, for example, mind and containers, and because they map one domain onto the other, proposing to see one in terms of the other, metaphors as linguistic constructs can change the way we see and think of reality. And because these metaphors are transmitted, received, and shared among speakers and hearers in social contexts of communication, they are also discursive constructs that can reinforce the discursive habits of the group when they are used repeatedly, and thus take on a reality that starts permeating the group members' culture (see, e.g., Tannen, 1998). Semiotic relativity is thus indissociable from linguistic and discursive relativity.

9.5   Linguistic Relativity, or How Speakers of Different Languages Think Differently When Speaking

The linguistic relativity hypothesis has recently been revisited in a different form on the typological/grammatical and on the lexical/semantic levels. The grammatical level has been investigated recently by Dan Slobin and his associates in a large-scale cross-cultural project in cognitive linguistics (Berman & Slobin, 1994; Slobin, 1996, 2000). Slobin builds on Boas' insight that "in each language, only a part of the complete concept that we have in mind is expressed," and that "each language has a peculiar tendency to select this or that aspect of the mental image which is conveyed by the expression of the thought" (Boas [1911] 1966, pp. 38–9). But he replaces Sapir/Whorf's static nominal phrase "thought-and-language," with the more dynamic phrase "thinking-for-speaking." We cannot prove, he notes, that language and thought are co-extensive, nor that language determines our worldview, but we can show that, in order to speak at all, speakers have to attend to those dimensions of experience that are enshrined in the grammatical categories of the language they speak. In order to utter the English sentence "The man is sick," a Siouan would have to indicate grammatically whether the man is moving or at rest, a Kwakiutl speaker would have to specify whether the man is visible or non-visible to the speaker, a Spanish speaker would need to know whether the man is temporarily or chronically sick (Slobin, 1996, p. 71).

Slobin compares the stories told by children 3–11 years of age in different countries about the same sequence of 24 pictures without words, *Frog where are you?* He focuses on expressions of temporal and spatial orientation in the narrations of speakers of English, German, Spanish, Hebrew, and Turkish. (2000, p. 111). His findings reveal, for all age groups, "a different online organization of the flow of information and attention to the particular details that receive linguistic expression" (p. 78). Here are examples from three of the pictures. Picture 1: A boy climbs a tree to look in a hole while a dog stands next to a beehive. Picture 2: An owl flies out of the tree and knocks the boy down, and the dog is pursued by the bees. Picture 3: A deer takes the boy on his antlers and throws him into the river.

To encode temporal relations in the first two pictures and their sequel, both English and Spanish speakers have a perfective aspect to express a punctual, completed event in the past ("the owl flew away"), but English speakers only have a gerund to express a non-punctual, durative event ("the wasps were chasing him"), whereas Spanish speakers have both an imperfective aspect (*le perseguían al perro las avispas* 'the dog was being chased by the wasps') and a gerundive expression (*el perro salió corriendo* 'the dog came out running') to encode that same event.

To encode spatial relations, English speakers tend to express the path taken by a motion in space through particles and prepositions added to one single verb such as in "the bird flew down from out of the hole in the tree," or "[he] threw him over the cliff into a pond." Speakers of German do the same, e.g., *Der Hirsch nahm den Jungen auf sein Geweih und schmiB ihn den Abhang hinunter genau ins Wasser* 'The deer took the boy on his antlers and hurled him down from the cliff right into the water'. By contrast, Spanish speakers tend to express directionality through syntactic constructions like relative clauses, as in *El ciervo le llevo hasta un sitio, donde debajo habia un rio* 'the deer took him until a place, where below there was a river', or a combination of several verbs: *el pajaro salio del agujero del arbol volando hacia abajo* 'the bird exited of the hole of the tree, flying towards below' (Slobin, 2000, p. 112).

Slobin calls languages like English, German, or Dutch, satellite-framed languages (or S-languages), because motion path is given by a satellite to the verb – in English, a verb particle – while manner is bundled up with the verb. For example: English *an owl flew out of the hole in the tree*, German *da kam ne Eule rausgeflattert*, Dutch *dan springt er een uil uit het gat*. In these examples the particles give the path "out of" – *raus* 'out' – and the main verb depicts manner of motion "fly" – *flattert* 'flaps', *springt* 'jump'. By contrast, languages like French, Spanish, or Turkish are verb-framed (or V-languages) because motion path is indicated by the main verb in a clause – verbs like 'enter', 'exit', 'cross' (e.g., Fr. *le hibou il sort de son trou* 'the owl exits its hole', Sp. *sale un buho* 'exits an owl'), and manner is expressed by adding an element or phrase to the sentence (Slobin, 2000, p. 112).

What does this tell us about the way these speakers think? Slobin (2000) claims that

> users of V-languages build mental images of physical scenes with minimal focus on manner of movement, and with rather different conceptualizations of manner when it is in focus. Thus, when they hear or read stories, or newspaper reports, or gossip, they might end up with quite different mental representations than users of S-languages. These differences are exceptionally difficult to pin down, but the considerable range of evidence examined here is at least suggestive of rather divergent mental worlds of speakers of the two language types. (p. 133)

He is careful however, to restrain his claims "to what Sapir called 'the relativity of concepts' at the interface between experience and its expression in language" (Slobin, 2000, p. 133), and not to extend them to all the other thought processes that may occur beyond this interface. And indeed, not all thought is encoded linguistically, and Whorf was the first to admit it. However, as Pavlenko comments, the fact that "speakers of satellite-framed languages represent manner and directed motion as a single conceptual event, while users of verb-framed languages build mental images of physical scenes with minimal focus on the manner of movement" has important consequences for research on the interaction of language and thought in bi-and multilingual individuals (Pavlenko, in press).

Research in gestural communication lends support to Slobin's findings. David McNeill, who researches the role of hand gestures as windows to the mind (McNeill, 1992), found clear correlations between the storytelling gestures and the linguistic structures used by speakers of various languages (McNeill & Duncan, 2000), thus supporting Slobin's claim that speakers of V- and S-languages differ in their conceptualization of motion events. It should be interesting to study the relation of thought and gestures in multilingual speakers.

The semantic level of linguistic relativity has been explored recently most systematically by Anna Wierzbicka (1992). She too is inspired by von Humboldt and Sapir/Whorf as she searches for a natural semantic metalanguage that could explain conceptual differences among languages, since "it is impossible for a human being to study anything – be it cultures, language, animals, or stones – from a totally extra-cultural point of view." She tries to identify "universal semantic primitives out of which thoughts and complex concepts are constructed and in terms of which all complex concepts [and the culture-specific aspects of meaning] in any language can be explained" (1992, p. 25). For example she compares concepts like Russian *dusha* or *serdce*, German *Seele*, and English *soul*, *mind* or *heart* by exploring their associative networks and their connotations, and by decomposing each concept into parts whose names have simple English equivalents. So, for example:

Mind
one of two parts of a person
one cannot see it
because of this part, a person can think and know (p. 45)

Seele
one of two parts of a person
one cannot see it
it is part of another world
good beings are part of that world
things are not part of that world
other people can't know what things happen in that part of a person
sometimes the person doesn't know what these things are
these things can be good or bad
because of this part, a person can be a good person (p. 37)

Dusha
one of two parts of a person
one cannot see it
because of this part, things can happen in a person that cannot happen in
    [anyone else]
these things are good or bad
because of this part, a person can feel things that [no one else] can feel
other people can't know what these things are if the person doesn't say it

a person would want someone to know what these things are
because of this part, a person can be a good person
because of this part a person can feel something good toward other people
   (p. 59)

Through this metalanguage, Wierzbicka is able to describe the linguistic relativity of culture-specific human concepts in culture-specific configurations, i.e., their dependence for meaning on their social and historical contexts of use. She concludes, like Slobin, with cautious claims:

> Although lexical differences of this kind can be misinterpreted and exaggerated, nonetheless they do mean something, and if carefully and cautiously interpreted, they can indeed be regarded as clues to the different cultural universes associated with different languages . . . In the case of English, the decline and fall of the word soul, and the ascendancy of the word mind, seem to provide particularly significant evidence for cultural history and for prevailing modern ethnophilosophy.   (p. 63)

9.6   Discursive Relativity, or How Speakers of Different Discourses (across Languages or in the Same Language) Have Different Cultural Worldviews

The idea that "verbal discursive practices affect some aspects of thinking either by modulating structural influences or by directly influencing the interpretation of the interactional context" (Lucy, 2000, p. x) underlies much recent research in linguistic anthropology, language socialization studies, and cultural psychology, as mentioned in Section 9.3. This kind of research draws not on rationalist theories of mind, but on theories that account for the interaction of mind, language, and social/cultural action in communicative practices of everyday life. I focus here on the work of three linguistic anthropologists who have had a particularly great influence on bringing discursive relativity to the attention of applied linguists. All three could subscribe to Joel Scherzer's remark that "[discourse] is the nexus, the actual and concrete expression of the language-culture-society relationship. It is discourse which creates, recreates, modifies, and fine tunes both culture and language and their intersection" (Scherzer, 1987, p. 296).

Parallel to the work of Lakoff and Johnson in cognitive linguistics, and following along the lines of Malinowski and Boas, John Gumperz has shown the importance of contextualization cues to make sense of what is going on in conversation (Gumperz, 1992, p. 231). Contextualization cues are those features of speech that "relate what is said at any one time and in any one place to knowledge acquired through past experience, in order to retrieve the

presuppositions [participants] must rely on to maintain conversational involvement and assess what is intended" (1992, p. 230). Such cues may be phonological (choice of intonation, stress, and pitch), paralinguistic (gestures, facial
expressions), or linguistic (choice of code, choice of lexical forms or formulaic
expressions). They link what is said to what is thought and to how the
world is perceived by the participants. Gumperz gives an example of
miscommunication between a graduate student and his informant in an
ethnographic survey, due to the inability of the student to pick up the relevant
contextualization cues:

> The graduate student has been sent to interview a black housewife in a low
> income, inner city neighborhood. The contact has been made over the phone by
> someone in the office. The student arrives, rings the bell, and is met by the
> husband, who opens the door, smiles and steps towards him:
>   Husband: So y're gonna check out ma ol lady, hah?
>   Interviewer: Ah no. I only came to get some information. They called from the
> office.
>   (Husband, dropping his smile, disappears without a word and calls his wife.)
>   The student reports that the interview that followed was stiff and quite
> unsatisfactory. Being black himself, he knew that he had "blown it" by failing to
> recognize the significance of the husband's speech style in this particular case.
> (Gumperz, 1982a, p. 133)

Contextualization cues are part of a larger class of discourse elements called
"indexicals" that indirectly refer to, or "index," the personal, social, cultural,
and ideological subject position of the speaker and require interpretation on
the part of the participants (Gumperz, 1996). Indexicality is a powerful way of
researching the intersection of patterns of language use and concommitant patterns of thought and culture. Hanks (1996) gives evidence of the way linguistic
structures index both thought processes and social alignments in speech events.
His analyses of Mayan communicative practices in Yucatan show how linguistic forms derive their meaning not only from their selection among the
many forms provided by the code, but from the way members combine and
engage these forms in the course of their social conduct. For example, when
Yuum comes to the house of the shaman Don Chabo to get a blessing, the following dialogue ensues between Yuum, standing outside, and Don Chabo's
daughter-in-law Margot, standing inside her kitchen, through the open window:

> Yuum: kul a an wa don caabo
> *Is Don Chabo seated?*
> Margot: sen tol o, taan uy uk; ul. Seen to ic nah o
> *Go over there. He's drinking. Go over there inside.*
>   (Hanks, 1996, p. 157)

Hanks shows in exquisite detail how each of the indexicals in these two utterances – deictics like *over there, you, he, inside, go,* and verbs with indexical value

like *seated* (meaning: 'in session') or *drinking* (meaning: 'having dinner') – refer to the social, economic, gender divisions between Margot's kitchen and her father-in-law's house, to the power relationships between shamans and their clients, and to the whole spatial and temporal organization of social life in Yucatan Mayan communities (1996, pp. 155–66).

Thus, language as communicative practice is tied to a person's position in time, space, social and historical relations, and his/her social and emotional identity. How do children learn language as communicative practice? In a programmatic article titled "Linguistic resources for socializing humanity" (1996), Elinor Ochs examines what it takes to become "a speaker of culture" (see Ochs, 2002). Drawing on her fieldwork on child language socialization in a Samoan village and her extensive research in developmental pragmatics, she found that, through language and other symbolic tools, children and adults construct the culture they live in by publicly signalling the actions they are performing, the stances they are displaying, i.e., their evaluation of their own and others' feelings and beliefs, the social identities they put forward, and the sequence of actions, or activities, in which they are engaged. Language acquisition is, in part, a process of socialization, "a process of assigning situational, i.e., indexical, meaning . . . to particular forms (e.g., interrogative forms, diminutive affixes, raised pitch and the like)" (1996, pp. 410–11; see also Ochs & Schieffelin, 1984). Ochs' work brings together insights from Deacon, Lakoff, Johnson, and Slobin by showing how language, as both symbolic system and communicative practice, is intimately linked to spatial and temporal orientation, to the speakers' subject positioning vis-à-vis these events, and to the actions taken. By focusing on activity, rather than on speaker utterance, as the unit of analysis, Ochs is able to closely connect the linguistic, the cognitive, and the social in children's development.

9.7   Language Relativity in Applied Linguistic Research

Research on all three forms of language relativity has been carried out pretty much independently of research on second language acquisition (SLA), which forms a large area of the field called "applied linguistics." The brief survey that follows recapitulates the history of SLA research from the perspective of language relativity.

Prior to the emergence of applied linguistics in the late fifties/early sixties, the combination of structural linguistics and behavioral psychology led to contrastive analysis approaches in language acquisition study and to behavioristic methods of language teaching (repetition, habit formation, translation). The first cognitive revolution in educational psychology brought about by Jerome Bruner and his colleagues in the fifties reinstated the autonomy of the thinking subject (Bruner, Goodnow, & Austin, 1956), at the same time as the linguistic revolution brought about by Noam Chomsky (1957) reinstated the autonomy of the speaking-hearing subject, thus liberating the learner from behavioral conditioning and political manipulation. Both western psychology and linguistics have implicitly adopted the rationalist, Cartesian view that language reflects thought and thought is expressed through language, but also that psychological processes exist independently of language and of the social activities in which language is used.

Through the eighties, SLA research was not interested in linguistic relativity. The classical texts in the field (Ellis, 1986; Spolsky, 1989; Larsen-Freeman & Long, 1991; Lightbown & Spada, 1993; V. Cook, 1993) don't even mention the concept. Researchers within the formal linguistic tradition sought to discover universal aspects of second language (L2) acquisition based on the principles of Universal Grammar and its language-specific parameters, or on universally valid psycholinguistic processes of L2 development. Researchers within the functionalist tradition of SLA sought to discover L2-specific rules of communicative competence including the deployment of communicative strategies and the management of conversations in social contexts. Researchers within the pragmatics strand of SLA explored the realization of speech acts across languages.

In neither of these cases was language relativity on the agenda. Although SLA research was concerned with the social context of language learning (see e.g., Ellis, 1987), it viewed the social as a stable, pre-existing fixture, existing outside the individual, not constructed by an individual's psychological and linguistic processes. By relying on the standard (national) native speaker as a benchmark for language acquisition, it seemed to equate, like Herder and von Humboldt, one language with one national community and one national culture. This is particularly noticeable in interlanguage pragmatics (Kasper & Rose, 2001), which investigates the realization of speech acts across "cultures." For researchers in this area of applied linguistics, a speaker of Japanese or Hebrew is seen as a representative of "the" Japanese or Israeli national culture. "Culture" is most of the time essentialized into monolithic national cultures on the model of monolithic standard national languages. Such a synchronic mapping of language onto culture seems unduly deterministic, even though it is explained by its different research tradition. It is also noticeable in the area of contrastive rhetoric, that still influences much of ELT today (see Section 9.9 below).

The overwhelming focus of SLA research on the (standard) linguistic aspects of communicative competence and the (universal) cognitive aspects of learning, as well as its inability to deal satisfactorily with social and cultural variation, foreclosed any possibility of taking into consideration semiotic, linguistic, and discursive relativity in language development. What has been missing is a consideration of the historical dimension of the relation of language, thought, and culture – a dimension that sociocultural approaches to SLA have brought back into the equation by taking a historically and socially relativistic perspective on language development.

The social and cultural turn in SLA within the last ten years (e.g., Kramsch, 1993; Lantolf, 2000) has made the language relativity principle more relevant in applied linguistics. It is implicit in recent environmental or ecological theories of SLA (e.g., Larsen-Freeman, 2002; Lemke, 2002; van Lier, 2000), and in the return of a phenomenological tradition of inquiry (Kramsch, 2002a). It can be seen in language socialization research, in sociolinguistic strands of applied linguistics (e.g., Rampton, 1997), and in neo-Whorfian perspectives on bi- and multilingualism (Pavlenko, in press),

The seeds are now there to deal with individual, social, and cultural variation within SLA research. Efforts to eschew rigid dichotomies like input vs. output, acquisition vs. learning, and to replace them by more holistic concepts like affordances, collaborative dialogue, or mediated activity leave open the possibility of placing language relativity at the core of language acquisition and use (Lantolf, 2000). So does the recent emphasis on creativity and play in language development (Cook, 2000), ritual and symbolic interaction (Rampton, 2002) and on the conceptual and subjective make up of multilingual speakers and learners (Pavlenko, 1999; Kramsch, forthcoming). Interest in language relativity can also be found in the increased attention devoted in linguistic anthropology to verbal art, poetic patterning, and the "poetic imagination." All these recent developments focus on the way individual and collective thoughts and sensibilities are co-constructed, shaped, and subverted through language as communicative and representational practice.

From a methodological perspective, the principle of language relativity suggests adopting an ecological/phenomenological approach to research in applied linguistics (Kramsch, 2002b). As such it is both inspirational and risky. Because it enables applied linguists to recapture the early holistic view of language, thought, and culture envisaged by Boas and Sapir, it feels more valid than positivistically oriented research approaches that have to reduce the evidence to what is rationally researchable. On the other hand, it might be much less reliable, if by reliable we mean evidence that can be replicated to support universal claims to truth. However, the research reviewed above shows that it is possible to relate language to thought and culture in ways that adhere to the criteria of sound and rigorous research in the social sciences, especially in cognitive linguistics and linguistic anthropology. Taking into account language relativity will require taking into account phenomena that have remained too long under the radar of applied linguistic research, i.e., cultural knowledge and its reproduction, and "the more chaotic and inchoate sides of language and social life" (Hill & Mannheim, 1992, p. 398). It will require greater use of long-term longitudinal studies, ethnographic methods of data collection, cross-linguistic discourse analyses, and a willingness to draw on social and cultural theories to illuminate the relationship between macro- and micro-level phenomena (for an example of a research agenda for the study of bilingualism and thought from a relativistic perspective, see Pavlenko, in press).

9.8   Language Relativity in Educational Practice

The critical test of applied linguistics as a research field is, of course, education, in the broadest sense of the bringing about of social and cultural change. Henry Widdowson pointed to this problem when he wrote: "It is the responsibility of applied linguists to consider the criteria for an educationally relevant approach to language" (1980, p. 86). But what is "educationally relevant"? Jerome Bruner answers:

> [Education] is not simply a technical business of well-managed information processing, nor even simply a matter of applying "learning theories" to the classroom or using the results of subject-centered "achievement testing." It is a complex pursuit of fitting a culture to the needs of its members and their ways of knowing to the needs of the culture.   (Bruner, 1996, p. 43)

The needs of the culture, as perceived and formulated by teachers, school administrators, and textbook writers and publishers may not be the same as those formulated by researchers, nor is the discourse of all practitioners or of all researchers homogeneous. Culture, in an individual, as in society at large, is plural, changing, and often conflictual. The problem here is the conflict between the desire of the practitioner and the constraints of the institution, e.g., between the culture of teaching and the culture of testing, or between the culture of the students and the culture of native speakers. The conflict is expressed in three questions that can be raised by the principle of language relativity in educational linguistics.

First, isn't applied linguistic theory itself subjected to the principle of language relativity? The case has been made for the teaching of English around the world that is supported by an applied linguistic theory very often born out of an Anglo-Saxon view of communication and interaction (e.g., Pennycook, 1994; Canagarajah, 1999; and others). Yet such a view is only partially true, for applied linguistic theory is multiple, even though not all theories are equal before the laws of demand and supply on the economic textbook market. Moreover if applied linguistic theory is both universally valid and contingent upon the cultural conditions of its enunciation, so is educational theory.

Second, isn't educational culture inherently inhospitable to the principle of language relativity, since its ultimate goal is to discriminate between educated and non-educated segments of the population through the imposition of the same formal norms to everyone? The reason why (non-relativistic) grammar is taught as a formal system, apart from the fact that it is more easily "testable," is precisely because of a positivistic, information-processing educational culture that imposes its own rationalistic frames on what is acceptable teaching at what level for what age group, and what is not. It is this educational culture that has trained the teachers and the teacher-trainers. Its rationale is to be found in the historical, cultural, political traditions of the institution. It is often associated with noble goals of educational equity, objectivity, fairness, etc. in a mass education system, but this only exacerbates the dilemma. Since the principle of language relativity acknowledges the presence of both universal and culture-specific forms of knowledge, the question is really: How can an educational system make explicit what is universal and what is culture-specific in the knowledge it dispenses?

Third, can language relativity be taught directly or can it only be modelled? This is the key question. Suggestions have been made to make teachers and students aware of the relevance of the linguistic relativity principle in its Vygotskyan, diachronic form, both with regard to their L1 and the L2 (Kramsch, 1993, 1998). Teachers can show their students, for example, how the English grammar encourages its speakers to attend to reality in a certain way when they speak. They can explain the multiple ways in which "culture" is constructed through language, and how else it could be constructed through that same language. They can make their syllabus, teaching methods, and teaching goals more transparent, by telling students what "culture" they have learned by learning to talk and write in a foreign language. They can take every opportunity to link language use to a speaker's or writer's thought, i.e., stance and point of view, and to link that point of view to that of other speakers and writers of the same national, social, or cultural discourse community (Kramsch, 2001). However, teachers should be aware that linking language, thought, and culture in language teaching is not without risk, as I show below.

9.9   The Danger of Stereotyping and Prejudice

However attractive the notion of language relativity might be for research, (even though it poses problems of methodology), it is not without risks when used in educational practice. In an influential essay on cross-cultural rhetoric, Robert Kaplan, 30 years ago, advanced the theory that speakers of different languages write according to different rhetorical logics. Kaplan's views echo those of Sapir and Whorf:

> It is apparent but not obvious that, at least to a very large extent, the organization of a paragraph, written in any language by any individual who is not a native speaker of that language, will carry the dominant imprint of that individual's culturally-coded orientation to the phenomenological world in which he lives and which he is bound to interpret largely through the avenues available to him in his native language.   (Kaplan, 1972, p. 1)

In diagrams ("doodles") that have since become famous, Kaplan suggested that "each language and each culture has a[n expository] paragraph order unique to itself, and that part of the learning of a particular language is the mastering of its logical system," or of the "logos immanent in the language" (1972, p. 63). Thus, the English paragraph is represented by a straight downward arrow, the

Oriental (here Chinese and Korean, but not Japanese) paragraph by a spiral circling toward the center, the Romance paragraph by a downward crooked arrow broken up by several horizontal "digressional" plateaux.

It is easy to see why so many ESL (English as a second language) teachers of writing extrapolated from the nature of the students' native language to the logic of their paragraphs, and, from there, to the innate logic of their minds and the intrinsic nature of their characters. Even though this was of course not what Kaplan had intended, many believed that Americans were direct and straightforward, Chinese devious and roundabout, and the French illogical and untrustworthy, and that those qualities were the direct result of the language they spoke.

Kaplan did later disavow these undue extrapolations (1987), but he still maintained his original position that "the acquisition of a second language really requires the simultaneous acquisition of a whole new universe and a whole new way of looking at it" (1972, p. 100). Like Whorf, he continued to link cultural differences to the structure of the language itself: "rhetorical and stylistic preferences are culturally conditioned and vary widely from language to language" (p. 103), thus equating one (standard) language with one (national? professional? educational?) culture. The problem, however, is that it is not the English (written) language itself that is more direct than, say, the French, but the preferred styles of essayist prose inculcated by the current educational system of each country. It is the educational institution, not the language itself, that decides what counts as an effective "expository paragraph" and that imposes its definition of the genres of power on those it is charged with schooling. The semantic categories of literacy are themselves culturally and socially inflected. Thus the following statement for English teachers rests on cultural assumptions of genre that might not be shared by all, not even among native speakers of English:

> If, for example, one wishes to produce texts to be read by village women in sectors of Southeast Asia, what organization of text is most likely to introduce that audience to basic child nutrition in the most effective manner, and how will that rhetorical structure differ from one intended to serve the same purposes for women in sectors of the Arab Middle East?   (Kaplan, 1987, p. 20)

This paragraph assumes, for example, that "basic child nutrition" is a public topic that can be aired through a text destined for a large audience that needs to be "introduced to it" in the most "effective" manner. But neither the concept of basic child nutrition nor the concept of effectiveness are likely to be categories that mean quite the same for all speakers of English, Chinese, and Arabic around the world. So the problem is not one of rhetorical organization, but, as genre researchers have shown (e.g., Swales, Bazerman), of communicative purpose. If texts have different organizations, it is because they have different purposes, and their readerships have different expectations. As Wierzbicka would say, an essay is not an essay is not an essay when written in different languages for different audiences with different purposes in mind. Language relativity, like no other axiom, confronts applied linguistics with its intrinsic boundary nature between language theory and educational practice.

9.10   Instead of Language-Thought-and-Culture: Speakers/Writers, Thinkers, and Members of Discourse Communities

As we have seen, the principle of language relativity shifts the focus away from static concepts like language, thought, and culture toward more dynamic notions of speakers/writers, thinkers, and members of discourse communities. Language is only one of many semiotic systems with which learners make sense of the world expressed in a different language. The acquisition of another language is not an act of disembodied cognition, but is the situated, spatially and temporally anchored, co-construction of meaning between teachers and learners who each carry with them their own history of experience with language and communication. Culture is not one worldview, shared by all the members of a national speech community; it is multifarious, changing, and, more often than not, conflictual.

Language relativity suggests reorienting the focus of language teachers from what they do to who they are. Whether the language they teach is the language they grew up with, or a foreign language, they themselves have had to grapple with language relativity. It has, no doubt, put into question their own worldview, it has made them conscious of what got lost in translation. They have to resonate to the foreign words with the sensibility of both a native speaker and a non-native speaker. Most of all, now fluent as they are in the language they teach, they have to remember what it felt like to learn a new language, the linguistic and culture shocks experienced, the challenges and rewards encountered along the way. This sensitivity to language relativity, this sense of wonder at the mysteries of the untranslatable, cannot be taught directly. It has to be modelled by the language teacher herself.

When considering the implications of language relativity for educational practice, it is important to make the difference between language relativity and moral relativism. It is not because we can no longer uphold universal values that our language would impose on speakers of other languages that we are no longer entitled to the values that our language both creates and reflects. The principle of language relativity enables us to understand to a certain degree how speakers of other languages think and what they value. It does not mean that it obliges us to agree with or to condone these values. But it does commit us to "see ourselves amongst others, as a local example of the forms human life has locally taken, a case among cases, a world among worlds, [a view] without which objectivity is self-congratulation and tolerance a sham" (Geertz, 1983, p. 16).

9.11   Conclusion: The "Incorrigible Diversity" of Applied Linguistics

This essay has drawn on several disciplines besides linguistics, such as psychology, sociology, and anthropology and new cross-disciplinary fields like cognitive linguistics, cultural psychology, linguistic anthropology, to illuminate the relationship of language, thought, and culture in applied linguistics. The question arises as to whether the field is done a service or a disservice by becoming "hybridized" to such an extent. Not every applied linguist agrees that it is a good thing for applied linguistics to draw on so many feeder disciplines without the possibility of developing a unified applied linguistic theory. Yet, it seems that research on language as cognitive, social, and cultural practice cannot but draw on a multiplicity of disciplines, even though it does not make the methodology of applied linguistics research any easier.

In an essay titled "Culture, Mind, Brain/Brain, Mind, Culture," Clifford Geertz takes a cautiously optimistic view of the hybridization of psychology and anthropology in the last 20 years

> the mental nature of culture, the cultural nature of mind, have haunted anthropology since its inception . . . Our brains are not in a vat, but in our bodies. Our minds are not in our bodies, but in the world. And as for the world, it is not in our brains, our bodies, or our minds: they are, along with gods, verbs, rocks, and politics, in it.   (Geertz, 2000, pp. 204–5)

We could say in turn that the role of applied linguistics, as the study of speakers, writers, and members of discourse communities, is less a matter of "hybridizing disciplines, putting hyphens between them, than it is of reciprocally disequilibrating them" (Geertz, 2000, p. 199). In this respect, we could benefit from Geertz' encouraging words:

> What seems to be needed is the development of strategies for enabling Bruner's "different construals of [mental] reality" to confront, discompose, energize, and deprovincialize one another, and thus drive the enterprise erratically onward. Everything that rises need not converge: it has only to make the most of its incorrigible diversity.   (p. 199)

Constructing a useful applied linguistics means making the most of its incorrigible diversity. It is about cross-pollinating different construals of linguistic, mental and cultural reality in light of the problems of the practice. In so doing, it just might change these construals.

See also 5 DISCOURSE ANALYSIS, 14 LANGUAGE AND POLITICS, 21 INDIVIDUAL DIFFERENCES IN SECOND LANGUAGE LEARNING, 32 CRITICAL APPLIED LINGUISTICS.

REFERENCES

Bakhtin, M. (1981) *The dialogic imagination: four essays*. Ed. M. Holquist, trans. C. Emerson & M. Holquist. Austin, TX: University of Texas Press.

Bakhtin, M. (1986) *Speech genres and other late essays* (ed. C. Emerson & M. Holquist, trans. Vern W. McGee). Austin, TX: University of Texas Press.

Becker, A. L. (2000) *Beyond translation: essays toward a modern philology*. Ann Arbor: University of Michigan Press.

Berman, R. & Slobin, D. (1994) *Relating events in narrative: a crosslinguistic developmental study*. Hillsdale, NJ: Lawrence Erlbaum.

Bernstein, B. (1971) *Class, codes and control*. Vol. 1. London: Routledge & Kegan Paul.

Boas, F. ([1911] 1966) Introduction. *Handbook of American Indian languages*, vol. 1: *Bureau of American Ethnology Bulletin*, 40, 5–83.

Bruner, J. (1996) *The Culture of education*. Cambridge, MA: Harvard University Press.

Bruner, J. S., Goodnow J. J., & Austin, G. A. (1956) *A study of thinking*. New York: John Wiley and Sons.

Canagarajah, A. S. (1999) *Resisting linguistic imperialism in English teaching*. Oxford: Oxford University Press.

Chomsky, N. (1957) *Syntactic structures*. The Hague: Mouton.

Cook, G. (2000) *Language play, language learning*. Oxford: Oxford University Press.

Cook, V. (1993) *Linguistics and second language acquisition*. New York: St. Martin's Press.

Deacon, T. (1997) *The symbolic species: the co-evolution of language and the brain*. New York: W. W. Norton.

Duranti, A. & Goodwin (eds.) (1992) *Rethinking context: language as an interactive phenomenon*. Cambridge: Cambridge University Press.

Edwards, D. & Potter, J. (eds.) (1992) *Discursive psychology*. London: Sage.

Ellis, R. (1986) *Understanding second language acquisition*. Oxford: Oxford University Press.

Ellis, R. (ed.) (1987) *Second language acquisition in context*. Englewood Cliffs, NJ: Prentice-Hall.

Fairclough, N. (ed.) (1992) *Critical language awareness*. London: Longman.

Fauconnier, G. (1985) *Mental spaces: aspects of meaning construction in natural language*. Cambridge, MA: MIT Press.

Friedrich, P. (1986) *The language parallalax: linguistic relativism and poetic indeterminacy*. Austin, TX: University of Texas Press.

Geertz, C. (1983) *Local knowledge*. New York: Basic Books.

Geertz, C. (2000) *Available light: anthropological reflections on philosophical topics*. Princeton: Princeton University Press.

Gumperz, J. J. (1982a) *Discourse strategies*. Cambridge: Cambridge University Press.

Gumperz, J. J. (ed.) (1982b) *Language and social identity*. Cambridge: Cambridge University Press.

Gumperz, J. J. (1992) Contextualization and understanding. In A. Duranti & C. Goodwin (eds.), *Rethinking context: language as an interactive phenomenon* (pp. 229–52). Cambridge: Cambridge University Press.

Gumperz, J. J. (1996) The linguistic and cultural relativity of inference. In J. J. Gumperz & S. C. Levinson (eds.), *Rethinking linguistic relativity* (pp. 374–406). Cambridge: Cambridge University Press.

Gumperz, J. J. & Levinson, S. C. (1996) *Rethinking linguistic relativity*.

Cambridge: Cambridge University Press.

Halliday, M. A. K. (1978) *Language as social semiotic*. London: Edward Arnold.

Hanks, W. (1996) *Language and communicative practices*. Boulder, CO: Westview Press.

Herder, J. G. von ([1772] 1960) *Sprachphilosophische Schriften*. Hamburg: Felix Meiner Verlag.

Hill, J. & Mannheim, B. (1992) Language and worldview. *Annual Review of Anthropology*, 21, 381–406.

Holquist, M. (1990) *Dialogism: Bakhtin and his world*. London: Routledge.

Hymes, Dell (1996) *Ethnography, linguistics, narrative inequality: toward an understanding of voice*. London: Taylor & Francis.

Jacoby, S. & Ochs, E. (1995) Co-construction: an introduction. *Research in Language and Social Interaction*, 28(3), 171–84.

Jaworski, A. & Coupland, N. (eds.) (1999) *The discourse reader*. London: Routledge.

Johnson, M. (1987) *The body in the mind: the bodily basis of meaning, imagination, and reason*. Chicago: University of Chicago Press.

Kaplan, R. B. (1972) *The anatomy of rhetoric: prolegomena to a functional theory of rhetoric*. Philadelphia, PA: Center for Curriculum Development.

Kaplan, R. B. (1987) Cultural thought patterns revisited. In U. Connor & R. Kaplan (eds.), *Writing across languages: analysis of L2 text* (pp. 9–22). Reading, MA: Addison-Wesley.

Kasper, G. & Rose, K. (2001) *Research methods in interlanguage pragmatics*. Mahwah, NJ: Erlbaum.

Kramsch, C. (1993) *Context and culture in language teaching*. Oxford: Oxford University Press.

Kramsch, C. (1998) The privilege of the intercultural speaker. In M. Byram. & M. Fleming (eds.), *Foreign language learning in intercultural perspective* (pp. 16–31). Cambridge: Cambridge University Press.

Kramsch, C. (2001) Language, culture, and voice in the teaching of English as a foreign language. *NovELTy. A journal of English language teaching and cultural studies in Hungary*, 8(1), 4–21. (http://www.novelty.hu)

Kramsch, C. (2002a) Introduction: How can we tell the dancer from the dance? In C. Kramsch (ed.), *Language acquisition and language socialization: ecological perspectives* (pp. 1–30). London: Continuum.

Kramsch, C. (ed.) (2002b) *Language acquisition and language socialization: ecological perspectives*. London: Continuum.

Kramsch, C. (forthcoming) The multilingual subject. In I. de Florio-Hansen & A. Hu (eds.), *Mehrsprachigkeit und multikulturelle Identitaet* [Multilingualism and multicultural identity]. Tuebingen: Stauffenburg Verlag.

Labov, W. (1972) *Language in the inner city*. Philadelphia: University of Philadelphia Press.

Lakoff, G. (1987) *Women, fire, and dangerous things: what categories reveal about the mind*. Chicago: University of Chicago Press.

Lakoff, G. (1992) Metaphor and war: The metaphor system used to justify war in the Gulf. In H. Kreisler (ed.), *Confrontation in the Gulf: University of California professors talk about the war* (pp. 1–19). Berkeley, CA: Institute of International Studies.

Lakoff, G. & Johnson, M. (1980) *Metaphors we live by*. Chicago: University of Chicago Press.

Lakoff, R. T. (1990) *Talking power: the politics of language*. New York: Basic Books.

Lakoff, R. T. (2000) *The language war*. Berkeley: University of California Press.

Lantolf, J. (ed.) (2000) *Sociocultural theory and second language learning*. Oxford: Oxford University Press.

Larsen-Freeman, D. (2002) Language acquisition and language use from a chaos-complexity perspective. In C. Kramsch (ed.), *Language acquisition and language socialization: ecological perspectives* (pp. 33–46). London: Continuum.

Larsen-Freeman, D. & Long, M. (1991) *Introduction to second language acquisition research*. London: Longman.

Lemke, J. (2002) Language development and identity: Multiple timescales in the social ecology of learning. In C. Kramsch (ed.), *Language acquisition and language socialization: ecological perspectives* (pp. 68–87). London: Continuum.

Levinson, S. (1997) From outer to inner space: linguistic categories and non-linguistic thinking. In J. Nuyts & E. Pederson (eds.), *Language and conceptualization* (pp. 13–45). Cambridge: Cambridge University Press.

Lightbown, P. M. & Spada, N. (1993) *How languages are learned*. Oxford: Oxford University Press.

Lucy, J. (2000) Introductory comments. In S. Niemeier & R. Dirven (eds.), *Evidence for linguistic relativity* (pp. ix–xxi). Amsterdam: John Benjamins.

Lucy, J. & Wertsch, J. (1987) Vygotsky and Whorf: A comparative analysis. In M. Hickmann (ed.), *Social and functional approaches to language and thought* (pp. 67–86). New York: Academic Press.

Malinowski, B. (1923) The problem of meaning in primitive languages. Supplement 1 in C. K. Ogden & I. A. Richards, *The Meaning of meaning: a study of the influence of language upon thought and of the science of symbolism* (pp. 451–510). London: Kegan Paul.

Malinowski, B. (1935) *Coral gardens and their magic*, vol. 2. London: Allen & Unwin.

McNeill, R. (ed.) (1992) *Hand and mind: what gestures reveal about thought*. Chicago: University of Chicago Press

McNeill, R. & Duncan, S. D. (2000) Growth points in thinking-for-speaking. In R. McNeill, (ed.), *Language and gesture* (pp. 141–61). Cambridge: Cambridge University Press.

Moerman, M. (1988) *Talking culture: ethnography and conversation analysis*. Philadelphia: University of Pennsylvania Press.

Morson, G. & Emerson, C. (1990) *Mikhail Bakhtin: creation of a prosaics*. Stanford: Stanford University Press.

Niemeier, S. & Dirven, R. (eds.) (2000) *Evidence for linguistic relativity*. Amsterdam: John Benjamins.

Ochs, E. (1988) *Culture and language development: language acquisition and language socialization in a Samoan village*. Cambridge: Cambridge University Press.

Ochs, E. (1996) Linguistic resources for socializing humanity. In J. J. Gumperz & S. C. Levinson (eds.), *Rethinking linguistic relativity* (pp. 407–37). Cambridge: Cambridge University Press.

Ochs, E. (2002) Becoming a speaker of culture. In C. Kramsch (ed.), *Language acquisition and language socialization: ecological perspectives* (pp. 99–120). London: Continuum.

Ochs, E. & Schieffelin, B. (1984) Language acquisition and socialization: three developmental stories. In R. A. Shweder & R. A. LeVine (eds.), *Culture Theory: essays on mind, self, and emotion* (pp. 276–320). Cambridge: Cambridge University Press.

Pavlenko, A. (1999) New approaches to concepts in bilingual memory.

Bilingualism: Language and Cognition, 2(3), 209–30.

Pavlenko, A. (in press) Bilingualism and thought. In A. de Groot & J. Kroll (eds.), *Handbook of bilingualism: psycholinguistic approaches*. Oxford: Oxford University Press.

Pennycook, A. (1994) *The cultural politics of English as an international language*. London: Longman.

Pennycook, A. (1998) *English and the discourses of colonialism*. London: Routledge.

Pennycook, A. (2001) *Critical applied linguistics*. Mahwah, NJ: Erlbaum.

Pinker, S. (1994) *The language instinct: how the mind creates language*. New York: Harper & Row.

Rampton, B. (ed.) (1997) Retuning applied linguistics. Special issue of the *International Journal of Applied Linguistics*, 7(1).

Rampton, B. (2002) Ritual and foreign language practices at school. *Language in Society*, 31(4), 491–525.

Romaine, S. (1995) *Bilingualism* (2nd edn.). Oxford: Blackwell.

Sapir, E. (1962) *Culture, language and personality: selected essays*. Ed. David Mandelbaum. Berkeley: University of California Press.

Scherzer, J. (1987) A discourse-oriented approach to language and culture. *American Anthropologist*, 89(2), 295–309.

Schieffelin, B. & Ochs, E. (1986) *Language socialization across cultures*. Cambridge: Cambridge University Press.

Schultz, E. A. (1990) *Dialogue at the margins: Whorf, Bakhtin, and linguistic relativity*. Madison, WI: University of Wisconsin Press.

Shore, B. (1996) *Culture in mind: cognition, culture and the problem of meaning*. Oxford: Oxford University Press.

Silverstein, M. (1976) Shifters, linguistic categories, & cultural description. In K. Basso & H. Selby (eds.), *Meaning in anthropology* (pp. 11–55). Albuquerque: University of New Mexico Press.

Slobin, D. I. (1996) From "thought and language" to "thinking for speaking." In J. J. Gumperz & S. Levinson (eds.), *Rethinking linguistic relativity* (pp. 70–96). Cambridge: Cambridge University Press.

Slobin, D. I. (2000) Verbalized events. A dynamic approach to linguistic relativity and determinism. In S. Niemeier & R. Dirven (eds.), *Evidence for linguistic relativity* (pp. 108–38). Amsterdam: John Benjamins.

Spolsky, B. (1989) *Conditions for second language learning*. Oxford: Oxford University Press.

Stigler, J. W., Shweder, R. A., & Herdt, G. (eds.) (1990) *Cultural psychology: essays on comparative human development*. Cambridge: Cambridge University Press.

Tannen, D. (1998) *The argument culture*. New York: Random House.

Turner, M. (1996) *The literary mind: the origins of thought and language*. Oxford: Oxford University Press.

Van Lier, L. (2000) From input to affordance: Social-interactive learning from an ecological perspective. In J. Lantolf (ed.), *Sociocultural theory and second language learning* (pp. 245–60). Oxford: Oxford University Press.

Varela, F. J., Thompson, E., & Rosch, E. (1991) *The embodied mind: cognitive science and human experience*. Cambridge, MA: MIT Press.

Von Humboldt, W. ([1836] 1988) *On language: the diversity of human language structure and its influence on the mental development of mankind* (trans. P. Heath). Cambridge: Cambridge University Press.

Vygotsky, L. ([1934] 1962) *Thought and language*. Ed. and trans. E. Hanfmann & G. Vakar. Cambridge, MA: MIT Press.

Vygotsky, L. (1978) *Mind and society: the development of higher psychological processes* (ed. M. Cole, V. John-Steiner, S. Scribner, & E. Souberman). Cambridge, MA: Harvard University Press.

Vygotsky, L. (1981) The genesis of higher mental functions. In J. V. Wertsch (ed.), *The concept of activity in Soviet psychology* (pp. 144–88). Armonk, NY: Sharpe.

Wertsch, J. V. (ed.) (1985) *Culture, communication and cognition: Vygotskian perspectives*. Cambridge: Cambridge University Press.

Whorf, B. L. ([1940] 1956) *Language, thought, and reality: selected writings of Benjamin Lee Whorf*. Ed. J. B. Carroll. Cambridge, MA: MIT Press.

Widdowson, H. (1980) Applied linguistics: the pursuit of relevance. In Robert B. Kaplan (ed.), *On the scope of applied linguistics* (pp. 74–87). Rowley, MA: Newbury House.

Wierzbicka, A. (1992) *Semantics, culture, and cognition: universal human concepts in culture-specific configurations*. Oxford: Oxford University Press.

FURTHER READING

Lucy, J. (1992) *Language diversity and thought: a reformulation of the linguistic relativity hypothesis*. Cambridge: Cambridge University Press.

McNeill, R. (ed.) (2000) *Language and gesture*. Cambridge: Cambridge University Press.

10 Conversation Analysis

ROD GARDNER

10.1 Introduction

The primary focus of research in Conversation Analysis (CA) is talk rather than language. Talk is understood to be an occasion when people act out their sociality (cf. Schegloff, 1986). The emphasis within CA on the social can be traced historically to its emergence within the discipline of sociology in the 1960s. In the decades since, it has become cross-disciplinary. CA scholars can now being found working not only within sociology, but also within anthropology, social psychology, communication studies, linguistics, and applied linguistics. Within these disciplines CA has always remained a minority, if not marginal, interest. The reason for this can be seen partly in the nature of the object of enquiry. Talk is a complex activity, where language (and other paralinguistic and visual semiotic systems), cognition, and sociality meet. Its study can thus be seen as being located somewhere in the no man's land between the disciplines of linguistics, psychology, and sociology/anthropology. Despite, or perhaps because of, this position, its importance and influence has gradually grown over recent decades as the isolation of the various social sciences has, at least in part, been eroded.

What makes talk a worthy focus of study for social scientists from such a diversity of backgrounds? Talk is, first, "what appears to be the primordial site of sociality" (Schegloff, 1986, p. 112). This is an important notion with its implication that it is talk above all else that allows us to transcend isolation and to share our lives with others. Talk is a crucial activity at the center of world-changing events: summit meetings between world leaders, policy decisions in board rooms of multinational companies, international conferences on environmental policies. It is also a means we use to do the mundane and routine in life: the exchange of greetings with a neighbor, polite chit-chat with workmates during a break, ordering a snack at lunch time. At the more personal level, the important life events of courtship, divorce, and death are pivotally talked through. Indeed they would not exist as specifically human activities without talk. Life's experiences – the ordinary and the everyday, the profound and the momentous – are first and foremost experiences that are shared socially through the activity of talk.

It might be argued that talk is but one of a number of modes of communication and interaction available to humans, and so why privilege talk above, for example, writing or electronic modes? After all, virtually no complex modern activity – in politics, law, education, commerce, the electronic media, defense, finance, medicine, sport – can take place without written documents or computerized communication. The main question, however, is about which of these modes is most fundamentally human. Of these modes, only talk exists in all human social groups. Historically, and almost certainly phylogenetically, talk came first. And last but not least, talk is ontogenetically primary: children learn talk by mere exposure to their caregivers, whereas literate and electronic forms of communication need to be actively taught.

Whilst it can be argued that talk is the basic site of human sociality, this does not say why it may be of particular interest to applied linguists. Obviously language is a central and essential component of talk. This is made plain by talk on the telephone, which lacks the visual and the full audial channel, and is particularly heavily reliant on language. Also complex communication is impossible without language, even though, as all travelers know, certain basic needs can be met without language. One of the central concerns of applied linguists has been to understand how language is used for communication, therefore it follows that an understanding of how language is used in talk must be a central foundation for the discipline.

CA is one of a number of approaches to the study of spoken language. It differs from other approaches in respect to certain theoretical assumptions, methodological principles, and analytic techniques. In terms of the object of the enquiry, there are certain aspects of talk that have, from the beginning, been central to CA to a greater extent than for other approaches. The first of these is the notion of interaction. Whilst most approaches to discourse tend to focus on the speaker, in CA talk is seen as a jointly accomplished activity, with the listener and the speaker given equal status as co-constructors of the emerging talk. Speakers design their contributions specifically for the recipients of the talk, and listeners in turn influence the speaker by the responses they give. Each unit of talk builds upon the prior talk, and is understood by participants in light of their understanding of that prior talk. To take a simple example, if an utterance is understood by a listener to be a first greeting, then there are expectations that the most likely next utterance will be another greeting. It is in this way that talk is seen as co-constructed by listeners and speakers.

The second and related aspect of talk that CA pays particular attention to is temporality. One outcome of this is a focus on two sides of the "time" coin: silence and simultaneous talk in conversation. Thus a silence can profoundly affect how some talk that precedes or follows it is understood, and simultaneous talk may be indicative of how speakers are understanding or feeling about each other. A consideration of time also opens up questions relating to how talk emerges moment by moment, is highly locally organized, with participants showing split-second sensitivities to others' contributions. These are evident in, for example, the onset of a speaker's turn, or a mid-utterance change in the formulation of an emerging turn.

These features of talk work together in complex ways. One of the major objectives of CA is to describe how the various sub-systems of talk combine, and to provide an account of the mechanics of talk. Such an account will then provide a focus not only on how speakers' utterances are constructed prosodically, grammatically, and lexically – turn design – but also on how speakers overwhelmingly cooperate in an orderly taking of turns, and how these turns are sequenced into sets of actions, as adjacent pairs and more extended sequences.

10.2   Foundations of CA

One of the basic precepts of CA is that ordinary everyday conversation is most basic to human interaction and sociality. Other forms of talk, such as interviews in work or media settings, medical consultations, courtroom inter-action, classroom talk, and any other forms of institutional talk, derive from and are a simplification of ordinary conversation in terms of the organization of the speech exchange system, and of the types of actions sanctioned. This is based on an observation that turn-taking, for example, is at its most complex in ordinary conversation, even though the basic rules of conversation are relatively simple. In institutional talk in media, educational, legal, medical settings, in contrast, there are usually constraints on who talks at what point, and who has rights to select next speakers. There are also usually constraints on what kinds of actions a particular participant may undertake, such as who asks the questions and who provides the answers. In the early years of CA there was therefore a focus on what was considered the more basic form of talk, namely conversation, deriving from an assumption that in order to understand how something works, the best place to start is with the most fundamental form of that thing. It was not until the 1980s that CA scholars began to turn their attention extensively to non-conversational forms of talk. The prevailing belief was that it was necessary first to lay a certain descriptive foundation, before turning analytic attention to the derived forms of talk that are its institutional forms.

It can thus be seen that a basic claim in CA is that ordinary conversation is the default version of talk (and by implication perhaps of language too), and that all other forms of talk-in-interaction are derived from ordinary con-versation, and are thus culturally and socially restricted. For example, modes of talk in education, in law, in the media, in medicine, are likely to be derived from local (cultural) needs and contingencies, and adaptations of talk will encompass these. The corollary of this is that ordinary conversation is likely, at least in many of its practices, to be universal. This latter claim remains to be demonstrated empirically, but on the basis of research so far, there are no compelling grounds to suspect that this view is wrong.

10.2.1 Historical foundations

10.2.1.1 Garfinkel and Goffman: ethnomethodology and the study of the interaction order

CA is historically linked to ethnomethodology, and indeed many of the precepts of the latter were espoused by Harvey Sacks and Emanuel Schegloff in the emergent days of CA in the 1960s. Ethnomethodology had its roots in the late 1940s and 1950s with Harold Garfinkel, a sociologist who started by studying jury deliberations in the USA. He was asking questions about how juries came to their decisions: about what constitutes an adequate account of an event, or an adequate description, or adequate evidence in and for what they were doing. He found that mainstream sociology of the day did not help him much. He was unhappy with the privileged position of the scientist, which claimed access to social reality that is denied the "ordinary" person, given to the scientist through a belief that social scientific method is superior to ordinary, everyday common sense. As Heritage (1984) puts it, there is a belief in the cognitive superiority of science.

Simultaneously in ethnomethodology there is a denial of a model of an external social reality consisting of a set of fixed norms, beliefs, and values. Garfinkel's challenge to the mainstream was to put the pursuit of an understanding of a common sense and a locally achieved everyday construction of reality at the center of his research agenda. In other words, he sought to investigate how the ordinary person interactively and reflexively achieves an understanding of everyday practical life, its "policies, methods, risks, procedures, strategies," and thus to explicate "the rule governed activities of everyday life" (Garfinkel, 1967, p. 35).

A second important figure to influence Sacks was Ervin Goffman (Sacks was a student of both Goffman and Garfinkel). Goffman (e.g., 1959, 1967) was probably the first major social scientist to look in close detail at people interacting. His particular genius was to be able to make acute observations of human interactions without the aid of electronic recordings. He helped pave the way for the study of human sociality at the micro-level (individuals interacting with other individuals, small group interactions), in reaction to the prevailing concerns of contemporary sociology with macro-level phenomena.

These two major pioneers were ground breakers for the emergence of CA in the 1960s, with its own distinct agenda.

10.2.1.2 Early CA

CA developed as a distinctive intellectual movement in the 1960s, yet still sharing much of its philosophical base with ethnomethodology. One such shared base is the examination of practical reasoning in everyday life, exemplified through what is considered to be the key instantiation of this: talk-in-interaction. CA is the study of sequences of actions and their interactional products, with the starting point being the "unique adequacy" of such an instance, what it is that makes some talk just that which it is, and nothing else. It is not, initially at least, and in its practice as ethnomethodology, a search for generalizations, but a description of how an interaction works in and of itself. In practice, over years of accumulation of descriptions of turn-taking practices, the organization of repairs to conversational troubles, or the ways in which actions build into sequences, some generalizations have emerged, but nevertheless CA is characterized by great caution in this respect, and an insistence on beginning an analysis of an instance of talk with a description of what is going on uniquely, rather than from assumptions of practices based on prior research.

In its origins, CA borrows from ethnomethodology three basic themes: accountability, reflexivity, and indexicality (cf. Garfinkel, 1967). Accountability refers to members' own methods for making their actions visible and reportable to other members – that is, accountable as ways of doing everyday activities. It is assumed (and has turned out to be massively so in talk) that these activities are orderly, observable, ordinary, oriented to, rational, and describable. Accounts are possible because practices underlying social actions, including talk, can be reproduced and can be learned, for example by the very young, or by a non-member.

Reflexivity refers to a conviction that such accountability reflects the talk in all its aspects: the field of action, the settings, the practices of talk, the actions and activities of a social interaction. Members' accounts of ordinary social actions reflect the social actions themselves.

Indexicality refers to a belief that meanings in language are dependent upon the locus in which they are used. This extends the notion of deixis in linguistics to claim that *all* language is indexical, or less radically, that all utterances are adequate only if they are suited to the local conditions in which they are being used. It thus rejects a context-free characterization of language (or of situated practice) as inadequate and unrealizable. This ethnomethodological side of CA can be seen as an attempt to ask the question about how actors make adequate sense and adequate reference in their social field. It is an "inside-out" rather than an "outside-in" attempt at understanding talk.

These Garfinkelian beginnings have led on the one side to ethnomethodological studies of work. The other main development has been CA, which has diverged in a number of significant ways from ethnomethodology. A full discussion of Sacks' early career and his intellectual influences can be found in Schegloff, 1992a and 1992b. Much of the following discussion is indebted to this source. In the early days, Harvey Sacks studied suicide prevention meetings, group therapy sessions, phone conversations, and dinner conversations as a way of getting into the study of natural, spontaneous social activities. Goffman's anecdotal and insightful studies of face-to-face interaction were influential in these early stages, though mainly in that they had shown that face-to-face interaction was a valid object of study, rather than that they influenced strongly the methodology that Sacks developed to study conversation. His influences were very wide, and included, perhaps surprisingly, Chomsky, some of whose early lectures he attended. It became apparent that parties in conversations can achieve coherent, rational, mutually comprehensible interactive talk despite a preponderance of apparently vague and imprecise language. He and Schegloff came to see conversation as something that could be examined as an object of inquiry in its own right. Talk was itself action, and not a mere window to other processes, social or cognitive or linguistic. The early years of the emergence of the study of conversation and talk is, fortunately, largely captured in Sacks' lectures between 1964 and 1972, published as a collection edited by Gail Jefferson in 1992.

One way of putting the question that CA addresses is, "How can you provide an adequate description of any event?" The next section provides an account of CA's attempt to answer that question.

10.2.2 *Methodological issues in CA*

A basic belief in CA is that society is constituted first and foremost through conversation and talk-in-interaction, of which language is a crucial facet. CA is a search for order in talk, which is seen as one (the most important one) of "the rule governed activities of everyday life" (Garfinkel, 1967, p. 35). The fundamental way in which we accomplish our lives is through talk-in-interaction: the routine and the abnormal, the trivial and the profound, the mundane and the extraordinary. CA proposes an examination of the fine detail of talk, of the underlying structures that members of the social group draw upon to constitute their social world. It takes a highly empirical approach to analysis. A conversation analyst would eschew intuitive interpretations of data based on native speaker competence. Instead the goal is to discover how participants themselves understand and interpret what they are doing. The analyst does this with an approach which Psathas (1990) has called "unmotivated looking." One examines the data with as few assumptions and preconceptions about what is going on as possible, and with nothing being dismissed a priori as disorderly, accidental, or trivial. Ethnographic information is of secondary importance, in the sense that no assumptions are made based on, for example, institutional roles (mother, doctor, colonel, witness) or gender or institutional position, unless it can be demonstrated that these factors are invoked or displayed or made relevant by participants through the talk. The analysis also demotes to secondary importance any retrospective, recollected description of events, as it is assumed that the recording captures more reliably what happened than memory can (whilst granting, of course, that recordings are themselves imperfect). Neither are macro-social assumptions about how, for instance, doctors or women or bosses can be expected to behave taken as primary sources for analysis. In practice, of course, such "unmotivated looking" is difficult, if not impossible, to achieve completely. The point, however, is to reduce, as far as possible, the influence of one's preconceptions on what one hears and sees. The achievement of this skill is part of the training of a conversation analyst.

The way into the data, as developed initially by Sacks, is to take a short piece of real interaction for study, consider it for the effects achieved through it, and then ask how this was done, i.e., what underlying methods and procedures are used. Such an approach does not enable an account in any generalizable or comprehensive way of the necessary conditions for the doing of an action, for example an invitation, but is a partial account of a situated instance of such an action. Correspondingly, the way into the data is not through an appeal to some extra-interactional phenomenon, such as notions of politeness or assumptions about the influence of gender, or a set of rules describing generalized conditions for the production of an utterance, but by an examination of an utterance as one within a sequence of utterances, each of which exhibits links of relevance to those preceding and following it.

The implication of this is also that the roles, relationships, and characteristics of participants in a conversation are not invoked in the analysis, unless they are perceivably relevant in the data. In the case of ordinary conversation, a participant's gender would be deemed relevant only if the participants themselves invoked gender as relevant to the talk. Even in the case of, for instance, a doctor–patient consultation, the role "doctor" or "patient" is not assumed, though in most (but not all) cases it quickly becomes apparent that the participants themselves are oriented to their particular roles. But it is to be noted at the same time that the constants in these instances are the roles and constellations of "doctor" or "patient," whilst the individuals themselves are ephemeral, in the sense that sooner or later they will slip into other roles, such as parent, shopper, or friend, and also during the doctor–patient consultation there may be phases when the institutional roles are backgrounded. The payoff for this approach is that the methodology demands of the analyst a constant attention to what is demonstrably occurring in the interaction without interpreting certain actions as being accountable for by the assumed characteristics of a person as "woman" or "doctor" or "punk."

The procedures of the project of CA are accomplished through analysis based on the evidence of the talk that is produced by members of a conversational community incorporating certain roles, followed up by discussion of findings amongst the community of analysts. The way to study this talk is through recordings in audio or video of naturally occurring events: conversations, talk in classrooms, interviews in the media, trials in courtrooms, meetings in offices, consultations in doctors' surgeries, surveys in call centers. A requirement is that these talk events should be natural, that is, they would have taken place in pretty much the same way had they not been recorded. The analysis takes place by playing the recording repeatedly, and whilst one is listening, transcribing it. In this way, the analyst becomes increasingly familiar with the data, both through the repeated listening and through the close transcribing process. Transcription follows a system largely developed by

Gail Jefferson (e.g., Jefferson, 1984). This process is to be seen not as a means to capture the data for later analysis, but as a tool to become as closely familiar with the object of inquiry as possible, thereby turning the act of transcription into an act of analysis.

It is not surprising that such an austere, even reductionist, approach to discourse will attract its critics. It has been said, for example, that the focus on the local, the "micro," or the "molecular" has the consequence that the larger socioeconomic and historical context is neglected. However, this criticism can be turned around to ask how it is possible to provide an adequate description of any event. As Sacks (1963) put it, when comparing the validity of different descriptions in social science:

> The feature of any description that it will not only be incomplete but that (a) it could be indefinitely extended and (b) the extension cannot be handled by a formula for extrapolation, implies that any description can be read as far from complete, or as close to complete, as any others. From simply reading two descriptions of variant length, style, etc., one could conclude that while one is more elaborate the other is more terse, while one is more extensive the other more intensive, etc.

The procedure, then, is to begin with a detailed description at the micro-level, without the presumption of attempting comprehensiveness or any attempt at a definitive description. One describes only what is hearable and seeable in the data, interpreted through the context of the talk.

The notion of context in CA requires some explication: it is the context of the actions in the talk. Any utterance is both context-shaped and context-renewing. It is context-shaped by the "immediately local configuration of preceding activity," and by the "larger environment of activity," and context-renewing in that each utterance functions "to renew (i.e., maintain, adjust, or alter) any broader or more generally prevailing sense of context" (Drew & Heritage, 1992, p. 18). In other words, what is said in the unfolding talk will be interpreted in the light of what has just been said (context-shaped), and will in turn provide the context for the interpretation of the next utterance (context-renewing). Although this raises largely what might be called the textual or discourse context, aspects of the spatio-temporal situation can also be invoked, through what is made noticeable or salient by the speakers' talk. Thus ethnographic information will be considered relevant contextual information only if it is displayed by participants as being relevant. For instance, it is not considered important that one interactant is a male unless there are recoverable features in the talk that display the relevance of that person's role as male, through the explicit, or at least recoverable, orientation of participants to the maleness of the person.

A metaphor for this approach to context is Bateson's "blind man with a stick," which "takes as a point of departure for the analysis of context the perspective of the participant(s) whose behavior is being analyzed" (Goodwin

& Duranti, 1992, p. 4). Bateson's question asked what, when describing an act of a blind man walking through a city, would be the relevant contextual features. Potentially these are vast, and in terms of Sacks' view of description, could be indefinitely extended and could not be handled by any formula. They could include the total social, physical, and historical environment, including places for pedestrians, vehicles, traffic lights, traffic regulations, buildings, air temperature, pollution levels, descriptions of other pedestrians, their personal histories, what happened on this street a year ago, a century ago, and so on ad infinitum. Following Goodwin and Duranti, though, a principled approach to context would be to describe only what is specifically invoked in the talk, what the talker or walker makes relevant by making it perceptible, seeable/ hearable through the talk, or through the tapping of the stick, and following how this changes from moment to moment. There is, though, a sense in which Bateson's blind person metaphor is limited when it comes to describing context: in talk participants are not only in the event, but they are also creating the event.

Schegloff (1988) has provided perhaps the most succinct summary of the CA approach to context. He says of it:

> I refer . . . not to social contexts like offices, classrooms or families, but sequential contexts formulated in terms of more or less proximately preceding talk and the real jobs of projecting further talk which utterances can do, for which they can be inspected by their recipients, an inspection to which speakers must therefore be reflexively attentive. Such prior and prospective contexts are inescapably implicated in the real-life projects, however humble or exalted, which are being prosecuted through the talk. These real-life projects, and the sequential infrastructure of talk-in-interaction, are involved in the production and analysis of talk by the parties in such intimate detail that we are only beginning to understand it. But it is clear that temporality and sequentiality are inescapable; utterances are in turns, and turns are parts of sequences; sequences and the projects done through them enter constitutively into utterances like the warp of a woven fabric.

Context can thus be seen not as a "set of variables that statistically surround strips of talk," but as standing in "a mutual reflexive relationship [to talk], with talk, and the interpretive work it generates, shaping context as much as context shapes talk" (Goodwin & Duranti, 1992, p. 31).

10.3   Principal Findings in CA

The body of findings in CA has grown to a large corpus over the decades since the late sixties. An attempt at summarizing the main findings must therefore remain partial. In this section, there is a sketch of some important findings in the fields of turn-taking, sequence organization, repair, turn design, and prosody.

10.3.1 *Turn-taking*

The seminal paper in CA on turn-taking is the paper by Sacks, Schegloff, and Jefferson that appeared in 1974, "A simplest systematics for the organization of turn-taking for conversation." Whilst the initial claims made in that paper have been refined over the years, for example concerning what constitutes a turn constructional unit (the basic unit of talk), or what the notion of turn completion means, the set of characteristics and rules of turn-taking have remained the definitive statement on the phenomenon. In particular, the rules for turn allocation in conversation have stood the test of time, despite criticism that they are derived from the turn-taking conventions of middle-class male America. However, as a basic set of rules they have thus far been shown to shed light on turn-taking practices across a range of languages and cultures, including Thai, Japanese, Finnish, and German. This is not to say there are no differences. Some variations in practice derive, for example, from the grammar, e.g. clause-final particles in Japanese, or the end placement of the main verb in German. It has also been claimed that cultural differences in the tolerance of simultaneous talk or of silence will entail differences in turn-taking practices, with Italian frequently cited as an example of a linguistic culture with "everyone talking at the same time," and Australian Aboriginal culture as one where very extended periods of silence are tolerated. These claims notwithstanding, there do not appear to be any studies on languages other than American English that are based on a close analysis of actually occurring conversations which show that speakers do not (1) orient to transition relevance places at points of possible completion, (2) include both speaker selection of next speaker or self-selection by next speaker, (3) have various devices (many of which have been described) for extending or curtailing turns at talk or current speakership, or dealing with simultaneous talk when it occurs.

The rules as set out by Sacks, Schegloff, and Jefferson (1974) are as follows. A TRP is a transition relevance place, which is the place in the turn at which it becomes relevant or legitimate for another party in the conversation to begin speaking. C is current speaker and N is next speaker.

Rule 1 – applies initially at the first TRP of any turn
(a) If C selects N in current turn, then C must stop speaking, and N must speak next, transition occurring at the first TRP after N-selection.
(b) If C does not select N, then any (other) party may self-select, first speaker gaining rights to the next turn.
(c) If C has not selected N, and no other party self-selects under option (b), then C may (but need not) continue (i.e. claim rights to a further turn-constructional unit).

Rule 2 – applies to all subsequent TRPs
When rule 1(c) has been applied by C, then at the next TRP Rules 1(a)–(c) apply, and recursively at the next TRP, until speaker change is effected.

These rules constitute a context-free set, which are applicable to any conversation. They are also context-sensitive, in the sense that they are applied locally in any conversation. Two points can be noted about these rules. First, they have built into them a mechanism that privileges speaker change, as only if rules 1(a) and 1(b) are not applied can the current speaker continue to speak. Second, these are rules to be oriented to, not slavishly followed. They are a set of expectations about conversational turn-taking behavior, which can be temporarily revoked by a speaker if they deem that local exigencies of the conversation require it. This can result, for example, in the occurrence of interruptions or other forms of simultaneous talk.

It also needs to be noted that these rules are for ordinary conversation, and not for other forms of talk, such as classrooms, courtrooms, media interviews, or committee meetings. What one invariably finds in such institutional settings is that the rules are simplified, so that for example one speaker alone (the teacher, the judge, the interviewer, the chairperson) has rights for speaker selection, and there is no sanctioned self-selection by other participants.

The strength of these rules is that they are simple, yet robust, and they can be shown to account not only for orderly turn-taking behavior, but also for apparent breakdowns in orderliness. But conversations rarely break down completely. This is in part because the turn-taking rules provide an organizational bedrock for orderliness in talk, without them being a straitjacket, so that cultural, gender, class or other differences can be encompassed within conversational turn-taking behaviors without the rules, as a set of basic practices, being abandoned.

10.3.2   *Adjacency pairs and sequence organization*

A second level of orderliness in the organization of talk is that of the sequencing of actions in talk. At one level this deals with the obvious: a question tends to be followed by an answer, a greeting by a greeting, an offer by an acceptance or a rejection. This basic pairing of actions in conversation has led to the notion of adjacency pairs. The basic rules for the production of adjacency pairs were formulated early in the history of CA, by Schegloff and Sacks (1973).

> Given the recognizable production of a first pair part, at its first possible completion its speaker should stop, a next speaker should start, and should produce a second pair part of the same pair type.

Thus adjacency pairs are composed of two turns by different speakers, and speakers orient to them being placed adjacently. Typical first pair parts include questions, requests, offers, invitations, advice, and informings. Typical second pair parts include answers, acceptances, rejections, declines, agreements, and disagreements. There are constraints on these pairings, thus questions take answers, greetings take return greetings, and requests take grants or rejects. A way of expressing these constraints is to say that a first pair part is sequentially implicative of a second pair part. If, upon the utterance of a first pair part, the second pair part is missing, its absence is noticeable, and regularly remarked on by speakers. As Schegloff (1990) put it, the second pair part becomes officially absent.

Adjacency pairs constitute a basic sequencing occasion in talk, in which chains of adjacency pairs can often be located. Basic adjacency pairs can, though, also be expanded at any point: before the first pair part, between the two parts, or after the second pair part. These expansions can become very elaborate, with sometimes several minutes of talk hung on a single adjacency pair.

Expansions are usually adjacency pairs in their own right. In pre-expansions an adjacency pair may pave the way for the main adjacency pair. Before an invitation, for example, an enquiry about availability is regularly made, as in "What are you doing?" which may be followed by a "go-ahead" in the form of "Nothing." This adjacency pair is subsidiary to the actual invitation and its response, as in, "Want a drink?" – "Why not." Such pre-sequences pre-monitor the actions that are projected. A plausible reason can be found in a consideration of the observation that very many first pair parts have two principal possible second pair parts. In the case of an invitation, these are an acceptance or a rejection. It has also been observed that there is a structurally inbuilt preference of one of these responses, which may be glossed as the positive response. In the case of invitations, the preferred response is the acceptance rather than a decline, in the case of a self-deprecation, it would be a rejection rather than an acceptance of that self-deprecation, in the case of an assessment it would be an agreement with the assessment rather than a disagreement. The description of preference organization is based not through appeal to some notion such as politeness, or what a speaker would "prefer" to do, but on the observation that preferred responses to a first pair part are done differently to dispreferred ones. Thus acceptances of invitations are, overwhelmingly, straightforward, immediate, and brief. Declines of invitations, on the other hand, are frequently delayed, both temporally through a longer than normal silence before the response, and also sequentially, in that they may be preceded by some other action, such as a turn-initial "well" or "uhn," or an account for why the invitation is going to be rejected, or a thanks for the invitation. Similar kinds of preference organization are found for other "bipolar" first pair parts. Thus requests show a preference for a grant over a reject, offers for an accept over a decline (though very generous offers show a preference for a decline over an accept), compliments for a reject over an accept, announcements for an alignment with the announcement rather than a disalignment.

An explanation for some pre-sequences is that they can avoid dispreferred second pair parts. Thus if the response to "What are you doing?" is "I'm busy," then the prospective inviter can see that certain conditions for an invitation are not met, and thus an invitation is unlikely to follow, and the dispreferred response of a decline is avoided. Indeed many pre-sequences avoid the potential for some future trouble. A "generic" summons-answer pre-sequence, used to engage the attention of a co-present person, as in "Gary," followed by "Yeah," is used to avoid the potential trouble of lack of attention. A preliminary to preliminaries (cf. Schegloff, 1980), as in "Can I ask you a question?" which is followed by the provision of essential background information before the question is asked, is used to avoid the potential trouble of lack of knowledge on the part of the recipient. A pre-story, as in "Did you hear what happened to Jill yesterday?" can be used to avoid the potential trouble both of the story being old news to the recipients, and also the potential trouble of transition relevance, for once a story is underway, it is important that the storyteller is not interrupted at every transition relevance place.

Adjacency pairs can also be expanded between the first and second pair parts, or after the second pair part. Insertion sequences often occur as repairs to an actual or potential misunderstanding of the first pair part, to clear up a mishearing or ambiguity or non-comprehension, before doing the second pair part. They may also seek more information, such as finding out the reason for an invitation or a request before accepting or granting it. Post expansions may also be repairs, to clarify a potential or actual misunderstanding of a second pair part. They may also do things such as acknowledge a second pair part, or express thanks for it, or expand on it is some way.

Any adjacency pair can be expanded. One finds, for instance, insertion sequences within pre-sequences, or post-sequences to insertion sequences, so that some sequences of talk can become extremely complex. However, even the most complex of sequences are still organized around adjacency pairs.

10.3.3   *Repair*

Repairs can occur as adjacency pairs. They then constitute a very particular kind of pair, one that is used to deal with troubles of hearing, production, or understanding in talk. One astonishing feature of talk is how unusual breakdown is. This is not to say, of course, that total understanding is the norm in conversation, nor that it is not, but it is to claim that generally the organization, structures, and coherence of talk are maintained, and that when that orderliness is threatened with breakdown, overwhelmingly that threat is dealt with very quickly, and orderliness is restored.

Most repairs do not in fact occur as sequences, but are achieved by a speaker dealing with a problem him- or herself during the production of a turn. These self-repairs in the same turn take the form of a replacement or insertion or deletion of a piece of talk, or of a reordering of the elements of a turn. Other repairs are achieved more collaboratively. The recipient of some talk may indicate difficulty with it. This can take the form of a "Pardon?" or a "Who?" or "Did you say X?" In such cases initiation of repair takes place in the turn subsequent to the turn in which the source of the trouble occurs. More rarely, a speaker may not realize there is trouble until a response has been heard, and thus initiate repair in the third turn. Even rarer is initiation in the fourth turn. Beyond that turn, no repair initiation has been described.

There is also a preference for the speaker of the trouble turn to do the repair (cf. Schegloff, Jefferson, & Sacks, 1977). That is, whilst another speaker regularly initiates repair, which is then typically done in the third turn by the trouble source speaker, it is comparatively rare for another speaker to actually carry out the repair. Thus problems of understanding are overwhelmingly dealt with efficiently, mostly by the speaker of the trouble source, and mostly very close to the source of the trouble.

10.3.4   Turn design

A more recent strong focus in CA has been turn design, in particular the aspects of grammar or the way in which a turn at talk, or a turn constructional unit, is put together. This is an area of inquiry in which linguists have obvious credentials to make a contribution. Rather than approach the grammar of a sentence as a psychological phenomenon, it can be considered as something that is constructed in response to the contingencies of the local meaning and social requirements of the emerging talk. This is, more or less, the old question about the relationship between form and function: the morphosyntax and lexis of an utterance, and the action it is designed to achieve.

Early CA was somewhat naive in its understanding of grammar, which is perhaps not surprising, given that the practitioners were sociologists. The unit of talk (the turn constructional unit, or TCU) was considered to be a word, a phrase, a clause, or a sentence (Sacks, Schegloff, & Jefferson, 1974), but the importance of prosody was at least recognized. More recently some linguists have focused on grammar in conversational talk, notably West Coast Functionalists in the USA (e.g., Ono & Thompson, 1995; Ford & Thompson, 1996). Their approach has been to look at how people construct utterances in real time, and in particular the way in which they use regular, patterned, grammatical schemas under the constraints of having to talk in interaction. Their view is that syntactic constructional schemas need to be flexible enough to be subordinated to local interactional contingencies. Ono and Thompson suggest that syntactic schemas are abstract prototypes, which speakers and listeners orient to in a rough and ready and tolerant way. The research agenda is to demonstrate how certain constructions are chosen to achieve particular actions, and how these choices are motivated, in part at least, by local interactional contingencies.

It also raises questions about what constitutes a unit of talk. A turn can be from a single morpheme (or even a phoneme or a non-verbal/non-vocal element), to a complex of several clauses. Turns are packaged as intonational units, and are further chunked into units of meaning, or pragmatic units. So there is broad agreement that a unit of talk is phonological (units of intonation), grammatical (clauses, clause complexes, or sub-clausal units) and pragmatic (action or meaning units). But many questions remain unanswered (Schegloff, 1996). What elements make up a TCU? How do you deal with repetitions or revisions, or with mid-turn silences? Where do turns start? Is a pre-turn inbreath part of the TCU? Where do they end? What is the relationship between a TCU and the previous TCU, and the following one?

Ford & Thompson (1996) have proposed an answer to a few of these questions. They found, for example, that speaker change occurs most regularly where there is a coincidence of pragmatic, intonational, and syntactic completion, but that syntactic completion regularly occurs without the other two, and is not, in itself, a good predictor of speaker change. Their conclusion is that these three systems work together to determine where a unit of talk begins and ends.

Much remains to be done to work out the complex relationship between the form of a turn, and the action it is designed to do. There is reason to believe that a study of grammar in talk can help to understand in a principled way the relationship between the grammatical resources available in a language, for example the many possible ways to ask a question, and the sequential position of an action, for example whether this is an only question, or the first in a series, or a later one in a series.

10.3.5   *Prosody in talk*

Another area in which linguists have contributed to the broader CA project is prosody, in particular a group of German linguists engaged in what they call "interactional linguistics" (e.g., Auer & di Luzio, 1992; Couper-Kuhlen & Selting, 1996; Selting & Couper-Kuhlen, 2001). Whilst their interest is not restricted to prosody, and they are not the only scholars looking at prosody in conversation, they have made a particularly strong contribution to the area, one which has traditionally been a weak point in CA studies (but see Local & Kelly, 1986; Kelly & Local, 1989). Their studies have included descriptions of intonational and other prosodic forms and practices in relation to grammatical phenomena in interactional settings such as indirect speech, questions, clause subordination, the beginnings of stories, emphatic speech, focusing on features such as pitch level, the level of onset at the beginning of a unit of talk, terminal pitch direction, and rhythm in conversational talk. They have opened up systematic studies in this highly complex area.

10.4   CA and Applied Linguistics

The discussion of the foundations and principles of CA so far has not addressed its relevance to applied linguistics in any detail, though it should be clear that the fundamental subject matter of CA is also of interest to applied linguistics. For example, in the field of language teaching, the nature of language as a communication, or language in use, has been a central issue at least since the 1970s. Conversation and talk in general are the home of language in use. In both CA and applied linguistics, despite their different home disciplines and some obviously different foci of attention and terminology, there is a concern to understand how people communicate with each other, and how people use language-as-talk to accomplish certain actions.

This common ground was recognized quite early by some university educators. In some MAs in Applied Linguistics from the late 1970s in Britain and North America, with a changing understanding of the nature language, which included psychological and social aspects, an indebtedness can be traced to a number of disciplines beyond linguistics, including ethnomethodology for CA. Thus a generation of applied linguists emerged with an awareness of, if not a training in, CA.

In the 1990s the cross-over between sociology and applied linguistics became particularly strong at UCLA, California, where many applied linguistics graduate students were given a strong training in CA through departmental links to the conversation analysis program in sociology. Today this cross-disciplinary training has spread, notably to Finland, but also to Denmark, Germany, and Australia. The 1990s saw the emergence of a growing, though still small, corpus of published research from these students in what can be called applied conversation analysis, in the fields of second language education, language testing, second language acquisition, and second language discourse. There are two main areas of interest for applied linguists from the work of CA. First, the study of institutional talk has increased our understanding of language in use in a variety of settings. Second, more recent studies have contributed more directly, albeit in a small way so far, to central traditional areas of applied linguistics, such as language teaching, language testing, and second language acquisition.

10.5   Applications of CA

10.5.1   *Institutional talk*

When we are dealing with organizations, either as agents or professionals, or as clients, patients, or customers, we engage in institutional talk. This talk is the means by which practical tasks and activities are performed in pursuit of organizational goals. Indeed, a CA approach to such talk is that the institution does not provide a context for a particular type of talk (the "bucket" theory of context), but that the institutional context is talked into existence by the participants: they build the context in their talk and through their talk (Heritage, 1997).

The main thrust of work in CA on talk in institutional or work settings has focused on the methods and practices by which parties in institutional talk orient to and play out their institutional identities, in particular through turn-taking practices and the types of actions performed by the speakers (Drew & Sorjonen, 1997). Commensurate with basic methodological and theoretical principles in CA, the approach has been to examine in detail at a micro-level how participants in institutional talk manifest their institutional conduct through the talk they produce (Drew & Heritage, 1992). One manifestation of this is an observable orientation of participants to the institutional goals: there is a more or less stable understanding about the objectives of the task at hand, both by the institutional professionals and the lay participants, though these can differ and even clash, as professionals are likely to have knowledge and understanding of the institution that are not made explicit for the lay person.

A second manifestation is that constraints are placed on participants. This is very noticeable in a courtroom, where people have clearly defined roles, but is also present, less rigidly, in other kinds of institutional interaction, such as medical consultations. The degree of constraint and institutionality may vary according to the phase of the encounter. Information gathering and diagnosis may follow routines closely, whilst a closing phase may be very like ordinary conversation.

A third manifestation is the ways in which participants think or make inferences as they make their ways through the interaction. For example, news interviewers withhold response tokens such as *uh huh*, probably because the main recipients of the talk are the audience, and it is recipients who do response tokens. Doctors generally withhold *ohs*, which can be indicative of "newness" or "surprise," and might be construed as prefatory to bad news. Together these three features of institutional talk leave a "fingerprint" that is identifiably that of a particular interaction.

Specific resources for achieving an institutionality to the talk include the ways in which speakers refer to themselves and others (e.g., job titles, collective "we" for the institution), lexical choice (e.g., the specialist vocabulary of a specialist field), grammatical form (e.g., choice of grammar for questions in different phases of a medical interview), turn-taking and sequencing (e.g., media interviewer holding back a question and interviewee holding back an answer until the end of a complex turn).

Once certain characteristic ways of talking in particular institutional settings have been described, it is possible to compare these with description of other settings. For example, Heritage and Sorjonen (1994) found that many questions in medical encounters between health visitors and new parents were prefaced with an *and*, but only in certain phases of the interview. By comparing the different phases, they were able to show that *and*-prefaced questions occur when routine questions (for form-filling) are being asked. The resources used to "make institutional" some talk that participants may be engaged in do not appear to be restricted to a particular institutional setting, but they may be used in a certain frequency, in certain sequential positions, in certain combinations, that together constitute the institutionality of the talk.

There is now an emerging literature on talk in institutional settings: medical, counseling, educational, legal, media, business, administrative, service encounters. There has also recently been an emerging literature in which conversation analysts, particularly those with an applied linguistic training, have published studies in language education, testing, and second language acquisition. Below is a selection of some CA work that might be seen as being of special relevance to applied linguistics.

10.5.2 *CA and media, medical, and legal talk*

A considerable quantity of attention has been paid by conversation analysts to talk in the media (in particular news interviews), in medicine (in various types of interactions), and in law. These studies have shown that speech exchange systems vary across different types of talk in institutional settings. Usually one participant has special rights in choosing the next speaker: the interviewer in the news interview, the doctor in a consultation, the judge in a courtroom. Also the types of activities undertaken by participants are shown to be constrained. Interviewers ask questions by and large, but don't, in the normal course of events, give answers, and doctors in certain phases of consultations provide advice, but rarely complain, whilst witnesses give factual answers, but don't ask questions. Certain practices are found to be common in particular types of institutional talk. There are techniques widely used by doctors to break bad news to patients. News interviewers make special use of the adjacency pair rule, in relation to the institutional expectations that they ask the questions. They regularly take the opportunity to use the first part of their turn to do something other than ask a question, such as provide background information for the question, or set up incriminating evidence or claims. Interviewees, unlike participants in ordinary conversation, generally go along with this by not beginning their turn until a question has been asked.

A general underlying trend found in many of these studies is that very few practices discovered in institutional talk are exclusive to that type of talk. What seems to happen prevailingly is that the frequency of a practice may be higher (or lower) to meet the demands of talking in an institution. The adaptations usually appear as simplifications of ordinary conversation practices, to the extent that turn-taking or types of actions done are more restricted than in ordinary conversation.

10.5.3 *CA and education settings*

In an early study using CA methodology in an educational setting, McHoul investigated turn-taking in formal classrooms, and proposed a set of turn-taking rules derived from Sacks, Schegloff, & Jefferson (1974), which laid out rules which allowed "that only teachers can direct speakership in any creative way" (McHoul, 1978, p. 188). In a subsequent paper on repair in the classroom (McHoul, 1990), the author found that in the classrooms he investigated, similar types of repair were found to those described for ordinary conversation (Schegloff, Jefferson, & Sacks, 1977), but that other initiation (by the teacher) in the next turn was notably frequent, though self-repair, rather than other-repair, remained the preferred type. A later investigation of repair in language classrooms is Seedhouse (1999). Mehan (1985) looked at how classroom discourse is structured, and in one of the few studies of non-English classrooms, He (1995) investigated the way in which ambiguity was dealt with in Chinese heritage language classrooms in the USA. There have, though, been few investigations of classroom interaction using CA.

However, in recent years a number of young scholars have researched some other domains of language in education. In 1998 a collection of papers appeared (Young & He, 1998) which included CA papers on talk in language proficiency interviews (LPIs) and other testing environments, comparing miscommunication in LPIs and ordinary conversation, in particular in how repairs are accomplished (Egbert, 1998), and answering questions in LPIs (He, 1998). The previous year Lazaraton (1997) had examined preference organization in similar oral proficiency tests. Earlier still, Filipi (1995) looked at aspects of the sequence of actions, particularly expansions of base adjacency pairs in an Italian oral proficiency interview, and also at interviewers' use (or non-use) of silence, response tokens, and other accommodative resources in the same interviews (Filipi, 1994).

Some CA researchers have also turned their attention to the evaluation of teaching materials, in particular the authenticity of the dialogues presented. Wong (1984) found that a number of features found in naturally occurring telephone conversations were missing, incomplete, or problematic in the eight textbooks she examined. Meanwhile Gardner (1999) argued that the representation of ways of disagreeing (dispreferred responses) were inadequately represented in the ESL textbooks he examined.

10.5.4   CA and second language learning and second language talk

For many years CA used monolingual, native speaker talk as its data, with researchers in the vast majority of cases studying their own languages and cultures. The assumption appeared to be that in order to get at the practices of members of a community of speakers, one needed as researcher to be a member of that community. Thus English native speakers would study English, Dutch would study Dutch, and Finns would study Finnish. In recent years there has been some weakening of this position, together with an emergent interest in second language talk. It seemed that CA had reached a point where enough was known about basic practices of conversation in certain language communities to make it possible and worthwhile to investigate conversations involving non-native speakers.

This raised interest too in the talk of language learners. A series of papers, in particular from Denmark (e.g., Wagner, 1996; Firth & Wagner, 1997), set out a challenge to SLA, criticizing the lack of sophistication in the conceptualization of interaction in SLA studies. This led to a lively series of papers, mostly in the same issue of the *Modern Language Journal* in 1997. A major reaction to Firth and Wagner from SLA researchers was that acquisition is a psychological phenomenon, to which interaction is a secondary issue. A challenge went out for conversation analysts to demonstrate through research how talk and interaction might be of importance to SLA (e.g., Long, 1997). Since then a book has appeared on SLA and CA (Markee, 2000), and a collection of papers is in preparation of studies on second language talk and second language learning in a variety of languages (Gardner & Wagner, in preparation).

10.6   Future Directions

CA is about explicating the complexities, local nature, and quiddity of instances of talk. It has shown these to be subtle and highly variable, adding layers of social, contextual, and interactional complexity to the already complex phenomenon of language as studied by applied linguists. One may be able to draw some general conclusions about, for example, the ways in which the allocation of turns at talk are achieved, but this is a long way from anything like a comprehensive description of the ways in which human talk-in-interaction is conducted.

The next few years are likely to see a continuing attention to ordinary conversation, about which there is still a lot to be learned. Heritage (2000) argues that CA needs to build upon the groundwork of the first 35 years of establishing and describing basic practices and mechanisms in talk-in-interaction. Some of the empirical findings will be of a sufficient breadth to support statistical analysis. Studies of talk in institutional settings will continue to appear. In the field of applied linguistics, it can be expected that studies on second language talk and second language learning, classroom language, and language in testing environments will increase.

See also 5 DISCOURSE ANALYSIS, 11 LANGUAGE AND THE LAW, 12 LANGUAGE AND GENDER.

REFERENCES

Auer, P. & Di Luzio, A. (eds.) (1992) *The contextualization of language.* Amsterdam: Benjamins.

Couper-Kuhlen, E. & Selting, M. (eds.) (1996) *Prosody in conversation. interactional studies.* Cambridge: Cambridge University Press.

Drew, P. & Heritage, J. (1992) Analyzing talk at work: an introduction. In P. Drew & J. Heritage (eds.), *Talk at work: interaction in institutional settings* (pp. 3–65). Cambridge: Cambridge University Press.

Drew, P. & Sorjonen, M.-L. (1997) Institutional dialogue. In T. van Dijk (ed.), *Discourse as social interaction. Discourse studies: a multidisciplinary introduction*, vol. 2 (pp. 92–118). London: Sage.

Egbert, M. (1998) Miscommunication in language proficiency interviews of first-year German students: a comparison with natural conversation. In R. Young & A. He (eds.), *Talking and testing* (pp. 147–69). Amsterdam: Benjamins.

Filipi, A. (1994) Interaction or interrogation? A study of talk occurring in a sample of the 1992 V.C.E Italian Oral Common Assessment Task. Unpublished MA thesis, University of Melbourne, Australia.

Filipi, A. (1995) Interaction in an Italian oral test: the role of some expansion sequences. In R. Gardner (ed.), *Spoken interaction studies in Australia.* ARAL Series S, no. 11, 119–36.

Firth, A. & Wagner, J. (1997) On discourse, communication, and (some) fundamental concepts in SLA. *Modern Language Journal*, 81, 285–300.

Ford, C. & Thompson, S. (1996) Interactional units in conversation: syntactic, intonational, and pragmatic resources for the management of turns. In E. Ochs, E. Schegloff, & S. Thompson (eds.), *Interaction and grammar* (pp. 134–84). Cambridge: Cambridge University Press.

Gardner, R. (1999) Resources for delicate maneuvers: learning to disagree. In E. Alcón (ed.), *Discourse and language teaching.* ARAL Series S, no. 16, (pp. 31–47).

Gardner, R. & Wagner, J. (eds.) (in preparation) *Second language talk.*

Garfinkel, H. (1967) *Studies in ethnomethodology.* Englewood Cliff, NJ: Prentice-Hall.

Goffman, E. (1959) *The presentation of self in everyday life.* Garden City, NY: Doubleday.

Goffman, E. (1967) *Interaction ritual: essays in face to face behavior.* Garden City, NY: Doubleday.

Goodwin, C. & Duranti, A. (1992) Rethinking context: an introduction. In A. Duranti & C. Goodwin (eds.), *Rethinking context: language as an interactive phenomenon* (pp. 1–42). Cambridge: Cambridge University Press.

He, A. (1995) Practices in Chinese heritage language classes. *Discourse Studies*, 3(1), 73–96.

He, A. (1998) Answering questions in LPIs: a case study. In R. Young & A. He (eds.), *Talking and testing* (pp. 101–16). Amsterdam: Benjamins.

Heritage, J. (1984) *Garfinkel and ethnomethodology.* Cambridge: Polity.

Heritage, J. (1997) Conversation analysis and institutional talk: analysing data. In D. Silverman (ed.), *Qualitative research: theory, method, practice* (pp. 161–82). London: Sage.

Heritage, J. (2000) Conversation analysis at century's end: practices of talk-in-interaction, their distributions, and their outcomes. *Research on Language and Social Interaction*, 32(1 & 2), 69–76.

Heritage, J. & Sorjonen, M.-L. (1994) Constituting and maintaining activities across sequences: and-prefacing as a feature of question design. *Language in Society*, 23, 1–29.

Jefferson, G. (1984) Transcription conventions. In J. Atkinson & J. Heritage (eds.), *Structures of social action* (pp. ix–xvi). Cambridge: Cambridge University Press.

Kelly, J. & Local, J. (1989) On the use of general phonetic techniques in handling conversational material. In D. Roger & P. Bull (eds.), *Conversation: an interdisciplinary perspective* (pp. 197–212). Clevedon, UK: Multilingual Matters.

Lazaraton, A. (1997) Preference organization in oral proficiency interviews: the case of language ability assessments. *Research on Language and Social Interaction*, 30(1), 53–72.

Local, J. & Kelly, J. (1986) Notes on phonetic and conversational structure. *Human Studies*, 9, 185–224.

Long, M. (1997) Construct validity in SLA research: a response to Firth and Wagner. *The Modern Language Journal*, 81(3), 318–23.

McHoul, A. (1978) The organization of turns at formal talk in the classroom. *Language in Society*, 7, 183–213.

McHoul, A. (1990) The organization of repair in classroom talk. *Language in Society*, 19, 349–77.

Markee, N. (2000) *Conversation analysis.* Mahwah, NJ: Erlbaum.

Mehan, H. (1985) The structure of classroom discourse. In T. A. Dijk (ed.), *Handbook of discourse analysis,* vol. 3 (pp. 120–31). New York: Academic Press.

Ono, T. & Thompson, S. (1995) What can conversation tell us about syntax? In P. Davis (ed.), *Alternative linguistics: descriptive and theoretical modes* (pp. 213–72). Amsterdam: Benjamins.

Psathas, G. (ed.) (1990) *Interaction competence.* Washington, DC: University Press of America.

Sacks, H. (1963) Sociological description. *Berkeley Journal of Sociology*, 8, 1–16.

Sacks, Harvey (1992) *Lectures in conversation* (ed. Gail Jefferson), vols 1 & 2. Oxford: Blackwell.

Sacks, H., Schegloff, E., & Jefferson, G. (1974) A simplest systematics for the organization of turn-taking for conversation. *Language*, 50, 696–735.

Schegloff, E. (1980) Preliminaries to preliminaries: "Can I ask you a question?" *Sociological Inquiry*, 50(3–4), 104–52.

Schegloff, E. (1986) The routine as achievement. *Human Studies*, 9, 111–51.

Schegloff, E. (1988) Presequences and indirection: applying speech act theory to ordinary conversation. *Journal of Pragmatics*, 12, 55–62.

Schegloff, E. (1990) On the organization of sequences as a source of "coherence" in talk-in-interaction. In B. Dorval (ed.), *Conversational organization and its development* (pp. 51–77). Norwood: Ablex.

Schegloff, E. (1992a) Introduction. In H. Sacks (ed.), *Lectures in conversation,* vol. 1 (pp. ix–lxiv). Oxford: Blackwell.

Schegloff, E. (1992b) Introduction. In H. Sacks (ed.), *Lectures in conversation,* vol. 2 (pp. ix–lii). Oxford: Blackwell.

Schegloff, E. (1996) Turn organization: one intersection of grammar and interaction. In E. Ochs, E. Schegloff, & S. Thompson (eds.), *Interaction and Grammar* (pp. 52–133). Cambridge: Cambridge University Press.

Schegloff, E., Jefferson, G., & Sacks, H. (1977) The preference for self-correction in the organization of repair in conversation. *Language*, 53(2), 361–81.

Schegloff, E. & Sacks, H. (1973) Opening up closings. *Semiotica*, 8, 289–327.

Seedhouse, P. (1999) The relationship between context and the organization of repair in the L2 classroom. *IRAL*, 37, 59–78.

Selting, M. & Couper-Kuhlen, E. (2001) Forschungsprogramm "Interaktionale Linguistik." *Linguistische Berichte*, 187, 257–89.

Young, R. & He, A. (eds.) (1998) *Talking and Testing.* Amsterdam: Benjamins.

Wagner, J. (1996) Foreign language acquisition through interaction – a critical review of research on conversational adjustments. *Journal of Pragmatics*, 26, 215–35.

Wong, J. (1984) Using conversational analysis to evaluate telephone conversations in English as a second language textbooks. Unpublished master's thesis, University of California, Los Angeles.

FURTHER READING

Atkinson, J. M. & Drew, P. (1979) *Order in court: the organization of verbal interaction in judicial settings.* London: Macmillan.

Atkinson, J. M. & Heritage, J. (eds.) (1984) *Structures of social action*. Cambridge: Cambridge University Press.

Boden, D. & Zimmerman, D. (eds.) (1991) *Talk and social action*. Cambridge: Polity.

Button, G. & Lee, J. (eds.) (1987) *Talk and social organization*. Clevedon, UK: Multilingual Matters.

Clayman, S. & Maynard, D. (1995) Ethnomethodology and conversation analysis. In P. ten Have & G. Psathas (eds.), *Situated order: studies in the social organization of talk and embodied activities* (pp. 1–30). Washington, DC: University Press of America.

Coulter, J. (ed.) (1991) *Ethnomethodological sociology*. London: Elgar.

Drew, P. (1990) Conversation analysis: who needs it? *Text*, 10(1–2), 27–35.

Drew, P. & Asher, K. (1994) *Conversation analysis. The encyclopedia of language and linguistics*. London: Pergamon.

Drew, P. & Heritage, J. (1992) *Talk at work: interaction in institutional settings*. Cambridge: Cambridge University Press.

Duranti, A. & Goodwin, C. (eds.) (1992) *Rethinking context: language as an interactive phenomenon*. Cambridge: Cambridge University Press.

Heritage, J. (1987) Ethnomethodology. In A. Giddens & J. Turner (eds.), *Social theory today* (pp. 224–72). Cambridge: Polity.

Hutchby, I. & Drew, P. (1995) Conversation analysis. In J. Verschueren, J.-O. Östman, & J. Blommaert (eds.), *Handbook of pragmatics* (pp. 182–90). Amsterdam: Benjamins.

Hutchby, I. & Wooffit, R. (1998) *Conversation analysis: principles, practices and applications*. Cambridge: Polity.

Lynch, M. (2000) The ethnomethodological foundations of conversation analysis. Text, 20(4), 517–32.

Lynch, M. & Bogen, D. (1994) Harvey Sacks' primitive natural science. *Theory, Culture and Society*, 11, 65–104.

Moerman, M. (1988) *Talking culture: ethnography and conversation analysis*. Pennsylvania: University of Pennsylvania Press.

Nofsinger, R. (1991) *Everyday conversation*. Newbury Park: Sage.

Ochs, E., Schegloff, E., & Thompson, S. (eds.) (1996) *Interaction and grammar*. Cambridge: Cambridge University Press.

Pomerantz, A. & Fehr, B. (1997) Conversation analysis: an approach to the study of social action as sense making practices. In T. A. van Dijk (ed.), *Discourse: a multidisciplinary introduction*, (pp. 64–91). London: Sage.

Psathas, G. (ed.) (1979) *Everyday language: studies in ethnomethodology*. New York: Irvington.

Psathas, G. (1995) *Conversation analysis: the study of talk-in-interaction*. Thousand Oaks: Sage.

Schegloff, E. (1968) Sequencing in conversational openings. *American Anthropologist*, 70, 1075–1095.

Schegloff, E. (1993) Reflections on quantification in the study of conversation. *Research on Language and Social Interaction*, 26(1), 99–128.

ten Have, P. (1999) *Doing conversation analysis: a practical guide*. London: Sage.

ten Have, P. & Psathas, G. (eds.) (1995) *Situated order: studies in the social organization of talk and embodied activities*. Washington, DC: University Press of America.

Young, R. & He, A. (eds.) *Talking and testing*. Amsterdam: Benjamins.

11   Language and the Law

JOHN GIBBONS

11.1   Introduction

In Gibbons (2001) I suggest that the applied linguistic enterprise has three main stages – a revealing and analysis of a language problem or issue (*reflection*), the development of some form of treatment (*action*), and *evaluation* of the success of the treatment. This approach to applied linguistics frames the following discussion of language and the law.

Since this paper is in English, I shall talk mostly of the Common Law system. It is important to note however that many more people are subject to versions of the Roman Law system, including most of Asia (including China, South-East Asia, and Japan), Latin America, and continental Europe, and that Shariah law is also widespread.

11.2   Legal Language

The language of the law is an important arena for applied linguistics, because the law is such an important and influential institution, and because it is packed with language problems. Most of our common everyday activities are carried out within a legal frame. A bus ticket is a legal contract, and virtually any form of transport, particularly driving a car, is similarly hedged about with legal issues. Employment too is a legislative domain. Our family relations are subject to family law, and the media we use are similarly controlled. Law intrudes into almost every aspect of modern life. If we examine the law however, it is the most linguistic of institutions. Legislation is a linguistic entity, with no existence outside of language. Equally police investigation and court proceedings are overwhelmingly linguistic processes, mainly spoken rather than written in Common Law systems. What makes these of significance for applied linguistics is that the linguistic aspects of the law raise many issues and difficulties. The written language of legislation and regulation is difficult to understand for lay people – there is a profound communication problem – yet lack of understanding of the law is not a defense in court.

For applied linguistic purposes we need to understand the nature of legal language, and possible sources of communication difficulty (the reflection stage), and to work out ways of overcoming the problem in so far as this is possible (action). The analysis here examines four major sources of possible problems. The first is the specialized text structures and procedures used in the law – the *genre* issue in short. The second is the extreme *writtenness* of many legal documents: some are virtually impossible to read aloud in a meaningful way. The third is the *technicality* of much legal discourse: the law and its practitioners have developed a range of unique legal concepts, and these can be expressed efficiently only by using legal jargon. The fourth is the *interpersonal* arena, where power disparities and hyper-formality are produced by the essentially controlling nature of the legal system.

Looking first at genres, the highly institutionalized, and sometimes ritualized discourse of the law often follows regular patterns; organized sequences of elements which each play a role in achieving the purpose of the discourse. Following Bhatia (1993), Halliday & Hasan (1985), and Martin (1992) among others, these are termed genres. It is well established in reading theory that a knowledge of the genre that one is reading is important, and sometimes essential for understanding (Wallace, 1990; Weaver, 1988). This is in part why legal documents can be difficult for lay readers to understand, while lawyers have less difficulty. This is well illustrated in the discussion between the eminent linguist Charles Fillmore, and some legal authorities reported in *Washington University Law Quarterly*, volume 73 (1995, pp. 922–31), particularly the discussion of the following sentence from a contract.

> After this marriage in the absence of any agreement to the contrary the legal relations and powers as regards to property might, by reason of some change in our domicile or otherwise, be other than those of our present domiciles or other than those which we desire to apply to our relationship powers and capacities.

Charles Fillmore finds this "incompetent" and unintelligible. The lawyers however were able to draw on their knowledge of the genre of contracts of this type, to say that such a clause is inserted at the beginning of many such contracts to cover the contingency of the parties moving to another state where the law is different. Despite the chronically poor drafting of this language, their knowledge of the genre enabled the lawyers to understand it, and to be in agreement concerning its meaning.

One of the most fundamental genres is that of narrative. An important issue arising from genres is the notion developed in some depth by Bennett and Feldman (1981), Jackson (1991), and Stygall (1994) that the competing (prosecution or plaintiff vs. defense) versions of events in a trial are in fact competing narratives. Bennett and Feldman (1981) describe these as competing "stories." Courtroom narratives are not limited to the particular events under litigation, they may be stories of the witness's life, loves, and previous contacts with the law. This narrative interpretation both facilitates analysis, and problematizes the process. For example, narratives mostly follow a simple linear time sequence, yet life is rarely simple or linear – events happen at the same time and relationships between them may be subtle and complex. However some of the authors in Papke (1991) provide evidence from trials that a simple narrative structure easily intelligible to jurors may be preferred to a more complex account that is closer to the facts. Again the risks of injustice inherent in such language behavior are troubling.

Courtroom proceedings and police procedures can also be seen to follow genre structures. Indeed in the case of trials, the sequence of stages through which they pass is regulated. Maley (1994, p. 16) provides a helpful chart listing the main genres used in the legal process. Once more a knowledge of these genres is helpful in understanding and participating in what is happening. Hall (forthcoming) makes a convincing case that the possible different purposes of police interviews, seeking the truth of events or attempting merely to get a result by means of a confession, demand different genre structures, and the current prescribed genre structure of police interviews in New South Wales inadvertently favors the second. In this case the form of the applied linguistic treatment is obvious: change the genre and train police officers in its use.

Turning now to the written/spoken dimension, it is worth remembering that all legal systems have oral origins – the Roman legal system, the source of most continental and Asian legal systems, was an oral system for most of the existence of the Roman empire; the Common Law system used in the English-speaking world has its origins in Germanic tribal law; Shariah, the Islamic legal system, developed in part from the orate systems of desert Arabs – indeed the Prophet Mohammed (PBUH) was probably illiterate. Danet & Bogoch (1994) provide a convincing account of the movement from an oral to a written mode. The linguistic consequences are far reaching. They include the possibility of extremely long and complex sentence structures (often between 70 and 100 words), which are virtually impossible to read aloud meaningfully or to understand when heard. With written language, however, we have the luxury of multiple recasts to construct them, and multiple readings to decode them, so that they become possible, if perhaps undesirable. These very long sentences are often used to package together a number of core concepts or prescriptions, along with all the conditions in which they apply (Bhatia, 1994). Legal language also tends to use long and complex noun phrases; Crystal and Davy (1969, p. 205) give the following example: "The payment to the owner of the total amount of any installment then remaining unpaid of the rent herinbefore reserved and agreed to be paid during the term . . ." Halliday (1989) and Halliday & Hasan (1985) shows that this process, particularly the creation of abstract nouns from other parts of speech ("grammatical metaphor") is a consequence of literacy. An illustration of these phenomena can be found in the short extract from a contract given previously. It is a sentence of 55 words, with a fairly complex structure including a number of prepositional phrases and a long complex phrase following "be." There are also numerous abstract nouns, including "absence," "agreement," and "capacities." Police investigation and court proceedings can also suffer from this problem, although to a lesser degree, since oral interaction includes the possibility of the face-to-face negotiation of meaning. The problem is that there is psycholinguistic evidence (Felker et al., 1981) that complex sentence and phrasal structures, and the use of grammatical metaphor, make texts difficult to understand.

Another part of the difficulty of legal language is its technicality. Maley (1994) among others has pointed out that the law consists to some degree of legal concepts, and therefore words to express these concepts are essential. It is part of a wider objective of legal language, that of being as precise and decontextualized as possible. Some legal terms are used almost exclusively to refer to legal contexts, for instance "estoppel" and "magistrate." Others are words with non-legal meanings that are used with a particular meaning in legal contexts, such as "party" (one side in a court case), "damages," and "restraint" (as in "restraint of trade"). Legal English has borrowed a range of terms from Norman French and Latin, and many of these terms are still in wide use: for example *habeas corpus* and *voir dire*. Jargon is also characteristic of the legal language of other European languages, and to a lesser extent of legal Japanese. Legal Chinese, on the other hand, uses mostly everyday language with specialist meaning. In general, laws and contracts are intended to apply to specific behaviors and entities/people in specific circumstances, and legal language attempts to spell out precisely what these are, in order to avoid hostile interpretations. Legal drafters often combine all these elements in a single sentence, which explains the extreme length mentioned earlier.

The language problem that arises from technicality is that legal terms limited to the legal domain may not be known to lay people, and legal terms with non-legal meanings may be understood in their everyday sense. For example, Diamond & Levi (1996, p. 232) mention jurors misunderstanding the legal term "aggravating" to mean "irritating," and thereby being in danger of incorrectly imposing the death penalty. If legal jargon is in some cases unknown or poorly known to non-lawyers, it clearly has the potential to impair their understanding of and their participation in the legal process. This accentuates the problems of complexity discussed above.

One source of this difficulty is that legal discourse may be addressing two audiences, both a lay audience and a legal audience. For instance, police cautions must not only communicate to the person being cautioned, they must also be admissible in court as having fully performed the function of cautioning. This explains in part inertia and even resistance when it comes to using plain language for legal purposes. Another source of resistance among police and lawyers is their understanding of the types of social message conveyed. Most work in this area has assumed that only propositional information is communicated. It is clear however that complex and technical language also carries a social message concerning the power and authority of the person using it. Resistance to a lessening of this power and authority is not surprising.

The "action" taken to resolve this problem is the adoption of plain language principles, which attempt to make the language of the law as simple and comprehensible as possible, while ensuring that the legal language continues to perform its task of being as explicit and watertight as possible (see for example Law Reform Commission of Victoria, 1987; Steinberg, 1991). There are active plain legal language movements in the USA, Britain, and Australia, and in a range of other countries. In Britain they have recently achieved a significant success in persuading the government and mainstream English law authorities to implement change toward plain language. They have assisted the Master of the Rolls Lord Woolf in producing the 1998 *Civil Procedure Rules* (SI 1998 3132) which provide clearer equivalents for many forms, documents, and procedural wordings. Many of the idiosyncrasies of legal language have been addressed. A number of arcane legal terms have been replaced: for instance a *plaintiff* is now a *claimant*, a *pleading* is now a *statement of case*. Law Latin has been replaced with English – *ex parte, inter partes, in camera* and *sub poena* have become *with notice, without notice, in private*, and a *summons*. Proper names such as an *Anton Piller order* have been replaced with more transparent titles such as a *search order*. These changes have yet to be adopted elsewhere, and critical evaluations of them are emerging.

Gibbons (2001) demonstrates some of the problems caused by the linguistic complexity of police cautions, discusses the sometimes tortuous process of simplifying them, and provides evaluations of the revisions. However the editing involved in the process can carry risks, as Davies (forthcoming) shows: in the removalist's contract that she discusses some of the legal content is lost in a plain language version.

When we examine interaction in legal contexts, another issue arises – extreme power asymmetry. The legal system is by its very nature an instrument of control and power, and in a democratic society this power is ceded to the legal system to maintain order and some degree of fairness within society. However, the power ceded to police and lawyers runs a constant risk that people will be coerced into saying things they do not mean or know to be untrue or incomplete. This interpersonal power is manifested and exerted to a significant degree through language. It can be seen in the forms of address used: Your Honour, Your Worship, Your Lordship, My Learned Friend, etc. Among police officers it may lead to the use of unnecessarily elaborate "copspeak" to maintain status: Maley & Fahey (1991, p. 8) give the following example from a police sergeant's courtroom testimony.

Police Officer:	I was unable to maintain the light being illuminated.
Counsel:	To keep the torch on?
Police Officer:	To keep the torch on.

Power relations in both courtrooms and police stations affect turn taking. In a court it is illegal for people to speak without being allotted a turn by the judge, and illegal for them not to speak when questioned, unless they have a specific "right to silence." While judges have the right to speak whenever they wish, lawyers in general must take turns (Atkinson & Drew, 1979). Turn-taking in courtrooms has therefore become regulated and institutionalized along power hierarchy lines. Equally police officers when interviewing will often refuse to answer questions, and will expect answers. The coercive nature of courtroom questioning has also received considerable attention from linguists – see for example Danet et al. (1980), Harris (1984), Phillips (1987). Eades (1994) gives the following example of highly coercive questioning when an Aboriginal witness remained silent during cross-examination:

> Counsel: . . . I'd suggest the reason to you, because you don't want everyone to know the little criminal that you are, do you? That's the reason, isn't it? Isn't it? Your silence probably answers it, but I'll have an answer from you. That's the reason, isn't it?

The core information "you are a little criminal" is deeply embedded in the grammatical structure, so that it is very difficult to deny directly – a negative response would be a denial that this is the reason for silence, not a denial that he is a criminal. Furthermore there are multiple question tags such as "isn't it" used as coercive devices. Eades argues that the content of any answer to such a question would be suspect. Lawyers use many such linguistic strategies to control the responses of witnesses.

Critical discourse analysis is an emerging focus. For instance Vasilachis de Gialdino (1997) examined an Argentinian labor reform bill rooted in neo-liberalism, describing the language used within labor courts in Argentina, discussion of the reform in the parliament and the executive, and the treatment of these in the local press, showing in the latter (Vasilachis de Gialdino, 1997, pp. 270–1) that workers were not discussed, unionists were portrayed as violent and irrational, and reduced protection for workers was portrayed as a positive move toward globalization, modernization, and flexibility. There is also a growing debate concerning gender and language in the law, often showing an interaction between legal power and male–female power relations (see particularly Matoesian, 1997). This is related to language and disadvantage before the law (see below).

The problem is clear, in that truth may be the casualty when questioning takes place in situations of high power asymmetry in which the witness is open to manipulation. It is difficult to find thoroughgoing solutions. The actions taken so far are to alert and educate lawyers and judges to the risks involved in such questioning, to change the rules of courtroom procedure to reduce the use of coercive questioning, and where particularly vulnerable witnesses are involved (such as children, the intellectually handicapped, and the deaf) to allow the presence of a "friend" to support and help them. However the problem is deeply rooted in the adversarial nature of Common Law legal systems, and in the notion that evidence must be "tested."

The language of witnesses may also manifest power or its absence. O'Barr (1982) and O'Barr & Conley (1990) did an important series of studies which revealed a set of linguistic markers of power (such as hesitation, low coherence, and use of emphatics and mitigators), and demonstrated that witnesses and defendants whose language is less powerful were less likely to be believed – a worrying indicator of the linguistic means by which social injustice may be reproduced. There were even indications that people who use less powerful language might receive less financial compensation from an offender.

The nature of the language of the law poses other applied linguistics challenges. How can it be taught? How can it be translated or interpreted into other language?

11.3   Teaching the Language of the Law

We have seen in previous sections the extreme complexity and unusual nature of legal language. This poses a substantial problem, particularly for the many countries where the language of the law is not the mother tongue of those involved in the legal system. In India and much of anglophone Africa, for example, lawyers in training need help to master not only technicalities and the legal concepts that they represent, but also the convoluted grammatical structures in which much legislation is framed. This places considerable demands upon the teachers and curriculum designers responsible for teaching English to these law students. They themselves may have trouble in understanding the cognitive complexity of legal documents, and the linguistic realization of that complexity. Once understood, training students to master it is a pedagogical challenge. Teachers may also need to train law students in oral interactive techniques to master the power laden language of the court. There are also ethical issues involved in both the promulgation of this register that excludes so many ordinary people, particularly second language speakers, and in training people to use language to manipulate and distort the testimony of others.

11.4   Legal Interpreting and Translation

Turning first to legal interpreting and translation, we have already touched on the possible disadvantage suffered by minorities who cannot cope easily with the complexity and power of the language of the law. People who have only a limited command of the language used for legal proceedings are also likely to suffer severe disadvantage before the law if (1) an interpreter/translator is not provided and (2) if the interpreting/translation does not accurately convey what is said/written. Although most legislations will provide such services in some circumstances, the basic Common Law situation is that it is at the discretion of the judge. Since judges are rarely qualified language testers, there is chronic underprovision of interpreters in some jurisdictions. For instance Carroll (1995) describes some courts where interpreters are provided in less than 10 percent of the cases where they are needed. Gibbons (2001) describes a similar situation for police under-use of interpreters. Some jurisdictions (such as the state of New Jersey in the USA) have adopted laws which address this issue, by making interpreters available for all second language speakers unless there is evidence from a qualified language tester that the person has sufficient command of the courtroom language to fully participate in proceedings.

There may also be a problem with interpreter supply, particularly for languages of low demand, or where legal interpreter training is unavailable. The paradigm case is that of tribal minorities whose languages have small numbers of speakers, where there may be no highly proficient bilinguals, or no appropriate interpreter training available in the community. Medium term solutions include the training of para-professional interpreters to provide at least some service to the community, and long term solutions will involve investment in education, and the development of alternatives such as minority language courtrooms.

Berk-Seligson (1990), Hale and Gibbons, (1999) and many others have documented the extreme difficulty of providing accurate interpreting in courtroom contexts, where even minor inaccuracies may lower the standards of justice. The conditions that make this process particularly difficult are the pressure to use as little time as possible (by its very nature interpreted testimony takes twice as long), and the lack of understanding of interpreting among some lawyers, who may for example interrupt during interpreting, or demand a literal word-for-word translation. In order to avoid such problems interpreters are often reluctant to use dictionaries, or to ask what is meant when there are two candidate translations. All these factors can reduce the accuracy of interpreting. Particular linguistic problems include the interpreting of address forms (e.g., *señor* in Spanish), passivization, discourse markers such as "umm," "well," "you know," and tag questions (there are no exact equivalents of English tags in other languages, but as we saw in the example from Eades given above, they are an important feature of cross-examination). In many jurisdictions these problems can be exacerbated by inadequate training and sub-professional rates of pay. Clearly adequate resourcing is a basic first step in resolving this issue, with more training for both lawyers and interpreters, but the very nature of interpreting and translation is that it is not an exact process – a consequence of the differences between human languages and cultures.

Turning now to legal translation, the problems do not lie with the interactive phenomena discussed in relation to interpreting, but rather in the extreme complexity and technicality discussed earlier. For example Vlachopoulos (forthcoming) discusses the translation of an English language legal document into Greek, and documents the challenge posed by Common Law concepts (and the terms used to refer to them), which in a number of cases do not exist in Greece's continental legal system, and therefore lack a corresponding Greek term. When we add in the conceptual complexity and delicacy of many legal texts, the task becomes even more daunting. Vlachopoulos proposes a range of solutions including the use of terms which are close in conceptual content from non-legal registers, including everyday language. Otherwise one is obliged to use extensive footnoting and discussion of the translation itself.

Apart from the language of the law, there are a number of other areas where language issues emerge in the legal arena. Important among these are language legislation, including language crimes, and linguistic evidence.

11.5 Language Legislation

There is legislation on many language issues. One area is that of language rights. A language issue that underlies many armed conflicts around the world (for instance Macedonian in Kosovo, or Kurdish) is the right to use a language for public purposes such as education, law, and with government agencies, and even to speak it in private. There has been a movement in the European Union toward the acceptance of many more languages as public languages – for instance Catalan and Basque in Spain. An indication of how far this has gone is that judges in the Basque country must learn Euskara, or else employ an Euskara interpreter at their own expense. In the USA, on the other hand, most states now have legislation to prevent the use of minority languages for public purposes (González & Melis, 2001). The basic argument seems to be between the role of the dominant language in sustaining national unity and including all members of society in its processes, and the rights of minorities to access public institutions in a language they fully understand, and to maintain their language and culture. US English proponents do not seem to take sufficiently into account the evidence that for children a high level of bilingualism is viable and achievable, while for adult migrant learners of the second language high levels of proficiency are rarely attained and therefore services in their mother tongue are needed to avoid social disadvantage. The actions taken to support or suppress the use of particular languages in national life consist of the passing and enforcing of legislation or regulations. The evaluation of their success can be seen in long term language shift, maintenance, and loss.

There is also a type of language legislation by means of which certain kinds of language behavior are criminalized to become "language crimes." Examples are bribery, threats, and perjury. Shuy (1993) provides a thorough analysis of the linguistic nature of such crimes, and also reveals the difficulty and delicacy of demonstrating in court that such crimes have or have not been committed. For example he shows that for the successful achievement of bribery there is a genre consisting of: an opening; a discussion of the briber's "problem" and checking that the bribee has the capacity to intervene in the problem; a proposal, which may involve some negotiation of both action and reward; an acceptance or rejection of the bribe; if the bribe is accepted the possible discussion of future "business"; and a closure. For bribery to take place both the proposal and the acceptance are essential stages. Shuy shows that it is not uncommon for cases to come to court in which it is clear that the bribee did not accept the bribe, but is being prosecuted for being part of a bribery event. His painstaking analysis is a prerequisite for action, in this case appearing in court and showing as appropriate that the language crime of bribery did or did not take place. Green (1990) documents a case where a young man was accused of conspiracy to distribute cocaine. The question in this case was whether the young man participated in a drug deal. Green shows through a careful and detailed discourse analysis of pronoun use and the man's contributions to the discussion, including markers of cooperation (such as "yeah"), answers to questions, topic management, clarification requests, interruptions, turn-taking, as well as incomprehension markers, that he never actively participated in the deal itself. The evaluation of the success of such intervention by forensic linguists is usually whether their evidence is accepted by the court, and is affirmed if they are also on the winning side.

Another type of language crime is that of using offensive language, mostly swearwords. For example, the NSW 1988 Summary Offences Act states:

(1)   A person shall not –

      . . .

      (b)   use offensive language in or near, or within hearing from, a public place or a school.

(2)   It is sufficient defense to a prosecution for an offence under this section if the defendant satisfies the court that the defendant had a reasonable excuse for conducting himself or herself in the manner alleged in the information for the offence.

Previously the maximum punishment of this offence was up to three months in prison, changed to a fine in 1993. The question asked by Walsh (1995) is "What is offensive?" The test proposed by the courts is "whether reasonable persons in the relevant place and at the relevant time, and in the circumstances there and then prevailing, would be likely to be seriously alarmed or seriously affronted." It is noticeable that this test depends on the immediate context, including the participants and their schemas. It provides little real information, leaving it open to the magistrate to determine who is a reasonable person, and what is likely to alarm or affront them. There is also a defense of a "reasonable excuse," for instance if someone drops a hammer on their foot. On reflection, the extreme discretion within this legislation is dangerous, since in 1993 Amnesty International reported that it was used overwhelmingly to imprison or fine Aborigines, and to a lesser extent younger and working-class people. Around 5,000 people a year were found guilty of this offence in the mid 1990s. The applied linguistic action adopted by Taylor (1995) was to reveal the hypocrisy of law makers and law enforcers, by gathering well-documented instances of police officers and politicians using swearwords themselves. Indeed one aboriginal man was prosecuted for saying to police "Don't tell me to get fucked." Even if one deplores the use of offensive language, in these circumstances to legislate against it is unfair and unrealistic, and questionable given the history of such legislation in oppressing minorities.

Vilification is another type of language crime. This can take the form of libel or slander of individuals, or of group vilification. To be prosecuted, libel and slander of individuals need evidence of untruth and of harm to the recipient, but in law there may be no need to prove intent, i.e., that the harm was deliberate. So the definitions of slander in normal dictionaries normally include intent, for instance the *Oxford Dictionary* definition has "maliciously", while law dictionaries exclude this element: another case where legal constructions differ from those of everyday language and culture. Interestingly, in the USA freedom of speech considerations have taken precedence, and there is little litigation concerning libel and slander, at least in cases involving the media. However in other Common Law jurisdictions where freedom of speech is not constitutionally guaranteed there are many more court cases.

Group vilification is mostly legislated against in terms of ethnicity, but there is also legislation against vilification on the grounds of religion, disability, or sexual orientation. Group vilification usually takes the path of constructing an "us" and a "them" (often on little real basis), and then negatively portraying "them" (see for example van Dijk, 1987, 1993). The problem is that vilification, as well as causing distress to its recipients, can lead to discrimination and even violent action. The Nazis for instance consistently portrayed the Jews in words and images as vermin, and this served as a rationalization for extermination. However the legislative action to be taken is hotly debated, with the USA largely refusing to inhibit freedom of speech, while some other legislations do so (Freedman & Freedman, 1995). Evaluation of the success of such legislation has shown that it tends to lead to coded expression of vilification in place of overt expression.

11.6   Linguistic Evidence

Finally, another major area where language intersects with the law is that of linguistic evidence. The paradigm case is where a linguist or applied linguist gives evidence on a language issue in court. However such evidence may also be provided to police, lawyers and intelligence agencies, and in a range of other contexts. Various types of expert and expertise may also be involved, including anthropologists and sound technicians.

One issue that must be addressed is the admissibility of linguistic evidence. In Roman Law based legal systems there is usually a system for accrediting experts. After rigorous examination, an expert is accepted or rejected as competent to give evidence in a certain field, and if accepted, his or her evidence will be taken without further demur in subsequent court cases. In Common

Law systems the competence of expert witnesses is challenged each time they appear in a case, and their evidence is accepted or rejected on the following grounds: expertise – whether their knowledge is specialized and beyond "common-sense" knowledge; validity – whether their expertise and evidence is fully relevant to the issue on which they are testifying; and reliability – whether it is scientifically derived. (Bowe & Storey, 1995, pp. 188–9) point out concerning the expertise of forensic linguists that

> While many people are quite capable of identifying or eliminating unknown speakers in a[n earwitness] line-up, they are generally unable to say why . . . Linguistically trained analysts on the other hand are in a position to give a detailed description of differences or similarities noted in two voice samples, together with an explanation of how and why these differences or similarities occur.

Evidence may range across many linguistic levels, including phonology, grammar, discourse and conversational phenomena, and sociolinguistic variation. Linguistic evidence falls into two main areas – communication and identification. We will examine these in turn, beginning with communication, and moving through the linguistic levels.

11.6.1   *Communication*

Looking first at the role of pronunciation in communication, a linguist may be called upon to uncover what someone said. For example I have been involved in two cases where some form of secret language or "pig Latin" was used, where my role was to decode it. This may not always be as simple as one might imagine, for example in one case, during early hearings of a tape recording it was difficult to crack the oral code used in expressions such as [bəpəkəpoz əpin əpə kəpʊpl əpov məpʊns]. It emerged that every vowel has an [əp] inserted before it (it reads "because in a couple of months"). Linguists may also be called upon to say whether an accent or a poor quality recording causes intelligibility problems.

At the level of vocabulary and grammar, linguists may be able to say both what is meant by a particular wording, or whether particular complex lexical and/or grammatical forms make a text difficult to understand. Levi (1994, pp. 16–17) discusses her evidence in a case where the information given to recipients of "public aid" was done in language that was virtually unintelligible to them. She writes

> my analysis included commentary on such problems as use of bureaucratic jargon, crucial terms left vague or undefined, needlessly complex syntax, anaphora (e.g., demonstrative pronouns like *this*) with obscure antecedents, related information scattered throughout nonadjacent sections, incoherent sequencing of topics, blatant omissions of critical (and legally-mandated) information, and an intimidating and obfuscating graphic presentation.

(From this it can be seen that Levi also examined discourse phenomena.) The success of Levi's intervention can be seen in the fact that the agency involved was ordered to pay US$20 million to the recipients, and to rewrite its documents in a way intelligible to them.

McMenamin (1993) documents a case where the issue was the meaning of the words "syndrome," "accident," and "disease." McMenamin testified on behalf of parents whose child died of Sudden Infant Death Syndrome (SIDS) at the age of 18 months. The child's life was protected by the father's life and accident insurance, which included the statement "The plan pays a benefit for losses resulting from any kind of accident . . ." The insurance company denied the claim initially, saying that the policy did not cover deaths from illness or disease. McMeniman's reading of the medical literature and dictionary definitions revealed that "syndrome" is distinguished from "disease" in that a "syndrome" groups together patterns of incidents, but there is no explanation in terms of physical malfunctioning, particularly that caused by bacteria, viruses, etc., while "diseases" exist at a specific time in a specific person, between health and either restored health or death ("syndromes" do not share this quality). As McMeniman says "'disease' is a temporally bound state between health and death. A diseased person either gets well or becomes chronically diseased and dies. SIDS is something a healthy infant either has or does not have. The result, even with a 'near-miss', is health or death, nothing in between." Hence SIDS cannot be classified as a disease. McMeniman's evidence was accepted. Solan (1995) makes a case that linguists could be involved in decisions concerning the meaning and application of legislation in particular cases (legal interpretation) on the basis of grammatical and lexical analysis, but this is challenged by lawyers (see the debate in the special edition of the *Washington Law Journal* in which Solan's paper appears).

Over the last 20 years Diana Eades and Michael Walsh among others have carefully documented communication problems between Australian Aborigines and the law (see for instance Eades, 1994, 1995; Walsh, 1994). They describe the problems that speakers of Aboriginal English have with the legal process. An underlying issue is what as known as the "knowledge economy" in Aboriginal society. In traditional Aboriginal societies material goods were mostly held in common, and status, rather than deriving from wealth, came from the possession of secret knowledge (this situation is also found in other indigenous communities). The result is that much knowledge is not to be shared freely. Some of it is available only to those who have been ceremonially initiated into it. It may be the property of only women or men (women's/men's "business"). The consequence is that questioning in Aboriginal societies is generally done with great caution, often indirectly by raising a topic, and leaving it open to the interlocutor to contribute what knowledge she or he is willing to share. Direct questioning is regarded as rude and intrusive. Answering is not obligatory, since a direct answer may involve secret material or may grant the questioner unearned status. The clash with police questioning and courtroom examination is evident. Police investigation and court trials are largely dependent on the right to question and the obligation to answer. Eades has testified in court on a number of occasions concerning the resulting lack of communication.

11.6.2 *Identification*

Identification may involve comparing two or more language samples, and saying whether they were produced by the same person or not; alternatively it may involve profiling the person who produced the language – there may be indicators of age, class, occupation, gender, mother tongue, and so on. Perhaps the best known area of identification is that of speech sounds – there are many papers on this topic in the journal *Forensic Linguistics*, and Hollien (1990, 2001) provides detailed and convincing description and illustration of the issues involved. Perhaps the most tendentious issue is whether machine analysis is superior to the expert ear. There was a period when "voiceprints" (more correctly spectograms) were widely used in the USA, often by people poorly trained to produce and interpret them. Not surprisingly much of this evidence was discredited subsequently, which led to considerable suspicion of such methods in courtrooms. Hollien (1990) provides spectograms of a particular utterance, where two different speakers had almost identical spectographic profiles, and a single speaker produced markedly different profiles. In recent years the techniques and technology have developed, and much more caution is used in drawing conclusions. In particular certain vowel formants can be a strong contributor to voice identification, provided that the recording on which they are based is of adequate quality. Hollien notes however that there are many points where recording quality can be lost. Identification becomes particularly difficult if one of the samples for analysis is recorded in such a way that much of the signal is affected, for example over the telephone, or on poor recording equipment, or in a poor recording situation (for instance one involving background noise): since many police recordings of voices are covert, it is unlikely that these will be of high quality. Sometimes therefore the human ear is a better indicator than a machine, particularly when, for example, one is attempting to distinguish between regional accents (in our current state of knowledge this task cannot be performed by a machine). Often a combination of the two techniques is effective. Courts still tend to prefer machine based analysis, since it is more overtly "scientific." The untrained ear is unreliable in voice identification, earwitness identification being even less reliable than eyewitness identification.

Where speech sound data may be reliable is in the negative. It is often possible to say with certainty that two samples come from *different* speakers (even if it not always possible to say with certainty that two speech samples come from the *same* speaker). Labov and Harris (1994) describe the Prinzivalli case, in which Labov says that there was no doubt that Prinzivalli could not have made a bomb threat phone call because the bomb threat voice had an unmistakable New England (Boston area) accent, while Prinzivalli had an equally unmistakable New York accent. His main problem was convincing the court of this (see Labov & Harris for a clear exposition); in essence he had to train the court to hear the pronunciation differences. The evidence was accepted and Prinzivalli was acquitted.

Similar in nature are various identificatory elements of the written language. Handwriting can be distinctive, and peculiarities of spelling and punctuation can be strong identifiers. In a recent case I was able to profile a writer as probably coming from a Central European background, since his English misspelling shared many characteristics with cognate words in Central European languages, but other misspellings also indicated that the man spoke English with an Australian accent. This narrowed the likely range of writers considerably.

A related area is that of trade names. Here the linguist may be asked whether there is a likely confusion between two trade names, for example I was asked to decide whether there was a possibility that two drugs, "Alkeran" and "Arclan" might be confused in Australian English (particularly if "Alkeran" were pronounced beginning with a long "a" – [ɑ]). My conclusion, based in part on evidence of processes such as metathesis, and exchanges of [r] and [l], was that it was unlikely but possible. Since such a confusion could be life threatening, this issue was important. Similarly, Oyanadel & Samaniego (1999) were able to determine that the second part of a trade name for baby cream "Fasaglos" had been derived from an established brand "Hipoglos," by studying the morpheme -*glos* in Spanish.

In the area of vocabulary and grammar there are two main approaches used in identification or profiling. The first is essentially probabilistic analysis, usually performed by computer programs. There is a widespread belief, based in part on literary studies, that there are certain grammar features and vocabulary choices that are used more by one person than another. It is important to note that this works only when register variables such as topic, formality, and genre type are held constant, since these features also have a strong impact on both grammatical structure and vocabulary choice. I am still unconvinced that such forms of analysis are effective, but this may reflect my own lack of understanding of their statistical basis. Even supporters of such methods nowadays caution against excessively strong statements based on them.

The second type of analysis is based on any peculiarities in grammatical structure or vocabulary. Sometimes these are non-standard usages, and they may come from a limited proficiency in either the register or the language that the person is using. Coulthard (1997, and elsewhere) has presented evidence that when police fabricate evidence, they sometimes slip into police jargon and the hyper-elaboration discussed earlier. This phenomenon can be detected and revealed by a linguist. I have testified that a transcript was not a faithful record of a second language speaker because the transcript contained a range of tenses that he had not mastered.

Eagleson (1994) shows how a range of linguistic features, including spelling, syntax, morphology, and punctuation provided evidence concerning the authorship of a letter which purported to be a suicide note. Police believed the letter had been written by the woman's husband, who was suspected of murdering her. Eagleson compared samples of the husband's and the wife's writing, and was able to show a range of features that were found in the man's writing and the disputed letter, but not in the woman's writing, particularly "assult" (for assault), "carring" (carrying), "thier" (their), and "treat" (threat); the omission of the third person -s (e.g., "he give"); the intrusive apostrophe; the omission of past tense -ed (e.g., "he never really believe her"); and long poorly structured stretches of language with no punctuation dividing them. The man changed his plea to guilty when confronted with this evidence.

In the notorious Australian kidnapping case of Kerry Whelan, Robert Eagleson and I were able to determine that the ransom letter, which masqueraded as coming from an Asian gang, had probably been written by a native speaker of English on the basis of the use of low frequency elaborate vocabulary, and complex grammatical patterns. There were also indications from the patterning and format of the letter that the writer may have had some experience in writing radio advertisements (there were signs of intertextuality). This type of profiling, while it is not conclusive in its identification, may avoid the expenditure of resources following misleading indications.

Coulthard (1994) gave important evidence on cohesion phenomena to the appeal of the Birmingham Six, which showed on the basis of the nature of the discourse that the police records of interviews contained fabrication. For instance they contained repeated reference to a "white plastic bag" in that full form, rather than beginning with the full form, and then using only "bag" thereafter, which would be normal in spoken discourse. This hyper-elaboration is typical of legal language, rather than everyday speech. Another feature was that the man consistently referred to his friends by their first name, or their first name plus surname, while in the contested samples, they were referred to by surname only. Coulthard also examined a range of other features. The Birmingham Six were subsequently released and paid compensation.

The best evaluation of such evidence comes when the person identified on linguistic grounds later confesses to producing the language – see for example Eagleson (1994).

11.7   Conclusions

Language and the law (sometimes also known as Forensic Linguistics) is an important and fast developing area of applied linguistic concern. All the issues discussed here are of major significance to those involved, whether they are people who cannot understand the legislation impacting on their lives, witnesses whose testimony is distorted by linguistic pressure tactics, minorities whose language cannot be used or who are subjected to group vilification, or the guilty or innocent convicted by language evidence. All these areas are open to examination and action by applied linguists.

See also 5 Discourse Analysis, 13 Stylistics.

REFERENCES

Atkinson, J. M. & Drew, P. (1979) *Order in court: the organisation of verbal interaction in judicial setting*. London: Macmillan.

Bennett, W. L. & Feldman, M. S. (1981) *Reconstructing reality in the courtroom*. London: Tavistock Publications.

Berk-Seligson, S. (1990) *The bilingual courtroom: court interpreters in the judicial process*. Chicago, IL: The University of Chicago Press.

Bhatia, V. K. (1993) *Analysing genre: language use in professional settings*. Harlow: Longman.

Bhatia, V. K. (1994) Cognitive structuring in legislative provisions. In J. Gibbons (ed.), *Language and the law* (pp. 136–55). Harlow: Longman.

Bowe, H. & Storey, K. (1995) Linguistic analysis as evidence of speaker identification: demand and response. In D. Eades (ed.), *Language in evidence issues confronting aboriginal and multicultural Australia* (pp. 187–200). Sydney: University of New South Wales Press.

Carroll, J. (1995) The use of interpreters in court. *Forensic Linguistics*, 2(1), 65–73.

Coulthard, M. (1994) Powerful evidence for the defence: an exercise in forensic discourse analysis. In J. Gibbons (ed.), *Language and the Law* (pp. 414–27). Harlow: Longman.

Coulthard, M. (1997) A failed appeal. *Forensic Linguistics*, 4(2), 287–302.

Crystal, D. & Davy, D. (1969) *Investigating English style*. London: Longman.

Danet, B. & Bogoch, B. (1994) Orality, literacy, and performativity in Anglo-Saxon wills. In J. Gibbons (ed.), *Language and the Law* (pp. 100–35). Harlow: Longman.

Danet, B., Hoffman, K. B., Kermish, N. K., Rafn, H. J., & Stayman, D. G. (1980) An ethnography of questioning. In R. Shuy & A. Shnukal (eds.), *Language use and the uses of language: papers from the Fifth NWAV* (pp. 222–34). Washington, DC: Georgetown University Press.

Davies, E. C. (forthcoming) Register distinctions and measures of complexity in the language of legal contracts. In J. Gibbons, V. Prakasam, & K. V. Tirumalesh (eds.), *Language and justice*. Delhi: Longman Orient.

Diamond, S. S. & Levi, J. N. (1996) Improving decisions on death by revising and testing jury instructions. *Judicature*, 79(5), 224–32.

Eades, D. (1994) A case of communicative clash: aboriginal English and the legal system. In J. Gibbons (ed.), *Language and the law* (pp. 234–64). Harlow: Longman.

Eades, D. (1995) Language and the law: white Australia vs Nancy. In M. Walsh & C. Yallop (eds.), *Language and culture in aboriginal Australia* (pp. 181–190). Canberra: Aboriginal Studies Press.

Eagleson, R. (1994) Forensic analysis of personal written texts: a case study. In J. Gibbons (ed.), *Language and the law* (pp. 363–73). Harlow: Longman.

Felker, D. B., Pickering, F., Charrow, V. R., Holland, V. M., & Redish, J. C. (1981) *Guidelines for document designers*. Washington, DC: American Institutes for Research.

Freedman, M. H. & Freedman, E. M. (eds.) (1995) *Group defamation and freedom of speech: the relationship between language and violence*. Westport, CT: Greenwood Press.

Gibbons, J. (2001) Revising the language of New South Wales police procedures: applied linguistics in action. *Applied Linguistics*, 22(4), 439–69.

González, R. D. & Melis, I. (eds.) (2001) *Critical perspectives on the official English movement*, vol. 2: *History, theory and policy*. Champaign-Urbana, IL: NCTE/Laurence Erlbaum.

Green, G. M. (1990) Linguistic analysis of conversation as evidence regarding the interpretation of speech events. In J. N. Levi & A. G. Walker (eds.), *Language in the judicial process* (pp. 247–77). New York: Plenum Press.

Hale, S. & Gibbons, J. (1999) Varying realities patterned changes in the interpreter's representation of courtroom and external realities. *Applied Linguistics*, 20(2), 203–20.

Hall, P. (forthcoming) Prone to distortions?: undue reliance on unreliable records in the NSW Police Service's formal interview model. In J. Gibbons, V. Prakasam, & K. V. Tirumalesh (eds.), *Language and justice*. Delhi: Longman Orient.

Halliday, M. A. K. (1989) Some grammatical problems in scientific English. *Australian Review of Applied Linguistics Series*, S(6), 13–37.

Halliday, M. A. K. & Hasan, R. (1985) *Language, context and text: aspects of language in a social-semiotic perspective*. Geelong, Vic.: Deakin University Press.

Harris, S. (1984) Questions as a mode of control in magistrates' courts. *International Journal of the Sociology of Language*, 49, 5–27.

Hollien, H. (1990) *The acoustics of crime: the new science of forensic phonetics*. New York, NY: Plenum.

Hollien, H. (2001) *Forensic voice identification*. New York: Academic Press.

Jackson, B. S. (1991) Narrative models in legal proof. In D. R. Papke (ed.), *Narrative and legal discourse: a reader in storytelling and the law* (pp. 158–78). Liverpool, UK: Deborah Charles Publications.

Labov, W. & Harris, W. A. (1994) Addressing social issues through linguistic evidence. In J. Gibbons (ed.), *Language and the law* (pp. 265–305). Harlow: Longman.

Law Reform Commission of Victoria (1987) *Plain English and the law. Report no. 9*. Melbourne: F. D. Atkinson Government Printer.

Levi, J. (1994) Language as evidence: the linguist as expert witness in North American courts. *Forensic Linguistics*, 1(1), 1–26.

Maley, Y. (1994) The language of the law. In J. Gibbons (ed.), *Language and the law* (pp. 3–50). Harlow: Longman.

Maley, Y. & Fahey, R. (1991) Presenting the evidence: constructions of reality in court. *International Journal for the Semiotics of Law*, 4(10), 3–17.

Martin, J. R. (1992) *English text: system and structure*. Amsterdam/ Philadelphia: John Benjamins.

Matoesian, G. (1997) "You were interested in him as a person?" Rhythms of domination in the Kennedy Smith rape trial. *Law and Social Inquiry*, 22(1), 55–91.

McMenamin, G. R. (1993) *Forensic stylistics*. Amsterdam: Elsevier.

O'Barr, W. M. (1982) *Linguistic evidence: language power and strategy in the courtroom*. New York: Academic Press.

O'Barr, W. M. & Conley, J. (1990) *Rules versus relationships: the ethnography of legal discourse*. Chicago, IL: University of Chicago Press.

Oyanadel, M. & Samaniego, J. L. (1999) *Aplicaciones de la lingüística al campo legal*. Paper presented at the 13th Congreso de la Sociedad Chilena de Lingüística, SOCHIL, La Serena, Chile.

Papke, D. R. (ed.) (1991) *Narrative and legal discourse: a reader in storytelling and the law*. Liverpool, UK: Deborah Charles Publications.

Phillips, S. (1987) On the use of wh questions in American courtroom discourse: a study of the relation between language form and language function. In L. Kedar (ed.), *Power through discourse* (pp. 83–111). Norwood, NJ: Ablex.

Shuy, R. (1993) *Language crimes: the use and abuse of language evidence in the courtroom.* Oxford: Blackwell.

Solan, L. M. (1995) Judicial decisions and linguistic analysis: is there a linguist in the court? *Washington University Law Journal,* 73(3), 1069–83.

Steinberg, E. T. (ed.) (1991) *Plain language – principles and practice.* Detroit, MI: Wayne State University Press.

Stygall, G. (1994) *Trial language: differential discourse processing and discursive formation.* Amsterdam and Philadelphia: John Benjamins.

Taylor, B. (1995) Offensive language: a linguistic and sociolinguistic perspective. In D. Eades (ed.), *Language in evidence: issues confronting aboriginal and multicultural Australia* (pp. 219–58). Sydney: University of New South Wales Press.

van Dijk, T. A. (1987) *Communicating racism: ethnic prejudice in thought and talk.* Newbury Park, CA: Sage.

van Dijk, T. A. (1993) *Elite discourse and racism.* Newbury Park, CA: Sage.

Vasilachis de Gialdino, I. (1997) *Discurso Político y Prensa Escrita.* Barcelona: Editorial Gedisa.

Vlachopoulos, S. (forthcoming) Translating the untranslatable? The impact of cultural constraints on the translation of legal texts. In J. Gibbons & V. Prakasam (eds.), *Justice and Language.* Delhi: Longman Orient.

Wallace, C. (1990) *Reading.* Oxford: Oxford University Press.

Walsh, B. (1995) Offensive language: a legal perspective. In D. Eades (ed.), *Language in evidence issues: confronting Aboriginal and multultural Australia* (pp. 203–18). Sydney: University of New South Wales Press.

Walsh, M. (1994) Interactional styles in the courtroom. In J. Gibbons (ed.), *Language and the law* (pp. 217–33). Harlow: Longman.

Weaver, C. (1988) *Reading process and practice: from socio-psycholinguistics to whole language.* Portsmouth, NH: Heinemann Educational.

FURTHER READING

Eades, D. (ed.) (1995) *Language in evidence: linguistic and legal perspectives in multicultural Australia.* Sydney: University of New South Wales Press.

Edwards, J. (1994) *Multilingualism.* London: Routledge.

Forensic Linguistics: the International Journal of Speech, Language and the Law.

Gibbons, J. (ed.) (1994) *Language and the law.* Harlow: Longman.

Gibbons, J. (2003) *Forensic linguistics: an introduction to language in the*

judicial system. Oxford: Basil Blackwell.

Levi, J. N. & Walker, A. G. (eds.), (1990) *Language in the judicial process.* New York: Plenum.

Matoesian, G. (1993) *Reproducing rape: domination through talk in the courtroom.* Chicago, IL: The University of Chicago Press.

Tiersma, P. M. (1999) *Legal language.* Chicago, IL: The University of Chicago Press.

12   Language and Gender

SUSAN EHRLICH

12.1   Introduction

Debates over the nature of gender identity and its social construction, originating in feminist work of the 1990s, have in recent years informed research in sociolinguistics generally and feminist linguistics more specifically. In particular, conceptions of gender as categorical, fixed, and static have increasingly been abandoned in favor of more constructivist and dynamic ones. Cameron (1990, p. 86), for example, makes the point (paraphrasing Harold Garfinkel) that social actors are not sociolinguistic "dopes," mindlessly and passively producing linguistic forms that are definitively determined by social class membership, ethnicity, or gender. Rather, Cameron argues for an understanding of gender that reverses the relationship between linguistic practices and social identities generally posited within the quantitative sociolinguistics or variationist paradigm. Work within this tradition (at least, in the 1970s and 1980s) typically focused on establishing correlations between linguistic variables and social factors such as age, race, ethnicity, and sex, implicitly assuming that these aspects of social identity exist prior to and are determinate of linguistic behavior (and other social behavior). By contrast more recent formulations of the relationship between language and gender, following Butler (1990), emphasize the performative aspect of gender: linguistic practices, among other kinds of practices, continually bring into being individuals' social identities. Under this account, language is one important means by which gender – an ongoing social process – is enacted or constituted; gender is something individuals *do*, in part through linguistic choices, as opposed to something individuals *are* or *have* (West & Zimmerman, 1987). Cameron's comments are illustrative:

> Whereas sociolinguistics would say that the way I use language reflects or marks my identity as a particular kind of social subject – I talk like a white middle-class woman because I am (already) a white middle-class woman – the critical account

suggests language is one of the things that *constitutes* my identity as a particular kind of subject. Sociolinguistics says that how you act depends on who you are: critical theory says that who you are (and taken to be) depends on how you act. (Cameron, 1995, pp. 15–16, emphasis in original)

The idea that individuals' linguistic practices do not simply arise from a set of permanent and invariant social traits that are fixed in childhood and adolescence means, among other things, that we are all continually involved in the work of "doing gender" Linguistic resources, culturally coded as feminine or masculine, are continually drawn upon in the enactment of gender, and according to Butler (1990, p. 49), "congeal over time to produce the appearance of substance, of a 'natural' kind of being." Indeed, the very existence of gendered identities that do not correspond to dominant notions of masculinity and femininity attests to the "constructed," as opposed to the "natural," character of gender and to the greater agency ascribed to social actors under the "performativity" thesis. Nonetheless, social constructionist approaches to gender not only elucidate the "constructed" nature of gendered identities (i.e., gender as performance), but also the "rigid regulatory frame" within which certain performances become intelligible or as Bucholtz (1999, p. 7) says "are made to make cultural sense." Butler (1990, p. 17) argues that the coherence of "gendered" subjects does not depend on the actual features of individuals (what she calls the "logical or analytic features of personhood"), but upon "socially instituted and maintained norms of intelligibility" that define and police normative constructions of gender. An adequate account of language and gender, then, requires not only attending to the way that social actors linguistically constitute themselves as gendered but also to the regulatory norms that "define what kinds of language are possible, intelligible and appropriate resources for performing masculinity or femininity" (Cameron, 1997a, p. 49). Such regulatory norms make certain performances of gender seem natural, that is, in Butler's words, they seem to "congeal over time"; these same cultural norms render other gendered identities inappropriate or unintelligible, and often subject to social and physical sanctions and penalties (e.g., homophobia, gay bashing, the "fixing" of intersexed infants).

In this chapter, I begin by tracing the development of social constructionism within the field of language and gender. I then go on to consider empirically-based investigations of language and gender in relation to the theoretical constructs introduced above. While many language and gender researchers writing in the 1990s and beyond have embraced a social constructionist approach to gender, Stokoe and Smithson (2001, pp. 218–19) make the point that some of this work "blends a constructionist stance with cultural (essentialist) feminism." That is, in determining how speakers "do femininity" or "do masculinity," Stokoe and Smithson suggest that analysts at times interpret their data in terms of stereotypical categories of femininity and masculinity – categories and norms that perpetuate traditional gender dualisms rather than interrogating them. My goal, then, in this chapter is twofold: to theorize empirically-based studies that have not necessarily been contexualized within a social constructionist framework and to give empirical substance to theoretical notions that have often remained abstract in feminist philosophical discussions.

12.2 Historical Overview: From "Dominance" and "Difference" to Social Constructionism

Much language and gender research in the 1970s and 1980s took "difference" between women and men as axiomatic and as the starting point for empirical investigations. That is, either implicitly or explicitly, it was assumed that women and men constituted dichotomous and internally-homogenous groups and the goal of research was both to characterize the difference in their linguistic behavior and to *explain* its occurrence. The first kind of explanation, characterized as the "dominance" approach (Cameron, 1992), viewed male dominance as operative in the everyday verbal interactions of women and men, in turn giving rise to linguistic reflexes of dominance and subordination. Lakoff (1975), for example, in her classic work *Language and Woman's Place*, argued that women use linguistic features of tentativeness and powerlessness (e.g., tag questions, declaratives with rising intonation) in line with their subordinate status relative to men. In influential subsequent work, West and Zimmerman (for example, 1983) identified interruptions as a site of men's conversational dominance, while Fishman (1983) documented the "conversational shitwork" women perform in order to sustain conversations with men. A second type of explanatory account, characterized as the "difference" or the "dual-cultures" approach (Cameron, 1992), suggested that women and men learn different communicative styles based on the segregated same-sex peer groups they play in as children (see Maltz & Borker, 1982; Tannen, 1990). A crucial point for Tannen (1990, p. 47), in her popularized and best-selling version of the dual-cultures model – *You Just Don't Understand: Women and Men in Conversation*, was the legitimacy of both men's and women's conversational styles: "misunderstandings arise because the styles [women's and men's] are different" and "each style is valid on its own terms." In fact, it has often been the so-called innocence of the communicative differences underlying male–female communication that has been critiqued by scholars advocating a "dominance" rather than a "difference" or "dual-cultures" approach. (See, for example, Freed, 1992; Henley & Kramarae, 1991; Troemel-Ploetz, 1991; and Uchida, 1992.)

Influenced by feminist scholarship more generally, feminist linguistics in the 1990s began to challenge the homogeneous and static nature of the categories taken as foundational to much research within the "dominance" and "difference" approaches. That is, assumptions about the categories of "women" and "men" as binary opposites with little internal heterogeneity were critiqued on both empirical and political grounds. Henley & Kramarae (1991) argued, for example, that focusing on differences rather than similarities between women and men functions to exaggerate and reinforce gender polarities – arguably, a focus that does not serve the interests of feminism – and abstracts gender away from the specificities of its social context. Indeed, many of the claims about gender-differentiated language that emerged from studies in the 1970s and 1980s – the most notable being that women's speech styles are cooperative, while men's are competitive – were based on studies that did just this: they were based on limited populations – white, North American and middle class – engaged in cross-sex conversation, where as Freeman and McElhinny (1996) note, gender is probably maximally contrastive, yet their results were overgeneralized to all women and men. Freed and Greenwood (1996) provided an important corrective to these kinds of overly-general claims. Their subjects, women and men involved in same-sex dyadic conversations with friends, displayed strikingly similar linguistic behavior – behavior typically associated with the so-called cooperative speech style of women. They concluded that it was the demands of a particular type of talk – friendly conversations with same-sex individuals – and *not* gender that was responsible for the emergence of this speech style. What becomes clear from such a study is the importance of considering communicative settings and tasks as possible determinants of linguistic behavior that has more typically, and perhaps too simplistically, been treated as the effect of a speaker's gender.

12.3 Social Constructionist Approaches to Language and Gender

In contrasting essentialism and social constructionism, Bohan (1997, p. 33) considers the difference between "describing an individual as friendly and describing a conversation as friendly." While the gendering of "friendly" for an essentialist would mean that one gender, say, women, is more friendly than the other, a social constructionist would argue that the differential exposure of men and women to friendly-eliciting contexts leads to a social agreement whereby "friendly" is gendered as feminine. In other words, for a social constructionist, it is not that friendliness is an intrinsic characteristic of individuals; rather, it becomes connected to femininity because women are more often associated with situations or contexts that are friendly. Indeed, the Freed and Greenwood study described above is revealing of the process by which "cooperative speech styles" have become gendered (in both the scholarly literature and the popular imagination). It may be the case that in western cultures women, more than men, are associated with same-sex friendly conversations – situations and contexts that seem to encourage a cooperative speech style. In turn, a social understanding and agreement develops (or empirical research is conducted) that links cooperative speech styles with women, thereby gendering cooperative speech styles as feminine. Thus, while seemingly intrinsic to individuals, gendered traits are social and cultural constructs that may more accurately be described as "contextually determined" (Bohan, 1997, p. 39). Perhaps not surprising, then, is Goodwin's (1990) finding, based on an ethnographic study of urban African American children in Philadelphia, that activity-type (i.e., context) was a better predictor of speech style than gender. That is, in certain activities, all-girl groups adopted hierarchical speech styles similar to those adopted by the all-boy groups. On the basis of such findings, Goodwin suggests that stereotypes about women's speech collapse when talk in a whole range of *activities* is examined.

While Goodwin (1990, p. 9) argues that "situated activities" are the "relevant unit for the analysis of cultural phenomena, including gender," Eckert and McConnell-Ginet (1992a; 1992b; 1999) suggest that gender should be investigated in "communities of practices" – a somewhat larger analytic domain than "activities" (McElhinny, 2003). Like Goodwin and social constructionist approaches to gender more generally, Eckert and McConnell-Ginet do not view gender as an attribute of an individual, but rather something that emerges out of individuals' engagement in a complex set of social practices; put another way, individuals produce themselves as gendered by habitually engaging in certain practices (i.e., communities of practice) that are linked practically and/or symbolically to cultural understandings of gender. In Eckert and McConnell-Ginet's (1992b; 1995) words: "gender is produced (and often reproduced) in differential membership in communities of practice." Like Butler's performativity thesis, then, the communities of practice framework views gender as an *effect* of participating in certain kinds of social practices, and not a cause.

That the relationship between language and gender is almost always mediated by social activities or practices is a point probably first made in the language and gender literature by Ochs (1992, p. 340) when she claimed that "few features of language directly and exclusively index gender." For Ochs, a *direct* indexical relationship between linguistic forms and gender is exemplified in personal pronouns that denote the sex/gender of an interlocutor. To say, by contrast, that language *indirectly* indexes gender is to say that the relationship is mediated by the social stances, acts, activities, and practices (e.g., friendly activities) that are gendered in a particular community. In Japanese, for example, there are certain sentence-final particles that index assertiveness and intensity, and others that index uncertainty and hesitancy (Inoue, 2002); moreover, there is a symbolic association in Japanese culture between men and assertiveness, on the one hand, and women and uncertainty, on the other hand. (See Inoue (2002) for a historical account of this indexing process.) Consider further the example of tag questions in English: tag questions may display or index a stance of uncertainty or tentativeness, as Lakoff (1975) suggested, and, in turn, a stance of uncertainty may in some English-speaking communities be associated with femininity. It is in this sense that a linguistic form, such as a sentence-final particle or a tag question, could be said to *indirectly* index femininity. As Ochs says, however, this is not an exclusive or direct relationship; in fact, given the multifunctionality of linguistic forms, a linguistic form such as a tag question uttered by a cross-examining lawyer in a trial context may index a verbal act of coercion (e.g., Sir, you did go to your girlfriend's house on the night of her murder, didn't you?) which, in turn, may be associated with masculinity in some communities. What the preceding discussion reveals, among other things, is the greater agency imputed to social actors under social constructionism. If gendered linguistic practices are not fixed traits but social and cultural constructs indirectly and symbolically associated with gender (but more accurately linked to certain contexts, stances, acts, activities, or practices), then individuals can presumably construct their gendered identities (or interpret others' identities) by drawing upon (or interpreting) these symbolic resources in various ways. Such an account leaves open the possibility of "gendered" linguistic practices being variable across communities and cultures, and variable across individuals of the same sex/gender within a given culture. Indeed, such an account allows for the possibility that individuals can appropriate linguistic practices that do not correspond to the normative expectations for their particular social group. In what follows, I consider empirical studies that have attended (either explicitly or implicitly) to the mediating variable of social practice (or social activity or social context) in investigations of language and gender. In so doing, I demonstrate the variability in women's and men's linguistic practices that emerge from such investigations and the way in which linguistic practices that become "gendered" may be (more accurately) grounded in particular social activities or contexts.

12.4 Variation across Cultures: Language and Gender in Bilingual and Multilingual Settings

This section describes the findings of several ethnographic studies that have sought to understand gender-differentiated language use and acquisition in bilingual and multilingual settings. Given that the relationship between language and gender is, as argued above, not a direct one, but one mediated by the social practices and activities that come to be "gendered" in particular communities or cultures, then investigations of gender and bilingualism are most fruitfully carried out in relation to those culture- or community-specific social practices and activities. Indeed, in what follows I have attempted to categorize these studies according to social practices in different cultures/communities that seem to have consequences for gender-differentiated language use and acquisition.

12.4.1 *Restricted exposure to the prestigious language*

Hill (1987) investigates gender differences in the use of an indigenous language (Mexicano) and Spanish (a former colonial language) in rural communities located in the central Mexican states of Puebla and Tlaxcala. These communities are characterized by increasing proletarianization, that is, "members are shifting from a base of subsistence agriculture and associated rural pursuits such as woodcutting, supplemented seasonally by migratory labor, to integration into a regional and national system of wage labor" (Hill, 1987, p. 123). Women are much less likely than men to participate in regular wage labor and, on this basis, one might speculate that women would be less proficient in Spanish than men. Indeed, members of the community believe just this: Women are said to "lag" linguistically, that is, they are believed to be more often monolingual in Mexicano, their Mexicano is believed to be less influenced by Spanish, and their Spanish is believed to be more influenced by Mexicano. However, Hill's findings regarding women's speech reveal a somewhat more complex picture. In some ways, women's speech is less Spanish than men's; for example, women's Spanish is "more likely to be conspicuously interlingual than the Spanish of men and on many variables they exhibit 'less hispanization of their Mexicano usage than do men'" (Hill, 1987, p. 134). In other ways, by contrast, women seem to exhibit a high sensitivity to Spanish norms, for example, in their use of Spanish stress patterns on borrowed Spanish nouns in Mexicano. (Men are more likely to use Mexicano stress patterns on borrowed Spanish nouns.) Hill concludes with the following comments:

> Rather than think of the speech norms of women as marginal to a core of male norms, we might instead think of women's speech as highly constrained within a narrow range of possibilities, at the same time less Mexicano and less Spanish than male's speech, whereas men are able to use the full range of code variation. (1987, p. 158)

That is, women's Spanish is generally poorer than men's because women do not have access to wage labor and the marketplace where Spanish is spoken. At the same time, women's Mexicano is in certain respects more Spanish than men's because women are excluded from certain male social practices, in particular, the discourse of solidarity embraced by the men. According to Hill, men resist their integration into mainstream Spanish culture by emphasizing their Mexicano identities linguistically. This fact explains women's greater use of Spanish stress patterns in Spanish nouns borrowed into Mexicano: the Mexicano stress pattern is a salient marker of an authentic and pure variety of Mexicano and thus a means by which men signal their solidarity with their indigenous culture.

Like Hill (1987), Harvey (1994) investigates the gender-differentiated use of an indigenous language, Quechua (in Ocongate, a small Andean town in Southern Peru), relative to the former colonial language of Peru, Spanish. Whereas the majority of men (76 percent) are either fully bilingual or fluent in Spanish with heavy influences from Quechua, 46 percent of women are monolingual Quechua speakers or have extremely limited Spanish. (This is only true of 10 percent of the men.) To a large extent, this asymmetry in the acquisition of

Spanish can be explained in terms of differential exposure to the prestige language: historically, women were less likely than men to be educated or to be involved in migrant labor. Harvey notes that in recent years more and more women are learning Spanish in recognition of the connection between bilingualism and positions of authority in the community. Women bilingual speakers, however, are much more reluctant than men to use Spanish. This is because of the quite severe social costs that accompany women's abdication of tradition: women's use of Spanish is ridiculed and ostracized in the same way that women's abandoning of traditional dress is. Like Hill, Harvey describes the ambivalent relation that the community's men have to bilingualism given the loss of indigenous traditions that may go hand in hand with integration into mainstream Spanish culture. Cameron (1992) makes the following general remarks about bilingual situations analogous to those described by Hill and Harvey:

> Although matters are very complex, it seems men may feel threatened by women's becoming bilingual. Why should that be? One suggestion is that minority men are dealing with their own ambivalence about the loss of indigenous traditions. Assimilation brings certain economic rewards, but it also undermines the continuity of one's way of life and thus one's identity. In a male dominated society, men can resolve this problem by taking the rewards of cultural change for themselves while requiring the community's women to be living symbols of the tradition. (Cameron, 1992, p. 202)

In addition to having restricted access to Spanish, women's use of Spanish in the Peruvian community of Ocongate seems also to be restricted by the women's position "as the living symbols of tradition."

12.4.2 *Women as cultural brokers*

Not all postcolonial or postimperial situations result in women's restricted access to, or use of, the colonial or imperial language. In some communities, women are expected to not only be the "guardians" of the traditional language and culture (Burton, 1994) but also to mediate between the dominant and minority cultures. Medicine (1987) coins the term "cultural broker" to characterize the role that women often assume in Native American communities. In describing the effects of white domination on the Lakota Sioux, Medicine (1987, p. 163) reports that it was typically the women who were "recruited to work in the houses of missionaries and of other agents of change" and as a result they became more proficient in English than men. At the same time, women were also expected to be the major socializers of children and taught them, according to Medicine, "that interaction in two different worlds required entirely different languages."

In her exploration of language and social identity among women in an East Harlem Puerto Rican community, Zentella (1987) comments on the conflicts experienced by Puerto Rican women in New York City who are expected both to preserve a Spanish-speaking tradition and to mediate between the dominant and minority cultures. This "cultural broker" role, not surprisingly, had linguistic consequences: Zentella (1987, p. 177) reports that her data and that of Poplack (1980) "showed that the most prolific intrasentential code-switchers were also the best speakers of English and Spanish and that these were usually women." Thus, we see that both Medicine and Zentella portray situations in which women are both the conservators of a traditional language and innovators in English, a role not unlike that assumed by men in the communities described by Hill.

12.4.3   *Women as innovators in social change*

Although a number of researchers have characterized women's role in bilingual communities as that of "guardians" of the traditional language and, by extension, ethnic identity, Gal (1978) describes a different kind of situation, one in which young women reject Hungarian, the language associated with the traditional culture. Gal focuses on the Hungarian-German bilingual community of Oberwart, Austria, exploring the effects of urbanization and industrialization on women's and men's choice of Hungarian versus German. Young peasant women are leading in the shift from Hungarian to German in this community, because, Gal argues, the peasant lifestyle associated with Hungarian is one they wish to reject. Although for men a peasant life offers self-employment, independence, and autonomy, for women it consists of strenuous and time-consuming manual labor. Thus, Gal explains young women's linguistic choices in terms of their desire to distance themselves from a life that is symbolically and practically associated with Hungarian. We see here that the motivation and incentives for learning a second language may differ for women and men, depending on the types of opportunities that a second language creates or makes available to them in particular communities. It is noteworthy that the women in Oberwart had access to the Hungarian, but rather than assuming a "cultural broker" role, they strategically employed German in order to escape their social position as peasants.

The studies described above are meant to illustrate the variability that exists cross-culturally with respect to gender and bilingualism and the extent to which this variability is tied to the social practices of local communities. While cross-cultural variability is of little surprise to linguistic anthropologists, there nonetheless exists a fairly robust generalization in the second language acquisition literature regarding the superiority of female learners. (See Ehrlich (1997) for a detailed discussion and critique of this literature.) By contrast, the studies described in this section demonstrate the difficulty of drawing generalizations about the precise way that gender – or the social practices that constitute gender in particular communities – interact with second language acquisition and bilingualism. What do become apparent, however, are the kinds of social practices that may produce gender differentiation in acquisition outcomes. Hill and Harvey, for example, describe communities in which women were less proficient than men in the dominant, postcolonial language of Spanish because of women's restricted access to Spanish and/or the cultural expectation that they would be the preservers of the indigenous traditions. (Hill also describes the women of Puebla and Tlaxcala as more constrained in terms of code variation.) By contrast, within Medicine's and Zentella's investigations, women, more often than men, were the proficient bilinguals because they assumed a "cultural broker" role in their communities. That is, in addition to being the preservers of the indigenous traditions, women in these communities were also expected to mediate between the dominant and minority communities. Gal describes yet another kind of situation: young women in Oberwart were leading in the community's shift from Hungarian to German. Indeed, Gal's study shows women actively reconstructing themselves as German speakers as a way of resisting the norms of femininity associated with Hungarian peasant life. In the terms of Butler's performativity thesis, the young women of Oberwart were exercising a certain degree of agency in drawing upon linguistic resources that signaled a different kind of femininity – one that would facilitate their escape from a peasant way of life. A similar kind of resistance has been described by Siegal (1994, 1996) in a foreign language acquisition context. In an ethnographic study of four white women learning Japanese, Siegal (1994, p. 648) found that the learners "created their own language based on their perceptions of Japanese women's language and demeanor and their awareness of their position in Japanese society." Siegal's work portrays female foreign language learners as active agents who abandon honorifics and sentence-final particles associated with Japanese women's language to resist a social positioning that is thrust upon them. That is, in the same way that the Hungarian women of Oberwart made linguistic choices in order to resist their identities as peasant wives, so Siegal's learners drew upon the interactional resources of Japanese to resist Japanese constructions of femininity.

Hill notes that the Mexicano women of her study, like the women of Gal's study, would also have benefited from the symbolic resources of the urban elite, in their case, Spanish. Yet, ultimately, Hill concludes that the material realities of Mexicano culture militated against women's access to Spanish: "If the uncompensated labor of these women is a pivotal component of the regional system of industrial wage labor, it seems unlikely that the educational opportunities and other support that would enable the women of the Malinche Volcano to fulfill their potential change will be made available to them" (Hill, 1987, p. 159). Hill's comments point to the kinds of material conditions that can impede women's access to prestigious symbolic resources, thereby making impossible the "performances" of counter-hegemonic femininities that were possible for the young women of Oberwart. Indeed, what emerges from the Hill and Harvey studies more generally is an understanding of some of the political economic factors that adversely affect women's exposure to valuable symbolic resources.

12.5 Variation within Gender Categories: Variation Theory and Communities of Practice

In spite of the tendency for sociolinguistic work within the variationist or quantitative sociolinguistics tradition to use "female" and "male" as oppositional and unanalyzed speaker variables (Cheshire, 2002), as far back as 1983, Nichols determined that different groups of women in an all-black speech community on the coast of South Carolina behaved differently with respect to the adoption of standard linguistic variants. In fact, contrary to the prevailing view of the time (and a view that persists among some in variationist circles) – that women are more sensitive to and make greater use of prestige variants than men – Nichols found that women's linguistic behavior was driven by their relation to the local labor market, rather than by "some generalized response to the universal condition of women" (Nichols, 1983, p. 54). Indeed, while younger mainland women in the community Nichols studied were leading in the community's shift from a low-prestige linguistic variety, Gullah, to standard English, older mainland women were the heaviest users of Gullah. Because older mainland women, like their male counterparts, were restricted to workplaces where they were generally not exposed to standard English, they maintained their use of the low-prestige Gullah. On the other hand, younger mainland women had access to new employment opportunities in white-collar sections of the labor market where they were required to use standard English. Their relation to the labor market, then, provided them with the opportunity and incentive to use standard English. Given that in western industrialized societies, more generally, standard varieties are often more crucial to women in the workplace (Eckert & McConnell-Ginet, 1999) in jobs such as teacher, secretary, receptionist, flight attendant, etc. it is perhaps not surprising that women have been found (and are thought) to use standard linguistic variants more than men. What is important to note about such a generalization, however, is that linguistic behavior more accurately linked to certain kinds of *contexts* (i.e., certain kinds of employment opportunities), becomes gendered as feminine because women in western industrialized societies are more often in these contexts. Indeed, Nichols' work demonstrates that older mainland women who did not have access to the kinds of employment contexts that necessitated the use of standard English were the heaviest users of the non-standard variety, Gullah. Although not explicitly articulated within a social constructionist framework, Nichols' work considers the linguistic practices of men and women in relation to their social practices, or more specifically, their workplace practices. And, as I have argued above, attending to the social contexts or activities or communities of practice that men and women participate in helps to make transparent the process by which certain linguistic styles and/or varieties become socially constructed as feminine or masculine.

Eckert (1989, 2000) also finds generalizations about women's greater use of prestige forms to be untenable in light of her work on Detroit suburban adolescents. Undoubtedly influenced by work such as Nichols', in 1989 Eckert published a devastating critique of variationist approaches to language and the independent variable of sex. Specifically, her critique centered on the variationist practice of classifying speakers according to the binary and oppositional category of sex. Arguing that such a practice belies the complexity of a social phenomenon such as gender, Eckert (1989, p. 265) concluded that "most [variationist] analyses [of sex differences] have fallen short . . . in the confusion of social meaning with the analysts' demographic abstractions." While it is only later that Eckert (with McConnell-Ginet) introduces the notion of "communities of practice" into the area of language and gender, the seeds of such an innovation are apparent in her 1989 article as she highlights the importance of understanding gender as a complex social practice. Certainly, one of the great advantages of the "community of practice" framework is its examination of gender, not in isolation, but in relation to other social variables. Rather than adopting a notion of community based on location or population, a community of practice "focuses on a community defined by social engagement . . . A community of practice is an aggregate of people who come together around mutual engagement in some common endeavor" (Eckert & McConnell-Ginet, 1992b, p. 95). Indeed, Eckert (1989, 2000) found that the linguistic behavior of adolescent girls and boys in a Detroit high school interacted in interesting ways with two class-based communities of practice – jocks and burn-outs. Not surprisingly, the jocks, a middle-class community committed to engagement in school-sponsored activities (Eckert & McConnell-Ginet, 1995, p. 475), had more standard pronunciations than the burn-outs, a working-class community whose activities were defined in terms of their "autonomy from the school" (Eckert & McConnell-Ginet, 1995, p. 474). But, it was not the case that the girls in both groups had more standard pronunciations than the boys. (Note that this might be expected given women's so-called greater sensitivity to prestige norms.) What did distinguish the girls from the boys in both groups, however, was their extreme use of variables signaling their community memberships. That is, while the jock girls had the most standard pronunciations of the four groups, the burn-out girls had the least standard pronunciations. As Eckert & McConnell-Ginet (1999, p. 195) note, "standard language usage seems to be actively pursued by those young women who identify themselves with the school's corporate culture (and the middle class aspirations it supports); it is roundly avoided by those who reject such an identification." Such a finding, of course, does not unequivocally support the generalization that women's use of standard variants is greater than men's; rather, the generalization seems to be that girls, more than boys, are expressing their category membership through the symbolic resources of language. Thus, in attending to gender as a complex social practice, and, in particular, to its relation to workplace-based/class-based communities of practice, both Nichols and Eckert expose the premature generalizations that can result from abstracting gender away from the specific social practices of local communities.

12.6   Similarity across Gender Categories: Drawing upon "Masculine" and "Feminine" Repertoires

As noted above, the "difference" or "dual-cultures" approach to language and gender presupposes the existence of differences in men and women's linguistic behavior and attempts to locate the origins of such differences in the same-sex peer groups of childhood. Applying Gumperz' (1982a, 1982b) work on cross-cultural communication to male–female communication, Maltz and Borker (1982), and later Tannen (1990), suggest that women and men, like members of different cultural groups, learn different communicative styles because of the segregated girls' and boys' peer groups they play in as children. Indeed, women are said to develop cooperative speech styles because of the non-hierarchical nature of all-girl groups, whereas men are said to develop competitive speech styles because "boys play in larger, more hierarchically organized groups than do girls" (Maltz & Borker, 1982). While abandoning many of the essentialist assumptions of Maltz and Borker's work (i.e., that women and men are destined to act out conversational traits developed and fixed in childhood), Coates (1996, 1997), in her research on women's and men's same-sex talk among friends, nonetheless determined that women's talk tended to be more collaborative than men's. Assuming that women and men share interactional resources, Coates (1997, p. 126) argues that her subjects drew upon them differently in "doing same-sex friendship." Specifically, the male friends avoided interruptions and overlaps and adhered scrupulously to a one-at-a-time floor, thereby producing conversations characterized by a series of monologues. The women friends, by contrast, employed a collaborative mode of conversational interaction, privileging the voice of the group over the voice of the individual.

Coates' findings are somewhat at odds with those of Freed and Greenwood (1996). Recall that Freed and Greenwood conducted an experimental study involving same-sex friends in casual conversations that produced similar linguistic behavior – a cooperative speech style – in both female and male speakers. In contemplating the emergence of similarities where other researchers have found differences, Freed (1996, p. 66) speculates that the particular research design used by Freed and Greenwood (1996) may have "inadvertently created an experimental space which is *symbolic* of what our society views as a 'female space'" (emphasis in original). Consistent with social constructionist approaches to gender, Freed sees the particular context generated by Freed and Greenwood's experimental conditions to be conventionally associated with femininity in western cultures and, in turn, the speech style produced in this context to be concomitantly "gendered" as feminine. Indeed, in naturalistic settings, like those investigated by Coates (1996, 1997) women may be more likely to be found in contexts symbolically associated with femininity and men, likewise, in contexts symbolically associated with masculinity. As Freed points out, however, an experimental setting that positioned women and men in symmetrical social relations, performing identical tasks, elicited in the women and men the same kind of talk. A question that arises from such a study, then, concerns the possibility of a comparable *naturalistic* setting (i.e., where men and women are positioned symmetrically and are performing the same tasks) generating similar kinds of talk in women and men.

McElhinny's (1995) study of the interactional styles of male and female police officers in Pittsburgh offers a particularly striking example of such a setting. In moving into a traditionally masculine workplace, female police officers did not adopt an empathetic and warm interactional style associated with many traditionally female workplaces (e.g., nursing, secretarial work, social work), as might be expected; rather they appropriated a masculine (linguistic) identity in dealing with the public. More specifically, McElhinny (1995, p. 220) argues that both women and younger, college-educated men in the police force adopted a "bureaucratic" interactional style – a rational, emotionless, and efficient interactional style associated with middle-class masculinity. That is, engaged in the same workplace practices, the women and the younger, college-educated men of the Pittsburgh police force adopted similar interactional styles.

By investigating the linguistic practices of women working in a traditionally *masculine* workplace, McElhinny's work also sheds light on the "performative" nature of gender. If gender is something individuals do, as opposed to something individuals are, then venturing into contexts traditionally associated with the other gender can bring with it social practices, including linguistic practices, that are also associated with the other gender. For the female police officers in Pittsburgh, appropriating working-class masculine practices based on physical force and aggression may not have been an option; however, according to McElhinny, the women were able to create a space for themselves in a largely masculine workplace by challenging "the hegemonic definition of a police officer (and of working-class masculinity) as centered on displays of physical force and emotional aggression" and orienting to an alternative kind of masculinity – one that "centered on mental ability and cool efficiency" (p. 238).

More extreme appropriations of linguistic practices not normatively associated with one's own gender can be discerned in a series of recent studies involving individuals who transgress sex/gender norms in much more dramatic ways than the female police officers of Pittsburgh. (See, for example, Barrett, 1999; Gaudio, 1997; Kulick, 1998.) In Butler's words, such individuals are "incoherent" gendered beings because they "fail to conform to gendered norms of cultural intelligibility" (1990, p. 17). A striking example of this "cultural unintelligibility" and its social consequences is embodied in the Hindi-speaking *hijras* of India – the subjects of much of Kira Hall's work (Hall, 1997; Hall & O'Donovan, 1996). The hijras are regarded as a "third sex" in India and, for the most part, live in segregated communities due to their socially marginal and ostracized status. Because the majority of hijras are born and raised as boys, their entry into a hijra community involves learning to perform a new gender identity: an identity, according to Hall and O'Donovan (1996, p. 239) "which distances itself from masculine representations in its appropriation of feminine dress, social roles, gesture and language." (Hall & O'Donovan report that more than 75 percent of the hijras living in India today have undergone genital surgery (i.e., castration).) While it might be expected that well-socialized and experienced hijras would always linguistically gender themselves and other hijras as feminine (Hindi has an extensive and obligatory morphological system signaling gender), Hall and O'Donovan found this not to be the case. Rather, they determined that the hijras made variable use of the grammatical gender system depending on whether they wished to convey social distance from a referent or addressee or solidarity with a referent or addressee. Indeed, consistent with the cultural meanings associated with masculinity and femininity in India, the hijras employed the *grammatical* markings of masculinity and femininity to convey such meanings: masculine grammatical markings to signal social distance and feminine grammatical markings to signal solidarity. As Cameron (1996, p. 46) observes about this description of the hijras' linguistic practices, there is an important sense in which "we are all like the hijras." That is, we all make variable use of linguistic forms, styles, and/or genres that are culturally and ideologically coded as masculine or feminine in order to construct our identities from moment to moment, and from context to context. The men of Freed and Greenwood's study, for example, drew upon an interactional style culturally associated with femininity when discussing the topic of close friendships (a topic, perhaps, gendered as feminine) in an experimental setting orchestrated by two self-professed feminists. In a similar way, the women of the Pittsburgh police force drew upon an emotionless and hyper-rational interactional style associated with middle-class masculinity when constructing their identity in a primarily male and masculine workplace. What the hijras make transparent, then, is the variable use that "ordinary" men and women make of linguistic repertoires conventionally associated with the other gender. Such variability is testimony to the greater agency ascribed to individuals under Butler's performativity thesis.

12.7   Institutional Coerciveness

While the theorizing of gender as "performative" has succeeded in problematizing essentialist and static notions of gender, for some feminist linguists (e.g., Wodak, 1997) Butler's formulation ignores the power relations that impregnate most situations in which gender is performed and hence affords subjects unbounded agency. For Cameron (1997b), by contrast, Butler's (1990) discussion of performativity does acknowledge these power relations, that is, by alluding to the "rigid regulatory frame" within which gendered identities are produced. Kulick (forthcoming) also defends Butler's work against such charges; he says that early criticisms of her framework were based on an inaccurate reading of the social actor "as an entirely self-aware and volitional subject who could choose to put on or take off genders the way people put on or take off clothes." Like Cameron, Kulick argues that such a characterization of Butler's work ignores how subjects become constituted as intelligible or unintelligible, coherent or incoherent, given the matrices of power and the regulatory norms that define and police normative constructions of gender. The problem may be, as Cameron (1997b, p. 31) suggests, that philosophical discussions of Butler's "rigid regulatory frame" often remain very abstract. That is, the routine enactment of gender is often, perhaps always, subject to what Cameron calls the "institutional coerciveness" of social situations; yet, too often in feminist philosophical discussions "gender . . . floats free of the social contexts and activities in which it will always be . . . embedded." In other words, dominant gender ideologies have considerable influence on the linguistic practices of women and men, facilitating the production of certain kinds of gendered identities and thwarting or inhibiting others.

Addressing the tensions between local and more universal accounts of language and gender, Bergvall (1999) emphasizes the need to analyze dominant gender ideologies that pre-exist and structure local (linguistic) enactments of gender. That is, while more local and contextual accounts of language and gender (e.g., Eckert & McConnell-Ginet, 1992a, 1992b, 1999) move us away from overarching and excessive generalizations about women, men and "gendered" talk, Bergvall (1999, p. 282) suggests that we also consider the force of socially ascribed gender norms – "the assumptions and expectations of (often binary) ascribed social roles against which any performance of gender is constructed, accommodated to, or resisted." Likewise, Woolard and Schieffelin (1998, p. 72) argue that we must connect the "microculture of communicative action" to what they call "macrosocial constraints on language and behavior." Certainly, the examination of language and gender within institutions elucidates some of the macro-constraints that pre-exist local performances of gender. Indeed, Gal (1991) argues that because women and men interact primarily in institutions, such as workplaces, families, schools, and political forums, the investigation of language and gender in informal conversations, outside of these institutions, has severe limitations. It "creates the illusion that gendered talk is mainly a personal characteristic" (p. 185), whereas, as much feminist research has revealed, gender is also a structuring principle of institutions.

Consistent with this emphasis on institutions and their ability to influence or "coerce" performances of gender is the view of ethnomethodologists that identities are interactionally *co-constructed*. That is, rather than viewing the construction of an identity as achieved exclusively through the actions of an individual speaker, such a view suggests that they also emerge through the way a self is positioned by other speakers. Drawing on data from sexual assault trials, Ehrlich (2001) explores some of the interactional processes by which gendered identities can be co-constructed in institutions or, put somewhat differently, the way that institutional discourse can "coerce" performances of gender (Ehrlich, 2003). Trial discourse is notable for its question-answer format; moreover, given the institutionally-sanctioned power accorded to questioners in such contexts (e.g., lawyers and judges), witnesses are "systematically disabled" from asking questions or initiating turns (Hutchby & Wooffitt, 1998, p. 166). Ehrlich analyzes the presuppositions of questions asked of complainants in sexual assault trials and argues that, when taken together, such presuppositions formed a powerful ideological frame through which the events under investigation were understood and evaluated. That is, although no longer codified in law in the United States or Canada, the "utmost resistance standard" – the idea that complainants did not resist the accused "to the utmost" – circulated discursively in the sexual assault adjudication processes analyzed by Ehrlich. And, in response to innumerable questions whose presuppositions embodied the utmost resistance standard, the complainants involuntarily cast themselves as ineffectual agents: their strategic attempts to resist the perpetrators of sexual assault were transformed into ineffectual acts of resistance within the discourse of the trial. Put another way, the identities "performed" by the complainants in these contexts – as passive and lacking in appropriate resistance – were "coerced" performances of gender, given the dominant discourse (i.e., the utmost resistance standard) that structured their linguistic acts of identity.

The idea that sexist linguistic practices can adversely influence the kinds of gendered identities women are able to produce was a major impetus behind non-sexist language reform efforts in the 1970s and 1980s. Early work on sexist language, for example, pointed to the detrimental effects, both practical and symbolic, of masculine generics such as *he* and *man* – forms, it was argued, that render women invisible. Indeed, a substantial body of empirical evidence showed, among other things, that *he/man* generics readily evoke images of males rather than females, have negative effects on individuals' beliefs in women's ability to perform a job, and have a negative impact on women's own feelings of pride, importance, and power. (For a review of this work see Henley, 1989.) While recent work in feminist linguistics has witnessed a broadening in its conception of sexist linguistic representations beyond single words and expressions to discursive practices (see Cameron, 1998a, 1998b) for discussion), the "coercive" effect of such representations continues to be of concern to language and gender researchers. Cameron (1998a) demonstrates how a range of linguistic features, none of which would be deemed problematic by a word-based critique of sexist language, can together function to construct rape in sexist and androcentric ways. And Benedict (1992, 1993) and Clark (1998) demonstrate the pervasiveness of rape reports in the media that portray rapists as crazy, evil, sexual deviants and fiends, rather than as women's husbands, partners, family members, etc., in spite of the fact that women are much more likely to be raped by husbands, lovers, and dates than by strangers. As Clark (1998) comments, "the intense hyperbole of fiend naming focuses a self-righteous fury on stranger attacks, which are actually a very small area of male/female violence." Indeed, Benedict argues that rape reporting in the mainstream media is socially controlling to the extent that it simultaneously curtails women's freedom by fostering a fear of violence in public spaces and creates a false sense of security around the situations wherein women are most vulnerable.

That this type of social control and regulation can have linguistic consequences for women is a point made persuasively by Polanyi (1995) in her ethnographic study of American university students in a Russian study-abroad program. Focusing on reports of sexual harassment documented by the female students, Polanyi shows that the routine sexual harassment and assault experienced by the women created target language interactions (with Russian men) in which they were reduced to silence or made to feel humiliated and degraded. In contrast to the silence and degradation experienced by the young women in their encounters with Russian men, Polanyi cites the journal of a young man whose pleasant flirtation with a Russian woman resulted in an evening of increased linguistic fluency: "My Russian felt good, and her ongoing barrage of smiles certainly helped . . . We joked and chatted . . . My Russian was smooth and flexible" (Polanyi, 1995, p. 281). Clearly, target language interactions in which learners are encouraged to speak by, among other things, an "ongoing barrage of smiles" will produce a different kind of output in the target language (i.e., output that is "smooth and flexible") than interactions which involve harassment. In fact, Polanyi makes the point that when "faced with complex interpersonal situations" the young women in the study-abroad program were acquiring the linguistic skills to cope: some reported learning useful vocabulary for dealing with sexually harassing situations; others reported that their linguistic ability to deal effectively with harassing situations in Russian became a point of pride. In spite of the considerable linguistic and sociolinguistic competence acquired by these women, however, the linguistic skills developed in response to the sexually harassing situations were not the focus of language proficiency tests. Thus, not surprisingly, Brecht, Davidson, and Ginsberg (1995, p. 56), in their long-term study of the predictors of language gain in the same Russian study-abroad programs, found that women made fewer gains than men in listening and speaking skills and that men were more likely to "cross the crucial divide between Intermediate+ to Advanced level" than women. It is important to note that the young women performed as well as the young men on Russian tests before the study-abroad program. The problem, according to Polanyi, is *not* that the young women were less gifted language learners than the young men. Rather, despite the fact that the women were subject to sexist and androcentric practice in the foreign language learning situation, the tests that measured their proficiency took as their norm men's linguistic activities and practices – activities and practices that did not involve sexual harassment.

Translated into the terms of this discussion, the linguistic identities performed by these young men and women were saturated by the gendered ideologies and power relations that characterized the foreign language learning situation. In contrast to the women of Siegal's (1994, 1996) study (see Section 12.4.3), who exercised a considerable degree of agency in resisting aspects of Japanese "women's language" that they perceived as overly humble and self-deprecating, the women in Polanyi's study constructed a linguistic identity in Russian that was not primarily of their own making. Positioned as victims of sexual harassment, the young women developed a linguistic proficiency (i.e., identity) in direct response to this positioning. Hence we see the way that identities are subject to "institutional coerciveness" and thereby co-constructed, or put another way, the way that dominant gender ideologies form the backdrop "against which any performance of gender is constructed, accommodated to, or resisted" (Bergvall, 1999, p. 282).

12.8   Conclusion

At the outset of this chapter, I observed that an adequate account of language and gender must be attentive to the way that identities are constructed and constituted through linguistic practices, as well as the way that dominant gender ideologies and power relations can constrain such constructions of gender. Indeed, I have attempted to show the importance of recognizing the dynamic and performative nature of (linguistic) gendered identities; at the same time, I have demonstrated the way that institutional forces such as legal and media representations of violence against women (and in Polanyi's work, actual instances of violence against women) can shape the identities that women (and men) are able to produce.

While the study of language and gender has traditionally been divided into two separate (but related) strands of research – (1) the study of language use: how women and men use language (differently) and (2) the study of sexist language: how sexism manifests itself linguistically – this chapter has shown the impossibility of maintaining what was once a significant distinction in the language and gender literature. (See also Cameron (1998b) for a discussion of this issue.) That is, if discursive representations that encode culturally-dominant notions of gender can influence the linguistic practices (and other types of social practices) that women and men engage in, then linguistic investigations of gender performances would benefit from more systematic contextualization within investigations of dominant gender ideologies, as they are manifest in and outside of language.

See also 9 Language Thought, and Culture, 14 Language and Politics, 22 Social Influences on Language Learning, 30 Language Planning as Applied Linguistics.

REFERENCES

Barrett, R. (1999) Indexing polyphonous identity in the speech of African American drag queens. In M. Bucholtz, A. C. Liang, & L. Sutton (eds.), *Reinventing identities: the gendered self in discourse* (pp. 313–31). New York: Oxford University Press.

Benedict, H. (1992) *Virgin or vamp: how the press covers sex crimes*. New York: Oxford University Press.

Benedict, H. (1993) The language of rape. In E. Buchwald, P. Fletcher, & M. Roth (eds.), *Transforming a rape culture* (pp. 101–5). Minneapolis: Milkweed Press.

Bergvall, V. (1999) Toward a comprehensive theory of language and gender. *Language in Society*, 28, 273–93.

Bohan, J. (1997) Regarding gender: essentialism, constructionism and feminist psychology. In M. Gergen & S. Davis (eds.), *Towards a new psychology of gender* (pp. 31–47). London: Routledge.

Brecht, R., Davidson, D., & Ginsberg, R. (1995) Predictors of foreign language gain during study abroad. In B. Freed (ed.), *Second language acquisition in a study abroad context* (pp. 37–66). Amsterdam: John Benjamins.

Bucholtz, M. (1999) Bad examples: transgression and progress in language and gender studies. In M. Bucholtz, A. C. Liang, & L. Sutton (eds.), *Reinventing identities: the gendered self in discourse* (pp. 3–24). New York: Oxford University Press.

Burton, P. (1994) Women and second language use: an introduction. In P. Burton, K. Dyson, & S. Ardener (eds.), *Bilingual women: anthropological approaches to second language use* (pp. 21–9). Oxford: Berg.

Butler, J. (1990) *Gender trouble: feminism and the subversion of identity*. New York: Routledge.

Cameron, D. (1990) Demythologizing sociolinguistics. In J. Joseph & T. Taylor (eds.), *Ideologies of language* (pp. 79–93). London: Routledge.

Cameron, D. (1992) *Feminism and linguistic theory*. New York: St. Martin's Press.

Cameron, D. (1995) *Verbal hygiene*. London: Routledge.

Cameron, D. (1996) The language-gender interface: challenging co-optation. In V. Bergvall, J. Bing, & A. Freed (eds.), *Rethinking language and gender research: theory and practice* (pp. 31–53). London: Longman.

Cameron, D. (1997a) Performing gender identity: young men's talk and the construction of heterosexual masculinity. In S. Johnson & U. Meinhof (eds.), *Language and masculinity* (pp. 47–64). Oxford: Blackwell.

Cameron, D. (1997b) Theoretical debates in feminist linguistics: questions of sex and gender. In R. Wodak (ed.), *Gender and discourse* (pp. 21–36). London: Sage.

Cameron, D. (1998a) Introduction: why is language a feminist issue? In D. Cameron, (ed.), *The feminist critique of language: a reader* (pp. 1–28). London: Routledge.

Cameron, D. (1998b) Gender, language, and discourse: a review essay. *Signs: Journal of Women in Culture and Society*, 23, 945–73.

Cheshire, J. (2002) *Handbook of language variation and change* (pp. 423–43). Oxford: Blackwell.

Clark, K. (1998) The linguistics of blame: representations of women in *The Sun*'s reporting of crimes of sexual violence. In D. Cameron (ed.), *The feminist critique of language: a reader* (pp. 183–97). London: Routledge.

324 *Susan Ehrlich*

Coates, J. (1996) *Women talk*. Oxford: Blackwell.

Coates, J. (1997) One-at-a-time: the organization of men's talk. In S. Johnson & U. Meinhof (eds.), *Language and masculinity* (pp. 107–29). Oxford: Blackwell.

Eckert, P. (1989) The whole woman: Sex and gender differences in variation. *Language Variation and Change*, 1, 245–67.

Eckert, P. (2000) *Linguistic variation as social practice*. Oxford: Blackwell.

Eckert, P. & McConnell-Ginet, S. (1992a) Think practically and look locally: language and gender as community-based practice. *Annual Review of Anthropology*, 21, 461–90.

Eckert, P. & McConnell-Ginet, S. (1992b) Communities of practice: where language, gender, and power all live. In K. Hall, M. Bucholtz, & B. Moonwomon (eds.), *Locating power: proceedings of the Second Berkeley Women and Language Conference* (pp. 89–99). Berkeley, CA: Women and Language Group.

Eckert, P. & McConnell-Ginet, S. (1995) Constructing meaning, constructing selves: snapshots of language, gender and class from Belten High. In K. Hall & M. Bucholtz (eds.), *Gender articulated: language and the socially constructed self* (pp. 469–508). New York: Routledge.

Eckert, P. & McConnell-Ginet, S. (1999) New generalizations and explanations in language and gender research. *Language in Society*, 28, 185–201.

Ehrlich, S. (1997) Gender as social practice: implications for second language acquisition. *Studies in Second Language Acquisition*, 19, 421–46.

Ehrlich, S. (2001) *Representing rape: language and sexual consent*. London: Routledge.

Ehrlich, S. (2003) Coercing gender: language in sexual assault adjudication processes. In J. Holmes &

M. Meyerhoff (eds.), *The handbook of language and gender* (pp. 645–70). Oxford: Blackwell.

Fishman, P. (1983) Interaction: the work women do. In B. Thorne, N. Henley, & C. Kramarae (eds.), *Language, gender and society* (pp. 89–101). Newbury, MA: Newbury House.

Freed, A. (1992) We understand perfectly: a critique of Tannen's view of cross-sex communication. In K. Hall, M. Bucholtz, & B. Moonwomon (eds.), *Locating power: proceedings of the Second Berkeley Woman and Language Conference*, (pp. 144–52). Berkeley, CA: Berkeley Women and Language Group.

Freed, A. (1996) Language and gender research in an experimental setting. In V. Bergvall, J. Bing, & A. Freed (eds.), *Rethinking language and gender research: theory and practice*. (pp. 54–76). London: Longman.

Freed, A. & Greenwood, A. (1996) Women, men, and type of talk: what makes the difference? *Language in Society*, 25, 1–26.

Freeman, R. & McElhinny, B. (1996) Language and gender. In S. L. McKay & N. H. Hornberger (eds.), *Sociolinguistics and language teaching* (pp. 218–80). Cambridge: Cambridge University Press.

Gal, S. (1978) Peasant men can't get wives: language change and sex roles in a bilingual community. *Language in Society*, 7, 1–16.

Gal, S. (1991) Between speech and silence: the problematics of research on language and gender. In M. di Leonardo (ed.), *Gender at the crossroads of knowledge* (pp. 175–203). Berkeley, CA: University of California Press.

Gaudio, R. (1997) Not talking straight in Hausa. In A. Livia & K. Hall (eds.), *Queerly phrased: language, gender and sexuality* (pp. 430–60). New York: Oxford University Press.

Goodwin, M. (1990) *He-said-she-said: talk as social oganization among black children*. Bloomington, IN: Indiana University Press.

Gumperz, J. (ed.) (1982a) *Discourse strrategies*. Cambridge: Cambridge University Press.

Gumperz, J. (ed.) (1982b) *Language and social identity*. Cambridge: Cambridge University Press.

Hall, K. (1997) "Go suck your husband's sugarcane!": hijras and the use of sexual insult. In A. Livia & K. Hall (eds.), *Queerly phrased: language, gender and sexuality* (pp. 430–60). New York: Oxford University Press.

Hall, K. & O'Donovan, V. (1996) Shifting gender positions among Hindi-speaking hijras. In V. Bergvall, J. Bing, & A. Freed (eds.), *Rethinking language and gender research: theory and practice* (pp. 228–66). London: Longman.

Harvey, P. (1994) The presence and absence of speech in the communication of gender. In P. Burton, K. Dyson, & S. Ardener (eds.), *Bilingual women: anthropological approaches to second language use* (pp. 44–64). Oxford: Berg.

Henley, N. (1989) Molehill or mountain? What we know and don't know about sex bias in language. In M. Crawford & M. Gentry (eds.), *Gender and thought: psychological perspectives* (pp. 59–78). New York: Springer-Verlag.

Henley, N. & Kramarae, C. (1991) Gender, power and miscommunication. In N. Coupland, H. Giles, & J. Wiemann (eds.), *Miscommunication and problematic talk* (pp. 18–43). Newbury Park, CA: Sage.

Hill, J. (1987) Women's speech in modern Mexicano. In: S. Philips, S. Steele, & C. Tanz (eds.), *Language, gender and sex in comparative perspective* (pp. 121–60). Cambridge: Cambridge University Press.

Hutchby, I. & Wooffitt, R. (1998) *Conversation analysis*. Cambridge: Polity Press.

Inoue, M. (2002) Gender, language and modernity. *American Ethnologist*, 29, 392–422.

Kulick, D. (1998) *Travesti: sex, gender and culture among Brazilian transgendered prostitutes*. Chicago: University of Chicago Press.

Kulick, D. (forthcoming) No. *Language and communciation*.

Lakoff, R. (1975) *Language and woman's place*. New York: Harper & Row.

Maltz, D. & Borker, R. (1982) A cultural approach to male-female miscommunication. In J. Gumperz (ed.), *Language and social identity* (pp. 196–216). Cambridge: Cambridge University Press.

McElhinny, B. (1995) Challenging hegemonic masculinities: female and male police officers handling domestic violence. In K. Hall & M. Bucholtz (eds.), *Gender articulated: language and the socially constructed self* (pp. 217–43). New York: Routledge.

McElhinny, B. (2003) Theories and methods for studying gender in linguistics. In J. Holmes & M. Meyerhoff (eds.), *The handbook of language and gender* (pp. 21–42). Oxford: Blackwell.

Medicine, B. (1987) The role of American Indian women in cultural continuity and transition. In J. Penfield (ed.), *Women and language in transition* (pp. 159–66). Albany, NY: State University of New York Press.

Nichols, P. (1983) Linguistic options and choices for Black women in the rural South. In B. Thorne, N. Henley, & C. Kramarae (eds.), *Language, gender and society* (pp. 54–68). Newbury, MA: Newbury House.

Ochs, E. (1992) Indexing gender. In A. Duranti & C. Goodwin (eds.), *Rethinking context: language as an interactive phenomenon* (pp. 335–58).

Cambridge: Cambridge University Press.

Polanyi, L. (1995) Language learning and living abroad: stories from the field. In B. Freed (ed.), *Second language acquisition in a study abroad context* (pp. 271–91). Amsterdam: John Benjamins.

Poplack, S. (1980) Sometimes I'll start a sentence in Spanish y termino en espanol: towards a typology of code-switching. *Linguistics*, 18, 581–618.

Siegal, M. (1994) Second-language learning, identity and resistance: white women studying Japanese in Japan. In M. Bucholtz, A. Liang, L. Sutton, & C. Hines (eds.), *Cultural performances: proceedings of the Third Berkeley Women and Language Conference* (pp. 642–50). Berkeley, CA: Berkeley Women and Language Group.

Siegal, M. (1996) The role of learner subjectivity in second language sociolinguistic competency: western women learning Japanese. *Applied Linguistics*, 17, 356–82.

Stokoe, E. & Smithson, J. (2001) Making gender relevant: conversation analysis and gender categories in interaction. *Discourse and Society*, 12, 217–44.

Tannen, D. (1990) *You just don't understand: women and men in conversation.* New York: Morrow.

Troemel-Ploetz, S. (1991) Review essay: selling the apolitical. *Discourse and Society*, 2, 489–502.

Uchida, A. (1992) When "difference" is "dominance": a critique of the "anti-power-based" cultural approach to sex differences. *Language in Society*, 21, 547–68.

West, C. & Zimmerman, D. (1983) Small insults: A study of interruptions in cross-sex conversations between unacquainted persons. In B. Thorne, N. Henley, & C. Kramarae (eds.), *Language, gender and society* (pp. 103–18). Newbury, MA: Newbury House.

West, C. & Zimmerman, D. (1987) Doing gender. *Gender and Society*, 1, 25–51.

Wodak, R. (1997) Introduction: some important issues in the research of gender and discourse. In R. Wodak (ed.), *Gender and discourse* (pp. 1–20). London: Sage.

Woolard, D. & Schieffelin, B. (1998) Introduction: language ideology as a field of inquiry. In B. Schieffelin, K. Woolard, & P. Kroskrity (eds.), *Language ideologies: practice and theory* (pp. 3–47). New York: Oxford University Press.

Zentella, A. (1987) Language and female identity in the Puerto Rican community. In J. Penfield (ed.), *Women and language in transition* (pp. 167–79). Albany, NY: State University of New York Press.

FURTHER READING

Bergvall, V., Bing, J., & Freed, A. (eds.) (1996) *Rethinking language and gender research: theory and practice.* London: Longman.

Bucholtz, M., Liang, A. C., & Sutton, L. (1999) *Reinventing identities: the gendered self in discourse.* New York: Oxford University Press.

Cameron, D. (ed.) (1998) *The feminist critique of language: a reader.* London: Routledge.

Campbell-Kibler, K., Podeswa, R., Roberts, S., & Wong, A. (2002) *Language and sexuality: contesting meaning in theory and practice.* Palo Alto: CSLI Publications.

Coates, J. (ed.) (1998) *Language and gender: a reader*. Oxford: Blackwell.

Crawford, M. (1995) *Talking difference: on gender and language*. London: Sage.

Eckert, P. & McConnell-Ginet, S. (2003) *Language and gender*. Cambridge: Cambridge University Press.

Frank, F. & Treichler, P. (1989) *Language, gender and professional writing*. New York: Modern Language Association of America.

Hall, K. & Bucholtz, M. (1995) *Gender articulated: language and the socially constructed self*. New York: Routledge.

Holmes, J. & Meyerhoff, M. (2003) *Handbook of language and gender*. Oxford: Blackwell.

Johnson, S. & Meinhof, U. (eds.) (1997) *Language and masculinity*. Oxford: Blackwell.

Kramarae, C. & Treichler, P. (1985) *A feminist dictionary*. London: Pandora Press.

Livia, A. & Hall, K. (eds.) (1997) *Queerly phrased: language, gender and sexuality*. New York: Oxford University Press.

Mills, S. (ed.) (1995) *Language and gender: interdisciplinary perspectives*. London: Longman.

Mills, S. (1995) *Feminist stylistics*. London: Routledge.

Talbot, M. (1998) *Language and gender: an introduction*. Cambridge: Polity Press.

Tannen, D. (ed.) (1993) *Gender and conversational interaction*. New York: Oxford University Press.

Wilkinson, S. & Kitzinger, C. (eds.) (1995) *Feminism and discourse: psychological perspectives*. London: Sage.

Wodak, R. (ed.) (1997) *Gender and discourse*. London: Sage.

13 Stylistics

JOHN MCRAE AND
URSZULA CLARK

13.1 Introduction

Stylistics has always caused controversy: there are those who deny its usefulness, and those for whom it is an essential branch of applied linguistics. This is
partly because it has proved notoriously difficult to define, since it functions
as an umbrella term, covering a range of different stylistic approaches to the
study of texts. A further difficulty is that although stylistic analysis originated
as a way of applying linguistic models to literary texts, it has become clear that
such models can be applied to the analysis of any type of text: to non-literary
registers as well as the literary (e.g., Bex, 1996). Consequently, the range of
texts with which stylistics concerns itself has extended from an initial preoccupation with "literary" texts to include any kind, written or spoken. Furthermore, the range of disciplines from which stylistic theory and practice draws
is no longer limited to linguistics, as was the case at its inception, but also
includes pragmatics, literary theory, psychology, and social theory. What draws
all these different aspects of stylistics together, though, is the centrality of the
language of the text – be it poem, advert or E-text – to the consideration of its
possible interpretation(s).

13.2 What is Stylistics?

In recognition of the difficulties in defining precisely what constitutes stylistics,
many textbooks in the field begin with an attempt at definition (e.g., Short,
1988). One such definition (Thornborrow & Wareing, 1998, p. 4) identifies
three key aspects of stylistics. These are:

1 the use of *linguistics* (the study of language) to approach *literary texts*;
2 the discussion of texts according to *objective criteria* rather than according to
  purely subjective and impressionistic values;

3   an emphasis on the *aesthetic* properties of language (for example, the way rhyme can give pleasure).

Even so, Thornborrow and Wareing proceed immediately to qualify their definition, as the remainder of this section demonstrates.

13.2.1   *Linguistics and literary texts*

Concerning the first key aspect, the use of linguistics in approaching the study of literary texts, Thornborrow and Wareing note that although initially stylistics may have concerned itself with the analysis of literary texts, it has become clear that the kinds of texts which lend themselves to stylistic analysis exceed the boundaries of what is commonly taken to be "literary." Furthermore, as Thornborrow and Wareing point out, stylistics may have begun as a way of explaining how "meaning" in a text was created through a writer's linguistic choices, but in recent years this position has shifted somewhat. Thanks to research in the field of pragmatics, even linguists have come to realize that meaning is not stable and absolute, but depends as much upon the processes of interpretation undertaken by a reader or listener as upon the actual linguistic structures that are used. Consequently, account has to be taken of contextual factors, which had been ignored in the past, such as the cultural background of the reader, the circumstances in which the particular text is read, etc. Rather than concern themselves exclusively with finding out "what a text means," stylisticians have become "more interested in the systematic ways language is used to create texts which are similar or different from one another, and . . . [to] link choices in texts to social and cultural context" (Thornborrow & Wareing, 1998, p. 5).

This is not to say that stylisticians are no longer concerned with discovering meanings in a text, but that they have begun to take greater account of the relationship between the text and the context in which it is both produced and received, and to consider the text as a part of discourse, rather than apart from it (e.g., Carter & McCarthy, 1994). In this way, stylistics has shifted away from the Saussurian structuralism with which it was once commonly associated, and which saw the text as predominantly monologic, stable, and self-referential, toward a more Bakhtinian notion of dialogism and the recognition that artistic form and meaning emerge from the exchange of ideas between people (Carter & McCarthy, 1994, p. 10). Widdowson (1975) was among the first to examine such textual features as the speaker's role in shaping meaning (the "I" of the text), point of view, and reader response, all of which have become focal points of later stylistic analysis, while issues of "literariness" and the place of imagination in text production and reception have become major areas of study.

13.2.2   *Objective criteria*

In terms of the second key aspect identified by Thornborrow and Wareing above, stylisticians hoped that by insisting that texts were discussed and interpreted according to objective criteria, rather than through the application of subjective and impressionistic values, they would avoid many of the pitfalls associated with early-to-mid-twentieth-century literary criticism. Such criticism was (and in many cases, still is) based upon reading a text closely, and selecting features from it to comment on and analyze, with a view to forming judgments in terms of literary worth. However, the principle of selection at work was highly personalized, and often seemed to allow individual literary critics the power to select whatever criteria they wished in judging how "good" or "bad" a text was. Thus, two literary critics, say, could select two entirely different sets of criteria and reach diametrically opposite judgments concerning the merits of the same text. Consequently, stylistics was intended to provide a less intuit-ive, less personalized method of analysis, and one which was deliberately based upon the scientific discipline of linguistics in order to generate the necessary observable and replicable categories of description. As Thornborrow and Wareing point out, "By concentrating on the language of the text, and accepted linguistic methods of categorising and interpreting, it was argued that stylistics did not reflect the views of the individual critic, but an impersonal, reproducible 'truth.' Anyone approaching the text and conducting the same stylistic procedure ought to arrive at the same results" (Thornborrow & Wareing, 1998, p. 5).

Throughout the 1970s, and again more recently in the 1990s, stylisticians' claims to objectivity have been much criticized, principally on the grounds that the selection of procedures from a given range, whatever its source – from linguistics as much as literary criticism – inevitably introduces a degree of subjectivity through the process of selecting from the various options. But as Wales points out below, few people today *would* claim that stylistics is totally objective, precisely because the decisions regarding which elements of a text anyone chooses to scrutinize are themselves subjective ones. Furthermore, the process of interpretation is made even more subjective when a variety of other intangible factors are taken into consideration which vary from reader to reader, such as their educational, social, and cultural backgrounds.

13.2.3   Aesthetic properties of the text

Thornborrow and Wareing's third key aspect, the aesthetic properties of a text, may represent an area of interest for many stylisticians, but this is by no means true for all of them. Again, stylistics may have originated in trying to provide a description of aesthetics derived from linguistics, particularly in terms of the analysis of the sounds associated with poetry. Such an approach may generally form a part of the stylistic analysis of the formal properties of a text, particularly poetry. However, as the range of texts to which stylistic analysis can be applied has been extended, this approach no longer forms such an essential part of all analysis. Rather, as with so much else in stylistics, its continued role will depend upon a combination of the particular purpose of the stylistic analysis, and the type of text to which it is applied.

13.3   Text, Context, and Interpretation

Several other scholars have tried to define the term "stylistics," though it is not surprising that an agreed definition remains elusive. Wales, in the first edition of her *Dictionary of Stylistics* (2001, pp. 437–8), offers the following attempt:

> STYLISTICS: The study of style . . . Just as style can be viewed in several ways, so there are several stylistic approaches. This variety in stylistics is due to the main influences of linguistics and literary criticism . . . By far the most common kind of material studied is literary; and attention is largely text-centred . . . The goal of most stylistics is not simply to describe the formal features of texts for their own sake, but in order to show their functional significance for the interpretation of text; or in order to relate literary effects to linguistic "causes" where these are felt to be relevant . . .

In the second edition of the text, Wales (2001) reiterates her definition of stylistics as being a discipline principally concerned with describing the *formal* features of texts and the *functional* significance of these features in relation to the *interpretation* of the text. As such, it continues to have as much in common with literary criticism, especially practical criticism, as it does with linguistics. She points out that "Intuition and interpretative skills are just as important in stylistics as in literary criticism; however, stylisticians want to avoid vague and impressionistic judgements about the way formal features are manipulated (not that good literary criticism is necessarily vague or impressionistic" (2001, p. 373).

For their part, literary critics take issue with what they see as an "objective" approach to the interpretation of literary texts (e.g., see: Fowler, 1996; Mackay, 1996, 1999; for responses from stylisticians, see Short et al., 1998; Short & van Peer, 1999). Consequently, Wales (2001, p. 373) qualifies the earlier 1989 definition by saying that "Stylistics is only 'objective' (and the scare quotes are significant) in the sense of being methodical, systematic, empirical, analytical, coherent, accessible, retrievable and consensual."

Short (1988) claims that it is not the purpose of stylistic analysis to come up with a "definitive" reading or interpretation of a text, but that undertaking an "objective" linguistic analysis of a text is one way of limiting the scope of possible interpretations, including misinterpretations. Stylistics, then, no longer pretends to lay any claim it might once have done to an objectively discovered "meaning" in a text based solely on the derivation of descriptive categories drawn from linguistics. Rather, it has moved away from this position to acknowledge the fact that linguistic categories by themselves are not sufficient, or the only factors which need to be considered in the act of interpretation.

As a branch of applied linguistics, then, stylistics drew upon developments in descriptive linguistics (especially in its earlier stages), and particularly so in relation to grammar, through which it developed many of its models and "tools" for analysis. Throughout the latter half of the twentieth century and now into the twenty-first, it has also drawn upon developments in literary theory, and has been particularly indebted to reception theory for its shift in focus to include not only considerations thrown up by the *text*, but also to recognize how we as *readers* shape a text and in turn are shaped by it. Added to this have been developments in *cognitive linguistics*, which draws upon psychological theories of processing. Similarly, the study of *pragmatics* demands that the act of interpretation takes into account the structures of language actually in use. These issues are particularly important for an analysis of the language of drama, and also when considering interactional and contextual aspects of linguistic behaviour, including speech act theory and conversational analysis.

A further aspect of textual analysis with which some stylisticians concern themselves, and which others oppose, is the study of the extent to which inter-pretation is influenced by the perceived existence of tensions between the text and its reception in the wider *context* of social relations and sociopolitical structures in general: i.e., the ideology underlying the text (see: Fairclough, 1989; Kress, 1989; Mills, 1995). Stylistic analysis thus becomes embedded within a framework of *critical discourse analysis* (CDA). In this way, explorations of authority, power, and inequality feature as part of stylistic analysis, which pays attention to the formal features of the text and its reception within a reading community in relation to ideology. Haynes' *Introducing Stylistics* (1992) and Mills' *Feminist Stylistics* (1995) are two examples of such an approach. However, this development has been the subject of much controversy, not least because *all* texts chosen for analysis are generally selected in ways which inevitably throw up ideological considerations: e.g., newspaper reports, doctor–patient conversations, etc. (Fairclough, 1996; Toolan, 1997; Widdowson, 1995). Furthermore, the framework for textual analysis at an ideological level is nowhere near as fully developed as those which deal with its more formal, linguistic levels, and with which stylistics is more usually associated. Nevertheless, despite such criticisms, CDA has been the first attempt so far to formalize a methodology, which seeks to articulate the relationship between a text and the context in which it is produced and received.

From its earlier formalist and structuralist beginnings, then, stylistics has broadened to include three distinct but interrelated strands, any of which can independently form the primary focus of study, or lend them-selves to viable combination with either or both of their alternatives. These strands are:

1   that which is concerned with the recognizably formal and linguistic properties of a text existing as an isolated item in the world;
2   that which refers to the points of contact between a text, other texts, and their readers/listeners;
3   that which positions the text and the consideration of its formal and psychological elements within a sociocultural context.

13.3.1 *Formal and linguistic properties*

The first area of study, which centers upon the formal and linguistic properties of a text, includes, for example, consideration of the ways in which writers (or speakers): make selections from the linguistic potentials of a given language so as to create an artefact manifesting certain formal properties (e.g., foregrounding); construct cohesion and coherence within a text so as to give it a dynamic (e.g., narrative structure); position themselves (and their characters) vis-à-vis their potential readers (e.g., modality, transitivity, point of view).

Of the three strands, this first one – being the oldest – has the most developed conceptual vocabulary and frames of reference. In the stylistics classroom, a common language or metalanguage exists for learning activities centerd around the metaphorical concept of the stylistician's "toolbox," and includes the use of "checklists" of the kind offered by writers of textbooks in stylistics such as McRae (1997), Short (1988, 1996), and as is discussed further below (see Section 13.4.1). As Short (1988) points out, the techniques often associated with teaching English Language to non-native students of English are often employed in teaching these areas of stylistics to both native and non-native-speaking students. And, because this is the most developed area within stylistics, it tends to dominate pedagogic practice. Even so, there are other scholars, such as Carter and Long (1991), Clark (1996), and McRae (1997), who would argue that the value of a stylistic approach – as opposed to one drawn purely from English Language teaching – is that it allows for consideration of the cultural and social contexts implicit in the language of the text. Consequently, it provides much more scope for "reading between the lines," and for considering what is absent or implicit in a text, than would a reading which focused solely on the linguistic codes governing the explicit use of language.

13.3.2 *Point of contact*

The second strand considers the point of contact between the text and the reader as an interactive, communicative act. It includes such considerations as the ways in which writers draw attention to other texts, both antecedent and contemporaneous (intertextuality), and studies how readers track texts during the act of processing (e.g., anaphoric devices). Here, as research into this area becomes more developed, a common metalanguage is beginning to emerge within the field of cognitive stylistics (see Section 13.5).

13.3.3 *Text and sociocultural context*

Finally, the third strand considers the text within its sociocultural context and considers, for example, the ways in which the readers "place" texts within a social framework (e.g., genre studies), and how texts mediate authority, power, and control (e.g., critical discourse analysis, feminist stylistics). At this point in the debate, critics like Fish (1980) bring the concept of the interpretative community into the discussion, and this has had a major impact on affective stylistics. The particular concerns, philosophical outlook, and general worldview which the reader brings to bear on the text will obviously play a tremendous role in colouring her or his search for meaning in a text, and it is essential that this influence is acknowledged when applying the objective criteria that are deployed through the checklists of linguistic features contained within a text (see Section 13.4.1).

This strand shifts the point of focus away from a static and monologic view of the text which exists in its own world as a self-sufficient entity, toward one which is much more dynamic, cognitive, intertextual, and interpersonal. However, precisely how this third category fits in with or relates to the other two strands is an area which – as Toolan (1997) demonstrates – has yet to be fully explored, and this ambiguity is sometimes used as an excuse for failing to engage with it.

These categories of the areas of focus given above are not intended to be exhaustive and, quite clearly, within these various concentrations, stylisticians will concern themselves to a greater or lesser extent with detailed study of particular texts, working within the various frames of reference provided by some (but not all) of them.

13.4   Stylistics and Pedagogy

The pedagogic value of stylistics in terms of the teaching of representational language and how this works within a text, in both native speaker and non-native speaker contexts, has been defined by Short in these terms:

> Stylistic analysis, unlike more traditional forms of practical criticism, is not interested primarily in coming up with new and startling interpretations of the texts it examines. Rather, its main aim is to explicate how our understanding of a text is achieved, by examining in detail the linguistic organization of a text and how a reader needs to interact with that linguistic organization to make sense of it. Often, such a detailed examination of a text does reveal new aspects of interpretation or helps us to see more clearly how a text achieves what it does. But the main purpose of stylistics is to show how interpretation is achieved, and hence provide support for a particular view of the work under discussion. (Short, 1995, p. 53)

Style in any context – but more particularly in the verbal, linguistic and literary context – has generally been defined rather vaguely and subjectively, so Short's practical way of looking at the issue is salutary.

13.4.1   Checklists

Stylistics has developed a plethora of checklists covering the linguistic features of texts and tools used by an author which can give a fingerprint to any text – clues as to *how* it means rather than simply what it means. As Short suggests above, stylistics goes beyond meaning and content to examine how effects are created and achieved, and variations on this kind of checklist can be found in several textbooks (Clark, 1996; McRae, 1997; Simpson, 1997; Thornborrow & Wareing, 1998; Toolan, 1998). What they have in common is an intention to elucidate the *processes* in writing and reading, empowering the reader to develop language awareness, text awareness, and cultural awareness in the reading of all texts, whether "literary" or not.

13.4.2   *Literature in a foreign language*

Since stylistics deals essentially with the linguistic features of a text, its methods have been extensively applied to teaching literature in English for non-native speakers. For the remainder of this study, the term "L1" denotes native speakers, and "L2" non-native speakers.

Most L1 stylisticians ignore or are unaware of the problems of teaching English to non-native speakers as a second or a foreign language. Stylistics in an L2 context has entirely different dimensions and ranges of usefulness when compared with its possible application in language teaching generally, and then again, the differences between a second language teaching situation and a foreign language teaching situation lend further complexities to the issue. Literature in any shape or form was largely ignored in English as a second language (ESL) and English as a foreign language (EFL) until the publication of McRae and Boardman in 1984 and which, almost 20 years on, is still among the most widely used textbooks containing literary materials for language learning and development.

McRae's distinction between *referential* and *representational* language use repositions the "literariness" of texts in relation to the processes the reader brings to bear on the text in the overall cognitive relationships between production and reception. In this way of thinking, *referential* language is purely transactional, with no requirement for processing and interpretation – the kind of language, in fact, usually provided in most textbooks for the teaching and learning of English as a second or foreign language. *Representational* language refers to any use of language, which makes an appeal to the imagination or to the affective side of the interlocutors: imagery, idioms, advertisements, modality, text worlds are all textual elements which are crucial to the processing of this linguistic material.

Pedagogic stylistics introduces representational language from the outset of language learning, and thus the discipline is intended to develop ongoing language awareness (of the target language and any other known languages), text awareness (genre, text-type and function, etc.), and wider cultural awareness. This attempted integration is now known as "Five Skills English," moving on from the basic functional skills of listening, speaking, reading, and writing which have dominated communicative language teaching for three decades.

This use of imaginative materials does not necessarily involve the use of literature as such, but has come to be identified as "literature with a small 'l'" (McRae, 1997). The approach can involve the study of an idiomatic line such as, "This is not my cup of tea," which would be difficult to imagine in a non-representational context, and can be deployed to help open up any kind of text, from the simplest decoding of a bus ticket to the highest literary expression. What the reader brings to the text is fundamental to the process of creating meaning.

Textual analysis, a mainstay of first language stylistics, is given less importance in a second or foreign language context. However, the linguistic tools of stylistics are precisely what EFL/ESL learners need in order to develop their approaches to reading any text, be it literature with a small "l" or institutionally-defined literary study. The checklist approach is the first systematic step toward the goal of acquiring this awareness.

Checklists featured in EFL textbooks using stylistics are similar to those described above, and commonly include some or all of the following: lexis, syntax, cohesion, semantics, phonology, graphology, dialect/variety, register, period/intertextuality, and function, among others.

What is developed in students as a result of routine reference to this kind of checklist are their capacities for *language awareness*, *text awareness*, and *cultural awareness*, all of which had been largely ignored in language teaching until the mid-1990s. L2 learners inevitably have a different kind of language awareness from that of L1 speakers; indeed, native speakers' language awareness is often very limited. Most L1 speakers would not know that the verb "to go" is conjugated as "go/went/gone"; all L2 learners know this from the outset of their learning. Similarly the problem areas of English for learners, such as the present perfect tense or phrasal verbs, are simply taken for granted by native speakers. It has been noticeable in recent years that approaches developed in the EFL/ESL context are coming to be more widely applied in first language teaching (e.g., Carter et al., 2001).

However, a significant difference between the application of stylistics in L1 and L2 context is its *purpose*. The texts, which might be studied and analyzed using stylistic approaches actually mean *differently* for non-native learners. The reasons for reading and studying the texts are of a different order. *Process* becomes the key word. As before, there is no single correct interpretation which has to be excavated from somewhere in the depths of the text – no hidden secrets. Neither is there any single "correct" way of analyzing and interpreting the text, nor any single correct stylistic approach. In this sense the appropriate method is very much a hands-on approach taking each text on its own merits, using what the reader knows, what the reader is aiming for in his or her learning context, and employing all of the available tools, both in terms of language knowledge and methodological approaches.

13.4.3 *Approaching the text: analyzing the formal and linguistic properties*

In an L2 context, a first-year EFL class of near-beginners obviously has fewer linguistic tools than an advanced learners, but that should not preclude them from using stylistic approaches when reading texts. The use of stylistic approaches in a non-native speaker context is not vastly different from the approaches to reading and analysis in the native speaker context. One of the first things often demonstrated in a non-native speaker context is how very little should ever be taken for granted by either instructor or student.

For example, readers in Bangladesh interpreted the poem by Wordsworth commonly known as "Daffodils" without knowing what daffodils were, and read them as possibly being beautiful birds, "fluttering and dancing in the breeze" and "tossing their heads in sprightly dance" (see Appendix 1, lines 6, 12; also McRae, 1998, pp. 33–5.) This is simply a question of unfamiliar lexis, but the reading serves in a connotational sense to show how over-familiarity with predetermined lexical meaning can deny the reader the potential of meanings beyond lexical definitions.

A closer look quickly reveals that the poem contains many words – even pairs of words and longer phrases – which are highly charged: "golden," "dancing," "bliss," and "pleasure" represent only a few. Productive analysis can result from allowing a class to discuss the differences between words like "crowd" (line 3) and "host" (line 4); between "host" and "company" (line 16). Students could be invited to consider the contrast between the actions performed by the speaker (the aimless "wandering" of line 1 and the recumbent position described in lines 19–20) and the "fluttering" and "tossing" of the daffodils' "sprightly dance" (lines 6, 12). Similarly, they might reflect upon the inherent tensions between phrases like "little thought" and "pensive mood" (lines 17 and 20). How would they account for the contradiction between the "lonely" mood of the speaker in line 1 and "the bliss of solitude" in line 22? (Indeed, the students could eventually be asked to evaluate the assertion that the whole text should be read as charting a movement from that psychological state of loneliness to the appreciation of the bliss of solitude.) And of course students engaged in such an exercise would be encouraged to find other lexical tensions/binary oppositions of their own.

The poem's syntax, too, can be a useful tool, as demonstrated – to give but one example – in line 11 ("Ten thousand saw I at a glance") with its shift from the traditional subject-verb-object relationship. This is known as *foregrounding*, in that more emphasis is placed upon the word that should be the object – the daffodils in this case, "present" here in the elliptical omission. The reader must also ask the obvious question here: how many daffodils did the speaker see? The figure of "Ten thousand" does not represent the literal number (and indicates still less that the speaker actually *counted* them!), but rather serves to confirm the word "host" in line 4. What matters most linguistically is that the daffodils are now in "subject position" within the reader's consciousness, and the "I" of the speaker is relegated to the less important "object position."

Attention could also be paid to Wordsworth's use in stanzas 2–4 of the cohesive pronouns "them" and "they," which take the place of the noun "daffodils." The "I" disappears, too, becoming "a poet" in line 15: a less personal, more general referent. Line 15 ("A poet could not but be gay") is in many ways one of the most significant lines in the whole text. The word "gay" here means joyful or happy (a synonym for "jocund" in the next line), but the syntax suggests ambiguity: is the poet gay or isn't he? The answer, of course, is "yes" – the positive meaning emerges despite the negative-seeming construction: he could not be anything but gay. It should, however, be noted how static the text has become by the end of this stanza with any verbs of movement firmly associated with the daffodils. The fact that the speaker only "gazes" is stated twice in one line (17), along with the suggestion that at this point in the account he is not even thinking.

Another important development in this third stanza is the change in verb tense in line 18 with "had brought" – a time shift which bridges the narrative past tense of the first three stanzas and the present tense we will find in the final stanza. The word "For" (line 19) opening stanza 4 is also vital here; as is so often the case, this connector carries the thrust of the text's movement forward, underscoring the contrast between "little thought" and what has actually happened after the speaker saw the daffodils (and still continues to happen for him).

As the paragraphs above suggest, by the time the reader reaches the last stanza she or he has encountered several sets of linguistic signals which have worked together to communicate a sense of movement that is occurring on many levels within the poem: the change in nature of the physical motions described by the speaker; the shift in focus from the passivity of the speaker to vibrant activity of the flowers; the shift in time from past to present; the fluctuation in the speaker's emotional barometer from sadness, through a kind of cautious cheerfulness to outright blissful serenity, etc. This process reaches its culmination in stanza 4, as the daffodils become unmistakable as the active subject of the text, as "they flash upon that inward eye" of the speaker (line 21). The "I" is in a completely passive, Zen-like state, ready to receive whatever might happen. The daffodils have taken him over: this happens "oft," and the connectors of time tell us the sequence, with "oft" (line 19) leading directly to "when" in the same line, which in turn leads to the main verb "flash" in line 21. Line 22 ("Which is the bliss of solitude") takes us inward and ends with a semi-colon, leading on to a "then" in line 23, thus completing a sequence through which the reader has traveled from the past tense of narrative preceding line 18, into the speaker's present experience (and presumably onward into his expectations for the future). Likewise, the reference to "that inward eye" represents the end of another journey initiated at the opening of the text when the speaker's eye looked outward, thus confirming the shift in focus already noted from outer- to inner-self. The movement is completed only in the last line of the poem, where the climax of pleasure and harmony is reached – indicating the speaker's arrival at a "place" about as far away as it is possible to get from the lonely wandering of line 1.

This type of analysis reveals how much more than a mere description of natural beauty the poem "Daffodils" really is, making as it does significant points in the final stanza about the nature of human perception and the importance of remaining open to our impressions, for the sake of both our general happiness and ongoing spiritual development. But as highly worthy as that achievement is, that result represents a secondary objective for the exercise. The primary purpose of stylistics is to improve students' sensitivities toward language usage through the analysis of specific texts: a goal that would yield enormous benefits in both L1 and L2 contexts. To return to the case of Bangladeshi students, readers who do not know what daffodils are will undoubtedly have a very different experience of the Wordsworth text. But through the type of analysis outlined above, they would also receive a number of fundamental tools which would prove invaluable for unlocking the meanings of linguistic codes of all sorts, and which by doing so would also place in its true perspective their initial mistake of interpreting "daffodils" to mean "beautiful birds." And that lexical error, of course, raises another question which all future students of the poem – both L1 and L2 – should be asked to consider: do the objects described in the poem have to be flowers? Would the experience that the poem describes be substantially changed if we substituted another object for the daffodils, and if so, how?

13.4.4 *Approaching the text: the re-writing exercise*

The technique described above, in Section 14.4.3, represents the traditional literary activity of "close reading," coupled with a new emphasis on language awareness. Similarly, stylisticians also employ the technique of heuristic rewriting of texts as a pedagogic aid, rather than an end in itself (see Durant & Fabb, 1990, pp. 98, 186; and Pope, 1995). One of the most widely used texts in this area is the William Carlos Williams poem "This is Just to Say." Such an exercise often begins with the cross-genre "translation"/paraphrasing of a poetic text into the form of a prose note, followed by the formal analysis of every aspect of the adapted text as a basic part of the teaching and learning process, before the text is rewritten back into poetic form and compared with the Williams original. Such rewriting is an aid in particular to text awareness – helping learners into an awareness of how the text means rather than just what it means. The same technique can be applied by removing words, phrases, lines, or whole paragraphs/stanzas from a given text and analyzing what differences the changes would make.

A similar type of classroom activity became part of the focus of a recent study (Zyngier, 2000). On this occasion, the selected text was "I, too, sing

America," a poem by Langston Hughes (see Appendix 2). Students in Brazil, Eastern Europe, and England were asked to discuss a list of questions compiled by the PEDSIG members, half of which were aimed at eliciting a close analysis of the language of the poem: tenses, use of time, agency, referents, conjunctions, etc. The other half were related to the events and feelings related in the poem, and finished with a consideration of the poem's historical and social context, including the period in which it was written. The teacher, in summing up the session, commented that:

> students reached the end of the discussion by providing five possible contexts: One group thought the poem was about North and South Americans divided by economical and political stages . . . Another group considered the black and white ever discussed theme, in which black people are said to be inferior to white people . . . Finally, others mentioned the contrast between rich/poor, employer/ employee and Americans/immigrants . . . This activity helped students talk about the many interpretations a poem can have and enabled them to develop their power of argumentation by using examples from the text that conformed to their opinion . . .   (Zyngier, 2000, p. 5)

The different possible interpretations center around one theme: that of prejudice. In the words of one student, "my group found that we had a kind of debate in the class as each group had a different interpretation. It was very interesting because, even though the interpretations were different, all the groups found that the poem was about prejudice . . ." (Zyngier, 2000, p. 5).

Following on from the discussion, students explored topics, which might lend themselves to expression in a similar style and highlighting similar tensions in historical context. The students were then asked to write such a poem themselves and – when finished – were invited to reflect upon this process. Typically, the main function of such an exercise is for students to experience for themselves the subtleties of language use evident in a text under discussion, by attempting to write either a text in a similar style, as was the case in this lesson, or to re-write it in a different one: a poem as prose, or a narrative from a different character's perspective, for example. By engaging in such an activity, students' intuitive knowledge of the linguistic structures associated with writing are brought to the surface or, conversely, explicitly-taught structures may become absorbed into a more intuitive layer of students' consciousness.

One student responded to this exercise with the following contribution – an original poem and prose commentary:

Revenge!

Yesterday I was a student
Sitting behind the class
I thought that I couldn't
Do the exercises best

Tomorrow I will be a teacher
Standing in front of a class
My students will think they can't reach
The same things that I have passed.

First of all, I have used the contrast between past and future disposed in two different stanzas. The first stanza was written in the past tense and the second in the future. My intention was to show all my feelings as a student now, and then I thought about how teachers work, what they do and I could only see all the time that it looks like a revenge. So, I thought that it sounded not only a good and funny idea, but also a perfect title for my poem . . . I wanted to show my own feelings, as I am studying to be a teacher, someone who deals with these two sides: students' minds and a teacher's thoughts. I have noticed that it is easier to show feelings without hurting other people's ideas through the alteration of time. (Zyngier, 2000, pp. 6–7)

Regardless of the reactions recorded above, however, the primary function of such an exercise is still that of sensitizing students to language use, and more specifically to its complexity and capacity for referentiality (see also McRae, 1998). The by-product of such an activity may well be an improvement in the students' own linguistic competence in a specific context but, as with pedagogical stylistics generally, and as argued in Section 13.4.3 above, this is not its primary or overarching purpose. Nor can the undertaking of such an activity guarantee transference of linguistic skill from one pedagogic context to another. The primary focus is on creativity and multiplicity of meaning produced through and by patterns of language rather than upon the patterns of language themselves, or any consequent accuracy on the part of students in their reproduction. Instead, learning, understanding, making explicit patterns of language are emphasized as primary and necessary steps toward a stylistic interpretation of a text, and part of the process of textual interpretation rather than ends in themselves. Furthermore, the act of interpretation and the context within which it occurs are themselves located in a network of other contexts – social, cultural, economic, political – which all play a part, regardless of whether they remain implicit or are made explicit. It is these contexts, which are brought into play when a poem such as "I, too, sing America" is studied in a classroom, and account for the different nuances of discussion and interpretation made by students in the three recorded settings of South America, Eastern Europe, and England.

13.5 New Directions

Recently the second strand of stylistics identified in Section 13.3.2 above – namely, the point of contact between a reader, a text, other texts, and other readers – has been the focus of much attention. The spread of stylistic approaches is now moving more and more into the area of cognitive stylistics. This is the most positive development in the field, both for native and non-native speakers, since it expands Short's aims into what Stockwell (forthcoming, 2002, pp. 6–7) describes as

> a social and critical model for augmenting stylistic analysis . . . an analytical procedure that can account for what has long been the holy grail of stylistics: a rigorous account of reading that is both individual and social, and genuinely recognises the text as an intersubjective phenomenon and the literary work as a product of craftedness and readerly cognition.

This keen awareness of the sociopolitical background, which inevitably affects the production and reception of texts, is illustrated in the fact that areas such as deixis and modality have been attracting more and more attention within stylistics in recent years. The term deixis in linguistics "refers generally to all those features of language which orientate or 'anchor' our utterances in the context of proximity of space (here vs. there; this vs. that), and of time (now vs. then)," and is concerned with the "multi-dimensional nature" of texts and their dependence for meaning upon the situation or context in which they developed (Wales, 2001, p. 99). Similarly, modality reflects the increased interest in discourse analysis, and the growing fascination in the way texts contain, record, and sustain the variety of interpersonal relationships between authors, implied authors, narrators, and readers (Wales, 2001, p. 256). This focus upon the subtleties that shape our notions of/reactions to "point of view," and the deictic elements of texts, are represented in the discussion of classroom practices in Sections 13.4.3 and 13.4.4 above.

Consequently, those working in the field of stylistics are increasingly coming to recognise the interactive nature of roles played by the reader and the text in the activity of analysis and the construction of an interpretation. The text – for stylisticians as well as literary critics – is a heteronomous object, which only comes to life through a receiving consciousness. Learners often want there to be only one meaning to any text: stylistics gives them the tools, both linguistic and affective, cognitive, analytical and expressive, to explore the ranges of meaning potential and how that meaning is achieved.

See also 1 LANGUAGE DESCRIPTIONS, 2 LEXICOGRAPHY, 5 DISCOURSE ANALYSIS.

REFERENCES

Bex, T. (1996) *Variety in written English: texts in society, societies in text*. London: Routledge.

Carter, R. & Long, M. N. (1991) *Teaching literature*. Harlow: Longman.

Carter, R. & McCarthy, M. (1994) *Language as discourse: perspectives for language teaching*. London: Longman.

Carter, R., Goddard, A., Reah, D., Sanger, K., & Bowring, M. (2001)

Working with texts: a core book for language analysis (2nd edn.). London: Routledge.

Clark, U. (1996) *An introduction to stylistics*. Cheltenham: Stanley Thornes.

Durant, A. & Fabb, N. (1990) *Literary studies in action*. London: Routledge.

Fairclough, N. (1989) *Language and power*. Harlow: Longman.

Fairclough, N. (1996) A reply to Henry Widdowson's "Discourse analysis: a critical review." *Language and Literature*, 5(1), 49–56.

Fish, S. (1980) *Is there a text in this class?: the authority of interpretive communities.* Cambridge, MA and London: Harvard University Press.

Fowler, R. (1996) On critical linguistics. In C. Caldas-Coulthard & M. Coulthard (eds.), *Texts and practices* (pp. 3–14). London: Routledge.

Haynes, J. (1992) *Introducing stylistics* (2nd edn.). London: Routledge.

Kress, G. (1989) *Linguistic processes in sociocultural practice*. Oxford: Oxford University Press.

Mackay, R. (1996) Mything the point: a critique of objective stylistics. *Language and Communication*, 16(1), 81–93.

Mackay, R. (1999) There goes the other foot: a reply to Short et al. *Language and Literature*, 8(1), 59–66.

McRae, J. (1997) *Literature with a small "l"* (2nd edn.; 1st edn. 1991). London: Macmillan/Prentice-Hall.

McRae, J. (1998) *The language of poetry*. London: Routledge.

McRae, J. & Boardman, R. (1984) *Reading between the lines*. Cambridge: Cambridge University Press.

Mills, S. (1995) *Feminist stylistics*. London: Routledge.

Pope, R. (1995) *Textual intervention*. London: Routledge.

Short, M. (ed.) (1988) *Reading, analysing and teaching literature*. Harlow: Longman.

Short, M. (1995) In P. Verdonk & J. J. Weber (eds.), *Twentieth-century fiction from text to context*. London: Routledge.

Short, M. (1996) *Exploring the language of poems, plays and prose*. Harlow: Longman.

Short, M. & van Peer, W. (1999) A reply to Mackay. *Language and Literature*, 8(3), 269–75.

Short, M., Freeman, D., van Peer, W., & Simpson, P. (1998) Stylistics, criticism and mythrepresentation again: squaring the circle with Ray Mackay's subjective solution for all problems. *Language and Literature*, 7(1), 39–50.

Simpson, P. (1997) *Language through literature: an introduction*. London: Routledge.

Stockwell, P. (2002) *Cognitive stylistics*. London: Routledge.

Thornborrow, J. & Wareing, S. (1998) *Patterns in language: an introduction to language and literary style*. London: Routledge.

Toolan, M. (1997) What is critical discourse analysis and why are people saying such terrible things about it? *Language and Literature*, 6(2), 83–104.

Toolan, M. (1998) *Language in literature: an introduction to stylistics*. London: Arnold.

Wales, K. (2001) *A dictionary of stylistics* (2nd edn.; 1st edn. 1989). Harlow: Longman.

Widdowson, H. G. (1975) *Stylistics and the teaching of literature*. Harlow: Longman.

Widdowson, H. G. (1995) Discourse analysis: a critical review. *Language and Literature*, 4(3), 157–72.

Zyngier, S. (2000) Critical pedagogy and stylistics in the EFL context: reappraising and prospecting. Unpublished conference paper prepared for the 20th Annual International PALA Conference, Goldsmith's College, London, UK, June 30 to July 2, 2000.

FURTHER READING

Arnold, J. (ed.) (2000) *Affect in language teaching*. Cambridge: Cambridge University Press.

Carter, R. (ed.) (1982) *Language and literature: an introductory reader in stylistics*. London: Edward Arnold.

Carter, R. & Brumfit, C. (eds.) (1986) *Literature and language teaching*. Oxford: Oxford University Press.

Carter, R. & Burton, D. (eds.) (1982) *Literary text and language study*. London: Edward Arnold.

Carter, R. & Long, M. N. (1987) *The web of words*. Cambridge: Cambridge University Press.

Carter, R. & McRae, J. (eds.) (1996) *Language, literature and the learner*. Harlow: Longman.

Clark, U. & Zyngier, S. (forthcoming) Towards a pedagogical stylistics. *Language and Literature*, 12.

Cluysenaar, A. (1976) *Introduction to literary stylistics*. London: Batsford.

Duchan, J. F., Bruder, G. A., & Hewitt, L. E. (eds.) (1995) *Deixis in narrative: a cognitive science perspective*. Hillsdale, NJ: Lawrence Erlbaum.

Fabb, N. (1997) *Linguistics and literature*. Oxford: Blackwell.

Fairclough, N. (1995) *Media discourse*. London: Edward Arnold.

Fowler, R. (1986) *Linguistic criticism*. Oxford: Oxford University Press.

Fowler, R. (1991) *Language in the news: discourse and ideology in the press*. London: Routledge.

Goatly, A. (2000) *Critical reading and writing: an introductorycoursebook*. London: Routledge.

Green, K. (ed.) (1995) *New essays in deixis: discourse, narrative, literature*. Amsterdam: Rodopi.

Leech, G. N. & Short, M. H. (1981) *Style in fiction*. Harlow: Longman.

McRae, J. (1992) *Wordsplay*. London: Macmillan.

McRae, J. & Pantaleoni, L. (1990) *Chapter and verse*. Oxford: Oxford University Press.

McRae, J. & Vethamani, M. E. (1999) *Now read on: a course in multi-cultural reading*. London: Routledge.

Montgomery, M., Durant, A., Fabb, N., Furniss, T., & Mills, S. (2000) *Ways of reading* (2nd edn.). London: Routledge.

Nash, W. (1990) *Language in popular fiction*. London: Routledge.

Semino, E. (1997) *Language and world creation in poems and other texts*. London: Longman.

Simpson, P. (1993) *Language, ideology and point of view*. London: Routledge.

Talbot, M. M. (1995) *Fictions at work: language and social practice in fiction*. London: Longman.

Toolan, M. (1989) *Narrative: a critical linguistic introduction*. London: Routledge.

Traugott, E. C. & Pratt, M. L. (1980) *Linguistics for students of literature*. New York: Harcourt Brace Jovanovich.

Werth, P. (1999) *Text worlds: representing conceptual space in discourse*. Harlow: Pearson.

Wright, L. & Hope, J. (1996) *Stylistics: a practical coursebook*. London: Routledge.

APPENDIX 1

I wandered lonely as a cloud
    That floats on high o'er vales and hills,
When all at once I saw a crowd,
    A host, of golden daffodils;
Beside the lake, beneath the trees,   5
Fluttering and dancing in the breeze.

Continuous as the stars that shine
And twinkle on the Milky Way,
They stretched in never-ending line
    Along the margin of a bay: 10
Ten thousand saw I at a glance,
Tossing their heads in sprightly dance.

The waves beside them danced, but they
    Out-did the sparkling waves in glee:
A poet could not but be gay,   15
    In such a jocund company:
I gazed – and gazed – but little thought
What wealth the show to me had brought.

For oft, when on my couch I lie
    In vacant or in pensive mood,   20
They flash upon that inward eye
    Which is the bliss of solitude;
And then my heart with pleasure fills,
And dances with the daffodils.   William Wordsworth (1807)

APPENDIX 2

I, too, sing America.

I am the darker brother.
They send me to eat in the kitchen
When company comes,
But I laugh,   5
An' eat well,
And grow strong.
Tomorrow,
I'll eat at the table
When company comes.   10
Nobody'll dare
Say to me,
"Eat in the kitchen,"
Then.

Besides,   15
They'll see how beautiful I am
And be ashamed.

I, too, am America.   Langston Hughes (1925)

14 Language and Politics

JOHN E. JOSEPH

14.1 Beginnings: The Politics of Linguistic Correctness and Persuasion

The study of language and politics is aimed at understanding the role of linguistic communication in the functioning of social units, and how this role shapes language itself. From early in the history of western thought, language and politics have defined what it is to be human. Aristotle's *Politics* famously describes man as by nature a political animal, and his *On Interpretation*, read in the context of his *History of Animals*, shows that what essentially separates man from beast is articulate language signifying by convention. The fact that the word "politics" derives from Greek *polis* 'city' is significant. The city as an organized social unit depends on linguistic communication for its functioning, and urban life places functional demands on language that are substantially different from those in a sparsely populated rural setting. Country folk depend on the land for their living, city folk on one another. Politics is the art, and language the medium, whereby they position themselves to get what they need, and beyond that, what they want.

This morning Crispin, aged 3 years 4 months, showed me a toy that needed mending. "Bring it me," I said, to which he replied disdainfully, "Dada, bring it *to* me." My smile of interest at this early attempt to enforce a linguistic norm no doubt encouraged his incipient pedantry – unwise on my part, since similar corrections made to his nursery classmates may produce not pleasure but teasing or a thumping. If they see the correction as Crispin's attempt to show himself superior to them, their instinctive reaction will be to bring him down a peg. Still, presuming he survives bloodied but unbowed, the research literature suggests that his use of "standard" forms will make him the more persuasive speaker when it comes to convincing the teacher that he did not start the fight, and this persuasiveness may well carry on throughout his life.

The "correction" in question is of a usage over which native speakers disagree, both across and within dialects. "Bring me it" is acceptable to many but not all speakers; "Bring it me" is likewise semi-acceptable, but only in parts of England. "Bring them them" is fine for me in spoken usage, though not in writing, and most native speakers seem to reject it in either mode. What matters for present purposes is that any given speaker you might ask is unlikely to respond that all these forms are perfectly fine. They will normally be quite certain that one is right, another possible but bad, a third simply meaningless. This is true even of people who might be quite non-judgmental on non-linguistic matters.

This singular capacity of language to be a locus of disagreement over what is correct is at the center of its social functioning. Issues of linguistic correctness go far deeper than the particular grammatical or lexical quibble at hand. They are interpreted as reflecting the speaker's intelligence, industry, social worthiness, level of exposure to the elders of the tribe. In modern societies, exposure to tribal elders has been institutionalized into systems of "education," but the fundamental principle remains unchanged from the earliest human groups and existing non-human primate groups.

Interpreting language use in this way is a political act. It determines who stands where in the social hierarchy, who is entrusted with power and responsibility. There is a further linguistic-political dimension in how those in power, or desiring power, deploy language in order to achieve their aims. This is traditionally the domain of rhetoric, defined by Aristotle as the art of persuasion. In modern times, particularly in the climate of twentieth-century ideas about the unconscious mind and the possibility of thought control, it has come to be classified under the still more loaded rubric of "propaganda." Applied linguistics, as the study of language in use, can be thought of as the approach to language that takes its political dimension directly into considera-tion, whereas theoretical linguistics attempts to abstract it away. Language teaching and learning, which occupy a privileged place within applied linguistics, are political in the sense that they always involve two languages with differing cultural prestige in the world at large and in the particular situation in which the teaching and learning are taking place. These differences are mirrored in the relationship of teacher and learner, and in the discourses they generate.

In the twentieth century, the understanding of language and politics was shaped by an ongoing conflict and tension between structuralism (and later "poststructuralism"), which treats language as a system of signs given in advance and structuring the unconscious minds of the members of a speech community, and a range of Marxist (and "post-Marxist") approaches focused on the social production and reproduction of signs and their political con-sequences. Since not everyone engaged in this "Marxist" line of enquiry has been a Marxist by political affiliation, and since official Marxist doctrine on language has repeatedly shifted, the label should be read as indicating intellectual genealogy only.

14.2   The Structuralist vs. Marxist Divide

Posthumously assembled and published in 1916, the *Course in General Linguistics* by Ferdinand de Saussure (1857–1913) would within a decade and a half assume the status of foundational text for structuralist linguistics. Saussure declared that *langue*, a language, is a social fact, and that social force holds the system together so powerfully that no individual can change the language. Changes occur in *parole* 'speech,' and if eventually the social community accepts the change, the system moves to a new state, a new *langue*. But the social space which language occupies for Saussure is not political: every member of the speech community possesses the language, he says, in identical form. There is no scope for one speaker to manifest power over another, for *langue* has no individual dimension – that belongs entirely to *parole*. Despite the apolitical nature of his analysis, the shadow of Saussure would loom large in subsequent attempts at a political account of language. If not reacting against Saussure's idealization of a homogeneous speech community, such attempts are likely to be based on a methodology deriving from the structuralism Saussure is credited with founding, or perhaps reacting against that very structuralism.

Nowhere did Saussure's *Course* have a deeper influence in the decade following its publication than in Russia, where it was initially received as consistent in spirit with the "formalism" then in vogue. But in the course of the 1920s serious questions were raised about the commensurability of formalism with the basic Marxist view that every central facet of human experience is *social* in its origin and operation. The widest-ranging critiques of the structuralist approach to language were launched by Mikhail Bakhtin (1895–1975) and members of the intellectual circle he led. The one who took on Saussure most directly was Valentin N. Voloshinov (1895–1936), in *Marxism and the Philosophy of Language* (1973, originally published 1929). Here, as in certain other works by those close to Bakhtin, his ideas are so closely interwoven with theirs that it remains unclear to what extent Bakhtin should be considered the co-author or indeed the author (see Todorov, 1984).

For Voloshinov, Saussure's *Course* represents the most striking and thoroughly developed form of what he disparagingly terms "abstract objectivism" (Voloshinov, 1973, p. 58). It defines the boundaries of language to include "not the relationship of the sign to the actual reality it reflects nor to the individual who is its originator, but the *relationship of sign to sign within a closed system* already accepted and authorized" (p. 58, italics in original). Rather than deal with actual utterances, it considers only the language system abstracted away from them. (For Saussure's part, he had insisted that the language system is not abstract but concrete because it is "psychologically real" for speakers.) Saussure does at least move beyond the Romantic view of language as facet of individual consciousness. Yet his refusal to engage with "history," in the Marxist sense of the actions of actual people (the "base," as opposed to "superstructure"), denies his approach any claim to genuine social substance in the Marxist sense. For Voloshinov,

> Every sign, as we know, is a construct between socially organized persons in the process of their interaction. Therefore, *the forms of signs are conditioned above all by the social organization of the participants involved and also by the immediate conditions of their interaction.*   (1973, p. 21)

Signs are ideological in their very nature, and social existence is not merely reflected in them but "refracted" by them. For the sign is not like a smooth mirror, but one with a cracked and irregular surface, created by the "differently oriented social interests within one and the same sign community, i.e., *by the class struggle*" (Voloshinov, 1973, p. 23). When Voloshinov declares that "Sign becomes an arena of the class struggle" (p. 23), he makes language central to the "base," a Marxist declaration that language and politics are inseparable, maybe even indistinguishable. "*Linguistic creativity . . . cannot be understood apart from the ideological meanings and values that fill it*" (p. 98).

No speech act is individual; they are always social, even if the addressee exists only in the speaker's imagination. And indeed, every word we utter is generated in interaction with an imagined audience in our mind, before any real audience ever hears or reads it. Thus, according to Voloshinov and Bahktin, language is inherently "dialogic," and it is a fundamental error and illusion of "bourgeois" linguistics to conceive of it as monologic, generated simply by the individual psychology of a speaker. The discrete systems that linguists normally study co-exist with a multiplicity of different ways of speaking that are constantly intermingling with each other, a condition for which Bakhtin (1981, written 1934–5) introduces the term "heteroglossia."

> A unitary language is not something given but is always in essence posited – and at every moment of its linguistic life it is opposed to the realities of heteroglossia. But at the same time it makes its real presence felt as a force for overcoming this heteroglossia, imposing specific limits to it . . .   (Bahktin, 1981, p. 270)

This tension constitutes the arena of the class struggle where voices and signs are concerned.

Voloshinov's and Bakhtin's writings fell into obscurity until their rediscovery in the 1960s. By this time, many of their ground-breaking ideas had been arrived at independently by later Marxists, post-Marxists, and even non-Marxists, and when their work began to be translated into French and English, they seemed perfectly contemporary despite the 40-year remove. Thus Voloshinov (1973) is not historically the master text for as much modern thinking about language and politics as might superficially appear, though it is still the most important book on the subject yet written. (For a fuller account of Marxist theories of language, see Minnini, 1994b.)

Saussure and Voloshinov offer two clearly differentiated modes for approaching the social and political in language. Saussure's is based on an understanding of the social as what binds people together, Voloshinov's as what keeps them apart. The latter accords better with what "social" has now come to signify in sociolinguistics and the social sciences generally. Yet so relentlessly does Voloshinov pursue the argument that language is ideological from top to bottom that he makes the terms "language" and "politics" appear tautological – it ceases to be clear what one can say about the relationship between them that would be meaningful.

The most interesting perspectives on language and politics of recent decades have come neither from linguistics or structuralism narrowly conceived, nor from orthodox Marxist thought, but from combining what is enlightening in each. From Saussure, a recognition that our very way of talking about "a language" implies a powerful social cohesion; from Voloshinov, that utterances come first, and that languages as abstract systems are artifacts of the analysis of politically contextualized utterances. From Voloshinov, a keen awareness of language as a field of political struggle; from Saussure, an admission that the arbitrariness of the link between signifier and signified, and the existential break between the signified (a concept) and things in the world, ultimately means that these political struggles are not directly tied to any sort of historical necessity, Marxist or otherwise.

14.3 Politics in Discourse: Approaches in the Marxist Line

In the English-speaking world, the connection between language and politics was first brought to general attention in a 1946 article by George Orwell (the pen name of Eric Arthur Blair, 1903–50), that anticipates the core problem of language he would address so memorably three years later in his novel *Nineteen Eighty-Four*.

> Modern English, especially written English, is full of bad habits which spread by imitation and which can be avoided if one is willing to take the necessary trouble. If one gets rid of these habits one can think more clearly, and to think clearly is a necessary first step towards political regeneration . . . This invasion of one's mind by ready-made phrases . . . can only be prevented if one is constantly on guard against them, and every such phrase anaesthetizes a portion of one's brain. (Orwell, 1946, pp. 252–3, 263)

The linguistic "bad habits" consist of strings of words that form well-worn patterns, coercing their users to think in certain ways. "Clear thinking" demands that one start from mental images, visualizing things then finding words to describe them. Starting with words is likelier to produce purely abstract thinking.

The detachment of language from observable reality is what makes it possible for a political party to maintain an orthodoxy among its followers, and in the most extreme cases, to dupe those it wishes to enslave. If the party uses language in a way that prevents concrete mental pictures from being called up, people will not understand what is happening to them, and they cannot rebel against what they do not understand. Orwell is not against abstract thinking so long as it is grounded in observable reality. Too great a distrust of abstractions can have catastrophic political consequences of its own. Tyranny and freedom, after all, are abstract concepts, yet resisting the one and defending the other is a matter of life and death.

In Orwell's *Nineteen Eighty-Four* (1949), Newspeak is English re-engineered through massive vocabulary reduction and shifts of meaning. It is controlled by the Party, whose head, Big Brother, is a symbol rather than an actual person. A small Inner Party use Newspeak to control the minds of the larger Outer Party. The aim of Newspeak is "to make all other modes of thought impossible." For instance, according to the Party, 2 + 2 = 5. The hero of the novel, Winston Smith, realizes from the evidence of his own eyes that this is wrong, but the Party already has enough control over his thought and language that he cannot put together the argument he intuitively knows would prove its falsity. The same is true with the Party's operation for rewriting history, in which Winston himself is engaged, and indeed with its three slogans, "WAR IS PEACE / FREEDOM IS SLAVERY / IGNORANCE IS STRENGTH."

Propaganda can only be combated by rational analysis and argument. This entails rephrasing propagandistic statements in a different form. If such rephrasing were made impossible through the loss of alternative words in which the same idea might be given a different linguistic shape, then it might no longer be possible to question the truth of any statement. As the ultimate language for the suppression of thought, Newspeak represents the horrific end of the road that Orwell (1946) describes English as traveling, where standardization of language goes hand in hand with standardization of thought. (For more on Orwell on language, see Joseph, Love, & Taylor, 2001, ch. 3.)

A socialist writing squarely in the tradition of Marxist concerns about language, Orwell was nevertheless as critical of the Soviet politics of his time as he was of fascism or indeed his own country's imperialism. Indeed, he can be read as turning Marxist linguistic thought against Stalin. Although by the time of his death in 1953 few in the west would claim any intellectual allegiance to Stalin, the radical left never forgave Orwell the enormously successful novels that so brilliantly exposed the linguistic means by which the totalitarian USSR maintained its tyranny. Even the Cambridge professor and novelist Raymond Williams (1921–88), the most intelligent and catholic of Marxist thinkers (see Williams, 1977), was deeply ambivalent toward Orwell, and Williams' followers, such as Tony Crowley and Marnie Holborow, who do not maintain his arm's length distance from Marxist orthodoxy, are openly antipathetic to Orwell. Williams' most significant legacy to his followers was perhaps a sense of the crucial importance of the revolution within Marxism that had been introduced by Antonio Gramsci (1891–1937) and his concept of "hegemony," which holds that political control is exerted even in the absence of direct rule, through the operation of an invisible hegemonic power structure (see Lo Piparo, 1979; Minnini, 1994a). Crowley (1989, 1996) and Holborow (1999) have analyzed the phenomenon of Standard English in these terms, and the following passage encapsulates some of the key issues:

> In the nineteenth century, the ideology of Standard English was part of a wider ruling-class project to extend its hegemony over a growing working class and to meet the demands of mass education on its own terms. However, this ruling-class ideology ran up against the narrowness of its social base, which, in the case of language, could be seen in the reality of the continued existence of non-standard forms used by the vast majority of society. (Holborow, 1999, p. 185)

By this view, in the nineteenth century there were rulers and workers, with the former using education and the ideology of Standard English to extend their hegemony over the latter. But what about the steadily growing middle class of the period – are they all meant to be part of the ruling class? What about the system of schools they created that made it possible for talented children of workers to rise to the ruling class – is this to be taken as part of the latter's hegemony? Yes, the Marxist would answer, following Gramsci: the hegemonic structure being what it is, everything that happens, short of working-class revolution, works to the advantage of the ruling class. Any material improvement in the lot of workers is a means of co-opting them into the bourgeoisie, and thus is *against* the interest of the working class. So too with Standard English and education: indoctrinating all working-class children to speak and write like the ruling class would represent the latter's ultimate triumph over the former. But, says Holborow, this ruling-class ideology failed because its social base was too narrow – the vast majority of society resisted and won by continuing to use non-standard forms.

Obviously, this is not the only possible interpretation of the facts. There is good reason to think that general education did not serve the interests of the important segment of the ruling class that depended upon the availability of a plentiful and pliable labor force. It was part of a longer-term improvement in quality of life that it would be utterly perverse to look upon as contrary to the interests of the working class. There is equally good reason to believe that many in the ruling class would have been horrified if the children of workers had begun *en masse* to speak just like their own children. If the "ideology of Standard English" was aimed at ensuring that such linguistic homogeneity did *not* happen, it succeeded. Language standards function precisely by running contrary to what most native speakers' intuitions would predict. It is by mastering these arbitrary norms that an individual displays the will and the wherewithal to occupy a particular place in the social hierarchy.

In continental Europe, significant contributions to a Marxist account of language would be made by Ferrucio Rossi-Landi (1921–85) and Michel Pêcheux (b. 1938) (Rossi-Landi, 1975, 1983; Pêcheux, 1982). However, the most important turn in the Marxist line has been that of someone who is clearly post-Marxist,

Jürgen Habermas (b. 1929) (see Habermas, 1998). He was trained in the Frankfurt School, which took as one of its intellectual starting points the reformulation of Marxist theory by Georg Lukács (1885–1971). By rethinking the relationship of theory to practice, Lukács led the way to a less deterministic and mechanistic form of Marxism than Marx himself had instituted. Linking theory to practice has been at the center of Habermas' thinking, not least in what has been described as his "leading idea," namely "that human language and human communication in general already contain implicit intersubjective norms" (Jarvis, 1999, p. 435). In these norms of everyday language use, Habermas argues, lie the grounds for universal values and principles – in short, for truth. Habermas' contribution has been less in analyzing the political content of language use than in establishing why it should be the central topic of philosophical concern. Since the Middle Ages philosophers have sought universal truth in logic-based theories of propositions and grammatical structures, while dismissing what people do with language as trivial. In arguing for the primacy of practice, Habermas has remained in the Marxist line, where the politics of language use is real, and its analysis trivial insofar as it is abstracted away from this reality.

14.4   Politics in Grammar and Discourse: Approaches in the Structuralist Line

In the 1920s the mainstream of linguistics shifted from the historical enquiry of the nineteenth century to the "structuralist" analysis of language systems at a given point in time, following the inspiration of Saussure. It was not therefore congenial to a political understanding of language, and the linguists who occasionally touched upon the subject, such as Benjamin Lee Whorf (1897–1941) and Alan S. C. Ross (1907–80), did so in popular writings rather than in articles for linguistics journals. Not until the 1950s did structuralist enquiry start to find a place for the political content of language.

In France, this was the period in which structuralism ascended from a linguistic method to a general intellectual paradigm, propelled by the great success of Lévi-Strauss (1955) (see Joseph, 2001). The two French structuralists who would have the most profound and lasting impact on language and politics, Michel Foucault (1926–84) and Pierre Bourdieu (1930–2002), would seem on the surface to have as much in common with the post-Marxist line represented by Habermas as with linguistic structuralism. There are indeed important points in common with Habermas, especially in Bourdieu's case. But what essentially distinguishes Foucault from his Marxist counterparts is his belief that the objects of knowledge, including language as well as the concepts that constitute its signifieds, are not produced by subjects thinking, speaking, and acting intersubjectively. Rather, they are produced by "power" itself, with which they have a mutually constitutive relationship.

We should admit that power produces knowledge . . . ; that power and knowledge directly imply one another; that there is no power relation without the correlative constitution of a field of knowledge, nor any knowledge that does not presuppose and constitute at the same time power relations . . . In short, it is not the activity of the subject of knowledge that produces a corpus of knowledge, useful or resistant to power, but power–knowledge, the processes and struggles that traverse it and of which it is made up, that determines the forms and possible domains of knowledge.   (Foucault, 1977, pp. 27–8)

Foucault is often misrepresented by his enemies – a category that runs the gamut from Marxists to conservative "anti-relativists" – as holding that neither power nor knowledge nor any other reality is anything more than a linguistic construct. His critique of western thought is actually much more subtle than this. Power, operating through language, determines the parameters of what is knowable (the *episteme*), which change from epoch to epoch (see Foucault, 1970).

Bourdieu (1991) attempts to reconnect the Marxist and structuralist lines by renouncing the structuralist dismissal of the human "subject." He conceives of every area of human activity as a socially charged "field," in which the players are neither signs as in earlier structuralism, nor manifestations of power as in Foucault, nor the more traditional conceptions of the Romantic individual or the Marxist social subject, but instead instances of what he terms *habitus*, a "location" within a system, inhabited by an active human subject who is defined by the system but, crucially, not merely its passive object, but engaging in exchanges of symbolic power.

Independently of developments in France, a minority of linguists in the Anglo-American world began "politicizing" structuralism. The first linguist to acknowledge the relevance of Orwell to the general understanding of language was J. R. Firth (1890–1960), a self-proclaimed non-Saussurean, whose complex systemic analyses of language nonetheless share certain features with contemporary structuralisms (see Firth, 1950, 1951). It would be Firth's students, notably M. A. K. Halliday (b. 1925), who would pave the way toward a form of text analysis based upon uncovering the hidden ideologies that structure the use of language. Halliday is both a Marxist and a structuralist – the perception of the two as opposed ideologies faded in the 1960s, when the prominent Marxist theorist Louis Althusser (1918–90) came to be labeled as a structuralist by everyone but himself. (Still, even now some Marxists, Holborow for example, insist that (post-)structuralism is the direct opposite of their own doctrine because it situates reality in language rather than uniquely in the class struggle.) By developing a "systemic–functional grammar" aimed at comprehending both the social and semiotic dimensions of texts, Halliday (see e.g., Halliday, 1978) provided the tools for the "critical linguistics" developed by Roger Fowler (1938–99) in collaboration with a group of younger scholars (see Fowler, 1987; Fowler, Hodge, Kress, & Trew, 1979). This in turn led to the "critical discourse analysis" (CDA) of Fairclough (1989, 1992), which marries critical linguistics with the perspectives of Foucault and Bourdieu, and sees itself as capturing the "dynamic" nature of both power relations and text production by uncovering the hegemonic structures within texts. This is in contrast with earlier analyses, including those of critical linguistics, which concerned themselves with static relations and how they are encoded.

In the United States, structuralism was "politicized" by two papers delivered at conferences in 1958, one of which, Ferguson (1959), will be considered in Section 5. The other, "The Pronouns of Power and Solidarity," was co-written by psychologist Roger Brown (1925–97) and Shakespeare scholar Albert Gilman (1923–89). The paper (Brown & Gilman, 1960) presented the distinction between familiar and deferential pronouns of address (Spanish *tu/Usted*, French *tu/vous*, German *du/Sie*, etc.) as a system for establishing and maintaining interpersonal relations that is directly embedded into grammar. It is an implicit critique of the structuralist view of the language system as autonomous and aloof from the mundane politics of *parole*, reminiscent of the then-forgotten Voloshinov's conception of language as the arena of the class struggle, except that Brown and Gilman consider only interpersonal relations and not the broader political picture. They show how the *tu*-type forms are used to keep social inferiors in their place, but also to manifest tender intimacy to a child or a lover, political solidarity with one's peers, or a personal bond to God. It can, in other words, function to break down the social boundaries between individuals as much as to maintain them, the meaning of each utterance being dependent upon the surrounding political context. Brown and Gilman paved the way for much research into such phenomena across a wide range of languages, and led ultimately to the "politeness theory" of another Brown, Penelope, and her co-author Levinson (1987).

The other major figure in American "late structuralism," Noam Chomsky (b. 1928) has written a great deal about "propaganda" that might be considered in the (post-)Marxist line (see e.g., Chomsky, 1992). He is an "anarcho-syndicalist" and counts Orwell among his key early influences (1992, p. 21). But he has always insisted that there is no connection between his political writings and his linguistics, and though some have questioned this (e.g., Sampson, 1979; Joseph, 2002, ch. 9), superficially at least his syntactic and phonological analyses are in the true structuralist line. Nevertheless, among the group of talented students who broke away from him in the 1960s to practice what was loosely called "generative semantics" were George and Robin Lakoff, each of whom would go on independently to start a line of enquiry into the political dimensions of language. George examined metaphors and how they pervade language and thought, often injecting a political dimension into discourse that is not political in a literal sense. For example: "LOVE IS WAR. He is known for his many rapid *conquests*. He *overpowered* her. She is *besieged* by suitors" (Lakoff & Johnson, 1980, p. 49). Political discourse itself is conditioned by certain master metaphors such as that of the "race" for a political position, inter-party rivalry as a sort of "match" between "teams" who sometimes drop the "political football."

Robin Lakoff (1973, 1975) argues that languages, in both their structure and their use, mark out an inferior social role for women and bind them to it. As with deferential address and interpersonal relationships, gender politics is incorporated directly into the pronoun systems of English and many other languages, through the use of the masculine as the "unmarked" gender (as in "Everyone take his seat"). Lakoff's book fed into a movement to change such usage, so that now it is more common to say "his or her" or use "their" as a singular pronoun, a usage formerly considered solipsistic but now on its way to acceptability. Lakoff points to features that occur more frequently in women's than in men's English, such as tag questions, hedges, intensifiers, and pause markers, which as marks of insecurity and of the role women are expected to occupy are fundamental to maintaining the status quo in gender politics. Her interpretations received independent support from conversation analysis data (Sacks, Schegloff, & Jefferson, 1974; Sacks, 1992; Tannen, 1993) showing that in discussions involving both men and women, the occurrence of interruptions is very unequal, with women many times less likely to interrupt men than the other way round.

O'Barr (1982) would argue that in fact the features Lakoff identified should not be considered part of "women's language," but of "powerless language," since their occurrence is in fact greater among men *or* women who occupy low-prestige jobs and are less well-educated, than among persons of the same sex with a higher level of education and more prestigious employment. O'Barr's particular concern was with the effects which "powerless" and "powerful" language produce in the courtroom situation; his data show that juries generally give more weight to testimony that does not include the features Lakoff pointed out, although this depends somewhat on their preconceptions of where the witness testifying ought to be on the sociolinguistic scale. O'Barr's findings have been taken as suggesting that the fairness of trial by jury is compromised by the inherent politics of language, though it is not at all clear that any attempt at remedying this would be either equitable or indeed possible.

Robin Lakoff's work was soon followed up by Thorne and Henley (1975) and Spender (1980), and led both to the discourse analyses of women's language practiced by Tannen (1994), and to the more politically oriented work of Cameron (1992, 1995). Tannen (1990), an international best-seller, would give rise to a very considerable industry of personal and marital therapy based upon the notion that men's and women's different modes of conversing box them into separate cultures, the walls of which need to be broken through in order for genuine communication to occur and the politics of marriage to be kept peaceful and productive. This is wholly inimical to the Marxist view that gender differences are trivial, class distinctions being the only ones that matter. But even many non-Marxists question whether it is ultimately in the interests of women or other "powerless" groups to insist on their cultural difference, rather than working for integration.

The conversation analysis practiced by Harvey Sacks (1935–75) and his collaborators, mentioned briefly above, have contributed greatly to the understanding of the politics of everyday language within the structuralist tradition, as have the vast amounts of work on language attitudes carried out by the social psychologists Wallace Lambert (b. 1922), Howard Giles, and their students (for a fuller account see Bradac et al., 2001), and on language variation by Willam Labov (b. 1927) and his associates and students (see Joseph, Love, & Taylor, 2001, ch. 10).

14.5   The Politics of Language Choice

Within the structuralist linguistic tradition, the cultural politics of language was introduced by Charles Ferguson (1921–98) in a 1959 article entitled "Diglossia." Ferguson originally proposed a "narrow" definition of diglossia as

> a relatively stable language situation in which, in addition to the primary dialects of the language (which may include a standard or regional standards), there is a very divergent, highly codified (often grammatically more complex) superposed variety, the vehicle of a large and respected body of written literature, either of an earlier period or in another speech community, which is learned largely by formal education and is used for most written and formal spoken purposes but is not used by any sector of the community for ordinary conversation. (Ferguson, 1959 [1972], pp. 244–5)

The core examples Ferguson examines are Arabic, Modern Greek, Swiss German, and Haitian Creole. Other examples which he cites are Tamil, Chinese, and Latin in relation to the emerging Romance languages in the Middle Ages and Renaissance. He specifically excludes the standard-language-plus-dialects configuration familiar from western European languages as not encompassing the same level of "divergence" either structurally or functionally. Standard French is used for "ordinary conversation" in France, where it is not therefore in a diglossic relation with non-standard French dialects. Whereas, in Haiti only Haitian Creole is used in ordinary conversation, and therefore it *is* in a diglossic relation with Standard French. In such a case he calls Haitian Creole the L ("low") and Standard French the H ("high") language.

Within a few years, however, Ferguson's narrow definition had been abandoned – because those who used it found that the differences of linguistic structure were of trivial importance compared to the cultural-political factors implicit in the functional differentiation of L and H. The new "broad" definition of diglossia, asserted for example by Fishman (1967), encompassed every case of a multilingual or multidialectal community in which the varieties used occupy different functional domains and have different levels of prestige. Subsequent investigation has suggested that every linguistic community fits this description.

The Marxist analysis of Standard English as a tool of class dominance has been discussed in Section 14.3. There is, however, another line of political attack on the phenomenon of standard languages, based upon the fact that historically they have with few exceptions been the languages of nations or even empires. A recurrent theme in recent work by sociolinguists and linguistic anthropologists interested in language and national identity (Gal, 1998; Silverstein, 2000; Joseph, 2003) is that Anderson (1991) got only half the story right when he called the nation an "imagined political community" whose existence is built crucially upon a shared language. What is missing is an awareness that languages too are "imagined communities" whose very existence and maintenance depend on the belief in the nation. Language and nation are myths that construct each other reciprocally, rather than one constructing the other.

In reconsidering the relationship of linguistic to national identity, it is worth going back, as Anderson did, to Ernest Renan (1823–92), who said:

> A nation is a soul, a spiritual principle. Two things that are actually one make up this soul, this spiritual principle. One is in the past, the other in the present. One is the common ownership of a rich legacy of memories; the other is the present-day agreement, the desire to live together, the will to continue validating the heritage that has been inherited jointly.   (Renan, 1882, p. 26, my translation)

This astute insight into the general classical western European idea of the nation is grounded in the context of wars against external enemies. But when the memories are of great battles against *internal* enemies – usually divided along religious or sectarian lines – the national memories themselves became a textual battleground.

The national language becomes a major front in the battle, for its own symbolic sake and also because the text of memory will be constructed and transmitted in it. In the classical situation of the founding of a modern European nationalism, the "language war" takes the form of a *questione della lingua* [language question], the Italian term having been generalized because it was in Italy that the first really significant struggle of this kind took place, starting already in the early fourteenth century (see Joseph, 1987; Milroy & Milroy, 1991). Similar debates about which particular dialect would be the basis of the national language raged during the Renaissance in France, the Iberian peninsula, Germany, Scandinavia, and the British Isles, and later in the Balkans, Poland, Turkey, and India, to name just a few of the most important cases. Their ferocity would defy belief, were it not that the location of the common "soul" was at stake.

It is in this sense that powerful "ideologies of language" may be said to condition language choice, from the level of selecting a national language down to what one will speak, and how, in a given conversational situation. For studies of specific cases of such ideologies in operation, and their interaction with the linguistic identities of speakers, see Edwards (1985), Gal (1989), Joseph and Taylor (1990). Further studies of the political issues involved in language choice can be found in Inglehart and Woodward (1967), Fishman,

Ferguson, and Das Gupta (1968), Mazrui (1975), Nelde (1980), Weinstein (1983, 1990), Wolfson and Manes (1985), Kachru (1986). The politics of language choice in the specific context of education is the subject of Hoyke and Parker (1994), Tollefson (1995), Cummins (2000). For each of the topics discussed in this paragraph, additional sources are included in the further reading section below.

In recent years, a fierce debate has raged within applied linguistics concerning the spread of English and its cultural and political consequences. Phillipson (1992) has very influentially promulgated the idea that the spread of English is being brought about through "English linguistic imperialism," a set of practices through which "the dominance of English is asserted and maintained by the establishment and continuous reconstitution of structural and cultural inequalities between English and other languages" (Phillipson, 1992, p. 47). He calls English linguistic imperialism an example or sub-type of "linguicism," defined as "ideologies, structures, and practices which are used to legitimate, effectuate, and reproduce an unequal division of power and resources . . . between groups which are defined on the basis of language" (p. 47). However, in his treatment no other examples or sub-types are discussed. Phillipson follows closely Galtung's (1971) cultural imperialism theory, which is based upon a division of the world into Center and Periphery. Hegemonic force means that the Center is always dominating the Periphery. When members of the "peripheral" population are themselves the ones opting for education in the "center" language or promoting it for their countrymen, this merely means that they have been co-opted into linguicism themselves; they are internal colonialists.

One of the most powerful tools of linguicism, according to Phillipson, is language teaching and multilingual education. "Linguicism occurs . . . if there is a policy of supporting several languages, but if priority is given in teacher training, curriculum development, and school timetables to one language" (1992, p. 47). Skutnabb-Kangas, the other most important applied linguist working in the area of "linguistic human rights" (see Skutnabb-Kangas & Phillipson, 1995), regularly asserts that "Languages are today being killed and linguistic diversity is disappearing at a much faster pace than ever before in human history" (Skutnabb-Kangas, 2000). The perpetrators are globalization, which she calls "a killing agent," and education. "Schools are every day committing linguistic genocide" (2000).

The basic premises of this movement have entered mainstream applied linguistics through work such as that collected in Graddol and Meinhof (1999). However there have also been serious criticisms of it from both "center" (Davies, 1996) and "periphery" (Bisong, 1995; Makoni, 1995), as well as from Marxists who see Phillipson as trying to reassert the nationalistic identities that stand in the way of class consciousness (thus Holborow, 1999). But the most significant development in opposition has been the concept of "linguistic hybridity" (see Pennycook, 1998). Hybridity denies that the spread of English wipes out other languages and cultures, providing evidence instead of how resilient and adaptative languages and cultures are to intermingling. Rajagopalan (1999) argues that, because societies will always be stratified, language too will always be politically stratified. "There is violence in language because human relations are fraught with power inequalities" (1999, p. 203); "it is in the very nature of human languages, all of them, to be driven by power inequalities" (p. 205). To imagine that society could ever be otherwise is a romantic dream. To imagine that resistance to the spread of English could ever bring this dream about is delusional – it rests upon a notion of cultural and linguistic "authenticity" no longer relevant to the post-World War II world, in which large-scale migrations from the south to north have demolished the framework within which concepts like "native speaker" arose. The world today is one of "mestiza identities" in which multilingualism is the norm rather than the exception. Although the loss of local and regional languages occasioned by the spread of English is alarming, it is the direct result of political forces beyond the capacity of applied linguists and language teachers to do anything about.

Refuting this hybridity-based view, Canagarajah (1999) asserts that it leads to, and appears to justify, a passive stance toward inequality. He accuses Rajagopalan of misrepresenting the views of Phillipson and his followers, who "argue against English not because they believe in a new world where there will be no power inequalities, but because the exercise of unquestioned power is harmful" (Canagarajah, 1999, p. 208). Ultimately, "Though [his] purpose . . . may have been to liberate us from the paralyzing guilt complexes that hamper our work, Rajagopalan ends up making us even more powerless" (p. 211). Canagarajah's principal strategy for combating the global hegemony of English is to (re)incorporate mother tongues into the teaching of the target language. This not only validates the mother tongue in the students' eyes, but also helps challenge English by encouraging the encroachment of mother tongue structures into "the very grammatical and discourse system of English" (p. 212).

It seems that both sides of the linguistic imperialism debate are converging onto a view that hybridity is the answer, and disagree over whether it occurs spontaneously or needs to be brought about through acts of "resistance." Such acts, as Canagarajah describes them, certainly challenge the most basic traditional assumptions of what language teaching is about. In so doing they are in line with the idea of a "critical pedagogy" (Rampton, 1999; Pennycook, 2001) that aims to make language teaching a vehicle of freedom rather than submission to hegemony. However, many question how well a pedagogy that encourages the encroachment of mother tongue structures into the target language really serves the interests of "peripheral" students, when educational systems and society at large continue to measure achievement in traditional target-defined ways.

The political dimensions of language are far more extensive than it has been possible to cover in this brief chapter. For other general treatments of the subject, each from a somewhat different perspective, see O'Barr & O'Barr (1976), Shapiro (1984), Chilton (1994).

See also 11 Language and the Law, 15 World Englishes, 30 Language Planning as Applied Linguistics, 32 Critical Applied Linguistics.

REFERENCES

Anderson, B. (1991) *Imagined communities: reflections on the origin and spread of nationalism* (2nd edn.). London & New York: Verso.

Bakhtin, M. (1981) Discourse in the novel. In M. Holquist (ed.), *The dialogic imagination: four essays by M. Bakhtin* (trans. C. Emerson & M. Holquist) (pp. 259–422). Austin: University of Texas Press. (Original work written 1934–5, first published 1975).

Bisong, J. (1995) Language choice and cultural imperialism: a Nigerian perspective. *ELT Journal*, 49, 122–32.

Bourdieu, P. (1991) *Language and symbolic power* (ed. J. B. Thompson, trans. G. Raymond & M. Adamson) Cambridge, MA: Harvard University Press. (Original work published 1982.)

Bradac, J. J., Cargile, A. C., & Hallett, J. S. (2001) Language attitudes: retrospect, conspect, and prospect. In W. P. Robinson & H. Giles (eds.), *The new handbook of language and social psychology* (pp. 137–55). Chichester & New York: John Wiley & Sons.

Brown, P. & Levinson, S. C. (1987) *Politeness: some universals in language usage*. Cambridge: Cambridge University Press.

Brown, R. & Gilman, A. C. (1960) The pronouns of power and solidarity. In T. A. Sebeok (ed.), *Style in language* (pp. 253–76). Cambridge, MA: MIT Press. (Reprinted in P. P. Giglioli (ed.), (1972), *Language and social context* (pp. 252–82). Harmondsworth: Penguin).

Cameron, D. (1992) *Feminism and linguistic theory* (2nd edn.). Basingstoke: Macmillan.

Cameron, D. (1995) *Verbal hygiene*. London & New York: Routledge.

Canagarajah, A. S. (1999) On EFL teachers, awareness, and agency. *ELT Journal*, 53, 207–14.

Chilton, P. A. (1994) Politics and language. In R. E. Asher (ed.), *Encyclopedia of language and linguistics* (pp. 3214–21). Oxford: Pergamon.

Chomsky, N. (1992) Language in the service of propaganda. In *Chronicles of dissent* (interviews with David Barsamian) (pp. 1–22). Stirling, Scotland: AK Press.

Crowley, T. (1989) *The politics of discourse: the standard language question in British cultural debates*. Basingstoke: Macmillan.

Crowley, T. (1996) *Language in history: theories and texts*. London & New York: Routledge.

Cummins, J. (2000) *Language, power and pedagogy: bilingual children in the crossfire*. Clevedon, UK: Multilingual Matters.

Davies, A. (1996) Ironising the myth of linguicism. *Journal of Multilingual and Multicultural Development*, 17, 485–96.

Edwards, J. (1985) *Language, society, and identity*. Oxford: Blackwell.

Fairclough, N. (1989) *Language and power*. London: Longman.

Fairclough, N. (1992) *Discourse and social change*. Cambridge: Polity.

Ferguson, C. A. (1959) Diglossia. *Word*, 15, 325–40. (Reprinted in P. P. Giglioli, (ed.), (1972). *Language and social context* (pp. 232–52). Harmondsworth: Penguin.)

Firth, J. R. (1950) Personality and language in society. *Sociological Review*,

42, 37–52. (Reprinted in J. R. Firth (1957), *Papers in linguistics, 1934–51* (pp. 177–89). London: Oxford University Press.)

Firth, J. R. (1951) Modes of meaning. *Essays and Studies* (The English Association), 118–49. (Reprinted in J. R. Firth (1957), *Papers in linguistics, 1934–51* (pp. 190–215). London: Oxford University Press.)

Fishman, J. (1967) Bilingualism with and without diglossia; diglossia with and without bilingualism. *Journal of Social Issues*, 32, 29–38.

Fishman, J., Ferguson, C. A., & Das Gupta, J. (eds.) (1968) *Language problems of developing nations*. New York: Wiley.

Foucault, M. (1970) *The order of things: an archaeology of the human sciences*. London: Tavistock. (Original work published 1966.)

Foucault, M. (1977) *Discipline and punish: the birth of the prison* (trans A. Sheridan). Harmondsworth: Penguin. (Original work published 1975.)

Fowler, R. (1987) Notes on critical linguistics. In R. Steele & T. Threadgold (eds.), *Language topics: essays in honour of Michael Halliday* (vol. 2). Amsterdam & Philadelphia: John Benjamins.

Fowler, R., Hodge, R., Kress, G., & Trew, T. (1979) *Language and control*. London: Routledge & Kegan Paul.

Gal, S. (1989) Language and political economy. *Annual Review of Anthropology*, 18, 345–67.

Gal, S. (1998) Multiplicity and contention among language ideologies. In B. B. Schieffelin, K. A. Woolard, & P. V. Kroskrity (eds.), *Language ideologies: practice and theory* (pp. 445–9). New York and Oxford: Oxford University Press.

Galtung, J. (1971) A structural theory of imperialism. *Journal of Peace Research*, 8(2), 81–117.

Giglioli, P. P. (ed.) (1972) *Language and social context*. Harmondsworth: Penguin.

Graddol, D. & Meinhof, U. (eds.) (1999) English in a changing world. *AILA Review*, 13.

Habermas, J. (1998) *On the pragmatics of communication*. Cambridge, MA: MIT Press.

Halliday, M. A. K. (1978) *Language as social semiotic: the social interpretation of language and meaning*. London: Edward Arnold.

Holborow, M. (1999) *The politics of English: a Marxist view of language*. London: Sage.

Hoyke, M. & Parker, S. (eds.) (1994) *Who owns English: English language and education*. Buckingham & Philadelphia: Open University Press.

Ingelhart, R. F. & Woodward, M. (1967) Language conflicts and political community. *Comparative Studies in Society and History*, 10, 27–40, 45. (Excerpts reprinted in P. P. Giglioli, (ed.), *Language and social context* (pp. 358–77). Harmondsworth: Penguin.)

Jarvis, S. (1999) The Frankfurt School and critical theory: introduction. In S. Glendinning (ed.), *Edinburgh encyclopedia of continental philosophy* (pp. 429–37). Edinburgh: Edinburgh University Press.

Joseph, J. E. (1987) *Eloquence and power: the rise of language standards and standard languages*. London: Frances Pinter; New York: Blackwell.

Joseph, J. E. (2001) The exportation of structuralist ideas from linguistics to other fields: an overview. In S. Auroux, E. F. K. Koerner, H.-J. Niederehe, & K. Versteegh (eds.), *History of the language sciences: an international handbook on the evolution of the study of language from the beginnings to the present* (vol. 2) (pp. 1880–1908). Berlin & New York: Walter de Gruyter.

Joseph, J. E. (2002) *From Whitney to Chomsky: essays in the history of American linguistics.* Amsterdam & Philadelphia: John Benjamins.

Joseph, J. E. (2003) *Language and identity: national, cultural, personal.* Basingstoke & New York: Palgrave Macmillan.

Joseph, J. E. & Taylor, T. J. (eds.) (1990) *Ideologies of language.* London & New York: Routledge.

Joseph, J. E., Love, N., & Taylor, T. J. (2001) *Landmarks in linguistic thought II: The Western tradition in the twentieth century.* London & New York: Routledge.

Kachru, B. (1986) The power and politics of English. *World Englishes*, 5(2/3), 121–40.

Lakoff, G. & Johnson, M. (1980) *Metaphors we live by.* Chicago: University of Chicago Press.

Lakoff, R. (1973) Language and woman's place. *Language in Society*, 2, 45–80.

Lakoff, R. (1975) *Language and woman's place.* New York: Harper & Row.

Lévi-Strauss, C. (1955) *Tristes tropiques.* Paris: Plon. (English translation (four chapters omitted) by John Russell, London: Hutchinson, 1961; full English translation by John & Doreen Weightman, London: Cape, 1973.)

Lo Piparo, F. (1979) *Lingua, intellettuali, egemonia in Gramsci.* Bari: Laterza.

Makoni, S. (1995) Linguistic imperialism: old wine in new bottles. *British Association of Applied Linguistics Newsletter*, 50, 28–30.

Mazrui, A. A. (1975) *The political sociology of the English language: an African perspective.* The Hague & Paris: Mouton.

Milroy, J. & Milroy, L. (1991) *Authority in language: investigating language prescription and standardisation* (2nd edn.). London & New York: Routledge.

Minnini, G. (1994a) Hegemony. In R. E. Asher (ed.), *Encyclopedia of language and linguistics* (pp. 1541–2). Oxford: Pergamon.

Minnini, G. (1994b) Marxist theories of language. In R. E. Asher (ed.), *Encyclopedia of language and linguistics* (pp. 2390–3). Oxford: Pergamon.

Nelde, P. H. (ed.) (1980) *Languages in contact and in conflict.* Wiesbaden: F. Steiner.

O'Barr, W. M. (1982) *Linguistic evidence: language, power, and strategy in the courtroom.* San Diego: Academic Press.

O'Barr, W. M. & O'Barr, J. F. (eds.) (1976) *Language and politics.* The Hague: Mouton.

Orwell, G. (1946) Politics and the English language. *Horizon*, 13 (April), 252–65.

Orwell, G. (1949) *Nineteen eighty-four.* London: Secker & Warburg.

Pêcheux, M. (1982) *Language, semantics and ideology.* London: Macmillan.

Pennycook, A. (1998) *English and the discourses of colonialism.* London & New York: Routledge.

Pennycook, A. (2001) *Critical applied linguistics: a critical introduction.* Mahwah, NJ: Lawrence Erlbaum.

Phillipson, R. (1992) *Linguistic imperialism.* Oxford: Oxford University Press.

Rajagopalan, K. (1999) Of EFL teachers, conscience, and cowardice. *ELT Journal*, 53, 200–6.

Rampton, B. (1999) Dichotomies, difference, and ritual in second language learning and teaching. *Applied Linguistics*, 20, 316–40.

Renan, E. (1882) Qu'est-ce qu'une nation? In H. Psichari (ed.), *Œuvres complètes d'Ernest Renan* (vol. 1) (pp. 887–906). Paris: Calmann-Lévy, 1947–61.

Rossi-Landi, F. (1975) *Linguistics and economics.* The Hague: Mouton.

Rossi-Landi, F. (1983) *Language as work and trade.* South Hadley, MA: Bergin & Garvey.

Sacks, H. (1992) *Lectures on conversation* (ed. Gail Jefferson) (2 vols). Oxford & Cambridge, MA: Blackwell.

Sacks, H., Schegloff, E. A., & Jefferson, G. (1974) A simplest systematics for the organization of turn-taking for conversation. *Language*, 50, 696–735.

Sampson, G. (1979) *Liberty and language*. Oxford: Oxford University Press.

Saussure, F. de. (1983) *Course in general linguistics* (trans R. Harris). London: Duckworth; La Salle, IL: Open Court. (Original work published 1916.)

Shapiro, M. J. (ed.) (1984) *Language and politics*. Oxford: Basil Blackwell.

Silverstein, M. (2000) Whorfianism and the linguistic imagination of nationality. In P. V. Kroskrity (ed.), *Regimes of language: ideologies, polities, and identities* (pp. 85–138). Santa Fe, N.: School of American Research Press.

Skutnabb-Kangas, T. (2000) *Linguistic genocide in education – or worldwide diversity and human rights?* Mahwah, NJ: Lawrence Erlbaum.

Skutnabb-Kangas, T. & Phillipson, R. (eds.) (1995) *Linguistic human rights: overcoming linguistic discrimination*. Berlin: Mouton de Gruyter.

Spender, D. (1980) *Man made language*. London: Routledge & Kegan Paul.

Tannen, D. (1990) *You just don't understand: women and men in conversation*. New York: Morrow.

Tannen, D. (ed.) (1993) *Gender and conversational interaction*. New York: Oxford University Press.

Tannen, D. (1994) *Gender and discourse*. New York: Oxford University Press.

Thorne, B. & Henley, N. (eds.) (1975) *Language and sex: difference and dominance*. Rowley, MA: Newbury House.

Todorov, T. (1984) *Mikhail Bakhtin: the dialogical principle* (trans W. Godzich). Minneapolis: University of Minnesota Press. (Original work published 1981.)

Tollefson, J. W. (ed.) (1995) *Language policy and educational inequality*. Cambridge: Cambridge University Press.

Voloshinov, V. N. (1973) *Marxism and the philosophy of language* (trans L. Matejka & I. R. Titunik). Cambridge, MA & London: Harvard University Press. (Original work published 1929.)

Weinstein, B. (1983) *The civic tongue: political consequences of language choices*. New York: Longman.

Weinstein, B. (ed.) (1990) *Language planning and political development*. Norwood, NJ: Ablex.

Williams, R. (1977) *Marxism and literature*. Oxford: Oxford University Press.

Wolfson, N. & Manes, J. (eds.) (1985) *Language of inequality*. Berlin & New York: Mouton.

FURTHER READING

Blommaert, J. (ed.) (1999) *Language ideological debates*. Berlin & New York: Mouton de Gruyter.

Canagarajah, A. S. (1999) *Resisting linguistic imperialism in English teaching*. Oxford: Oxford University Press.

Dua, H. R. (ed.) (1996) *Language planning and political theory*. Special issue of *International Journal of the Sociology of Language* (no. 118). Berlin: Mouton de Gruyter.

Fairclough, N. (1995) *Critical discourse analysis: the critical study of language*. London: Longman.

Grillo, R. D. (1989) *Dominant languages: language and hierarchy in Britain and France*. Cambridge: Cambridge University Press.

Hodge, R. & Kress, G. (1993) *Language as ideology* (2nd edn.). London & New York: Routledge.

Kibbee, D. A. (ed.) (1998) *Language legislation and linguistic rights*. Amsterdam & Philadelphia: John Benjamins.

Kroskrity, P. V. (ed.) (2000) *Regimes of language: ideologies, polities, and identities*. Santa Fe, NM: School of American Research Press.

Landau, J. M. (ed.) (1999) *Language and politics: theory and cases*. Special issue of *International Journal of the Sociology of Language* (no. 137). Berlin & New York: Mouton de Gruyter.

Ng, S. H. & Bradac, J. J. (1993) *Power in language: verbal communication and social influence*. London: Sage.

Parakrama, A. (1995) *De-hegemonizing language standards: learning from (post)-colonial Englishes about "English."* London: Macmillan.

Pennycook, A. (1994) *The cultural politics of English as an international language*. London: Longman.

Ricento, T. (ed.) (2000) *Ideology, politics and language policies: focus on English*. Amsterdam & Philadelphia: John Benjamins.

Schieffelin, B. B., Woolard, K. A., & Kroskrity, P. V. (eds.) (1998) *Language ideologies: practice and theory*. New York & Oxford: Oxford University Press.

Schiffman, H. F. (1996) *Linguistic culture and language policy*. London & New York: Routledge.

Schmid, C. L. (2001) *The politics of language: conflict, identity, and cultural pluralism in comparative perspective*. Oxford: Oxford University Press.

Tollefson, J. W. (1991) *Planning language, planning inequality: language policy in the community*. London & New York: Longman.

Wodak, R. & Corson, D. (1997) Language policy and political issues in education. *Encyclopedia of language and education* (vol. 1). Dordrecht, Boston, & London: Kluwer Academic Publishers.

15 World Englishes

KINGSLEY BOLTON

15.1 Introduction

The expression "world Englishes" is capable of a range of meanings and interpretations. In the first sense, perhaps, the term functions as an umbrella label referring to a wide range of differing approaches to the description and analysis of English(es) worldwide. Some scholars, for example, favor a discussion of "world English" in the singular, and also employ terms such as "global English" and "international English," while others adopt the same terms in their plural forms. Indeed, in recent years, a plethora of terminology has come into use, including: English as an international (auxiliary) language, global English(es), international English(es), localized varieties of English, new varieties of English, non-native varieties of English, second language varieties of English, world English(es), new Englishes, alongside such more traditional terms as ESL (English as a Second Language) and EFL (English as a Foreign Language).

In a second narrower sense, the term is used to specifically refer to the "new Englishes" found in the Caribbean and in West African and East African societies such as Nigeria and Kenya, and to such Asian Englishes as Hong Kong English, Indian English, Malaysian English, Singaporean English, and Philippine English. Typically studies of this kind focus on the areal characteristics of national or regional Englishes, with an emphasis on the linguistic description of autonomous varieties of Englishes. In a third sense, world Englishes refers to the wide-ranging approach to the study of the English language worldwide particularly associated with Braj B. Kachru and other scholars working in a "world Englishes paradigm." The Kachruvian approach has been characterized by an underlying philosophy that has argued for the importance of inclusivity and pluricentricity in approaches to the linguistics of English worldwide, and involves not merely the description of national and regional varieties, but many other related topics as well, including contact linguistics, creative writing, critical linguistics, discourse analysis, corpus linguistics, lexicography, pedagogy, pidgin and creole studies, and the sociology of language (Bolton, 2002a).

Underlying each of these three broad approaches is an evident concern with monocentrism versus pluricentrism, i.e. one *English* (with all its geographical and social varieties), or multifarious *Englishes* (deserving consideration and recognition as autonomous or semi-autonomous varieties of the language). This tension between the centrifugal and centripetal dynamics of international English(es) also finds expression in discussions of "world English" versus "world Englishes." Butler (1997), for example, writing as lexicographer, claims that in most contexts where English is establishing itself as a "localized" or "new" English "[t]here two major forces operating at the moment... The first is an outside pressure – the sweep of American English through the English-speaking world," which Butler regards as synonymous with *world English*, because "[t]his force provides the words which are present globally in international English and which are usually conveyed around the world by the media" (Butler, 1997, p. 107). The other dynamic, at the level of *world Englishes*, is "the purely local – the wellspring of local culture and a sense of identity" (p. 109). Thus at the level of lexis, items like *cable TV, cyberpunk, high five*, and *political correctness* might be identified with "world English," whereas items like *bamboo snake, outstation, adobo*, and *sari-sari store* would be items found in "world Englishes," more specifically "Asian Englishes."

When Kachru and Smith took over the editorship of the journal *World Language English* in 1985, it was retitled to *World Englishes*, and Kachru and Smith's explanation for this was that *World Englishes* embodies "a new idea, a new credo," for which the plural "Englishes" was significant:

> "Englishes" symbolizes the functional and formal variation in the language, and its international acculturation, for example, in West Africa, in Southern Africa, in East Africa, in South Asia, in Southeast Asia, in the West Indies, in the Philippines, and in the traditional English-using countries: the USA, the UK, Australia, Canada, and New Zealand. The language now belongs to those who use it as their first language, and to those who use it as an additional language, whether in its standard form or in its localized forms.   (Kachru & Smith, 1985, p. 210)

In an early article on this topic, McArthur (1987) postulates a core variety of "World Standard English," which he then contrasts with the wide range of geographical Englishes used worldwide. This contrast between a common core of international "English" and geographically distinctive "Englishes" is currently maintained by a number of other commentators (notably Crystal, 1997).

In the last two decades, there has been a substantial change in approaches to English studies in recent years; a paradigm shift that began in the early 1980s. At that time, various branches of linguistics, including English studies, sociolinguistics, and applied linguistics, began to recognize and describe the remarkable spread of English worldwide which was then in progress. Early scholarship in this area included Kachru's (1982) *The Other Tongue* and (1986)

The Alchemy of English, Pride's (1982) *New Englishes*, Noss' (1983) *Varieties of English in Southeast Asia*, and Platt, Weber, and Ho's (1984) *The New Englishes*. The volume edited by Noss included a number of position papers, including one by Llamzon on the "Essential features of new varieties of English." According to Llamzon, new varieties of English are identifiable with reference to four essential sets of features: ecological, historical, sociolinguistic, and cultural (Llamzon, 1983, pp. 100–4). In the last context, Llamzon discusses *cultural features* with reference to creative writing and a local literature in English, arguing that "works by novelists, poets and playwrights have demonstrated that the English language can . . . be used as a vehicle for the transmission of the cultural heritage of Third World countries. The appearance of this body of literary works signals that the transplanted tree has finally reached maturity, and is now beginning to blossom and fructify" (p. 104). The horticultural metaphor also finds expression in his conclusion, where he argues that a "new variety of English may likened . . . to a transplanted tree," which, if properly nurtured "will grow into a healthy and vigorous plant and contribute to the beauty of the international landscape not only by virtue of its lush verdant branches and leaves, but more importantly by its fruits – the literary master-pieces of novels, short stories, poems, dramas and songs of its speakers and writers" (pp. 105–6).

Llamzon's reference to the importance of creative writing and literatures in this context is significant. In many Asian societies, including India, Singapore, and the Philippines, there is a body of creative writing in English that reaches back to the colonial era, and since the early 1980s Commonwealth and postcolonial writers from a range of developing societies have increasingly won acclaim from the international literary world. The emergence of "new Englishes" in the early 1980s thus overlapped with and was influenced by the "new literatures" that were then gaining recognition (see, for example, King, 1980; Hosillos, 1982; Lim, 1984). In the 1980s, such postcolonial creative writing began to attract the interest of both the reading public and academics, and the end of the decade saw the publication of *The Empire Writes Back* (Ashcroft, Griffiths, & Tiffin, 1989). By 1993, the title of their book had been appropriated for a *Time* magazine cover story and feature article, which detailed the successes of the Booker nominees and prize-winners, such as Salman Rushdie and Vikram Seth (both of Indian parentage), as well as Kazuo Ishiguro (of Japanese descent), Timothy Mo (Anglo-Chinese), Michael Ondaatje (Sri Lankan), Ben Okri (Nigerian), and Nobel prize-winner Derek Walcott (Caribbean). In this article Pico Iyer describes such writers as "transcultural," because "they are addressing an audience as mixed up and eclectic and uprooted as themselves." Iyer argues for "a new postimperial order in which in which English is the lingua franca," and quotes Robert McCrum to the effect that "There is not one English language anymore, but there are many English languages . . . each of these Englishes is creating its own very special literature, which, because it doesn't feel oppressed by the immensely influential literary tradition in England, is somehow freer" (Iyer, 1993, p. 53).

The last three decades have seen a rapid growth of interest in the study of the "world Englishes" as well as a number of related fields, however these are glossed: English as an international language, global English(es), international English(es), localized varieties of English, new varieties of English, non-native varieties of English, and world English(es), etc. At present there are at least three international academic journals devoted primarily to this branch of linguistics (*English Today, English World-Wide*, and *World Englishes*), which have been supplemented by a substantial number of books on the subject. Currently, a number of distinct albeit overlapping, approaches to research (and publications) in the field of "world English(es)," "new Englishes," and "new varieties of English" may be identified. These include the following (1) the English Studies approach, (2) sociolinguistic approaches (sociology of language, features-based, Kachruvian, pidgin and creole studies), (3) applied linguistic approaches, (4) lexicographical approaches, (5) the popularizers approach, (6) critical approaches, and (7) the futurology approach. These are discussed in some detail in the following sections of this chapter.

15.2   The English Studies Approach

The "English Studies" approach to world Englishes has developed historically from the description of English tradition, which dates back at least to the late nineteenth century and the work of scholars such as Henry Bradley (1845–1923), Otto Jespersen (1860–1943), Daniel Jones (1881–1967), Charles Talbut Onions (1873–1965), Henry Sweet (1845–1912), and Henry Wyld (1870–1945). More recently, this approach may be exemplified by the work of contemporary British linguists, such as Robert Burchfield, David Crystal, Sidney Greenbaum, Tom McArthur, Randolph Quirk, and John Wells.

Randolph Quirk was one of the first in the contemporary period to discuss varieties of English and the notion of "standards" of world English in his 1962 book, *The Use of English*. His *Grammar of Contemporary English* (Quirk et al., 1972) also surveyed varieties of English, although here the aim was to differentiate the "common core" of the language from such classes of variety as "regional," "educational," "social," as well as varieties according to "subject matter," "medium," "attitude," and "interference" (pp. 13–32). Quirk later (1990) assumed the role of a guardian of international "standards" of English and was drawn into a celebrated debate with Braj Kachru on "liberation linguistics," but one obvious irony here is that Quirk seems to have begun his academic life as a "linguistic liberal," with his 1962 essay arguing for tolerance and noting that:

> English is not the prerogative or "possession" of the English ... Acknowledging this must – as a corollary – involve our questioning the propriety of claiming that the English of one area is more "correct" than the English of another. Certainly, we must realize that there is no single "correct" English, and no single standard of correctness.   (Quirk, 1962, pp. 17–18)

Some 20 years on, his 1990 paper was to see him arguing a rather different case, urging overseas teachers of English to keep in constant touch with "native speaker" norms, and praising the merits of a world "Standard English."

In the mid-1980s, a number of books on world English(es) in the "English studies" tradition were published, including Burchfield's influential *The English Language* (1985), Greenbaum's *The English Language Today* (1985), and Quirk and Widdowson's *English in the World: Teaching and Learning the Language and Literatures* (1985). Each of these attempted to address issues related to the learning and use of English from a global perspective. Burchfield (1985) attracted much attention when he discussed the possible fragmentation of English along the lines earlier seen with Latin:

> The most powerful model of all is the dispersal of speakers of popular forms of Latin in various parts of western Europe and the emergence in the early Middle Ages of languages now known as French, Italian, Spanish, Portuguese, and of subdivision (like Catalan) within these languages, none easily comprehensible to the others . . . English, when first recorded in the eighth century, was already a fissiparous language. It will continue to divide and subdivide, and to exhibit a thousand different faces in the centuries ahead . . . The multifarious forms of English spoken within the British Isles and by native speakers abroad will continue to reshape and restyle themselves in the future. And they will become more and more at variance with the emerging Englishes of Europe and of the rest of the world.   (Burchfield, 1985, pp. 160, 173)

Burchfield's comparison of the dispersal of Latin in the Middle Ages with English in the 1980s provides the starting-point for Quirk's (1985) discussion of "The English language in a global context," in which Quirk argues the case for normativity, declaiming at one point that "the fashion of undermining belief in standard English had wrought educational damage in the ENL [English as a native language] countries" and that there is no justification for such an attitude to be "exported" to societies where English has the status of a second or foreign language: "The relatively narrow range of purposes for which the non-native needs to use English (even in ESL countries) is arguably well catered for by a single monochrome standard form that looks as good on paper as it sounds in speech" (Quirk, 1985, p. 6). By the mid-1980s, it seems that Quirk had transcended the linguistic radicalism of his youth, and that he was anxious to join battle on behalf of both "Standard English" and "standards" of English. His 1985 paper also represents a rehearsal for a later engagement against the forces of "liberation linguistics," an engagement that would pit Quirk in debate against Kachru some five years later in the pages of *English Today*.

Another significant figure in this field since the 1980s has been Tom McArthur, the founding and current editor of *English Today* (from 1985), and the editor of *The Oxford Companion to the English Language* (1992). McArthur's (1987) paper on "The English languages?" sets out part of his theoretical agenda for the study of world Englishes. As the title of the article suggests, the notion of plural Englishes is foregrounded in the discussion, and McArthur asks "If there are by now 'English literatures' can the 'English languages' be far behind?" (McArthur, 1987, p. 9). Over the two decades, *English Today* has had a substantial impact on the discussion and debate about "English languages" around the world with many articles having a geographical focus (Africa, the Americas, Asia, Europe, etc.), while others have dealt with such issues as corpus linguistics, grammar and usage, history of English, language and gender, and English lexicography worldwide, etc. McArthur has also influenced scholarship on world English(es) greatly with his editorship of *The Oxford Companion to the English Language* (1992), a volume entitled *The English Languages* (1998), and the recently-published *Oxford Guide to World English* (2002).

A third influential figure in the 1980s and 1990s was Manfred Görlach, whose orientation has been described as "the study of varieties of English in a world-wide context" (Schneider, 1997a, p. 3). Görlach's intellectual lineage was derived of "Anglistik" in the German academic tradition, and he rose to prominence in the field as the founding editor of *English World-Wide*, which began publication in 1980, and publishes a wide range of articles on dialectology, pidgins and creoles, and the sociolinguistics of English throughout the world. Görlach himself has identified his approach as part of "English studies," commenting that: "As a sub-discipline of English Studies, a consideration of English as a world language would provide an ideal opportunity to expand the social, historical and geographical aspects of English Studies and . . . might well serve to enhance the appeal of a traditional and somewhat ageing discipline" (Görlach, 1988, pp. 37–8). Since Görlach's retirement as general editor of *English World-Wide* in 1998, he has been succeeded by Edgar W. Schneider, who has also published widely in this field (e.g., Schneider, 1997a, 1997b).

Others following similar approaches include Quirk's former colleagues on the Survey of English Usage, David Crystal and Sidney Greenbaum. Crystal's early work centered on academically-oriented English studies (e.g., Crystal & Quirk, 1964; Crystal, 1969, 1975), but by the mid-1980s Crystal was moving away from detailed empirical research and embarking on his present career of academic entrepreneur, encyclopedist, broadcaster, and "popularizer" (see section 15.6 below). Greenbaum's (1985) volume on *The English Language Today* was an important work at the time, and from 1990 until his death in 1996, Greenbaum also directed the International Corpus of English (ICE) research project, which is being run in around 15 countries worldwide (Greenbaum, 1996; Nelson, Wallis, & Aarts, 2002). Other British-based scholars include Wells (1982), Burchfield (1985, 1994), Graddol, Leith, and Swann (1996), and Goodman (Goodman & Graddol (1996). From the United States, further contributions to the study of varieties of English worldwide have also come from John Algeo (1991), Richard W. Bailey (1991), and Frederick Cassidy (1985).

15.3 Sociolinguistic Approaches to World Englishes

Sociolinguistic approaches to world English(es) may be regarded as subsuming four types of studies: (1) the sociology of language (Fishman, Cooper, & Conrad, 1977; Fishman, Conrad, & Robal-Lopez, 1996); (2) "features-based" approaches to world English(es) (Cheshire, 1991a; Trudgill & Hannah, 1994, etc.); (3) Kachruvian studies (Kachru, 1992, etc.); and (4) pidgin and creole studies (Todd, 1984, etc.).

15.3.1 *The sociology of language*

Two books by Joshua A. Fishman and his associates (Fishman, Cooper, & Conrad, 1977 and Fishman, Conrad, & Rubal-Lopez, 1996) have provided sociologically-detailed treatments of "the spread of English" and "post-imperial English" respectively. These studies were published 20 years apart, and the data cited, and commentaries given, chart a number of developments in the spread of English in the world. The 1977 volume addressed a number of topics, and also attempted to identify the relevant sociopolitical predictors of the use of English in postcolonial societies (former anglophone colonial status, linguistic diversity, religious composition, and educational and economic development). Fishman also noted that the "international sociolinguistic balance" at that time rested on three factors: (1) the spread of English; (2) the control of English; and (3) the fostering of vernacular languages (Fishman, 1977, p. 335).

Twenty years later in *Post-Imperial English* Fishman and his colleagues (Fishman, Conrad, & Rubal-Lopez, 1996) returned to a consideration of some of the same issues. In the first chapter ("Introduction: Some empirical and theoretical issues"), Fishman (1996a) poses three questions: is English "still" spreading in the non-English mother tongue world? (yes); is that continued spread in any way directly orchestrated by, fostered by, or exploitatively beneficial to the English mother tongue world? (to be judged); and, third, are there forces or processes that transcend the English mother tongue world itself and which also contribute to the continued spread and entrenchment of English in non-English mother tongue countries? (ditto). Fishman suggests that English is now less "an imperialist tool" and more "a multinational tool":

> Multinationals are pro-multinational rather than pro one or another imperial or national metropolitan center, and English can serve them parsimoniously almost everywhere. In this sense, English may well be the lingua franca of capitalist exploitation without being the vehicle of imperialism or even neo-imperialism *per se*. Perhaps, just as neo-colonialism has become merely a form of the world capitalist system rather than a form of imperialism itself, so English may need to be re-examined precisely from the point of view of being post-imperial . . . not directly serving purely Anglo-American territorial, economic, or cultural expansion without being post-capitalist in any way? (Fishman, 1996a, p. 8)

Fishman then goes on to claim that there is evidence to support the view that the world economy has entered a new capitalist phase, which has led to increased living standards globally; that in this new order the growth of English may be not necessarily at the expense of local languages; and that one effect of anglophone imperialism has been "the rise of local elites and counter-elites who became interested in both English and their local vernaculars in order to communicate with different constituencies." With the end of the cold war, Fishman suggests, our thinking on English should also be "de-ideologized," as it is possible that "the impact of English on cultures and societies throughout the world has been a variable one," not one that can be summarized in "simple moralistic terms" (pp. 9–10).

Partly in response to Philippson's *Linguistic Imperialism* (1992) (see section 15.6 below), Fishman also discusses English in the context of economic globalization:

> Economically unifying and homogenizing corporate and multinational forces are increasingly creating a single market into which all societies – former colonial and non-colonial states alike – can be and, indeed, for their own self-interests' sake, usually seek to be integrated. The language of these forces is now most frequently English . . . On the other hand, a similarly powerful trend is occurring in the opposite direction, in the direction of asserting, recognizing, and protecting more local languages, traditions, and identities – even at the state level – than ever before in world history.   (Fishman, 1996b, p. 639)

The former British and American colonies that Fishman surveys are, he asserts, "participating in both trends, in various degrees and with differing priorities"; to characterize the former trend as "the imperialism of English" is both "antiquated" and "erroneous" (p. 639).

15.3.2   *"Features-based" approaches*

In contrast to the sociology of language approach to world Englishes, a "features-based" approach has typically involved the linguist in identifying and making statements about the distinctive features of varieties in terms of pronunciation or "accent" (phonology), vocabulary (lexis), or grammar (morphology and syntax). One leading example of this approach is Trudgill and Hannah's *International English* (1994, first edition published 1982) which describes "standard varieties" of English in terms of "differences at the level of phonetics, phonology, grammar and vocabulary" (p. 3). *International English* uses tape-recordings of English speech from Australia, India, Ireland, New Zealand, North America, Scotland, South Africa, Wales, West Africa, and the West Indies. The third edition added an expanded section on creoles, as well as descriptions of Singapore and Philippine English.

However, the merits of an approach based on a notional "standard" have been queried by linguists such as Cheshire, who asserts that:

Current descriptions, whether of a non-standard dialect, a "new" variety or even of a hypothetical international standard variety, are all too often given as lists of assorted departures from southern British standard English or from American standard English, with no attempt at determining the extent to which the local linguistic features function as part of an autonomous system.   (Cheshire, 1991b, p. 7)

In the introduction to her own book on world Englishes, *English Around the World* (1991a), Cheshire advocates an approach based on empirical socio-linguistic research. The case studies included in this volume usually focus on the analysis of sociolinguistic variation and many might be more accurately described as "variation studies" (in the Labovian paradigm) rather than studies of linguistic features per se. Cheshire argues that in the case of "second language" varieties of English, sociolinguistic analysis can answer the question of where errors stop and where "legitimate features of a local variety" start (p. 11).

15.3.3   *The Kachruvian approach*

The work of Braj B. Kachru in this field is of central and enduring importance, and the influence of the Kachruvian approach to world Englishes (WE) extends across a range of subdisciplines including applied linguistics, critical linguistics, descriptive linguistics, discourse analysis, and educational linguistics. Indeed, the coining and promotion of the term "world Englishes" is chiefly associated with Braj Kachru, Yamuna Kachru, Larry Smith, and a sizable number of other academics who have adopted a world Englishes approach to research and teaching in this field. Kachru himself has had an enormous influence on such work. In addition to his many books and articles and his editorship of *World Englishes*, Kachru is also responsible for anchoring the annual conferences on world Englishes held by the *International Association for World Englishes* (IAWE), which provide a forum for research, discussion, and debate.

Historically, there is general agreement that the study of world Englishes can be dated from the two conferences on English as a world language that took place in 1978, one in April at the East-West Center in Hawai'i, and the second in June–July at the University of Illinois at Urbana-Champaign, and Braj Kachru played a major role in both conferences (see Smith, 1981; and Kachru, 1982). These conferences discussed the sociopolitical contexts of English in the world; the use of English in former anglophone colonies; the processes of "nativization" and "acculturation" in such societies; and the description of varieties of English (Kachru, 1992, p. 1). Throughout the 1980s, other conferences were organized through the auspices of such organizations as IATEFL (International Association for the Teaching of English as a Foreign Language), TESOL (Teachers of English to Speakers of Other Languages), the Georgetown University Round Table, and the East-West Center, and by the mid-1980s the term "world Englishes" was gaining currency (Kachru, 1985;

Kachru & Smith, 1988; Kachru, 1992, p. 2). The justification for the adoption of this term, Kachru argues, is that:

> The term symbolizes the functional and formal variations, divergent sociolinguistic contexts, ranges and varieties of English in creativity, and various types of acculturation in parts of the Western and non-Western world. This concept emphasizes "WE-ness," and not the dichotomy between *us* and *them* (the native and non-native users). (Kachru, 1992, p. 2)

In Kachru's (1992) survey of "World Englishes: approaches, issues and resources," he summarizes the study of world Englishes in terms of 11 related and overlapping issues, identified as: the spread and stratification of English; characteristics of the stratification; interactional contexts of world Englishes; implications of the spread; descriptive and prescriptive concerns; the bilingual's creativity and the literary canon; multi-canons of English; the two faces of English: nativization and Englishization; fallacies concerning users and uses; the power and politics of English; and teaching world Englishes (Kachru, 1992, p. 2). In his discussion of the first issue, "the spread and stratification of English," Kachru argues in favor of the strength of his model of the spread of English in terms of "three concentric circles," *the inner circle* (ENL societies), *the outer circle* (ESL societies) and *the expanding circle* (EFL societies). In the second section on the "characteristics of the stratification," Kachru critically examines such sociolinguistic metalanguage as "lect" and "cline," before proceeding to a discussion of the "interactional contexts of world Englishes" and the "implications of the spread" of world Englishes for the outer and expanding circles in linguistic, cultural, terms.

The notion of "descriptive and prescriptive concerns" for Kachru involves a critical evaluation of such "sacred cows" of theoretical and applied linguistics as "interference," "interlanguage," "error," "speech community," the "native speaker," and the "ideal speaker-hearer" of English. In addition there are issues linked to questions of the models, norms, and standards for English in the outer and expanding circles. In this context, Kachru distinguishes three types of varieties: First, the *norm-providing* varieties of the inner circle, including American English, British English, and the less-preferred varieties of Australian and New Zealand English. Second, the *norm-developing* varieties of the outer circle, where the localized (or "endocentric") norm has a well-established linguistic and cultural identity, as in, e.g., Singapore English, Nigerian English, and Indian English. And third, the *norm-dependent* varieties of the expanding circle, e.g. as in Korea, Iran, Saudi Arabia, where the norms are external (or "exocentric," i.e., American or British). Two other concerns relate to the identification of "errors" (as opposed to "innovations"), as well as the "variables of intelligibility" in world Englishes.

The issue of "the bilingual's creativity and the literary canon" refers to the existence and development of the "new literatures in English" of Africa, Asia, and the Caribbean, and the extent to which these "contact literatures in

English" have undergone *nativization* and *acculturation*. Kachru argues that in South Asia, West Africa, and Southeast Asia, these literatures are thus "both nativised and acculturated" as instanced by the work of the 1986 Nobel Prize winner Wole Soyinka from Nigeria, and Raja Rao of India, and that the issue of the bilingual's creativity is an important area for linguistic, literary, and pedagogical research. The notion of "multi-canon" attempts to accommodate the current sociolinguistic reality in world English where speakers of a wide range of first languages communicate with one another through English, so that, "a speaker of a Bantu language may interact with a speaker of Japanese, a Taiwanese, an Indian, and so on" (Kachru, 1992, p. 7). As a result English has become acculturated in many "un-English" sociolinguistic contexts, in many African and Asian societies where there is no shared Judeo-Christian or European cultural heritage, or shared literary canon. English then becomes multi-canonical English.

The issue concerning "the two faces of English: nativization and English-ization" focuses on the reciprocal effects of language contact: i.e., the effect on English in a localized context (nativization), and the effect on local languages in the same situation (Englishization). Instances of the borrowing of English vocabulary into local languages include Hong Kong, Japan, the Philippines, and many other societies around the world, but Englishization also extends to the level of grammar, as in the adoption of impersonal constructions in Indian languages; or the use of the passive constructions with a "by" equivalent in Korean, both of which have been traced to English. Finally, in the 1992 article, Kachru notes the pedagogical importance of world Englishes to the teaching of language, literature, and teaching methodology, emphasizing the need for a two-fold paradigm shift:

> First, a paradigm shift in research, teaching, and application of sociolinguistic realities to the functions of English. Second, a shift from frameworks and theories which are essentially appropriate only to monolingual countries. It is indeed essential to recognize that World Englishes represent certain linguistic, cultural and pragmatic realities and pluralism, and that pluralism is now an integral part of World Englishes and literatures written in Englishes. The pluralism of English must be reflected in the approaches, both theoretical and applied, we adopt for understanding this unprecedented linguistic phenomenon. (Kachru, 1992, p. 11)

Kachru's enthusiasm for the teaching of world Englishes was not shared by everyone in the early 1990s. In a landmark paper, Randolph Quirk, by then Vice-Chancellor of London University, was becoming increasingly worried by what he termed the "half-baked quackery" of English teachers preaching the gospel of "varieties of English," and published a polemical paper taking issue with those he thought to be undermining the importance of Standard English (Quirk, 1990). This involved an attack on the growing study and teaching of "varieties," and was to lead him into a celebrated debate against Kachru.

Central to Quirk's (1990) paper, "Language varieties and standard language" was the distinction between *non-institutionalized* varieties and those varieties that are *institutionalized* (i.e., being fully described and with defined standards). Here he claims that: "Of the latter, there are two: *American English* and *British English*; and there are one or two others with standards rather informally established, notably *Australian English*" (Quirk, 1990, p. 6). Quirk then argues strongly that the distinction between a "native" variety and a "non-native" variety is crucial, or in his own words "the one that seems to be of the greatest importance educationally and linguistically" (p. 6). He also excludes the possibility that any non-native variety can be institutionalized, asserting that: "I exclude the possibility only because I am not aware of there being any institutionalized non-native varieties." Quirk asserts that "[t]he implications for foreign language teaching are clear: the need for native teacher support and the need for non-native teachers to be in constant touch with the native language," commenting that the research suggested that the "internalizations" of natives were radically different from those of non-natives. He later concludes that "the mass of ordinary native-English speakers have never lost their respect for Standard English, and it needs to be understood abroad too . . . that Standard English is alive and well, its existence and its value alike clearly recognized" (p. 10).

Kachru's (1991) riposte to Quirk, "Liberation linguistics and the Quirk concern," sets out to challenge a number of Quirk's "concerns," arguing (1) "that the recognition of a range of variation for English is a linguistic manifestation of underlying ideological positions"; (2) "that there is confusion of types of linguistic variety"; (3) "that the use of the term 'institutionalized variety' with the non-native varieties of English is inappropriate"; (4) "that there is a recognition of variation within a non-native variety"; (5) "that there is a widely recognized and justified sociolinguistic and pedagogical distinction between ESL and EFL"; and (6) "that there is recognition of the 'desirability of non-native norms'" (p. 5). Kachru also questions a number of Quirk's other arguments which are seen as grounded in a rejection of "sociolinguistic realities," and the adoption of a perspective based on monolingual contexts. The actual realities of multilingual societies, Kachru argues, are *linguistic realities, sociolinguistic realities*, and *educational realities* that are quite distinct from those in Britain or North America, and here the core of his argument is that Quirk ignores the central issue of "sociolinguistic realities" in outer-circle societies and fails to specify how he might produce a "pragmatically viable proposal" for the "international codification" of English (pp. 11–12).

15.3.4   Pidgin and creole studies

There have been periodic discussions in the last 20 years in the field of world Englishes about the relationship between such new Englishes and the study of English-based pidgins and creoles. As the study of world English(es) took off in the 1980s, the specialist journals in the field had to decide on how to deal with pidgin and creole varieties. Görlach (1980, p. 6) argues that because of the continua that exist in many societies linking pidgins and creoles with standard languages, their study "can therefore with some justification be regarded as being part of English or French or Portuguese studies, as is the study of the respective dialects," citing Krio, Tok Pisin, and Sranan as cases in point. Over the years, Görlach published many such papers on English-based pidgins and creoles, and McArthur's *English Today* has opted for a similar editorial policy, as has the journal *World Englishes*, with at least one special issue devoted to the topic (Mufwene, 1997). Other work in this field includes Todd (1984, 1995) who has commented on the indeterminacy of varieties in pidgin and creole contexts, noting, for example, in the case of Nigeria that:

> The unidealised truth seems to be . . . that for many speakers in Nigeria it is now extremely difficult, if not impossible, to separate Nigerian English Pidgin from pidginised Nigerian English or anglicised Nigerian Pidgin. Today, in the spoken medium and in the writings of Aik-Imoukhuede, Oyekunle and Saro-Wiwa, we find not compartmentalized English and Pidgin, not even a continuum from basilectal through mesolectal to acrolectal, but a linguistic amalgam where the interinfluencing is so complete that even articulate linguists are not always certain which varieties they are using or why. (Todd, 1995, p. 37)

It seems clear that "creolistics" overlaps to an extent with the study of world Englishes, although even commentators such as Görlach remain ambivalent on this issue. In a 1996 paper entitled "And is it English?," Görlach discusses the existence of varieties such as code-switching, pidgins, creoles, cants, and mixed languages. In the case of pidgins and creoles, Görlach asserts that these are "independent languages on all counts," noting that varieties which are "marginally English" may persist as "one of the more messy facts of life" (p. 171).

15.4 Applied Linguistic Approaches

One of the first "applied linguistic approaches" to varieties of world English began in the 1960s with the work of Halliday, MacIntosh, and Strevens (1964), who sought to apply insights derived from "the linguistic sciences" to the newly-emergent field of applied linguistics, which in Britain and the USA was broadly concerned with theories of language learning, language teaching, and language pedagogy. In section 6 of the book the authors discussed the use of varieties of English around the world, noting that "during the period of colonial rule it seemed totally obvious and immutable that the form of English used by professional people in England was the only conceivable model for use in education overseas" (Halliday, MacIntosh, & Strevens, 1964, p. 292). By the 1960s, they argued, things were very different, and now there was choice available between American, British, Australian, and other regional variants. Thus, they argue (and this has a very contemporary ring) that:

> English is no longer the possession of the British, or even the British and the Americans, but an international language which increasing numbers of people adopt for at least some of their purposes . . . In West Africa, in the West Indies, and in Pakistan and India . . . it is no longer accepted by the majority that the English of England, with RP as its accent, are [sic] the only possible models of English to be set before the young.   (p. 293)

The publication of the Halliday, McIntosh, and Strevens (1964) book, and the expression of similar viewpoints in other academic papers, prompted Clifford Prator to publish a spirited yet historically misplaced attack on what he called "The British heresy in TESL" (Prator, 1968). This paper is of interest because it pre-dates the Kachru–Quirk debate (see above) by some 20 years; and also because of the fact that some of the issues it raises are still discussed today (see Romaine, 1997). Prator's central argument is that "in a country where English is not spoken natively but is widely used as the medium of instruction, to set up the local variety of English as the ultimate model to be imitated by those learning the language" is "unjustifiable intellectually and not conducive to the best possible results" (Prator, 1968, p. 459). He identifies seven fallacies associated with the British heresy: (1) that second language varieties of English can legitimately be equated with mother tongue varieties; (2) that second language varieties of English really exist as coherent, homogeneous linguistic systems, describable in the usual way as the speech of an identifiable social group; (3) that a few minor concessions in the type of English taught in schools would tend to or suffice to stabilize the language; (4) that one level of a language, its phonology, can be allowed to change without entailing corresponding changes at other levels; (5) that it would be a simple matter to establish a second language variety of English as an effective instructional model once it had been clearly identified and described; (6) that students would long be content to study English in a situation in which, as a matter of policy, they were denied access to a native speaker model; and that (7) granting a second language variety of English official status in a country's schools would lead to its widespread adoption as a mother tongue.

Peter Strevens was one of those singled out for opprobrium by Prator; and it is evidently true that Strevens consistently argued for a varieties-based approach to TESL and TEFL during his academic career (see Strevens 1977, 1980, 1985). Both his 1977 book *New Orientations in the Teaching of English* and his 1980 volume *Teaching English as an International Language* gave substantial coverage to what he glossed as "localized forms of English" (LFEs), arguing that:

> in ESL areas where local L2 forms have developed and where they command public approval it is these forms which constitute the most suitable models for use in schools, certainly more suitable than a British or American L1 model . . . the native speaker of English must accept that English is no longer his possession alone: it belongs to the world, and new forms of English, born of new countries with new communicative needs, should be accepted into the marvelously flexible and adaptable galaxy of "Englishes" which constitute the English language. (Strevens, 1980, p. 90)

High heresy indeed, but over the next two decades the influence of such heresy was to change the way that many applied linguists would approach their subject, particularly at the level of theory. Thus, throughout the 1980s and 1990s, issues related to world Englishes began to be communicated regularly to an applied linguistics audience through such publications as *The Annual Review of Applied Linguistics, Applied Linguistics, English Language Teaching Journal, TESOL Quarterly*, and other journals in the field.

15.5 The Lexicographical Approach

The domestic English dictionary tradition as exemplified by Samuel Johnson's (1755) *A Dictionary of the English Language* and J. A. H. Murray's *Oxford English Dictionary* (1884–1928) embodied two principles: (1) the potential of dictionaries for "fixing" and standardizing the language (however unrealistic this might turn out to be); and (2) the identification of a "nucleus" or core of the language, defined according to "Anglicity."

Arguably, the first dictionaries of world Englishes were glossaries produced in the United States at the beginning of the nineteenth century. These included Pickering (1816), Bartlett (1848), etc. Noah Webster, by contrast, was concerned to produce a national dictionary, for reasons partly if not wholly political, because "As an independent nation, our honor requires us to have a system of our own, in language as well as government." Webster further predicted that: "These causes will produce, in a course of time, a language in North America, as different from the future language of England, as the modern Dutch, Danish and Swedish are from the German, or from one another" (1789, pp. 220–3).

His first dictionary appeared early in the nineteenth century (1806), but it was not until 1828 that his major work, *An American Dictionary of the English Language*, was published. In the twentieth century, Webster's was complemented by a number of other works on American English including Craigie and Hulbert (1938–44), Mathews (1951), and a number of dialect dictionaries including Cassidy (1985). Earlier dictionaries of Canadian English include Avis (1967), which has recently been superseded by *The Canadian Oxford Dictionary* (Barber, 1999). Australian lexicography can be traced back to Morris (1898), which was intended as a supplement to the *OED*, and to the list that Lake compiled as a supplement to Webster's (1898) (cited in Görlach, 1995). It is only in recent years that Australia has had its own "inclusive" national dictionary, *The Macquarie Dictionary* (edited by Susan Butler), which was first published in 1981. In 1988, Oxford University Press published *The Australian National Dictionary*, subtitled *A Dictionary of Australianisms on Historical Principles*. In 1997, the *Dictionary of New Zealand English* appeared, edited by Orsman (1997). South Africa has its own dictionary tradition, starting with Pettman (1913), and continuing to the present with Branford (1987), and Silva's (1998) *A Dictionary of South African English on Historical Principles*.

India developed its own tradition of glossaries and wordlists, including Whitworth's *An Anglo-Indian Dictionary* (1885) and Yule and Burnell's *Hobson-Jobson: A Glossary of Anglo-Indian Words and Phrases* ([1886] 1969). Later works have included Rao (1954) and Hawkins (1984), but as yet no fully autonomous national dictionary for India or other South Asian societies has appeared. In West Africa, there have been plans for a number of years to complete a *Dictionary of West African English*, but so far this project remains incomplete (Banjo & Young, 1982). For the Caribbean, there is Cassidy and Le Page's *Dictionary of Jamaican English* (1967), and Holm and Schilling's *Dictionary of Bahamian English* (1982), as well as the recent *Dictionary of Caribbean English Usage* (Allsopp, 1996).

Dictionaries are profoundly important for the recognition of world Englishes. As Quirk (1990) has pointed out, it is only when a world variety of English is supported by codification (chiefly expressed through national dictionaries) that one can make a strong claim that such a variety is "institutionalized." Perhaps the best example of this in recent times has been the case of Australia where the *Macquarie Dictionary* has been largely accepted as a "national dictionary" or, in their own words, as "Australia's own." By the 1990s the editors of *Macquarie* had also become activists for the promotion of world Englishes in Asia, and are now planning a dictionary focusing on English in the Asian region with extensive coverage of the vocabularies of the new Englishes of Southeast Asia, particularly those of Hong Kong, Malaysia, Singapore, and the Philippines. Susan Butler, *Macquarie's* editor, argues that:

> this dictionary will shift attitudes in the region to English. Rather than being seen as an alien language, and a conduit of Western culture, it will be evident that English can also express Asian culture. The flexibility of English, its ability to serve as a vehicle for the expression of local culture, has been one of its great characteristics since it left English shores.   (Butler, 1997, p. 123)

15.6   The Popularizers, Critical Linguists, and Futurologists

15.6.1   *The popularizers*

During the 1980s, at the same time as interest in the study of international varieties of English was quickly growing within universities in the west, a number of popular accounts of the spread of English were being published in Britain and North America. The best-known of these was perhaps McCrum, Cran, and MacNeil's (1986) *The Story of English*, which was accompanied by the worldwide broadcast of a nine-part BBC documentary on the history of the English language. Although the series and the book were a popular success in both Europe and North America, they provoked a strong reaction from both linguists intolerant of descriptive inaccuracies, and from cultural critics resentful of the perceived triumphalism.

That the charges of triumphalism were somewhat justified seems hard to deny. The first part of the television series, "An English-speaking world," contained such clichés in Robert MacNeil's commentary as "World War II was the finest hour for British English"; "The sun set on the Union Jack, but not on the English language"; and "English, the language of the skies, is now becoming the language of the seven seas"; with the American newspaper pundit William Safire declaiming: "I think it's a glorious language . . . it's growing, it's getting more expressive, it's getting more global, getting more accepted around the world." The book, largely authored by McCrum, fiction editor at Faber and Faber and a novelist in his own right, was somewhat more restrained, and McCrum, Cran, and McNeil do at times temper their celebration of English with mention of "[t]he darker, aggressive side of the spread of global English," which includes the elimination of linguistic diversity and "the attack on deep cultural roots" (p. 44), as in Québec. Later they are moved to explain the "peculiar genius" of English, which it emerges, is essentially democratic and freedom-loving:

> Its genius was, and still is, essentially democratic. It has given expression to the voice of freedom from Wat Tyler, to Tom Paine, to Thomas Jefferson, to Edmund Burke, to the Chartists, to Abraham Lincoln, to the Suffragettes, to Winston Churchill, to Martin Luther King. It is well equipped to be a world language, to give voice to the aspirations of the Third World as much as the inter-communication of the First World.   (pp. 47–8)

Another eminent popularizer from the late 1980s to the present, has been David Crystal, whose first work in a popular vein was the (1988) Penguin paperback, *The English Language*. This was followed by his (1995) *The Cambridge Encyclopedia of The English Language*, and the (1997) *English as a Global Language*, and it was this last work which probably attracted the most criticism. As Crystal himself explains in his introduction, the book was originally prompted by the suggestion of Mauro Mujica, one of the leaders of the US English campaign in the United States. Its aim was to "to explain to members of his organization [US English], in a succinct and factual way, and without political bias, why English has achieved such a worldwide status" (1997, p. ix). Crystal also explains that the report was intended originally for private circulation, but he later decided to rework and expand it into a book for wider circulation. In spite of the fact that the suggestion for the study came from Mujica, Crystal claims that "this book has not been written according to any political agenda," and that he was chiefly concerned to present an account of "the relevant facts and factors" relating to the description of a "world language," the place of English, and the future of English as a global language (1997, p. x). This slim book is distinguished by a number of arguments, including his assertion that the "remarkable growth" of English is, simply stated, explicable largely in terms of the fact that "it is a language which has repeatedly found itself in the right place at the right time" (1997, p. 110). In a similar vein, most arguments in Crystal's analysis of the future of "global English" are reducible to the evocative slogan of "having your cake and eating it," a phrase for which Crystal *qua* popularizer appears to have a particular fondness (1997, p. 138).

The book drew particular flak from Robert Phillipson, who took Crystal to task in a lengthy review in the journal *Applied Linguistics*, charging that the work was "Eurocentric" and "triumphalist," accusations that Crystal countered in a response in the same journal (Phillipson, 1999; Crystal, 2000). By this time, Phillipson had already established himself as one of the leading critical linguists in this field.

15.6.2   Critical linguists

In fact, the discourse on world English(es) changed gear dramatically in 1992 with the publication of Phillipson's book *Linguistic Imperialism*. Whereas the 1980s saw relatively restrained arguments from Kachru and other enthusiasts in the world English(es) "movement" on the need for a paradigm shift in the study of English as an international language, this discourse was formulated according to the game-rules of an essentially western liberal perspective. Phillipson's arguments, however, represent a harder-edged Marxian, if not Marxist, response to the subject.

At the core of Phillipson's theoretical approach to "linguistic imperialism" are a series of arguments about the political relations between what Phillipson characterizes as the "core English-speaking countries" (Britain, the USA, Canada, Australia, and New Zealand) and the "periphery-English countries" where English either has the status of a second language (e.g., Nigeria, India, Singapore), or is a foreign and "international link language" (e.g., Scandinavia, Japan) (1992, p. 17). The nature of this relationship, Phillipson argues, is one of structural and systemic inequality, in which the political and economic hegemony of western anglophone powers is established or maintained over scores of developing nations, particularly those formerly colonies of European powers. The political and economic power of such nations in the Third World is, moreover, accompanied by "English linguistic imperialism," defined by Phillipson in the following terms:

> A working definition of *English linguistic imperialism* is that *the dominance of English is asserted and maintained by the establishment and continuous reconstitution of structural and cultural inequalities between English and other languages* . . . English linguistic imperialism is seen as a sub-type of linguicism.   (1992, p. 47, original emphasis)

Finally, Phillipson asks whether ELT can help create "greater linguistic and social equality," and whether "a critical ELT" can help fight linguicism (p. 319). In the final chapter on "Linguistic imperialism and ELT," Phillipson asks who has been responsible for the global spread of English in recent decades, and for the "monolingual and anglocentric" professionalism that has accompanied its teaching worldwide. The "allies in the international promotion of English" were Britain and the USA, but they, or their political leaders and cultural agencies (such as the British Council and United States Information Service (USIS)), have only been partly responsible, as the main force, Phillipson claims, has been structural and he charges that: "The ELT policy-makers themselves, in Center and Periphery, in Ministries of Education, universities, curriculum development centers and the like are part of a hegemonic structure" and that "The structure of academic imperialism has ensured that Center training and expertise have been disseminated worldwide, with change and innovative professionalism tending to be generated by the Center" (p. 305).

Phillipson's book attracted an immediate response from applied linguists and sociolinguists. Fishman and Spolsky, two heavyweights active in both disciplines, gave favorable reviews, and *World Englishes* even devoted a special issue to a symposium on the book (Kachru, 1993). Less favorable reviews varied from the "mixed" (McArthur, 1993, p. 50, "painstaking, fascinating, informative, frustrating but patently well-meant book"), to the dismissive (Conrad, 1996, p. 27, "a kind of toothless Marxism").

Another important theorist and commentator from a critical perspective has been Alastair Pennycook. Pennycook's (1994) *The Cultural Politics of English as an International Language* endorses Phillipson's critique of the role of applied linguistics and ELT in "helping to legitimate the contemporary capitalist order" (1994, p. 24), and seconds his view that anglophone countries (Britain and America) have promoted English throughout the world "for economic and political purposes" and "to protect and promote capitalist interests" (p. 22). The final chapter calls for a radical pedagogy, concerned with the creation of "counter-discourses," "insurgent knowledges," "common counter-articulations" so that "critical English language educators" (formerly known as English teachers) join the struggle for "a critical, transformative and listening critical pedagogy through English" (p. 326). Throughout his other writings, Pennycook has sought to advance and refine a critical perspective on both world Englishes and applied linguistics. In his latest book, *Critical Applied Linguistics* (2001), he explains that:

> Critical applied linguistics . . . is more than just a critical dimension added on top of applied linguistics: It involves a constant skepticism, a constant questioning of the normative assumptions of applied linguistics and presents a way of doing applied linguistics that seeks to connect it to questions of gender, class, sexuality, race, ethnicity, culture, identity, politics, ideology and discourse. (Pennycook, 2001, p. 10)

Both Phillipson and Pennycook have been influential in establishing the agenda for the critical discussion of world English(es) is the last ten years or so. Related work by other authors includes Tollefson (1995, 2002), Eggington & Wren (1997), Holborow (1999), Ricento (2000), and Skutnabb-Kangas (2000).

15.6.3   *Futurology*

Two fairly recent works that have attempted to discuss the future prospects for English in the world are Crystal (1997) and Graddol (1997). Crystal, in the final chapter of *English as a Global Language,* highlights a number of issues related to the "future of global English." The issues he discusses include the anxiety about the mother tongue in societies such as India, the debate about the official English movement in the USA, and the existence and growth of the new Englishes. The first issue he addresses is that of "ownership," noting that "when even the largest English speaking nation, the USA, turns out to have only about 20 percent of the world's English speakers . . . it is plain that no one can now claim sole ownership" of English, and that "[t]his is probably the best way of defining a genuinely global language" (Crystal, 1997, p. 130). There are those, he continues, especially in Britain, who are "uncomfortable" about this, but they have no alternative:

> Within ten years, there will certainly be more L2 speakers than L1 speakers. Within fifty years, there could be up to 50 percent more. By that time, the only possible concept of ownership will be a global one . . . An inevitable consequence of this development is that the language will become open to the winds of linguistic change in totally unpredictable ways. The spread of English around the world has already demonstrated this, in the emergence of new varieties of English in the different territories where the language has taken root. The change has become a major talking point only since the 1960s, hence the term by which these varieties are often known: "new Englishes."   (pp. 130–1)

Instead of fragmented unintelligible varieties, however, Crystal identifies a new, unifying dialect, that of "World Standard Spoken English" (WSSE), which he now sees developing worldwide:

> People would still have their dialects for use within their own country, but when the need came to communicate with people from other countries they would slip into WSSE . . . People who attend international conferences, or who write scripts for an international audience, or who are "talking" on the Internet have probably already felt the pull of this new variety. It takes the form, for example, of consciously avoiding a word or phrase which you know is not going to be understood outside your own country, and of finding an alternative form of expression . . . it is too early to be definite about the way this variety will develop. WSSE is still in its infancy. Indeed, it has hardly yet been born. (pp. 137–8)

  Graddol's (1997) *The Future of English?* was commissioned and published by the British Council's English 2000 project, the final section of which is devoted to "English in the future." Graddol identifies two major issues linked to the notion of "world standard English": (1) whether English will fragment into many different languages (the Quirk/Kachru debate); and (2) whether US and

British English will continue to serve as models of correctness, or whether a "new world standard" will emerge. In contrast to Crystal, Graddol rejects world standard English and predicts a "polycentric" future for English standards in the future, presenting a number of analyses of the economic and sociopolitical effects of the spread of English. Graddol's "state-of-the-art" report on English also illustrates the rapid shift in the last 30 years from a focus on "the linguistic" (as in early studies of varieties of English) to an increasing preoccupation with "the extra-linguistic," e.g., the socioeconomics of globalization in Graddol, and the Marxism, dependency theory, and postcolonial theorizing of Phillipson and Pennycook.

15.7 Endword: From Theory to Practice

The review of the literature in the preceding section demonstrates just how far the debates and discourses on world English(es) and new Englishes have come since the identification of this topic in sociolinguistics and applied linguistics in the late 1970s and early 1980s. As is indicated above, there are currently a number of overlapping and intersecting approaches to this field of inquiry. What also emerges from this survey, however, is a changing disciplinary and discoursal map, marked by a series of paradigm shifts in the last 20 years. In this final section, we might now pause to consider the implications of such approaches for applied linguistics. The kinds of responses that are possible in this context will depend on a range of factors, including different under-standings of the field of "applied linguistics."

For some, applied linguistics has the status of an independent discipline associated with its own body of theory and methodologies, while, for others, it is seen as "mediating" between such parent disciplines as education, linguistics, psychology, sociology, etc. and various forms of problem-solving activities, especially those associated with language learning and language teaching. In this latter context, for example, Widdowson has commented that applied linguistics is "an activity which seeks to identify, within the disciplines concerned with language and learning, those insights and procedures of enquiry which are relevant for the formulation of pedagogic principles and their effective actualization in practice" (1990, p. 6, cited in Cook & Seidlhofer, 1995, p. 8). For the purposes of this short conclusion, I will assume that the term is capable of two broad definitions: in the first sense, as a wide-ranging area of interdisciplinary theory and activity of relevance to such fields as linguistics, psycholinguistics and sociolinguistics; and, in a second sense, as a rather narrower field of activity mainly concerned, following Widdowson, with pedagogic principles and practices.

The significance of world Englishes for applied linguistics in the first and wider sense is profound, challenging the discipline to come to terms with a wide range of issues, descriptive and theoretical, linked to the unprecedented impact of English throughout the world. Current estimates suggest that there are now an estimated 375 million users of English in inner-circle societies, 375 million in outer-circle (ESL) societies, and around 750–1,000 million in the expanding (EFL) circle (McArthur, 2001). Other statistics suggest that in Asia alone the number of English users now totals over 600 million people, including over 300 million in India, and over 200 million in China. Virtually every Asian city has an English language newspaper, and many societies in the region also provide English language programs on radio and television. English is also an important pan-Asian lingua franca in the business world, so that, for example, when a factory manager from Vietnam sells garments to a Singaporean merchandiser, the language of choice is usually English. The dominant trend over recent decades is that more and more Asian people are speaking more and more English, and they are speaking it mainly to other Asians (Kachru, 1997b).

The vast majority of teachers of English as a second and foreign language in the world today are "non-native" teachers working in a wide range of settings in outer-circle and expanding-circle societies. The number of secondary school teachers of English in China alone now totals around 500,000 (Bolton, 2003). In outer-circle Asian societies such as Hong Kong, India, Malaysia, Singapore, and the Philippines (as well as a host of African societies), such teachers operate in sociolinguistic contexts where English has established de facto intranational norms, often at variance with the exonormative targets of traditional teaching materials. In situations such as these, the maintenance of traditional target norms of English proficiency may not only lack realism but may also contribute to the stigmatization of the norms of local users (including teachers and learners), contributing to a "culture of complaint" rather than "a culture of confidence" (Bolton, 2002b).

In addition, the "nativization" of English in many such societies has been accompanied by the "Englishization" of many indigenous languages, leading to complex patterns of contact linguistics, including lexical transfer, code-switching and code-mixing, and discoursal and syntactic change and accommodation. The interface of English with both local languages and national vernaculars throughout many parts of the world presents applied linguistics (in "sense 1") with a series of challenges: *linguistic* (the description and analysis of language systems), *sociolinguistic* (providing adequate accounts of context and language use), and *psycholinguistic* (in assessing or reformulating extant models of first and second language acquisition). In this latter context, the notion of "native speaker" has come under increasing scrutiny (Davies, 1991; Singh, 1998).

At the same time, despite the greater recognition accorded to the Englishes of Africa and Asia in recent years, considerable problems for applied linguistics still exist in the area of pedagogic principles and practices (applied linguistics in "sense 2" terms). In many outer-circle societies, questions linked to norms and codification are typically unresolved. For example, even though some educationalists in societies such as Hong Kong and the Philippines have started to recognize local norms of educated speech, official attitudes frequently remain ambivalent at best. Attitudes vary considerably from one society to the next, with Filipino teachers often rejecting the imposition of American norms, while Hong Kong teachers continue to express deference to the norms of the "native speaker." Nor is it clear that that the official endorsement of "local standards" would necessarily further the world Englishes cause, especially when one considers that varieties are typically caught not taught, and questions of norms and standards are invariably embedded in the particular language cultures and traditions of such societies. One possible innovation that might be considered here, however, is a much-increased provision of courses on "language awareness" (dealing with issues related to world Englishes) for teachers, teacher trainers, and other educators not only in outer- or expanding-circle societies, but also for comparable groups in such inner-circle societies as the USA, UK, Australia, Canada, etc. The expanded accessibility of programmes of this kind may help to clear the space for new and creative approaches to language education and the teaching of English, in a range of contexts worldwide.

Kachru himself discusses these and related issues in a 1990 paper entitled "World Englishes and applied linguistics," where he notes the limitations of traditional applied linguistics perspectives on world Englishes, suggesting that these had been skewed by the ethnocentrisms of inner-circle practitioners, reliance on interlanguage and error analysis frameworks, and misconceptions concerning the sociolinguistic realities of multilingual outer-circle societies (Kachru, 1990). A later paper by Kachru and Nelson (1996) goes on to explore the ways in which the world Englishes approach might be adopted within the language classroom, suggesting a number of imaginative strategies that might be employed in teaching Englishes across a variety of educational settings, including multicultural education, the teaching of discourse pragmatics, and the teaching of new literatures in English (see also Kachru, 1997a).

Brown (2000) surveys the resources for research and teaching in the field, and suggests a range of research and applied agendas for world Englishes. At the level of applied linguistics research, these include longitudinal studies of values and attitudes, textual studies in multicultural communities, empirical studies of attitude development and change, and world Englishes-based research on second language acquisition. Related educational research might then involve comparative classroom-based studies across the three circles (what have elsewhere been dubbed ENL, ESL, and EFL contexts), and the evaluation of learning/teaching materials. Brown also suggests an activist role for world Englishes scholars in organizing conferences, publishing, designing texts and curricular, and playing a leadership role in professional communities world-wide (see also, Kachru, 1997a; and Matsuda, 2002).

In the last ten years or so, there has been a growing awareness of the world Englishes paradigm among applied linguists and others in outer-circle English-using African and Asian societies. There has also been an evident response to the world Englishes paradigm in many academic circles in the USA, partly in resonance, one speculates, to the relatively high levels of immigration to the United States from Asian societies in recent years, and a nascent awareness of world Englishes in an immigrant context (Lippi-Green, 1997). In other educational settings, such as Europe, with its own crowded ecology of former colonial languages such as French, German, and Spanish, the academic response to the world Englishes paradigm has been mixed.

One particularly acute problem at present remains the center-periphery domination in what has been called "English language industry" (McArthur, 2001) throughout the world. Academic publishing and textbook publishing in both applied linguistics and English language teaching is largely controlled by a small number of publishing houses based in the UK and USA, who rely on a relatively small number of experts for their expertise and professionalism. Historically, however, applied linguistics in both these societies did not arise in a sociopolitical vacuum, but came out of two rather different sets of experiences. In the case of Britain, applied linguistics emerged as a discipline during the 1960s and 1970s when significant numbers of English language specialists were recruited to assist in various educational projects in decolonizing Commonwealth societies. In the USA, in recent decades, the greatest impetus to applied linguistics and TESOL has come from immigrant education and ESL programs in the college and university context. Both approaches seem now to have coalesced around a body of shared practices, professionalism, and theory (see, for example Candlin & Mercer, 2001; Carter & Nunan, 2001; Kaplan, 2002). Despite what may be the best intentions of western practitioners to develop an unbiased or at least politically neutral applied linguistics at the level of theory as well as pedagogic principles, it is difficult to ignore the imbalance between the developed and developing world in many of the contexts of English language teaching today. English language teachers in many of the outer-circle and expanding-circle contexts face difficulties in terms of conditions, facilities, and resources undreamed of in comparable western institutions. Academics from these societies have parallel difficulties in finding a voice in major journals in the field (although notable exceptions include *English Today* and *World Englishes*), as well as in book production.

In this context, the Kachruvian approach offers a politics that is balanced between the pragmatic recognition of the spread of English(es) and the critical scrutiny of native speaker ideologies from the inner circle. It also affirms the pluricentricity and inclusivity signposted by Kachru and Smith in their first editorial statement for the *World Englishes* journal: "The editorial board considers the native and non-native users of English as equal partners in deliberations on uses of English and its teaching internationally.... The acronym WE, therefore aptly symbolizes the underlying philosophy of the journal and the aspirations of the Editorial Board" (Kachru & Smith, 1985, p. 210). Whether that vision is realizable depends partly on the flow of ideas and insights in at least two directions. A consideration of world Englishes is important to applied linguistics for a range of reasons. Not least because researchers and teachers from Europe and North America may have much to learn from the experiences of the outer and expanding circles, both at levels of theory and description, and in the consideration of pedagogic "principles" and "practice."

At an individual level, the English language now plays an important role in the lives of a rapidly increasing proportion of the world's population. From a global perspective, the sociolinguistically complex sites of English-using African and Asian societies are no mere exotic sideshow, but important sites of contact, negotiation, and linguistic and literary creativity. From the perspective of applied linguistics, perhaps the major challenge from world Englishes is how the center-periphery balance might be best redressed, or "re-centered" and "pluricentered." This however is likely to be no easy task, given the continuing tendency at present, within both academia and publishing, toward the apparent commodification and homogenization of much of the work in this field, both theoretical and pedagogical.

See also 9 LANGUAGE THOUGHT, AND CULTURE, 14 LANGUAGE AND POLITICS, 17 THE NATIVE SPEAKER IN APPLIED LINGUISTICS, 20 SECOND LANGUAGE LEARNING, 30 LANGUAGE PLANNING AS APPLIED LINGUISTICS.

REFERENCES

Algeo, J. (1991) A meditation on the varieties of English. *English Today*, 7, 3–6.

Allsopp, R. (1996) *The dictionary of Caribbean English usage*. Oxford: Oxford University Press.

Ashcroft, B., Griffiths, G., & Tiffin, H. (1989) *The empire writes back*. London: Routledge.

Avis, W. S. (1967) *A dictionary of Canadianisms on historical principles*. Toronto: Gage.

Bailey, R. W. (1991) *Images of English*. Ann Arbor: The University of Michigan Press.

Banjo, A. & Young, P. (1982) On editing a second-language dictionary: the proposed dictionary of West African English (DWAE). *English World-Wide*, 3, 87–91.

Barber, K. (1999) *The Canadian Oxford dictionary*. Oxford: Oxford University Press.

Bartlett, J. R. (1848) *Dictionary of Americanisms: a glossary of words and phrases usually regarded as peculiar to the United States*. New York: Bartlett and Welford.

Bolton, K. (2002a) World Englishes: approaches, issues, and debate. Paper presented at the 11th International Association of World Englishes (IAWE) Conference, University of Illinois at Urbana-Champaign, October 17–20, 2002.

Bolton, K. (2002b) Hong Kong English: autonomy and creativity. In K. Bolton (ed.), *Hong Kong English: autonomy and creativity* (pp. 1–25). Hong Kong: Hong Kong University Press.

Bolton, K. (2003) *Chinese Englishes: a sociolinguistic history*. Cambridge: Cambridge University Press.

Branford, W. (1987) *The South African pocket Oxford dictionary*. Cape Town: Oxford University Press.

Brown, K. (2000) World Englishes and the classroom: research and practice agendas for the year 2000. In E. Thumboo (ed.), *The three circles of English* (pp. 371–82). Singapore: UniPress.

Burchfield, R. (1985) *The English language*. Oxford: Oxford University Press.

Burchfield, R. (1994) *The Cambridge history of the English language*, vol. 5:

English in Britain and overseas: origin and development. Cambridge: Cambridge University Press.

Butler, S. (ed.) (1981) *The Macquarie dictionary*. Sydney: Macquarie Dictionary Company Limited.

Butler, S. (1997) Corpus of English in Southeast Asia: implications for a regional dictionary. In M. L. S. Bautista (ed.), *English is an Asian language: the Philippine context* (pp. 103–24). Manila: The Macquarie Dictionary.

Candlin, C. N. & Mercer, N. (2001) *English language teaching in its social context*. London: Routledge.

Carter, R. & Nunan, D. (eds.) (2001) *The Cambridge guide to teaching English to speakers of other languages*. Cambridge: Cambridge University Press.

Cassidy, F. G. (1985) *Dictionary of American regional English*. Cambridge, MA: Harvard University Press.

Cassidy, F. G. & Le Page, R. (1967) *Dictionary of Jamaican English*. Cambridge: Cambridge University Press.

Cheshire, J. (ed.) (1991a) *English around the world: sociolinguistic perspectives*. Cambridge: Cambridge University Press.

Cheshire, J. (1991b) Introduction: sociolinguistics and English around the world. In J. Cheshire (ed.), *English around the world: sociolinguistic perspectives* (pp. 1–12). Cambridge: Cambridge University Press.

Conrad, A. W. (1996) The international role of English: the state of the discussion. In J. A. Fishman, A. W. Conrad, & A. Rubal-Lopez (eds.). *Post-imperial English* (pp. 13–36). Berlin, New York: Mouton de Gruyter.

Cook, G. & Seidlhofer, B. (eds.) (1995) *Principles and practice in applied linguistics. Studies in honour of H. G. Widdowson*. Oxford: Oxford University Press.

Craigie, W. A. & Hulbert, J. R. (1938–44) *A dictionary of American English on historical principles*. Chicago: University of Chicago Press.

Crystal, D. (1969) *Prosodic systems and intonation in English*. Cambridge: Cambridge University Press.

Crystal, D. (1975) *The English tone of voice: essays in intonation, prosody and paralanguage*. London: Edward Arnold.

Crystal, D. (1988) *The English language*. London: Penguin Books

Crystal, D. (1995) *The Cambridge encyclopedia of the English language*. Cambridge: Cambridge University Press.

Crystal, D. (1997) *English as a global language*. Cambridge: Cambridge University Press.

Crystal, D. (2000) On trying to be crystal-clear: a response to Phillipson. *Applied Linguistics*, 21, 415–23.

Crystal, D. & Quirk, R. (1964) *Systems of prosodic and paralinguistic features in English*. The Hague: Mouton.

Davies, A. (1991) *The native speaker in applied linguistics*. Edinburgh: Edinburgh University Press.

Eggington, W. G. & Wren, H. (1997) *Language policy: dominant English, pluralist challenges*. Amsterdam/Canberra: John Benjamins/Language Australia.

Fishman, J. A. (1977) English in the context of international societal bilingualism. In J. A. Fishman, R. L. Cooper, & A. W. Conrad (eds.), *The spread of English: the sociology of English as an additional language* (pp. 329–36). Rowley, MA: Newbury House.

Fishman, J. A. (1996a) Introduction: some empirical and theoretical issues. In J. A. Fishman, A. W. Conrad, & A. Rubal-Lopez (eds.), *Post-imperial English* (pp. 3–12). Berlin, New York: Mouton de Gruyter.

Fishman, J. A. (1996b) Summary and interpretation: post-imperial English 1940–1990. In J. A. Fishman, A. W.

Conrad, & A. Rubal-Lopez (eds.), *Post-imperial English* (pp. 623–41). Berlin, New York: Mouton de Gruyter.

Fishman, J. A., Conrad, A. W., & Rubal-Lopez, A. (eds.) (1996) *Post-imperial English*. Berlin, New York: Mouton de Gruyter.

Fishman, J. A., Cooper, R. L., & Conrad, A. W. (eds.) (1977) *The spread of English: the sociology of English as an additional language*. Rowley, MA: Newbury House.

Goodman, S. & Graddol, D. (eds.) (1996) *Redesigning English: new texts, new identities*. London: Routledge.

Görlach, M. (1980) Editorial. *English World-Wide*, 1, 3–7.

Görlach, M. (1988) English as a world language – the state of the art. *English World-Wide*, 10, 279–313.

Görlach, M. (ed.) (1995) Dictionaries of transplanted Englishes. In M. Görlach (ed.), *More Englishes: new studies in varieties of English 1988–1994* (pp. 124–63). Amsterdam/ Philadelphia: John Benjamins.

Görlach, M. (1996) And is it English? *English World-Wide*, 17, 153–74.

Graddol, D. (1997) *The future of English?* London: The British Council.

Graddol, D., Leith, D., & Swann, J. (1996) *English: history, diversity and change*. London: Routledge.

Greenbaum, S. (ed.) (1985) *The English language today*. Oxford: Pergamon.

Greenbaum, S. (ed.) (1996) *Comparing English worldwide*. Oxford: Clarendon Press.

Halliday, M. A. K., MacIntosh, A., & Strevens, P. (1964) *The linguistic sciences and language teaching*. London: Longman.

Hawkins, R. E. (1984) *Common Indian words in English*. Delhi: Oxford University Press.

Holborow, M. (1999) *The politics of English: a Marxist view of language*. London: Sage.

Holm, J. & Shilling A. W. (eds.) (1982) *Dictionary of Bahamian English*. Cold Spring, New York: Lexik House.

Hosillos, L. (1982) Breaking through the Wayang Screen: literary interdependence among new literatures in Southeast Asia. In B. Bennett, E. T. Hong, & R. Shepherd (eds.), *The writer's sense of the contemporary: papers in Southeast Asia and Australian literature* (pp. 59–62). Nedlands: Centre for Studies in Australian Literature, University of Western Australia.

Iyer, P. (1993) The empire writes back. *Time*, February 8 (6), 48–53.

Johnson, S. (1755) *A dictionary of the English language*. London: Printed by W. Strahan, for J. & P. Knapton.

Kachru, B. B. (ed.) (1982) *The other tongue: English across cultures*. Urbana, IL: University of Illinois Press.

Kachru, B. B. (1985) Standards, codification and sociolinguistic realism: the English language in the outer circle. In R. Quirk & H. G. Widdowson (eds.), *English in the world: teaching and learning the language and literatures* (pp. 11–30). Cambridge: Cambridge University Press.

Kachru, B. B. (1986) *The alchemy of English: the spread, functions, and models of non-native Englishes*. Oxford: Pergamon Press.

Kachru, B. B. (1990) World Englishes and applied linguistics. *Studies in Linguistic Sciences*, 19, 127–52.

Kachru, B. B. (1991) Liberation linguistics and the Quirk concern. *English Today*, 25(7.1), 3–13.

Kachru, B. B. (1992) World Englishes: approaches, issues and resources. *Language Teaching*, 25, 1–14.

Kachru, B. B. (ed.) (1993) Symposium on linguistic imperialism. *World Englishes*, 12, 335–73.

Kachru, B. B. (1997a) World Englishes 2000: resources for research and teaching. In L. E. Smith &

M. L. Forman (eds.), *World Englishes 2000* (pp. 209–51). Honolulu: University of Hawai'i Press and the East-West Center.

Kachru, B. B. (1997b) English as an Asian language. In M. L. S. Bautista (ed.), *English is an Asian language: the Philippine context* (pp. 1–23). Manila: The Macquarie Library.

Kachru, B. B. & Nelson, C. (1996) World Englishes. In S. L. Mckay & N. H. Hornberger (eds.), *Sociolinguistics and language teaching* (pp. 71–102). Cambridge: Cambridge University Press.

Kachru, B. B. & Smith, L. E. (1985) Editorial. *World Englishes*, 4, 209–12.

Kachru, B. B. & Smith, L. E. (1988) World Englishes: an integrative and cross-cultural journal of WE-ness. In E. Maxwell (ed.), *Robert Maxwell and Pergamon Press: 40 years' service to science, technology and education* (pp. 674–48). Oxford: Pergamon Press.

Kaplan, R. (ed.) (2002) *The Oxford handbook of applied linguistics.* New York: Oxford University Press.

King, B. (1980) *The new English literatures: cultural nationalism in a changing world.* London: Macmillan.

Lake, J. (1989) *Webster's international dictionary, Australasian supplement.* Springfield, MA: G. & C. Merriam.

Lim, S. (1984) Gods who fall: Ancestral religions in the new literatures in English from Malaysia and Singapore. *Commonwealth Novel in English*, 3(1), 39–55.

Lippi-Green, R. (1997) *English with an accent: language, ideology, and discrimination in the United States.* London/New York: Routledge.

Llamzon, T. (1983) Essential features of new varieties of English. In R. B. Noss (ed.), *Varieties of English in Southeast Asia.* Singapore: Regional Language Centre.

Mathews, M. M. (1951) *Dictionary of Americanisms on historical principles.* Chicago: University of Chicago Press.

Matsuda, A. (ed.) (2002) Symposium on world Englishes and teaching English as a foreign language. *World Englishes*, 21(3), 421–55.

McArthur, T. (1987) The English languages? *English Today*, July/September, 9–11.

McArthur, T. (1992) *The Oxford companion to the English language.* Oxford: Oxford University Press

McArthur, T. (1993) The sins of the fathers. *English Today*, 35(9:3), 48–50.

McArthur, T. (1998) *The English languages.* Cambridge: Cambridge University Press.

McArthur, T. (2001) World English and world Englishes: trends, tensions, varieties, and standards. *Language Teaching*, 34, 1–20.

McArthur, T. (2002) *The Oxford guide to world English.* Oxford: Oxford University Press.

McCrum, R., Cran, W., & MacNeil, R. (1986) *The story of English.* London: Faber & Faber, BBC publications.

Morris, E. E. (1898) *Austral English: A dictionary of Australasian words, phrases and usage.* London: Macmillan.

Mufwene, S. S. (1997) Introduction: understanding speech continua. *World Englishes*, 16, 181–4.

Murray, J. A. H. (ed.) (1884–1928) *A new English dictionary on historical principles.* Re-edited and re-titled, *The Oxford English dictionary* (from 1933). Oxford: Oxford University Press.

Nelson, G., Wallis, S., & Aarts, B. (2002) *Exploring natural language: working with the British component of the International Corpus of English.* Amsterdam: John Benjamins.

Noss, R. B. (ed.) (1983) *Varieties of English in Southeast Asia.* Singapore: Regional Language Center.

Orsman, H. (1997) *The dictionary of New Zealand English: a dictionary of*

New Zealandisms on historical principles. Auckland: Oxford University Press.

Pennycook, A. (1994) *The cultural politics of English as an international language*. London: Longman.

Pennycook, A. (2001) *Critical applied linguistics*. New Jersey: Lawrence Erlbaum.

Pettman, Rev. C. (1913) *Africanderisms. A glossary of South African words and phrases and of place and other names*. London: Longmans, Green & Co.

Phillipson, R. (1992) *Linguistic imperialism*. Oxford: Oxford University Press.

Phillipson, R. (1999) Linguistic imperialism re-visited – or re-invented. A rejoinder to a review essay. *International Journal of Applied Linguistics*, 9, 135–42.

Pickering, J. (1816) *A vocabulary or collection of words and phrases which have been supposed to be peculiar to the United States of America*. Boston: Cummings & Hilliard.

Platt, J., Weber, H., & Ho, M. L. (1984) *The new Englishes*. London: Routledge.

Prator, C. (1968) The British heresy in TESL. In J. A. Fishman, C. Ferguson, & J. Das Gupta (eds.), *Language problems of developing nations* (pp. 459–76). New York: John Wiley & Sons.

Pride, J. B. (1982) *New Englishes*. Rowley, MA: Newbury House.

Quirk, R. (1962) *The use of English*. London: Longman.

Quirk, R. (1985) The English language in a global context. In R. Quirk & H. G. Widdowson (eds.), *English in the world: teaching and learning the language and literatures* (pp. 1–30). Cambridge: Cambridge University Press.

Quirk, R. (1990) Language varieties and standard language. *English Today*, 21, 3–21.

Quirk, R. & Widdowson, H. G. (eds.) (1985) *English in the world: teaching and learning the language and literature*.

Cambridge: Cambridge University Press.

Quirk, R., Greenbaum, S., Leech, G., & Svartvik, J. (1972) *A grammar of contemporary English*. London: Longman.

Rao, G. S. (1954) *Indian words in English: a study in Indo-British cultural and linguistic relations*. Oxford: Clarendon.

Ricento, T. (2000) *Ideology, politics, and language politics: focus on English*. Amsterdam/Philadelphia: John Benjamins.

Romaine, S. (1997) The British heresy in ESL revisited. In S. Eliasson & E. H. Jahr (eds.), *Language and its ecology: essays in memory of Einar Haugen* (pp. 417–32). Berlin/New York: Mouton de Gruyter.

Schneider, E. W. (1997a) Introduction. In E. W. Schneider (ed.), *Englishes around the world* (vol. 1) (pp. 15–17). Amsterdam and Philadelphia: John Benjamins.

Schneider (1997b) *Englishes around the world*, vol. 1: *General studies, British Isles, North America*. Amsterdam: John Benjamins.

Schneider (1997c) *Englishes around the world*, vol. 2: *Caribbean, Africa, Asia, Australasia*. Amsterdam: John Benjamins.

Silva, P. (1998) *A dictionary of South African English on historical principles*. Oxford: Oxford University Press.

Singh, R. (ed.) (1998) *The native speaker: multilingual perspectives*. New Delhi: Sage.

Skutnabb-Kangas, T. (2000) *Linguistic genocide in education, or worldwide diversity and human rights*. Mahwah, NJ/London: Lawrence Erlbaum.

Smith, L. E. (ed.) (1981) *English for cross-cultural communication*. London: Macmillan.

Strevens, P. (1977) *New orientations in the teaching of English*. Oxford: Oxford University Press.

Strevens, P. (1980) *Teaching English as an international language*. Oxford: Pergamon.

Strevens, P. (1985) Standards and the standard language. *English Today*, 2, 5–8.

Todd, L. (1984) *Modern Englishes: pidgins and creoles*. Oxford: Blackwell.

Todd, L. (1995) Tracking the homing pidgin: a millennium report. *English Today*, 41, 33–43.

Tollefson, J. W. (ed.) (1995) *Power and inequality in language education*. Cambridge/New York: Cambridge University Press.

Tollefson, J. W. (ed.) (2002) *Language policies in education: critical issues*. Mahwah, NJ/London: Lawrence Erlbaum.

Trudgill, P. & Hannah, J. (1994) *International English: a guide to varieties of standard English* (3rd edn.). London: Edward Arnold.

Webster, N. (1789) *Dissertations on the English language*. Boston: Isaiah Thomas; facs. Reprinted Menston: Scolar, 1967.

Webster, N. (1806) *A compendious dictionary of the English Language*. Hartford, CN: Sidney's Press for Hudson & Goodwin and for Increase Cooke & Co.

Webster, N. (1828) *An American dictionary of the English language* (2 vols). New York: S. Converse. Facsimile reprint, San Francisco: Foundation for American Christian Education, 1967.

Wells, John C. (1982) *Accents of English* (3 vols). Cambridge: Cambridge University Press.

Whitworth, G. C. (1885) *An Anglo-Indian dictionary: a glossary of Indian terms used in English, and of such English or other non-Indian terms as have obtained special meanings in India*. London: Kegan Paul, Trench & Co.

Widdowson, H. G. (1990) *Aspects of language teaching*. Oxford: Oxford University Press.

Yule, H. & Burnell, A. C. ([1886] 1969) *Hobson-Jobson: a glossary of Anglo-Indian words and phrases*. London: John Murray. New edition 1903, reprinted 1969, London: Routledge & Kegan Paul.

FURTHER READING

Smith, L. E. & Forman, M. L. (eds.) (1997) *World Englishes 2000*. Honolulu: University of Hawai'i Press and the East-West Center.

Thumboo, E. (ed.) (2001) *The three circles of English*. Singapore: UniPress.

16 The Philosophy of Applied Linguistics

KANAVILLIL RAJAGOPALAN

16.1 Introduction

Upon being asked to explain what philosophy was all about, the English philosopher G. E. Moore is famously said to have gestured toward his crowded bookshelves and remarked: "It is what all these are about." Philosophy has no precise boundaries. Almost anything under the sun (or, for that matter, above it) will lend itself to a philosophical treatment. Now, what this also shows is that professional philosophers are likely to disagree about almost everything. A philosopher will most certainly say that the expression "philosophy of x," where the x stands for an object (as in "philosophy of mind"), a practice (as in "philosophy of religion"), a phenomenon (as in "philosophy of language"), a topic or a subject matter (as in "philosophy of human rights"), or a field of inquiry (as in "philosophy of history") is multiply ambiguous. Incidentally, even this way of putting things is unlikely to satisfy everyone concerned. For instance, someone might argue that the mind is an epiphenomenon rather than an object properly speaking, or that religion has to do more with belief systems than a set of ritual practices or, for that matter, that mind, religion, language, and so forth are all fields of inquiry, just as much as history is.

The expression "philosophy of history," for instance, may be understood to mean: (1) a philosophically informed account of actual events as they get played out along the path of history; (2) a philosophically illuminating overview of history insofar as it constitutes a distinctive and clearly demarcated field of inquiry, with special emphasis on its academic and scientific credentials; or (3) an examination of the philosophical underpinnings of a particular academic discipline, namely history, with a view to teasing out unresolved or poorly resolved issues of a philosophical nature and discussing possible ways of better addressing them.

As only to be expected, the term "philosophy of applied linguistics" is capable of being interpreted in any one of the three senses distinguished above as well. It may be understood to mean a philosophically informed account of the nature of applied linguistics (hereafter AL) as well as of the important landmarks in the history of its development over the years. For instance, an interesting topic in the philosophy of AL understood in this sense might be the philosophical import of the way the field evolved from an initial preoccupation to define itself as an appendix to linguistics proper – primarily concerned with applying insights from linguistic theory to a set of practices, notably language teaching – to an autonomous field of inquiry concerned with a broad range of questions involving language.

The term "philosophy of AL" may also be understood to mean philosophy of science with its attention riveted on AL as a scientific discipline in its own right. On this interpretation, the term refers to the investigation of all those questions that are relevant to an appraisal of the scientific status of AL as a field of inquiry. Among the questions raised in this regard will inevitably be the one that most researchers in the area have been concerned with ever since AL became an autonomous field of inquiry: What precisely is the nature of the relation between AL and its parent discipline, theoretical or general linguistics? Is AL destined to remain forever subaltern to its parent discipline, dependent upon the latter for its theoretical sustenance as well as claims of scientific credibility? Or could it be the case that exaggerated subservience to its parent discipline has only stifled the growth of AL and its potential for expansion into as yet uncharted territories? Alternatively, has the time come for scholars in AL to look for other sources for inspiration and, possibly, chalk out a brand new research program for it, based on a multitude of neighboring disciplines, but with goals, methods, and priorities fashioned in entirely independent terms?

Finally, the term "philosophy of AL" may also be understood to cover a broad range of philosophically important issues that have of late begun to capture the attention of scholars in AL in their efforts to, on the one hand, reflect upon how they have traditionally conducted themselves in their scientific practices and, on the other, redefine their research priorities in light of new challenges and rethink the very scope of their field. On this third interpretation, questions such as the underlying ethics of certain professional practices (methods used in collecting data, for instance), the desirability or otherwise of making sure that the researcher's political commitments are kept at bay and not allowed to interfere with the work of analysis, the responsibility – including possible ties of moral indebtedness – of field workers vis-à-vis their informants, etc., begin to take center stage. Needless to say, discussion of these and other issues of cardinal importance is bound to affect future developments in AL and possibly result in major changes in the way researchers currently view their own work as well as research priorities.

Before proceeding to unpack each of these distinct senses of the expression "philosophy of AL," it is important to point out that they overlap partially. For instance, the growing concerns among the practitioners of AL with the ethical implications of their work may be discussed as belonging to the "philosophy of AL" in any one of the three senses distinguished above. Beyond the shadow of a doubt it constitutes an important landmark in the history of the discipline. Equally truly, one can discuss the issue of whether or not ethical issues can be directly addressed within the remit of AL without jeopardizing its claims to being a science. Finally, it hardly needs pointing out that to raise the thorny issue of ethics is to call forth an entire range of other philosophically loaded questions.

16.2 Landmarks in the History of AL and Their Significance

16.2.1 Early beginnings

Just when AL became a field of inquiry in its own right is difficult to pin down, as indeed it is with practically every other field of academic inquiry. As Giddens (1995, p. 5) has perspicaciously remarked: "All disciplines have their fictive histories, all are imagined communities which invoke the myths of the past by means of both charting their own internal development and unity, and also drawing the boundaries between themselves and their neighboring disciplines." Some of the earliest recorded uses of the term, for example in the title of a book called *World Economy: An Essay in Applied Linguistics* by Lockhart – mentioned by the editors of *Language Learning*, subtitled *A Quarterly Journal of Applied Linguistics*, in its very first issue (cited in van Els et al., 1984, p. 11) – bear little resemblance to the contemporary understanding of the term. For this reason, Howatt (1984) well advisedly takes the year 1948 – when the journal just referred to was itself launched – as the date of birth of the modern discipline of AL. On the other hand, it is an acknowledged, though seldom remembered (or, conveniently forgotten?), fact that some of the very ancient works of grammar such as Panini's trail-blazing *Asthadhayi* (? fourth century BC) were undertaken with a keen interest in the preservation and teaching of the Sanskrit language (Lyons, 1968) – in other words, in the application of the results of the study to practical goals, which is clearly one way of describing what AL is all about. The indisputable point often made that Panini's work is "about as far removed as could be from one's [present day] conception of a teaching grammar" (Robins 1967, p. 144) does not detract from the force of the argument being advanced here. In fact, a case can be made that the very enterprise of theoretical linguistics itself was, from a historical perspective, born of eminently practical concerns such as the one that inspired Panini.

It has also been observed by many scholars that the history of modern linguistics, especially in the USA, was directly influenced by the perceived prospects for immediate application of its findings to such matters of strategic interest as designing and conducting crash courses in unfamiliar languages for soldiers selected for overseas assignments during World War II, automatic machine translation and the cracking of enemy military codes, etc. Arguably then, the history of modern linguistics itself (as indeed that of perhaps every other discipline) has been, in some measure, determined by purely pragmatic factors such as the channeling of public funds to specific areas of practical concern where there was hope of immediate returns for the money invested (Newmeyer & Emonds, 1971, pp. 300–1).

Considerations of the sort made in the two paragraphs above properly belong to so-called "sociology of knowledge" rather than "philosophy of science," because what is being claimed is that some of the major developments in the history of linguistics were the result of factors not intrinsic to the study of language itself, but primarily having to do with the sociopolitical milieu prevailing at given historical moments. While such observations do make sense as far as they go, there can be little doubt either that the operation by which AL came to be viewed as a fall-out from its putatively more "scientific" parent discipline, namely theoretical linguistics, rather than the other way round as the actual history of events would seem to suggest, is very much of a piece with the positivist thought – or what Holliday (1996) calls the "culture of positivism" – that dominated linguistics as it rose to the status of the "queen of human sciences" in the early decades of the twentieth century. And, by and large, scientists with a theoretical frame of mind have been given to thinking that genuine scientific work can only be carried out by keeping at bay practical considerations, or for that matter the consequences of their discoveries on other spheres of human concern.

Having said that, it is important to register that it is from the enormous prestige of theoretical linguistics in the first half of the twentieth century that AL initially borrowed its scientific credentials (Mackey, 1966, p. 197). And, from its early stages until fairly recently, AL was practically identified with language teaching. Robert Lado's book *Language Teaching* bore the carefully chosen subtitle *A Scientific Approach* (Lado, 1964). Allen and Corder (1975) began their editorial preface to volume 2 of the *Edinburgh Course in Applied Linguistics* with the following words:

> Our aim in AL is to make use of the knowledge and insights gained from scientific investigations into the nature of language, in the hope that we may solve some of the problems which arise in the planning and implementation of language teaching programs.

In his contribution to that landmark volume of papers, Corder did note that "AL in its broadest sense is concerned with many activities apart from language teaching," but made a point of stressing that "[t]he starting point of every application of linguistics to any practical tasks is a description of the language or languages involved in the task" (Corder, 1975, p. 5), thus reiterating the classic position assumed by Halliday, McIntosh, and Strevens (1964).

In so characterizing the nature of AL, Halliday, McIntosh, and Strevens and Corder presumably had at the back of their mind the way descriptive linguistics, principally in the USA, had been put to the service of foreign language teaching in the first half of the twentieth century – although it must be noted that Corder (1973, p. 276) did recognize the importance of researchers in AL keeping pace with developments in linguistics. In the heyday of American structural linguistics, the field linguists were primarily concerned with describing, classifying, and cataloguing native Indian languages, many of which were on the verge of extinction. When all of a sudden called upon to face the challenge of designing and implementing crash courses in foreign languages, these linguists naturally transferred the kind of professional expertise they had accumulated over the years to the unfamiliar task of teaching fellow Americans to speak little-known languages. Another field of practical concern that came to be strongly influenced by structural linguistics was translation. The translator, claimed Nida (1969, p. 79), "goes through a seemingly round-about process of analysis, transfer, and restructuring." Since so much of the emphasis in those days was on an accurate description of living languages to be followed by an effort to classify them in accordance with their common structural properties, it was but a small step to conclude that the key to the learning of other languages – and, *mutatis mutandis*, translating from one language to another – was primarily a matter of perceiving structural differences between them and the learner's own mother tongue.

Teaching methods and techniques were developed by focusing on the sim-ilarities and dissimilarities between the learners' native language (in general, English) and the language that was to be taught. This explains why so-called contrastive analysis became the mainstay of AL in its infancy. The underlying assumption was that the closer the two languages in terms of their structural similarities, the easier would be the learning process. Dissimilarities, on the other hand, would induce negative transfer or interference. This meant that language teachers would optimize their efforts by concentrating on those areas of the grammar of the language being learned (L2) which showed marked differences with the grammar of the learners' native language (L1).

Teaching techniques such as pattern practice which were developed and perfected as part of so-called audiolingual method during those days also drew inspiration from behaviorist psychology which many prominent linguists like Leonard Bloomfield had come to embrace. Referring to the materials pre-sented in their book *English Pattern Practices*, Lado and Fries (1943, p. xv) claimed: "We offer them with confidence in their extraordinary efficiency." And two decades later, Lado (1964, p. 6) still spoke enthusiastically of "the powerful idea of pattern practice" which he went on to define as "practice that deliberately sets out to establish as habits the patterns rather than the indi-vidual sentences, particularly where transfer from the native language creates learning problems." The contrastive approach also gave theoretical sustenance to the technique of error analysis – the analysis of the kind of errors made by language learners with a view to devising appropriate remedial measures – although, the technique itself, in its modified versions, long survived interest in the approach (Richards, 1974). Work done in subsequent years also uncovered the enormous potential of error analysis for providing insights into the processes involved in the learning of second and foreign languages (Selinker, 1992).

16.2.2   The Chomskyan revolution and its impact

But all this was thrown into total disarray with the appearance of Noam Chomsky on the scene. With the introduction of Generative Grammar, the very rationale behind behavioristically oriented structural linguistics was rejected and, along with it, teaching methods and techniques based on that approach to the study of language were also discredited. Here we have yet another proof of how AL, at least in its early stages, evolved in tandem with its parent discipline, theoretical linguistics. Every major development in theoretical linguistics was bound to have immediate repercussions in AL.

However, Chomsky's theoretical stance also presented some insuperable problems to AL. If, on the one hand, it helped dethrone an entire language teaching methodology based on insights from an earlier way of doing linguistics, on the other hand, it held little promise of anything like a new method based on it. In point of fact, some of the claims made by Chomsky and his followers seemed to indicate precisely the impossibility of ever coming up with one. For a central element of Chomsky's conception of language was the claim that one does not *learn* a language (one's first language) as such; instead languages manifest themselves as part of an individual's natural growth from infancy to adulthood. To make matters worse, Chomsky himself contributed to the prevailing state of perplexity by confessing to being "rather skeptical about the significance, for the teaching of languages, of such insights and understanding as have been attained in linguistics and psychology" (Chomsky, 1966, p. 43).

The full impact on AL of the growing suspicion that Chomskyan linguistic theory, concerned primarily with native speakers and how they acquired their first language, may have precious little to contribute to how adults learn a second language (let alone problems of language teaching, be it the first or a second language) can only be gauged by taking into account the fact that many scholars concerned with second language teaching and learning had by then come to take it for granted that, despite obvious differences, the two processes followed identical paths. In fact, in spite of Chomsky's own reservations on the matter, many Chomskyans persisted on sticking to that line of inquiry. As Schachter (1988, p. 219) points out, the idea had been entertained by Corder (1967) as a working hypothesis, subsequently transformed into a claim by Dulay and Burt (1974) and Krashen (1981), and finally elevated to the status of an "article of faith" by Krashen (1985) and Cook (1985). The following remark by Cook (1994, p. 45) shows just how noble the research goals had been all along, yet how paltry turned out to be the actual results: "Universal Grammar is concerned with the core area of language acquisition; its very centrality means that it can be taken for granted and *much of it does not need to be taken into account in language teaching, which has other more pressing concerns*" (emphasis added).

Some theoretically oriented scholars have opted to found a separate subdiscipline – of theoretical linguistics – called second language acquisition (SLA), leaving problems related to teaching and other matters to specialists in AL. Thus Gregg considers it a mistake to classify L2 learning research as "part of a field called AL" and argues that "progress in L2 acquisition theory, as in any other scientific discipline, comes by focusing on the explanatory problem, and not by looking over one's shoulder at the possible applications." (Gregg, 1996, pp. 74–5). They invoke the authority of other researchers like Newmeyer and Weinberger (1988) who, in Gregg's words, "nowhere belittle the importance of practical applications of science," and "merely make the claim, which is supported by empirical evidence from the history of science, that successful sciences divorce themselves from direct concern with practical applications" (Gregg, 1989, pp. 289–90). In the words of Ritchie and Bhatia (1996, p. 18):

> By the mid-1980s, inquiry into SLA had emerged as a basic discipline with an agenda of research and methodology fully distinct from its applied sister discipline. This agenda was (and is) theory-driven with close relationships to basic research in other domains, including research on the structure and use of language, the study of L1 acquisition, of language variation and change, and human cognition in general.

That SLA continues to be an intensely disputed territory can be verified by Larsen-Freeman's (2000, p. 165) equally confident assertion that it is by all means one of the sub-fields of AL.

No doubt, over the years there have been several other attempts to tone down the thrust of Chomsky's remark (Newmeyer, 1987) and to rehabilitate generative linguistics as a prime source of inspiration and new insights for language teachers, but with limited or little appreciable success. The state of affairs portrayed in the following remark by Cook (1985, p. 16) does not seem to have changed significantly since then: "A recent characteristic of AL has been its dissociation from contemporary theoretical linguistics; a bare handful of articles have attempted to relate the Chomskyan position to AL..." Such complaints have only helped create annoyance in some quarters at the self-reassuring "reference to a specialization as though it were the whole field" (Edge, 1993, p. 44).

In retrospect, perhaps a more lasting but sadly deleterious impact of Chomsky's revolution in linguistics on developments in AL, especially from the 1960s to the 1980s, was what I have elsewhere referred to as "the apotheosis of the native speaker" (Rajagopalan, 1997). In part, this was the result of a precipitate transformation of a linguistic rule of thumb into a pedagogic motto. Even before Chomsky appeared on the scene, descriptive linguists had always looked to the native speaker as "the only true and reliable source of language data" (Ferguson, 1983, p. vii). What underwent a dramatic change as a result of Chomsky's influence was the way linguists began to look upon the native speaker: as not merely a source of indispensable data but also as someone who was uniquely privileged to analyze the data introspectively – a practice which the structural linguists used to condemn in the name of scientific objectivity.

Now, to claim that the native speaker has an intuitive knowledge of his/her language of which she/he is (in principle) a consummate speaker and that such knowledge ought to count as data for linguistic analysis is one thing; to jump from there to the rather smug conclusion that a native speaker is, *eo ipso*, a person ideally qualified to *teach* that language to speakers of other languages is a totally different thing. Unfortunately, many language educators fell into the trap of thinking that the second claim logically followed from the first. It took some years before the realization dawned on them that there was more to language teaching than was dreamt of in the highly abstract and sophisticated theories about language that professional linguists are wont to propose every now and then. As we shall see later, the idea that "knowledge of *what*" is sufficient to guarantee "knowledge of *how*" has been one of the most enduring dogmas of rationalist thought and is largely responsible for the widespread belief that applied sciences are eternally dependent on knowledge produced by their "pure" counterparts.

A welcome consequence of the "dethronement" of the native speaker in language teaching was ably summed up by Davies (1989, p. 169) in the following words: "If it is accepted that the native speaker is no longer at the center of communicative competence, then that liberates language teaching because it means that worthwhile goals are suddenly accessible – intermediate goals perhaps, but at least not unlike the knowledge/ability of many native speakers." Davies' use of the term "communicative competence" also testified to a growing dissatisfaction amongst AL practitioners with Chomsky's more abstract and idealized notion. What finally led to disenchantment among language teachers with the Chomskyan paradigm in linguistics was its exaggerated and exclusive emphasis on the *knowledge* of language – or "linguistic competence," as Chomsky called it – to the utter neglect of what the speakers actually do when they put such knowledge to real use in communicating with fellow members of the particular speech community to which they belong. In 1979, Brumfit and Johnson (1979, p. 3) summed up the state of the art when they wrote:

> Linguistics – in Chomsky as in Bloomfield – is by and large the study of language structure. Perhaps this is why transformational grammar, so revolutionary in linguistics, has had such little effect on language teaching. After all, the most it can offer is alternative strategies for teaching grammar – new ways of teaching the same thing.

16.2.3   Post-Chomskyan developments

In the late 1960s, the American anthropologist-cum-linguist Dell Hymes advanced the notion of "communicative competence" in opposition to Chomsky's "linguistic competence." Roughly around the same time, in Britain, Michael Halliday was engaged in elaborating what was later to become known throughout the world as the "systemic-functional linguistic theory." Both

Hymes and Halliday approached language from a broader perspective and claimed that speaking a language was not simply a matter of putting to use an abstract set of rules a speaker has internalized, largely in virtue of an innate endowment called "universal grammar," as Chomsky had insisted. In a seminal paper entitled "Language as social semiotic," Halliday (1974, p. 17) announced a radical departure from Chomsky's more restrictive view of linguistics as a branch of cognitive psychology when he wrote:

> Probably the most significant feature of linguistics in the seventies is that man has come back into the center of the picture. As a species, of course, he was always there; his brain, so the argument ran, has evolved in a certain way – *ergo*, he can talk. But truly speaking man does not talk; *men* talk. People talk to each other; and it is this aspect of man's humanity, largely neglected in the dominant linguistics of the sixties, that has emerged to claim attention once more.

Halliday was referring to an earlier period in the history of linguistics, especially in Britain, when language was studied as "part of the social process" (Firth, 1957, p. 180), anticipating developments in the 1970s and 1980s.

The so-called communicative approach to language teaching was in large measure a response to these developments in linguistics. More and more scholars were being won over to the position that language teaching cannot be reduced to the teaching of grammatical structures. To learn a (second) language successfully is to be able to perform real-life activities with and through it and not simply to internalize a set of grammatical rules. Thus Widdowson (1972, p. 16) proposed a distinction between *signification* and *value*, the former referring to the meaning "which language items have as elements of the language system" and the latter to "that which they have when they are actually put to use in acts of communication." Widdowson went on to argue that, instead of expending their energies on exploring the signification of language items, language teachers should focus on the communicative value of those items, making the students familiar with the specific communicative functions those items have in given situations of actual use. The new emphasis on the functions of language as embodied in so-called notional and functional syllabuses also drew on important work done in the philosophy of language (Austin, 1962; Searle, 1969) that, from 1960s on, had begun to make its impact felt on theoretical linguistics.

Yet, as early as the 1980s, scholars were slowly becoming aware of the fact that the adoption of a theoretical stance was itself no guarantee of success when it came to actual practice in the classroom. Canale (1983, p. 5) for one lamented that the term "communicative competence" had become a buzzword and that "[t]he distinction between communicative competence and actual communication remains poorly understood and, somewhat surprisingly, of marginal interest in the second language field." Newmeyer (1982, p. 97) complained that the term was an unfortunate one in that "it creat[ed] a pernicious ambiguity where none existed previously." Proposals for teaching based on the notion of communicative competence also came under scathing attack from scholars like Swan (1985) who argued that some of the theoretical claims made on their behalf had been largely exaggerated or grossly mistaken. However, the majority of applied linguists did agree on one thing, namely that "[t]he introduction of the notion of communicative competence solved a problem, that of the chilly inadequacy of linguistic competence" (Davies, 1989, p. 157).

Armed with hindsight, one may today put forward the following as a possible explanation for what had apparently gone wrong: One major problem with the way Hymes' concept of "communicative competence" was received by the scholarly community was that it was widely interpreted to mean just another kind of competence. This meant that, far from being understood as a concept advanced in opposition to Chomsky's concept of "linguistic competence" as Hymes had originally intended it to be, it was seen by many as good old Chomskyan competence, duly enriched in order to accommodate considerations about communication and speech community (Taylor, 1988, p. 163). Hymes' own idea of "what is 'possible'," which he offered as a way of describing "linguistic competence" in contradistinction to "what is 'feasible'" as a way of adequately describing his own "communicative competence" (Hymes, 1972), easily lent itself to an interpretation according to which the latter was nothing but a function (in the mathematical sense) of the former or alternatively, the latter was to be derived from the former by taking into account limitations imposed by the condition of feasibility (along much the same lines as Chomsky had taken pains to distinguish "competence" from "performance" – i.e., knowledge of language as opposed to its use in real-life situations). A case in point is the following remark by Johnson (1982, p. 12): "What is communicative competence? Clearly it is something which involves systemic competence – the ability to form grammatically correct sentences. . . . Systemic competence is a part (and a very important part) of communicative competence, whether we are talking about the student learning a foreign language or the child learning its first language."

Such a limited and limiting view of communicative competence evidently came into conflict with a growing body of work done in the tradition of error analysis, in particular on what is referred to as the second language learner's "interlanguage" (Selinker, 1972, 1992; Corder, 1981; Kasper & Blum-Kulka, 1993). Drawing on Weinreich's groundbreaking study on languages in contact (1953), the defenders of the interlanguage hypothesis and its variants argued that learners do construct their own makeshift grammars whose distinctive characteristics include a tendency toward fossilization (when learners stop progressing after having reached a reasonable degree of proficiency in the target language) and overgeneralization of rules. As noted early on by Candlin (1974, p. viii), results from research done in error analysis and on interlanguage "raise issues of validity of the competence/performance distinction." In other words, there was a growing awareness in some quarters that what was urgently needed was not simply to build on a view of language already in place (namely, the generativist conception of language, centered on the knowledge of language as possessed by an ideal speaker), hoping to make it suit the requirements of practical issues such as second language learning and teaching, but to look for ways of breaking new ground, untrammeled by theories that, for all their prestige and penetration, only seemed to stand in the way. In the eyes of many, the need of the hour was a complete overhaul of the theoretical apparatus used so far, not a partial repair or superficial refurbishing.

But the apologists of the theory-first approach to AL – the approach centered on the key belief that applied fields such as AL depended on the prior availability of ready-made theories that were themselves formulated with no concern for their possible application – still managed to hold on to their ground by strategically conceding that such practical matters as language teaching were in general far too complex and multifaceted to be handled by any one theory or, for that matter, any one field of inquiry. Once admitted, such a claim would allow for the possibility that a theory of SLA could still be claimed to be valid and perfectly in order as it is only useful for purposes of language teaching and other practical matters to the extent its lessons are used in conjunction with results from other fields of inquiry (to wit, cognitive science, social psychology, pedagogy, and so forth). Thus it was that, from the 1980s on, more and more researchers in AL were being won over to the idea that theirs was a cross-/multi-/interdisciplinary field.

16.2.4   Coming of age in AL

Initially at least what the claim of interdisciplinarity effectively meant was that AL was from now on to be viewed as a discipline at the meeting point of several other, independently constituted disciplines that did not otherwise communicate to one another. No doubt, the move from a bridge discipline to what now came to be regarded as a crossroads discipline was salutary, inasmuch as it gave expression to a growing perception among AL practitioners that they needed to look to a wider range of disciplines instead of hoping to derive all the theoretical sustenance from theoretical linguistics alone.

Although not many scholars seem to have realized it, there was some irony in the fact that talk of interdisciplinarity, in part at least as a way of getting AL out of its exclusive subservience to its parent discipline, was still in large measure encouraged by developments within mainstream linguistics itself, as well as such kindred areas as cognitive psychology. By the early 1980s, the thesis of modularity of mind, already anticipated in some of Chomsky's earlier writings, had become part of the received wisdom in linguistics, especially within the generative paradigm (Fodor, 1983; Chomsky, 1984). Succinctly put, the thesis of modularity is a claim to the effect that our knowledge of language is modular, that is, made up of distinct sub-systems or modules. For a full understanding of how the mind functions, the contribution of every module is absolutely necessary, although none is sufficient on its own. From modularity as a thesis in the philosophy of mind to interdisciplinarity as a claim in the philosophy of AL it was but a small step.

It is because of this somewhat timid and rather conciliatory nature of the thesis of interdisciplinarity that the idea of transdisciplinarity, which replaced it in the 1990s, is philosophically significant in the history of the evolution of AL as an autonomous discipline. We shall look into the full implications of this development in the next section.

16.3   The Status of AL as a Science

16.3.1   *The road to autonomy*

We have already seen that, in its early stages, AL flourished in the shadow of theoretical or general linguistics. The very name of the burgeoning field, as well as its self-assumed status as a sub-discipline, underscored the prevailing mood among its practitioners that they only stood to gain by association, albeit one of subservience, with their colleagues on the theoretical side of the divide constantly providing them with the theoretical anchorage that they so badly needed lest their own reflections should be seen as going adrift with no principle or sense of direction.

But it is important to point out that even as early as the early 1970s there were some scholars who felt that the relation between AL and its parent discipline should not be thought of in such straightforward or totally unproblematic terms. Wilkins went as far as conceding that "[f]or the teacher's practical purposes there may not be much in a linguist's description that he did not already know" and "[w]hat seems good linguistics might turn out to be bad psychology" (Wilkins, 1972, pp. 3, 216). But he stopped short of dismissing the usefulness of linguistics to the language teacher. Thus, the last two sentences of his book read as follows: "It is possible that linguistics is not even one of the most important elements in the preparation of a language teacher. The value of linguistics is that, by increasing his awareness of language, it makes him more competent and therefore a better language teacher" (Wilkins, 1972, p. 229).

"Linguistics," wrote Widdowson (1979, p. 215), "stands in need of interpretation," proceeding to explain his claim saying "linguistics . . . requires the mediation of an interpreter for its potential usefulness to language teacher to be realized" (p. 217). In Widdowson's view, the process by which such mediation was to be achieved was "one of adaptation" which would consist in "the selection of insights from the whole range of theoretical and descriptive studies of language, stripping them of their formal integuments where these are cumbersome" (p. 217). In other words, AL was to be, from now on, viewed as essentially a "bridge" or "link" discipline, serving as an intermediary between linguists and language teachers (and all others working at the applied end of the chain).

What these and several other remarks by the leading applied linguists of that period reveal is that a certain consensus was beginning to emerge among scholars with regard to the importance and relevance of theoretical linguistics to those who work in AL. In the words of Brumfit (1980, p. 161): "if AL were to be considered *merely* the application of linguistics to anything to which it could be applied, then it would be no more than a mirror for linguists to peer into – for the only issues which linguists can confront are linguistic issues, not applied ones." There was a general perception that insights borrowed from the parent discipline did not on their own guarantee success in the SL classroom. Some empirical studies such as an ambitious survey referred to in the literature as the "Pennsylvania Project," designed to test the efficacy of teaching methods inspired by work in theoretical linguistics, turned out exactly the opposite results, to the utter dismay and disappointment of the researchers involved (Diller, 1971). While, no doubt, scholars were cautious enough not to jump to precipitate conclusions, these studies did help fuel the already growing suspicion that uncritical transfer of insights from theoretical linguistics to applied domains such as language teaching could no longer be justified.

Yet the earliest reactions from scholars in AL were rather timid and betrayed a somewhat ambivalent attitude toward the parent discipline. Most were reluctant to announce anything like a total break with linguistics. But they also felt that it was no longer possible to tie the fortunes of AL to the whims and fancies of those who did "pure" research and the new models of grammatical analysis they came up with every once in a while. Spolsky (1970, p. 145) expressed the prevailing mood when he suggested that the term AL itself was partly to blame: "The term 'applied linguistics' is not particularly a happy one: in one way, it is too broad, failing to suggest what linguistics is applied to; in another, it suggests a level of practicality that lacks the dignity of 'pure linguistics'." Although Spolsky himself did not plead for a break with linguistics, which he felt had a lot to contribute to AL, he did suggest "educational linguistics" as an alternative designation for the field (Spolsky, 1978). To judge by its continued acceptance by others over the following several years (cf. Stubbs, 1986; van Lier, 1994), the term did enjoy a fairly respectable lease of life. In van Lier's words "the linguistics in AL has veered off in the direction of theory (in a sense, therefore, has left AL), leaving pedagogy to cope with the practical side of things" (van Lier, 1994, p. 203). But, if the original term was too broad, as Spolsky alleged, one might equally well object that its substitute is too narrow and excludes a number of other areas – to wit, translation, lexicography, bi- (or multi-) lingualism, speech pathology, forensic analysis of texts, literacy, language planning, language teacher education, and so forth – which one would want to see under the rubric of AL.

Be that as it may, the time was now ripe for AL researchers to declare the autonomy of their discipline. As Edge (1989, p. 407) put it: "As far as English language teaching is concerned, AL may be seen to have grown out of a desire to liberate language teaching from an intellectual subservience to linguistics." That such a decisive move did send some alarm signals to many scholars in mainstream linguistics is evidenced by early admonitions from researchers like Newmeyer (1982) who urged that AL still had a lot to gain from linguistics, its principal if not sole feeder discipline until then.

16.3.2   Signs of maturity

From the perspective of philosophy of science, what the declaration of AL's autonomy meant was that researchers recognized the need to turn to disciplines such as sociology, anthropology, education, cognitive science, and so forth in addition to linguistics in order to formulate their own theoretical frameworks suited to their applied goals. In other words, AL was slowly being transformed into an *interdisciplinary* field, which was no longer exclusively tied to developments in theoretical linguistics. This was indeed a far cry from an earlier attitude best summed up in Corder's famous dictum: "The applied linguist is a consumer, or user, not a producer, of theories" (1973, p. 10). However, there were skeptics too who saw in the new development a claim to the effect that "language teachers should not rely on linguistics to inform its practice" (Flynn, 1991) – which it by no means was. It is noteworthy that even nearly a decade after talk of interdisciplinarity had become common currency in AL, Phillipson (1992, p. 256) could still complain: "AL drew heavily on linguistics, and only lightly on education, cultural theory, sociology, international relations etc. This still appears to be the case."

The 1990s were however marked by a growing awareness of the need to conceive of AL as a *trans*disciplinary field of inquiry. This meant traversing (and, if it comes to the push, *transgressing*) conventional disciplinary boundaries in order to develop a brand new research agenda which, while freely drawing on a wide variety of disciplines, would obstinately seek to remain subaltern to none. The move from interdisciplinarity to transdisciplinarity highlights, in addition, a growing awareness on the part of AL practitioners that it was not enough to look for inspiration in a number of neighboring disciplines. The challenge to AL, as Fairclough (1997, p. 4) put it, "is to reshape its tradition in engaging with and trying to 'operationalize' new thinking about language – including post-structuralist and postmodernist thinking – *in new ways of analyzing language*" (emphasis added).

Rampton (1995, p. 233) has observed that there is a clearly discernible tendency in AL, especially in Great Britain, to move away from the influence of linguistics, pedagogy, and psychology to areas such as sociology, anthropology, media studies, and so forth as the source of inspiration and fresh ideas. Writing specifically about the teaching of English as an international language, McKay (2002, p. 128) emphasizes the need for being "culturally sensitive to the diversity of contexts in which English is taught and used." Rampton's sharp criticism of the notion of native speakerhood and its implications for teaching English as a foreign language (Rampton, 1990) and Cook's idea of "multi-competent language users" (Cook, 1999) give us a clue as to how far scholars are willing to go after relinquishing wisdom inherited from mainstream theoretical linguistics in order to attend to the new realities that have come into existence as a result of large-scale migratory movements across the globe and the resultant cultural intermixing currently taking place at an unprecedented level. If these developments are any clear indication, one could hazard the guess that AL is on the verge of a major paradigm shift in the sense of Kuhn (1962).

16.3.3   Neo-empiricist turn

From the perspective of philosophy of science, there can be little doubt that AL is currently going through some radical changes. Worth special mention in this regard is the emergence of corpus linguistics. Interested in looking at the use of language in real-life situations and arriving at inductive generalizations concerning tendencies in progress, corpus linguistics may be seen as a fine example of the empiricism that has been the hallmark of British thought. Small wonder, therefore, that it is in Great Britain that corpus linguistics is today most robustly consolidated as a research program with significant results already made available to the scholarly community and promises of more in the pipeline (Aimer & Altenberg, 1991; McEnery & Wilson, 1996; Biber, Conrad, & Reppen, 1998).

What corpus linguistics produces are snapshots of language in a constant process of evolution. Rather than purport to capture the putative "essence" of, say, word meanings, its findings point to statistical tendencies of collocation, colligation, and so on, which are subject to constant change and are thus by definition unstable. In lexicography, which is one area that stands to benefit directly from work done in corpus linguistics, this new development has meant a corresponding diminution of the importance of lexicology understood as a branch of intensional lexical semantics (semantics of word meanings explicated in terms of language-internal relations). The thoroughly applied nature of lexicography was highlighted by Hartmann (1981, p. 297) when he affirmed "that lexicography is linguistics applied hardly needs debating, but we should try to argue and possibly agree on what kind of linguistic (and non-linguistic) knowledge the dictionary compiler draws and what purpose he hopes to serve."

Corpus linguistics entails an entirely new approach not only to lexicography (Sinclair, 1987), but to every other realm of practical concern to which its findings are applied. It is true of even grammar, considered the *pièce de résistance* of modern linguistics ever since the Chomskyan revolution (Sinclair, 1990). An early breakthrough was signaled by the publication of the landmark book *A Comprehensive Grammar of the English Language* (Quirk et al., 1985), based on a corpus of data manually assembled by a team of experts under the pioneering leadership of Sir Randolph Quirk from 1953 on.

It is important to register that the history of corpus linguistics provides some crucial evidence as to how advances in theoretical linguistics have not always necessarily been salutary to developments in AL. For, if anything, the advent of generative linguistics in the late 1950s actually put a damper on work in corpus linguistics, whose practitioners could only go full steam ahead with their project after it had become clear that the Chomskyan paradigm was itself of limited relevance as far as practical affairs involving language (such as language teaching) were concerned and also after computer technology had become sophisticated enough to perform the kind of laborious tasks that needed to be undertaken at a fraction of the time it would otherwise take.

It is interesting at this juncture to recall that, when some two decades ago Strevens (1980) defined AL as "what applied linguists do," not everyone thought that such a definition went a long way toward explaining what AL was about. According to Evensen (1997, p. 35), the author even "earned considerable ridicule." What Strevens' detractors failed to realize was that he was simply being faithful to that long tradition of British empiricism and sober, down-to-earth sense of practicality of which Moore's gesture (mentioned at the outset of this chapter) of pointing at his bookshelves in response to a request for a definition of philosophy is a fine example. Empiricism in this sense is thoroughly opposed to the "theory-first" attitude that characterizes much of Continental rationalism which in turn harks back to the "definition-first" attitude reflected in the notoriously annoying insistence by the Socrates of Plato's earlier dialogues that one can be said to know what x is all about just in case one is able to provide a definition for x beforehand.

The neo-empiricist swing in AL today is an unmistakable and, from the looks of it, irreversible trend – at least as far the foreseeable future is concerned. As more and more AL scholars are becoming convinced that the theory-first approach has only stood in the way of real progress in the field, there has been an increasing concern with thinking of new ways to bring theory and practice closer together. As we have already seen, perhaps nowhere else is the interest in practice as a pretext for doing theory more evident than in SLA. This has prompted many applied linguists to demand a thorough rethinking of past attempts to make theory and practice mesh with each other. Thus, in response to the claim made by Gregg (1989, p. 15) that "[t]he ultimate goal of SLA is the development of a *theory* of SLA" (emphasis added), van Lier (1991, p. 78) contends that such a position in medicine would lead to "statements such as 'The ultimate goal of AIDS research is the development of a theory of AIDS' rather than the understanding of the disease and its prevention." On his part, Gregg (1993) remains unrepentant and continues to insist that without a proper theory of the disease no cure would be forthcoming. On the strength of his conviction that "theoretical linguistics is currently in a stagnation of crisis proportions," de Beaugrande (1997, p. 279) has argued that the applicability of a theory to actual practice should be one of the criteria to be used for judging the very validity of that theory. Evensen (1997, p. 39) points to "a fundamental dialectic between applied and basic research which still remains to be properly understood." Among recent attempts to address the issue is that of Davies (1989) who makes a convincing case for foregrounding reflective personal experience while "doing being applied linguists."

16.4   Some Philosophical Issues Arising from AL

16.4.1   *The ethical question*

Of particular significance in the recent history of AL is the growing interest among scholars in the ethical implications of work done in the field. Now, there is a long and respectable tradition in western thought according to which ethical considerations are to be made at the level of practical reasoning, leaving pure theory entirely free from them. It is grounded on the assumption that pure knowledge knows no ethics, which only makes its presence felt when one is dealing with human action and agency. In philosophy, this tradition often asserts itself in the form of an injunction, discussed at some length by David Hume, against attempting to derive moral conclusions (such-and-such *ought* to be the case) from factual premises (such-and-such *is* the case) or vice versa. In his *Principia Ethica*, Moore was to condemn the non-observance of the distinction between "facts" and "values" as the *naturalistic fallacy*. It is hardly surprising therefore that theoretically oriented linguists have typically tended to shy away from the ethical considerations arising out of their work. When asked if there were any possible links between his scientific writings and his political activities, Chomsky (1977, p. 3) categorically denied that there was any "direct connection" between the two.

Given its early self-image as an activity rather than a field of theoretical inquiry (Corder, 1973, p. 10), one would expect that AL is the privileged space for raising ethical issues which it no doubt is. In fact many on the theoretical side of the divide appear to be perfectly happy to leave ethical issues to the care of those concerned with applied matters. But recent research in AL indicates that any such complacence may be misguided. It is increasingly becoming clear that work done in AL can have important implications for mainstream theoretical linguistics. That is to say, theory may have important lessons to learn from practice. Corpus linguistics is a case in point. As Halliday (1993, p. 1) has remarked:

> Work based on corpus studies has already begun to modify our thinking about lexis, about patterns in the vocabulary of languages; and it is now beginning to impact on our ideas about grammar. In my view, this impact is likely to be entirely beneficial. Corpus linguistics brings a powerful new resource into our theoretical investigations of language.

The emergence in the last two decades or so of what is variously referred to as "critical linguistics" (Fowler and Kress, 1979; Hodge and Kress, 1979), "linguistic criticism" (Fowler, 1986), "critical language awareness" (Fairclough, 1992), "critical discourse analysis" (Fairclough, 1989, 1995; Cameron et al., 1992) or "critical applied linguistics" (Pennycook, 2001) may be viewed as a major development in this regard inasmuch as it goes against the time-honored tradition of keeping ethical questions at bay while doing science. In fact, what these scholars have demonstrated is that the very line separating theory and practice is blurred. Today, more and more researchers are actively engaged in critically examining practices that for long seemed exempt from ideological or political connotations. A case in point is language testing. Scholars are increasingly becoming aware of the important consequences of testing on language teaching and learning – the so-called "washback" effect (Davies, 1990). More recently, Shohamy (2001) has made a compelling case for her thesis that tests are not isolated events, nor for that matter events that unproblematically partake of the process of language teaching/learning, but are embedded in wider contexts brimming over with social, political, and ideological meanings.

Central to the critical orientation is the conviction on the part of its advocates that linguistic analysis ought to move beyond the mere discovery of the structural configurations in given texts to uncovering the ideological forces that help maintain those structures and in so doing contribute to correcting historically instituted social injustices and pave the way for the emancipation of those on the seamy side of the social order. To achieve this, critical linguists undertake a thorough ideology critique, for their point of departure is the claim that all texts are shot through with ideological connotations. In this sense, contemporary critical turn in AL is heir to the so-called Critical Theory that became the hallmark of the *Institut für Sozialforschung* (Institute for Social Research), better known as the Frankfurt School, founded in the wake of World War I. The working motto of critical theorists is summed up in Horkheimer's celebrated observation that, unlike traditional theory which consisted in "the sum-total of propositions on a subject, the propositions being so linked that a few are basic and the rest derive from there," critical theory is "the unfolding of a single existential judgment," namely, "that it need not be so; man can change reality" (Horkheimer, 1972).

The philosophical significance of the critical turn in AL can hardly be overestimated. Following a tradition going back to Kant, Hegel, and Marx, among others, critical theorists are intent on bridging the proverbial gap between theory and practice. Instead of treating the latter as a mere handmaiden to the former, they endeavor to bring the weight of dialectical thinking to bear on the task of coordinating theory and practice. In the context of AL, this has meant rethinking the very relation between linguistic theory and the various practices involving language. There is an emerging consensus that theory with no practical goal is just as worthless as practice devoid of solid theoretical foundation.

Assuming a Foucauldian perspective, Cameron et al. (1992) insist that social science is never neutral or value-free and that, thanks to the inevitable interplay of knowledge and power, social science research helps constitute distinctive "regimes of truth" which in turn help legitimate certain social prejudices and stereotypes by creating classificatory grids like "criminality," "sexual deviance," and "teenage motherhood." In other words, the construction of theories is itself a form of social practice (Cameron, 1994).

Rampton (1997) argues that the key to an appreciation of the critical role of theorists is the recognition of their "situatedness." In his words, "researchers can't help being socially located, with biographies and subjectivities that are brought to bear at every stage of the research process, influencing in some form or another the questions they ask and the way they try to find the answers" (p. 11).

16.4.2   The road ahead

There is still a long way to go and many stubborn resistances (cf. Widdowson, 2000) to be overcome. As Corson (1997, p. 167) puts it:

> AL began to flourish well before any hermeneutic, critical, or postmodern epistemology had become influential in setting the course for inquiry in the human sciences . . . Although many applied linguists are deeply involved with issues of human emancipation, these interests have been rather muted and have had little abiding impact on AL generally. This is especially true of its central language teaching functions . . . Indeed, just this perception that "language teaching" is its central function, may have distorted the epistemological foundations of AL in general.

Still, if one may hazard a guess, the critical orientation of AL is here to stay. And, from the looks of it, it is now the turn of theoretical linguistics to be influenced by these exciting new developments in the applied domain – thus fulfilling, who knows, what was always already its destiny (Rajagopalan, 1999). No doubt, there are immense challenges ahead, not the least urgent of which is the threat posed by globalization to local cultures and regional and minority languages (Celani, 2000). The following words by Martin (2000, pp. 123–4) may be seen as providing a fitting conclusion to this chapter:

> Developing an adaptive framework for AL is one great challenge for a new millennium! The other great challenge, along with keeping their own house in order, is that applied linguists will have the job of resuscitating linguistics as a discipline – one with a more socially responsible role to play in a post-colonial, post-modern world.

See also 14 Language and Politics, 17 The Native Speaker in Applied Linguistics, 19 Research Methods for Applied Linguistics, 20 Second Language Learning, 24 Fashions in Language Teaching Methodology, 26 Language Teacher Education, 32 Critical Applied Linguistics.

ACKNOWLEDGMENTS

Thanks are due to Maria Antonieta Alba Celani, and Luiz Paulo da Moita Lopes for helpful comments.

REFERENCES

Aijmer, K. & Altenberg, B. (eds.) (1991) *English corpus linguistics. studies in honour of Jan Svartvik.* London: Longman.

Allen, J. P. B. & Corder, S. P. (1975). Editors' preface. In J. P. B Allen & S. P. Corder (eds.), *Papers in applied linguistics. The Edinburgh course in applied linguistics* (vol. 2) (pp. xi–xii). Oxford: Oxford University Press.

Austin, J. L. (1962) *How to do things with words.* Oxford: Clarendon Press.

Beaugrande, R. de (1997) Theory and practice in applied linguistics: disconnection, conflict, or dialectic? *Applied Linguistics,* 18, 279–313.

Biber, D., Conrad, S., & Reppen, R. (1998) *Corpus linguistics: investigating language structure and use.* Cambridge: Cambridge University Press.

Brumfit, C. J. (1980) Being interdisciplinary – some problems facing applied linguistics. *Applied Linguistics,* 1, 158–64.

Brumfit, C. J. & Johnson, K. (1979) *The communicative approach to language teaching.* Oxford: Oxford University Press.

Cameron, D. (1994) Putting our practice into theory. In D. Graddol. & J. Swann (eds.), *Evaluating Language* (pp. 15–23). Clevedon, UK: Multilingual Matters/BAAL.

Cameron, D., Frazer, E., Harvey, P., Rampton, B., & Richardson, K. (1992) *Researching language: issues of power and method.* London: Routledge.

Canale, M. (1983) From communicative competence to communicative language pedagogy. In J. C. Richards & R. W. Schmidt (eds.), *Language and communication* (pp. 2–27). London: Longman.

Candlin, C. (1974) Preface. In J. C. Richards (ed.), *Error analysis:*

perspectives on second language acquisition (pp. viii–x). London: Longman.

Celani, M. A. A. (2000) "You've snatched the carpet from under my feet"; courses as contexts for change in in-service language teacher education. In AILA 1999 Tokyo Organizing Committee (eds.), *Selected papers from AILA '99* (pp. 242–58). Tokyo: Waseda University Press.

Chomsky, N. A. (1966). Linguistic theory. Language teaching: broader contexts. In *Report of NE conference on the teaching of foreign languages* (pp. 43–9). Wisconsin.

Chomsky, N. A. (1977) *Language and responsibility.* New York: Pantheon Books.

Chomsky, N. A. (1984) *Modular approaches to the study of mind.* San Diego: San Diego State University Press.

Cook, V. J. (1985) Chomsky's universal grammar and second language learning. *Applied Linguistics,* 6, 2–18.

Cook, V. J. (1994) Universal grammar and the learning and teaching of second languages. In T. Odlin (ed.), *Perspectives on pedagogical grammar* (pp. 25–48). Cambridge: Cambridge University Press.

Cook, V. J. (1999) Using SLA research in language teaching. *International Journal of Applied Linguistics,* 9(2), 267–84.

Corder, S. P. (1967) The significance of learner's errors. *International Review of Applied Linguistics,* 9, 147–59.

Corder, S. P. (1973) *Introducing applied linguistics.* Harmondsworth: Penguin.

Corder, S. P. (1975) Applied linguistics and language teaching. In J. P. B. Allen & S. P. Corder (eds.), *Papers in applied linguistics. The Edinburgh course in applied linguistics* (vol. 2) (pp. 1–15). Oxford: Oxford University Press.

Corder, S. P. (1981) *Error analysis and interlanguage*. Oxford: Oxford University Press.

Corson, D. (1997) Critical realism: an emancipatory philosophy for applied linguistics? *Applied Linguistics*, 18(2), 166–87.

Davies, A. (1989) Communicative competence as language use. *Applied Linguistics*, 10, 157–70.

Davies, A. (1990) *Principles of language testing*. Oxford: Blackwell.

Diller, K. C. (1971) *Generative grammar, structural linguistics, and language learning*. Rowley, MA: Newbury House.

Dulay, H. & Burt, M. (1974) A new perspective in the creative construction process in child second language acquisition. *Language Learning*, 24, 253–78.

Edge, J. (1989) Ablocutionary value: on the application of language teaching to linguistics. *Applied Linguistics*, 10, 407–17.

Edge, J. (1993) The dance of Shiva and the linguistics of relativity. *Applied Linguistics*, 14, 43–55.

Evensen, L. (1997) Applied linguistics within a principled framework for characterizing disciplines and transdisciplines. *AILA Review*, 12, 31–41.

Fairclough, N. (1989) *Language and Power*. London: Longman.

Fairclough, N. (ed.) (1992) *Critical language awareness*. London: Longman.

Fairclough, N. (1995) *Critical discourse analysis*. London: Longman.

Fairclough, N. (1997) Discourse across disciplines: discourse analysis in researching social change. *AILA Review*, 12, 3–17.

Ferguson, C. (1983) Language planning and language change. In J. Cobarrubias & J. Fishman (eds.), *Progress in language planning* (pp. i–xii). Berlin: Mouton.

Firth, J. R. (1957) Personality and language in society. In J. R. Firth (ed.), *Papers in linguistics 1934–1951* (pp. 180–7). Oxford: Oxford University Press.

Flynn, S. (1991) The relevance of linguistic theory for language pedagogy: debunking the myths. In J. E. Alatis (ed.), *Georgetown University roundtable on language and linguistics* (pp. 18–32). Washington, DC: Georgetown University Press.

Fodor, J. A. (1983) *The modularity of mind*. Cambridge, MA: MIT Press.

Fowler, R. (1986) *Linguistic criticism*. London: Oxford University Press.

Fowler, R. & Kress, G. (1979) Critical linguistics. In R. Fowler, R. Hodge, G. Kress, and T. Trew (eds.), *Language and control* (pp. 54–69). London: Routledge & Kegan Paul.

Giddens, A. (1995) *Politics, sociology, and social history*. Palo Alto: Stanford University Press.

Gregg, K. R. (1989) Second language acquisition theory: the case for a generative perspective. In S. M. Gass & J. Schachter (eds.), *Linguistic perspectives on second language acquisition* (pp. 69–78). Cambridge: Cambridge University Press.

Gregg, K. R. (1993) Taking explanation seriously; or, let a couple of flowers bloom. *Applied Linguistics*, 14, 276–94.

Gregg, K. R. (1996) The logical and developmental problems of second language acquisition. In W. C. Ritchie & T. K. Bhatia (eds.), *Handbook of second language acquisition* (pp. 50–81). New York: Academic Press.

Halliday, M. A. K. (1974) Language as social semiotic: towards a general sociolinguistic theory. In A. Makkai & V. B. Makkai (eds.), *The first LACUS forum 1974* (pp. 17–46). Columbia, SC: Hornbeam Press.

Halliday, M. A. K. (1993) Quantitative studies and probabilities in grammar. In M. Hoey (ed.), *Data, description, discourse: papers on the English language in honour of John McH Sinclair* (pp. 1–25). London: HarperCollins.

Halliday, M. A. K., McIntosh, A. & Strevens, P. (1964) *The linguistic sciences and language teaching*. London: Longman.

Hartmann, R. (1981) Dictionary, learners, users. Some issues in lexicography. *Applied Linguistics*, 2, 297–303.

Hodge, R. & Kress, G. (1979) *Language as ideology*. London: Routledge.

Holliday, A. (1996) Developing a sociological imagination: expanding ethnography in international English language education. *Applied Linguistics*, 17, 234–55.

Horkheimer, M. (1972) Traditional and critical theory. In M. Horkheimer (ed.), *Critical theory: selected essays* (pp. 99–102). New York: Herder & Herder.

Howatt, A. P. R. (1984) *History of English language teaching*. Oxford: Oxford University Press.

Hymes, D. (1972) On communicative competence. In J. B. Pride & J. Holmes (eds.), *Sociolinguistics* (pp. 269–85). Harmondsworth: Penguin.

Johnson, K. (1982) *Communicative syllabus design and methodology*. Oxford: Pergamon Press.

Kasper, G. & Blum-Kulka, S. (1993) *Interlanguage pragmatics*. Oxford: Oxford University Press.

Krashen, S. (1981) *Second language learning and second language acquisition*. Oxford: Pergamon Press.

Krashen, S. (1985) *The Input Hypothesis: issues and implications*. New York: Longman.

Kuhn, T. (1962) *The structure of scientific revolutions* (2nd enlarged edn.). Chicago: University of Chicago Press.

Lado, R. (1964) *Language teaching: a scientific approach*. New York: McGraw-Hill.

Lado, R. & Fries, C. C. (1943) *English pattern practices*. Ann Arbor: The University of Michigan Press.

Larsen-Freeman, D. (2000) Second language acquisition and applied linguistics. *Annual Review of Applied Linguistics*, 20, 165–81.

Lyons, J. (1968) *Introduction to theoretical linguistics*. Cambridge: Cambridge University Press.

Mackey, W. (1966) Applied linguistics: its meaning and use. *English Language Teaching*, 22, 261–74.

Martin, J. R. (2000) Design and practice: enacting functional linguistics. *Annual Review of Applied Linguistics*, 20, 116–26.

McEnery, T. & Wilson, A. (1996) *Corpus linguistics*. Edinburgh: Edinburgh University Press.

McKay, S. L. (2002) *Teaching English as an international language*. Oxford: Oxford University Press.

Newmeyer, F. J. (1982) On the applicability of transformational-generative grammar. *Applied Linguistics*, 8, 89–120.

Newmeyer, F. J. (1987) The current convergence in linguistic theory: some implications for second language acquisition research. *Second Language Research*, 3, 1–19.

Newmeyer, F. J. & Emonds, J. (1971) The linguist in American society. *Papers from 7th Regional Meeting, Chicago Linguistic Society* (pp. 285–303).

Newmeyer, F. J. & Weinberger, S. H. (1988) The ontogenesis of the field of second language learning research. In S. Flynn & D. O'Neil (eds.), *Linguistic theory in second language acquisition* (pp. 34–45). Dordrecht: Kluwer.

Nida, E. A. (1969) Science of translation. In A. S. Dil (ed.) (1975) *Linguistic structure and translation* (pp. 79–101). Stanford: Stanford University Press.

Pennycook, A. (2001) *Critical applied linguistics: a critical introduction*. Mahwah, NJ: Lawrence Erlbaum.

Phillipson, R. (1992) *Linguistic imperialism*. Oxford: Oxford University Press.

Quirk, R., Svartvik, J., Leech, G., & Greenbaum, S. (1985) *A comprehensive grammar of the English language*. London: Longman.

Rajagopalan, K. (1997) Linguistics and the myth of nativity: comments on the controversy over "new/non-native" Englishes. *Journal of Pragmatics, 27,* 225–31.

Rajagopalan, K. (1999) Tuning up amidst the din of discordant notes: on a recent bout of identity crisis in applied linguistics. *International Journal of Applied Linguistics, 9,* 99–119.

Rampton, M. B. H. (1990) Displacing the native speaker: expertise, affiliation, and inheritance. *ELT Journal, 44,* 97–101.

Rampton, M. B. H. (1995) Politics and change in research in applied linguistics. *Applied Linguistics, 16,* 233–56.

Rampton, M. B. H. (1997) Retuning in applied linguistics. *International Journal of Applied Linguistics, 7,* 3–25.

Richards, J. (1974) *Error analysis: perspectives on second language acquisition*. London: Longman.

Richie, W. C. & Bhatia, T. K. (1996) Second language acquisition: introduction, foundations, and overview. In W. C. Ritiche & T. K. Bhatia (eds.), *Handbook of second language acquisition* (pp. 1–46). New York: Academic Press.

Robins, R. H. (1967) *A short history of linguistics*. London: Longman.

Schachter, J. (1988) Second language acquisition and its relation to universal grammar. *Applied Linguistics, 9,* 219–35.

Searle, J. R. (1969) *Speech acts: an essay in the philosophy of language*. Cambridge: Cambridge University Press.

Selinker, L. (1972) Interlanguage. *IRAL, 10,* 147–63.

Selinker, L. (1992) *Rediscovering interlanguage*. London: Longman.

Shohamy, E. (2001) *The power of tests: a critical perspective on the uses of language tests*. London: Longman.

Sinclair, J. (1987) *Collins COBUILD English language dictionary*. London: HarperCollins.

Sinclair, J. (1990) *Collins COBUILD English language grammar*. London: HarperCollins.

Spolsky, B. (1970) Linguistics and language pedagogy – applications or implications? In J. E. Alatis (ed.), *Linguistics and the teaching of English to speakers of other languages or dialects* (pp. 143–53). Washington, DC: Georgetown University Press.

Spolsky, B. (1978) *Educational linguistics: an introduction*. Rowley, MA: Newbury Press.

Strevens, P. (1980) Who are applied linguists and what do they do? In R. B. Kaplan (ed.), *A British point of view: upon the establishment of AAAL* (pp. 17–20). Rowley, MA: Newbury House.

Stubbs, M. (1986) *Educational linguistics*. Oxford: Blackwell.

Swan, M. (1985) A critical look at the communicative approach (parts 1 & 2). *ELT Journal, 39*(2–12), 76–87.

Taylor, D. S. (1988) The meaning and use of the term "competence" in linguistics and applied linguistics. *Applied Linguistics, 9,* 148–68.

van Els, T., Bongaerts, T., Extra, G., van Os, C. & Jansen-van Dieten, A.-M. (1984) *Applied linguistics and the learning and teaching of foreign languages*. London: Edward Arnold.

van Lier, L. (1991) Doing applied linguistics: towards a theory of practice. *Issues in Applied Linguistics, 28,* 78–81.

van Lier, L. (1994) Educational linguistics: field and project. In J. E. Alatis (ed.), *Georgetown University round table on language and linguistics* (pp. 199–209). Washington, DC: Georgetown University Press.

Weinreich, U. (1953) *Languages in contact.* Publication of the Linguistic Circle of New York, no. 1.

Widdowson, H. G. (1972) Teaching of English as communication. *The ELT Journal,* 27(1), 15–19.

Widdowson, H. G. (1979) *Explorations in applied linguistics.* Oxford: Oxford University Press.

Widdowson, H. G. (2000) On the limitations of linguistics applied. *Applied Linguistics,* 21, 3–25.

Wilkins, D. A. (1972) *Linguistics in language teaching.* London: Edward Arnold.

FURTHER READING

Davies, A. (1999) *An introduction to applied linguistics: from practice to theory.* Edinburgh: Edinburgh University Press.

Dinneen, F. B. (ed.) (1974) *Linguistics, teaching and interdisciplinary relations.* Washington, DC: Georgetown University Press.

Kaplan, R. B. (ed.) (1980) *On the scope of applied linguistics.* Rowley, MA: Newbury House.

Wilkins, D. (1994) Applied linguistics. In R. E. Asher (ed.), *The encyclopedia of language and linguistics* (vol. 1) (pp. 162–72). Oxford: Pergamon Press.

Part II
Applied-Linguistics (A-L)

Introduction to Part II: Applied Linguistics (A-L)

CATHERINE ELDER

As with the first part of this volume, we have organized the 16 chapters in this A-L component of the volume on a cline, this time, in the opposite direction starting from what we have classed as "weak" A-L (i.e., drawing on multiple disciplinary sources often including linguistics; concerned to some extent with practical issues but not ameliorative in its goals) and moving toward "strong" A-L (again transdisciplinary, but concerned little if at all with linguistics and focused predominantly on corrective action or praxis) at the end. Putting both parts of the volume together this can also be viewed as moving from the most linguistic – Chapter 1 – to least linguistic – Chapter 32. There are five sections divided as follows.

Section 7 contains three chapters linked to one another by virtue of their concern with the problem of definition and categorization. These chapters draw together different disciplinary strands to create taxonomies or frameworks which explain phenomena central to work in applied linguistics: the native speaker (in a chapter by Alan Davies), language minorities (by John Edwards), and research methodology (by JD Brown). There would certainly be a case for putting the Edwards and Davies chapters in Section 3 of the L-A bundle, since both explore the connection between speakers and their language, but each of these authors expressly frames his contribution in terms of its applicability to other A-L research efforts.

Davies opens his chapter with the question "How useful is the concept of native speaker to applied linguistics?" and offers definitions of the concept from both sociolinguistic (native speaker as user) and psycholinguistic (native speaker as font of knowledge) perspectives. He draws on these definitions to deconstruct and illuminate discussions of such issues as linguistic imperialism, the status of world Englishes and their speakers, and the validity of non-native models as standards for English teaching, arguing that all of them boil down to the question of identity, or that sense of self which "is closely associated with the power that being a native speaker gives." Disagreement about these issues stems, in his view, from different interpretations of the native speaker concept which functions as both "metaphor and embodiment of the language-parole and of the competence-performance distinctions."

Any investigation of minority groups and languages is, as John Edwards points out, a central theme for a number of disciplines – he includes sociology, political science, and social philosophy on his list. All are concerned with what constitutes groupness, with notions of pluralism, and with the problems posed by inter- and intragroup tensions. Edwards, like Davies, links the A-L study of minority groups to issues of identity which, he argues, are at the heart of any investigation concerned with the social life of language. He sees language minorities as a special case of the social, worthy of attention because of their fragility, but also because their group dynamics offer information which is generalizable to the larger applied linguistic enterprise. His chapter deals at the outset with issues of definition and categorization, highlighting the importance of both geographical and temporal dimensions as well as structural relations in making distinctions between majority/minority and indigeneous/immigrant groups. Edwards offers his tentative typology of minority language situations not as an explanatory model of social behavior, as would a linguist concerned with building a theory, but as a kind of checklist which other researchers can use to locate their particular activities within a broader research context.

JD Brown has in common with the previous two authors his desire to impose some kind of external order on a very broad field of enquiry. Research in A-L, as he defines it, is united only by a common interest in language related problems and comprises an extraordinarily diverse range of investigations embracing multiple methods of enquiry. What this chapter does is to sketch the parameters of this diversity, with the aim of assisting applied linguists to locate their endeavors at one or other point on the various continua he identifies (quantitative/qualitative, interventionist/non-interventionist and so on) and to ensure optimum fit between the approach they adopt and the relevant institutional context. In the absence of any unity of approach (of the kind that one might find in certain areas of L-A), what becomes important is a set of standards or principles against which this highly amorphous field can be held accountable. Ethics, he says, "is an area where all research methods and techniques come together and tend to agree."

The four chapters in Section 8 (by Littlewood, Ellis, Barkhuizen, and Williams respectively) share a common concern with language learning, although in the case of Williams' chapter on literacy studies, the process of learning to read and write is only one of a range of issues he engages with. The considerable weight given in this volume to language learning (and even more so to language teaching – see Section 9) was dictated by its status as one of the most central and commonly investigated issues or "problems" in applied linguistics. Language learning is here located toward the weak end of the A-L continuum, both because it continues to rely at least partly on linguistic description and because it does not necessarily involve institutional intervention.

William Littlewood's chapter frames second language learning in practical terms: his fundamental purpose is to explain the phenomenon in the interests of improving the learning outcomes and, where relevant, enhancing the effectiveness of teaching. Explanations of language learning, as Littlewood points out, range widely, some invoking general learning principles derived from educational psychology and sociology and others focusing on language itself. Littlewood sketches some of the major processes involved in acquisition (transference, generalization, simplification, and imitation) and some typical developmental sequences. In addition, alongside these linguistically-oriented accounts, he looks more globally at a number of cognitive and contextually based models or theories which attempt to explain the task confronting the learner.

The chapter by Rod Ellis, INDIVIDUAL DIFFERENCES IN LANGUAGE LEARNING, reviews research into learner-related variables – both cognitive and affective – that help explain why second language learning proceeds in very different ways, at varying rates, and with different degrees of success from one learner to another. Again, the starting point is the language problem: the variability of language learning attainment. Ellis reminds us that the driving force behind early research efforts in this area was the need to select (via measures of aptitude, motivation, and the like) those learners most likely to benefit from language instruction. Educational ideology has now changed and, as he notes, the impetus for current individual difference research is more often the need to choose the best instructional approach for the learner, rather than the reverse – hence the current proliferation of studies on individual learner strategies and styles. Ellis is also interested in whether individual differences are amenable to change, posing practical questions such as "How successful are pedagogic interventions directed at training learners to use specific strategies?" Here we see evidence of the quintessentially A-L concern with intervention. In this sense Ellis sets himself apart from second language acquisition researchers in the L-A tradition (e.g., see Birdsong in Part I). He is nevertheless aware that adequate explanations of the rate and success of learning rely on theory. His vision for individual difference research is an ambitious one, involving the building of an overarching model which accounts for the relative contributions of acquisitional processes, opportunities for learning, abilities, strategies, cognitions, and consciousness in an individual's learning, while at the same time accepting that language learning is always situated and that these factors will configure differently for different learning tasks and in different settings.

This yearning for an all embracing model of SLA is also implicit in the chapter by Gary Barkhuizen, although one may surmise that he would give more weight to the social in such a model than would Ellis. His SOCIAL INFLUENCES ON LANGUAGE LEARNING offers "a broad overview of the many dialogues which have tried to explain how language learning and the social context in which it takes place relate to each other," again with the express A-L type aim of improving the efficiency of learning. He touches on various dimensions of the social (e.g., age, social class, ethnicity, and gender) and reviews models of language learning (e.g., Schuman's acculturation theory,

Giles' intergroup model, and Norton's social identity model) which emphasize the complex interactions between learners and their social environment. Barkhuizen's discussion of contextual influences and constraints incorporates language education and language-in-education policies, with particular reference to current efforts in South Africa to redress past linguistic imbalances by actively promoting the learning and use of African languages. His interest in educational intervention takes him beyond the realms of SLA as traditionally conceived and puts him squarely within the realm of A-L.

What is notable in the more socially embedded approaches to language learning of the kind described in Barkhuizen' chapter is the marginal role they accord to linguistics as a feeder discipline. This is nowhere more true than in the case of recent literacy research, dealt with in the review of literacy studies prepared by Eddie Williams. Although Williams, as already noted, concentrates mainly on mainstream cognitive approaches to the study of literacy which do concern themselves with the language system, he gives some space is his chapter to the work of Street and his followers and to their distinction between "autonomous" and "ideological" research traditions. The latter, which views literacy as a social practice, eschews the study of the component skills or processes involved in reading and writing, dismissing such research as narrowly focused, decontextualized, and apolitical. Discussions of pedagogy amongst literacy researchers in the ideological tradition tend to deemphasize the skills of decoding, focusing mainly on mastery of the discourse conventions of powerful genres along with the ability to contest and critique these conventions. Williams, while conceding that there is merit in such approaches, argues that there is a continuing and important role for the "autonomous literacy" model in language teaching "in the sense that if one cannot read, then one cannot read anything" whether critically or otherwise.

Section 9 deals more explicitly with issues of pedagogy than Section 8 and hence moves a little closer to the strong end of the A-L continuum since the issue under investigation is what is done with/for/to learners, rather than how learning unfolds. This section includes a discussion of fashions in language teaching methodology by Bob Adamson, of computer-assisted language learning" (CALL) by Paul Gruba, of language teacher education by Richard Johnstone, of LSP (Languages for Specific Purposes) by Helen Basturkmen and Catherine Elder, and of bilingual education by Heather Lotherington. CALL is included with teaching rather than learning because the introduction of technology as a teaching tool can be said to turn learning into a form of instruction. The focus of the LSP chapter is also on delivery, both in classrooms and test situations, and hence fits better here than with other work in L-A (such as LANGUAGE AND THE LAW) which we noted was oriented more toward language description than intervention.

Discussion of developments in language teaching methodologies are often cast as evolutionary, moving from early misguided attempts involving grammar-translation toward more sophisticated approaches which aim to produce autonomous learners able to use language effectively in a range of communicative contexts. Adamson's chapter on FASHIONS IN LANGUAGE TEACHING METHODOLOGY is skeptical, making the point (also mentioned by Rajagopalan in Part I) that the advent of different methods is often a matter of historical accident rather than intelligent design, and stems from the ideologies and imperatives which arise in different social contexts. His outline of the history of English language teaching approaches in China makes this point very clearly. Adamson's strongly relativist view of methodology and his attempt to give coherence to the field by offering flexible guidelines rather than a one-size-fits-all recipe, is akin to Brown's proposal (above) that ethical guidelines or standards be used as a means of unifying the highly disparate repertoire of research methods within A-L.

The objective of CALL, as characterized in Gruba's chapter, is again one of amelioration: to enhance language learning and teaching using computerized means. To do so CALL draws insights selectively from a range of disciplines including psychology, artificial intelligence, computational linguistics, instructional technology and human–computer interaction. Gruba's discussion of CALL encompasses four key areas: the role of computers, students, teachers, and researchers. Theories and approaches to CALL, according to Gruba, tend to follow on the heels of those in language teaching (moving from structuralism and behaviorist inspired models toward more holistic, communicative, and socially-embedded approaches). Again, however, these developments are constrained by context, perhaps even more so than is the case with teaching methodology, because the implementation of CALL relies utterly on access to technology. Gruba notes that, despite the proliferation of CALL activity within the language teaching profession, thus far there have been few attempts to evaluate CALL achievements or indeed to critique the ideological underpinnings of the CALL enterprise.

Language teacher education (LTE) is an obvious example of A-L as practical intervention, in this case by teacher educators (sometimes in collaboration with teacher practitioners and language researchers) to further the goals of successful language teaching and learning. Johnstone, like Adamson, stresses that LTE is necessarily constrained by and responsive to local conditions, supporting this contention with examples from a variety of European contexts. There are two problems which LTE must address: namely, the what (of the LTE curriculum) and the how (of delivery). After sketching the areas of knowledge and competence teachers might be expected to master in the process of becoming professional, Johnstone outlines the factors likely to influence the provision of these inputs (international support, teacher supply, access to professional contact, working conditions). He goes on to discuss issues of ideology and process (teacher beliefs, novice–expert interactions, links between LTE and SLA research), highlighting the problematic relationship between knowing/reflecting and doing and the role of LTE in mediating this divide.

The instrumental orientation of A-L appears in high relief in Basturkmen and Elder's chapter THE PRACTICE OF LSP. The activity of LSP, as they have construed it, is motivated by the need to teach and test language efficiently and in a way which fits as closely as possible with the needs of the students or test-takers in the academic or professional contexts in which they are required to operate. Working out what language skills are required of students or teachers or tour guides or doctors and then teaching or testing those skills is reliant to some extent on prior linguistic descriptions or characterizations of the relevant genres (of the kind referred to in some of the L-A chapters in this volume). But the A-L challenge is not only to identify the critical features of communication in the relevant domain, it is also to reconstruct them in the form of classroom or test tasks which are subject to their own sets of contextual constraints. This bridging process is sometimes fraught with difficulty, as the authors acknowledge, pointing to problems in determining and prioritizing needs, in achieving appropriate levels of task authenticity, and getting the right balance between specificity and generality. While the LSP enterprise has been dismissed by some as overly pragmatic, the authors argue that the practice of LSP invites reflection about the value of considering language skills separately from other equally important aspects of professional or academic communication, thereby contributing to theories of language in use.

The issue of language as object versus language as medium for communication of academic content knowledge is also central to the study of bilingual education, although Lotherington defines bilingual education rather more broadly, as any educational arrangement in which two languages are used instructionally, regardless of whether language is the object or vehicle of instruction. Thus her discussion embraces a vast range of social contexts and institutional arrangements for teaching languages, including limited exposure second language instruction programs for majority learners in primarily monolingual contexts and minority language maintenance programs for indigenous and immigrant groups in language contact situations. One of the key foci of A-L research into bilingual education over the years has been the practical question: does it actually work? But, as Lotherington notes, research findings on this topic are controversial. This is partly due to the ideological nature of the bilingual education debate (also discussed by Lo Bianco – see below), but also to the problem of determining what constitutes success in programs with very different goals and to the difficulty of extrapolating from one institutional context to another, given the multiple variables involved.

Section 10 is concerned with language based institutional arrangements or practices which are more broadly focused than language teaching (although they may also encompass teaching concerns). Chapters included here are those by Anne Pauwels on language maintenance, by Joseph LoBianco on language planning and by Tim McNamara on language testing. Investigation of these practices requires, as always in A-L, an understanding of a range of issues beyond language and draws on different disciplines and modes of enquiry.

Discussions of language maintenance, according to Pauwels, bring together "(sub)disciplines such as sociology, sociology of language, anthropology, in particular anthropological linguistics, social psychology, sociolinguistics, contact linguistics and applied linguistics as well as others such as (linguistic) demography and political science." Pauwels takes what she identifies as an A-L stance in her treatment of this topic, considering the question of how and why languages are or are not maintained and what action can be taken to foster maintenance in situations where they are endangered. (Such actions may involve individual strategies such as the application of the "one parent one language" principle for raising children in the home, or institutional intervention to introduce the language as medium of instruction for compulsory education.)

One might ask how language maintenance, as characterized by Pauwels, differs from language attrition, which we have classified as L-A and which is in some sense the mirror image of maintenance/revival. One answer would be that attrition studies are less likely to be concerned with corrective action and more likely to focus on the linguistic code rather than non-linguistic factors. Linguistics, writes Lo Bianco, because of its choice to "reify language as a subject of analysis within the formal conceptual apparatus of autonomous linguistic science, is an inadequate basis for characterizing a discipline involving action for intervention". Lo Bianco is here talking about language planning, which he locates within A-L because it aims beyond understanding or explanation toward what he terms "scholarly legitimization of particular courses of public action." He critically reviews past and current attempts to define and theorize the discipline and sketches different forms of language planning activity (both current and historical). The diversity of goals and conflicting interests he uncovers in his analysis of language planning efforts and the constraining and shaping effects of context lead him to question the feasibility of a "unified ethics of practice". He nevertheless sees the need for reconceptualizing and revitalizing this ever-expanding field. He proposes that language planning frameworks should add new conceptual models to their repertoire, including critical and political linguistics as well as those areas of enquiry that deal with the professional identity formation of the actors engaged in the process of planning and with the discourses whereby language planning problems are formulated and resolved.

Language testing, dealt with in the chapter by McNamara, is generally agreed to be at the "strong" end of the A-L continuum because the impetus for its activity is typically practical – tests offer an efficient means of solving institutional imperatives such as the need to select suitably proficient foreign students to enrol in English-medium universities or to evaluate the effectiveness of particular language policies or approaches to language teaching. Language testers also draw on various disciplinary sources (for example psycholinguistics, discourse analysis, educational measurement) in deciding how to elicit and measure the relevant language abilities and in their efforts at validation. Current models of test validation, as McNamara indicates, require testers to adduce multiple sources of evidence and argument to support score inferences, paying due attention to the values and ideologies underpinning test constructs and to the consequences of test use. The process of validation is thus the tester's means of "scholarly legitimization of particular courses of public action," as LoBianco puts it (see above). The tendency of these stronger forms of A-L is to theorize the very process of doing.

However, as with many of the other A-L topics in this volume, the focus is not merely practical, and cross-disciplinary links are bidirectional. McNamara declares that language tests also play a critical role in operationalizing and inviting reflection on theoretical models (or constructs) of language ability, thereby informing the research areas from which these models are drawn (a point also raised in the chapter on LSP).

Section 11 contains a single chapter, CRITICAL APPLIED LINGUISTICS, by Alastair Pennycook, which could be seen as performing a similar function to the philosophy chapter at the end of Part I, in that it stands back and reflects on the meaning and purpose of A-L activity.

Pennycook gives examples of significant work in an emergent area which he claims is "pushing forward the intellectual and empirical boundaries of the discipline." Amongst the domains he considers are critical discourse analysis and critical literacy, critical approaches to translation, language education and language testing, language planning and language and literacy in workplace settings. The themes identified as central include poverty, racism, gender difference, and inequality. The role of critical applied linguistics, as he puts it, is to "make applied linguistics matter" and he makes no bones about declaring linguistics as irrelevant to this goal. The intellectual underpinnings of critical applied linguistics are also discussed and what it means to be critical defined in opposition to liberal humanist and neo-Marxist formulations. Pennycook concludes his chapter with a biting rebuttal of attacks on critical applied linguistics mounted by his critics.

The very existence of a transgressive critical applied linguistics which attacks the foundations and goals of applied linguistics is perhaps a sign that applied linguistics is a discipline which has come of age. It has matured to a point where it has spawned an *enfant terrible* who bites the hand that has fed it. Critical applied linguistics both sets itself in opposition to applied linguistics, seeing any normative discipline as complicit in perpetuating unequal relations of power, and spurns the very notion of discipline as unifying force, defining itself as anti-disciplinary. Pennycook's characterization of the critical applied linguistics agenda is ameliorative, but not in the traditional A-L sense of attempting to reflect upon, intervene in, and where possible remedy particular language problems. Critical applied linguistics aims to uncover the ideological forces and discoursal practices which underlie the very formulation of language problems and defines itself as socially transformative in a more radical and far-reaching sense. Quite how this social transformation will take place remains unclear since Pennycook's characterization of this emergent field shies away from any attempt to formulate a *modus operandi*, arguing the case for what he terms "movable praxis," which evolves and reshapes itself in response to the multiple contexts in which it operates.

17 The Native Speaker in Applied Linguistics

ALAN DAVIES

17.1 Introduction

In this chapter, I discuss the role of the native speaker in applied linguistics and set out the different interpretations of the concept. I begin with the issue of the native speaker as identity; then I consider various definitions of the concept. I then examine the relation between the native speaker and the non-native speaker and raise the question of whether a second or foreign language learner who starts learning after puberty can become a native speaker of the target language. This brings us back to the issue of identity: I consider four ways of coping with the issue of loss of identity as a native speaker. I conclude that the native speaker concept remains ambiguous, necessarily so, since it is both myth and reality.

17.2 Native Speaker as Identity

The concept of native speaker occupies a curious position in applied linguistics. On the one hand it is widely used as a benchmark for knowledge of a language (and as such attracts opposition because it excludes those who are not native speakers), and as a criterion for employment; on the other hand a definition of the native speaker is elusive. How useful is the concept of native speaker to applied linguistics? That is the theme of this chapter.

Ferguson comments: "Linguists . . . have long given a special place to the native speaker as the only true and reliable source of language data" (Ferguson, 1983, p. vii). He continues:

> much of the world's verbal communication takes place by means of languages which are not the users' mother tongue, but their second, third or nth language, acquired one way or another and used when appropriate. This kind of language use merits the attention of linguists as much as do the more traditional objects of their research.   (p. vii)

This is a plea from sociolinguistics. But is Ferguson right to conclude as follows: "In fact the whole mystique of native speaker and mother tongue should preferably be quietly dropped from the linguist's set of professional myths about language" (p. vii). As my discussion shows, there is no doubt about the myth-like properties of the native speaker idea. The question remains, however, of whether it is also a reality. I attempt to answer that question.

Theoretically, as we shall see, the native speaker concept is rich in ambiguity. It raises, quite centrally, the issue of the relation between the particular and the universal. Chomsky, as a protagonist of the universalist position, conveys to Paikeday's questioning approach about the status of the native speaker (Paikeday, 1985) the strongest possible sense of the genetic determinants of speech acquisition which, as he sees it, must mean that to be human is to be a native speaker.

What Chomsky does is to equate language development with other normal human development, finding no value in questions about developmental states or stages which he regards as contingent and essentially of no theoretical interest. In the same vein Chomsky finds distinctions between synchronic states of language or languages and dialects uninteresting, "the question of what are the 'languages' or 'dialects' attained, and what is the difference between 'native' and 'non-native' is just pointless" (Chomsky quoted in Paikeday, 1985, p. 57). Chomsky's whole argument depends on a rationalist opposition to "incorrect metaphysical assumptions: in particular the assumption that among the things in the world there are languages or dialects, and that individuals come to acquire them" (Paikeday, 1985, p. 49). This is the argument from psycholinguistics (or cognitive linguistics).

And so Chomsky must conclude that "everyone is a Native Speaker of the particular language states that the person has 'grown' in his/her mind/ brain." In the real world, that is all there is to say" (p. 58). Chomsky's view is uninfluenced by any social factor or contextual constraint. Variety and context, he seems to argue, are trivial. This is a thoroughgoing unitary competence view of language in which language use is contingent and the native speaker is only a realization of that competence at a linguistic and not a language-specific level. For Chomsky, like many theoretical linguists, is not interested in languages: what he studies is language.

For our present purpose, however, we note that Chomsky does in fact acknowledge the real individual, living, as he says, in the real world, whose speech repertoire is multiple. His view may take no account of social or sociolinguistic analysis or parameters, but he is not unaware that the real word consists of complex variation. Our concern in this chapter is to explore the real-world parameters of the native speaker since it is there that applied linguistics has its role.

The native speaker/non-native speaker distinction is hardly as dramatic as the difference between the sexes; and it does not contain the crucial genetic difference. If we accept the model of Universal Grammar (UG), different languages are the same language (or set of principles) but with different parameter settings. From this point of view it has been maintained that languages differ essentially in terms of vocabulary. I can express the argument as follows. A child draws on UG to construct his/her first language (L1) on the basis of input from parents or other caretakers using their L1. The child is then in time socialized into a standard language (see below). Parameters are set and reset at all points. The same procedure is said to apply to the second language (L2) learner, who first regresses to UG and then adds or exchanges one L1 for another L1 through resetting of parameters.

A child may be a native speaker of more than one language as long as the acquisition process starts early and necessarily prepuberty. After puberty (Felix, 1987), it becomes difficult – not impossible, but very difficult (Birdsong, 1992) – to become a native speaker. Unlike male/female differences, native speaker/ non-native speaker differences are not innate but learnt, but the learning is so well imprinted that the "membership" it bestows is real and fixed. What this means is that the concept of the native speaker is not a fiction, but has the reality that "membership," however informal, always gives. The native speaker is relied on to know what the score is, how things are done, because she/he carries the tradition, is the repository of "the language." The native speaker is also expected to exhibit normal control especially in fluent connected speech (though in writing only after long schooling), and to have command of expected characteristic strategies of performance and of communication. A native speaker is also expected to "know" another native speaker, in part because of an intuitive feel, like for like, but also in part because of a characteristic systematic set of indicators, linguistic, pragmatic, and paralinguistic, as well as an assumption of shared cultural knowledge.

The native speaker, who remains a learner of new words and new registers (not to mention additional languages) and who is able to balance that role with the proper authority role necessarily attained, can only be a valued resource for others. McCawley (1986) notes the difference between the native and the non-native speaker as learner since the native speaker has to combine being also the authority. Indeed, we might hazard that a non-native speaker can claim that they have achieved the steady state of being a native speaker in the second language when they are prepared to accept the fragility of the knowledge they have so carefully acquired, acknowledging that there is always more to learn. Adulthood as a native speaker is no different from being an adult in any other field.

By remaining a learner, the native speaker gains access to the standard language. Note that it is membership of the group of native speakers that determines behaviour, in this case, adoption of the standard language, rather than the other way round of behaviour determining membership. And it is membership as a native speaker that determines the choice of the code to be used in an encounter, including the standard language.

Such a stress on identity relates this view of the native speaker to the work in social identity theory of Henri Tajfel. His comment on the typical majority-minority situation is relevant: "minorities are often defined on the basis of criteria originating from, and developed by, the majorities. They are different from something which, itself, need not be clearly defined" (Tajfel, 1981, p. 317). There is a relief in this saving comment that allows us to admit that a failure to define the native speaker may indicate that, like other majorities, native speakers define themselves negatively as not being non-native speakers. To be a native speaker means not being a non-native speaker. Such a conclusion reminds us of the central importance to all discussions of language behaviour of the non-native speaker. Before we consider the non-native speaker, what is it we know about the native speaker?

17.3   Definitions of the Native Speaker

Let us rehearse what seems to be agreed about the native speaker:

- Everyone is a native speaker of his/her own unique code: this allows us to reject as illogical the notion of semilingualism (Martin-Jones & Romaine, 1986).
- Everyone accepts and adheres to the norms of a standard language, either an informal (standard) language, which might be a dialect, or a codified standard (typically called a language). The relation between informal (standard) language(s) and a codified standard is that the codified standard is flexible enough to permit a good deal of tolerance to the informal (standard) language(s), except in situations where for extraneous cultural or political or religious reasons there is norm conflict leading to misunderstandings and refusal to communicate. Examples of informal (standard) languages might be Singapore English and Newfoundland English.
- Those near what Bartsch (1988) called the "point" that is the centre or model of the standard language, are favored and advantaged. They suffer less from insecurity, are less likely to practice hypercorrection, and above all have less of a learning problem in using the standard language for public purposes (for example in education) because their home language use is nearer to the standard language. Meanwhile those near the extremes are disfavored and disadvantaged, they are more likely to feel insecure and to have their version of the standard language stigmatized, as well as to stigmatize it themselves. In public uses (such as education) they have more of a learning problem. It is possible (though this is quite unclear) that they may also have a cognitive problem because they have learnt to think in their own variety of the standard language, a difficulty compounded by possible lack of intelligibility of input by teachers whose standard language may be nearer the point. Nevertheless, this is the situation of social life and of a non-homogeneous community and it is possible, if difficult, for those disadvantaged initially by their own L1 to accumulate and later gain full access to a more central version.

- Native speakers all do indeed have intuitions about their standard language, but in those cases where there is tolerance but flexibility it is likely that their knowledge of and performance in those norms will be shaky. And where they are uncertain they will guess, or admit ignorance, or fall back on some basic UG principle. What this means is that intuitions are learnt not innate: the grammar of the standard language is not built into the head of the child any more than is the grammar of his/her own individual idiolectal version of the standard language.
- All native speakers have access to some kind of language faculty, which may be called UG and which has to operate at a very high level of abstraction. The apparent polar arguments seeking to explain acquisition, whereby the learner moves across from an L1 (some version of the old contrastive analysis model) or regresses to the primary UG state and then moves forward again into an L2, are in a serious sense non-arguments since both must be true. Since the L1 grammar is a version of UG and underlying it is UG, then it is a matter of generative arrangement how I draw the connection between L1 and L2 since UG must occur there somewhere.

The native speaker (and this means all native speakers) may be defined in the following six ways (Davies, 1991, 2003):

1 The native speaker acquires the L1 of which she/he is a native speaker in childhood.
2 The native speaker has intuitions (in terms of acceptability and productiveness) about his/her idiolectal grammar.
3 The native speaker has intuitions about those features of the standard language grammar which are distinct from his/her idiolectal grammar.
4 The native speaker has a unique capacity to produce fluent spontaneous discourse, which exhibits pauses mainly at clause boundaries (the "one clause at a time" facility) and which is facilitated by a huge memory stock of complete lexical items (Pawley & Syder, 1983). In both production and comprehension the native speaker exhibits a wide range of communicative competence.
5 The native speaker has a unique capacity to write creatively (and this includes, of course, literature at all levels from jokes to epics, metaphor to novels.
6 The native speaker has a unique capacity to interpret and translate into the L1 of which she/he is a native speaker. Disagreements about the deployment of an individual's capacity are likely to stem from a dispute about the standard or (standard) language.

17.4   Native Speaker or Native Speaker-Like?

To what extent can the L2 learner become a target language native speaker? We will consider this question in relation to L2 learners in general. Let us again consider the six criteria in section 17.3 above:

1 *Childhood acquisition*   No, the second language learner does not acquire the target language in early childhood. If she/he does, then she/he is a native speaker of both L1 and the target language (TL), or in her/his case of L1x and L1y; that is, she/he is a bilingual native speaker.

2 *Intuitions about idiolectal grammar*   Yes, it must be possible, with sufficient contact and practice, for the second language learner to gain access to intuitions about his/her own idiolectal grammar of the target language (although, as I will show, this makes an important assumption about criterion 1, childhood acquisition).

3 *Intuitions about the standard language grammar*   Yes again, with sufficient contact and practice the second language learner can gain access to the standard grammar of the target language. Indeed in many formal learning situations it is exactly through exposure to a target language standard grammar that the target language idiolectal grammar would emerge, the reverse of L1 development.

4 *Discourse and pragmatic control*   In practice it is very difficult for a non-native speaker to gain the discourse and pragmatic control of a native speaker; difficult but not impossible in special cases.

5 *Creative performance*   Yes again, with practice it must be possible for a second language learner to become an accepted creative artist in the target language. Among writers, there are of course well-known examples of such cases – Conrad, Becket, Senghor, Narayan. There is also the interesting problem of the acceptability to the L1 community of the second language learner's creative writing; this is an attitudinal issue, but so too is the question of the acceptability to the same community of a creative writer writing not in the standard language but in a non-codified (standard) language, e.g., Scots. Equally in doubt is the acceptability of a standard variety of a language to readers from other standard varieties: too American or too Australian, a Brit might say; and, of course, the reverse.

6 *Interpreting and translating*   Yes again, this must be possible although international organizations generally require that interpreters should interpret into their L1. (It remains, of course, unclear what judgments are made of an applicant for an interpreter's post; no doubt proficiency tests are carried out, but it might be difficult to deny the claim of an applicant that she/he is a native speaker.)

All except (1) are contingent issues. In that way the question: Can a second language learner become a native speaker of a target language? reduces to: Is it necessary to acquire a code in early childhood in order to be a native speaker of that code? Now the answer to that question, and this is where the circularity lies, is to ask a further question: What is it that the child acquires in acquiring his/her L1? But I have already answered that question in my criteria (2)–(6) above, and so the question again becomes a contingent one.

We need in (2) and (3) above to ensure a cultural dimension since the child L1 acquirer has access to the resources of the culture attached to the language and particularly to those learnt and encoded or even imprinted early. The post-puberty second language learner does not have this experience, which puts a question mark against my assertion about gaining access to intuitions about the idiolectal grammar if those intuitions lack a childhood cultural component. Still, having said that, what of sub-cultural differences between, for example, the Scots and the English; of different cultures with the same standard language (for example the Swiss, the Austrians, the West Germans, and the East Germans); or of different cultures with different standard languages (for example the British and the American)? What too of International English and of an isolated L1 in a multilingual setting (for example Indian English)?

Given the interlingual differences and the lack of agreement on norms that certainly occur among such groups it does appear that the post-pubertal second language learner has a difficult but not an impossible task to become a native speaker of a target language which can contain such wide diversities. The answer to the question of whether L2 learners can evolve into native speakers of the target language must therefore be "Yes": but the practice required, given the model of the child L1 acquirer who for five to six years spends much of his/her time learning language alone, is so great that it is not likely that many post-pubertal second language learners ever become native speakers of their target language. The analogy that occurs to me here is that of music, where it is possible to become a concert performer after a late start but the reality is that few do. The more exact analogy of learning to play the piano as a child and switching to, say, the cello later on is common and is perhaps more relevant.

Coppieters' empirical investigation (Coppieters, 1987) into the differences between native speakers of French and advanced learners of French in grammatical judgments produced results which indicated a significant difference between the two groups. She concluded that the difference between native speakers and non-native speakers repeats the elaborated/restricted code difference which Bernstein (1971–5) reported and with the same implication. For what holds back the non-native speaker (like the speaker of a restricted code) is the early acquired generalizing capacity.

It is difficult for an adult non-native speaker to become a native speaker of a second language precisely because I define a native speaker as a person who has early acquired the language. However, the limitations imposed by the later acquisition, when it is very successful, are likely to be psycholinguistic rather than sociolinguistic. The adult non-native speaker can acquire the communicative competence of the native speaker; she/he can acquire the confidence necessary to membership. Leaving aside the matter of accentual difference, what is more difficult for the non-native speaker is to gain the speed and the certainty of knowledge relevant to judgments of grammaticality. But as with all questions of boundaries (for the native speaker is a boundary that excludes), there are major language differences among native speakers. Native speakers may be prepared to make judgments quickly about grammaticality but they do not necessarily agree with one another. And so I am left asking to what extent it matters. If a non-native speaker wishes to pass as a native speaker and is so accepted, then it is surely irrelevant if she/he shows differences on more and more refined tests of grammaticality. That may be of interest psycholinguistically, but for applied linguistic purposes I maintain that it is unimportant.

The differing positions of the psycholinguistic and the sociolinguistic are probably irreconcilable. For the psycholinguist no test is ever sufficient to demonstrate conclusively that native speakers and non-native speakers are distinct: once non-native speakers have been shown to perform as well as native speakers on a test, the cry goes up for yet another test. For the sociolinguist there is always another (more) exceptional learner who will, when found, demonstrate that (exceptional) non-native speakers can be equated to native speakers on ultimate attainment. The problem is that we cannot finally and absolutely distinguish non-native speakers from native speakers except by autobiography. So Cook (1999) is right to make a strong case for the native/non-native speaker distinction being one above all of biography. However, making the cut by biography shows only some problems and hides away the exceptions, the bilinguals, the movers away, the disabled intellectually, the exceptional learners. The fact is that mother tongue is not gender, it is not a given from the womb. It is, classically, social, just as culture is. We cannot distinguish between native speakers and non-native speakers because our premises are inherently flawed, as Hyltenstam and Abrahamsson (2000) point out, since there are different views of what being a native speaker means. They include:

1 native speaker by birth (that is by early childhood exposure),
2 native speaker by virtue of being a native user,
3 native speaker (or native speaker-like) by being an exceptional learner,
4 native speaker through education in the target language medium,
5 native speaker through long residence in the adopted country.

What is at issue is whether claiming to be a native speaker, to "own" the language, requires early childhood exposure. Let us consider this issue of ownership with regard to English.

17.5   Losing a Native Speaker Identity

The global expansion of English in the twentieth century has been widely discussed and analyzed (Crystal, 1997; Holborow, 1999; Graddol, 1999). It has been seen in both a favourable and in a critical light. Those who regard the expansion favourably (Fishman, Cooper, & Conrad, 1975; MacArthur, 1999) comment on the empowering role of English, the values of openness it brings, the access it provides both to knowledge and to markets. Those who regard the expansion negatively discuss the hegemonizing of the weak by the strong, the ways in which English is used by the powerful west and their allies to dominate through globalization, much as they dominate through economic and military means. They also point to the loss of choice, first linguistic, and then, inevitably it is suggested, cultural. What the spread of English does, it is argued (Phillipson, 1992), is to squeeze other languages into less and less central roles, eroding their functions until eventually they are marginalized to the private and the home and finally lost. That, it is suggested, is what is happening in a society such as Singapore where English is now the only school medium of instruction for all Singaporeans. It is what has already happened in Guyana. And this destruction of the local language(s) is not confined to the Third World, to poor countries which do not have the resources at hand to combat the rise of English. It applies equally to the developed world, where it remains for the present possible to operate a language policy of the local language plus English in countries such as Denmark, the Netherlands, Sweden. Such countries are often held up as models of successful language learning and teaching: successful because they succeed in acquiring the foreign language, English, and becoming proficient in it while at the same time not losing their first language, Danish, Swedish, Dutch, and so on. But the picture of easy (and stable) bilingualism in these western countries is queried by observers such as van Els (2000), who take the view that English in these settings could well be the cuckoo in the European nest, meaning that in another couple of generations, these local languages could be in terminal decline. That, of course, is the problem with the argument from function: if language is primarily a matter of functional distinction and adequacy, then once a world language such as English starts to encroach on the local language functions, there is really nothing to stop it from taking over all functions. Except sentiment of course, except the sense of distinctness, except the concern that it is possible to be truly oneself (a Dane, a Swede, a Singaporean) only in the local language or in one of the local languages (Holborow, 1999; wa' Thiongo, 1986). At the back of such a sentiment is the two-fold awareness of language in personal and in group identity. On one side there is the central role accorded to language as the transmitter and carrier of the sense of self, both inclusiveness to the in-group and exclusiveness to those who are seen to belong to other ethnicities. On the other side is the meaning attached to the local language(s) itself, meaning that derives from its cognitive and psychological importance in the ontogenetic growth of cognition and other aspects of "normal" development. The first of these concerns what you do with language, its sociolinguistics, the second with what language does to you, its psycholinguistics.

Both have to do with the sense of self which is, or seems to be, bound up with the language(s) in which one grew up as a child, one's first language, mother tongue. The sense of self, one's personal identity is, on this basis, closely associated with the power that being a native speaker gives. Such power is very hard to attain in any additional acquired language, however successful the acquisition.

And that identity is threatened by the sense of not being valued for one's self (one's language is perceived as not good enough), of someone else's language being presented not just as different (so much is obvious), but as better than yours, and of the pervading feeling that whatever you do you will never achieve "proper" command over the incoming language, that "inferiority complex" of which Medgyes (1994, p. 10) wrote.

One's personal sense of identity is bound up with one's language: this is true both for the social aspects – sharing being a native speaker with others (and the opposite, not sharing it with those who do not belong); and the psycholinguistic aspects – mapping one's way through the basic interpersonal communicative skills (BICS) and cognitive/academic language proficiency (CALP) that are claimed to be necessary to effective cognitive development (Cummins, 1984).

This being so, or rather if this is so, then we would expect the growth of English to be condemned as an aspect of postcolonial imperialism because it erodes the pride of native speakerness appertaining to local languages and never somehow replaces it with the gift (or the attainment) of being a native speaker in the acquired and desired English. Here, the stereotyped attitude of the excolonialists to themselves, native speakers of English, is not dissimilar to the attitude the British took in their colonial heyday: the attitude that allowed the "natives" to remain native, that accorded them large measures of local autonomy (indirect rule) but which took for granted that it was never going to be possible for the colonized to become British.

Underlying many of the remarks by postcolonial apologists is their failure to acknowledge that English in the world at the start of the twenty-first century is a special case, if only because the inferiority complex, to which we have referred, is more likely to be found in relation to a global language such as English than to a language of more limited provenance. This denial of a special status for native speakers of English is surely ideological, belonging to an argument about the role of English in a world filled with new or world Englishes, where most speakers of English are second language learners. In this context there is a political point to be made in comparing the privileged position of the Old Variety of English (OVE) speaker, say of British or American English, and the New Variety of English (NVE) speaker, say of Nigerian or Indian English. Rajagopalan maintains that: "the quest for the pure native is part of a larger agenda that in other epochs manifested itself – and in some quarters still does – as the quest for the pure race" (1997, p. 229). Since there are no "viable and fool-proof criteria for identifying a native" (p. 228), then all that is left is the "myth of nativity" (p. 229).

Are such sentiments specific to English because English is a special case? Or are the sentiments generalizable? Would these critics make the same point about Welsh or Basque or Menomini or Kikuyu? Clearly they are making a political point and an understandable one, given the inequities of the world. It is worth remembering that English is not itself a cause of those inequities, rather, it is a correlative. There are after all countries and societies with high levels of English (e.g., Kerala) which remain very poor. But that said, if native speakers' privilege is controlled, by for example choosing a different language for schooling, as happened in Malaysia in the 1970s, English still appears today to enjoy a special status. True, Graddol writes of the "decline of the native speaker" and asks the "tantalising question: . . . large numbers of people will learn English as a Foreign Language in the 21st century . . . But will they continue to look towards the native speaker for authoritative norms of usage?" (1999, p. 68).

It is this question of authority that worries Greenbaum when he writes of the inherent instability of a New Variety of English (NVE) and wonders whether the real question is the acceptance of the national characteristics and their institutionalization (Greenbaum, 1985).

Where does this leave the postcolonial English speaker, such as the native speaker/user of Singaporean English? James (1999) maintains that there is good documentary evidence for the existence of Singapore English, a view attested to by Gupta (1994). Surely, the answer is that it leaves Singapore English exactly where it leaves, say, Glasgow English. Singapore is in fact in a stronger position: it has statehood and therefore is a centralizing force for language planning and norms. We might speculate on what would be the position of English if Scotland became independent. Would there be a deliberate scotizing of norms? Or would Scotland go the way of Ireland? There, the rich vein of creative writing in English has never been supported by – or itself supported – the demand for the development of a Standard Irish English. True, there has been research into and discussion of Hiberno-English (Harris, 1985), but little sign of different norms for education and publishing and the media (as in the USA, Australia). Perhaps Ireland – the oldest British colony – has had enough confidence not to insist on making that difference explicit. Or perhaps the presence of the Irish Gaelic language has provided a sufficiently separate identity and taken up the space that a Standard Irish English movement might have filled.

The theoretical debate about native speakers may be unresolved, but in the daily practice of language teaching and testing resolution is necessary and agreement on a model and a goal required. Even so Leung, Harris, and Rampton (1997, p. 1) argue for flexibility: "Little development of such an expanded pedagogy is possible without the displacement of conventional notions of the 'native speaker' of English (what we here label the 'idealised native speaker')." While this approach makes sense for individuals it is hard to see how it would lead to a language teaching policy for whole populations. Cook (1999) argues for the second language (the non-native speaker) model to replace the native speaker in order to consider the harmful effects of privileging an inappropriate communication model in countries such as Japan.

What both Rajagopalan (1999) and Canagarajah (1999) helpfully do is to argue strongly (as Medgyes, 1999, does) for the valorizing of the L2 teacher of English while at the same time reassuring professional colleagues that in teaching English as a Foreign Language (or indeed English as a Second Language) they are not acting as instruments of linguistic imperialism. Rajagopalan attacks the "alarmist thesis that the teaching of English to speakers of other languages is an outrageous act of aggression" (1999, p. 202). And Canagarajah, a doughty critic of the power of English in the periphery, makes very clear that scholars and teachers in the periphery are not dupes, that they are perfectly capable of operating "subtle forms of resistance to English," appropriating from it what they need (1999, p. 3). And he puts a question mark against the absolutist strategy advocated by the Kenyan writer James Ngugi (Ngugi wa' Thiongo) who renounced English as his medium in order to write in his first language, Kikuyu: "there are many reason why [his] oppositional strategy may be ill conceived . . . this is not a solution to the ideological challenges, but an escape from it. (Canagarajah, 1999, p. 177). This is the argument presented by Agnihotri and Khanna (1997) following their survey of young people in India's views on "the space of English in tomorrow's India" (p. 50). They conclude that English is indeed an Indian language and needs to be problematized in the Indian context, that it must be accorded its proper role within the "complementarity" of the English language (p. 139).

17.6   Four Ways of Coping with Loss

This sense of loss of identity as a native speaker of one's own language through domination by English (or, of course, of any other widely spoken language) attracts four kinds of comment. The first is that of the attack on the cult of the native speaker, usually as teacher of his/her L1. This reminds us of the Paikeday argument (1985) and is presented typically by those who have suffered from discrimination on the grounds of themselves not being regarded as native speakers. The second comes from the special case of so-called world Englishes, the term used to legitimate the Englishes spoken in the British non-white colonies (Indian English, Malaysian English, Kenyan English, and so on). The position taken up here is again one that complains of discrimination against users of world Englishes by those who are native speakers of metropolitan English varieties (British English, American English, and so on). The third concern with identity takes the world English critique further. It presents the linguistic imperialism argument which states that English (and by implication any world language) rides roughshod over all local languages with which it comes in contact and particularly those in the ex-colonies: so now the critique is not just of the attitude of native speakers of metropolitan English to new Englishes, but also to all other languages. These three attacks are all on the sociolinguistic side, claiming that belonging to desired groups is made difficult by the loss of or denial of native speaker status. The fourth attack takes on the psycholinguistic argument and concerns the claimed need for all normal development to take place in the language of the home. It is an argument for the rewarding of first language importance in child development and therefore may be regarded as a claim not just for the fact of native speaker status but for its pre-eminence.

Commentators take up very different positions on the issue of native speaker power. But we can, I think, postulate that they separate into those writing from the foreigner perspective and those writing from the "other-native" perspective. The foreigner view is of two kinds, "traditional" and "revisionist." The traditional view is that native speakers have special advantages but that these advantages are not unfair, just given; and in any case it is possible for non-natives working in professions such as language teaching to gain high levels of proficiency and to use their own learner background to deploy particularly relevant pedagogic skills. Medgyes (1999) provides an excellent summary of this type of view, as do several of the contributors to Braine (1999). They argue that being a non-native-speaking teacher of English is a powerful position to be in.

17.6.1   *The traditional foreigner*

Medgyes looks for cooperation between native and non-native-speaking teachers "The ideal NEST [native English-speaking teacher] and the ideal non-NEST arrive from different directions but eventually stand quite close to each other" (Medgyes, 1999, p. 74). Or as Kramsch and Lam (in Braine, 1999) make clear from the title of their chapter ("Textual identities: the importance of being non-native") being a non-native has advantages. This is an appealing view, given the fact that by far the majority of the world's language teachers are teaching what is to them a foreign language. A supportive view, though not directly concerned with the language of teachers, is found in Mohanan (1998), who takes a very traditional line: "For a given speaker, a non-native system is one that s/he has acquired after the acquisition and stabilisation of some other linguistic system" (p. 50). And he challenges those who argue the issue from the position of righting social justice: "the plea for 'endonormative' standards as a means of preventing social injustice contains a logical contra-diction. We should be willing to abolish all standards or to accept exonormative standards" (p. 53).

What Mohanan is drawing our attention to here is how even a variety which is subordinate to a distant standard (say Singapore English to British English) has the tendency to assume a dominant normative status with respect to some marginalized speakers (e.g., of Singlish) in Singapore. And Annamalai makes a similar point with regard to the relation between Telugu and Tamil in India and ponders whether bilingual speakers of both may be regarded as native speakers of Tamil: "Nativity . . . is a shifting construct and is correlated with political perceptions" (Annamalai, 1998, p. 154).

Holborow (1999) offers a similar argument from a Marxist perspective. "Often attempts to revive and impose a former national language can be a nationalist cloak under which new rulers' interests are hidden" (Holborow, 1999, p. 79). The traditional foreigner view is, at bottom, an acceptance of the strong view, that the native speaker is so by virtue of early childhood experience. That is seen to be an inescapable fact and it is pointless to pretend otherwise.

17.6.2   The revisionist foreigner

Observing the sense of deprivation of which Medgyes writes, Seidlhofer (2000) takes the bold step of recommending the abandonment of the traditional native speaker model, echoing Kramsch who suggests that it is time to "take our cues not from monolingual native speakers . . . but from the multilingual non-native speakers that constitute the majority of human beings on the planet" (1993, p. 49). The problem with such boldness is that it takes learners into a mapless setting. For indeed the state of mind she describes among non-native speakers of English as a lingua franca is surely one of anomie. Seidlhofer quotes Medgyes on non-native-speaking teachers of English: "We suffer from an inferiority complex caused by glaring defects in our knowledge of English. We are in constant distress as we realize how little we know about the language we are supposed to teach" (Medgyes, 1994, p. 10). (Skeptics among us might wonder how far this lament applies to native speakers also.) But the point Medgyes is making is that native speakers do not need this knowledge in an explicit form, while non-native speakers do because that is their way into the language.

And so Seidlhofer recommends that attention be given to the variety of English used by speakers of English as a Lingua Franca (EliF) communicating with one another. She claims that the appeal to the native speaker as model for all English is not appropriate now that the numbers of EliF speakers far outnumber the English L1 speakers, especially since the L1 model is neither desired by nor relevant to communication between EliF speakers, "it is important to realise that native-speaker language use is just one kind of reality, and not necessarily the relevant one for lingua franca contexts" (Seidlhofer, 2000, p. 54). So it is English as a lingua franca that needs to be investigated and described, now that EliF is spreading "with a great deal of variation but enough stability to be viable for lingua franca communication" (p. 54).

Seidlhofer proposes a research project which works toward "mapping out and exploring the whole spectrum of Englishes across the world" (p. 65). Such a project may be thought timely now that the methodology exists for the compilation of a corpus of English as a lingua franca. Indeed, work on such a corpus (the Vienna EliF corpus) has already begun. The end point of the research is to provide a description of EliF use which "would have potentially huge implications for curriculum design and for reference materials and textbooks."

It is understandable that Seidlhofer should wish to overturn the native speaker model. "There is" she claims "really no justification for doggedly persisting in referring to an item as 'an error' if the vast majority of the world's L2 English speakers produce and understand it" (p. 65). As she points out, her iconoclasm is widely shared in the linguistic imperialism English postcolonialist literature (Paikeday, 1985; Phillipson, 1992; Medgyes, 1994; Canagarajah, 1999).

17.6.3   *The other native*

The "other native" view is very well represented in both the Braine (1999) and Singh (1998) volumes. A number of the contributors to the Braine volume are involved in teaching English in North America where they have met with prejudice about their lack of native speaker status. And so the prevailing theme of the book is critical, protesting at not being accorded the same status as native speakers. This was, it will be remembered, the complaint of Thomas Paikeday (1985), pointing to his experience of job discrimination. But it is worth noting that such discrimination is typically found in mother tongue English settings. In the great majority of situations where English (or any language) is taught, the teachers are not native speakers, but members of the local community who themselves have acquired the language they teach as a foreign language. What the argument is really about is whether language use in a NVE setting, which involves English and no doubt other languages as well, provides participants with sufficient exposure to English to make them native users and furthermore in so doing gives them everything that the traditional native speaker has acquired in absorbing the language from childhood. Such native users – this is agreed – speak a different variety of English, a NVE, but this is, it is argued, in no way inferior to the variety spoken by those brought up in the UK or in any other setting Kachru (1982) has called the inner circle. And it therefore follows, so the argument runs, that there should be no discrimination (in teaching or in any other occupation) on the grounds of group membership of such NVEs.

This is the argument that Singh (1998) puts forward. It is the postcolonial argument. It is the argument that says that American English is different from British English and yet is not regarded as being full of errors. Therefore, Indian English (etc.) should be considered different, not inferior. It is an argument that appeals to social justice. So much is clear. But is it an argument that convinces in applied linguistic terms?

Singh (1998) is not comfortable with the term "native speaker," preferring to speak of "native user." In this his approach is similar to that of Ikome (1998) and Kandiah (1998). For Ikome, "native speaker" is a political designation for social empowerment or for peer recognition (p. 37). Kandiah attacks: "the mainstream discourse on the native speaker (which) can be seen to be a strongly normative discourse that is heavily invested ideologically against considerable numbers of people on our globe." (1998, p. 92). He insists that "it ought not to be necessary to repeat here the demonstration that these varieties of English [the NVEs] are the equal of any other variety of the language, being not mere hodge-podges of errors, mere deviations from the norms of the 'mother' language, but viable rule-governed systems in their own right which sustain and are sustained by speech communities of their native users" (p. 93).

He admits that the argument is not fundamentally about what distinguishes one variety from another, nor about whether a variety of native users (rather than native speakers), maintained by a speech community largely made up of non-monolingual speakers of English whose English has not necessarily been acquired as their first childhood language, should be regarded as "the equal of any other variety." What the argument is about is whether the boundary between the NVE and the OVE is seen to be a real boundary by the NVE native users.

This is the appeal to the Barth social boundary theory (Barth, 1970) and ultimately is about the attitudes of native users to their own NVE: "The critical feature of the group then becomes self-ascription and ascription by others on the basis of features, signs, signals, value orientations and standards which the actors themselves regard as significant and by which they judge themselves and expect others to judge them" (1970, p. 96). Barth's model of ethnicity is helpful here, since what it does is to emphasize, as Kandiah realizes, membership before content. This is the conclusion that Medgyes comes to, quoting Davies (1991, pp. 8, 16): "I believe that (native speaker) membership is largely a matter of self ascription, not of something being given ... We should bear in mind, however, that such a choice carries responsibilities in terms of confidence and identity."

Medgyes is concerned with the status of an individual near-native speaker, unlike Kandiah whose concern is for group membership. The confidence Medgyes refers to applies equally to both. But while the Medgyes individual near native needs to identify with the norms of English, both in a linguistic and a cultural sense, which in his case means the norms of OVEs, the identity Kandiah is concerned with is identity with the NVE group; and confidence for him means asserting that the English variety which his NVE members speak relates to the norms of their own NVE. This is the postcolonial imperative, that just as the Australian native speaker of English no longer admits allegiance to the norms of British English, similarly the NVE native user (say of Singapore English) no longer takes account of the norms of British English.

How far the norms differ is an empirical question, but it seems likely that as far as the written language is concerned, the differences are minimal. I am still of the opinion I expressed in 1991, that: "on linguistic grounds Singaporean English does not exist, but nor of course does British English ... what does exist is the individual speaker. If a speaker identifies him/herself as a native speaker of Singaporean English then that is a sociolinguistic decision" (Davies, 1991, p. 67). Which means, of course that it is a decision about identity.

17.6.4   *International English*

We have considered three ways of coping with the sense of losing one's identity as a native speaker – the traditional foreigner, the revisionist foreigner, and the other native. There is a fourth way, that of a globalized international language. One approach would be via an artificial language such as Esperanto or Idaho, where everyone gives up their national identity (or adds to it) for the sake of an international ideal of community. The other approach is via an existing lingua franca, such as English, and here we are close to the revisionist foreigner position where we discussed the proposal of Seidlhofer. The difference between that and what has come to be known as International English is that International English is not just for L2 users, but for all. The question which arises for applied linguistics is whether International English (Smith, 1983; Kachru, 1985; Davies, 1989) means a special variety of English with its own norms which are distinct from any national official standard English, or whether it means a use of English in international conferences and settings, for example the United Nations, academic conferences, trade missions, business negotiations. If the latter, then International English becomes like EliF. My own view is that International English usually means using one or the other standard English in international settings. Therefore, from an applied linguistic point of view, it is more appropriate to designate the activity as English as an International Language rather than as International English. The emphasis is then firmly put on the use of English and not on a separate language.

17.7   Conclusion

Disputes and differences of opinion about the native speaker arise because the concept is interpreted differently. That is why it has been referred to as both myth and reality (Davies, 2003). Discussions of the native speaker concept get trapped in the very different ideas of what is being talked about. One main type of approach sees the native speaker as the repository and guardian of the true language – this is the linguistic view; the other, the social view, concerns the native speaker as the standard setter. The two views are related and merge into one another. But what they reflect is that different positions can be taken on the basis of interest in and concern for the same phenomenon, because what is at issue is the individual speaker in relation to his/her social group, and to its community norms, i.e., the standard language. At bottom the native speaker is both metaphor and embodiment of the language/parole and of the competence/performance distinctions.

See also 3 SECOND LANGUAGE ACQUISITION AND ULTIMATE ATTAINMENT, 15 WORLD ENGLISHES, 18 LANGUAGE MINORITIES, 20 SECOND LANGUAGE LEARNING, 31 LANGUAGE TESTING.

REFERENCES

Agnihotri, R. K. & Kanna, A. Y. (1997) *Problematizing English in India*. New Delhi: Sage.

Annamalai, E. (1998) Nativity of language. In R. Singh (ed.), *The native speaker: multilingual perspectives* (pp. 148–57). New Delhi: Sage.

Barth, F. (ed.) (1970) *Ethnic groups and boundaries*. London: George, Allen & Unwin: Bergen: Universitets Forlaget.

Bartsch, R. (1988) *Norms of language.* London: Longman.

Bernstein, B. (1971–5) *Class, codes and control* (vols 1–5). London: Routledge & Kegan Paul.

Birdsong, D. (1992) Ultimate attainment in second language acquisition. *Language,* 68, 706–55.

Braine, George (ed.) (1999) *Non-native educators in English language teaching.* Mahwah, NJ: Lawrence Erlbaum.

Canagarajah, S. (1999) *Resisting linguistic imperialism in English teaching.* Oxford: Oxford University Press.

Cook, V. (1999) Going beyond the native speaker in language teaching. *TESOL Quarterly,* 33(2), 185–209.

Coppieters, R. (1987) Competence differences between native and near-native speakers. *Language,* 63, 544–73.

Crystal, D. (1997) *English as a global language.* Cambridge: Cambridge University Press.

Cummins, J. (1984) *Bilingualism and special education: issues on assessment and pedagogy.* Clevedon, UK: Multilingual Matters.

Davies A. (1989) Is international English an interlanguage? *TESOL Quarterly,* 23(3), 447–67.

Davies, A. (1991) *The native speaker in applied linguistics.* Edinburgh: Edinburgh University Press.

Davies, A. (2003) *The native speaker: myth and reality.* Clevedon, UK: Multilingual Matters.

Felix, S. W. (1987) *Cognition and language growth.* Dordrecht: Foris.

Ferguson, C. (1983) Language planning and language change. In H. Cobarrubias & J. Fishman (eds.), *Progress in language planning: international perspectives* (pp. 29–40). Berlin: Mouton.

Fishman, J. A., Cooper, R. L., & Conrad, A. W. (1975) *The spread of English.* Rowley, MA: Newbury House.

Graddol, D. (1999) The decline of the native speaker. In D. Graddol &

U. H. Meinhof (eds.), *English in a changing world* (pp. 57–68). *AILA Review,* 13.

Greenbaum, S. (1985) Commentary on Braj B. Kachru "Standards, codification and sociolinguistic realism: the English language in the outer circle." In R. Quirk & H. G. Widdowson (eds.), *English in the world: teaching and learning the language and literatures.* (pp. 31–2). Cambridge: Cambridge University Press and the British Council.

Gupta, A. F. (1994) *The step-tongue: children's English in Singapore.* Clevedon, UK: Multilingual Matters.

Harris, J. (1985) *Phonological variation and change: studies in Hiberno-English.* Cambridge: Cambridge University Press.

Holborow, M. (1999) *The politics of English: a marxist view of language.* London: Sage.

Hyltenstam, K. & Abrahamsson, N. (2000) Who can become native-like in a second language? All, some or none? On the maturational constraints controversy in second language acquisition. *Studia Linguistica,* 54(2), 150–66.

Ikome, Otto M. (1998) Language "nativization" in West Africa: acculturation and acquisition of "native" speakers in Cameroon. In R. Singh (ed.), *The native speaker: multilingual perspectives* (pp. 62–78). New Delhi: Sage.

James, J. (1999) Linguistic realities and pedagogical practices in Singapore: another perspective. In Gopinathan et al., *Language, society and education in Singapore: issues and trends* (2nd edn.) (pp. 99–116). Singapore: ASEAN/RELC.

Kachru, B. B. (ed.) (1982) *The other tongue: English across cultures.* Urbana, IL: University of Illinois Press.

Kachru, B. B. (1985) Standards, codification and sociolinguistic realism: the English language in the outer circle. In. R. Quirk & H. G. Widdowson (eds.), *English in the world: teaching and learning the language and literatures* (pp. 11–30). Cambridge: Cambridge University Press and the British Council.

Kandiah, T. (1998) Epiphanies of the deathless native user's manifold avatars: a post-colonial perspective on the native speaker. In R. Singh (ed.), *The native speaker: multilingual perspectives* (pp. 79–100). New Delhi: Sage.

Kramsch, C. (1993) *Context and culture in language teaching*. Oxford: Oxford University Press.

Kramsch, C. & Lam, W. S. E. (1999) Textual identities: the importance of being non-native. In G. Braine (ed.), *Non-native educators in English language teaching* (pp. 57–72), Mahwah, NJ: Lawrence Erlbaum.

Leung, C., Harris, R., & Rampton, B. (1997) The idealised native-speaker, reified ethnicities, and classroom realities: contemporary issues in TESOL. *Working papers in urban language and literacies*, no. 2. King's College, London.

MacArthur, T. (1999) On the origin and nature of Standard English. *World Englishes*, 18(2), 61–170.

Martin-Jones, M. & Romaine, S. (1986) Semilingualism: a half-baked theory of communicative competence. *Applied linguistics*, 7(1), 26–38.

McCawley, J. D. (1986) Review of *The native speaker is dead!* by T. M. Paikeday. *Linguistics*, 24(6), 1137–41.

Medgyes, P. (1994) *The non-native teacher*. London: Macmillan.

Medgyes, P. (1999) *The non-native teacher* (revised 2nd edn.). Ismaning, Germany: Hueber Verlang.

Mohanan, K. P. (1998) On new/ non-native Englishes: a quartet:

second response. In R. Singh (ed.), *The native speaker: multilingual perspectives* (pp. 50–3). New Delhi: Sage.

Paikeday, T. M. (1985) *The native speaker is dead!* Toronto and New York: Paikeday Pub. Co.

Pawley, A. & Syder, F. H. (1983) Two puzzles for linguistic theory: naturelike selection and naturelike fluency. In J. C. Richards & R. Schmidt (eds.), *Language and communication* (pp. 191–226). Harlow: Longman.

Phillipson, R. (1992) *Linguistic imperialism*. Oxford: Oxford University Press.

Rajagopalan, K. (1997) Linguistics and the myth of nativity: comments on the controversy over "new/non-native" Englishes. *Journal of Pragmatics*, 27, 225–31.

Rajagopalan, K. (1999) Of EFL teachers, conscience and cowardice. *ELT Journal*, 53(3), 200–6.

Seidlhofer, B. (2000) Mind the gap: English as a mother tongue versus English as a lingua franca. University of Vienna Department of English, *Views*, 9(1), 51–68.

Singh, R. (ed.) (1998) *The native speaker: multilingual perspectives*. New Delhi: Sage.

Smith, L (ed.) (1983) *Readings in English as an international language*. Oxford: Pergamon Press.

Tajfel, H. (1981) *Human groups and social categories*. Cambridge: Cambridge University Press.

van Els, T. J. M. (2000) The European Union, its institutions and its languages: some language political observations. Final Public lecture University of Nijmegen, The Netherlands, 22 September.

wa' Thiongo, N. (1986) *Decolonising the mind: the politics of language in African literature*. London: Heinemann.

FURTHER READING

Bialystok, E. (1997) The structure of age: in search of barriers to second language acquisition. *Second language research*, 13, 116–37.

Coulmas, F. (ed.) (1981) *Festschrift for native speaker*. The Hague: Mouton.

Graddol, D. (1997) *The future of English*. London: The British Council.

Kaplan, A. (1993) *French lessons: a memoir*. Chicago: University of Chicago Press.

18 Language Minorities

JOHN EDWARDS

18.1 Introduction

On his arrival in England in 1930, Gandhi was asked by a journalist what he thought of modern civilization. His famous response: "That would be a good idea." Less well known, perhaps, is his observation (made to his biographer, Louis Fischer, in 1946) that "civilization is to be judged by its treatment of minorities." Such a litmus test has often been suggested and, more broadly, many writers have argued that the moral standing of societies can best be appraised through a consideration of how they treat their poorest members, the most socially disadvantaged, those marginalized by accident or by design. If, indeed, we pay attention to the *gaps* between the "haves" and the "have-nots" (however defined), we often add substantially to cruder views based upon overall wealth, power, and productivity. Modern rhetoric about "leveling the playing fields" or "equal access" reflects some of the salient concerns here, concerns that are, in fact, central to liberal-democratic sensitivities. Traditional liberal attitudes – such as the desire to ameliorate social conditions so that individuals may have the best opportunity to fulfill their potentials, to enjoy self-defined lives – are of course relevant here. There have been recent attempts to reconcile such attitudes, which traditionally remained neutral as to the *contents* of the good or fulfilling life, with selective attention to *groups* rather than individuals – a reconciliation that allegedly extends liberalism in ways that do not damage its philosophical core. Kymlicka (1995) has argued, for instance, that some groups require extra attention for the continuation of their culture; these are typically collectivities that have suffered at the hands of more powerful neighbors, or rivals, or colonizers. He further suggests that indigenous groups have a stronger claim on this attention than do immigrant populations. And, while he discusses a variety of *types* of groups, his main concern is for ethnocultural ones. Indeed, if we are interested in "non-mainstream" groups that are differentiated by language, we are virtually always talking about ethnic communities.

Aside from considerations of fairness or justice that motivate attention to those outside the social mainstream, the study of ethnolinguistic minority groups can be rewarding in broader ways. The basic issue, for instance, in ethnocultural continuity is one of identity maintenance, and it is naturally more poignant when the group in question feels itself (its language, its culture) to be at risk. This is why settings involving minority groups often show things in the boldest fashion. But it would be an error to imagine that the matter is one of "minority" interest alone; *all* groups – large or small, weak or powerful – have stakes here. We can see this more clearly once we realize that struggles for the maintenance of group identity are not only to be understood in *inter*-group terms: there is also an *intra*-group dimension. Quite apart from whether or not groups stand in fear of neighboring cultures, there exists the difficulty of preserving valued traditions in a world increasingly full of homogenizing pressures. A desired continuity, one that stresses the original, the pure, the authentic – highly-charged words, to be sure, and not always appropriate – must contend with an equally desired modernization (for example), with broader and broader access, with mobility of every description.

A more or less modern perspective was provided by Saussure. In describing the spread of language, he referred to two conflicting tendencies, *la force d'intercourse* and *l'esprit de clocher*; he felt, however, that what obtained for language obtained generally:

> The laws that govern the spread of linguistic phenomena are the same as those that govern any custom whatsoever, e.g., fashion. In every human collectivity two forces are always working simultaneously and in opposing directions: individualism or *provincialism* [*esprit de clocher*] on the one hand and *intercourse* – communications among men – on the other.   (Saussure, [1916] 1960, pp. 205–6)

Provincialism is what keeps communities faithful to their original habits, but at the price of immobility and narrowness (*il rend les hommes sédentaires*); "intercourse," by contrast, obliges people to move about and forces them out of the shadow of the village belfry.

Tensions between the village and the town, between the traditional and the modern, between minorities and majorities, are obviously very old indeed, but it is surely reasonable to suggest that they now have greater force than ever before. Opposing centrifugal and centripetal pressures can be observed across a wide range of settings and have been described, in fact, as the "axial principles of our age" (Barber, 1992, p. 53). These pressures have been discussed in recent times by many writers, using many different dichotomies to try and capture their essence. Among these are "roots and options," "civism and pluralism," "state and community," "tribalism and globalism." And of course there is the classic distinction, first drawn by the German sociologist, Ferdinand Tönnies, between *Gemeinschaft* and *Gesellschaft*. Not all of these dichotomies are exactly synonymous, but all reflect the tension inherent in desires to retain something "small," or "valued," or "traditional" in the face of larger, overarching, more impersonal forces. The operative question can often be stated as some variant of "How can I or my group keep what is held dear without forfeiting access to a wider world?"

We are talking here, at the broadest level, of matters of *pluralism* and *assimilation*, and the fact that contemporary sociologists and social historians have coined phrases like *pluralistic integration, participationist pluralism, modified pluralism, liberal pluralism, multivariate assimilation* (and other such unwieldy and jargonistic terms) suggests that, in many different social settings, some intermediate position has been (or could potentially be) achieved between complete, seamless assimilation into a mainstream and social segregation. This is the tension underlying many minority–majority contacts.

For monolingual majority-group speakers in their own "mainstream" settings, the instrumentality and the symbolism of language coincide and, for most such individuals, the language-identity linkage is not problematic – indeed, it is seldom considered. Minority-group speakers, however, may lack this luxury; for them, matters of language and culture are often more immediate. There is often the possibility – and, in many instances, the inevitability – of a split between the communicative and the symbolic functions of language: you may have to live and work in a new language, a medium that is not the carrier of your culture or the vehicle of your literature. In these sorts of settings the study of minority groups, and their identities, clearly has general illuminative value. Identities, like everything else, are thrown into sharper relief when threats are perceived. Minority attitudes and actions can also galvanize others, and may remind a larger and often unreflective society that matters of language and identity are not relevant for "ethnics" and "minorities" alone.

The three great contemporary themes of sociolinguistics and the sociology of language are the relationship between language and identity, endangered languages, and the new ecolinguistics – which is, above all, concerned with the preservation of diversity. Always important strands, they take center stage now, in part, because of the transitional times in which we live. This is because identity is the heart of the matter, and because concern for it is unsurprisingly greatest when it, and the languages associated with it, become most susceptible to change. Since one is tempted to say that matters of identity are important in *all* areas of what might simply be termed the "social life of language," they are clearly central to much of applied linguistics in particular. With what has been said above about the particular poignancy of small-group contexts, it follows that language minorities and minority languages will be of special interest – both intrinsically and for the generalizable information that they can reveal. In this chapter, I will comment upon some of the most salient features in this connection. In Section 18.2, definitions – of both immigrant and indigenous minority groups and their languages – are considered. In Section 18.3, the meaning and implications of language maintenance, decline, shift and revival are dealt with, with some particular attention given to the role of linguists as advocates as well as scholars (here I also touch upon contemporary thrusts under the heading of the "ecology of language"). Bilingualism is the theme of Section 18.4, since it is commonly seen as the key to the co-existence of smaller and larger varieties. Following that in Section 18.5 are remarks on the categorization of minority languages – together with some justification of the utility of typological exercises; in this section I return once more to modern ecology-of-language matters. The final section, 18.6, presents a summary and conclusions in which, once again, an argument is made for the particular relevance of minority dynamics for the larger applied linguistics enterprise.

18.2   Minority Groups

The position of minority groups and the maintenance of their languages are very much in the news today. Regarding indigenous minorities, consider the case of continental Europe: as it moves – sometimes erratically – toward federalism, its minorities and its "stateless" peoples are pressing for increased and improved attention. About 20 years ago, in fact, the European Parliament began to provide such recognition and, since then, there have been further developments (see Baetens Beardsmore, 1993, 1994; Edwards, 1994a; Sikma & Gorter, 1991). Important here was the establishment in 1982 of the Dublin-based Bureau for Lesser Used Languages. Its Secretary-General recently observed that: "If our languages have been ignored in the past by European institutions this is no longer the case. The European Community is positive towards the cause of our languages and now includes in its budget a provision of 3.5 million ECU to promote regional and minority languages and cultures" (Breathnach, 1993, p. 1). The phrase "Europe of the Regions" is increasingly heard and discussed, and minorities are looking to link their own concerns with those of others (see Dekkers, 1995, and other publications of the Fryske Akademy). In eastern Europe and the former Soviet Union, as well, minority issues are firmly on the agenda as once-smothered ethnicities are reasserted (Ignatieff, 1993; Moynihan, 1993).

Turning to immigrant minority groups, we can observe recent agitations in the United States over multiculturalism (for critical treatments, see Hughes, 1993; Schlesinger, 1992) as well as the continuing saga of the "US English" movement, clearly aimed at reducing the perceived "threat" of Spanish (Baron, 1990; Crawford, 1992; Marshall, 1986). In Canada, the ongoing struggle between English and French has concentrated minds wonderfully – but interested observers insufficiently appreciate how this debate has drawn in *all* groups (including aboriginal and allophone populations) and has occasioned intense scrutiny of officially-sponsored policies of bilingualism and multiculturalism (Edwards, 1994b, 1995a, 1997).

What *is* a minority group or a minority language? Certainly, the agreed context is important here. Is, for instance, French in Canada a minority language? It depends on the geographic perspective – provincial, regional, continental – that one adopts. (Indeed, one could say the same about English: there is much current debate about whether Québec anglophones are a "real" minority.) Such definitional difficulty applies to many minority languages in which a concentration of population has a long- or well-established homeland within some larger political boundaries. This also raises issues about the breadth and variability of allegiance, about state and nation, and about – more specifically – the fact that state and national borders need not coincide. (Much current Canadian confusion, for instance, arises because Québec sovereigntists feel themselves to be, above all, *un peuple*, a nation denied its proper autonomy, while others see them as a provincial component of federalism – an obviously distinct component, to be sure, but not of national status.) Even where borders *do* coincide, minority status may attach to the group's language, usually indicating previous historical movement (e.g., Irish in Ireland). Some might also want to point here to languages which have majority status within a state but which, not being so-called "languages of wider communication," have in some sense a minority role on a continental or global stage (Bulgarian could be illustrative here). This leads directly to the issues of power, prestige, and dominance which are often more salient than mere numbers in determining majority or minority status. Numbers (and concentrations of numbers) themselves are important, of course. Indigenous people in Canada, for example, now number just over one million, thus constituting only about 3.8 percent of the total population (see Edwards, 1998, for broad coverage of recent Canadian language issues). Furthermore – since it would clearly be inappropriate to consider "aboriginals" as some monolithic entity – we should also bear in mind that this overall number is broken down into more than 50 language groups, only three of which have more than 5,000 speakers (Edwards, 1995b; Foster, 1982). But numbers alone are not the whole story – nor, indeed, its most important element. Native language groups in South Africa vastly outnumber speakers of English and Afrikaans, but have historically been of "minority" status in terms of power and prestige.

There is, too, the question of minorities *within* minorities – the aboriginal groups in Québec come to mind, as do national groups within the ex-Soviet republic of Georgia. Bitter recent experience teaches us that possession of minority status does not necessarily sensitize groups to the perceived plight of other, smaller entities. For example, the nationalists in Québec who argue that it is their democratic right to secede, following a successful provincial referendum, would generally deny that same course of action to the James Bay Cree. *Quod licet Jovi non licet bovi.*

These are examples of indigenous varieties. Very often, although of minority status, such groups – by virtue of cohesion, or concentration, or geographical remoteness or isolation – do have the advantage of a homeland or heartland. This is denied to immigrant minorities whose problems may therefore be exacerbated. (There are important variations, of course. The French in the northeastern United States, and the Spanish in the southwest are, unlike others, just a metaphorical step away from their "heartland." Indeed, the effect of their migration has often been simply to expand that heartland so that it transcends political boundaries.)

It is important to understand the temporal dimension here: the very distinction between indigenous and immigrant soon becomes arguable. In the Canadian context, for example, would we restrict the term "indigenous" only to Amerindian varieties (whose speakers were themselves migrants at one time, some crossing via "Beringia," for instance)? Should we consider English and French to be indigenous (now, if not always)? What about some of the languages that came with immigration – Gaelic, for example, which arrived in Canada in the late eighteenth century? Similarly, what are the indigenous languages of Australia or the United States? In the latter context, both English and Vietnamese could be considered non-indigenous; would we want to make a case, in some circumstances at least, for English being somehow *more* indigenous than Vietnamese? Can it ever be correct to establish linguistic indigenity with the forming of a country, with the emergence of a new state? If we leave the so-called "receiving" countries and consider, say, Europe, we can still find difficulties in assessing indigenity. Stephens (1976), in his treatment of European linguistic minorities, attempted to distinguish between "indigenous" (apparently meaning native to a place, with length of residence unspecified) and "autochthonous" (with its more aboriginal, from-the-soil connotations). Does this simplify or confuse things? We might agree that the Welsh and the Bretons are indigenous minorities, but are they autochthonous? How will we regard the apparently permanent *gastarbeiter* groups in western Europe five hundred years hence? As another non-European example, consider the Tamils of Sri Lanka. Some came to the island a thousand years ago, others from the mid-nineteenth century. Are some indigenous and some not; are some more indigenous than others?

How long must residence be established before a new homeland emerges? Obviously this matter can dissolve into absurdity, and in most cases, perhaps, we might find generally accepted conventions. But I have two serious points to make here. First, it is well to remind ourselves of the temporal perspective generally since, on the one hand, it may decrease the immodesty of some of our flamboyant claims about which minority groups have "seniority" over others, whose land is whose, and so on. On the other hand, it underscores the dynamic, not static, nature of the human tide. We might even hope to remind ourselves here of the altogether too neat dichotomies of oppressor/oppressed, victor/vanquished, and even moral/immoral, divisions that often reflect an allegiance to a black-and-white view of history, a view which denies a more complicated reality. Second, and more immediately, the theoretical difficulty of establishing indigenity leads to the possibility that all minorities, whatever their provenance, may exhibit certain common features. Thus, a typology of minority language situations (see below) might link indigenous with immigrant minorities, however defined.

It is also necessary to bear in mind that minority communities and, more particularly, minority languages and identities – however defined – are by definition always at least at a *potential* risk. This is, perhaps, the one unifying feature, the one constant, across contexts. Because of the importance of *power* and *status* – of greater moment, as already noted, than numbers, concentrations, and geographical placement – minority-group stability cannot simply be assured through official recognition. Romansch may be official in Switzerland, but it is not on the same footing as German, French, or Italian. French in Québec, the province's official language (and one increasingly supported in all sorts of ways), is still spoken by only six million in a North American anglophone ocean 40 times greater. Irish is the official language of Ireland, but rather than being the Celtic triumph which some hoped statehood would produce, it illustrates the relative inadequacy of bureaucratic sanction alone. There are, of course, some success stories. Catalan is one, but it would be simplistic to assume that the possession of regional-autonomy status within Spain was the prime cause of this success: it was necessary, perhaps, but certainly not sufficient.

The preceding discussion is hardly exhaustive, but it does at least suggest something of the terminological and other difficulties that complicate the study of minority cultures and languages. It also prompts the Orwellian observation that some minorities are more minor than others. As Allardt (1984, p. 203) put it, "*ils sont plus minorisés.*"

18.3 Maintaining Minority Varieties

The idea of "language maintenance" is also less than crystal clear. Must it always imply vernacular oral maintenance? Could a language preserved in written form, but spoken by few (or none) on a regular basis, be considered "maintained"? In most instances, of course, maintenance *does* imply a continuity of the ordinary spoken medium and this, in turn, highlights the importance of uninterrupted domestic language transmission from one generation to the next. If this transmission is sustained, then language maintenance – at some level – is assured; if this transmission falters or ends, then the language becomes vulnerable and its maintenance threatened (see Fishman, 1990). This is another way of saying that the home is perhaps the most important of all language *domains* – but it is immediately apparent that for this central domain to continue, there must usually exist extra-domestic settings within which the language is necessary or, at least, of considerable importance. Furthermore, not all domains are of equal weight or value in terms of supporting linguistic continuity. While it is impossible to be categorical here, it is possible to identify – for a given variety, at a given time, in a given context – what one might call *domains of necessity*. These domains are typically, of course, related to the most central aspects of people's lives, and so one could single out settings such as the home, the school, and the workplace. On the other hand, domains in which participation is voluntary, or sporadic, or idiosyncratic, are not likely to be so important for broad language maintenance. In summary, then, the maintenance of a language is on a surer footing if it, and it alone, is required in domains of central and continuing salience.

Language maintenance is not, of course, an issue equally germane for all groups. It is, rather, one which assumes greater importance when a group and its language are at some risk of assimilation; thus, discussions of language minorities and language maintenance naturally coincide. In such discussions, furthermore, language maintenance almost always involves at least some element of language *revival*, for it is only when a variety begins to lose ground (or is seen to be at some risk of doing so) that attention becomes focused upon it. It is useful to bear in mind here that revival does not simply and solely mean a restoration to life after death. ("Language death," incidentally, is another term which is less straightforward than it might first appear.) Revival can also, quite legitimately, refer to reawakening and renewal, to the restoration of vigor and activity, to the arresting of decline or discontinuity.

How, in this sense, can language maintenance be effected; how can decline and discontinuity be halted? There are two major and interrelated factors involved, one tangible and one more subjective. The first we have already mentioned: the continuing existence of important domains within which the use of the language is necessary. These domains depend, of course, upon social, political, and economic forces, both within and without the particular language community. Although the details will clearly vary from case to case, of general relevance are issues of linguistic practicality, communicative efficiency, social mobility, and economic advancement. These four constitute the greatest advantages associated with "large" languages, and the greatest disincentives for the maintenance of "small" ones. In many cases of language contact between varieties that are unequal in important ways, some bilingual accommodation is often sought, but bilingualism itself can be an unstable and impermanent way-station on the road to a new monolingualism (in the dominating variety; see also below). Formal language planning on behalf of beleaguered languages often can do very little to stem the forces of urbanization, modernization, and mobility, the forces which typically place a language in danger and which lead to language shift. A decline in the existence and attractions of traditional life styles also inexorably entails a decline in languages associated with them. Of course, linguistic standardization and modernization efforts are always theoretically possible, but they are not always practicable, nor do they necessarily change in any substantial way the status-based balance of dominance among competing forms. "Small" varieties which have developed to national language levels (for example, Somali and Guaraní) remain less broadly useful than (for example) English and Spanish.

It should always be remembered that, historically and linguistically, change rather than stasis is the norm. Environments alter, people move, and needs and demands change – and such factors have a large influence upon language. The desire for mobility and modernization is, with some few notable exceptions, a global phenomenon. Whether one looks at the capitalist world or the erstwhile communist one, at contemporary times or historical ones, at empires or small societies, at immigrant minorities or indigenous groups, one sees a similarity of pressures which take their toll, force change, and throw populations into transitional states that have, naturally, unpleasant consequences (at least in the short term). Language decline and shift are most often *symptoms* of contact between groups of unequal political and economic power. Decline, then, is an effect of a larger cause, and it follows that attempts to arrest it are usually very difficult. One does not cure measles by covering up the spots; one cannot maintain a language by dealing with language alone. A logical approach to language maintenance, and the halting of decline and shift, is to unpick the social fabric that has evolved and then reweave it in a new pattern. This is, again, theoretically possible (as with revolutionary upheavals), but it is significant here that most who are concerned with language maintenance usually want only *some* reworking of social evolution, not wholesale revolution. It is a considerable understatement to say that this is a difficult and delicate undertaking.

The other, more intangible aspect of language maintenance is the matter of the collective *will* to stem discontinuity, to sustain vigor in the face of the factors just discussed. This brings us to the larger question of *identity*. Nahir (1977) has pointed out that revival – and, we could also say, efforts at language maintenance generally – presupposes the existence of a variety with which a group identifies, and it is from this source that the will to act arises. The language in question typically possesses powerful *symbolic* value in addition to its more purely communicative functions. Rabin's (1971) view that revival efforts are both radical and "extralinguistic" seems correct – radical, inasmuch as a significant change to the *status quo* is intended; extralinguistic, since maintenance/revival activity must centrally involve social considerations and forces.

Given the powerful elements already mentioned, the formidable attractions associated with "large" languages and "large" societies, it is not surprising that *active* moves for language maintenance are usually the preserve of only a small number of people. There are, of course, practical reasons why the masses cannot usually involve themselves in maintenance efforts, and it is a common-place to find that a broad but rather passive goodwill exists at this level. To galvanize this inert quantity has always been the most pressing issue for activists who, by logical extension, are often rather atypical of those for whom they speak and act. Many years ago, in commenting upon efforts to sustain Irish, Moran (1900, p. 268) made a point which is still relevant in many quarters: "Without scholars [the revival] cannot succeed; with scholars as leaders it is bound to fail."

Language maintenance is usually a parlous enterprise. By the time a "small" variety is seen to stand in need of it, the precipitating social pressures have often assumed large proportions. It is interesting that, traditionally, linguists themselves have seen, in most cases of language decline and shift, a "natural-ness" which effectively precludes any useful intervention, even if it were thought broadly desirable (see Bolinger, 1980). Some contemporary scholars (particularly sociolinguists and sociologists of language), however, have not shied away from engagement in what might be called the "public life" of language. Fishman is a good example here. He has noted that regret over mother tongue loss – among groups who "have not capitulated to the massive blandishments of western materialism, who experience life and nature in deeply poetic and collectively meaningful ways" (1982, p. 8) – has brought many academics into linguistics and related fields. This self-proclaimed "founding father" of sociolinguistics makes no secret of his own commitment here, and has recently (1990, 1991) devoted considerable attention to the question of "reversing language shift" – an undertaking he deems a "quest" of "sanctity." Fishman implicitly and explicitly endorses a view of applied linguistics as *both* scholarship and advocacy; this stance may perhaps be thought to involve some dangers (see Edwards, 1995b).

In 1992, Krauss made a pointed argument, one which continues to set the tone for much contemporary debate. Linguists, he noted, will be "cursed by future generations" if they do not actively intervene to stem the "catastrophic destruction" now threatening nine out of ten of the world's languages (pp. 7– 8). More traditional linguistic documentation is seen to be insufficient; social and political action and advocacy are required. Linguists should go well beyond the usual academic role of description and documentation, he argued, "promote language development in the necessary domains . . . [and] learn . . . the techniques of organization, monitoring and lobbying, publicity, and activism" (p. 9). A response by Ladefoged, arguing for a continuation of the linguist-as-disinterested-scientist role, ensured that the debate would continue. Adopting what is perhaps a more traditional stance, he noted that the linguist's task is to present the facts, and not to attempt to persuade groups that language shift is a bad thing *per se*; not all speakers of threatened varieties see their preservation as possible or even always desirable:

> One can be a responsible linguist and yet regard the loss of a particular language, or even a whole group of languages, as far from a "catastrophic destruction" . . . statements such as "just as the extinction of any animal species diminishes our world, so does the extinction of any language" are appeals to our emotions, not to our reason.   (Ladefoged, 1992, p. 810)

A third participant in this debate (in *Language*) was Dorian, who noted that all arguments about endangered languages are political in nature, that the low status of many at-risk varieties leads naturally to a weakened will-to-maintenance, that the loss of any language is a serious matter, and that the laying out of the "facts" advocated by Ladefoged is not a straightforward matter, since they are inevitably intertwined with political positions. At the very least, Dorian notes, this is an "issue on which linguists' advocacy positions are worth hearing" (1993, p. 579; fuller details here can be found in Edwards, 1994c). We have, indeed, heard more and more of these positions, and important contemporary collections include those of Brenzinger (1992, 1998),

Dorian (1989), Grenoble & Whaley (1998a), Nettle & Romaine (2000), and Robins & Uhlenbeck (1991); see also Crystal (2000).

Apart from anthologies dealing with endangered varieties, we should note here that several organizations are now devoted to the preservation of diversity, to the "ecological" perspective, to active intervention on behalf of threatened languages. They include the Endangered Language Fund, the Committee on Endangered Languages and Their Preservation, and Terralingua: Partnerships for Linguistic and Biological Diversity (based in the United States); the Foundation for Endangered Languages (in England); Germany's Gesellschaft für bedrohte Sprachen; and the International Clearing House for Endangered Languages (Japan). Similar concerns motivate the European programs of Linguasphere and the Observatoire Linguistique (Dalby, 2000) as well as those whose more pointed purpose is language rights legislation. Fuller details may be found in Crystal (2000) and Maffi (2000).

It is clear that this is a very contentious area. What some would see as inappropriate and unscholarly intervention, others would view as absolutely necessary. Any combination of scholarship and advocacy is fraught with potential danger, but one might reasonably argue that one of the "facts" to be presented to groups and policy-makers is the very commitment of at least some in the academic constituency. Groups whose languages are at risk might profit from the knowledge that the issues so central to them are also seen as important by "outsiders." At the end of the day, though, we should remember that the actions of linguists – whether fervently pro-maintenance in tenor or more "detached" – are likely to pale when compared with the realities of social and political pressures. These realities should at least suggest a sense of perspective.

18.4   The Bilingual Solution

Those who wish to see an extended future for the small languages of the world no longer propose – if, indeed, they ever seriously did – that Welsh or Frisian, Haida or Mi'kmaq, will be sufficient for their speakers' purposes and aspirations across all domains. Accommodation with "bigger" languages increasingly recommends itself and this leads to an emphasis upon bilingualism as a longer-term solution for small or threatened languages. This position is particularly prominent within contemporary ecology-of-language frameworks. Mühlhäusler (1996), for instance, argues for what he calls an "equitable" bilingualism. Maffi (2000) notes the desirability of a stable and non-subtractive bilingualism that links mother tongues with languages of wider communication. Wurm says the same, endorsing the "possibility of speakers of . . . endangered languages being bilingual in their own language and a given large metropolitan language" (1998, p. 194). And Crystal observes that the duality is "perfectly possible, and . . . highly desirable. Because the two languages have different purposes – one for identity; the other for intelligibility [*sic*] – they do not have to be in conflict" (2000, p. 29); he also expands upon the *modus vivendi* offered by "healthy" bilingualism – i.e., one in which languages are complementary and not competitive.

Bilingualism is, in fact, a reasonable solution – reasonable on theoretical grounds, and reasonable in the *de facto* sense that more people in the world are bilingual (or multilingual) than are monolingual. It is also worth restating the truisms that bilingualism *per se* involves no cognitive penalties, that it is a capacity that can be almost effortlessly acquired by the youngest of children, and that the lack of education (and, indeed, illiteracy) of most of the world's multilinguals further attests to its unexceptional character. Bilingualism is not rocket science. It is a rational and practical response to diversity; indeed, it is an obvious one. The question here is not whether bilingualism *can* allow people to alleviate linguistic and cultural pressures – the answer is clear. The question is whether bilingualism *will* have this function, particularly where small languages are involved.

Diglossia between smaller and larger varieties is difficult to ensure, especially in times of change. In Austro-Hungary, Mühlhäusler (2000) tells us, lack of mobility reinforced linguistic ecological stability. On the other hand, we recall that migrations – from the old to the new world, for example – have generally exacted linguistic and cultural tolls. Is the implication that stasis is the price of ethnolinguistic continuity? And mobility is not only a physical phenomenon – there is movement, for instance, that either consists of, or is assisted by, education and literacy. Is it any wonder, then, that the contemporary ecological viewpoint sometimes has difficulty endorsing literacy, and champions localized and oral cultures? While the latter is reasonable *per se*, we should surely be wary of arguments which even begin to suggest that language maintenance might be purchased at the expense of literacy.

Of course, if people are willing to remain in an isolated condition – physically or psychologically – the possibilities for long-term bilingualism are more propitious. Indeed, isolation has not only stabilized bilingualism, it has very often accounted for the endurance of monolingualism in the original variety. Twenty years ago, Fishman noted:

> Stable bilingualism and biculturism cannot be maintained on the basis of open and unlimited interaction between minorities and majorities. Open economic access and unrestricted intergroup interaction may be fine for various practical and philosophical purposes. Indeed, they strike most of us as highly desirable legal and social principles; but they are destructive of minority ethno-linguistic continuity. (Fishman, 1980, p. 171)

This seems to summarize the situation quite well. Here is an avowed supporter of minority languages, of stable bilingualism, of "ethnolinguistic continuity," suggesting that the price of stability is higher than most have evidently been willing to pay. Curious, to say the least, that open access and interaction are seen as "fine" – these are the sorts of things that people struggle and migrate for, not simply desirable principles. Would we advocate voluntary minority-group self-segregation – as has appealed only to a handful of groups, generally along religious lines – or would we take steps to ensure that Gaelic speakers never get off Cape Breton, remaining in their island fastness for the sake of their language and culture?

18.5 Categorizing Minority Languages

Minority language situations are usually socially and politically complex, and it is sometimes said that a further difficulty arises because every setting is different. Of course each is unique – but this is not because its elements are found nowhere else; in fact, basic constituents are remarkably similar across contexts. The uniqueness of each arises, rather, through particular combinations and weightings of essentially the same building blocks. The implication is clear: things can be generalized, providing our data are comprehensive and we have some comparative framework on which to array them. A typology, then, suggests itself.

Some commentators, it is true, have expressed doubts about typological exercises. In several reviews, for instance, Williams (who has severely criticized the current state of the sociology of language in general and minority language matters in particular) has questioned the utility of typologies (see, for example, his 1980 review of Allardt's comparative study of European minorities). More specifically, he has claimed (1986) that typologies reflect "implicit theoretical assumptions" while perhaps having "limited analytical usefulness" (p. 509). In 1988, he repeated these observations, adding: "I fail to understand the preoccupation of students of language with typologies" (p. 171). I think Williams' points are of interest, but they do not necessarily sound a death knell for typologies. All endeavors proceed from implicit assumptions, but the constraints these imply can be greater or lesser depending, among other things, upon the comprehensiveness of the undertaking; a broader typology with many elements is thus more likely to be useful than a narrower approach. Also, whatever the verdict on the purely analytic utility of a typology, it would seem that simply having a broad listing of potentially important elements is worthwhile.

Roberts, a colleague of Williams, has also criticized the *use* of typologies in language policy/conflict situations. They "are born out of static, descriptive accounts of situations, and imply permanent relationships" (1987, p. 311). They can provide "snapshot accounts of particular language situations, but the tendency to 'fit' the parameters of a given typology onto a language situation results in some serious limitations" (p. 312). They take no account of the "historically specific dimensions of a language situation" and are constrained by their "inability to pinpoint the dynamic (and frequently contradictory) interrelationships between different elements" (p. 312). A specific difficulty is that their application "forces discussion of societal bilingualism as a stable state" (p. 321).

I have provided the citations here because they reflect reasonable cautions. In response, however, it should be said that a typology *per se* need not imply permanence (typological models can be reworked as necessary, for example); that *any* account will necessarily be a "snapshot"; that it is only misuse of a model which would lead to a forcing of parameters; that there is no good reason why a typology cannot explore historical dimensions; that a good model could actually elucidate relationships among variables; and that a typological treatment of bilingualism which permitted discussion of it only as a stable state would be obviously flawed.

My general point is this: since there is every reason to assume that people will continue to interest themselves in language situations, and wish to describe and account for their dynamics, since it makes no sense to assume that different contexts are unique in every element, and since we are inevitably and rightly drawn to the task of theory construction or, at least, classification/description, then a comprehensive and well-specified typology may serve as a useful guide. Cross-context comparisons might well be facilitated, for example, if attention was given to the same variables in all settings; any student in the area will have experienced frustration in attempting comparisons and contrasts where this sort of attention has not been paid (see Ferguson, 1991).

Finally here, we can simply observe that many respected workers in the field – Haugen, Stewart, Kloss, and Ferguson among them – have found it meaningful to employ a typological approach. Haugen's concern, for example, was that:

> most language descriptions are prefaced by a brief and perfunctory statement concerning the number and location of its speakers and something of their history. Rarely does such a description really tell the reader what he ought to know about the social status and function of the language in question. Linguists have generally been too eager to get on with the phonology, grammar, and lexicon to pay more than superficial attention to what I would like to call the "ecology of language." (Haugen, 1972, p. 325)

Besides linguists, educationalists, sociologists, psychologists, historians, and others have also often failed to give sufficient treatment to ecological variables. As well, it seems to me that useful sociolinguistic forays into minority language matters – and many others, too – must be interdisciplinary; we can no longer afford the luxury of simply remaining within our own narrow boundaries, particularly since their location is very much open to debate.

Various typologies and part-typologies already exist, of course – one thinks of the valued work of Ferguson (1962, 1966), Haugen (1972), Kloss (1967, 1968), Stewart (1962, 1968), and others. These have not, however, been systematically exploited, and a more comprehensive approach could integrate and expand upon previous insights. In formulating a typology of minority language settings, it is necessary, then, to list, categorize, and intercorrelate many elevant variables – in a word, to try and understand something of the interrelationships that give a setting its unique tenor. The result would be a framework clarifying contexts of language maintenance and language shift. One could imagine, as well, that such a scaffolding could be used to inform and guide relevant policies. If minority communities are described in a formalized or semi-formalized way, they can better understand their own situation (and how it compares to others elsewhere), and can more accurately present their case. Similarly, if particular responses are desired from some larger, or external, or "mainstream" authority, the latter should be given the best and most candid information available; otherwise inaccurate, inadequate, or inappropriate interventions may result, actions that will consequently have little likelihood of success.

More specifically, for what follows I am making several assumptions. First, a comprehensive, multidisciplinary analysis of ethnic minority language situations will be intrinsically useful context by context. Second, emerging generalities may be found which will permit comparison and classification of different contexts under certain rubrics. I have already pointed out that the uniqueness of situations arises from the *combination* of shared components – and anyone who has ever attempted a contrastive analysis, or who has cited different examples to make a general point, has in effect argued that some features are constant or at least similar enough across contexts to lead to generalization. Third, information thus obtained may produce a useful socio-political picture of minority settings from the perspectives of *both* minority and majority communities. Fourth, this in turn might enable predictions to be made about language maintenance and shift and, indeed, might even serve as an indicator of what is desirable, what is possible, and what is likely.

Considering the utility of a geographical underpinning for more socially orientated investigation, it is interesting that there are actually rather few such basic frameworks (see Edwards, 1991), although several writers have informally drawn attention to specific points of similarity across contexts. A useful model to build upon is that proposed in 1987 by White; it involves three basic distinctions. The first is among minority languages which are unique to one state, those which are non-unique but which are still minorities in all contexts in which they occur, and those which are minorities in one setting but majority varieties elsewhere. This initial distinction gives rise to the terms *unique, non-unique,* and *local-only* minority. The second categorization deals with the type of connection between speakers of the same minority language in different states; are they *adjoining* or *non-adjoining*? Finally, what degree of spatial cohesion exists among speakers within a given state? Here, the terms *cohesive* and *non-cohesive* can be used. Given that the adjoining/non-adjoining distinction does not apply to unique minorities, it follows that a ten-cell model emerges. White's framework, as initially adapted (Edwards, 1991) dealt with *indigenous* minority language settings only; in an extension, however (Edwards, 1992), the model was enlarged to cover *immigrant* scenarios as well – so ten cells become twenty. Table 18.1 illustrates the model. There are, of course, problems with this model (as with any other); some of these are discussed in

Table 18.1 Examples of minority language situations

Type	Indigenous minorities	Immigrant minorities
1 Unique Cohesive	Sardinian (Sardinia) Welsh (Wales) Friulian (Friuli-Venezia-Giulia)	Dialect communities (often religiously organized) in which the variety is now divergent from that in the region of origin (e.g., Pennsylvania "Dutch")
2 Unique Non-cohesive	Cornish (Cornwall)	As above, but where speakers are scattered
3 Non-unique Adjoining Cohesive	Occitan (Piedmont and Liguria, and in France) Basque (France, and in Spain) Catalan (Spain, and in Andorra)	Enclaves of immigrants found in neighboring states
4 Non-unique Adjoining Non-cohesive	Saami (Finland, Norway, Sweden and Russia)	Scattered immigrants in neighboring states
5 Non-unique Non-adjoining Cohesive	Catalan (Spain, and in Sardinia)	Welsh (Patagonia) Gaelic (Nova Scotia)
6 Non-unique Non-adjoining Non-cohesive	Romany (throughout Europe)	Scattered immigrants of European origin in "new-world" receiving countries
7 Local-only Adjoining Cohesive	French (Valle d'Aosta, and in France)	French (in New England town enclaves) Spanish (southwest USA) Italian *gastarbeiter* (in Switzerland)
8 Local-only Adjoining Non-cohesive	German (Piedmont, and in Switzerland)	French (scattered throughout New England)
9 Local-only Non-adjoining Cohesive	French (Apulia, and in France)	Immigrant enclaves in "new-world" countries
10 Local-only Non-adjoining Non-cohesive	Albanian (throughout the Mezzogiorno, and in Albania)	As above, but where speakers are scattered

Source: Based on Edwards (1992). With kind permission by John Benjamins Publishing Company, Amsterdam/Philadelphia. www.benjamins.com.

Edwards (1992). However, it may possess some utility. Indeed, a geographical framework alone might be quite useful – for example, other things being equal (which they seldom are) or, indeed, unequal, the strength of a minority language will vary along the three dimensions of the model. A purely geographical approach must, nevertheless, have a severely limited significance, and in order to more fully apprehend the complexities of minority languages and their speakers, further information from a variety of sources is clearly required.

Ferguson and Stewart, to cite two well-known examples, have presented classificatory information concerning language types, functions, status, and degrees of use. Thus, Ferguson (1962, 1966) treats patterns of language dominance, extent of standardization and degree/type of language use; Stewart (1962, 1968) outlines language *types* (vernacular, standard, classical, etc.) and *functions* (in education, religion, officialdom, cross-group communication, and so on). These schemes, valuable as they are – and, by the way, relatively neglected as they are, at least outside that group of "typologically-inclined" scholars – clearly deal with an incomplete subset of the important features. There is little attention given to social-status elements for example, or to what Haugen would term "ecological" variables (i.e., those describing and illuminating interactions among languages, speakers, and environments).

Haugen's (1972) own ecology-of-language approach embraces linguistic, sociological, sociolinguistic, and other aspects, and directs attention to such matters as language domains, use, traditions, politics, and attitudes. Haarman (1986) built upon Haugen's perspective, expanding it considerably in terms of greater specificity of variables. However, while both Haugen and Haarmann move in the right directions, there remain some difficulties; these are addressed in Edwards (1992), but can be conveniently summarized here: first, there is insufficient specificity of variables – both schemes sketch out important areas, but lack of precision clearly detracts from typological utility; second, some important matters are almost entirely neglected – little is said, for example, about historical, psychological, educational, and geographic dimensions. One could respond to these points by noting that neither model restricts amplifications and expansions. Nevertheless, the fact remains that many points of detail are not explicitly presented, and I take this to be a failing in frameworks supposed to facilitate cross-situational comparability. Also, the introduction of neologisms and the use of terms which show considerable overlap are unfavorable features (although I must admit that my own scheme, in its present incarnation at least, is also less than perfect in these respects).

A recent typological approach from a psychological point of view is found in the "ethnolinguistic vitality" model. Giles, Bourhis, and Taylor (1977) outlined three factors – demography, status, and institutional support – seen to contribute to group viability. Bourhis, Giles, and Rosenthal (1981) extended this "objective" scheme to one of perceived or subjective vitality; they made the reasonable argument that groups' *perceptions* of vitality may be at variance with objective reality, and that such perceptions may be important determinants of individual and group behavior. They thus presented a 22-item "subjective vitality questionnaire" based upon the three factors just noted. Again, however, there are difficulties (see Edwards, 1985, 1992). As with the Haugen and Haarmann models, the vitality conception contains elements which are too general, and it neglects altogether some vital features. In presenting the original, "objective" format, Giles, Bourhis, and Taylor (1977) do provide useful discussion of the three factors, and they acknowledge that their analysis is not exhaustive. Nonetheless, they point out that the three-factor scheme meaningfully deals with linguistic minorities, and the subsequent expansion into "subjective" vitality assessment might be seen as a premature solidification of factors in the 22-item arrangement. In this latter format, dimensions such as the historical, economic, religious, political, and educational are assessed by only one question each; it is thus inevitable that only a very rudimentary overview can result.

The subjective vitality questionnaire has been used by Giles and his associates in quite a number of settings over the last few years, leading Young, Bell, and Giles (1988, p. 288) to note that "sufficient and necessary exploratory groundwork therefore has been laid down now for a more systematic programme of cross-national empirical research to be undertaken. Therein, a vitality theory can be formulated." Based upon points made above (see also Edwards, 1992), it will be clear, however, that I have some reservations. These revolve around what I consider to be inadequate and incomplete delineation of variables. Perhaps the most important aspect of any typology is comprehensiveness. Without this, it may have superficial plausibility and it may, indeed, enable separation and categorization of groups. It will, however, be limited in exactly the same way that a factor-analytic program is constrained by the appropriateness and breadth of input.

Of particular contemporary interest – and having the potential, perhaps, to embrace earlier and more limited approaches – is an ecological framework. Haarman (1986) has rightly pointed out that scholars had been conducting "ecological" investigations long before the birth of Haugen's outline (see above). Implicit in the earliest conceptions of this "economy of nature" is the scientific investigation of the "natural conditions" constituting environments and, from this perspective, ecological awareness (broadly speaking) is very old. It can be traced, for instance, at least to Aristotelian concepts of "design in nature" and the idea that the world is essentially ordered, it attracted further philosophical and religious elaborations (which argued, for example, that God was the designer), and it underpins contemporary secular science which replaces divinity with natural laws. In a predictable extension of a concept which initially focused upon plants and animals, an ecological anthropology folded culture into the mix, reminding us of the reciprocity between what is given and what is constructed. But again, what is sometimes taken as a modern idea has longstanding roots: Plato and Aristotle, after all, thought that climate was an important factor in human affairs and, in the eighteenth century, Montesquieu built an elaborate philosophy on this basis, a philosophy linking climate (and topography) to all manner of individual and collective traits – from exploratory activity to religion.

Apparently, the first specific reference to the ecology of language is found in a chapter by Voegelin, Voegelin, and Schutz (1967), but the term is particularly associated with Haugen (see his 1972 collection). His intent, as we have seen here, was to emphasize the interconnectedness of languages with their environments; more particularly, through his ecological model, Haugen endorsed linguistic diversity. Since his time, the breadth of the ecology-of-language view – a breadth that would logically follow from its parent discipline – has been progressively reduced and the label of ecology increasingly co-opted. Ecology traditionally involved adaptation and struggle within relationships ranging from the "beneficial" to the "inimical." In this sense, earlier non-interventionist linguistic views – now sometimes discredited on the grounds that it is wrong to simply stand aside and watch – were fuller than later ones, since the former often acknowledged a Darwinian sort of linguistic struggle. While there are some contemporary researchers who would claim an ecological perspective reflecting a broad spectrum of possibilities (from linguistic health all the way to extinction, perhaps) – see the recent chapter by Mufwene (2000), for instance – the field now generally argues for more pacific interaction. As Mühlhäusler (2000, p. 308) has noted in a recent review article, "functioning ecologies are nowadays characterized by predominantly mutually beneficial links and only to a small degree by competitive relationships . . . metaphors of struggle of life and survival of the fittest should be replaced by the appreciation of natural kinds and their ability to coexist and cooperate." As in ecology writ large, so in the ecology of language. We have a view of a world in which there is room for all languages, where the goodness of diversity is a given. The "new ecology" is motivated chiefly by the accelerated loss of languages; it is an environmentalism that makes a specific case for diversity and, while this is clearly a legitimate stance *per se*, it is not unreasonable to have some misgivings about an area that styles itself very broadly while marshalling its activities along rather more specific lines (for further details see Edwards, 2001, 2002).

I have mentioned here the work of Haugen, Haarmann, Giles, and others, and have tried to indicate that much further analysis of existing literature is needed before anything approaching a comprehensive typology is produced. Suggestions were also made (in Edwards, 1992) about further developments which would logically follow upon the construction of a more complete "checklist"; these include attempts to provide relative weightings for variables, probing for *meanings* attached to elements by respondents (i.e., going beyond measurement of *belief* to assessment of *attitude*, in the usual psychological meaning of these terms), factor-analytic reduction exercises, and the general formulation of an instrument which could be used for both "objective" and "subjective" purposes.

The present stage of development is clearly quite elementary – except, perhaps, for the basic geographic framework – but several important elements have suggested themselves. We could consider, on the one hand, three quite basic categories – speakers, language, and setting (these recall, of course,

Haugen's ideas of ecological relationships) and, on the other, a number of substantive perspectives (demography, sociology, linguistics, psychology, history, politics/law/government, geography, education, religion, economics/business/industry and media, for example). With cross-tabulation of these categories and perspectives, a scaffolding of 33 cells emerges which might serve as a useful starting point. (See Edwards, 1992 for fuller details, for an outline of some of the areas on which such a framework would focus, and for notes on some difficulties and overlaps.)

Space does not permit fuller elucidation of the current status of this typological model – which, in any event, remains incomplete. Apart from my own papers on the matter (referred to here), there are several recent discussions of the model which readers may find useful. These include Grenoble and Whaley (1998b) and King (2001). The former relates it to earlier work by Hyltenstam and Stroud (1991, 1996), as well as to Fishman's (1990, 1991) more restricted scheme for assessing and reversing language shift. The latter closely examine the typology and, while acknowledging some of its strengths, also note weaknesses and underdevelopments. Two of their critical comments are particularly apposite (and, indeed, I anticipated them in earlier work). First, the typology as it stands does not attend sufficiently to the *weighting* of variables, to their relative rankings; these will of course be of central importance in all applications. Second, some of the factors are, in themselves, insufficiently delineated – particularly those dealing with settings or situations; for example, in assessing the degree to which minority groups have autonomy or any measure of "special" rights or status, closer specification of the area or region in which these may apply is obviously required.

Quite apart from the utility of this particular typology, however, I am convinced that efforts to generalize across situations are worthwhile. There is ample evidence that the literature remains characterized more by height than by depth; that is, we have an ever-increasing number of case studies, regional assessments, minority language evaluations, treatments of linguistic contact and conflict, analyses of planning and policies, and so on – but we have relatively few investigations that try to establish links across cases, areas, and groups. It is hard to see – critics of typologies notwithstanding – how further careful work here could fail to be useful. And not all of this need be theoretically elaborate; more modest undertakings will repay the effort. As Ferguson observed: "It is frustrating to read a stimulating case study and find that it lacks information on what the reader regards as some crucial points . . . what I have in mind is not so much a well developed theoretical frame of reference as something as simple as a checklist of points to be covered" (1991, p. 230).

18.6   Conclusion

The study of minority groups and languages is, for the reasons I have discussed here, a central theme in several contemporary literatures – in sociology, political science, and social philosophy, for example. Of great intrinsic interest, minority issues can also serve to highlight matters of more general concern. The *intra*group tensions that can interfere with the cultural continuity of all groups – large or small, dominant or subordinate – are examples here, as are the opposing forces of parochialism and intercourse (to return to Saussure's terms). All this is particularly timely in a world where English becomes more and more powerful and where, consequently, more and more groups feel the cold winds of change. The globalizing forces for which English is the primary vehicle push themselves relentlessly into all corners, of course, intent on selling shoes, soft drinks, and sex to everyone from Boston to Bhutan – but we should recall that there are equally powerful "pull" factors at work here. Globalization and its ramifications are often welcomed by many who see in them upward mobility – physical, social, and psychological. Apologists for the "authentic" life can easily forget, it seems, the advantages, the advances, and the freedoms that larger cultures may offer, and that have historically had great appeal to the huddled masses. It is a complicated picture we are looking at here.

Besides – and, in part, because of – the unprecedented strength of modern homogenizing pressures, there is also a deeper concern now with the treatment of minority groups and their cultures. Of course, liberal democracies must, by definition, pay attention here, but the continued importance of minority issues – which have shown a persistence that has sometimes surprised political observers and complicated their systems – has encouraged a finer focus. (All the "rational" philosophies, from liberalism to Marxism, have had to deal with the continuing "problem" of nationalism, for instance.) The work of philosophers and political scientists is now attempting to consider such matters in broader and more general perspective. Two of the centrally recurring themes involve the rights, linguistic and otherwise, that minority groups might warrant at a collective level, and the related question of how groups might qualify, as it were, for these. It has been argued, for instance – as I noted at the beginning of this chapter – that indigenous or aboriginal groups might plausibly deserve more, in these regards, than immigrant populations. There are great difficulties, on various levels, with such approaches, but it is certain that these efforts at generalization and the elucidation of underlying principles are a distinct advance over the more isolated and specialized arguments of the past. They are also, in their own way, attempts at categorization. Efforts to better understand minority language groups, in order (for example) to suggest reasoned variations in government policy or official interventions, involve organization, cross-context comparison and, indeed, many (perhaps all) of the elements outlined in the previous section. It is hard to escape the conclusion that advances in this area necessarily involve typological work of one sort or another.

See also 7 Assessing Language Attitudes, 14 Language and Politics, 17 The Native Speaker in Applied Linguistics, 28 Bilingual Education, 29 Language Maintenance, 30 Language Planning.

472   *John Edwards*

REFERENCES

Allardt, E. (1984) What constitutes a language minority? *Journal of Multilingual and Multicultural Development*, 5, 195–205.

Baetens Beardsmore, H. (1993) An overview of European models of bilingual education. *Language, Culture and Curriculum*, 6, 197–208.

Baetens Beardsmore, H. (1994) Language policy and planning in Western European countries. In W. Grabe et al. (eds.), *Annual review of applied linguistics, 14: language policy and planning* (pp. 93–110). New York: Cambridge University Press.

Barber, B. (1992) Jihad vs McWorld. *Atlantic*, 269(3), 53–63.

Baron, D. (1990) *The English-only question.* New Haven: Yale University Press.

Bolinger, D. (1980) *Language: the loaded weapon.* London: Longman.

Bourhis, R., Giles, H., & Rosenthal, D. (1981) Notes on the construction of a "Subjective Vitality Questionnaire" for ethnolinguistic groups. *Journal of Multilingual and Multicultural Development*, 2, 145–55.

Breathnach, D. (1993) If your language should die. *Contact Bulletin*, 9.

Brenzinger, M. (ed.) (1992) *Language death.* Berlin: Mouton de Gruyter.

Brenzinger, M. (ed.) (1998) *Endangered languages in Africa.* Köln: Rüdiger Köpp.

Crawford, J. (1992) *Hold your tongue: bilingualism and the politics of "English Only."* Reading, MA: Addison-Wesley.

Crystal, D. (2000) *Language death.* Cambridge: Cambridge University Press.

Dalby, D. (2000) Linguasphere unites a thousand world voices. *Times Higher Education Supplement*, 26 May.

Dekkers, A. (1995) *Teacher training of minority languages for primary and secondary education.* Ljouwert: Fryske Akademy.

Dorian, N. (ed.) (1989) *Investigating obsolescence.* Cambridge: Cambridge University Press.

Dorian, N. (1993) A response to Ladefoged's other view of endangered languages. *Language*, 69, 575–9.

Edwards, J. (1985) *Language, society and identity.* Oxford: Blackwell.

Edwards, J. (1991) Socio-educational issues concerning indigenous minority languages: terminology, geography and status. In J. Sikma & D. Gorter (eds.), *European lesser used languages in primary education* (pp. 207–26). Ljouwert: Fryske Akademy.

Edwards, J. (1992) Sociopolitical aspects of language maintenance and loss: towards a typology of ethnic minority language situations. In W. Fase, K. Jaspaert, & S. Kroon (eds.), *Maintenance and loss of ethnic minority languages* (pp. 37–54). Amsterdam/Philadelphia: John Benjamins.

Edwards, J. (1994a) European language and identity in the 1990s. Paper presented at International Conference on Nations and Languages and the Construction of Europe, Leuven.

Edwards, J. (1994b) Ethnolinguistic pluralism and its discontents: a Canadian study, and some general observations. *International Journal of the Sociology of Language*, 110, 5–85.

Edwards, J. (1994c) What can (or should) linguists do in the face of language decline? In M. Harry (ed.), *Papers from the Seventeenth Annual Meeting of the Atlantic Provinces Linguistic Association* (pp. 25–32). Halifax: Saint Mary's University.

Edwards, J. (1995a) Monolingualism, bilingualism, multiculturalism and identity: lessons and insights from recent Canadian experience. *Current Issues in Language and Society*, 2, 5–37.

Edwards, J. (1995b) *Multilingualism*. London: Penguin.

Edwards, J. (1997) French and English in Canada: before and after the Québec referendum of October 1995. In P. Weber & W. Wölck (eds.), *Recent studies in contact linguistics* (pp. 101–9). Bonn: Dümmler.

Edwards, J. (ed.) (1998) *Language in Canada*. Cambridge: Cambridge University Press.

Edwards, J. (2001) The ecology of language revival. *Current Issues in Language Planning*, 2, 231–41.

Edwards, J. (2002) Forlorn hope? In J.-M. Dewaele, A. Housen, & Li Wei (eds.), *Opportunities and challenges of bilingualism* (pp. 25–44). Berlin: Mouton de Gruyter.

Ferguson, C. (1962) The language factor in national development. In F. Rice (ed.), *Study of the role of second languages in Asia, Africa, and Latin America* (pp. 8–14). Washington, DC: Center for Applied Linguistics.

Ferguson, C. (1966) National sociolinguistic profile formulas. In W. Bright (ed.), *Sociolinguistics* (pp. 309–15). The Hague: Mouton.

Ferguson, C. (1991) Diglossia revisited. *Southwest Journal of Linguistics*, 10, 214–34.

Fishman, J. (1980) Minority language maintenance and the ethnic mother-tongue school. *Modern Language Journal*, 64, 167–72.

Fishman, J. (1982) Whorfianism of the third kind. *Language in Society*, 11, 1–14.

Fishman, J. (1990) What is reversing language shift (RLS) and how can it succeed? *Journal of Multilingual and Multicultural Development*, 11, 5–36.

Fishman, J. (1991) *Reversing language shift*. Clevedon, UK: Multilingual Matters.

Foster, M. (1982) Indigenous languages in Canada. *Language and Society* (Ottawa), 7, 20–4.

Giles, H., Bourhis, R., & Taylor, D. (1977) Towards a theory of language in ethnic group relations. In H. Giles (ed.), *Language, ethnicity and intergroup relations* (pp. 307–48). London: Academic Press.

Grenoble, L. and Whaley, L. (eds.) (1998a) *Endangered languages*. Cambridge: Cambridge University Press.

Grenoble, L. & Whaley, L. (1998b) Toward a typology of language endangerment. In L. Grenoble & L. Whaley (eds.), *Endangered languages* (pp. 22–54). Cambridge: Cambridge University Press.

Haarmann, H. (1986) *Language in ethnicity: a view of basic ecological relations*. Berlin: Mouton de Gruyter.

Haugen, E. (1972) *The ecology of language*. Stanford: Stanford University Press.

Hughes, R. (1993) *Culture of complaint*. Oxford: Oxford University Press.

Hyltenstam, K. & Stroud, C. (1991) *Språkbyte och Språkbevarande*. Lund: University of Lund Press.

Hyltenstam, K. & Stroud, C. (1996) Language maintenance. In H. Goebl, P. Nelde, Z. Starý, & W. Wölck (eds.), *Contact linguistics* (pp. 567–78). Berlin: Walter de Gruyter.

Ignatieff, M. (1993) *Blood and belonging*. Toronto: Viking/Penguin.

King, K. (2001) *Language revitalization processes and prospects*. Clevedon, UK: Multilingual Matters.

Kloss, H. (1967) Types of multilingual communities. In S. Lieberson (ed.), *Explorations in sociolinguistics* (pp. 7–17). Bloomington: Indiana University Press.

Kloss, H. (1968) Notes concerning a language-nation typology. In J. Fishman, C. Ferguson, & J. Das Gupta (eds.), *Language problems of developing nations* (pp. 69–85). New York: Wiley.

Krauss, M. (1992) The world's languages in crisis. *Language*, 68, 4–10.

Kymlicka, W. (1995) *Multicultural citizenship*. Oxford: Oxford University Press.

Ladefoged, P. (1992) Discussion note: another view of endangered languages. *Language*, 68, 809–11.

Maffi, L. (2000) Language preservation vs. language maintenance and revitalization. *International Journal of the Sociology of Language*, 142, 175–90.

Marshall, D. (1986) The question of an official language: Language rights and the English Language Amendment. *International Journal of the Sociology of Language*, 60, 7–75. (See also the 18 comments on Marshall's paper that complete this number of *IJSL*.)

Moran, D. (1900) The Gaelic revival. *New Ireland Review*, 12, 257–72.

Moynihan, D. (1993) *Pandaemonium: ethnicity in international politics*. Oxford: Oxford University Press.

Mufwene, S. (2000) Language contact, evolution and death. In G. Kindell & M. Lewis (eds.), *Assessing ethnolinguistic vitality* (pp. 39–64). Dallas: Summer Institute of Linguistics.

Mühlhäusler, P. (1996) *Linguistic ecology*. London: Routledge.

Mühlhäusler, P. (2000) Language planning and language ecology. *Current Issues in Language Planning*, 1, 306–67.

Nahir, M. (1977) The five aspects of language planning. *Language Problems and Language Planning*, 1, 107–23.

Nettle, D. & Romaine, S. (2000) *Vanishing voices*. Oxford: Oxford University Press.

Rabin, C. (1971) A tentative classification of language planning aims. In J. Rubin & B. Jernudd (eds.), *Can language be planned?* (pp. 277–9). Honolulu: University Press of Hawai'i.

Roberts, C. (1987) Political conflict over bilingual initiatives. *Journal of*

Multilingual and Multicultural Development, 8, 311–22.

Robins, R. & Uhlenbeck, E. (eds.) (1991) *Endangered languages*. Oxford: Berg.

de Saussure, F. ([1916] 1960) *Course in general linguistics* (trans. W. Baskin). London: Peter Owen.

Schlesinger, A. (1992) *The disuniting of America: reflections on a multicultural society*. New York: Norton.

Sikma, J. & D. Gorter (eds.) (1991) *European lesser used languages in primary education*. Ljouwert: Fryske Akademy.

Stephens, M. (1976) *Linguistic minorities in Western Europe*. Llandysul: Gomer.

Stewart, W. (1962) An outline of linguistic typology for describing multilingualism. In F. Rice (ed.), *Study of the role of second languages in Asia, Africa, and Latin America* (pp. 15–25). Washington, DC: Center for Applied Linguistics.

Stewart, W. (1968) A sociolinguistic typology for describing national multilingualism. In J. Fishman (ed.), *Readings in the sociology of language* (pp. 531–45). The Hague: Mouton.

Voegelin, C., Voegelin, F., & Schutz, N. (1967) The language situation in Arizona as part of the southwest cultural area. In D. Hymes & W. Bittle (eds.), *Studies in southwestern ethnolinguistics* (pp. 403–51). The Hague: Mouton.

White, P. (1987) Geographical aspects of minority language situations in Italy. Paper presented at International Seminar on Geolinguistics, Stoke-on-Trent.

Williams, G. (1980) Review of *Implications of the Ethnic Revival in Modern Industrialized Society* (E. Allardt). *Journal of Multilingual and Multicultural Development*, 1, 363–70.

Williams, G. (1986) Language planning or language expropriation? *Journal of Multilingual and Multicultural Development*, 7, 509–18.

Williams, G. (1988) Review of *Third International Conference on Minority Languages: General Papers* and *Third International Conference on Minority Languages: Celtic Papers* (eds. (both volumes), G. MacEoin, A. Ahlquist, & D. Ó hAodha). *Language, Culture and Curriculum*, 1, 169–78.

Wurm, S. (1998) Methods of language maintenance and revival, with selected cases of language endangerment in the world. In K. Matsumura (ed.), *Studies in Endangered Languages* (pp. 191–211). Tokyo: Hituzi.

Young, L., Bell, N., & Giles, H. (1988) Perceived vitality and context: a national majority in a minority setting. *Journal of Multilingual and Multicultural Development*, 9, 285–9.

FURTHER READING

Ammon, U., Mattheier, K., & Nelde, P. (eds.) (1990) *Minderheiten und Sprachkontakt (Sociolinguistica*, 4). Tübingen: Niemeyer.

Fase, W., Jaspaert, K., & Kroon, S. (eds.) (1992) *Maintenance and loss of minority languages*. Amsterdam: Benjamins.

Fase, W., Jaspaert, K., & Kroon, S. (eds.) (1995) *The state of minority languages*. Lisse: Swets & Zeitlinger.

Haugen, E., McClure, J., & Thomson, D. (eds.) (1981) *Minority languages today*. Edinburgh: Edinburgh University Press.

19 Research Methods for Applied Linguistics: Scope, Characteristics, and Standards

JAMES DEAN BROWN

19.1 The Scope of Applied Linguistics Research

Over the past two decades, books on applied linguistics research have often failed to define the term *research*, perhaps because the focus of such books was so narrow that a definition of *research* seemed self-evident. Some books (Anshen, 1978; Hatch & Farhady, 1982; Butler, 1985; Woods, Fletcher, & Hughes, 1986; Brown, 1988; Hatch & Lazaraton, 1991; Rietveld & van Hout, 1993; Scholfield, 1995) focused almost exclusively on statistical research. Other books focused on the research methodology involved in language teacher research (Freeman, 1998), language classroom research (van Lier, 1988; Allwright & Bailey, 1991), action research (Wallace, 1998; Burns, 1999), survey research (Brown, 2001), research methods in text and discourse analysis (Jenner, 2000), or research methods in pragmatics (Kasper & Dahl, 1991). Recently, collections of articles have also begun to appear that are focused on a specific type of research, like teacher research (Griffee & Nunan, 1997; Hornberger & Corson, 1997), or qualitative research (Bailey & Nunan, 1997).

Other research-oriented books in applied linguistics have been more inclined to grapple with the notion of what *research* is, perhaps because they were somewhat more general in nature, usually surveying a variety of different types of research. The earliest of these explored the differences between qualitative and quantitative research (Seliger & Shohamy, 1989). A few years later, Johnson (1992) covered correlational approaches, case-study approaches, survey research, ethnographic research, experimental research, and what she called multisite/multimethod research, and Nunan (1992) explained experimental method, ethnography, case study, classroom-observation research, introspection methods, elicitation techniques, interaction analysis, and program evaluation. Still more recently, McDonough and McDonough (1998) dealt with observation, introspection, diary studies, experiments, interviews, question-naires, numerical techniques, and case study research, and Brown and Rodgers (2002) included chapters on case study research, introspection research, classroom observation and interaction research, descriptive statistics research, correlational research, quasi-experimental research, and course or program evaluation.

19.1.1 Defining applied linguistics research

In Brown (1992), I reported on a survey of hundreds of members of the Teachers of English to Speakers of Other Languages (TESOL) organization around the world. One of the questions I asked them was how they defined research. The diversity of answers was staggering, ranging from short, ideal-istic answers about what research is (e.g., "Careful, thorough study" and "The search for the truth") to very cynical answers (e.g., "Something that profs at universities that grant advanced degrees do because they don't teach and need to publish" and "Ignoring the obvious"). The approaches to defining research differed in fairly systematic ways, falling generally into four categories as follows:

1 *Definitions that listed the types of research* (e.g., "An investigation of a particu-lar topic, or problem, through a document search and/or empirical study (the conducting of experiments) and analysis" and "Investigation through the reading of literature, experimentation and/or any other type of data gathering . . .")
2 *Definitions that listed the topics of research* (e.g., "In its widest sense, to seek new ways to improve language education and intercultural com-munication training" and "Searching for information on how students process information, internalize data and retain it for communicative purposes.")
3 *Definitions that covered the purpose of research* (e.g., "The search for informa-tion that will help practitioners (in this case, teachers) better carry out their jobs . . ." and "Systematic study of language issues and use in order to improve delivery of services to our students.")
4 *Definitions that enumerated the steps in the process of research* (e.g., "Working toward truth, proving theories, trying out new approaches – and then compiling results, analyzing results and sharing with colleagues" and "Stating a hypothesis; gathering data; testing the hypothesis; relating the conclusions to issues at hand.")

Given the scope of applied linguistics research indicated in these responses, finding a single definition general enough to include all possibilities, yet clear enough to be meaningful seemed to me to be a major challenge. In a conversa-tion with Donald Freeman many years ago, he suggested that research might be defined simply as "any principled inquiry." That definition seemed to me

to be broad enough to fit the many types of research done in applied linguistics, but also remained meaningful. For the purposes of this chapter, I will
expand that definition slightly to fit *applied linguistics research* as I see it today:
any systematic and principled inquiry in applied linguistics. I have added the
word *systematic* because to me research must not only be *principled*, but also
orderly, methodical, precise, and well organized, all of which are listed as
synonyms for *systematic* in my computer's dictionary.

Such a broad definition of research allows the flexibility to include many
different types of research under one umbrella, but can also cause considerable
confusion unless the similarities and differences among the many research
types are clearly understood.

19.1.2 *Options in applied linguistics research*

In Brown (1988), I naively categorized the different types of research as shown
in Figure 19.1 into two categories that my librarian mother taught me years
ago: secondary research (derived from the research and writings of others)
and primary research (derived from original data of some sort). I further
subdivided primary research into case studies and statistical research and then
subdivided statistical research into survey and experimental research. In the
mid-eighties, I apparently viewed the types of research going on in applied
linguistics in such simplistic binary terms.

After a decade or so of experiences like the TESOL survey (discussed above
and reported in Brown, 1992), I expanded my view of the types of research in
applied linguistics to include more categories. As shown in Figure 19.2 (from
Brown, 2001), the secondary/primary dichotomy still seemed appropriate, but
those two categories were further subdivided with considerably more detail
provided. In this case, secondary research included library research (research
heavily dependent on secondary sources, often associated term papers in school)
and literature reviews (more sophisticated reviews of some aspect of the

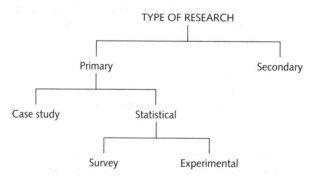

Figure 19.1 Very broad categories of research (Nunan, 1992 interpretation of Brown,
1988)

© Cambridge University Press.

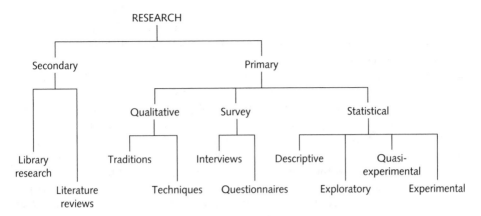

Figure 19.2   Broad categories of research (adapted from Brown, 2001)
© Cambridge University Press.

literature of the field, which contributed new knowledge to the field). Primary research included three general sub-categories: qualitative, survey, and statistical research. Qualitative research involved many different traditions (see Table 19.3 below) and data gathering techniques (including at least case studies, introspection, discourse analysis, interactional analysis, and classroom observations). Survey research included interviews and questionnaires. Statistical research included descriptive studies, exploratory research, quasi-experimental studies, and experimental research. Recognizing the different types of applied linguistics research is all well and good, but fully identifying the distinguishing characteristics of those different types of research remained a challenge.

19.2   Characteristics of Applied Linguistics Research

Applied linguistics research can be described from many different perspectives including at least (1) the contextual factors involved in applied linguistics research, (2) van Lier's parameters of educational research design, (3) Grotjahn's data collection methods, data types, and data analysis procedures, (4) other sets of research characteristics, and (5) the qual–quant continuum.

19.2.1   Contextual factors in applied linguistics research

Brown and Rodgers (2002, pp. 14–16) summarized a number of contextual factors that influence applied linguistics research at international, national, professional, institutional, local, and personal levels:

1   *International and national contexts.* International and national organizations and governmental bodies support a fair amount of applied linguistics research. Since they control the money, their political priorities tend to influence who will do such research and how.

2   *Professional contexts.* Within applied linguistics, the types of research that are popular at any given time vary; for a few years, interest in one type of research may increase at the expense of another, then interest may be rekindled for that latter type. In other words, even research can have its trends and fads.

3   *Institutional contexts.* Institutional contexts in applied linguistics research can refer to everything from entire school districts, to individual language programs, or even to very specific individual tutoring situations. Within these institutional contexts a number of factors can influence the type and quality of research: the size of the institution, availability of resources to support research, institutional policies and priorities, the institution's past experiences with researchers, and even the personalities of the various administrators and teachers involved.

4   *Local contexts.* Local contexts refer to the specific circumstances in which the research will take place. The context may be a classroom, laboratory, private home, Internet bulletin board, or even a coffee shop. A number of factors in the local context may turn out to be important to the success or failure of a research study:
    (a) *physical context* (e.g., class size, layout of the school, etc.),
    (b) *time context* (e.g., minutes per class, classes per day, etc.),
    (c) *social context* (e.g., language backgrounds, ethnic mix of the students, etc.),
    (d) *pedagogical context* (e.g., teaching methods used, preferred learning styles of the students and teachers, etc.),
    (e) *psychological context* (e.g., comfort level of participants with regard to research studies, etc.).

5   *Personal contexts.* Individual researchers have certain preconceptions about the aspects of applied linguistics that ought to be researched, the form that research should take, and their role in the research process. Such preconceptions and preferences arise from individual differences in abilities, personalities, motivations, priorities, training, etc. and may influence the types of research a particular individual or group will be interested in doing.

Johnson (1992, p. 217) examined a wider variety of the contextual factors involved in research as shown in Figure 19.3. She started with five factors that I would group together as *influences that initially shape research*: (1) the socio-political and sociocultural contexts, (2) purposes and goals, (3) initiators/ impetus, (4) support and funding, and (5) institutional setting. Some of the details of these categories are similar to what Brown and Rodgers (2002) discussed as contextual factors, though Johnson provided considerably more detail. She also presented the *characteristics of the research process* itself in Figure 19.3

Sociopolitical and Sociocultural Contexts National and cultural groups Status and roles of teachers and researchers		
Purposes and Goals Contribute to knowledge Professional growth Emancipation Change practice/working conditions Democratize inquiry		
Initiators/Impetus Grassroots: teachers Professional organizations University-based researchers Schools: inservice training	**Support and Funding** Professional organizations Federal, public Networks, groups Released time	
Institutional Settings Own class, school, institute Collaboration across settings		
Characteristics of Research Process Topic (teacher-generated, other-generated) Participants (teachers, researchers, students) Particular perspectives of participants Resources available (time, videos, etc.) Methodology (ethnographic, quasi-experimental) Data sources Standards for quality Scope		
Audiences Self Institution Teachers Wider communities Support groups Administrators	**Diffusion** Books Newsletters Conferences Professional organizations	**Use of Results** Student growth Reflection Professional growth Change practice Change structures Planning

Figure 19.3 Issues in teacher inquiry (from Johnson, 1992, p. 217)
© 1992 Pearson Education. Reprinted/adapted by permission of Pearson Education Ltd.

and then provided three categories that I would group together as the *uses of the output of the research process*: audience, diffusion, and use of results.

19.2.2 Van Lier's parameters of educational research design

As shown in Figure 19.4 (from van Lier, 1988) research can also be described in terms of an *intervention* axis (i.e., degree of intervention, from intervention

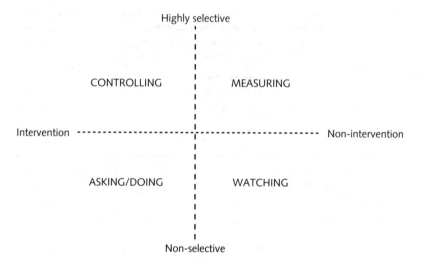

Figure 19.4   Parameters of educational research design (van Lier, 1988, p. 57) © Pearson Education. Reprinted by permission of Pearson Education Ltd.

to non-intervention) and a *selectivity* axis (i.e., selectivity of focus, from highly selective to non-selective). For example, on the intervention axis, research can take the form of a formal experimental design with a randomly assigned treatment and control groups, which would be an *intervention* study, or it can take the form of a series of informal classroom observations, which would be more in the direction of a *non-intervention* study. On the selectivity axis, research can be *highly selective* in focus (e.g., obligatory use of the definite article by immigrant Chinese adolescent men from Guangdong province), or *non-selective* (e.g., all language related behaviors observed of all participants in a population of students).

The selectivity and intervention axes also create what van Lier calls four territories:

1   *controlling*, in which the researcher conducts a carefully planned experiment restricted both in participants and content focus;
2   *measuring*, in which intervention is minimal but the data focus is highly restricted;
3   *asking/doing*, in which the researcher might intervene to ask participants to talk about what they are thinking;
4   *watching*, in which the researcher just observes with both intervention and selectivity kept to a minimum.

Each of these territories accounts for different types of research and has different potential audiences (what he calls audience *inhabitants*).

19.2.3 Grotjahn's data collection methods, data types, and data analysis procedures

According to Grotjahn (1987), research can be classified in terms of *data collection methods* (i.e., experimental vs. non-experimental), *data types* (i.e., qualitative vs. quantitative), and *data analysis procedures* (statistical vs. interpretive). Table 19.1 shows his analysis of these three factors. Notice that he has classified the research types as pure or mixed exploratory-interpretive or analytical-nomological, and that together the pure and mixed types represent all possible combinations of data collection methods, data types, and data analysis procedures. At first, some of Grotjahn's combinations may be difficult to envisage. For example, I initially had trouble imagining number 3 "experimental-qualitative-interpretive" and number 5 "exploratory-qualitative-statistical." However, with a little reflection, I was able to think of existing applied linguistics studies that were predominantly experimental in nature but included some qualitative interpretations. I was also able to think of studies that were predominantly exploratory and qualitative in nature but included some statistical analysis to support the interpretations.

19.2.4 Other sets of research characteristics

The topics discussed above (i.e., contextual factors, intervention and selectivity, data collection methods, data types, and data analysis procedures) are all interesting and useful ways of characterizing applied linguistics research, but unfortunately, such research is far more complicated than any of those sets of categories would suggest because it also includes at least the following additional concerns: time orientation, theory generation, variable description, and researcher perspective.

19.2.4.1 Time orientation

Another way to classify research is according to *time orientation*, or the amount of time invested in gathering data. Along those lines, studies are sometimes classified as either cross-sectional or longitudinal (e.g., see Larsen-Freeman & Long, 1991). *Cross-sectional* studies are those conducted over a short period of time, often with a relatively large number of participants. For instance, a study might gather language proficiency data (using a test), motivation data (using a questionnaire), and personal information data (on the same questionnaire) from 300 students in a one-shot cross-sectional study.

In contrast, *longitudinal studies* are typically carried out over a relatively long period of time, often with a small number of participants. For example, a study might dedicate five years to following five students of varying backgrounds, making careful observations of their language proficiency growth, their motivation to learn languages, their personal characteristics, etc.

Table 19.1 Different possible research designs

Paradigm	Data collection method	Resulting data type	Type of data analysis
Pure			
1 Exploratory-interpretive	Non-experimental design	Qualitative data	Interpretive analysis
2 Analytical-nomological	Experimental or quasi-experimental design	Quantitative data	Statistical analysis
Mixed			
3 Experimental-qualitative-interpretive	Experimental or quasi-experimental design	Qualitative data	Interpretive analysis
4 Experimental-qualitative-statistical	Experimental or quasi-experimental design	Qualitative data	Statistical analysis
5 Exploratory-qualitative-statistical	Non-experimental design	Qualitative data	Statistical analysis
6 Exploratory-quantitative-statistical	Non-experimental design	Quantitative data	Statistical analysis
7 Exploratory-quantitative-interpretive	Non-experimental design	Quantitative data	Interpretive analysis
8 Experimental-quantitative-interpretive	Experimental or quasi-experimental design	Quantitative data	Interpretive analysis

Source: Adapted from Grotjahn (1987, pp. 59–60)

Other ways of describing the time orientation have recently surfaced like *prolonged engagement* (observations and involvement with a group of people over a long period of time), *persistent observations* (frequent observations over that long period of time), and the *cyclical nature* (data collection, analysis, interpretation, followed by further data collection, analysis, interpretation, etc.) of longitudinal studies in the exploratory-interpretative tradition (see especially, Davis, 1995, pp. 444–5).

19.2.4.2 Theory generation

Studies can also differ in terms of *theory generation*, which can take two forms: hypothesis forming and hypothesis testing. *Hypothesis forming* research may begin with some very general framing questions, but will typically have no hypotheses to start with. In such a study, the researcher will make every effort to keep an open mind and form hypotheses about what is going on only after a great many observations of various sorts. The resulting hypotheses are typically considered part of the interpretation, and the researcher often goes back to the participants to ask them if the hypotheses are reasonable (in a process called *member checking*). One of the great strengths often cited for qualitative research is its potential for forming new hypotheses.

In contrast, *hypothesis testing* research begins with a set of research questions and hypotheses. Sometimes the hypotheses are stated; more often they are implicit in the research questions. The statistical analyses in such studies are designed to formally test the probability that the hypotheses are true and typically include some form of probability statement, like $p < 0.01$, which indicates that there is less than a one percent probability that the observed difference (or relationship) is a chance fluctuation. One of the strengths often cited for quantitative research is its potential for hypothesis testing.

19.2.4.3 Variable description

Similarly, *variable description* can take two forms in applied linguistics research: variable definition and variable operationalization. In *variable definition* research, the researcher attempts to begin with no preconceived notions of what the important variables in the study will be, or how they will be defined. As the study progresses, the process of discovering and describing variables serves to gradually define them.

In *variable operationalization* research, the researcher clearly outlines the variables of interest from the outset (particularly the dependent, independent, and moderator variables) and explains how each one was *operationalized*, that is, how each one was observed or measured and quantified. For instance, the variable Japanese language proficiency might be operationalized as scores on a particular Japanese proficiency test, or the variable nationality might be operationalized as 1 for Chinese, 2 for Japanese, and 3 for Korean based on asking each of the participants what passport they hold, etc.

19.2.4.4   Researcher perspective

The *researcher's perspective* is sometimes described as either emic or etic. Researchers adopting the *emic perspective* make every effort to understand the point of view of the participants and to examine how the interpretations drawn from the research relate to those views through practices such as member checking (getting the participants' reactions to the interpretations drawn from the research). Researchers assuming the *etic perspective* take an outsider's view during the data gathering process, often attempting to be as objective as possible (for more on the emic/etic distinction, see Davis, 1995, p. 433).

19.2.5   The qual–quant continuum

For some applied linguistics the key distinction among the different types of research is that between qualitative and quantitative research. Indeed, in the Department of Second Language Studies at the University of Hawai'i, where I work, the research courses begin with an introductory course that introduces the basic concepts of qualitative and quantitative research methods. Then the students can take courses in one of two strands: one series for those interested in qualitative research and another for those who want to learn about quantitative research methods.

19.2.5.1   The qualitative versus quantitative dichotomy

Reichardt and Cook (1979, p. 10) summarize the differences between qualitative and quantitative research as shown in Table 19.2. Notice that the column on the left in Table 19.2 is labeled "Qualitative paradigm" and that the column to the on the right is labeled "Quantitative paradigm," with each column containing adjectives and adjectival phrases describing each "paradigm." A number of these distinctions are uncontroversial and make eminent sense; for example, the fact that the qualitative paradigm advocates qualitative methods and the quantitative paradigm advocates quantitative methods and the fact that the qualitative paradigm is typically naturalistic where the quantitative paradigm would more accurately be characterized as controlled.

However, I disagree with other distinctions, especially those that begin with *un-*. "Uncontrolled observation" and "ungeneralizable" both seem to me to be unfair characterizations of qualitative research. The observations in qualitative research are often well planned and structured in their own ways, as in a well-designed interview schedule, a classroom observation checklist, or a carefully planned discourse coding scheme. "Ungrounded" appears to me to be an equally unfair characterization of quantitative research because such research is sometimes quite exploratory. I would also argue that the use of the terms *subjective* and *objective* has become outdated partly because the two terms have become highly loaded over the years (Porter, 1998) and partly because those loaded meanings do not accurately characterize the two types of research. For example, is it not reasonable to classify some aspects of qualitative research as

Table 19.2 Characteristics of qualitative and quantitative "paradigms"

Qualitative paradigm	Quantitative paradigm
Advocates the use of qualitative methods	Advocates the use of quantitative methods
Phenomenologism and verstehen: "concerned with understanding human behavior from the actor's own frame of reference"	Logical-positivism: "seeks the facts or causes of social phenomena with little regard for the subjective states of individuals"
Naturalistic and uncontrolled observation	Obtrusive and controlled measurement
Subjective	Objective
Close to the data; the "insider" perspective	Removed from the data; the "outsider" perspective
Grounded, discovery-oriented, exploratory, expansionist, descriptive, and inductive	Ungrounded, verification-oriented, confirmatory, reductionist, inferential, and hypothetico-deductive
Process-oriented	Outcome-oriented
Valid; "real," "rich," and "deep" data	Reliable; "hard," and replicable data
Ungeneralizable; single case studies	Generalizable; multiple case studies
Holistic	Particularistic
Assumes a dynamic reality	Assumes a stable reality

Source: Reichardt & Cook (1979), p. 10)
© Sage Publications Inc. Reprinted by permission of Sage Publications Inc.

objective? Is it not true that subjectivity is considered a positive characteristic by some qualitative researchers (see for instance Glesne & Peshkin, 1992, pp. 100–6)? Is it not possible that some aspects of quantitative research are quite subjective (e.g., the subjective decisions made in designing quantitative studies, creating the measures, interpreting the data, etc.)?

In addition, I feel the labeling in Table 19.2 of the two types of research as separate "paradigms" and the listing of characteristics in pairs of opposites is a disservice because such a qualitative-versus-quantitative approach leads readers to see the two types of research as mutually exclusive alternatives. As I will explain below, such a strong and even adversarial distinction between qualitative and quantitative research may be an unnecessarily polarizing and even inaccurate characterization of the relationships among the various types of research in applied linguistics.

19.2.5.2   General problems with the qualitative versus quantitative dichotomy

Such a qualitative versus quantitative approach also has a number of general problems:

1 Dichotomizing qualitative versus quantitative research leaves out altogether secondary research types like literature reviews.
2 It treats as monolithic at least seven very distinct qualitative research *techniques* (case study research; introspection research; discourse analysis research; interactional analysis research; classroom observation research; interviews; and questionnaires).
3 It represents as monolithic at least ten qualitative research *traditions* that come from a variety of other fields like anthropology and theology (see Table 19.3, adapted slightly from Lazaraton, 1995, p. 460).
4 It presents as monolithic at least six very different quantitative research techniques (interviews; questionnaires; descriptive; exploratory; quasi-experimental; and experimental).
5 It ignores the way survey research, including interviews and questionnaires, is both qualitative and quantitative.
6 It ignores the ways researchers often combine qualitative and quantitative research techniques (as shown above in the Grotjahn's analysis in Table 19.1).
7 It confuses *research methods* (interpretive, survey, and statistical) and *research techniques* (like those listed in the second and fourth points above).

19.2.5.3   The qual–quant interactive continuum

Perhaps a more constructive and accurate approach would be to view qualitative and quantitative research as a matter of degrees, a continuum, rather than a clear-cut dichotomy like the one shown in Table 19.2. As Newman and

Table 19.3 Qualitative research traditions

Qualitative research traditions	Their disciplinary roots
Holistic ethnography	Anthropology
Ethnography of communication	Anthropology, sociolinguistics
Cognitive anthropology	Anthropology, linguistics
Discourse analysis	Linguistics
Phenomenology	Philosophy
Ecological psychology	Psychology
Symbolic interactionism	Social psychology
Heuristics	Humanistic psychology
Ethnomethodology	Sociology
Hermeneutics	Theology, philosophy, literary criticism

Source: adapted from Lazaraton (1995, p. 460)

Benz (1998) put it, "All behavioral research is made up of a combination of qualitative and quantitative constructs" (p. 9). They advocate the notion of a *qual–quant research continuum*, as opposed to a dichotomy, and insist that the continuum be considered "interactive."

Accordingly, I present the qual–quant research continuum as the first one in bold-faced type in Figure 19.5. I then array the research characteristics described in the previous section below the qual–quant continuum in additional continua. Hence, each of the characteristics is represented by a continuum that ranges from the qualitative-exploratory end of the qual–quant continuum to the quantitative-experimental end. As in Newman and Benz (1998), these continua should be viewed as interactive. They are interactive in the same sense that van Lier's (1988) two research parameters, selectivity and intervention (see Figure 19.4), were interactive. *Interactive* in this case means they can act together in all possible combinations to varying degrees.

Van Lier (1988) was able to show how two parameters (selectivity and intervention) interact in applied linguistics research. Grotjahn (1987) was able to show how three dichotomous research dimensions (data collection method, resulting data type, and type of data analysis) can interact, or combine, as shown in Table 19.1. However, in this chapter, I am not trying to show how two or three characteristics interact, but rather how 12 characteristics interact. Thus, a diagram like van Lier's will not suffice because such graphical representations can only show two dimensions or at most three dimensions at a time and because, in any case, most humans cannot readily visualize twelve-dimensional space. Nor can I show how the 12 characteristics interact by using a table like Grotjahn's because it would take 12 columns and 2^{12}, or 4,096, rows to show all possible combinations. Such a huge table would be unwieldy and difficult for any reader to understand. In any case, Grotjahn's approach would

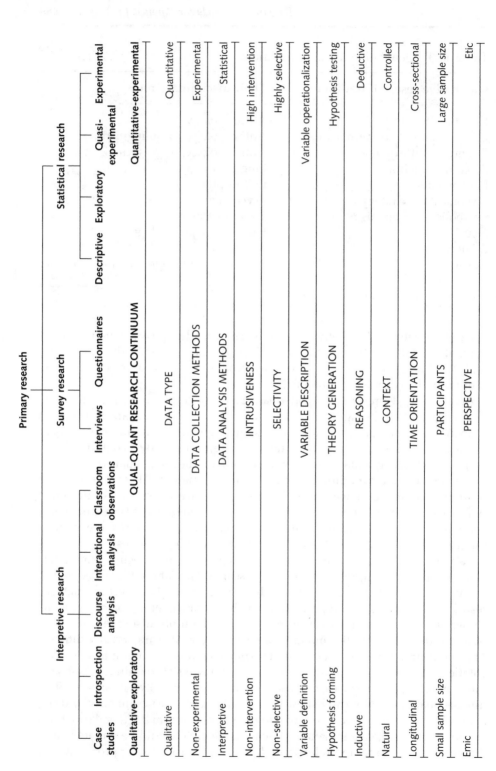

Figure 19.5 Primary research characteristics continua

force me to treat the research characteristics as dichotomies, which I prefer to avoid. I have instead chosen to represent each as a continuum and describe those continua as interactive.

In short, any particular research project can be viewed as combining any possible combinations of the points along the 12 research characteristics continua. For example, one research project might be characterized as being in the middle of the data type continuum because it uses both quantitative and qualitative data in equal proportions; the same research project might be leaning toward the non-experimental end of the data collection methods (say 20 percent along it) because it is largely observational but uses one set of test scores; the project might also be considered 60 percent along the data analysis methods continuum because the analyses are somewhat more statistical than interpretive; and so forth. In short, Figure 19.5 allows discussion of research that varies from qualitative-exploratory to quantitative-experimental in an almost infinite number of possible combinations of characteristics. Indeed, Figure 19.5 shows how 12 research characteristics can be combined to create an almost infinite number of possible interrelationships and thus to describe a wide variety of different research types.

Notice that the tree above the research characteristics continua restricts itself to primary research (because secondary research has a whole set of different characteristics), then shows three general primary research methodologies (interpretive, survey, and statistical) and the many different research techniques (ranging from case studies to experimental) in applied linguistics that *tend* to array themselves from the qualitative-exploratory to the quantitative-experimental end of the qual–quant continuum. I emphasize the word *tend* in order to allow for the possibility that any of these various research techniques could have research characteristics anywhere along the various continua. In short, the research techniques ranging from case studies to experimental are convenient categories that can help us to understand the world of applied linguistics research, but at the same time, they may lead us to oversimplify the true state of affairs.

19.3 Standards for Sound Applied Linguistics Research

The qual–quant not only provides an interactive continuum useful for characterizing applied linguistics research but can also serve as a basis for understanding the standards that researchers use in judging the soundness of such research. This discussion will again focus on primary research, leaving secondary research out because it involves a separate set of issues. Because I consistently started with the qualitative-exploratory end of the continuum in the previous section, out of fairness, I will start with the quantitative-experimental end in this section.

19.3.1 The quantitative-experimental end of the continuum

Researchers at the quantitative-experimental end of the continuum value the concepts of reliability, replicability, validity, and generalizability. Generally speaking, those are the standards quantitative researchers hold up in judging the soundness of their research.

19.3.1.1 Reliability

The standard of *reliability* in quantitative research requires researchers to demonstrate both (1) the reliability of the instruments used in their studies and (2) the reliability of the results of their studies. *Reliability of instruments* is concerned with the degree to which the results of a questionnaire, test, or other measuring instrument are consistent. Addressing this issue typically means answering the question: To what degree would the results be the same if the instrument were administered repeatedly? Similarly, the *reliability of the results* of a study is concerned with the degree to which the results would be likely to reappear if the study were replicated under the same conditions. Any expectation that the instruments or the results of a study would ever be 100 percent reliable would be unreasonable. However, the reliability of quantitative research can be maximized by carefully designing, piloting, and validating any measures involved and by carefully planning and designing the research from the beginning. In addition, ample statistical tools exist to help researchers study and report the degree to which their measures are consistent (e.g., Cronbach alpha, K-R20, etc.; see Brown, 1996 for ways to calculate and interpret such reliability coefficients) and to help researchers estimate the probability that the results of their studies are consistent, or will be the same in replication (e.g., the $p < 0.05$ sorts of statements associated with many statistical tests; for ways to interpret such p values, see Brown, 1988 or Hatch & Lazaraton, 1991).

19.3.1.2 Replicability

The standard of *replicability* in quantitative research requires researchers to provide enough information about a study to allow other researchers to replicate or repeat the study exactly as it was originally conducted. The replicability of a quantitative study can be improved by thorough and complete descriptions of: (1) the participants in the study and how they were selected, (2) the instruments used in the study as well as arguments for their reliability and validity, and (3) the procedures followed in collecting the data, scoring or coding the instruments, and analyzing the results (see Brown, 1988, ch. 5 for a more complete discussion of what should be included to make a study adequately replicable).

19.3.1.3   *Validity*

The standard of *validity* in quantitative research requires researchers to demonstrate both internal and external validity. *Internal validity* is the degree to which the results of a study can be accurately interpreted as meaning what they appear to mean. *External validity* is the degree to which the results of a study are contrived or artificial, or put another way, the degree to which the results apply to the outside world. Listed below are a number of issues identified by Campbell and Stanley (1963) as potential threats to the internal and external validity of a study:

Internal validity
1   History
2   Maturation
3   Testing
4   Instrumentation
5   Statistical regression
6   Selection bias
7   Experimental mortality
8   Selection-maturation interaction

External validity
9   Reactive effects of testing
10   Interaction of selection biases and the treatment
11   Reactive effects of experimental arrangements
12   Multiple treatment interference.

The internal and external validity of a quantitative study can be improved by consciously guarding against all of these threats when planning and conducting research (for more on controlling these potential threats, see Campbell & Stanley, 1963; Brown, 1988, 1997; or Hatch & Lazaraton, 1991).

19.3.1.4   *Generalizability*

As mentioned above, the standard of *generalizability* in quantitative research requires researchers to show the degree to which the results of a study can justifiably be generalized, or applied, to a larger population or to other similar groups. A study can be extremely well designed, controlled, and internally valid, but lack external validity. The problem is that controls, when introduced, may make the study artificial and thus limit the external validity. In one sense of the word, generalizability is clearly related to the concept of external validity discussed in the previous paragraph. In another sense of the word, generalizability is about the degree to which the sample used in a study is representative of the population to which the results will ultimately be applied, or put another way, the degree to which the results can justifiably be generalized to a larger population or to similar groups. The generalizability of a quantitative study can be improved by consciously guarding against threats to external validity (numbers 9–12 at the bottom of the list above) while designing a study that approximates as nearly as possible the conditions that would occur in the real world and by using a sample that is representative of the population to which the researcher wishes to generalize (for more on sampling and generalizability, see Brown; 1988, 1997; or Hatch & Lazaraton, 1991).

19.3.2   The qualitative-exploratory end of the continuum

Researchers at the qualitative-exploratory end of the continuum value the concepts of dependability, confirmability, credibility, and transferability. Generally speaking, those are the standards qualitative researchers hold up in judging the soundness of their research.

19.3.2.1   Dependability

The standard of *dependability* in qualitative research requires that researchers account for (1) any shifting conditions directly related to the people and things they are studying and (2) any modifications they have made in the design of their study as it has progressed. The purpose of such accounting is to help researchers and their readers get a more exact understanding of the context. Dependability is roughly analogous to the concept of reliability (described above) in quantitative studies. The dependability of a qualitative study can be improved by using such techniques as stepwise replications, overlapping methods, and/or inquiry audits (for more on these concepts, see Davis, 1992, 1995; or Brown, 2001).

19.3.2.2   Confirmability

The standard of *confirmability* in qualitative research requires that researchers fully reveal the data they are basing their interpretations on, or at least make those data available. The point is that, whether or not anybody actually takes the researchers up on it, they should make their data available so that other researchers could examine them and confirm, reject, or modify the original interpretations. The confirmability of a qualitative study is approximately analogous to the concept of replicability (described above) in quantitative studies. Confirmability can be improved by using audit trails (as described briefly in Davis, 1992, 1995; Brown, 2001; or in more detail in Lincoln & Guba, 1985).

19.3.2.3   Credibility

The standard of *credibility* in qualitative research requires researchers to show that they maximized the accuracy of their definitions and their characterizations of the people or things under investigation – especially as the various participants in the study judged those interpretations. Credibility is more or less analogous to the concept of internal validity (described above) in quantitative studies. The credibility of qualitative studies can be enhanced by using such techniques as member checking, negative case analysis, peer debriefing, persistent observations, prolonged engagement, referential analysis, and/or triangulation (for more on these techniques, see Davis, 1992, 1995; or Brown, 2001).

19.3.2.4 Transferability

The standard of *transferability* in qualitative research requires researchers to describe the research design, context, and conditions so well that the readers can decide for themselves if the interpretations apply to another context with which they are familiar. Transferability in qualitative research is approximately analogous to the concept of generalizability (described above) in quantitative studies. Transferability can be enhanced by using thick description (for more on this notion, see Davis, 1992, 1995; Lazaraton, 1995; or Brown, 2001).

19.3.3   How interactive are the standards of sound research?

Figure 19.6 is my attempt to represent the interactive relationships among the various standards continua. Recall that earlier, I defined *interactive* as all possible combinations of the points along the continua. In other words, for each of the standards continua in Figure 19.6, a study may need to focus entirely on the standard at the qualitative-exploratory end of the continuum or the standard at the quantitative-experimental end. In other cases, researchers may need to balance their concern for standards at both ends of the continuum to varying degrees. For example, one team of researchers might need to demonstrate the dependability, confirmability, credibility, and transferability of their study, while another might need to stress the reliability, replicability, validity, and generalizability their study. A third team might need to combine all eight standards, while a fourth team might choose to stress primarily reliability, replicability, validity, and generalizability, but also feel that confirmability and transferability should be addressed briefly. And so forth.

   Notice, as in Figure 19.5, the tree above the standards continua shows how the many different research techniques in applied linguistics *tend* to array themselves across the qual–quant and various standards continua. Again, I emphasize that they *tend* to do so because to do otherwise would be to negate the possibility that any of these various research techniques might require standards at one end or the other or both to varying degrees. Nonetheless, Figure 19.6 should help in understanding how the standards of sound research can interact in the world of applied linguistics research.

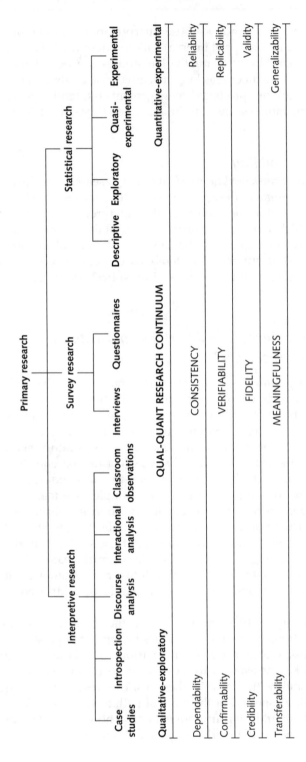

Figure 19.6 Standards of research soundness continua for primary research

19.3.4 *Ethical considerations*

General social sciences research ethics have been discussed from many points of view (for an overview of this work, see Kimmel, 1988). Periodically over the years various national and international organizations have even attempted to provide guidelines for their memberships (e.g., the American Psychological Association, which has provided various sets of guidelines for the ethical conduct of research: 1953, 1982, 1994).

Kimmel (1988) discussed some of the sorts of ethical problems that arise in social sciences research:

1 The complexity of a single research problem can give rise to multiple questions of proper behavior.
2 Sensitivity to ethical issues is necessary but not sufficient for solving them.
3 Ethical problems are the results of conflicting values.
4 Ethical problems can relate to both the subject matter of the research and the conduct of the research.
5 An adequate understanding of an ethical problem sometimes requires a broad perspective based on the consequences of research.
6 Ethical problems involve both personal and professional elements.
7 Ethical problems can pertain to science (as a body of knowledge) and to research (conducted in such a way as to protect the rights of society and research participants).
8 Judgments about proper conduct lie on a continuum ranging from the clearly unethical to the clearly ethical.
9 An ethical problem can be encountered as a result of a decision to conduct a particular study or a decision not to conduct the study.

Instead of dwelling on the potential problems that unethical behavior can cause in research, I would prefer to simply delineate some of the steps that can be taken to avoid ethical pitfalls in applied linguistics research anywhere along the qual–quant continuum. Some of the most important ethical and professional responsibilities fall into three categories (adapted from Brown, 1997): participant issues, analysis responsibilities, and concerns for the audience of a study:

With regard to *participant issues*, it is important to:

1 Avoid abusing the participants in a study in any way, including at least abuses of their persons, time, or effort; it may also be important to obtain the participants' informed consent in writing.
2 Avoid abusing any colleagues by collecting data from their students without their permission or by using too much of their precious class time.
3 Reward the cooperation and efforts of all participants and colleagues, at very least by giving them feedback or information on what happened in the study.

In terms of the *analysis responsibilities*, it is crucial to:

4   Guard against consciously or subconsciously modifying data or interpretations so they support personal views and prejudices.
5   Select the appropriate research method and technique(s) and best possible interaction of research characteristics for the purposes of the particular research project involved.
6   Select the most appropriate interaction of standards possible for the purposes of the particular research project involved.

As for *concerns for the audience* of a study, it is essential to:

7   Explain the research clearly so it can be understood by the readers.
8   Organize the report using traditional sections, headings, and other conventions (e.g., see American Psychological Association, 1994; or Brown, 2001, ch. 6) so readers can easily follow the study.
9   Interpret results very carefully while guarding against any temptation to over-interpret, or generalize beyond what the data and results can support.

Since ethics is an area where all research methods and techniques come together and tend to agree, I will end here. However, I would like to mention one further set of considerations that is seldom listed in discussions of research ethics. In my view, all researchers in applied linguistics have two overriding ethical responsibilities: (1) to continue reading, learning, and growing as researchers in order to better serve the field, and (2) to design research that is effective and fits well into the particular institutional contexts involved by selecting those characteristics and standards along the qual–quant continuum that will best interact to provide systematic and principled answers to the many important questions that remain to be answered in applied linguistics.

REFERENCES

Allwright, D. & Bailey, K. M. (1991) *Focus on the language classroom: an introduction to classroom research for language teachers*. Cambridge: Cambridge University Press.

American Psychological Association (1953) *Ethical standards of psychologists*. Washington, DC: American Psychological Association.

American Psychological Association (1982) *Ethical principles in the conduct of research with human participants*. Washington, DC: American Psychological Association.

American Psychological Association (1994) *Standards for educational and psychological testing* (4th edn.). Washington, DC: American Psychological Association.

Anshen, F. (1978) *Statistics for linguists.* Rowley, MA: Newbury House.

Bailey, K. M. & Nunan, D. (eds.) (1997) *Voices from the language classroom.* Cambridge: Cambridge University Press.

Brown, J. D. (1988) *Understanding research in second language learning: a teacher's guide to statistics and research design.* Cambridge: Cambridge University Press.

Brown, J. D. (1992) What is research? *TESOL Matters,* 2(5), 10.

Brown, J. D. (1996) *Testing in language programs.* Upper Saddle River, NJ: Prentice-Hall Regents.

Brown, J. D. (1997) Designing a language study. In D. Nunan & D. Griffee (eds.), *Classroom teachers and classroom research* (pp. 109–21). Tokyo: Japan Association for Language Teaching.

Brown, J. D. (2001) *Using surveys in language programs.* Cambridge: Cambridge University Press.

Brown, J. D. & Rodgers, T. (2002) *Doing applied linguistics research.* Oxford: Oxford University Press.

Burns, A. (1999) *Collaborative action research for English language teachers.* Cambridge: Cambridge University Press.

Butler, C. (1985) *Statistics in linguistics.* Oxford: Blackwell.

Campbell, D. T. & Stanley, J. C. (1963) *Experimental and quasi-experimental designs for research.* Chicago: Rand McNally.

Davis, K. A. (1992) Validity and reliability in qualitative research on second language acquisition and teaching: another researcher comments . . . *TESOL Quarterly,* 26, 605–8.

Davis, K. A. (1995) Qualitative theory and methods in applied linguistics research. *TESOL Quarterly,* 29, 427–53.

Freeman, D. (1998) *Doing teacher research: from inquiry to understanding.* Boston, MA: Heinle & Heinle.

Glesne, C. & Peshkin, A. (1992) *Becoming qualitative researchers: an introduction.* London: Longman.

Griffee, D. T. & Nunan, D. (eds.) (1997) *Classroom teachers and classroom research.* Tokyo: JALT.

Grotjahn, R. (1987) On the methodological basis of introspective methods. In C. Færch & G. Kasper (eds.), *Introspection in second language research* (pp. 54–81). Clevedon, UK: Multilingual Matters.

Hatch, E. & Farhady, H. (1982) *Research design and statistics for applied linguistics.* Rowley, MA: Newbury House.

Hatch, E. & Lazaraton, A. (1991) *The research manual: design and statistics for applied linguistics.* Rowley, MA: Newbury House.

Hornberger, N. H., & Corson, D. (eds.) (1997) *Encyclopedia of language and education,* vol. 8: *Research methods in language and education.* Dordrecht: Kluwer Academic.

Jenner, B. (trans.), Tilscher, S., Meyer, M. & Wodak, R. (2000) *Methods of text and discourse analysis.* Thousand Oaks, CA: Sage.

Johnson, D. M. (1992) *Approaches to research in second language learning.* New York: Longman.

Kasper, G. & Dahl, M. (1991) *Research methods in interlanguage pragmatics* (NFLRC Technical Report no. 1). Honoluolu: National Foreign Language Resource Center, University of Hawai'i Press.

Kimmel, A. J. (1988) *Ethics and values in applied social research.* Newbury Park, CA: Sage.

Larsen-Freeman, D. & Long, M. H. (1991) *An introduction to second language acquisition research.* London: Longman.

Lazaraton, A. (1995) Qualitative research in applied linguistics: a progress report. *TESOL Quarterly*, 29, 455–72.

Lincoln, Y. & Guba, E. (1985) *Naturalistic inquiry*. Beverly Hills, CA: Sage.

McDonough, J. & McDonough, S. H. (1998) *Research methods for English language teachers*. London: Edward Arnold.

Newman, I. & Benz, C. R. (1998) *Qualitative-quantitative research methodology: exploring the interactive continuum*. Carbondale, IL: Southern Illinois University Press.

Nunan, D. (1992) *Research methods in language learning*. Cambridge: Cambridge University Press.

Porter, T. M. (1998) *Trust in numbers: the pursuit of objectivity in science and public life*. Princeton, NJ: Princeton University Press.

Reichardt, C. & Cook, T. (1979) Beyond qualitative versus quantitative methods. In T. Cook & C. Reichardt (eds.), *Qualitative and quantitative methods in education research*. Beverly Hills, CA: Sage.

Rietveld, T. & van Hout, R. (1993) *Statistical techniques for the study of language and language behaiour*. Berlin: Mouton de Gruyter.

Scholfield, P. (1995) *Quantifying language: a researcher's guide to gathering language data and reducing it to figures*. Clevedon, UK: Multilingual Matters.

Seliger, H. W. & Shohamy, E. (1989) *Second language research methods*. Oxford: Oxford University Press.

van Lier, L. (1988) *The classroom and the language learner: ethnography and second language classroom research*. London: Longman.

Wallace, M. J. (1998) *Action research for language teachers*. Cambridge: Cambridge University Press.

Woods, A., Fletcher, P., & Hughes, A. (1986) *Statistics in language studies*. Cambridge: Cambridge University Press.

FURTHER READING

For overviews on research methods, I would recommend Brown & Rodgers (2002), Johnson (1992), McDonough & McDonough (1998), Nunan (1992), or Seliger & Shohamy (1989). Unfortunately, books focusing on qualitative research methods in applied linguistics are rare. Brown & Rodgers (2002) devotes about half of its content to that type of research. However, to find books focused on qualitative research methods, readers must turn to sources outside the field. I recommend Glesne & Peshkin (1992), Lincoln & Guba (1985), and Newman & Benz (1998). Books that I recommend on classroom and action research are much more common, including at least Allwright & Bailey (1991), Burns (1999), Freeman (1998), and Wallace (1998). For more information on statistical research, I would suggest reading Brown (1988 and 2001), Hatch & Lazaraton (1991), Rietveld & van Hout (1993), or Scholfield (1995).

20 Second Language Learning

WILLIAM LITTLEWOOD

20.1 Introduction

Debate about second language learning has been going on for many centuries now. In the first century AD, for example, the Roman rhetorician Quintilian discussed the optimal age for second language learning. He favored an early start because "by nature we retain best what is learned in our tenderest years." Around 400 AD, St Augustine supported what we would now call intrinsic motivation, in the belief that "free curiosity has a more positive effect on learning than necessity and fear." He also advocated an inductive approach to learning, since "we cannot hope to learn words we do not know unless we have grasped their meaning . . . by getting to know the things signified" (all quotations are from Kelly, 1969). The same issues that occupied Quintilian and St Augustine are still alive today, and opinions are still divided.

Usually the debate has had, to a greater or lesser degree, a practical purpose: to improve the success of learning and the effectiveness of teaching. Thus, if learning in our "tenderest years" leads to better retention, it may be advisable to start teaching as early as possible; if intrinsic motivation is most effective, it may be more important to create interesting learning conditions than to rely on external rewards and punishments; and so on. It is therefore not surprising that in the last 50 years, as international contacts have increased and ever more people have needed to learn a second language, we have seen a corresponding increase in the efforts to reach a more thorough and systematic understanding of second language learning. In the 1950s these efforts consisted mainly in seeking ways to explain second language learning by appealing to general learning principles, notably those derived from behaviorist psychology (Rivers, 1964, is a classic critical survey). Gradually, as the special nature of language learning became clearer, second language learning established itself as a field of enquiry in its own right. Since the 1970s in particular, research into second language learning – often referred to as "second language acquisition research" or the abbreviated "SLA research" – has increased dramatically and even developed sub-fields, each with its own concepts and methods. One survey of the overall field of SLA research (Ellis, 1994) runs to over 800 pages.

Today, then, the study of second language learning is an immensely rich and varied enterprise. Most participants in this enterprise still see its ultimate justification in terms of the desire to improve learning and teaching. In this respect the study of second language learning is one important branch of the overall field of "applied linguistics," the purpose of which is "to solve or at least ameliorate problems involving language" (Davies, 1999, p. 1). Since the mid-1980s, however, an increasing amount of research in the field has moved away from the practical purposes that first initiated it and many researchers now approach second language learning as a problem-area in its own right. They explore it and address theoretical problems within it independently of whether these problems have practical significance, simply because second language learning is a domain of human experience that merits scientific study (examples of this development are the contributions to Ritchie and Bhatia, 1996, and the journal *Second Language Research*). Of course we should not draw strict dividing lines, because such "non-applied" research is also likely to improve the basis for making practical decisions. Conversely, a review of classroom-oriented SLA research since 1985 (Lightbown, 2000) cautions us against over-hasty attempts to apply the results of this research to teaching, since they are only one amongst several sources of knowledge that teachers draw on in shaping their expectations and practice.

20.1.1   Some terms clarified

In this chapter the term "second language" refers to any language that is learnt when the first language system is already in place. No distinction is made between the "second," "third," or even "fourth" (etc.) language that a person learns. This does not mean that it is irrelevant whether a person has already learnt one or more other "second" languages before being exposed to the one currently being learnt – indeed the ways in which language learning may be affected by previously learnt languages other than the first language is an area of enquiry in its own right (Cenoz, Hufeisen, & Jessner, 2001). However it would be impossible to sustain the distinction in any review of second language research, since this research itself rarely distinguishes between subjects who are learning a new language for the first time and those who have already experienced the process. It seems intuitively likely, indeed, that a large proportion of the "second" language learners who have been studied are in reality learning a third or fourth language.

Some writers make a distinction between a "second" language, which has societal functions in the community where it is learnt (e.g., English in India or English as learnt by an immigrant to the USA), and a "foreign" language, which is learnt for contact outside the community (e.g., French as learnt in the UK). In this article the term "second language" is used as a cover term and refers to an additional language, which is learnt in either kind of situation.

Finally the term "language" itself – the goal of second language learning – needs elaboration. In the early days of second language learning studies, this goal was conceived primarily in terms of grammar and vocabulary – literally, then, in terms of *language* elements. However, subsequent developments in linguistics and related disciplines have led to a much wider conceptualization of the knowledge and abilities that second language learners need to acquire (see for example the seminal article of Canale & Swain, 1980). The goal is now usually recognized as including various aspects of "communicative competence," for example:

- linguistic competence, which includes the knowledge of vocabulary, grammar, semantics, and phonology that have been the traditional focus of second language learning;
- discourse competence, which enables speakers to engage in continuous discourse, e.g., by linking ideas in longer written texts, maintaining longer spoken turns, participating in interaction, opening conversations and closing them;
- pragmatic competence, which enables second language speakers to use their linguistic resources in order to convey and interpret meanings in real situations, including those where they encounter problems due to gaps in their knowledge;
- sociolinguistic competence, which consists primarily of knowledge of how to use language appropriately in social situations, e.g., conveying suitable degrees of formality, directness and so on;
- sociocultural competence, which includes awareness of the background knowledge and cultural assumptions which affect meanings and which may lead to misunderstandings in intercultural communication.

Most research into the dynamics of second language development has focused on linguistic and (to a lesser extent) discourse competence. In the area of pragmatic competence, research has studied the communication strategies used by second language speakers (Kasper & Kellerman, 1997) but rarely how these strategies develop. In the areas of sociolinguistic and sociocultural competence, important areas of study have been how second language speakers perform speech acts and how misunderstandings may arise when they transfer first language strategies and assumptions to their second language use (Cohen, 1996).

20.1.2 Scope of this chapter

This chapter approaches the study of second language learning as part of the broader field of applied linguistics and sees it as aiming ultimately to increase our capacity to learn and teach second languages more effectively. Viewed from this perspective, however, there are three important areas which are not dealt with here. The two areas of second language research, which have perhaps the most important implications for language pedagogy, are the ways in which learning is affected by *social factors* and *individual differences*. These two areas are the subjects of separate chapters in this volume (and respectively) and will therefore not be dealt with here. This means also that this chapter does not deal with one of the main arenas in which individual differences and social factors play their role, namely, *learners' motivation* (see Dörnyei, 2001, for an up-to-date survey).

To those people who have grown up in situations dominated by one majority language and learnt another language for communication abroad or with foreign visitors, the prototypical setting for second language learning may seem to be the classroom. A feature of second language research since the 1970s has been that it has paid attention not only to learning in the classroom but also to so-called "natural," "informal," or "untutored" learning which takes place outside classrooms, either simultaneously with classroom learning (as in the case of students who take vacation English courses in the UK or the USA) or as the main source of learning (as with many immigrants or child second language learners). From this broader perspective, the overall field of study is the process of second language learning as it may occur in any context; the influence of classroom instruction on this process is just one important aspect of this field of study. This is the perspective taken in this article.

Resources for conducting research are obviously more available in some countries than in others and, equally obviously, this has affected the range of specific languages for which we have data. Since we have far more information about English than other languages and since English is a language, which all readers of this handbook understand, most of the specific examples will involve English. Of course it is hoped that the processes and principles, which these examples illustrate, will apply equally to the learning of other languages.

The chapter is structured as follows. Section 20.2 discusses what research has shown about some of the major processes involved in second language learning. Section 20.3 then discusses what we know about typical sequences of learning and what might cause them. Section 20.4 looks at how learning is affected by classroom instruction, which focuses on formal aspects of language. Section 20.5 outlines some of the most important theoretical positions which are currently adopted by those involved in the study of second language learning. Section 20.6 summarizes diagrammatically the key elements and processes of second language learning that have been mentioned in the chapter.

20.2   Processes of Second Language Learning

One of the principles of all learning is that we make sense of new information and ideas by relating them to our previous knowledge. There are two main kinds of previous language knowledge which second language learners can use in order to make sense of the new language they encounter: the first is their knowledge of their mother tongue and the second is the knowledge they already possess about the second language itself. In the first case it is common to talk about "transfer" and in the second case about "generalization." These processes will be discussed in this section. The section will then include brief discussion of two processes which are less creative in nature but which also appear to play an important role in the overall second language learning process, namely, simplification and imitation.

When a learner produces language, which conforms to native speaker norms, it is obvious that learning has taken place but not usually possible to know what kind of learning it was. For example, if a learner says *I don't know how to do it*, there is no way of knowing if he or she has mastered a complex set of English rules or simply memorized a set pattern. One way of trying to catch a clearer glimpse into the second language learner's mind is to look not only at the correct forms that he or she produces, but also at the errors (Corder, 1967; James, 1998; Richards, 1974). We will see below how the study of learners' errors has been a particularly rich source of insights into the processes by which second language learning takes place.

20.2.1   Transfer

Particularly when the second language shares a wide range of structures with the mother tongue, transfer is a powerful process that can already take the learner deep into the new system (Odlin, 1989). For example, when French native speakers begin to learn English, they already know how word order usually signals meaning; how the logical object becomes the grammatical subject when the passive voice is used; the basic principles that underlie the uses of the definite and indefinite articles; the main patterns for forming relative clauses; and so on. They already possess the cognitive habit of paying attention to (and signaling) number each time they use a noun, or tense each time they use a verb. Sometimes of course, even within the domains just mentioned, they may transfer knowledge which is not appropriate and leads them into error. For example, they may say *I am actor*, omitting the article on the pattern of French *je suis acteur*, or they may over-use the present perfect tense in *Yesterday I have sold my car* under the influence of French *Hier j'ai vendu ma voiture*. Overall, however, they can transfer a large body of relevant mother tongue knowledge, which makes the second language learning process easier and quicker. Indeed, errors such as those just mentioned illustrate even more clearly than their correct utterances that the process of transfer is taking place.

The extent to which transfer helps French native speakers to learn English becomes clearer if we consider the problems encountered by native speakers of a language which does not share so many features with English. This Chinese native speaker, for example, has learnt English for over ten years but still shifts almost randomly between tenses as she tells of her experience last summer: *At the start of the holiday, I try hard to find a summer job. Luckily, I was employed by an audit firm. Although I have worked for three months only, I learnt a lot of things.* Similarly, many advanced Chinese learners experience difficulty with the basic relative clause construction (e.g., *The first feeling comes into my mind is that I need to pay a lot of money*), the use of articles (e.g., *Rabbit is an animal which is very small*) or the passive (which is often avoided completely – in one set of 17 essays on general topics, written by students with over ten years' English learning experience, it does not occur at all). In addition to these aspects of learning where transfer seems to be less available to the Chinese than to the French native speaker, there are also clear instances when transfer does take place, sometimes leading to errors (e.g., *There had stuffy air* and *Although I love playing so much, but I play only in my free time*, which reflect Chinese patterns in existential constructions and concessive clauses respectively). However we may assume that for the Chinese learner, too, transfer usually performs a helpful role, for example by providing awareness of basic word order conventions or the distinctions between major word classes.

The examples just given show the process of transfer operating at the level of the learners' linguistic competence. This is the domain on which most research has concentrated. However the same process operates at higher levels of discourse (Littlewood, 2001; Takahashi, 1996). For example, a common transfer error in the discourse of Chinese learners of English is caused by different conventions for using "yes" or "no" in reply to negative questions. In this exchange, the Chinese native speaker (B) was understood by the native English speaker (A) as meaning that she does indeed live with her parents:

A: Don't you live with your parents then?
B: Yes.

– until B continued with the words:

B: I live on my own. I rent a flat.

– where it emerges that B is in fact transferring into English the normal Chinese discourse strategy of replying to the speaker's assumption (*"Yes, you are right – I don't* live with them") rather than to the proposition itself, as is normal in English discourse (in this case, *"No, I don't* live with them").

Until the 1960s, it was generally assumed that transfer (often labeled negatively "interference") was not only a hindrance to learning but also the only major cause of error (Brooks, 1960). We will now see that in fact many errors are not due to transfer but to another basic learning process, namely, generalization.

20.2.2   Generalization

The ability to go "beyond the information given" in experience and make generalizations, which can then be used to understand and create new instances of experience, is fundamental to learning (Bruner, 1973). There are many terms which refer to aspects of this same process but from different theoretical perspectives, e.g., rule-formation, pattern-perception, schema-construction or the establishment of neural networks. Any of these terms can also be used in referring to second language learning. The process means, for example, that second language learners do not need to learn separately, for each verb, how it can be used to express time in the past: once they know the underlying pattern that creates *walked* from *walk* and *danced* from *dance*, they can also create *jumped* from *jump* and *stepped* from *step*. At the level of sentence structure, once they have a rule that enables them to make the logical object of one action into the subject and topic of a sentence by means of the passive, they can do it for a whole range of other logical objects. As with transfer, then, although we cannot actually observe generalization taking place, we may assume that it is operating all the time and is almost always helpful to learning. Indeed, if this were not the case, second language learners would never be able to use the structures of the language creatively to understand or express new meanings.

Again as with transfer, the process of generalization becomes clearest when it leads not to correct forms but to errors, that is, when it becomes *overgeneralization*. For example, the same process of generalization that allows learners to associate *jumped* and *jump* may also lead them to hear *hoist* as a past participle similar to *jumped* (presumably from a verb *hois'* with no final "t"), leading to the common announcement in Hong Kong that *The number one typhoon signal is hoist.* Alternatively, if a learner generalizes from *waited* and *wanted* to *expected*, she may say how *touch-ted* she feels by a movie she has just *watch-ted*. Many other examples of overgeneralization can be found in the speech and writing of second language learners. Here, for example, a learner overgeneralizes an English rule for inverting subject and object in questions: *Tell me what can I do.* Here another learner overgeneralizes in the opposite direction: *Why I tell you I am an optimistic youngster?* The next learner is familiar with the common "I am + adjective + to" pattern as in "I am eager (willing, ready, etc.) to . . ." and uses it inappropriately with "easy to . . .": *I am so easy to cry but always keep back my tears.* Finally, this learner knows that words like "buy" are normally followed by objects and produces the deviant utterance *Health is your wealth that you cannot buy it.* All of these forms were produced by Chinese-speaking learners of English but, in principle, could have been produced by learners of any mother tongue, since they are based on the learners' previous experience with the second language itself rather than with their mother tongue.

As with transfer, generalization and overgeneralization errors occur not only within the learner's developing linguistic competence but also at higher levels of discourse. For example, the phrase *What's the matter?* is often overgeneralized by Chinese speakers in Hong Kong from situations where a person is in some difficulty to other situations where help is requested. Thus one may enter a travel agency in Hong Kong and be greeted not with (say) "Can I help you?" but with *What's the matter?*

20.2.3   *Transfer and generalization combined*

In the above two sections transfer and generalization are treated as two distinct processes. As I indicated earlier, however, they are related in that each is a way of using prior knowledge to make sense of what is new. We would therefore expect to encounter many instances where previous mother tongue knowledge and previous second language knowledge combine to offer the learner a similar way of making sense of new second language data. Thus when a German speaker says *I would have it done* to express the past conditional (i.e., in the sense of "I would have done it"), is this a transfer of the German word order rules which, in the translation equivalent, would move the past participle to the end of the phrase (*Ich hätte es gemacht*)? Or is it a case of influence from the English pattern "to have something done"? When an Italian native speaker says *I think to go to Spain*, is this a case of transfer of the Italian pattern "pensare + infinitive" or is it overgeneralization of the English pattern after verbs such as "I want" or "I intend"? It seems likely that both influences are at work and indeed reinforce each other.

20.2.4   *Simplification*

Transfer and generalization are ways of actively making sense of a new language in terms of what is already known. A third process that often takes place, especially in the early stages of learning, is more reductionist in nature. This is the process of simplification, in which a speaker omits elements that are redundant and produces something similar to the "telegraphic speech" found in early mother tongue acquisition. For example, a Chinese native speaker in Hong Kong saw that I had some photocopying to be done and informed me *Photocopier broken*. On another occasion, after I had paid in advance for a cup of tea at the cash desk of a canteen and was going to the wrong counter to collect it, the cashier corrected me with an appropriate gesture and *Sir! . . . tea there*. Simplification may be supported here by transfer, since the Chinese equivalents of these utterances would not require a copula.

Such simplified utterances enable a speaker to convey essential meanings with a minimum of linguistic competence. Indeed it is debatable whether they are best seen as products of the speaker's developing linguistic system or simply as one-off strategies designed to solve an immediate communication problem. From a developmental perspective, perhaps an important function is that they enable the second language learner to engage in interaction at an early stage and thus be exposed to a wider range of language.

20.2.5   *Imitation*

In the behaviorist perspective that dominated in the 1950s, imitation (leading through repetition to memorization) was a cornerstone of the learning process. In the reaction against behaviorism its importance was widely rejected

(Dulay & Burt, 1973), but it is now again generally recognized as a significant process.

The clearest evidence for the role of imitation is provided by set phrases ("formulaic speech") that learners often produce as a means of coping with common or important situations in their environment. Evidence that the phrases result from imitation comes from the fact that the learner's other output shows no evidence that he or she has mastered the grammar that underlies them. Thus a learner may regularly use phrases such as the one mentioned earlier – *I don't know how to do it* – at an early stage of learning, when he or she never otherwise uses either the full negative "I don't . . ." or "how + infinitive . . ." as productive patterns.

Formulaic speech is an important feature of second language use and learning (Wray, 1999). On the one hand, like simplification, it gives speakers the linguistic tools for coping with situations that would otherwise be beyond their competence. On the other hand it may provide them with a memorized store of "language samples" which they can process internally, so that the underlying rules gradually become incorporated into their developing linguistic competence. There is evidence that some second language learners are more disposed than others to follow this route.

20.2.6 *Conscious and unconscious learning processes*

The four processes mentioned in this section – transfer, generalization, simplification and imitation – may all occur either subconsciously or consciously. In natural situations, we may expect them to occur almost always subconsciously, while the second language learner/speaker focuses on the meanings which are communicated. In formal learning situations, it is of course very common for these processes to be raised to consciousness (Rutherford, 1987). For example, a teacher may highlight a rule so that the learners can generalize it more easily, or a learner may consciously try to imitate, repeat, and memorize a useful utterance in a dialogue. The relationship between conscious and unconscious learning processes is an area of lively debate, which we will encounter again in later sections.

20.3 Sequences of Development

As we have seen, the analysis of learners' errors has contributed much to our understanding of second language learning. However, since it focuses attention mainly on structures, which learners have not yet fully acquired at a particular time, it does not tell us much about the actual progression of learning. For example, in the case of the learner who asked *Why I tell you that I am an optimistic youngster?*, how did he reach that point and how is he likely to develop further? If we hear a speaker use the simplified *I no want it*, does that tell us anything about where he or she stands in relation to gradual mastery of negative structures? To answer questions such as these, we need to consider the development of individual learners over time. This was done first in the context of first language acquisition and subsequently by second language researchers (e.g., Bailey, Madden, & Krashen, 1974; Dulay & Burt, 1973; contributors to Hatch, 1978). A small selection of the results is presented here.

20.3.1   *Acquisition of the negative*

Learners with a wide range of mother tongues have been found to follow a similar sequence of development in acquiring the negative:

1 At first learners simply place a negative particle outside the main sentence structure (*No very good*).
2 Then comes a stage when the particle is placed inside the sentence but before the verb (*I no want it; I not like that*).
3 The first instances of placing the particle after the verb occur with auxiliary verbs such as "is" and "can" (*He was not happy; You can't tell her*). "Don't" may be used, but it is not marked for number or tense (*She don't like it*).
4 Finally the particle is placed after a part of "do," which is also marked for number and tense (*It doesn't swim*).

These stages are not clear-cut but overlap with each other. Thus a learner who has moved to stage 3 in most of her language may sometimes also produce forms typical of stage 2. Furthermore, there is some variation within the stages. Some of this may result from transfer. At stage 2, for example, Spanish learners prefer to use *no* whereas Norwegian learners prefer *not*, influenced by the sounds of their mother tongue; also, stage 2 persists longer for many Spanish learners than for others, presumably because their own language places the particle before the verb (as in *Carmen no es de Madrid*). In general, however, the studies show remarkable similarity in how learners gradually develop their mastery of the negative.

20.3.2   *Acquisition of the interrogative*

As with negatives, there seems to be a typical sequence of stages in the development of interrogatives. Here only wh-interrogatives will be mentioned:

1 At first learners simply place the question word in front of the sentence, without inverting the subject and verb (*Why we not live in Scotland?*).
2 At the next stage inversion takes place with the copula (*Where is the sun?*).
3 Inversion later comes to be made with "do," which is marked for number and tense (*What do you say?*)
4 Later still, complex questions occur such as negative questions (*Why can't he come?*) and embedded questions (*Tell me why you can't do it*).

20.3.3 *Acquisition of morphemes*

It was the so-called "morpheme studies" in first language research that drew widespread attention to the possibility of natural developmental sequences (Brown, 1973). This research examined the sequence in which 14 grammatical morphemes were acquired by several children and found that the sequence was basically the same. These findings stimulated a series of second language studies (reported, e.g., in Dulay, Burt, & Krashen, 1982), which examined the same phenomenon. They took large groups of learners and measured how accurately they produced the different morphemes in their speech or writing. This "accuracy order" was assumed to be the same as the order in which the morphemes are acquired (an assumption which has however been questioned). The studies found a noticeable similarity amongst the second language learners from different language backgrounds. The accuracy order suggests that all learners first acquire a group of morphemes comprising present progressive "-ing," plural "-s," and copula "to be"; the second group consists of auxiliary "to be" and the articles "the" and "a"; then come irregular past forms; and the fourth group includes regular past with "-ed," third person singular "-s," and possessive "-s."

20.3.4 *A built-in syllabus?*

Although only a few structures have been studied from this perspective (others include relative clauses, past tense markers, and German word order), the results combine to suggest that for some structures at least, the sequence of acquisition may to some extent be pre-programmed in the learner's mind. This reinforces the idea, already suggested by the results of error analysis, that learners may operate with a "built-in syllabus" (Corder, 1967): that is, they not only work on the input with processes such as generalization, transfer, simplification, and imitation, but are also disposed to develop their internal grammar in natural, predictable sequences. Furthermore, these same sequences have been observed even in the spontaneous output of classroom learners who have been taught the correct target forms, suggesting that the internal syllabus often overrides the external syllabus which the teacher or course-book tries to impose.

The processes discussed in Section 20.2 are not in themselves specific enough to explain natural sequences. They do not explain, for example, why one rule rather than another is generalized, why questions and negatives are acquired in the particular sequence observed, or why plural "-s" is acquired before third person singular "-s." Various additional explanations have been proposed. One is that a form is more likely to be learnt if it is supported by more than one process, for example, by both generalization and transfer, or by both transfer and simplification. A target form may also become established more quickly if it is more frequent in the input (this has been suggested for the morphemes discussed above), more salient perceptually in the speech that learners hear, or more important in communication (this seems to be the case with formulaic speech). A more technical suggestion is that the development of some structures may be governed by psycholinguistic "processing constraints," so that the achievement of one stage is a prerequisite for achieving the next (Pienemann, 1989). This may explain the sequences of negatives and interrogatives, in which each stage requires the learner to perform more (or more complex) operations on the basic "subject – verb – object" pattern.

20.4   The Effects of Classroom Instruction

In the previous section it was mentioned that the learner's "built-in syllabus" seems in some ways to be independent of the effects of instruction: similar errors and similar sequences have been observed in both natural and instructed learners. This discovery led some researchers to posit that the built-in syllabus may be powerful enough to override the effects of instruction. They raised the question of how instruction affects learning, if indeed it does at all (Long, 1983).

It is clear that instruction has effects on learning in the case of those many second language speakers whose ability comes only from classroom instruction, supplemented perhaps by a limited amount of outside-class practice. In studies which have compared learners who experience only natural exposure with learners who experience both exposure and classroom instruction, the results (though less conclusive) also indicate that instruction improves learning. The issue remains, however, of exactly *how* classroom instruction affects the learning process. For example, does it affect the course that learning takes? Or does it affect only the rate of progress along a pre-determined course? To what extent is it helpful if teachers focus learners' attention explicitly on the forms of the language they are learning (e.g., on its grammar and vocabulary), or should the main focus always be on the communication of meanings? Can we identify the conscious learning strategies which seem most helpful to learning? These are some of the key questions, which will be considered in this section.

A teacher often asks a group of learners to repeat and practice a complex structure during a lesson and, in that controlled situation, they become able to produce the structure in response to the teacher's stimulus. Intensive patterns drills are based on this procedure. However this production often results from conscious manipulation rather than genuine learning. Here we are concerned not with this kind of performance but with whether the learners can still use a structure in their spontaneous use of language some time *after* the instruction has taken place.

20.4.1   The rate and course of learning

Several studies have provided evidence that instruction can accelerate the rate of learning. In one of these (Doughty & Varela, 1998), learners were given instruction in forming relative clauses at a stage when they were considered ready to acquire them. They acquired the rules more quickly than learners who were exposed to input containing the structures but received no instruction. In another study (Pienemann, 1989), English-speaking learners of German were taught German word-order rules. All the learners were at "stage 2" in the developmental sequence that the researchers had observed with other students. Some stage 2 learners were taught rules from stage 3 and others were taught rules from stage 4. It was found that the first group benefited from instruction and moved quickly into stage 3, but that the second group were unable to "skip" a natural stage: they either remained at stage 2 or moved into stage 3. These and similar findings are the main evidence for Pienemann's "learnability" or "teachability" hypothesis, according to which instruction (in some areas of language at least) can accelerate the rate of learning but not cause learners to skip a natural stage. Other areas of language may be more flexible and teachable at any time.

20.4.2   Focus on form

The studies just mentioned already provide evidence that learning can benefit from instruction which focuses on form (often called "consciousness-raising"). Other important evidence comes from French immersion programs in Canada. The students in these programs attend classes in "content" (i.e., non-language) subjects in the medium of French. From a language learning perspective, therefore, they are learning in a natural environment without explicit instruction. They achieve a high degree of fluency in French, to the extent that these programs have often been cited as support for adopting a "natural approach" to language teaching in which there is no error-correction or explicit focus on form. However, closer examination revealed that though the students emerge as fluent communicators, there are some aspects of French grammar that they do not master (Harley & Swain, 1984), perhaps because these aspects are not essential to communication in the classroom setting (where all the participants except the teacher are fellow native English speakers). In a number of experimental studies, aspects of grammar (e.g., the conditional and the different uses of the past continuous and simple past tenses) have been taught explicitly to groups of learners, whose performance has later been compared with learners who have received no instruction. The overwhelming evidence is that explicit focus on formal aspects of language is helpful and produces lasting improvement in performance (Doughty & Williams, 1998; Spada, 1997).

20.4.3   Conscious learning strategies

So far in this section we have considered how learning might be affected by action initiated by the teacher. Another line of exploration has focused on action initiated by the learner. Many researchers have investigated the conscious strategies that learners use in order to plan and carry out their learning (O'Malley & Chamot, 1990; Oxford, 1990).

The so-called "good language learner" studies of the 1970s (notably Naiman et al., 1995 [1978]) laid the foundations for this research by investigating some of the qualities that characterize successful language learners. These learners are characterized above all by strategies for active involvement: for example, they repeat silently to themselves what the teacher or other students say; they think out their own answer to questions which the teacher puts to other students; they pay close attention to the meaning of the language they are practicing; and they seek opportunities to use the language outside class, for example by reading or seeking personal contacts. Subsequent research (surveyed in McDonough, 1999) has confirmed that sucessful learners generally use a greater number of active learning strategies. It has identified strategies which fall into four broad categories: metacognitive strategies (e.g., planning one's learning time), cognitive strategies (e.g., techniques for memorizing vocabulary), affective strategies (e.g., ways to deal with frustration and increase motivation), and social strategies (e.g., joining a group as a peripheral participant and pretending to understand). A practical aim of this research is to identify in more detail the strategies which lead to more successful learning, so that these strategies can be introduced to less successful learners. It is generally accepted, however, that the specific strategies which best suit one learner will not necessarily be those that best suit another learner.

20.5   Theories of Second Language Learning

So far this chapter has presented some of the findings of second language research together with some of the explanations that have been proposed. These have been essentially "local" or "lower-level" explanations, in the sense that they have tried to account for specific aspects of the learning process, such as the kinds of error that learners make or the natural sequences of development that have been observed, by means of specific notions such as transfer, processing constraints, or the frequency of items in the input. In this section we will move to a higher level and look at some of the more global explanations that have been proposed for the human capacity to learn a second language. These explanations are variously called "hypotheses," "models," or "theories," depending on the scope and depth of the explanatory power that their proponents claim for them, but these terms will not be kept rigorously distinct here.

Theories of second language learning fall broadly into two categories: those which take as their starting point the *cognitive processes* that underlie second language learning and those that start from the *context* of learning. Of course no cognition-oriented theory can ignore the context in which the cognitive processes are activated and no context-oriented theory can ignore the processes which convert input into learning. It is a question of emphasis.

A complete theory would integrate satisfactorily both the cognitive and contextual bases of learning into a single framework which would accord appropriate weightings to both sets of factors and illuminate the relationships between them. Such a theory is not yet available and (in view of the complexity of second language learning and the different forms that it takes) there is even some doubt as to whether it would be desirable or possible. What we have at present are therefore "middle-level" rather than comprehensive theories of second language learning.

20.5.1   Cognition-oriented theories

This section looks first at three related hypotheses, which develop a conception of language learning as occurring through innate mechanisms which exist specially for this purpose. It then looks at how other researchers have proposed to account for language learning within the wider framework of cognitive learning theory.

20.5.1.1   The creative construction hypothesis

Much of the early research in the 1970s was guided by the conception (stimulated by work in first language acquisition) of a "language acquisition device," which facilitates a process of "creative construction" in the mind of the learner. Partly in reaction to behaviorist ideas that second language learning is a process of habit-formation in which the major obstacle to learning is interference from the mother tongue, many researchers (e.g., Dulay & Burt, 1973) set out to show that second language as well as first language learners are endowed with innate mechanisms for processing language and creating their own internal grammar. Some of this work was described in Sections 20.2 and 20.3 above. The grammar that learners construct is often called their "interlanguage" (i.e., a language located somewhere on a continuum between their mother tongue and the target language) (Selinker, 1972) or "transitional competence" (i.e., a competence which is in a state of transition, as it develops in the direction of the target language) (Corder, 1967). However it does not generally become identical with the target language, as some non-target features become "fossilized" in the learner's grammar. In this theory (variously called the "creative construction hypothesis" or "interlanguage theory"), it is usually claimed that many of these innate mechanisms are specific to language learning rather than of a general cognitive nature, since the input does not contain enough evidence for general cognitive mechanisms to work on. The input acts primarily as a "trigger" to activate the mechanisms.

20.5.1.2   The input hypothesis

An attempt to formulate a more comprehensive theory, which incorporates the creative construction hypothesis, is the "input hypothesis" (also called the "monitor model") formulated by Krashen (1982). In this model the most important distinction is between "acquisition" and "learning." "Acquisition" is subconscious and guided by the learner's innate mechanisms along natural developmental sequences. It occurs as a result of exposure to comprehensible input, is not accessible to conscious control or instruction, and occurs best when the "affective filter" (e.g., level of anxiety) is low. "Learning" is conscious and often occurs through instruction or error correction. "Acquired" language is most important and forms the basis for spontaneous communication. Language that has been "learnt" plays only a subsidiary role as a "monitor" of speech or writing and can never pass through into the acquired system. Many of the claims of this model cannot be proven (e.g., the strict separation of acquisition and learning), but it has attracted many supporters and continues to inspire much discussion (see McLaughlin, 1987, for a detailed critique).

20.5.1.3   The Universal Grammar hypothesis

The language acquisition device, which is postulated as driving the creative construction process, is largely a "black box." Some of what it contains can be hypothesized on the basis of learners' errors and sequences of development discussed earlier in this article – mechanisms such as transfer, procedures such as paying attention to saliency, the constraints on learnability, and so on. Another approach is based on the linguistic theory of "universal grammar" (UG) associated with Noam Chomsky's school of thought. The theory of UG claims that there is a set of principles which govern all languages and are already wired into the human brain when we are born. The principles themselves are universal, but they allow for variation in the form of certain parameters that need to be set. For example, there is a "structure-dependency" principle, which specifies that every language is organized hierarchically, such that each component not only forms part of a higher-level structure but also (down to the individual morpheme) has its own internal structure. Thus a phrase is part of the structure of the sentence, but also itself has a head element and subordinate elements (i.e., a complement). The structure-dependency principle has a "head parameter," which specifies whether the head element in a phrase is placed before or after the other elements. In some languages (e.g., English) the head comes first, in others (e.g., Japanese) it comes last. The child learner's task is to discover how this parameter should be "set" for the particular language he or she encounters. Once it has been set, the child has information relevant to all parts of the language to which the head parameter applies. These principles and parameters thus explain how the child learns much more about the language than he or she could have learnt form the input alone. They could explain this for the second language learner, too, if they are still available "the second time round." Whether they are indeed still available is an area of lively debate, often highly technical, involving issues such as whether a second language learner acquires knowledge which would not be available directly from the input (e.g., because it would require negative as well as positive evidence) and whether learning one aspect of language sometimes leads to knowledge of some other aspect which is related to the same principle and parameter (Towell & Hawkins, 1994, present a detailed application of UG theory to second language acquisition).

20.5.1.4   The cognitive skill-learning model

The cognition-oriented approaches described so far in this section regard language learning (whether first or second) as a unique form of learning which requires explanations specific to itself. Many researchers do not accept this view: they argue that general principles of cognitive psychology are sufficient to account also for second language learning (Johnson, 1996). Communicating through language is regarded as a complex skill in which, as with other skills, overt performance is based on a hierarchy of cognitive plans. Let us say, for example, that a man intends to ask his friend to lend him his car tomorrow. At the highest level of the hierarchy he needs to select an overall strategy (e.g., direct request? prepare the ground by asking if his friend will be travelling anywhere himself?). If he decides on the first strategy, he must select one of many possible ways of formulating a request (depending on factors such as the nature of their relationship and how much inconvenience the request is likely to cause). Formulating the request involves selecting a grammatical plan and, within that plan, individual components such as noun phrases and verb phrases. These have to be filled with specific lexical items which involve articulatory plans, which are in turn realized by appropriate motor skills. In skilled performance, only the higher-level plans require conscious attention (through "controlled processing"), whilst those at the lower levels are realized subconsciously (through "automatic processing"). Since human attention capacity is limited, fluent performance depends on the establishment of a repertoire of lower-level plans which can be processed automatically, so that sufficient attention can be given to higher-level decisions (e.g., communicative intention and meaning). At the early stages of learning, however, conscious attention has to be devoted even to lower-level plans such as grammatical structuring or word selection, leading to performance which is non-fluent and/or contains errors. Learning consists of moving these lower-level plans into the domain of automatic processing, so that they can unfold fluently in response to decisions at the higher levels.

The creative construction model (together with the related input hypothesis and UG hypothesis) sees language learning as proceeding in natural sequences as a result of internal mechanisms which are "triggered" by input from the environment. The cognitive skill-learning model just described sees second language learning as a less specialized process, one which is more amenable to control, and one in which productive performance has a clearer role. Both models seem to capture important aspects of different people's learning experience and may represent alternative routes by which language may enter a person's communicative competence. In some kinds of situation, one kind of learning may predominate (e.g., the creative construction model in natural learning environments, the cognitive skill-learning in instruction), but the other will not be excluded. In many schools, for example, high priority is given to engaging learners in communicative activity which will activate their natural learning mechanisms.

20.5.2   Context-oriented theories

In the theories described so far in this section, the external context performs a necessary role but the focus is on the internal mechanisms that process the information that it provides. This section will look at theories and hypotheses, which shift attention to the context itself and to the ways in which it facilitates the process of learning.

20.5.2.1   The interaction hypothesis

The "interaction hypothesis" is a development of the input hypothesis discussed above (Long, 1985). The prerequisite for learning is still seen as comprehensible input, but attention is now drawn to the conditions that enable comprehensible input to be made available. The hypothesis argues that this is most likely to occur in situations of social interaction. These provide opportunities for the negotiation of meaning, requests for clarification, and comprehension checks. As a result, it is more likely that the input will be tuned to the current level of competence of the individual learner and thus become "intake" which is available for learning. Researchers have shown that increased opportunities for negotiation are indeed likely to lead to increased comprehension. They have also studied the kinds of classroom interaction task that are most likely to lead to the negotiation of meaning (e.g., pair-work tasks in which both learners have information and must reach a decision or a solution to a problem). However, the assumed causal link between increased opportunities for negotiation and improvement in learning has not yet been demonstrated empirically.

20.5.2.2   The output hypothesis

Natural second language learners often go through a "silent period" when they listen and respond, but do not actually produce language themselves. Nonetheless they develop knowledge of the language which can later serve as a basis for their own production. In the input hypothesis described earlier, this leads to the claim that acquisition occurs through processing "comprehensible input," in which forms occur from the learner's next natural developmental stage. Language production (including oral or written practice in class) is not necessary to learning and can be simply left to develop naturally, when learners feel they are ready. The "output hypothesis" argues (partly on the basis of the French immersion classes mentioned earlier, in which massive input still does not lead to accuracy in all aspects of grammar) that input is not sufficient and that output too plays a significant role in acquisition (Swain, 1995). The need to speak or write makes learners pay attention to aspects of grammar which they would not need for comprehension purposes alone and thus makes them notice gaps in their knowledge. It gives them opportunities to make hypotheses about how the grammatical system works and (when meanings are negotiated) they get feedback about whether these hypotheses are correct. It stimulates them to discuss the language with others and thus "scaffold" each other (see Section 20.5.2.3) in their efforts to understand the language. Furthermore, from a cognitive skill-learning perspective, output helps to automate the cognitive plans that underlie language production.

20.5.2.3   *The scaffolding hypothesis*

In the interaction hypothesis, social interaction plays a mediating role: it facilitates the provision of input, which in turn triggers acquisition. In what we will call here the "scaffolding hypothesis," social interaction provides the substantive means by which learning occurs. The hypothesis is based on sociocultural theory, which goes back to the work of Vygotsky in the 1930s and holds that social interaction is the most important stimulus for all learning. Two central concepts are "scaffolding" and the "zone of proximal development." "Scaffolding" refers to the way in which, with support from others, learners can reach levels of achievement which they would be unable to reach independently. This support often comes from an expert (e.g., a teacher), but learners themselves may also provide it for each other. The "zone of proximal development" is the domain of performance that a learner cannot yet achieve independently but is capable of achieving with the help of scaffolding. The expectation is that what is currently possible through scaffolding will later become possible without it. Researchers have shown how learners who help each other during interaction may, together, produce language that neither could produce alone. They have also shown how language items which learners produce on one occasion with the help of scaffolding may subsequently be incorporated into their independent discourse (see the contributions to Lantolf, 2000).

20.5.2.4   *The acculturation model and social identity theory*

The interaction hypothesis and the scaffolding hypothesis both focus on the immediate context in which social interaction takes place. Brief mention will be made here of two theories which extend the perspective outward to the wider sociopolitical context of learning. Both are concerned mainly with the experience of immigrants in their new host country. According to the "acculturation model" associated with John Schumann (1978), language learning involves a process of acculturation and is therefore heavily dependent on the degree of social and psychological distance that learners perceive between themselves and the speakers of the target language. This distance is smaller (and the conditions for learning are correspondingly more favorable) when, for example, the learner's own community shares social facilities and has regular contacts with the target language community. The "social identity model" (Norton, 2000) is based on the mutual influences that link language and identity: language is one means by which identity is constructed and identity affects the ways in which we use language. This identity is seen as dynamic and, as a person consolidates his or her identity in a new community, so his or her ability to speak and learn the language increases.

With these last two models we have begun to consider the influence on learning of wider social factors, which are the subject of Chapter 22 in this volume.

20.6   Conclusion

The various elements and processes of second language learning that have been described in this article are summarized in Figure 20.1. This diagram reminds us at level 1 that much second language learning (particularly in the second language environment) takes place in a wider social and sociopolitical context where it is one aspect of acculturation and identity construction. All second language learning (except some forms of self-instruction) takes place in an immediate context (level 2), which contains varying degrees of social interaction and instruction. These provide stimuli for learning which include those mentioned at level 3 of the diagram, where "output" comprises both spontaneous language use and controlled practice. These stimuli are processed subconsciously and/or consciously by internal mechanisms, some of which may be specific to language learning, others part of our general cognitive endowment. The former produce developmental sequences, which are to some extent predetermined, and the latter enable controlled plans to become automatic and fluent. Both kinds of learning serve to develop an ever-greater store of subconscious and conscious elements, which the learner can use for second language communication.

It should be stressed that, in reality, the various concepts in Figure 20.1 are not all rigidly distinct. Many are probably better conceived as the two extremes of a continuum (e.g., subconscious and conscious, since there can be varying degrees of consciousness) and others may be mingled in actual situations (e.g., instruction involves particular kinds of social interaction). The diagram should therefore be viewed more as a simplified summary of key elements and processes in second language learning than as an attempt to model the actual details of social, cognitive, and psycholinguistic reality.

See also 1 LANGUAGE DESCRIPTIONS, 21 INDIVIDUAL DIFFERENCES IN SECOND LANGUAGE LEARNING, 22 SOCIAL INFLUENCES ON LANGUAGE LEARNING.

1 The wider context

Acculturation	–	Identity construction

– – –

2 The immediate context

Social interaction	–	Instruction

– – –

3 Stimuli for development

Input	Scaffolding	Output	Consciousness-raising	Conscious strategies

– – –

4 Levels of processing

Subconscious processing	–	Conscious processing

– – –

5 Learning processes and constraints

Language acquisition mechanisms/Universal Grammar	Processing constraints	Cognitive skill-learning mechanisms

– – –

6 Learning progression

Natural developmental sequences	–	Automation of cognitive plans

– – –

7 Transitional communicative competence

Subconscious and conscious elements in the learner's interlanguage

Figure 20.1   Elements and processes of second language learning

REFERENCES

Bailey, N., Madden, C., & Krashen, S. (1974) Is there a "natural sequence" in adult second language learning? *Language Learning*, 24, 235–43.

Brooks, N. H. (1960) *Language and language learning: theory and practice*. New York: Harcourt.

Brown, R. (1973) *A first language: the early stages*. Cambridge, MA: Harvard University Press.

Bruner, J. S. (1973) *Beyond the information given: studies in the psychology of knowing*. (Selected, edited and introduced by J. M. Anglin.) New York: Norton.

Canale, M. & Swain, M. (1980) Theoretical bases of communicative approaches to language teaching and testing. *Applied Linguistics*, 1, 1–47.

Cenoz, J., Hufeisen, B., & Jessner, U. (eds.) (2001) *Cross-linguistic influence in third language acquisition: psycholinguistic perspectives*. Clevedon, UK: Multilingual Matters.

Cohen, A. D. (1996) Speech acts. In S. L. McKay & N. H. Hornberger (eds.), *Sociolinguistics and language teaching* (pp. 383–420). Cambridge: Cambridge University Press.

Corder, S. P. (1967) The significance of learners' errors. *International Review of Applied Linguistics*, 5, 161–9.

Davies, A. (1999) *An introduction to applied linguistics*. Edinburgh: Edinburgh University Press.

Dörnyei, Z. (2001) *Teaching and researching motivation*. London: Longman.

Doughty, C. & Varela, E. (1998) Communicative focus on form. In C. Doughty & J. Williams (eds.), *Focus on form in second language acquisition* (pp. 114–38). Cambridge: Cambridge University Press.

Doughty, C. & Williams, J. (eds.) (1998) *Focus on form in second language acquisition*. Cambridge: Cambridge University Press.

Dulay, H. & Burt, M. (1973) Should we teach children syntax? *Language Learning*, 24, 245–58.

Dulay, H., Burt, M., & Krashen, S. (1982) *Language two*. New York: Oxford University Press.

Ellis, R. (1994) *The study of second language acquisition*. Oxford: Oxford University Press.

Harley, B. & Swain, M. (1984) The interlanguage of immersion students and its implications for second language teaching. In A. Davies, C. Criper, & A. P. R. Howatt (eds.), *Interlanguage* (pp. 291–311). Edinburgh: Edinburgh University Press.

Hatch, E. M. (ed.) (1978) *Second language acquisition: a book of readings*. Rowley, MA: Newbury House.

James, C. (1998) *Errors in language learning and use: exploring error analysis*. London: Longman.

Johnson, K. (1996) *Language teaching and skill learning*. Oxford: Blackwell.

Kasper, G. & Kellerman, E. (1997) *Communication strategies: psycholinguistic and sociolinguistic perspectives*. London: Longman.

Kelly, L. G. (1969) *25 centuries of language teaching: an inquiry into the science, art and development of language teaching methodology, 500 B.C.–1969*. Rowley, MA: Newbury House.

Krashen, S. (1982) *Principles and practice in second language acquisition*. Oxford: Pergamon.

Lantolf, J. P. (ed.) (2000) *Sociocultural theory and second language learning*. Oxford: Oxford University Press.

Lightbown, P. M. (2000) Classroom SLA research and second language teaching. *Applied Linguistics*, 21, 413–62.

Littlewood, W. (2001) Cultural awareness and the negotiation of meaning in intercultural communication. *Language Awareness*, 10, 189–99.

Long, M. (1983) Does second language instruction make a difference? *TESOL Quarterly*, 17, 359–82.

Long, M. (1985) Input and second language acquisition theory. In S. M. Gass & C. G. Madden (eds.), *Input in second language acquisition* (pp. 377–93). Rowley, MA: Newbury House.

McDonough, S. H. (1999) Learner strategies. *Language Teaching*, 32, 1–18.

McLaughlin, B. (1987) *Theories of second-language learning*. London: Edward Arnold.

Naiman, N., Fröhlich, H., Stern, H., & Todesco, A. (1995 [1978]) *The good language learner*. Clevedon, UK: Multilingual Matters.

Norton, B. (2000) *Identity and language learning: gender, ethnicity and educational change*. London: Longman.

Odlin, T. (1989) *Language transfer: cross-linguistic influences in language learning*. Cambridge: Cambridge University Press.

O'Malley, J. & Chamot, A. (1990) *Learning strategies in second language acquisition*. Cambridge: Cambridge University Press.

Oxford, R. (1990) *Language learning strategies: what every teacher should know*. Rowley, MA: Newbury House.

Pienemann, M. (1989) Is language teachable? Psycholinguistic experiments and hypotheses. *Applied Linguistics*, 10, 52–79.

Richards, J. C. (1974) *Error analysis: perspectives on second language acquisition*. London: Longman.

Ritchie, W. C. & Bhatia, T. K. (eds.) (1996) *Handbook of second language acquisition*. San Diego: Academic Press.

Rivers, W. M. (1964) *The psychologist and the foreign language teacher*. Chicago: Chicago University Press.

Rutherford, W. (1987) *Second language grammar: learning and teaching*. London: Longman.

Schumann, J. (1978) The acculturation model for second language acquisition. In R. Gingras (ed.), *Second language acquisition and foreign language teaching* (pp. 27–50). Arlington, VA: Center for Applied Linguistics.

Selinker, L. (1972) Interlanguage. *International Review of Applied Linguistics*, 10, 209–31.

Spada, N. (1997) Form-focussed instruction and second language acquisition: a review of classroom and laboratory research. *Language Teaching*, 30, 73–87.

Swain, M. (1995) Three functions of output in second language learning. In G. Cook & B. Seidlhofer (eds.), *Principles and practice in applied linguistics* (pp. 234–50). Oxford: Oxford University Press.

Takahashi, S. (1996) Pragmatic transferability. In G. Kasper (ed.), *The development of pragmatic competence* (pp. 189–224). Special issue of *Studies in Second Language Acquisition*.

Towell, R. & Hawkins, R. (1994) *Approaches to second language acquisition*. Clevedon, UK: Multilingual Matters.

Wray, A. (1999) Formulaic language in learners and native speakers. *Language Teaching*, 32, 213–31.

FURTHER READING

Baker, C. & Prys Jones, S. (1998)
Bilingualism and second language
acquisition. In C. Baker & S. Prys
Jones, *Encyclopedia of bilingualism and
bilingual education* (pp. 635–64).
Clevedon, UK: Multilingual Matters.

Cook, V. J. (2001) *Second language
learning and language teaching*
(3rd edn.). London: Arnold.

Corder, S. P. (1981) *Error analysis and
interlanguage*. Oxford: Oxford
University Press.

Ellis, R. (1997) *Second language acquisition*.
Oxford: Oxford University Press.

Larsen-Freeman, D. & Long,
M. H. (1991) *An introduction to second
language acquisition research*. London:
Longman.

Lightbown, P. & Spada, N. (1999)
How languages are learned (2nd edn.).
Oxford: Oxford University Press.

Littlewood, W. (1984) *Foreign and second
language learning: language acquisition
research and its implications for the*
classroom. Cambridge: Cambridge
University Press.

McLaughlin, B. & Robbins, S. (1999)
Second language learning. In
B. Spolsky (ed.), *Concise encyclopedia
of educational linguistics* (pp. 540–52).
Amsterdam: Elsevier.

Mitchell, R. & Myles, F. (1998) *Second
language learning theories*. London:
Arnold.

Sharwood Smith, M. (1994) *Second
language learning: theoretical foundations*.
London: Longman.

Skehan, P. (1998) *A cognitive approach to
language learning*. Oxford: Oxford
University Press.

Spolsky, B. (1989) *Conditions for second
language learning*. Oxford: Oxford
University Press.

Williams, M. and Burden, R. (1997)
Psychology for language teachers.
Cambridge: Cambridge University
Press.

21 Individual Differences in Second Language Learning

ROD ELLIS

21.1 Introduction

Learners vary enormously in how successful they are in learning a language. This is true for both first language (L1) and second language (L2) acquisition, although there is an important difference. In the case of L1 acquisition, children vary in their rate of acquisition but all, except in cases of severe environmental deprivation, achieve full competence in their mother tongue; in the case of L2 acquisition (SLA), learners vary not only in the speed of acquisition but also in their ultimate level of achievement, with a few achieving native-like competence and others stopping far short. How can we explain these differences in achievement? Broadly speaking, three different sets of explanatory factors have been identified; social, cognitive, and affective. This chapter, however, will consider only those factors that lie inside the learner – the cognitive and affective factors – and will focus on L2 learning.

Individual difference research has a considerable history in applied linguistics. Horwitz (2000a), reviewing publications in *The Modern Language Journal* from the 1920s up to the end of the 1970s, documents how interest in L2 learners' differences evolved over the decades. She notes a marked change in the labels used to refer to individual differences: "The terms *good and bad, intelligent and dull, motivated and unmotivated* have given way to a myriad of new terms such as *integratively and instrumentally motivated, anxious and comfortable, field independent and field sensitive, auditory and visual*" (p. 532, original emphasis). Horwitz characterizes these changes as evolutionary rather than revolutionary, but they seem to reflect a radical shift in the way learners are viewed; whereas earlier they were seen in absolute terms, as either innately endowed with or lacking in language learning skills, in more recent research they are characterized in more relative terms, as possessing different kinds of abilities and predispositions that influence learning in complex ways.

This change of perspective over the years reflects a development in the role of individual difference research in applied linguistics. In earlier periods, the primary concern was to provide a basis for selecting which learners should be chosen to receive foreign language instruction. To this end, the main purpose of individual difference research was to *predict* which learners would succeed. This led ultimately to the development of tests of language aptitude such as the Modern Language Aptitude Battery (Carroll & Sapon, 1959). More recent research on motivation or on learning strategies, however, has sought to *explain* why some learners succeed more than others and has been seen as complementary to mainstream research in SLA. This later research continues to have an "applied" side, however. It has been used to identify the characteristics of "good language learners" as a basis for learner training (i.e., providing guidance in how best to learn). It has also served as a basis for aptitude–treatment interactions (i.e., matching learners to different types of instruction so as to maximize learning).

Interest in individual differences has grown since the 1970s to the point where it has become a major area of enquiry in SLA. This interest is reflected in numerous articles published in all the major SLA journals (in particular *Language Learning* and *The Modern Language Journal*), in several major surveys of individual differences (e.g., Skehan, 1991), and, increasingly, in full-length books devoted to specific factors responsible for individual differences (e.g., Dörnyei's 2001 book on motivation). Research into individual differences has taken place alongside and separate from mainstream SLA research, where the primary concern has been the processes responsible for L2 acquisition (e.g., noticing, chunking, restructuring). One reason for this is that universalist and differential approaches have distinct agendas, the former seeking to explain the mechanisms responsible for the commonalities observed in the process of language learning (e.g., the "natural" order and sequence of L2 acquisition), the latter directed at examining how and why learners differ. This separation, however, is unfortunate, as it results in a piecemeal approach to understanding L2 acquisition that inhibits the development of an integrated theory to account for how and to what extent learners allocate resources to different learning mechanisms. As Breen (2001) emphasizes, an essential feature of psycholinguistic processes is that they are *selective*. The task facing researchers, therefore, must be to identify not just what the psycholinguistic processes involved in L2 acquisition are or what motivates individual learner selectivity, but how selectivity and processes interact in the performance of different tasks.

This review will be in two main parts. The first part will discuss the methods that have been used to investigate individual differences, in particular the instruments for measuring the various factors. The second part will consider a number of factors that have been found to contribute to individual differences in learning and will provide a review of the main research findings relating to each factor.

21.2   Methodology and Instrumentation

Research into individual difference has relied predominantly on quantitative methods. The favored method is a survey questionnaire consisting of Likert scale items that require learners to self-report on some aspect of their language learning. In some cases, such as the Group Embedded Figures Test (GEFT), established tests from the field of psychology have been used. The data obtained from questionnaires and tests are submitted to correlational analysis (e.g., Pearson Product Moment correlation, exploratory and confirmatory factor analysis, or multiple regression), the purpose of which is to identify relationships among individual difference variables and/or the relationship between a specific factor (such as motivation) and a measure of L2 achievement or proficiency.

In such research, much depends on the validity and reliability of the questionnaires and tests used. Do they measure what they purport to measure? Do they do so consistently? As a result, considerable effort has gone into the development of questionnaires and there now exist a number of well-established instruments, which are shown in Table 21.1. It should be noted, however, that doubts about these instruments, especially about their validity, continue to be voiced. Researchers who view learning from a social-constructionist perspective have argued that how learners approach and respond to learning an L2 can only be considered in relation to the specific learning activities they engage in and that methods that require them to report general tendencies are inherently flawed. This problem is evident when learners are asked to agree/disagree with statements like "I ask questions in English," which they will find difficult to respond to because the behavior in question varies dynamically according to context. The construct validity of some of the most popular instruments has also been challenged. For example, there is controversy over what the GEFT measures. Does it measure the extent to which learners are field independent (i.e., the perceptual ability to distinguish the details that comprise a whole), or is it simply a measure of general intelligence, as Griffiths and Sheen (1992) claim? Further, the statistical analysis of learners' responses to questionnaires does not always support the theoretical constructs that underlie their design. For example, the Strategy Inventory for Language Learning (SILL) (Oxford, 1990), from which the statement above comes, was designed to measure six categories of learning strategies comprising two major groups (direct and indirect), but factor analytic studies have consistently failed to demonstrate either the two groups or the specific categories (Robson & Midorikawa, 2001). Another problem is that different instruments for measuring the same factor exist (reflecting attempts to solve the validity problems referred to above), making it difficult to compare results across studies. A final problem lies in the limitation of correlational analysis; this can only demonstrate the relationship between variables, not causality. Thus, if a relationship is found between a specific factor, such as motivation, and language achievement there is no easy way of telling what the independent and dependent variables are, although some statistical treatments (such as path analysis) purport to overcome this difficulty. Despite these problems, researchers have continued to use the instruments in question.

Table 21.1 Frequently used instruments in researching individual difference factors in SLA

Individual difference factor	Research instrument	Brief description
Language aptitude	Modern Language Aptitude Test (MLAT) (Carroll and Sapon, 1959)	A battery of tests measuring phonemic coding ability, grammatical sensitivity and rote learning ability.
Learning style	Group Embedded Figures Test (Witkin et al., 1971)	A test requiring learners to identify geometrical shapes embedded in larger figures.
	Perceptual Learning Style Preference Questionnaire (Reid, 1987)	Questionnaire measuring four perceptual learning styles (visual, auditory, kinesthetic, tactile) and two social styles (group and individual).
Motivation	Attitude Motivation Index (Gardner, 1985)	A questionnaire designed to measure learner attitudes, orientations, desire to learn the L2 and motivational intensity.
Anxiety	Foreign Language Classroom Anxiety Scale (Horwitz, Horwitz & Cope, 1986)	A questionnaire measuring the degree and sources of learners' classroom language anxiety.
	Input Anxiety Scale, Processing Anxiety Scale and Output Anxiety Scale (MacIntyre & Gardner, 1994)	Three short questionnaires designed to investigate learners' anxiety at three levels of processing.
Personality	Eysenck Personality Inventory (Eysenck & Eysenck, 1964)	A psychological questionnaire measuring different personality traits, including extraversion/introversion.
Learner beliefs	Beliefs about Language Learning Inventory (Horwitz, 1987a)	Questionnaire investigating five areas of learner beliefs; language aptitude, difficulty of language learning, the nature of language learning, effective learning and communication strategies, and motivation.
Learning strategies	The Strategy Inventory for Language Learning (Oxford, 1990)	Questionnaire that exists in several forms (e.g., for learners of English as a second language (ESL) and for English speaking learners of foreign languages) measuring direct and indirect learning strategies.

The over-reliance on quantitative methods in individual difference research is unfortunate. In an interesting discussion of research methods, Spolsky (2000) reports that Wallace Lambert, who originated the use of motivation questionnaires in the 1950s, once suggested that "the best way to learn about someone's integrative motivation was probably to sit quietly and chat with him over a bottle of wine for an evening" (p. 160). The limitations of quantitative approaches have led some researchers to dismiss them and to argue in favor of the exclusive use of qualitative methods (see, for example, Spielman and Radnofsky's (2001) peremptory dismissal of the use of questionnaires for examining the role of anxiety in L2 learning). A better approach, however, as Spolsky suggests, is to use quantitative methods alongside such qualitative approaches as interviews, learner diaries, and learner autobiographical narratives. A hybrid approach is likely to provide a much richer and more personalized account of the factors responsible for learner difference. A good example of such research can be found in Schumann's (1997) account of how the neurobiological structure of the brain influences the learner's affective response to learning an L2. However, there are few such examples in the published literature on individual differences, doubtlessly because this kind of research is very time consuming.

21.3   Individual Difference Factors: A Review of the Research

What are the factors responsible for individual differences in L2 learning? A brief study of the literature affords a daunting array of factors. However, it is possible to see the wood for the trees. There are a number of key factors that figure repeatedly. In Table 21.2 these are grouped according to whether they constitute "abilities" (i.e., cognitive capabilities for language learning), "propensities" (i.e., cognitive and affective qualities involving preparedness or orientation to language learning), "learner cognitions about L2 learning" (i.e., conceptions and beliefs about L2 learning), or "learner actions" (i.e., learning strategies).

Readers will note that "age" is not included in Table 21.2. This might seem surprising given that the age when a learner starts learning an L2 has been found to impact strongly on a learner's ultimate level of achievement. However, "age" itself does not belong to any of the four categories; rather, it potentially affects learners' abilities, propensities, cognitions, and actions (as do other factors such as previous learning experiences and the learning situation). Possibly, too, age affects the actual psycholinguistic processes involved in learning, with younger learners able to access a "language acquisition device" and older learners reliant on general cognitive learning strategies – the Fundamental Difference Hypothesis (Bley-Vroman, 1989). This, however, remains an area of controversy in SLA, and in any case does not account for how

Table 21.2   Factors responsible for individual differences in L2 learning

Category	Factors	
1 Abilities	(a)	Intelligence
	(b)	Language aptitude
	(c)	Memory
2 Propensities	(a)	Learning style
	(b)	Motivation
	(c)	Anxiety
	(d)	Personality
	(e)	Willingness to communicate
3 Learner cognitions about L2 learning	(a)	Learner beliefs
4 Learner actions	(a)	Learning strategies

individual differences arise in language learning before or after any supposed "critical period." The question of the role played by age in L2 acquisition warrants an entirely separate treatment and will not be considered here.

21.3.1   Abilities for language learning

Table 21.2 identifies three cognitive abilities hypothesized to be involved in L2 learning – intelligence, language aptitude, and memory. These are clearly related. For example, all tests of language aptitude have included a measure of memory for words, normally in the form of a paired-associates test. Links between the analytic ability involved in identifying grammatical patterns and intelligence have also been identified. Skehan (1990) administered language aptitude tests to the children in the Bristol Language Project after they had reached secondary school. He found that a range of aptitude measures, especially that measuring analytic language learning ability, were significantly correlated with L1 measures (in particular, measures of the auxiliary system and pronominalization). Language aptitude was also strongly related to measures of foreign language ability. Interestingly, however, there was no relationship between L1 measures based on the children's speech and any of the L2 measures. Skehan explained these results by proposing that the aptitude tests measured both an underlying language learning capacity, which was similar in L1 and L2 learning, and also an ability to handle decontextualized material, such as that found in the formal language tests he used to measure L2 learning. The latter is the same ability tapped by intelligence tests. Sasaki (1996), in a study that factor-analyzed the scores of Japanese learners of English on a language aptitude test and a test of verbal intelligence, reported three first-order factors, reflecting different aspects of language aptitude, but a single second-order factor, on which measures of both language aptitude and verbal intelligence loaded. These studies suggest that language aptitude, notably the ability to analyze linguistic structure (but less so ability to discriminate sounds and memory), and intelligence are related, but also that there are other aspects of language aptitude that are distinct.

Language aptitude is one of the "big two" individual difference factors (the other being motivation). Research based on tests such as the MLAT has revealed consistent correlations with language achievement in the order of 0.40 or higher. For example, Sparks, Ganschow, and Patton (1995) found that language aptitude measured by the MLAT was one of the two best predictors of the grades achieved by school foreign language learners, the other being native language (English) grades.

Carroll's early research into language aptitude identified four aspects of language aptitude, although the test he and Sapon designed (MLAT) measured only three of these (i.e., there was no measure of inductive learning ability). The four aspects are:

1   phonemic coding ability (i.e., the ability to code foreign sounds in a way that they can be remembered later),
2   grammatical sensitivity (i.e., the ability to recognize the grammatical functions of words in sentences),
3   inductive learning ability (i.e., the ability to identify patterns of correspondence and relationships involving form and meaning),
4   rote learning ability (i.e., the ability to form and remember associations between stimuli).

Although this model of language aptitude was designed at a time when the prevailing instructional approach was audiolingual in nature, it has withstood the test of time remarkably well, the MLAT (or tests based on a very similar model of language aptitude) continuing to be the preferred instrument in current research. Carroll (1991) announced that he was "somewhat skeptical about the possibilities for greatly improving foreign language aptitude predictions beyond their present levels" (p. 27). More recently, however, Skehan (2002) has suggested how a model of L2 acquisition might be used to identify additional aptitudinal aspects, in particular the ability to attend to form in the input and to access language material from memory.

Evidence for the construct validity of the MLAT comes from a number of studies that have shown aptitude scores are related to both formal, test-like measures of L2 proficiency and to more informal measures based on communicative performance. Horwitz (1987b), for example, found that MLAT scores correlated significantly with scores on a discrete-point grammar test and with scores derived from relatively spontaneous oral production. Thus, Krashen's (1981) claim that language aptitude would only be related to "learning" and not to "acquisition" has been shown to be unfounded. Further counter evidence can be found in a number of recent experimental studies that have examined the relationship between language aptitude and implicit/explicit learning. In these studies, implicit learning was operationalized as exposure to sentences exemplifying a specific structure with the instruction to memorize the sentences, while explicit learning involved asking learners to actively look for the rule or, in some cases, to process the sentences after they have received an explanation of the rule. Studies (e.g., Robinson, 1997) indicate that language aptitude is implicated in both types of learning. It could be argued, however, that the implicit learning condition in these studies does not correspond to the natural environment in which Krashen argued "acquisition" takes place. The "incidental" condition in Robinson's (1997) study, where the learners were instructed to just try to understand the sentences they were exposed to, is closer perhaps to a natural learning situation. Interestingly, correlations between MLAT and the learning that occurred in this condition were much lower and statistically non-significant. A reasonable interpretation is that language aptitude is implicated in L2 learning when learners are paying attention to form but not when they are focused exclusively on meaning. It is also possible that different aspects of language aptitude are involved in informal and formal learning. For example, if, as Grigorenko, Sternberg, and Ehrman (2000) suggest, intelligence is a factor in explicit learning, we might expect measures of linguistic-analytic ability to be important here, while the phonemic-coding and memory abilities may play a bigger role in informal learning.

These more recent studies demonstrate how the study of language aptitude is being incorporated into some of the current concerns of SLA. Robinson (2001) argues for a research program that systematically examines the interactions between task demands, language aptitude and language learning. He suggests that "the information processing demands of tasks draw differentially on cognitive abilities" (p. 386) and that we need to discover how this affects learning outcomes. There have, in fact, been surprisingly few studies that have examined language aptitude in relation to specific pedagogical tasks as opposed to general achievement. An exception is Nagata, Aline, and Ellis (1999) who examined learners' performance on a one-way information gap task involving listening to and carrying out instructions that contained new L2 words – a task directed at incidental acquisition. They reported moderate but statistically significant correlations between measures of sound-symbol association, grammatical-semantic sensitivity and memory for words on the one hand, and comprehension of the instructions on the other. In contrast, only memory for words was systematically related to post-test measures of the acquisition of the new words. This study suggests that different aspects of language aptitude may be implicated in different kinds of language processing. It also reinforces the point made above, namely, that language aptitude is involved in incidental acquisition but only when the task requires attention to the target forms in question.

There have been proposals for new models of language aptitude. Skehan (1998) suggests that Carrol's original four-part model can be collapsed into a three-part one by incorporating grammatical sensitivity and inductive language learning ability into a single "language analytic ability." He argues that these three aptitudes operate differently during the course of adult language learning. Language analytic ability, which is closely related to general intelligence, is involved throughout, while phonemic-coding ability plays a major role only in the early stages. Memory ability is involved in all stages, but in the case of exceptional learners it is enhanced allowing them to achieve a more or less native-like level of proficiency. In a later publication Skehan (2002) suggests the need to relate different components of aptitude to four macro-stages in language acquisition; noticing (e.g., phonemic coding and working memory), patterning (e.g., language analytic ability), controlling (memory retrieval processes), and lexicalizing (e.g., memory abilities).

Grigorenko, Sternberg, and Ehrman (2000) go further in offering an entirely new model of language aptitude based on an analysis of "acquisition processes." However, their test appears to perform very similarly to earlier tests. When factor-analyzed, scores loaded on two factors – an intelligence related factor and a language-specific factor, with considerable overlap between the two, while correlations with measures of language learning were of the same order as those reported for the MLAT. However, this test does afford the possibility of achieving a closer match between specific aptitudes and specific psycholinguistic processes and, as such, may provide a useful tool for implementing the research program Robinson (2001) advocates.

Finally, Sternberg (2002) suggests that the theory of "successful intelligence" he has developed through general research on native-speaking students may also be applicable to L2 learning. This theory distinguishes three types of aptitude: analytical intelligence (i.e., the ability to analyze, compare, and evaluate), creative intelligence (i.e., the ability to produce novel solutions to problems), and practical intelligence (i.e., the capacity to adapt to, to shape, and to select environments suited to one's abilities). Sternberg argues that tests have generally targeted analytic and, to a lesser extent, creative intelligence, largely because teaching methods have typically emphasized these. He argues that instruction needs to be matched to the particular type of ability a learner is strong in and emphasizes that practical ability, typically neglected by both testers and teachers, is trainable.

Thus, there has been a notable reawakening of interest in language aptitude in recent years. Some researchers, such as Skehan and Grigorenko, have been concerned to develop new models based on theories of L2 acquisition or of psycholinguistic processing. Other researchers, such as Sternberg, have argued for a more differentiated view of aptitude that recognizes the importance of tacit as well as analytic knowledge.

In contrast to the extensive study of language aptitude there has been a paucity of research that has been directed specifically at memory abilities, although it is not difficult to see how memory might influence acquisition. Individual differences in memory are likely to affect learners' ability to notice and also their ability to rehearse what they have noticed. The results of Nagata et al.'s study reported above lend support to this claim. Miyake and Friedman (1998) found that a measure of working memory (the English Listening Span Test) predicted syntactic comprehension that required the Japanese subjects to draw pictures to show the thematic roles of nouns in sentences. They argue that their study demonstrates that learners with a larger working memory are better placed to take advantage of word order information because they can hold more information in their minds. Mackey et al. (2002) utilized tests of both Phonological Short Term Memory (STM) and Verbal Working Memory (using a test of listening span). They found that listeners who reported less noticing of question forms as they performed tasks tended to have low working memory capacities while those that reported more noticing tended to have high capacities. However, the learners' developmental stage was also a factor; less-advanced learners with high Phonological STM noticed more than more advanced learners with similar levels of Phonological STM. Both Miyake and Friedman and Mackey et al. also note, not surprisingly, that working memory scores correlate with measures of language aptitude. A key issue, therefore, is to what extent it is to be considered a separate individual difference factor.

To sum up, there is now ample evidence that cognitive abilities, as measured in particular by language aptitude tests, can account for a substantial proportion of the variance in achievement scores in L2 learners. More interestingly, there is growing evidence that they are implicated differentially in the pscyholinguistic processes involved in learning under incidental, implicit, and explicit learning conditions. Future research is likely to be directed at identifying which abilities are related to which processes. A question of considerable interest is whether learners with distinct language aptitude profiles (e.g., strong in language-analytic abilities or strong in memory and practical ability) can achieve success in different ways, as Skehan (1998) and Sternberg (2002) propose.

21.3.2   Propensities for language learning

There are major differences between "abilities" and "propensities." Whereas the former are, to a considerable extent, a matter of innate endowment and relatively fixed, the latter involve personal preference and consequently are more fluid. Also, propensities such as learning style allow for the possibility of a continuum, with success in learning achievable in more than one way.

21.3.2.1   Learning style

Learning style has both a cognitive and an affective dimension and thus reflects "the totality of psychological functioning" (Willing, 1987); it refers to an individual's preferred way of processing information and of dealing with other people. There are a large number of psychological models of learning style but the distinction that has attracted the greatest attention in SLA is that between field dependence and field independence.

Field-dependent people see things "holistically" and thus have difficulty in identifying the parts that make up a whole. However, they are people-oriented and find social interaction easy and pleasurable. Field-independent people, in contrast, see things more "analytically," by distinguishing the parts that make up a whole, but are more individualistic and less inclined to social interaction. Two hypotheses have been advanced regarding L2 learning. The first is that field-dependent learners will do better in informal language learning because of their greater interpersonal skills. The second is that field-independent learners will be advantaged in more formal learning because of their enhanced analytic skills. Early studies, based on the GEFT (see Table 21.1), produced no clear support for the first hypothesis and only weak support for the second. They showed that measures of field independence (there being no separate measure of field dependence) correlated weakly, often non-significantly, with measures of communicative language use and performance on discrete-item tests. Also, as we have already noted, the theoretical construct itself came under attack.

The dismissal of field dependence/independence may be premature, however. The failure of the earlier research to find any relationship between GEFT scores and measures of L2 proficiency/performance may have arisen because of methodological problems in the design of the studies, in particular with how communicative language use was measured. Johnson, Prior, and Artuso (2000) argue that in many of the earlier studies the measurement of communicative ability was confounded with formal aspects of language use. They report a study in which significant negative correlations (in the order of –0.50) were found between GEFT scores and measures derived from conversations with an interviewer and some lower but still significant negative correlations (–0.30) between GEFT scores and teachers' ratings of the learners' pragmatic competence. The negative correlations indicate that learners who were field dependent, and thus scored poorly on the GEFT, achieved higher scores in communicative language use, as predicted by the theory. Interestingly, they found near zero correlations between GEFT scores and measures of academic language proficiency.

Other researchers have made use of other models of learning style. These typically involve more than a single dimension of style. Willing (1987), in a factor-analytic study of ESL learners' responses to a questionnaire, distinguished two intersecting dimensions of style: holistic versus analytic (similar to the field dependence/independence distinction) and active versus passive. This realized four basic learning styles, which Willing characterized as "concrete," "analytical," "communicative," and "authority-oriented." Reid (1987) examined the learning styles of ESL and native speakers of English in the US, again by means of a specially designed questionnaire. She distinguished four perceptual learning modalities (visual, auditory, kinesthetic, and tactile) and two social styles (group and individual).

Attempts have also been made to relate learning style to a model of information processing. Skehan (1998) shows that the various styles identified by different researchers can be slotted into a framework based on three stages of acquisition (input, central processing, and output/retrieval) and on whether the focus is information processing or knowledge representation. This indicates how different models of learning style give emphasis to different aspects of language acquisition. Johnson, Prior, and Artuso (2000) draw on a theory of selective attention to explain why field-dependent learners achieve higher levels of communicative proficiency. They suggest that field-dependent learners are not so well equipped with "control executives" responsible for the allocation of mental capacities such as attention as are field-independent people. In tasks that have no distracting aspects, such as the conversational tasks in their study, field-dependent learners do better. In other words, field-dependent learners are adept at the kind of holistic learning of chunks that aids communicative fluency.

There are some fairly obvious ways in which language pedagogy can benefit from an understanding of learning style. One is through attempts to match the kind of instructional activities to learners' preferred learning styles. Another is through encouraging learners to identify their own natural way of learning to ensure that they can learn efficiently. A third application is to help learners to see the advantages of learning styles other than the one they incline to and thereby to become more flexible in the way they learn.

21.3.2.2   *Motivation*

Motivation is more of an affective than a cognitive factor and, even more so than learning style, is adaptable. It is the second of the "big two" individual factors, accounting for only slightly less of the variance in learners' achievement scores than language aptitude. Not surprisingly teachers recognize the importance of motivation, both with regard to the motivation that students bring to the language classroom (extrinsic motivation) and the motivation that is generated inside the classroom through the choice of instructional activities (intrinsic motivation). Similarly, motivation has attracted increasing attention from researchers, reflected in a growing number of theoretical models of L2 motivation and in consequent research studies. In the last decade, motivation has attracted more attention from teachers and researchers alike than any other individual difference factor, a reflection not just of its importance for understanding language learning but also of the potential for maximizing its success.

The serious study of motivation in language learning began with Lambert and Gardner's work on the social psychology of language learning in the bilingual context of Canada. The theory they developed and the research it spawned is described fully in Gardner (1985). Crucial to understanding the sociopsychological perspective is the distinction between "orientation" and "motivation." "Orientation" refers to the long-range goals that learners have for learning a language. Two broad types of orientation were distinguished: an "integrative orientation," involving a wish to develop an understanding of and possibly become part of the target language culture, and an "instrumental orientation," consisting of a felt need to learn the target language for some functional purpose (e.g., to obtain a job). "Motivation" was defined primarily in terms of "motivational intensity" (i.e., the effort learners were prepared to make to learn a language and their persistence in learning). Thus learners might demonstrate particular orientations but be weakly and strongly motivated to achieve their goals. Lambert and Gardner's early work in Canada suggested that integrative motivation correlated most strongly with measures of L2 achievement but subsequent research has shown that in some teaching contexts (e.g., the Philippines or India) an instrumental motivation was more important. In his later publications, Gardner acknowledges that both motivations are important and that they can co-exist in the same learner population.

Lambert and Gardner's work continues to be influential. However, there is now general acceptance that orientations cannot be narrowly defined as either "integrative" or "instrumental." Further research in Canada has shown that francophone learners display a number of different orientations. Kruidenier and Clement (1986), for example, found a number of different orientations – travel, friendship, prestige, and knowledge. Moreover, it is quite likely that learners' orientations change over time, reflecting both shifting societal patterns and technological developments. Thus, in a replication of the Kruidenier and Clement study, using a sample drawn from the same population, Belmechri and Hummel (1998) found some of the same orientations (e.g., travel and friendship) but also some new ones (e.g., self-understanding and instrumental). Other studies have demonstrated that some learners appear to be characterized by a lack of any orientation at the beginning of a prescribed course of study but may develop orientations during it. In short, learners' orientations are varied, depending on the situational and temporal context, and also dynamic. What may be important is not what orientation this or that learner has but rather the extent to which they are prepared to pursue their learning goal (i.e., motivational intensity and perseverance).

During the 1990s the sociopsychological perspective on motivation was challenged for a number of reasons. First, it was seen as failing to acknowledge the resultative dimension of motivation. Gardner viewed motivation as causative (i.e., it led to L2 achievement), but a number of studies indicated that, in some learners, motivation resulted from success in learning. Second, related to this point, it was seen as presenting motivation in too static a way, failing to acknowledge that motivation was dynamic, shifting all the time as a result of learners' learning experiences and, no doubt, countless other purely personal factors. Third, and from a pedagogic perspective most important, the sociopsychological perspective was seen as too deterministic – motivation was treated as something that learners brought to the task of learning an L2 that determined their success. It did not allow for the possibility that learners could develop intrinsic interest in the process of their attempts to learn. For this reason, in particular, the theory was seen as lacking in pedagogic relevance (Crookes & Schmidt, 1991).

Subsequent developments in the study of motivation have attempted to address these criticisms. Reflecting what is a general trend in applied linguistics, researchers have increasingly gone beyond the confines of SLA itself to consider theories of motivation from general psychology. This has undoubtedly enriched our understanding of the role that motivation plays in language learning but has also led to a bewildering array of theoretical positions. Dörnyei (2001) identifies ten "contemporary motivation theories" of potential relevance to L2 learning, noting that "the list is far from complete" (p. 9). Dörnyei's point in presenting this plethora of theories is that classrooms are such complex places that no single motivational principle can account for what goes on in them. Thus "in order to understand why students behave as they do, we need a detailed and most likely eclectic construct that represents multiple perspectives" (p. 13). There is a grave danger, however, that the construct so arrived at will lack both clarity and coherence. Little is to be gained by simply listing motivational principles.

With regard to recent developments in theories of L2 motivation, two proposals are of particular interest. The first concerns an attempt to build a theory that acknowledges the dynamic, multidimensional nature of motivation. Dörnyei's (2001) process model of learning motivation for the L2 classroom distinguishes a "preactional stage" involving "choice motivation," which relates closely to the idea of orientation; an "actional stage" involving "executive motivation," which concerns the effort the learner is prepared to invest to achieve the overall goal and is heavily influenced by the quality of the learning experience; and a "postactional stage" involving "motivational retrospection," where the learner forms attributions out of the learning experience which influence the preparedness to continue. Such a model is able to account for how motivation changes over time and, as such, is far superior to the static models of motivation that have dominated research to date.

The second development concerns the important distinction between extrinsic and intrinsic motivation. Noels et al. (2000) provide a detailed model for these two types of motivation. They define extrinsically motivated behaviors as "those actions carried out to achieve some instrumental end" (p. 61) and distinguish three types: (1) external regulation, which involves behavior motivated by sources external to the learner such as tangible benefits and costs; (2) introjected regulation, which involves behavior that results from some kind of pressure that individuals have incorporated into the self; and (3) identified regulation, consisting of behavior that stems from personally relevant reasons. Intrinsic motivation is defined as "motivation to engage in an activity because it is enjoyable and satisfying to do so" (p. 61). Again, three types are distinguished; (1) knowledge (i.e., the motivation derived from exploring new ideas and knowledge), (2) accomplishment (i.e., the pleasant sensations aroused by trying to achieve a task or goal), and (3) stimulation (i.e., the fun and excitement generated by actually performing a task). Noels et al. also consider amotivation – the absence of any motivation to learn. A factor-analytic study based on responses to a questionnaire by anglophone learners of L2 French in Canada largely confirmed this model of motivation, clearly distinguishing the extrinsic and intrinsic motivations. As expected, amotivation was negatively correlated with measures of perceived competence and intention to continue study. Interestingly, the measures of intrinsic motivation were more strongly correlated with the criterion measures than the measures of extrinsic motivation. Noel et al. interpret the results in terms of self-determination theory, arguing that the more self-determined a learner's motivation is, the greater the achievement. This study, then, bears out the general claim that intrinsic motivation contributes strongly to L2 learning.

Both of these developments in motivational theory hold out promise for language pedagogy. Whereas it was difficult to see how teachers could have much effect on their students' motivational orientations, it is much easier to envisage them influencing their "executive motivation" by providing the conditions that promote intrinsic motivation. But how exactly are they to achieve this? One of the most promising recent advances in the study of motivation from an applied perspective is the attention being paid to how teachers can motivate their students. Drawing on this research (and perhaps even more so on his common sense), Dörnyei (2001) proposes 35 strategies for the language classroom. These are divided into strategies for developing the basic motivational conditions (e.g., "create a pleasant and supportive atmosphere in the classroom"), for generating initial motivation (e.g., "increase the students' expectancy of success in particular tasks and in learning in general"), for maintaining and protecting motivation (e.g., "make learning stimulating and enjoyable for the learners by enlisting them as active task participants"), and for encouraging positive self-evaluation (e.g., "offer rewards of a motivational nature"). Dörnyei emphasizes that although the efficacy of many of these strategies remains to be confirmed, "there is no doubt that student motivation can be consciously increased by using creative techniques" (p. 144).

21.3.2.3 Anxiety

Learners may have an inbuilt tendency to feel anxious (trait anxiety) but they may also, irrespective of their personalities, experience anxiety in particular contexts (situational anxiety). Foreign language classroom anxiety constitutes a particular kind of situational anxiety, one that is distinct from classroom anxiety in general because being required to use an L2 when proficiency is limited constitutes a threat to learners' "language-ego." Early work on foreign language classroom anxiety was carried out by means of analyzing learners' diary studies. It showed that classroom learners often did experience anxiety, especially when they felt themselves to be in competition with other learners (see Bailey, 1983). Later research has adopted a quantitative approach based on questionnaires. The Foreign Language Classroom Anxiety Scale (Horwitz, Horwitz, & Cope, 1986) focused on general foreign language classroom anxiety (emphasizing oral communication). It has been followed by additional questionnaires to measure L2 reading anxiety and L2 writing anxiety.

A number of studies have shown that anxiety, whether of the speaking, reading, or writing kind, is negatively related to L2 achievement. However, as with motivation, a key issue is whether anxiety is the *cause* of poor achievement or the *result*. This issue has aroused considerable debate. Based on a series of studies of foreign language classroom learning, Sparks, Ganschow, and Javorsky (2000) promulgated the Linguistic Coding Difference Hypothesis, which claims that success in foreign language learning is primarily dependent on language aptitude and that students' anxiety about learning an L2 is a consequence of their learning difficulties. They dismiss the research carried out by Horwitz and her associates as "misguided." Not surprisingly, Horwitz (2000b) has reacted strongly to this dismissal of her work, arguing that while processing difficulties may cause anxiety in some learners, they are not the cause in all learners, as even advanced, successful learners have reported experiencing anxiety. The two positions, however, are not as contradictory as they appear to be. As the research on language aptitude shows, learners' abilities do affect achievement, which in turn can induce anxiety (in the case of failure or perceived difficulty), as Sparks et al. argue. However, the anxiety that learners experience can in turn impact on their future learning, often in a debilitating manner (as claimed by Horwitz). In short, what is needed is a dynamic model that shows how cognitive abilities and the propensity for anxiety interact in contributing to L2 achievement.

The dynamic aspect of L2 learning, not easily captured through questionnaires, is evident from the early diary studies and also from Spielman and Radnofsky's (2001) ethnographic study of the "tension" generated in a highly intensive residential French course for adults. This study shows that anxiety cannot be examined in purely quantitative terms (as more or less intense), but that it has a qualitative dimension as well. They propose that anxiety can be "euphoric/non-euphoric" (i.e., an event can be viewed as stressful but still viewed as positive or at least as not possessing negative characteristics) or dysphoric/non-dysphoric (i.e., a stressful event can be viewed negatively or as lacking in positive attributes). They document how the students they studied experienced euphoric tension as the product of their attempts to re-invent themselves in the target language. Dysphoric tension arose largely as a result of the mismatch between the instructional program and the students' own ideas about how best to learn and their need to be treated as adult, thinking people. The authors conclude that the causes of anxiety defy systematization, but suggest that a pedagogic program needs not just to avoid dysphoric tension but also maximize the benefits to learning from euphoric tension.

The study of anxiety can also be linked to a model of psycholinguistic processing. MacIntyre and Gardner (1994) propose that language anxiety occurs at each of the three principal stages of the language acquisition process. In the input stage, anxiety is a function of the learner's ability to handle unfamiliar external stimuli, in the central processing stage it is aroused when the learner attempts to store and organize input, and in the output stage, anxiety occurs as a result of the learner's attempts to retrieve previously learned material. In each stage, anxiety can inhibit the functioning of the key processes. MacIntyre and Gardner developed a questionnaire, consisting of three separate scales, to investigate anxiety in relation to the three acquisitional stages. Onwuegbuzie, Bailey, and Daley (2000) conducted a study to investigate the psychometric properties of this questionnaire, reporting that it manifested high construct validity (i.e., a factor analysis found one specific factor for each of the three scales).

Anxiety, like motivation, is a learner factor that is amenable to pedagogic influence. However, it is probably far too simplistic to work on the assumption that less is better. As Spielman and Radnofsky's study shows, there is a positive side to anxiety. Pedagogic intervention needs to be directed at achieving the right level and type of anxiety. Relating anxiety to a processing model, as proposed by MacIntyre and Gardner, may ultimately help teachers to fine-tune their interventions by focusing on specific sources of anxiety.

21.3.2.4   Personality

Intuitively, personality is a key factor for explaining individual differences in L2 learning. Not surprisingly, therefore, a number of personality variables have been investigated, including anxiety (as a trait), risk-taking, tolerance of ambiguity, empathy, self-esteem, and inhibition (see Ellis, 1994, for a review of the earlier research). The aspect of personality that has received the greatest attention, however, is extraversion.

Generally speaking, extraversion is viewed as a factor having a positive effect on the development of L2 basic interpersonal skills, as extraverted learners are likely to interact more and more easily with other speakers of the L2. However, introspective learners may also experience an advantage: they may find it easier to study the L2 and thereby develop higher levels of cognitive academic language proficiency. In general, however, there has only been weak support for these hypotheses. Studies (e.g., Carrell, Prince, & Astika, 1996) have found only weak and generally non-significant correlations between personality and measures of L2 proficiency.

Two surveys of the research, however, suggest that extraverted learners may indeed have an advantage when the criterion measure is "natural communicative language." Strong (1983) reviewed the results of 12 studies that had investigated extraversion or similar traits and showed that, in 6 of the 8 studies that included a measure of spontaneous oral language, extraverted learners did better. Dewaele and Furnham (1999) reviewed some 30 studies of personality and concluded: "Extraverts were found to be generally more fluent than introverts in both the L1 and L2. They were not, however, necessarily more accurate in their L2, which reinforced the view that fluency and accuracy are separate dimensions in second language proficiency" (p. 532). They point out that an effect for extraversion only becomes evident on measures of oral communicative speech and that the strength of the relationship depends on the task – the more complex the task, the stronger the relationship. Drawing on Eysenck's theory of personality, they claim that extraverts are less easily distracted when operating from short-term memory, are better equipped physiologically to resist stress, and thus have lower levels of anxiety, which allows for greater attentional selectivity. They suggest that extraverts and introverts may make different choices in the accuracy/speed tradeoff, especially when they are required to perform in the L2 under pressure. Again, then, we see an attempt to relate a factor responsible for individual differences to an information processing view of L2 acquisition.

21.3.2.5   *Willingness to communicate*

A propensity factor that has attracted recent attention is "willingness to communicate" (WTC), defined as "the intention to initiate communication, given a choice" (MacIntyre et al., 2001, p. 369). This factor is of obvious interest to communicative language teaching (CLT), which places a premium on learning through communicating; learners with a strong WTC are likely to benefit more from CLT while those who are not so willing may learn better from more traditional instructional approaches. Interestingly, McIntyre et al. report that WTC inside the classroom correlated strongly with WTC outside in anglophone learners of L2 French in Canada, demonstrating that WTC is a stable, trait-like factor. However, Dörnyei and Kormos (2000) found that Hungarian students' WTC in the classroom was influenced by their attitudes to the task. Strong, positive correlations were found between a measure of WTC and the amount of English produced while performing a communicative task in the case of learners who expressed positive attitudes to the task but near zero correlations in the case of learners with low task attitudes. It would seem then that learners' WTC depends in part on their personality and in part on their intrinsic motivation to perform specific classroom activities. Again, then, this suggests that teachers can enhance their students' WTC by ensuring they hold positive attitudes to the tasks they are asked to perform.

21.3.3   *Learner cognitions*

Since Horwitz's (1987a) original study of language learner beliefs, there has been a steadily growing body of research investigating the constructs that L2 learners hold about such matters as the difficulty of the language they are learning, their own aptitude for learning a L2, and the best way to learn (see, for example, the special issue of *System*, 23(2), Dickinson & Wenden, 1995). These constructs can be usefully divided into higher-order "conceptions" (epistemology) and lower-order "beliefs." Benson and Lor (1999) define "conceptions" as "concerned with what the learner thinks the objects and processes of learning are," whereas "beliefs" are "what the learner holds to be true about these objects and processes" (p. 464). A number of studies, including that of Benson and Lor who investigated Chinese undergraduate students at the University of Hong Kong, suggest that learners hold conceptions about what language is and how to learn and that these conceptions fall into two broad categories, which can be glossed as "quantitative/analytic" and "qualitative/experiential." These categories bear a close resemblance to the learning styles discussed above (e.g., the distinction

Table 21.3 Learners' cognitions about language and language learning

Conception	Nature of language	Nature of language learning
Quantitative/analytic	Learning an L2 is mostly a matter of learning grammar rules.	To understand the L2 it must be translated into my L1.
	In order to speak an L2 well, it is important to learn vocabulary.	Memorization is a good way for me to learn an L2.
Qualitative/experiential	Learning an L2 involves learning to listen and speak in the language.	It is okay to guess if you do not know a word.
	To learn a language you have to pay attention to the way it is used.	If I heard a foreigner of my age speaking the L2 I would go up to that person to practice speaking.

between field independent and field dependent). Table 21.3 indicates the kinds of beliefs related to each. It should be noted that these two general conceptions are not mutually exclusive; learners can and often do hold a mixed set of beliefs. A number of studies also suggest a third general conception – "self-efficacy/confidence" in language learning. This conception has more to do with how learners perceive their ability as language learners and their progress in relation to the particular context in which they are learning.

There is much to play for in the study of learner cognitions. Key issues (1) are the relationship between learners' beliefs about language learning and their beliefs about learning in general, (2) the extent to which beliefs are culturally determined, (3) the relationship between learner cognitions and success in learning an L2, and (4) the extent to which learners' beliefs change over time. Mori (1999) found that Japanese university students' general beliefs about learning and language learning beliefs were relatively unrelated. He explains the apparent autonomy of belief dimensions in terms of the differential influence of background and achievement factors. There is mixed evidence regarding the effect of cultural background on beliefs. In some areas, at least, there seems to be a surprising unanimity of beliefs. For example, Schulz (2001) found that Columbian learners of English in Columbia and American learners of foreign languages in the US both placed great store on explicit grammar study and error correction (evidence of a primarily quantitative/analytic conception). Interestingly, Schulz did find a difference between the learners' and teachers' beliefs, the teachers demonstrating much less confidence in the efficacy of error correction than their students. In general, the relationship between stated beliefs and L2 achievement/proficiency appears to be a weak one. Mori reports that beliefs were generally not strongly related to measures of learning. Tanaka and Ellis (2003) report almost no relationship between Japanese learners' beliefs and their TOEFL scores, although they did find a statistically significant relationship between experiential beliefs and performance on an oral interview test. In this study, there was also no relationship between changes in beliefs after a three-month period of study abroad and gains in proficiency. However, it is perhaps not surprising that the relationship between beliefs and proficiency is so weak as the fact that learners hold a particular belief is no guarantee they will act on it; situational constraints or personal reasons may prevent them. Finally, as Tanaka and Ellis demonstrate, learners' beliefs are dynamic. The study abroad experience had a marked effect on the learners' beliefs, especially those relating to qualitative/experiential and self-efficacy/confidence conceptions.

The study of learner cognitions can serve as a basis for learner training/ education. Teachers need to be aware of what their learners' beliefs are as this will enable to assess their readiness for autonomy. They also need to determine whether their beliefs are functional (i.e., being acted on) or dysfunctional. As Benson and Lor (1999) suggest, any attempt to modify learners' beliefs must tackle their underlying conceptions and take into account the specific learning context. In some situations, at least, teachers appear to play a significant role in the development of their students' conceptions about language learning (see Williams & Burden, 1999).

21.3.4   *Learner actions*

Learner actions define the approach learners adopt in learning an L2. This is influenced directly by learners' cognitions and their explicit beliefs about how best to learn. In particular, learners' actions are governed by self-efficacy beliefs as, quite naturally, they opt for an approach they feel comfortable with and able to implement, and avoid actions that they consider exceed their ability to perform. A number of studies have shown a fairly strong relationship between self-efficacy beliefs and learners' actions. Yang (1999), for example, found that Taiwanese university students' self-efficacy beliefs were strongly related to their reported use of learning strategies, especially functional practice strategies (i.e., the stronger their belief in their ability to learn English and the more positive their attributions of learning English, the greater their reported use of strategies).

Learner actions have been variously labeled – behaviors, tactics, techniques, and strategies. The term most commonly used is "learning strategies," defined as "behaviors or actions which learners use to make language learning more successful, self-directed and enjoyable" (Oxford, 1989). Learning strategies are generally viewed as problem-oriented (i.e., learners deploy them to overcome some learning problem) and conscious. Considerable effort has gone into classifying the strategies that learners use. Oxford (1990), for example, distinguishes direct and indirect strategies and sub-categories of each. Chamot (1987) distinguishes three broad categories: (1) metacognitive, which involve an attempt to regulate learning through planning, monitoring and evaluating; (2) cognitive, which involve analysis, transformation, or synthesis of learning materials; and (3) social/affective, which concern ways in which learners interact with other users of the L2. These classifications are not without problems. As we have already noted, the taxonomies may not be supported by the results of factor analyses of learners' responses to questionnaires. In particular, the distinction between metacognitive and cognitive strategies seems problematic, as is widely acknowledged in the general educational literature on learning strategies.

The study of learning strategies has been motivated by both the wish to contribute to SLA theory by specifying the contribution that learners can make to L2 learning and by the applied purpose of helping learners to learn more efficiently by identifying strategies that "work" and training them to make use of these. Early research on learning strategies took the form of "good language learner" studies. Naiman et al. (1978), for example, carried out a double-barreled study of highly successful adult L2 learners and adolescent classroom learners of L2 French, using intensive face-to-face interviews with the former and classroom observation with the latter. Like other studies they found that interviewing learners was more effective than observation as many of the strategies learners use are mental and so not directly observable. Also like other studies, Naiman et al. found that successful language learners use a mixture of analytic strategies for attending to form and experiential strategies for realizing language as a means of communication. A comprehensive review of the "good language learner" studies can be found in Ellis (1994, pp. 546–50). Looking back at these studies, two points seem to stand out. The first is that they were considerably more illuminating and of practical value to the teaching profession than the survey-based, quantitative studies that dominate the scene today. The second is that what seems to characterize successful learners above all is the flexible use of learning strategies. Good language learners have a range of strategies at their disposal and select which strategies to use in accordance with both their long-term goals for learning the L2 and the particular task to hand. This suggests that generally little is to be gained by trying to identify and train learners in specific strategies.

There is, however, one advantage of the currently dominant survey approach to the study of learning strategies. It allows for a systematic investigation of the various factors that influence strategy use. These factors include learner age, stage of learning, gender, the target language, learner cognitions, learning style, cultural background, personality, previous experience of language learning, and the setting in which learning is taking place. Studies have shown that all these factors impact on learners' choice of learning strategies. For example, Wharton (2000) examined bi- and multi-lingual university students studying French and Japanese as foreign languages in Singapore.

Using the SILL, she found that students studying French had a higher overall mean for strategy use than students studying Japanese, that overall reported strategy use was lower than that in second language learning situations, that affective strategies in particular were less preferred, that motivation was most strongly related to reported strategy use, and that students who considered their proficiency to be "good" or "fair" reported significantly greater use of strategies than those who considered it "poor." However, contrary to other studies, which have shown greater strategy use by females, Wharton found no effect for gender. Studies such as this demonstrate that different populations of learners employ strategies in different ways and thus help to guard against ethnocentric bias in definitions of good language learning strategies. They provide further evidence against directing learner training at specific strategies and they lend support to a sociocultural perspective on learning strategies, which emphasizes that choice of strategy is the result of how learners construct the activity they are engaged in and is under continual revision (see Donato & McCormack, 1994).

How successful are pedagogic interventions directed at training learners to use specific strategies? Chamot (2001) reviews the research to date. The results are mixed and tend to bear out the comments made above, namely, that strategy use depends on contextual factors and is necessarily relative. Thus, whereas there is support for teaching the use of some strategies, such as the key-word method for learning vocabulary, there is also evidence to suggest that learners will resist using the strategies they are taught if they feel their existing strategies are effective. Further, there may be developmental constraints on learners' ability to learn new strategies. In general, more proficient learners make greater use of strategies than less proficient learners. This is often interpreted as indicative of the role that learning strategies play in advancing proficiency. But an alternative view is that it is learners' proficiency that dictates the strategies they are able to use. Halbach (2000), in a qualitative study based on learner diaries, found that it was the better students that benefited from strategy training, leading her to question the value of such training for weaker students.

Learning strategies have proved a gold mine to which many researchers have rushed. However, the results to date are somewhat disappointing. One reason for this is the lack any theoretical account of how learning strategies relate to the psycholinguistic processes involved in L2 acquisition.

21.4   Conclusion

A recurrent theme of the preceding review of research into individual differences in L2 learning is the need for an overarching theory to explain how these factors influence both the rate/success of learning and the processes involved.

The theory will need to acknowledge the *situated* nature of L2 learning. That is, it must reflect the fact that the role of individual learner factors is influenced by the specific setting in which learning takes place and the kinds of tasks learners are asked to perform in the L2. It will also need to account for how individual learner factors influence: (1) *opportunities for learning*, and thereby the quantity and quality of the L2 data that learners have to work with; and (2) the *acquisitional processes* responsible for interlanguage development. Further, the theory will have to specify the relationships and interactions among the various individual difference factors. In particular, it will need to indicate how a learners' *abilities* and *propensities* help to shape their *cognitions* about language and language learning and how these, in turn, affect their choice of *learning strategies*. The theory will need to grapple with what is perhaps the overriding issue in SLA today – the *role of consciousness*. It will need to specify, for example, whether the influence of individual difference factors such as motivation and language aptitude is mediated by learner cognitions and learning strategies, which by definition are conscious actions performed by the learner, or whether they have a more direct effect on opportunities to learn and acquisitional processes that arise without awareness on the part of the learner. Finally, the theory will need to explain how different aspects of a learner's L2 proficiency (e.g., fluency as opposed to accuracy) are influenced by the various factors.

Not surprisingly, perhaps, there is no such theory at the moment. Researchers have preferred to focus their efforts on discrete factors resulting in disparate literatures dealing with this and that, as reflected in the preceding review of the research. The result is a lot of illumination but somewhat limited explanation. It is clear that learners contribute hugely not just to how fast they learn or how successful they are but also, selectively, to the acquisitional processes through which learning takes place. The goal of future research should be the development of a comprehensive theory to account for the nature of this contribution.

See also 3 SECOND LANGUAGE ACQUISITION AND ULTIMATE ATTAINMENT, 20 SECOND LANGUAGE LEARNING, 22 SOCIAL INFLUENCES ON LANGUAGE LEARNING.

REFERENCES

Bailey, K. (1983) Competitiveness and anxiety in adult second language learning: looking at and through the diary studies. In H. Seliger & M. Long (eds.), *Classroom-oriented research in second language acquisition* (pp. 67–103). Rowley, MA: Newbury House.

Belmechri, F. & Hummel, K. (1998) Orientations and motivation in the acquisition of English as a second language among high school students in Quebec City. *Language Learning*, 48, 219–44.

Benson, P. & Lor, W. (1999) Conceptions of language and language learning. *System*, 27, 459–72.

Bley-Vroman, R. (1989) The logical problem of second language learning. In S. Gass & J. Schachter (eds.), *Linguistic perspectives on second language acquisition* (pp. 41–68). Cambridge: Cambridge University Press.

Breen, M. (2001) Overt participation and covert acquisition in the language classroom. In M. Breen (ed.), *Learner contrributions to language learning* (pp. 112–40). Harlow: Longman.

Carrell, P., Prince, M., & Astika, G. (1996) Personality types and language learning in an EFL context. *Language Learning*, 46, 75–99.

Carroll, J. (1991) Cognitive abilities in foreign language aptitude: then and now. In T. Parry and C. Stansfield (eds.), *Language aptitude reconsidered* (pp. 11–29). Englewood Cliffs, NJ: Prentice-Hall.

Carroll, J. & Sapon, S. (1959) *Modern Language Aptitude Test – Form A.* New York: The Psychological Corporation.

Chamot, A. (1987) The learning strategies of ESL students. In A. Wenden and J. Rubin (eds.), *Learner Strategies in Language Learning* (pp. 71–83). Englewood Cliffs, NJ: Prentice-Hall.

Chamot, A. (2001) The role of learning strategies in second language acquisition. In M. Breen (ed.), *Learner contrributions to language learning* (pp. 25–43). Harlow: Longman.

Crookes, G. & Schmidt, R. (1991) Language learning motivation: reopening the research agenda. *Language Learning*, 41, 469–512.

Dewaele, J. & Furnham, A. (1999) Extraversion: the unloved variable in applied linguistic research. *Language Learning*, 49, 509–44.

Dickinson, L. & Wenden, A. (1995) *Autonomy, self-direction and self access in language teaching and learning.* Special issue of *System*, 23(2).

Donato, R. & McCormack, D. (1994) A sociocultural perspective on language learning strategies: the role of mediation. *The Modern Language Journal*, 78, 453–64.

Dörnyei, Z. (2001) *Motivational strategies in the language classroom.* Cambridge: Cambridge University Press.

Dörnyei, Z. & Kormos, J. (2000) The role of individual and social variables in oral task performance. *Language Teaching Research*, 4, 275–300.

Ellis, R. (1994) *The study of second language acquisition.* Oxford: Oxford University Press.

Eysenck, H. & Eysenck, S. (1964) *Manual of the Eysenck Personality Inventory.* London: Hodder & Stoughton.

Gardner, R. (1985) *Social psychology and second language learning: the role of attitude and motivation.* London: Edward Arnold.

Griffiths, R. & Sheen, R. (1992) Disembedded figures in the landscape: a reappraisal of L2 research on field dependence/independence. *Applied Linguistics*, 13, 133–48.

Grigorenko, E., Sternberg, R., and Ehrman, M. (2000) A theory-based approach to the measurement of foreign language learning ability: the Canal-F theory and test. *The Modern Language Journal*, 84, 390–405.

Halbach, A. (2000) Finding out about students' learning strategies by looking at their diaries: a case study. *System*, 28, 85–96.

Horwitz, E. (1987a) Surveying student beliefs about language learning. In A. Wenden & J. Rubin (eds.), *Learner strategies in language learning* (pp. 119–29). New York: Prentice-Hall.

Horwitz, E. (1987b) Linguistic and communicative competence: reassessing foreign language aptitude. In B. VanPatten, T. Dvorak, & J. Lee (eds.), *Foreign language learning: a research perspective* (pp. 146–57). New York: Newbury House.

Horwitz, E. (2000a) Teachers and students, students and teachers: an ever-evolving partnership. *The Modern Language Journal*, 84, 523–35.

Horwitz, E. (2000b) It ain't over till it's over: on foreign language anxiety, first language deficits, and the confounding of variables. *The Modern Language Journal*, 84, 256–9

Horwitz, E., Horwitz, M., & Cope, J. (1986) Foreign language classroom anxiety. *The Modern Language Journal*, 70, 125–32.

Johnson, J., Prior, S., & Artuso, M. (2000) Field dependence as a factor in second language communicative production. *Language Learning*, 50, 529–67.

Krashen, S. (1981) *Second language acquisition and second language learning*. Oxford: Pergamon.

Kruidenier, B. & Clement, R. (1986) *The effect of context on the composition and role of orientations in second language acquisition*. Québec: International Centre for Research on Bilingualism.

MacIntyre, P. & Gardner, R. (1994) The subtle effects of induced anxiety on cognitive processing in the second language. *Language Learning*, 44, 283–305.

MacIntyre, P., Baker, S., Clement, R., & Conrod, S. (2001) Willingness to communicate, social support, and language learning orientations of immersion students. *Studies in Second Language Acquisition*, 23, 369–88.

Mackey, A., Philp, J., Egi, T., Fujii, A., & Tatsumi, T. (2002) Individual differences in working memory, noticing of interactional feedback and L2 development. In P. Robinson and P. Skehan (eds.), *Individual differences in L2 learning* (pp. 181–209). Amsterdam: John Benjamins.

Miyake, A. & Friedman, N. (1998) Individual differences in second language proficiency: working memory as language aptitude. In A. Healy and L. Bourne (eds.), *Foreign language learning: pyscholinguistic studies on training and retention*

(pp. 339–64). Hillsdale, NJ: Lawrence Erlbaum.

Mori, Y. (1999) Epistemological beliefs and language learning beliefs: what do language learners believe about their learning? *Language Learning*, 49, 377–415.

Nagata, H., Aline, D., & Ellis, R. (1999) Modified input, language aptitude and the acquisition of word meanings. In R. Ellis (ed.), *Learning a second language through interaction* (pp. 133–49). Amsterdam: John Benjamins.

Naiman, N., Fröhlich, M., Stern, H., & Todesco, A. (1978) *The good language learner*, research in education series no. 7. Toronto: The Ontario Institute for Studies in Education. (Also republished in 1996 by Multilingual Matters, Clevedon, UK.)

Noels, K., Pelletier, L., Clement, R., & Vallerand, R. (2000) Why are you learning a second language? Motivational orientations and self-determination theory. *Language Learning*, 50, 57–85.

Onwuegbuzie, A., Bailey, P., & Daley, C. (2000) The validation of three scales measuring anxiety at different stages of the foreign language learning process: the input anxiety scale, the processing anxiety scale, and the output anxiety scale. *Language Learning*, 50, 87–117.

Oxford, R. (1989) Use of language learning strategies: a synthesis of studies with implications for teacher training. *System*, 17, 235–47.

Oxford, R. (1990) *Language learning strategies: what every teacher should know*. Rowley, MA: Newbury House.

Reid, J. (1987) The learning style preferences of ESL students. *TESOL Quarterly*, 21, 87–111.

Robinson, P. (1997) Individual differences and the fundamental similarity of implicit and explicit adult language learning. *Language Learning*, 47, 45–99.

Robinson, P. (2001) Individual differences, cognitive abilities, aptitude complexes and learning conditions in second language acquisition. *Second Language Research*, 17, 368–92.

Robson, G. & Midorikawa, H. (2001) How reliable and valid is the Japanese version of the strategy inventory for language learning (SILL)? *JALT Journal*, 23, 202–26.

Sasaki, M. (1996) *Second language proficiency, foreign language aptitude, and intelligence*. New York: Lang.

Schulz, R. (2001) Cultural differences in student and teacher perceptions concerning the role of grammar instruction. *The Modern Language Journal*, 85, 244–58.

Schumann, J. (1997) *The neurobiology of affect in language*, vol. 48: *Language learning monograph series*. Ann Arbor MI: University of Michigan & Blackwell.

Skehan, P. (1990) The relationship between native and foreign language learning ability: educational and linguistic factors. In H. Dechert (ed.), *Current trends in European second language acquisition research* (pp. 83–106). Clevedon, UK: Multilingual Matters.

Skehan, P. (1991) Individual differences in second language learning. *Studies in Second Language Acquisition*, 13, 275–98.

Skehan, P. (1998) *A cognitive approach to language learning*. Oxford: Oxford University Press

Skehan, P. (2002) Theorising and updating aptitude. In P. Robinson (ed.), *Individual differences and instructed language learning* (pp. 69–93). Amsterdam, John Benjamins.

Sparks, R., Ganschow, L., & Javorsky, J. (2000) Déjà vu all over again: a response to Saito, Horwitz, and Garza. *The Modern Language Journal*, 84, 251–9.

Sparks, R., Ganschow, L., & Patton, J. (1995) Prediction of performance in first-year foreign language courses: connections between native and foreign language learning. *Journal of Educational Psychology*, 87, 638–55.

Spielman, G. & Radnofsky, M. (2001) Learning language under tension: new directions from a qualitative study. *The Modern Language Journal*, 85, 259–78.

Spolsky, B. (2000) Anniversary article: language motivation revisited. *Applied Linguistics*, 21, 157–69.

Sternberg, R. (2002) The theory of successful intelligence and its implication for language aptitude-testing. In P. Robinson (ed.), *Individual differences and instructed language learning* (pp. 13–43). Amsterdam, John Benjamins.

Strong, M. (1983) Social styles and second language acquisition of Spanish-speaking kindergarteners. *TESOL Quarterly*, 17, 241–58.

Tanaka, K. & Ellis, R. (2003) Study abroad, language proficiency and learner beliefs about language learning. *JALT Journal*, 25, 63–85.

Wharton, G. (2000) Language learning strategy use of bilingual foreign language learners in Singapore. *Language Learning*, 50, 203–43.

Williams, M. & Burden, R. (1999) Students developing conceptions of themselves as language learners. *System*, 83, 193–201.

Willing, K. (1987) *Learning styles and adult migrant education*. Adelaide: National Curriculum Resource Centre.

Witkin, H., Oltman, O., Raskin, E., & Karp, S. (1971) *A manual for the Embedded Figures Test*. Palo Alto, CA: Consulting Psychology Press.

Yang, N. (1999) The relationship between EFL learners' beliefs and learning strategy use. *System*, 27, 515–35.

FURTHER READING

Arnold, J. (ed.) (1999) *Affective language learning*. Cambridge: Cambridge University Press.

Benson, P. (2000) *Teaching and researching autonomy in language learning*. Harlow: Longman.

Dörnyei, Z. (2001) *Teaching and researching motivation*. Harlow: Longman.

Larsen-Freeman, D. (2001) Individual cognitive/affective learner contributions and differential success in second language acquisition. In M. Breen (ed.), *Learner contributions to language learning* (pp. 12–24). Harlow: Longman.

Robinson, P. (ed.) (2002) *Individual differences and instructed language learning*. Amsterdam: John Benjamins.

Skehan, P. & Dörnyei, Z. (in press) Individual differences in second language learning. In C. Doughty and M. Long (eds.), *Handbook of second language acquisition*. Oxford: Blackwell.

Wenden, A. (1991) *Learner strategies for learner autonomy*. London: Prentice-Hall.

Williams, M. & Burden, R. (1997) *Psychology for language teachers*. Cambridge: Cambridge University Press.

22 Social Influences on Language Learning

GARY BARKHUIZEN

Actual talk does not occur like a travelogue, with the scene and the narration separate.

(Mehan & Wood, 1983, p. 140)

22.1 Introduction

Learning an additional language is a difficult and complex endeavor. There exists not only the awesome task of mastering the grammatical system of the language, but also the job of learning how to utilize this system appropriately and effectively when actually communicating in real-life situations. Describing and explaining this process is perhaps even more difficult. There is obviously something going on inside the heads of language learners. But this remains unobservable. Matters are further complicated when the outcomes of that learning, now observable, are examined within any social context. An infinite number of variables suddenly come into play. The work of applied linguists includes the disentanglement of this complex web of cognitive and social arrangements.

Applied linguists, however, are concerned with more than answering an intriguing question. They do not spend their time grappling with this mystery in order to further their understanding of what language is all about; that is, "to further a linguistic theory" (Davies, 1999, p. 6). Instead, their work is "grounded in real-world language-driven problems and concerns" (Kaplan & Grabe, 2000, p. 4), a position supported by Widdowson (2000, p. 3) who says that applied linguistics is a mediating activity which "seeks to accommodate a linguistic account to other partial perspectives on language so as to arrive at a relevant reformulation of 'real world' problems." If it were possible to discover how people learn an additional language, and how they do so most economically and efficiently, there would be enormous and very useful implications for those involved in actually *teaching* additional languages. Of course, societal problems with which applied linguists engage themselves go beyond those associated with learning and teaching languages, both outside and inside classrooms. Language learning, however, is the focus of this chapter. More specifically, it aims to provide a broad overview of the many proposals which have tried to explain how language learning and the social context in which it takes place relate to each other.

The title of this chapter, "Social Influences on Language Learning," needs some explaining. It is not as straightforward as it seems. There are three components to the title, each in its own way problematic: (1) social influences, (2) language learning, and (3) on. The challenge with the first of these is mainly one of definition. Instinctively we all feel we know what is meant by "social," but scanning the literature on language learning produces a range of definitions which seldom describe the same thing. For example, in his chapter on *social factors* and second language acquisition (SLA) (in a section on *external factors* and SLA), Ellis (1994) distinguishes between *social context* and *social factors*. The former refers to "the different *settings* in which L2 [second language] learning can take place" (p. 197), or to put it another way, "each *setting* can be seen as a *context* in which constellations of *social factors* typically figure to influence learning outcomes" (p. 197). His examples of *social factors* are age, sex, social class, and ethnic identity, and *contexts* could be either natural settings, where informal learning occurs, or educational settings, where formal learning takes place. Elsewhere, Ellis has referred to social *aspects* (1997, p. 37), social *determinants* (Ellis & Roberts, 1987, p. 26), *situational domains* and *situational contexts* (Ellis & Roberts, 1987, p. 7), *situational variables* (Ellis, 1992), learning *environments* (Ellis, 1990) and *external constraints* (Ellis, 1999, p. 461). Brown and Fraser (1979) use the term *situation*, dividing it into *scene* and *participants*, with scene in turn divided into *setting* and *purpose*. Long (1998, p. 93) uses both *social settings* and *environment*, apparently interchangeably. Stern (1983, p. 269) describes the social context "as a set of *factors* that is likely to exercise a powerful influence on language learning," also referred to as *environmental factors* which generate *environmental influences* (p. 270), thereby hinting at the direction of the influential force; i.e., from social to learning. He also refers to the relationship between *social milieu* (p. 271) and language learning, which on other occasions occurs within a *social climate* (p. 426). In a final example, Spolsky (1989), too, refers to social factors as a subset of the social context, a relationship which becomes manifest in a number of *conditions* for language learning.

In other words, language learning takes place in a social context which consists of a number of influential social factors. These factors include the physical scene or setting and the participants, including the learner, which together establish the conditions or the environment for language learning.

The meaning of the second component of the title of this chapter, *language learning*, is easier to explain. The first question to be asked is whether this refers to learning one's first language, an additional language, or more than one language simultaneously in some bilingual/multilingual arrangement. In this chapter the focus will be on learning a second or an additional language. What this means sounds simple enough, but becomes slightly more complex when the process is discussed in terms of *acquiring* another language. Krashen's (1981) distinction between the two, learning as consciously studying the language and acquisition as subconsciously internalizing it, has been found to be problematic by researchers and SLA theorists but popular with teachers. In most cases the distinction has been abandoned and the terms used interchangeably. Evidence of what has been learned/acquired (i.e., interlanguage – see Section 22.2.3) can be found in the learner's output (see Section 22.2.2). SLA researchers who look at the development and use of interlanguage and output are interested in both the product of the learning (the form of the actual language used by learners) and the process of learning (the psychological processes that occur during learning and the social context factors that interact with the learning process; see, e.g., a review in Kormos, 1999). In this chapter I make a distinction between the product/processes of language acquisition/learning on the one hand, and *language education* on the other. Language education refers to the practices, procedures, and provision of language learning. Associated with these are language-in-education policies and the concomitant variable opportunities for learning. In other words, it is social context in a broader sense.

Finally, the smallest part of the chapter's title, *on*, links the other two components, but exactly how, is the difficult question. There are two issues involved, both of which will be examined in more detail later. Firstly, it seems obvious that there must be a relationship between social context and language learning; learning does not and cannot take place in a social vacuum. But it is the nature and strength of this relationship which provides language learning theorists with a challenge. A related question concerns the extent to which the relationship should be considered in explanations of SLA. Tarone (2000, p. 182) raises this question as follows:

> The central question has been whether a theory of SLA must account only for the psycholinguistic processes involved in acquiring an interlanguage (IL), or, alternatively, whether social and sociolinguistic factors influence those psycholinguistic processes to such an extent that they too must be included in such a theory. It seems very clear that SLA *is* a psycholinguistic process. But to what extent are those psycholinguistic processes affected by social context?

Secondly, what is the direction of the relationship? In the early years of SLA research and theorizing, the dominant discourse seemed to indicate that social context influences learning; i.e., that they are separate entities with the former having an effect on the latter (e.g., Beebe & Zuengler, 1983). Questions, however, have been asked about whether what was spoken about as language learning was actually language *use* rather than language or interlanguage *development*. Tarone and Liu (1995) demonstrate progress with this dilemma in their report of a study which shows that "interaction in different social contexts can influence both interlanguage use *and* overall interlanguage development" (p. 108). A more recent discourse in the field has emphasized the *sociality* of language development, whereby learners and learning are socially, historically and politically constructed (Toohey, 2000). So, instead of learning being described as something which happens to learners as they interact in their relative social contexts, they themselves are partly constitutive of those contexts, which at the same time reflexively organize who they are (their identities) and their language learning.

The title of this chapter, then, quite clearly announces a relationship which is complex, and one which attracts the interest not only of those involved in SLA theory and research but also those in linguistics, psychology, philosophy, and education, including language teachers. It is to be expected, therefore, that multiple perspectives on language learning will be evident and that solutions to some of the problems raised will be hard to find. Larsen-Freeman (2000, p. 174) sums up this thought in the following prediction:

> A major contribution of SLA/AL [applied linguistics] over the next decade lies in coming to terms with our differences – not so that we all agree, but so that the field can become more inclusive, when justified, and so that the complexity of the SLA process and learners is duly respected. A coherent epistemology would be a remarkable contribution of the next decade. Should we fail to accomplish this, I fear that we will experience continued internecine feuding and fragmentation.

The remainder of the chapter is concerned with the three main components of its title: the definition of social context, the nature of language learning and language education, and the complex relationship between the two. In some parts they will be addressed directly and in others they will be implicitly referred to in the ideas and research presented.

22.2   A Basic Model of Language Learning

Learning an additional language necessarily involves at least five elements, or to put it another way, any explanatory model of language learning must take into account at least the following five elements (see Figure 22.1): To start off, there has to be a *learner*, the person learning the language. No language learning will take place if the learner is not exposed to *input*, some form of the language being learned, and one of many constituents of the *social context*. In the process of learning the language, a systematic representation of that knowledge, an *interlanguage*, develops inside the learner's head. Learning is evident in *output*, a display of the learner's ability in the language.

The aim of SLA research is to discover how these obligatory elements fit together; that is, what arrangements would most adequately explain how languages are learned. For instance, in Figure 22.1, simply adding an arrow-head, converting a solid line into a dotted line, subdividing any of the elements, or giving them different names would be making a comment on theory. My purpose in this section is to provide an overview of attempts to explain how the social context element relates to the other four. In the following section a selection of models or theories of SLA which incorporate some configuration of social context will be presented.

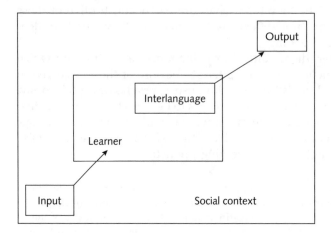

Figure 22.1   Necessary elements for learning an additional language

22.2.1   *The learner*

Ellis (1994) provides a thorough review of social factors, mediated through learner attitudes, which affect language learning. These are to be distinguished from individual learner differences such as learner beliefs, affective variables, learning strategies, and cognitive styles. Ellis covers four factors, age, sex, social class, and ethnic identity – and warns that it is not these factors "that determine L2 proficiency, but rather the social conditions and attitudes associated with these variables. Also, the factors interact among themselves, and their effect on learning depends to a large extent on the setting. Any conclusions, therefore, must be cautious" (1994, p. 211).

Ellis (1994) sums up his review of age-related research by indicating that younger learners are generally more successful at learning languages than older learners. A more recent review of research (Marinova-Todd, Marshall, & Snow, 2000) includes this finding as one of three misconceptions about age and L2 learning, the others being a misattribution of conclusions about language proficiency to neurobiological factors and a misemphasis on unsuccessful adult language learners at the expense of those who do achieve native-like proficiency levels. The authors ascribe some of these misconceptions to aspects of the social context, such as the environment in which the learners (of all ages) find themselves and their levels of motivation which develop as a result of their interaction with their social worlds.

The relationship between language learning and gender (Wodak & Benke, 1997), has recently received considerable attention. Ellis (1994) points out that sociolinguistic research has shown that men use a higher frequency of non-standard forms than women but that women tend to be at the forefront of linguistic change. He adds that "both principles suggest that women might be better at L2 learning than men; they are likely to be more open to new linguistic forms in the L2 input and they will be more likely to rid themselves of interlanguage forms that deviate from target-language norms" (1994, p. 202). He concludes his summary of the research by saying, however, that although the results have been mixed, females generally do better than males in classroom settings, and they also have more positive attitudes to learning (see also Freeman & McElhinny, 1996). More recently research has moved away from the restrictive designs of sociolinguistic variationist studies to "broad-based ethnographic investigations and an examination of discourse and conversation where language is studied in genuine communicative contexts" (Freed, 1995, p. 3; see also Eckert & McConnell-Ginet, 1992; Norton Peirce, 1995). These studies mirror research approaches which draw on poststructuralist theory and which are being adopted in other fields, such as education. They explore the changing subject positions of individuals as they relate to others in their groups and communities within variable relations of power. Nelson (1999), drawing on queer theory, uses this approach in her examination of sexual identities in an ESL (English as a second language) classroom. Although she does not directly address implications for language learning (focusing instead on pedagogy), the possibilities for future research are encouraging.

Ellis (1994) comments that there have been few studies which have investigated social class and L2 learning, and summarizes the findings of those that he reviewed as follows:

> The results to date suggest that middle-class children achieve higher levels of L2 proficiency and more positive attitudes than working-class children when the programme emphasizes formal language learning. This may be because they are better able to deal with decontextualized language. However, when the programme emphasizes communicative language skills, the social class of the learners has no effect.   (1994, p. 206)

Belonging to or being labeled a member of a particular social class means that an individual will experience life in a particular way. Wong (2000), for instance, reports that in the US the social stratification of school children begins in the first grade. Children from the highest achieving reading groups are "tracked" into college-bound course in secondary school, and those from lower-level reading groups are tracked into the industrial and technical classes. The former are typically children who come from middle-class homes where storytelling and educational-type toys abound. The latter are typically working-class children from a diverse range of ethnic, linguistic, and cultural homes. Once the children are placed in their respective reading groups they experience varying quality of instruction, coupled with different sets of expectations. Dropping out of school and moving on to college are the opposing outcomes. The place of L2 students in this scenario (and no doubt in other similar contexts) is unclear. L2 students may, for example, be classified as intellectually deficient because of low English proficiency and tracked into inappropriate courses.

This uncertainty serves to illustrate the complexity of social factor arrangements; age, gender, social class, and ethnicity "are not experienced as a series of discrete background variables, but are all, in complex and interconnected ways, implicated in the construction of identity and the possibilities of speech" (Norton, 2000, p. 13). The poststructuralist tone of this comment will be taken up later, but for now its message is relevant to the following comments about ethnicity and language learning.

Fishman's (1997) extended definition and historical overview of the concept of *ethnicity* encapsulates the difficulty in pinning down exactly what it is. Its unsatisfactory comparisons with race, nationality, and culture over time make it even more challenging to find connections between ethnicity and language learning. In its various guises, however, Ellis (1994) states that there is general agreement that ethnic identity plays an important role in language learning. The influence can take three possible forms (Ellis, 1994): a normative view of the relationship which emphasizes the influence of ethnic group membership on L2 learning; a sociopsychological view of the relationship which emphasizes the role of the attitudes learners have to learning a particular L2; and a sociostructural view which also considers the role of attitudes in language learning, but this time in inter-ethnic communication (ethnolinguistic identity theory, Giles & Johnson, 1987, will be examined when considering theories of SLA below). An alternative approach, already hinted at by Norton (2000) above, is one which takes a critical stance that emphasizes the dynamic experience of identity and subjectivity in the process of being or becoming a member (including learning the language) of a particular group. Ibrahim (1999), in his study of francophone African youths learning BESL (Black ESL) in a Canadian setting, for example, asks, inter alia, the following questions: "Who do we as social subjects living within a social space desire to be or to become? And whom do we identify with, and what repercussions does our identification have on how and what we learn?" (p. 352). Such an approach does not lend itself to linear connections between ethnicity and language learning.

22.2.2   Input and output

Input refers to the type of language input received by learners when listening or reading in the target language. Whether in a language classroom (Ellis, 1990; Wong-Fillmore, 1985), a natural setting (Parks & Maguire, 1999), or an SLA experimental laboratory (Mackey, 1999; Toth, 2000), the relationship between input and interlanguage development has attracted the attention of SLA researchers for the past few decades. The relevance of the connection for this chapter lies in the fact that input, however generated, is part of the social context. A mentalist view of language learning, for example that associated with Universal Grammar, however, dramatically plays down the role of input, suggesting that minimal exposure to input is all that is needed to trigger the cognitive acquisition system. Krashen's (1985) Input Hypothesis and Long's (1983) Interaction Hypothesis initiated a steady stream of studies focusing on input and learners' interaction with it and its providers. Further research classified input into, inter alia, baseline, premodified, and interactionally modified (Ellis & He, 1999) and it was also hypothesized that input and output worked together in developing interlanguage. Swain's (1985) Comprehensible Output Hypothesis, for example, claims that acquisition may occur when learners have to make efforts to ensure that their output is comprehensible, a claim not always supported by research (e.g., Izumi & Bigelow, 2000).

Sociocultural perspectives propose a zone of proximal development within which learners and more knowledgeable input-providers together socially construct opportunities for language learning. Perspectives which foreground the role of the learner's social identity and relations of power within the target language community would paint a very different picture of what input and output are, how they are (co-)constructed and their role in language learning. Thus, in Norton Peirce's (1989) account of the learning and use of People's English in South Africa during the struggle against apartheid, output is not perceived to be merely the appropriate use of linguistic forms. It is, rather, a source of resistance, a political tool. Although it is clear that written and spoken input are external to the learner and that access to them is gained through interaction, in modified, negotiated, or scaffolded forms, it is less clear what the effect of input is on language learning (Ellis, 1999; Spada, 1997).

22.2.3 *Interlanguage*

One goal of language learning is to construct a mental system of L2 knowledge, what is referred to, in a number of different ways, as an interlanguage (IL). Another goal is to utilize this IL for effective communication. Very broadly, IL research asks the following questions: What does this system look like? How is it used? How does it change? Attempts to answer these questions have drawn on a range of different perspectives, from psycholinguistic on the one hand to sociolinguistic and co-constructionist on the other. Tarone (2000), in a review which reminds us of the complex relationship between social context and L2 acquisition, points out that "neither strand of SLA research has consistently and systematically set out to gather the sort of data which might show whether social factors affect cognitive processes of *acquisition* in specific ways" (2000, p. 186, my emphasis). What studies within these traditions do more successfully, however, is to show how social factors affect IL *use*. There is a distinction between IL use and IL development; the first being synchronic variation and the second diachronic variation. There is some disagreement in the literature, however, as to the extent to which this variation is systematic (as opposed to free variation), and how important it is for understanding L2 acquisition (see Preston, 1996).

Tarone and Liu (1995) report on data which indicates that participation in different interactional contexts results not only in differential IL use but also in differential IL development. Bob, a young Chinese boy, was observed over a period of 26 months in a range of contexts with peers and teachers at school and with the researcher. Interactions with the researcher were most product-ive with regard to both rate and route of acquisition. The authors interpret this finding as stemming from the nature of the researcher's input (since his sessions with Bob were one-on-one, the input was finely tuned to his needs) and from Bob's attempts to produce comprehensible output. What this study does is to show quite clearly the connection between all the elements in the basic model of SLA illustrated in Figure 22.1.

Young (1999), in a review of sociolinguistic approaches to SLA, points out that pragmatics has been attracting much research activity. It is easy to see why. Pragmatics is the study of how language is used to communicate in different social contexts. Researchers concerned with IL development, therefore, would not only want to know how linguistic knowledge is acquired, but also how linguistic knowledge relates to the ability to communicate successfully and appropriately. Kasper (2001) provides an assessment of four approaches to the study of IL pragmatics. They range from those which grapple with finding a place in IL for pragmatic ability in relation to grammatical ability and communicative competence to sociocultural and language socialization approaches. Kasper (2001, p. 525) concludes as follows:

> I advocate multiple theoretical and empirical perspectives to the acquisition of pragmatic ability as a domain in SLA. I do not advocate an unprincipled "anything goes" approach. Progress in developmental interlanguage pragmatics requires that practitioners continue to examine critically the fit between research goals and investigative approaches as well as the compatibility of candidate theories.

This comment is perhaps relevant to SLA research more generally, and will be addressed in the next section.

22.3   Language Learning

Contrary to those working within mentalist paradigms of SLA research, Selinker & Douglas (1985, p. 190) believed that "until we are able to come to grips with the notion 'context' in a doable research framework, our work on IL will be at least incomplete, and perhaps wrong." Fifteen years later Tarone (2000) declared that we are still wrestling with context in interlanguage theory. Dur-ing that time a captivating debate took place which considered, sometimes quite vitriolically and possibly unproductively, the role of social context in SLA theory. It was ignited by a Firth and Wagner (1997) article which claimed in the abstract that "methodologies, theories, and foci within SLA reflect an imbalance between cognitive and mentalistic orientations, and social and contextual orientations to language, the former orientation being unquestionably in the ascendancy" (1997, p. 285). Aligned with the mentalistic perspective is a research approach which gives pre-eminence to "coding, quantifying data, and replicating results. It prioritizes explanations of phenomena in terms of underlying cognitive processes over descriptions of phenomena" (Firth & Wagner, 1997, p. 288), reminiscent of laboratory-located, experimental research. The same authors conclude by calling for a more balanced, "holistic" consideration of both cognitive and social factors in SLA theorizing and research approaches. A number of responses within the same journal followed (e.g., Gass, 1998; Kasper, 1997), but the lengthiest (and most entertaining) came from Long (1998). He justifies his defense as follows:

> Paying too much attention to our besiegers risks legitimizing some of the woollier critics of SLA, who might be better simply ignored, as well as some of their more absurd criticisms. Worse, it could gradually create a siege mentality and isolate the field from its constituents and from neighboring disciplines. On the other hand, completely ignoring all the current assaults (and insults) also seems ill advised.   (Long, 1998, p. 112)

Long's main concern with regard to the social context debate is that critics of the more established psycholinguistic approaches to SLA have failed so far to produce any evidence of their own that social factors influence language acquisition, as opposed to use, which, he believes, is hardly the "explanandum for SLA" (p. 91).

It is a lack of this sort of evidence, too, which is common to the following models or theories of SLA. I have selected them here because they represent different perspectives (i.e., cultural, sociopsychological, and poststructural) on the relationship between social context and the process of language learning. A brief description of each theory, with illustrative examples of research, will make this relationship evident. Different selection criteria could have included the following: (1) Gardner's (see 1988) socio-educational model which was developed to explain language learning in classroom settings, (2) sociocultural theory approaches to SLA associated with the ideas of Russian psychologist Vygotsky (see Lantolf & Pavlenko, 1995 for an overview), and (3) Larsen-Freeman's (1997) discussion of the parallels between complex non-linear systems occurring in nature and language acquisition.

22.3.1   *The acculturation model*

Schumann's (1978, 1986) acculturation model has as its main ingredient the learner adapting to a new culture. It was established to explain the acquisition of an additional language by immigrants in naturalistic majority language contexts. The theory emerged from a now famous case study of a 33-year-old Costa Rican named Alberto who failed to acculturate to the target language community and thus developed only a "pidginized," early-stage form of English. Schumann (1978, p. 34) explains the finding as follows: "Second language acquisition is just one aspect of acculturation and the degree to which a learner acculturates to the target-language group will control the degree to which he acquires the second language." Acculturation is expressed in terms of social distance (becoming a member of a target language group) and psychological distance (how comfortable learners are with the learning task). The model has been very influential over the years and still generates research to this day. Welsh (2001), for example, using an acculturation framework, investigated English learners' perceptions of their language learning within a homestay environment in New Zealand. All the students were studying at a tertiary institution and all had high expectations of improving their English by living in a homestay, which Welsh (2001, p. 4) defines as "an accommodation which includes full board and lodging for students studying in a foreign country through which they may be exposed to the culture, language and social structures of that country." For many of the students their expectations were not met, and although language learning was not actually measured, the study did provide useful insights into the connection between acculturation (or lack thereof) of international students and their experiences of language learning.

For some theorists, one limitation of the acculturation model, as a theory of SLA, is that it does not explain the internal mechanisms of how an L2 is acquired; it is a sociopsychological model rather than a cognitive-processing model. Another claimed limitation is that the model does not consider the language learner "as having a complex social identity that must be understood with reference to larger, and frequently inequitable social structures which are reproduced in day-to-day social interaction" (Norton Peirce, 1995, p. 13). It focuses instead on group differences between the language learner's group and the group associated with the target language.

22.3.2   *The intergroup model*

These criticisms could be leveled against Intergroup Theory (Giles & Byrne, 1982), a theory which also takes into account the relationship between the learner's group (the ingroup) and the target language group (the outgroup). However, unlike the acculturation model, which sees the relationship between the groups as static or changing very slowly, Intergroup Theory emphasizes the dynamic nature of the *interaction* between the groups; specifically, groups with different ethnolinguistic identities. According to Giles and Byrne (1982), language learners are more likely to define themselves in ethnic terms and adopt strategies for linguistic divergence, and are less likely, therefore, to acquire the L2, to the extent that they (1) identify strongly with their own group, which considers language an important symbol of its identity; (2) make insecure social comparisons with the outgroup; (3) perceive their own group's vitality to be high (i.e., having institutional support and a high status, and being relatively large); (4) perceive their ingroup boundaries to be hard and closed; and (5) identify strongly with few other social categories. Ethnolinguistic convergence, on the other hand, will lead to more successful social integration as well as L2 proficiency. In considering the relevance of ethnolinguistic identity theory for SLA in the context of the work of social psychologists (mostly psychologists) and applied linguists (SLA researchers), Beebe & Giles (1984, p. 17) make the following observation: "Neither field can succeed in explaining second language data without the other. Interdisciplinary research, merging the interests and findings of the two approaches, will enable us to inspect data from a broader, more balanced perspective." Intergroup Theory, probably because of a lack of any research evidence to support its claims, particularly with regard to interlanguage development, as well as the two criticisms mentioned above, never really got off the ground. Its strength, however, lies in its emphasis on ethnicity (and, although downplayed, issues of social inequality) as a social factor in L2 learning.

Using ethnolinguistic identity theory as a framework, a study by Barkhuizen and de Klerk (2000) investigated the inter-ethnolinguistic interactions of the personnel in a multilingual army camp in the Eastern Cape Province in South Africa. Although English was the official language of communication and instruction in the camp, Xhosa, the majority language in the region, was actually the most widely used (albeit mainly for non-work-related functions) because of the ethnolinguistic demographics of the camp (40 percent of the 279 personnel who participated in the study were Xhosa-speaking). In South Africa there is a relatively static view of the relationship between language and ethnicity, one which perpetuates "the myth of linguistically and culturally homogeneous communities within Southern Africa" (Herbert, 1992, p. 2). This differs from interpretations such as those offered by Rampton (1997, p. 9), who argues that "people don't sit contentedly in the social group categories that society tries to fix them in, and they don't confine themselves only to those identities that they are expected to have legitimate or routine access to." All personnel in the camp were members of the army. As such they worked together to accomplish the goals of the army. They shared certain beliefs, duties, values, and motivations. But they were also members of other groups; different ethnic groups in which they interacted with their families and close friends when not in the army. The research attempted to discover to what extent army personnel identified with the superordinate identity of the army, its "armyness," in order for the army to function as a successful social institution, and how being in the army affected their language behavior, including their perceptions of their language learning.

Findings show that the personnel who could speak English (including L2 speakers) were quite happy to do so, and that those who could not speak Xhosa were willing to learn the language. Many did so successfully, as the following exchange shows (I = interviewer; T = trainee; TS = trainees):

I: Okay, but you speak Zulu so you can understand Xhosa and speak it quite well, but what about North Sotho or Tswana?

TS: [laugh] They forced to speak Xhosa.

I: So they are forced to speak Xhosa because you are in this area where everybody speaks Xhosa?

TS: Yes, that's right.

I: Is there anybody here [14 trainees] who hasn't learned any Xhosa this year?
T1: I think all they learn Xhosa.
T2: All they know it.

The following comments from trainees further reveal their motives:

Nowadays we work together like here in the army, so I think where there are different people from other tribes and so on I think it is very interesting to speak those languages whereby we try communication. We are different nations. All over South Africa we are like this now.   (T, Xhosa speaker)

Well I can say the main thing to make most of the other language [speakers] to learn Xhosa is just because of when we start to get the passes and start to go out we already know that here in Grahamstown there stay Xhosa speakers, so when we go in to look for some cherries [female companions] we are going to suffer when we don't know Xhosa. That's the main thing to make us learn Xhosa; the girlfriends.   (T, non-Xhosa speaker)

The reformulated and extended version of ethnolinguistic identity theory (Giles & Johnson, 1987) takes into account situational variables in inter-ethnolinguistic interaction, such as the concern to maintain communicational efficiency, and the interactants' perception of overlap between themselves in terms of shared group membership. Both these variables may help to explain the patterns of language behavior and language learning in the army camp. Although this study does not address interlanguage acquisition, it does provide useful insights into the dynamic nature of ethnicity, and the multiple, changing social (and context-bound) identities of individual language learners.

22.3.3   *Social identity and investment*

McNamara (1997, p. 566) states that the "centrality of the notion of social identity to current work on language learning reflects a renewed theoretical and political concern for the social dimension of language learning." He adds, however, that applied linguists "have drawn variously on different conceptualizations of social identity, making no reference to the existence of alternatives" (p. 565). The wide array of articles in Norton's (1997a) edited special-topic issue of *Tesol Quarterly* illustrates this point only too well. Norton's own work (1997b, 2000; Norton Peirce, 1995) presents perhaps the clearest and certainly most accessible account of the relationship between social identity and SLA theory. She argues that "a person negotiates a sense of self within and across different sites at different points in time, and it is through language that a person gains access to – or is denied access to – powerful social networks that give learners the opportunity to speak" (Norton, 2000, p. 5). Identity is not constant, but multiple, fluid, and often contradictory. A person is both "subject of and subject to relations of power" (Norton Peirce, 1995, p. 15) in any particular social interaction. He or she takes up a certain subject position, but this positioning is changeable, it can be challenged. In Norton's view of the relationship between social context and L2 acquisition, then, learners and their learning are socially constructed. Her main criticism of SLA theory is that it has not developed a comprehensive theory of social identity which integrates the language learner and the social context in which that learning takes place. It has been concerned with questions such as who is learning language, what they are learning, and how they are doing it. But it has not examined these questions in relation to the social and cultural practices of the language learner and target language communities.

Central to Norton's ideas on language learning is the concept of 'investment," which refers to learners' commitment to learning the L2, the level of commitment being tied to their perceptions of their relationship to the social world; in other words, it is an investment in the target language as well as in their social identity. Norton (2000, p. 10) explains:

> If learners invest in a second language, they do so with the understanding that they will acquire a wider range of symbolic and material resources, which will in turn increase the value of their cultural capital. Learners expect or hope to have a good return on that investment – a return that will give them access to hitherto unattainable resources.

Norton's study of adult immigrant learners of English in Canada (see Norton, 2000, for a full account of the study) provided the data on which she based her perspectives on SLA theory. As her own study demonstrates, she recommends research which adopts qualitative methods and which emphasizes analysis of how L2 learners make sense of their experiences of learning the language. She also invites researchers (language learners and their teachers) to participate in collaborative classroom-based social research which collapses "the boundaries between their classrooms and their communities" (Norton Peirce, 1995, p. 26).

Toohey (2000), who acknowledges the flimsiness of these boundaries, nevertheless focuses her study on classroom activities and practices. The participants were a small group of children from minority language backgrounds in Canada. During their time in kindergarten and Grades 1 and 2, Toohey examined, through observation and interviews, the practices of the school with respect to assigning identities to the children, how participation in physical, material, and intellectual practices determined access to classroom resources (including conversations with peers and the teacher), and how discourse practices "regulated children's access to possibilities for appropriation of powerful and desirable voices in their community" (2000, p. 3). Her findings are couched in a discussion of theoretical ideas which expose the intimate and complex nature of the relationship between language learners and their identities, their learning and their educational environments.

Kapp (2001), in a very different educational context, addresses the politics of English in her examination of ESL classroom discourses in a South African school. The school is located 15 kilometers away from central Cape Town in a township which, during the apartheid years, was designated for African people. The township has a very high unemployment rate and Kapp (2001, p. 129) points out that it is one of the most dangerous areas in Cape Town:

> I was always tense and fearful as I drove from my relatively safe, middle-class, racially mixed suburb, past the working-class "colored" townships. A thick pall of wood-fire smoke hanging over the bridge signaled arrival in the township. This area does not exist on my street map of Cape Town. As one turns left into the unmarked main street, the huge police station dwarfs the semi-detached houses (commonly known as "matchboxes"). The main road is filled with litter and potholes and is devoid of trees and shrubs . . . There is a middle-class sector in the township where some of the teachers live, a section inhabited by hostel dwellers, and an informal settlement inhabited by more recent migrants to Cape Town. The latter consist of wood and iron shacks. According to the 1996 census data, 58% of households in the township have electricity and running water.

The school has 30 classrooms and approximately 1,600 students, almost all of whom live in the township. In order to develop the thick qualitative data endorsed by both Toohey and Norton, Kapp explored, through longitudinal observation, informal interviews and student writing, students' and teachers' attitudes to English in relation to Xhosa, the predominant home language; language practices across the curriculum; school culture and local social conditions; and regional and national policy-making and language debates. Using critical classroom discourse analysis, Kapp paints an incredibly vivid picture of how township life, school life, English-classroom life, and the aspirations and realities of the ESL teachers and their students all intersect in the process of constructing their identities and their learning and teaching. She says, in her abstract (Kapp, 2001, p. ii):

> The study describes and explains a number of contradictions with regard to English. It explores the ways in which students' complex, seemingly contradictory language attitudes and classroom practices are intimately linked to their attempts to define appropriate roles and identities in relation to the unstable school and township environment, as well as their construction of their place in the world within and beyond the township. It also highlights the contradictions of the English curriculum, which emphasizes the centrality of language for learning and student-centered pedagogy; but values "banking" of facts and functional, oral communication in its assessment practices. It explores teachers' negotiation of these contradictions, their constructions of their students and their notions of learning English.

Kapp's study explores SLA research in order to examine the social context of language learning. It demonstrates quite clearly that the relationship between learning and context is not a simple, linear one: besides the psychological and social components of this relationship, there are also very powerful political processes involved. Kapp's study, like those of Norton and Toohey, shows that in order to gain a fuller understanding of SLA they cannot be ignored.

22.4   Language Education

I refer to language education as the practices, procedures and provision of language learning. Associated with these are language-in-education policies and the variable opportunities for learning which they provide. As the studies described immediately above indicate, the contexts of language learning are always complex, and boundaries between naturalistic language learning settings and educational (or formal) ones are necessarily soft and multidimensional. Distinctions have, nevertheless, been made. Judd (1978, described in Ellis, 1994), for example, distinguishes between three broad types of natural L2 learning contexts: (1) L2 learning in majority language contexts (e.g., Mexican migrants in the United States learning English or army personnel learning Xhosa in an army camp in the Eastern Cape Province in South Africa); (2) L2 learning in official language contexts (e.g., learning English in Nigeria or India); (3) L2 learning in international contexts (e.g., English for business, academic work, science, the media and tourism in many countries around the world). Ellis (1994) summarizes four broad types of educational contexts distinguished by Skuttnab-Kangas (1988): segregation, mother tongue maintenance, submersion, and immersion. In what follows, I consider factors inside and outside of classrooms and show how they operate collaboratively to determine the success or not of language learning. I use as a framework for the discussion five of the twelve questions asked by Kaplan (2000, pp. viii–x) in his elaboration of the myths and political realities associated with language teaching, and I use language teaching and learning within the school system in South Africa to conceptualize my discussion. I choose South Africa because it is a context with which I am more familiar, but it is by no means a special case. Other multilingual countries, such as India, Nigeria, and Papua New Guinea, face similar concerns and have also been involved in very lively, multi-faceted debates.

During the apartheid era, language-in-education policy in South Africa was directly reflective of apartheid ideology. Under the current government, the main sociopolitical and ideological principles underlying the constitution of the country are given as the promotion of democracy for all South Africans, the reconstruction of South African society (by addressing past imbalances and discriminatory practices), and the reconciliation of the peoples of South Africa. Such ideological concerns are manifest in decisions regarding both language policy and language-in-education policy. Central themes in the national language policy are: (1) societal multilingualism as a national resource that is an integral part of nation building and the creation of access, (2) the linguistic equality of all South African languages, and (3) the need for actively promoting African languages, which were, unlike English and Afrikaans, neglected in the past, and through such redressive action facilitating the empowerment of the majority of the country's people. While English and Afrikaans continue to enjoy official status, nine African languages now also enjoy equal official status at the national level. The nine provinces are free to choose which of these eleven official languages are to be declared official at regional level.

Language-in-education policy is reflective of the language policy as a whole (Kamwangamalu, 1997), and has at its core the following two principles: (1) redressing past linguistic imbalances and encouraging educational multilingualism, the purpose of the latter being to promote the educational use of African languages at all levels of education against the continued dominance of English and Afrikaans, and (2) ensuring linguistic freedom of choice for learners in terms of language as subject and medium of instruction in the context of gaining democratic access to broader society.

(1) *What language(s) will be taught in the public school system?* and (2) *Who will be taught these languages?* Under apartheid (pre-1994), the advancement of the indigenous African languages as subject and medium of instruction was used as a central instrument of the policy of divide and rule. Linguistic difference was not only used as a tool for dividing racial groups in the country, but was also exploited to divide the African people themselves. There was a specific attempt to create and foster an ethnolinguistic nationalism amongst pre-identified ethnic groupings. The primary goal of mother tongue education was thus not educational but ideological (achieved, for instance, by forcing children to attend specific schools created exclusively for those groups). Besides these general factors, there was a gross disparity in the language-in-education policies of black and white schools, policies which had their origins in general apartheid concerns (see Hartshorne, 1987). For white students, the medium of instruction was exclusively either English or Afrikaans. Because English speakers had to attend English schools and Afrikaners Afrikaans schools, a division within the privileged white group itself was created. For black students, on the other hand, the situation existed where the enforced mediums of instruction were, for different subjects, English, Afrikaans, and an African language. Integral to the motivation of this policy appeared to be the perspective that blacks had to function as effective servants of the white state and therefore had to be competent in both official "white" languages. As far as language as subject is concerned, black children were expected to learn not only the two official languages (at the time, English and Afrikaans) as white children had to do, they also were required to study an African language (their mother tongue). Given the deprivations of apartheid education, instruction and learning in all these languages suffered.

Implementation of new state and regional language-in-education policies has lagged behind the ambitious policy statements made over the past ten years. The main reasons have been lack of funding for human and material resources, an interest in matters more pressing than linguistic ones (e.g., provision of education generally and vast curriculum changes such as the introduction of an outcomes-based mode of teaching and learning), and the language attitudes of educators, students, and their parents. There is little motivation, for example, to learn African languages as formal school subjects as they are perceived largely as horizontal codes (languages of everyday interaction and solidarity) rather than as vertical codes (languages of educational and societal access).

(3) *Who will teach these languages?* Any language-in-education policy decisions have to be supported by appropriate language teacher education. Pre-service teacher education, in the past, was notorious for its lack of success in training language teachers. The segregated teacher education system produced black teachers who were hopelessly under-qualified with regard to modern language teaching methods, a problem which continues today, especially with regard to African languages (Barkhuizen, 2000). The English proficiency of those who taught English was woefully inadequate. Some would argue that this situation has hardly changed in South African schools, most of which are under-resourced, crowded, and rural. In the past, white teachers received a much better training and their schools were better resourced, and of course they typically taught their own mother tongue, English or Afrikaans. With recent calls for a multilingual approach to language education the nature of teacher education has had to change accordingly. The lack of resources for this, both human and material, presents further barriers to quick and effective change. The majority of language classrooms in the country are, in any case, still monolingual (i.e., made up of students who speak the same mother tongue). The minority would be in former white, typically urban schools, which have attracted students whose mother tongue is not English or Afrikaans, and which still have the better qualified teachers, who are able to implement syllabus changes and new assessment practices.

(4) *How will success be determined?* Success in learning (and teaching) is determined by how well students do on various forms of internal (including continuous) and external assessment (see Barkhuizen, 1995; Kapp, 2001). Results dictate whether or not students move from one grade to the next, what jobs they get and whether or not they go to university. The relationship between assessment and teaching practices in South Africa has been carefully planned and monitored since the gradual introduction in the mid-1990s of the controversial outcomes-based education curriculum. Historically, assessment practices in South Africa have been very complicated, the situation being compounded by unfamiliarity with the new curriculum and poor provincial level administration. In the past, different languages had their own examinations, the languages were examined as first, second, and third languages, and these in turn were examined at higher, standard, and sometimes even lower grade levels. With recent curriculum changes, these distinctions are beginning to disappear. Whether or not students are successful will depend to some degree on answers to the following questions: (a) How many languages will students be required to study as subjects? The popular suggestion is that at least two and preferably three of the official languages (including one African language)

be studied. (b) Will results from language assessment (including external examinations) count for purposes of promotion from one grade to the next? (c) Will there be specific language requirements for admission to tertiary education institutions? (d) In terms of other school subjects, will students be allowed to answer examination questions in the language of their choice? This could mean, for example, that a student may choose to answer an examination question in Xhosa, even if English was used as the language of learning for that subject.

(5) *What is the best methodology for teaching these languages?* The methodology deemed to be the most appropriate for South African school children has been communicative language teaching (this refers particularly to teaching English and Afrikaans; very few students learn African languages as additional languages). A communicative approach has been endorsed in syllabus documents since the early 1980s (and reinforced in a range of new syllabuses that emerged post-1994) but it was rarely implemented with any effect. Many black students, for example, endure endless grammar lessons working steadily through outdated language textbooks, mainly because their teachers are themselves unable to communicate very efficiently in the target language. The grammar exercises (and answer books) provide teachers with a crutch for getting through the classes. In some cases, where communicative language teaching is attempted, it is interpreted as oral practice only, typically in groups, and often results in code-switching or use solely of the mother tongue. Since 1995, and coinciding with the new political dispensation, communicative language teaching goals have been reinforced through special emphasis in syllabus documents, the purpose being to empower language (especially English) learners to be successful users of the language in situations outside of the classroom, particularly for further study and in the job market. Recently, language-in-education planners have also been responsible for a critical language awareness (CLA) thread running through the curriculum, an innovation which South African language education should certainly welcome. Consistent with the goals of CLA, their objective is to instil in South African language learners the ability to question and resist the content and composition of the texts they encounter in language classrooms, something which had no place in earlier syllabuses. Whether teachers are able to grasp the principles behind CLA and to implement them appropriately in the classroom, and whether appropriate materials are going to be produced, is another matter.

22.5   Concluding Remarks

In the opening paragraph of this chapter I pointed out that learning an additional language is a difficult task, and that describing and explaining the process of language learning is probably just as difficult. Those who attempt to do so, that is, applied linguists, have to decide where their focus should be. As I have shown in this chapter, it is sometimes the case that commentators and researchers have different starting points: some concentrate their efforts on the psychological aspects of language learning, some pay attention to the social context in which learning takes place, and others believe that both these perspectives should be considered in relation to the broader sociopolitical contexts of language learning, contexts in which learners are positioned and position themselves. At the same time, the work of language learning researchers has important implications for language-in-education planners, teachers, and material developers; their work has practical implications but the complexity of language learning, the difficulty of describing and explaining the learning process, and the responsibility associated with the implications of the work does not make what they do easy.

It is the complex nature of the language learning task and the different perspectives adopted in trying to explain learning which have been the central theme of this chapter. My basic model of language learning illustrated in Figure 22.1 mirrors almost exactly the four major variables which Breen (2001, p. 1) believes have to be accounted for in any explanation of how people learn a language: "(1) what the learners contribute to the process; (2) the language data made available to the learners in the communicative environment in which the learning occurs; (3) the interaction between learners and the environment in terms of the situated learning process; and (4) the actual outcomes from the learning."

At the start of the chapter I named five elements necessary for language learning: the learner, input, interlanguage, output, and social context. Throughout the chapter I presented the ideas of SLA theorists and the findings of SLA researchers who have also referred to these elements. They may have given them different names, they may have identified a different number of elements, they may have stressed their relative importance in varying ways, and they may have configured their interrelationships differently. What they have in common, however, is their connection, a connection which, in whatever form, is displayed in a social context. How we define the elements and explain the processes which connect them is the work of those who contemplate the social influences on language learning.

See also 12 LANGUAGE AND GENDER, 20 SECOND LANGUAGE LEARNING, 21 INDIVIDUAL DIFFERENCES IN SECOND LANGUAGE LEARNING, 30 LANGUAGE PLANNING, 32 CRITICAL APPLIED LINGUISTICS.

REFERENCES

Barkhuizen, G. P. (1995) Setting examinations: implications for English second language speakers. *Journal for Language Teaching*, 29, 110–19.

Barkhuizen, G. P. (2000) *Learners' perceptions of the teaching and learning of Xhosa first language in Eastern and Western Cape high schools*. Pretoria: Pan South African Language Board.

Barkhuizen, G. P. & de Klerk, V. (2000) Language contact and ethnolinguistic identity in an Eastern Cape army camp. *International Journal of the Sociology of Language*, 144, 95–117.

Beebe, L. M. & Giles, H. (1984) Speech-accommodation theories: a discussion in terms of second-language acquisition. *International Journal of the Sociology of Language*, 46, 5–32.

Beebe, L. M. & Zuengler, J. (1983) Accommodation theory: an explanation for style shifting in second language dialects. In N. Wolfson & E. Judd (eds.), *Sociolinguistics and language acquisition* (pp. 195–213). Rowley, MA: Newbury House.

Breen, M. P. (ed.) (2001) *Learner contributions to language learning: new directions in research*. Harlow: Longman.

Brown, P. & Fraser C. (1979) Speech as a marker of situation. In K. Scherer & H. Giles (eds.), *Social markers in speech* (pp. 33–62). Cambridge: Cambridge University Press.

Davies, A. (1999) *An introduction to applied linguistics: from practice to theory*. Edinburgh: Edinburgh University Press.

Eckert, P. & McConnell-Ginet, S. (1992) Think practically and look locally: language and gender as community-based practice. *Annual Review of Anthropology*, 21, 461–90.

Ellis, R. (1990) *Instructed second language acquisition: learning in the classroom*. Oxford: Basil Blackwell.

Ellis, R. (1992) Learning to communicate in the classroom. *Studies in Second Language Acquisition*, 14, 1–23.

Ellis, R. (1994) *The study of second language acquisition*. Oxford: Oxford University Press.

Ellis, R. (1997) *Second language acquisition*. Oxford: Oxford University Press.

Ellis, R. (1999) Item versus system learning: explaining free variation. *Applied Linguistics*, 20, 460–80.

Ellis, R. & He, X. (1999) The roles of modified input and output in the incidental acquisition of word meanings. *Studies in Second Language Acquisition*, 21, 285–301.

Ellis, R. & Roberts, C. (1987) Two approaches for investigating second language acquisition. In R. Ellis (eds.), *Second language acquisition in context* (pp. 3–30). Englewood Cliffs, NJ: Prentice-Hall.

Firth, A. & Wagner, J. (1997) On discourse, communication, and (some) fundamental concepts in SLA research. *Modern Language Journal*, 81, 285–300.

Fishman, J. A. (1997) Language and ethnicity: the view from within. In F. Coulmas (ed.), *The handbook of sociolinguistics* (pp. 327–43). Oxford: Blackwell.

Freed, A. F. (1995) Language and gender. *Annual Review of Applied Linguistics*, 15, 3–22.

Freeman, R. & McElhinny, B. (1996) Language and gender. In S. L. McKay & N. H. Hornberger (eds.), *Sociolinguistics and language teaching* (pp. 218–80). Cambridge: Cambridge University Press.

Gardner, R. (1988) The socio-educational model of second language learning: assumptions, findings and issues. *Language Learning*, 38, 101–26.

Gass, S. (1998) Apples and oranges: or, why apples are not oranges and don't need to be. A response to Firth and Wagner. *Modern Language Journal*, 82, 82–90.

Giles, H. & Byrne, T. (1982) An intergroup approach to second language acquisition. *Journal of Multilingual and Multicultural Development*, 3, 17–40.

Giles, H. & Johnson, P. (1987) Ethnolinguistic identity theory: a social psychological approach to language maintenance. *International Journal of the Sociology of Language*, 68, 69–99.

Hartshorne, K. B. (1987) Language policy in African education in South Africa, 1910–1985, with particular reference to the issue of medium of instruction. In D. Young (ed.), *Bridging the gap between theory and practice in English second language teaching* (pp. 62–81). Cape Town: Maskew Miller Longman.

Herbert, R. K. (1992) Language in a divided society. In R. K. Herbert (ed.), *Language and society in Africa: The theory and practice of sociolinguistics* (pp. 1–19). Johannesburg: Witwatersrand University Press.

Ibrahim, A. (1999) Becoming black: rap and hip-hop, race, gender, identity, and the politics of ESL learning. *TESOL Quarterly*, 33, 349–69.

Izumi, S. & Bigelow, M. (2000) Does output promote noticing and second language acquisition? *TESOL Quarterly*, 34, 239–78.

Kamwangamalu, N. M. (1997) Multilingualism and education policy in post-apartheid South Africa. *Language Problems and Language Planning*, 21, 234–53.

Kaplan, R. B. (2000) Foreword. In J. K. Hall & W. G. Eggington (eds.), *The sociopolitics of English language teaching* (pp. vii–xiv). Clevedon, UK: Multilingual Matters.

Kaplan, R. B. & Grabe, W. (2000) Applied linguistics and the *Annual Review of Applied Linguistics*. *Annual Review of Applied Linguistics*, 20, 3–17.

Kapp, R. L. (2001) The politics of English: a study of classroom discourses in a township school. Unpublished doctoral dissertation, University of Cape Town, South Africa.

Kasper, G. (1997) "A" stands for acquisition: a response to Firth and Wagner. *Modern Language Journal*, 81, 307–12.

Kasper, G. (2001) Four perspectives on L2 pragmatic development. *Applied Linguistics*, 22, 502–30.

Kormos, J. (1999) Monitoring and self-repair in a second language. *Language Learning*, 49, 303–342.

Krashen, S. (1981) *Second language acquisition and second language learning*. Oxford: Pergamon.

Krashen, S. (1985) *The input hypothesis: issues and implications*. London: Longman.

Lantolf, J. P. & Pavlenko, A. (1995) Sociocultural theory and second language acquisition. *Annual Review of Applied Linguistics*, 15, 108–24.

Larsen-Freeman, D. (1997) Chaos/complexity science and second language acquisition. *Applied Linguistics*, 18, 141–65.

Larsen-Freeman, D. (2000) Second language acquisition and applied linguistics. *Annual Review of Applied Linguistics*, 20, 165–81.

Long, M. (1983) Native speaker/non-native speaker conversation and the negotiation of comprehensible input. *Applied Linguistics*, 4, 126–41.

Long, M. (1998) SLA: Breaking the siege. *University of Hawai'i Working Papers in ESL*, 17, 79–129.

Mackey, A. (1999) Input, interaction, and second language development. *Studies in Second Language Acquisition*, 21, 557–87.

Marinova-Todd, S. H., Marshall, D. B., & Snow, C. E. (2000) Three misconceptions about age and L2 learning. *TESOL Quarterly*, 34, 9–34.

McNamara, T. (1997) What do we mean by social identity? Competing frameworks, competing discourses. *TESOL Quarterly*, 31, 561–7.

Mehan, H. & Wood, H. (1983) *The reality of ethnomethodology*. Malabar, FL: Robert E. Krieger.

Nelson, C. (1999) Sexual identities in ESL: Queer theory and classroom inquiry. *TESOL Quarterly*, 33, 371–91.

Norton, B. (ed.) (1997a) Special topic issue: Language and identity. *TESOL Quarterly*, 31.

Norton, B. (1997b) Language, identity, and the ownership of English. *TESOL Quarterly*, 31, 409–29.

Norton, B. (2000) *Identity and language learning: gender, ethnicity and educational change.* Harlow: Longman.

Norton Peirce, B. (1989) Toward a pedagogy of possibility in the teaching of English internationally: people's English in South Africa. *TESOL Quarterly*, 23, 410–20.

Norton Peirce, B. (1995) Social identity, investment, and language learning. *TESOL Quarterly*, 29, 9–31.

Parks, S. & Maguire, M. (1999) Coping with on-the-job writing in ESL: a constructivist-semiotic perspective. *Language Learning*, 49, 143–75.

Preston, D. R. (1996) Variationist perspectives on second language acquisition. In R. Bayley & D. R. Preston (eds.), *Second language acquisition and linguistic variation* (pp. 1–45). Amsterdam: John Benjamins.

Rampton, B. (1997) Cross-talk and language crossing: Indian English, interactional sociolinguistics and late modernity. *Southern African Journal of Applied Language Studies*, 5, 1–20.

Schumann, J. (1978) *The pidginization process: a model for second language acquisition.* Rowley, MA: Newbury House.

Schumann, J. (1986) Research on the acculturation model for second language acquisition. *Journal of Multilingual and Multicultural Development*, 7, 379–92.

Selinker, L. & Douglas, D. (1985) Wrestling with "context" in interlanguage theory. *Applied Linguistics*, 6, 190–204.

Skuttnab-Kangas, T. (1988) Multilingualism and the education of minority children. In T. Skuttnab-Kangas & J. Cummins (eds.), *Minority Education.* Clevedon, UK: Multilingual Matters.

Spada, N. (1997) Form-focussed instruction and second language acquisition: A review of classroom and laboratory research. *Language Teaching*, 30, 73–87.

Spolsky, B. (1989) *Conditions for second language learning.* Oxford: Oxford University Press.

Stern, H. H. (1983) *Fundamental concepts of language teaching.* Oxford: Oxford University Press.

Swain, M. (1985) Communicative competence: Some roles of comprehensible input and comprehensible output in its development. In S. Gass & C. Madden (eds.), *Input in second language acquisition* (pp. 235–53). Rowley, MA: Newbury House.

Tarone, E. (2000) Still wrestling with "context" in interlanguage theory. *Annual Review of Applied Linguistics*, 20, 182–98.

Tarone, E. & Liu, G-Q. (1995) Situational context, variation, and second language acquisition theory. In G. Cook & B. Seidlhofer (eds.), *Principle and practice in applied linguistics* (pp. 107–24). Oxford: Oxford University Press.

Toohey, K. (2000) *Learning English at school: identity, social relations and classroom practice.* Clevedon, UK: Multilingual Matters.

Toth, P. D. (2000) The interaction of instruction and learner-internal factors in the acquisition of L2 morphosyntax. *Studies in Second Language Acquisition*, 22, 169–208.

Welsh, A. K. (2001) Homestay: the perceptions of international students at a tertiary institution in New Zealand. Unpublished MA thesis, University of Auckland, New Zealand.

Widdowson, H. G. (2000) On the limitations of linguistics applied. *Applied Linguistics*, 21, 3–25.

Wodak, R. & Benke, G. (1997) Gender as a sociolinguistic variable: new perspectives on variation studies. In F. Coulmas (ed.), *The handbook of sociolinguistics* (pp. 127–50). Oxford: Blackwell.

Wong, S. (2000) Transforming the politics of schooling in the US: a model for successful academic achievement for language minority students. In J. K. Hall & W. G. Eggington (eds.), *The sociopolitics of*

English language teaching (pp. 117–36). Clevedon, UK: Multilingual Matters.

Wong-Fillmore, L. (1985) When does teacher talk work as input? In S. M. Gass & C. G. Madden (eds.), *Input in second language acquisition* (pp. 17–50). Cambridge, MA: Newbury House.

Young, R. (1999) Sociolinguistic approaches to SLA. *Annual Review of Applied Linguistics*, 19, 105–32.

FURTHER READING

Barkhuizen, G. P. & Gough, D. (1996) Language curriculum development in South Africa: what place for English? *TESOL Quarterly*, 30, 453–71.

Cook, V. (1991) *Second language learning and language teaching*. London: Edward Arnold.

Gregg, K. (1990) The variable competence model for second language acquisition, and why it isn't. *Applied Linguistics*, 11, 364–83.

Larsen-Freeman, D. & Long, M. (1991) *An introduction to second*

language acquisition research. London: Longman.

McLaughlin, B. (1987) *Theories of second language learning*. London: Edward Arnold.

Nunan, D. (2001) Second language acquisition. In R. Carter & D. Nunan (ed.), *The Cambridge guide to teaching English to speakers of other languages* (pp. 87–92). Cambridge: Cambridge University Press.

Swann, J. (1992) *Girls, boys and language*. Oxford: Basil Blackwell.

23 Literacy Studies

EDDIE WILLIAMS

23.1 Overview

Literacy studies in the English-speaking world present a disparate scene, reflecting a variety of interpretations of the term "literacy." To facilitate presentation, this review will divide the work into two traditions, the "narrow" and the "broad." The narrow tradition is typified by the standard dictionary definition of literacy as "the ability to read and write." This definition, which is implicit in much public discourse, focuses upon individual capacities, yielding research topics which include theories of initial reading and writing, reading as comprehension, and writing as composition, in both first and additional languages.

Literacy in the broad interpretation, on the other hand, examines the deployment of literacy practices in society, and has its origins in sociology and anthropology. This interpretation is part of an intellectual movement which came to the fore from the 1980s onward, and which turned away from a focus on the individual, characteristic of the previous psychological approaches, and toward a focus on the social. The broad approach accordingly concentrates upon the meanings and values of literate behavior in social contexts. It is compatible with the notion of communicative competence, although it espouses a more critical perspective.

It goes without saying that the boundary of such a narrow/broad division is not absolute, with "crossing" in both directions. (Other metaphorical extensions of literacy, such as emotional literacy, political literacy, etc., will not be dealt with here as they have no direct basis in written language.) This review will devote more space to the narrow tradition, hitherto the more heavily theorized and researched area.

Since the child's acquisition of initial literacy raises issues that are specific to children at that stage of development, it is convenient to deal with initial reading and initial writing under a single heading, rather than attempt to accommodate the two skills separately into the narrow/broad divisions. Much of the work on initial literacy has been concerned with what might be termed "alphabetization," that is, the process by which children come to master the orthographic system of English. Pedagogy in this field has been considerably politicized around the relative efficacy of the so-called "phonic" methods as against the "real" books (latterly "good" books) methods. To say that the jury is still out would be to imply that one day the verdict will be returned and accepted, an unlikely eventuality. The weight of opinion (e.g., Adams, 1990), would appear to be that both sets of methods have their place, although research suggests that children of average and below average reading ability appear to benefit from systematic attention to "phonics." It is not, however, the aim of this review to pass judgment on the efficacy of teaching methods, but rather to focus on research and theoretical issues while noting, where appropriate, their relationship to pedagogy.

Despite the fact that "reading and writing" are invariably joined in definitions of literacy, most work has tended to separate the two. Our account of the narrow approach will reflect this, treating reading and writing separately, although more attention will be given to reading, where the bulk of the work has been carried out (as early as 1908, Edward Huey in his magisterial work claimed that "there is too much work in reading to review"). The fact that reading has received more attention may reflect the view that it is regarded as more "basic" than writing – Venezky (1990, p. 9) for example, claims that "reading is clearly primary to any definition of literacy."

Within the "narrow" tradition, work in reading has been preoccupied with characterizing what knowledge and competencies readers need, and how these are deployed in the construction of meaning. Reader proficiency in the language of the text plays a crucial role, and in the applied linguistics perspective, a great deal of attention has been devoted to the relative importance of "reading ability" and "language proficiency" in second/foreign language reading. Work on the process, rather than the product of reading has yielded reading strategies and skills "beyond language," and has also complemented the research on the componentiality of reading.

Studies of mainstream English writing focused very much in the sixties and seventies on the linguistic aspect of the product, and analyzed school writing from the point of view of linguistic development, while writing in English as a second language (ESL) provided ready grist to error analysis (or was simply language practice whose effects were largely unresearched). Subsequently mainstream English studies of writing at primary school level began to look at written production as evidence of personal growth and of sensitivity to audience. Studies at higher levels, including ESL, became preoccupied with the process approach to writing, to the extent that voices were raised that product was being neglected, and that, in academic writing, students were being misled by writing courses which didn't teach them to write according to the expected linguistic and rhetorical norms for their academic discipline, the reason for this neglect being a supposed excess of sensitivity to cultural and linguistic imperialism. That debate continues.

This review will first look at children's early literacy, then move to the narrow approaches to literacy studies, dealing first with reading, then with writing. We then move to the broad approaches to literacy, and close by pointing very briefly to some areas for future research in literacy.

23.2   Children's Early Literacy

Written literacy is indispensable to modern institutions, and powerfully supported by social attitudes, and especially by educational practices. Indeed, some educationists (e.g., Kress, 1997) have expressed skepticism of formal schooling's emphasis on written literacy to the neglect of other forms of meaning representation, and have urged that children's acquisition of literacy be studied as one of the range of semiotic activities. It is an issue foreshadowed almost a century earlier by Huey:

> [P]edagogically, what sort of symbols . . . are the most effective instruments for thinking the earth (*sic*), its divisions and dependencies? . . . are words, though totally unlike their objects, the best manipulators of meaning? And what is the order in the development of capacity and interest, in the child . . . for the various modes of symbolic presentation . . . ?   (1908/1968, p. xliii)

The traditional concern of education, however, has been written language, with research on early literacy concentrating on the child's acquisition of the alphabetic principle (i.e., the sound–letter correspondence) in English spelling. It has of course been complicated by the perception, largely justified, that English spelling is "chaos." It is certainly a notoriously mixed system: it is partly alphabetic and phonemic, thus providing guidance on pronunciation in words such as *bat, fed, hop.* It is also partly morphophonemic, providing information about syntactic and semantic relations such as the past tense morpheme, spelled as *-ed* in *learned, looked,* and *loaded,* although pronounced differently, or the plural morpheme spelled as *-s* in *books* and *balls,* and again pronounced differently. There are unfortunately a host of other irregular features of English spelling, historical in origin, which have nothing to do with morphophonemic alternation, for example the realization of initial /n/ in *knee, gnaw,* and *nip.* Although spelling-to-sound rules have been devised, they are complex, and not totally accurate, while sound-to-spelling rules are equally complex and accurate in fewer than half the cases (Berniarsky, 1969, cited in Adams, 1990, p. 389). Orthographic systems such as English which have poor sound–spelling correspondences are termed "orthographically deep," while those that have good correspondences are termed "orthographically shallow."

The learner's acquisition of the alphabetic principle has generated a great deal of research interest (e.g., Goswami & Bryant, 1990; Byrne, 1998), with particular importance attached to phonological awareness (also labeled phonemic awareness, and phonic awareness), as an important factor in facilitating acquisition of the alphabetic principle. Phonological awareness refers to the learner being aware that words are made of a fixed set of "sounds": this enables appreciation of the principle whereby, at least for "regularly spelled" words, a letter corresponds to one of this set of sounds.

The term "decoding" invariably arises in work on letter–sound correspondence, but it is a rather troublesome one: for some people (e.g., Chall, 1967), it refers to simply "sounding out" and "blending together" the letters of a word, then "saying the word aloud" without necessarily understanding. For others, decoding refers not only to the above process, but additionally, and crucially, to recognizing the word, when the reader matches the phonological representation to an item in their mental lexicon. Since it is not possible for all initial readers to be taught to read every word individually, then clearly such a process is important in allowing these learners to have independent access to words that they know, but which they have never before seen in print. Successful decoding in such cases is more likely with words which have regular one-to-one sound–spelling correspondence. This has led to the view (e.g., Downing, 1973, p. 109) that children learn to read more quickly in languages with a relatively shallow orthography (e.g., Spanish, Swahili) than they do in those with a deep orthography (e.g., English, French).

The complexity of English orthography has lead to a number of proposals that the system be regularized in order to help initial reading. In the 1960s, the initial teaching alphabet (i t a) was one such proposal, implemented in the UK and US. However, a thorough evaluation (Warburton & Southgate, 1969), concluded that, although i t a helped children in the early stages, there was, after three years, no difference (with respect to reading performance on traditional orthography) between children taught through i t a and traditional orthography. There was also a suspicion that i t a had an adverse effect upon traditional spelling.

Despite the "chaos" of English orthography, it is widely accepted that through practice learners eventually move from mediated access (i.e., via the spelling of the words) of word recognition to achieve direct access through "automatic recognition" of the word. It is also clear that even initial readers may, for certain salient and regularly encountered written words, (e.g., a well-known product brand, or their own name) have direct access through recognizing the appearance of the words, a process which has been likened to learning hieroglyphics. Both the ability to recognize whole words and the ability to analyze words phonetically are said to be important in the development of fluent reading (Vellutino & Scanlon, 1982, p. 194).

Studies of children's ideas about written language suggest that at a very early age (before 2), children from a range of social and national backgrounds are sensitive to its formal features and functions, and distinguish between a drawing and a piece of writing, and also between the activities of drawing and writing. There is also evidence that children's writing displays developmental regularities, although researchers vary in the way they divide and label this continuum. Tolchinsky (1998) lists the following stages:

1   undifferentiated and unconstrained, where the "writing" produced by the child appears as the same regular "scribble" – often of the "teeth of the saw" form;
2   formally constrained where children limit the quantity and consecutive repetition of letters in words;
3   syllabic, where there is a correspondence between the number of syllables in a word and the number of letters in the child's written version;
4   alphabetic (for languages that employ the alphabetic principle), where children are aware that phonemes can be systematically represented by letters.

In children's emergent writing the names of letters (e.g., "bee" for B/b, "tea" for T/t), as well as the sounds conventionally given to the letters when pronounced in isolation (respectively roughly "buh" and "tuh"), can mislead initial writers, to yield spellings such as "tract" for "tractor," where the final letter "t" in the child's view adequately represents the final syllable, since both are pronounced in the same way. In addition, it has also been found (e.g., Read, 1971) that early spelling in English is affected by phonological regularities which are not apparent in conventional spelling. Thus when English children write initial *chr-* for conventional *tr-* in words such as *treat* they realize that the *tr-* of treat is closer to the alveolar affricate of *ch-* in *cheat* than to the alveolar plosive *t-* in *team*. (This specific example, of course will not be true for all varieties of English, but the general principal holds.)

How children eventually acquire conventional spelling in English is uncertain; Goswami and Bryant (1990, p. 53), suggest that children use different principles, since they seem to realize quite early that spelling does not depend entirely on a phonological code whereby there is a one-to-one letter–sound correspondence. Children generally use the letter "s," for example, not the letter "z," at the end of words like "balls," thus revealing a grasp of "s" as the realization of the orthographic rule for plural morphemes, despite the differing pronunciations. As children get older they seem to have a growing appreciation of the fact that the phonological code is not the only one, and begin to use other rules in the orthographic code (such as the effect of final "e" in words like "cap" and "cape"), as well as visual memory for word spellings.

The relationship between children's early spelling and reading development is not clear. Goswami and Bryant (1990, p. 148) claim that children separate these processes. They appear, for example to be more willing to take account of sounds when they spell, rather than when they read, most dramatically demonstrated in cases where children can spell words which they cannot read. Further research is needed to attempt to establish these connections, as well as the possibility that different children may acquire these skills by different pathways.

23.3   Reading

Reading, as has been mentioned, is generally regarded as the "basic" literacy skill, and it is difficult to conceive of an adult who could write reasonably but could not read at all, whereas the converse is attested (thus reading the Bible, but not writing, was important for many Protestants, and seventeenth-century Swedes had to be able to read the Lutheran Bible in order to marry (Graff, 1995, p. 21)). The psycholinguistic tradition of reading research falls into two approaches, one which is interested in establishing the components necessary for the reading process, and a second which attempts, rather more ambitiously, to model the process by specifying components and the relations between them.

23.3.1   *Component approaches*

Simple two-component models of reading propose what may be roughly characterized as a reading component, and language component. More elaborate models list a variety of other components, with a world knowledge usually featuring. Since work done on reading skills deals in similar components, skills studies may be regarded as an extension of the component approach.

Prominent advocates of the two-component view of reading are Hoover and Tunmer (1993, p. 1) who say "this view holds that reading consists of only two components, one that allows language to be recognized through graphic representation, and another that allows language to be comprehended." In the case of initial readers, they see word recognition as occurring indirectly through phonological coding followed by a matching of the resulting representation to an item in the mental lexicon. In the case of fluent readers, however, the graphic representation of the word is mapped directly onto its representation in the mental lexicon. This is similar to the pathways for reading proposed in phonological awareness studies, with the difference that Hoover and Tunmer give prominence to the construction of meaning through language knowledge. In short, they are making the intuitively appealing claim that in order to understand a written text, the two necessary components are the ability to read, and competence in the language of the text.

23.3.1.1   *Language competence in reading*

Among the strongest claims for the role of language is that of Vellutino and Scanlon (1982, p. 196) who assert that "reading is primarily a linguistic skill . . . it is the linguistic components of printed words that imbue them with meaning and substance." A number of studies have broken down language into syntax and lexis, and examined how they contribute separately to the construction of meaning through reading. Other studies have looked at the effect of "language" in undifferentiated terms, perhaps more in accordance with our intuitions of how we read (that syntactic decoding operates in a lexical vacuum, or vice versa, is rather implausible).

23.3.1.2 Syntax

In the case of first language (L1) readers, studies of the effect of syntactic competence are scarce. The reason seems to be, as Fries (1963, p. 70) pointed out, a general assumption that "grammatical meanings are intuitive" and therefore their effects did not need to be studied, a view supported by Schlesinger (1968) who concluded after a series of experiments that, for first language readers, syntax did not significantly affect the reading process.

However, psychologists working with young readers suggest that syntax is indeed important in first language reading. Vellutino and Scanlon (1982, p. 236) conclude from their review that competence in syntax facilitates the process of identifying written language, as it provides immediate feedback if a "reading" is at variance with the grammatical context, and thereby allows self-correction. They also report work which found that, faced with sentences such as *John promised Mary to shovel the driveway*, poor readers tended to see *Mary* as doing the shoveling. Such misinterpretation is explained by the so-called "minimum distance principle," where the noun phrase closest to a preceding infinitive verb is judged as the implicit subject, possibly generalized from sentences such as *John told/wanted/asked Mary to shovel the driveway*. A decade later Rayner and Pollatsek (1989) introduced the very similar "garden path" principle according to which less proficient readers structure written sentences in the most "economic" manner, by trying to relate new items syntactically to preceding items. Thus in sentences such as: (1) *Because Tim always eats a whole chicken this doesn't seem much to him*, as opposed to (2) *Because Tim always eats a whole chicken is just a snack for him* it is predicted that the first sentence is easier to process than the second, since the "default" path is to attach "a whole chicken" to "eats" as the object of a transitive verb. Although Vellutino and Scanlon's review finds correlations between syntactic proficiency and reading ability, they also point out that syntactic competence does not necessarily cause reading ability, and suggest that syntactic weaknesses could be signs of problems in other areas of language.

In second language (L2) studies of syntax in reading, there is, despite the small number of studies, universal acceptance of the view that a degree of second language syntactic competence is necessary. Berman (1984) for example, after conducting a series of studies with Israeli students at tertiary level concludes that "efficient FL readers must rely – in part, though not exclusively – on syntactic devices to get at text meaning." However, Berman's note of reserve is in order. It may well be the case that successful processing of text may be achieved with less than native speaker competence in syntax, through a combination of lexical knowledge and background knowledge. In other words, readers may "guess" at a structural meaning, as they may "guess" at lexical meaning.

23.3.1.3 Vocabulary

There is a great deal of work with L1 English primary school readers which provides support for the relationship between lexical development and reading ability. A number of such studies are cited by Vellutino and Scanlon (1982), who find substantial correlations between measures of vocabulary and reading achievement. In addition, early work on readability, as well as research into L2 academic reading, has indicated the importance of vocabulary, while surveys among second language learners invariably and predictably reveal vocabulary to be an important reading concern.

There is some inconsistency in vocabulary research, arising from the difficulty of defining "a word." While some studies deal only with lexical words, others includes both structural and lexical words. The phrases "head words" and "word families" are also used inconsistently, although generally accepted current usage is that "head word" refers to a single word lexeme, while "word family" refers to a base word, inflected forms, and derived forms. Two other important vocabulary issues are what constitutes "knowing a word," and what words are likely to be "most useful." While from the perspective of speaking, knowing a word includes knowledge of meaning, pronunciation, grammatical association, and collocation, what is crucial from a reading perspective is being able to attribute appropriate meaning in the given context. The meaning that a reader can attribute to a word, however, may vary from zero, through a vague notion of associated topics or domains, to "complete mastery."

For the "usefulness" of lexical items in reading, a major criterion has been frequency. A consistent finding is that the 2,000 most common words (including grammatical function words) account for approximately 80 percent of the total number of words in most prose texts. However, the other 20 percent of these texts is made up of the remaining words of the English language (several hundred thousand). There is thus a "frequency paradox" in that, since the 2,000 most frequent words are common to most texts, a crucial contribution to the message uniqueness of texts is not the 2,000 most common words, but rather the words that constitute the remaining 20 percent, some of which may be extremely infrequent. Low levels of vocabulary knowledge, especially in the case of second language readers, have implications for the advice that readers should guess the meanings of unknown words from context: in order to be able to do this, it has been estimated that readers need to know approximately 95 percent or more of the other words in a text.

23.3.1.4   *Background knowledge*

"Background knowledge" has, particularly under the label "schema theory," received a great deal of attention in the applied linguistics/ESL view of reading, following research in the USA in the 1970s. There are terminological variations, with "script" and "framework" being used for what is essentially the same notion as "schema."

A "schema" (pl. "schemata") is defined as an abstract structure representing concepts, which is stored in memory: current usage suggests that knowledge of objects, of routine behavior, as well as of belief systems, all qualify as "schemata." In addition, some writers (e.g., Carrell, 1984) have used the phrase "formal schema" to refer to the structure of texts, such that there are different structures for a narrative, a description, comparison, etc. Because of its all-embracing nature, the term "schema" is now widely judged to have little theoretical value, and the term "background knowledge" is often preferred. However it may be referred to, the effects of prior knowledge have been frequently demonstrated in both first and second language reading.

Anderson et al. (1977), for example, in a classic experiment, explain different interpretations of the same concocted ambiguous texts in terms of different schemata that are invoked by different L1 readers, which in turn are associated with differing personal interests. Thus one group of music students interpreted a text as being about a musical performance, while another group of non-musicians interpreted the same text as being about a game of cards, the variation being triggered by alternative explanations of word such as "key" and "score." Academic background has likewise been demonstrated to have an effect on reading comprehension. Alderson and Urquhart (1988) report on two ESL studies which show that a student's background discipline affects performance on reading tests. However, although Alderson and Urquhart concluded that academic background can indeed have an effect on reading comprehension, the results did not allow the stronger conclusion that academic background determines comprehension. In terms of cultural schemata, Steffensen and Joag Dev (1984) carried out a cross-cultural comparison of two groups of readers, one from the US, and one from India, and showed how recall is affected by familiarity with culturally specific practices (in their case "traditional" American weddings as opposed to traditional Indian ones).

23.3.1.5   "Reading ability" in second language reading

While the view that language proficiency is important for reading is generally accepted, there has been considerable debate about the relative contributions to second language reading of, on the one hand, reading ability, as manifested in first language reading, and on the other, general proficiency in the second language.

Some have argued that L2 reading depends crucially on L1 reading, that "reading is only learned once" and that poor L2 reading is in part due to poor L1 reading skills or failure to transfer such skills. However, it is a matter of simple observation that many people *only* learn to read in their chronological L2 or learn to read in L2 *first* (both common occurrences with minority groups whether indigenous or migrant). The view that L2 reading depends on L1 reading therefore cannot be taken too literally.

The converse view is that reading ability in L2 is largely a function of proficiency in that language, and that a minimal level of proficiency in L2 is needed before L1 reading skills will transfer (the "language threshold" hypothesis of second language reading). It is pertinent to note at this point, however, that the terms "first language" or "mother tongue" may be inappropriate in cases where learners have "bilingualism as a first language," or undergo a shift in language dominance (such that their chronologically first language atrophies and they achieve greater fluency in their second language), or indeed in cases where learners have acquired literacy almost entirely through a second language, as is the case in much of Sub-Saharan Africa. A number of studies have investigated the relative contributions of "reading ability" and "language proficiency" to reading.

Bernhardt and Kamil (1995) administered reading tests in English and Spanish to 187 English L1 speakers at three levels of Spanish instruction, and concluded that both factors were important, although they found that language proficiency played a greater part than did ability in first language reading. Carrell (1991) administered reading tests in English and Spanish to 45 native speakers of Spanish and 75 native speakers of English. She concluded that while both first language reading ability and second language proficiency level are significant in second language reading ability, the relative importance of the two factors varied: for the Spanish group reading English texts, differences in reading ability in the first language (Spanish) appeared to be more important than differences in proficiency in English. However, for the English group reading Spanish texts, the position was reversed, with proficiency levels in the second language (Spanish) being more important than were differences in reading ability in their first language (English). Thus the results of the Spanish group tend to support the transfer of skills hypothesis, while the results of the English group support the language proficiency hypothesis. The reason advanced for this is that the English group was below the "language threshold" required by the Spanish test, and not in a position to utilize their reading skills; the Spanish group, on the other hand, were above the level required by the English texts, and accordingly the "language threshold" was not in evidence in their results.

The effect of differential language proficiency was also explored by Lee and Schallert (1997). They investigated 809 Korean middle-school students, and concluded that the contribution of L2 proficiency is greater than the contribution of L1 reading ability in predicting L2 reading ability. They also found that there was a much stronger relationship between L1 and L2 reading at higher levels of L2 proficiency. The importance of language proficiency in reading was confirmed by Verhoeven's (1990) longitudinal study of Dutch and Turkish children. He found that in the first two grades, Turkish children were less efficient in reading Dutch than their monolingual Dutch peers, and concludes that at this level reading comprehension appears to be most strongly influenced by "children's oral proficiency in the second language." (p. 90). Again these findings are in line with the general conclusion that in second language reading, L2 knowledge plays a more significant role at low levels of proficiency, while L1 reading is more influential at high levels of L2 proficiency.

Educational surveys confirm what could be predicted from experimental findings, namely that using an unfamiliar (usually a second) language in reading at primary school level tends to produce poor results. Elley (1994) reports on a survey of 32 countries which found that children whose home language differed from the school language performed less well on reading tests than those who were tested in their home language. The situation in sub-Saharan

Africa where ex-colonial languages (mainly English, French, and Portuguese) dominate the education system from the primary level onward, gives particular cause for concern: in Zambia there is ample evidence that most primary school pupils are not able to read adequately in the official language of instruction, English (Nkamba & Kanyika, 1998; E. Williams, 1996), while in Zimbabwe, Machingaidze, Pfukani, & Shumba (1998, p. 71) conclude that at year 6 over 60 percent of pupils did not reach "the desirable levels" of reading in English.

There are, however, counter claims to the view that children will have greater success in reading if they are taught in their mother tongue. In Morocco Wagner, Spratt, & Ezzaki (1989) traced Berber L1 and Arab L1 children from years 1 to 5, administering annual tests of Arabic reading. Although there were differences in favor of the Arab L1 children in year 1, these differences had almost disappeared by year 5, and Wagner et al. dispute the view that learning to read in a first language is more beneficial to achievement than learning to read in a second language. However, it is clear that the Berber L1 children were using Arabic informally outside the school, as well as formally inside, and that it had probably become their dominant language by year 5.

The well-known French-medium immersion programs in Canada are also adduced as evidence that students can acquire native-like proficiency in literacy skills in a second language. Evaluation suggests that while this is true for reading and listening, it is not the case for writing or speaking (Cummins & Swain, 1986, p. 49). It would also be misleading to generalize from Canadian immersion, given the special factors (parents deliberately opted for the immersion schools, and could withdraw their children if they experienced problems; additionally the schools were well provided for, and all the teachers were trained).

23.3.1.6   Reading for language learning

Rather than consider the language proficiency thresholds necessary for "successful" reading, language pedagogy has tended to look at how reading may improve language proficiency. "The best way to improve your knowledge of a foreign language is to go and live amongst its speakers. The next best way is to read extensively in it," proclaims Nuttall (1996, p. 128). Extensive reading (i.e., independent reading of relatively long self-selected texts with minimal teacher intervention) has long enjoyed such support. (We omit here consideration of intensive classroom reading, where reading is incidental to language or skill development.) Theoretical justification for extensive reading comes from Krashen's input hypothesis (e.g., Krashen, 1989) which suggests that the crucial factor in second language acquisition is exposure to adequate amounts of comprehensible input. However, research into the effects of extensive reading has yielded mixed results.

Studies of incidental vocabulary learning through extensive reading have been frequent (see Coady, 1997). While a number have yielded positive results (Horst, Cobb, & Meara, 1998; Day, Omura, & Hiramatsu, 1991; Hafiz & Tudor, 1990), others have revealed little vocabulary learning (Pitts, White, & Krashen,

1989), and the intuitively appealing notion that extensive reading will increase reader vocabulary is clearly subject to other conditions.

In terms of general language development, research results are again divided. Several studies, (including Walker, 1997; Hafiz & Tudor, 1989; Mason & Krashen, 1997) claim that extensive reading resulted in improvement in the readers' linguistic proficiency. Less positive research findings are reported by Lai (1993) in one of the largest investigations, which involved 18 schools in Hong Kong. Lai does, however, suggest that the program benefits those students who otherwise have little exposure to English, and also benefits high ability students with high motivation.

Other research findings on the effect of extensive reading on writing are generally positive: a number of studies claim it improves writing (e.g., Hafiz & Tudor, 1990), but there is, surprisingly, no strong evidence that it improves spelling. The view that extensive reading promotes positive attitudes to reading is widespread (Elley, 1991), although attitude assessment does not seem to have been carried out in a rigorous manner.

While claims for the potential of extensive reading are intuitively appealing, it would appear to be difficult for programs to meet all the conditions necessary for "success." To cite but two of these, at the cultural level, extensive reading presupposes the acceptability of reading as a leisure activity, while at the linguistic level, the vocabulary demands of the text relative to the vocabulary knowledge of the reader is a crucial factor. Hirsh and Nation (1992) suggest that some 98 percent of the text's vocabulary has to be known to prevent reader frustration. The traditional answer to this has been the production of simplified and simple reading texts (Davies, 1984), but "matching" of individual texts and readers in terms of language and interest is problematic.

23.3.1.7 Reading skills

Work carried out on reading skills may be regarded as an extension of the component approach to reading. The overall coherence of the field has been marred by inconsistent application of the term "skill," and the introduction of "strategy" often as an undifferentiated alternative. It has been suggested that a skill be regarded as an acquired ability, which has been automatized, and operates subconsciously, whereas a strategy is a conscious procedure carried out in order to solve a perceived problem. The presence or absence of consciousness, however, is difficult to detect, and readers may achieve the same goal through "a strategy" or "a skill." Thus for beginner readers, phonological encoding may be a strategy whereby they deliberately "sound out" a word they do not recognize, in order to gain clues as to its identity. A fluent reader, on the other hand, who generally employs the skill of automatic word recognition, may still resort to the strategy of phonological encoding when faced with an unfamiliar word.

A number of reading skills taxonomies were produced in the sixties and seventies. Typical is Davis (1968) who listed: (1) identifying word meanings, (2) drawing inferences, (3) identifying writer's technique and mood, (4) finding answers to questions. Thorndike (1971) has a shorter list, namely (1) memory for word meanings, (2) reasoning in reading. However, many items featured in such lists are not intrinsic to the reading process, but are rather part of the product. Other "reading skills" lists go further, to include reading styles such as scanning, skimming, intensive and extensive reading, which again are not intrinsic to the reading process.

A careful attempt to investigate reading sub-skills was made by Lunzer and his associates (Lunzer, Waite, & Dolan, 1979). They administered English reading tests to 257 native speaker English primary school pupils, and concluded that "one must reject the hypothesis that the several tasks used in the tests of reading comprehension call on distinct sub-skills which can be differentially assessed and taught" (1979, p. 59). Their results "would seem to be entirely consistent with a hypothesis of unitary aptitude of comprehension" (1979, p. 62). A similar conclusion was reached by Rost (1993), who administered a German reading comprehension test to 222 German elementary school pupils, and found that results could be accounted for by "one broad factor, general reading competence" (Rost, 1993, p. 87). (However, a vocabulary dimension to reading skills is detectable even in these studies; Lunzer, Waite, & Dolan observe that "word meaning" scores in their tests do not appear to be entirely consistent with the "unitary" process view, while Rost suggests an alternative two-factor explanation of his results, one factor being "inferential reading comprehension" and the other "vocabulary." Such comments suggest that knowledge of vocabulary may be significant, but that it tends to be masked if readers are being tested in their first language.)

The theoretical issue of whether reading is made up of a number of separate sub-skills or of a single skill would seem to have implications for pedagogy, since in the former case the skills may be separately taught through appropriate exercises in intensive reading lessons, while in the latter case the most appropriate course of action would be for participants to undertake individualized self-access extensive reading.

23.3.2   Process models of reading

These models attempt not only to specify relevant components, but also to specify the relationships between them. Reviews of reading often give separate treatment to three psycholinguistic process models, labelled "bottom-up," "top-down," and "interactive." Although the order of presentation implies an historical evolution, with each succeeding view replacing its predecessor, the prototypical representative of the "bottom-up" model (Gough, 1972), appeared five years later than Goodman's "psycholinguistic guessing game" approach to reading (Goodman, 1967), generally regarded as the champion of the "top-down" view.

However, rather than embrace the unidirectionality suggested by the terms bottom-up and top-down, it might be more accurate to employ the terms data-driven and concept-driven, and see the debate in terms of differing foci of interest, the data-driven focus being on text as a point of departure, the concept-driven on the reader's cognitive state and capacities. The interactive model, of course, views reading as a process whereby the reader is engaged in the continuous construction of meaning based on input from the text. The debate has a long history: in ancient Greece, Aristotle's "intromission" theory maintained that letters sent out rays that entered the reader's eyes, while the "extromission" theory, championed by Euclid, claimed that the reader reached out to the page by means of a "visual spirit." It was left to the eleventh century Iraqi scholar al-Hasan ibn al-Haytham (Alhazen) to propose an interactive view (see Manguel, 1996, pp. 28–32).

23.3.2.1   *Data-driven models*

Gough's (1972) bottom-up model of reading holds that the reader takes in data from the page in sequence, and proposes that reading involves a letter-by-letter and word-by-word analysis of the orthographic words, processed through various nodes: the "scanner," the "decoder," and the "librarian," culminating in the transfer of the input from "Primary Memory" to a device (labeled "Merlin") which applies linguistic knowledge to determine the meaning of the input. The crucial feature of this model, which justifies its label, is that it is unidirectional, and that the higher level processes concerned with the construction of meaning do not affect the lower level processes. In pedagogy, the model lent support to a phonics-based approach to initial reading which stressed letter-by-letter "sounding out," and included decontextualized exercises requiring learners to distinguish items in orthographic minimal pairs such as "park/bark," "tap/top."

The specificity of Gough's model means that it is susceptible – and has proved vulnerable – to empirical evaluation. Experimental evidence and informal observation yield the same criticism of data-driven models, namely that they fail to account for a variety of context effects. Thus readers, especially initial readers reading in their L1, make miscues (i.e., mistakes or deviations from what is actually written on the page) which would appear to be generated by their knowledge of language, but are only partially explicable by bottom-up processing, for example an English native speaker child aged 5 reading aloud *Rabbit went* for *Rabbit won't* or *He won't bother about* . . . instead of *He won't bother today* . . .

23.3.2.2   *Concept-driven models*

Rather than seeing Goodman's psycholinguistic approach to reading as a reaction against the bottom-up *model* proposed by Gough, it is more appropriate to see him as reacting against phonics-based pedagogic *methods* in the teaching of initial reading. The proponents of concept-driven models hold that text is sampled and that predictions which are meaningful to the reader are made on the basis of their prior knowledge, especially, although not exclusively, their language knowledge. Hence the "psycholinguistic guessing game" in the words of Goodman's well-known title (Goodman, 1967).

While Goodman's account lacks specificity compared with that of Gough, the view of reading as a process of "guessing" based on the reader's state of knowledge is powerful in accounting for context effects, which are readily attested whenever one listens to initial readers reading aloud in their first language. The model exerted considerable influence in applied linguistics and the pedagogy of initial reading in the USA and the UK, particularly through the advocacy of Smith (e.g., Smith, 1978).

23.3.2.3   Interactive models

This model was elaborated by Rumelhart (1977), and proposes that graphemic input (i.e., the marks on the page) passes to a visual information store, where a feature extraction device extracts "critical features." The information thus extracted passes to a "pattern synthesizer," where it is operated upon by various kinds of knowledge related to language, namely syntactic knowledge, semantic knowledge, lexical knowledge, orthographic knowledge as well as pragmatic information "about the current contextual situation." The crucial point about this interactive model is that the knowledge sources operate in parallel: the information in the pattern synthesizer is scanned to yield the "most probable interpretation," and the higher level processing of meaning may affect the lower level processing of the orthographic word (i.e., there is "top-down" as well as "bottom-up" processing).

The compensatory interactive model (Stanovich, 1980) similarly represents reading as resulting from the interaction between bottom-up and top-down processing. In addition there is in this model, interaction between the knowledge schemata themselves. These schemata include knowledge of orthographic conventions and of the relevant language, and extend beyond information from the "current contextual situation" to encompass background knowledge. The compensatory element in Stanovich's model claims that reader deficiency at one level may be compensated for by proficiency at another. Thus a reader may compensate for deficiencies at word meaning level by relying more heavily on an appropriate schema. Such a view has obvious appeal in second language reading.

23.3.2.4   Reinstating the bottom

There have, however, been considerable arguments not only against "concept driven" top-down views, but also "interactive approaches" to the extent that they rely on "the top." Support for the importance of attending to the written words comes from Mitchell (1982) who claims word recognition is automatic in good readers, while Stanovitch (1986) reviews studies suggesting that it is in fact poor readers who the most use of contextual redundancy to facilitate word recognition.

Just and Carpenter (1987) found that even skilled readers do not fixate on one out of every three or four words, as had previously been supposed, but on over 80 percent of content words, and around 65 percent of syntactic words. In their model, lexical access, syntactic analysis, and semantic analysis work in parallel to yield comprehension. Readers interpret successive words as they encounter them, integrating the new information with what they have learned from the text, and with what they already know about the topic and the genre. Just and Carpenter refer to this strategy as "immediacy of interpretation" (rather than a "wait and see" strategy, which they claim is only used when unavoidable). The strength of their approach is that it takes into account the generally automatic nature of skilled reading, in which many of the processes are sufficiently automatic to be carried out in parallel. The high rates of fixation are supported by the results of a long series of experiments by Rayner and Pollatsek (1989), who claim that in "normal" reading there is a fixation every 1.1 words on average, and that fixation duration is 200–270 milliseconds.

It would appear that "guessing" is a strategy of unskilled readers, and also occurs developmentally in initial readers. Advice to "guess" has remained, nonetheless prominent in L2 reading (although here we might note that L2 readers are being urged to guess the *meaning* of unknown words, rather than, as is the case for L1 readers, the *identity* of known, but unrecognized, words).

23.3.3 *Reading styles*

The degree to which a reader attends to the text yields different "reading styles," those commonly identified being scanning (rapid and partial search reading for specific information), skimming (rapid sample reading to obtain general gist), intensive reading (deliberate reading and re-reading to extract detailed information), extensive reading (relatively rapid and complete reading, as favored for "extensive reading" programm). These styles are clearly behavioral responses to text, mediated by the reader's purpose and the degree to which the purpose (reading for information, pleasure, etc.) is facilitated by the text. Equally clearly, these "reading styles" are not discrete categories, and although much has been made of them in ESL/EFL reading materials, there is little research into their validity, or indeed whether they are subject to consistent developmental sequence. Terminology is again inconsistent with "skills" being an alternative label to "styles."

23.4 Writing

Most people write less than they read, and much "real-life" writing that people routinely indulge in is either the production of brief texts (shopping lists, notes, etc.) for self-consumption, or so-called "reproductive writing" in response to an existing text (filling in forms, competition details, completing cheques, etc.). The creation of new texts for non-personal consumption, sometime referred to as "productive writing," is an activity which a relatively small proportion of the population is believed to engage in (Kress, 1982, p. 3). It is of course possible that in recent years, interaction via electronic writing, such as emailing, phone texting, or Internet chat room writing, has proportionately increased productive writing. However, Crystal (2001), among others, sees Internet communication as a "third medium," intermediate between speech and writing. The applied linguistic work that has been done on the Internet is for the moment limited, but it is a field is likely to receive considerable attention in the near future.

23.4.1   *Language development in writing*

While responsive writing generally consists of single words or phrases, productive writing is a more complex business. It is prescriptively regulated, not only with respect to spelling, but with respect to the requirement for "complete sentences" which, furthermore, are normally to be written in standard English. It is a commonplace of linguistics that much spontaneous spoken language does not occur in sentences (i.e., at least one main clause, with the option of various subordinate clauses), but rather in elliptical utterances or information chunks, which may or may not be clauses, but are perfectly comprehensible because of the physical or conversational context in which they occur. The "complete sentence" would appear to be an artifact of written language.

Linguistic development was a preoccupation for studies of children's writing development in the 1960s and 1970s: longitudinal studies include that by Loban (1976) who looked at the progress of 211 Californian children over 13 years, with similar results to other surveys, namely a gradual increase over time in terms of fluency (as measured by number of words), and grammatical complexity (as measured by subordinate clauses). Likewise in the UK, Harpin (1973) investigated the work of 290 primary school children over six terms, and found that the amount of writing produced increased, that sentences became longer, and that syntax (again in terms of subordination) became more complex, although it slowed down somewhat in the fourth year of junior school.

There is relatively little work in the UK on the acquisition of standard language in the writing of speakers of dialect (or non-standard) varieties. Schooled literacy, however, is acknowledged to be an important influence in the dissemination of standard language. Children who start their schooling already speaking the standard variety have an advantage in the early years, but research by Williams (1994), using an apparent time model, suggests that most speakers of dialect forms acquire control over standard English by the end of their eighth or ninth year of schooling. This obviously disadvantages them for any assessments involving writing that occur before then. In the US, studies have for the most part concentrated on speakers of vernacular black English: at college level there is little evidence of dialect forms in writing. Whiteman (1981) concluded that, although dialect features were present in black and white children's writing, this could not be attributed entirely to dialect influence, but was partly a function of the children's writing development.

23.4.2 Personal growth in writing

Such linguistic development is not surprising, and Wilkinson (1986) criticized such studies as not being concerned with context or meaning. To make good this deficiency, he developed an assessment technique along four dimensions, cognitive, affective, moral, and stylistic, intending to assess "personal growth." He concluded from a cross-sectional investigation of 150 children aged 7, 10 and 13 that they had advanced on all dimensions except the moral. Stylistically it was found that text became better organized, there was greater inter-sentential cohesion, and a more exact use of lexis.

Britton et al. (1975), who were also interested in personal growth rather than linguistic development, claimed that children's writing first develops expressive function and then develops two further functions, the transactional ("getting things done" in practical terms) and the poetic (where language itself is the focus of attention). While the work of Britton et al. was influential at the time, being incorporated into the UK Bullock Report on primary schooling, it was criticized on the grounds that the identification of the three functions was entirely subjective. It was also pointed out that that there was no psycholinguistic or linguistic basis for any developmental sequence from expressive to transactional or poetic. A more lasting educational legacy of Britton et al.'s work is awareness of audience as a criterion for assessing a writer's development: their theory of written communication, and indeed many subsequent theories, place writing styles along a continuum ranging from writing for oneself at one pole, to writing for an unknown audience at the other.

23.4.3 Writing as composing

A recurring theme in the ESL perspective, namely interest in cross-cultural rhetorical organization, was stimulated by Kaplan in 1966. After analyzing approximately 600 foreign students' compositions in English, Kaplan claimed that Semitic, Oriental, and Romance cultures produced different thought patterns, resulting in specific paragraph structures, marked respectively by "parallel construction," "indirection," and "digression." "English" thought patterns, however, according to Kaplan, were "linear." Although the *naiveté* of this view was widely criticized, it prompted sustained research in contrastive rhetoric and the development of "testable hypotheses about writing patterns in many cultures and languages" (Connor, 1996, p. 32). The pedagogic response, however, which leant toward teaching students to write according to the claimed "English" model, was to be criticized from a sociopolitical perspective.

Within L1 pedagogy, the cognitively oriented work of Flower and Hayes (1981) was very influential. Rejecting the prescriptive "stage" models of composition writing which center on "plan, write, re-write" and take the final product as their reference point, they instead studied thinking processes in writing through analysis of protocols ("think aloud" verbalizations) of good and poor writers, and developed a model which sees writing as involving a set of thinking processes. Although Flower and Hayes' basic process of planning, translating, and reviewing seems to have much in common with "stage" models, their work did cause a shift in the teaching of writing away from concern with the final product, and toward teacher intervention in the process.

This stress on process rather than product was questioned by Horowitz (1986) who, while sympathetic to the pedagogical intent of process approaches, claimed that they fell short in preparing students for academic writing tasks such as laboratory reports or examination writing. Obviously, unprepared students may be penalized for failing to create a product acceptable to the relevant academic sub-culture. Despite such views, the dominance of the "English" model was further questioned, particularly in the US. Raimes (1991) for example, evoked the notion of "the politics of pedagogy" and expressed concern that ESL writers may see their writing styles as inferior. Others argued that ESL writing programs neglected to see writing as a social artifact with political as well as social implications. At the heart of the debate is the issue of whether ESL students should be taught to write according to the discourse norms of the target community (university departments in the English-speaking world in this case), or whether that discourse community should become more tolerant of non-standard patterns. The answer from many in the ESL camp (Zamel, 1997; McKay, 1993) was that there should be tolerance. However, it is questionable whether EAP (English for Academic Purposes) practitioners can persuade academics working in other disciplines to amend their beliefs of what constitutes appropriate academic discourse. For the foreseeable future empowerment of the disempowered is likely to be achieved precisely through enabling them to master the literacy norms of the powerful, rather than expecting the powerful to embrace the norms of the powerless.

23.5   Broad Interpretations of Literacy

Broad interpretations of literacy are concerned not with the psycholinguistic process of reading and writing, nor with the adequacy of reading comprehension or written production in terms of a prescribed educational standard, but rather with literacy as social practice. An important distinction in the broad approach is the distinction between the "autonomous literacy" model and the "ideological literacy" model (Street, 1984). The autonomous model sees literacy as a value-neutral set of skills, detached from social context, which it is assumed can bring about certain cognitive and social consequences. Much of what has been dealt with above as the "narrow" approach to literacy is in the "autonomous" tradition. The "autonomous" nature of schooled literacy has long been an issue of concern, as instanced by W. B. Hodgson's essay of 1867 (see Graff, 1995), where he queries the value of the ability to read with no consideration given to the value of what is read.

Much of the impetus for literacy studies in this perspective arises from the belief that literacy in formal education is a restrictive and decontextualized attempt to "teach literacy" without reference to society. The "ideological" model of literacy, in contrast, is concerned with literacy practices related to specific social contexts; the multiplicity of contexts inevitably generates a multiplicity of literacies, which are not simply neutral, but are associated with power and ideology. The ideological model, it is claimed, leads to a better understanding of how literacy is embedded in other human activity – in brief "literacy" does not exist outside of human action, and the strong may manipulate institutions concerned with literacy in ways that disadvantage the weak.

23.5.1   Consequences of literacy

Proponents of the ideological model of literacy claim that a number of invalid claims are made for "autonomous literacy," two of the main ones being (1) that literacy, as an "autonomous agent," leads to logical and scientific thinking, and (2) that literacy leads to social and economic development.

The first claim (made by the anthropologist Goody rather than educationists) is challenged by the research of Scribner and Cole (1981), who studied the Vai people in Liberia, where one group were literate in the Vai script, another group had literacy in reading the Koran, and a third group was literate in English, the medium of education. The conclusions that Scribner and Cole drew from their test results are frequently cited to demonstrate that it is not literacy (in this case "the ability to read") itself, that produces cognitive changes, but schooling, since the schooled group, literate in English, were superior in reasoning power. Although this work is presented as a naturally occurring experiment, it is clear that literacy is not isolated as a variable; nonetheless the view that there are unlikely to be cognitive benefits simply from being able to read and write, irrespective of what is read and written, is persuasive. (Vai literacy is not of course "autonomous literacy" since their practices were themselves embedded in Vai culture – the term refers to a model of literacy, and not, by definition, to a practice of literacy.)

As concerns literacy and economic development, there has long been a belief that investment in education would have an effect in developing countries, similar to that claimed for developed countries – Denison (1962), for example, claimed that between 1930 and 1960, 23 percent of annual growth in the US national income was attributable to education. In the same vein C. A. Anderson (1966) estimated that an adult literacy rate of about 40 percent was needed for economic development, although he adds that that level would not be sufficient if societies lacked other support systems. Indeed, the failure of the Experimental World Literacy program, organized by UNESCO in 11 countries from 1967 to 1972, provided evidence that literacy alone cannot be a causal factor in development. Reflecting upon the failure, UNESCO observes that, if development is to occur, then literacy, economic and social reforms must be integrated (Lind & Johnson, 1990, pp. 71–5).

Nonetheless, although literacy may not be a sufficient condition for economic development, there is ample evidence that it is a necessary condition: thus Azariadis and Drazen (1990), who looked at the development history of 32 countries from 1940 to 1980, concluded that not one of the countries where the threshold level of labor force educational quality, including literacy, was not met, managed to achieve rapid growth. Moock and Addou (1994) suggest that this threshold represents a level of education where literacy and numeracy skills attained are sufficient to be retained and rewarded in later life. The current consensus is that literacy is a necessary contributory factor in development, but that, in line with the ideological model of literacy, it is not an independent causal factor. (That said, however, it must be admitted that in the work on development, "literacy" and "education" are inevitably confounded.)

23.5.2   *Social dimensions in literacy*

In their focus on the social role of literacy, the new literacy studies involve detailed ethnographic work on reading and writing practices in specific communities, such as Heath's (1983) seminal work on literacy in three communities in the US, Barton and Hamilton's (1998) description of various literacy practices in Lancaster, and Martin-Jones and Jones' (2000) documenting of a variety of bilingual literacies. While there is a range of locations, the focus is consistently upon practice and value. For example, Street's (1984) research on literacy in Iranian villages identifies three sets of literacy practices: traditional literacy associated with the primary Quranic school; schooled literacy from the modern state school; commercial literacy associated with selling fruit. He notes that, contrary to expectation, commercial literacy was mainly undertaken by those who had Quranic literacy, since they had the status within the village that those with schooled literacy lacked. The perspective on literacy in such work is to relate it to notions of identity, of power, and of solidarity, rather than to identify components of literacy as in a psycholinguistic approach, or assess methods of enhancing literacy, as in an educational approach.

A second branch of interest in the broad approach to literacy is critical reading, deriving from critical discourse analysis, which attempts not only to describe texts, but also to interpret and explain them. Critical readings of texts are typically concerned with one or more of the following:

1   linguistic issues, such as choice of vocabulary, the manipulation of grammar (e.g., the expression or suppression of agency in verb phrases),
2   rhetorical issues such as the overall text structure and organization,
3   issues of text type and discourse convention (e.g., an advertisement, a newspaper robbery report).

Such reading critiques not only the language and sentiments expressed in texts, but also the ideological and/or the historical assumptions underpinning them as filtered through the writer, whether with or without the writer's intent. It is socially engaged in that it claims to reveal how readers may be unwittingly manipulated by powerful, and especially capitalist, forces.

The broad approach to literacy presents a strong moral argument, in the socialist tradition of Raymond Williams (e.g., Williams, 1961). However, the enthusiasm of its proponents occasionally lead to incomplete representations of the psycholinguistic tradition. Gee, for example, claims that the psycholinguistic position is that there is a "right" interpretation for texts that "is (roughly) the same for all competent readers" (Gee, 1996, p. 39). In fact this notion has been widely contested by applied linguists of a psycholinguistic persuasion (e.g., Cohen et al., 1988; Urquhart, 1987). Likewise Gee's point that readers from different cultures interpret texts differently had long been established in reading studies by such as Steffenson & Joag Dev (1984). Finally, Gee's interpretation that the warning on the aspirin bottle functions as a legal safeguard on the part of the company, rather than a benevolent concern for the safety of the public, certainly has merit. However, if one cannot read – in the psycholinguistic sense – one will not be able to make any kind of interpretation of the aspirin bottle, nor indeed any other text. There is thus an argument that "autonomous literacy" is a valid model, in the sense that if one cannot read, then one cannot read anything. Equally, the "ideological literacy" model is valid in the sense that the converse proposition "If one can read, then one can read everything" is clearly wrong.

New literacy studies, however, have brought centre-stage the social dimension, that had previously been adduced mainly to account for educational failure. It has made its point that literacy practices are ideologically laden, and often manipulated by powerful institutions. Future developments would appear to include applying these views to mainstream education. "Weak" proposals for application suggest, for example, that educational institutions can contribute to students' writing if they draw on writing practices in the community, as well as teaching more academic and statusful types of writing, while maintaining a critical watch over the whole (Ivanic & Moss, 1991).

A "stronger" project for implementing a pedagogy of literacy has come from the New London Group (a group of educationists who first met in New London, US: see Cope & Kalantzis, 2000). Having developed the basic concept of "Design" (capitalization *sic*), which refers to conventions of meaning (linguistic, visual, audio, gestural, and spatial), the group proposes the following four sequential components of pedagogy: "Situated Practice", which draws on the experience of meaning-making in lifeworlds; "Overt Instruction," through which students develop an explicit metalanguage of Design; Critical Framing, which interprets the social context and purpose of Designs of meaning; and Transformed Practice, in which students, as meaning makers, become designers of social futures" (Cope & Kalantzis, 2000, p. 9). It is not clear, however, that such a highly abstract approach, which is based solely on the analysis of social practices, would provide a sufficient basis for literacy, since it seems to lack any theory of learning. As Street (2000: 29) says of the new literacy studies their "sternest test . . . is that of practical applications in the field of mainstream education."

Although there is for the moment no work in mainstream education that integrates comunity literacy practices into school literacy teaching, there are studies which have investigated the relationship between family literacy practices and school literacy teaching. In the UK, Gregory and Williams (2000) document a range of home and school practices in a multicultural urban area of London, and found that children from relatively poor economic backgrounds draw on home literacy practices, as well as those of the school, in learning to read, and that older siblings and grandparents as well as parents, can be important mediators of literacy. Snow et al. (1991) report on work in the US which also looked at home-school literacy in poor families, and came to the conclusion that, for the people with whom they were working, there was a need for holistic family literacy programs involving "bridge building" support for both caregivers and children. The differing conclusions of these two pieces of research highlight the importance of local contexts.

23.6   The Future?

Looking into the future, the studies that await research are of great variety, which guarantees that literacy will continue to present a disparate scene. The psycholinguistics of reading is beginning to explore the field of memory, while the effects of ageing on reading and writing has hardly been touched; in both areas interdisciplinary studies with neurology could be profitable. The incipient work into multimodal literacy, exploring arrangements of graphics and visuals in communication, will certainly make progress. Further interdiciplinary work is likely from the investigation of the links between numeracy and literacy. The communication revolution has implications for individual and global practices in literacy. Electronic literacy is already being explored from a range of perspectives, and this is sure to increase.

On a larger scale, economic and cultural globalization means the movement of goods, services and people across the globe, with implications for literacy in both rich and poor countries. The role of literacy in human and economic development in poor communities is attracting renewed attention, as well as the literacy practices and needs of migrants in rich countries. Grassroots literacy of poor villagers, those neglected denizens of the global village, also merits further documentation and research. There are still answers waiting to be explored for the questions "What is literacy?" and "What is literacy for?" And no doubt there are different questions waiting to be discovered.

See also 1 Language Descriptions, 22 Social Influences on Language Learning, 28 Bilingual Education, 32 Critical Applied Linguistics.

REFERENCES

Adams, M. J. (1990) *Beginning to read: thinking and learning about print.* Cambridge MA: MIT Press.

Alderson, J. C. & Urquhart, A. H. (1988) This test is unfair: I'm not an economist. In P. L. Carrell, J. Devine, & D. E. Eskey (eds.), *Interactive approaches to second language reading* (pp. 168–82). Cambridge: Cambridge University Press.

Anderson, C. A. (1966) Literacy and schooling on the development threshold: some historical cases. In C. A. Anderson & M. J. Bowman (eds.), *Education and economic development* (pp. 347–62). London: Frank Cass.

Anderson, R. C., Reynolds, R. E., Schallert, D. L., & Goetz, E. T. (1977) Frameworks for comprehending discourse. *American Educational Research Journal*, 14, 367–82.

Azariadis, C. & Drazen, A. (1990) Threshold externalities in economic development. *The Quarterly Journal of Economics*, 2, 501–26.

Barton, D. & Hamilton, M. (1998) *Local literacies.* London: Routledge.

Berman, R. A. (1984) Syntactic components of the foreign language reading process. In J. C. Alderson & A. H. Urquhart (eds.), *Reading in a Foreign Language*, (pp. 139–59). London: Longman.

Bernhardt, E. B. & Kamil, M. L. (1995) Interpreting relationships between L1 and L2 reading: consolidating the linguistic threshold and linguistic interdependence hypotheses. *Applied Linguistics*, 16, 15–34.

Britton, J., Burgess, T., Martin, N., Macleod, A., & Rosen, H. (1975) *The development of writing abilities (11 to 18).* London: Macmillan Educational.

Byrne, B. (1998) *The foundation of literacy: the child's acquisition of the alphabetic principle.* Hove: The Psychology Press.

Carrell, P. L. (1984) The effects of rhetorical organisation on ESL readers. *TESOL Quarterly*, 18, 441–69.

Carrell, P. L. (1991) Second language reading: reading ability or language proficiency? *Applied Linguistics*, 12, 159–79.

Chall, J. S. (1967) *Learning to read: the great debate.* New York: McGraw-Hill.

Coady, J. (1997) L2 vocabulary acquisition. In J. Coady & T. Huckin (eds.), *Second language vocabulary acquisition* (pp. 225–37) Cambridge: Cambridge University Press.

Cohen, A., Glasman, H., Rosenbaum-Cohen, P. R., Ferrara, J., & Fine, J. (1988) Reading English for specialised purposes: discourse analysis and the use of student informants. In P. L. Carrell, J. Devine, & D. E. Eskey (eds.), *Interactive approaches to second language reading* (pp. 152–67). Cambridge: Cambridge University Press.

Connor, U. (1996) *Contrastive rhetoric.* Cambridge: Cambridge University Press.

Cope, B. & Kalantzis, M. (eds.) (2000) *Multiliteracies: literacy learning and the design of social futures.* London & New York: Routledge.

Crystal, D. (2001) *Language and the internet.* Cambridge: Cambridge University Press.

Cummins, J. & Swain, M. (1986) *Bilingualism in education.* London: Longman.

Davies, A. (1984) Simple, simplified and simplification: what is authentic? In J. C. Alderson & A. H. Urquhart (eds.), *Reading in a foreign language* (pp. 181–95). London: Longman.

Davis, F. B. (1968) Research in comprehension in reading. *Reading Research Quarterly*, 3, 499–545.

Day, R. R., Omura, C., & Hiramatsu, M. (1991) Incidental EFL vocabulary learning and reading. *Reading in a Foreign Language*, 7, 541–52.

Denison, E. F. (1962) *The sources of economic growth in the United States and the alternatives before us*. New York: Committee for Economic Development.

Downing, J. (ed.) (1973) *Comparative reading*. London: Collier Macmillan.

Elley, W. B. (1991) Acquiring literacy in a second language: the effect of book-based programmes. *Language Learning*, 41, 375–411.

Elley, W. B. (1994) *The IEA study of reading literacy: achievement and instruction in thirty two school systems*. Oxford: Pergamon.

Flower, L. & Hayes, J. R. (1981) A cognitive process theory of writing. *College Composition and Communication*, 32, 365–87.

Fries, C. C. (1963) *Linguistics and reading*. New York: Holt, Reinhart & Winston.

Gee, J. (1996) *Social linguistics and literacies*. London: Routledge/ Falmer.

Goodman, K. S. (1967) Reading: a psycholinguistic guessing game. *Journal of the Reading Specialist*, 6, 126–35. (Reprinted in H. Singer & R. B. Ruddell (eds.) (1994) *Theoretical models and processes of reading* (pp. 470–96). Newark: International Reading Association.)

Goswami, U. & Bryant, P. (1990) *Phonological skills and learning to read*. Hove: Lawrence Erlbaum.

Gough, P. B. (1972) One second of reading. *Visible Language*, 6, 291–320.

Graff, H. J. (1995) *The labyrinths of literacy*. Pittsburgh: University of Pittsburgh Press.

Gregory, E. & Williams, A. (2000) *City literacies*. London: Routledge.

Hafiz, F. M. & Tudor, I. (1989) Extensive reading and the development of language skills. *ELT Journal*, 43, 4–13.

Hafiz, F. M. & Tudor, I. (1990) Graded readers as an input medium in L2 learning, *System*, 18, 31–42.

Harpin, W. S. (1973) *Social and educational influences on children's acquisition of grammar*. Swindon: Social Science Research Council, Report 757.

Heath S. B. (1983) *Ways with words: language life and work in communities and classrooms*. Cambridge: Cambridge University Press.

Hirsh, D. & Nation, I. S. P. (1992) What vocabulary size is needed to read unsimplified texts for pleasure? *Reading in a Foreign Language*, 8, 689–96.

Hoover, W. A. & Tunmer, W. E. (1993) The components of reading. In G. B. Thompson, W. E. Tunmer, & T. Nicholson (eds.), *Reading acquisition processes* (pp. 1–19). Clevedon, UK: Multilingual Matters.

Horowitz, D. (1986) Process, not product: less than meets the eye. *TESOL Quarterly*, 20, 783–97.

Horst, M., Cobb, T., & Meara, P. (1998) Beyond "A Clockwork Orange": acquiring second language vocabulary through reading. *Reading in a Foreign Language*, 11, 207–23.

Huey, E. B. (1908/1968) *The psychology and pedagogy of reading*. Cambridge, MA: MIT Press. (Originally published 1908 by Macmillan.)

Ivanic, R. & Moss, W. (1991) Bringing community writing practices into education. In D. Barton & R. Ivanic (eds.), *Writing in the community* (pp. 193–223). London: Sage Publications.

Just, M. A. & Carpenter, P. A. (1987) *The psychology of reading and language comprehension*. Boston, MA: Allyn and Bacon.

Kaplan, R. B. (1966) Cultural thought patterns in inter-cultural education. *Language Learning*, 16, 1–20.

Krashen, S. 1989. We acquire vocabulary and spelling by reading: additional evidence for the input hypothesis. *Modern Language Journal*, 73, 440–64.

Kress, G. (1982) *Learning to write.* London: Routledge & Kegan Paul.

Kress, G. (1997) *Before writing: rethinking the paths to literacy.* London: Routledge.

Lai, F.-K. (1993) The effect of a summer reading course on reading and writing skills. *System*, 21, 87–100.

Lee, J.-W. & Schallert, D. L. (1997) The relative contribution of L2 language proficiency and L1 reading ability to L2 reading performance: a test of the threshold hypothesis in an EFL context. *TESOL Quarterly*, 31, 713–39.

Lind, A. & Johnson, A. (1990) *Adult literacy in the third world.* Stockholm: Swedish International Development Authority.

Loban, W. (1976) *Language development: kindergarden through grade 12.* Urbana, IL: NCTE.

Lunzer, E., Waite, M., & Dolan, T. (1979) Comprehension and comprehension tests. In E. Lunzer & K. Gardner (eds.), *The effective use of reading* (pp. 37–71). London: Heinemann Educational.

Machingaidze, T., Pfukani P., & Shumba, S. (1998) *The quality of education: some policy suggestions based on a survey of schools: Zimbabwe* (SACMEQ, Policy Research Report no. 3). Paris: International Institute for Educational Planning, UNESCO.

Manguel, A. (1996) *A history of reading.* London: Harper Collins.

Martin-Jones, M. & Jones, K. (eds.) (2000) *Multilingual literacies.* Amsterdam & Philadelphia: John Benjamins.

Mason, B. & Krashen, S. (1997) Extensive reading in English as a foreign language. *System*, 25, 91–102.

McKay, S. L. (1993) Examining L2 composition ideology: a look at literacy education. *Journal of Second Language Writing*, 2, 65–81.

Mitchell, D. C. (1982) *The process of reading.* New York: Wiley.

Moock, P. R. & Addou, H. (1994) Agricultural productivity and education. In *International encyclopaedia of education* (vol. 1) (pp. 244–54). Oxford: Pergamon Press.

Nkamba, M. & Kanyika, J. (1998) *The quality of education: some policy suggestions based on a survey of schools: Zambia* (SACMEQ Policy Research Report no. 5). Paris: International Institute for Educational Planning, UNESCO.

Nuttall, C. (1996) *Teaching reading skills in a foreign language.* Oxford: Heinemann.

Pitts, M., White, H., & Krashen, S. (1989) Acquiring second language vocabulary through reading. *Reading in a Foreign Language*, 5, 271–5.

Raimes, A. (1991) Out of the woods: emerging traditions in the teaching of writing. *TESOL Quarterly*, 25, 407–30.

Rayner, K. & Pollatsek, A. (1989) *The psychology of reading.* Englewood Cliffs, NJ: Prentice-Hall.

Read, C. (1971) Pre-school children's knowledge of English phonology. *Harvard Educational Review*, 41, 1–34.

Rost, D. H. (1993) Assessing the different components of reading comprehension: fact or fiction? *Language Testing*, 10, 79–92.

Rumelhart, D. E. (1977) Towards an interactive model of reading. In S. Dornic (ed.), *Attention and performance: VI* (pp. 573–0603). Hillsdale, NJ: Erlbaum.

Schlesinger, I. M. (1968) *Sentence structure and the reading process.* The Hague: Mouton.

Scribner, S. & Cole, M. (1981) *The psychology of literacy.* Cambridge, MA: Harvard University Press.

Smith, F. (1978) *Reading.* Cambridge: Cambridge University Press.

Snow, C. E., Barnes, W. S., Chandler, J., Hemphill, L., & Goodman, I. F. (1991) *Unfulfilled expectations: home and school influences on literacy.* Cambridge, MA: Harvard University Press.

Stanovich, K. E. (1980) Towards an interactive compensatory model of individual differences in the development of reading fluency. *Reading Research Quarterly*, 16, 32–71.

Stanovich, K. E. (1986) Matthew effects in reading: some consequences of individual differences in the acquisition of literacy. *Reading Research Quarterly*, 21, 360–406.

Steffensen, M. S. & Joag Dev, C. (1984) Cultural knowledge and reading. In J. C. Alderson & A. H. Urquhart (eds.), *Reading in a foreign language* (pp. 48–61). London: Longman.

Street, B. V. (1984) *Literacy in theory and practice*. Cambridge: Cambridge University Press.

Street, B. (2000) Literacy events and literacy practices. In M. Martin-Jones & K. Jones (eds.), *Multilingual literacies*. Amsterdam: John Benjamins.

Thorndike, E. L. (1971) Reading as reasoning: a study of mistakes in paragraph reading. *Journal of Educational Psychology*, 8, 323–32.

Tolchinsky, L. (1998) Early writing acquisition in Catalan and Israeli communities. In A. Y. Durngunoglu & L. Verhoeven (eds.), *Literacy development in a multilingual context* (pp. 289–98). Mahwah, NJ: Lawrence Erlbaum.

Urquhart, A. H. (1987) Comprehensions and interpretations. *Reading in a Foreign Language*, 3, 387–409.

Vellutino, F. R. & Scanlon, D. M. (1982) Verbal processing in poor and normal readers. In C. J. Brainerd & M. Pressley (eds.), *Verbal processes in children* (pp. 189–264). New York: Springer-Verlag.

Venezky, R. L. (1990) Definitions of literacy. In R. L. Venezky, D. A. Wagner, & D. S. Cilberti, (eds.), *Towards defining literacy* (pp. 2–16). Newark, DE: International Reading Association.

Verhoeven, L. (1990) Acquisition of reading in a second language. *Reading Research Quarterly*, 25, 90–114.

Wagner, D. A., Spratt, J. E., & Ezzaki, A. (1989) Does learning to read in a second language always put the child at a disadvantage? Some counter-evidence from Morocco. *Applied Psycholinguistics*, 10, 31–48.

Walker, C. (1997) A self access extensive reading project using graded readers. *Reading in a Foreign Language*, 11, 121–49.

Warburton, F. W. & Southgate, V. (1969) *i t a: an independent evaluation*. London: Murray & Chambers.

Whiteman, M. F. (1981) Dialect influence in writing. In M. F. Whiteman (ed.), *Writing, the nature, development and teaching of written communication*. Hillsdale, NJ: Lawrence Erlbaum.

Wilkinson, A. (1986) *The quality of writing*. Milton Keynes: Open University Press.

Williams, A. (1994) Writing in reading: syntactic variation in children's school writing in Reading, Berkshire. In G. Melchers & N.-L. Johannesson (eds.), *Non-standard varieties of language*. Stockholm: Almqvist & Wiksell International.

Williams, E. (1996). Reading in two languages at year 5 in African primary schools. *Applied Linguistics*, 17, 182–209.

Williams, R. (1961) *The long revolution*. London: Chatto.

Zamel, V. (1997) Toward a model of transculturation. *TESOL Quarterly*, 31, 341–52.

FURTHER READING

Alderson, J. C. (2000) *Assessing reading.* Cambridge: Cambridge University Press.

Baynham, M. (1995) *Literacy practices: investigating literacy in social contexts.* Harlow: Longman.

Bernhardt, E. B. (1991) *Reading development in a second language: theoretical, empirical and classroom perspectives.* Norwood, NJ: Ablex.

Day, R. R. & Bamford, J. (1998) *Extensive reading in the second language classroom.* Cambridge: Cambridge University Press.

Durngunoglu, A. Y. & Verhoeven, L. (eds.) (1998) *Literacy development in a multilingual context.* Mahwah, NJ: Lawrence Erlbaum.

Huckin, T., Haynes, M., & Coady, J. (eds.) (1993) *Second language reading and vocabulary learning.* Norwood, NJ: Ablex.

Kern, R. (2000) *Literacy and language teaching.* Oxford: Oxford University Press.

Street, B. V. (1995) *Social literacies: critical approaches to literacy in development, ethnography, and education.* Harlow: Addison Wesley Longman.

Urquhart, A. H. & Weir, C. J. (1998) *Reading in a second language: process, product and practice.* London: New York.

Wallace, C. (1992) *Reading.* Oxford: Oxford University Press.

24 Fashions in Language Teaching Methodology

BOB ADAMSON

24.1 Introduction

Language teaching, as this volume amply demonstrates, is a complex undertaking. It is an enterprise that is shaped by views of the nature of language, of teaching and learning a language specifically, and of teaching and learning in general; and by the sociocultural settings in which the enterprise takes place. Thanks to its multidisciplinary nature, applied linguistics has contributed research- and practice-based ideas that have helped to shape these views, and promoted understanding of the diversity and commonalities of the settings. One product of applied linguistics has been attempts to crystallize the theoretical views of language, education, and language education into prescribed teaching materials and strategies, or methods. The abundance of methods derived from different theoretical standpoints has led to the emergence of a field of study – methodology. Another product of applied linguistics has been the heightened awareness in the literature of the significant role of the sociocultural context in which language education is occurring, which in turn undermines the notion of generalizability on which methods are premised. Despite the claims of proponents of some methods, no consensus has emerged, nor is likely to emerge, as to the "best" or "right" way to teach a language – indeed there have been calls to abandon the search for what Richards (2001, p. 167) calls the "supermethod" and to concentrate on equipping teachers with a repertoire of methods and skills that can be used selectively in different contexts.

The term "methodology" tends to be employed loosely in language teaching. It is commonly used interchangeably with "method" and "pedagogy." Methodology denotes the study of the system or range of methods that are used in teaching, while a method is a single set of practices and procedures, derived from theory or theorization of practice, that impinges upon the design of a curriculum plan, resources, and teaching and learning activities. Language teaching methodology encompasses such methods as the direct method, audiolingualism, and Crazy English, but the field of study is not limited to those methods that are widespread in application or that have achieved a degree of recognition in the field. Methodology also includes methods that might be developed and employed by just one teacher, provided there is a principled rationale from which the set procedures of the method have been distilled – the popularity of some methods is not necessarily an indication of their inherent quality. The essential difference between methodology and pedagogy is that methodology is more narrowly focused and tends to be more dogmatic in its application, as it targets language learning as its main goal, is largely based on individual theoretical insights, and is deemed applicable in different contexts; whereas pedagogy has broader educational goals, is influenced by a wider range of theories and curricular influences and tensions, and is more rooted in and responsive to the practical realities of a particular classroom. This distinction is important and, as discussed later in this chapter, has led to a major critique of the value of methodology.

As methods link theory and practice, they thus represent a key contribution of applied linguistics to language education. They do not necessarily arise from a priori theorizing: they could also be derived from successful practice (Krashen, 1987). Some methods offer an all-embracing package that promises comprehensive language learning; others offer strategies for achieving particular objectives. Richards and Rodgers (1986, 2001) describe methods in terms of three levels: approach, design, and procedure. The *approach* refers to the underpinning theory of language and of language learning; the *design* covers the specification of linguistic content and the roles of the teacher, learners, and instructional materials; while *procedure* means the techniques and activities that are used in the classroom. This suggests that methods can be analyzed as scientific constructs – the products of theorizing or reflective practice; or, alternatively, methods can be viewed as curricular resolutions, given the interplay between methods and aspects of the curriculum, such as planned objectives, syllabus specifications, types of resources, the roles of teachers, learners and materials, and actual teaching and learning practices. A third perspective is to consider methods as sociocultural artifacts, the products and reflections of their times.

This chapter considers these perspectives by addressing a number of questions concerning language teaching methodology. Where do methods originate? What are the salient features of methods that have been widely promoted? How do they gain acceptance? Does methodology still have relevance in postmodernist contexts? To suggest answers to these questions, I will draw not just on the literature that is available to me (largely limited to materials written in English), but also on my teaching and research experiences in mainland China and Hong Kong. In this chapter I argue that no method is inherently superior to another; instead, some methods are more appropriate than others in a particular context. I reject the notion that methods have been evolving toward perfection, preferring to share the view of Rowlinson (1994, p. 7) that

[i]t is easy, and rather dangerous, to view language-teaching methodology, and indeed other aspects of education also, as a continuous upward progress through history. The fact that some methods have achieved a high degree of adoption (if not actual implementation) is due to an element of serendipity, and very few are truly innovative.

24.2   The Origins of Methods

Language teaching methods, as noted above, are derived from a range of standpoints. These include views of language, of language learning in general, and of second or foreign language learning in particular. The variety of origins has produced a plethora of methods. Language has been perceived in the literature as a codified linguistic structure underpinned by established rules (e.g. Honey, 1997) or as a mediated social semiotic (e.g. Halliday, 1973; Lantolf, 2000). Language learning has been variously described in terms of behaviorist habit formation (Skinner, 1957), of an innate language acquisition device and a universal grammar (Chomsky, 1965), or of being meaning-oriented rather than form-oriented (Mitchell, 1994). Second or foreign language learning has been equated with first language learning (Gouin, 1892) or has been depicted as a process that is very different from first language learning (Stern, 1970). In this section, some of the methods that have been propounded on the strength of these perspectives are outlined. The majority are methods that are among those most commonly described in historical overviews of language teaching (e.g. Titone, 1968; Rivers, 1981; Tang, 1983; Howatt, 1984; Larsen-Freeman, 1986; Richards and Rodgers, 1986; Knight, 2001). This does not suggest that the attention in the literature accorded to a method is proportional to its effectiveness in bringing about language learning. The dissemination of methods is facilitated by itinerant teachers, publications in various media and training opportunities for teachers. The proponents of the more famous methods have had access to, or influence over, these channels, and adoption tends to occur when the methods have values that are in harmony with those of major stakeholders in a particular educational initiative, whether this is at the state level, school level, or classroom level.

Until the middle of the twentieth century, the grammar-translation method was the predominant method for language teaching in most educational contexts. This method was derived from the learning of Latin and Greek, which were the classical languages taught in Europe. Grammar as a discipline had its roots in Greek and Roman scholarship and was revived during the Renaissance. The objective of the method was to instill intellectual rigor and to transmit the cultural values embodied in the literary canons to a new generation. Language was thus viewed as an academic discipline, rather than as a means for conducting everyday social interactions. Priority was given to the written language, with comprehension achieved through translation from the target language into the mother tongue, and competence developed through translation from the mother tongue into the target language, underpinned by mastery of the grammar system through parsing and other form-focused exercises, and memorization of lexical items. Oral skills were fostered though the use of dictations, rote-learning of texts, and reading aloud. The teacher's role was that of expert linguist, with the learner as recipient of knowledge.

The limited practicality of the grammar-translation method for communicating in everyday situations created dissatisfaction toward the end of the nineteenth century among language teachers in Europe. In France, Gouin proposed a method, called a Series, which was based on interactions from daily life. The teacher models a series of statements describing the steps of the interaction in sequence; the learners imitate (Roberts, 1999). Gouin's Series focused interest on everyday language and on children's acquisition of the mother tongue, which, it was believed, came about initially through listening and speaking (Richards & Rodgers, 1986). Another French scholar, Marcel, distinguished between the four skills (speaking, listening, reading, and writing), a distinction which was viewed as important in later approaches that placed communication at a premium, and investigated ways of structuring learning with a focus on meaning (Roberts, 1999). There were calls for a more scientific approach to language learning, most notably from the Reform Movement that was founded in the 1880s (Knight, 2001). Investigations into various aspects of language produced innovations such as the International Phonetic Alphabet in 1888, based on the work of Henry Sweet. The direct method expounded in Jespersen (1904), and championed by Charles Berlitz, was a product of this movement. The direct method is premised on the belief that, as with first language learning, total immersion in the target language is conducive to rapid progress in communicating. The teacher's role is to supply contextual support for the learners, without recourse to the learners' mother tongue, as far as possible. Listening and speaking skills precede reading and writing. Grammar learning is inductive and restricted in scope to forms that are commonly used in the spoken language (Rivers, 1981).

Experimentation in psychology in the middle of the twentieth century, most notably Skinner's work with animals and his behaviorist principles of learning, produced the audiolingual method. The method sees learning as being brought about by positive reinforcement of correct behavior or utterances (in the case of language learning), with the correctness being instilled by repetition or drilling. It also builds on earlier work by scholars such as Fries and Bloomfield in the field of structural linguistics, which was concerned with compiling descriptive rather than prescriptive grammars of languages. The audiolingual method focuses primarily on oral skills, with the teacher modeling utterances. Learners are drilled to produce correct responses – errors are not tolerated – with a strong emphasis on habit formation. The utterances are organized into structures commonly used to realize speech acts in daily situations, with the learners' attention being drawn (through contrastive analysis) to differences between the target language and the mother tongue, so as to minimize confusion and error. The mechanical learning entailed in the audiolingual method led to the popularity of language laboratories, which afforded opportunities for both teacher-led and independent study.

The synthesis of behaviorism and structural linguistics was criticized by scholars such as Rivers (1964) and Carroll (1965), but other methods linking psychology with language teaching appeared in the 1960s and 1970s. The Silent Way, propounded by Caleb Gattegno, relies on problem-solving by the learners. The goal is to get learners to produce the target language, but they must do so with minimal assistance from the teacher. The teacher uses charts and colored blocks to establish the meaning of model utterances, but the learners have to apply inductive and self-monitoring techniques to build their own structural knowledge of the target language. The total physical response method designed by James Asher does not incorporate a specific linguistic model, being primarily a teacher-dominant approach, with the learner responding physically to instructions, generally in the form of simple structures. Another method is Suggestopedia, created by Georgi Lozanov in Bulgaria. Borrowing principles from yoga and research into psychotherapy carried out in the former Soviet Union, Suggestopedia teachers seek to reduce the psychological barriers of learner anxiety by providing a relaxed, comfortable, and caring learning environment, often with soothing background music. Community Language Learning, developed by Charles Curran, similarly sought to reduce learner stress by adapting techniques from psychological counseling (Knight, 2001). A later method with psychological origins, which appeared in China in the 1990s, addresses the problem of anxiety from a different angle. Identifying the fear of losing face as a major cultural obstacle to language learning, Li Yang's "Crazy English" method involves learners shedding their inhibitions by shouting slogans such as "I enjoy losing face!," "Welcome setbacks!" and "Relish suffering!," and by using techniques similar to those of the total physical response method (Bolton, 2002). The language content is the mastery of sentence patterns and vocabulary lists.

An alternative starting point for the development of language teaching methods is to view language essentially as social practice, and the goal of language teaching as engendering the learner's competence to communicate in the target language. Communication is viewed as social interaction and therefore dynamic and influenced by the cultural context, rather than being a fixed linguistic system existing in a vacuum. Toward the end of the twentieth century, great attention was given to the "Communicative Approach," or "Communicative Language Teaching," although in reality these are more an umbrella term for a range of curriculum design principles and teaching methods all sharing the underlying philosophy than a single, specific method. Bygate, Skehan, and Swain (2001, p. 2) argue that the Communicative Approach "was explicitly a post-method approach to language teaching . . . in which the principles underlying the use of different classroom procedures were of paramount importance, rather than a package of teaching materials." The pluralism of the Communicative Approach could be seen as united by common principles, which include a view of language as principally serving as an expression of meaning at the discourse level (not just the word or sentence level), where appropriacy is as important as accuracy; a view of language learning as best brought about by involving learners actively in communication related to real-life contexts; and a view of the teacher as a facilitator and motivator, as well as source of knowledge.

One development that spurred the acceptance of the Communicative Approach principles was the Functional-Notional Approach, which organized the syllabus according to language functions (everyday interactions, such as buying food, giving directions, or offering advice) and notions (concepts, such as time, quantity, and location), but offered little explicit advice on appropriate teaching methods. A method known variously as the presentation-practice-production (P-P-P) method or the Five Steps method (adding Revision as the first step before Presentation, and Consolidation as the fifth step) was promoted in curriculum documents, teacher education courses, and handbooks (e.g. Hubbard et al., 1983), but this later became associated with "weak" forms of the Communicative Approach, as it tends to be used in conjunction with syllabuses that focus on the mastery of discrete linguistic items – albeit in realistic contexts of use – rather than on holistic language, which represents the "strong" form (Howatt, 1984).

Task-based learning was appropriated from other subject areas in the curriculum (such as issues-based teaching in social sciences) and from experiments in Bangalore by N. S. Prabhu, and promoted as a "strong" form of the Communicative Approach, as it emphasizes holistic language. Drawing on constructivist views of learning, particularly those of Vygotsky and Bruner, task-based learning advocates a learner-centered curriculum and teaching methods that have a strong element of group-work and autonomous activities: thus it appears to mesh well with communicative views of language learning that stress the development of various competences – communicative, strategic, cultural, etc. – by the individual learner. The notion of tasks has been widely interpreted, and there has been discussion concerning the best ways to realize task-based learning in the classroom, in terms of task type and learner interaction (see Ellis, 2001). Bygate, Skehan, and Swain (2001, p. 11) define a task as "an activity which requires learners to use language, with emphasis on meaning, to attain an objective," adding that the task might be "influenced by learner choice" and "susceptible to brief or extended pedagogic intervention." In some contexts, such as the Target Oriented Curriculum, an initiative in Hong Kong in the 1990s, task-based learning in English language is seen as aiding the achievement of cross-curricular goals that go beyond language learning per se. In this initiative, tasks are described as having a purpose that involves more than a display of knowledge or practice of discrete skills; having a tangible or intangible product that is holistic, realistic, and linked to settings beyond the classroom; involving a process of thinking and doing by the learners; and requiring some of the following generic skills: problem-solving, reasoning, inquiring, conceptualizing, and communicating (Hong Kong Government Education Department, 1994, p. 18).

The interest in the social dimensions of language contributed to the development of genre pedagogy, which evolved from Halliday's work on Systemic-Functional Linguistics (e.g. Halliday, 1973) and follows the spirit of critical approaches to education championed by Paolo Freire in *Pedagogy of the Oppressed* (1970) and the work on power and discourse by Michel Foucault. Genre pedagogy is concerned with providing learners with access to what are perceived as the most powerful genres of written and spoken text in society (Dufficy, 2000). Genres (of which reports and recounts are examples) are social processes: they are texts possessing certain regular features arising from the regularity of their use in specific social situations (Kress, 1993). Texts are constructed through grammar, which is viewed as performing a semantic function (Martin & Rothery, 1993). To empower learners, genre pedagogy employs a procedure of explicit instruction by the teacher to initiate the learners in the construction of a text through analysis of the subject matter, or "field"; the interlocutor relationship, or "tenor"; and the channel, or "mode" (Martin, 1993). This is followed by collaborative text construction, and finally autonomous text production by the learners (Dufficy, 2000).

This brief and highly selective overview of methods demonstrates the challenge and problem facing language teaching methodology. The challenge is to devise a methodology that takes into account the diverse epistemologies of relevant theories; the problem is that this challenge is almost certainly a fruitless endeavor.

24.3   Methodology and Curriculum

This section explores the relationship between language teaching methodology and different aspects of curriculum. Defining the term "curriculum" is problematic, but for current purposes, the working definition adopted by Marsh and Willis (1995, p. 10) is used: "an interrelated set of plans and experiences that a student undertakes under the guidance of the school." Marsh and Willis (1995) distinguish between the "planned" or "intended" curriculum, which is the product of design and development by various agencies, such as educational bureaus at the state level, or educational publishers; the "enacted" curriculum, which refers to the educational content and activities that are provided in a classroom; and the "experienced" curriculum, which is what individual learners actually gain from the process.

At the intended level, the methodological approach to language teaching promoted in a curriculum initiative is informative as it reflects the orientation of the curriculum toward particular goals. Specific language teaching methods can be linked to values systems that incorporate sociopolitical and philosophical thought (Clark, 1987). For instance, the grammar-translation method, which is concerned with literary texts and grammatical knowledge about the target language, is associated with a Classical Humanist curriculum orientation, which Clark (1987, p. 91) describes as ". . . elitist, concerned with the generalizable intellectual capacities and with the transmission of knowledge, culture, and standards from one generation to another." A second values system, Social and Economic Efficiency, focuses on human capital and the needs of society. Language teaching, according to this philosophy, provides the learner with a social skill that is also valuable in the job market (thus determining the languages that are included in the curriculum). Methods associated with the Communicative Approach would, to a large extent, be promoted in such a curriculum, as the methods are oriented toward enabling the learners to function in social situations. Progressivism is a values system that emphasizes individualism rather than societal needs. It celebrates diversity and seeks to develop the whole person through generic learning skills and attention to individual needs, ability, and interests. Task-based learning, as can be seen from the Hong Kong example given in the previous section, has been linked with Progressivism. A fourth values system is Social Reconstructionism. This philosophy problematizes society and identifies inequalities and iniquities, and views education as a means to achieve social amelioration and justice through awareness-raising and empowerment. Genre Pedagogy would be an apposite method for a curriculum with a Social Reconstructionism agenda.

This is not an exhaustive list of values systems, and it has a broadly western flavor, but it is sufficient to demonstrate that language teaching methodology is subject to philosophical and political controversies. A number of dualities are evident: the individual versus society; past versus future; intellect versus whole person; permanence versus change, and so on. Methods may be promoted for philosophical or political reasons rather than for their inherent educative value. The politics of education can polarize methods. Government support for educational reform tends to be forthcoming if a crisis is perceived, such as a need to get "back to basics" or to stop "stifling creativity," resulting in oscillations in promoted methods. It is ironical that curricular innovations in language teaching tend to adopt a monotheistic approach by promoting a fashionable teaching method and demonizing others, while there exists a pantheon of methods derived from theory and/or practice that could usefully contribute to the teaching and learning process.

Also at the planned curriculum level are published resources – textbooks and other educational media. Publishers promote a particular method for a number of reasons. In education systems that maintain a degree of control over the content of resources (for example, those with a government committee that vets materials to ensure that the content is suitable and that there is adequate coverage of the set syllabus), publishers will generally follow the method that is explicitly or implicitly promoted in official curriculum documents. Another reason might be that the publisher wants to be seen as being at the cutting edge, pioneering a new trend, or at least in line with current fashions. A third motivation is market forces – providing the end-user (who might be the teacher or the learner) with the resources for them to teach or learn according to their preferred method, which might or might not be in harmony with the officially promoted method. Technology may also dictate the selection of method. A lack of alternative resources to the book helps to encourage the primacy of reading skills and those methods, such as the grammar-translation method, that are reading-oriented. Audio-lingualism benefited from the availability of technological advances, such as tape recorders and filmstrip projectors, and itself gave rise to the extensive use of language laboratories (which once installed at considerable expense were difficult to remove, thus contributing to the enduring promotion of the method). The growing popularity of personal computers has resulted in the development of various computer-assisted language learning methods that are delimited by the possibilities of the available hardware and software. Textbooks and other resources might also have an implicit or explicit political agenda (Apple & Christian-Smith, 1991) or convey social, moral, or cultural messages that were not originally part of the planned curriculum.

There is often slippage between the planned, enacted, and experienced curriculum (Marsh & Willis, 1995). Curriculum enactment often involves a process of adaptation as teachers take account of the chalkface realities that they face. Morris (1996) identifies several factors that are powerful influences on teachers' pedagogical choices, which may or may not be in harmony with the method promoted in the intended curriculum. These influences include the available resources; physical and logistical constraints; the desire to maintain control of a class; the demands of public examinations (and the expectations of stakeholders, such as learners, their families, the local community, educational authorities and colleagues, in this regard); the prevailing culture of the subject; the ethos of the school (or whatever the educational setting might be); teacher isolation in settings that do not offer a supportive environment for handling the challenges of methodological change; and career factors – for example, whether the promotion system rewards or discourages teachers who experiment with innovative teaching methods. In language education, another influence on teachers' pedagogy is their own language competence. Those who are weak in the target language may tend to use the mother tongue to compensate. Similarly – and this is a result of the large-scale employment of native-speaking teachers – those who do not have a high degree of competence in the learners' mother tongue may prefer to select features of the direct method. In both cases, the reasons for choosing the particular approaches might not be for deeply held educational convictions on the part of the teachers. As a result, it is unsurprising that there is "little evidence that methods are realised at the level of classroom action in the ways intended by their creators" (Nunan, 1991, p. 3). How learners experience the various methods depends on a host of factors, including intelligence, aptitude, personality, motivation and attitudes, learner preferences, learner beliefs, age of acquisition, and the nature of the activity (Lightbown & Spada, 2001). The complexity of classroom realities virtually renders invalid any "one-size-fits-all" approach to method selection.

24.4   Methods as Sociocultural Artifacts

As well as reflecting contemporary theoretical ideas and practices in language learning, language teaching methods are sociocultural artifacts. Rowlinson (1994, p. 7) argues that

> What is taught and how it is taught is a product of [the ideas of the time], as well as of the conditions in which it is to be taught. It is society that determines the content of education, in the light of the dominant philosophy and (more recently) scientific concept. Many, perhaps most, new approaches are rediscoveries of old methods neglected and left in the shade, now re-illuminated by the light of social need. Language teaching, like all other teaching, reflects the temper of the times.

In this section, the linkages between espoused methods, curriculum orientation, and society are investigated with particular reference to the English language curriculum in the People's Republic of China. There are two main reasons for selecting English language teaching in China. The country is on the expanding circle of English-speaking nations, using Kachru's (1985) classification of the "inner" (core), "outer," and "expanding" (peripheral) circles, and offers a non-Eurocentric perspective. Second, China has a very long history of educational thought that has differed in emphasis from western traditions (Marton, 2000).

The predominant English language teaching method in China before and immediately after the Communist revolution in 1949 was the grammar-translation method (Tang, 1983; Dzau, 1990; Penner, 1991; Adamson & Morris, 1997). The method was promoted in the official secondary school curriculum and widely implemented in the classroom at secondary and tertiary levels. Intensive reading was a common component in the curriculum of institutions of higher education. The grammar-translation method was deemed suitable for China in the 1950s for several reasons. First, although it had been introduced into China by missionaries and other teachers from overseas, it resembles indigenous methods for teaching and learning Chinese (Ford, 1988; Dzau, 1990) in that the stress is on word study and grammar, rote-learning is a key strategy, and texts embodying moral and or cultural values are used. The method has been widely used in public schools in Europe and is based on approaches to learning Ancient Greek and Latin that value these languages for the intellectual rigor and cultural initiation that they offer learners, rather than for their utility in daily life. Second, the emphasis on reading skills was apposite for the post-revolution era in China, when the state was allied with the Soviet Union in the face of anti-communist hostility from many English-speaking nations, since the main role ascribed to English was to gain access to scientific and technical knowledge through western journals (Ministry of Education, People's Republic of China, 1950). Third, the roles of the teacher, as transmitter of knowledge, and of the learners, as initiates into the academic discipline, prescribed by the grammar-translation method closely corresponded to the roles of teachers and learners in Chinese pedagogical traditions. The learning process that was promoted with the grammar-translation method was known as the Five Steps – review old materials, orient new materials, explain new materials, consolidate newly learned materials, give assignments (Penner, 1991). These Five Steps were derived from the work of a Soviet educator, I. A. Kairov, who had written an influential book on pedagogy that had been translated into Chinese. In the official secondary school textbooks, the sequence of the presentation of tenses was also informed by Soviet approaches to language learning.

The Sino-Soviet schism in the early 1960s resulted in China being more open to western ideas and collaboration, as the nation pursued economic rather than political goals. The Chinese authorities decided that economic modernization would require oral competence in the workforce as well as strong reading skills. A taskforce was set up to study foreign teaching methods, and this investigation led to experiments with the audiolingual method, which had been introduced to China by teachers from overseas. At that time, the audiolingual method had established a significant position in the international market, as it was easily packaged into commercial courses for self-study or classes, and its use of modern technology was appealing to teachers and learners who wished to feel that they were at the cutting edge. The method had grown in the USA from the need in World War II to train personnel rapidly in order to cope with military situations that would require foreign languages, such as questioning captured soldiers or administering displaced persons. The language drills developed for this purpose were then allied to Skinner's work on Behaviorism with animals. Once again, the choice of this method was seen as appropriate for China as learning through repetition was similar to common approaches to learning Chinese characters.

The social upheaval of the Great Proletarian Cultural Revolution, 1966–76, again turned the English language curriculum into a predominantly political propaganda tool, but with distinct regional variations. In Beijing, Shanghai, and Guangzhou, textbooks from this time continue to reflect a blend of the grammar-translation and audiolingual methods, as these major cities still engaged in international trade, especially after President Nixon's visit to China in 1972 ushered in a degree of détente. However, in the hinterland, which was closed to foreigners, the textbooks reverted to political propaganda using the grammar-translation method, as this method lends itself readily to transmissive modes of teaching, and the method was more suited to the teaching styles of the available teachers, most of whom would not have had much exposure to spoken English.

When China embarked upon another economic modernization drive in 1978, with an Open Door policy to encourage foreign investment, the emphasis was placed on communicative goals. The official English language curriculum for secondary schools issued in 1983 incorporated a Functional-Notional syllabus, which was a recent trend in foreign language curriculum design. The Functional-Notional syllabus originated in a project sponsored by the Council of Europe to establish a threshold level outlining the basic linguistic requirements for language learners in common situations (van Ek, 1975). This approach suited China's need to train interpreters for international trade and tourism, and to prepare scholars to travel overseas for further studies. In the 1990s, the secondary school syllabus promoted the Five Steps variant of the P-P-P approach to teaching and learning (which had strong similarities to Kairov's Five Steps and was therefore consonant with the experiences of many teachers in China). The choice of this approach was the result of interaction between the curriculum developers and a foreign publisher, with the latter being well versed in the P-P-P approach, as it was popular in textbook series for the international market at that time. When reforming the English language curriculum for secondary schools in 1993, the Ministry of Education openly acknowledged the limitations of methodology by urging teachers to use the officially espoused Five Steps as far as possible, but to feel free to amend their approaches to suit the particular teaching context. In the most recent curriculum initiative in the secondary school curriculum, task-based learning is promoted. The rationale is partly frustration with the limitations of the Five Steps approach, with the tendency of its practitioners to focus on the mastery of discrete linguistic components, and partly to follow the trends in China toward whole-person education. This matches the rationale for task-based learning elsewhere, particularly in post-industrial societies. The rapidity of change brought about by globalization and modern technology makes the planning of future human capital needs very difficult. Vocational training for particular careers is increasingly replaced by a focus on more generic skills and the ability to cope with change. Task-based learning, it is believed, can be tailored to cater for individual needs, interests, and abilities in this regard, and learning through the target language can assist whole-person development.

What emerges from the historical overview is not only the endurance of long-standing indigenous methods – which are characterized by their focus on literary texts, grammatical parsing, rote-learning of passages, and memorization of vocabulary, spelling and grammatical paradigms – but also the tendency of Chinese educators to graft foreign ideas (such as Kairov's Five Steps, Audio-lingualism, or the Functional/Notional Approach) to these methods. It suggests that methods only cross-cultural boundaries easily if they can be appropriated in a form consistent with the values and beliefs of the community adopting and adapting the methods. The values and beliefs might shift in emphasis over time (as China's policies moved from a political to an economic orientation), which will engender a reassessment of the appropriated methods. The overview also indicates that promoted methods are mirrors of the contemporary sociocultural climate and of the priorities of the major stakeholders.

24.5   Beyond Methods

Nunan (1991, p. 3) has strong reservations about the value of methods:

> Despite their diversity, all methods have one thing in common. They all assume that there is a single set of principles which will determine whether or not learning will take place. Thus they all propose a single set of precepts for teacher and learner classroom behavior, and assert that if these principles are faithfully followed, they will result in learning for all. Unfortunately, little evidence has been forthcoming to support one approach rather than another, or to suggest that it is the method rather than some other variable which caused learning to occur.

In fact, world-weary cynicism from teachers often greets the promotion of new methods by curriculum reformers. When researching teachers' understandings of task-based learning in a Hong Kong primary school, I was told by one English language teacher that she half-heartedly embraced the innovation, as she found the learners were rapidly bored with the same approach, "but a task a day keeps the inspector away." So why has methodology failed to provide a clear set of precepts to language teachers? One reason is that language and education are both highly complex phenomena riven with tensions that defy an all-embracing theory. As Ellis (1994, p. 15) remarks, "Second language acquisition is a complex, multifaceted phenomenon and it is not surprising that it has come to mean different things to different people." The purposes of second language learning are also diverse – people may need to acquire knowledge of, about, and/or through a second language. All this makes it very difficult for the proponents of a method to claim that it will suit all learning styles and purposes, although curriculum reform is often couched in terms that castigate previous practices as "traditional," "teacher-centered," or other watchwords of contemporary pedagogical incorrectness.

Teachers' cynicism reveals their frustration that methods – even methods as widely conceived as task-based learning – fail to take into account the totality of learning contexts, which are embedded in macro-, meso-, and micro-sociocultural conditions that defy the generalizations that lie behind the promotion of particular methods. Also, systemic pressures, such as examination changes or school inspections, may bring about superficial adjustments to a teacher's pedagogy, but many teachers resent being asked or forced to discard beliefs about methods that they have acquired through experience at the chalkface. This resistance has been magnified by the regularity of reforms, many of which are dismissive of methods that were formerly promoted with great vigor by the same stakeholders, and by a shift toward critical interrogation of established practices that is a feature of postmodernist approaches to academic inquiry. Language teaching methodology has been critiqued to the point where its value as a central support for teachers' pedagogy has been queried. Stern (1992, p. 277) observes: "It is particularly important that in the development of a policy for teaching procedures we learn to operate with flexible sets of concepts which embody any useful lessons we can draw from the history of language teaching but which do not perpetuate the rigidities and dogmatic narrowness of the earlier methods concept."

The inability of methodology to cater for the diverse contexts in which second or foreign languages are learnt has given rise to attention in the literature to the different domains of learning, recognizing the formal and unnaturalistic characteristics of most language education settings and attempting to understand how second language learning takes place in such settings. This has been accompanied by an emphasis on the teacher as mediator of learning experiences, as reflective practitioner, as action researcher, and as eclecticist. These ascribed roles are not new (a perusal of "The Analects" reveals that Confucius articulated and demonstrated all these qualities), but they are a product of the times in which language teaching has assumed great importance in the trends toward economic globalization. The teaching of English in particular has been boosted by its status as an international language, but there is concern in many quarters about the concomitant negative effects of linguistic and cultural imperialism, and, as Canagarajah notes (1999, p. 3): "[t]he realization that education may involve the propagation of knowledges and ideologies held by dominant social groups has inspired a critical orientation to pedagogical paradigms." The goals of critical pedagogy are to ensure, at least, the appropriateness of methods that are selected for use in a given setting, and more radically – adopting a Social Reconstructionist paradigm – to provide a corrective toward social equality.

So does this disaffection sound the death-knell for methodology? The answer is surely "no," for just as the current sociocultural climate has produced the diminished role and status of rigid methodology in many – but by no means all – educational settings, methods are still useful props for teachers in constructing their own pedagogy. Some educationalists suggest that teachers' pedagogy should be comprised solely of methods, carefully selected to match the needs of the context in which they shall be employed. For example, Rivers (1981, p. 55) describes teachers using a principled eclectic approach as trying

> to absorb the best techniques of all the well-known language-teaching methods into their classroom procedures, using them for purposes for which they are most appropriate. True eclecticists, as distinguished from drifters who adopt new techniques cumulatively and purposelessly ... adapt their methods to the changing objectives of the day and to the types of students who pass through their classes. They gradually evolve a method which suits their personality. To be successful, an eclectic teacher needs to be imaginative, energetic, and willing to experiment. With so much to draw from, no eclecticist need lack for ideas for keeping lessons varied and interesting.

Kumaravadivelu (1994) argues that eclectic use of existing methods is not enough, as methods cannot take account of classroom realities. Instead, teachers need to move to a "postmethod" condition, in which they act as principled pragmatists, shaping the classroom learning through informed teaching and critical reflection. This classroom-centered pedagogy can involve selected borrowing from existing methods, but also involves the teachers in constructing creative solutions to address the issues that they face in their daily work. To assist teachers to develop a systematic, coherent, and relevant pedagogy, Kumaravadivelu outlines ten macro-strategies for teachers to employ, in order to reconcile the theoretical insights of methods (which are usually generated and promoted at the center of power) with the realities of the disempowered periphery:

1   *Maximize learning opportunities* by taking account of the local context and specific needs, interests, and abilities of all the learners.
2   *Facilitate negotiated interaction* by actively involving all learners in classroom discourse.
3   *Minimize perceptual mismatches* by closing the gap between the implemented and the experienced curriculum.
4   *Activate intuitive heuristics* by encouraging learners to make educated guesses in inferring grammatical rules.
5   *Foster language awareness* by raising the learners' sensitivity to language and its role in human life.
6   *Contextualize linguistic input* in order to provide essential pragmatic clues to meaning.
7   *Integrate language skills* as they are interrelated and mutually reinforcing.
8   *Promote learner autonomy* by helping learners to understand and utilize effective learning strategies.
9   *Raise cultural consciousness* by valuing the contributions of learners as cultural informants.
10 *Ensure social relevance* by making learners aware of the social, political, economic, and educational environment in which language learning takes place.

Kumaravadivelu's framework itself can be critiqued as a theoretical construct, as it is underpinned by specific views of language and language education; and as a sociocultural artifact, as it reflects social and educational values, and it might not be applicable in all contexts – particularly those in which a teacher's scope for autonomous decision-making is constrained by systemic and other factors. Although both principled eclecticism and pragmatism offer pedagogical strategies to teachers to respond to particular circumstances, the need for autonomy to employ these strategies is often in tension with systemic forces (such as the prescribed syllabus or the focus of examinations), with the design of available resources, and with many teachers' limited access to relevant knowledge on which they might base their informed professional decisions. Nonetheless, by seeking a flexible alternative to rigid methods to help teachers address the challenges of the language education classroom, these ideas do recognize the real concerns of teachers that underlie the cynicism that greets the promotion of new methodological innovations.

24.6   Conclusion

This chapter has examined language education methodology from different perspectives and has identified the shortcomings of the field. Methods are developed from diverse origins; reflect the contemporary context from which they emerged; are promoted for political, social, and economic as well as educational reasons; and have limited practical application in specific environments. The attention of applied linguistics is increasingly turning to the teacher and the learner, and the ways in which they can operate effectively in their educational context, instead of offering generalized, pre-packaged solutions in the shape of teaching materials and strategies.

In postmethod contexts, applied linguistics can make a telling contribution to the development of teachers' principled eclecticism or pragmatism by providing the principles that lay the foundations of a teacher's informed choice. Another challenge for applied linguistics is to advocate that teachers are provided with the pedagogical space and support for them to operate as principled eclecticists or pragmatists. Given the powerful political and economic forces that are brought to bear on education systems, and which tend to restrict and confine teachers, this challenge is significant.

See also 20 SECOND LANGUAGE LEARNING, 21 INDIVIDUAL DIFFERENCES IN SECOND LANGUAGE LEARNING, 22 SOCIAL INFLUENCES ON LANGUAGE LEARNING, 26 LANGUAGE TEACHER EDUCATION.

REFERENCES

Adamson, B. & Morris, P. (1997) The English language curriculum in the People's Republic of China. *Comparative Education Review*, 41(1), 3–26.

Apple, M. & Christian-Smith, L. K. (1991) The politics of the textbook. In M. Apple & L. K. Christian-Smith (eds.), *The politics of the textbook* (pp. 1–21). London: Routledge.

Bolton, K. (2002) Chinese Englishes: from Canton jargon to global English. *World Englishes*, 21(2), 181–99.

Bygate, M., Skehan, P., & Swain, M. (2001) Introduction. In M. Bygate, P. Skehan, & M. Swain (eds.), *Researching pedagogical tasks: second language learning, teaching and testing* (pp. 1–20). Harlow: Longman.

Canagarajah, A. S. (1999) *Resisting linguistic imperialism in English teaching.* Oxford: Oxford University Press.

Carroll, J. B. (1965) The contribution of psychological theory and educational research to the teaching of foreign languages. *Modern Language Journal*, 49, 273–81.

Chomsky, N. (1965) *Aspects of the theory of syntax.* Cambridge, MA: MIT Press.

Clark, J. L. (1987) *Curriculum renewal in school foreign language learning.* Oxford: Oxford University Press.

Dufficy, P. (2000) Through the lens of scaffolding: genre pedagogy and talk in multilingual classrooms. *TESOL in Context*, 10(1), 4–10.

Dzau, Y. F. (1990) Historical background. In Dzau, Y. F. (ed.), *English in*

China (pp. 11–39). Hong Kong: API Press.

Ellis, R. (1994) *The study of second language acquisition*. Oxford: Oxford University Press.

Ellis, R. (2001) Second language acquisition: research and language pedagogy. In C. N. Candlin & N. Mercer (eds.), *English language teaching in its social context* (pp. 44–74). London: Routledge.

Ford, D. J. (1988) *The twain shall meet: the current study of English in China*. Jefferson: McFarland & Company.

Freire, P. (1970) *Pedagogy of the oppressed*. New York: The Continuum Publishing Company.

Gouin, F. (1892) *The art of teaching and studying languages* (trans. H. Swan & V. Bétis). London: George Philip & Son (Original work published 1880.)

Halliday, M. A. K. (1973) *Explorations in the functions of language*. London: Edward Arnold.

Honey, J. (1997) *Language is power: the story of standard English and its enemies*. London: Faber & Faber.

Hong Kong Government Education Department (1994) *General introduction to target oriented curriculum*. Hong Kong: Government Printer.

Howatt, A. P. R. (1984) *A history of English language teaching*. Oxford: Oxford University Press.

Hubbard, P., Jones, H., Thornton, B., & Wheeler, R. (1983) *A training course for TEFL*. Oxford: Oxford University Press.

Jespersen, O. (1904) *How to teach a foreign language*. London: George Allen & Unwin.

Kachru, B. (1985) Standards, codification and sociolinguistic realism: the English language in the outer circle. In R. Quirk & H. G. Widdowson (eds.), *English in the world: teaching and learning the language and literatures* (pp. 11–30). Cambridge: Cambridge

University Press in association with The British Council.

Knight, P. (2001) The development of EFL methodology. In C. N. Candlin & N. Mercer (eds.), *English language teaching in its social context* (pp. 147–66). London: Routledge.

Krashen, S. D. (1987) *Principles and practice in second language acquisition*. Englewood Cliffs, NJ: Prentice-Hall.

Kress, G. (1993) Genre as social process. In B. Cope & M. Kalantzis (eds.), *The powers of literacy: a genre approach to teaching writing* (pp. 22–37). London: The Falmer Press.

Kumaravadivelu, B. (1994) The postmethod condition: (e)merging strategies for second/foreign language teaching. *TESOL Quarterly*, 28(1), 27–48.

Lantolf, J. P. (2000) Introducing sociocultural theory. In J. P. Lantolf (ed.), *Sociocultural theory and second language learning* (pp. 1–26). Oxford: Oxford University Press.

Larsen-Freeman, D. (1986) *Techniques and principles in language teaching*. Oxford: Oxford University Press.

Lightbown, P. & Spada, N. (2001) Factors affecting second language learning. In C. N. Candlin & N. Mercer (eds.), *English language teaching in its social context* (pp. 28–43). London: Routledge.

Marsh, C. & Willis, G. (1995) *Curriculum: alternative approaches, ongoing issues*. Englewood Cliffs, NJ: Merrill.

Martin, J. R. (1993) A contextual theory of language. In B. Cope & M. Kalantzis (eds.), *The powers of literacy: a genre approach to teaching writing* (pp. 116–36). London: The Falmer Press.

Martin, J. R. & Rothery, J. (1993) Grammar: making meaning in writing. In B. Cope & M. Kalantzis (eds.), *The powers of literacy: a genre approach to teaching writing* (pp. 137–53). London: The Falmer Press.

Marton, F. (2000) Afterword – the lived curriculum. In B. Adamson, T. Kwan,

& K. K. Chan (eds.), *Changing the curriculum: the impact of reform on primary schooling in Hong Kong* (pp. 277–92). Hong Kong: Hong Kong University Press.

Ministry of Education, People's Republic of China (1950) *Gaodeng waiyu jiaoxue jihua (cao'an)* [Draft foreign language teaching plan for tertiary institutions]. Beijing: Ministry of Education.

Mitchell, R. (1994) The communicative approach to language teaching: an introduction. In A. Swarbrick (ed.), *Teaching modern languages* (pp. 33–42). London: The Open University.

Morris, P. (1996) *The Hong Kong school curriculum: development, issues and policies*. Hong Kong: Hong Kong University Press.

Nunan, D. (1991) *Language teaching methodology*. New York: Prentice-Hall.

Penner, J. (1991) *Opening the door with the English key – foreign involvement in EFL teacher education in China: an annotated bibliography*. Vancouver: University of British Columbia (mimeograph).

Richards, J. C. (2001) Beyond methods. In C. N. Candlin & N. Mercer (eds.), *English language teaching in its social context* (pp. 167–79). London: Routledge.

Richards, J. C. & Rodgers, T. S. (1986) *Approaches and methods in language teaching*. Cambridge: Cambridge University Press.

Richards, J. C. & Rodgers, T. S. (2001) *Approaches and methods in language*

teaching (2nd edn.). Cambridge: Cambridge University Press.

Rivers, W. M. (1964) *The psychologist and the foreign-language teacher*. Chicago: The University of Chicago Press.

Rivers, W. M. (1981) *Teaching foreign-language skills* (2nd edn.). Chicago: The University of Chicago Press.

Roberts, J. T. (1999) *Two French language teaching reformers reassessed: Claude Marcel and François Gouin*. Lewiston, NY: Edwin Mellen Press.

Rowlinson, W. (1994) The historical ball and chain. In A. Swarbrick (ed.), *Teaching modern languages* (pp. 7–17). London: The Open University.

Skinner, B. F. (1957) *Verbal behavior*. New York: Appleton-Century-Crofts.

Stern, H. H. (1970) *Perspectives on second language teaching*. Toronto: Ontario Institute for Studies in Education.

Stern, H. H. (1992) *Issues and options in language teaching*. Posthumous edition edited by P. Allen & B. Harley. Oxford: Oxford University Press.

Tang Lixing (1983) *TEFL in China: methods and techniques*. Shanghai: Shanghai Foreign Language Education Press.

Titone, R. (1968) *Teaching foreign languages: an historical sketch*. Washington, DC: Georgetown University Press.

van Ek, J. A. (1975) *The threshold level in a European unit/credit system for modern language learning for adults*. Strasbourg: Council of Europe.

FURTHER READING

Asher, J. (1965) The strategy of the total physical response: an application to learning Russian. *International Review of Linguistics*, 3, 291–300.

Brown, H. D. (1994) *Principles of language learning and teaching* (3rd edn.).

Englewood Cliffs, NJ: Prentice-Hall Regents.

Crookes, G. & Gass, S. (eds.) (1993) *Tasks and language learning: integrating theory and practice*. Clevedon, UK: Multilingual Matters.

Curran, Charles (1972) *Counseling-learning: a whole-person model for education*. New York: Grune & Stratton.

Curran, Charles A. C. (1976) *Counseling-learning in second languages*. Apple River, IL: Apple River Press.

Ellis, R. (1990) *Instructed second language acquisition: learning in the classroom*. Oxford: Blackwell.

Gattegno, C. (1972) *Teaching foreign languages in schools: the Silent Way* (2nd edn.). New York: Educational Solutions.

Holliday, A. (1994) *Appropriate methodology and social context*. Cambridge: Cambridge University Press.

Lozanov, Georgi (1978) *Suggestology and outlines of suggestopedy*. New York: Gordon & Breach.

McDonough, J. & Shaw, C. (1993) *Materials and methods in ELT: a teacher's guide*. Oxford: Blackwell.

Nunan, D. & Lamb, C. (1996) *The self-directed teacher: managing the learning process*. Cambridge: Cambridge University Press.

Pennycook, A. (1994) *The cultural politics of English as an international language*. London: Longman.

Phillipson, R. (1992) *Linguistic imperialism*. Oxford: Oxford University Press.

Prabhu, N. S. (1987) *Second language pedagogy*. Oxford: Oxford University Press.

Wilkins, D. A. (1976) *Notional syllabuses*. Oxford: Oxford University Press.

25 Computer Assisted Language Learning (CALL)

PAUL GRUBA

25.1 Introduction

Simply stated, Computer Assisted Language Learning (CALL) can be defined as "the search for and study of applications of the computer in language teaching and learning" (Levy, 1997, p. 1). Although earlier practitioners relied on acronyms such as CAI (computer-aided instruction), CAL (computer-assisted learning), CELL (computer-enhanced language learning) and TELL (technology-enhanced language learning), CALL is now widely regarded as the central acronym to refer to studies concerned with second language and computer technology. Other terms, however, continue to be introduced to focus on particular uses of the computer. For example, individual learning through adaptive computer systems, promoted as intelligent CALL (ICALL), and web-enhanced language learning (WELL), is used by educators who promote Internet-based activities. A European Community group has formed under the banner ICT4LT (Information and Communication Technologies for Language Teachers). For their part, Warschauer and Kern (2000) prefer to use the term NBLT (net-worked-based language teaching) to encompass a broader range of the inter-connected computers; whereas Debski (2000) has coined the term PrOCALL (project-oriented CALL) to highlight large-scale collaborative activities. Chapelle (2001), on the other hand, employs the acronym CASLA (computer applications in second language acquisition) to serve as an umbrella phrase that pulls together research in CALL, computer-assisted language assessment (CALT), and computer-assisted second language acquisition research (CASLR).

Overall, the main objective of CALL is to "improve the learning capacity of those who are being taught a language through computerized means" (Cameron, 1999a, p. 2). Note that such a definition focuses particularly on language learning, not language teaching, while at the same time the use of the computer forces reconsideration of traditional stakeholder roles: learners, teachers, and researchers have each had to adapt to the demands and opportunities afforded by a range of new technologies. With the advent of networked computers and the Internet, in particular, learners are increasingly called upon to design and execute their own computer-based activities.

The growing availability of Internet access has prompted CALL instructors to move away from stand-alone workstations and more toward networked computers (e.g., Debski, 2000; Warschauer & Kern, 2000). Socio-collaborative approaches to teaching and learning are replacing communicative ones, and debates about pedagogy now center on aspects of learner autonomy, collaborative project design, and appropriate assessment practices. CALL educators are also being challenged to keep pace with rapid change and innovation to meet concerns about evolving technologies, professional development, and rising student levels of electronic literacy. Issues of power, access, and equity are also gaining wider prominence and debate in the CALL community (Warschauer, 1998).

Much of the current debate amongst CALL researchers concerns the establishment of a coherent agenda for research. The lack of a clear theoretical framework has long dogged the maturation of CALL (Levy, 1997) and investigators are now seeking to "take stock" of what has been accomplished (Cameron, 1999a, p. 9) in order to strengthen methodological approaches and define priorities for investigation (Chapelle, 1997; Motteram, 1999; Salaberry, 1999).

To put current issues of CALL into perspective, this chapter begins with an attempt to locate the disciplinary influences on this emerging area of study. A history of CALL, roughly divided into Structural, Communicative, and Integrative stages, is then presented. In turn, the chapter then examines the roles of computers, students, instructors, and researchers in CALL, and concludes with a critical discussion of recent developments.

25.2   Overview of CALL

As with the broader field of applied linguistics, CALL can be located at the crossroads of a number of disciplines. Levy (1997, pp. 47–75) regards the studies in psychology, artificial intelligence, computational linguistics, instructional technology, and human–computer interaction as primary influences. Although Levy is aware that the area can be framed somewhat differently, he draws on these five cross-disciplinary fields to as a way to structure the knowledge base. Studies in psychology, for example, contribute insights about programmed instruction and cognition as they relate to CALL; research in computational linguistics informs work to do with machine translation, natural language processing, and concordance.

In her extensive review, Chapelle (2001, pp. 27–43) places CALL within six computer-related sub-disciplines: educational technology, computer-supported collaborative learning (CSCL), artificial intelligence, computational linguistics, corpus linguistics, and computer-assisted assessment. Unlike Levy (1997), Chapelle argues that studies in human–computer interaction have had little impact on CALL and sees educational technology as a much more significant influence. In her view, the area became distinct in the mid-1980s with the formation of professional organizations and journals specifically devoted to the emerging field. According to Chapelle (2001, p. 15), the Australian journal *On-CALL* appeared in the mid-1980s. Across the Atlantic, *ReCALL* first appeared in 1988, and this was followed by *Computer Assisted Language Learning: An International Journal* two years later. In North America, *CÆLL Journal* specifically targeted computer use in English as a second language (ESL) contexts from its release in 1989. Other journals that helped frame CALL research include *The CALICO Journal* and *IALL Journal of Language Learning Technologies*. Annual professional conferences, most prominently *Euro-CALL*, have also helped to solidify the emerging field.

25.2.1 A brief history

Although Delcloque (2000) has embarked on an ongoing project to detail the history of CALL, sections of three books (Ahmad et al., 1985, pp. 27–44; Chapelle, 2001, pp. 1–26; Levy, 1997, pp. 13–46) provide extensive accounts of developments in the area. Ahmad et al. (1985) consider the work conducted in the United States and Britain in the years 1965–85. In one early project carried out at Stanford University, instructors created self-instructional materials for Slavic language learning and delivered them via a mainframe computer. Another group at the University of Illinois developed a system named Programmed Logic for Automated Teaching Operations (PLATO), in which teachers were able to write a Russian-English translation course. The computer program was able to provide both drills and marking for student work as well as an authoring component for instructors. The PLATO system later expanded to include a number of foreign languages and offered them in increasingly technically sophisticated ways. Although high costs prohibited their widespread use, mainframe computer applications throughout the 1960s and 1970s were developed to the point of interactive features to help students read specialist scientific texts. With the arrival of the "microcomputer boom" in the late 1970s, however, expensive mainframe computer usage was phased out. Developers and instructors alike began to shift their attention to personal computers.

From the early 1980s, increased computer availability fuelled a growing interest in CALL. Teachers were able to write or modify computer applications to suit specific language learning situations; as a result, more and more students were exposed to them both at home and on campus. In his review, Levy (1997) highlights the Time-Shared, Interactive, Computer Controlled Information Television (TICCIT) project initiated at Brigham Young University in 1971 as one of the first examples of multimedia-based instruction. Here, computers had the capacity to integrate text, audio, and video that could be controlled by the learner. The TICCIT system was based on an explicit theory of instructional design that allowed instructors to add content but, unfortunately, not to decide how to teach with the now programmed materials.

Levy (1997) also singles out the Athena Language Learning Project based at Massachusetts Institute of Technology (MIT). In this project, communicative approaches to language teaching underpinned the development of a multimedia authoring environment and an integration of techniques based on research in artificial intelligence. One significant part of this project was the full integration of language teachers in the development process; that is, project managers promoted teaching and learning with computers above software design and instructional theory.

As personal computers became easier to use, *Storyboard* and *HyperCard* became influential authoring programs during the early 1980s. Levy pays particular attention to teacher-programmers as they began to work out their own CALL practices. Materials were often designed as single activities and included simulation, text reconstruction, gap-filling, speed-reading, and vocabulary games (Levy, 1997, p. 23). By the end of the 1980s, CALL practitioners had produced a substantial body of work that focused mainly on pedagogical computer use. Critics at the time, however, began to question the effectiveness of such practices and suggested a much deeper examination of CALL activities and materials (Dunkel, 1991, pp. 24–5).

From the start of the 1990s, teachers began to make greater use of networked computers, and by mid-decade the explosive growth of the Internet prompted CALL educators to increasingly adopt socio-collaborative modes of learning. In her recent overview, Chapelle (2001) notes that Internet usage prompted not only a much greater access to resources, but also provided the motivation for developers to create sophisticated materials that would hopefully attract large audiences. Classroom-based CALL activities could include learner communities throughout the world through email, virtual environments, and shared domains. Pedagogical discussions of CALL have thus shifted to exploration of such communities and their use of collaborative activities (e.g., Debski & Levy, 1999; Warschauer & Kern, 1999) but, once again, research in this era was critiqued for its absence of a focused agenda (Chapelle, 1997). In the mid-1990s, an Australian national report found that "With minor exceptions, the application of technology in language teaching and learning has been fragmented, frequently idiosyncratic, topic oriented and largely based on distributive technologies" (Australian National Board of Employment, Education and Training, 1996, p. 195). On a similar note, Chapelle (2001, p. 175) concluded with that the twentieth century was "a time of idiosyncratic learning, quirky software development, and naive experimentation" for second language learning and computers.

25.2.2   Major theoretical perspectives

Trends in CALL roughly parallel those in other areas of applied linguistics. Starting with the structural and behaviorist models that manifested in audio-lingual approaches to language learning, CALL educators then explored aspects of communicative approaches to language learning. Socio-cognitive theories of instruction are now an integral part of CALL. Table 25.1 summarizes key aspects of CALL over 30 years. This table provides a way to organize

Table 25.1 Key aspects of theoretical perspectives in CALL

	Structural CALL (1970s–1980s)	Communicative CALL (1980s–1990s)	Integrative CALL (twenty-first century)
Role of the computer	Information carrier; as a "tutor"	Workstation; as a "pupil"	Unified information management system; as a "toolbox"
Technology focus	Materials delivery	Cognitive augmentation	Group orchestration
Theory of learning	Behaviorist	Information processing theory; cognitive constructivist learning	Sociocultural theories of learning
Model and process of instruction	Programmed instruction; assimilation	Interactive, discovery-based learning; interaction	Collaborative learning; "intra-action"
View of second language acquisition	Structural (a formal system)	Cognitive (a mentally constructed system)	Socio-cognitive (developed in social interaction)
Dominant approaches to second language teaching	Grammar-translation & audiolingual	Communicative language teaching	Content based; specific purposes
Learner status	Dependant	Independent	Collaborative
Principal use of computers in CALL	Drill and practice	Communicative exercises	Authentic discourse
Principal learning objective of CALL	Accuracy	And fluency	And agency
Primary research concern	Instructional efficacy, instructional competence	Instructional transfer, learner proficiency	Instruction as enacted practice, team "coficiency"

Source: Based on Warschauer (2000a), with Crook (1994), Koschmann (1996), Ullmer (1994)

the rather fluid categories that characterize the development of CALL. Practitioners in the era of structural CALL placed a strong emphasis on grammar and they employed the use of mainframe computers to help students gain accuracy in their language usage. Grammar-translation and audio-lingual methods, grounded in behaviorism, went hand in hand with programmed instruction. Students were able to repeat drills with the seemingly tireless and patient computer-as-tutor, and instruction appeared to be at an upmost efficiency. Crook (1994, p. 12) sees the tutorial metaphor as a central preoccupation in the "computer-assisted instruction" (CAI) tradition of educational technologies. The goals of CAI developers were centered on making responses uniquely fitted to individual learner needs and delivering helpful, customized feedback through "intelligent tutorial systems."

Crook (1994, pp. 13–16) examines the tutorial role of computers and the popularity of drill exercises. First, he notes, computers never truly became "intelligent" because of the inherent difficulties in constructing algorithms that could sensitively respond to learner profiles. At the time, the sophisticated hardware needed to attempt this goal was available almost exclusively in military and industrial training contexts. Nonetheless, Crook writes, tutorial drills have a continued appeal to educators for two reasons: (1) teachers uncomfortable with innovative uses in technology "may well adopt the comparatively easy solution of focusing their commitment on straightforward, self contained programs" (p. 14); and (2) many instructors feel that repeated exposures to certain practices and structures are beneficial to students.

Crook's observations can be applied to the CALL context. Indeed, Decoo and Colpaert (1999, p. 56) point out that there is "a mass of learners who are deeply embedded in fixed educational structures and who are asking for and welcoming effective forms of tutorial CALL matching those structures." They urge researchers to re-evaluate the role of the computer in drills and practice for classroom activities which are time-consuming and repetitive.

Richmond (1999) argues that a true picture of CALL resembles a split between "dedicated" and "integrated" streams. Much more widely practiced, "dedicated CALL" largely consists of using stand-alone programs to drill and practice items of grammar, vocabulary, and syntax. Richmond argues that the complexity and costs of software, as well as a host of technical problems, has shied teachers and students away from more integrated uses of the computer. The popularity of "dedicated CALL" has prompted researchers to continue to develop increasingly sophisticated tutorial applications that aid vocabulary acquisition, improve the writing in character-based languages, and build sustained interactions with target materials (e.g., Hamburger, Schoelles, & Reeder, 1999). Over the long term, Richmond predicts, the increased ease of software use and greater access to networks will bring the "dedicated" practices closer to "integrated" ones.

Following an overall shift in teaching methods aligned with cognitive constructivist theories of learning, practices in communicative CALL sought to help students develop their own mental models through use of the target language. Exercises were designed to guide meaningful peer interactions and promote fluency. Esling (1991), created a series of task-based CALL activities to promote productive email exchanges between ESL students at two Canadian universities. In these activities, for example, students were directed to describe photographs, give directions, or express an opinion. The role of computer software was to help deliver visual materials for description, process word documents, or provide interactive simulations. In another project, Abraham and Liou (1991) studied the spoken language of learners at workstations to compare the talk elicited by different types of computer applications and to see if the talk was more useful and productive than would otherwise be the case in non-computer situations. In their conclusion, they report that the talk elicited by the different programs did not vary widely, nor was it significantly different than in non-computer situations.

Integrative CALL seeks to make full use of networked computers as a means to engage learners in meaningful, large-scale collaborative activities (Debski, 2000; Warschauer & Kern, 2000). Instructors promote close ties between learning processes, objectives, and a student ownership of the outcomes. As with mainstream computer-supported collaborative learning (e.g., Bonk & King, 1998; Koschmann, 1996; Land & Hannafin, 2000), meaningful interaction and authentic project work are highlighted. Authentic discourse provides the basis for learning material. Students are taught techniques in online publishing, and are urged to produce their own texts. Fostering learner *agency*, or "the satisfying power to take meaningful action and see the results of our own decisions and choices" (Murray, 1997, p. 126 cited in Warschauer, 2000b, p. 524), is a primary goal of integrative CALL. The key distinction between communicative CALL and integrative CALL is that, in the former, learner choice and self-management of activity are driven by task-based approaches to syllabus design. At its most liberal interpretation, a syllabus in integrative CALL simply represents a "dynamic blueprint" where learning occurs through "accidents" generated by projects (Barson, 1999). In contrast, a syllabus in communicative CALL is likely to be discrete and related to a set of curricular guidelines that have been defined in advance of learner needs (Corbel, 1999).

In practice, however, the realization of integrative CALL may lie beyond the realm of language learning institutions constrained by a lack of resources, embedded teaching practices, and large class sizes. Such is the case in adult migrant education centers in Australia, for example (Taylor & Corbel, 1998) or in educational centers in South Africa (Oberprieler, 1999). At such sites, students are generally directed to access online materials alone, teachers are not free to alter a syllabus based on established curriculum guidelines. Students may not have the means to make use of the Internet outside limited class times.

25.3   Key Areas: The Roles of Computers, Students, Teachers, and Researchers

Broadly speaking, CALL is made possible through an interdependent relationship among computers, students, and instructors. The use of computers, for example, influences the nature of student activities which in turn affects how teacher may set goals and construct the learning environment. The aim of this section is to provide a detailed examination of the roles computers, learners, and teachers play in CALL settings.

25.3.1   *Roles of the computers*

In the structural stage of CALL, educators characterized the computer as a "tutor" who patiently delivered repetitive drills. In this way the computer could engage the independent student in individualized, self-paced instruction through efficient materials delivery. Later, in communicative CALL, the computer was seen as a "pupil" that was trained to navigate through "microworlds" (Papert, 1980). Communicative CALL practitioners also used the computer to stimulate conversations amongst small groups of students who sat in front of it. In recent integrative CALL approaches, the computer acts like a "unified information manager" (Ullmer, 1994), that comes equipped with a host of applications, or a "toolbox," that stand ready to be used in the construction of projects. More and more, a computer environment can create a "social space" in which to conduct purposeful interactions through virtual reality (Toyoda & Harrison, 2002).

With the widespread use of computers in the 1980s, concern grew about their effectiveness (Kulik, Kulik, & Schwalb, 1986). Significantly, critics sought justification of claims that computers help to raise test scores and speed language acquisition (Dunkel, 1991) or otherwise promote cognitive augmentation through carefully designed materials (Clark & Sugrue, 1991). Such concerns were raised against a background of comparison studies which pitted computer-assisted instruction against other modes of learning and often concluded there was "no significant difference" between the types of presentations (Russell, 1999).

Although claims are still made that computers in education are "oversold and underused" (Cuban, 2001), many educators now see their use as an expected and necessary part of learning (Debski & Gruba, 1999; Pennington, 1999a). These days, the computer is likely to be seen in the "subservient role of tool in the service of the larger goals and contexts of instructional communities" (Meskill, 1999, p. 141). That is, most educators now downplay the centrality of computers and simply acknowledge their integrated use in classroom management, materials presentation, and learner interactions.

In light of studies which view motivation as a key factor in language learning success (for an extensive review, see Dörnyei, 2001), CALL practitioners have been keen to point out that computer environments themselves can motivate many student (Soo, 1999). According to Pennington (1996), learners gain motivation through computer use because they are less threatened and thus take more risks and are more spontaneous. With reference to computer-based writing, Pennington (1999a, p. 289) credits positive attitudes toward computing as a key factor in student motivation to produce high quality materials. Increased access to authentic materials, email usage, and collaborative activities have also been seen to spur student motivation to learn language (e.g., Biesenbach-Lucas & Weasenforth, 2001; Warschauer, 1995).

Despite a general enthusiasm for computers, student resistance to their use can potentially reduce motivation through activities which promote isolation, dull creativity, and otherwise contribute to learner frustrations (Lewis & Atzert, 2000).

One key role of computers is to deliver materials. Indeed, in structural CALL, efficient materials delivery was a prime focus of the technology. Sophisticated applications have been designed to adapt and fit individual learner needs. Materials in communicative CALL served as prompts for both discussion and practice. Increasingly, Internet access to foreign newspapers, specialized websites, and other forms of media has shifted a view of materials as authentic discourse. Specifically because they help make available such a wide range of authentic materials, Kramsch and Anderson (1999, p. 31) write that "computers seem to realize the dream of every language teacher – to bring the language and culture as close and as authentically as possible to students in the classroom." However, they remind us, even though digitized materials give the appearance of authenticity, such media reshape the context of language use. That is, it is important for the consumers of multimedia to remember that such materials create their own unique symbol system through the juxtaposition, selection, and filtering of complex aural and visual elements (Potter, 2001; Salomon, 1979).

Computers also permit the creation of electronic materials. Davies (1998) provides a succinct four-part overview of multimedia authoring packages for language teachers. In the first of his categories, he cites products which align with the "Keep it Simple and Stupid" school of design. The popularity of this approach rests with its relative ease of use. Secondly, an integrated approach using a full authoring suite can be utilized for materials production. A third approach is to use a multipurpose application and then later move and adapt materials into related computer environments. In his fourth "Generic CALL" category, Davies writes about the formation of a European Community project, known as MALTED (Multimedia Authoring for Language Tutors and Educational Development), that aims to create an authoring environment which specifically meets the requirements of language teachers. Participating project members are set to develop the means of authoring multimedia courseware that can be shared and revised according to the requirements of local contexts. By using an open framework, the project hopes to encourage contributions based on a range of instructional design approaches. Similar work is underway in the Information and Communications Technology for Language Teachers (ICT4LT) community.

Levy (1999a) pulls together theory, research, and evaluation throughout the process of CALL materials design. He singles out audience awareness, unbridled creativity, and a clear understanding of development tools as the most fundamental characteristics of good designers. From there, designers need to determine the focal use of an element and ground its intended use in either holistic or discrete language learning activities. At the same time, they must determine where their materials will sit along the computer as a tutor or as a unified information system continuum.

With reference to the broader CASLA agenda, Chapelle (2001) urges the production of software tools that are designed specifically for language acquisition use and research. Of course, such tools could also be productively applied to language teaching situations in order to provide an authentic educational experience to research participants. At present, Chapelle observes, there is no single tool that can perform functions such as task difficulty estimates and yet support a structure for learner models. Table 25.2 provides Chapelle's list of desired functions and their purposes.

As shown by its frequent mention in Table 25.2, the nature of technology-mediated tasks for language acquisition and assessment is a particular point of interest for CALL (Chapelle, 2001; Hoven, 1999a). The basic definition of pedagogical tasks is "a focused, well-defined activity, relatable to pedagogic decision making, which requires learners to use language, with an emphasis on meaning, to attain an objective, and which elicits data which may be the basis for research" (Bygate, Skehan, & Swain, 2001, p. 12).

Such a definition of tasks in computer environments, particularly in regard to integrative CALL, may well change. For example, as Driscoll (2000) points out, social constructivist approaches to instruction prefer that tasks not be "well-defined" so that learners themselves can work out how to meet the challenges of a particular "problem space." In Debski (2000), for example, it is argued that collaborative learners themselves need to negotiate what to do and how to complete activities. That is, task definition in and of itself is an opportunity for learning in an ill-defined domain. The optimal role of "objectives," too, may require consideration because they may change within the context of a group project. Authenticity must be re-examined as lines blur between the class-room and the world beyond (Chapelle, 1999). Further, future definition of technologically-mediated tasks may well need an explicit view of mode of presentation as a way to acknowledge the effects of medium on comprehension.

Significantly for CALL educators, computers have the potential to help students with special needs, for example, in their use of screen readers, Braille devices, or other assistive technologies. The goal of "web access initiative" projects is to make all objects available in "gracefully depreciating" forms so that however they are to be used, they are still accessible (LeLoup & Ponterio, 1997). Awareness about the provision and design of accessible materials, however, is very low amongst CALL practitioners. Discussions focused on

Table 25.2 Functions needed in CASLA software tools and their purposes

Software function	Purpose
Estimate task difficulty	Select appropriate level of task for intended learners Provide feedback for task development
Analyze learners' linguistic output	Assess task authenticity Assign point value and collect diagnostic data for language assessment Gather learner data for research
Analyze the language of objects (written text, audio, video)	Assess task authenticity Assess linguistic complexity of input
Support objects ordered in a database	Store examples of a variety of content and genres to be used directly or as models for language tasks
Gather process-oriented data	Assess participation in learning condition Assess learner characteristics in specific tasks
Support a structure for a learner model	Store learner data for intelligent tutoring, assessment Explore the nature of learner models for research
Author learning conditions	Develop tasks for instruction and research and operationalize SLA theory

Source: From Chapelle (2001, p. 171). Reproduced with the permission of Cambridge University Press and the author.

design issues (Levy, 1999a; Peterson, 2000) neglect to mention accessibility. Potentially, inattention to accessible materials design may prompt legal challenges. In the case of Australia, for example, Commonwealth legislation requires *anyone* who publishes on the Internet to ensure that resources are accessible (Nevile, 1999). Fortunately, the tools and the means for making the content accessible are improving.

One aspect of computer usage, however, is its potential to exacerbate existing differences in society (Warschauer, 2000b; 2002). The costs of buying, using, and maintaining computers also impacts upon how a language learning program is perceived. In this way, computers are for more than just learning: they shape the perception of the program and attract students eager to be seen using the latest technologies (Cuban, 2001).

25.3.2   *Roles of the learner*

In each of the three stages of CALL, the role of students changes in tandem with shifts in learning theory, the capabilities of computers, and instructional processes. In structural CALL, students were dependent on programs of instruction that efficiently delivered grammar and vocabulary materials. Communicative CALL practices sought to place learners in independent relationships with the computer, as students progressed through interactive work with applications. Within integrative CALL, students are expected to work collaboratively and utilize the computer as a "toolbox" for group project work. Increasing student familiarity with computers now challenges CALL educators to direct their use for the specific purposes of language learning (Chapelle, 2001). To better understand the relationship of students to the computer, CALL researchers have explored learner strategies, examined the status of learners, and begun to characterize the skills and practices required to work effectively in computer environments.

Generally, applied linguists hold a strong interest in learner strategies (Chamot, 2001). In CALL, this interest has been directed to looking at student behaviors regarding online reading, listening, speaking, and writing (Hegelheimer & Chapelle, 2000; Liou, 2000), particularly in regard to the comprehension of second language multimedia. Chun and Plass (1997) framed the key issues of "multimedia comprehension" based on studies of online reading and visual interpretation. Hoven (1999b), too, proposed a model for learners' listening and viewing skills in multimedia environments.

Based on transcripts of verbal report protocols of Australian learners of Japanese, Gruba (1999) created a framework for understanding second language digital video comprehension. He concluded that visual elements work in a number of ways that go beyond merely "supporting" verbal elements; they are better thought of as integral resources to comprehension whose influence shifts from primary to secondary importance as a listener develops a mature understanding of the videotext.

Though far from perfect, speech technologies for language learning are rapidly developing (Ehansi & Knodt, 1998; Goodwin-Jones, 2000a) as educators seek to make student learning more engaging within the computer environment. With an emphasis on pronunciation, Aist (1999) provides a solid outline of current developments in speech recognition software for language learning. Essentially, the student can interact through speech in three general ways. The first, Aist denotes, is in the form of "visual feedback," which shows a student a display of intonation and loudness patterns. When a student utterance is compared to that of a native speaker and scored automatically, a "template-based" approach is used. A third way to assist students with pronunciation is to have a "model-based" approach. By building up a model of mispronunciations through comparison to native speaker utterances or predicted common errors, students gain specific feedback on errors and a guide on how to correct them.

As the production of mainstream educational journals like *Computers and Composition* attest, computer-assisted writing has been a fertile ground for the observation of strategic student use of word-processing and email applications (Pennington, 1999b). One of the major findings in this area is that students produce longer compositions and are more positive about writing when they use computers. Pennington (1999a) attributes such positive attitudes primarily to the ease of generating text, clarity of the copy, and the cyclical nature of critical text-generation-and-revision processes. When negative attitudes emerge, they are likely to stem from a low student awareness of word-processing capabilities and quickly manifest themselves as feelings of intimidation, frustration, and a dislike of mechanics.

Although Blin (1999) found that few CALL studies have researched autonomous learner processes, one direction in the move toward integrative CALL is to allow for, and promote, learner autonomy throughout a course of instruction. Certainly, the recent descriptions of PrOCALL projects (Debski, 2000) make a strong case for self-directed student work. Within the context of CALL, learner autonomy can be defined as "the development of a capacity for engagement with and critical reflection on the learning process" (Shield & Weininger, 1999, p. 100). Aligned more with socio-collaboration, autonomy "involves the development of interdependence through which a group of learners and teacher will collaboratively take responsibility for and control of their learning/teaching environment" (Blin, 1999, p. 134). Demonstration of autonomous behavior can be found by examining how students negotiate, make use of resources, set goals, and sustain learning.

Hoven (1999a) clearly places the learner in control of his or her own learning. She believes that the learner needs to be in control of the "content, mode, order, pace, and level of self-direction of the package" (p. 150). An advocate of integrative CALL, Hoven argues that syllabus design should be framed in a sociocultural theoretical perspective in which the texts are negotiated, mediated, and made to be interactive. In her principles for implementing a "learner-centered CALL" syllabus, she suggests that any allocation of control to the learners needs to be accompanied by awareness-raising activities that encourage responsible management. As part of this, she argues that sophisticated online help facilities coupled with effective navigation elements may help foster learner control.

Although exactly what defines "literacy" is debatable (for an extensive review, see Kern, 2000), in the context of CALL the term seeks to describe the range of technical skills and embedded social practices students need before they can productively engage in computer-based activities. As the range of tools continues to expand in this area (Goodwin-Jones, 2000b), it is a lack of computer skills, of course, that may discourage full participation in CALL classrooms (Lewis & Atzert, 2000); conversely, students proficient with computers may gain new status and ways to use language beyond those of their peers (Johnson, 1991, p. 78). Although Corbel (1997) promoted "computer literacy" as a way to examine such practices, Shetzer and Warschauer (2000) discredit the term because of its relatively narrow focus on technical aspects of usage. For their part, "electronic literacy" is a preferred term to encompass the skills and practices regarding how to find and organize information as well as how to read and produce it (Shetzer & Warschauer, 2000, p. 173; Warschauer, 1998).

Accordingly, Shetzer and Warschauer (2000) divide the electronic literacy framework into three overlapping areas: communication, construction, and research. Thus, to become adept at communication via computer, the learner must be able to interact and collaborate in decentered, asynchronous ways. For skillful construction, students need to master hypertext authoring in order to blend written text, graphics, audio, and video together in coherent narratives. They must also learn to collaborate effectively, and take into account responses from both intended and Web-based unintended audiences. Students conducting research via the Internet need to hone their critical skills in order to evaluate both the validity and appropriate interpretation of source materials. In summary, Shetzer and Warschauer argue that learners engaged in electronic literacy practices must ultimately become autonomous and take charge of their own learning. One role for instructors, then, is to promote independent lifelong learning strategies.

25.3.3 Roles of the instructor

The integration of CALL into the classroom has challenged instructors to become familiar with new technologies and redefine their views of teaching. Indeed, according to Kramsch (1993, p. 201):

> The enormous educational potential of the computer is confronting teachers with their pedagogic responsibilities as never before. Never before have teachers so urgently needed to know what knowledge they want to transmit and for what purpose, to decide what are the more and the less important aspects of that knowledge, and to commit themselves to an educational vision they believe in.

Not only have computers shifted instructional practices, they have changed the way materials are designed, assessment is conducted, and how programs are evaluated. Although once the realm of specialists, CALL techniques and practices have become an integrated part of professional development programs.

Not surprisingly, a major portion of CALL literature focuses on classroom practices. Chapelle (2001, p. 8), for example, provides a list of 13 CALL teaching handbooks published in the early 1980s. More recently, Cameron (1999b),

Debski and Levy (1999), Egbert and Hanson-Smith (1999), Jager, Nerbonne and Van Essen (1998), and Pennington (1996), Warschauer and Kern (2000) have produced substantial collections of CALL material largely aimed at pedagogical theory and practice. In Felix's (2001) collection, an interactive CD-ROM of online language learning resources is included. One central theme of much of the literature concerns the role of the instructor within a CALL setting.

In both structural and communicative CALL, the teacher often served as a mediator between the computer and students throughout the learning process. Although computer usage generally fostered a "programmed" approach to instruction, instructors were nonetheless reminded to stay on hand to keep things running smoothly. In a study of learner talk elicited by computers, Abraham and Liou (1991, p. 104) suggested that teachers "need to make sure that students understand instructions and can supply the kind of responses required to make the program advance." Even in today's Internet-focused settings, teachers still can act as a "reintermediary" (Corbel, 1999; Tapcott, 1999) in order to mediate between learners and the resources available outside.

Within integrative CALL, teachers are encouraged to take on a less intrusive role. In classrooms described in the PrOCALL Project (Debski, 2000), for example, students are asked to nominate their own projects and, at the same time, take responsibility for shaping the objective, syllabus, and assessment components of the subject.

Here, Lewis and Atzert (2000) found that an extensive use of computers fostered anxiety in some students and thus detracted from language learning goals. To counter such anxieties, Lewis and Atzert suggest that teachers situate computer technologies in a historical and cultural context in such a way that students can form a critical perspective of their use.

Technological environments can be seductive, Kramsch and Anderson (1999) write, particularly because multimedia can seemingly dull the capacity to be critical. That is, sophisticated productions can lead us into believing that what appears real on the screen is real in life. Because of this, one responsibility for teachers regarding students is to "deepen their understanding of the relationship between text and context when teaching language as communicative practice" (Kramsch & Anderson, 1999, p. 39) in order to avoid portraying multimedia in simplistic ways.

To prepare teachers for professional development workshops, Hatasa (1999) provides a 16-point checklist for self-evaluation of technological literacy. Although somewhat simplistic and focused on technological aspects, Hatasa nonetheless lays the foundation for discussion on what types of skills should be required for proficient CALL instructors.

Debski and Gruba (1999) undertook a qualitative survey into foreign language instructors' attitudes toward integrative CALL. Key perceptions included a primary teacher concern for authenticity and recreating real-life situations. The instructors saw computers as a way to encourage social interaction so that

Table 25.3   Suggested areas of professional development for integrative CALL educators

Area	Reference(s)
Assist students to overcome anxieties fostered by extensive computer usage	Lewis & Atzert, 2000
Initiate and sustain student activity and interaction through computers; encourage creative, autonomous learning	Debski, 2000; Warschauer & Kern, 2000
Design new criteria for assessment that ensures equitable marking of group projects, accounts for computer skills and contends with individual learning goals	Barson, 1999; Debski & Gruba, 1999
Take an active role in research and evaluation projects	Lynch, 2000; Motteram, 1999; Shetzer & Warschauer, 2000
Consider the sociopolitical impact of computer usage beyond the classroom	Warschauer, 1998, 2002
Acquire electronic literacy skills, including multimedia texts interpretation, basic materials design and production	Bickerton, 1999; Corbel, 1993; Hatasa, 1999; Kramsch & Anderson, 1999; Levy, 1999; Shetzer & Warschauer, 2000

the computers acted as "active partners" rather than "passive assistants" to the instructional process (p. 232). The classroom instructors were critical of "instructional uses of technology" in situations where computers either did not encourage or simply stifled social interactions. Such a perception of computers had made some teachers abandon CALL altogether.

Professional development for teachers (see Table 25.3), particularly those who believe in and can implement socio-collaborative theories embodied in integrative CALL, is an ongoing challenge to the educational community. Increased student levels of electronic literacy and commonplace use of computers will make keen "early adopters" of technology less rare. The innovations they have pioneered, however, will flounder without a wider base of instructors who are able to sustain innovative practices in ways that are sensitive to local contexts.

25.3.4   *Establishing CALL research priorities*

Primary research concerns in CALL shift with each stage. Within structural CALL, investigators examined ways in which the use of the computer helps with the efficacy of instruction (see, for example, Dunkel, 1991). Such concerns were moved aside as researchers began to examine the total environment of learning. Under communicative views of instruction, studies investigated the variety of factors which were thought to influence the "distributed cognition" amongst computers, learners, and instructors (e.g., Salomon, 1993). In the current stage of integrative CALL, sociocultural theories of language learning are moving to the center of research agendas (Belz, 2002) and discussion continues about the use of second language acquisition as a basis for CALL research (Chapelle, 1997, 2001; Salaberry, 1999).

Chapelle (1997, p. 21) sparked debate when she argued that cohesive research agenda required a "perspective on CALL which provides appropriate empirical research methods for investigating the critical questions about how CALL can be used to improve instructed SLA [second language acquisition]". In Chapelle's view, cross-disciplinary contributions to empirical CALL research were found wanting and published studies had often vaguely described key definitions. She identified two key research questions: (1) "What kind of language does a learner engage in during a CALL activity?" and (2) "How good is the language experience in CALL for L2 learning?" (Chapelle, 1997, p. 22). Essentially, Chapelle sees attempts to answer the first question as descriptive. That is, they provide a basis for decisions creating a syllabus. The second question is evaluative in that it aims to examine the quality of learner language. Although Chapelle points out that these questions, of course, are not the only ones that could be explored in the CALL classroom, she concluded her call for a research agenda focused on aspects of instructed SLA.

In reply to Chapelle (1997), Salaberry (1999) argued that SLA theory was too narrow to support a basis for CALL research, and that work that embraced a sociocultural perspective of learning may be more productive. Salaberry pointed out that a more comprehensive agenda would examine the medium of presentation in CALL activities and more closely examine psycholinguistic assumptions, and concluded that "the analysis of computer mediated communication, including the analysis of learners' use of technical components that render CMC possible, deserves to be at the forefront of future research agenda" (Salaberry, 1999, p. 106).

In the area of educational media research, the dismissal of media comparison approaches led to a rise of investigations concerned with "media attributes" (Wetzel, Radtke, & Stern, 1994). Educational media researchers (e.g., Clark, 1994; Kozma, 1994) now urge investigators to consider those variables that cluster around "media" (e.g., speed of presentation, familiarity, editing style, clarity of images, topic). Additionally, researchers need to examine those associated with "method" (e.g., instructor behavior, repeated viewings, length of exposure, motivational attitudes) as a way to account for differences in performance. In a similar vein, Tatsuki (1993) claims that CALL research has also suffered because of significant flaws that include exceedingly small sample sizes, a lack of control groups, a tendency to overgeneralize, and a failure to operationalize key variables. As with Dunkel (1991), Tatsuki (1993) called on researchers to abandon comparative designs in favor of more "basic research into how learners learn language and how specific media affect language learning" (p. 24). Fortunately, such advice has been largely heeded and researchers now look more closely at how the interactions of computers, learners, and instructors influence the process of language learning.

In regard to the examination of learner behaviors, or strategies, CALL researchers need to explore the framework of "constructively responsive" readers set out by Pressley and Afflerbach (1995). This perspective, based on the underpinnings of cognitive constructivism (for an overview, see Driscoll, 2000), regards comprehenders as flexible, concerned with main ideas, and, most importantly, responsive to the presentation of textual resources as they attempt to build a coherent macro-structure. There are a number of reasons to advocate this approach. First, unlike perspectives of learner behavior established on information-processing models of cognition (e.g., O'Malley & Chamot, 1990), its theoretical foundation remains current and defensible in light of the recent construction-integration model of comprehension proposed by Kintsch (1998). Secondly, the framework is sufficiently complex to accommodate a wide range of interactions with electronic texts that, no doubt, exist. The complexity of this framework can help investigators go far beyond the relatively narrow conceptualizations of learner behaviors offered by the three-category "cognitive, metacognitive and social/affective" framework of O'Malley and Chamot (1990). Importantly, as Pressley and Afflerbach (1995) point out, their framework is far from being "saturated" and thus permits its use as a cornerstone for investigations. CALL theorists can proceed with confidence that use of the framework does not first require justification as a conceptual point of departure.

With these foundations laid, researchers could concentrate on the investigation of specific features of electronic literacy practices. Indeed, Pressley and Afflerbach's (1995) use of reading literature as the basis for their framework accords with Chun and Plass' (1997) proposition that reading theory be used as a basis for multimedia comprehension research. Combined with the current drive to integrate constructivist approaches to instructional media design (e.g., Levy, 1999), the common ground shared between constructively responsive reading theory and trends in educational software development could form a strong foundation for continued in-depth research on multimedia text comprehension.

The need for evaluation of CALL projects and activities is a recurrent theme in the literature and has become more urgent as the field expands (Chapelle, 2001, p. 26). As Motteram (1999) has observed, CALL researchers appear to have focused on finding ways to justify large investment in computers. Several factors, however, are merging to strengthen CALL evaluation research. Broadly speaking, the increased emphasis on computer-based learning throughout education has produced new tools for analysis, increased funding, and widened interest.

Work in CALL evaluation, however, is sparse and may require new research techniques to better understand how practitioners shape their projects, design materials, and go about teaching with computers (Goodfellow, 1999; Levy,

1997). Lynch (2000) provides one example of CALL program evaluation. Based on evaluative work on network-based classrooms (Bruce, Kreeft-Peyton, & Baston, 1993) and on his own context-adaptive model (Lynch, 1996), Lynch first establishes the goals, audiences, and preliminary thematic framework of the PrOCALL project before embarking on an initial data collection system. In this study, data was gathered from a range of sources including classroom documents and observations, teacher logs and interviews, student focus group sessions, and quality of teaching surveys. He then worked with the project director and teachers to revise evaluation and research goals in a cyclical fashion.

Lynch (2000) organized and coded his data with the help of qualitative data analysis software (NUD•IST 4.0, for *Non-numerical unstructured data indexing searching and theorising*; 1997). Although Lynch concluded that most students were positive about the PrOCALL innovation, he found that some were frustrated by such an approach to language teaching and learning. A low threshold of computer skills and language abilities was a key factor in frustrations. Lynch notes that proponents of integrative CALL must be careful to strike appropriate balances between those activities which focus on electronic literacy skills and those which provide opportunities for language learning. Future evaluation efforts, he recommends, should be ongoing and involve all stakeholders connected to the project.

25.4 Discussion

Because of large-scale computer-based tests, student work styles and the increasingly commonplace use of information technologies, Chapelle (2001) predicts "anyone concerned with second language teaching and learning in the 21st century needs to grasp the nature of the unique technology-mediated tasks learners can engage in for language acquisition and how such tasks can be used for assessment" (p. 2). Interpreted broadly, Chapelle's comment foreshadows a time in the near future when computers will occupy a much more central position in applied linguistics.

Clearly, the networked-based and socio-cognitive approaches that mark integrative CALL are here to stay. Mainstream educators have widely examined such learning environments (Jonassen & Land, 2000); CALL specialists need to draw from these experiences and make them relevant to second language contexts. Although the interdisciplinary nature of CALL makes it an unwieldy area of research on occasion, a wider exploration of related literature should nonetheless be encouraged. The journal *Computer Supported Cooperative Work*, for example, contains a number of articles salient to those interested in socio-cognitive aspects of CALL; other journals of interest include *Journal of the Learning Sciences, Journal of Asynchronous Learning Networks, Journal of Educational Computing Research, Journal of Computing in Higher Education*, and *Educational Technology*. For those interested in online writing instruction, the journal *Computers and Composition* is a valuable forum of discussion on issues.

Notably, integrative CALL practitioners have been at a loss to deal with assessment issues. As Barson (1999, p. 25) observes, there is a "troubling lack of correlation between standard achievement tests and the complex of values requiring assessment and appreciation in self-realization learning." For their part, those who seek to improve CALL pedagogical practices must necessarily begin to address assessment concerns, particularly through collected volumes of work that focus on specific techniques of instruction. Because large-scale language examinations such as the Test of English as a Foreign Language (TOEFL) are now available as computer-based versions, language testing specialists will continue to gain insights into the use and implications of computers in language assessment (see, for example, Ginther, 2001; Taylor et al., 1998). CALL educators will need to work alongside these language testing professionals to develop integrated assessment practices, particularly in cases such as web-based testing (Roever, 2001). As Barson (1999) recognizes, there is a major challenge ahead to create classroom-based and teacher-supported instruments that can accurately capture foreign language proficiency in the context of computer-supported collaborative learning.

Given the increasing centrality of technologies to applied linguistics, it is disappointing to see recent attempts to define pedagogic tasks (Bygate, Skehan, & Swain, 2001) ignore the role of computers. The absence of technology in such discussions limits the insights about task design and research solely to traditional classrooms. For their part, advocates of integrative CALL must establish guidelines for project-based tasks similar to those which can be found in mainstream activities (e.g., Jonassen & Land, 2000). Arguably, too, progress can be made in online TBLT (Task Based Language Teaching) by drawing from the field of instructional design, particularly in regard to "task analysis procedures" (Jonassen, Hannum, & Tessmer, 1999) that could encourage researchers to think more systematically about the reusability of objects across an entire language program.

CALL research both needs to be conducted in a wider variety of organizations and over longer periods of time. All too often, as Levy (2000) points out, investigations are situated in well-resourced tertiary institutions and provide only a snapshot of complex events. As Corbel (1993) reminds us, however, each particular setting has its own peculiar approaches to change management, work styles, institutional culture, and management structures that themselves all contribute to particular views of educational computer usage.

Finally, as Warschauer (1999; 2000b; 2002) examines the impact of computers beyond the classroom and begins to unpack the "digital divide," other CALL researchers need to be urged to read more widely in areas of social informatics, cyber-cultures, and cultural studies. One notable absence in the framing of "critical applied linguistics" (Pennycook, 2001), for example, was a lack of discussion of the impact of technologies in the field. A stronger critique of technologies could only strengthen CALL and move it further away from a tendency to paint somewhat troublefree and utopian visions of technology in education.

See also 20 SECOND LANGUAGE LEARNING, 22 SOCIAL INFLUENCES ON LANGUAGE LEARNING, 23 LITERACY STUDIES.

REFERENCES

Abraham, R. & Liou, H-C. (1991) Interaction generated by three computer programs: analysis of functions of spoken language. In P. Dunkel (ed.), *Computer-assisted language learning and testing: research issues and practice* (pp. 85–109). New York: Newbury House.

Ahmad, K., Corbett, G., Rogers, M., & Sussex, R. (1985) *Computers, language learning, and language teaching*. Cambridge: Cambridge University Press.

Aist, G. (1999) Speech recognition in computer-assisted language learning. In K. Cameron (ed.), *CALL: media, design and applications* (pp. 165–81). Lisse: Swets & Zeitlinger.

Australian National Board of Employment, Education and Training (1996) *The implications of technology for language teaching*. Canberra: Australian Government Publishing Service.

Barson, J. (1999) Dealing with double evolution: action-based learning approaches and instrumental technology. In R. Debski & M. Levy (eds.), *World CALL: global perspectives on computer assisted language learning* (pp. 11–32). Lisse: Swets & Zeitlinger.

Belz, J. (2002) Social dimensions of telecollaborative foreign language learning. *Language Learning and Technology*, 6, 60–81.

Bickerton, D. (1999) Authoring and the academic linguist: the challenge of multimedia CALL. In K. Cameron (ed.), *CALL: media, design and applications* (pp. 59–79). Lisse: Swets & Zeitlinger.

Biesenbach-Lucas, S. & Weasenforth, D. (2001) E-mail and word processing in the ESL classroom: how the medium affects the message. *Language Learning and Technology*, 5, 135–65.

Blin, F. (1999) CALL and the development of learner autonomy. In R. Debski & M. Levy (eds.), *World CALL: global perspectives on computer assisted language learning* (pp. 133–47). Lisse: Swets & Zeitlinger.

Bonk, C. J. & King, K. S. (eds.) (1998) *Electronic collaborators: learner-centered technologies for literacy, apprenticeship, and discourse*. Mahwah, NJ: Lawrence Erlbaum.

Bruce, B., Kreeft-Peyton, J., & Batson, T. (eds.) (1993) *Networked-based classrooms: promises and realities*. New York: Cambridge University Press.

Bygate, M., Skehan, P., & Swain, M. (2001) Introduction. In M. Bygate, P. Skehan, & M. Swain (eds.), *Researching pedagogic tasks: second language learning, teaching and testing* (pp. 1–20). Harlow, UK: Pearson.

Cameron, K. (1999a) Introduction. In K. Cameron (ed.), *CALL: media, design and applications* (pp. 1–10). Lisse: Swets & Zeitlinger.

Cameron, K. (ed.) (1999b) *CALL: media, design and applications*. Lisse: Swets & Zeitlinger.

Chamot, A. (2001) The role of learning strategies in second language acquisition. In M. Breen (ed.), *Learner contributions to language learning* (pp. 25–43). Harlow: Longman.

Chapelle, C. A. (1997) CALL in the year 2000: Still in search of research paradigms? *Language Learning and Technology*, 1(1), 19–43.

Chapelle, C. A. (1999) Theory and research: investigation of "authentic" language learning tasks. In J. Egbert & E. H. Smith (eds.), *CALL environments: research, practice and critical issues* (pp. 101–15). Alexandria: TESOL.

Chapelle, C. A. (2001) *Computer applications, in second language acquisition.* Cambridge: Cambridge University Press.

Chun, D. M. & Plass, J. L. (1997) Research on text comprehension in multimedia environments. *Language Learning and Technology*, 1, 60–81.

Clark, R. E. (1994) Media will never influence learning. *Educational Technology Research & Development*, 42, 21–9.

Clark, R. E. & Sugrue, B. M. (1991) Research on instructional media, 1978–1988. In G. Anglin (ed.), *Instructional technology* (pp. 327–43). Englewood, CO: Libraries Unlimited.

Corbel, C. (1993) *Computer-enhanced language assessment.* Sydney: National Centre for English Language Teaching and Research.

Corbel, C. (1997) *Computer literacies: working efficiently with electronic texts.* Sydney: National Centre for English Language Teaching and Research.

Corbel, C. (1999) Task as *tamogotchi*: ESL teachers' work in the emerging hypermedia environment. *Prospect*, 14, 40–5.

Crook, C. (1994) *Computers and the collaborative experience of learning.* London: Routledge.

Cuban, L. (2001) *Oversold and underused: computers in the classroom.* Cambridge, MA: Harvard University Press.

Davies, G. (1998) Four approaches to authoring CALL materials. Keynote presentation at EUROCALL 98; University of Leuven, Belgium, September.

Debski, R. (ed.) (2000) Project-oriented CALL: implementation and evaluation. *Computer Assisted Language Learning* (special edition), 13(4–5).

Debski, R. & Levy, M. (eds.) (1999) *World CALL: global perspectives on computer assisted language learning.* Lisse: Swets & Zeitlinger.

Debski, R. & Gruba, P. (1999) A qualitative survey of tertiary instructor attitudes towards project-based CALL.

Computer Assisted Language Learning, 12(3), 219–39.

Decoo, W. & Colpaert, J. (1999) User-driven development and content-driven research. In K. Cameron (ed.), *CALL: media, design and applications* (pp. 35–58). Lisse: Swets & Zeitlinger.

Delcloque, P. (ed.) (2000) *A history of computer-assisted language learning web exhibition.* Available: http://historyofcall.tay.ac.uk/

Dörnyei, Z. (2001) *Motivational strategies in the language classroom.* Cambridge: Cambridge University Press.

Driscoll, M. (2000) *Psychology of learning for instruction* (2nd edn.). Boston: Allyn & Bacon.

Dunkel, P. (ed.) (1991) Computer-assisted language learning and testing: Research issues and practice. New York: Newbury House.

Egbert, J. & Hanson-Smith, E. (eds.) (1999) *Computer-assisted language learning: research, practice, and critical issues.* Alexandria, VA: TESOL.

Ehansi, F. & Knodt, E. (1998) Speech technology in computer-assisted language learning: limitations of the new CALL paradigm. *Language Learning & Technology*, 2, 45–60.

Esling, J. H. (1991) Researching the effects of networking: evaluating the spoken and written discourse generated by working with CALL. In P. Dunkel (ed.), *Computer-assisted language learning and testing: research issues and practice* (pp. 111–31). New York: Newbury House.

Felix, U. (2001) *Beyond Babel: language learning online.* Melbourne: Language Australia.

Ginther, A. (2001) *Effects of the presence or absence of visuals on TOEFL CBT listening-comprehensive stimuli* (TOEFL Research Report no. 66). Princeton, NJ: Educational Testing Service.

Goodfellow, R. (1999) Evaluating performance, approach and outcome. In K. Cameron (ed.), *CALL: Media,* design and applications (pp. 109–40.) Lisse: Swets & Zeitlinger.

Goodwin-Jones, B. (2000a) Emerging technologies: speech technologies for language learning. *Language Learning and Technology*, 3, 6–9.

Goodwin-Jones, B. (2000b) Emerging technologies: literacies and technology tools/trends. *Language Learning and Technology*, 4, 11–18.

Gruba, P. (1999) The role of digital video media in second language listening comprehension. Unpublished dissertation, Department of Linguistics and Applied Linguistics, University of Melbourne.

Hamburger, H., Schoelles, M, & Reeder, F. (1999) More intelligent CALL. In K. Cameron (ed.), *CALL: media, design and applications* (pp. 183–202). Lisse: Swets & Zeitlinger.

Hatasa, K. (1999) Technological literacy for foreign language instructors. In R. Debski & M. Levy (eds.), *World CALL: global perspectives on computer assisted language learning* (pp. 339–53). Lisse: Swets & Zeitlinger.

Hegelheimer, V. & Chapelle, C. (2000) Methodological issues in research on learner-computer interactions in CALL. *Language Learning and Technology*, 4, 41–59.

Hoven, D. (1999a) CALL-ing the learner into focus: towards a learner centered model. In R. Debski & M. Levy (eds.), *World CALL: global perspectives on computer assisted language learning* (pp. 149–67). Lisse: Swets & Zeitlinger.

Hoven, D. (1999b) A model for listening and viewing comprehension in multimedia environments. *Language Learning and Technology*, 3, 88–103.

Jager, S., Nerbonne, J., & Van Essen, A. (eds.) (1998) *Language teaching and language technology*. Lisse: Swets & Zeitlinger.

Johnson, D. M. (1991) Second language and content learning with computers: research in the role of social factors.

In P. Dunkel (ed.), *Computer-assisted language learning and testing: research issues and practices* (pp. 61–83). New York: Newbury House.

Jonassen, D. & Land, S. (2000) *Theorectical foundations of learning environments*. Mahwah, NJ: Lawrence Erlbaum.

Jonassen, D. H., Hannum, W. H., & Tessmer, M. (1999) *Task analysis methods for instructional design*. Mahwah, NJ: Lawerence Erlbaum.

Kern, R. (ed.) (2000) Literacies and technologies. *Language Learning and Technology* (special issue), 4, 2.

Kern, R. & Warschauer, M. (2000) Introduction: theory and practice of networked-based language teaching. In M. Warschauer & R. Kern (eds.), *Network-based language teaching: concepts and practice* (pp. 1–19). Cambridge: Cambridge University Press.

Kintsch, W. (1998) *Comprehension: a paradigm for cognition*. Cambridge: Cambridge University Press.

Koschmann, T. (1996) Paradigm shifts in instructional technology: an introduction. In T. Koschmann (ed.), *CSCL: theory and practice of an emerging paradigm* (pp. 1–23). Mahwah, NJ: Lawrence Erlbaum.

Kozma, R. B. (1994) Will media influence learning? Reframing the debate. *Educational Technology Research & Development*, 42, 7–19.

Kramsch, C. (1993) *Context and culture in language teaching*. Oxford: Oxford University Press.

Kramsch, C. & Anderson, R. (1999) Teaching text and context through multimedia. *Language Learning and Technology*, 2, 31–42.

Kulik, C. C., Kulik, J. A., & Schwalb, B. J. (1986) The effectiveness of computer-based adult education: a meta-analysis. *Journal of Educational Computing Research*, 2, 235–52.

Land, S. M. & Hannafin, M. J. (2000) Student-centered learning envrronments. In D. H. Jonassen & S. M. Land (eds.), *Theoretical foundations of learning environments* (pp. 1–23). Mahwah, NJ: Lawrence Erlbaum.

LeLoup, J. W. & Ponterio, R. (1997) Language education and learning disabilities. *Language Learning and Technology*, 1, 2–4.

Levy, M. (1997) *Computer-assisted languagelearning: context and contextualisation*. Oxford: Oxford University Press.

Levy, M. (1999) Design processes in CALL. In K. Cameron (ed.), *CALL: media, design and applications* (pp. 83–107). Lisse: Swets & Zeitlinger.

Levy, M. (2000) Scope, goals and methods in CALL research: questions of coherence and autonomy. *ReCALL*, 12, 170–95.

Lewis, A. & Atzert, S. (2000) Dealing with computer-related anxiety in the project-oriented CALL classroom. *Computer Assisted Language Learning*, 13, 377–95.

Liou, H-C. (2000) Assessing learner strategies using computers: new insights and limitations. *Computer Assisted Language Learning*, 13, 65–78.

Lynch, B. K. (1996) *Language program evaluation: theory and practice*. Cambridge: Cambridge University Press.

Lynch, B. K. (2000) Evaluating a project-oriented CALL innovation. *Computer Assisted Language Learning*, 13, 417–40.

Meskill, C. (1999) Computers as tools for sociocollaborative learning. In K. Cameron (ed.), *CALL: media, design and applications* (pp. 141–62). Lisse: Swets & Zeitlinger.

Motteram, G. (1999) Changing the research paradigm: qualitative research methodology and the CALL classroom. In R. Debski & M. Levy (eds.), *World CALL: global perspectives on computer assisted language learning* (pp. 201–12). Lisse: Swets & Zeitlinger.

Murray, D. (1997) *Hamlet on the holodeck: the future of narrative in cyberspace*. Cambridge, MA: MIT Press.

Nevile, L. (1999) Universal web accessibility: a significant mindshift beyond current practice. *Proceedings of the AusWeb99 Conference, East Ballina, NSW*. (http://ausweb.scu.edu.au/aw99/papers/nevile/paper.html)

NUD•IST 4.0 (1997) (computer application) Melbourne: QSR Incorporated.

Oberprieler, G. (1999) Outcomes-based learning and the role of CALL in South Africa. In R. Debski & M. Levy (eds.), *World CALL: global perspectives on computer assisted language learning* (pp. 185–200). Lisse: Swets & Zeitlinger.

O'Malley, J. M. & Chamot, A. U. (1990) *Learning strategies in second language acquisition*. Cambridge: Cambridge University Press.

Papert, S. (1980) *Mindstorms: children, computers and powerful ideas*. New York: Basic Books.

Pennington, M. C. (1996) The power of the computer in language education. In M. C. Pennington (ed.), *The power of CALL* (pp. 1–14). Houston: Athelstan.

Pennington, M. C. (1999a) The missing link in computer-assisted writing. In K. Cameron (ed.), *CALL: media, design and applications* (pp. 271–92). Lisse: Swets & Zeitlinger.

Pennington, M. C. (ed.) (1999b) *Writing in an electronic medium: research with language learners*. Houston: Athelstan.

Pennycook, A. (2001) *Critical applied linguistics: a critical introduction*. Mahwah, NJ: Lawrence Erlbaum.

Peterson, M. (2000) Directions for development in hypermedia design. *Computer Assisted Language Learning*. 13, 253–70.

Potter, W. J. (2001) *Media literacy* (2nd edn.). Thousand Oaks, CA: Sage.

Pressley, M. & Afflerbach, P. (1995) *Verbal protocols of reading: the nature of constructively responsive reading.* Hillsdale, NJ: Lawrence Erlbaum.

Richmond, I. M. (1999) Is your CALL connected? Dedicated software vs. integrated CALL. In K. Cameron (ed.), *CALL: media, design and applications* (pp. 295–314). Lisse: Swets & Zeitlinger.

Roever, C. (2001) Web-based language tests. *Language Learning and Technology,* 5, 84–94.

Russell, T. L. (1999) *The no significant difference phenomenon.* Chapel Hill, NC: Office of Instructional Telecommunications, University of North Carolina.

Salaberry, R. (1999) CALL in the Year 2000: still developing the research agenda. *Language Learning and Technology,* 3, 104–7.

Salomon, G. (1979) *Interaction of media, cognition, and learning.* San Francisco: Jossey-Bass.

Salomon, G. (ed.) (1993) *Distributed cognitions.* Cambridge: Cambridge University Press.

Shetzer, H. & Warschauer, M. (2000) An electronic literacy approach. In M. Warschauer & R. Kern (eds.), *Network-based language teaching: concepts and practice* (pp. 171–85). Cambridge: Cambridge University Press.

Shield, L. & Weininger, M. (1999) Collaboration in a virtual world: group work and the distance language learner. In R. Debski & M. Levy (eds.), *World CALL: global perspectives on computer assisted language learning* (pp. 99–116). Lisse: Swets & Zeitlinger.

Soo, K.-S. (1999) Theory and research: learning styles, motivation, and the CALL classroom. In J. Egbert & E. Hanson-Smith (eds.), *CALL environments research, practice and critical issues* (pp. 289–301). Alexandria, VA: TESOL.

Tapcott, D. (1999) *Creating value in the network economy.* Boston: Harvard Business Review Press.

Tatsuki, D. H. (1993) Interactive video and hypermedia: where's the beef? *The Language Teacher,* 17, 19–24.

Taylor, C., Jamieson, J., Eignor, D., & Kirsch, I. (1998) *The relationship between computer familiarity and performance on computer-based TOEFL test tasks* (TOEFL Research Report 61). Princeton, NJ: Educational Testing Service.

Taylor, T. & Corbel, C. (1998) *Online for all? Evaluating current and potential use of Internet-based activities for AMEP students.* Sydney: NCELTR Special Research Project 98/1.

Toyoda, E. & Harrison, R. (2002) Categorization of text chat communication between learners and native speakers of Japanese. *Language Learning and Technology,* 6, 82–99.

Ullmer, E. J. (1994) Media and learning: are there two kinds of truth? *Educational Technology Research and Development,* 42, 21–32.

Warschauer, M. (1995) *E-mail for English teaching.* Alexandria, VA: TESOL Publications.

Warschauer, M. (1998) Researching technology in TESOL: determinist, instrumental, and critical approaches. *TESOL Quarterly,* 32, 757–61.

Warschauer, M. (1999) *Electronic literacies: language, culture and power in online education.* Mahwah, NJ: Lawrence Erlbaum.

Warschauer, M. (2000a) The death of cyberspace and the rebirth of CALL. Keynote address given to the IATEFL/ESADE CALL in the 21st Century. (Available at http://www.gse.uci.edu/markw/cyberspace.html)

Warschauer, M. (2000b) The changing global economy and the future of English teaching. *TESOL Quarterly,* 34, 511–35.

Warschauer, M. (2002) *Technology and social inclusion: rethinking the digital divide*. Cambridge, MA: MIT Press.

Warschauer, M. & Kern, R. (eds.) (1999) *Network-based language teaching: concepts and practice*. Cambridge: Cambridge University Press.

Warschauer, M. & Kern, R. (eds.) (2000) *Network-based language teaching: concepts and practice*. Cambridge: Cambridge University Press.

Wetzel, C. D., Radtke, P. H., & Stern, H. W. (1994) *Instructional effectiveness of video media*. Hillsdale, NJ: Lawrence Erlbaum.

FURTHER READING

Bell, D. & Kennedy, B. M. (2000) *The cybercultures reader*. London: Routledge.

Cole, R. A. (ed.) (2000) *Issues in web-based pedagogy: a critical primer*. Westport, CN: Greenwood Press.

Hamelink, C. J. (2000) *The ethics of cyberspace*. London: Sage.

Herring, S. C. (1996) *Computer-mediated communication: linguistic, social and cross-cultural perspectives*. Amsterdam: John Benjamins.

Holland, M., Kaplan, J., & Sams, M. (eds.) (1995) *Intelligent language tutors: theory shaping technology*. Mahwah, NJ: Lawrence Erlbaum.

Kearsley, G. (2000) *Online education: teaching and learning in cyberspace*. Belmont, CA: Wadsworth Thompson Learning.

Koschman, T., Hall, R., & Miyake, N. (eds.) (2002) *CSCL 2: carrying forward the conversation*. Mahwah, NJ: Lawrence Erlbaum.

Littleton, K. & Light, P. (eds.) (1999) *Learning with computers: analyzing productive interactions*. New York: Routledge.

O'Malley, C. (ed.) (1995) *Computer supported collaborative learning*. Berlin: Springer-Verlag.

Thompson, P. (1995) Constructivism, cybernetics, and information processing: implications for technologies of research on learning. In L. Steffe & J. Gale (eds.), *Constructivism in education* (pp. 123–33). Hillsdale, NJ: Lawrence Erlbaum.

Wilson, B. G. (1996) *Constructivist learning environments: case studies in instructional design*. Englewood Cliffs, NJ: Educational Technology Publications.

Windschitl, M. (1998) The WWW & classroom research: what path should we take? *Educational Researcher, 27*, 28–33.

26 Language Teacher Education

RICHARD JOHNSTONE

26.1 Introduction

Much of the recent discussion of language teacher education (LTE) has focused on inner, "mental" process concerned with language teacher knowledge and learning, e.g., Freeman (2002). However, before my own thoughts on this area are offered, it is necessary to address two sorts of contextual factor: first, "social, political, and cultural factors" which highlight the range of different jobs that LTE has to do in a diverse world, and then "provision factors" which not only constrain what LTE can achieve but also have implications for who "owns" it. There follows a discussion of ideology and process including teachers' knowledge, learning, and beliefs; then an account of novice and expert languages teachers and of possible progression from the one to the other; and finally an exploration of the possible relationship between LTE and applied linguistics research.

26.2 Social, Political, and Cultural Background

It takes only a small number of instances to suggest how diverse are the contexts in which LTE is situated. In his account of LTE in Spain, Portugal, Ireland, the USA, and England and Wales, Byram (1994, p. 7) argues that "the situation in teacher training reflects the historical development of an education system, of a socioeconomic system and of the political character of a country." In Spain a policy of decentralization since the mid-1980s had led to the rise of autonomous regions and the establishment of teachers' centers as the main location for continuing education courses. In Portugal, the rights of teachers to continuing education within normal working hours had been established by law, along with the right to apply for sabbatical leave in order to take a higher degree or do research which would be of professional benefit. In Ireland the emphasis in initial teacher education (ITE) was on the teacher as a teacher rather than as a subject specialist, which led to some languages teaching being undertaken by teachers without a formal language qualification or expertise, and with a consequent role for in-service of compensating for ITE.

More recently, in many parts of the "developed world" LTE has become more problematical than at any time in its past, as a new political and managerial ideology of education overtakes it. Mitchell (2000) for example claims that in "developed" countries such as the UK, USA, and Australia educational policy-making has become increasingly political, with increasing state intervention in matters previously seen as professional, leading to the standardized delivery of a teaching product and to a prioritization of measurable, evidence-based outcomes over processes. Underlying this trend has been a feeling among politicians in power that not only has teaching at school failed to deliver a fully satisfactory product, but also that teacher education must shoulder much of the blame.

With reference to the "developing" world, Hallemariam, Kroom, and Walters (1999) describe the languages situation in Eritrea, where there are major challenges of textbook preparation, teacher training, low salaries, difficult living conditions, and ambivalent languages attitudes of parents of language minority children, since some prefer Arabic to their own vernaculars. The emerging post-independence policy supports the equality of the various nationalities and a multilingual approach based on recognizing each of the nine Eritrean languages, with mother tongue education at the center. Bruthiaux (2000) argues that in the developing world, with a major need to improve living standards, "language education" and "development economics" should go hand in hand, but in fact "language education has managed to stay aloof from mainstream economics" (p. 273). Nonetheless, three positive examples are given from different parts of the developing world: micro-lending in Bangladesh, property rights in Egypt, and agronomic research in Latin America. These are not based on abstract knowledge deployed top-down by the state's technical and educational agencies, but on a more bottom-up approach which "takes as its starting point forms of knowledge embedded in local experience [and involving] small-scale projects designed to respond directly to practical needs and involving elementary literacy in local vernaculars" (p. 288).

Even as brief and selective an account as this shows that LTE has to confront conditions which are specific to the context in which it is located, whether these are changes in political orientation and internal organization (e.g., Spain), the rights of teachers by law (e.g., Portugal), the balance between teaching for generic and for specialist purposes (e.g., Ireland), difficult living conditions and inter-ethnic issues (e.g., Eritrea); the challenge in conditions of destitution for LTE to link closely with economic development and vernacular cultures (various); and the attempt to convert LTE into an instrument which serves broader political needs and to hold it to account for delivery of an imposed agenda (e.g., UK, USA, Australia).

Issues such as those highlighted above give LTE an important and specific job to do and allow it to become usefully "engaged" with matters of pressing national concern, but in another sense they imply that LTE should also have a less "accepting" role which consists if necessary of providing a critical challenge to the assumptions on which this "engagement" is based.

The context for LTE is not determined solely by conditions specific to any one state, and all states are affected by globalization. In most states where English is not a national or official language there is an increasingly perceived need to equip many if not all citizens with a command of international English. This in turn can have negative consequences for the uptake of other "foreign" languages and also for local heritage or community languages. On the other hand, in many states where English is the dominant language, there may be relatively little motivation for learning or maintaining any other language at all. In their White Paper (1995) the European Commission recommended that all member states of the European Union (EU) should equip all students at school with a working command of three languages by the end of compulsory schooling, so that all students across the EU would be in a position to benefit from "mobility" (which is a fundamental political right of all citizens of the EU) and to participate meaningfully in "citizenship" at European as well as at local and national level.

Thus, as a result of globalization or Europeanization, LTE is immediately "engaged" in diverse ways. These may include the promotion of international English, the promotion of other major languages in order to restrain or at least complement the seemingly irresistible rise of international English, the maintenance and revitalization of lesser-used heritage or community languages, and the development of a strategy for "languages education" which brings together first language and additional language development within a broad framework of international mobility and citizenship

26.3   Aspects of Provison

26.3.1   A framework for LTE provision

Table 26.1 suggests how diverse LTE provision is. The framework of LTE provision it illustrates is too comprehensive to be discussed here but it suggests that LTE can be many different things and is unlikely to be embraced within one ideology or one set of processes. Gone are the days when LTE would be "owned" by one group called "LTE providers." In fact, the "ownership" of LTE may be plotted across three phases.

In phase 1, it was "owned" by LTE professionals who in keeping with professionals generally were trusted to put their particular expertise at the service of society, e.g., Nixon et al., 1997. It is possible that some LTE courses for TESOL still fall into this category, taking students from many different countries, giving them what the staff consider will be a good LTE experience, and then sending them back home but without any real accountability for their capacity to use these experiences in a professionally productive way.

Table 26.1 A framework for LTE provision

Aspects of provision	Particular instances
Stage of LTE	• Pre-service (whether concurrent as part of a first degree, or consecutive in the form of a postgraduate certificate) • On-the-job • In-service (often nowadays called CPD or continuing professional development)
For which sector	• Pre-school • Elementary (or, primary) school • Secondary school • Further or higher education • Vocational education • Informal education
Status	• An accredited professional award in one particular country (e.g., qualifying to teach Spanish in England and Wales) • More general (e.g., obtaining a general qualification for TESOL that is not tied to the requirements of any one country). • Non-award-bearing
Types of provision	• 1-day seminars • Conferences • Short courses • Undergraduate programmes • Higher degrees (generic but with languages element), e.g., MEd; EdD, Higher degrees (specialist), e.g., MSc in Applied Linguistics (by research or taught), PhD
Modes of provision	• Direct contact • Mixed-mode (open learning) • Mixed mode (including web-based components) • Web-based
Providers	• Higher Education (e.g., Faculties of Education, Departments of Applied Linguistics, Language Departments or Languages Centres) • Teachers (as tutors, mentors or in other roles) • National authorities including inspectors • Regional or local authorities

Table 26.1 (*cont'd*)

Aspects of provision	Particular instances
	• Accredited agencies • Private consultants • International organizations (e.g., British Council; Goethe Institut; Alliance Française) • Professional associations, trades unions
Receivers	• Students preparing to become teachers • Teachers • Teacher educators • School management • Regional and national decision-makers
Stakeholders	• Teacher education providers • Students preparing to become teachers • Parents • Staff in schools • Employers, e.g., regional authorities • Students learning languages • National Ministries of Education • Inspectors • Politicians
Functions	• Training • Education • Personal development
Relation with generic issues	• Languages Teacher Education (LTE) on its own • LTE embedded within more generic issues of Teacher Education
Key provision factors (examples)	• International and national agencies • Teacher supply • Continuous professional contact • Adequate conditions of work • Supportive institutional ethos

In phase 2, LTE professionals are considered as "providers" in a provider–client relationship and are held accountable for the extent to which they satisfy "customers" such as Ministries, local authorities, and schools. Some TESOL LTE courses fall into this category, as special arrangements are made with ministries in particular countries for delivering a "customized" package of LTE, designed to be professionally relevant to the students' subsequent professional context. Much LTE for modern or second languages is also to be found here, with the "buyers" in the form of ministries exercising considerable downward pressure on what the "provider" will deliver.

Finally, in phase 3, LTE is viewed as not being owned exclusively by any one group but as jointly owned by a range of stakeholders. As a consequence, curriculum, processes, and outcomes have to be negotiated. In principle this is an excellent development, reflecting a democratic and accountable society, and one advocated by such reputed authorities on teacher education as Brown & McIntyre (1993). It can, and often does, however, often make life uncomfortable for LTE providers who may feel that their special expertise, some of which derives from the discipline of applied linguistics, is insufficiently valued or understood. LTE providers then may be required to develop skills whereby they are able to justify the distinctive contribution which they think they can make from their particular expert knowledge base.

26.3.2   *What is provided*

What then is the distinctive contribution that LTE providers might make from a knowledge base that is informed by applied linguistics? They can support language teachers, student teachers, and others in respect of:

- the implications of particular languages policies and guidelines, e.g., on new curricula and examinations;
- proficiency in the languages they teach;
- pedagogy, assessment, and evaluation;
- first and additional language development and the relation of this to multiple literacy and to cognitive, emotional, and personal development;
- language structure (including discourse), function, and use;
- intercultural development;
- autonomy, including learner and teacher development;
- ICT (information and communications technology);
- affective characteristics of learners, e.g., attitudes, motivation, anxiety;
- cognitive characteristics of learners, e.g., aptitude, learning strategy, verbal and other ability;
- specific issues such as "special needs," "differentiation," or "early language learning";
- languages in society, including issues of multilingualism, needs analysis, "minority" language maintenance and revival, languages and economic regeneration, languages and social inclusion and citizenship;
- teachers as researchers and as users of research.

Even a list as incomplete as this suggests three sorts of challenge to LTE provision.

First, it is unlikely that all of the above can be provided or absorbed in one course or program, so there is an issue as to how these various topics might relate to each other over the course of a language teacher's period of study, training, and professional career.

Second, many LTE programs are not self-contained but form only a part of a broader program leading to an initial qualification to teach or offering continuing professional development to qualified teachers. As such they sit alongside more generic academic and professional topics such as bullying, gender, stereotyping, self-esteem, identity and self-emancipation, social inclusion, emotional intelligence, multiple intelligence, curriculum development, general pedagogy, assessment, evaluation, quality assurance, school effectiveness and improvement, team-building, management and administration. There is therefore an issue as to how much space LTE can obtain in a curriculum to which new generic policy-related elements are regularly added.

Third, given the multiple ownership of LTE, it is conceivable that particular "stakeholders" such as national or regional inspectors, or schoolteachers themselves, may hold strong views on particular topics which may be built into official guidelines for schools and for LTE and which may pose problems for LTE specialists. In the UK, for example, official guidelines on grammatical progression do not sit easily with the findings of second language acquisition research. Because of the new accountability, LTE specialists may be obliged to ensure that their students are prepared for "delivering" the official guidelines while at the same time coming to understand their limitations.

Many specific provision factors can exercise a positive or a negative influence on LTE. Five of these are briefly discussed.

26.3.2.1 *International and national agencies*

The European Commission has invested very large sums of money in programs which have helped internationalize LTE by bringing together networks of language teacher educators from different member states. One such network draws on Scotland, Spain, Austria, Italy, England, and Germany in order to develop strategies and materials suitable for the pre-service education of languages teachers in primary (elementary) schools. Of similar value have been the international workshops for LTE staff put on by the Council of Europe, dealing with major policy priorities such as the reintroduction of modern languages at primary school. The Council of Europe's Common European Framework of Reference is intended to be equally relevant to all 50+ participating states, serving as an international tool applicable to all languages and levels of proficiency and providing invaluable input to LTE courses.

By helping to internationalize LTE, the European Commission and the Council of Europe allow for the exchange of new ideas, for collaboration on joint projects, for bringing insights and skills into parts of Europe where previously there had not been a tradition of research and development or indeed a tradition of political democracy, and they afford those involved a healthy degree of critical detachment from the policies and pressures which may be bearing down on them in their own countries.

Other agents which serve to promote transnational developments in LTE across the world are "cultural institutes" such as the British Council, the French Institute, the Goethe Institute, and the Cervantes Institute, and other cultural bodies associated with particular consulates. Each of these are organizations of one particular country, but they have many bases across the world with a mission to promote their particular languages and the cultures associated with them. Within this mission there has always been an important LTE function which they implement at times on their own, but often in partnership with national or local agencies. In many parts of the world where LTE is not highly developed nationally, bodies such as these may be just about the only international source of LTE available to practitioners. Although their contribution has been widely welcomed, there are some senses in which it may be seen as a mixed blessing, for example if also perceived to be associated with the promotion of one global language at the expense of other more local languages and their associated cultures.

Another major source of input to LTE are those academic or professional journals which serve different disciplines. Within the discipline of applied linguistics, LTE staff and students may of course refer to international research journals which promote theory development, such as *Language Learning* or *Studies in Second Language Acquisition*, but of at least equal value for LTE are those other journals which while maintaining theoretical perspectives also reflect a wider range of more pragmatic and professional concerns, for example *The Modern Language Journal*, *TESOL Quarterly*, *Babel*, *Language Learning Journal*, and the *Canadian Modern Language Review*. Journals of this sort play a vital role in helping LTE staff to see themselves as belonging to a national and an international community which has an identity, a history and which shares its concerns about its present and its future.

Underlying this section is a reservation which I have about much of the otherwise excellent literature on LTE. It tends to present teachers as individuals, and to highlight concepts such as "the reflective practitioner," when in fact they belong to a community of practice. Teachers have a professional as well as a personal identity, and the above agencies – along with professional associations such as ALL (Association for Language Learning (UK)) and IATEFL (International Association of Teachers of English as a Foreign Language) plus distinguished organizations such as CILT (Centre for Information on Language Teaching and Research (UK)), Language Australia, OISE (Ontario Institute for Studies in Education (University of Toronto, Canada)), and ECML (European Centre for Modern Languages (Graz, Australia)) – are key agents in ensuring that an informed languages voice is not obliterated by more powerful political or generic educational considerations.

26.3.2.2   *Teacher supply*

A key aspect of provision must be the supply of an adequate number of adequately educated and trained teachers. However, this is often a major problem. Central to this provision must be a combination of good teaching and of adequate proficiency in the languages concerned, but often this combination is not available. Rahman (2001, p. 251) exemplifies this dilemma when writing of English language teaching in Pakistan, claiming that English is hardly ever used outside the class and that the "formal training of teachers appears to me to be far less important than their command of the language." The survey of outcomes and provision for early foreign language learning across member states of the European Union by Blondin et al. (1998) reveals a similar problem. Given the almost exponential rate at which early language teaching has been introduced across Europe, the demand for good teachers often far outstrips the supply. In fact the very policy itself can founder on this "bread and butter" issue of "teacher supply," either failing to meet the demand or meeting the demand inadequately by putting teachers in place who do not possess the combination of knowledge and skills to make a success of it.

26.3.2.3   *Continuous professional contact*

Writing about teacher education generally, Fullan (1991, p. 53) claims that "teachers do receive information literature, and must attend workshops here and there, but they do not have the opportunity for continuous professional contact, which would become necessary for becoming aware of and following up of innovative ideas." Widdowson (1990, p. 65) similarly argues in respect of in-service courses that "the participants are inspired by the social and professional intensity of the event but find that they have little to carry home with them except a heady sense of general enlightenment which is often quickly dispersed on its contact with reality." If languages teachers then are so busy that the most they can manage are a few "one-off" continuing professional development (CPD) events, then however successful these may seem at the time, the lack of provision for continuous professional contact is likely to mean that relatively little mid- to longer-term impact is achieved.

Brown & McIntyre (1993, p. 13) claim a major flaw with in-service courses has been that "almost always, in-service has been based on a 'deficit model' of teaching. . . . The emphasis has been on the identification of what it is thought teachers ought to be doing and are not doing, and an appropriate action to remedy matters." They claim this deficit model makes it difficult for teachers to recognize their own skillfulness and discourages them from considering their own teaching analytically. A more "bottom-up" alternative, antagonistic to the "deficit model," is outlined by Legutke (1994, p. 57) who argues that there is often "a striking discrepancy between what is claimed by experts descending into conference assemblies of language teachers, and what actually happens in the majority of foreign language classrooms." He reports on an in-service project which brought the participating teachers into regular professional contact with each other, whereby they reviewed their own teaching and learnt through the teaching of other teachers. An outside expert was still needed, but in a "process" approach such as this, as opposed to one based on "transmission," it was less predictable when input would be needed and what forms it should take. Legutke concludes (1994, p. 62) that "attempts at implementing classroom innovation are bound to fail unless teachers take an active part in its design and evaluation, and unless they act as both learners and researchers." However, the provision of an infrastructure which would support regular professional contact of this sort is a major challenge which unfortunately many ministries and authorities are not prepared to meet, either because they prefer the top-down dissemination of national policy or because they consider the resource implications are too high.

26.3.2.4   *Adequate conditions of work*

Crookes (1997a, 1997b) believes that the general working conditions of many second and foreign language teachers are unsatisfactory, with the consequence that the relationship between teaching and research is almost non-existent. They often have far less autonomy than in other professions, and "there are grounds for grave concern when we consider the factors influencing second and foreign language teachers and teaching in many parts of the world" (1997a, p. 67). These include long classroom hours, lack of preparation time, lack of funds for materials and equipment, and limited time for reading, writing, or reflection. This exhausts teachers' energy and increases their dependence on experiential knowledge for day-to-day coping. He concludes (1997b, p. 109) that "the work conditions of second and foreign language teachers, the conception of a teacher's responsibilities, and the conception of schools' responsibilities in sustaining professional practice, must be changed."

26.3.2.5   *Supportive ethos*

Another factor which strongly influences LTE is the provision of a supportive ethos within the academic institution where LTE is located. Where a supportive ethos does not exist and priorities lie elsewhere, then the quality of LTE can be compromised. Many LTE staff, for example, work in universities, where increasingly there is severe pressure to achieve high-quality research and publication. This can create unresolvable conflicts within their minds: Do I do a really good job on my LTE program? Do I spend less time on this in order to concentrate on research? Can I obtain sufficient research funds to allow me to "buy myself out" of some of my LTE, but if so what will this mean for the quality of the LTE program? In an ideal world, all LTE staff would themselves be engaged in research of some sort, but the world is not ideal and very often a support structure does not exist which would enable them to achieve all of their aims. Another conflict of priorities can arise between LTE and other domains for which an organization might be responsible.

26.4   Ideology and Process

Freeman's (2002) excellent review of teacher knowledge and teacher learning traces the emergence of a view of teaching as "mental activity" over the past 25 years, proceeding through three phases. In the first phase, pre-1980, the notion of "mental activity" was absent, as the content and the methodology of a teacher's task existed in two totally separate and "given" domains (one influenced by university courses in the target language and the other by broad methodologies of language teaching) which seemed self-evident and which teachers were not expected to reconcile. Then in the years 1980–90 there came a phase in which what was happening inside a teacher's head became worthy of research and development interest, as teachers came to be seen as decision-makers, albeit ones who operated on a still behavioral process-product basis, taking decisions about processes which seemed conducive to the delivery of particular learning products. Finally, in the last ten years of the decade, a more subtle and multi-layered view developed as language teachers were understood as seeking to bring content and methodology together and to reconcile different images which were operating simultaneously, including not only an image of the self as teacher at present, and of the learners who were being taught, but also as embodied in a number of former and potential selves, for example as trainee teacher, as learner, as future expert.

Another perspective on the evolution of thinking about LTE is provided by Schulz (2000), writing mainly about the United States. Teaching was viewed in the early part of the twentieth century as an art and teachers were born and not made, with little if any formal training required and an accurate pronunciation considered the most fundamental of all teacher attributes. By 1941, however, language teacher development had become an established field, concerned with methods, foreign languages at elementary school, training and supervision of teaching assistants in university foreign language departments. Recent innovations figured highly, for example language laboratory, tape-recorder, closed-circuit television, video, micro-teaching. Schulz argues that today teaching is no longer viewed exclusively as an art. The creative element is still important but importance also attaches to principles, processes, skills, behaviors, techniques, strategies, beliefs, and attitudes which impact on teaching and learning and which can be empirically studied and taught. Before 1966, teacher education was mainly in the hands of literary scholars, but today it is in the domain of applied linguistics or foreign language education specialists. They are no longer exclusively concerned with methods but seek a wider and deeper knowledge base drawing on interdisciplinary connections with second language acquisition (SLA), psychology, linguistics, anthropology, and education. Schulz argues that we are nonetheless still discussing many of the issues which were discussed over 80 years ago and to which we have still not found convincing solutions. "Foreign language teacher preparation is still long on rhetoric, opinions and traditional dogma, and short on empirical research that attempts to verify or test these opinions or practices" (pp. 516–17).

Thinking about LTE has often been expressed in terms of "models" or "theories" which compete with and possibly succeed one another. Wallace (1991) for example identifies three such models: the craft or apprenticeship model; the applied science, or theory-practice model; and the reflective model. Writing about language teaching at present, Crandall (2000) perceives a shift from transmission, product-oriented theories to constructivist, process-oriented theories of learning, teaching, and teacher learning. In parallel there is a change of focus from methods to methodology. "Methods" courses may be innovative, e.g., Silent Way, or traditional, e.g., grammar-translation, audiolingual, communicative, but "methodology" on the other hand is more flexible and constructivist, involving exploration of the nature of teaching and learning and discovering the strategies of successful teachers. Van Patten (1997) claims it is not well known or documented how language teachers use class time, what types of arrangement they provide to students, what the theoretical and other underpinnings of their decisions are, and thus it is not clear how language teaching is "constructed." He suggests however that this can be investigated at two levels. At the micro-level the key question is how they construct class time, how their philosophies of teaching develop, how decisions are made. At the macro-level the object of research is language teaching as a profession, for example trends in textbooks, the context in which teachers teach, notions of change and innovation, and there is a need to deal with the multiplicity of multiple issues which impinge on languages teachers all at the same time, to help practitioners construct their own "coherence" systems.

Underlying much of the recent discussion of LTE has been a somewhat polarized debate which views LTE as being either competency-based or reflection-based.

26.4.1   Competency-based LTE

On this approach competences are specified which relate to practice. They are not derived exclusively or even mainly from research, but tend more often to reflect pragmatic discussion among stakeholders, with inputs not only from teacher educators but also teaching and management staff in schools or other institutions, accrediting bodies, parents' representatives, researchers, and ministry or local officials. The competences constitute a checklist of specific functional objectives toward which the trainee aspires.

Although in the USA and the UK they undoubtedly reflect political and bureaucratic demands for control and accountability (e.g., Roberts, 1998), they can also offer benefits. As Grenfell (1998) indicates, by being available to and indeed "owned" by all stakeholders, including students, competences can reflect an open and de-mystifying process of negotiating and sharing what it is that teachers at different stages of their career should know and be able to do. The approach can however bring its own problems. Good language teaching is a highly complex activity and may be distorted if reduced to a checklist of separate, observable components. It is easy to fall into the trap of "reification," assuming that competences are objects which have their own existence and can be measured, whereas in fact what one is observing is adjectival ("competent teaching") or adverbial ("teaching competently"). Moreover, if one accepts the notion of "competences" in LTE, one should ask how often and in how many different contexts one should see (say) a student teacher teaching competently in a particular way before he or she may be said to have acquired a particular "competence." In addition, lists of competences can grow and grow, and their volume can restrict an individual's scope for personal initiative.

26.4.2   *Reflection-based LTE*

To some extent, a reflective approach is a reaction against the forces of bureaucracy, centralization, and control which have been descending on teacher education. Teachers in fact should not be seen simply as "deliverers" of a fixed "curriculum," but should be valued as reflective professionals who frame and re-frame problems and test out their interpretations and solutions. Underlying this view is an assumption that teachers' knowledge is not arrived at purely by scientific means, but that "professionals display skills for which they cannot state the rules and procedures" (Schön, 1983, p. 50). For Schön there can be both reflection-on-action (before and after a teaching episode) and also reflection-in-action whereby teachers draw spontaneously on the implicit craft knowledge which they have gradually acquired. Some doubt has been cast about practitioners' capacity to engage in "reflection-in-action" when busily engaged in real-time teaching. This seems fair comment up to a point, but many of the best languages teachers I have witnessed have been able to vary the pace of their lessons, for example by creating pauses for reflection, or by slowing certain episodes down, or by creating episodes in which the teacher does no talking, or simply by pausing for a while before responding to a learner's utterance in order to decide on whether to respond in relation to meaning, grammar, pronunciation, or some other consideration. In this way it does seem possible to build reflection into the very fabric of language teaching. If so, it becomes central to LTE courses on classroom pedagogy.

At the same time, however, some have argued, e.g., Brown & McIntyre (1993), that unless handled well reflection can prove problematical in Initial Teacher Education, since a prior concern may have to be a "survival strategy" based on the development of lesson plans and of pedagogical routines. It can however play an important role in ITE also, e.g., Van Lier (1996), if students receive a curriculum in which concrete teaching experiences and time for input and reflection are closely integrated, since this may allow them to reflect on the specific experiences in which they have been engaged. Van Lier (1996) has also raised a possible problem with "the content of the reflecting," arguing it is often impossible to separate what goes on in class from what goes on elsewhere in the worlds of the students and their teachers. It may be difficult or impossible to access relevant information of this sort so as to be able to reflect on it, and some teachers may feel reluctant to engage fully with the policy or administrative issues which directly or indirectly affect what happens in class. On the other hand Crookes (1997b) argues that if LTE can draw teachers into action research and if the understanding of action research to be used is critical and participatory, this can take them "from immediate technical problems to collaborative investigations of the social conditions that prevent them from being professional" (p. 109).

Finally, if reflection is really to work for teachers, it needs its own discipline. If teachers are to reflect, for example, on what their students appear to have learnt during a lesson, some commitment to a research mentality is needed, e.g., "How may I elicit a sufficient range of spontaneous utterances?" "By what criteria will a judgement be made about these utterances when elicited?" and "What do these utterances tell us about a student's state of interlanguage development, attitude, self-confidence etc.?" If reflection simply equates to "In my professional judgement, they did well (or badly)," then it adds nothing.

26.4.3   *Teachers' knowledge and beliefs*

If a reflective approach is to be beneficial, teachers must be able to reflect not only on what they and their students are doing but also on what they think they know, understand, believe, and see. LTE clearly has an important role in encouraging teachers to explore and refine their own belief systems.

Richards and Lockhart (1994) argue that teachers' belief systems are derived from a number of sources: their own experience as language learners; experience of what works best; established practice; personality factors; educationally-based or research-based principles (e.g., cooperative learning); principles derived from an approach or method (e.g., communicative language teaching). In order to make coherent sense of beliefs emanating from sources as diverse as these, teachers need time away from the pressures of "real-time" teaching in order to allow the particles of belief from these sources to form a belief system which they can then monitor and further adapt. Freeman (1991) suggests that articulation is a process through which teachers clarify tensions in their professional practice and he outlines three sorts of implication. First, there is the importance of articulation in connecting personal knowledge to empirical knowledge, allowing students opportunities to make sense of things by filtering them through experiential knowledge gained as learners and teachers. To foster self-examination of this sort, teacher educators can ask teachers to assess their values, write autobiographies, and identify images of teaching. Second, articulation can help in fostering reflection which contextualizes teachers' knowledge; that is, reflection in response to their own classrooms as they become ethnographers of their own situations. Third, articulation can support the role of emotions and moral beliefs in the sense-making process. This arises from a supportive community in which assumptions can be questioned and in which participants can examine contradictions in their own behavior. In understanding teachers' beliefs it is useful to recognize the power of stories. Articulation of this sort helps teachers not only to sort out their experiences, but also to become more aware of consequences and possible alternative explanations.

Breen et al.'s (2001) study of experienced language teachers (of adults and of children) in Australia is significant both for its methodology of exploring teachers' beliefs and for its findings. Aiming to discover the relationship between their thinking and their actions, their research was based on the observation of classroom behavior directly followed by a one-hour interview. "We cannot deduce language pedagogies on the basis of teachers' accounts of how they work without reflecting with them upon *actual* instances of practice" (p. 498). From this they established the key principles that each teacher operated, for example "Learners must take responsibility for their own learning," and the specific practices that were used in order to realize each principle, for example "Encourages, and at times insists, that students do things for themselves" and "Explicitly teaches students, especially boys, to manage themselves" (p. 488). They found that across the 18 teachers some but not all of the principles were shared. One very common principle was: "Taking account of differences between students and/or the specific characteristics of individual students." This one principle realized 26 different practices across the teachers of adults and 13 across the teachers of children. The findings also worked in reverse because one particular practice could realize more than one principle, for example "Explicit modelling or explanation of language" was justified across 18 teachers in terms of 29 principles. In total over 300 principles were described. Experienced teachers appeared to differ from each other in the principles they currently hold and the practices they attribute to them, almost exactly echoing Brown & McIntyre's (1993) similar conclusion in relation to expert teachers more generally.

Research of the above sort has considerable potential for LTE, for example serving as topics for discussion which will prompt other groups of practitioners to reflect in relation to themselves. Of particular interest is the strategy of asking teachers to reflect on specific instances of their own actual teaching. In this sense, the use of video-recordings of teachers' own practice can be an excellent stimulus for them to articulate and share their interpretations of what was going on and of why they acted in the ways they did.

Central to the above is the promotion of teacher as learner which Freeman (2002) argues is the core activity of teacher education and which cannot thrive in a culture of prescription and transmission. For Freeman, teachers' mental lives represent the hidden side of teacher education, and the challenge is to create a sociocultural environment in which these mental lives can be richly fulfilled. In Barnett's (2000) terminology, a "complex" world has become "supercomplex." Problems – in language education as elsewhere – have multiple and unpredictable rather than single meanings and cannot be solved in any absolute sense, September 11, 2001 providing a telling example. What is needed is a disposition to interpret situations multidimensionally, to think flexibly and to act with purpose but also to engage in a constant process of monitoring and negotiation.

26.5 From Novice to Expert

For LTE to be effective over the course of a teacher's career, it helps if there is a clear view of what the different stages in a career might yield. Richards

(1998) plots three such stages on a continuum of language teacher development. First, inexperienced teachers require the technical competence of proven principles (a science-research conception); second, with more experience they can begin to interpret their classroom practice and shape it to fit certain theories (a theory-philosophy conception); third, they construct their own personal theories and progress to an art-craft approach, matching their teaching to the demands of their learners and the particular classroom situations in which they find themselves. On this view, teacher development is an evolutionary process of self-discovery and self-renewal.

LTE has a central role in helping teachers learn how to record, reflect on, and profit from their own thoughts in relation to their practice, and to use this for their own professional development from novice to expert. Two "diary" studies are revealing in this sense. Antonek, McCormick, and Donato (1997) argue that student teacher portfolios can do more than inform teacher educators about what student teachers have been doing and thinking; they can also help student teachers form a professional identity. Characteristics of working portfolios are that they are developed over time and allow the author to take risks. They are also socially constructed, because they derive from the student's interacting with learners, fellow students, teachers, teacher educators, and others. The two foreign language student teachers in their study revealed very different routes to the ability to teach and the identities of each were "woven from a combination of knowledge about affect, teaching, human relations and subject matter" (p. 24). Neither mentioned SLA theories in their portfolios but focused on interpersonal relationships and effectiveness of activities. In her account of 26 diary studies of novice Englsih as a second language (ESL) teachers in the USA, Numrich (1996) found that their early preoccupations were with their own teaching needs, for example creating a suitable classroom atmosphere by making the classroom a comfortable, safe environment, establishing control when students talk, being creative and varied in their teaching. The diaries revealed aspects which replicated their own second language learning, such as integrating culture into the language teaching process and giving students a need to communicate; but they also identified areas where the novice teacher consciously departed from her own second language learning, for example they were less prone to correcting errors or to teaching grammar than their own teachers had been with them. The diaries also revealed that the novices made some unexpected discoveries, such as that positive learning can take place outside the classroom and that some students do in fact want error correction on pronunciation and grammar.

Both of the above studies then challenge any view that with student teachers or novice teachers the agenda is necessarily limited to "survival" or to the development of technical competence, but suggest instead that from a very early point reflection and the construction of a personal identity as a languages teacher are involved, and that LTE has a major role in encouraging these processes.

There seems to be very little published research on how student teachers, new teachers, and expert teachers of languages differ from each other. An exception is Olshtain and Kupferberg's (1998) study comparing 15 expert, 15 new, and 15 student teachers, the findings of which are of clear relevance to LTE. The expert teacher trained her class to follow her own explicit code of conduct and provided opportunities for the generation of optimal input and output. Two of her key principles in realizing the above were: "Every student, even the weakest in the class, should get a chance to create individual discourse during the lesson," and "All students should be exposed to an abundance of language input, both from the teacher and other students" (p. 189). A distinction was made between "realis" and "irrealis" statements in the respondents' discourse. "Realis" showed that events were true, thereby anchoring their beliefs in actual professional experience, while "irrealis" referred to potential events that may have been likely or desired but that had thus far not been realized. Of the three groups, the experts made most use of realis statements and the student teachers most use of irrealis. The experts sometimes concatenated two or more realis so as to focus simultaneously on subject matter and general pedagogical issues (a strategy which echoes the findings of Breen et al. above). Integration of this sort hardly occurred in the new teachers and did not occur in the student teachers.

Johnston and Goettsch (2000) examined the knowledge base on which experienced teachers draw in their work when concerned with grammar. This was on the assumption that "there are certain forms of knowledge possessed by experienced practising teachers in the field, and language teacher education would do very well to incorporate these into its curricula" (p. 443). They focused on three categories: content knowledge (e.g., of English grammar); pedagogical content knowledge (e.g., explanations of particular grammar points); knowledge of learners (e.g., teachers' constructions of what students know about grammar and how they learn). These were found to interact with each other in complex ways as the teachers taught. This interrelated knowledge was most easily realized in stories of actual teaching events, that is, narrative knowledge built up from their personal and professional experience. There seemed to be two key features of the teachers' knowledge: it seemed highly process-oriented, a process of interaction leading to a gradual understanding rather than the transfer of information; and it drew on the three categories at once. Even at present it is common to find the three categories treated separately: content knowledge covered in classes on language structure; pedagogical content in methods courses; knowledge of learners in courses on SLA. "Yet, this very modularisation of knowledge becomes problematic" (p. 463). This points to the need for a significantly more integrated approach to LTE. They claim that this modularization applies not only in the USA but in many other countries also.

The studies and views in the present section reveal important insight into what makes expert or experienced teachers tick. It is not the case, however, that the process of moving from inexperienced teacher to expert is entirely one of extending and refining one's repertoire. Some, though not all, inexperienced teachers display a wider and more imaginative repertoire of teaching than do their more experienced seniors. In some senses the experienced teachers "get by" and achieve good results not only on the basis of how they teach but also on the basis of who they are perceived to be. Over the years they assemble a history and a status, and it is these things as much as what they actually do which influence their students' language learning. Viewed in this way then, language teacher development becomes in part a process of widening one's repertoire but also one of narrowing down and of creating personal and routinized combinations of principle and process which work within an identity that the teacher constructs. This can cause difficulties when experienced teachers act in the role of mentors to students in training, since they may expect in those students the same repertoire which they themselves have routinized. This situation is not inevitable but it suggests that mentors themselves may need support in helping their students explore the potentialities which are within them rather than "copy the master." It also suggests an important continuing role for LTE tutors in bringing their more widely contextualized insights and experience into a triangulated discussion with student teachers and their school-based mentors.

26.6   LTE and Applied Lingustics Research

It has already been suggested that in many if not all LTE programs there may be competition for space. Potential input from applied linguistics research may have to compete with more generic input from educational policy, theory, and research and also with mixtures of insight and ignorance deriving from language teachers' and other stakeholders' personal ideology or professional experience. If the discipline of applied linguistics is to "defend its corner" and maintain a respected place in LTE, then what sort of case may be made?

The case is not completely straightforward. For example, a number of eminent researchers in SLA have cautioned against any assumption that there is a direct connection between SLA research and language pedagogy (LP). Mitchell (2000) for example claims that, at least in relation to modern languages at secondary school in the UK, it is not possible to make firm research-based prescriptions from applied linguistics about the detail of "what works" in foreign language grammar pedagogy. Ellis (1997) in fact claims that the discourses of SLA and LP are in potential conflict with each other because they represent different social worlds with different values, beliefs, and attitudes: "SLA and LP have different goals – theory-building versus practical action – and draw on different epistemologies – technical versus professional knowledge. A simple transfer of information from one discourse to the other is, therefore, simply not possible" (1997, p. 88), and he suggests that "SLA is likely to be more helpful in informing the general context of action rather than in identifying specific pedagogical actions" (p. 78).

None of the above suggests, however, that applied linguists should be diffident about their possible contribution to LTE. Below, five roles within LTE are suggested to which applied linguistics research might make a key contribution. One example is provided to illustrate each role, but many further examples are possible. Each role is headed by a brief statement in italics designed to offer a "way in" to a possibly contested discussion among LTE stakeholders so that a voice informed by applied linguistics research may be heard.

(1)   A *"But it's not quite like that"* role. In many countries across Europe and elsewhere there is a massive policy commitment to the early introduction of an additional language. In some cases this has been justified by the claim that young children are better adapted for additional language learning than are older children, adolescents, or adults. In fact, in the recent past a number of reviews have been published of research on the "critical period hypothesis" (CPH) in respect of learning an additional language, e.g., Marinova-Todd, Marshall, & Snow (2000), Scovel (2000), Singleton (2001). All of them recommend caution. If the early learning of an additional language is to be justified, then this should not be based on an uncritical acceptance of the CPH, and several key conditions should be met.

(2)   A *"Maybe this is worth considering"* role. Here, LTE staff might draw on applied linguistics research in order to discuss with languages teachers the possibility of trying out new ideas deriving from applied linguistics research. While I accept the argument that SLA and LP have different discourses, I would nonetheless be interested to see what happened if, for example, Van Patten & Cadierno's (1993) "input-processing" approach or Swain's (1985) "comprehensible output" approach were tried out. The actual language teaching which I have observed in Scotland and several other countries hardly ever contains these features, and so to some extent the gap between SLA research and LP persists because these invaluable research-based insights have been investigated in a relatively small number of small-scale classroom experiments designed for SLA research purposes. They do not generally appear to have been incorporated into the cluster of pedagogical principles and practices which successful teachers seem to have implicitly acquired and which reflective practice might help them evaluate in terms of their perceived effectiveness rather than as valid or invalid hypotheses about SLA. If so, more's the pity.

(3)   A *"How might we evaluate/analyze/measure/better understand our practice?"* role. A major example of large-scale teacher participation in action research, with clear benefits to LTE, is given by Burton (1997). The project embracing 200 languages teachers in Australia on LIPT (languages in-service programme for teachers) had a high LTE element in that it involved language teachers researching their own classrooms as a means of personal professional renewal, within the supportive framework of a research community. The teachers received action research training and were further supported through structured network groups for peer assistance and trained leadership. The program ran

for four years, providing a rare opportunity for sustained personal growth, as opposed to the more usual short fix. As a result, the languages teachers opened up their classrooms both to other teachers and to other learning specialists in new ways. It gave them the confidence to pursue a personal research topic. Their publications showed that the action research component generated hypotheses and theorizing from experience to personal sets of generalizations about teaching. It helped establish a critical community, whereby teachers pooled data and incorporated this wider group experience. However, the teachers concluded they could not manage this kind of professional networking and researching alone. These processes required sufficient and regular support, suggesting a continuing and appropriately funded role for LTE.

(4)   A *"Can we analyze what we really think about/mean by this?"* role. This is an area in which LTE staff have a vital role to play in helping teachers and other stakeholders explore, interrogate, and refine their own knowledge, learning, and beliefs. In this they may act as link between the different discourses of applied linguistics and of common-sense languages pedagogy. Everybody has a sense of what is meant by "communication" or by "motivation" for example, to name only two key concepts, but this does not necessarily mean that their more precise technical meanings as derived from the research literature are as widely understood. It could be helpful to busy practitioners and other stakeholders if they had opportunities to access these more precise technical meanings. To make this point is not to suggest that the influence should be one-way, with research meanings informing common-sense meanings. As has been suggested already in this paper, practitioners' own common-sense meanings which may be implicit and gradually acquired through experience may contain their own relevance and wisdom which in due course may inform the knowledge base which research builds up.

(5)   A *"But haven't we been here before, so what are we going to do about it this time?"* role. During the 1960s and 1970s there were several attempts at introducing modern foreign languages in primary (elementary) school education, in some cases, e.g., Burstall et al. (1974), with negative evaluations. A key factor contributing to the lack of success was identified as lack of "continuity" from primary to secondary education, with secondary schools failing to take account of what their first-year students had learnt from their three years of French at primary school. During the 1990s there has been a major reemergence of modern foreign languages in primary (elementary) education, yet the review of recent research on this across the European Union (Blondin et al., 1998) shows clearly that "continuity" remains a major problem, one that has to be solved before languages at primary school can make a significant impact on subsequent language learning and use. Applied linguistics research has a major responsibility to point such findings out, especially as policymakers may have invested large sums of money in supporting their early language learning projects and may have a vested interest in obtaining "favorable" findings. LTE staff have a correspondingly important role in

ensuring that research findings of this sort become well known and that key factors such as "continuity" are cogently drawn to the attention of policy-makers and are thoroughly incorporated into courses which help teachers from primary (elementary) and secondary sectors to engage in a common dialogue and to negotiate agreed ways of ensuring that a negative history does not repeat itself.

There is no suggestion that there are only five such roles, those sketched out above. Taken together, however, they do suggest that LTE has a vital part to play in mediating between applied linguistics research and the professional practices of language teaching and of languages policy development. They suggest also that LTE is itself an important domain within Teacher Education research.

See also 22 SOCIAL INFLUENCES ON LANGUAGE LEARNING, 24 FASHIONS IN LANGUAGE TEACHING METHODOLOGY.

REFERENCES

Antonek, J. L., McCormick, D. E., & Donato, R. (1997) The student teacher portfolio as autobiography: developing a professional identity. *The Modern Language Journal*, 81(1), 15–27.

Barnett, R. (2000) *Realizing the university in an age of supercomplexity*. Milton Keynes: OH Press.

Blondin, C., Candelier, M., Edelenbos, P., Johnstone, R., Kubanek-German, A., & Taeschner, T. (1998) *Foreign languages in primary and pre-school education: a review of recent research within the European Union*. London: CILT.

Breen, M., Hird, B., Milton, M., Oliver, R., & Thwaite, A. (2001) Making sense of language teaching: teachers' principles and classroom practices. *Applied Linguistics*, 22(4), 470–501.

Brown, S. & McIntyre, D. (1993) *Making sense of teaching*. Buckingham: The Open University Press.

Bruthiaux, P. (2000) Supping with the dismal scientists: practical interdisciplinarity in language education and development economics. *Journal of Multilingual and Multicultural Development*, 21(4), 269–091.

Burstall, C., Jamieson, M., Cohen, S., & Hargreaves, M. (1974) *Primary French in the balance*. Windsor: NFER Publishing.

Burton, J. (1997) Second language teachers as researchers of their own practice. *The Canadian Modern Language Review*, 54(1), 84–109.

Byram, M. (1994) Training for language teachers: views from elsewhere. *Language Learning Journal*, 10, 6–8.

Crandall, J. (2000) Language teacher education. *Annual Review of Applied Linguistics*, 20(2000), 34–8.

Crookes, G. (1997a) What influences What and How second and foreign language teachers teach? *The Modern Language Journal*, 81(1), 67–99.

Crookes, G. (1997b) SLA and language pedagogy. *Studies in Second Language Acquisition*, 19, 93–116.

Ellis, R. (1997) SLA and language pedagogy: an educational perspective.

Studies in Second Language Acquisition, 19, 69–92.

European Commission (1995) *White paper: teaching and learning. Towards the learning society*. Luxemburg: Office for Official Publications of the European Commission.

Freeman, D. (1991) "To make the tacit explicit": teacher education, emerging discourse, and conceptions of teaching. *Teaching and Teacher Education*, 7, 439–54.

Freeman, D. (2002) The hidden side of the work: teacher knowledge and learning to teach. A perspective from north American research on teacher education in English language teaching. *Language Teaching*, 35, 1–13.

Fullan, M. (1991) *The new meaning of educational change*. London: Cassell.

Grenfell, M. (1998) *Training teachers in practice*. Clevedon, UK: Multilingual Matters.

Hallemariam, C., Kroon, S., & Walters, J. (1999) Multilingualism and nation-building: language and education in Eritrea. *Journal of Multilingual and Multicultural Development*, 20(6), 475–93.

Johnston, B. & Goettsch, K. (2000) In search of the knowledge base of language teaching: explanations by experienced teachers. *Canadian Modern Language Review*, 56(3), 437–69.

Legutke, M. (1994) Teachers as researchers and teacher trainers: an inservice project for German in Pacific Northwest. *Deutsche Unterrichtspraxis*, 1/94, 56–76.

Marinova-Todd, S. F., Marshall, D. B., & Snow, C. (2000) Three misconceptions about age and L2 learning. *TESOL Quarterly*, 34(1), 9–31.

Mitchell, R. (2000) Applied Linguistics and evidence-based classroom practice: the case of foreign language grammar pedagogy. *Applied Linguistics*, 21(3), 281–303.

Nixon, J., Martin, J., McKeown, P., & Ransom, S. (1997) Towards a learning profession: changing codes of occupational practice within the new management of education. *British Journal of Sociology of Education*, 18(1), 5–28.

Numrich, C. (1996) On becoming a language teacher: insights from diary studies. *TESOL Quarterly*, 30(1), 131–53.

Olshtain, E. & Kupferberg, I. (1998) Reflective-narrative discourse of FL teachers exhibits professional knowledge. *Language Teaching Research*, 2(3), 185–202.

Rahman, T. (2001) English-speaking institutions in Pakistan. *Journal of Multilingual and Multicultural Development*, 22(3), 242–61.

Richards, J. C. (1998) *Beyond training. Perspectives on language teacher education*. Cambridge: Cambridge University Press.

Richards, J. C. & Lockhart, C. (1994) *Reflective teaching in second language classrooms*. Cambridge: Cambridge University Press.

Roberts, J. (1998) *Language teacher education*. London: Arnold.

Schön, D. A. (1983) *The reflective practitioner: how professionals think in action*. New York: Teachers College.

Schulz, R. A. (2000) Foreign language teacher development: MLJ perspectives – 1916–1999. *The Modern Language Journal*, 84(4), 495–522.

Scovel, T. (2000) A critical review of the critical period research. *Annual Review of Applied Linguistics*, 20, 213–23.

Singleton, D. (2001) Age and second language acquisition. *Annual Review of Applied Linguistics*, 21, 77–89.

Swain, M. (1985) Communicative competence: some roles of comprehensible input and comprehensible output in its development. In S. M. Gass &

C. Madden (eds.), *Input in second language acquisition* (pp. 235–53). Rowley, MA: Newbury House.

Van Lier, L. (1996) *Interaction in the language curriculum: awareness, autonomy and authenticity*. New York: Longman.

Van Patten, B. (1997) How language teaching is constructed. Introduction to the special issue. *The Modern Language Journal*, 81(1), 1–5.

Van Patten, W. & Cadierno, T. S. (1993) Explicit instruction and input processing. *Studies in Second language Acquisition*, 15, 225–43.

Wallace, M. J. (1991) *Training foreign language teachers: a reflective approach*. Cambridge: Cambridge University Press.

Widdowson, H. G. (1990) *Aspects of language teaching*. Oxford: Oxford University Press.

FURTHER READING

Freeman, D. & Johnson, K. (1998) Reconceptualising the knowledge-base of language teacher education. *TESOL Quarterly*, 32, 397–417.

Freeman, D. & Richards, J. C. (eds.) (1996) *Teacher learning in language teaching*. New York: Cambridge University Press.

Johnson, K. (2001) *An introduction to foreign language learning and teaching*. London: Longman.

Klapper, J. (2001) Shifting perspectives in language teacher education. In J. Klapper (ed.), *Teaching languages in Higher Education* (pp. 15–34). London: CILT.

Oxford, R. & Nyikos, M. (1997) Interaction, collaboration and cooperation: learning languages and preparing language teachers. Introduction to the special issue. *The Modern Language Journal*, 81(4), 440–2.

Richards, J. C. & Nunan, D. (1990) *Second language teacher education*. Cambridge: Cambridge University Press.

Roberts, J. (1999) Personal construct psychology as a framework for research into teacher and learner thinking. *Language Teaching Research*, 3(2), 117–44.

27 The Practice of LSP

HELEN BASTURKMEN AND
CATHERINE ELDER

27.1 Introduction

The chapter outlines some key issues in the practice of LSP (Language for Specific Purposes) both from a teaching and testing perspective. In Sections 27.2–5 of the chapter we offer a general description of LSP followed by an overview of key issues in the field. The chapter also documents recent developments in the teaching of LSP, including the influence of genre-based research on syllabus design and methodology and practitioners' efforts to come to terms with the critical turn in applied linguistics which sees LSP as both conservative and disempowering.

Sections 27.6–8 deal with LSP testing, which follows on the heels of trends in LSP teaching with a move away from discrete-item linguistically oriented approaches in the direction of better contextualized performance-based measures and a greater concern with fair testing practice. Some purposes of LSP tests are outlined and a rationale for this approach to measurement is offered. Two key problems facing LSP testers, those of specificity and authenticity, are then discussed. While LSP testing, like teaching, is largely driven by practical needs, we show how investigations of construct validity drawing on an analysis of test data can offer insight into theories of language use in context, thereby making an important contribution to research in applied linguistics.

27.2 What Is LSP?

LSP is generally used to refer to the teaching and research of language in relation to the communicative needs of speakers of a second language in facing a particular workplace, academic, or professional context. In such contexts language is used for a limited range of communicative events. For example, in a university context, spoken language is typically used by students in events such as participating in seminars and tutorials, presenting papers, and asking and answering questions in class. Analysis of language in such events generally reveals that language is used in constrained and fairly predictable ways. Thus, the analysis of questions in university lectures reveals the frequent use of a four-part routine (asking for clarification, interpretation check, digression, and challenge) (McKenna, 1987).

LSP courses usually focus on the specific language needs of fairly homogeneous groups of learners in regard to one particular context referred to as the target situation. For example, LSP courses may involve a group of language learners who all intend to study at university, work as engineers, or aim to work as nurses in the future. The aim of such courses is to help the learners deal with the linguistic demands of their academic, workplace, or professional target situations. LSP courses can be "pre-experience" or "post-experience" (Robinson, 1991). The former refers to courses designed for learners aspiring to enter particular workplace, academic, or profession situations. In these cases the courses aim to teach the learners the language skills and knowledge they will need in order to gain entrance. The latter refers to courses designed for learners already involved in the target situation. In these cases the courses aim to help the learners become better equipped linguistically to cope with the communicative demands they face in their work or study situations. Major divisions in LSP are Language for Academic Purposes, and Language for Occupational Purposes, the latter comprising Language for Professional Purposes and for Vocational Purposes (Dudley-Evans & St John, 1998).

LSP courses can be highly specific or more general, referred to as narrow and wide angled respectively. For example, teaching Language for Academic Purposes may involve one of two options: Language for General Academic Purposes or Language for Specific Academic Purposes (Blue, 1993; Jordan, 1997; Dudley-Evans & St John, 1998). In the former, students from a range of disciplines are grouped together and instruction focuses on their common academic needs and skills, such as note taking skills, lecture comprehension, seminar skills, the structure of an argumentative essay, and so forth. In the latter, students are grouped according to their disciplines and instruction focuses on features of language use and the language skills critical for successful communication in them. So, for example, instruction for law students might focus on specific genres significant in legal studies, such as the legal problem answer (Bruce, 2002). There are numerous examples of highly specific LSP courses designed in response to the needs of one particular group of learners. For example, Shi, Corcos, and Storey (2001) describe an English for Medical Purposes course developed to help medical students prepare for their junior clerkship in the first part of their clinical training in a Hong Kong university hospital.

LSP has tended to be driven largely by practical rather than theoretical concerns (Dudley-Evans & St John, 1998; Basturkmen, 2002), such as the pressing need to set up language courses for specific groups of learners of a second language. Sullivan & Girginer (2002) report a typical sequence of events. They found themselves in the position of setting up an English course for future pilots and air traffic controllers in Turkey. Finding the available instructional materials inadequate and the description of language use in aviation insufficient for the task, they collected and analyzed a corpus of spoken discourse transactions between pilots and air traffic controllers (obtained from the nearby international airport) and interviewed a number of air traffic controllers and pilots. From examination of the data in conjunction with the professionals, the teacher-researchers identified a number of critically important features of language use in aviation, such as the formation of requests. They then used their analysis of the authentic discourse from the target situation as a basis for the development of instructional materials.

27.3   Key Features of LSP

Two central aspects of LSP are needs analysis and description of language use in target situations. Generally needs analysis is recognized to be a key feature of LSP (Hutchinson & Waters, 1987; Robinson, 1991; Dudley-Evans & St John, 1998; Flowerdew & Peacock, 2001b). Conventional approaches have defined needs analysis as the attempt to systematically collect information about the communicative demands faced by those in the target situation. This includes information about language use in specific academic, professional, or vocational groups, the linguistic skills used most frequently in the target situation, and the difficulties second language learners experience there. This information is then used in designing second language courses tailored to help second language learners meet those demands. The reason for this close association between analysis of needs in the target situation and LSP course design is two-fold. Firstly, instruction geared to target situation needs is believed to be more efficient in getting learners from point A to point B, and this is particularly important given that LSP courses, unlike many general second language courses, are often short term. Secondly, it is argued (Bloor & Bloor, 1986) that learners perceive LSP courses to be highly motivating because they can see the point of the instruction relating closely to their actual needs. Because the learners find the content of the courses motivating, they learn more effectively.

Generally needs analysis has been seen as the attempt to identify the gap between what students know and can do at the present point of time and what they need ideally to be able to do in the target situation. This type of analysis is referred to as deficiency analysis (West, 1997). The information yielded is used by the course developer to design a language course bridging the gap between the two points (Graves, 1996). Bosher and Smalkoski (2002) report on a needs analysis project carried out to determine the source of language difficulties experienced by non-English-speaking background students enrolled on a nursing degree program in the US. The needs analysis identified target situation demands and the present situation of the student nurses' language skills. They found that the main difficulty the student nurses faced was that of communication with clients and colleagues in clinical settings. Based on this information, an English as a second language (ESL) course was developed targeting this area of communication.

The above example illustrated a needs analysis and course design based on language skills. Some writers have argued the usefulness of basing LSP course designs on an analysis of the tasks learners need to perform in the target situation (Long & Crookes, 1992; Jasso-Aguilar, 1999). Tasks regularly performed in the target situation are identified and a course of instruction designed around them. Dudley-Evans & St John (1998) describe the use of a "deep-end strategy" in conjunction with task-based teaching. The strategy involves students' performance of the task as the point of departure for instruction. Input and information from the teacher about language points or communication skills may be provided after the task performance if necessary. For example, analysis of an engineering target situation may reveal that engineers need to read technical manuals in English and derive from them sets of operating instructions for workers. The LSP instructor provides task specifications and a technical manual and requires the students to prepare the instructions using whatever language and conceptual knowledge they already possess. Following the production of the safety instructions, the teacher provides feedback. Such an instructional approach is particularly applicable to post-experience LSP as it can be assumed that the students already have a body of conceptual knowledge and can perform a number of target situation tasks in their first language. The main element missing for the learner is how to express that conceptual knowledge he or she already has in the second language.

A further key feature of LSP is the focus on description of language use in target situations (Flowerdew & Peacock, 2001a). Numerous pedagogically oriented research studies have been carried out with the aim of describing how language is used in specific academic, professional, or workplace contexts. Pinto dos Santos (2002) reports an analysis of a corpus of letters of negotiation faxed between a Brazilian pharmaceutical company and two European companies. The research aimed to identify the rhetorical features of the letters, the schematic structure of this genre of business communication, and any cross-cultural differences between how both parties structured this genre in English. Findings from the study were used to inform the development of instructional materials in teaching business communication. Soler (2002) examines the use of adjectives in texts in biochemistry to identify various uses, such as, to describe and qualify phenomena observed in experiments and to signal the writer's anticipation of peer agreements and opposition to the claims made. Based on the findings, Soler suggests ways university students can be guided in reading and writing research articles. Ferguson (2001) examines the use of conditionals in three genres of medical English (medical journal articles, medical journal editorials, and doctor–patient consultations), and finds considerable variation, the most obvious being the use of polite directives in medical consultations, which are absent from the other two genres. The implication of this variation is that LSP instructors should link instruction on conditionals to the genres most relevant to their learners.

27.4   Issues in LSP Teaching

One debate amongst LSP practitioners centers on the question of how specific LSP teaching should be. Ferris (2001) outlines two viewpoints in the teaching of writing in English for Academic Purposes (EAP). Advocates of the first viewpoint argue the case for instruction focusing on generalized academic writing skills. Learners from diverse disciplines can be taught these generalized skills together and it is hoped the learners will then transfer the skills to writing in their own specific disciplines. Advocates of the second viewpoint argue the case for discipline specific EAP writing instruction. They argue that learners need to be taught how to analyze and imitate the norms of the specific disciplines they wish to enter. Instruction should involve groups of learners studying the same discipline. Thus those studying English for Finance would be taught separately from, say, those studying English for Legal Purposes.

Hyland (2002), a proponent of specificity in LSP, argues that generic labels such as scientific language, business English or academic skills, are misleading in that they disguise and misrepresent the discursive complexity and variation between how different groups in those broad bands use language and their aims in doing so. Although different groups may use the same labels, for example, most academic disciplines use the term lecture or research report, what these communicative practices involve in terms of language use or the social action they are expected to fulfill varies widely between groups or disciplines. A recent research study supporting this argument is that of Samraj (2002), who identifies ways research article introductions from the two related fields, wildlife behavior and conservation biology, vary in their schematic structure and communicative aims.

A second issue concerns the meaning of the term "language for specific purposes" (Bloor & Bloor, 1986; Flowerdew & Peacock, 2001a). One view is that a specific purpose language is a restricted repertoire of a general language system. According to this view, the second language learner first needs to learn the basic core of the second language and after this can learn additional elements, such as items that feature strongly in the target situation of interest (for example, features of language use in engineering). This view is based on the notion of a generative base of language (structures and words) underpinning all language use. The common core is seen as a variety-less language and knowledge of it as a prerequisite for learning additional specific purpose elements. Specific registers (for example, language for medicine, language in business communications) are understood to all be grounded in this basic core.

Another view (Bloor & Bloor, 1986) is that languages for specific purposes are varieties of language and that there is no such thing as general-purpose language. All language exists as one variety or another because all language is used in specific situations. While the different varieties may not be totally distinct from one another and there are features of language use common to all varieties, there is no "basic" variety-less language. From this perspective the idea of beginning language study with a common core before adding a repertoire of context-specific features makes no sense. The learner can acquire the common elements from studying any variety of a language while at the same time learning the specific forms and conventions appropriate to that variety.

A third issue which has provoked controversy concerns the type of needs analysis that should be conducted and whose voice should be listened to. Conventionally proposals for needs analysis have been based on objective assessments of communicative demands (skills, tasks, etc.) in target language situations. More recently there have been calls for consideration of subjective views. West argues that an essential feature of a good needs analysis is that it takes into account the preferences of the learners in terms of both what to learn and styles of learning (1997). Uvin (1996) reports on the development of a language course for health care purposes for Chinese-origin health care workers in a USA hospital. Uvin carried out a rigorous objective needs analysis followed by design and implementation of a course closely linked to target situation language competencies. However, the response of the health care workers to the course was poor and it was discontinued until a subsequent subjective needs analysis made it possible to re-orientate the course more to the learners' wants and preferences. Of course, in the event of conflicting views of language needs, the analyst faces the dilemma of whose interpretation to select. Hull (1996) reports her experiences of designing language courses for company executives in a situation where the clients (the companies she was dealing with), the students (the company executives), and the language instructors who taught on in-house courses all had differing perspectives of what was needed and what could be done. For example, the clients' expectations about what communication skills for business should be taught was seen by the language instructors as unreasonable within the time frame of the proposed language course. The problem of reconciling the different perspectives of language and non-language professionals is a perennial concern for LSP practitioners and is discussed further in relation to testing (see below).

27.5 The Widening Agenda of LSP Teaching

Although needs analysis and descriptions of language use in target situations remain the major items on the LSP teaching agenda, recent years have seen the development of approaches to LSP indicating that the agenda is broadening. Two of these approaches, each of which offers a different perspective on the role of LSP, are detailed below.

27.5.1 Genre-based approaches

Genre-based approaches to teaching LSP have emerged in the last two decades. Genres are described and defined in terms of the communicative purposes they serve and are labelled by the communities from which they emerge. For example, many academic discourse communities have communicative events labelled as the "research article," the "dissertation," the "seminar," and so on. The task of genre analysis in LSP is to identify the genres used in the target situations and to offer descriptions of them to the second language learner. To this end, the approach to genre analysis developed by Swales (1990) has been particularly influential and has been used as the basis for a number of LSP motivated studies (see, for example, Bhatia, 1993; Zhu, 1997; Henry & Roseberry, 2001). Swales defines a genre as a recognizable communicative event characterized by a number of communicative purposes. The members of the professional or academic community in which the genre regularly occurs can easily identify and understand these purposes. A genre is a structured and conventionalized form of communication and there are constraints on the component elements in terms of their intent, positioning, and function. Analysis involves steps such as identification of the moves typically making up the genre and the communicative purposes of each move, investigation of the strategies different writers or speakers use to achieve the moves, examination of linguistic choices writers and speakers make, and the social influences influencing genre formation.

Genre-based approaches to teaching LSP have moved beyond the conventional focus on the surface linguistic forms which characterize communication in professional, workplace or academic situations and now attempt to raise learners' awareness of the social influences and functions of genres and to help them understand the values placed on these genres by the target communities (Dudley-Evans, 1994; Hirvela, 1997). Dudley-Evans (1994, p. 229) states that genre-based approaches can be exploited in teaching for the purposes of "demystification of the epistemological conventions" of subject disciplines. In this respect, genre based LSP teaching represents a form of acculturation, an attempt to help learners understand the social and cultural context in which the genres operate, the community's purposes for using the genre, and the institutional expectations placed on it.

27.5.2   *Critical approaches*

A second and more radical departure from conventional approaches to LSP is currently being advocated in the field of EAP. Over the years, there have been developments in the types of needs analysis carried out and in the approaches taken to description of language use. However, the underlying goal has remained constant: to help language learners meet the expectations and demands of the target situation and gain entrance and acceptance in those situations. This has entailed the attempt to get second language learners to fit in with the norms and conventions of those target situations. This is now being challenged and a number of writers argue that LSP is too passive and ready to accept the institutional practices and precepts established in the target situations. It is argued that LSP should not unquestioningly lead second language learners to simply accept the communicative norms and status quo of target situations, but should empower them by helping them develop a critical perspective on those norms. Notable proponents of these views, such as Pennycook (1997) and Benesch (1996, 1999, 2001) argue that the established communicative practice of in-groups such as those in target situations should not be seen as the inevitable facts of the target situation, but rather that second language learners should be helped to view them critically and seek changes if necessary.

The emergence of critical approaches has led to debate in EAP. In the late 1990s this debate was seen in articles written by Pennycook and Allison that appeared in the journal *English for Specific Purposes*. Allison (1996) argued that English for Specific Purposes should continue its essentially pragmatic function (needs analysis, course and materials development, etc.), and warned of the dangers of a confrontational stance. Pennycook (1997), on the other hand, argued against what he termed "vulgar pragmatism" (the exclusive focus on everyday practical concerns). He argued that LSP needed to go beyond everyday concerns (such as course and materials design) and address broader social and political issues, for example, what LSP is doing and why. Pennycook argued that LSP has been a force for accommodation. By maintaining a conservative stance toward institutions and privileged members of established groups (those in the target situations), LSP was in effect upholding the values of those dominant groups and maintaining the established status quo.

In line with emerging critical approaches to LSP, Benesch (1996) argues the case for a critical approach to needs analysis. Conventional approaches to needs analysis in LSP, maintains Benesch, can give the misleading impression of being neutral undertakings that set out simply to identify objectively lists of skills or languages required for competent performance in target situations. In reality, however, needs analysis have been biased toward institutional viewpoints and the perspectives of those already in the target situation. Benesch argues that needs analysis must recognize the fact that institutions are hierarchical and that there is a need to afford those at the bottom of the hierarchy more power than they have by giving more priority to their version of needs.

Benesch (1996, 1999) reports on her approach to needs analysis in a paired ESL writing/psychology class in the US. The aim was to identify the needs of her students in coping linguistically with their psychology lectures, but also to explore ways to use the findings from her analysis of needs to transform the target situation (psychology classes). Benesch's analysis revealed that the students were experiencing difficulties with the amount of reading for the psychology paper. In conventional approaches to needs analysis, this finding would most usually be acted upon by the LSP instructors in terms of offering provision of reading skills instruction and teaching strategies for effective extensive reading, and so on. In short, the problems would be seen as residing with the second language learners and the onus for change and development would be placed on them. The response of Benesch to the problem was (1) to provide typical EAP reading support language activities, (2) to encourage the learners to act to transform the target situation to better meet their needs (Benesch ran a number of classes as a platform from which the students wrote proposals to the psychology professor suggesting how the lectures could be changed), and (3) to raise the students' awareness of their rights in regard to getting the information they needed from the psychology lecture (for example, by showing the students how to ask questions to get necessary information).

A less strident version of critical pedagogy in EAP is reported in Swales et al. (2001). The writers describe the design and implementation of an EAP course for postgraduate students of architecture. One event in the postgraduate architecture program leading to high levels of anxiety for the writers' EAP students was the "critique" or design jury. This event, which has been extensively criticized in the literature on education in architecture, involves students in presenting and justifying their designs to a jury of faculty and professionals. Swales et al. (2001) present instructional material developed for the EAP classroom. The material, entitled "critical analysis of critique," sets up a forum for discussion on the problems of the event and aims to help the students become more aware of its educational context. The writers also report practical means they developed to empower the students in these events. For example, to help the students maintain some control over the interaction some instruction in the EAP class focuses on ways to hold the floor in a discussion.

27.6   LSP Testing

We now turn to a consideration of issues in LSP testing. Although there are early examples of LSP tests with clearly defined vocational or academic purposes dating back to the first half of this century (Spolsky, 1995), the testing of language for specific purposes came into its own from the 1970s onward in the wake of the communicative teaching movement with its focus on learner needs and its emphasis on ability for use rather than on discrete items of linguistic knowledge. General proficiency tests, which are broadly focused and cater for all comers, have typically placed more emphasis on grammar and vocabulary knowledge, which can be regarded as core components of language ability and therefore provide information which allows for generalization across a range of different domains. LSP tests on the other hand, which serve a more homogeneous population (e.g., a group of students, doctors, or business managers), are more often than not performance-based, in the sense that they involve test-takers in actively using the language to achieve particular communicative functions rather than in simply displaying their linguistic knowledge. They tend also to be more narrowly focused with tasks designed to simulate the demands of particular real-world situations. Thus, a test of academic language will look quite different from a test of medical language or business communication and will also, in theory at least, engage different kinds of knowledge and skill from the test-taker. As is the case for LSP teaching, LSP testing activity is premised on the assumption that different domains of language use draw on different areas of knowledge and are associated with distinct varieties of language, the characteristics of which can be identified through needs analysis. Proponents of LSP testing maintain that, because the test tasks share critical language features of tasks in the target domain of language use and draw on content knowledge which is part and parcel of effective communication in that domain, the scores derived from the test will give a more accurate prediction of the candidate's language ability in the field of interest. Further, just as LSP teaching is regarded as more motivating because of its relevance to learner needs, LSP testing may also be more acceptable to stakeholders because there is a more transparent relationship between tasks on the test and tasks performed in the relevant occupational setting. While test appeal (or face validity) is not important in its own right, it may mean that test-takers engage more actively with the test tasks and that receiving institutions take the test results more seriously. Such tests are also claimed to have positive washback, in the sense that teachers who have the task of preparing students to take these tests will be more likely to involve the learners in authentic communicative activities which are conducive to improving their ability to function in the target situation.

27.7   Test Purposes

LSP tests, whether in English or other languages, are typically used for selection or accreditation purposes, for example, to determine readiness for academic study, as is the case with the widely used IELTS (International English Language Testing System); to license foreign health professionals to practice in an English medium environment (McNamara, 1997); to assess the Japanese language skills of those applying to work in the tourism and hospitality industry (Brown, 1993); to select teachers who have the skills needed to work effectively in Spanish-English bilingual programs (Grant, 1997); or, to cite an unusual and even more specific purpose, to evaluate the listening translation ability of linguists employed to assist with telephone-tapping activities initiated by US law enforcement agencies (Wu & Stansfield, 2001).

One of the problems with using LSP tests for selection purposes is that testees cannot always be expected to have acquired the specialist knowledge and skills required for effective performance *before* they enter the particular professional or academic community. Whereas the "deep end" approach, which confronts learners with unadulterated real-world tasks, may be an effective strategy in some teaching situations (see above), a specific-purpose approach to test design in pre-experience contexts may be both unfair to the test-taker and inefficient in the sense that it fails to predict future performance accurately. Clapham (2000) makes this point strongly in relation to pre-university EAP tests, suggesting that what is really needed in devising selection tools for tertiary study are indirect measures of academic aptitude rather than of language proficiency, given that learners may have received little instruction in writing academic essays or in listening to lectures in a school learning environment. On the other hand, a stronger case for assessing domain-specific proficiency can be made in a high stakes professional contexts such as medicine or air traffic control, where the test-taker's current command of the relevant skills is critical to patient well-being or passenger safety.

Thus far most of the published literature on LSP assessment has focused on high stakes proficiency testing. Locally designed LSP assessments for placement, diagnosis or evaluation of in-house LSP training programs have been less well documented. Recent exceptions are Feak and Salehzadeh's (2001) description of the process of developing a "home-grown" EAP video listening placement assessment at the University of Michigan, Davidson and Cho's (2001) account of the evolution of a placement measure for ESL students enrolled at the University of Illinois, and Brindley and Ross' (2001) report on how tests were used in the evaluation of an EAP program at Kwansei Gakuin University in Japan. The latter study combines the use of proficiency tests with locally developed achievement tests tailored to the content of the courses concerned. Alderson (2000) argues that greater effort needs to be expended on developing such context-sensitive measures of progress in EAP programs, rather than relying on proficiency measures which are likely to under-represent these programs' achievements.

Also rare in the LSP literature are reports on the assessment of subject-specific language acquired in mainstream education contexts where language is the vehicle for teaching different school subjects (but see Butler (1997) on the development of tasks to assess the academic language proficiency in history and social science for minority students K-12 and Cohen and Gómez (forthcoming) for an account of a test designed to measure the academic language acquired in science lessons in the context of a primary school Spanish immersion program). In fact this kind of context is not generally considered in discussions of LSP testing, although it is arguably relevant given its concern with delimited domains of discipline-specific language use.

Occasionally LSP tests may be used to promote the use of a minority language in a majority language environment. The Mäori Language Commission in New Zealand has embarked on the development of a series of Mäori language proficiency tests with occupation-specific tasks designed to elicit the language used for job-related tasks in different work settings. The first of these is a Mäori test for the Public Sector (Te Taura Whiri i te Reo Mäori, 2002). Salary incentives are offered to those who reach a specified threshold on this test in the hope that this will encourage use of the Mäori language in the public domain and thereby foster language revival. In Australia, a telephone-mediated test measuring the kinds of language used in health care settings has been devised in both Cantonese and Vietnamese, for the purpose of building a register of bilingual hospital workers able to use their language skills in inter-action with immigrant patients and, where command of technical language proves adequate, to explain treatment options and/or elicit informed consent from those about to undergo an operation (Grove & Whelan, 2001).

27.8 Issues in LSP Testing

The major debates in LSP covered in the first part of this paper (the issue of generality versus specificity, the nature of the LSP construct, and the problematic role of needs analysis in defining the target domain) loom even larger for language testers; first, because these issues are encapsulated within a single set of tasks or items administered within a very brief time span, and second, because questions of fairness to test-takers and efficiency for institutions are paramount in any testing situation. However tests also serve the useful purpose of operationalizing LSP constructs in a form which is open to scrutiny, and involve, by their very nature, the gathering of quantifiable empirical data whereby key research hypotheses can be put to the test. The following section will deal with two practical problems facing LSP test developers, namely, that of specificity and authenticity, and will report on the insights into these problems offered by test-based research.

27.8.1 *Specificity*

The issue of what constitutes a specific purpose domain and how this can be defined and distinguished from other real-world domains crops up in any LSP test development project. Language testers, like those responsible for LSP course design, more often than not use some kind of needs analysis (or job analysis as it is sometimes termed) as a point of reference in drawing up test specifications. Characterizations of specific areas of language use are become increasingly sophisticated with, for example, the advent of digitized corpuses such as the TOEFL Spoken and Written Academic Corpus (Biber et al., 2002) and the English for Academic Purposes Spoken Data Collection (Simpson et al., 2000), which can be mined for test development purposes. However, although methods of defining an LSP domain have become more sensitive, they still fail to address the basic problem identified by Alderson (1988) in his critique of the elaborate Munby-type needs analysis conducted by Weir in preparation for the TEEP (Test of English for Educational Purposes). The inventories or taxonomies derived from these analyses tend to be unwieldy because the range of "allowable contributions" (Swales, 1990) in any specific domain of language use is generally too broad to be fully captured in a teaching syllabus, let alone in a one-off test. In addition, there is no agreed method for determining which combination of skills, functions, or knowledge areas are critical for effective performance in the domain of interest. The limitations of needs analysis are further highlighted by Hawthorne (1997), who considers the plethora of communication demands facing migrant engineers and nurses who succeed in finding employment in the Australian workforce and concludes that "test designers have minimal capacity to produce occupation-specific tests which take a genuine account of issues such as cross-cultural effectiveness and field specialization" (p. 16). Elder (2001) illustrates the sampling problems faced by test developers in designing language proficiency tests for teachers, following a needs analysis identifying the range of language functions performed by teachers both inside and outside the classroom. Some of the requisite language skills were not specific to teaching and others varied according to the teaching situations (e.g., primary versus secondary, immersion versus language instruction) and indeed to different kinds of lessons and teaching topics. Even if systematic language variation between these different teaching situations is empirically demonstrable, it is clearly impractical to design a test for each situation or indeed, taking specificity to its logical conclusion, for each individual. Opting for a common core approach based on those language behaviors that occur in all teaching situations can also be unsatisfactory because it necessitates abstraction from the real world to a point where test tasks may be too decontextualized to elicit the language behavior appropriate to the teaching domain. More specific tests, which select tasks corresponding to those occurring in actual teaching situations, may be more meaningful, but the performances derived from them may have limited generalizability beyond the particular classroom event they refer to.

In addition, too much specificity may result in under-representation of the construct, since even a tightly delimited domain characterized by highly routinized language forms may be subject to unpredictability. Aeronautical radiotelephony communications, for example, may rely largely on standardized phraseologies, but even here, in addition to unexpected emergency situations, there are many non-routine but not highly unusual circumstances which are not catered for by these phraseologies. A test which is too specific in the language it elicits might not accommodate such eventualities, with fearful consequences in this instance.

In sum, while there is ample research evidence for the existence of language varieties (some of which was alluded to in the first half of this paper), these varieties, as noted earlier, may overlap. They may also lack internal coherence in the sense that there are often subdivisions within each variety. In selecting test tasks the LSP test designer must therefore settle for a compromise solution, based on common sense decisions.

Decisions regarding the specificity or otherwise of a test must nevertheless be supported by substantive empirical evidence if claims are to be made regarding the validity of inferences drawn from test scores. It is here that test-based research offers useful insights which, as it happens, do not always support the case for specificity. A convincing example is the painstaking investigation undertaken by Clapham (1996) into candidate performance on the subject-specific modules of the IELTS test. These modules were included on the assumption that candidates with particular disciplinary specialisms would do better on reading comprehension tests related to their particular field of expertise because they could bring their subject-specfic knowledge and language skills to bear while performing the tasks. Clapham's results revealed that this was not necessarily the case and that background knowledge of the reading topic in fact accounted for an extremely small proportion of the variance in test scores. The low-scoring students were too hampered by limited language proficiency to make use of their background knowledge and the high-scoring students, she speculates, were proficient enough not to have to draw on this knowledge to make sense of the texts concerned. The intermediate level students were the only ones for whom subject-specific knowledge appeared to make a difference. An earlier large-scale study by Hale (1988), although revealing a significant relationship between subject-specific reading passages and major field of study, concluded that the effect was negligible in terms of its practical impact on overall TOEFL scores. While the findings of research in this area are somewhat equivocal and may be partly attributable to the test designers' failure to choose texts or tasks which are unambiguously located within a particular disciplinary field, they give some grounds for the conclusion reached by Davies (2001) that "the discipline path is in fact a garden path" (p. 141) and lead Fulcher (1999) to assert that "Unless future research . . . can provide measurable definitions of 'specific' it may no longer be appropriate to talk about tests of English for Academic Purposes, but rather of test of English through Academic Contexts (EAC)" (pp. 214–15).

Research outcomes such as these have contributed to the decision (taken in 1995) to abandon the discipline-specific modules on the IELTS in favor of generic academic reading tasks. Whether this shift from a specific to a more general common core approach to language proficiency testing will be mirrored in other professional and vocational assessment contexts remains uncertain.

27.8.2   *Authenticity*

Another thorny issue at the heart of LSP testing is that of authenticity, a term which is used with reference to the content and format of the test, on the one hand, and, on the other, to the nature of the test-taker's response and to the way this response is judged. Authenticity, now regarded as a critical validity requirement of LSP testing, can only be said to have been achieved if there is a demonstrable correspondence between the task on a test and the corresponding target language use situation, such that the task succeeds in engaging the relevant language abilities of the test-taker.

To increase the chance that relevant context-specific behaviors will be elicited in test performance, Douglas (2000) offers a framework (adapted from Bachman and Palmer's (1996) taxonomy of test method facets) to assist in matching the characteristics of test tasks to features of the target language use situation. He also advocates the involvement of subject specialist informants with insider knowledge of the domain of interest to help with understanding and interpreting the communicative event or situation which the test is designed to represent (Douglas, 2000, p. 101).

Wu and Stansfield (2001) follow suit, proposing a model of "Verification of Authenticity in Test Development" (p. 199), which involves dialogue between the test development team and expert informants at all stages of the test development process. They illustrate this model with reference to the chain of design decisions involved in the development of their Listening Translation Test for linguists hired by law enforcement agencies to decipher conversations between persons under criminal investigation, claiming that the application of this model has resulted in a test which corresponds very closely in its demands to what linguists in these situations are normally required to do.

The quest for authenticity in LSP also raises the issue of how to formulate appropriate criteria for assessment purposes. In designing a test of Japanese for tour guides, Brown (1994) draws on the insights of industry informants with experience of tour guiding as a basis for criteria (e.g., enthusiasm, empathy, and persuasiveness) for assessing the quality of communication on role plays designed to simulate typical occupational encounters. These "indigenous criteria" (Douglas, 2001) are used in conjunction with more traditional linguistic ones, to produce job-specific task-related profiles of language competence. Jacoby and McNamara (1999) go further to propose that ethnographic studies be conducted to document the means by which members of a particular group are socialized into field-specific discourse practices and that these methods be used as the basis for critiquing existing test criteria and establishing more authentic ones.

The requirements of test fairness, usefulness, and practicality nevertheless place considerable limits on all dimensions of authenticity in the test encounter. For example, in the case of the aforementioned listening translation test, test designers were, for obvious reasons, obliged to use actors "who were able to talk like criminals, if the conversation required it" (Wu & Stansfield, 2001, p. 195), rather than actual criminal subjects. While the credibility of these conversations was verified by "experts" with insider knowledge of "criminal-speak," the conversations were inevitably less than authentic in some respects.

Feak and Salehzadeh (2001) and Read (2002) point to the difficulties created by a "free-wheeling" approach to eliciting multi-party conversation on tests designed to measure the language proficiency characteristic of academic seminars. With very few exceptions, academic listening tests involve the use of "doctored" scripts, to ensure that these contain material that is rich enough to allow for a variety of challenging comprehension questions to be asked, short enough (without too many pauses and digressions) to satisfy efficiency requirements, as well as simple and audible enough not to place unreasonable demands on the test-taker. (Such modifications, it should be noted, are also very common on materials produced for LSP teaching, although there are stronger arguments for using natural speech segments in the teaching context.)

McNamara (1997), writing about the development of the Occupational English Test (OET) for health professionals, describes a number of ways in which job simulations "may distort the reality of professional communication when implemented under test conditions" (p. 35). One example was the requirement that test-takers (in the role of medical practitioner) organize the notes they took on recorded case histories under specific content headings. This was deemed necessary to achieve a scoreable performance, although in the corresponding real-world setting doctors' note-taking practices vary widely and may be extremely cursory, especially in situations where the diagnosis is clear.

Conversely, when test simulations do end up producing highly authentic interactions this may be a source of unfairness, as Lumley and Brown (1996) point out in their analysis of discourse data from the OET nurse–patient role-plays. Some role-plays on this test were designed to introduce a deliberate point of conflict on the grounds that such tension was a normal feature of many hospital interactions. Test interlocutors, in the role of patient, were sometimes found to be over-enthusiastic in their response to the instruction "be persistent" on their role play card by interrupting, disputing what was said by the candidate (in the role of nurse), and preventing her from completing an explanation (1996, p. 124). The authors point out that while such behaviors often occur in real-world settings and were deemed to be authentic by expert informants, they may be counterproductive in the test situation, resulting in a loss of confidence and, in some cases, making candidates appear less proficient.

The problems associated with job-specific role-plays are also discussed by Elder (2001). She reports on the suspension of disbelief required to simulate the teacher role in the test situation, due to the absence of a student audience and the presence of an interlocutor who occupies the role of judge, facilitator, and audience simultaneously. Some test-takers, she notes, may be unfairly penalized for their inability or unwillingness to conform to the script assigned to them, whereas others, with quite limited language proficiency but good communication skills or acting ability, may be rewarded for giving a convincing teacher-like performance on the test.

This raises the issue of the success criteria used in judging task performance, which McNamara (1996, pp. 43–5) characterizes as being either weak (i.e., where underlying language skills are assessed independently of the context in which they are elicited) or strong (i.e., where the fulfillment of the task demands is assessed in it own right, with all the skills – linguistic and non-linguistic – that this entails). On a test of teacher proficiency, for example, a strong approach to LSP assessment will give priority to communication strategies such as simplification and repetition which might be required of a teacher in order to get the message across effectively to a student audience. Elder (2001), however, reports that scores given to test-takers with a good command of such strategies were sometimes at odds with those derived from more traditional linguistic criteria focusing on the range and complexity of linguistic resources, resulting in anomalous measurements where both strong and weak criteria were incorporated within a single rating scheme. Douglas (2001) also acknowledges that it is not a simple matter to make the transition from the indigenous (and arguably more authentic) criteria applied in judging real-world communication to those that will employed in an LSP testing context. The criteria may be too local and too task-specific to allow generalizability across the range of task performances. Involving subject specialists or occupational experts in the rating process may be valuable in that it accommodates the view of end users, but it may also be hazardous given studies which show that such raters orient themselves differently to the task of rating than do linguists or ESL teachers, may lack the metalinguistic knowledge to identify relevant linguistic features of performance, and may sometimes be less reliable (e.g., see Elder, 1993a; Brown, 1995; Lumley, 1998; Daborn & Calderwood, 2000; Douglas & Myers, 2000; Grove & Whelan, 2001). Again, some kind of compromise is needed. Hamp-Lyons and Lumley (2001, p. 128) suggest that getting the right balance between input from content specialists and from linguists as one of the key challenges facing LSP testing.

Thus, while the profession now takes for granted the value of assessing language in meaningful "life-like" contexts, it must also be acknowledged that absolute authenticity is unobtainable on a test and indeed a misguided ambition in that it confuses the criterion with the method of measurement. Current research tends to focus on how more or less authentic test delivery modes, response formats, or scoring procedures (e.g., tape- versus video-mediated listening texts, stand-alone writing versus integrated reading and writing tasks, machine versus human scoring) affect test performance, exploring the implications of any differences for construct validity. Evidence that a more authentic test leads to better predictions of real-world performance is however lacking. The most commonly conducted studies are those exploring the capacity of EAP tests to predict future academic success and thus far these have furnished little evidence to the effect that the type of language proficiency instrument used is what makes a difference to the strength of the correlation between test scores and academic outcomes. Any differences which emerge from such studies may have as much to do with differences in the reliability of the instruments concerned, the diverse nature of the populations tested, the different cut-off points prescribed for entry to academia in different contexts, and the variability of the criteria used to measure academic success (see Elder, 1993b; Graham, 1987; and Criper & Davies, 1988 for further discussion).

Until such evidence is forthcoming (and for methodological reasons such studies are hard to conduct), the strongest practical arguments for LSP testing are political and pedagogical. First, LSP tests make the goals, methods, and outcomes of assessment more transparent and hence more convincing to end users (although this, as Alderson (2000) suggests, is itself a matter for empirical research). Second, high stakes LSP tests are more likely to generate teaching activity which is seen by learners as relevant to their needs (although whether this is true and whether such courses actually serve the learners better than more general common core proficiency courses remains, as we saw earlier, the subject of debate). Nevertheless, while in many ways the LSP testing endeavor is an act of faith, rather than an empirically defensible practice, the journey from indirect to increasingly direct contextualized measures of language behavior has resulted in greater reflection about the nature of language ability as it is enacted in the world (rather than as a static competence which resides within the mind of the test-taker) and about the value of separating language ability from other aspects of communication which may be equally important for performance in both academic and professional encounters.

27.9   Conclusion

Trends in LSP teaching as described in this chapter are paralleled closely by those in LSP testing. Both teaching and testing are now informed by richer conceptualizations of what specific purpose language ability entails. These constructs now draw on increasingly sophisticated characterizations of the domains of interest, described not only in terms of linguistic features, but also in terms of the conventions, cultural values, and belief systems operating within the relevant discourse communities. Both language teaching and language testing have responded to the demands and needs of LSP, teaching more adventurously, no doubt, because it can more easily than testing take account of the local and the contingent, while testing needs to be more generally accountable. Two challenges remain to be answered by both endeavors. The first is why LSP (teaching and testing): is it a theoretical or a practical (and face validity) matter? The vote so far seems to favor the practical explanation. The second challenge arises – ironically – because in responding to LSP user needs and target behaviors, both teaching and testing stand accused of accommodating to current inequitable power relations. This raises wider political and ethical issues and is taken up both in the introduction to this volume and in Chapter 32.

See also 4 Language Corpora, 5 Discourse Analysis, 24 Fashions in Language Teaching Methodology, 31 Language Testing, 32 Critical Applied Linguistics.

REFERENCES

Alderson, J. C. (1988) New procedures of validating proficiency tests of ESP? Theory and practice. *Language Testing*, 5(2), 220–232.

Alderson, J. C. (2000) Testing EAP: progress? achievement? proficiency? In G. M. Blue, J. Milton, & G. Saville (eds.), *Assessing English for academic purposes* (pp. 21–47). Switzerland Peter Lang.

Allison, D. (1996) Pragmatist discourse and English for academic purposes. *English for Specific Purposes*, 15(2), 85–103.

Bachman, L. & Palmer, A. (1996) *Language testing in practice: designing and developing useful language tests.* Oxford: Oxford University Press.

Basturkmen, H. (2002) Towards a theory for analyzing theory and practice in

LSP. *International Review of Applied Linguistics*, 40, 23–35.

Benesch, S. (1996) Needs analysis and curriculum design in EAP: an example of a critical approach. *TESOL Quarterly*, 30(4), 723–38.

Benesch, S. (1999) Rights analysis: studying power relations in an academic setting. *English for Specific Purposes,* 18(4), 313–27.

Benesch, S. (2001) *Critical English for academic purposes: theory, politics and practice*. Mahwah, NJ: Erlbaum Associates.

Bhatia, V. K. (1993) *Analyzing genre: language use in professional settings*. London: Longman.

Biber, D., Conrad, S., Reppen, R., Byrd, P., & Helt, M. (2002) Speaking and writing in the university: a multidimensional comparison. *TESOL Quarterly*, 36(1), 9–48.

Bloor, M. & Bloor, T. (1986) *Languages for specific purposes: practice and theory*. Centre for Language and Communication Studies Occasional Papers, 19. Dublin: Trinity College, Centre for Language and Communication Studies.

Blue, G. (1993) (ed.) *Language, learning and success: studying through English*. *Developments in ELT*. Hemel Hempstead: Phoenix ELT.

Bosher, S. & Smalkoski, K. (2002) From needs analysis to curriculum development: Designing a course in health-care communication for immigrant students in USA. *English for Specific Purposes*, 21(1), 59–79.

Brindley, G. & Ross, S. (2001) EAP assessment: issues, models and outcomes. In J. Flowerdew & M. Peacock (eds.), *Research perspectives on English for academic purposes*. Cambridge: Cambridge University Press.

Brown, A. (1993) The role of test-taker feedback in the test development process: test-takers' reaction to a tape-mediated test of spoken Japanese. *Language Testing*, 10(3), 277–303.

Brown, A. (1994) LSP testing: the role of linguistic and real-world criteria. In R. Khoo (ed.), *LSP: problems and prospects* (pp. 202–18). Singapore: SEAMEO Regional Language Center.

Brown, A. (1995) The effect of rater variables in the development of an occupation-specific language performance test. *Language Testing*, 12(1), 1–15.

Bruce, N. (2002) Dovetailing language and content: teaching balanced argument in legal problem answer writing. *English for Specific Purposes*, 21(4), 321–45.

Butler, F. (1997) Academic language proficiency tasks for K-12 minority students: a prototype test development effort. *Language Testing Update*, 22, 25–6.

Clapham, C. (1996) *The development of IELTS: a study of the effect of background knowledge on reading comprehension*. Cambridge: Cambridge University Press.

Clapham, C. (2000) Assessment for academic purposes: Where next? *System*, 28(4), 511–21.

Cohen, A. D. & Gómez, T. (forthcoming) Towards enhancing academic language proficiency in a fifth-grade Spanish immersion classroom. In D. Brinton & O. Kagan (eds.), *Heritage language: a new field emerging*. Mahwah, NJ: Lawrence Erlbaum.

Criper, A. & Davies, A. (1988) *ELTS Validation Project Report, English Language Testing Service Research Report 1/1*. Cambridge: British Council and UCLES.

Daborn, E. & Calderwood, M. (2000) Collaborative assessment of written reports: electrical engineering and EFL. In G. M. Blue, J. Milton, & G. Saville (eds.), *Assessing English for academic purposes* (pp. 21–47). Switzerland: Peter Lang.

Davidson, F. & Cho, Y. (2001) Issues in EAP test development: what one institution and its history tell us. In J. Flowerdew & M. Peacock (eds.), *Research perspectives on English for academic purposes* (pp. 286–97). Cambridge: Cambridge University Press.

Davies, A. (2001) The logic of testing languages for specific purposes. *Language Testing*, 18(2), 133–47.

Douglas, D. (2000) *Assessing languages for specific purposes*. Cambridge: Cambridge University Press.

Douglas, D. (2001) Language for specific purposes assessment criteria: where do they come from? *Language Testing*, 18(2), 171–85.

Douglas, D. & Myers, R. (2000) Assessing the communication skills of veterinary students: whose criteria? In A. J. Kunnan (ed.), *Fairness and validation in language assessment: selected papers from the 19th Language Testing Research Colloquium, Orlando, Florida* (pp. 60–81). Cambridge: Cambridge University Press.

Dudley-Evans, T. (1994) Genre analysis: An approach for ESP. In M. Coulthard (ed.), *Advances in written text analysis* (pp. 219–22). London: Routledge.

Dudley-Evans, T. & St John, M. J. (1998) *Developments in English for specific purposes*. Cambridge: Cambridge University Press.

Elder, C. (1993a) How do subject specialists construe classroom language proficiency? *Language Testing*, 10(3), 235–354.

Elder, C. (1993b) Language proficiency as predictor of performance in teacher education. *Melbourne Papers in Language Testing*, 2(1), 68–89.

Elder, C. (2001) Assessing the language proficiency of teachers: are there any border controls? *Language Testing*, 18(2), 149–70.

Feak, C. & Salehzadeh, J. (2001) Challenges and issues in developing an EAP video listening placement assessment: a view from one program. *English for Specific Purposes*, 20(1), 477–93.

Ferguson, G. (2001) If you pop over there: a corpus-based study of conditionals in medical discourse. *English for Specific Purposes*, 20(1), 61–82

Ferris, D. (2001) Teaching writing for academic purposes. In J. Flowerdew & M. Peacock (eds.), *Research perspectives on English for academic purposes* (pp. 298–314). Cambridge: Cambridge University Press.

Flowerdew, J. & Peacock, M. (2001a) Issues in EAP: a preliminary perspective. In J. Flowerdew & M. Peacock (eds.), *Research perspectives on English for academic purposes* (pp. 8–24). Cambridge: Cambridge University Press.

Flowerdew, J. & Peacock, M. (2001b) The EAP curriculum: issues, methods and challenges. In J. Flowerdew & M. Peacock (eds.), *Research perspectives on English for academic purposes* (pp. 177–94). Cambridge: Cambridge University Press.

Fulcher, G. (1999) Assessment in English for academic purposes: putting content validity in its place. *Applied Linguistics*, 20(2), 221–26.

Graham, J. (1987) English language proficiency and the prediction of academic success. *TESOL Quarterly*, 21(3), 505–21.

Grant, L. (1997) Testing the language proficiency of bilingual teachers: Arizona's Spanish proficiency test. *Language Testing*, 14(1), 23–46.

Graves, K. (ed.) (1996) *Teachers as course developers*. Cambridge: Cambridge University Press.

Grove, E. & Whelan, A. (2001) Conflicting perspectives: linguistic and professional judgments of oral communication skills. *Melbourne Papers in Language Testing*, 10(2), 1–20.

Hale, G. A. (1988) Student major field and text content: interactive effects on reading comprehension in the test of English as a foreign language. *Language Testing*, 5(1), 49–61.

Hamp-Lyons, L. & Lumley, T. (2001) Assessing language for specific purposes. *Language Testing*, 18(2), 127–32.

Hawthorne, L. (1997) Defining the target domain: what skills are required of engineers and nurses? *Melbourne Papers in Language Testing*, 6(1), 44–52.

Henry, A. & Roseberry R. L. (2001) A narrow-angled analysis of moves and strategies of the genre: "Letter of Application." *English for Specific Purposes*, 20(2), 153–67.

Hirvela, A. (1997) Disciplinary portfolios and EAP instruction. *English for Specific Purposes*, 16(2), 83–106.

Hull, L. (1996) A curriculum framework for corporate language programs. In K. Graves (ed.), *Teachers as course developers* (pp. 176–202). Cambridge: Cambridge University Press.

Hutchinson, T. & Waters, A. (1987) *English for specific purposes*. Cambridge: Cambridge University Press.

Hyland, K. (2002) Specificity revisited: how far should we go now? *English for Specific Purposes*, 21(4), 385–95.

Jacoby, S. & McNamara, T. (1999) Locating competence. *English for Specific Purposes*, 18(3), 213–41.

Jasso-Aguilar, R. (1999) Sources, methods and triangulation in needs analysis: a critical perspective in a case study of Waikiki maids. *English for Specific Purposes*, 18(1), 27–46.

Jordan, R. R. (1997) *English for academic purposes: a guide and resource book for teachers*. Cambridge: Cambridge University Press.

Long, M. & Crookes, G. (1992) Three approaches to task-based syllabus design. *TESOL Quarterly*, 26(1), 27–56.

Lumley, T. (1998) Perceptions of language-trained raters and occupational experts in a test of occupational English language proficiency. *English for Specific Purposes*, 17(4), 347–65.

Lumley, T. & Brown, A. (1996) Specific-purpose language performance tests: task and interaction. In G. Wigglesworth & C. Elder (eds.), *The testing cycle: from inception to washback. Australian Review of Applied Linguistics*, series S no. 13 (pp. 105–36). Canberra, Australian National University.

McKenna, E. (1987) Preparing foreign students to enter discourse communities in US. *English for Specific Purposes*, 6(3), 187–202.

McNamara, T. (1996) *Measuring second language performance*. London, Longman.

McNamara, T. (1997) Problematising content validity: the Occupational English Test (OET) as a measure of medical communication. *Melbourne Papers in Language Testing*, 6(1), 19–43.

Pennycook, A. (1997) Vulgar pragmatism, critical pragmatism and EAP. *English for Specific Purposes*, 16(4), 253–69.

Pinto dos Santos, V. B. M. (2002) Genre analysis of business letters of negotiation. *English for Specific Purposes*, 21(2), 167–99.

Read, J. (2002) The use of interactive input in EAP listening assessment. *Journal of English for Academic Purposes*, 1, 105–19.

Robinson, P. (1991) *ESP Today: a practitioners' guide*. New York: Prentice-Hall.

Samraj, B. (2002) Introductions in research articles: Variations across disciplines. *English for Specific Purposes*, 21(1), 1–17.

Shi, L., Corcos, R., & Storey, A. (2001) Using student performance data to develop an English course for clinical training. *English for Specific Purposes*, 20(3), 267–91.

Simpson, R. C., Briggs, S. L., Ovens, J., & Swales, J. M. (2000) The Michigan Corpus of Spoken Academic English. Ann Arbor, MI: The Regents of the University of Michigan. (Available online at www.lsa.unmich.edu/eli/micase/micase.htm)

Soler, V. (2002) Analysing adjectives in scientific discourse: an exploratory study with educational applications for Spanish speakers at advanced university level. *English for Specific Purposes*, 21(2), 145–65.

Spolsky, B. (1995) *Measured words: the development of objective language testing.* Oxford: Oxford University Press.

Sullivan, P. & Girginer, H. (2002) The use of discourse analysis to enhance ESP teacher knowledge: an example using aviation English. *English for Specific Purposes*, 21(4), 397–404.

Swales, J. (1985) *Episodes in ESP.* Oxford: Pergamon.

Swales, J. M. (1990) *Genre analysis: English in academic and research settings.* Cambridge: Cambridge University Press.

Swales, J. M., Barks, D., Ostermann, A. C., & Simpson, R. C. (2001) Between critique and accommodation: reflections on an EAP course for Masters of Architecture students. *English for Specific Purposes*, 20, Supplement 1, 439–58.

Te Taura Whiri i te Reo Māori (2002) *National Māori Language Proficiency Examinations/Whakamātauria Tō Reo Māori*, Candidate Handbook for Public Sector Māori (PSM) and Level Finder Examination (LFE). Wellington, NZ: Te Taura Whiri i te Reo Māori.

Uvin, J. (1996) Designing workplace ESOL courses for Chinese health-care workers at a Boston nursing home. In K. Graves (ed.), *Teachers as course developers* (pp. 39–62). Cambridge: Cambridge University Press.

West, R. (1997) Needs analysis: state of the art. In R. Howard & G. Brown (eds.), *Teacher education for LSP* (pp. 68–79). Clevedon, UK: Multilingual Matters.

Wu, M. W. & Stansfield, C. W. (2001) Towards authenticity of task in test development. *Language Testing*, 18(2), 187–206.

Zhu, Y. (1997) An analysis of structural moves in Chinese sales letters. *Text*, 17(4), 543–66.

FURTHER READING

Alderson, J. C. (1988) Testing English for specific purposes – how specific can we get? In A. Hughes (ed.), *Testing English for university study* (pp. 16–28). London: Modern English Publications in association with The British Council.

Clapham, C. (2001) Discipline specificity and EAP. In J. Flowerdew & M. Peacock, (eds.), *Research perspectives on English for academic purposes* (pp. 84–100). Cambridge: Cambridge University Press.

Davies, A. (1986) Indirect ESP testing: old innovations. In Portal, M. (ed.), *Innovations in language testing* (pp. 55–67). Windsor: NFER/Nelson.

Douglas, D. (2001) Three problems in assessing language for specific purposes: authenticity, specificity and inseparability. In C. Elder, A. Brown, E. Grove, K. Hill, N. Iwashita, T. Lumley, T. McNamara, & K. O'Loughlin (eds.), *Experimenting with uncertainty: essays in Honour of Alan Davies* (pp. 45–52). Cambridge:

UCLES/Cambridge University Press.

Johns, A. M. (1997) *Text, role, and context: developing academic literacies.* Cambridge: Cambridge University Press.

Paltridge, B. (2001) Linguistic research and EAP pedagogy. In J. Flowerdew & M. Peacock, (eds.), *Research perspectives on English for academic purposes* (pp. 55–70). Cambridge: Cambridge University Press.

Skehan, P. (1984) Issues in the testing of English for specific purposes. *Language Testing,* 1(2), 202–20.

Widdowson, H. (1983) *Learning purpose and language use.* Oxford: Oxford University Press.

28 Bilingual Education

HEATHER LOTHERINGTON

28.1 Introduction

The world of the twenty-first century is inescapably multicultural. Twentieth-century technological innovations, particularly during the past quarter century, have revolutionized human and information transfer creating radically new opportunities for cross-cultural human communication in both real and virtual time. With the aid of fast, efficient and economical air travel, immigration patterns have shifted, rendering even those nations assumed to be fundamentally monocultural and monolingual into culturally complex societies. Supranational political and trading blocks have formed, dissolved, and reformed, and with them have come languages of wider, intercultural communication. Our shrinking political boundaries have brought with them everyday social encounters no one thought possible a mere half century ago, when increasing human mobility was beginning to challenge concepts of citizenship, nationality, and cultural identity.

Over the past half century, as societies have become increasingly multicultural, many demands for specific language and literacy proficiencies have arisen in terms of maintaining, revitalizing, and archiving the languages of non-dominant cultures and in acquiring languages of wider or official communication. In response, experimental bilingual and multilingual education programs have been developed, and they have grown into well-researched educational alternatives that are now familiar options in schools around the world.

28.2 A Brief Historical Introduction to Bilingual Education

Bilingual education has become a very popular educational option, but it is not a new phenomenon. According to Mackey (1978), bilingual education is thousands of years old, predating even the invention of the alphabet. Lewis (1976) points out that prior to the Christian era, the three linguistic ascendancies of Akkadian, Aramaic, and Greek brought with them consequent widespread bilingualism requiring bilingual education for minority functionaries.

The history of language contact shows that languages of strongest influence are those which have been supported by powerful institutions: religion, education, government, and the professions. The close relationship between religion, language, and literacy pervades civilization, and continues to sustain instruction of and in languages of liturgical significance, including classical languages such as Hebrew and Arabic, and languages of contemporary missionary focus. Indeed, as Crystal notes, it is a common religious tenet that a divine being has bestowed language on humanity (1997, p. 338).

In earliest days, the relative rarity of literate languages drove the need for formally studying in a language other than that spoken at home (Mackey, 1978). Prior to the Industrial Revolution, which fueled a need for a literate working force, education was the domain of the privileged, often conducted, at least partly, in a classical language. In classical Rome, Greek was taught to elite children, but, as Genesee points out (1987, p. 2), not without controversy about possible cognitive and linguistic effects of simultaneous bilingual instruction, a debate still heard today. In western Europe, the dominant language of scholarship was Latin until a just a few centuries ago (Genesee, 1987).

Not until the invention of the printing press were vernacular languages a viable literary alternative (Lewis, 1976). Even after education began to be taught in "national" languages, such as English and French, rather than classical languages, there were home-school language schisms owing to dialect differences (Genesee, 1987), a situation also known in contemporary bilingual education.

Mass education is a relatively recent social phenomenon, dating back only a century or two, and the teaching of languages has now moved from being the study of classical and foreign languages by a small elite for largely academic purposes to a being a basic social and economic necessity. What we see in the mid-twentieth century is the coming together of this tradition of classical language education with new developments and expectations in democratic education through vernacular languages. That marriage explains the assumption behind bilingual education that the cultural enrichment claimed for the classics could be achieved through any modern language, while at the same time offering cognitive empowerment by giving the status of language medium to the vernaculars.

Contemporary forms of bilingual education find their roots in experimental classrooms of the 1950s and 1960s, including importantly, the St Lambert French immersion kindergarten (Québec, 1965), the Dade County two-way immersion program (Florida, 1963), and the first European School (Luxembourg, 1957).

28.3   Current State of Debate

28.3.1   *Bilingual immersion education*

The longest standing debate about bilingual education is simply, "Does it work?" The reasons for instituting bilingual education depend on the sponsoring communities and ultimate program goals. Balances in the introduction of the languages of instruction can vary widely depending on choices made. However, parents and community members want to be reassured that children in bilingual education programs will not abandon their first language and culture, will learn the second language, and will not sacrifice curricular learning in any way.

A strong bilingual education program growing rapidly in popularity is *bilingual immersion* in which at least 50 percent of curricular content is delivered through the medium of the second language. The first bilingual immersion program was a French immersion kindergarten instigated by the St Lambert Protestant Parents for Bilingual Education (Lambert & Tucker, 1972). In the early 1960s, prior to the 1969 declaration of the Official Languages Act in Canada, the province of Québec was in a state of high political tension over issues of linguistic and cultural recognition of the majority francophone population. In an English-speaking pocket of the greater Montréal area, a group of concerned parents began a sustained planning, consulting, and public lobbying effort for better quality, more effective French as a second language education for their children. These parents "felt their children were being shortchanged and should have the opportunity to become 'bilingual' within the school system . . ." (Lambert & Tucker, 1972, p. 220). They had many reservations, however, that eventually shaped the format of their experimental program. The Québec provincial education system was segregated by both language and religion, with resulting French Catholic, French Protestant, English Catholic, and English Protestant schools. Many parents did not want to jeopardize their cultural and religious backgrounds by sending their children to French Catholic or even the "academically weaker French Protestant" schools (Lambert & Tucker, 1972, p. 221). Nor did they want an enrichment program of the sort offered at the Toronto French School in the neighboring province of Ontario, where French and Russian were offered with goals and examinations directed to external qualifications, such as the French baccalauréat. "They wanted 'normal' education, with one exception – it should lead to bilingualism by the end of elementary school, with no deficit in the mother tongue" (Lambert & Tucker, 1972, p. 231).

The program proposed by the St Lambert Protestant Parents for Bilingual Education was a radical paradigm shift in second language education; there was nothing like it in Canadian French as a second language education (Swain & Johnson, 1997). Children were taught by a French-speaking teacher; introduction to English was delayed until grade 2 when English literacy skills were first introduced to them. The amount of English gradually increased until grade 6 at which point 50 percent of the curriculum was given in each language (Swain & Johnson, 1997).

Four decades later, following the success of the French immersion kindergarten experimentally organized for anglophone children in St Lambert in 1965, the pedagogical model first described as "immersion in a 'language bath'" (Lambert & Tucker, 1972, p. 225) has spread globally, and recent accounts of immersion education describe programs in Africa, Asia, Australia, Europe, North America, and the Pacific (Johnson & Swain, 1997). However, incongruously, side by side with the increase in schools proposing immersion language courses internationally, are movements in the United States of America actually banning bilingual education in favor of "English only" administrations (Crawford, 1992; Schmid, 2001).

28.3.2   Bilingualism and nationalism

According to Hornberger, the concept of one nation one language, signaling the unification of a nation-state through a common language, emerged relatively recently in human history, following the establishment of eighteenth- and nineteenth-century nation-states in Europe and the Americas (2001, p. 31). Since the twentieth century, however, this marginalizing ideology has been pressured by globalization, ethnic fragmentation, multinational trade, and supranational political blocs. Furthermore, denationalization has occurred for a number of major world languages such as English, Spanish, and Russian, which have been appropriated as languages of wider communication (Lewis, 1976).

Bilingual education is rooted in a political ideology that rejects a singularity of cultural vision and works toward understanding across cultural and linguistic difference. Although bilingual education is generally lauded as an enriching educational experience, this is not a universal opinion. Given the range of political perceptions of multilingualism, from economic bonus to political threat, and the influence of social policies on public views and expectations of citizens' language competencies, opportunities for and attitudes toward bilingual education vary widely.

The volatile "English only" movement snowballing in the United States promotes a highly deterministic link between language, culture, and nation. Within this philosophy, American culture is firmly anchored in use of the English language, and cultural and linguistic diversity are drawn as intolerable threats to political unity (LoBianco, 2001). This ethnocentric mentality is bolstered by the growing prominence of English as a global language for purposes of business and intercultural communication, and the immensity of the American economy in global financial markets. Acquisition of English is thus rationalized economically with relative ease, and under the additional political weight which vilifies minority tongues as un-American, other languages are drawn through a sort of cost-benefit analysis as irrelevant, interfering, and best abandoned.

Within this political climate, bilingual education runs the gamut from culturally remedial to barely legal, if at all. Nonetheless, innovative bilingual programs, including formative, locally developed programs such as two-way immersion, are taking place in the United States, many of them socially and culturally grounded in ardent opposition to current political platforms.

The case of Ebonics is illustrative. Ebonics, or African American Vernacular English (AAVE) is a recognized variety of English spoken by a majority of inner city African Americans. It is a variety of language that has been studied by sociolinguists; AAVE has a consistent grammar, vocabulary, and phonology and is as capable a medium for logical reasoning as any other (Schmid, 2001). The genesis of AAVE is debated but there is some speculation that it has roots in a creole spoken by some of the first inhabitants, which has been increasingly affected by mainstream English (Crawford, 1992; Crystal, 1997).

An Ebonics-English bilingual education program was instituted in Oakland, California to vociferous debate in the 1990s. The pro-lobby saw Ebonics-medium education as a means of better reaching children and of introducing "standard" American English to them not as a perpetual correction of their competent AAVE language but as a parallel language variety: one of wider communication. In essence, this lobby believed that nurturing individual bilingualism would facilitate emergent literacy and successful entry into mainstream English-speaking society by linguistically differentiating Ebonics from standard American English. The opposition balked at conferring recognition on a non-standard vernacular. Some assumed their children would be prevented from learning standard English, or feared that children were being stigmatized through school use of their home vernacular (Schmid, 2001). Despite the fact that the debate came to national and international media attention, involving professional associations such as the American Association of Applied Linguistics (AAAL), the Linguistic Society of America (LSA), and Teachers of English to Speakers of Other Languages (TESOL) in public debate on the matter, resistant attitudes remained (Murray, 1999). Within a year, California had moved toward politically curtailing all bilingual education.

28.3.3 *Language ecology and revitalization movements*

> *It is for this reason that those who seek to defend a threatened linguistic capital, such as knowledge of the classical languages in present-day France, are obliged to wage a total struggle. One cannot save the value of a competence unless one saves the market, in other words, the whole set of political and social conditions or production of the producers/consumers.*
> (Bourdieu, 1991, p. 57)

Tove Skutnabb-Kangas estimates the number of oral languages (i.e., excluding sign languages) around the world to number approximately 6,700 (2000, p. 31).

However, the world's languages, like other resources, are very unevenly distributed. Of the world's oral languages, over 5,000 are spoken in just 22 countries, which have the highest per capita linguistic diversity (2000, p. 34). However, many of these languages are under severe threat of imminent extinction. According to Daniel Nettle, 11.5 percent of the world's languages have fewer than 150 speakers; a further 30 percent have fewer than 1,000 speakers (1999, p. 114).

Close to half of the population of the earth speaks just a handful of the world's languages; Nettle and Romaine, citing the 1996 Ethnologue, number these at 15: Mandarin Chinese, English, Spanish, Bengali, Hindi, Portuguese, Russian, Japanese, German, Wu Chinese, Javanese, Korean, French, Vietnamese and Telegu (2000, p. 29). Skutnabb-Kangas includes Arabic in the top five as well (2000, p. 38). Some of these major world languages have been labeled "killer languages." Their swelling ranks of speakers through educational and administrative coercion signal minority language shift. Of these, English is usually accorded top place as killer of linguistic diversity.

Bilingual education can be both saboteur and guardian of what Nettle and Romaine term: "biolinguistic diversity" (2000, p. 13). Bilingual education is a tool for spreading world languages, and this is seen very much in the international popularity of English in bilingual programs and second language courses. At the same time, bilingual education is a vehicle for language maintenance programs where children's home languages are reinforced through literate study at school. Furthermore, bilingual education can be a critical mainstay in language revitalization programs where children are educated in a threatened language, offering a means of language regeneration.

Skutnabb-Kangas (2000, p. 6) quotes Joshua Fishman as repeatedly indicating that schools alone cannot save endangered languages, but they can kill them. The political engineering of language and literacy competencies through educational and economic reward can be to the detriment as well as the support of language revitalization and maintenance efforts.

Papua New Guinea has the highest linguistic diversity on earth, as home to over 850 languages from a number of distinct language families. The Summer Institute of Linguistics has been active in the development and teaching of vernacular language education in Papua New Guinea for decades, notably with the Viles Tok Ples Skuls project which began in 1980 in response to parental fears about the socially alienating effects of English medium schooling on their children (Litteral, 1999). Villagers wanted education for their children that reinforced their *Tok Ples* (literally: "talk place" meaning vernacular language), and prepared them well academically. The provincial government supported parents' expressed concerns and instituted the Viles Tok Ples Skuls: vernacular medium preparatory schools. By 1993, the indigenous education project had extended to 250 languages (Litteral, 1999, p. 3), despite the decimating effects of the Bougainville civil war, and vernacular language preparatory schools were spreading to other provinces across the country. The Viles Tok Ples Skuls provide preparatory vernacular literacy to grade one where English is introduced in a bridging year; maintenance of the vernacular through content-based study of non-core subjects to grade 6, and vernacular activities in secondary and tertiary education (Litteral, 1999, p. 4).

In Aotearoa-New Zealand, a landmark Maori-English bilingual program has gone some way toward *revitalizing* Te Reo Maori (the Maori language), which, only a generation ago, was under serious social threat, with less than 5 percent of Maori schoolchildren found to be able to speak their language in 1975 (Durie, 1997, p. 16). Maori-speaking children, like many minority language children worldwide, were punished for speaking Te Reo Maori at school prior to the 1970s. The prevailing assimilationist policies reinforced English monolingualism in education as in the larger society. Trial Maori-English bilingual programs began in the late 1970s. In 1982 the first Kohanga Reo, or language nest, was established. This early total immersion kindergarten program has been very successful, and a range of follow-up Taha Maori (Maori enrichment) and Kura Kaupapa Maori (language immersion) programs allows children to continue language acquisition and maintenance as they progress through school (Durie, 1997). By 1995, close to 50 percent of all Maori children were enrolled in Kohanga Reo (1997, p. 18), and the language nest model was being applied to other Pacific languages spoken in Aotearoa-New Zealand.

28.4   Contexts of Bilingual Education

28.4.1   *Sociocultural*

Language signals and encodes cultural identity. Contemporary cultural identities are very complex. People's identities mediate personal, social, cultural, and language affiliations through their language repertoire. Many people see themselves as intrinsically bicultural.

Bilingual education is socioculturally targeted. Learning through the media of two languages is not random. It is essential that students understand at least one of the languages through which they will be taught. Nonetheless, the language backgrounds of students enrolled in bilingual education include a range of knowledge bases, from monolingual to bilingual or multilingual in an assortment of high and/or low status languages.

The contexts supporting bilingual education are endlessly variable. The micro-context of the home could be monolingual and monocultural, monolingual but bicultural, bilingual and bicultural, or multilingual, with generations of family members having different language competencies and preferences. The language/s of the home may also have variable levels of status within the community, which itself might function in a variety of languages, despite the national language profile. In California, for example, where bilingual education has been politically barred, there are extensive and well-established neighborhoods in which languages such as Spanish, Cantonese, and Korean thrive.

How and where students fit into the dominant sociocultural context of the bilingual education program is highly salient. The onus on a student who has recently settled in a country and needs to learn the majority language for all aspects of survival is something quite different from that on a student enrolled in an enrichment program out of intellectual curiosity. Not only do expectations and assessments of students' success rates vary considerably with the relative social importance of the languages, but also the vitality of the languages themselves may be at stake. For instance, in a recent study in Australia, students in a variety of bilingual courses were found to have the following range of possible language backgrounds (Lotherington, 2001):

1   recent arrivals to Australia who had been educated in the target language (TL),
2   those who had an oral and literate grounding in the TL,
3   those who had an oral background in the TL,
4   those who had a passive knowledge of the TL,
5   dialect speakers,
6   those with a cultural but not a language background in the TL,
7   monolinguals with no language background in the TL,
8   bi- and multilinguals with no language background in the TL.

28.4.2   *Political*

28.4.2.1   *Language policy*

The treatment of cultural pluralism in national policy is a determining factor in languages-in-education policies and programs.

National political reactions to cultural diversity range from multiculturalism, where cultural pluralism is welcomed as an asset (e.g., Australia), to assimilation, where minority cultural populations are expected to abandon their linguistic heritages and melt into majority language and cultural norms (e.g., the United States of America), to disaggregating polarities, where cultural groups are isolated and maintained separately from each other, with attendant unequal civil rights (e.g., the former apartheid regime of the Republic of South Africa) (Baker, 2001).

Accordingly, language can be politically perceived as a problem, a right, or a resource (Ruiz, 1984). For instance, a nation with a political agenda of assimilation sees cultural and linguistic pluralism as incompatible with national unity, and as such understands language diversity to be a problem. Bilingualism in nations of this political character is seen as neither a normal nor indeed desirable social trait, but running contrary to historical legacy, or to a non-negotiable cultural identity. In the American "melting pot," bilingualism is envisioned as a *transitional* state through which minority language speakers must pass en route to majority language adoption. As such, *subtractive bilingualism*, where the second language (L2) is intended to replace the first language (L1), is reinforced. In effect this is *language shift* rather than any kind of bilingualism.

Nations espousing multiculturalism may look upon language diversity as a right of citizens and provide constitutional protection. Where societal languages have been accorded the status of citizenship rights in officially bilingual and multilingual countries, protective legislation provides for education as well as other designated legal, institutional, and administrative functions. For instance, in Canada, where English and French have been accorded status as official languages, bilingual education programs are widely available. *Additive bilingualism*, where the L2 is added to the L1, is encouraged in such a political climate; however, as equivalent constitutional protection is not accorded to all minority and indigenous languages in the country, selective language shift can easily occur if minority language speakers shift from speaking their unprotected minority languages in the home and community to the official languages of the country. In this case, where individual and societal languages are not equally supported, bilingual education can be either additive or subtractive, depending on the learner's L1.

Multicultural nations may further view linguistic diversity as a resource that socially and economically enriches the culture as a whole, and actively promote acquisition and maintenance of additive bilingualism through educational means. For example, in the state of Victoria, Australia, options for credit study of over 50 languages have been possible for a number of years now (Department of Education, 1997). Indeed, in a case study of a suburban high school in Melbourne in 1998, ten community languages were being taught as credit subjects: Arabic, Chinese, Khmer, French, German, Greek, Italian, Japanese, Spanish, and Vietnamese; two of these languages (Vietnamese, Chinese) through immersion programs (Lotherington, 2001).

28.4.2.2 Language planning

Language policy is a combination of explicit public policy (as in the declaration of official languages), and less obvious implicit social norms. Language policy may be directed to the language code itself, as in corpus planning, or to status planning, where the place of language in society, rather than the language code, is engineered.

Status planning affects bilingualism and bilingual education by facilitating the study of languages of high or protected status. Language can be accorded official status, as in the case of Bislama, the variant of Melanesian Pidgin spoken in Vanuatu. Bislama's official status alters public opportunities for using the language for administrative, institutional, and business purposes, which, in turn, positively affects attitudes toward the language. Language can be given special priority in government planning as well. For example, in Victoria, Australia, eight key languages are educationally prioritized: Chinese, French, German, Greek, Indonesian, Italian, Japanese, and Vietnamese (Clyne, 1997, p. 104).

Corpus planning affects bilingual education insofar as it mandates language standards. The Académie française, a seventeeth-century institution that safeguards French language and culture, is an example of corpus planning.

Another is Te Tauru Whiri i te Reo Maori (the Maori Language Commission) in Aotearoa (New Zealand).

28.4.2.3   Language standards

Defining what a language is emerges as a problem where language norms and standards are drawn for educational and publishing purposes. Some language communities do not name their language. This is not only true of indigenous languages but also of vernacular languages, particularly of pidgins and creoles, which are typically held in low social esteem. As Lisa, a bilingual Jamaican Patois-English speaker, and a graduate student of Education points out:

> My mother would never consider herself bilingual because she honestly thinks that she speaks English and only English. If you were to ask my mother what other languages are spoken in Jamaica other than English, she would be very offended. How could you ask such a question when the official language in Jamaica is English and Patois is only "bad" English? People are upset by the notion that what they think is English is not what others think is English. (personal communication, Lisa Tomlinson, York University, Toronto)

The question of who sets the standard involves a historical quest. Languages of large speech communities, especially world languages, are lexically indexed in dictionaries that note regional, temporal, and social variations; they are preserved in bodies of published literature, and broadcast through mass media. However smaller languages, especially preliterate languages, are open to debate on whether they should be educationally recognized. This debate about recognition is driving the anti-bilingualism lobby in California vis-à-vis the teaching of Ebonics in school. At a metropolitan school in Toronto, the teachers note that they don't know what the students are speaking and assume it is Ebonics. It is pointed out that children are using Jamaican Patois. The children themselves do not necessarily understand that this is essentially a different language.

Establishing a recognized orthography for a language is imperative. In the Micronesian republic of Nauru, children speak Nauruan or an English lexifier Pidgin as lingua franca with others on the island. However, they are expected to cope with formal education in English, using a curriculum imported from Australia. English is not spoken colloquially by Nauruans. Their widely used Pidgin is not acknowledged as a distinct language. Codification of the Nauruan language is a further political issue: orthographic conventions have not been agreed upon. This essentially prevents any opportunity to introduce English through bilingual education for Nauruan schoolchildren (Lotherington, 1998).

28.4.3   Psychological

An L1 always develops within a natural context: no one "teaches" their child to speak, despite the claims of errant caretakers. Acquisition of an L2 does not exactly parallel L1 development; otherwise we would all be able to endlessly and relatively effortlessly acquire new languages. However, we do know that L1 development provides an important basis for L2 learning in formal, serial language learning (Cummins, 2000).

28.4.3.1 Attitudes

The attitudes held by students with the regard to the languages they are learning, the cultural context/s of those languages, and their speakers affect learners' success in becoming bilingual.

Attitudes toward their own cultural identity can affect learners' L2 acquisition, L1 maintenance, and intergenerational language transmission. Second language learners with a positive sociocultural identity are more likely to maintain their L1 and to add an L2 to their linguistic repertoire than L2 learners who have a negative sociocultural identity, and may see *second language acquisition* (SLA) as an avenue for replacing the L1 rather than adding to it.

Students' motivations for acquiring or maintaining a second language through bilingual study include both intrinsic and extrinsic influences. Parents, other relatives, and teachers may act as extrinsically motivating forces on those learning or maintaining a minority language. Learners may also have an intrinsic interest in the language.

A teacher in a Hebrew immersion program in Canada asks how she can improve students' motivations for learning Hebrew when it is seldom heard outside of the confines of the school. She wants her students to feel part of a social collective; to feel *integratively* motivated to belong. However, she despairs that Israeli youth seem to want to learn more English, so it is difficult to sell modern Hebrew as the language of contemporary Jewish culture to young Canadians when the Israeli teenagers they are likely to meet want to learn more English.

Meanwhile a teacher of Mandarin Chinese in Australia is busily selling her content-based bilingual program on the basis that knowledge of Chinese is an important asset for both local business and foreign trade. She is highlighting an *instrumental motivation* to learn Chinese: knowing the language will be socially, academically or economically facilitative.

28.5 Models of Bilingual Education

28.5.1 Learning a second language

An L2 can be learned naturalistically, or "picked up" through contextual circumstances, or it can be formally learned through conscious application. SLA has been extensively studied by applied linguists and psychologists in an effort to sort out quite why and how learning an L2 varies from learning an L1 and how we can better teach second languages. Variability in SLA is endless, situated in linguistic, contextual, individual, social, political, cultural, and pedagogical factors. However, there is systematicity in SLA as well and theoretical findings have informed the field on learner characteristics, variations in linguistic environments, and interlanguage development (Long, 1994). Nonetheless, there are still gaps in fundamental theoretical understanding.

The term L2 captures fundamental differences in the process of language learning rather than in the temporal sequence of language acquisition. *Foreign language* (FL) is a term sometimes used instead of *second language* (SL). This is a political label denoting the FL as a language of exogenous linguistic and cultural norms. The use of the term *foreign language* in the educational context is culturally isolating; indeed such usage is increasingly being replaced by less alienating terms such as *international language* (Canada), and *community language* (Australia).

Stern (1983) details the history of second language pedagogy from the late 1870s to the early 1980s, during which period languages were taught through a variety of methods, but essentially as linguistic artifacts: subjects where focus on the grammar and vocabulary, whether oral or written, constituted learning the language. Only in the 1970s did the field turn to the more communicative approaches to language learning that underscore contemporary bilingual education.

Most descriptors of L2 learners denote deficit. Acronyms used to describe L2 learners of English, which is predicted to be more widely spoken in the world as L2 than L1 within the next 50 years (Graddol, 1999), are marked forms against an underlying unmarked native English speaker: ESL (English as a second language), EFL (English as a foreign language), ESOL (English to speakers of other languages), NESB (non-English-speaking background), LEP (limited English proficiency), LOTE (language other than English). Bilingual education, in its strong forms, avoids these negative labels by introducing the languages of study in a more democratic academic context.

28.5.2   Bilingual and multilingual education

Bilingual education refers to education in which two languages are used instructionally. It is a growing international phenomenon. Recent volumes on bilingual education have documented programs operating on all continents; for example, Africa (Ghana, Kenya, Nigeria, South Africa, Tanzania); Asia (Brunei, China, Hong Kong, India, Indonesia, Japan, Malaysia, Singapore); Europe (Belgium, Denmark, Finland, Germany, Hungary, Ireland, Italy, Netherlands, Norway, Slovak Republic, Slovenia, Spain, Sweden, United Kingdom); the Middle East (Lebanon); North America (Canada, Jamaica, Mexico, United States); South America (Paraguay, Peru); and the Pacific region (Australia, Hawai'i, New Zealand, South Pacific Islands). These documented case studies describe a variety of programs oriented to learning a majority language, a minority language, an international language, or an indigenous language (including revitalized languages) addressed variously to national minority groups, migrant populations, dominant language groups, indigenous groups, and deaf and hard-of-hearing groups (Christian & Genesee, 2001; Cummins & Corson, 1997; Johnson & Swain, 1997; Paulston, 1988). This is a staggering testimony to the range and popularity of bilingual education.

There are a number of types of bilingual, and increasingly multilingual, education, some intended for children who are just learning one of the two languages used educationally, and others for children who are already bilingual. Bilingual education programs may be oriented either toward transition to the second language or toward maintenance of the first language. Baker (2001) characterizes education programs for bilingual learning as *strong* and *weak*. In strong bilingual education programs, additive bilingualism and biliteracy are the intended outcomes of the program. In education programs only weakly oriented to bilingualism, additive bilingualism is not an intended outcome of the program.

Bilingual education programs may be aimed at:

1 enrichment education for majority language speakers (L2 = minority language),
2 maintenance education for bilingual speakers (L2 = minority language),
3 compensatory education for minority language speakers in a majority context (L2 = majority language),
4 transitional education for minority language speakers in a majority context (L2 = majority language),
5 revitalization education in an endangered language (L2 = endangered minority language).

28.5.2.1 *Strong bilingual education programs*

Content-based learning is an approach to second language instruction in which the L2 is used as the medium of instruction to teach and learn curricular content. Content-based learning is theoretically based on *communicative competence*, which emphasizes the socially appropriate and meaningful use of language, that is, knowing how to effectively use language rather than knowing about language. The term *content-based language teaching* normally refers to programs in which less than 50 percent of the curriculum is taught through the medium of the L2; where 50 percent or more of the curriculum is taught using the L2, the term *immersion* is used.

Bilingual immersion, the best-known form of content-based bilingual education, has been very widely researched. According to Swain and Johnson (1997, pp. 6–8), the core features of an immersion program include:

1 use of the L2 as medium of instruction,
2 a curriculum parallel to that used in the L1,
3 overt support for the L1,
4 additive bilingualism as program aim,
5 exposure to the L2 being largely confined to the classroom,
6 students entering the program with similar, limited levels of L2 proficiency,

7   bilingual teachers,
8   the classroom culture being that of the local L1 community.

Variable features of immersion programs include (Swain & Johnson, 1997, pp. 8–11):

1   educational level at which immersion is introduced,
2   the extent of language immersion,
3   the ratio of L1 to L2 at different stages of the program,
4   continuity of the program across the school system,
5   bridging support for students,
6   resources,
7   commitment,
8   attitudes toward the L2 culture,
9   status of the L2,
10   evaluation of program success.

Total immersion programs introduce the second language immediately and use it for 100 percent of course work for a specified period of time leading to gradual introduction of the first language. For a program to be designated *partial immersion* requires that at least 50 percent of subjects are taught in each language.

There are several entry points into an immersion program. In early immersion programs, children begin on school entry. Middle entry to immersion is normally at around grade 4, and tends to be partial. Late entry immersion is typically around grade 7. There is some evidence to indicate that students in early total French immersion programs graduate with slightly better L2 proficiencies, although more mature learners have been shown to be cognitively better prepared to learn selected aspects of the second language (Swain, 1997; Swain & Lapkin, 1982).

Aimee, Clarence, Gary, and Brittany are four grade 8 students at Meadowvale Senior Public School in North Toronto. (All names are pseudonyms.) They are students in a late entry partial immersion program known as: "extended French." The large middle school they attend receives children from several elementary feeder schools including two which offer total immersion. The high desirability of the total immersion programs in public elementary schools bolsters the real estate value of homes in school catchment areas.

Meadowvale Senior Public School (MSPS) is a triple track school: children coming from total French immersion programs, whether early or middle entry, can continue to work in French immersion at MSPS and carry on their French immersion program at the regional high school. Children wishing access to late-entry partial immersion are provided with the extended French program in which French, history, geography, art, health, computer studies, and physical education are taught in French; and English, math, science, music, and swimming are taught in English. In the core French stream, children are taught only French language in French.

Although French immersion was developed for anglophone students, these four French immersion students represent to a small degree Toronto's staggering linguistic and cultural diversity. All children are fluent in English but only Brittany has a monolingual English background. Clarence's background is Jamaican, Gary's German-English, Aimee's Polish-Canadian. Other children in their class come from diverse language backgrounds, including Chinese, Greek, Hebrew, Russian, and Serbian. They are typical of contemporary immersion students in present-day metropolitan areas, who are far more culturally and linguistically complex than the learners of the 1960s for whom bilingual immersion was originally designed.

In Australia, 14 different immersion programs, involving a host of different languages, were operating in Victorian schools in 1998. Compared to the bottom-up evolution of immersion education in Canada, the impetus for bilingual education in Australia has been quite top-down. Many schools, aware of the international increases in bilingual and multilingual education, and inspired by the success of a number of well-established, local bilingual programs, have been funded under state educational initiatives to trial experimental bilingual courses. As in all trial programs, they are facing a number of difficulties, including hiring suitably qualified bilingual teachers and providing follow-up bilingual programs in the same language combinations to consolidate early learning.

Two-way immersion programs integrate a majority and a minority language community in a bilingual, bicultural program providing instruction through the media of both languages. This model of bilingual education is designed for bicultural rather than multicultural social contexts. Successful two-way Spanish-English bilingual programs are inspiring like programs across the USA (Rhodes, Christian, & Barfield, 1997).

Two-way immersion programs aim to provide quality education in two languages. Specific program goals are to promote academic success, second language achievement, positive cross-cultural attitudes, and high self-esteem, created by equal validation of both a minority and a majority language and opportunities for minority language children to act as models to majority language children (Rhodes, Christian, & Barfield, 1997).

Maintenance education is designed to provide minority language children with the opportunity to maintain a literate engagement with their minority language. Maintenance programs follow on from transitional education, normally through courses in which the language itself is formally studied, rather than being the medium for other content learning. This model works with well-defined populations, but it is not practical for very heterogeneous school populations. Educational support for the L2 is minimized in a maintenance program.

As Fishman points out, language maintenance is not possible without intergenerational mother tongue transmission, but maintenance is essentially a post-transmission process (1991, p. 113). However, without the reinforcement of literacy, normally learned in school, *fossilization* of the minority language and eventual loss in proficiencies are likely to occur. As such, bilingual programs are an essential, if not a sufficient contributor to language vitality. Home is the primary domain for L1 maintenance; opportunities for maintenance also exist in larger social circles and through mass media.

28.5.2.2   *Multilingual education*

Multilingual education entails the teaching and learning of multiple languages. Research reports on multilingual programs operating in the Basque country, Bolivia, Canada, Eritrea, Luxembourg, Peru, and the Philippines attest to the growing popularity of trilingual education (see Cenoz & Genesee, 1998). Multilingual education is by nature very complex, so it is consequently demanding in terms of administration, materials, and staffing. There are various multilingual education program models in existence, the introduction and incorporation of languages depending on contextual and linguistic needs and resources.

A foundational paradigm of multilingual education is the European School model, first trialled in Luxembourg in 1957. *Dual stream bilingual education,* where two or more majority languages are used as classroom media, such as in the European Schools (Baetens Beardsmore, 1993) is oriented to multilingualism within a supra-national European identity. Mainstream bilingual education is accomplished through a melding of the principles of both immersion and maintenance education. Children's distinct cultural identities are maintained through instruction in their L1. Formal study of a second language then leads to transitional use of the second language as an additional medium for content study. Study of a further language is required as well.

Luxembourg has developed a universal trilingual education system, involving the language spoken by Luxembourgers, Lëtzebuergesch (Luxembourgish) and two exoglossic languages of neighboring countries: French and German. Through its unique education system, Luxembourg supports triglossia: the socially complementary use of three languages. Luxembourger children begin nursery school at age 4 in Lëtzebuergesch, and are introduced to German in grade 1, which they learn intensively and progressively move toward using for the main medium of instruction until grade 6. They are introduced to French in grade 2, and teaching through the medium of French increases systematically in the high school grades. All languages are maintained throughout school, and other foreign and classical languages are introduced as well. Thus, Luxembourger children have studied several languages by the time they leave secondary school (Hoffman, 1998): truly multilingual education.

28.5.2.3   *Weak second language education programs*

It is also important to discuss weak programs ostensibly oriented to bilingualism, in order to be aware of their problematic natures.

Some programs that do not hold to the basic principles of immersion education attempt to designate themselves immersion. If the aims of L2 medium education are not additive bilingualism, then the program is, in effect, *submersion.* Language submersion is the opposite of immersion in that it provides no L1 support for children being "immersed" in an L2. In submersion education, the curriculum is taught through the medium of a high status second language. This L2 may be a majority language in the country or it may be a language of wider communication not actually used at the community level. Submersion programs offer a "sink or swim" approach to language and literacy acquisition. Children thus receive minimum pedagogical support for the crucial acquisition of literacy skills and a threshold level of the L2 sufficient to support further schooling. Such submersion programs are found in colonial contexts – both intranational as well as international.

National language policy in the Solomon Islands states that children are to be educated in English. The country is highly multilingual; Pijin is used for cross-linguistic communication. Given that English is a colonial language, not spoken at a colloquial level by the general population, the language must be learned in the classroom (Lotherington, 1996). English is spoken in the classroom according to policy, but in practice, teachers, understandably, often rely on vernacular communication. In many cases, teachers, who are themselves survivors of submersion education, are unconfident of their competencies in English. Children are expected to acquire literacy skills in English to a threshold level enabling them to do cognitively demanding work through an English print medium in classrooms where there is insufficient oral support, all but predestining them to failure (Lotherington, 1998). This is submersion.

Transitional education treats bilingualism as a transient phenomenon, in accordance with the political aims of assimilation. Transitional education aims to introduce basic literacy and numeracy in the minority L1 alongside introduction to the majority L2. Learners are provided with a limited bridging period during which they are expected to acquire a threshold level of the L2 and proceed onto content learning through the medium of the L2. Transitional programs assume linguistic homogeneity in classes and may even teach a high status version of the students' true vernacular as their L1.

In Fiji, two languages taught transitionally are Fijian and Hindi. However, Bauan Fijian, which has evolved through a complex political history as the national standard of Fijian, is not the home dialect of many Fijian children, who speak a spectrum of local communalects. Therefore, many Fijian children are learning to read in Bauan as a second dialect in what are intended to be vernacular medium classes (Mugler, 1996). The case is even more disturbing for Indo-Fijian children, who learn Standard Hindi in the vernacular classroom but speak a preliterate Hindi koine in the community (Shameem & Read, 1996). Therefore, only in some Fijian transitional classes, and in no Hindi transitional classes, are children actually learning in their L1.

Language object programs offer formal language study; however, the L2 is not used as a medium for content learning. Exposure to the L2 is limited in this model, and traditionally focused on form rather than meaning. Although only limited enrichment has occurred with language object programs in most contexts, Baker (2001, p. 200) points out that Scandinavians have often achieved high levels of fluency in English with this sort of traditional language program.

He credits students' motivation to learn the language and its economic imperative in the society as positive influences.

28.6　Evaluation of Bilingual Education

> *[B]ilingualism is not just a societal resource, it is also an individual*
> *resource that can enhance aspects of bilingual children's academic,*
> *cognitive and linguistic functioning.*
>
> (Cummins, 2000, p. 175)

28.6.1　Assessment and evaluation practices

An enduring problem in assessing and evaluating bilingual education programs is in defining bilingual proficiency. How much and what kind of each language is enough to warrant the label of bilingual? The question taken back a notch in languages seems ridiculous: how well must a person know an L1 in order to be considered proficient? Is there an end point or determining set of skills in language proficiency?

Bilingualism is neither a monolithic nor a static state; bilingual language proficiencies are complex, functionally complementary, and dynamic. However, language and literacy competencies may be differentially evaluated, educationally, socially, and politically. The stakes are high. Without acquiring the language and literacy competencies contemporary society sees as fundamental to linguistic functioning, students are deemed to have failed educationally. Political assessments of language value and literacy proficiencies are typically understood in limited terms of economic potential.

Social and pedagogical biases in educational measurement mean that L2 proficiencies tend to be judged against monolingual L1 standards, and a deficit picture formed rather than a more humanistic and sociolinguistically realistic picture of the individual's particular skills in each language (Cenoz & Genesee, 1998). "Indeed bilinguals, in and outside school, are usually evaluated according to the 'monolingual' competence in their non-native languages" (Cenoz & Genesee, 1998, p. 18).

Strong bilingual education programs have as their aim additive bilingualism: the acquisition and maintenance of both languages. This means that student assessment and program evaluation must take account of proficiencies in both languages. However, in subtractive models, such as transitional education, assessment typically focuses on the majority language to the detriment of the minority language.

As Swain (1983) has noted, appropriate assessment is critical to effective bilingual teaching. Academic literacy practices in the high status languages of schooling, whether L1 or L2 for the individual child, typically drive assessment and accountability in educational practice. The case of Rosemount High School is illustrative. In a study of a pilot content-based Chinese-English bilingual education course in this suburban high school in Melbourne, Australia, two discernible orientations to bilingual education emerged, owing partly to the backwash effects of assessment practices (Lotherington, 2001).

The students in the grade 9 and 10 bilingual English-Chinese stream at Rosemount High School were culturally and linguistically heterogeneous. Some were recent newcomers from China; others had a Chinese cultural heritage, but were not speakers of Mandarin; still others had no cultural or linguistic connection to Chinese. This diversity reflected a wide range of background knowledge, attitudes toward Chinese, and motivations for enrolling in the content-based bilingual program. The participating teachers, whose Chinese cultural origins also differed, both independently developed an enrichment approach to Chinese bilingual education.

State assessment of the subject Ms Lau was responsible for teaching through the medium of Chinese was in English. This drew serious concerns from her as the year progressed; she felt she was spending too much time on terminology and was insecure about the students' functional command of the subject as a whole. Ms Zhao, on the other hand, taught Chinese language as well as an optional subject that did not require state assessment. This affected teaching, with Ms Lau emphasizing content over language learning, with the result that more and more English was used in her classroom at the expense of Chinese, and Ms Zhao working across the curriculum to provide maximum Chinese language and literacy learning opportunities for her students. In the final analysis, only Ms Zhao was teaching a content-based bilingual program (Lotherington, 2001).

Evaluating bilingual education is complicated; assessment needs to take account of multiple viewpoints, including those of the individual child, the class as a whole, the school, and the type of educational program. Measures of success in bilingual education programs are dependent on the aims and goals of the program. As Baker (2001) points out, evaluation leans toward quantitative outcomes; insufficient attention is paid to qualitative approaches to data gathering which may provide richer evidence of the workings of a bilingual program. However, bilingual education is an ideology; it is not socially, educationally, or politically neutral. The kind of evidence which is gathered and the way such evidence is interpreted may be governed by researchers' and examiners' political agendas.

28.6.2 *Benefits of bilingual education*

Although much research has been conducted, there have been volatile debates on the merits of bilingual education in North America over the past few decades. As noted by Cummins (2000), the research evidence in applied linguistics has been strongly supportive of bilingual education. Vocal opponents of bilingual education tend to come from other research backgrounds.

Twenty years ago, Swain and Lapkin candidly discussed frequently asked questions of French immersion programs, which included (1982, pp. 16–23):

1 What happens to the development of students' first language (English) skills?
2 Do the immersion students learn more French than students in a core French program? How does their French compare to that of native speakers of French?
3 Are the immersion students able to keep up with their English-educated peers on subject content taught to them in French?
4 Does participation in the immersion program hinder general intellectual or cognitive growth?
5 How do children with below average IQ fare in an immersion program?
6 How do children with learning disabilities fare in an immersion program?
7 What are the social and psychological consequences of participation in immersion programs?

Bilingual immersion education has been widely researched and answers to these questions are available, although, as always, educational success and particular problems experienced vary with contextual constraints. Vis-à-vis French immersion in Canada, research indicates that immersion education is beneficial, and that any L1 developmental literacy lags and gaps in content knowledge are temporary and disappear once a certain functional language threshold has been reached. Cognitive, social, and psychological benefits are also in evidence. Children's identity has not proven to be at risk and their attitudes to francophone society are more positive and less rigidly stereotyped. Achieving native-like proficiency speaking and writing in the L2 has been somewhat more problematic, with grammatical accuracy and accent issues noted, though these tend to be more obvious in contexts where children have little access to French outside of the school context (Baker & Hornberger, 2001; Swain & Lapkin, 1982). Professionals continue to work with accuracy issues, and have introduced a focus on form into the communicatively-focused immersion model.

Several decades after the first experimental French immersion program took place in St Lambert, Québec, a number of positive social, educational, and economic effects have accrued from the societal incorporation of the values of official bilingualism. The status of French has changed dramatically; according to a recent economic analysis of language (Breton, 1998), official language bilinguals in Canada have increased both their earning power and their earnings. Although non-official language bilinguals have not seen their economic value increased in the same way, the increasing popularity of bilingual education and the introduction of trilingual programs augurs well for positive change in this direction.

Cummins enumerates applied linguistics researchers' common findings about bilingual education (2000, pp. 202–3):

1 Bilingual programs for students from minority and majority language backgrounds have been implemented successfully in countries around the world.

2 Bilingual education, by itself, is not a panacea for students' underachievement.
3 The development of literacy in two languages entails linguistic and perhaps cognitive advantages for bilingual students.
4 Significant positive relationships exist between the development of academic skills in L1 and L2.
5 Conversational and academic registers of language proficiency are distinct and follow different developmental patterns.

After a half century of researching bilingual and multilingual education, covering the gamut from ambitious multilingual programs, such as the European Schools, to two-way bilingual and bicultural immersion models, to bilingual immersion, to content-based teaching, to language studies of more modest proportions, applied linguistics researchers know that bilingual education does work. This knowledge comes from research that spans the globe. How well bilingual education works depends on how bilingual proficiency is defined and assessed. We know that if both (or all) languages are educationally supported, children will profit educationally, linguistically, and socially; indications are that they will also profit cognitively and economically.

Although bilingual education has been a part of human civilization for thousands of years, it has taken on a new life over the past half century. Bilingual and multilingual education programs are spreading rapidly worldwide; it remains to be seen whether humans can effectively promote better ecological language practices through such educational innovations. Certainly, the groundwork has been provided for such success.

See also 18 LANGUAGE MINORITIES, 22 SOCIAL INFLUENCES ON LANGUAGE LEARNING, 29 LANGUAGE MAINTENANCE, 30 LANGUAGE PLANNING AS APPLIED LINGUISTICS.

REFERENCES

Baetens Beardsmore, H. (ed.) (1993) *European models of bilingual education.* Clevedon, UK: Multilingual Matters.

Baker, C. (2001) *Foundations of bilingual education and bilingualism* (3rd edn.). Clevedon, UK/Philadelphia: Multilingual Matters.

Baker, C. & Hornberger, N. (eds.) (2001) *An introductory reader to the writings of Jim Cummins.* Clevedon, UK: Multilingual Matters.

Bourdieu, P. (1991) *Language and symbolic power* (trans. G. Raymond &

M. Adamson). Cambridge, MA: Harvard University Press.

Breton, A. (ed.) (1998) *Economic approaches to language and bilingualism.* Ottawa, Ontario: Canadian Heritage.

Cenoz, J. & Genessee, F. (1998) Psycholinguistic perspectives on multilingualism and multilingual education. In J. Cenoz & F. Genesee (eds.), *Beyond bilingualism: multilingualism and multilingual education* (pp. 16–32). Clevedon, UK: Multilingual Matters.

Christian, D. & Genesee, F. (eds.) (2001) *Bilingual education*. Alexandria, Virginia: Teachers of English to Speakers of Other Languages, Inc.

Clyne, M. (1997) Managing language diversity and second language programmes in Australia. *Current Issues in Language and Society*, 4(2), 94–119.

Crawford, J. (1992) *Hold your tongue: bilingualism and the politics of English only*. Reading, MA: Addison-Wesley.

Crystal, D. (1997) *The Cambridge encyclopedia of language* (2nd edn.). Cambridge: Cambridge University Press.

Cummins, J. (2000) *Language, power and pedagogy: bilingual children caught in the crossfire*. Clevedon, UK: Multilingual Matters.

Cummins, J. & Corson, D. (eds.) (1997) *Encyclopedia of language and education, vol. 5: Bilingual education*. Dordrecht: Kluwer.

Cummins, J. & Danesi, M. (1990) *Heritage languages: the development and denial of Canada's linguistic resources*. Toronto: Our Schools/Our Selves Education Foundation.

Department of Education (1997) *Languages other than English in government schools, 1996*. Melbourne: State of Victoria.

Durie, A. (1997) Maori-English bilingual education in New Zealand. In J. Cummins & D. Corson (eds.), *Encyclopedia of language and education, vol. 5: Bilingual education*. Dordrecht: Kluwer.

Fishman, J. A. (1991) *Reversing language shift*. Clevedon, UK: Multilingual Matters.

Genesee, F. (1987) *Learning through two languages*. Cambridge, MA: Newbury House.

Graddol, D. (1999) The decline of the native speaker. In D. Graddol & U. H. Meinhof (eds.), *English in a changing world* (pp. 57–68). *AILA Review*, 13.

Hoffman, C. (1998) Luxembourg and the European schools. In J. Cenoz & F. Genesee (eds.), *Beyond bilingualism: multilingualism and multilingual education* (pp. 143–74). Clevedon, UK: Multilingual Matters.

Hornberger, N. (2001) Multilingual language policies and the continua of biliteracy: an ecological approach. *Language Policy*, 1(1), 27–51.

Johnson, R. K. & Swain, M. (eds.) (1997) *Immersion education: international perspectives*. Cambridge: Cambridge University Press.

Lambert, W. E. & Tucker, G. R. (1972) *Bilingual education of children: the St. Lambert experiment*. Rowley, MA: Newbury House.

Lewis, E. G. (1976) Bilingualism and bilingual education: the ancient world to the Renaissance. In J. A. Fishman (ed.), *Bilingual education: an international sociological perspective* (pp. 15–200). Rowley, MA: Newbury House.

Litteral, R. (1999) Language development in Papua New Guinea. *SIL Electronic working papers 1999–2002*, February. http://www.sil.org/silewp/1999/002/SILEWP1999-002.html

LoBianco, J. (2001) Officialising language: a discourse study of language politics in the United States. Unpublished doctoral dissertation, Australian National University.

Long, M. H. (1994) The least a second language acquisition theory needs to explain. In H. D. Brown & S. Gonzo (eds.), *Readings on second language acquisition* (pp. 470–88). Upper Saddle River, NJ: Prentice-Hall Regents.

Lotherington, H. (1996) A consideration of the portability and supportability of immersion education: a critical look at English immersion in Melanesia. *Journal of Multilingual and Multicultural Development*, 17(5), 349–59.

Lotherington, H. (1998) Trends and tensions in post-colonial language education in the South Pacific. *International Journal of Bilingual Education and Bilingualism*, 1(1), 65–75.

Lotherington, H. (2001) A tale of four teachers: a study of an Australian late-entry content-based program in two Asian languages. *International Journal of Bilingual Education and Bilingualism*, 4(2), 97–106.

Mackey, W. F. (1978) The importation of bilingual education models. In J. E. Alatis (ed.), *International dimensions of bilingual education. Georgetown University round table on languages and linguistics* (pp. 1–18). Washington, DC: Georgetown University Press.

Mugler, F. (1996) Vernacular language teaching in Fiji. In F. Mugler & J. Lynch (eds.), *Pacific languages in education* (pp. 273–87). Suva: Institute of Pacific Studies and Department of Literature and Language/Vanuatu, Pacific Languages Unit.

Murray, D. E. (1999) Whose "standard"? What the Ebonics debate tells us about language, power and pedagogy. In J. E. Alatis & A.-H. Tan (eds.), *Georgetown round table on languages and linguistics 1999: language in our time* (pp. 281–91). Washington, DC: Georgetown University Press.

Nettle, D. (1999) *Linguistic diversity.* Oxford: Oxford University Press.

Nettle, D. & Romaine, S. (2000) *Vanishing voices: the extinction of the world's languages.* Oxford: Oxford University Press.

Paulston, C. B. (ed.) (1988) *International handbook of bilingualism and bilingual education.* Westport, CN: Greenwood Press.

Rhodes, N. C., Christian, D., & Barfield, S. (1997) Innovations in immersion: the Key School two-way model. In

R. K. Johnson & M. Swain (eds.), *Immersion education: international perspectives* (pp. 265–83). Cambridge: Cambridge University Press.

Ruiz, R. (1984) Orientations in language planning. *NABE Journal*, 8(2), 15–34.

Schmid, C. L. (2001) *The politics of language: conflict, identity, and cultural pluralism in comparative perspective.* New York: Oxford University Press.

Shameem, N. & Read, J. (1996) Administering a performance test in Fiji Hindi. In G. Wigglesworth and C. Elder (eds.), *The language testing cycle: from inception to washback* (*Australian Review of Applied Linguistics*, series S/13). Canberra: Applied Linguistics Association of Australia.

Skutnabb-Kangas, T. (2000) *Linguistic genocide in education – or worldwide diversity and human rights.* Mahwah, NJ: Lawrence Erlbaum.

Stern, H. H. (1983) *Fundamental concepts of language teaching.* Oxford: Oxford University Press.

Swain, M. (1983) Large-scale communicative language testing: a case study. *Language Learning and Communication*, 2(2), 133–47.

Swain, M. (1997) French immersion programs in Canada. In J. Cummins & D. Corson, (eds.), *Encyclopedia of language and education*, vol. 5: *Bilingual education* (pp. 261–9). Dordrecht: Kluwer.

Swain, M. & Johnson, R. K. (1997) Immersion education: a category within bilingual education. In R. K. Johnson & M. Swain (eds.), *Immersion education: international perspectives* (pp. 11–16). Cambridge: Cambridge University Press.

Swain, M. & Lapkin, S. (1982) *Evaluating bilingual education: a Canadian case study.* Clevedon, UK: Multilingual Matters.

FURTHER READING

Baker, C. (2000) *A parents' and teachers' guide to bilingualism* (2nd edn.). Clevedon, UK: Multilingual Matters.

Baker, C. & Prys Jones, S. (eds.) (1998) *Encyclopedia of bilingualism and bilingual education.* Clevedon, UK: Multilingual Matters.

Beligan, A., Clyne, M., & Lotherington, H. (1999) *Growing up with English plus* (video). Melbourne: Language Australia.

Cenoz, J. & Genesee, F. (eds.) (1998) *Beyond bilingualism: multilingualism and multilingual education.* Clevedon, UK: Multilingual Matters.

Churchill, S. (1998) *Official languages in Canada: changing the language landscape.* Ottawa: Canadian Heritage.

Corson, D. (1993) *Language, minority education and gender: linking social justice and power.* Clevedon, UK: Multilingual Matters; Toronto: OISE.

Day, E. M. & Shapson, S. (1996) *Studies in immersion education.* Clevedon, UK: Multilingual Matters.

Döpke, S. (1992) *One parent, one language: an interactional approach.* Amsterdam: John Benjamins.

Edwards, V. (1998) *The power of Babel: teaching and learning in multilingual classrooms.* Stoke-on-Trent: Trentham Books.

Fishman, J. (ed.) (1999) *Handbook of language and ethnic identity.* New York: Oxford University Press.

Fishman, J. (2001) *Can threatened languages be saved? Reversing language shift revisited: a 21st century perspective.* Clevedon, UK: Multilingual Matters.

Garcia, O. & Baker, C. (eds.) (1995) *Policy and practice in bilingual education: a reader extending the foundations.* Clevedon, UK: Multilingual Matters.

Genesee, F. (ed.) (1994) *Educating second language children: the whole child, the whole curriculum, the whole community.* Cambridge: Cambridge University Press.

Grosjean, F. (1982) *Life with two languages: an introduction to bilingualism.* Cambridge, MA: Harvard University Press.

Lotherington, H. (2000) *What's bilingual education all about? A guide to language learning in today's schools.* Melbourne: Language Australia.

Romaine, S. (1995) *Bilingualism* (2nd edn.). Oxford: Blackwell.

29 Language Maintenance

ANNE PAUWELS

29.1 Defining Language Maintenance

In the study of language maintenance (henceforth LM) the term "LM" is closely linked to the term "language shift" (LS). In fact investigating language maintenance is often done through the identification of domains and situations in which the language is no longer used or is gradually making way for the use of another language. Whilst it is difficult to find a definition of either term which is accepted unanimously among scholars in the field there is nevertheless a common understanding that *language shift* implies the change (gradual or not) by a speaker, a group of speakers, and/or a speech community from the dominant use of one language in almost all spheres of life to the dominant use of another language in almost all spheres of life. The term *language maintenance* is used to describe a situation in which a speaker, a group of speakers, or a speech community continue to use their language in some or all spheres of life despite competition with the dominant or majority language to become the main/sole language in these spheres.

29.2 LM and LS in the Context of Language Contact

Both phenomena emerge in the context of language contact. Although language contact does not always involve linguistic competition in which only one language survives, there are many situations of language contact in which one language (gradually) loses ground in the face of another language. This "losing ground" can have several consequences for the language and the speech community in question. The most drastic effect is undoubtedly *language death*. This occurs in situations where an entire speech community stops using the language for a variety of reasons. The language dies because it no longer has a community of users (including speakers) and all its functions or uses have been usurped by another language. More drastic reasons for language death include cases where an entire speech community is wiped out as a consequence of disease, of genocide, or other disaster. Examples include the death of American Indian and Australian Aboriginal languages as a result of invasion, colonization, and settlement by Europeans in those territories (e.g., Grenoble & Whaley, 1998; Robins & Uhlenbeck, 1991). Language death is usually irreversible, especially for those languages of which no written and/or oral records exist. In some cases *language revival* or *language revitalization* are possible either because of existing records of the language or through reconstruction based on similarities with neighboring languages or dialects.

A less drastic effect is often known as *language shift*. In the case of LS a speech community (gradually) gives up or loses the use of its language and/or of many functions of the language and shifts to the use of another language for most, if not all its communicative and other cultural, symbolic needs. The language itself, however, survives because it continues to be used in other contexts or communities. Language shift is usually signaled by a period of transitional (unstable) bilingualism in which the competing languages are used side by side in a community, with one language progressively intruding into all spheres of the other language. Migration (forced or voluntary) often results in a language situation characterized by LS: individuals or groups belonging to speech community A migrate to a territory in which the language of speech community B dominates. Whilst speech community A continues using its language in a variety of settings, it needs to acquire the language of speech community B in order to survive in that community. Over time many members of speech community A abandon the use of their language and embrace the language of speech community B. The massive migration movements from Europe to the United States, Canada, Australia, and New Zealand and later from Asia to these countries have provided fertile ground for studying LM and LS (e.g., Clyne, 1991; Cummins, 1986; Edwards, 1998; Fishman et al., 1966; Haugen, 1953; Holmes, 1997). Other studies have focused on the migration of so-called "guestworkers" from Greece, Turkey, and Northern Africa to Northern Europe (e.g., Extra & Verhoeven, 1993a) and on the settlement of people from former British and Dutch colonies in Britain and the Netherlands respectively (e.g., Extra & Verhoeven, 1993b; Linguistic Minorities Project, 1985). Perhaps the most studied context for LS is that affecting indigenous linguistic minorities across the world: for example, Catalan in Spain, Quechua in South America, Aboriginal languages in Australia, Maori in New Zealand, Ainu in Japan, Navajo in the US. The linguistic minority status often arises as a consequence of a community being displaced by a more dominant group or community which dictates cultural, social, economic, and linguistic policies. Details about linguistic minorities (both indigenous and non-indigenous) can be found in Chapter 18 of this volume. Linguistic groups and communities threatened by LS can or may undertake efforts of various kinds to reverse LS or to maintain their language in all or some spheres of usage.

29.3   LM and LS as Cross- and Interdisciplinary Fields of Research

The study of LM and LS is a multidisciplinary and interdisciplinary enterprise involving and/or bringing together (sub)disciplines such as sociology, sociology of language, anthropology (in particular anthropological linguistics), social psychology, sociolinguistics, contact linguistics, and applied linguistics as well as others such as (linguistic) demography and political science. Each (sub)discipline brings its own focus, goals, theories, and methods to the enterprise of studying language maintenance and language shift.

For the purpose of this chapter, which is embedded in a handbook of applied linguistics, the focus is on those aspects of the study of LM (and LS) which are of particular relevance to the field of applied linguistics and which highlight contributions applied linguists have made to the study of LM and LS. This comprises an overview of the main research methods and tools used and a discussion of research focusing on identifying factors and forces which may influence LM and/or LS patterns in speech communities, as well as a discussion of LM efforts. This chapter is closely linked to other chapters in the volume due to the interrelatedness of the topic of LM and LS to many other issues covered in this volume. Chapter 7 on language attitudes and Chapter 18 on language minorities will complement the discussion of factors influencing LM. The discussion on LM efforts will need to be read in conjunction with Chapter 30 on language planning, Chapter 28 on bilingual education, and Chapter 18 on language minorities.

29.4   Researching LM and LS: Methods, Tools, and Data

Given the multidisciplinary nature of the study of LM and LS it is not surprising that it is characterized by a plethora of research methods and tools ranging from survey techniques to participant observation and in-depth interviewing. Although the preference for one method over another is usually the result of a researcher's primary disciplinary association, an increasing number of researchers combine several methods in the study of LM and LS. Below I describe the main methods and data used to examine the issue of LM factors and to explore LM efforts.

29.4.1   *The use of census and other large-scale surveys*

Census surveys which include questions about language use, language proficiency, or language choice can provide useful data on LM and LS. Although census data on language use can be powerful tools in the study of LM and LS, they can also be fraught with problems reducing their value and validity (e.g., Clyne, 1991; Fasold, 1984; Lieberson, 1967; Nelde, 1989). Their main shortcomings include that they are almost always based on self-reports and self-assessments with people often over-estimating or under-estimating their usage patterns or practices. Furthermore, difficulties surrounding the interpretation of terms and words like "language," "home language," "mother tongue," and "language use" can limit the usefulness of language questions in the census. Notwithstanding these weaknesses, analyses of language data from census and other large-scale surveys are helpful in studying the process and dynamics of language shift. This is particularly so when data can be gathered from subsequent censuses and when these data can be cross-tabulated with socio-demographic variables such as place of birth, age, sex, and ethnicity. Census and other large-scale data are apt at identifying if LS is taking place in one or several speech communities and the extent of LS by comparing intra- and intergenerational language use as well as comparing data from several censuses. Such survey data are also able to cast some light on possible factors contributing to LS and/or LM: for example the extent to which LS is linked to degree of urbanization, levels of income, education, or place of birth (in the case of immigrant minorities). If researchers have access to data from several subsequent censuses they may be able to identify to what extent LS has accelerated over time or whether there are signs of reversing LS. Amongst the most detailed investigations of census data is the work of the Australian sociolinguist, Michael Clyne, who has undertaken extensive analyses of the 1976, 1986, 1991, and 1996 Australian Census including cross-census comparisons (e.g., Clyne, 1982, 1991, 2001; Clyne & Kipp, 1997, 1999; Kipp, Clyne, & Pauwels, 1995). These analyses have revealed to what extent different migrant speech communities in Australia, as well as different vintages and different generations of these groups, are resistant to LS. Further explorations have highlighted the impact of exogamy on LS as well as the relationship between sex (gender) and LS and between age and LS. Comparisons across the census data allowed Clyne and Kipp (1997) to investigate whether LS had increased or whether there were signs of LS reversal. With very few exceptions, the overall picture was one of increased LS in all communities and in both overseas and Australia-born generations. The analyses also assisted in identifying factors which promote or impede LM or LS in the Australian immigrant context. For example, on the basis of their comparative analysis Clyne and Kipp (1997, p. 472) were able to assert that "Factors such as cultural distance, ethnolinguistic vitality, population concentration and community dynamics in the context of the socio-political situation in Australia and beyond" are operative in determining rates of LS or LM. Increasingly the results of census surveys are used as the starting point for in-depth studies of specific factors (e.g., gender, marital patterns, generation) affecting LM or LS across or in particular speech communities.

29.4.2   Questionnaires

The questionnaire (often administered via an interviewer) is another prominent tool in the study of LM and LS. Questionnaires have been used to document various features crucial to LM and LS. These include investigating the language use patterns of bi- or multilingual persons in specific context (domain analysis), their language proficiency, and their attitudes toward the languages and LM/LS. The documentation of language use is usually done through a domain analysis. *Domain* is a crucial concept in the study of LM as it allows for the identification of contexts in which the minority language or language under threat is best maintained and in which situations it is least maintained. The term was proposed by Fishman (1964) to describe institutional contexts in which the use of one language variety was seen to be more appropriate than another. Domains are seen to be configurations of particular participants (interlocutors), places and time (locales), and topics. Typical domains include the family or home domain, the friendship domain, the neighborhood domain, the school domain, the work domain, and the religious or church domain. Each domain is made up of a typical set of interlocutors, who interact with each other in typical locales about typical topics. For example, a "normal" configuration for the work domain would be colleagues or employees interacting with each other about work-focused topics in the office or workplace. This normal configuration of a domain would usually trigger the use of a particular language. Diversions from the normally configurated domain may lead to the use of another language. For example, if colleagues in the office talk about their weekend leisure activities this may cause a switch to a language typically used in the friendship domain rather than in the work domain. Greenfield's (1972) domain analysis of the use of Spanish and English in the Puerto-Rican community in New York has become a model for many other studies adopting the domain approach. Although the questionnaire is not the sole tool for undertaking a domain analysis – this can also be done through participant observation – it is nevertheless a common one because of its ability to obtain detailed data on a sizeable number of language users within a reasonable time frame. A domain analysis is of particular use to the study of LM and LS, not only because it identifies which language(s) is/are used in a particular situation or domain, but also because it identifies domains (and their constellations of interlocutors, locales, topics) which are central to LM and domains which are prone to intrusion from another language and thus act as an agent of shift.

Results of domain analyses in a variety of communities characterized by "unstable" or transitional bi- or multilingualism point to the crucial importance of the home or family domain in the maintenance of a minority language. If the minority language is no longer used in a family context it is unlikely to be passed on to the next generation, eventually leading to a complete shift to the majority/dominant language. Edwards (1997, p. 34) makes another distinction between *domains of necessity* (domains which relate to the most central aspects of a person's life, e.g., home, school, work) and domains in which a person's participation is more voluntary or sporadic. He asserts that "the main-tenance of a language is on a surer footing if it, and it alone, is required in the domains of central and continued salience" (Edwards, 1997, p. 34).

Questionnaires have also been used to obtain self-assessments of proficiency in the languages involved. Typically informants are asked to rate their pro-ficiency in the four major skills: speaking, listening/understanding, reading, and writing. In most cases they are given a rating scale ranging from *excellent/ very good* to *non-existent*. Language proficiency assessments assist in identifying the degree of LS or language attrition an individual or a group is experiencing. They also contribute to informing what actions and efforts are needed to ensure or foster LM.

Language attitudes (see also Chapter 7, this volume) also play a crucial role in the study of LM, and LS and are often examined through questionnaires (e.g., Dorian, 1981; Linguistic Minorities Project, 1985; Romaine, 1989). The exploration of language attitudes in the context of bilingualism, LM and LS frequently focuses on establishing the role of language as a symbol of group identity. In some cases participants are asked to respond to direct and open-ended questions seeking their opinion about LM such as "Do you think that schools should assist in the maintenance of minority languages?" In other cases questions regarding language attitudes take the form of an evaluative statement to which the informant is asked to respond often making use of an agreement–disagreement rating scale. Bennett's (1990) work on LM and ethnic identity among second generation Dutch-Australians uses many such questions to explore language attitudes.

The open-ended and closed-ended questions allow the researcher to probe individual or group attitudes to the role, functions, and relevance of the ethnic/minority language in the marking of that group's identity. The findings of such studies are then used to make prognoses about LM or LS in that community. For example, if a community or group believes it can maintain its group identity without its members speaking the group/ethnic language then the prognosis for long-term LM is slim. On the other hand, if they hold positive attitudes toward the importance and/or relevance of the ethnic language as a marker of group identity then the likelihood for LM is greater.

Attitudes can also be studied in other more indirect ways: for example, the matched-guise technique coupled with a semantic-differential response rating scale is often used to examine whether specific values (e.g., status, solidarity, prestige, friendliness) are associated more with one language than with another. The outcomes regarding values may be connected to a desire to maintain or not maintain a language. Chapter 7 in this volume provides an in-depth description of the technique and its value for linguistic attitudinal research.

29.4.3   *Participant observation*

In-depth studies of LM and LS affecting specific communities or groups often rely heavily on participant observation and other forms of researcher participation in the community under investigation. Such studies focus on documenting the linguistic choices that individuals make in their community and on exploring the reasons why they make these choices or which factors/ forces shape their choice or usage patterns. Researchers frequently become "part" of the community by living and working there for a considerable period of time or by regular engagement with the group/community over an extended period of time. They observe and frequently audio-tape and/or video-record a variety of linguistic interactions which are then subjected to multiple analyses (e.g., domain analysis, analysis of discourse, linguistic analysis) which can shed light on the questions of LM or LS. Gal's (1979) detailed study of LS in the bilingual village of Oberwart in Austria, Zentella's (1997) longitudinal study of Spanish LM among the Puerto Rican community in New York, as well as Heller's (1999) study of the language practices (French, English and other) in a school in Ontario, Canada are well-known examples of studies relying heavily on the participant observation/full participation methods to gather their data.

29.4.4 *Integrative and multi-method approaches to LM and LS research*

Not unlike practices in other fields of applied linguistics, scholars in the field of LM and LS also often prefer to combine methods or to adopt an integrative approach to research methods because of the perceived advantages of such a combination in examining and understanding the phenomena of LM and LS. Besides the above mentioned methods, the following methods and procedures also frequently feature in LM and LS studies: collection of personal narratives (e.g., written and verbal stories, diaries), test procedures, archival methods, and focus groups.

29.5 Factors and Forces Promoting LM or LS

For applied linguists a key objective of studying LM and LS is to be able to address the questions: how can LS be halted or reversed (e.g., Fishman, 1991) and/or how can LM be effected? This objective is linked to what many applied linguists see as one of their crucial roles: advocacy. Making their expertise and knowledge available to inform and assist individuals, groups, communities, and indeed governments in relation to linguistic matters, including LM, is seen as pertinent to being an applied linguist. Addressing the question of LM efforts relies on the identification of factors and forces which operate to promote LM and those which tend to slow down or even halt the process of LS.

The multitude of studies investigating questions of LM and LS in a diverse range of situations has led to the development of some theories and frameworks which try to "predict" or explain factors and forces conducive to LM or

LS. Unfortunately this chapter won't be able to do justice to the depth and breadth of this enterprise and readers will be referred to other sources for a more in-depth discussion.

29.5.1   Clear-cut and ambivalent factors promoting LM

A prominent approach among sociologists of language working on immigrant language settings involves the categorization of factors into clear-cut factors which promote LM or LS unambiguously. Kloss' (1966) work on German-American LM in the US became the basis or inspiration for many studies in the US (e.g., Fishman et al., 1966) and Australia (e.g., Clyne, 1982). He identified a range of factors which he categorized as either *clear-cut* (clearly promoting LM) or *ambivalent* because they could promote either LM or LS. The presence of one or more clear-cut factors would predict stronger LM in a group than the lack of such factors. Kloss' clear-cut factors include

1   early point of immigration,
2   the existence of linguistic enclaves,
3   membership of a denomination with parochial schools,
4   pre-emigration experience with LM.

The ambivalent factors identified by Kloss (1966) include both individual and group factors:

1   Educational level of the immigrant: a higher level of education could mean greater cultural and linguistic activity around the minority language but it could also mean greater ease of integration into the majority group because of lesser difficulties with language and educational barriers.
2   Numerical strength of the group: large groups may be better placed to engage in LM efforts. However, if they are very large and dispersed there may not be a sense of community, which may hamper LM efforts.
3   Linguistic and cultural similarity with the dominant group: linguistically and culturally similar groups may have more difficulty preserving their linguistic and cultural identity because of their relative ease of integration with the dominant group. However, the ease of integration may mean that they have more time to devote to LM.
4   Attitude of the dominant or majority group toward the language and/or group: although a positive and supportive attitude of the majority is generally found to give minority groups more chances at LM, there is also evidence that some groups are moved to greater LM efforts in the context of suppression and even persecution.
5   Sociocultural characteristics of the group: Kloss introduced this factor to alert to other inter-ethnic differences in LM not explained by the above.

This may refer to language being seen as a "core value" in the group (see Section 29.5.2) or language being seen as a symbol of ethnic identity.

Kloss' factors have been tested in the Australian context by Clyne (1982, 1991). His work highlights the contextual nature, not only of the factors themselves but also of their type. For example, Clyne (1991, p. 87) comments that in Australia the clear-cut factor "early point of immigration" only promotes LM if it is combined with the presence of linguistic enclaves. Similarly parochial schools only lead to LM if the schools are bilingual. The factor "pre-emigration experience with LM" is not a clear-cut but an ambivalent factor in the Australian context. Kloss' distinction of clear-cut vs. ambivalent factors has inspired some scholars to test other factors in terms of this distinction. Clyne (1982) identifies the presence of grandparents with limited or no English skills as a factor clearly conducive to LM. *Exogamy* (especially involving marriage between a member of the ethnolinguistic minority and the linguistic majority) has been found to be clearly LS promoting (e.g., Pauwels, 1985). Additional factors whose status in the promotion of LM or LS have been or are being explored include *language variety* (e.g., Pauwels, 1986, 1988b), *gender/sex* (Holmes, 1993; Pauwels, 1997), *political situation in the homeland* (Clyne, 1982), *ethnic denominations* (e.g., Klarberg, 1983), all of which seem to be ambivalent.

Although there is a certain usefulness in an approach that identifies a series of factors or forces which promote LM, this approach does not address issues such as the dynamics between factors in terms of promoting LM.

29.5.2   Language as a core value

Another model seeking to explain why certain groups maintain their language better than other groups is the "core value" theory whose main proponent is Smolicz (e.g., 1980; 1981). Inspired by humanistic sociology (Znaniecki, 1968), Smolicz' theory is built around the notion that each group subscribes to a particular set of cultural values which are vital to its continued existence as a separate entity. In some groups language is identified as a prime core value whereas in others it is seen as less central to continued existence. Consequently LM is assumed to be more important to those groups for which language is a core value. The core value theory continues to exert substantial influence as a theory, especially in the immigrant context, despite several shortcomings being pointed out by scholars such as Clyne (1988, 1991) and Kouzmin (1988).

29.5.3   Ethnolinguistic vitality

The concept "ethnolinguistic vitality" is linked to the social psychological approach to the study of language and intergroup contact (e.g., Giles, Bourhis, & Taylor, 1977; Giles & Johnson, 1981; Tajfel, 1974, 1982). Not unlike the core value theory, the theory of ethnolinguistic vitality is concerned with identifying factors (i.e., vitality factors) which a group needs or relies on in order to operate as a separate and distinctive entity, especially in intergroup situations. A group with high ethnolinguistic vitality will continue to operate as a distinctive entity whereas a group with low ethnolinguistic vitality is less likely to maintain itself as a distinctive entity or group. Giles, Bourhis, & Taylor (1977) list a range of variables/components which comprise *objective* ethnolinguistic vitality. There are *status* variables: economic status, self-perceived social status, status of the language. There are *demographic* variables including numerical strength and geographic distribution of the group. *Institutional support* variables concern to what extent the language is represented in institutions such as schools, government, courts. In addition to these variables of objective ethnolinguistic vitality, Giles, Bourhis, & Taylor stress the importance of perceived or subjective ethnolinguistic vitality. This refers to the perception the group has of its own vitality. This may in fact be a more reliable indicator than the objective vitality factors as many of these correspond with Kloss' (1966) ambivalent factors and are therefore equally limited in explaining LM patterns. Furthermore the variables or dimensions which make up objective ethnolinguistic vitality have come under fire for being "too crude, not independent of one another, and not differentiated enough with regard to their overall weighting" (Pauwels, 1988a, p. 12; see also Edwards, 1985; Husband & Saifullah Khan, 1982).

29.5.4   *The market value of language*

A range of scholars (e.g., Haugen, 1980; Jaspaert & Kroon, 1988; Tandefelt, 1988) working on minority language settings have drawn attention to the fact that language can be considered a socioeconomic resource which has a market value (see also Bourdieu's (1982) notion of the linguistic marketplace). In a contact setting it is the language or languages which are perceived as useful in a socioeconomic sense that will persist. This theory may explain, for instance, why there are class differences in LM patterns within the same ethnolinguistic groups: if the maintenance of the minority language can lead to socioeconomic improvements (i.e., better employment) then it is likely to be maintained. Within the context of LM studies this theory has, however, under-estimated the symbolic value of language and its power in driving LM (see, e.g., Fishman et al., 1985 on ethnic revival in the US).

29.6   LM Efforts: Community and Individual Strategies and Initiatives

Studies of LM and LS not only advance our insight into LM or LS factors but also reveal attempts, successful or not, at LM. The latter helps us to identify initiatives and strategies to maintain a language "under threat." LM efforts can cover a very wide range of strategies and initiatives and can have variable goals and outcomes (e.g., Fishman, 2001; Grenoble & Whaley, 1998). The variability in goals and outcomes is often a result of the state in which the minority language finds itself as well as the social and political contexts within which the maintenance efforts take place. For example, a minority language with a sizeable number of "active" speakers and with access to a literary heritage may have a broader scope for LM than a minority language with few, if any remaining speakers. Similarly, the scope of LM efforts may go beyond the personal and private if the sociopolitical context is characterized by tolerance or support, whereas an oppressive environment may severely restrict the scope of LM.

A comprehensive and useful model within which to describe LM efforts is Fishman's (1991) work on *Reversing Language Shift*. He proposes an eight-stage model to provide insights into the necessary steps which need to be taken by a community in order to reverse LS (see Figure 29.1). The number of stages is related to the "severity of intergenerational dislocation" (Fishman, 1991, p. 393) and is subdivided into two groupings. Stages 8 to 5 represent those which are needed to attain diglossia, that is, the continued use of the minority language as the low (L) variety, with the majority language representing the high (H) variety (Ferguson, 1959).

Stages 4 to 1 are seen to be necessary to "transcend diglossia" (Fishman 1991, p. 395) and strive for "increased power-sharing" (p. 401) and a more officially recognized status of the language (e.g., formal recognition as a national language alongside others, formal recognition as the dominant language in a

---

Stages of Reversing Language Shift: Severity of Intergenerational Dislocation (read from bottom up)

1   Education, work sphere, mass media and governmental operations at higher and nationwide levels.
2   Local/regional mass media and governmental services.
3   The local/regional (i.e., non-neighborhood) work sphere, both among Xmen and among Ymen.
4a Public schools for Xish children, offering some instruction via Xish, but substantially under Yish curricular and staffing control.
4b Schools in lieu of compulsory education and substantially under Xish curricular and staffing control.
II *RLS to transcend diglossia, subsequent to its attainment*

5   Schools for literacy acquisition, for the old and for the young, and not in lieu of compulsory education.
6   The intergenerational and demographically concentrated home-family-neighborhood: the basis of mother tongue transmission.
7   Cultural interaction in Xish primarily involving the community-based older generation.
8   Reconstructing Xish and adult acquisition of XSL.
I   *RLS to attain diglossia (assuming prior ideological clarification)*

Note: Xish refers to minority language, Yish refers to the majority language.

Figure 29.1   Fishman's model for reversing language shift (Fishman, 1991, p. 395)

specific region/territory). These latter four stages cannot be undertaken by the ethnolinguistic community alone but involve direct interaction with the official authorities. After all, the goal of these stages is either the "intrusion" of a minority language into a sphere or domain considered to be the exclusive or dominant province of the majority language or the "reclamation" of such domains for the minority language. Gaining access for the minority language to the domains represented in stages 4 to 1 represents an increasing level of power sharing of the minority language with the majority language. Within an applied linguistic framework it is the field of language policy and language planning which focuses on this pursuit by ethnolinguistic minorities (see Chapter 30, this volume).

Stages 8 to 5 are more likely to be undertaken without majority involvement or assistance, although they can of course be part of official language policies (e.g., the protection of endangered languages). Stage 8 is needed when language death has occurred or when LS is complete. In the case of language death it may be necessary to reconstruct the language from available sources (in some cases by borrowing from related languages) (e.g., Dorian, 1988). The role of linguists and applied linguists is quite substantial in this stage: they often undertake the linguistic reconstruction of a language as well as devise materials to re-introduce the language. If the situation is one of complete LS with the language still being used elsewhere, it may be possible to revive its use by importing specialist resources (both speakers and materials). The aim of this stage is to have a language that can be maintained and to have at least some "fluent" adult speakers. This stage describes the situation of some extinct Australian Aboriginal languages, and Amerindian languages as well as Basque and perhaps even Irish.

Stage 7 describes a situation in which the elderly members of a community are still speakers of the language and use it primarily for ethno-cultural functions (festivals, rituals).

Stage 6 describes the most crucial stage in the LM process (or the process of reversing LS) – the reinforcement of the language in the home, the family, the neighborhood, and the community. Fishman is joined by the majority of LM scholars in identifying these domains or sites as constituting the linchpin for LM. Without continued language use in these domains further stages (5 to 1) will not enhance the intergenerational linguistic transmission process.

Stage 5 refers to community initiatives and efforts to impart literacy in the minority language to both younger and older members of the speech community. My discussion of LM efforts and initiatives will focus on Fishman's stages 6 and 5.

29.6.1   *Language maintenance efforts in the family, home, and neighborhood domains*

As stated before, the ultimate survival of a language (other than as a fossilized language for specialized use, e.g., Latin or Coptic) depends on intergenerational transfer. The language practices of parents, grandparents, and other relatives or kin considered important in child rearing are crucial in laying the foundations for the maintenance of a minority language among future generations. This is especially the case when there is no or limited opportunity to use the language outside the "home" due to sociopolitical or other environmental factors. Considerable effort has gone into describing models and strategies to assist parents, families, and indeed communities in maintaining the minority language in the family. Often based on (their own) detailed scholarly descriptions of children's bilingual upbringing and family bilingualism (e.g., Arnberg, 1987; De Houwer, 1994; Döpke, 1993; Leopold, 1939, 1947, 1949a, 1949b; Saunders, 1982, 1988) applied linguists as well as advocates of bilingualism provided practical assistance to parents through bilingual guidebooks, bilingual family newsletters, and other publications as well as through seminars, workshops, and community involvement. For example, the *Bilingual Family Newsletter* published by Multilingual Matters provides support to bilingual families through discussion of new research findings, of reports by individual families on successful and not so successful practices, and through exchange of information on useful resources or new developments. In Australia applied linguists have been actively involved in the promotion of LM in the family not only by offering workshops for families and communities on bilingual upbringing of children but also by speaking to professional groups such as childcare workers, health care and medical staff, teachers and school principals to inform them about the nature of childhood bilingualism and to try to eliminate a range of negative myths about early bilingualism (e.g., Janssen & Pauwels, 1993; Clyne, 2001).

There is no single model for LM in the family or for childhood bilingualism which has proved to be universally more successful than others. This is a consequence of there being too many extralinguistic factors which can affect the outcome of any effort at LM in the family and home. Besides the "minority language = home language" model in which families aim to use the minority language as exclusive or at least dominant language in the home, the "one parent – one language" model based on Leopold's pioneering study is gaining greater currency, especially among families where one partner speaks the majority language. Most studies of LM in the family show that LM efforts are especially successful among young (pre-school-age) children. School-age children are more prone to LS, especially if their schooling excludes or prohibits the use of the home language in the school or in public. This often impacts adversely on their use of the minority language in the home: they stop being active users of the home language and become receptive bilinguals only.

The LM efforts of the home and family can be strengthened through language practices and efforts in the neighborhood. The presence of community-based childcare, playgroups, and playgrounds will give (young) children the opportunity to use or at least hear the minority language outside a home environment. Similarly the presence of shops, small businesses, and markets operated by members of the ethnolinguistic minority who (can) use the minority language with their customers act as a reinforcement for LM in the home. Of course the impact of the neighborhood is most significant where there is a significant concentration of minority group members. This applies to a range of indigenous minorities who are concentrated in a specific region as well as to some immigrant minorities such as Puerto Ricans in New York (e.g., Fishman, Cooper, & Ma, 1971; Zentella, 1997) or Greeks in Melbourne (e.g., Clyne, 2001). If the ethnolinguistic minority has a dispersed pattern of settlement, then such neighborhood efforts are not only more difficult to institute but also less effective.

Other community-based efforts which transcend the neighborhood include the establishment of cultural and social organizations (clubs/societies), the development of media services (printed and electronic media) in the minority language as well as the continuation of ethno-religious practices which further LM. The exact purpose and impact of these organizations and initiatives on intergenerational language transfer will vary from context to context. This is discussed in detail by contributors from across the world in Fishman (2001).

29.6.2   *LM in the educational domain*

Communities and scholars agree that minority language teaching is an important tool for language maintenance. Although some parents take the responsibility for developing literacy in the minority language in their children, it is more common for this to happen through a form of minority language education organized by (a sector of) the ethnolinguistic community. Of course the minority group can also exert pressure on the official majority to provide such education (see stages 4a and 4b in Fishman's 1991 model) within the mainstream schooling system. If this is successful, community-based initiatives are either replaced or complemented by public or government-supported programs. These include, for example, bilingual education (for more details see Lotherington), minority language classes offered to minority language children only within mainstream schooling, the availability of community languages to all children irrespective of ethnolinguistic background, as well as teaching the minority language as a foreign language in the mainstream school system (e.g., Clyne, 1991; Jaspaert & Kroon, 1991; Reich, 1991; Skutnabb-Kangas & Cummins, 1988; Spolsky 1986; and Chapter 30, this volume).

Community-based minority language education which does not replace compulsory education (i.e., Fishman's stage 4) also takes different forms across different communities. Besides the home, other bodies and groups act as agencies of literacy acquisition. These include social and cultural clubs and centers, religious organizations, parental groups, as well as neighborhood networks. For example, in Peru the Evangelical Church of Peru promotes Quechua literacy, albeit "with a primary goal of socialization to Christianity" (Hornberger & King, 2001, p. 177). For Australia, Clyne (1991, p. 129) notes that "778 ethnic organizations, principally clubs, churches and parent associations" conduct part-time ethnic schools and insertion classes (language classes provided by the community in mainstream schools) in more than 50 languages. Most such classes incorporate language and culture and in some cases also religious instruction. In the case of Basque, the formerly clandestine and underground schools – *ikastolak* – have become publicly funded institutions which offer both full and partial immersion programs (Fishman, 1991, p. 165). For Frisian, Gorter (2001, p. 226) mentions that the Afûk organization plays a key role, especially since it has been modernized significantly in the past ten years. It offers specialized courses for specific groups such as legal and health professionals and foreigners. It is working on a general course in Frisian which will be available on CD-Rom.

The quality of the tuition also varies greatly depending on the linguistic and financial resources of the community. In some cases the classes are run by highly qualified teachers, whereas in other cases they are staffed by volunteers from the community with limited pedagogical and linguistic expertise. The latter scenario tends to adversely affect the continued participation of young and adolescent children in such classes, especially if the teaching modes are at odds with those of the mainstream school.

29.7   Concluding Remarks

In a globalizing world characterized by multinational expansions, increasing voluntary and involuntary transnational movements, and accompanied by the need or desire for a global communication code, there will be even greater pressures on and challenges for ethnolinguistic minorities if they wish to maintain their cultural, ethnic, or linguistic distinctiveness. It is hoped that applied linguistic expertise can assist such groups in making linguistically informed decisions and also assist them in LM efforts by drawing upon case studies from the past.

See also 7 ASSESSING LANGUAGE ATTITUDES, 8 LANGUAGE ATTRITION, 28 BILINGUAL EDUCATION.

REFERENCES

Note: The asterisked items in the reference list are also considered especially relevant for further reading.

Arnberg, L. (1987) *Raising children bilingually: the preschool years.* Clevedon, UK: Multilingual Matters.

Bennett, E. J. (1990) Attitudes of the second generation Dutch to language maintenance and ethnic identity. PhD Thesis, Monash University, Melbourne, Australia.

Bourdieu, P. (1982) The economics of linguistic exchanges. *Social Science Information*, 16, 645–68.

Clyne, M. (1982) *Multilingual Australia.* Melbourne: River Seine Publications.

Clyne, M. (1988) The German-Australian speech community: ethnic core values and language maintenance. *International Journal of the Sociology of Language*, 72, 67–83.

*Clyne, M. (1991) *Community languages: the Australian experience*. Cambridge: Cambridge University Press.

Clyne, M. (2001) Can the shift of immigrant languages be reversed in Australia? In J. Fishman (ed.), *Can threatened languages be saved?* (pp. 364–90). Clevedon, UK: Multilingual Matters.

Clyne, M. & Kipp, S. (1997) Trends and changes in the home language use and shift in Australia, 1986–1996. *Journal of Multilingual and Multicultural Development*, 18(6), 451–73.

Clyne, M. & Kipp, S. (1999) *Pluricentric languages in an immigrant context*. Berlin: Mouton De Gruyter.

*Cummins, J. (ed.) (1986) *Heritage languages in Canada: research perspectives*. Toronto: OISE.

De Houwer, A. (1994) *The acquisition of two languages from birth: a case study*. Cambridge: Cambridge University Press.

Döpke, S. (1993) *One parent – one language*. Amsterdam: John Benjamins.

Dorian, N. (1981) *Language death: the life cycle of a Scottish Gaelic dialect*. Philadelphia: University of Pennsylvania Press.

*Dorian, N. (ed.) (1988) *Investigating obsolescence: studies in language contraction and death*. Cambridge: Cambridge University Press.

Edwards, J. (1985) *Language, society and identity*. Oxford: Blackwell.

Edwards, J. (1997) Language minorities and language maintenance. *Annual Review of Applied Linguistics*, 17, 30–42.

*Edwards, J. (ed.) (1998) *Languages in Canada*. New York: Cambridge University Press.

*Extra, G. & Verhoeven, L. (eds.) (1993a) *Immigrant languages in Europe*. Clevedon, UK: Multilingual Matters.

Extra, G. & Verhoeven, L. (eds.) (1993b) *Community languages in the Netherlands*. Amsterdam: Swets & Zeitlinger.

Fasold, R. (1984) *The sociolinguistics of society*. Oxford: Blackwell.

Ferguson, C. (1959) Diglossia. *Word*, 15, 325–40.

Fishman, J. A. (1964) Language maintenance and language shift as a field of inquiry: a definition of the field and suggestions for its further development. *Linguistics*, 9, 32–70.

*Fishman, J. A. (1991) *Reversing language shift*. Clevedon, UK: Multilingual Matters.

*Fishman, J. A. (ed.) (2001) *Can threatened languages be saved?* Clevedon, UK: Multilingual Matters.

Fishman, J. A. et al. (eds.) (1966) *Language loyalty in the United States*. The Hague: Mouton.

Fishman, J., Cooper, R. L., & Ma, R. (eds.) (1971) *Bilingualism in the Barrio*. Bloomington: Indiana University Press.

Fishman, J. et al. (eds.) (1985) *Rise and fall of the ethnic revival*. Berlin: Mouton De Gruyter.

Gal, S. (1979) *Language shift: ocial determinants of linguistic change in bilingual Austria*. New York: Academic Press.

Giles, H., Bourhis, R., & Taylor, D. M. (1977) Towards a theory of language in ethnic group relations. In H. Giles (ed.), *Language, ethnicity and group relations* (pp. 307–438). London: Academic Press.

Giles, H. & Johnson, P. (1981) The role of language in ethnic group relations. In J. C. Turner & H. Giles (eds.), *Intergroup behaviour* (pp. 199–243). Oxford: Blackwell.

Gorter, D. (2001) A Frisian update on reversing language shift? In J. Fishman (ed.), *Can threatened languages be saved?* (pp. 215–33). Clevedon, UK: Multilingual Matters.

Greenfield, L. (1972) Situational measures of normative language views in relation to person, place and topic among Puerto Rican bilinguals. In J. Fishman (ed.), *Advances in the sociology of language* (vol. 2) (pp. 17–35). The Hague: Mouton.

*Grenoble, L. A. & Whaley, L. J. (eds.) (1998) *Endangered languages.* Cambridge: Cambridge University Press.

Haugen, E. (1953) *The Norwegian language in America* (2 vols). Philadelphia: University of Pennsylvania Press.

Haugen, E. (1980) Language fragmentation in Scandinavia. In E. Haugen, J. D. McClure, & D. Thomson (eds.), *Minority languages today* (pp. 100–19), Edinburgh: Edinburgh University Press.

Heller, M. (1999). *Linguistic minorities and modernity.* London: Longman.

Holmes, J. (1993) Women's role in language maintenance and language shift. *International Journal of Applied Linguistics,* 3(2), 159–79.

Holmes, J. (1997) Keeping tabs on language shift in New Zealand: some methodological considerations. *Journal of Multilingual and Multicultural Development,* 18/1, 17–39.

Hornberger, N. & King, K. A. (2001) Reversing Quechua language shift in South America. In J. Fishman (ed.), *Can threatened languages be saved?* (pp. 166–94). Clevedon, UK: Multilingual Matters.

Husband, C. & Saifullah Khan, V. (1982) The viability of ethnolinguistic vitality: some creative doubts. *Journal of Multilingual and Multicultural Development,* 3(3), 193–205.

Janssen, C. & Pauwels, A. (1993) *Raising children bilingually in Australia.* Melbourne: Monash University, Language & Society Centre.

Jaspaert, K. & Kroon, S. (1988) Social determinants of language shift by Italians in the Netherlands and Flanders. Paper presented at the International Symposium on the Loss

and Maintenance of Minority Languages, Noordwijkerhout, August.

*Jaspaert, K. & Kroon, S. (1991) Ethnic minority language teaching and language policy: introductory remarks. In K. Jaspaert & S. Kroon (eds.), *Ethnic minority languages and education* (pp. 7–14). Amsterdam: Swets & Zeitlinger.

Kipp, S., Clyne, M., & Pauwels, A. (1995) *Immigration and Australia's language resources.* Canberra: Australia Government Publishing Service.

Klarberg, M. (1983) The effect of ideology on language teaching. PhD Thesis, Monash University, Melbourne, Australia.

Kloss, H. (1966) German-American language maintenance efforts. In J. Fishman et al. (eds.), *Language loyalty in the United States* (pp. 206–52). The Hague: Mouton.

Kouzmin, L. (1988) Language use and language maintenance in two Russian communities in Australia. *International Journal of the Sociology of Language,* 72, 51–65.

Leopold, W. (1939) *Speech development of a bilingual child: a linguist's record* (vol. 1). Evanston: Northwestern University Press.

Leopold, W. (1947) *Speech development of a bilingual child: a linguist's record* (vol. 2). Evanston: Northwestern University Press.

Leopold, W. (1949a) *Speech development of a bilingual child: a linguist's record* (vol. 3). Evanston: Northwestern University Press.

Leopold, W. (1949b) *Speech development of a bilingual child: a linguist's record* (vol. 4). Evanston: Northwestern University Press.

Lieberson, S. (1967) Language questions in censuses. In S. Lieberson (ed.), *Explorations in sociolinguistics* (pp. 134–51) The Hague: Mouton.

*Linguistic Minorities Project (1985) *The other languages of England.* London: Routledge & Kegan Paul.

Nelde, P. (1989) Ecological aspects of language contact or how to investigate linguistic minorities. *Journal of Multilingual and Multicultural Development*, 10(1), 73–86.

Pauwels, A. (1985) The role of mixed marriages in language shift in the Dutch community. In M. Clyne (ed.), *Australia: meeting place of languages* (pp. 39–55). Canberra: ANU, Research School of Pacific Studies.

Pauwels, A. (1986) *Immigrant dialects and language maintenance in Australia.* Dordrecht: Foris Publications.

Pauwels, A. (1988a) Introducion: the future of ethnic languages in Australia. *International Journal of the Sociology of Language*, 72, 5–14.

Pauwels, A. (1988b) Diglossic communities in transition: the cases of the Limburgs and Swabian speech communities in Australia. *International Journal of the Sociology of Language*, 72, 85–99.

Pauwels, A. (1997) The role of gender in immigrant language maintenance in Australia. In W. Wölck & A. De Houwer (eds.), *Recent studies in contact linguistics* (pp. 276–85). Bonn: Dümmler.

Reich, H. H. (1991) Developments in ethnic minority language teaching within the European community. In K. Jaspaert & S. Kroon (eds.), *Ethnic minority languages and education* (pp. 161–74). Amsterdam: Swets & Zeitlinger.

*Robins, R. H. & Uhlenbeck, E. M. (eds.) (1991) *Endangered languages*. Oxford: Berg.

*Romaine, S. (1989) *Bilingualism*. Oxford: Blackwell.

Saunders, G. (1982) *Bilingual children: guidance for the family.* Clevedon, UK: Multilingual Matters.

Saunders, G. (1988) *Bilingual children: from birth to teens.* Clevedon, UK: Multilingual Matters.

*Skutnabb-Kangas, T. & Cummins (eds.) (1988) *Minority education: from shame to struggle.* Clevedon, UK: Multilingual Matters.

Smolicz, J. J. (1980) Language as a core value of culture. *Journal of Applied Linguistics*, 11(1), 1–13.

Smolicz, J. J. (1981) Core values and cultural identity. *Ethnic and Racial Studies*, 4, 75–90.

*Spolsky, B. (ed.) (1986) *Language and education in multilingual settings.* Clevedon, UK: Multilingual Matters.

Tajfel, H. (1974) Social identity and intergroup behaviour. *Social Science Information*, 13, 65–93.

Tajfel, H. (1982) Social psychology of intergroup relations. *Annual Review of Psychology*, 33, 1–39.

Tandefelt, M. (1988) *Mellan två sprak.* Uppsala: Acta Universitatis Uppsaliensis.

Zentella, A. (1997) *Growing up bilingual: Puerto Rican children in New York.* New York: Blackwell.

Znaniecki, F. (1968) *The method of sociology.* New York: Academic Press.

FURTHER READING

Alladina, S. & Edwards, V. (1991) *Multilingualism in the British Isles* (2 vols). London: Longman.

Appel, R. & Muysken, P. (1987) *Language contact and bilingualism.* London: Edward Arnold.

Edwards, J. (1995) *Multilingualism.* London: Penguin.

Fase, W., Kaspaert, K., & Kroon, S. (eds.) (1992) *Maintenance and loss of minority languages.* Amsterdam: John Benjamins.

Hornberger, N. (1989) *Bilingual education and language maintenance*. Dordrecht: Foris Publications.

Pavlenko, A., Blackledge, A., Piller, I., & Teutsch-Dwyer, M. (eds.) (2001) *Multilingualism, second language learning and gender*. Berlin: Mouton de Gruyter.

30 Language Planning as Applied Linguistics

JOSEPH LO BIANCO

30.1 Introduction

I take the theme of this volume to be that a distinction between applied linguistics and linguistics applied is useful and necessary and argue that scholarship on language policy and planning (hereafter LPP) substantiates this distinction and bolsters claims that applied linguistics is a coherent and distinctive academic discipline not dependent on formal linguistics (Brumfit, 1997; Davies, 1999). The main reason for this claim is that the practical nature of the problems that LPP deals with requires us to analyze specificities of policy-making in contexts where language is only a part. The abstractions of descriptive linguistics, and the abstractions of those kinds of applied linguistics that imagine a descent lineage from descriptive linguistics, and, further, the abstractions of those branches of sociolinguistics that derive conceptually from descriptive linguistics, lead to models for studying language planning that are weakly descriptive, a-social, and a-historical. Language problems always arise in concrete historical contexts and these inevitably involve rival interests reflecting "loaded" relations among ethnic, political, social, bureaucratic, and class groupings, and other kinds of ideological splits and controversies, including personal ones. To explain how language problems encapsulate or exacerbate such relations requires interdisciplinary research grounded in real-world data. Understood in this way, as a scholarly practice deeply embedded in sociology, history, ethnic relations, politics, and economics, LPP research is applied scholarship drawing on knowledge far beyond linguistics. The extent to which LPP draws on descriptive linguistics varies according to the kind of language planning activity being studied, and the particular tradition of linguistic description which is utilized.

However, studying and doing language planning also poses challenges to applied linguistics. A key challenge derives from the policy infused nature of knowledge (data, concepts, and relationships) that informs language policy-making processes. An "interested" or "motivated" character is inherent in LPP and needs to be theorized as a central feature of researching language policy. An early aspiration of language planning scholars for a science of the field – "Language planning as a rational and technical process informed by actuarial data and by ongoing feedback is still a dream, but it is by no means so farfetched a dream as it seemed to be merely a decade ago" (Fishman, 1971, p. 111) – has had to be discarded as all the human sciences acknowledge, if not enjoy, the philosophical logic of postmodernity with its insistence on the impossibility of interest-free knowledge. Research conducted to sustain policy development is organically invested with dilemmas about how knowledge designed for action, for application, in contexts of contending interests and ideologies, is implicated in these processes and cannot in any absolute sense rise above interests and ideology. This does not mean that "rational and technical" processes are not possible, just that we must theorize these in the context of persisting interests.

There is an almost complete lack of use of categories drawn from descriptive linguistic classification in actual policy-making, with the possible exception of some corpus planning work. Even applied linguistics, and indeed, even trained professional language planners and the body of knowledge that might be called language planning theory, are rarely called upon, as Fishman has noted ". . . very little language planning practice has actually been informed by language planning theory" (1994, p. 97).

Despite all this, LPP is probably the most dispersed practice of applied linguistics and as old as verbalized semiotics: universal and ancient. That public authorities make minimal use of scholarly studies of language problems in society is a contradiction addressed throughout this chapter. Perversely, it is not only the actual practice of language policy-making that neglects LPP theory and scholarship, but also some theorizations of applied linguistics and sociolinguistics. For example, Chambers' *Sociolinguistic Theory* (1995) reserves "sociolinguistics" essentially for variation theory and removes LPP out of language studies altogether, placing it under political science. Even in academic programs that include LPP studies it is marginal, underscoring Kaplan's observation that ". . . only a handful of universities in the world offers anything more than a random course in language policy/planning" (1994, p. 3).

30.2 Defining and Theorizing

A continuing search for an adequate definition in LPP writing reflects both the wide range of disciplines that inform the field and the diversity of activity that is called language planning. During its formative decades of the 1960s and 1970s language planning theory tried to be a "science," understanding "science" as empirical and quantitative data-driven replicability; difficult when the data and concepts of language planning scholarship are contingent, transdisciplinary, and often framed by interest and motivation. These characteristics don't mean LPP can't be empirical and quantitative, but that what count as empirical and quantitative processes requires energetic re-theorization related to the function of context, politics, and processes of iterative decision-making in public affairs related to language.

A frequently cited definition is Cooper's: "Language planning refers to deliberate efforts to influence the behavior of others with respect to the acquisition, structure, or functional allocation of their language codes" (1989, p. 45). Other definitions include what people do, think and believe about language: "Language policy can be defined as the combination of official decisions and prevailing public practices related to language education and use" (McGroarty, 1997, p. 1). In other definitions there is no place for the non-deliberate realm: "The match of national language capacity to need" (Brecht & Walton, 1993, p. 3).

Much early thinking sought to locate LPP close to the conventional policy sciences, aiming to generate a "rational matrix": an ordered sequence of bounded actions governed by an overarching design, itself a data-driven rational response to a pre-established problem. This was prominent in the work of Joan Rubin and Bjorn Jernudd (Jernudd, 1973) who make important contributions to systematizing the field. In their work, together and separately, they connected language planning research to the formulation of alternatives, understanding the essential task as normative intervention by those empowered to decide, but emphasizing that proposed alternative courses of action should be evaluated and contrasted. Both specified orderly and systematic procedures such as the "establishment of goals, selection of means and prediction of outcomes," however they were also sensitive to the role of interests and power. Not all scholars have been willing to concede space to interests and ideologies calling for pure technicism. Tauli (1984), for example, called language planning a failure for not asserting that the planner, as scientist, should prevail over the preferences of language users by insisting that scientific criteria of efficiency, modernity, and instrumentalism should prevail over "nostalgia and sentiment." In keeping with the prevailing intellectual climate of scientific optimism, only a minority of LPP pioneers were skeptical about any limits to technical protocols and many imagined banishing subjectivity and interests from consideration. While there are, in fact, orderly and sequenced kinds of LPP whose processes of research knowledge utilization are "rational" and "overt," and which collect data in systematic and publicly demonstrable ways, in reality the ordered "rational matrix" holds true for only a minority of actual LPP.

Some definitions do not limit the effects intended by policy intervention and encompass multiple kinds of collective action: "the organized pursuit of solutions to language problems, typically at the national level" (Fishman, 1973, pp. 23–4) and "authoritative allocation of resources to language" (Fishman, 1994, p. 92). Importantly some definitions (Neustupny, 1978, 1983) have also included even mundane practices of individual language use. The inclusion of an individual's language choices, processes of correction, modification and management of expressive alternatives is a radical move that takes LPP into relationship with consciousness and social psychology, raising issues about the degree of deliberateness required to classify practices as LPP.

Neustupny's useful distinction between approaches to language planning, one describing societies which plan language via *policy*, the other via *cultivation*, was further developed to distinguish between *correction* and *management* of language issues as the superordinate frame for describing language planning, with subordinate categories of *treatment* (organized and deliberate attention to language) and *planning* for those varieties of language treatment which seek to be theoretically structured and highly systematic. In his "correction model" Neustupny speaks of communication "inadequacies" which exist in both the communicative acts of individuals and the communicative system in general. Inadequacies lead to hypercorrection and an increase in the consciousness of the speaker. Problems in the communicative system lead to a meta-linguistic correction system of the teaching and the treatment systems, while individual speakers note discrepancies in the system or forms they are using, find a design for its removal, and decide whether to implement the identified change.

Neustupny's approach is interesting for this ambitious attempt to see through, initially by analogy and later by systematic structuring, a connection between individual and societal treatment of the LPP process; although he reserved the term language planning only for those treatments that draw on explicit LPP *theory* and which are characterized by systematicity and future orientation. An appealing alternative possibility is that LPP can be conceived not simply as the societal and conscious analogue of personal language correction processes, but that the personal and the societal are both instances of LPP located relationally along a single continuum of actions.

Fishman's many contributions have grounded LPP in social context and national setting, and have been especially prominent in examining LPP as intervention in language ecology (maintenance, revival, and shift). In a 1974 work Fishman conjoins in a single framework modernization and development models with LPP. Four language problems are characterized: selection, stability, expansion, and differentiation, each corresponding to LPP processes, respectively: policy-decisions, codification, elaboration, and cultivation. These result in the outcomes identified by Ferguson (1979), another pioneer of LPP theorization, as graphization, standardization, and modernization. This work exemplifies the continuing attempts to devise coherent relationships between societal and linguistic planning processes. Often the societal is identified as the base problem, stimulating the activity in the first place, with the resultant outcome characterized in language terms.

Fishman (2001) has also pioneered new areas of relevance for LPP and tied it to identity in ethnically plural settings, language beliefs and attitudes, religious and sacred experience, as well as to language regeneration efforts of indigenous and immigrant minorities. His Graded Intergenerational Dislocation Scale is an instrument for locating a language on a descending scale as a heuristic for intervention to regenerate and revitalize languages in various states of attrition, facilitating cost benefit analyses of reconstruction efforts. This is an important tool for LPP that combines community effort with expertise, and further ties LPP to the policy sciences.

30.3   The "Activity"

The term "language planning" became prominent in the work of Haugen (1966) who made it the overarching category encompassing societal intervention in language. Haugen's still popular systematization distinguishes between: *selection* of form, *codification* of the selected form, *implementation* of new norms, and their *elaboration* into various public domains, including institutional and cultural *cultivation* of language.

Kloss (1969) divided language planning into two branches of activity: *corpus* and *status planning*. Corpus planning refers to norm selection and codification and is usually undertaken by language experts, resulting in dictionaries, grammars, literacy manuals, and pronunciation and writing style guides. Status planning is rarely entrusted to language experts. The results of status planning are laws, clauses in constitutions prescribing the official standing of languages, and regulations for their use in public administration. This institutional and administrative focus is generally for nation-solidifying purposes and aims to secure a language, or its preferred orthography, over national territory or, in cases of imperial or economic expansion, to spread beyond it. Corpus planning is often undertaken to overcome communicative inefficiencies, usually driven by ideological imperative. Typically these ideologies have been nationalist postcolonial reconstruction, but social movements also advance political aims through modifications to the lexis and discourse patterns of language. Examples in English have been university campus speech codes promulgated in the interests of anti-racism and counter-sexism, indeed for most kinds of linguistic political correctness. Pursuing social change via linguistic reform is based on a sense that social power and representation correlate with language or are consonant with more performatively based understandings of language (Butler, 1997) that consider language constitutive of social identities and politics a lingually performed practice. Status and corpus planning are the major activities discussed in LPP literature, but three other activities are studied.

Acquisition planning (language-in-education) typically describes the languages teaching policies of states. Foreign or second language instruction can be motivated by humanistic rationales, by economic interest calculations, by assessments about national security or geo-political interest, or by responses to the needs, opportunities, and rights of linguistic minorities.

Usage planning refers to efforts to extend the communicative domains of a given language. This usually occurs in opposition to a replacing language after political reconstitution (administrative devolution, federalism, or national independence) but in more extreme cases usage planning forms part of regeneration efforts on behalf of dying languages.

Prestige planning involves elevating the esteem of a linguistic code. While this often accompanies status planning, there is an ancient history of poetic, philosophical, and religious involvement in attaching enhanced prestige to given codes that precedes formal planning processes and sometimes contradicts them. The production of canonical literature by poets, prose writers, and other cultural figures has effects that can be usefully discussed as language planning.

These five language planning actions are rarely separate. In practice they overlap and are mutually producing. Their goals are to alter or entrench the status, extend or modify the corpus, enhance or deepen the acquisition, disperse the usage and elevate the prestige of linguistic codes. I believe that we need to include an additional, critically oriented, activity: *discourse planning*.

Discourse planning refers to the influence and effect on people's mental states, behaviors and belief systems through the linguistically mediated ideological workings of institutions, disciplines, and diverse social formations. Although discourse is quintessentially dialogical, and by definition permits contest and negotiation, *planning* discourse refers to the efforts of institutions and diverse interests to shape, direct, and influence discursive practices and patterns. Often discourse planning seeks to represent as natural ways to think that are socially constructed, and therefore contestable, interested, and motivated, by influencing the predisposition of people to think in particular kinds of ways. At its extreme discourse planning approaches Orwellian thought control, more commonly it specifies the motivated, though not necessarily deliberate or conscious, use of speech acts to effect influence and persuasion. Some discourse planning is reflexive, aiming to influence how people think, behave, and value language itself. As such, discourse planning is the ideological accompaniment of other kinds of LPP practice, such as the persuasive discourses of public authorities engaged in status planning.

30.4 Modernization, Authenticity, Development, and Theory

For much of its contemporary history LPP theory focused on the particular needs of developing nations (Eastman, 1983) and on processes of modernization. A seminal text (Rubin & Jernudd, 1971) was subtitled "*Sociolinguistic Theory and Practice for Developing Nations.*" The standpoint suggests a little problematized notion of a "linguistically settled" end-point nation, suggesting an archetypal national order synonymous with western modernity, imagined as either uni-lingual, with uncontested orthographic conventions, in which the population is maximally literate, or at least not problematically plurilingual. This modernization involved progressive specialization in economic domains, lessening of clan, tribal, and ethnic bonds, and their substitution with the identities and relationships of liberal, industrial, and post-industrial consumerism in which standardized, codified national languages and near-universal literacy, predominate. The "normality" of the state modeled from Europeanized monolingual polities often collided with local realities and experiences of the relations between identity, polity, and communication (Mansour, 1993).

By foregrounding multilingualism as a problem, the logic of LPP had often been to place communication practices into hierarchically organized classifications, via differential status allocations, differential literacy elaborations, and different ideological associations. More persistent were assumptions that extensive multilingualism necessarily correlates with poverty and under-development. Pattanayak (1987) shows that a range of modern scholars has discussed multilingualism negatively, as causing backwardness and economic underdevelopment. The following maxim-like point exemplifies this: "a country that is linguistically highly heterogeneous is always undeveloped, and a country that is developed always has considerable language uniformity" (Pool, 1972, p. 213).

Fasold states: "It is obvious that multilingual states have problems that more nearly monolingual ones do not . . . difficulties in communication within a country can act as an impediment to commerce and industry and be socially disruptive" (1984, p. 4) and "there is a definite relationship between linguistic uniformity and economic development" (p. 7). Although he does indicate some benefits of multilingualism, he argues that linguistic "diversity is inversely related to development." Fasold concedes that such a relationship may not be causal, resulting from arbitrary postcolonial boundary setting (p. 134).

The modernization-developmental connection has lessened considerably in LPP writing, partly through increased prominence of Asian and African theorists positing new kinds of polity and asserting naturalness for linguistic pluralism, partly through exposure of the westernizing assumptions these connections carried, but also through new multilingual challenges becoming prominent in Europe and in the "new world" Europeanized states. Very rapid economic growth in China and parts of South India, based on high-tech innovation, will likely cause further modification to assumptions whose essential error has been to confound societal multilingualism with an absence of interlingual communication, an especially problematical assumption for sociolinguistics which foregrounds the idea of overlapping discourse com-munities and the functional specialization of speech and communication domains.

More broadly, patterns of economic modernization, especially in north Asia, have not necessarily reproduced the model of the developed nation typical of European economic modernization, challenging parts of the paradigm of classical LPP. Romanized writing is not inevitable for modernization (Gottlieb & Chen, 2001), new technological innovation allows voice instruction and renders less necessary any kind of alphabetization and even disrupts classical speech-writing hierarchies, but the modernization-language-development connection remains a crucial topic in LPP, especially prominently in light of global English (Lo Bianco, 2002).

30.5 Language Planning in History: No Unitary Purpose

LPP is as ancient as language itself, is expanding everywhere, and is used for many different purposes. Some early theorization (Eastman, 1983, p. 126) imagined a unitary disciplinary purpose: "a field that seeks to foster ethnic interaction, world communication, and national identity," but the vast diversity of its historical and actual practice belies such a possibility, and although it is theoretically possible that academic training in LPP could produce a unified ethics of practice, the field of language planning is not guided by common goals. Language planning serves multiple and conflicting interests. The subjectivity of planners is central for an account of LPP that seeks to comprehensively deal with its practices.

In the third century BC India's only Buddhist Emperor, Ashoka, pursued political unification via linguistic toleration while Qin Shihuangdi, first emperor of a united China, suppressed regional scripts (an opposite policy for a similar objective), selecting a single standardized writing variety (the Small Seal) and mandating its use (Ferguson, 1979/96). These ancient precedents have modern manifestations; India's constitution continuing Ashoka's pluralism and in China's unitary policy.

At a similar time in the west language planning exhibited language and world-view beliefs. Plato advocated free literacy to counter communal poetic recitation aiming to "break the power base of Homer and traditional culture" (Gee, 1996, pp. 32–5), believing that through dialogic language Athenians might be "disenchanted" from the blandishments of Homeric verse and its dangerous "magic" that made the citizenry pliable and unthinking.

The European language academies (Florence, 1582; France, 1635; Spain, 1713) aimed to cultivate prestigious literary culture, but also laid the basis for subsequent national politics. Cultivated literary languages merged with the idea of national culture, advocacy for unique and bounded states to reflect language borders followed (Hobsbawm, 1993), under industrialization, with standardized mass literacy in national languages. This long evolution of canonical literary forms, eloquence and scientific discourse, and mass basic literacy, supports Coulmas' (1989, 1994) argument that languages do not yield standard forms naturally (these are cultural achievements), and Joseph's (1987) analysis of "eloquence" and its power as culturally specific, and variable. Linguistic evidence for nationalist politics spawned new nations and revived old ones. The invention of the linguistic minority (Heller, 1999), the creation of border communities, the emergence of polycentric, national-variety, languages, and other fall-out from determining political space through notions of language and culture as much as through power and force, spawned an expansion of deliberate language engineering, cultivation, and propagation that continues unabated in Europe, as elsewhere, today.

The nation-language ideology served Apartheid's originators to legitimate forced relocation of African peoples. In processes not always self-conscious or deliberate, scholarship joined policy. Uninterrupted speech chains were ruptured, inventing languages just as interpretable as mutually intelligible varieties, devising different orthographic conventions, and attaching the results to a discourse of uni-lingual nation-entities; all constituting evidence of separateness necessitating divided geo-political space (Alexander, 1989, p. 22). Linguistic classification and "scientific" nomenclature can be saturated with politics. This served Apartheid's project of "breaking up the black people into a large number of conflicting and competing so called ethnic groups" (Alexander, 1989, p. 21). Since 1996 language planning serves a dramatically different meta-policy in a South Africa seeking to forge a trans-ethnic but multilingual state but which pits progressive constitutionalism against the market-driven power of English in a post-national globalization (Webb, 2002).

Several centuries earlier, LPP produced in Sweden the world's highest literacy rates (far higher for women than in many countries today), an outcome motivated not by any literacy motivation but by commitment about direct, unmediated, encounter with God's word (Gee, 1996). In the eighteenth and nineteenth centuries the world's biological and chemical terminologies were rationalized by Linnaeus and Berzelius (Dahlstedt, 1976). From such experiences the Swedish Academy has evolved a function independent of state, issuing rulings on terminology, pronunciation, and spelling that are accepted in popular and technical domains. This expert-driven and authoritative rationality is sustained by a "total Swedish societal ideology" (Dahlstedt, 1976). Altogether different is the "creation" of Modern Turkish, replacing its Ottoman predecessor, a process preceded by romanization, and combining cultural innovation, modernization, democratization, imposition, cultivation, and ongoing contest resulting in what, according to Lewis (1999), has been a "catastrophic success."

More like Turkey than Sweden, but particular as well, is Vietnam's evolution of its writing system (DeFrancis, 1977; Lo Bianco, 2001a), the only nation to romanize Chinese orthography. This "policy" is the fruit of millennial struggle against various colonialisms, with multiple language and writing alternatives at different times, shifting reactions of the mandarin scholar-gentry class, colonial administrators, revolutionary and conservative politicians, poets and writers, and peasantry to the language options imposed or favored by various dominating outsiders and internal collaborators.

Accounting for any of these experiences of LPP could never be adequate from a disciplinary source grounded in language study alone, much less from linguistics, however conceived, but needs to be informed by historical, political, educational, and economic scholarship. However, since history, economics, education, and political theorizing invariably neglect to account for the role of language over time, in resources, in instruction, and in relations of power, a distinctive transdisciplinary applied discipline, grounded in real-world data, is required, otherwise language policy histories are rendered subservient to broader analysis that cannot account for its specificities. Located between human sciences that pay scant attention to language, and linguistic accounts that pay scant attention to context, a transdisciplinary language planning theorization is essential. Its reach and methods must far exceed the limits both of descriptive accounts of language and of the invisibility of language to historians, economists, and political scientists. An account of the Vietnamese case needs analysis of the peculiar "micro-linguistics" of graphization, a tri-graphic hierarchy of three scripts: *Chu Han* (Chinese writing of Chinese), *Chu Nom* (indigenous adaptation of Chinese writing for Vietnamese), and *Quoc Ngu* (romanization of Vietnamese), along with romanized French, alongside analysis of the languages this tri-graphia favored or impeded (Chinese, Vietnamese-influenced Chinese, French and Vietnamese). And all this must be grounded in the real-world contexts of the social, political, cultural, and economic interests that were advanced or retarded, the development, modernization, revolution, mass or elite literacy that the tri-graphic hierarchy made possible or difficult. These language-specific inflections of history, economy, education, and revolutionary or reactionary politics can never be accounted for fully within a solely contextual analysis and yet will always be inadequately accounted for without reference to the enveloping context (Lo Bianco, 2001a).

Some dimensions of language policy-making, beyond direct language activism, are dispersed among communities and reside in the ordinary practices of language use, confirming and disconfirming promulgated norms, invoking and resisting identities, advancing or retarding ideologies. Language practices, inherited as tradition, and language itself, populated with the meanings, associations, and ideologies of past speakers and present usage, constitute what speakers inherit, the past "policy" of the language resource of a collectivity, and these enter into complex relation with assertive institutions and authorities. This account is influenced by ideas on language as voice and dialogue, from Voloshinov and Bakhtin (Dentith, 1995), and is crucial to the present claim that LPP needs revitalization with the inclusion of discourse planning as a legitimate field of LPP.

30.6 Critiques

Academic marginality has not shielded language planning from attack. Perhaps severest has been the allegation that LPP is complicit with social repression in the interests of state and class (Luke, McHoul, & Mey, 1990). Mühlhäusler (1995) holds that when applied by developed-country experts (operating with notions of "one national language") to intergenerationally stable multilingual nations in post-colonizing contexts, LPP can lead to the creation of hierarchical diglossia among existing languages and varieties, and in turn this can lead to erosion and the ultimate demise of minority languages. Relatedly, the spread of anglophone westernizing modernity can lead to the destruction of distinctive life-worlds and the depletion of the alternative worldviews that reside in diverse linguistic systems (Nettle & Romaine, 2000; Phillipson & Skutnabb-Kangas, 1996; Skutnabb-Kangas, 1995), the result of the absorption of poor and marginalized peoples into global consumerism.

Another allegation has been that LPP has entrenched economic inequalities for immigrants in first world societies by language educational schemes tracking immigrants into low-paid, marginal jobs (Tollefson, 1991). The methods of LPP have been criticized for depending on positivistic, rationalist epistemology (a "pretence to science") and for relying exclusively on technicist-scientistic techniques (Luke, McHoul, & Mey, 1990). For Moore (1996) LPP theorists adopt an uncritical stance toward their own practices and operate with excessively descriptive approaches. Moore uses Dorothy Smith's sociology, which implicates scholarly practices in "relations of ruling," naming others' lives and experiences, inscribing outsider appropriations into orders of action that impose "invented" categories on lived experience; scholarly "overwriting" as domination.

The archetypal methods of LPP such as the sociolinguistic survey, and the rational choice matrix, the latter an analogue of management formalism: (1) Identification of Problem (fact-finding); (2) Specification of Goals (development of policy); (3) Cost-Benefit Analysis (weighing up alternatives with rational demonstration of the ultimately preferred one) (4) Implementation (5) Evaluation (comparing predicted to actual outcomes), are criticized for "masquerading" as neutral information-collecting instruments and ordered action-sequences. Critical scholarship argues that these methods can produce the means for bureaucratic and technocratic management of the lives of minority communities. Outsider, scholarly, ways to know and represent can predominate over insider lived experience, and serve the interests of state agencies, corporations, statistical documentation practices, and even proselytizing religious orders (Sommer, 1991). Such criticisms allege that formal processes of analysis in the service of commissioning agencies manufacture "factive" representations over communities otherwise independent of centralizing and hegemonical apparatuses. Such representations are often framed as information required to "solve" social, educational, health, and occupational problems, invariably seeking to alleviate "disadvantage."

Fishman rejects the most extreme of these criticisms (1994) but calls on LPP scholars to adopt stances, conceding that LPP cannot reside in some ideology-free zone being used by "ethnicisers, nativisers and traditionalisers" who "engage in language planning for their own purposes" (Fishman, 1994, p. 96).

30.7 Problems

A distinctive dimension of LPP theorization has been its struggle with "problems." Much LPP theory adheres to a view that LPP scholarship starts with a response to predetermined language problems. Some scholars have attempted comprehensive characterizations of language problems, most impressively Dua (1985, 1986), who claims that the "systematic account of language problems of a speech community is a prerequisite to an adequate theory of policy formulation, language planning and language treatment" (p. 3). Dua's scheme specifies various categories of people who define problems, insiders/outsiders, politicians/bureaucrats, researchers/professionals, and "the people," and specifies four social needs that defined language problems reflect:

Normative needs: definitions in which professionals or experts dominate;
Felt needs: definitions in which affected groups or individuals prevail in the
   process of defining;
Expressed needs: those felt needs that are converted into action; and,
Comparative needs: establishing a contrast among needs such as temporal,
   situational or locational.

Dua's matrix further complicates according to how needs are handled, involving a series of oppositions, broadly/narrowly, deeply/superficially, precisely/vaguely, and rationally/irrationally. This desire to comprehensively characterize is also exemplified in Nahir (1984) who identifies eleven intended treatments for language problems: purification, revival, reform, standardization, spread, lexical modernization, terminology unification, stylistic simplification, interlingual communication, language maintenance, and auxiliary-code standardization.

Attempting to characterize the totality of language problems in taxonomies underscores the vast complexity of LPP. However, and quite problematically, which language problems are allocated policy treatment is embedded in conflict about interests, probably only identifiable from critical perspectives. LPP sometimes appears to take claims by public authorities about policy intentions at face value, failing to recognize what the scholars would, as citizens, ordinarily recognize, that political languge is inflated, and that LPP is framed by political discourse. How many times does it occur that in electoral debating concessions are made to certain publically demanded principles only to be denied in practice, witness the legendary status of the political promise. LPP is also politics.

Most LPP scholarship has not been naive about the problematic nature of problems; there has been insufficient attention to the ideological character of processes for the determination of which language problems are allocated policy attention. LPP has wanted to describe processes of status, corpus, prestige, and usage planning without adequate regard to the prior structuring processes of ideology, discursive politics, the contest about what representations of language, what language problems, will be constituted for state agency or authoritative intervention. In public policy literature, however, there has long been an acute sense of the politicized character of policy problems with Edelman (1988) arguing they are ideological constructions that "come into discourse and into existence as reinforcements of ideologies" (p. 12).

An exemplary instance of this is the politics that surround the official English movement in the United States. The moves legislate English as "official" is, at face value, a classic instance of status planning, but what is the problem that these expensive and extensive (and materially redundant?) efforts respond to? Is it "Hispanophobia" (Crawford, 1995), "war against diversity" (Crawford, 2000), a moralistic "Reagan renaissance" (Tarver, 1989), "civilization" for the "American underclass" (Gingrich, 1995), rolling back expensive leftish "official multilingualism," or the "need" to "protect English" (Lo Bianco, 2001b)? Most dramatically, is American democracy, founded on English libertarian principles, at risk and needing its House of Representatives and Senate to make a stark and historic choice between "Democracy or Babel!" (de la Pena, 1991)?

The language problem that precedes and shapes language policy and planning is no straightforward thing, immersed as it is in discursive politics.

30.8   Praxis as (Past) Planning

Planning is itself a problematical notion, since it suggests changing the future. Is what we ordinarily do, with language as with most other behavior, past planning in action? Is the "default" system with which we mostly operate in mundane life simply the operation of what was previously consciously determined, and is now praxis? In a longitudinal study of US bilingual teachers, Shannon (1999) comments on what happens when there is an absence of explicit policy formulations, apart from broad policy, and finds that "practice" becomes "policy." In the absence of overt or explicit detailed planning, teachers make recourse, through underlying beliefs and values, to patterns of behavior that reflect past accommodations or past policies, sometimes contradicting the broad policy altogether. Thus ideology operates as "default" policy.

Recent approaches to the study of attitudes, values, and beliefs as constituting an ongoing, daily politics of language ideology (Schieffelin, Woolard, & Kroskrity, 1998) sustain Shannon's approach. Bakhtin's conception of ideologically laden discourse, most evident in "authoritative" contexts, where discourse: "is indissolubly fused with its authority – with political power, an institution, a person . . ." (Bakhtin, 1981, p. 343) extends this thinking, suggesting that what is default is in fact powerfully shaped by authoritative extant discursive representations, institutionality in discursive practice, and praxis, what is routinely done, as its daily enactment or performance.

The language ideology connection can be demonstrated by different constructions of what two-language teaching in schools "means." Two-language education is found in all parts of the world, but it is rarely the same thing, sometimes being marked as progressive, interesting, or enriching, other times as oppressive and regressive. Australian bilingual education can be simple acknowledgment of minority children's educational potential (Djite, 1994), or a conspiracy by a self-serving "educational establishment" denying indigenous children English literacy (Lo Bianco, 1999). Canadian bilingual education can be a politicized concession to Québec nationalism, but also educational and social enrichment (Heller, 1999). US bilingual education can be anti-poverty measures for disadvantaged Mexican-American pupils (Schneider, 1976), or education that "integrates language minority and language majority students in the same classroom with the goal of academic excellence and bilingual proficiency for both" (Christian et al., 1997). Most extreme, the language policy aimed at teaching arithmetic and social studies in Afrikaans alongside English became "the immediate cause of the 1976 Soweto uprising" that resulted in the deaths of many students (Juckes, 1995). Two-language education, like any LPP measure, assumes specific political meaning at the conjunction of overarching ideologies and specific histories, in real-world settings of conflict, opportunity, resources, and relations among groups.

Discourse, in its naming and framing problems, contributes in forming epistemological bases for understanding the world and is constitutive of perception. A reinvigorated theorization of LPP requires the addition of discourse planning to adequately explain, even to discuss, policy action in which language is the object of attention, obviously most in those domains where there is contest, conflict, and dispute. The key aim is to account for the language of politics in language planning theory, how language problems are construed discursively for policy attention, a process that results in selective elevation of some language issues to policy attention, while silencing alternative claims. The inclusion of the political discursive realm within the remit of LPP seeks to understand the constitution of language problems as a performative practice, engaging both traditional notions of rhetoric and persuasive talk, but also the actual accomplishment of goals of language policy through ideological structuring.

Language is a deeply problematic object of the conscious processes of planning because it is also the medium for its constitution as an object for policy attention. Policy and planning are interventions into "natural" ecologies, disrupting processes of evolution, diversification, and standardization. The most general purpose of intervention is to assert deliberative control. The imposition of deliberative, consciously-intended ends onto semiotic practices that have ecological character as substantive fields with endogenous developmental processes and histories raises questions about control exercisable by intervention and the ambiguous effects of intervention. It also foregrounds the connection between personal language practices and the societal domain. The official English movement in the United States is salient because of the material absence of what classical language planning would constitute as a "language problem," or, better, the heavily ideologized character of the "language problems" advanced for policy treatment. Making central within LPP the analysis of policy discourses surrounding the constitution of language policy problems establishes the performative character of the disputation around the status of English in America. Some discourses demand acknowledgment of English as "the language of America," America understood as a political community, united by claims to a tradition of liberal individualism and enterprise. These claims are an indispensable part of policy-making, the state-talk that policy talk is seeking to enact, but the discourse seeks not only to stimulate legislative action, it is itself policy action, performance of an extended routine of naturalizing associations of English with national iconography and values.

Praxis, and discourse, here constitute and perform, through countless reiteration, over time and space, illocutions (speech acts whose effects are immediate if persuasive) and make available public perlocutions (effects dependent on the material responses of lawmaking).

30.9   Sciences of Language

Underlying the possibility of any kind of language planning is the notion that "language . . . is . . . subjected to human action and control . . . This insight is the basis for all language planning" (Bartsch, 1988, p. 147). This insight tells us that language is not static and uniform, but not what it actually is. Different sciences of language investigation have struggled to more or less strongly locate the linguistic sign in relation to context, system, inter-subjective iteration, and the material world.

Newmeyer (1986) contrasts "autonomous" linguistics with three conceptions of language that connect it to external non-language realities: sociolinguistics, Marxist-oriented linguistics, and "humanistic" aesthetics. He takes "autonomous" approaches to mean generative linguistics, alongside its structuralist forerunners deriving from Saussure. Newmeyer's search for a characterization of language and context aims to look past what he characterizes as linguistic "modernism," a goal shared by Pratt (1987) who claims that underlying the formalizations of autonomous linguistics are "utopias," idealized assumptions about community and shared identity. Both identify an oscillation in approaches to language description between greater and lesser contextualization, like Hanks (1996), who substitutes "communication practices" for "language" as the center of scholarly interest. This oscillation is inflected in each historical phase in the research questions that occupy expert scholars of language. The inflections mean that similarly underlying questions recur in specific, grounded instances in new times under the rubrics of linguistics and applied linguistics. Although this process reflects a wider intellectual history of alternating periods of universality and relativism, the pattern of oscillation within language theorization is influenced to a considerable degree by practical constraints that faced scholarship, with spoken, and "fleeting," language now more amenable to systematic study, freed as scholars are from the constraints that Voloshinov called the "cadavers" of abstract systems, the dead texts that animated the interests of philology (in Dentith, 1995).

Other kinds of linguistics offer alternative ways of "seeing" language, and ground discussion of grammar, correctness and norms, in theories that give rise to different dilemmas concerning normative knowledge. These dilemmas suggest particular connections between informing language theory and practices of language planning. If applied linguistics isn't linguistics applied, or isn't just linguistics applied, we still need to ask what is the linguistics that isn't or is only partially, or only occasionally, applied? Three different sciences of language producing different kinds of LPP are considered.

A view of socially-made meaning, social semiotics, is central in the Systemic Functional Linguistics of M. A. K. Halliday and yields theorizations of the practice of policy and planning intervention different from those that claim descent from descriptive linguistics. Specifically, in Halliday (1993), a different base notion of language generates an approach to LPP which sees the "meaning resources" of a community, its children in school, or its science, social relations, and politics as expandable, or restrictable, on the basis of explicit connections between structure and semiosis, deriving from his explicitly made interconnections between language and the material realm. Halliday distinguishes between institutional and systemic LPP. The latter is more innovative and follows from sema-history notions, that is, stages of history and the relations between language and materialism, class, sex, and race. The relation between evolution and intervention refers to limits posed by grammar's base, the relation between social structure and language in different phases of history, as well as its disjunctions. Hallidayan inspired LPP would differ from conventional theorizations in several ways because semantics, not form, would be the central issue for investigation. In contemporary LPP theory acquisition planning refers to the efforts states make to teach foreign or minority languages, occasionally to the adult literacy campaigns in postcolonial nations. Notions such as "expanding the meaning resources of learners" would count as the central practice of a Halliday influenced LPP, whereas much post-war LPP has neglected national literacy education. Although sometimes "intellectualization" is cited in conventional LPP as code-centered corpus planning in Hallidayan inspired LPP, this process of extending meaning potential would be the central issue of examination and not a marginal one.

The second language science that would produce a radically original LPP is located in the "identity" orientation that shapes the linguistics of Le Page and Tabouret-Keller. Le Page and Tabouret-Keller (1985) and Le Page (1988, 1993) propound a unique view of language as science, and of the sorts of intervention that create what they regard as "language." A key premise of their theorization is a highly dynamic inseparability of language, "a repertoire of socially marked systems" (Le Page & Tabouret-Keller, 1985, p. 116), from the practices and instances of its use, questioning the ontological status of many of the categories assumed by conventional linguistics and challenging the fixity of these categories (ethnic groups, languages, dialects, different languages). This challenge derives from the locus of language; which they find residing in individuals whose creative and massive variations in its use reflect constant negotiation and change. Every speech act involves the projection of the "inner universe" of the speaker "implicitly with the invitation to others to share it" (Le Page & Tabouret-Keller, 1985, p. 181). This projection produces adjustments ("focusing") based on the feedback from the interlocutor's response to the language projected, in some measure reinforcing the original or producing its modification as the original speaker accommodates to the feedback received. Projection involves a creative and constitutive set of operations whereas focusing involves progression from simple feedback to incorporation and institutionalization.

Individuals inhabit and create a "multidimensional symbolic universe" (Le Page, 1988, p. 32) surrounding them with a multitude of possible linguistic choices and selections based on the interplay of projection and focusing. Le Page distinguishes between standards as norms and as prescription. The former comes about through focusing, the dialogical process of fit between projection and feedback, and is largely unconscious. This process can account for language change and development and even for rigidities in some processes (monastic scriptoria). Prescriptive norms on the other hand derive from the awareness of stereotypes based on norms. Le Page argues for example that Received Pronunciation originated in the "close interaction" between public schools, Oxford and Cambridge, and the "Mandarin ranks of the civil service" in the latter part of the nineteenth century and early part of the twentieth. Projection and focusing are understandable as LPP processes that make dynamic reformulations of language commonplace, but also help to explain stable phenomena.

A third alternative LPP can be constructed from critical approaches to language. Critical linguistics is premised on the idea that language and ideological systems are inseparable, but that these connections are naturalized, made to seem like common sense, and therefore masquerade as normal when in fact they represent and carry interest. Fairclough (1989, 1995) argues that language is the prime locus of ideology, that this insight of critical and social theory (influenced by Bourdieu, Foucault, and Habermas) is evidenced by the "linguistic turn" in contemporary social theory and is critical precisely because it reveals connections of power and ideology with language that are otherwise concealed through "linguistics proper." For critical linguistics, a theory of social practice that does not reduce or overly elevate individual agency and creativity, nor the determinative power of convention or structure, is the defining parameter of the field.

This approach rejects the classic base of descriptive (or autonomous) linguistics, in the tradition of Saussure, as unacceptably a-social, overly formalistic, with the related stress on synchronic analysis and abstract characterizations. Furthermore, critical scholarship argues that conventional sociolinguistics only seeks correlative relations between social structures and aspects of language (running the risk of legitimizing such correlated forms by a-critically describing their contextual "appropriateness," when critical linguistics might seek to problematize such relationships). In this vein Gee (1996, p. 104) states that "Since language situates speakers and hearers within fields of status and solidarity, and since these are inherent social goods to humans, all language is always and everywhere ideological."

Political linguistics is a term that has arisen within LPP writings, especially among critically inclined scholars. In settings where language correlates with major economic inequality Calvet (1998) takes a strong approach: "All planning presupposes a policy, the policy of those in power . . . by intervening in languages, he becomes part of the power game" (Calvet, 1998, p. 203). For in vitro experimentation to succeed it must work in vivo and Calvet's view is that the actual position of the linguist is predictable, usually the linguist is to be found on . . . the side of power, even if he only considers himself as a technician or adviser . . . language officials . . . risk becoming servants of the state . . . intervention by planning tends to dispossess speakers of their own language: all planning is carried out by a handful of planners possessing all the power over a people who are planned. (p. 203)

His one way out seems to derive not at all from professional ethics or responsibility but from citizenship, since "language policy is a civil war of languages . . ." so a linguist must "behave as a citizen and keep democratic watch . . ." (1998, p. 203). This position precludes a place for a kind of systematic scholarship that may be aware of the interested and motivated nature of policy and planning but which may still be systematic, careful, and scholarly; and may even work counter to dominant forces.

For Blommaert the challenge for LPP is positionality:

Taking sides is unavoidable: it comes with doing a particular type of questioning of linguistic reality. An attempt at providing a history of language, which takes into account social and political factors, forces us to voice interpretations of these factors. And in social and political reality, interpretations are partisan, and they almost automatically align the one who formulated the interpretation with one or another political bloc. So be it. (Blommaert, 1999, p. 437)

For Blommaert and Bulcaen (1997) this constitutes what they call "political linguistics."

New intellectual forming sources for a reinvigorated LPP also come from critical sociology, such as the work of Bourdieu (1982, 1991) and his analysis of a kind of human subject that makes central the ideology of economy. Bourdieu has produced an analogue of the economic human within a symbolic market. In Bourdieu's scheme there are four kinds of capital available to interacting humans: *Economic Capital* (various kinds of material wealth and assets), *Cultural Capital* (knowledge, skill and education), *Symbolic Capital* (accumulated prestige or honor), and *Social Capital* (connections and group membership). Individuals are distributed according to the configurations and quanta of capital that they possess and how the capital stocks can be transformed in social life into advantage. Power is taken to be the capacity of individuals to mobilize the authority accumulated in a market by deploying their capital stocks. This kind of power is a symbolic transmutation of coercive force.

For Bourdieu "buying and selling" economies are located within a communication economy in which linguistic interchange is a critical social practice. His is both a metaphorical rendering of marketplace terms and practices of language and a real analysis of the actual interplay of communicative exchange. Within these communication economies symbolic domination is effected by asymmetrical capital endowments. These take the form of a *habitus* in which the social person operates not just at linguistic dimensions but also with consequences in material capital. Bourdieu's analysis of the historical unification of the French linguistic market from pre-revolutionary to Republican times shows the operation of symbolic domination processes so that state linguistic unification and formal officialization accompanied each other.

The constitutional enshrinement of French was bolstered and made possible by the officialization of Parisian in the symbolic marketplace. It was not just that the state required standardized forms of literate language to operate its technical mechanisms of nationing and administration, but that there was a "struggle for symbolic power in which what was at stake was the formation and re-formation of mental structures" (Bourdieu, 1991, p. 48). The legitimization and realization of the language of state, with its content shifts toward new terms of address enshrining new social relationships, new metaphors and euphemisms, was a political struggle for the kind of language that a new social order demanded. This centralizing, hierarchical and universalizing, involved marginalizing local differences in the interests of Republican citizenship. This approach to LPP reveals a clear connection between micro-linguistic performativity of the macro-sociopolitical change of authority for French.

Bourdieu points out that symbolic domination utilizes and indeed ends up being a practice of euphemization; in effect a kind of self-censoring, governmentality in Foucault's language. The market results in euphemization because of a process of *anticipation* (Thompson, 1991). Adapting to the pre-eminence of certain kinds of dominant linguistic capital creates a hegemonizing of the extant power relations. It gives effect at the interpersonal linguistic exchange to a wider societal project of language officialization. Persuasive powers are "obeyed" in *anticipation* of their deployment.

Foucault's conception of how chainings of meaning are discursively related and repress alternative formations, and how these are historically produced though loosely structured combinations of statements, is relevant here as a kind of "discourse planning." In policy work this occurs through specialized and powerful kinds of knowledge that policy science generates, knowledge designed for action; knowledge whose techniques of production stress precision and validity, and claim to remove ideology and interest. For Foucault "There is no power relation without the correlative constitution of a field of knowledge, nor any knowledge that does not presuppose and constitute at the same time, power relations" (1979, p. 27). These insights are relevant to a reconceptualized LPP in that they assist us to explain not only instances of *language planning* but also how the discipline itself arose and what particular interests it has.

30.10   Discourse Planning

In an attempt at a comprehensive post-World War II intellectual history of LPP, Ricento (2000) identifies three phases characterized by research questions, methodologies, and goals. Early work was predominantly technicist and technocratic with expert specialists promulgating solutions for newly emerging postcolonial states utilizing a "developing country approach," but with little problematization of methodology, "developed country" assumptions, or interests. The second phase is characterized as a kind of neo-colonial re-think after the failure of economic "take-off." The current phase is shaped by a realization that LPP is not "philosophically neutral" leading to a challenge to its base in autonomous linguistics and some of its cherished ideas: native speakers, mother tongues, diglossia, national languages, bounded literacy, languages as discrete and bounded entities (instead of "will to community"), finite grammars, among others. Ricento claims that LPP today shows alarm about linguistic imperialism, language extinction and sees language and literacy as plural, contingent, and hybridizing social practices. The Ricento approach is helpful in bringing together contextual factors, intra-discipline epistemological change, and periodization. Inevitably such schemas can only be suggestive since time boundaries are never absolute, and the third stage is less new theory and more position taking.

What is proposed here is the addition of a category of language planning analysis, *discourse planning*, which understands discourse as both shaped and performing. The spirit of the informing linguistics identified above, and the limitations of descriptive analysis, partially motivate this proposal. The examination of persuasion and politics in language is not new, what is called for is the inclusion within LPP of the discursive realm as the key domain for the performance of language planning praxis. When persuasion and politics become focused on language itself, LPP becomes reflexive, and cyclical, the language of persuasion becomes deployed in the interests of enacting policy on language as object. Language here is both the means and object of itself. By scrutinizing the language of policy-making, using insights and methods of ethno-methodology to undertake micro-examinations of how language issues are constituted as problems for treatment by policy, we can integrate, if not reconcile, approaches to the study of language policy which are both systematic and empirical with approaches that acknowledge the ideological character of discourse. The examination of policy discourses, especially how policy discourses constitute problems for policy treatment, is a neglected field that will extend the scholarly range and rigor of LPP.

Language or code focused linguistics makes a choice to reify language and subject it to analysis within the formal conceptual apparatus of autonomous linguistic science. Applied linguistics, on the other hand, tackles contexts in which language issues, or problems, are paramount and subjects these problems to analyses, both empirical and speculative in design, to reach coherent accounts and understandings. Applied linguistics therefore reifies particular social moments, those in which language issues are prominent, and which require active kinds of analysis, aiming beyond understanding, or even explanation, toward scholarly legitimizations of particular courses of public action. Language policy and planning is an exemplary kind of scholarship for action.

Language planning is normative action for intervention (change or anti-change), whose analysis requires a reinvigorated intellectual framework combining professional identity formation, meaning and informational practices, among interacting subjects. Critical and political linguistics offer useful conceptual information, as do the alternative linguistic sciences that identify coherent connections with identity as multiple, shifting (but also stable and persisting) and with the material and cultural context. These links (to culture, identity, and material realms) are enacted in verbalization and writing. Other fields of dialogue for the reinvigoration of LPP include the (political) subjectivity of language planners, systematic data collection and careful analysis methods that can operate within realistic incorporation of persisting ideologies, and interest in policy-making. Language policy and planning are ancient, extensive, and predictably expanding. Their understanding and explanation will be enhanced if in addition to more rigorous understandings of status attribution politics, corpus modification processes, esteem and prestige alteration, and impacts on usage, we include analysis of their discursive mediation and construction.

See also 5 Discourse Analysis, 15 World Englishes, 28 Bilingual Education, 29 Language Maintenance, 32 Critical Applied Linguistics.

REFERENCES

Alexander, N. (1989) *Language policy and national unity in South Africa/Azania.* Cape Town: Buchu Books, Creda Press.

Annamalai, E., Jernudd, B. H., & Rubin, J. (eds.) (1986) *Language planning; proceedings of an institute.* Mysore: Central Institute of Indian Languages; Hawai'i: Institute of Culture and Communications, East-West Center.

Bakhtin, M. (1981) *The dialogic imagination.* Austin: University of Texas Press.

Bartsch, R. (1988) *The norms of language.* London: Longman.

Blommaert, J. (ed.) (1999) *Language ideological debates.* Berlin: Mouton de Gruyter.

Blommaert, J. & Bulcaen, C. (eds.) (1997) *Political linguistics (Belgian Journal of Linguistics,* 11). Amsterdam: John Benjamins.

Bourdieu, P. (1982) The economics of linguistic exchanges. *Social Science Information,* 16, 645–68.

Bourdieu, P. (1991) *Language and symbolic power.* Cambridge, MA: Harvard University Press.

Brecht, R. D. & Walton, A. R. (1993) *National strategic planning in the less commonly taught languages.* Washington, DC: National Foreign Language Center, Johns Hopkins University.

Brumfit, C. (1997) Theoretical practice: applied linguistics as pure and practical science. In A. Mauranen & K. Sajavaara (eds.), *Applied linguistics across disciplines,* (pp. 18–30). *AILA Review,* 12, 1995/6.

Butler, J. (1997) *Excitable speech: a politics of the performative.* London: Routledge.

Calvet, L. J. (1998) *Language wars and linguistic politics.* New York: Oxford University Press.

Chambers, J. K. (1995) *Sociolinguistic theory.* Oxford: Blackwell.

Christian, D., Montone, C. L., Lindholm, K. J., & Carranza, I. (1997) *Profiles in two-way immersion education.*

Washington, DC: Center for Applied Linguistics and Delta Systems.

Cooper, R. L. (1989) *Language Planning and Social Change*. Cambridge: Cambridge University Press.

Coulmas, F. (1989) Democracy and the crisis of normative linguistics. In F. Coulmas (ed.), *Language adaptation* (pp. 177–93). Cambridge: Cambridge University Press.

Coulmas, F. (1994) Why is language standardisation necessary? Economic considerations. In *National language institutes around the world, diversity in language issues* (pp. 172–201). Tokyo: National Language Research Institute.

Crawford, J. (1995) *Bilingual education: history, politics, theory and practice*. Los Angeles: Bilingual Education Services.

Crawford, J. (2000) *At war with diversity: US language policy in an age of anxiety*. Clevedon, UK: Multilingual Matters.

Dahlstedt, K. H. (1976) Societal ideology and language cultivation: the case of Swedish. *International Journal of the Sociology of Language*, 10, 17–50.

Davies, A. (1999) *An introduction to applied linguistics: from practice to theory*. Edinburgh: Edinburgh University Press.

DeFrancis, J. (1977) *Colonialism and language policy in Vietnam*. The Hague: Mouton.

Dentith, S. (1995) *Bakhtinian thought*. London: Routledge.

de La Pena, F. (1991) *Democracy or Babel?* Washington DC: US English.

Djite, P. (1994) *From language policy to language planning*. Melbourne: Language Australia Publications.

Dua, H. R. (1985) *Language-planning in India*. New Delhi: Harnam Publications.

Dua, H. R. (1986) Language-planning and linguistic minorities In E. Annamalai, B. H. Jernudd, & J. Rubin (eds.), *Language planning: proceedings of an institute*. (pp. 133–73). Mysore: Central Institute of Indian Languages;

Hawai'i: Institute of Culture and Communications, East-West Center.

Eastman, C. M. (1983) *Language-planning: an introduction*. Novato, CA: Chandler & Sharp.

Edelman, M. J. (1988) *Constructing the political spectacle*. Chicago and London: The University of Chicago Press.

Fairclough, N. (1989) *Language and power*. London: Longman.

Fairclough, N. (1995) *Critical discourse analysis: the critical study of language*. London: Longman.

Fasold, R. (1984) *Sociolinguistics of society* (vol. 1). Oxford: Blackwell.

Ferguson, C. A. (1979) National attitudes to language planning. In T. Huebner (ed.), *Socio-linguistic perspectives: papers on language in society, 1959–1994* (pp. 295–303). New York: Oxford University Press.

Fishman J. A. (1971) The sociology of language. In J. A. Fishman (ed.), *Advances in the sociology of language* (vol. 1) (pp. 217–414). The Hague: Mouton.

Fishman, J. A. (ed.) (1974) *Advances in language planning*. The Hague: Mouton.

Fishman, J. A. (1973) Language modernization and planning in comparison with other types of national modernization and planning. *Language in Society*, 2(1), 23–44.

Fishman, J. A. (1994) Critiques of language planning: a minority languages perspective. *Journal of Multilingual and Multicultural Development*, 15(2 & 3), 91–9.

Fishman, J. A. (ed.) (2001) *Can threatened languages be saved?* Clevedon, UK: Multilingual Matters.

Foucault, M. (1979) *Discipline and punish: the birth of the prison*. New York: Vintage.

Gee, J. (1996) *Sociolinguistics and literacy: ideology in discourse*. London: The Falmer Press.

Gingrich, N. (1995) *To renew America*. New York: Harper Collins.

Gottlieb, N. & Chen, P. (eds.) (2001) *Language policy in East Asia: a reader.* London: Curzon Press.

Halliday, M. A. K. (1993) Language in a changing world. *Applied Linguistics Association of Australia; occasional paper 13.* Canberra: Australian National University Printing Services.

Hanks, W. F. (1996) *Language and communicative practices.* Boulder, CO: Westview Press.

Haugen, E. (1966) *Language conflict and language planning: the case of modern Norwegian.* Cambridge, MA: Harvard University Press.

Heller, M. (1999) *Linguistic minorities and modernity: a sociolinguistic ethnography.* London and New York: Longman.

Hobsbawm, E. J. (1993) *Nations and nationalism since 1780: programme, myth, reality.* Cambridge: Canto.

Jernudd, B. H. (1973) Language planning as a type of language treatment. In J. Rubin & R. Shuy (eds.), *Language planning: current issues and research* (pp. 11–23). Washington DC: Georgetown University Press.

Joseph, J. E. (1987) *Eloquence and power: the rise of language standards and standard languages.* London: Frances Pinter.

Juckes, T. J. (1995) *Opposition in South Africa.* Westport, CT: Praeger.

Kaplan, R. B. (1994) Language policy and planning: fundamental issues. *Annual Review of Applied Linguistics,* 14, 3–19.

Kloss, H. (1969) *Research possibilities on group bilingualism.* Québec: International Center for Research on Bilingualism.

Le Page, R. B. (1988) Some premises concerning the standardization of languages with special reference to Caribbean Creole English. *International Journal of the Sociology of Language,* 71, 25–36.

Le Page, R. B. (1993) Language, economy and tolerance: an interview with Benigno Fernandez Salgado. MS: University of Oxford.

Le Page, R. B. & Tabouret-Keller, A. (1985) *Acts of identity: Creole-based approaches to language and ethnicity.* Cambridge: Cambridge University Press.

Lewis, G. (1999) *The Turkish language reform: a catastrophic success.* Oxford University Press.

Lo Bianco, J. (1999) Policy words: talking bilingual education and ESL into English literacy. *Prospect,* 14(2), 40–52.

Lo Bianco, J. (2001a) Vietnam: Quoc Ngu, colonialism, and language policy. In N. Gottlieb & P. Chen (eds.), *Language policy in East Asia: a reader* (pp. 159–207). London: Curzon Press.

Lo Bianco, J. (2001b) Officialising language. a discourse study of language politics in the United States. Unpublished PhD thesis. Australian National University.

Lo Bianco, J. (ed.) (2002) *Voices from Phnom Penh: language and development.* Melbourne: Language Australia Publications.

Luke, A., McHoul, A. W., & Mey, J. L. (1990) On the limits of language planning: class, state and power. In R. B. Baldauf, Jr. & A. Luke (eds.), *Language planning and education in Australasia and the South Pacific* (pp. 25–44). Clevedon, UK: Multilingual Matters.

Mansour, G. (1993) *Multilingualism and nation building.* Clevedon, UK: Multilingual Matters.

McGroarty, M. (1997) Language policy in the USA: national values, local loyalties, pragmatic pressures. In W. Eggington & H. Wren (eds.), *Language policy: dominant english, pluralist challenges.* Canberra: Language Australia; Amsterdam: John Benjamins.

Moore, H. M. (1996) Language policies as virtual realities: two Australian examples. *TESOL Quarterly*, 30(1) (Autumn), 473–97.

Mühlhäusler, P. (1995) *Linguistic ecology, language change and linguistic imperialism in the Pacific region*. London and New York: Routledge.

Nahir, M. (1984) Language planning goals: a classification. *Language Problems and Language Planning*, 8(3), 294–327.

Nettle, D. & Romaine, S. (2000) *Vanishing voices: the extinction of the world's languages*. Oxford: Oxford University Press.

Neustupny, J. V. (1978) *Post-structural approaches to language: language theory in a Japanese context*. Tokyo: University of Tokyo Press.

Neustupny, J. V. (1983) Towards a paradigm for language planning. *Language Planning Newsletter*, 9(4).

Newmeyer, F. J. (1986) *The politics of linguistics*. Chicago: the University of Chicago Press.

Pattanayak, D. P. (1987) *Multilingualism and multiculturalism: Britain and India, occasional paper no.1*. London: International Association for Intercultural Education, Institute of Education, University of London.

Phillipson, R. & Skutnabb-Kangas, T. (1996) English only worldwide or language ecology? *TESOL Quarterly*, 30, 429–52.

Pool, J. (1972) National development and language diversity. In J. A. Fishman (ed.), *Advances in the sociology of language*, vol. II: *Selected studies and applications* (pp. 213–30). The Hague: Mouton.

Pratt, M. L. (1987) Linguistic utopias. In N. Fabb, D. Attridge, D. Durant, & C. McAbe (eds.), *The linguistics of writing* (pp. 49–66). Manchester: Manchester University Press.

Ricento, T. (2000) Historical and theoretical perspectives in language policy and planning. In T. Ricento (ed.), *Ideology, politics and language policies: focus on English* (pp. 9–25). Amsterdam: John Benjamins.

Rubin, J. & Jernudd, B. H. (eds.) (1971) *Can language be planned? Sociolinguistic theory and practice for developing nations*. Honolulu: University of Hawai'i Press.

Schieffelin, B. B., Woolard, K. A., & Kroskrity, P. V. (1998) *Language ideologies: practice and theory*. New York: Oxford University Press.

Schneider, S. G. (1976) *Revolution, reaction or reform: the 1974 Bilingual Education Act*. New York: LA Publishing Company.

Shannon, S. M. (1999) The debate on bilingual education in the US: language ideology as reflected in the practices of bilingual teachers. In J. Blommaert (ed.), *Language ideological debates* (pp. 171–201). Berlin: Mouton de Gruyter.

Skutnabb-Kangas, T. (1995) *Multilingualism for all*. Lisse, Netherlands: Swets & Zeitlinger.

Sommer, B. A. (1991) Yesterday's experts: the bureaucratic impact on language planning for Aboriginal bilingual education. *Australian Review of Applied Linguistics*, Series S, 8, 109–35.

Tarver, H. (1989) Language and politics in the 1980s, the story of US English. *Politics and Society*, 17 (2), 220–39.

Tauli, V. (1984) The failure of language planning research. In A. Gonzalez (ed.), *Language planning, implementation and evaluation: essays in honour of Bonifacio Sibayan*. Manila: Linguistic Society of the Philippines.

Thompson, J. (1991) Introduction. In P. Bourdieu (ed.), *Language and symbolic power* (pp. 1–30). Cambridge, MA: Harvard University Press.

Tollefson, J. W. (1991) *Planning language, planning inequality: language policy in the community*. New York: Longman Cheshire.

Webb, V. (2002) *Language in South Africa: the role of language in national transformation, reconstruction and development*. Amsterdam: Benjamins.

FURTHER READING

Ager, D. (2001) *Motivation in language planning and language policy.* Clevedon, UK: Multilingual Matters.

Baker, S. (ed.) (2002) *Language policy: lessons from global models.* Monterey, CA: Monterey Institute for International Studies.

Crawford, J. (1999) *Bilingual education, history, politics, theory and practice* (4th edn.). Los Angeles: Bilingual Education Services.

Davis, K. A. (1994) *Language planning in multilingual contexts. policies, communities and schools in Luxembourg.* Amsterdam/Philadelphia: John Benjamins.

Jaffe, A. (1999) *Ideologies in action: language politics on Corsica.* Berlin and New York: Mouton de Gruyter.

Lo Bianco, J. & Wickert, R. (eds.) (2001) *Australian policy activism in language and literacy.* Melbourne: Language Australia Publications.

31 Language Testing

TIM MCNAMARA

31.1 Introduction: The Place of Language Testing within Applied Linguistics

Language testing has undergone a rapid evolution in the past 50 years, mirroring the development of applied linguistics more broadly. The replacement in the immediate post-war period of traditional assessment techniques, such as the translation and the composition by "scientific" tests based on linguistics (structuralism) and psychology (behaviorism), paralleled the advent of audiolingualism within language teaching. Similarly, the introduction of communicative methods in the 1970s and 1980s was matched by a greater emphasis on performance tests within language testing, where candidates were required to display practical control of language knowledge under real-time processing conditions, and within specified contexts of use. Language testing received a great impetus from the development of specific purpose language teaching associated with the explosion of English language courses for students and professionals operating within an international context in the 1970s. Most recently, language tests are under somewhat of a challenge, as they respond to critiques of individualistic notions of performance and are increasingly being scrutinized for their social accountability, in line with the critical turn in applied linguistics generally.

There is a tendency at times for language testing to be seen as specialized and marginal: for example, in Pit Corder's famous *Introducing Applied Linguistics* (Corder, 1973), language testing is relegated to the last chapter, very much on the margin, and within the International Association of Applied Linguistics (AILA) there is no recognized special field of language testing; it is seen as a sub-category of language teaching. Despite this, there are in fact grounds for the view that language testing represents one of the core areas of applied linguistics. First, the development of a language test involves a careful definition of the domain of knowledge, skill, or ability it is targeting. The development of a test of general proficiency in a language, for example, thus requires a definition of the construct of proficiency in a language. As a result, language testers have been at the forefront of those working on definitions of communicative ability in a second language, and such definitions are of fundamental importance not only to language testers but also to the whole field of applied linguistics. Second, data from language tests can be used to reflect on the adequacy of models and constructs of particular aspects of second language knowledge and skill, which have been developed in other areas of applied linguistics, such as in second language acquisition. For example, language tests of vocabulary knowledge necessarily draw on thinking about the nature of vocabulary knowledge in the work of researchers on vocabulary acquisition. Language test data can in turn be used to reflect on the adequacy of the models used, and so feed back into research in the areas from which the models are drawn. Third, research in many of the fields of applied linguistics requires language tests as tools for research. The role of language testing in validating constructs in applied linguistics has been discussed extensively over the years: important examples include Lado (1961), Davies (1977, 1990), Bachman (1989), and Bachman and Cohen (1998).

Finally, the importance of language tests is a function of the social and political roles they play. Language tests have marked social relevance in the contemporary world, as they play a role in socially very significant institutional and political processes. The idea of formal tests of knowledge or ability emerged in traditional China, where they were used for the selection of individuals who would go on to be trained to be the ruling elite. Tests thus played a crucial role in constructing the fundamental character of Chinese cultural and political life over many centuries (Fairbank & Goldman, 1998). In the modern world, language tests control access to international education by students studying through the medium of a second language (especially, but not exclusively, English), they play an important role in the management of the language education of the children of immigrants, they have been used as a weapon in intergroup conflicts, they act as controls in the mobility of professionals and other workers. They are used for certification of achievement in education, and in many countries control the transition between school and higher education. Given this social significance, language testing faces an ethical challenge: language testers need to make their language tests as fair as possible, and need to be aware of their social responsibilities in their work.

The importance of language testing is recognized institutionally within applied linguistics: language testing has its own journals, its own national and international conferences and an international professional association, the International Language Testing Association (ILTA).

Thinking about the character of language tests and responsibility for their development and use has been guided increasingly by theories of validity in general education, most recently the work of Messick (1989). But before considering validity we need to clear the ground a little by considering some characteristics of all tests, including language tests.

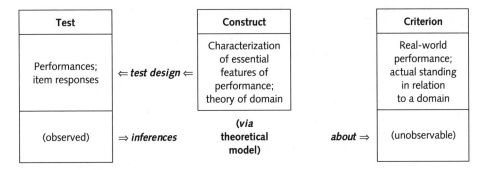

Figure 31.1   Test, construct, and criterion

31.1.1   *Reasoning in language tests*

Language testing is a process of gathering information about test-takers from observed performance under test conditions. This is done in order to draw inferences either about the likely quality of performance by the test-taker under non-test conditions, or about the test-taker's standing in relation to a relevant domain of knowledge and abilities (Figure 31.1). We thus make a distinction between the *test* (the means of drawing inferences) and the *criterion* (the target of test inferences). But because, in a testing version of Labov's Observer's Paradox, or Heisenberg's Uncertainty Principle, the criterion cannot be "known" in any direct sense, our inferences are necessarily mediated through test *constructs*, that is, our modeling of the criterion in terms of its essential features or characteristics. The relation of test, criterion and construct is set out in Figure 31.1.

For example, language tests are used throughout the world to control the entry of students into university settings where the language of instruction is not the student's first language. A language test is used to predict the student's ability to cope with the demands of the university settings. These demands need to be modeled: this involves considerable research into exactly what is required of international students in university settings, including both academic and social domains. This information (known as a job analysis) is then used to build a picture of the essential requirements of the target setting, the construct of academic language proficiency, and this is then reflected in the design of the test. Such a construct may be contested, for example in the degree to which the demands of specific areas of study are included, or ignored. In other cases, the source of our constructs will be work in areas of applied linguistics in which theories or models are built. For example, if we are interested in finding out about how bilinguals process vocabulary knowledge in each language, we will draw on models in psycholinguistics for our constructs, and build the test around them. Test constructs, then, are never themselves uncontroversial: they need to be articulated and defended as part of building a case for the validity of a test.

Often, there will be a need for a general or overall sense of the second language ability of the test-taker. Such tests are known as general proficiency tests. The need to articulate a construct of general proficiency in a second language, a need as much part of language curriculum design as it is of language testing, has seen some of the most fundamental work in applied linguistics on the nature of communicative competence. The field of language testing has been engaged in vigorous debate for many years on the modeling of the nature of general language ability, ever since the appearance of the model of communicative competence in a second language set out in a paper by Canale and Swain in 1980. This built on the work of Hymes (1972) on communicative competence in the mother tongue, which articulated an encompassing view of language knowledge and its relation to performance. Hymes was motivated by a concern for the needs of learners in schools who were experiencing learning difficulties, which he traced to gaps in underlying knowledge and skill in areas relevant to the particular social and cultural context of the classroom. Hymes saw the ability to take part in communicative events particular to a culture as a function both of knowledge of linguistic and sociolinguistic conventions, but also of personality factors, other kinds of know-ledge, motivation, and the like. This very broad view of competence was not adopted in discussions of second language communicative competence. Canale and Swain took a narrower view: they specifically excluded general perform-ance skills and focused on defining the dimensions of language knowledge underlying performance in second language communicative tasks. Following Hymes, they distinguished *sociolinguistic competence* (knowledge of the way language use is shaped by cultural conventions in particular communities of use) from *linguistic competence* (simple control of the linguistic system (including grammar, vocabulary and pronunciation) independently of its use in particular social and cultural contexts). Their model does include one aspect of perform-ance skill (although they classified it as an aspect of language knowledge): the ability to cope communicatively when one's linguistic resources are not fully adequate, a familiar problem for those communicating in their second language. They termed this *strategic competence*. (Canale (1983) later separately proposed the addition of another aspect of competence, which he called *discourse competence*, meaning the ability to construct coherent texts in speech and writing.)

The Canale and Swain model was taken up and modified by Bachman (1990) in his model of communicative language ability – what has come to be known as "the Bachman Model." Bachman elaborated aspects of the Canale and Swain model, reorganized it, and recognized that strategic competence was an aspect of general reasoning, and thus more properly understood as a general cognitive skill rather than an aspect of language knowledge.

Although such debates may appear at first sight rather technical and unrelated to real-world concerns, they have very real consequences for the design of language tests. For example, consider the case of a classroom teacher who wishes to be licensed to teach in a school setting where he/she will be operating through the medium of a second language. Now we all know that communicative skill as a teacher involves the whole personality of the teacher, not just what they may know of their subject matter, or of the language through which that subject matter is to be delivered, although these are both obviously crucial. If we exclude such qualities as rapport, maturity, creativity, and humor, which may be important in establishing a cooperative atmosphere for learning, then we may seriously underestimate the ability of the candidate to communicate what they know in the classroom. This is because communication is a shared responsibility between speaker and listener, and the listener's preparedness to understand, which in turn may be triggered by personal qualities in the speaker, can be an important component in communicative success. We may thus distinguish a broader and a narrower view of communicative ability: the broader view will incorporate the impact of factors other than simple knowledge of the language; the narrower view will exclude such factors. The tests resulting from these contrasting views will differ sharply in what they ask candidates to do and what is looked for in the candidate's performance. Tests adopting a broad view will present candidates with test tasks which seek to simulate the communicative demands of the target context, and evaluate performance in terms of criteria operating in that context. A test of second language communicative skill in doctors will present candidates with communicative tasks typical of clinical settings – explaining treatment options to patients or their relatives, for example – and criteria will include the overall communicative impact of the performance, and not just linguistic accuracy (McNamara, 1996 provides a detailed account of the development of such a test, the Occupational English Test). A test taking a narrower view would focus on aspects of linguistic skill in isolation: such an approach is represented in the Test of English for International Communication (TOEIC) (Woodford, 1982), designed ostensibly for the business world and used widely in Japan, which does not attempt to simulate tasks frequently encountered in business settings, but rather to isolate features of grammar and vocabulary, or listening and reading skills in contexts which are only superficially realistic.

Test design in other words rests on test constructs. As views on the nature of communicative competence in a second language are thus constantly evolving, and always contested, the nature of the language tests which they underpin will also change and be the subject of debate.

31.1.2 Theories of validity

Language tests, like other tests, are deliberate samples, in this case of an individual's language knowledge or language behavior, in order to reach a conclusion about the likely general state of that person's knowledge or ability. As with blood tests, or breath tests of drivers, language tests require technical expertise in their construction and application, in order to make the inferences that we draw from test results interpretable and supportable. The validation of

	TEST INTERPRETATION	TEST USE
EVIDENTIAL BASIS	Construct validity	Construct validity + Relevance/utility
CONSEQUENTIAL BASIS	Value implications	Social consequences

Figure 31.2   Facets of validity (from Messick, 1989, p. 20)

language tests refers to the process of gathering arguments and evidence in support of the interpretations and uses we may wish to make of test scores. As we will see, there are two basic processes involved: an articulation of the exact character of the knowledge we seek and of the purpose for which we seek it; and the gathering of empirical evidence (for example, investigating expected and unexpected patterns of responses as revealed in test scores) to support the interpretations we wish to make of candidate performance.

Messick (1989), in a seminal paper, set out the fundamental aspects of test validation in the form of a matrix (see Figure 31.2). The column "Test interpretation" involves considering the evidence of test validity outside any specific context of its deployment; the column "Test use" looks at the actual use of the test in a specific context. The point of this distinction is that while in principle a test may be soundly based on a theory of the abilities that it intends to measure, with good evidence from test data of its potential to make meaningful distinctions between candidates, the use of the test in a particular context might be inappropriate – for example, using on children a test designed for adults, or using a test designed to detect learning disabilities among children who speak English as a mother tongue on a population of children for whom English is a second language.

The horizontal rows distinguish two aspects of the defense of a test and its use. In the first row, logical argument and empirical evidence from test use are the basis for the claims we wish to make for the validity of the test. The bottom row introduces the notion that testing is not a value-neutral activity but always involves an implicit expression of (social) values. The social consequences of the actual deployment of tests are the focus of the final cell in the matrix.

Messick's approach represents a unified model of validation; previous approaches (e.g., Cronbach, 1964; Davies, 1977) had distinguished various kinds of validity: content validity, concerning the representativeness of test content; construct validity, concerning the coherence and defensibility of the theory (of knowledge, skill, and so on) on which the test is based; criterion-related validity, the extent to which measures produced by the test makes sense in the light of other relevant measures of skill, or predict outcomes associated with the skill being measured in the test, and so on. The scope of test validation, following Messick, is very broad, and may appear daunting. He requires of us that we think through the logic and meaning of our model of candidate abilities which is the target of the test, and be in a position to recognize and justify the values on which it is based; that we gather empirical evidence in support of the inferences we wish to make on the basis of test scores; and that we consider the consequences of its use.

31.2   Validation Research in Language Testing

Test validation is the process of investigating the meaningfulness and defensibility of the inferences we make about individuals based on their test performance. The need to defend our interpretations of the meanings of test scores is because of the necessarily indirect relationship between the test and what we ultimately want to know about, the candidate's standing in relation to the criterion. For example, take a group of students who have been admitted to a university setting on the basis of having achieved above a required threshold on a test of English for Academic Purposes. We would expect those who scored highly on the test to cope better with the communicative demands of their studies than those who scored less well, and that this would in part be reflected by their scores in academic subjects taken in the first semester of studies. We could thus seek empirical evidence in support of this expectation, and if the evidence supported the picture we had, then that evidence would be supportive of the validity of the inferences about test-takers' relative readiness to meet the communicative demands of university study made on the basis of their test scores. Such studies have been carried out in many different contexts in relation to a number of tests of academic language proficiency, with correlations between language test scores and subsequent performance in the order of 0.3 or better (Graham, 1987; Light, Xu, & Mossop, 1987). Such a figure indicates that differences in language test scores account for only about 10 percent of the variance in scores in academic subjects, suggesting that language plays a definite but limited role in the academic success of students in such settings – hard work, organization, and intelligence seem to be more powerful factors in predicting success.

Validation research is not always easy, or even feasible, even in cases where it is clear what we would like to know. Consider the case of the best-known international test of English for academic purposes, the Test of English as a Foreign Language (TOEFL), developed by the Educational Testing Service in Princeton. For many years, individuals working in universities receiving students selected on the basis of their scores on this test have noted anecdotally that scores appeared to correspond less and less well with the ability of these students to communicate in spoken English demonstrated by them once they had arrived in the English-speaking environment. This impression, if borne out in reality, might be due to better coaching of these students in test-taking techniques prior to their taking the test, for example in strategies for eliminating unlikely alternatives on multiple choice format test components. This coaching, designed simply to "beat the system" of the test, may have resulted in higher scores for students which do not reflect an increased ability to communicate in English. In order to investigate the reality and possible causes of this phenomenon of an apparent decline in the status of TOEFL scores as indicators of a candidate's overall proficiency in English, a careful validation study would seem to be called for, but its design poses difficulties. For example, you would need to find students whose initial performance on the test was poor, who subsequently improved through coaching, but whose subsequent performance in an English-speaking academic environment did not correspond to the proficiency level suggested by the score on the test (Douglas, 2003); and you would need to show that the predictive relationship between test scores and performance had worsened over the years.

In general, to the extent that the correlation for a particular test falls below what we might expect, it suggests that the test is failing to capture the essential communicative demands of the target setting, and the scores on the language test are less valid indicators of the proficiency in question. Such validation studies are complex and expensive to mount, but are justified when important decisions are taken on the basis of test scores.

A further example of the role of validation research in test score interpretation is to be found in the use of specific purpose language tests in occupational settings. Such tests are more closely targeted to the criterion than general proficiency tests. In Australia, nurses who have trained overseas in a language other than English are required to take an English language test as part of their registration for practice in Australia. The authorities permit the nurses to take either of two tests: (1) the Occupational English Test (OET) (McNamara, 1996), a test specifically designed for health professionals and which focuses on the communicative tasks facing health professionals in their workplace; or (2) the general training module of IELTS (International English Language Testing System), a more general proficiency test. Validity research would be directed at supporting the claims of the OET to be a better predictor of ultimate success in the workplace than the more general test. Of course there may be other reasons for the use of the more specific test, in particular in terms of its effect on teaching and learning as preparation for the test, the *wash-back* of the test.

In general, we can say that test scores are a way of coding numerically *claims* about the abilities of test-takers: for example, if two candidates get significantly different scores on a test, then this represents a claim that they differ significantly for example in their ability to communicate in the target setting. The design of tasks relevant to the target setting, and care in the management of the scoring of performances to ensure high levels of consistency, can in theory provide a strong basis for ensuring that the scores do represent a guide to the test-takers' underlying ability. Validation is the process of investigating the relationship between the claims of the test and evidence in support of these claims, both from the test scores themselves, or from independent evidence.

The process of validating tests can itself also provide evidence in support of the constructs on which the test is based. We will illustrate this from the case of a test of language aptitude.

Language aptitude is defined as "the extent to which an individual possesses specific language learning ability" (Davies et al., 1999, p. 10). It differs from language proficiency (current level of attainment in second language) in that language aptitude can be measured before an individual commences second language study. Language aptitude tests are designed to enable us to choose those with the greatest potential to benefit from language study, or to weed out those who will struggle to succeed. Organizations involved in the language training of military personnel in the UK, the US, and Australia often use language aptitude tests, particularly when selecting those who will be trained in a language such as Chinese, which has a complex writing system, and where mastery of tone distinctions is an important part of the learning task (Petersen & Al-Haik, 1976). Language aptitude tests have also been designed for use at school (Pimsleur Language Aptitude Battery (PLAB): Pimsleur, 1966; York Language Aptitude Test: P. Green, 1975) and university (Modern Language Aptitude Test (MLAT): Carroll & Sapon, 1959).

But what exactly is language aptitude? Psychologists and linguists have at various times tried to define the construct in terms of memory skills, ability to perceive patterns, ability to discriminate sounds, and the like (Carroll, 1962; Skehan, 1986, 1989; Cascallar, 1995; Sparks et al., 1998). Aptitude tests are necessarily based on one or other of these constructs. Data from the tests can then in turn be used to investigate the quality of these constructs. For example, predictive validity studies can be carried out to investigate the extent to which subsequent achievement is predicted by scores on the aptitude tests. Correlations of between 0.40 and 0.65 are reported between aptitude scores on MLAT or PLAB and end-of-course performance in intensive foreign language courses. While such correlations only account for between 16 percent and a little over 40 percent of the variation in the outcome scores, Skehan (1989) points out that this is the strongest of all causal variables studied, including motivation. The difficulty of prediction is illustrated by a counter-example (Harrington, 1990): it involves the York Language Aptitude Test (Green, 1975). A former teacher of Spanish at a Melbourne secondary college, Julie Harrington, routinely tested students beginning modern languages (French, German, and Spanish) using this measure, but did not use the results to select the students – she was motivated purely by interest. She then kept records of the students' progress over the course of a number of years, and by comparing the scores on the initial aptitude test with subsequent evidence of achievement in the various languages eventually concluded that the test had little potential to predict the outcomes of language study in this setting. This evidence leads us to wonder about the construct of language aptitude underlying the test: it is clearly not addressing some dimensions of what it takes to do well in language study at school. A further kind of validation research is to carry out statistical analyses on scores on individual test items and on test sub-components. This was the method used originally by Carroll to determine whether performance on test items from assumed components of aptitude clustered together, and has since been used in other studies of aptitude test data (Skehan, 1980, 1982).

Another way in which test constructs have been investigated is in the context of research on tests of the productive skills of speaking and writing, which involve judging processes using what are known as rating scales. In the assessment of speaking and writing in a second language, performances on a task are elicited and then evaluated by judges who have been trained to notice particular features of the performance. For example, in conversation-based spoken language tests, particular features such as fluency, pronunciation, grammatical correctness, interactive ability (being able to take the initiative, to respond appropriately to what has been said, and so on) may be evaluated. For each feature, the judge or rater may use a five or seven point scale to indicate how they would rate that aspect for the performance. Alternatively, an overall score may be given, again using a rating scale. Research has invest-igated the way in which judges use these scales. Are the scores for each aspect independent of one another, or does one aspect (e.g., grammar) "drive" the impressions recorded in the others? Are raters interpreting a particular category (e.g., "appropriateness of language") in a consistent way, and in accord with the way other raters are interpreting it? A wide variety of possible research methods are available, both quantitative (e.g., statistical analysis of score data), or qualitative, for example introspective studies using a technique known as "think aloud protocols." In this technique, raters engaged in the rating process are encouraged and trained to speak their thoughts aloud as they work, and a transcript of what they say is then analyzed to see how raters are interpreting scales, particularly when applied to performances that are difficult to judge in some way (Cumming, 1990; A. Green, 1997; Cumming, Kantor, & Powers, 2001; Lumley, 2000, 2002). Researchers have also used the methods of discourse analysis to understand better what is going on in interaction in oral tests (see, inter alia, Lazaraton, 1992, 1996; Ross, 1992; Young & He, 1998; for a recent survey, see McNamara, Hill, & May, 2002). Transcriptions are made of inter-action between interviewer and candidate, and features of the interaction (for example, the nature of the conversational support given to the candidate by the interlocutor, something which is not normally obvious but which can be revealed clearly through close analysis) are related to rater perceptions of the interaction. What this kind of investigation reveals is that raters often attribute to candidates the results of the action of the interlocutors; interlocutor behavior can thus be shown to be a source of invalidity in the raters' judgments (Brown, 2000, 2003).

In general then, the relationship between test construct and test perform-ance is a two-way street: tests are built on constructs, but can offer evidence of the validity of the constructs on which they are built. The investigation of these relationships is an important component of language test validation research.

31.3   Language Testing as Institutional Practice

Language tests play an important role at several important junctures in society. They thus have a fundamentally political character. Language tests often occur at gateways. They control access to opportunities within societies, and are used to control the flow of people between societies.

Within educational systems responsible for language education, language tests serve a number of functions (which they also share with other educational assessments). They are used for accountability within the system: they form the basis for reports to parents and students on the progress of individuals, and may be part of the assessment for prestigious certificates and degrees which themselves may be the key to unlocking social opportunities. Language tests, like other educational tests, form part of the procedure for decisions about the allocation of scarce resources at both a systemic and an individual level. For example, many language tests are used as evidence of achievement at school and may additionally be used as evidence of potential for further study at university level. They often form part of the assessment within the university system and may lead to the awarding of a degree.

The globalization of social structures makes the institutional function of language tests ever more far-reaching. For example, as Europe moves more and more in the direction of a single administrative unit, frameworks become necessary for the credentialing of students and workers across national boundaries. The *Common European Framework of References for Languages: Learning, Teaching and Assessment* (Council of Europe, 2001) establishes a unified framework for understanding the development of language proficiency in a growing number of languages within Europe, and its influence is being felt throughout language teaching in Europe, in school, university, and adult settings. Assessment becomes a primary mechanism whereby this framework is enforced. As globalization promotes the need for more efficient workforces and more flexible work practices, assessment of competency in vocational contexts becomes more and more a central arm of government policy (Brindley, 1998, 2001), and competency-based language assessments have emerged as a powerful feature of government policy. The increasing internationalization of education, particularly through the medium of English, has led to a greater dependence in educational systems on the recruitment of international students, and an accompanying demand for language tests to regulate the flow of students. The institutional character of language tests has been the subject of increasing analysis and critique, manifesting itself most clearly in the movement known as Critical Language Testing (Shohamy, 2001), which applies the perspectives of critical social theory to the institutional practices of language testing.

31.4   Language Tests and Identity

Ironically, concomitant with the use of tests to facilitate the movement of populations in the new globalized structures is the use of tests to resist the movement of peoples. Language tests have long been used as a form of border control, ever since the example of the Shibboleth test in the Bible (Judges 12: 4–6), in which defeated soldiers trying to pass as members of the victorious ethnic group were "outed" and slaughtered on the basis of a minor feature of their pronunciation of a particular consonant sound /ʃ/, for example as found in the word "shibboleth." Those trying to "pass" were required to say this word in order to check their pronunciation, and hence their identity. The use of language tests as part of a process of linguistic identification continues to this day. A recent example is a language test used to verify claims of German ethnicity. In the 1990s, people from minority German communities from former Eastern bloc countries wishing to emigrate to a reunited Germany faced a language test hurdle in the form of an oral interview in German with a trained interviewer. The interviewers welcomed evidence of the presence in the speech of the applicant of non-standard forms, indicating that they were speakers of a variety of German characteristic of German-speaking communities far removed from the main bulk of German speakers in Germany proper. The test acted as an effective means of reducing (by about half) the number of applicants who were successful; ironically, those families who had least resisted the vigorous efforts by the authorities in the countries concerned to hasten the linguistic assimilation of these minorities in the aftermath of World War II had their claims denied on the basis of the absence of the "required" linguistic evidence (McNamara, 2001b). Another contemporary example is the linguistic identification process used as part of the adjudication of claims to refugee status in a number of countries, including Australia. Members of minority communities who are subject to persecution in their homeland (for example, minorities within Afghanistan) have to establish that they have come directly from the area in which they suffer persecution and not from a first country of exile (for example, Pakistan), as under international law a second country of exile such as Australia has no obligation to grant refugee status if the first country of exile is not itself engaged in persecution of these refugees. Linguistic evidence becomes involved: applicants are interviewed in their mother tongue, and recordings of the speech sample so elicited are then subject to linguistic analysis. If a sample shows evidence of contact forms characteristic of the variety spoken among expatriate refugee communities outside the homeland, the applicant's claim to refugee status is denied (Eades et al., 2003).

The use of language tests as a form of border control is much more general than these examples suggest. In immigration contexts, language tests often feature as part of the procedure used in controlling entry. For example, proficiency in the language of the community the immigrant is about to enter is commonly used as a factor in considering a request for entry. Of course, this may be a rational matter, as where issues of refugee status are not involved, and countries seeking immigrants with more applicants than they can accept are in a position to be able to choose which immigrants to accept, it is argued that those with proficiency in the language of the country concerned are more likely to settle without difficulty and less likely to require government services. For this reason, applicants with high levels of proficiency in English and French are at an advantage in immigration selection procedures in Australia (Hawthorne, 1997) and Québec (Ambrose, 2003) respectively. Similar requirements have recently been introduced for certain categories of immigrant to the United Kingdom, including highly skilled immigrants (United Kingdom Home Office, 2003) and proposals are underway for this to be extended to other categories, for example ministers of religion (United Kingdom Home Office, 2002). Related issues have been raised in Germany (Ruebeling, 2002). The identity component of language proficiency tests for immigrants is perhaps clearer in the case of the inclusion of various forms of language tests in procedures for granting citizenship, for example in the United Kingdom (United Kingdom Home Office, 2002), and in the United States (United States Department of Justice, 2003), where procedures are variable and often rather informal. In Germany, recently introduced citizenship laws making it possible for the first time for people to acquire citizenship on the basis of residence rather than blood have included a language proficiency requirement. It is interesting to note that the most conservative states within Germany, who are required to administer this law, have been quick to seek the help of language testers to devise the required language tests, which are likely to stem the numbers applying for citizenship (Ruebeling, 2002).

The potential for the abuse of language tests in such contexts is most graphically illustrated in the case of the notorious Australian Dictation Test, which was used for about 30 years in the early twentieth century as an instrument of blatant racial and political exclusion (Dutton, 1998; Jones, 1998; McNamara, 2001b). People arriving in the country who were deemed undesirable on racial or political grounds were subjected to a test of dictation of 100 words in a language, which *it was assumed they did not understand*. They inevitably failed the test, which was then used as grounds for exclusion. Several thousand people were excluded by this means. The test was adopted in the newly independent Australian federation of former British colonies from 1901 as a means of achieving the goals of the so-called White Australia Policy. The Dictation Test was originally known as the Education Test, on the precedent of a similar test adopted in the colony of Natal in South Africa in the 1890s (Dutton, 1998). There was perhaps some advantage in displacement of the onus for exclusion onto a test of language or education, even though in this case the test provided only the most threadbare veil for the authorities' intentions. The use of technical means and the involvement of academics in the preparation of test materials in this case is a sobering reminder of the way in which technical expertise in language testing may be used as a cover for political motives in cases where the political and social agenda of language testing is less overt than here.

One response of the field to a growing realization of the political and institutional character of language testing is the emergence of a debate on the politics and ethics of language testing (Davies, 1997; ILTA, 2000). The emerging discussion of political issues, particularly within the emerging field of critical language testing, focuses on exposing the policies language tests are intended to serve; this is necessary in many cases because of the concealing function of language tests, discussed above. But such discussions do not always satisfy practitioners, not for the obvious reason that they might be by implication the subject of the critique, but because there will inevitably be disagreements over the values embodied in tests, even when they are clearly revealed. It is notable, for example, that since Voltaire in eighteenth-century France, tests have often been seen as fairer than less objective and less accountable procedures for making appointments, which otherwise were allocated on the basis of patronage and favoritism (Spolsky, 1995).

31.5   Language Testing Research and Language Learning

Given the gate keeping role of language tests, the functions they serve for institutions and the corresponding preparedness of institutions to invest in their development and validation, it is not surprising that the bulk of language testing research has focused on tests for admission and certification, in contexts such as international education, immigration, and employment. Examples include such major international tests as TOEFL in the United States and the British-Australian IELTS, each used to select international students for study at English-medium universities; tests used as part of immigration procedures in countries such as Australia and Canada; or employment related assessment schemes, targeted at particular groups such as teachers or health professionals, or at the general workforce, as in competency-based assessments. Relatively less attention has been paid to research on language assessment in the service of the needs of classroom teachers and learners. Where this has occurred, it has usually involved the development or implementation of curriculum-related scales and frameworks for describing student progress in language learning over time (McKay, 1994, 1995, 2000; Citizenship & Immigration Canada, 1995; Brindley, 1998, 2001). These frameworks have a dual purpose: to assist teachers in the task of assessment by providing guidance on the important dimensions of the development of learner competence, and to provide a common yardstick for reporting progress across an educational system in order to manage the system. Such scales and frameworks involve the teacher in the task of gaining evidence of learner achievement for management and accountability purposes, rather than leaving this to independently developed and validated external tests, although in some settings (such as England and the United States) formal testing has been introduced as a means of monitoring the attainment of educational outcomes. Research is scant on the impact on teachers and learners of these accountability measures, whether they are in the form of external tests or scales and frameworks to be used by teachers, although some excellent work has been done by Breen et al. (1997), Rea-Dickins and Gardner (2000), Teasdale and Leung (2000), Butler and Stevens (2001), Rea-Dickins (2001) and others. The scope and role of self-assessment has also been the subject of research over many years (Oskarsson, 1980; Oscarson, 1989; Ekbatani and Pierson, 2000), but there is a need for this research to be further developed in the light of the recent revival of interest in learner self-awareness, particularly within the context of the joint activity of learners (Swain, 2001; McNamara, 2001a).

Information from tests is sometimes used to inform language education policy. The clearest example is the way in which test scores are used as outcome measures, and information on improved outcomes is important to support policy initiatives, for example in the area of bilingual or immersion education, or the introduction of language programs in the early years of schooling (Hill, 2002; Elder, 2002; Hill & McNamara, in press). The information yielded by test scores is often crucial, for example in alerting authorities to the failure to achieve expected outcomes, or for reassuring nervous stakeholders that the outcomes are as desired. Information from test scores however is only one part of the picture as it cannot offer explanations for the outcomes so reported; it would be unwise to base decisions on the outcome measures alone. We need to consider the reasons for the results as often the problems are remediable. An example is the question of the ultimate benefit of second language education in the early years of schooling. Studies comparing the achievement of learners who begin second language study in the junior school compared with those who begin such study in the early years of secondary school have sometimes shown that whatever proficiency advantages there may be for those who have studied the language in the early years of education are wiped out within a year or two after the transition to secondary school (Brown, Hill, & Iwashita, 2000; Hill, 2002). The conclusion on the basis of this test score information that primary school language programs are not a sound investment of resources needs however to be approached with caution, as the reasons for the attrition of the differential proficiency and the differing goals of primary and secondary education need to be taken into account in explaining the results, along with many other contextual factors.

31.6 Current and Future Developments in Language Testing Research

Language testing is becoming increasingly sophisticated technically, with an increasing range of statistical tools available to investigate aspects of the validity of tests through analysis of patterns in test scores. Advances in measurement such as Generalizability Theory (Brennan, 1983; Bachman 1990) and Multi-Faceted Rasch Measurement (Linacre 1989; McNamara 1996) enable us to identify the components of variability in test scores associated with various aspects or facets of test performance conditions, particularly differences between raters in terms of their relative severity and consistency. The differential impact on individual raters of particular test tasks or categories of candidate (for example defined in terms of language background and gender) can now be systematically studied. Advances in the field of measurement known as Item Response Theory (Baker, 1997; McNamara, 1996), which allows powerful generalizations about candidates and items on the basis of the responses of samples of candidates to samples of items, has made possible the development of adaptive tests delivered by computer, which tailor the items presented to the candidate in the light of constantly upgraded estimates of the candidate's ability. Linking tests of differing overall levels of difficulty has enabled the construction of scales of, for example, reading ability as it develops over extended periods of time. The automation of scoring of writing and speaking is making rapid advances, to the point where computer assessments of the productive skills can in some cases match the reliability of human scorers (e.g., for writing, see Burstein & Chodorow, 2002; for speaking, see Bernstein, 1997). The delivery of test materials on the web is now also a reality; the potential advantages of this, for example the possibility of learner self-assessment on demand on-line, are now being explored in large-scale projects involving multiple languages in Europe such as DIALANG: http://www.dialang.org/english/index.html (Alderson, 2000) and in other applications.

In all these developments, the need for rigorous thinking about the validity of the resulting inferences about candidates remains paramount, including and perhaps especially the impact of the testing procedures on teachers and learners, and the social and political values they embody.

See also 16 The Philosophy of Applied Linguistics, 19 Research Methods for Applied Linguistics, 27 The Practice of LSP, 28 Bilingual Education, 32 Critical Applied Linguistics.

REFERENCES

Alderson, J. C. (2000) Technology and testing: the present and the future. *System*, 28(4), 593–603.

Ambrose, P. (2003) Québec selection criteria. At website http://www.canadaimmigrationlaw.net/Library/quebec.htm, accessed January 24, 2003.

Bachman, L. F. (1989) Language testing-SLA interfaces. *Annual Review of Applied Linguistics, 9,* 193–209.

Bachman, L. F. (1990) *Fundamental considerations in language testing.* Oxford: Oxford University Press.

Bachman, L. & Cohen, A. (eds.) (1998) *Interfaces between second language acquisition and language testing research.* Cambridge: Cambridge University Press.

Baker, R. (1997) *Classical test theory and Item Response Theory in test analysis. Language testing update, special report 2.* Lancaster: Centre for Research in Language Education, Lancaster University

Bernstein, J. (1997) Speech recognition in language testing. In A. Huhta, V. Kohonen, L. Kurki-Suonio & S. Luoma (eds.), *Current developemtns and alternatives in language assessment: Proceedings of LTRC 1996* (pp. 534–7). Jyväskylä, Finland: University of Jyväskylä.

Breen, M., Barratt-Pugh, C., Derewianka, B., House, H., Hudson, C., Lumley, T., & Rohl, M. (1997) *Profiling ESL children,* vol. 1: *Key issues and findings.* Canberra: Department of Employment, Education, Training and Youth Affairs.

Brennan, R. L. (1983) *Elements of generalizability theory.* Iowa City, IA: The American College Testing Program.

Brindley, G. (1998) Outcomes-based assessment and reporting in language programs: a review of the issues. *Language Testing,* 15, 45–85.

Brindley, G. (2001) Outcomes-based assessment in practice: some examples and emerging insights. *Language Testing,* 18(4), 393–407.

Brown, A. (2000) An investigation of the rating process in the IELTS oral interview. In R. Tulloh (ed.), *IELTS research reports* (vol. 3) (pp. 49–84). Canberra: IELTS Australia.

Brown, A. (2003) Interviewer variation and the co-construction of speaking proficiency. *Language Testing,* 20(1), 1–25.

Brown, A., Hill, K., & Iwashita, N. (2000) A longitudinal and comparative study: the attainment of language proficiency. *Melbourne Papers in Language Testing,* 9(1), 1–28.

Burstein, J. & Chodorow, M. (2002) Directions in automated essay analysis. In R. B. Kaplan (ed.),

The Oxford handbook of applied linguistics (pp. 487–97). Oxford: Oxford University Press.

Butler, F. A. & Stevens, R. (2001) Standardized assessment of the content knowledge of English language learners K-12: current trends and old dilemmas. *Language Testing,* 18(4), 409–27.

Canale, M. (1983) From communicative competence to communicative language pedagogy. In J. C. Richards and R. W. Schmidt (eds.), *Language and communication* (pp. 2–27). London: Longman.

Canale, M. & Swain, M. (1980) Theoretical bases of communicative approaches to second language teaching and testing. *Applied Linguistics,* 1(1), 1–47.

Carroll, J. B. (1962) The prediction of success in foreign language training. In R. Glaser (ed.), *Training and research in education* (pp. 87–136). Pittsburgh, PA: University of Pittsburgh Press.

Carroll, J. B. & Sapon, S. (1959) *Modern Language Aptitude Test – Form A.* New York: The Psychological Association.

Cascallar, E. (ed.) (1995) Special issue on language aptitude. *Language Testing,* 12(3).

Citizenship and Immigration Canada (1995) *Language benchmarks: English as a second language for adults.* Ottawa: Citizenship and Immigration Canada.

Corder, S. P. (1973) *Introducing applied linguistics.* Harmondsworth: Penguin Education.

Council of Europe (2001) *Common European framework of references for languages: learning, teaching and assessment.* Cambridge: Cambridge University Press

Cronbach, L. C. (1964) *Essentials of psychological testing.* Tokyo: Harper & Row.

Cumming, A. (1990) Expertise in evaluating second language

compositions. *Language Testing*, 7, 31–51.

Cumming, A., Kantor, R., & Powers, D. (2001) *Scoring TOEFL essays and TOEFL 2000 prototype writing tasks: an investigation into raters' decision making, and development of a preliminary analytic framework.* TOEFL Monograph Series. Princeton, NJ: Educational Testing Service.

Davies, A. (1977) Introduction. In J. P. B. Allen & A. Davies (eds.), *Testing and experimental methods: the Edinburgh course in applied linguistics* (vol. 4) (pp. 1–10). Oxford: Oxford University Press.

Davies, A. (1990) *Principles of language testing.* Oxford: Blackwell.

Davies, A. (ed.) (1997) Special issue: ethics in language testing. *Language Testing*, 14.

Davies, A., Brown, A., Elder, C., Hill, K., Lumley, T., & McNamara, T. (1999) *Dictionary of language testing.* Cambridge: Cambridge University Press.

Douglas, D. (2003) Re: Interpretability of TOEFL scores. Posting to discussion list LTEST-L, January 23. List address: LTEST-L@LISTS.PSU.EDU.

Dutton, D. (1998) Strangers and citizens: the boundaries of Australian citizenship 1901–1973. Unpublished PhD thesis, The University of Melbourne.

Eades, D., Fraser, H., Siegel, J., McNamara, T., & Baker, B. (2003) Linguistic identification in the determination of nationality: a preliminary report. Manuscript. Available at http://www-personal.une.edu.au/~hfraser/forensic/LingID.pdf.

Ekbatani, G. & Pierson, H. (eds.) (2000) *Learner-directed assessment in ESL.* Mahwah, NJ: Erlbaum.

Elder, C. (2002) Evaluating bilingual education: what place for language testing? Paper presented in the Symposium Assessment research and school-based language learning: the neglected interface, AILA, Singapore, December.

Fairbank, J. K. & Goldman, M. (1998) *China: a new history* (enlarged edn.). Cambridge, MA and London: Belknap Press of Harvard University Press.

Graham, J. (1987) English language proficiency and the prediction of academic success. *TESOL Quarterly*, 21(3), 505–21.

Green, A. J. K. (1997) *Verbal protocol analysis in language testing research.* Cambridge: Cambridge University Press.

Green, P. (1975) Aptitude testing: an ongoing experiment. *Audio-Visual Language Journal*, 12, 205–10.

Harrington, J. (1990) The York Language Aptitude Test: a predictor for achievement scores? Unpublished class paper, MA in Applied Linguistics, University of Melbourne.

Hawthorne, L. (1997) The political dimension of English language testing in Australia. *Language Testing*, 14(3), 248–60.

Hill, K. M. (2002) Between the cracks: the transition from primary to secondary school foreign language study. Paper presented in the Symposium Assessment research and school-based language learning: the neglected interface, AILA, Singapore, December.

Hill, K. & McNamara, T. F. (in press) Supporting curriculum initiatives in second languages: the roles of assessment research. In J. P. Keeves & R. Watanabe (eds.), *The handbook on educational research in the Asia Pacific region.* Amsterdam: Kluwer Academic.

Hymes, D. H. (1972) On communicative competence. In J. B. Pride & J. Holmes (eds.), *Sociolinguistics: selected readings* (pp. 269–93). Harmondsworth: Penguin.

International Language Testing Association (ILTA) (2000) *Code of ethics*

for foreign/second language testing.
Hong Kong: ILTA.

Jones, P. A. (1998) Alien acts: the White Australia Policy, 1901 to 1939. Unpublished PhD thesis, University of Melbourne.

Lado, R. (1961) *Language tests: the construction and use of foreign language tests.* London: Longman.

Lazaraton, A. (1992) The structural organization of a language interview: a conversation analytic perspective. *System*, 20, 373–86.

Lazaraton, A. (1996) Interlocutor support in oral proficiency interviews: the case of CASE. *Language Testing*, 13, 151–72.

Light, R. L., Xu, M., & Mossop, J. (1987) English proficiency and academic performance of international students. *TESOL Quarterly*, 21(2), 251–261.

Linacre, J. M. (1989) *Many-faceted Rasch measurement.* Chicago IL: MESA Press.

Lumley, T. J. N. (2000) The process of the assessment of writing performance: the rater's perspective. PhD thesis, University of Melbourne.

Lumley, T. J. N. (2002) Assessment criteria in a large-scale writing test; what do they really mean to raters? *Language Testing*, 19(3), 246–76.

McKay, P. (1994) *ESL development: language and literacy in schools*, vol. 1: *Teachers' manual* (2nd edn.). Canberra: AGPS.

McKay, P. (1995) Developing ESL proficiency descriptions for the school context: the NLLIA ESL bandscales. In G. Brindley (ed.), *Language assessment in action* (pp. 31–63). Sydney: National Centre for English Language Teaching and Research, Macquarie University.

McKay, P. (2000) On ESL standards for school-age learners. *Language Testing*, 17, 185–214.

McNamara, T. F. (1996) *Measuring second language performance.* London and New York: Longman.

McNamara, T. F (2001a) Language assessment as social practice:
challenges for research. *Language Testing*, 18(4), 333–49.

McNamara, T. F. (2001b) 21st century Shibboleth: Language tests, applied linguistics and the real world. Inaugural professorial address, University of Melbourne, October.

McNamara, T. F., Hill, K., & May, L. (2002) Discourse and assessment. *Annual Review of Applied Linguistics*, 22, 221–42.

Messick, S. (1989) Validity. In R. L. Linn (ed.), *Educational measurement* (3rd edn.) (pp. 13–103). New York: Macmillan.

Oscarson, M. (1989) Self-assessment of language proficiency: rationale and applications. *Language Testing*, 6(1), 1–13.

Oskarsson, M. (1980) *Approaches to self-assessment in foreign language learning.* Oxford: Pergamon.

Petersen, C. and Al-Haik, A. (1976) The development of the Defense Language Aptitude Battery (DLAB). *Educational and Psychological Measurement*, 36, 369–80.

Pimsleur, P. (1966) *Pimsleur Language Aptitude Battery (PLAB).* New York: Harcourt Brace Jovanovich.

Rea-Dickins, P. (2001) Mirror, mirror on the wall: identifying processes of classroom assessment. *Language Testing*, 18(4), 429–62.

Rea-Dickins, P. & Gardner, S. (2000): Snares and silver bullets: disentangling the construct of formative assessment. *Language Testing*, 17, 215–43.

Ross, S. (1992) Accomodative questions in oral proficiency interviews. *Language Testing*, 9, 173–86.

Ruebeling, H. (2002) Test Deutsch alfa: a German as a foreign language test for people who cannot read and write. Paper presented at the Language Assessment Ethics Conference, Pasadena, CA, May.

Shohamy, E. (2001), *The power of tests: a critical perspective on the uses of language tests.* London: Pearson.

Skehan, P. (1980) Memory, language aptitude and second language performance. *Polyglot*, 2, fiche 3.

Skehan, P. (1982) Memory and motivation in language aptitude testing. Unpublished PhD thesis, University of London.

Skehan, P. (1986) Where does language aptitude come from? In P. Meara (ed.), *Spoken language* (pp. 95–113). London: Centre for Information on Language Teaching.

Skehan, P. (1989) *Individual differences in second language learning*. London: Edward Arnold

Sparks, R., Arzer, M., Ganschow, L., Siebenhar, D., Plageman, M., & Paton, J. (1998) Differences in native-language skills, foreign-language aptitude, and foreign-language grades among high-, average- and low-proficiency foreign-language learners: two studies. *Language Testing*. 15(2), 181–216.

Spolsky, B. (1995) *Measured words*. Oxford: Oxford University Press.

Swain, M. (2001) Examining dialogue: another approach to content specification and to validating inferences drawn from test scores. *Language Testing*, 18, 275–302.

Teasdale, A. & Leung, C. (2000) Teacher assessment and psychometric theory: a case of paradigm crossing? *Language Testing*, 17(2), 165–86.

United Kingdom Home Office (2002) *Secure borders, safe haven: Integration with diversity in modern Britain*. White Paper, February. London: HMSO.

United Kingdom Home Office (2003) *Highly Skilled Migrant Programme (HSMP)*. London: Home Office, Immigration and Nationality Directorate. http://www.workpermits.gov.uk/default.asp?PageId=3631. Accessed January 30.

United States Department of Justice (2003) *Immigration and Naturalization Service: Naturalization*. http://www.ins.usdoj.gov/graphics/services/natz/index.htm. Accessed January 30.

Woodford, P. E. (1982) *An introduction to TOEIC: the initial validity study*. Princeton, NJ: Educational Testing Service.

Young, R. & He, A. W. (eds.) (1998) *Talking and testing: discourse approaches to the assessment of oral proficiency*. Amsterdam: John Benjamins.

FURTHER READING

Alderson, J. C. (2000) *Assessing reading*. Cambridge: Cambridge University Press.

Alderson, J. C. & Banerjee, J. (2001) Language testing and assessment (part 1). *Language Teaching*, 34(4), 213–36.

Alderson, J. C. & Banerjee, J. (2002) Language testing and assessment (part 2). *Language Teaching*, 35(2), 79–113.

Alderson, J. C., Clapham, C., & Wall, D. (1995) *Language test construction and evaluation*. Cambridge: Cambridge University Press.

Bachman, L. & Palmer, A. (1996) *Language testing in practice*. Oxford: Oxford University Press.

Brindley, G. (1989) *Assessing achievement in the learner centred curriculum*. Sydney: National Centre for English Language Teaching and Research.

Brown, J. D. & Hudson, T. (2002) *Criterion-referenced language testing*. Cambridge: Cambridge University Press.

Clapham, C. M. & Corson, D. (eds.) (1997) *Language testing and assessment*, vol. 7: *Encyclopaedia of language and education*. Dordrecht: Kluwer Academic.

Davidson, F. & Lynch, B. K. (2001) *Testcraft: a teacher's guide to writing and using language test specifications*. New Haven: Yale University Press.

Douglas, D. (2000) *Assessing languages for specific purposes*. New York: Cambridge University Press.

Henning, G. (1987) *A guide to language testing*. Cambridge, MA: Newbury House.

Hughes, A. (2003) *Testing for language teachers* (2nd edn.). Cambridge: Cambridge University Press.

McNamara, T. (1998) Policy and social considerations in language assessment. In B. Grabe (ed.), *Annual review of applied lingusitics*, 18, 304–19. New York: Cambridge University Press.

McNamara, T. (2000) *Language testing*. Oxford: Oxford University Press.

Norris, J., Brown, J., Hudson, T. & Yoshioka, J. (1998) *Designing second language performance assessments*. Honolulu: University of Hawai'i.

Shohamy, E. (1985) *A practical handbook in language testing for the second language teacher*. Ramat Aviv: Tel Aviv University.

Skehan, P. (1998) *A cognitive approach to language learning*. Oxford: Oxford University Press.

Stow, H. (1996) *Mark my words: assessing second and foreign language skills*. Parkville, Australia: NLLIA Language Testing Research Centre, University of Melbourne (videotapes).

Weigle, S. C. (2002) *Assessing writing*. Cambridge: Cambridge University Press.

32 Critical Applied Linguistics

ALASTAIR PENNYCOOK

32.1 Introduction

The emergence of various "critical" perspectives in applied linguistics since the mid 1980s has been welcomed by some and rejected by others. Some of these perspectives have emerged under overt banners of criticality: critical discourse analysis (CDA), critical literacy, or critical pedagogy; others are informed by general formations of critical work and theory: gender studies, queer theory, postcolonial studies, or anti-racist pedagogy. In this chapter I shall attempt an overview of this broad emergent orientation under the rubric of critical applied linguistics. This chapter will discuss significant themes in critical applied linguistics, covering developing approaches to issues in language policy and planning, translation and interpreting, language education, discourse analysis, literacy, language in the workplace, and other areas of applied linguistics. It will give an overview of current work in critical applied linguistics, showing how it is pushing forward the intellectual and empirical boundaries of the discipline. It will argue that recent work that has emerged under this rubric has been some of the most interesting and creative work in the field. It will focus in particular at some of the points of controversy in critical applied linguistics, showing how debates over notions such as ideology, discourse, identity, subjectivity, difference, and power shed light on the whole domain of applied linguistics.

In addition to summarizing, discussing, and critiquing recent work in critical applied linguistics, this chapter will raise a number of broader issues: First, critical applied linguistics needs to be understood as far more than just a critique of normative applied linguistics. Second, although the notion of *critical* is one that is greatly struggled over, critical applied linguistics needs both to avoid a normative politics, and to promote a particular political vision of what is meant by critical. Third, critical applied linguistics is more than just the sum of related critical approaches to language domains (CDA, critical literacy, critical pedagogy). Fourth, critical applied linguistics is also more than just the addition of a political/critical approach to applied linguistics; rather, it raises a host of different questions to be addressed, such as identity, sexuality, power, and performativity. And fifth, it therefore not only suggests a broad conception of applied linguistics, but it also pushes those boundaries further by drawing on a range of theoretical and empirical domains. The chapter will conclude by discussing some of the controversies and difficulties that have emerged as critical applied linguistics has developed.

For some, critical applied linguistics is little more than a critique of other orientations to applied linguistics. In the glossary of his introduction to applied linguistics, Davies (1999) provides the following definition: "a judgmental approach by some applied linguists to 'normal' applied linguistics on the grounds that it is not concerned with the transformation of society" (p. 145). For some applied linguists, critical applied linguistics probably does appear to be little more than a critique of mainstream work. But if it were indeed limited to such a role, it would surely be of only marginal interest. Indeed, elsewhere in his book, Davies (1999) is prepared to accord a broader role to critical applied linguistics as both a mode of critique, and, in critical pedagogy, as a mode of practice. From this point of view it "offers an alternative applied linguistics, known as critical applied linguistics (CAL). It does this in two ways, first by offering a critique of traditional applied linguistics . . . and second, by exemplifying one way of doing CAL, namely critical pedagogy" (p. 20).

In this broader vision, then, there are multiple ways of doing critical applied linguistics, of which critical pedagogy is only one. These definitions, however, still leave many concerns unaddressed. The two principal concerns I shall address below are, first, what domains of work might be considered to fall within the rubric of critical applied linguistics (a discussion which has obvious implications for more general considerations about the coverage of applied linguistics), and what constitute the different understandings of the "critical" in critical applied linguistics (a discussion that will take us beyond a view that critical applied linguistics is merely a critique of applied linguistics, and asks whether it is applied linguistics with a political conscience, or something else again).

32.2 Domains of Critical Applied Linguistics

It might be tempting to consider critical applied linguistics as an amalgam of related critical domains. From this point of view, critical applied linguistics would either be made up of, or constitute the intersection of, areas such as critical linguistics, critical discourse analysis, critical language awareness, critical pedagogy, critical sociolinguistics, and critical literacy. But such a formulation is unsatisfactory for several reasons. First, the coverage of such domains is rather different from that of critical applied linguistics; critical pedagogy, for example, is used broadly across many areas of education. Second, there are many other domains – feminism, queer theory, postcolonialism, to name but a few – that do not operate under an explicit critical label but which clearly have a great deal of importance for the area. Third, it seems more constructive to view critical applied linguistics not merely as an amalgam of different parts, a piece of bricolage, or a meta-category of critical work, but rather in more dynamic and productive terms. And finally, crucially, part of developing critical applied linguistics is developing a critical stance toward other areas of work, including other critical domains. Critical applied linguistics may borrow and use work from these other areas, but it should certainly only do so critically.

32.2.1   Critical discourse analysis and critical literacy

Nevertheless, there are clearly major affinities and overlaps between critical applied linguistics and other, named, critical areas such as critical literacy and critical discourse analysis. Critical literacy has often been overlooked in applied linguistics, largely because the narrowness of scope that has so often confined applied linguistics to questions of second languge education and cognitive processes has left little space for an understanding of critical theories and practices of literacy. It is possible, however, to see critical literacy in terms of the pedagogical application of CDA, and therefore a quite central concern for critical applied linguistics. CDA and critical literacy are sometimes also combined under the rubric of critical language awareness, since the aim of this work is to "empower learners by providing them with a critical analytical framework to help them reflect on their own language experiences and practices and on the language practices of others in the institutions of which they are a part and in the wider society within which they live" (Clark & Ivanic, 1997, p. 217).

Critical approaches to literacy, according to Luke (1997), "are characterized by a commitment to reshape literacy education in the interests of marginalized groups of learners, who on the basis of gender, cultural and socioeconomic background have been excluded from access to the discourses and texts of dominant economies and cultures" (p. 143). Luke and Freebody (1997) explain that "although critical literacy does not stand for a unitary approach, it marks out a coalition of educational interests committed to engaging with the possibilities that the technologies of writing and other modes of inscription offer for social change, cultural diversity, economic equity, and political enfranchisement" (p. 1).

Thus, as Luke (1997) goes on to argue, although critical approaches to literacy share an orientation toward understanding literacy (or literacies) as social practices related to broader social and political concerns, there are a number of different orientations to critical literacy, including Freirean-based critical pedagogy, feminist and poststructuralist approaches, and text analytic approaches. Critical discourse analysis would generally fall into this last category, aimed as it is at providing tools for the critical analysis of texts in context.

Summarizing work in CDA, Kress (1990) explains that, unlike discourse analysis or text linguistics with their descriptive goals, CDA has "the larger political aim of putting the forms of texts, the processes of production of texts, and the process of reading, together with the structures of power that have given rise to them, into crisis." CDA aims to show how "linguistic-discursive practices" are linked to "the wider socio-political structures of power and domination" (1990, p. 85). Van Dijk (1993) explains CDA as a focus on "the role of discourse in the (re)production and challenge of dominance" (p. 249). And Fairclough (1995) explains that CDA "aims to systematically explore often opaque relationships of causality and determination between (a) discursive practices, events and texts, and (b) wider social and cultural structures, relations and processes; to investigate how such practices, events and texts arise out of and are ideologically shaped by relations of power and struggles over power" (1995, p. 132).

Already, then, we can see a clear set of concerns across approaches to critical literacy and CDA: all are governed by a concern to understand texts and practices of reading and writing in relationship to questions of social change, cultural diversity, economic equity, and political enfranchisement. Whether as a mode of research (analyses of texts or of literacy contexts) or as a mode of pedagogy (developing abilities to engage in critical text analysis), these approaches are concerned with questions of power and of change. Nevertheless, there remain a number of unresolved concerns in this domain. These include the status of textual readings when no account is made of their interpretation by a wider audience; and the relationship between forms of linguistic and political analysis. Thus, while critical applied linguistic approaches to texts and textual practices need to avoid a view of socially underdetermined meaning that suggests that everything is open to interpretation, they also need to avoid forms of socially over-determined meaning that suggest that texts are mere reflections of a given social order. And while the amalgam of discourse analysis and theory has clearly produced a considerable body of interesting work, there is a need to explore the implications of poststructuralist frameworks for the status of both the linguistics and the politics (see Lee, 1996; Pennycook, 1994a, 2001; Poynton, 1997; and Threadgold, 1997).

32.2.2 Critical approaches to translation

Other domains of textual analysis related to critical applied linguistics include critical approaches to translation. Such approaches would not be concerned so much with issues such as "mistranslation" in itself, but rather the politics of translation, the ways in which translating and interpreting are related to concerns such as class, gender, difference, ideology, and social context. Hatim and Mason's (1997, pp. 153–9) analysis of a parallel Spanish and English text published in the UNESCO *Courier* is a good example of how a form of CDA across two texts reveals the ideological underpinnings of the translation.

In this case, as they argue, the English translation of a Spanish text on ancient indigenous Mexican cultures reveals in many of its aspects a very different orientation toward other cultures, literacy, and colonialism. When "antiguos mexicanos" [ancient Mexicans] becomes "Indians," "el hombre indígena" [indigenous man] becomes "pre-Columbian civilization," and "sabios" [wise men] becomes "diviners," it is evident that a particular discourse or ideology is at play. Hatim and Mason's analysis of lexical, cohesive, and other textual features leads them to conclude that the English translation here relays "an ideology which downplays the agency – and the value – of indigenous Mexicans and dissociates ... history from destiny" (pp. 158–9).

Looking more broadly at translation as a political activity, Venuti (1997) argues that the tendencies of translations to domesticate foreign cultures, the insistence on the possibility of value-free translation, the challenges to the notion of authorship posed by translation, the dominance of translation from English into other languages rather than in the other direction, the need to unsettle local cultural hegemonies through the challenges of translation, all point to the need for an approach to translation based on an "ethics of difference." Such a stance, on the one hand, "urges that translations be written, read, and evaluated with greater respect for linguistic and cultural differences" (p. 6); on the other hand, it aims at "minoritizing the standard dialect and dominant cultural forms in American English" in part as "an opposition to the global hegemony of English" (p. 10). Such a stance clearly matches closely the forms of critical applied linguistics I have been outlining: it is based on an anti-hegemonic stance, locates itself within a view of language politics, is based on an ethics of difference, and tries, in its practice, to move toward change.

Work on translation and colonial and postcolonial studies is also of interest for critical applied linguistics. Niranjana (1991), for example, argues that

> Translation as a practice shapes, and takes shape within, the asymmetrical relations of power that operate under colonialism ... In forming a certain kind of subject, in presenting particular versions of the colonized, translation brings into being overarching concepts of reality, knowledge, representation. These concepts, and what they allow us to assume, completely occlude the violence which accompanies the construction of the colonial subject. (pp. 124–5)

Postcolonial translation studies, then, are able to shed light on the processes by which translation, and the massive body of Orientalist, Aboriginalist, and other studies and translations of the Other, were, and still are, so clearly complicit with the larger colonial project. Once again, such work has an important role to play in the development of critical applied linguistics. It is indeed a shame that the monolingual biases of much mainstream applied linguistics have meant that translation has been marginalized as an applied linguistic domain. Critical approaches to translation might pose some very interesting challenges for applied linguistics.

32.2.3 Critical approaches to language education

Language teaching has been a domain that has often been considered the principal concern of applied linguistics. While my view of applied linguistics is a much broader one, language teaching nevertheless retains a significant role. I elsewhere (Pennycook, 1999) suggested that we can identify three main features that define critical work in language teaching: The domain or area of interest – to what extent do particular domains define a critical approach? A self-reflexive stance on critical theory – to what extent does the work constantly question common assumptions, including its own? And transformative pedagogy – how does the particular approach to education hope to change things? Thus, in trying to define critical applied linguistic work in language education, it is important to focus on the contextual concerns, be they issues of class, race, gender and so on, the ways in which the underlying framework relates to critical theory, and the ways in which the research or pedagogy is aiming to change what is going on. Again, we can see close parallels with the background concerns of critical literacy and CDA. There are also parallels with the distinction between research that turns a critical eye on an aspect of language education, and reports of critical practice.

Critical applied linguistic work in language education, then, may take as its central interest an attempt to relate aspects of language education to a broader critical analysis of social relations. Ibrahim (1999), for example, discusses how students from non-English-speaking African backgrounds studying in French schools in Canada "become Black" as they enter into the racialized world of North America. This process of becoming black, as he demonstrates, is intimately tied up with the forms of English and popular culture with which these students start to identify. Class is the principal concern addressed by Lin (1999) in her argument that particular ways of teaching English in Hong Kong (or elsewhere) may lead either to the reproduction or the transformation of class-based inequality. Ibrahim similarly asks what the implications are of his students identifying with marginality. Meanwhile questions of sexuality and sexual identity are the focus of Nelson's (1999) analysis of a period of discussion in an ESL (English as a second language) classroom about the implications of two women walking arm-in-arm down the street. Nelson argues that "queer theory may provide a more flexible, open-ended framework for facilitating inquiry, particularly within the intercultural context of ESL, than lesbian and gay theory does" (p. 377). Other authors take different configurations of power and inequality as their focus. For Brutt-Griffler and Samimy (1999), for example, it is the inequalities in the relationship between the constructs of the native and non-native speaker that need to be addressed, a concern that has become a major topic of discussion in recent years (e.g. Singh, 1998).

Canagarajah's (1993, 1999) use of critical ethnography to explore how students and teachers in the "periphery" resist and appropriate English and English teaching methods sheds important light on classroom processes in reaction to dominant linguistic and pedagogical forms: "It is important to understand the extent to which classroom resistance may play a significant role in larger transformations in the social sphere" (1999, p. 196). Other critical approaches to questions around language education include Norton's work on ways in which gender, power, and identity are interlinked in the process of language learning (1995, 2000). CDA and critical language education combine in much needed critical analysis of the interests and ideologies underlying the construction and interpretation of textbooks (see Dendrinos, 1992; Sunderland, 1994). Some have engaged in critical analysis of curriculum design and needs analysis, including a proposal for doing "critical needs analysis" which "assumes that institutions are hierarchical and that those at the bottom are often entitled to more power than they have. It seeks areas where greater equality might be achieved" (Benesch, 1996, p. 736). Benesch (2001) has now broadened this focus into a notion of Critical English for Academic Purposes, which "assumes that current conditions should be interrogated in the interests of greater equity and democratic participation in and out of educational institutions" (p. 64).

Turning more to research on, or accounts of, critical practice, a lot of work has not only discussed research on gender and language education (see Sunderland, 1994), but has focused on gender (in relationship to other forms of discrimination and inequality) in teaching practice. Sanguinetti (1992/3), Schenke (1991, 1996), and others have discussed various concerns in feminist pedagogy in English language teaching (ELT): "Feminism," Schenke argues, "like antiracism, is thus not simply one more social issue in ESL but a way of thinking, a way of teaching, and, most importantly, a way of learning" (1996, p. 158). Rivera (1999) and Frye (1999) discuss forms of participatory research and curricula in immigrant women's education in the USA. This focus on participatory education and research draws particularly on the work of Paulo Freire, and the subsequent developments of Freirean pedagogy in language and literacy education (see Auerbach, 1995, 2000; Auerbach & Wallerstein, 1987; Benesch, 2001; Graman, 1988). Basing her work in a similar tradition, Walsh (1991) talks of *critical bilingualism* as "the ability to not just speak two languages, but to be conscious of the sociocultural, political, and ideological contexts in which the languages (and therefore the speakers) are positioned and function, and the multiple meanings that are fostered in each" (p. 127).

Brian Morgan's (1997, 1998) work in a community center in Toronto also shows how critical practice in ESL can emerge from community concerns. As he suggests, "A community-based, critical ESL pedagogy doesn't mean neglecting language. It means organizing language around experiences that are immediate to students" (1998, p. 19).

32.2.4 Critical language testing

As a fairly closely defined and practically autonomous domain of applied linguistics, and one which has generally adhered to positivist approaches to research and knowledge, language testing has long been fairly resistant to critique. The main response to challenges about the "fairness" of language assessment has generally been to turn inward to questions of test validity rather than outward to the social, cultural, and political context of assessment. Spolsky (1995), however, in his history of the development of the TOEFL (Test of English as a Foreign Language) exam, is clear on the context in which this needs to be seen, suggesting that

> from its beginnings, testing has been exploited also as a method of control and power – as a way to select, to motivate, to punish. The so-called objective test, by virtue of its claim of scientific backing for its impartiality, and especially when it operates under academic aegis and with the efficiency of big business, is even more brutally effective in exercising this authority. (p. 1)

As he goes on to argue, the history of the TOEFL exam "best demonstrates the tendency for economic and commercial and political ends to play such crucial roles that the assertion of authority and power becomes ultimately more important than issues of testing theory or technology" (pp. 1–2).

While such an approach locates assessment within a broader critical analysis of its relation to authority and power, it still lacks a way of suggesting what critical applied linguistic practice might emerge in response. Kunnan (2000) goes some way toward this by considering not only questions of validity, but also issues of *access* (equitable financial, geographical, personal, and educational access to tests) and *justice*: "the notion of societal equity goes beyond equal validity and access and focuses on the social consequences of testing in terms of whether testing programs contribute to social equity or not and in general whether there are any pernicious effects due to them" (p. 4).

Shohamy (2000) pursues similar concerns when she insists that language testers need to take responsibility not only for their tests but also for the uses to which their tests are put: "Language testers cannot remove themselves from the consequences and uses of tests and therefore must also reject the notion of neutral language testing. Pretending it is neutral only allows those in power to misuse language tests with the very instrument that language testers have provided them" (pp. 18–19). Norton Peirce and Stein (1995) also point to concerns about the politics of testing when they suggest that "if test makers are drawn from a particular class, a particular race, and a particular gender, then test takers who share these characteristics will be at an advantage relative to other test takers" (p. 62).

Following on from this focus on responsibility for the uses to which tests are put, Shohamy (2001) has developed a notion of *critical language testing* (CLT) which "implies the need to develop critical strategies to examine the uses and consequences of tests, to monitor their power, minimize their detrimental force, reveal the misuses, and empower the test takers" (p. 131). CLT starts with the assumption that "the act of language testing is not neutral. Rather, it is a product and agent of cultural, social, political, educational and ideological agendas that shape the lives of individual participants, teachers, and learners"

(p. 131). She goes on to suggest several key features of CLT: test-takers are seen as "political subjects in a political context" and are encouraged to "develop a critical view of tests"; tests are viewed as "deeply embedded in cultural, educational and political arenas where different ideological and social forms are in struggle"; CLT asks whose agendas are implemented through tests, and suggests that there is no such thing as "just a test"; it demands that language testers ask what vision of society tests presuppose; it asks whose knowledge the test is based on and whether this knowledge is negotiable; it challenges the uses of tests as the only instrument to access knowledge (pp. 131–2). Shohamy's proposal for CLT clearly matches many of the principles that define other areas of critical applied linguistics: her argument is that language testing is always political, that we need to become increasingly aware of the effects and uses (consequential validity) of tests, and that we need to link preferred visions of society with an ethical demand for transformative practice in our own work as (critical) applied linguists.

32.2.5 *Critical approaches to language planning and language rights*

One domain of applied linguistics that might be assumed to fall easily into the scope of critical applied linguistics is work such as language policy and planning, since it would appear from the outset to operate with a political view of language. Yet, it is not enough merely to draw connections between language and the social world; a critical approach to social relations is also required. There is nothing inherently critical about language policy; indeed, part of the problem, as Tollefson (1991) observes, has been precisely the way in which language policy has been uncritically developed and implemented. According to Luke, McHoul, and Mey (1990), while maintaining a "veneer of scientific objectivity" language planning has "tended to avoid directly addressing larger social and political matters within which language change, use and development, and indeed language planning itself are embedded" (p. 27). Ricento (2000) has similarly taken much of the earlier work in language policy and planning to account for its apolitical naivety.

More generally, the whole domain of sociolinguistics has been severely critiqued by critical social theorists for its use of a static, liberal view of society, and thus its inability to deal with questions of social justice (see Williams, 1992). As Mey (1985) suggests, by avoiding questions of social inequality in class terms and instead correlating language variation with superficial measures of social stratification, traditional sociolinguistics fails to "establish a connection between people's place in the societal hierarchy, and the linguistic and other kinds of oppression that they are subjected to at different levels" (p. 342). Cameron (1995) has also pointed to the need to develop a view of language and society that goes beyond a view that language reflects society, suggesting that in critical theory language is treated as part of the explanation. Whereas sociolinguistics would say that the way I use language reflects or marks my identity as a particular kind of social subject . . . the critical account suggests language is one of the things that *constitutes* my identity as a particular kind of subject. Sociolinguistics says that how you act depends on who you are; critical theory says that who you are (and are taken to be) depends on how you act.   (1995, pp. 15–16)

Taking up Mey's (1985) call for a "critical sociolinguistics" (p. 342), therefore, critical applied linguistics would need to incorporate views of language, society, and power that are capable of dealing with questions of access, power, disparity, and difference, and which see language as playing a crucial role in the construction of difference.

Questions about the dominance of certain languages over others have been raised most tellingly by Phillipson (1992) through his notion of (English) linguistic imperialism, and his argument that English has been spread for economic and political purposes, and poses a major threat to other languages. The other side of this argument has then been taken up through arguments for language rights (e.g. Tollefson, 1991; Phillipson and Skutnabb-Kangas, 1996). As Skutnabb-Kangas argues (1998), "we are still living with linguistic wrongs" which are a product of the belief in the normality of monolingualism and the dangers of multilingualism to the security of the nation state. Both, she suggests, are dangerous myths. "Unless we work fast," she argues, "excising the cancer of monolingual reductionism may come too late, when the patient, the linguistic (and cultural) diversity in the world, is already beyond saving" (p. 12). What is proposed, then, is that the "right to identify with, to maintain and to fully develop one's mother tongue(s)" should be acknowledged as "a self-evident, fundamental *individual* linguistic human right" (p. 22). Critical applied linguistics, then, would include work in the areas of sociolinguistics and language planning and policy that takes up an overt political agenda to establish or to argue for policy along lines that focus centrally on issues of social justice.

Nevertheless, in spite of the importance of this work, there are several important concerns here. Phillipson's (1992) work, for example, needs to be understood for what it can and cannot do. As he suggests, the issue for him is "structural power" (p. 72), not intentions, and not local effects. He is interested in "English linguistic hegemony" which can be understood as "the explicit and implicit beliefs, purposes, and activities which characterize the ELT profession and which contribute to the maintenance of English as a dominant language" (p. 73). Thus, it is the ways that English is promoted through multiple agencies and to the exclusion of other languages that is the issue. What this of course lacks is a view of how English is taken up, resisted, used, or appropriated (Canagarajah, 1999; Pennycook, 1994b). Similarly we need to see both the power and the weaknesses of a language rights perspective. As Rassool (1998) asks: "in the light of these dynamic changes taking place globally and nationally can the argument for a universalizing discourse on cultural and linguistic pluralism be sustained?" (p. 98). I have elsewhere (Pennycook, 2001) tried to develop a notion of *postcolonial performativity* to move toward a rather different conceptualization of language in the world.

32.2.6   *Critical approaches to language, literacy, and workplace settings*

Another domain of work in applied linguistics that has been taken up with a critical focus has focused on language and literacy in various workplace and professional settings. Moving beyond work that attempts only to describe the patterns of communication or genres of interaction between people in medical, legal, or other workplace settings, critical applied linguistic approaches to these contexts of communication focus far more on questions of access, power, disparity, and difference. Such approaches also attempt to move toward active engagement with, and change in, these contexts. Examples of this sort of work would include Wodak's (1996) study of hospital encounters: "In doctor–patient interaction in the outpatient clinics we have investigated, discursive disorders establish certain routines and justify the actions of the powerful. Doctors exercise power over their patients, they ask the questions, they interrupt and introduce new topics, they control the conversation" (p. 170).

An important aspect of this work has been to draw connections between workplace uses of language and relations of power at the institutional and broader social levels. Recently, the rapid changes in workplace practices and the changing needs of new forms of literacy have attracted considerable attention. Gee, Hull, and Lankshear (1996), for example, look at the effects of "the new work order" under "new capitalism" on language and literacy practices in the workplace. Poynton (1993), meanwhile, draws attention to the danger that "workplace restructuring" may "exacerbate the marginalized status of many women," not only because of the challenge of changing workplace skills and technologies but also because of the failure to acknowledge *in language* the character and value of women's skills. Women's interactive oral skills, as well as their literacy skills, have often failed to be acknowledged in workplaces. Poynton goes on to discuss a project designed to change these workplace-naming practices.

One thing that emerges here is the way in which critical concerns are intertwined. Crawford's (1999) study of communication between patients, nurses, and doctors in Cape Town (RSA) health services, for example, highlights the complexities of relations between Xhosa-speaking patients, nurses operating as interpreters, and predominantly white doctors. The patients suffer as the linguistic and cultural gaps between them and the doctors are left to be bridged by nurses acting as unpaid interpreters. They in turn are caught between doctors' demands just to translate what the patient says and their need to deal with patients who feel alienated from this environment on many levels. And all this amid racial, cultural, and gender relations of long historical inequality.

Similar relations exist in court cases in Australia, where the lack of understanding of the pragmatic features of Indigenous Australians' English compounds the injustices of a long history of racism, poverty, and prejudice. As a recent study by Eades (2000) suggests, "silencing of witnesses was particularly evident in situations where the legal professionals did not understand some aspect of Aboriginal lifestyle and culture which the witness appeared to deem relevant to answering a question" (p. 190). In such contexts we can see not only the interrelationship between many of the domains of critical applied linguistics described above – critical approaches to discourse, translation, bilingualism, language policy, pedagogy – but also the interrelationships between these and underlying social relations of race, class, gender, and other constructions of difference.

32.3 Critical Frameworks

While the coverage, role, and orientation of applied linguistics remains contentious (see Candlin, 2001; Davies, 1999; McCarthy, 2001; Widdowson, 2000, 2001), so too does the notion of what it means to be "critical" or to do "critical" work. Apart from some general uses of the term – such as "Don't be so critical" – one of the most common uses is in the sense of "critical thinking" or literary criticism. Critical thinking is used to describe a way of bringing more rigorous analysis to problem solving or textual understanding, a way of developing more "critical distance" as it is sometimes called. This form of "skilled critical questioning" (Brookfield, 1987, p. 92), which has recently gained some currency in applied linguistics (see Atkinson, 1997), can be broken down into a set of thinking skills, a set of rules for thinking that can be taught to students. Similarly, while the sense of critical reading in literary criticism usually adds an aesthetic dimension of "textual appreciation," many versions of literary criticism have attempted to create the same sort of "critical distance" by developing "objective" methods of textual analysis. As McCormick (1994) explains,

> Much work that is done in "critical thinking" . . . – a site in which one might expect students to learn ways of evaluating the "uses" of texts and the implications of taking up one reading position over another – simply assumes an objectivist view of knowledge and instructs students to evaluate texts' "credibility," "purpose," and "bias," as if these were transcendent qualities. (p. 60)

According to Widdowson (2001), applied linguistics, as a discipline that mediates between linguistics and language teaching, "is of its nature a critical enterprise." In this sense, "to be critical means the appraisal of alternative versions of reality, the recognition of competing claims and perspectives, and the need to reconcile them" (p. 15). This means "taking a plurality of perspectives into account so as to mediate between them, seeking points of reciprocity, and correspondence as a basis for accommodation." Although there will inevitably be "partiality and prejudice in the process," these should be kept "under rational control" (p. 16). For Widdowson, then, being critical is a process of evaluating different perspectives on a topic. This vision of critical applied linguistics sits squarely within this first orientation toward the critical, a position based largely on a liberal and humanist politics and epistemology. But, apparently without any sense of irony, Widdowson also warns that there is another sense of the critical, namely "ideologically committed to a single perspective" (p. 15). Before discussing the perspective that Widdowson is here warning us about, however, there is another sense of critical that also needs to be considered.

One of the central goals of applied linguistics has been to place questions of language in their social context. This appears to be a foundational view for many applied linguists, and is epitomized by the tendency to decry theoretical linguistics (and its arch-demon Noam Chomsky) and to extol the virtues of socially oriented models of language (as epitomized in the work of demigods such as Dell Hymes). It is in this orientation to the socially relevant, the contextualized, the real, that we can find another version of the critical. In his plenary address to the Eighth World Congress of Applied Linguistics (AILA), Candlin (1990) asked "What happens when Applied Linguistics goes critical?" Candlin argued for a critical dimension to applied linguistics for two main reasons: First, because applied linguistics had started to lose touch with the problems and issues around language faced by ordinary language users. Applied linguistics, he argued, was becoming an arcane, sectarian, and theory-oriented discipline that was increasingly distanced from the everyday concerns of language use. Second, he suggested, a critical dimension was needed to reveal

> hidden connections . . . between language structure and social structure, between meaning-making and the economy of the social situation, but also connections between different branches of the study of language and their relationship to our central objective, the amelioration of individual and group existences through a focus on problems of human communication. A study of the socially-constituted nature of language practice.   (1990, pp. 461–2)

In this view, then, critical applied linguistics can be seen as an attempt to make applied linguistics matter, to remake the connections between discourse, language learning, language use, and the social and political contexts in which these occur.

Yet one of the shortcomings of work in applied linguistics generally has been a tendency to operate with "decontextualized contexts," that is to say, with only a very limited view of what constitutes the social. It is common to view applied linguistics as concerned with language in context, but the conceptualization of context is frequently one that is limited to an over-localized and under-theorized view of social relations. One of the key challenges for critical applied linguistics, therefore, is to find ways of mapping micro- and macro-relations (but also to go beyond this micro/macro formulation), ways of understanding a relationship between concepts of society, ideology, global capitalism, colonialism, education, gender, racism, sexuality, and class, on the one hand, and classroom utterances, translations, conversations, genres, second language acquisition, or media texts, on the other. Whether it is critical applied linguistics as a critique of mainstream applied linguistics, or as a form of critical text analysis, or as an approach to understanding the politics of translation, or as an attempt to understand implications of the global spread of English, a central issue always concerns how the classroom, text, or conversation is related to broader social cultural and political relations. But without an element of critique, such a view remains concerned only with "relevance": its vision of what it means to be critical is limited to relating the language to broad social contexts.

It is not enough, therefore, merely to draw connections between micro-relations of language in context and macro-relations of social inquiry. Rather, such connections need to be drawn within a critical approach to social relations. That is to say, critical applied linguistics is concerned not merely with relating language contexts to social contexts, but rather does so from a point of view that views social relations as problematic. While a great deal of work in sociolinguistics, for example, has tended to map language onto a rather static view of society (see Williams, 1992), critical sociolinguistics is concerned with a critique of ways in which language perpetuates inequitable social relations. From the point of view of studies of language and gender, the issue is not merely to describe how language is used differently along gendered lines, but to use such an analysis as part of social critique and transformation. A central element of critical applied linguistics, therefore, is a way of exploring language in social contexts that goes beyond mere correlations between language and society, and instead raises more critical questions to do with access, power, disparity, desire, difference, and resistance. It also insists on a historical understanding of how social relations came to be the way they are.

But the crucial question is: What sort of critical social theory? (See Table 32.1.) One version, based on various lines of thinking deriving from the great line of Marxist thought, we might call *emancipatory modernism*, based as it is on modernist frameworks of materialism and enlightenment. It reminds us that critical applied linguistics needs at some level to engage with the long legacy of Marxism, neo-Marxism, and its many counter-arguments. Critical work in this sense, which I am here categorizing as the third category of the critical, has to engage with questions of inequality, injustice, rights, wrongs. Looking more broadly at the implications of this line of thinking, we might say that critical here means taking social inequality and social transformation as central to one's work. Taking up Poster's (1989) comment that "critical theory springs from an assumption that we live amid a world of pain, that much can be done to alleviate that pain, and that theory has a crucial role to play in that process" (p. 3), critical applied linguistics might be viewed as an approach to language related questions that springs from an assumption that we live amid a world of pain, and that applied linguistics may have an important role in

Table 32.1   Four forms of the critical in applied linguistics

	Critical thinking	Social relevance	Emancipatory modernism	Problematizing practice
Goals	Detached appraisal	Language in social context	Ideology critique	Engagement with difference
Politics	Liberal-ostrichism	Liberal-pluralism	Neo-Marxism	Feminism, postcolonialism, queer theory, etc.
Theoretical base	Humanist-cognitive egalitarianism; critical distance	Constructivism, contextualization	Critical theory, macro-structures of domination	Post-occidentalism, anarcho-particularism
Focus of analysis	Emphasis on the individual, openness of textual meaning	Social contexts of language use; meanings in context	Critical text analysis, linguistic imperialism, language rights; emancipation	Discursive mapping, resistance and appropriation; engagement with difference
Weaknesses	Weak social theory; no means for dealing with difference, inequality or conflict	Social relevance assumed as adequate; no focus on transformation	Deterministic focus on structural inequality obscures agency and difference	Possible relativism, irrealism, and over-emphasis on discourse

either the production or the alleviation of that pain. But it is also a view that insists not merely on the alleviation of pain, but also the possibility of change.

While the sense of critical thinking I discussed earlier – a set of thinking skills, an ability to engage in detached appraisal – attempts almost by definition to remain isolated from political questions, from issues of power, disparity, difference, or desire, the sense of critical that I want to make central to critical applied linguistics is one that takes these as the *sine qua non* of our work. Critical applied linguistics is not about developing a set of skills that will make the doing of applied linguistics more rigorous, more objective, but about making applied linguistics more politically accountable. But as Dean (1994) suggests, the version of critical in Critical Theory is a form of "critical modernism," a version of critical theory that tends to critique "modernist narratives in terms of the one-sided, pathological, advance of technocratic or instrumental reason they celebrate" only to offer "an alternative, higher version of rationality" in their place (Dean, 1994, p. 3).

A great deal of the work currently being done in critical domains related to critical applied linguistics often falls into this category of emancipatory modernism, developing a critique of social and political formations but offering only a version of an alternative truth in its place: language rights replaces linguistic imperialism; critical readings of texts replace naive readings; teaching critical issues in the classroom replaces the avoidance of politics, and so on. This approach to critical applied linguistics, while directly relating questions of language use to issues of power and inequality, tends to maintain a belief in rationality, realism, and scientific endeavor, including the old Marxist divide between science and ideology. Thus, on the one hand, we have fairly traditional Marxian analyses of power in which "The relationship between social classes starts in economic production, but extends to all parts of a society," and such class relations have "a more fundamental status than others" (Fairclough, 1989, pp. 33–4). And, on the other hand, this political form of analysis insists on its rational scientificity. Phillipson (1992), for example, explains that he is aiming to develop a theory of linguistic imperialism, thereby "contributing to 'rational, scientifically-based discourse'" on the global spread of English, in the hope that "an adequate, theoretically explicit foundation for analyzing the issues has been provided" (p. 75). Summarizing work done in CDA, Kress (1990) insists that "while their activity is politically committed, it is nonetheless properly scientific, perhaps all the more so for being aware of its own political, ideological, and ethical stance" (p. 85), a sentiment echoed by Wodak (1996) when she argues that CDA is "a socially committed scientific paradigm. CDA is not less 'scientific' than other linguistic approaches" (p. 20).

Yet while claiming to be politically radical, this approach to critical applied linguistics is often intellectually conservative. My central point here is that just as critical work cannot be politically conservative but epistemologically radical (as some types of postmodernist analysis may be described), neither can it be politically radical but epistemologically critical (as some domains of critical work appear). As politically oriented academic work, it needs an interrelated critique of both domains. In place of this version of critical modernism, with its emphasis on emancipation and rationality, Dean (1994) goes on to propose what he calls a "problematizing" practice. This, he suggests, is a critical practice because "it is unwilling to accept the taken-for-granted components of our reality and the 'official' accounts of how they came to be the way they are" (p. 4). Thus, a crucial component of critical work is always turning a skeptical eye toward assumptions, ideas that have become "naturalized," notions that are no longer questioned. Dean (1994) describes such practice as "the restive problematization of the given" (p. 4). Drawing on work in areas such as feminism, anti-racism, postcolonialism, postmodernism, queer theory, or what has been called post-Occidentalism (see Mignolo, 2000), this approach to the critical seeks not so much the stable ground of an alternative truth, but rather the constant questioning of all categories.

From this point of view, critical applied linguistics is not only about relating micro-relations of applied linguistics to macro-relations of social and political power; nor is it only concerned with relating such questions to a prior critical analysis of inequality. Too much emancipatory modernist work operates by melding a fairly standard (applied) linguistic framework with a given political framework. A problematizing practice, by contrast, suggests a need to develop both a critical political stance and a critical epistemological stance, so that both inform each other, leaving neither the political nor the applied linguistic as static. Power, as Foucault (1991) suggested, should not be assumed as a given entity but rather should be explored as the very concern that needs explanation. Critical applied linguistics is a mixture of social critique and anarcho-particularism, questioning what is meant and maintained by many of the everyday categories of applied linguistics – language, learning, communication, difference, context, text, culture, meaning, translation, writing, literacy, assessment – as well as categories of social critique – ideology, race, gender, class, and so on.

Such a problematizing stance leads to another significant element that needs to be made part of any critical applied linguistics. If critical applied linguistics needs to retain a constant skepticism, a constant questioning of the givens of applied linguistics, this problematizing stance must also be turned on itself. As Spivak (1993) suggests, the notion of "critical" also needs to imply an awareness "of the limits of knowing" (p. 25). As I suggested above, one of the problems with emancipatory-modernism is its assurity about its own rightness, its belief that an adequate critique of social and political inequality can lead to an alternative reality. It is this position that Widdowson critiques as being "ideologically committed to a single perspective" (2001, p. 15). A postmodern-problematizing stance, however, needs to maintain a greater sense of humility and difference, and to raise questions about the limits of its own knowing. This self-reflexive position also suggests that critical applied linguistics is not concerned with producing itself as a new orthodoxy, with prescribing new models and procedures for doing applied linguistics. Rather it is concerned with raising a host of new and difficult questions about knowledge, politics, and ethics.

32.4   Concluding Concerns

The arrival of critical applied linguistics on the applied linguistic scene has, not surprisingly, caused some concern. Davies (1999) argues that "the influence of CAL is pervasive and can be unhelpful" (p. 139). He goes on to suggest that

> Modernist approaches (such as CDA) and postmodernist critiques (such as CAL) of applied linguistics are . . . seductive. They provide a useful debate on the nature of the discipline, they need to be taken into account. But they must not be allowed to take over, cuckoo-like. Because their interest at the end of the day is not primarily in . . . "real-world problems in which language is a central issue."
> And since this is what applied linguistics is about, it is difficult to consider

critical approaches as other than marginal to the applied-linguistics enterprise. (p. 142)

Davies is probably right to warn us of the seductiveness of critical approaches and the danger of their "taking over" the discipline (though this seems an unlikely scenario for enterprises that are "marginal" to applied linguistics), but it seems strange to suggest that the concerns I have discussed above – critical approaches to text, translation, language education, testing, language policy, or workplace settings – are not concerned with "real-world problems in which language is a central issue." We might want to argue about whose version of the real world is more real, or perhaps about what we mean by language, but it would seem hard to argue that language is not a central issue or that these are not real-world concerns.

Davies' comment also raises another issue: if critical applied linguistics provides "a useful debate on the nature of the discipline," it seems somewhat premature to seek closure by insisting that his definition defines "what applied linguistics is about." While critical applied linguistics, as I have suggested, does not appear to be opposed to a notion of being concerned with "real-world problems in which language is a central issue" (apart from questioning whose version of the real is put into play), it does seem to open up a broader debate about what constitutes applied linguistics. There are several important concerns here: First, as my overview above suggests, the domains of interest of critical applied linguistics are diverse, and certainly not limited to areas such as language education. It is certainly closer to Rampton's (1997) broad (though not unproblematic) vision for applied linguistics as "an open field of interest in language" (p. 14).

Second, by drawing on a far broader range of "external" domains than is often the case with applied linguistics, critical applied linguistics not only opens up the intellectual framework to many diverse influences, but also makes debates over "linguistics applied" versus "applied linguistics" at best of peripheral interest. Linguistics, in most of its current manifestations, is only of limited use to critical applied linguistics; and central concerns in critical applied linguistics have little to do with whether a fairly irrelevant body of knowledge about language can be applied directly or indirectly to domains of language use. Indeed, such a debate surely obscures many far more important issues to do with the applicability of a much broader range of knowledge to contexts of language use. And third, by taking not only a broad view on knowledge but also a political view on knowledge, critical applied linguistics takes us beyond a conception of applied linguistics as a fixed discipline, beyond even a view of applied linguistics as a domain of interdisciplinary work. Rather, part of the problematizing practice of critical applied linguistics is to take up an anti-disciplinary stance. While Davies (1999) may lament such a position as being "dismissive totally of the attempt since the 1950s to develop a coherent applied linguistics" (p. 141), critical applied linguistics must necessarily ask in whose interests such coherence has operated.

A further set of concerns has to do with normativity in critical applied linguistics. It might be objected that what I have been sketching out here is a problematically normative approach: by defining what I mean by "critical" and critical applied linguistics, I am setting up an approach that already has a predefined political stance and mode of analysis. Thus critical applied linguistics is open to Widdowson's (2001) critique of being committed ideologically to a single perspective. There is, of course, a certain tension here: an over-defined version of critical applied linguistics that demands adherence to a particular form of politics is a project that is already limited; but a version of critical applied linguistics that can accept any and every political view point is equally or even more limited. For Widdowson it is only the latter position that is tenable:

> Whose ethics are we talking about? Whose morals? And how can you tell a worthy cause from an unworthy one? Critical people, like missionaries, seem to be fairly confident that they have identified what is good for other people on the basis of their own beliefs. But by making a virtue of the necessity of partiality we in effect deny plurality and impose our own version of reality, thereby exercising the power of authority which we claim to deplore.   (2001, p. 15)

While there are good reasons to listen to these warnings of cuckoo-like take-overs and missionary zeal, there are also good reasons to challenge this denial of responsibility.

There are several weaknesses in Widdowson's own normative argument. According to Widdowson, not only do we need to avoid *misapplied linguistics* (2000), but we also need a "critical, not a hypocritical, applied linguistics to take us into the future" (2001, p. 16). It seems to me, that if we were to adopt Widdowson's dichotomy between critical and hypocritical applied linguistics (which I do not in fact wish to perpetuate), then it is the mainstream version that indeed is the hypocritical one on (at the very least) four important grounds.

- Hypocrisy number one: it is not uncommon from this stance to acknowledge the significance of political concerns (inequality, poverty, racism, and so on), but to argue either that these have nothing to do with academic or applied linguistic concerns, or (as above) that there is no way to decide between competing claims to ethical or political positions. Given the insistent claims by many who speak from more marginalized positions that racism, poverty, sexism, homophobia, and many other forms of discrimination have been central to their lives as language learners, educators, translators, and so on, it would seem hard to deny the importance of making these connections. Of course, we cannot and should not attempt to establish a correct or established position on these concerns, but we cannot avoid engagement with them. This is a hypocritical denial of ethical responsibility.
- Hypocrisy number two: critical work is often accused of adhering to a particular ideological stance, while those that make this critique claim some

neutral political and intellectual space. From a critical applied linguistic perspective, this denial of its own politics, this refusal to take into account broader social and political concerns, makes this an ostrich-like (head in the sand) approach to applied linguistics. This *liberal ostrichism* can be seen to run through many mainstream approaches to applied linguistics, making claims to neutrality while promoting a very particular vision of the world. This is a hypocritical denial of political responsibility.

- Hypocrisy number three: many of the attacks on critical applied linguistics suggest little understanding of critical theory, or the debates that surround domains such poststructuralism, postmodernism, postcolonialism, or queer theory. One does not have to agree with critical standpoints, but it is important at the very least to engage in the argument on a reasonable basis of understanding of the issues. This is a hypocritical denial of intellectual responsibility.
- Hypocrisy number four: the voices for change are coming from many quarters and with many different agendas. They are not just reducible to "postmodernism" or "critical pedagogy" or "critical discourse analysis" or "feminism"; rather, critical perspectives on applied linguistics are emerging from around the world with multiple agendas. To deny them is a hypocritical denial of social and cultural responsibility.

My purpose here has not been to establish and define critical applied linguistics as a fixed discipline, domain, or field, but rather to provide a glimpse of the *movable praxis* that is critical applied linguistics. I see critical applied linguistics as a constantly shifting and dynamic approach to questions of language in multiple contexts, rather than a method, a set of techniques, or a fixed body of knowledge. Rather than viewing critical applied linguistics as a new form of interdisciplinary knowledge, I prefer to view it as a form of *anti*-disciplinary knowledge, as a way of thinking and doing that is always problematizing. This means not only that critical applied linguistics implies a hybrid model of research and praxis, but also that it generates something that is far more dynamic. As with the notion of synergy as the productive melding of two elements to create something larger than the sum of its parts, it may be useful to view critical applied linguistics in terms of heterosis, as the creative expansion of possibilities resulting from hybridity.

This notion of heterosis, furthermore, opens up the possibility that critical applied linguistics is indeed not about the mapping of a fixed politics onto a static body of knowledge, but rather is about creating something new. As Foucault (1980) puts it, "the problem is not so much one of defining a political 'position' (which is to choose from a pre-existing set of possibilities), but to imagine and to bring into being new schemas of politicization" (p. 190). This is the political challenge for critical applied linguistics. Put more simply, my point here is that critical applied linguistics is far more than the addition of a critical dimension to applied linguistics, but rather opens up a whole new array of questions and concerns, issues such as identity, sexuality, access, ethics, disparity, difference, desire, or the reproduction of Otherness that have hitherto not been considered as concerns related to applied linguistics.

See also 12 LANGUAGE AND GENDER, 23 LITERACY STUDIES, 27 THE PRACTICE OF LSP, 30 LANGUAGE PLANNING AS APPLIED LINGUISTICS, 31 LANGUAGE TESTING.

REFERENCES

Atkinson, D. (1997) A critical approach to critical thinking in TESOL. *TESOL Quarterly*, 31(1), 71–94.

Auerbach, E. (1995) The politics of the ESL classroom: issues of power in pedagogical choices. In J. Tollefson (ed.), *Power and inequality in language education* (pp. 9–33). New York: Cambridge University Press.

Auerbach, E. (2000) Creating participatory learning communities: paradoxes and possibilities. In J. K. Hall and W. Eggington (eds.), *The sociopolitics of English language teaching* (pp. 143–64). Clevedon, UK: Multilingual Matters.

Auerbach, E. & Wallerstein N. (1987) *ESL for action: problem-posing at work.* Reading, MA: Addison Wesley.

Benesch, S. (1996) Needs analysis and curriculum development in EAP: an example of a critical approach. *TESOL Quarterly*, 30(4), 723–38.

Benesch, S. (2001) *Critical English for academic purposes: theory, politics, and practice.* Mahwah, NJ: Lawrence Erlbaum.

Brookfield, S. (1987) *Developing critical thinkers.* Milton Keynes: Open University Press.

Brutt-Griffler, J. & Samimy, K. (1999) Revisiting the colonial in the postcolonial: critical praxis for nonnative English-speaking teachers in a TESOL program. *TESOL Quarterly*, 33(3), 413–31.

Cameron, D. (1995) *Verbal Hygiene.* London: Routledge.

Canagarajah, S. (1993) Critical ethnography of a Sri Lankan classroom: ambiguities in student opposition to reproduction through ESOL. *TESOL Quarterly*, 27(4), 601–26.

Canagarajah, S. (1999) *Resisting linguistic imperialism in English teaching.* Oxford: Oxford University press.

Candlin, C. (1990) What happens when applied linguistics goes critical? In M. A. K. Halliday, J. Gibbons, & H. Nicholas (eds.), *Learning, keeping and using language.* Amsterdam: John Benjamins.

Candlin, C. (2001) Notes for a definition of applied linguistics in the 21st century. In D. Graddol, (ed.), *Applied linguistics for the 21st Century. AILA Review*, 14, 76–80.

Clark, R. & Ivanic, R. (1997) *The politics of writing.* London: Routledge.

Crawford, A. (1999) "We can't all understand the whites' language": an analysis of monolingual health services in a multilingual society. *International Journal of the Sociology of Language*, 136, 27–45.

Davies, A. (1999) *An introduction to applied linguistics: from theory to practice.* Edinburgh: Edinburgh University Press.

Dean, M. (1994) *Critical and effective histories: Foucault's methods and historical sociology.* London: Routledge.

Dendrinos, B. (1992) *The EFL textbook and ideology.* Athens: N. C. Grivas.

Eades, D. (2000) Silencing aboriginal witnesses in court. *Language in Society*, 29(2), 161–95.

Fairclough, N. (1989) *Language and power.* London: Longman

Fairclough, N. (1995) *Critical discourse analysis.* London: Longman.

Foucault, M. (1980) *Power/Knowledge: selected interviews & other writings, 1972–1977.* New York: Pantheon Books.

Foucault, M. (1991) *Remarks on Marx.* New York: Semiotext(e).

Frye, D. (1999) Participatory education as a critical framework for an immigrant women's ESL class. *TESOL Quarterly,* 33(3) 501–13.

Gee, J. Hull, G., & Lankshear C. (1996) *The new work order: behind the language of the new capitalism.* Sydney: Allen & Unwin.

Graman, T. (1988) Education for humanization: applying Paulo Freire's pedagogy to learning a second language. *Harvard Educational Review,* 58, 433–48.

Hatim, B. & Mason, I. (1997) *The translator as communicator.* London: Routledge.

Ibrahim, A. (1999) Becoming black: rap and hip-hop, race, gender, identity and the politics of ESL learning. *TESOL Quarterly,* 33(3), 349–69.

Kress, G. (1990) Critical discourse analysis. In W. Grabe (ed.), *Annual Review of Applied Linguistics* (vol. 11) (pp. 84–99).

Kunnan, A. (2000) Fairness and justice for all. In A. Kunnan (ed.), *Fairness and validation in language assessment: selected papers from the 19th Language Testing Research Colloquium, Orlando, Florida* (pp. 1–14). Cambridge: Cambridge University Press.

Lee, A. (1996) *Gender, literacy, curriculum: rewriting school geography.* London: Taylor & Francis.

Lin, A. (1999) Doing-English-lessons in the reproduction or transformation of social worlds? *TESOL Quarterly,* 33(3), 393–412.

Luke, A. (1997) Critical approaches to literacy. In V. Edwards and D. Corson (eds.), *Encyclopedia of language and education,* vol. 2: *Literacy* (pp. 143–51). Dordrecht: Kluwer Academic Publishers.

Luke, A. & Freebody, P. (1997) Critical literacy and the question of normativity: an introduction. In S. Muspratt, A. Luke, & P. Freebody (eds.), *Constructing critical literacies: teaching and learning textual practice* (pp. 1–18). St Leonards, NSW: Allen & Unwin.

Luke, A., McHoul, A., & Mey, J. L. (1990) On the limits of language planning: class, state and power. In R. B. Baldauf, Jr. & A. Luke (eds.), *Language planning and education in Australasia and the South Pacific* (pp. 25–44). Clevedon, UK: Multilingual Matters.

McCarthy, M. (2001) *Issues in applied linguistics.* Cambridge: Cambridge University Press.

McCormick, K. (1994) *The culture of reading and the teaching of English.* Manchester: Manchester University Press.

Mey, J. (1985) *Whose language? A study in linguistic pragmatics.* Amsterdam: John Benjamins.

Mignolo, W. (2000) *Local histories/ global designs: coloniality, subaltern knowledges, and border thinking.* Princeton, NJ: Princeton University Press.

Morgan, B. (1997) Identity and intonation: Linking dynamic processes in an ESL classroom. *TESOL Quarterly,* 31(3), 431–50.

Morgan, B. (1998) *The ESL classroom: teaching, critical practice and community development.* Toronto: University of Toronto Press.

Nelson, C. (1999) Sexual identities in ESL: queer theory and classroom inquiry. *TESOL Quarterly,* 33(3), 371–91.

Niranjana, T. (1991) Translation, colonialism and the rise of English.

In S. Joshi (ed.), *Rethinking English: essays in literature, language, history* (pp. 124–45). New Delhi: Trianka.

Norton, B. (2000) *Identity and language learning: gender, ethnicity and educational change.* London: Longman.

Norton Peirce, B. & Stein. P. (1995) Why the "Monkeys passage" bombed: tests, genres, and teaching. *Harvard Educational Review*, 65(1), 50–65.

Pennycook, A. (1994a) Incommensurable discourses? *Applied Linguistics*, 15(2), 115–38.

Pennycook, A. (1994b) *The cultural politics of English as an international language.* London: Longman

Pennycook, A. (1999) Introduction: critical approaches to TESOL. *TESOL Quarterly*, 33, 329–48.

Pennycook, A. (2001) *Critical applied linguistics: a critical introduction.* Mahwah, NJ: Lawrence Erlbaum.

Phillipson, R. (1992) *Linguistic imperialism.* Oxford: Oxford University Press.

Phillipson, R. & Skutnabb-Kangas, T. (1996) English only worldwide or language ecology? *TESOL Quarterly*, 30(3), 429–52.

Poster, M. (1989) *Critical theory and poststructuralism: in search of a context.* Ithaca: Cornell University Press.

Poynton, C. (1993) Naming women's workplace skills: linguistics and power. In B. Probert and B. Wilson (eds.), *Pink collar blues* (pp. 85–100). Melbourne: Melbourne University Press.

Poynton, C. (1997) Language difference, and identity. *Literacy and Numeracy Studies*, 7(1), 7–24.

Rampton, B. (1997) Retuning in applied linguistics. *International Journal of Applied Linguistics*, 7(1), 3–25.

Rassool, N. (1998) Postmodernity, cultural pluralism and the nation-state: problems of language rights, human rights, identity and power. *Language Sciences*, 20(1), 89–99.

Ricento, T. (2000) Historical and theoretical perspectives in language policy and planning. *Journal of Sociolinguistics*, 4(2), 196–213.

Rivera, K (1999) Popular research and social transformation: a community based approach to critical pedagogy. *TESOL Quarterly*, 33(3), 485–500.

Sanguinetti, J. (1992/3) Women, "employment" and ESL: an exploration of critical and feminist pedagogies. *Prospect*, 8(1&2), 9–37.

Schenke, A. (1991) The "will to reciprocity" and the work of memory: fictioning speaking out of silence in ESL and feminist pedagogy. *Resources for Feminist Research*, 20, 47–55.

Schenke, A. (1996) Not just a "social issue": teaching feminist in ESL. *TESOL Quarterly*, 30(1), 155–9.

Shohamy, E. (2000) Fairness in language testing. In A. Kunnan (ed.), *Fairness and validation in language assessment: selected papers from the 19th Language Testing Research Colloquium, Orlando, Florida* (pp. 15–19). Cambridge: Cambridge University Press.

Shohamy, E. (2001) *The power of tests: a critical perspective on the uses of language tests.* London: Longman

Singh, R. (1998) (ed.) *The native speaker: multilingual perspectives.* New Delhi: Sage Publications.

Skutnabb-Kangas, T. (1998) Human rights and language wrongs: a future for diversity? *Language Sciences*, 20(1), 5–28.

Spivak, G. C. (1993) *Outside in the teaching machine.* New York: Routledge.

Spolsky, B. (1995) *Measured words.* Oxford: Oxford University Press.

Sunderland, J. (ed.) (1994) *Exploring gender: questions and implications for English language education.* New York: Prentice-Hall.

Threadgold, T. (1997) *Feminist poetics: poiesis, performance, histories.* London: Routledge.

Tollefson, J. (1991) *Planning language, planning inequality: language policy in the community*. London: Longman.

van Dijk, T. A. (1993) Principles of critical discourse analysis. *Discourse and Society*, 4(2), 249–83.

Venuti, L. (1997) *The scandals of translation: towards an ethics of difference*. London: Routledge.

Walsh, C. (1991) *Pedagogy and the struggle for voice: issues of language, power, and schooling for Puerto Ricans*. Toronto: OISE Press.

Widdowson, H. G. (2000) On the limitations of linguistics applied. *Applied Linguistics*, 21(1), 3–25.

Widdowson, H. G. (2001) Coming to terms with reality: applied linguistics in perspective. In D. Graddol (ed.), *Applied linguistics for the 21st century*, *AILA Review*, 14, 2–17.

Williams, G. (1992) *Sociolinguistics: a sociological critique*. London: Routledge.

Wodak, R. (1996) *Disorders of discourse*. London: Longman.

FURTHER READING

Hall J. K. & Eggington, W. (eds.), *The sociopolitics of English language teaching*. Clevedon, UK: Multilingual Matters.

Norton Peirce, B. (1995) Social identity, investment, and language learning. *TESOL Quarterly*, 29, 9–31.

Index

courtroom interaction,
  and conversation analysis 264, 278
  see also juries, deliberations
courtrooms,
  interpreters and translators 291–3
  linguistic evidence 295–300
  narratives as competing stories 286–7
  powerless language in 357, 795
  sexual assault trials and institutional
    discourse 320
  transcription 110
  turn-taking 289–90
covariation 199
Cowie, Anthony 69, 70
Coxhead, A. 117
CPD *see* continuing professional
  development
CPH *see* critical period hypothesis
Craigie, W. A. 381
Cran, W. 382–3
Crandall, J. 659–60
Cranshaw, A. 91
Crawford, A. 794
Crazy English 605, 608
creative construction hypothesis 515,
  517
creativity 243, 251, 367
  bilingual 376–7
  and native speaker-likeness 436
Creber, C. 192
credentials, and language testing 773
creoles 379
creolistics 379
creolization 213
crimes, language 293–5
criteria, in language tests 765–7
  (Fig. 31.1); 768–9
critical applied linguistics 9, 24, 243,
  413–15, 430, 784–807
  aims of 430
  concerns 800–4
  and contrastive rhetoric 157
  definition 785
  domains 785–95
  and impact of technologies 642
  normativity in 802–3
  and world Englishes 385
critical approaches, to LSP teaching
  678–80

critical bilingualism 790
critical discourse analysis (CDA) 136,
  139–40, 158, 355–6, 413, 430, 784,
  785, 799
  and context of culture 146, 237
  and critical literacy 786–7
  and critical reading 596–7
  and function-internal description 147
  and genre 148–9
  interpretation debate 142
  of legal language 290–1
  and stylistics 332, 333
Critical English for Academic Purposes
  790
critical ethnography 789–90
critical frameworks 795–800
critical genre studies 148
critical language awareness (CLA) 158,
  243, 413, 570, 785, 786
critical language testing (CLT) 773, 776,
  790–2
critical linguistics 355–6, 413–14, 429,
  754, 758, 785
  and world Englishes 367, 384–5
critical literacy 430, 784, 785
  and critical discourse analysis 786–7
critical pedagogy 361, 617, 680, 784,
  785, 789–90
critical period hypothesis (CPH) 530,
  667
  and language attrition 219
  and ultimate attainment in SLA 83,
  87–9
critical reading 596–7, 795
critical sociolinguistics 785, 792–4, 797
critical sociology 755–6
critical theory 354, 414, 754, 789, 793,
  797, 798
  and gender identity 305
critical thinking, forms in applied
  linguistics 795, 797–8 (Table 32.1)
Crook, C. 628
Crookes, G. 658, 661–2
cross-cultural communication, discourse
  in 134
cross-cultural semantics 240
cross-referencing 41, 43
cross-sectional studies 483
Crowley, Tony 352, 353